The psychology of behaviour at work

Books by Adrian Furnham

Academic Books
Social situations (1981) (with Michael Argyle and Jean Graham)
The psychology of social situations (1981) (Edited with Michael Argyle)
Social behaviour in context (1986) (Edited)
The economic mind (1986) (with Alan Lewis)*
Culture shock (1986) (with Stephen Bochner)*
Personality psychology in Europe (1986) (edited with Alois Angleitner and Guus van Heck)
Lay theories (1988)*
The anatomy of adolescence (1989) (with Barrie Gunter)
The Protestant work ethic (1990)
Young people's understanding of society (1991) (with Barrie Stacey)
Consumer profiles: an introduction to psychographics (1992) (with Barrie Gunter)*
Personality at work (1992)
Biodata: biographical indicators of business performance (1993) (with Barrie Gunter and Russell
  Drakeley)
Corporate assessment: auditing a companies personality (1993) (with Barrie Gunter)
Business watching (1994) (with Barrie Gunter)
Social psychology at work (1995) (edited with Peter Collett)*
The new economic mind (1995) (with A. Lewis and P. Webley)
Why psychology? (1995) (with David Oakley)
Economic socialisation (1996) (edited with Peter Lunt)
All in the mind (1996)*
Complementary medicine (1997) (with Charles Vincent)
The psychology of behaviour at work (1997)*
Children as consumers (1998) (with Barrie Gunter)
The psychology of money (1998) (with Michael Argyle)*
Personality and social behaviour (1999) (with Patrick Heaven)*
Designing and analysing questionnaires and surveys (2000) (with Chris Jackson)
The psychology of culture shock (2001) (with Stephen Bochner & V. Ward)
Assessing potential (2001) (with Barrie Gunter)
Management incompetence (2003)
The dark side of behaviour at work (2004). (with John Taylor)
Personality and intellectual competence (2005) (with Thomas Chamorro-Premuzic)

Popular Books
Business watching (1994) (with Barrie Gunter)
The myths of management (1996)
Corporate culture shock (1997)
The psychology of managerial incompetence (1998)
Body language at work (1999)
The hopeless, hapless and helpless manager (2000)
The 3D manager: dangerous, derailed and deranged (2001)
Mad, sad and bad management (2003)
Management and myths (2004)
The people business (2005)

Specialist Monographs
Reaching for the counter (1993)
Children and advertising (2000)
Growing up with advertising (2002)*
Binge Drinking (2003)
Dishonesty at work (2005) (with John Taylor)

* Translated into at least one other language.

The psychology of behaviour at work

The individual in the organization

Adrian Furnham

University College London

Ψ Psychology Press
Taylor & Francis Group

HOVE AND NEW YORK

First published 2005 by Psychology Press
27 Church Road, Hove, East Sussex BN3 2FA

Simultaneously published in the USA and Canada
by Routledge Press Inc.
270 Madison Avenue, New York, NY 10061

Psychology Press is an imprint of the Taylor & Francis Group

Typeset in Times by RefineCatch Limited, Bungay, Suffolk
Printed and bound in Great Britain by MPG Books Ltd, Bodmin, Cornwall

Paperback cover design by Anú Design
Cover art by Steven Appleby

This publication has been produced with paper manufactured to strict
environmental standards and with pulp derived from sustainable forests.

British Library Cataloguing in Publication Data
A catalogue record for this book is available from the British Library

Library of Congress Cataloging-in-Publication Data
Furnham, Adrian.
    The psychology of behaviour at work : the individual in the organization /
Adrian Furnham. – 2nd ed.
        p. cm.
    Includes bibliographical references and index.
    ISBN 1–84169–503–3 (hardback) – ISBN 1–84169–504–1 (softcover)
1. Psychology, Industrial. I. Title.
    HF5548.8.P778 2005
    158.7 – dc22
    2004026387

ISBN 0-84169-503-3 (Hbk)
ISBN 0-84169-504-1 (Pbk)

For my beloved Benedict: Godspeed my fair one.

Contents

Preface

Updating a textbook is both an important and difficult task. The sheer volume of research papers published today makes it almost a full-time task for a textbook writer to keep up with what is going on. But it is also a matter of judgement about what to include, what to reduce and what to drop completely. The easiest option is just to add more, which is not a good idea. Other writers like to show how up to date they are by having lots of recent references. Some even hold the view that any reference, say before 1990, is outdated, worthless or wrong. I believe they are fundamentally wrong, even fashion victims.

In the second edition I have gone through chapter by chapter attempting first to prune or edit sections where I had originally perhaps been too self-indulgent or uncritical. Some whole sections have gone, others have been reduced. Next, I tried to locate books and papers which in my view had new, interesting and important things to say. That is of course a matter of judgement.

I have a friend whose publisher likes him to revise his (excellent and popular) textbook at least every two years. This clearly helps sales. To do this he consistently dedicates a day a week to the task. To keep up with the literature is a daunting task in any area of research these days. The problem is made worse by the fact that not only is there a fairly well defined and contained literature in applied psychology but one needs to read economics and, management and sociology journals as well. Scholarly books have an influence on popular books and vice versa. Both types have to be consulted, digested and considered.

In deciding what to include and exclude I tried always to keep a close eye on my readers. This book, now translated into Spanish, is a textbook in many European countries. It is used both as a (senior) undergraduate and post-graduate level for business and psychology students.

So the question is what do these students *want* and *need*. The reader I suppose expects the textbook writer to paint the big picture: to provide a map of the terrain and to address the most important questions. What are the issues, theories and research findings in the area?

Next, I think, the readers expect the writer to survey the available literature with a critical and selective eye. They see it as the writer's task to bring order and clarity into the morass of equivocal findings in the area. They expect theories to be both described and assessed. And they expect the author to understand their requirements and to deliver. The book must be comprehensive, critical and accessible. Well, I tried.

I wrote the preface to the last book on a beautiful island in the Phillipine archipelago during a monsoon-like storm. I am writing this one overlooking the stunning Indian ocean on holiday while visiting my mother. I rather enjoy writing and find it helps me to clarify my thinking. But I have rather too much a tinge of impulsivity for my own good and need, very desperately, to be more careful and obsessive in going over my hastily scribbled documents.

I am, as always and ever, grateful to my clever, stable and beautiful wife who often acts as my editor. She reads, corrects, queries and evaluates most of my popular writing for newspaper columns and some academic papers. Not only does she correct grammar and spelling, and improve my style, but most importantly she is an excellent sounding board for ideas. She is, after all, an experienced management consultant with a PhD (D.Phil. Oxon) in Psychology. She also puts up with my rather eccentric chronology which finds me in my office at 05.00 seven days a week.

The book is dedicated to my son. He might never read it and has already found the first edition more useful to prop up his computer than to be a source of wisdom. But you never know.

And, as I said in the first edition (and indeed all authors are bound to say), I have to take responsibility for errors, omissions and faux pas in this edition.

Adrian Furnham
Uvongo, KwaZulu Natal

1 Introduction

What is organizational or work psychology?

Most of us are born and die in organizations. We are educated and work in organizations. We spend a great deal of our in leisure time playing and praying in organizations. Furthermore, one of the largest and most powerful of organizations – the government or state – prescribes and proscribes how we should behave throughout our lives. We are shaped, nurtured, controlled, rewarded and punished by organizations all our lives. We are social animals who live in groups most of which might be called organizations.

Just after the Second World War, *work psychology* was conceived in terms of two simple and memorable epithets: "fitting the person to the job" and "fitting the job to the person". Today this would be called vocational and occupational psychology, management and ergonomics. But what do we understand work psychology to be today halfway through the first decade of the first century of the second millennium? Three ways of discovering the nature of work psychology is to look at definitions of it, how different academic disciplines contribute to it, and the subfields of work psychology.

Textbook *definitions* on the topic differ considerably. Consider the following:

- Cherrington (1989: 27): "The field of organizational behavior developed primarily from the contributions of psychology, sociology, and anthropology. Each of these three disciplines contributed ideas relevant to – organizational events that were combined into a separate study called organizational behavior. Three other disciplines that had a minor influence on the development of organizational behavior included economics, political science and history".
- Jewell (1985: 10): "Organizational behavior (work psychology) is a specialty area within the study of management. The difference between I/O [industrial/organizational] psychology as a subject for study and organizational behavior is not difficult to define conceptually. Industrial/organizational psychologists are interested in human behavior in general and human behavior in organizations in particular. Organizational behaviorists are interested in organizations in general and in the people component of organizations in particular. The basic distinction between I/O psychology and organizational behavior as academic areas of study is often difficult to maintain in applied organizational settings. The American Psychological Association formally recognized the interrelatedness of these two approaches to the same basic problems in 1973. At that time, the old designation of industrial psychology was replaced with the term now in standard use, industrial/organizational psychology".

- Baron & Greenberg (1990: 4): "The field of organizational behavior seeks knowledge of all aspects of behavior in organizational settings through systematic study of individual, group and organizational processes; the primary goals of such knowledge are enhancing effectiveness and individual well being".
- Spector (2003: 6): "The field of I/O psychology has a dual nature. First, it is the science of people at work. This aspect ties it to other areas of psychology, such as cognitive and social. Second I/O psychology is the application of psychological principles to organizational and work settings. There is no other area of psychology in which a closer correspondence between application and science exists. It covers many topics ranging from methods of hiring employees to theories of how organizations work. It is concerned with helping organizations get the most from their employees or human resources as well as which organizations take care of employee health and well-being".

As all students of the social sciences soon discover, definitions are of limited use, although they do highlight slightly different emphases between both writers and the disciplines they rely on most heavily. Certainly, there appears to be no shared and parsimonious definition of work psychology (or for that matter industrial and organizational psychology, or management science). Disciplines change and develop and encompass a very wide range of issues. However, the following may be proposed as a definition of organizational psychology:

> Organizational psychology is the study of how individuals are recruited, selected and socialized into organizations; how they are rewarded and motivated; how organizations are structured formally and informally into groups, sections and teams; and how leaders emerge and behave. It also examines how the organization influences the thoughts, feelings and behaviour of all employees by the actual, imagined or implied behaviour of others in their organization. Organizational psychology is the study of the individual in the organization, but it is also concerned with small and large groups and the organization as a whole as it impacts on the individual. Organizational psychology is a relatively young science. Like cognitive science, it is a hybrid discipline that is happy to break down disciplinary boundaries. From a psychological perspective, the major branches of the discipline to have influenced organizational psychology are experimental, differential, engineering and social psychology.

Another common way to understand work psychology is to look at its behavioural science *founder disciplines*, their contributions and special units of analysis. It is agreed that, of necessity, the subject of work psychology must be multidisciplinary. Psychology needs to take into consideration sociological factors; economics must take into consideration the foibles and idiosyncrasies so often researched by psychologists. So, work psychology is a *hybrid* that has borrowed (or stolen) ideas, concepts, methods and insights from some of the most established – subjects, particularly economics, psychology and sociology.

Figure 1.1 (based on Robbins, 1991: p. 14) illustrates the major contributory behavioural sciences. Four important points need to be made:

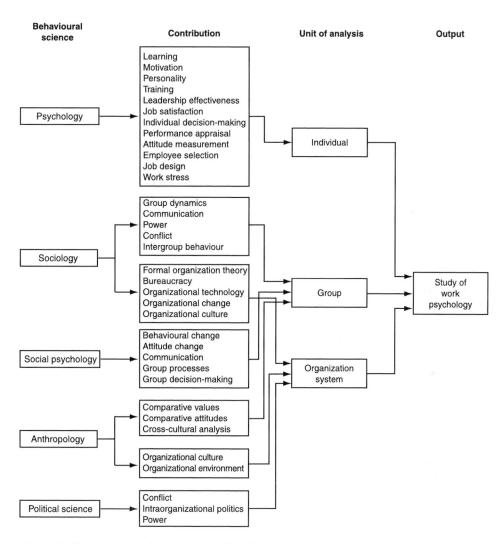

Figure 1.1 Towards a work psychology discipline. Adapted from Robbins (1991). Reproduced with the permission of Prentice-Hall, Inc.

- First, a good case could be made for including other disciplines, such as social administration/policy, industrial relations, international relations and computer science, although many of these are themselves hybrids.
- Secondly, the list of contributions in the second column are highly debatable – what is included and what not. Certainly, different writers would come up with different lists.
- Thirdly, the third column is very instructive; indeed, many textbooks are organized around the unit of analysis: the *individual* (intra- and interpersonal factors), the *group* (intra- and intergroup factors) and the *organization* (again inter- and intra-). Note that only psychology focuses on the individual, although branches of psychology focus not on "whole-person" research but some specific process such as memory or perception.

- Fourthly, this figure is too neat and it neglects to mention that various clashes or differences occur. Social psychologists and sociologists often study the same thing, but with different methods and assumptions. Economists and political scientists come to blows over ideology and epistemology. There is no neat slicing up of the cake of the natural phenomena of work psychology "carving-nature-at-her-joints". It is messier and more unhappy than suggested above. Academic disciplines have competing mutually exclusive theories and, rather than favouring eclecticism, prefer exclusivity.

However, what is important to remember is that many academic disciplines continue to contribute to the development of work psychology. This is because of the very large number of issues and problems that are traditionally covered by work psychology.

A third way of describing the field of work psychology is to list the various components or separate subfields covered by work psychology specialists. Thus, Muchinsky (1983) listed six different subspecialities in an attempt at conceptual clarification:

- Personnel psychology examines the important role of individual differences in selecting and placing employees, in appraising the level of employees' work performance, and in training recently hired, as well as veteran, employees to improve various aspects of their job-related behaviour.
- Organizational behaviour studies the impact of group and other social influences on role-related behaviours, on personal feelings of motivation and commitment, and on communication within the organizational setting.
- Organizational development concerns planned changes within organizations that can involve people, work procedures, job design and technology, and the structure of organizational relationships.
- Industrial relations concerns the interactions between and among employees and employers, and often involves organized labour unions.
- Vocational and career counselling examines the nature of rewarding and satisfying career paths in the context of individuals' different patterns of interests and abilities.
- Engineering psychology generally focuses on the design of tools, equipment and work environments with an eye towards maximizing the effectiveness of women and men as they operate in human–machine systems.

Lowenberg and Conrad (1998) suggest five slightly different areas based on a survey of working American psychologists. They are organizational development and change (examining structure and roles and their impact on productivity and satisfaction); individual development (mentoring, stress management, counselling); performance evaluation and selection (developing assessment tools for selection, placement, classification and promotion); preparing and presenting results (including research activities); and compensation and benefits (developing criteria, measuring utility and evaluating the level of accomplishment.

By giving one an idea of the specialities *within* work psychology, rather than the disciplines that contribute to it, it becomes easier to understand the range of issues dealt with by organizational psychologists.

Another way to discover the range of the disciplines is to examine the common topics covered on courses. The following is typical of the course topics covered in work psychology programmes (Dipboye, Smith, & Howell, 1994):

History and systems of psychology	Small group processes
Fields of psychology	Performance appraisal and feedback
Work motivation theory	Criterion measurement
Vocational choice	Personnel selection, placement and
Organizational development	classification
Attitude measurement and theory	Research methods
Psychometrics	Statistical methods and data analysis
Decision theory	Ethical and legal problems/issues
Human performance/human factors	Job and task analysis
Consumer behaviour	Cross-cultural differences
Measurement of personality and	Training theory: programme design and
individual differences	evaluation

However, there does appear to be agreement on some issues: that work psychology is essentially multidisciplinary; that it has various different facets/specialities; that it is comparatively new; and that it is both pure and applied. If the major areas of research in a discipline can be ascertained from the chapter headings of introductory textbooks, there does *not* appear to be a great deal of consensus as to the major topics in work psychology or indeed industrial/organizational psychology. For instance, Saal & Knight (1988) have a chapter on labour unions, whereas this topic is completely ignored by Baron & Greenberg (1990). Yet although the latter dedicate chapters both to stress and individual differences, the former effectively ignore this topic. To this extent it may be possible to distinguish between "*psychological work psychology*" and "*sociological work psychology*". That is, some researchers and textbook writers have been trained in sociological disciplines such as sociology or economics, which focus on group phenomena, whereas others come out of the individualistic tradition of psychology and ergonomics. Sociological work psychology is more closely linked to "management science" and tends to prefer generating theories or models to explain, describe or understand behaviour at work. Psychological work psychology looks very much like applied social psychology and tends to attempt field experiments to test quite specific hypotheses. Essentially, the former has as its unit the organization or a working group, and the latter has the individual as its unit of analysis. Given that work psychology is frequently a postgraduate rather than an undergraduate area of study, what probably determines whether someone is a sociological or psychological work psychology researcher is the core discipline within which they have been trained.

At the centre of the debate remains the question of the most appropriate unit of analysis in work psychology: the individual, the group or the organization. Most textbook writers in fact structure their work in terms of this threefold classification. That is, work psychology is considered to be the study of the *individual at work, working groups*, and the structure and behavioural *processes in organizations*. But there remains a tension at the heart of work psychology, as to what the central questions or boundaries are. For some, this tension provides the energy to work harder to resolve them; for others it signals the fragmentation of this new topic back into its original disciplinary conceptions. But most organizational problems do not fall neatly into the boundaries erected by zealous academics. So, for many these demarcation disputes are petty, irrelevant and ultimately damaging to the applied science aspects of work psychology. Managers want solutions to problems and are less interested in whether these are found by psychologists, sociologists or economists.

Assumptions and premises of work psychology

Psychologists are no more likely than economists to agree about many issues. This makes it difficult to try to specify any fundamental assumptions held by all of them. However, the following short list will possibly suffice as a starting point.

1   That organizations should produce those goods and services that fulfil the reasonable needs of people, considering both the physical welfare and the personal values of employers, employees, clients and the society at large.
2   That it is desirable to enhance the effectiveness of human involvement in the production and distribution of all goods and services. It is an article of faith that reasonable efficiency in such production of human talent in this process is therefore desirable and a major aim of all work psychology.
3   That in this process it is a desirable objective to maintain or enhance certain human values (health, safety, job satisfaction and work–life balance). It is an article of faith that the processes of producing such goods and services should be carried out in such a manner as to avoid any physical impairment of those involved and, if possible, to contribute positively to the personal satisfaction of all those so involved.
4   That marked disparities between the above objectives and their reasonable fulfilment are the sources of most of the human problems in all organizations.
5   That knowledge and insight of human behaviour gained through psychological research and through experience can contribute to the minimization of such problems.
6   The *modus operandi* of work psychology is to diagnose and identify both problems and opportunities to improve productiveness and satisfaction.

What do work psychologists do? Arnold, Robertson, & Cooper (1991: 32) suggested there are 12 distinct areas in which they work:

1   *Selection and assessment*: for all types of jobs by a variety of methods, including tests and interviews.
2   *Training*: identification of training needs; the design, delivery and evaluation of training.
3   *Performance appraisal*: identification of key aspects of job performance; design of systems for accurate performance assessment; training in appraisal techniques.
4   *Organizational change*: analysis of systems and relationships with a view to possible change; implementation of any such change (e.g. new technology).
5   *Ergonomics*: analysis and design of work equipment and environments to fit human physical and cognitive capabilities.
6   *Vocational choice and counselling*: analysis of a person's abilities, interests and values, and their translation into occupational terms.
7   *Interpersonal skills*: identification and development of skills such as leadership, assertiveness, negotiation, group working and relationships with other individuals.

8 *Equal opportunities*: monitoring, and if necessary enhancement, of opportunities for minority groups at work.
9 *Occupational safety and health*: examination of causes of accidents and the introduction of measures to reduce their frequency of occurrence.
10 *Work design*: allocation of tasks to make jobs as satisfying and motivating as possible.
11 *Attitude surveys*: design, conduct and analysis of surveys (e.g. by questionnaire or interview) of employee opinions and experiences at work.
12 *Well-being and work*: investigation of factors that lead to stress in work and unemployment, and identification of ways to prevent and manage stress.

What do work psychologists do?

Some years ago, the British Psychological Society listed 16 typical activities of work psychologists to give some sense of the depth and breadth of their activities.

1 *Selection and assessment* by interviews, personality and ability tests, or other means of all levels and types of personnel, including operators, supervisors, sales staff, managers, apprentices, civil servants, military personnel, clergy, and students. Selection should include monitoring and validating selection procedures to demonstrate their efficiency.
2 *Training*, including the identification and analysis of training needs, the design and development of training programmes, participation in training activities and, most importantly, the evaluation of the effectiveness of training. Training activities range from training for physical skills and machine operations to training for managers and supervisors in social skills and human interaction.
3 *Performance measurement and appraisal systems* require the examination of the human factors that lead to effective performance of a job, and the development of a system for monitoring this, that is fair and useful to both the employer and employee. Work psychologists get involved with the design, implementation and training for these systems.
4 *Organizational change and development* involves working with groups and individuals to enable them to understand their own and other people's motives and behaviour. It may also include an analysis of an organization, to determine whether its effectiveness can be improved by altering its structure or systems. Helping managers and staff cope with change is increasingly important.
5 *Industrial relations* involve psychologists working towards an understanding of trade unions, negotiations and many of the disputed fields of industrial relations systems, such as payment systems. Because trade unions are in decline, so is the area of endeavour.
6 *Ergonomics*, including the ergonomic analysis of jobs and their working environment, and their planning and redesign to take account of human capabilities. Ergonomics often involves psychologists working closely with engineers and physiologists. It may involve details of task and job design, for displays that are easily and accurately read (e.g. in an aircraft cockpit or power station control room) or for controls that are logically arranged and easy to identify (e.g. on a lathe or motor car). It also extends to the development of work and rest schedules that maintain efficiency and well-being, and reduce fatigue (e.g. shift systems).

7 *Occupational guidance and counselling* usually concern young people, but is more and more relevant to mid-career changes, especially when involving redundancy, unemployment, preparation for retirement and simple career moves. Work psychologists examine clients' own strengths and weaknesses, and help them to arrive at appropriate career decisions. This process usually involves the use of tests to measure aptitude, interests or personality, and an in-depth counselling interview to explain and interpret these.

8 *Career and management development* may be carried out from the individual's point of view, or from that of the organization, or both. Many of the skills required in occupational guidance, and in the performance appraisal, may be combined with analysis of training needs to achieve the manpower planning requirements of the organization and the career fulfilment of the individual.

9 *Occupational safety, health and welfare* examines the causes of accidents, methods of improving their prevention, the functioning of safety committees, and liaison with other parties concerned with health, risk and injury at work.

10 *Attitudes and opinion surveys* are used by many work psychologists who have developed special skills in the design and analysis of survey data. These techniques, and the use of statistical methods to reach decisions, help to determine the cause of events, and to evaluate the effectiveness of selection, training and many other sorts of procedure. They are often used to gauge morale through climate surveys.

11 *Stress management* is concerned with the identification of sources of stress as well as personal and organizational methods of preventing and managing stress. The area has grown substantially over the past few years.

12 *Equal opportunity at work* for women, ethnic minorities and other groups both in relation to organizational systems and structures (e.g. through the analysis and design of personnel policies) and to the individual (e.g. through the design of awareness training programmes for managers or assertiveness training for women). Changes in the typical demographic background of people at work have seen this area grow in importance.

13 *The design of new technology*, particularly the human aspects, concerns occupational psychologists from several aspects, such as the design of hardware, the introduction of new technology and the application of new technology in testing or training.

14 *Unemployment*: its management by organizations (e.g. redeployment or redundancy counselling), the facilitation of personal adjustment, job seeking, the use of leisure time and alternatives to unemployment are examples of the ways in which occupational psychologists have sought to ameliorate the effects of unemployment.

15 *Job, work and task design* in order to provide jobs that are individually more satisfying as well as being of benefit to the organization.

16 *Interpersonal, group and inter-group* processes and skills are wide-ranging; particular examples include leadership, assertiveness, conflict resolution and negotiation.

Professional accreditation

Work (or "occupational") psychology is defined by the Division of Occupational Psychology of the British Psychological Society (BPS) for the purposes of professional accreditation. To become a member of the Division, and a chartered occupational psychologist, candidates must (1) possess a recognized master's degree in occupational psychology; (2) demonstrate competence in five of the eight areas of professional practice, and (3) demonstrate the competence to practise independently. The eight areas of professional practice are as follows:

1 Human–machine interaction
2 Design of environments and work – health and safety
3 Personnel selection and assessment, including test and exercise design
4 Performance appraisal and career development
5 Counselling and personal development
6 Training – identification of needs, training design and evaluation
7 Employee relations and motivation
8 Organizational development and change

The following list provides a comprehensive but not an exclusive range of skills and knowledge related to the eight areas of professional practice:

1. Human–machine interaction
Acquiring techniques of:
- Functional analysis of a work system as a basis for the allocation of function in a human–machine interaction
- Work design
- Interface design
- Evaluation of software packages
- Task analysis: link analysis, error analysis, hierarchical task analysis, verbal protocol analysis
- Risk assessment: injury analysis, accident analysis, error analysis, anthropometry
- Physiological: electromyography, echocardiography/heart rate
- Psychological techniques: secondary tasks, skill tests
- Workplace design: information design – displays – controls; workplace layout
- System design: fault tree
- Knowledge of legislation and knowledge of design of a study
- Test of physical characteristics: eyesight, colour acuity, hearing, reaction time, heat tolerance

Practical application of knowledge and techniques
(a) Identification of needs and problems
(b) Analysis of needs and problems
- Review usability and comprehensibility of safety literature

(c) Formulation of solutions
- Design a simple work system based on functional analysis: (a) for differing individuals, (b) for people with disabilities

(d) Implementation of solutions
- Design and implement a safety training material display
- Redesign safety literature following its review
- Test usability of designed products

(e) Evaluation of outcomes
- Evaluate office equipment against legislation for visual display unit operators
- Evaluate the outcome of assessment and redesign of safety literature

2. Design of environments and work – health and safety
Acquiring techniques of:
- Measurement of the environment: light, heat, ventilation, workspace position/height, sources of threat
- Occupational stress inventories
- Risk assessment

Practical application of knowledge and techniques
(a) Identification of needs and problems
- Examining an accident/incident report and proposing changes in working practices to prevent a recurrence

(b) Analysis of needs and problems
- Carrying out risk analysis
- Undertaking work environment assessments and audits
- Carrying out a cost–benefit and cost-effectiveness analysis

(c) Formulation of solutions
- Using analyses to formulate solutions
- Recommend improvements in work environment by measuring analyses against legislation

(d) Implementation of solutions
- Modifying ambient conditions and work behaviour patterns
- Designing work settings

(e) Evaluation of outcomes
- Producing an accident/incident report following an investigation
- Evaluating workplace designs

3. Personnel selection and assessment, including test and exercise design
Acquiring techniques of:
- Psychometric training and assessment at Level A
- Psychometric training at Intermediate Level B
- Repertory grid techniques
- Acquiring techniques of and for the evaluation of an assessment centre; a selection procedure
- Critical incident techniques
- Development of competency techniques

Practical application of knowledge and techniques
(a) Identification of needs and problems

(b) Analysis of needs and problems
- Conducting a job analysis for a particular post or role
- Undertaking competency profiling

(c) Formulation of solutions
- Designing an assessment or development centre for a particular post or role, including: choice of exercises, design of matrix, administrative arrangements, and documentation for assessors/candidates
- Designing, drafting, and trialling assessment centre exercises and drafting support documentation for the exercises (for example, assessors' and role player's guidance notes)
- Designing, developing and delivering assessor training
- Designing and using application forms for selection; designing the short-listing process
- Designing an appraisal process
- Drafting job descriptions and person specifications
- Involvement in interview training
- Demonstrating awareness of good practice in interviewing

(d) Implementation of solutions
- Making decisions from an assessment centre
- Making decisions from data selection
- Giving feedback to participants from assessment/development centres
- Giving feedback from a psychometric exercise
- Conducting an appraisal
- Selecting, administering, scoring and interpreting two different psychometric ability and personality instruments
- Use of repertory grids as a data collection tool for competency profiling

(e) Evaluation of outcomes
- Statistical analysis of an assessment centre for monitoring purposes
- Evaluation and validation of an assessment centre
- Evaluation and validation of a selection/recruitment process

4. Performance appraisal and career development
Acquiring techniques of:
- Behaviourally anchored ranking scales (BARS)
- Behavioural expectancy scales (BES)
- Drawing up personal development plans (PDPs)
- Linking PDPs to business plans and attainment of competencies
- Use of 360-degree appraisal tools
- Executive development
- Appraisal skills and methods
- Career development planning
- Design of development centres
- Human resource planning
- Outplacement counselling

Practical application of knowledge and techniques
(a) Identification of needs and problems
(b) Analysis of needs and problems
(c) Formulation of solutions
(d) Implementation of solutions
  • Applying 360-degree appraisal tools
  • Appraisal of performance for motivation/development/goal setting/feedback/competence
  • Implementing development centres/human resource planning/career planning systems
  • Linking appraisal to human resource systems

(e) Evaluation of outcomes
  • Evaluating the effectiveness of development centres/human resource plans/career planning systems/career counselling

5. Counselling and personal development
Acquiring techniques of:
  • Listening skills
  • Counselling skills such as summarizing, reflecting back, etc.
  • Problem analysis
  • Using interest inventories
  • Report writing
  • Observation of career counselling and career development interviews
  • Career history interviews
  • Use and evaluation of computerized career choice systems and reports

Identification of needs and problems
(a) Analysis of needs and problems
  • Carrying out a career history interview
  • Using information from psychometric tests to identify the weaknesses and strengths of an individual

(b) Formulation of solutions
  • Identifying all the possible options available to solve a career crisis
  • Identifying stress management intervention options

(c) Implementation of solutions
  • Carrying out a career counselling/development interview based on analysis of psychometric information and other personal information provided
  • Outplacement counselling
  • Introducing stress management solutions into the workplace

(d) Evaluation of outcomes
  • Design and implementation of appropriate evaluation techniques and interventions

6. Training – identification of needs, training design and evaluation

Acquiring techniques of:

- To evaluate an existing training programme against training criteria
- Presentation techniques
- To design a training programme based upon a specified organizational outcome
- Validation techniques
- Training delivery skills

Practical application of knowledge and techniques

(a) Identification of needs and problems
- Review of a training course following evaluation and validation of results

(b) Analysis of needs and problems
- Involvement in undertaking a training needs analysis for a course

(c) Formulation of solutions
- Design of a training course for a specific need
- Involvement in the design of distance learning materials for a course
- Design of a specific learning package

(d) Implementation of solutions
- Delivery of a training course with evidence of the use of different styles, including formal input, facilitation, small group exercises, practical sessions, etc.

(e) Evaluation of outcomes
- Evaluation of a training course, including evaluation and validation of training

7. Employee relations and motivation

Acquiring techniques of:

- Sampling techniques
- Questionnaire design and analysis
- Focus group techniques
- Non-directive interviewing
- Motivation measurements
- Occupational stress analysis
- Knowledge of legal aspects of employee relations
- Team building
- Disciplinary actions
- Job design
- Negotiating and bargaining
- Conciliation, arbitration and mediation techniques

Practical application of knowledge and techniques

(a) Identification of needs and problems

   (b) Analysis of needs and problems
- Use of surveys
- Use of occupational stress inventories
- Repertory grid analysis
- Structured interviewing
- Use of focus groups
- Analysis of data elicited by the analytical tools

   (c) Formulation of solutions

   (d) Implementation of solutions
- Team-building activities
- Introduction of share ownership schemes

   (e) Evaluation of outcomes
- Evaluating the effectiveness of interventions

8. Organizational development and change
Acquiring techniques of:
- Contract formulation
- Consultation skills
- Negotiation and bargaining
- Sampling
- Questionnaire design
- Solution negotiation
- Use of organizational culture and climate measures
- Use of focus groups
- Management of change
- Leadership skills
- Negotiation techniques
- Decision-making supports

Practical application of knowledge and techniques
(a) Identification of needs and problems
- Identifying the need for change
- Identifying the underlying issues related to organizational change

(b) Analysis of needs and problems

(c) Formulation of solutions
- Aligning appraisal, training and personal development to organizational goals
- Aligning organizational goals and business plans

(d) Implementation of solutions
- Developing flexibility in the organization
- Implementing Investors in People

(e) Evaluation of outcomes
- Evaluating the impact of change

What, then, is an organization?

Organizations are human creations. They are entities in which interacting and mostly interdependent individuals work with a structure to achieve a common goal. They come in many forms and their goals are manifold and may not always be shared implicitly or explicitly by all members of the organization.

Most organizations have a formal *structure* that may be drawn on a chart. This specifies roles, titles, levels, ranks and reporting structure. The formal structure usually dictates the nature of specialization, centralization, standardization, formalization, and so on. The structure of an organization (tall/flat, centralized/decentralized) is a function of history, technology and the environment. Certainly, as the latter changes, particularly the market environment, so organizations have to change their structure (see Chapter 15).

But organizations cannot be described adequately on a chart. They are complex *systems* that have inputs and outputs of many sorts, and ways of transforming the former into the latter. There are many different systems in the organization operating at the same time, including the technology or production system and the social system. The systems way of looking at organizations stresses the interrelatedness and inter-active nature of organizations, although it may be wrong to suggest that these systems have a life of their own independent of the people in the system.

It is possible to look at organizations from many points of view – to stress the technology, the social system or culture, the external competitive environment, the formal versus informal structure of the organization, its accepted practices, and the employees and their characteristics. All are equally valid, although each, on its own, provides an incomplete picture of the organization. To emphasize this point, Morgan (1986) suggested that there are at least eight popular *metaphors* for the organization that represent very different ways of it:

- *as machine* – designed and operated as machinery and indeed making humans conform to their needs
- *as organism* – a live, adaptable mechanism like our bodies
- *as brains* – rational, problem-solving, self-critical and innovative
- *as culture* – a set of shared values, principles, attitudes and beliefs about what is important and how the world works
- *as political system* – an institution with set power, authority, responsibility, order; about control and influence
- *as psychic prison* – a collection of myths and fantasies that are confined by their own representation of themselves to the outside world
- *as flux and transformation* – a generative system that develops, grows and regenerates
- *as vehicle for domination* – a mechanism to impose its will on others by domination and control

These metaphors provide a simple, if restricted and restraining, way of looking at organizations. They are also ways in which organizations perceive themselves.

Work psychology is behaviour that occurs within the physical and/or psychological boundaries or contexts of organizations. Consider the person on the Clapham omni-bus. For eight hours of the day, he or she remains at work within a specified building and organization, in a culture that prescribes and proscribes all sorts of behaviour: verbal, non-verbal, spatial, and so on. After work this executive may go to a health club – also an organization with its own norms and rules. Thereafter, he or she may go home to a family, home for a meal and finally sleep. Is the home "an organization"? Does it have the features of an organization and if so what are they? Although it is true that all are in some sense organizations, work psychology is almost always specifically concerned with the *work* organization.

Cherrington (1989) has argued that an organization is an open social system (a set of interrelated elements that contains resources from the environment to which it "exports" some useful output product) that consists of the patterned activities of a group of people (relatively stable and predictable events that continue to occur with regularity) that tend to be goal directed. This definition seems to imply that a family unit (of whatever type) is indeed an organization. The question therefore remains: "What time is *not* spent under the behavioural influences of an organization?" Is all behaviour organizational behaviour? Is organizational behaviour different from "non-organizational" behaviour? And if so, what is the definition of the latter. Essentially, work psychology refers to behaviour at work, which is shaped, constructed and reinforced by the implicit and explicit needs of the organization.

Not all behaviour takes place within the "confines" of an organization, although it may remain shaped by an organization, or indeed, many organizations. Thus, the way people dress or talk outside the work organization might be shaped by the organization itself. But all sorts of factors shape, influence or determine behaviour, not only one's membership or experience of organizations. Indeed, one could argue that personality and ability factors determine both which organizations people choose to join and also how they behave in them. That is, there is evidence of reciprocal causation. In the Second World War, the British House of Commons was partly destroyed by bombing and Churchill demanded the building be rebuilt exactly as it had been because it had shaped and determined the particular (adversarial) nature of the behaviour within it! The implication is that we, through vocational choice, select organizations to work in that subsequently reward us for what we prefer to do. This may render organizational forces as consequences and not causes. Unless it can be demonstrated that organizational forces (culture, climate, implicit norms, explicit rules) are significant factors in determining behaviours within (working) organizations, it remains pointless to use the term and one might as well simply talk of behaviour (in organizations). On the other hand, if organizational behaviour is different from non-organizational behaviour, it merits keeping the term.

Organizations differ enormously along several dimensions: large–small, public–private, old–new. But to understand how they influence behaviour, climate and cultural variables need to be understood. Schein (1990) noted various organizational facets that prescribe how problems are solved: a common language and conceptual categories; consensus on group boundaries and criteria for inclusion and exclusion; criteria for the allocation of power and status; criteria for intimacy and friendship; and criteria for the allocations of rewards and punishments. In this sense, one may expect behaviour to differ very substantially between organizations. On the other hand, non-organizational behaviour is presumably less constrained and prescribed, and more determined by individual preferences and needs. It is no doubt for this reason that selectors ask candidates about their leisure pursuits, which are freely chosen and often unconstrained by organizational pressures, and hence supposedly, more accurately reflect the "true nature" of the individual. To answer this question one must know about the nature of the organization.

Organizations influence individual behaviour, but do individuals influence the behaviour of organizations? Work psychology theorists stress the importance of the socializing forces of an organization on the individual, preferring to focus on how organizational culture, climate, norms or structures shape individual behaviour. The individual level of analysis is exchanged for that of the organization. Yet individuals not only choose organizations (in line with their traits, values, preferences), they also change them to make them more habitable and comfortable to live in. Some organisms adapt to the environment they are given; others choose the preferred environment. People choose, but can change, their working environment to fit their needs and aspirations.

Organizations can only influence the behaviour of individuals within them if they are very powerful in the sense that various institutional rewards and punishments are in place to maintain a particular behaviour pattern. That is, either because of loyalty to organization values, roles and norms of behaviour, or because organizations demand strong conformity (such as armies, mental hospitals or religious institutions), individuals are strongly pressured into a homogeneous, "corporate culture", behavioural repertoire. Organizations can equally reward individuality, eccentricity and polymorphous perversity (such as universities) so that, in a paradoxical way, they can also strongly shape the behaviour of individuals in them by stressing individuality.

Terminological difference

A newcomer to work psychology soon becomes confused by the myriad terms that have been used synonymously: applied, industrial, occupational, organizational, vocational and work psychology are all used interchangeably; as well as related terms such as organizational behaviour, industrial/organizational psychology, ergonomics, and so on.

There are essentially three reasons why so many related terms exist. The first is *historical*: changes in both the focus of the research and the valence or value attached to various words. Hence, "industrial psychology" is a term seldom used these days, although it was popular for the first half of the twentieth century. Indeed, psychologists may now be more interested in non-manufacturing service industries than in large-scale heavy production industry. The world of cyberspace, the "virtual office" and cognitive ergonomics appear to interest work psychology specialists now more than manufacturing industries and production plants. Furthermore, the term "industry" is often pejorative and certainly is less favoured today.

The second reason is *ethnocentrism*. Different countries tended to choose and use different topics. Thus, the British (and many of her former colonies and dominions) used the term "occupational psychology", the Europeans "work psychology" and the Americans the clumsy "industrial/organizational psychology".

The third reason is largely *narcissism*. Much research offers eponymous fame or at least the possibility that a word or phrase attached to a test, a technique, a topic or a subdiscipline might offer the author lasting fame. Although this has been less true in this area, it may be one possible explanation for the proliferation of terms.

What are these many terms and how do they differ?

- *Applied psychology*: This is contrasted with pure psychology and it encompasses all psychology looking at the direct application of theory or methods from psychological research.
- *Business psychology*: A term occasionally used by consultants and management scientists to denote problems in everyday management. The term is gaining wider approval and may be used synonymously with organizational psychology. Critics might argue business psychology all too often takes the management, and not the workers', perspective.
- *Industrial psychology*: Perhaps the first term used in this area, it reflected the early interests of applied psychologists, many of whom were interested in environmental and physical factors at work (human factors), ergonomics and human groups. Ergonomics is now a thriving and expanding discipline.
- *Industrial/organizational (I/O) psychology*: An almost exclusively US term to include the older concerns of industrial psychology, and the more recent concerns of organizational psychologists. To a large extent it remains interchangeable with organizational psychology.
- *Occupational psychology*: Very much a British term referring to the whole area of organizational and industrial research. To some extent the term is misleading and has given way to the more common term of organizational psychology.
- *Organizational behaviour*: A term used to cover a multidisciplinary area with theories and methodologies borrowed from management science, psychology and sociology. In Britain and Europe, sociologists are probably in the majority in this area, whereas in the USA it is psychologists.
- *Organizational psychology*: Probably the most widely used term embracing the whole concept of work psychology and most facets of behaviour at work. This is probably the term that will "win" the etymological battle. However, non-psychologists naturally resent the "psychology epithet" and hence prefer the term behaviour.
- *Vocational psychology*: A term used to denote a quite specific area of research – mainly concerned with vocational choice, the "fit" between individual characteristics and job requirements, and the differences between people in different vocations.
- *Work psychology*: A relatively recent term, used mainly by European psychologists to encompass business, industrial, occupational, organizational and vocational psychology. Some use the term industrial, work and organizational psychology. Its simplicity is appealing, but once again it may be resisted by non-psychological researchers.

Personality–organizational interaction

A topic of great debate between work psychology and sociology psychology specialists is whether one can describe, explain or theorize at the level of the individual (personality, ability) as psychologists often do, or at the group or organizational level of the unique organization in a particular situation. The 1970s and 1980s saw personality psychology racked by the person–situation debate, which saw the emergence of three camps (relevant to this discussion):

- *Trait theorists* argued that a person's behaviour was cross-situationally consistent and that in the same situation predictable differences in social behaviour occurred. Supporters of this position would no doubt argue that work psychology was a function of the stable traits and abilities of people in the organization. That is, one can explain work psychology using psychological terms – particularly trait words, such as intelligence, competency and skill.

- *Situationists* believed behaviour varied considerably from situation to situation and that in "strong" situations (rule-bound, formal, goal-orientated) fewer major differences between individuals occurred. Thus, they would argue that work psychology was primarily a function of the organizational culture and climate and the everyday social situations that it prescribes and proscribes. That is, every organization is unique, and different sociological forces prescribe particular behaviour patterns in that organization.

- The advocates of *interactionism*, which was a compromise or synthesis position, argued that social behaviour was the function of a continuous process of multi-directional interaction between the person and the situation. Hence, supporters would argue from a personality theory and social psychological perspective that work psychology was a function of the interaction between traits and organization culture. That is, the particular contribution of specific people in a specific work group that led to observable behaviour patterns. This is a compromise, but an important one that suggests that it is the combination of particular individuals in particular circumstances that predicts all behaviour, including that in organizations.

The debate, often acrimonious and repetitive, hinged around certain issues: the fact that personality tests appeared poor at predicting any sort of behaviour (within or outside the organization); the average correlation between the same type of behaviour in different situations was always about 0.3; neither trait nor situational variables on their own appeared to account for more than 10% of the total variance. Many popular books, by highly successful businessmen and women, have led speculators to conclude that organizational success and failure is a function mainly of the personality (and ability) of its leaders (and followers). Such analyses grossly underestimate particular situational factors that play a major part.

The traditional trait or dispositional model (which accounted for behaviour in terms of personality variables) came under severe attack because it was argued that, quite simply, there was little or no empirical evidence to suggest that personality traits (such as extraversion) were manifest consistently over situations, stable over time or, indeed, little more than features in the eye of the beholder. Pervin (1984) has argued that after 15 years of research in this field we can be sure about what we do know and what we don't know. We know there is evidence of both personality and situational determinants of behaviour. No-one doubts that there is evidence for person consistency and situational variability in social behaviour; some people are more consistent than others; some situations have more powerful influences than others in reducing or maximizing the role of individual differences in behaviour; the amount of evidence for consistency of behaviour across situations and time depends on who is being studied, where, the personality variables being studied, and the measures used; all people observe their own behaviour as well as that of others and have systematic errors in reporting their own behaviour and that of others.

However, perhaps the most thoughtful review of this controversy has been that of Kenrick & Funder (1988), who note that nearly all of the arguments against personality traits being major determinants of social behaviour have turned out to be specious and yet we have not come full circle to the reacceptance of traits as they were understood 20 years ago. Current wisdom is summed up as follows:

> Other practical lessons have emerged from this controversy. The research now indicates quite clearly that anyone who seeks predictive validity from trait ratings will do better to use (a) raters who are thoroughly familiar with the person being rated; (b) multiple behavioral observations; (c) multiple observers; (d) dimensions that are publicly observable; and (e) behaviors that are relevant to the dimension in question. On the other hand, one should not expect great accuracy when predicting (a) behavior in "powerful" and clearly normatively scripted situations from trait ratings and (b) a single behavioral instance from another single behavioral instance. (Kenrick & Funder, 1988: 31)

This does imply that organizations with a strong culture in the sense of clear, enforced norms and rules shape individual behaviour more strongly than the personality of all the employees in that organization. But it also argues that if traits or personality variables are carefully selected (to be relevant) and measured, they can indeed be powerful predictors of individual and group organizational behaviour.

Various studies have been done in the p × s (personality × situation) traditional in the work psychology area. For instance, Newton & Keenan (1988) asked if work involvement was an attribute of the person or the environment and concluded that it was predominantly the latter. Yet there is a revival in interest and research in the disposition of personality determinants of organizational behaviour (Weiss & Adler, 1984), which has met with various criticism. Davis-Blake & Pfeffer (1989) have rehearsed some of the p × s debate but this time conceiving of it in terms of the p × o (personality × organization) debate. Their argument is essentially that organizations are strong settings that have a powerful effect on individual beliefs and behaviours; therefore, dispositions (personality traits, abilities, needs, etc.) are likely to have only limited effects on individual reactions in organizations. Such factors as well-defined organizational roles and strong corporate cultural norm or rule systems all minimize individual differences; to argue that individuals do not change and adapt requires an explanation (and evidence), as yet not forthcoming, as to why that is the case. Indeed, Davis-Blake & Pfeffer argued that all the evidence suggests that individuals are frequently affected by organizational structure and information. Organizations shape, discipline and socialize individuals to work in a particular way or style.

It is important to consider various reasons why this debate, now for all purposes settled in social and personality psychology, should be so powerfully discussed in the work psychology literature. This can be debated on sociological as well as psychological grounds. *First*, the idea that dispositions (abilities or skills) or personality traits predict organizational behaviour reduces work psychology theory and research to personality theory and psychometrics, something management scientists have a vested interest in not letting happen. *Secondly*, the work psychology literature seems to have neglected the dispositional approach for a longer period of time than the clinical literature, hence the sudden and belated revival of the topic. *Thirdly*, if the dispositional determinants' position is true, it makes organizational change more difficult, something work psychology specialists might not like to admit. That is, people are more difficult, if not impossible, to change than the organizations; hence, it is more satisfying to locate work psychology problems in the latter rather than the former.

No discipline is prepared to give up its level of analysis, style of theorizing or preferred methodology to another. Hence, sociologists resist and resent a psychological (inter- or intra-individual) level of analysis of management and organizational issues. Equally, psychologists are frequently hostile to sociological analysis, because they tend to focus on different issues. Thus, sociologists are interested in deviance because they assume conformity (to groups, norms, etc.) is the rule, whereas psychologists investigate conformity and obedience because they are puzzled by it, believing "deviance or uniqueness" to be normal. Thus, the tension that is apparent in work psychology may have benefits as well as drawbacks. Indeed, as the years go by and new researchers are trained initially in work psychology itself, rather than in psychology or sociology, these epistemological and methodological feuds may decline.

Management science, work psychology and common sense

To many laymen, the theories they come across in several social sciences – psychology, management, sociology, criminology – are common sense. That is, the theories or findings are already well known, and hence the research is thought to be a trivial, expensive and pointless exercise describing or proving what we already know. Four criticisms are often made:

1   Management science is little more than common sense. All findings and theories are unsurprising, uninformative, even tautological.
2   Management science debases common sense. It takes every simple, commonsense idea and through jargon renders it obscure.
3   Management science is often wrong. Its description of people and processes are simply not true.
4   Management scientists are dangerous. Their ideas and practices make them cynical manipulators of employees. Management scientists have political agendas.

Being sensitive to these criticisms, which is naturally seen as misplaced, social scientists have often confronted this point at the beginning of their textbooks, warning readers of the dangers of common sense, which lulls people into the false belief that they understand others. Some have even provocatively mentioned the term "uncommon sense" in their papers and titles. Thus, it is argued that common sense cannot tell us under which conditions each generalization is true; for that, scientific research is required (Fletcher, 1984). Others have attempted to persuade readers that *common knowledge* provides only inconsistent and misleading suggestions for understanding social behaviour by giving a short test.

Baron (1983) offers a similar quiz, where all the answers are *false*. Items include:

• Unpleasant environmental conditions (e.g. crowding, loud noise, high temperatures) produce immediate reductions in performance on many tasks.
• Directive, authoritative leaders are generally best in attaining high levels of productivity from their subordinates.

- In most cases, individuals act in ways that are consistent with their attitudes about various issues.
- Top executives are usually extremely competitive, hard-driving types.
- Most persons are much more concerned with the size of their own salary than with the salary of others.
- Direct, face-to-face communication usually enhances cooperation between individuals.
- Most persons prefer challenging jobs with a great deal of freedom and autonomy.

Box 1.1 illustrates another example.

Box 1.1 Common sense quiz

Much of what we "know" about the world is based on intuition. We have opinions, biases, hunches, and misinformation that we use both in making statements about others and in deciding what we do. The following 20 questions are designed to provide you with some feedback regarding what you "know" about human behaviour. Read each statement and mark T (true) or F (false).

True or false?
1. People who graduate in the upper third of their university class tend to make more money during their careers than do average students.
2. Exceptionally intelligent people tend to be physically weak and frail.
3. Most great athletes are of below average intelligence.
4. All people in Europe are born equal in capacity for achievement.
5. On the average, women are slightly more intelligent than men.
6. People are definitely either introverted or extraverted.
7. After you learn something, you forget more of it in the next few hours than in the next several days.
8. In small doses, alcohol facilitates learning.
9. Women are more intuitive than men.
10. Smokers take more sick days per year than do non-smokers.
11. 40-year-old people are more intelligent than 20-year-olds.
12. If you have to reprimand someone for a misdeed, it is best to do so immediately after the mistake occurs.
13. People who do poorly in academic work are superior in mechanical ability.
14. High-achieving people are high risk-takers.
15. Highly cohesive groups are also highly productive.
16. When people are frustrated, they frequently become aggressive.
17. Experiences as an infant tend to determine behaviour in later life.
18. Successful top managers have a greater need for money than for power.
19. Most people who work for the government are low risk-takers.
20. Most managers are highly democratic in the way that they supervise their people.
(Questions 1, 7, 10, 12, 16 and 17 are *true*: the rest are *false*.)

Source: Robbins (1991).

Some writers have explicitly contrasted "scientific" versus "lay" accounts of events (Reicher & Potter, 1985). Others have taken specific proverbs and attempted to test them. Sigelman (1981) attempted to test – using general social surveys – the folk proverb "ignorance is bliss". From his fairly extensive and well-analysed study he argued for the rejection of the age-old notion. On the other hand, Mischel & Mischel (1981) found that even 9- and 11-year-old children could predict some of the most basic empirical studies in psychological research.

Cynics and sceptics tend to argue that work psychology, as well as many of its parent disciplines – psychology, sociology, anthropology – are simply common sense dressed up as social science. However, Furnham (1983) has suggested that the "common sense objection" may take three forms. The *first* is that the findings and theories are well known, intuitive, unsurprising, uninformative and therefore are known to all. The *second* is partly the obverse – that is, academic disciplines which investigate issues that are the "stuff of personal experience" (job motivation, leadership) have tended – either by use of excessive jargon or technical language, or the focusing on minute, esoteric, trivial or irrelevant aspects of social behaviour – to debase or corrupt common sense. That is, topics that are amenable to common sense should have explanations in terms of lay language and not jargon, which excludes rather than facilitates everyday under-standing. A *third*, related objection occurs when experimental findings of social science, in this instance work psychology, appear to contradict widely held views of human nature. Many psychological studies, which have demonstrated that people are cruel, uninsightful, self-centred, compliant or antisocial, have been criticized more than those that have painted the opposite picture (Milgram, 1974, Zimbardo, Haney, Brooks, & Jaffe, 1973). That is, where findings are against the consensus, or common sense view, of people being basically good, altruistic, intelligent, and so on, objections are made. In this sense it seems most people have a preference for a Pollyanna perspective on work-ing individuals.

Stroebe (1980) has argued that many social psychological theories are intuitive and therefore not easily abandoned in the face of contradictory evidence. He mentions the complementary "needs" hypothesis (the idea that people with complementary needs such as dominance and submission should be mutually attractive), which has not been replicated or supported in over two dozen attempts to test it.

> Despite this devastating record, the theory is still presented in most attraction and social psychology textbooks. It just makes too much sense that, for example, some-body who loves to push people around should get along better with a spouse who prefers being pushed rather than pushing. (Stroebe, 1980: 186)

Equally we see Maslow's hierarchical theory of needs being repeated again and again in textbooks, conferences and reports, despite precious little evidence in favour of it. Indeed, many managers cling on to ideas and methods proved years ago to be both wrong *and* inefficient.

Similarly, as Brickman (1980) has pointed out, because social science, and particu-larly work psychology, returns its findings to the general culture in media reports, through articles in business magazines and seminars, they are apt to become more familiar and "commonsensical" over time:

> A finding in social psychology cannot remain non-obvious as people hear it again any more than a joke can remain funny to people who hear it again and again. More generally, we may propose that discoveries emerge from a region in which we disbelieve them into a zone in which we find them interesting, and then a zone in

which we find them obvious, and eventually perhaps, into a further region in which we are again oblivious to them. (Brickman, 1980: 12)

Textbooks in many of the social sciences continue to contrast science and common sense in a somewhat simplistic strawman way. Compare the way Kerlinger (1973: 35) contrasts the two along five dimensions:

1   While the man in the street uses "theories" and concepts he ordinarily does so in a loose fashion . . . The scientist, on the other hand, systematically builds his theoretical structures, tests them for internal consistency, and subjects aspects of them to empirical test . . .
2   . . . the scientist systematically and empirically tests his theories and hypotheses. The man in the street tests his "hypotheses" too, but he uses them in what might be a selective fashion . . . The – sophisticated social scientist knowing this "selection tendency" to be a common psychological phenomenon, carefully guards his research against his own preconceptions and predictions and against selective support of his hypotheses . . .
3   . . . the scientist tries systematically to rule out variables that are possible "causes" of the effects he is studying other than the variables that he has hypothesized to be the "causes". The layman seldom bothers to control his explanation of observed phenomena in a systematic manner . . .
4   . . . the scientist consciously and systematically pursues relations. The layman's preoccupation with relations is loose, unsystematic, uncontrolled. He often seizes, for example, on the fortuitous occurrence of two phenomena and immediately links them indissolubly as cause and effect . . .
5   The scientist, when attempting to explain the relations among observed phenomena, carefully rules out what have been called "metaphysical explanations".

Despite this vision of the heroic scientist versus the muddled layman, Kerlinger attempts to dispel erroneous stereotypes of science. However, his definition of scientific research was "systematic, controlled, empirical and critical investigation of hypothetical propositions about the presumed relations among natural phenomena" (p. 11). Not all social scientists are as dismissive of common sense in favour of disinterested empiricism (Hargreaves, 1981).

However, within the academic scientific community there is frequently antipathy to disciplines that investigate common sense, or by ignoring common sense rediscover it. Giddens (1987), who considered sociological research, argued that at the heart of objections to the discipline is the idea that sociologists state the obvious but with an air of discovery. Worse still, in that it offers explanations that do not ring true, sociology is doubly redundant because it not only tells us what we already know, but it parades the familiar in a garb that conceals its proper nature.

Giddens attempted to rebut these arguments thus: first, that common knowledge (Britain was particularly strike prone; there was a sharp rise in one-parent families) is frequently wrong and may lead to prejudice, intolerance and discrimination; secondly, correct knowledge may be the consequence of sociological research; thirdly, that common knowledge about behaviour differs from one group/milieu to another; fourthly, that people are normally able discursively to identify only a little of the complex conventional framework of their activities; fifthly, that behaviour may have unintended as well as intended consequences and that ways of acting, thinking and feeling may exist outside the consciousness of individuals; and sixthly, that ordinary language is too ambiguous for dispassionate analytic scientific description.

A major problem in the social, as opposed to the natural, sciences is that the theories and concepts invented by social scientists circulate in and out of the social worlds they are required to analyse. But while lay concepts obstinately intrude into the technical discourse of social science, the opposite is also true. Hence, the most interesting and innovative ideas in the social sciences risk becoming banal:

> The achievements of the social sciences tend to become submerged from view by their very success. On the other hand, exactly because of this we can in all seriousness make the claim that the social sciences have influenced "their" world – the universe of human social activity – much more than the natural sciences have influenced "theirs". The social sciences have been reflexively involved in a most basic way with those transformations of modernity which gives them their main subject-matter. (Giddens, 1987: 21)

In other words, the very popularity of work psychology may in some sense be its undoing. The more magazine and newspaper articles describe, discuss and deliberate on work psychology problems, theories and research, the more they become commonplace, obvious and commonsensical. However, it is likely that some findings that run counter to certain widely held beliefs will never be accepted. For instance, the idea that money has both limited and diminishing power to motivate work behaviour remains highly disputed by many lay people. Equally, lay people tend to underestimate the sheer number and type of human errors of judgement that are made by managers and workers in all sectors of the marketplace. Common sense can alas be very wrong at times. We need only look to the history of failed companies, failed products and even failed markets to see how common sense failed.

Knowledge about work psychology

Test your commonsense knowledge of the area before proceeding further. This is a simple, multiple-choice quiz about your knowledge about work and organizational psychology. It is divided into various sections and there are just over 10 questions in each section. Read each question through briefly, then circle a, b, c or d. Work fast; do not ponder too much over each question.

After each question has been answered, an estimate of the confidence level of how correct the answer is must be given. Your rating must be given as a percentage where 0% = "not at all confident" and 100% = "extremely confident".

SECTION 1

A. Current employee referrals (i.e. getting references) is a (an) ____ method of recruiting applicants.

(a) Ineffective
(b) Effective
(c) Expensive
(d) Useless

Your confidence rating, as % = _____

B. Newspaper advertisements and employment agencies are the worst sources of job applicants.

(a) True
(b) False

Your confidence rating, as % = _____

C. Imagine that you must conduct a job analysis for the job of Dog Bather. Which of the following would be helpful in completing the job analysis?

(a) Interview the supervisors of dog bathers
(b) Observe incumbents doing the job
(c) Personally give a dog a bath
(d) All of the above

Your confidence rating, as % = _____

D. Basically, job analysis yields two types of information and information about worker requirements. Job analysis techniques vary in the extent to which they emphasize one or the other type of information.

(a) True
(b) False

Your confidence rating, as % = _____

E. Job evaluation is

(a) Another term for job analysis
(b) A methodology used to assign monetary value to jobs
(c) Conducted by means of the critical incidents and job element techniques
(d) All of the above

Your confidence rating, as % = _____

F. Job analysis

(a) Provides information that is useful in benefit and compensation planning
(b) Is not usually needed when an organization develops training programmes
(c) Provides very little information about necessary worker qualifications
(d) Is a method for evaluating the monetary worth of jobs

Your confidence rating, as % = _____

G. The selection ratio at the bottom line refers to the number of people who were _____ compared with the number who _____.

(a) Hired; passed a test
(b) Tested; were interviewed
(c) Interviewed; applied
(d) Hired; applied

Your confidence rating, as % = _____

SECTION 2

A. Assessment centres may include a variety of psychological tests, including objective and projective personality tests.

(a) True
(b) False

Your confidence rating, as % = _____

B. Assessors in an assessment centre

(a) Are the applicants for the job
(b) May be outside consultants or from the organization's own staff
(c) Usually need no special training
(d) Must be licensed interviewers

Your confidence rating, as % = _____

C. The dimensions to be assessed in an assessment centre are best defined by

(a) The assessors
(b) The candidates
(c) Consultants
(d) A job analysis

Your confidence rating, as % = _____

D. The rationale of an assessment centre as a selection method is as follows: An applicant probably can perform the job, if he or she

(a) Can perform a sample of the job
(b) Has had experience in a similar job
(c) Can pass relevant psychological tests
(d) Has been recommended to participate in the assessment centre

Your confidence rating, as % = _____

E. Assessment centres

(a) Were introduced in the Second World War when the government needed a way to select secret service agents
(b) Are currently used mostly for selecting clerical employees
(c) Are based on the idea that past performance predicts future performance
(d) All of the above

Your confidence rating, as % = _____

F. Research shows that the evaluation of an applicant by an interviewer can be influenced by

(a) The evaluation of another applicant whom the interviewer saw previously
(b) Stereotypes about behaviour that are held by the interviewer
(c) The physical attractiveness of the applicant
(d) All of the above

Your confidence rating, as % = _____

G. The type of information obtained from applicants in selection interviews often varies from one applicant to the next. This is

(a) An advantage because the selection decision can then be made on the individual basis
(b) A problem that can be improved by structuring the interview
(c) Due to the deliberate misconduct of interviewers
(d) Solved by basing the interview questions on a careful reading of the résumés

Your confidence rating, as % = _____

H. Interviewing is

(a) Often not a valid method for making selection decisions
(b) More effective when the interview format is unstructured
(c) More effective if the interviewer is trying to assess personality traits
(d) Both b and c

Your confidence rating, as % = _____

I. The employment interview

(a) Is the best selection device we have at the present time
(b) Is used by most organizations
(c) Improves the quality of other selection devices
(d) All of the above

Your confidence rating, as % = _____

J. Writers of reference letters

(a) Usually prefer a structured reference form over an open-ended inquiry
(b) May have little ability to evaluate others
(c) Give too much information on the applicant
(d) Can be trusted to provide a fair and accurate evaluation

Your confidence rating, as % = _____

K. One way to improve the quality of application screening is to

(a) Use the same application form that is used by a business competitor
(b) Evaluate the application for evidence of the past behaviours that are required on the job
(c) Look for evidence of past exposure to similar jobs
(d) Have application forms completed by a recruiter rather than by an applicant

Your confidence rating, as % = _____

L. A personnel manager believes that the best way to select new employees is to look at the applicant's personal history of experiences. The manager is likely to

(a) Use such devices as application forms and biographical inventories for selection
(b) Develop special tests for each open position
(c) Rely on interviews for making selection decisions
(d) Require that applicants perform assessment centre activities

Your confidence rating, as % = _____

M. The personnel selection process

(a) Is reductionist
(b) Is accomplished typically through multiple hurdles
(c) Involves dropping some applicants from consideration at each stage of the process
(d) All of the above

Your confidence rating, as % = _____

SECTION 3

A. The polygraph/lie detector

(a) Has been used as an honesty test in employee selection
(b) Is no longer lawful for selection use
(c) Has not been shown to be valid for selection
(d) All of the above

Your confidence rating, as % = _____

B. Employee honesty

(a) Can be accurately assessed by either the polygraph or pencil-and-paper tests
(b) Is an important part of some jobs, such as those involving the handling of money
(c) Cannot be faked
(d) All of the above

Your confidence rating, as % = _____

C. According to research on the relationship of personality factors to job performance

(a) Conscientiousness can predict overall job performance
(b) Extroversion can predict performance in sales and managerial jobs
(c) Emotional stability can predict executive performance
(d) Both a and b

Your confidence rating, as % = _____

D. Most aptitude tests measure

(a) Both learned material and capacity for learning
(b) Only native ability
(c) The ability to think
(d) Verbal and mechanical comprehension

Your confidence rating, as % = _____

E. For good selection decisions, a selection instrument must be valid. This means that

(a) It must actually measure what it is supposed to
(b) Whatever it does measure must be relevant to the job
(c) It must not show differences between candidates
(d) Both a and b

Your confidence rating, as % = _____

F. Reliability

(a) Refers to the degree of consistency that exists between two or more supposedly similar measure
(b) May be assessed by testing and re-testing a sample with the same test
(c) May be assessed for judgement measures such as interview ratings
(d) All of the above

Your confidence rating, as % = _____

SECTION 4

A. Management training

(a) May focus on training the manager to lead
(b) Is offered by many companies to their supervisory employees
(c) Often includes communication skill training
(d) All of the above

Your confidence rating, as % = _____

B. Cross-cultural training

(a) Is offered by most international companies to their employees who go overseas
(b) Is meant to help employees deal with problems in interacting with people from another culture
(c) Probably does not help in the retention of employees who go overseas
(d) Usually is provided for overseas employees at least 6 months before their departure

Your confidence rating, as % = _____

C. Making university education more specifically oriented to a vocation means that

(a) The education is less likely to become work obsolete
(b) The graduate has greater flexibility in the kinds of jobs he or she can take
(c) The graduate is better prepared for a specific job
(d) All of the above

Your confidence rating, as % = _____

D. Imagine that you must train a group of people in the methods of statistical analysis. Several trainees have a negative attitude about statistics that prevents them from studying. Your best strategy in modifying this attitude is to

(a) Set up small groups in which the trainees adopt personal goals for studying and monitor each other's behaviour
(b) Demonstrate the correct solutions to problems before each study assignment is made
(c) Start each training session with a structured experience
(d) Include information in lectures about the necessity of practice for effective learning

Your confidence rating, as % = _____

E. Which of the following statements is not true?

(a) Feedback informs the performer as to whether an action needs to be modified

(b) For the greatest improvement in trainees' performance, the trainer should only provide positive feedback
(c) Giving trainees accurate information on how they are progressing is helpful
(d) At the start of the training, immediate is better than delayed feedback

Your confidence rating, as % = _____

F. Practice is

(a) Rehearsal or repetition of material to be learned
(b) Usually not necessary if training is done well
(c) Not motivating
(d) All of the above

Your confidence rating, as % = _____

G. An analyst is conducting a training needs assessment. He has looked at company records showing levels of turnover and absenteeism, and has studied existing job analyses to determine the kinds of work being done. His next step will be to

(a) Develop a programme that will meet both training and motivational needs
(b) Validate the training programme
(c) Survey the employees and their supervisors to determine individual needs
(d) Conduct an experiment to determine the department's real need

Your confidence rating, as % = _____

H. Which of the following situations most clearly indicates that an organization needs to provide training for employees?

(a) Employees are often absent from work
(b) The company has changed its product and bought new equipment
(c) Employees do not like their jobs
(d) Upper management thinks training would be helpful

Your confidence rating, as % = _____

SECTION 5

A. The post-appraisal interview

(a) Is often omitted in the workplace
(b) Has the potential of providing helpful feedback to employees
(c) Should be done frequently and involve participation of the employee
(d) All of the above

Your confidence rating, as % = _____

B. Research has shown that raters give better ratings to

(a) Same-race ratees
(b) Male ratees of the same race
(c) Different-race ratees
(d) Blacks

Your confidence rating, as % = _____

C. When selecting dimensions for a rating scale, the scale developer should

(a) Include dimensions used on other companies' scales
(b) Choose only dimensions that are relevant to the job being performed
(c) Choose general dimensions so as to make the scale as widely used as possible
(d) Include the dimensions of productivity, accuracy, neatness and initiative

Your confidence rating, as % = _____

D. Personnel data, such as ____, are sometimes used in performance evaluation.

(a) Performance ratings
(b) Counts of things produced
(c) Absenteeism and number of promotions
(d) Self-appraisals

Your confidence rating, as % = _____

E. Production measures of performance are disadvantaged in that they are

(a) Not objective
(b) Often based on a period of observation that is too short
(c) About the process of performance rather than the outcomes
(d) All of the above

Your confidence rating, as % = _____

F. Subordinate-evaluation of managers

(a) Is not effective because subordinates do not understand what managers must do
(b) Potentially can provide upward feedback to help a manager improve
(c) Is usually more positive than a manager's self-appraisal
(d) Is the most commonly used form of managerial appraisal

Your confidence rating, as % = _____

G. The advantage of using self-appraisal for performance evaluation is that

(a) It is more accurate than peer- or supervisor-appraisals
(b) The individual can identify his or her own needs for improvement
(c) It can be used with employees who work independently
(d) Both b and c

Your confidence rating, as % = _____

H. Peer appraisal is

(a) Sometimes used if the immediate supervisor has little contact with the employees
(b) More valid than supervisor appraisal
(c) Acceptable to employees even if the appraisal is negative
(d) Not as effective as self-appraisal

Your confidence rating, as % = _____

I. Performance evaluation information is used for

(a) Employee improvement
(b) Determining wage increases

(c) Evaluating training programmes
(d) All of the above

Your confidence rating, as % = _____

CORRECT ANSWERS:

Section 1:
A = b; B = a; C = a; D = b; E = a; F = d

Section 2:
A = a; B = b; C = d; D = a; E = a; F = d; G = b; H = a; I = b; J = b; K = b; L = a; M = d

Section 3:
A = d; B = b; C = d; D = a; E = d; F = d

Section 4:
A = a; B = b; C = c; D = a; E = b; F = a; G = a; H = b

Section 5:
A = d; B = a; C = b; D = c; E = b; F = b; G = d; H = a; I = d

How did you do? Give the test to a friend and test them. If you did well, was this due to simply common sense, knowledge, experience or wisdom? And if you think it is due to common sense, why do some people score so low? Where do you get common sense from?

Evolutionary psychology in business

Despite its popularity and growth in all the social sciences, evolutionary theory and socio-biology appears to have had little impact on organizational psychology. An important exception is the work of Nicholson. He argues that:

Our brains, hardwired to help us survive and reproduce in an ancient world, do things such as:

–   Make snap judgments based on emotions
–   Let one piece of bad news drive out a hundred pieces of good news
–   Take big risks when threatened and avoid risks when comfortable
–   Allow confidence to conquer realism to get what we want
–   Create opportunities for display and competitive contest
–   Classify things and people, dividing groups into "us" and "them"
–   Practice gossip and mind reading as key survival tools

The message of this book is not that we have to passively accept the costs of our instincts in the modern world. We need to understand them so we can manage them with insight. (Nicholson, 2000: 2)

Nicholson (2000) suggests that at work emotion controls reason not the other way around; that we are often over-confident when we should have no reason to be; that we expend more energy to avoid loss than seek gain; that we prefer classification over calculus, meaning we prefer stories (narratives) that "make sense" rather than the ambiguities of the truth; that we like contests and displays at work; and that we are natural discriminators against people of other groups. He sets out 13 myths and how evolutionary psychology dismisses them, for instance:

> Myth: Differences between men and women in work are solely the product of cultural brainwashing.
> Reality: Men and women have different hard-wired psychologies, so it is normal for them to want to do different things and to do the same things in different ways.

Nicholson's central point is that much of good, modern business practice is counter-productive because it is unnatural in the sense that it goes against the grain of human nature. These problems include:

1   Emotions are ignored and suppressed in the assumption that we are, or need to be, totally and coolly rational. So we need to honour emotion.
2   Business systems disempower, alienate and crush individuals who all ask for some control latitude and meaningful work. Thus we need to make hierarchies less rigid.
3   Politics at work nearly always lowers trust and a sense of community and commit-ment. Thus we need to deal with politics more openly.
4   Tribalism is normal: we are hard-wired to identify with groups; think in categorical terms; try to increase the status of our groups and notice visual group differences. Thus we need to make organizations more fluid.
5   Human groups and teams function well only under certain conditions; they are "small informal, egalitarian, inspired by shared goals, the knowledge that what they do is valued" (Nicholson, 2000: 56). Groups must therefore be more diverse.
6   Paradoxically, we are hard-wired for poor thinking – we have numerous, systematic errors in the way we make business decisions. What we notice, remember and consider is largely determined by how shocking, familiar or emotional the material is. Therefore, we need to put in place systems that counter our human biases.
7   We are highly sensitive and responsive to dominance, which can allow powerful people to abuse their power. Hence we need to devalue dominance.

Again, from an evolutionary and socio-biology perspective, Nicholson notes how natural forms of communication cause problems in business.

> Our instinctive patterns of communication are not rational, accurate, comprehen-sive, controlled or unemotional. What we really like to do is empathize, gossip, network, and tell stories. We have a strong oral preference. We love impromptu talking and listening. Many of the communications people find most satisfying are the least efficient for getting business done. Some people are better natural com-municators than others, but these are often not the people who are entrusted with key communications. Many business leaders lack confidence in this area. The skill people find most difficult is decentering – understanding what it must be like to be on the receiving end of a communication. We easily make the mistake of assuming that other people are like us in what they understand and want to hear.
>
> Communication networks in business are organic. They flow along the twisting channels of the rumour mill. These are formed by people's desire to give and receive information as a form of currency or grooming. This make networks politi-cal. It is a vain hope for executives to believe that a message poured down from the

top of the organizational tree will cascade down in an orderly fashion through all the tree's branches to its roots.

Our psychological capacity to network is limited. Once a business gets much beyond 150 members, it is difficult to maintain a unitary communications community. Sub-groupings assume greater significance. (Nicholson, 2000: 207)

Nicholson (2000) ends with seven predictions about what will NOT change in the future world of work:

1   We can adapt quite well to a semi-itinerant, mobile lifestyle. It takes us close to our origins, but it will be popular only where it is embedded in the context of a supportive surrounding community. Because this is not the norm in our culture, only a minority will opt for this type of work and lifestyle. Most people will retain a strong preference for more traditional forms of employment.

2   The traditional idea of the career is a modern invention to fit the linear hierarchy of organizations and occupations. But even if these structures disappear, people will still aspire to lifelong status advancement. If for no other reason, hierarchical career systems will be retained throughout the world of work. Some people will enjoy what are now being called "portfolio" careers, but those who can will stick with what they know best and like to do.

3   The separating boundary between work and home is also an artifice of recent times. We can well adapt to more integrated ways of living, for example through telecommuting, but this too will require a supportive context. People will prefer traditional working patterns if home working dislocates them from their employment community and takes them away from career opportunities.

4   So called virtual organizations will grow, in the sense that electronic linkages will become predominant *modus operandi*. But they will quickly succumb to the human instinct to organize hierarchically and clannishly. Networks of advantage, trust, and alliance will govern their conduct. They will not be preferred employers for the many people who want more direct experience of community.

5   People will always want to make and have "things." We cannot eat virtual breakfast and drink virtual water or fix cars with virtual tools. Much business will remain in highly traditional forms to make things we like and need to have. Forecasts of "the end of work" and the "death of jobs" are wild and false exaggerations. We will retain much that is familiar about occupational life.

6   People will always desire face-to-face dealings. No amount of virtuality will replace the irreducible experience of physically being in the presence of other people, especially in small groups. From boards of directors to project teams, meetings will continue to be conducted in this manner, even when there are highly sophisticated alternatives.

7   People will always want to congregate in common spaces. They will continue to want to go to work to see and experience the presence of other people. For the same reason that VCRs did not put movie theatres out of business and sports stadiums continue to fill up even when a game can be watched better on TV at home, people in business will find reasons to meet and gather physically.

(Nicholson, 2000: 275–276)

Theories, laws and models in work psychology

There is a range of possibly relevant terms that may be used to describe the theoretical aspects of work psychology. These include the following: adage, aphorism, attribution, axiom, belief, corollary, creed, definition, dictum, doctrine, explanation, guess, heuristic, hunch, hypothesis, idea, law, maxim, metaphor, model, motto, observation, paradigm, postulate, principle, proverb, rule, rumination, theory, truism, and so on. Although dictionary definitions may prove interesting, they are seldom very useful in making careful working distinctions. For instance, consider Chambers' *New English Dictionary* definitions of some of the more commonly used terms:

> *Hypothesis*: A proposition or principle put forth or stated (without any reference to its correspondence with fact) merely as a basis for reasoning or argument, or as a premise from which to draw a conclusion; a supposition. A supposition or conjecture put forth to account for known facts, especially in a science, a provisional supposition from which to draw conclusions that shall be in accordance with known facts and which serve as a starting-point for further investigation by which it may be proved or disproved and the true theory arrived at.

> *Law*: In the sciences of observation a theoretical principle deduced from particular facts, applicable to a defined group or class of phenomena, and expressible by the statement that a particular phenomenon always occurs if certain conditions be present.

> *Model*: A description of structure; something that accurately resembles something else; an archetypal image or pattern.

> *Paradigm*: A pattern, an example, an exemplar.

> *Principle*: A fundamental truth or proposition, on which many others depend; a primary truth, comprehending or forming the basis of, various subordinate truths; a general statement or tenet forming the (or a) ground of, or held to be essential to, a system of thought or belief; a fundamental assumption forming the basis of a chain of reasoning.

> *Theory*: A scheme or system of ideas or statements held as an explanation or account of a group of facts or phenomena; a hypothesis that has been confirmed or established by observation or experiment and is propounded or accepted as accounting for the known facts; a statement of what are held to be the general; laws, principles, or causes of something known or observed.

From the few terms selected, it would appear that these may be arranged in some sequential order reflecting developments. Hence, a hypothesis, which may contain a model or paradigm, precedes or is part of a theory that may or may not develop into a principle or law. Eysenck (1981: 2) in fact spelt out this relationship (see Figure 1.2). He writes:

> At an early age of development, we are reduced to fact-collecting on the basis of vague hunches, serendipitous discoveries of unforeseen regularities and inductive generalizations. When sufficient data have been collected along these lines, we are in the position of being able to put forward hypotheses of relatively small compass,

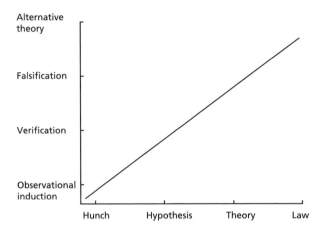

Figure 1.2 Demarcation theories of science: A unified point of view. Reprinted from Eysenck (1981) with the permission of Springer-Verlag.

and now the emphasis shifts to verification; unless we can verify these hypotheses, at least within the confines of certain parameter values, it is unlikely that they will be pursued further or interest other scientists. Given that this stage is successfully passed, we enter the realm of theory-making proper, and now falsification becomes the most important aspect of our experimental work. When a given theory is firmly established, it becomes a scientific law, and now the paradigm has become settled; only a revolution, sparked off by the accumulation of anomalous findings, and the emergence of an alternative theory, will dethrone such a theory. Thus, what constitutes a scientific approach will depend on the degree of development of a particular field; too rigorous a demand at too early a stage may well prevent the proper development of a discipline from ever taking place, just as too lenient a requirement at a later stage of development will prevent the discipline from growing up and assuming its rightful place.

However, it should be pointed out that there is no accepted agreement as to the use of these various terms. For instance, Valentine (1982) has provided rather different definitions for various terms: a *hypothesis* is a tentative law; a *postulate* is an assumption of a theory not intended to be subjected to empirical test; a *system* is a general theory plus meta-theoretical recommendations; a *law* refers to a relatively well-established statement of regular predictable relations among empirical variables. She appears to be satisfied with Marx's (1976) definition of a *theory* as a "provisional explanatory position, or a set of propositions, concerning some natural phenomena and consisting of symbolic representations of (1) the observed relationships among (measured) events, (2) the mechanisms or structures presumed to underlie such relationships or (3) inferred relationships and underlying mechanisms" (Valentine, 1982: 90). Similarly, she quotes Simon & Newell (1956) to distinguish models from theories: the former (models) are useful rather than true (heuristic aids, rather than complete descriptions), less data sensitive (disconfirming evidence is damaging to a theory but not necessarily to a model), and they are more susceptible to Type IIi errors (more liable to make false claims). The world of management training is full of models and particularly short on theories. Models *may* develop into theories but most often do not.

But terms such as model, paradigm, principle and theory may be used interchangeably by some writers, whichever suits their fancy and the current fad. Philosophers of science, on the other hand, in an attempt to bring order into this area, have attempted to taxonomize or specify different types of models, theories, and so on. For instance, Marx (1970) has distinguished between three types of theory (depending on the relationship between theory and data):

- *Deductive* theory – theoretical generalizations are induced from observations and predictions of future observations are deduced from theoretical hypotheses.
- *Functional* theory – which is a restatement of the data, with both data and theory being given equal weight.
- *Inductive* theory – where theoretical statements are simply summaries of empirical findings.

Lacy (1976: 110) noted that:

> Theory has various meanings: (i) One or more hypotheses or lawlike statements (either of first two senses), regarded as speculative. (ii) A law about unobservables is felt to be inevitably inconclusive. (iii) A unified system of laws or hypotheses, with explanatory force (not merely like a railway timetable). (iv) A field of study (e.g. in philosophy: theory of knowledge, logical theory). These senses sometimes shade into each other.

Another way of looking at definitions is to consider their function. Thus, Selltiz, Wrightsman, & Cook (1959: 481) note that "the intention of a theory in modern science is to summarize existing knowledge, to provide an explanation for observed events and relationships, and to predict the occurrence of as yet unobserved events and relationships on the basis of explanatory principles embodied in the theory". Valentine (1982) notes that theories serve to summarize and organize data by bringing order and coherence to material. They also are attempts at explanation and they serve a heuristic function of guiding research. However, she does note that some (particularly Skinner) have put forward a case against theories, arguing that they create new problems by giving a false sense of security.

Management scientists and consultants frequently talk about and produce "models" of such things as change processes, customer service or worker motivation. Most of these models are descriptive and heuristic; they are more like hypotheses about work psychology process, because they attempt to isolate the critical variables in the process and describe how they relate to one another causally. But they are seldom tested, rigorously or not. As a result, they remain hypotheses. And because they are not tested – indeed some may not be testable – there is no way of knowing if they are correct or not, or even – more importantly – how to choose between two competing hypotheses. In fact there are probably too many models or theories in work psychology and not enough attempts to validate them. Most of these models are process-specific and hence have limited general relevance. However, very few theories of models remain in work psychology that pretend to be inclusive or generalizable to many forms of work behaviour.

Another very thorny issue concerns whether work psychology is a science. This is not the place to debate such an issue. However, what does seem beyond debate is that researchers in the field adopt a scientific approach. Wexley & Yukl (1984) cited eight essential characteristics of the scientific approach:

- *Self-correcting:* There are built-in checks all along the way to obtaining scientific knowledge.
- *Empirical:* Perceptions, beliefs, and attitudes are carefully checked against objective reality.
- *Open to public inspection:* Procedures can be replicated (repeated) and results tested by other qualified researchers.
- *Objective and statistical:* Data collection is not biased, and a certain level of confidence can be placed in the results obtained.
- *Controlled and systematic:* Scientists try systematically to rule out alternative explanations for the results they obtain.
- *General theories:* Conceptual frameworks for organizing and explaining empirical observations also direct future research and suggest new hypotheses.
- *Tests hypotheses:* Tentative propositions about the relationships among various phenomena are evaluated in the light of empirical observations.
- *Aims to explain, understand, predict and change:* Only through explanation and understanding can industrial/organizational psychologists solve organizational problems efficiently and appropriately.

The direction of causality

The relationship between any two variables or factors can take many forms: it may be correlational or causal, and, if it is causal, different directions of causality are possible. Although an oft-repeated fact, it remains that both researchers and practitioners tend, wrongly, to infer cause from correlational data. Thus, any of the following relationships between personality (p) and organizational behaviour (or, indeed, other variables such as productivity and job satisfaction) may occur:

- *behaviour at work ~ p (no relationship between personality and behaviour at work):* This possibility would assume that there is no systematic relationship between any major personality factor and any dimension of behaviour at work. This may only appear to be so because the relationship that exists is too subtle to be measured, too unstable, or is frequently "washed out" or moderated by other more powerful and salient variables. Alternatively, it may be that there simply is no relationship between these two variables.
- *p → behaviour at work (personality "determines" behaviour at work):* This position assumes that some (but not all) personality traits determine, in some sense, various features of behaviour at work. People who adopt this position may well argue that various traits relate to, influence and determine various features of behaviour at work, or that some traits relate to all major work psychologies, or that most traits relate to one particular work psychology feature. The crucial axiom of this position is that personality traits "causally" determine behaviour at work, together perhaps with other related variables (e.g. non-verbal behaviour).
- *behaviour at work → p (behaviour at work "determines" personality):* This more

unusual position assumes that personality traits are, in some sense, a function of behaviour at work variables. This could be seen as a manifestation of the structurist–determinist position, in that organizational structure shapes ways of thinking and behaving that become set in behaviourally replicable traits. Precisely how this occurs, or which aspects of personality are shaped by which features of organizational structures and processes, is not clear, but what does appear to be at the core of this position is that personality traits and cognitive styles are primarily a function of external facets of the organization.

- *p ↔ behaviour at work (personality and behaviour at work are reciprocally determined)*: This somewhat more realistic synergistic view suggests that personality is a function of behaviour at work and vice versa; that is, there is bi-directional causality between personality and behaviour at work. This position allows for one direction of causality to be primary and the other to be secondary, so long as each has an influence on the other. There may also be differences within the position as to which aspects of personality and which of aspects of work psychology are singled out for reciprocal determinism.
- *p → behaviour at work; p_2 ↔ behaviour at work; p_3 ← behaviour at work; p_4 ≈ behaviour at work (mixed relationships)*: Some theorists may argue that, as both personality and behaviour at work are multifaceted, it is possible that all of the previous four relationships occur *simultaneously* – that is, some personality variables reciprocally determine specific behaviour at work variables; some personality variables uni-directionally determine some behaviour at work variables and vice versa; and, finally, some personality traits are not determined by, nor do they determine, behaviour at work, and some behaviour at work variables are neither determined by, nor determine, personality.
- *p × behaviour at work (personality and behaviour at work are moderated by other variables)*: This approach suggests that both personality and organizational behaviour are determined by another variable or group of variables. This moderator variable approach can take many forms, varying in the complexity of pathways and number of variables. Given the complexity of both work psychology and personality, it is hard to see how most theorists would opt for this "path-analysis" moderator variable approach. In a sense, this approach encapsulates all of the other models as well. Although it might well be true, there is certainly no agreement on the salient personality, occupational behaviour or moderator variables that are important, or on the precise causal links. Thus, while agreeing that the relationship is complex, multifaceted and multicausal, there are few explicit models of this process.

Understanding the cause or consequences of any behaviour at work process inevitably means looking at various variables concerning individuals (traits, abilities, needs), groups (cohesiveness, leadership communication pattern) and organizations (structure, culture, market). Like most behavioural issues, behaviour at work is multidetermined. Some variables have simple direct effects on behaviour at work; most interact with others to affect the behaviour. Some variables are causes, others consequences. Beware the simple model – it might be comprehensible but it is rarely comprehensive. The complexity of the forces that determine behaviour at work naturally require sophisticated models to reflect them.

Major methods of work psychology research

Academics and R&D (research and development) specialists are, by definition, engaged in scientific research. So, to a lesser extent, do consultants and managers themselves face problems? For the academic, research may or may not have an applied element to it – academic scientists may research an issue or problem out of curiosity. Indeed, some have been accused of indulging in what has been called "blue sky" research that has no known applications. Managers and R&D specialists, on the other hand, do research to solve highly specific problems. Their questions are thrown up by the organization and their justification for spending the research time is necessity. Although both groups may do excellent work, which can benefit each other, they have quite different models set out by Boehm (1980) in Figures 1.3 and 1.4.

Note that the academic researcher starts with an issue or problem that may interest them, whereas the applied researcher starts with an actual organizational problem. Note also that the practitioner needs to persuade others that the research is necessary and beneficial. Also, there are many more feedback loops in the practitioner model, which shows that the process is not as linear and simple as it is in pure academic research.

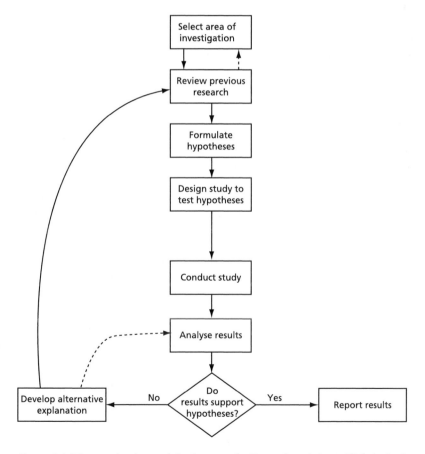

Figure 1.3 The academic model of research. Reproduced from Hakel, Sorker, Beek, & Moses (1982) with the permission of Sage Publications, Inc.

(a)

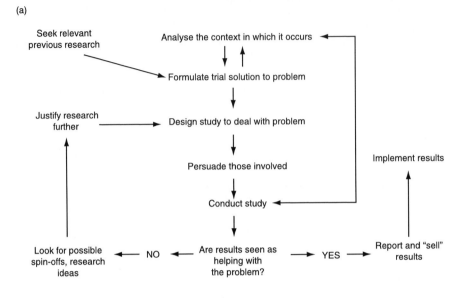

(b)

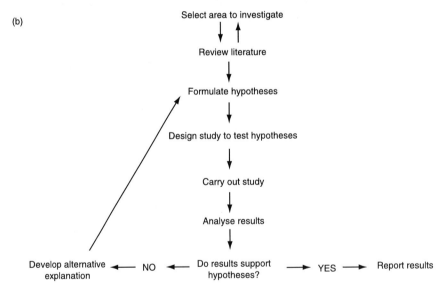

Figure 1.4 A model for the real-world enquiry process involved and, as a contrast, the traditional type of model given in most research methodological texts. Reproduced from Hakel, Sorker, Beek & Moses (1988) with the permission of Sage Publications, Inc.

Robson (2001) notes 16 characteristics that distinguish "real-world" applied research from pure research. In applied enquiry the emphasis tends to be on:

1 *solving problems* rather than *just gaining knowledge*;
2 *predicting effects* rather than *finding causes*;

3 *getting large effects* (looking for robust results) rather than *relations between variables* (and assessing statistical significance) and concern for actionable factors (where changes are feasible);

4 *developing and testing interventions, services and so forth* rather than *developing programmes and theories*;

5 *field* rather than *laboratory*;

6 *outside organization* (industry, business, school, etc) rather than *research institution*;

7 *strict time constraints* rather than *as long as the problem needs*;

8 *strict cost restraints* rather than *as much finance as the problem needs* (or the work is not attempted);

9 *little consistency of topic from one study to the next* rather than *high consistency from one study to the next*;

10 *topic initiated by sponsor* rather than *topic initiated by researcher*;

11 *often generalist researchers (need for familiarity with range of methods)* rather than *typically highly specialist (need to be at forefront of their discipline)*;

12 *little use of "true" experiments* rather than *much use of "true" experiments*;

13 *multiple methods* rather than *single methods*;

14 *orientated to the client* rather than *orientated to academic* peers (generally, and particularly in reporting);

15 *currently viewed as dubious by many academics* rather than *high academic prestige*;

16 *need for well-developed social skills* rather than *some need for social skills*.

(Robson, 2001: 11–12)

Robson further clarifies the distinction between laboratory, pure studies and applied research by citing actual published studies:

	Laboratory	**Real world**
Giving bad news	Subject has to inform next of kin in the lab	Coroner announcing death of partner
Interpersonal attraction	Anticipating interaction with a stranger: traits are listed as more or less similar to one's own	Fear and loathing at a college social function
Behaviour on a train	Response to an "implanted" crisis	Defense of common territory
Reactions to fear	Anticipating an electric shock	Learning first hand how to work on high steel in a 21-storey building
Superstition	Predicting sequence in which bulbs will light up	"Poker parlours" in California
Loosening of internal controls in response to anonymity	Students delivering shock when clothed in lab gowns and hoods	Tenants in high-rise housing exposed to danger
Impression formation	Students reading lists of adjectives	Folk-singers trying to "psyche out" an audience

Robson states:

> Cursory comparison of the models indicates several differences. As already stressed, the focus in real-world enquiry shifts from the usual scientific task to the

solution of a problem or resolution of an issue. The model is also substantially more complex, with a greater number of processes involved and increasingly complex interactions between the various stages. (Robson, 2001: 452)

Work psychology researchers are eclectic in their research methodology. Some very different methods are available to the work psychology researcher to investigate work psychology problems, test theories or explore ideas. To some extent, pragmatic and ethical issues dictate which method is used, although often it is the preferences and training of the researcher. Ideally, the research question should dictate which method is used and often that is the case. Each method has its advantages and disadvantages (Baron & Greenberg, 1990).

Work psychology in the laboratory

Is it possible to measure work psychology in a laboratory, such as how business people make decisions, the effects of group versus individual problem solving, and so on? The work psychology lab researcher's aim is to test the effects of one or more (manipulated) independent variables on one or more (measured) dependent variables. *Independent variables* in an experiment are those factors that are controlled or arranged by the experimenter and are often considered the cause of behaviour. *Dependent variables* refer to those behaviours of the participant that are observed or recorded by the experimenter. Thus, an independent variable may be *time* (short, intermediate and long periods) and the dependent variable *decision making*, so that one could test the effect of the time spent making decisions on the quality of these decisions.

Characteristic of the laboratory experiment is the investigator's ability to control the independent and dependent variables. Indeed, this aspect of control is one of the most important features of the laboratory experiment. Through this control, many extraneous complicating variables could be eliminated, so that one can measure the pure effect of one on the others.

In addition to control, the laboratory experiment also offers another important advantage: the ability to assign participants randomly to conditions. For an investigator to draw conclusions regarding cause and effect, he or she must be sure that the pattern of results was not attributable to some systematic difference in the groups being compared (i.e. all women in one group, or all volunteers in another). On average, *randomization* ensures an equality of participant characteristics across the various experimental conditions, so that we can be sure different groups are equivalent before the study takes place.

One other characteristic of the laboratory experiment should be mentioned: the *manipulation check* – a way of ensuring that the experiment has "worked" from the perspective of those taking part in it. Although experimenters are able to control the independent variable, it is still important for them to be sure that the participants in the experiment perceive the manipulation as it is intended.

Advantages

The advantages of the laboratory experiment as a means of acquiring knowledge have been largely summarized above. Principal among these is the ability of the experimenter to control the independent variables and to assign participants randomly to conditions. The two capabilities provide some basis for conclusions regarding cause and effect.

Furthermore, the laboratory allows the investigator to "sort out" factors – to simplify the more complex events of the natural world by breaking them down into their component parts.

Disadvantages

Although the laboratory experiment has some considerable advantages in terms of its ability to isolate and control variables, it has some substantial disadvantages. In recent years, these disadvantages have become the topic of considerable debate. Four major issues of concern have been the possible unnaturalness of the laboratory setting, the reactions of participants to the laboratory setting, the possible influence of experimenters on their results, and deception and ethics (Baron & Greenberg, 1990).

The issue of relevance concerns the artificiality of the laboratory setting and the fact that many of the situations created in the laboratory bear little direct relationship to the situations a person encounters in real organizational life. Aronson & Carlsmith (1968) have argued for the distinction between *experimental realism* and *mundane realism*. They contend that, in the laboratory, one can devise situations that have impact and that evoke valid psychological processes (experimental realism), even if the situation itself does not look like the real world (mundane realism). Yet, it remains true that many laboratory tasks appear suspiciously artificial and their *external validity* has not been demonstrated. External validity refers to the "generalizability" of research findings to other populations, treatment variables and measurement variables. It is naturally most important that the findings demonstrated in a laboratory can equally be demonstrated in the workplace.

A second criticism of the laboratory experiment focuses on the reactions of participants to the laboratory setting. These reactions may involve *demand characteristics* and *evaluation apprehension*. The first term refers to the fact that the experimental setting may evoke certain demands – that is, expectations on the part of participants to act in the way that they think the experimenter would wish (Orne, 1962). It may involve pleasing or displeasing the experimenter by doing what he or she expects (or the opposite). Evaluation apprehension refers to the concerns that a participant has about being observed and judged while in the laboratory setting. Because participants come to a laboratory experiment knowing that the investigator is interested in some aspect of their behaviour, they may be apprehensive or anxious about the way they are being observed and hence behave unnaturally. A third criticism of the laboratory experiment concerns *experimenter expectancies* (Rosenthal. 1966). It has been shown in a variety of situations that an experimenter, knowing the hypothesis of the study, can unknowingly influence the results of the study. The influence of these experimenter expectancies can be controlled to a large extent. For example, many experiments involve instructions that have been tape recorded in advance, thus assuring constancy in experimenter approach to all participants. Other techniques include the use of a "blind" experimenter, wherein the individual conducting the experiment is not informed of the experimental hypotheses and thus is less likely to exert a systematic bias on the results.

A fourth problem concerns the *ethics* of laboratory research, particularly when deception is involved. To ensure participants are naïve or unaware about the point of the study (and to reduce demand characteristics and evaluation apprehension), they are often deceived. Although they are fully de-briefed afterwards, the ethical problems must be faced.

Work psychology theories can be tested in laboratories, such as the efficacy of brain-storming (see Chapter 10), but the problems of ecological validity mean that it is often not the most ideal method.

Field experiment

In contrast to the laboratory experiment, the setting of the field experiment is a natural one and the participants are not generally aware that they are subjects in an experiment. Thus, for instance, one could study the effect on attractiveness or selection, or the effect of the response time to letters versus faxes versus e-mail in any organization by manipulating or measuring the independent variable carefully. Rather than contriving an artificial situation in a laboratory, the investigator who uses a field experiment to test a hypothesis is looking at behaviour in its natural setting. Like the laboratory experiment, in the field experiment the experimenter has control of the independent variables and the random assignment of participants to conditions.

Advantages

The advantages of the field experiment are that, by focusing on behaviour in a natural setting, the experimenter can be much more certain of the external validity of his or her findings. Furthermore, because participants are generally unaware of their status as subjects, the problems of reactivity and the participants' desire to be seen in a positive light are eliminated. In addition, because control over the independent variable and the principles of randomization are maintained, the field experiment allows the same possibilities for conclusions about cause and effect as does the laboratory experiment.

Disadvantages

Although the field experiment may seem to be an ideal combination of the application of the strict rules of experimentation with the realism of natural behaviour settings, it too has some disadvantages. These disadvantages relate to the nature of the independent variable, the nature of the dependent variable, the ethics of the experiment, and the practical difficulties involved. Because the experimenter is working in a complex natural setting where many events may be occurring simultaneously, the independent variable in the study must be quite obvious to the potential participant. Subtle manipulations of a variable may simply go unnoticed. The experimental independent variable is, in effect, competing with all of the other stimuli present in the setting.

The dependent variable in a field experiment needs to be selected carefully. The experimenters must be able to observe the dependent-variable behaviour readily and to judge it reliably. An additional problem in field experimentation concerns ethics. Is it reasonable for the investigator to involve individuals in an experiment without their knowledge or permission? Finally, the field experiment often poses practical problems. In contrast to the investigator in the laboratory, the investigator in the field has no control over the majority of events in the environment; unexpected events may reduce or destroy the effectiveness of the manipulation (Baron & Greenberg, 1990).

Quasi-experimental research

The defining characteristics of quasi-experimental research are that the investigator does not have full experimental control over the independent variables but does have extensive control over how, when and for whom the dependent variable is measured (Campbell & Stanley, 1966). Generally, these experiments involve behaviour in a natural setting and focus on the effect of intervention in a system of continuing behaviour.

In other cases, the intervention may be a natural disaster, such as flood, earthquake or tornado, a power blackout or the introduction of new laws. Other more common factors may be a strike or the compulsory change to new technology. The experimenter would have no control over the independent variable, but he or she could carefully select a set of dependent variables to measure the effect of the phenomenon.

Advantages

One unique advantage of quasi-experimental research conducted in a natural setting is that it allows for the study of very strong variables that cannot be manipulated or controlled by the experimenter. Often, too, quasi-experimental research deals with policy decisions that have consequences for very large numbers of people. The broad impact of such decisions gives added weight to the external validity of the study, in a manner that can rarely be matched in the more limited laboratory or field experiment.

Disadvantages

Because the investigator has no control over the primary independent variable in quasi-experimental research, it is always possible that other uncontrolled variables are affecting the dependent-variable behaviour. Also, random assignment of participants to conditions can rarely be assumed in the quasi-experimental design. Often such research must literally be done "on the run". Furthermore, the arbitrariness of events in the quasi-experimental world precludes the experimenter's ability to vary factors according to any theoretical model. The intensity of a stressful event, for example, might be an important variable in predicting the nature of response to stress. Nonetheless, it is clearly impossible for the experimenter to control such a variable, and hence the levels of intensity would need to be accepted as they naturally occurred.

Participant observation

These field studies are characterized by their in-depth consideration of a limited group of people. The investigator in this setting plays a more reactive role than in the field experiment. Rather than manipulate some aspect of the environment and observe the changes that occur, the investigator in the participant observer role records as much information as possible about the characteristics of that situation without altering it in any substantial way. Most often, people in the environment are aware of the investigator's presence and the general purpose of the investigation. The investigator is a *participant observer* – that is, someone actively engaged in the activities of the group while maintaining records of the group members' behaviours. They are not the classic time-and-motion observers shown in cartoons but part of the working group who monitor and observe as they work (Baron & Greenberg, 1990).

Observation is the key element of the field-study method. Considerable time must be devoted in advance to familiarizing oneself with the environment and becoming aware of the kinds of behaviours that are most likely to occur. Then, one must decide which types of behaviour are to be recorded, how, when and why.

Once categories of behaviour are selected for observation, the investigator must devise specific methods of recording the desired information. Finally, the observer must conduct a series of preliminary investigations to determine the *reliability* (or reproducibility) of the measures. In other words, it must be demonstrated that a series of *different* observers watching the same event and using the methods chosen to record observations will code the behaviour in the *same* way. Without such reliability, a coding system merely reflects one observer's biases and cannot be used as a basis for scientific statement.

Advantages

The major advantage of participant observation lies in its realism. The focus of the study is on events as they normally occur in a real-life setting. Furthermore, because most field studies take place over an extended period, they provide information about the sequence and development of behaviours that cannot be gained in the one-shot observation typical of field and laboratory experiments. Additionally, the duration of the field study generally allows for the collection of several different types of dependent measures.

Disadvantages

Although well conducted field studies furnish a wealth of data, the lack of control in such settings can be a problem. Because there is no controlled independent variable, it is difficult to form conclusions regarding cause and effect. Although there are some statistical techniques to assist in drawing causal conclusions, the process is a more difficult one than in the controlled experimental design. A second potential problem in the field study is the participants' awareness of the investigator's observations. When participants are aware of being observed, their behaviour may be *reactive* – that is, influenced by the process of observation. However, most experienced observers believe that in a long-term field study the participants become indifferent to the observer's presence, although the problem remains a serious one in briefer studies (Baron & Greenberg, 1990).

Archival research

Archival research refers to the analysis of any existing records that have been produced or maintained by persons or organizations other than the experimenter. In other words, the original reason for collecting the records was not a management study. Newspaper reports and government records of airplane fatalities, weather conditions and employment figures are forms of archival data. Other sources of material include books and magazines, folk stories of pre-literate societies, personal letters and speeches by public figures. Thus, one can examine from available records the effect of national unemployment on staff turnover or the effects of sunny weather (or cricket/tennis matches) on absenteeism.

Advantages

First, it allows the investigator to test hypotheses over a wider range of time and societies than would otherwise be possible. Many records date back centuries, a period of time that cannot be examined today using the other methods we have discussed. Demonstrating the validity of a hypothesis in several different cultures and historical periods, instead of being restricted to a specific group in the present time and place, gives us considerable confidence in the validity of that hypothesis as a test of human behaviour in general.

A second advantage of the archival method is that it uses *unobtrusive measures* – measures that did not cause reactivity in the participants at the time they were collected. Because the information used in archival research was originally collected for some other purpose, there is little or no chance that demand characteristics or evaluation apprehension will be problems for the present investigator.

Disadvantages

Although experimenters doing research did not collect the data personally and thus are spared some problems in terms of reactivity, they may encounter some difficulties in terms of data availability. A researcher will often not be able to locate the kind of data needed to test a hypothesis. Not being able to design the dependent measures, the investigator is left at the mercy of those who collected the data. Sometimes, of course, creativity and ingenuity will help the investigator to locate the kinds of data needed; in other cases, however, missing or inaccurate records will prevent an adequate experimental test. Even if the material is available, it is sometimes difficult to categorize it in the way necessary to answer the research question. Such procedures are time-consuming, although the development of computer programs has provided welcome assistance in some instances (Baron & Greenberg, 1990).

Simulation and role playing

Although the range of simulation studies is considerable, the aim of each is to imitate some aspect of a real-world situation to gain more understanding of people's psychological processes. Participants in these studies are typically asked to *role play* – to adopt a part and act as if they were in the real situation. Thus, one may ask a board of directors to role play a board meeting, or a working party to role play an important decision-making meeting. In advance of them taking part, the participants are fully informed about the situation and are asked to develop their part to the best of their ability.

Advantages

The success of simulation or a role-play study depends heavily on the degree of involvement that the role play can engender. If the participants get deeply involved in the setting, then the simulation may well approximate the real-life conditions that it intends to match. Furthermore, because participants are fully informed of the purposes of the study in advance, they basically take on the role of co-investigators, a role that is both ethically and humanistically more satisfying in many respects than the more typical experimental subject role in which the participant is unaware of many of the experimenter's intentions. An additional advantage of the simulation is that it may allow the investigator to study in the laboratory phenomena and situations that are difficult to study in the real world.

Disadvantages

In spite of their advantages, simulation and role playing are two of the most controversial methods used by behavioural scientists. Critics of the method claim that, when one asks participants to act as if they are in a certain role, they will do only what they think they *might* do and not necessarily what they *would* do in the real situation (Aronson & Carlsmith, 1968). In addition, the problems of experimental demands and evaluation apprehension, discussed earlier in relation to laboratory experiments, are even more serious when the participant is fully informed of the purposes of the study. On the other hand, proponents of role playing argue that, to some degree, the participants in an experiment are always playing a role in real life, whether it is the general role of subject or a more specific role defined by the investigator.

Surveys, questionnaires and interviews

Although many other methods in work psychology make use of questionnaires as part of their procedures, survey and interview methods rely *solely* on this type of information. In both cases, the investigator defines an area for research and designs a set of questions that will elicit the beliefs, attitudes and self-reported experiences of the respondent in relation to the research topic.

Designing a good questionnaire is difficult. Some considerations that enter into the design include the wording of questions, the provision of sufficient responses, and the format of the questionnaire itself. Considerable pre-testing is necessary to ensure that the questions are objective, unbiased, understandable to the average respondent, and specific enough to elicit the desired information (Baron & Greenberg, 1990).

When the questionnaire is being presented by an interviewer, additional precautions against biasing the responses are necessary. The issue of experimenter bias, discussed earlier in relation to laboratory experiments, can be a problem with the interview method if the interviewer consciously or unconsciously encourages some responses and discourages or seems uninterested in others. Thus, interviewers must be carefully trained to standardize the delivery of questions to respondents. In addition, the interview method requires some skills on the part of the interviewer in developing rapport, so that the respondent will be willing to answer questions in a straightforward and honest manner. Interviews are notoriously unreliable if not conducted by highly trained personnel.

In both questionnaire surveys and interviews, the investigator must be concerned with *sampling procedures*.

Advantages

A major advantage of both survey questionnaires and interviews is that they allow the investigator to formulate the issues of concern very specifically. Rather than devising a situation to elicit desired behaviour or finding a natural situation in which to observe that behaviour, constructors of questionnaires directly question people about the behaviour or area under investigation. Survey questionnaires are easier and more economical to use than interview procedures. In addition, they afford greater anonymity to the respondent, which is important in the case of sensitive or personal issues. Face-to-face interviews, on the other hand, allow the interviewer to gather additional information from observation. Furthermore, the interviewer can clarify questions that may be confusing to the respondent and ensure that the person intended to answer the questions is indeed the person responding.

Disadvantages

Perhaps the major difficulty with self-report data, whether from interviews or surveys, is the issue of accuracy. Other topics may lead to embellishments by respondents, who attempt to place themselves in a favourable light. As suggested earlier, survey questionnaires and interviews also have opposite sets of weaknesses. The survey questionnaire gives the investigator less control over the situation and cannot assure the conditions under which the questionnaire is being administered, who is answering it, and whether the respondent fully understands the questions. For its part, the interview is more costly, more time-consuming, and is more susceptible to examiner bias.

In summary, questionnaire and interview methods allow the investigator to ask directly about the issues of concern. Particularly in the case of questionnaires, very large-scale studies are possible, thus allowing greater generalizability of the results. However, both methods rely on the accuracy and honesty of the respondent and depend on self-reports of behaviour rather than observations of the behaviour itself.

One should not gain the impression, however, that work psychologists make an *either/or* choice of methods. They nearly always follow the *multi-trait, multi-method* approach advocated for so many years by measuring more than one trait (or behaviour pattern) by more than one method. Methods may be *combined* (e.g. questionnaires supplemented by means of interviews) or used *sequentially* (e.g. testing specific hypotheses in the laboratory and afterwards in the "real world" by means of field research).

To a large extent, the research question dictates the methodology. But there are other important considerations such as reliability and validity. Other methods may be used, not for research but for specific work psychology purposes. There are, for instance, various methods one could use to *select* people for a job. Cook (1990) lists ten methods and five criteria. Although not all would agree with this analysis, it provides a useful map for the work psychology practitioner (Table 1.1).

There is, of course, a difference between the use of tests for selection and the usefulness of the tests as methods for work psychology research. For instance, interviews can be most useful to understand how a management team might see the future, but, because of lying and self-presentational strategies, they do not make for a very good selection technique.

Conclusion

Even among the social sciences, work psychology is a young discipline. It is the child of a mixed marriage with many and varied relatives and, as a result, it has, or perhaps did have, something of an identity crisis. At one moment it leans heavily on the heritage of one parent (discipline), at another preferring the other parent. But this young child is

Table 1.1 Summary assessment of ten selection tests by five criteria

	Validity	Cost	Practicality	Generality	Legality
Interviews	Low	Medium/high	High	High	Untested
References	Moderate	Very low	High	High	A few doubts
Peer ratings	High	Very low	Very limited	Military only	Untested
Biodata*	High	Medium	High	High	Some doubts
Ability tests	High	Low	High	High	Major doubts
Personality tests	Low	Low	Fair	White-collar	Untested
Assessment centre**	High	Very high	Fair	Fairly high	No problems
Work sample	High	High	High	Blue-collar only	No problems
Job knowledge test	High	Low	High	Blue-collar only	Some doubts
Education	Low	Low	High	High	Major doubts

* Biodata are biographical information obtainable from classic application tests.
** This involves putting candidates through a wide range of procedures over an extended period.

Source: Cook (1990). Reproduced with the permission of John Wiley & Sons.

growing up. More and more people are being employed to understand it and, as a result, its future looks progressively secure. Work psychology is an applied science and as such has to answer the salient questions of the day. It is eclectic in its methodology to investigate issues.

Organizational or work psychology is the study of how organizations influence the thoughts (beliefs, values), feelings (emotions) and, most importantly, behaviours of all those working in the organization. Work psychology has both psychology and sociology as parents, and many other related disciplines as close relations. This mixed parentage has led to many different terms being used, often synonymously, to describe what work psychologists do. Their primary concerns are selection and training, appraisal and counselling, ergonomic design and occupational health, organizational change and development, industrial relations and communication, and work design.

Many central questions remain, of which many will not easily be answered: Is work psychology a science? What is an organization? How do events outside the organization influence behaviour within it? How do individuals within an organization influence it? How impartial and disinterested are work psychologists?

Some of the limitations and shortsightedness of researchers in the past are changing. The effects of culture are being more widely acknowledged, so that different perspectives are being considered. Work psychology is now more concerned with theory development and understanding the importance of historical trends on thinking, and both theories and methods are now reflecting the complex number of variables that together influence organizational behaviour.

One major difference between psychological and sociological work psychology researchers is the extent to which the former stress how individual differences and personality traits influence organizational behaviour, whereas the latter stress situational and organization features.

Both practitioners and academics from other disciplines have condemned work psychology as being no more than common sense. It is, through various quizzes, fairly easy to demonstrate this to be untrue; however, there are good reasons why ideas, theories and methods do percolate down to most people. The media is hungry for work psychology research, regularly reviews books and frequently interviews thinkers in the area. It is therefore easy to explain how "technical" ideas soon become well known.

There are few immutable laws of behaviour in work psychology, although many mini-theories have been tested. Most researchers in the area are eager to be scientific in their approach, adopting a wide range of methods. These methods vary from the most austere and controlled laboratory experiment to quasi-historical research in the archives. Some experiments are done in the natural setting and occasionally particular conditions (such as a strike) allow specific hypotheses to be tested. Sometimes researchers have to be participant observers by actually joining groups and closely recording their behaviour. Sometimes, role playing or simulating an actual past or imaginary future situation is used as a research method to understand the complex dynamics of organizational behaviour.

Surveys, questionnaires and interviews remain one of the most common research methods. As with each of the above techniques researchers have to be eclectic, choosing either the most appropriate or the best combination of methods. Using multiple methods has the advantage of replicating findings and combining disadvantages and artifacts associated with different methods.

Work psychology is nearly 100 years old! Starting out in a very small way and showing considerable growth and development over the past 50 years, it is now a healthy, vibrant discipline. Coinciding with the relatively sudden but significant increases in management education in business schools, it has become a popular area of research and study for many individuals.

A research perspective

Management gurus

A cynic once remarked that the term "guru" was applied to management thinkers because journalists could not spell "charlatan". Some of the acknowledged gurus are historical figures, such as the sixteenth-century Italian Machiavelli or those figures who were the founders of the discipline, such as Weber, Taylor, Fayol and others (see Chapter 2).

However, the growth of management science, business schools and management consultants since the 1960s has meant a sharp increase in the number of business gurus. Paradoxically, most of the gurus come from America and, to a lesser extent, Britain, both of which have seen a strong relative decline in their economic power and productivity. Nevertheless, gurus act as a useful catalyst for change and for challenging the efficacy of current practices.

Kennedy (1991) has reviewed the ideas of 33 gurus in the world of management. But let us consider just the ten most famous and their central ideas:

- *Adair*: Leaders of successful groups need to monitor three factors equally all the time – the *task* being set, the *team* and its morale and functioning, and the *individual* including oneself.
- *Bennis*: Leaders need a vision, need to communicate it (manage meaning in the organization), they need to be trusted and they need to manage themselves. Managers do things right, but leaders do the right thing.
- *de Bono*: Managers need to be creative by lateral thinking, which has five steps: escaping from fixed patterns of behaviour, challenging assumptions, generating alternatives, jumping to new ideas, and seeking to find entry points so that one can move forwards.
- *Deming*: The key to quality is reducing variation in production. Among his statistically derived recommendations (there were 14 in all) are: improve constantly and forever every

process of planning, production and service; eliminate quotas and numerical targets; and encourage education and self-improvement in everyone.

- *Drucker*: The originator of management by objective. Corporate goals should be divided into objectives and clearly assigned to units and individuals. Every organization should regularly inspect and assess the product, process, technology and service. Management of all organizations is essentially the same process akin to that of the conductor of an orchestra.
- *Kanter*: She first stressed the idea of empowering employees in the new "fast-entrepreneurial" flatter, decentralized organizations. She stresses cooperation above competition and the operation of business without the "crutch" of hierarchies.
- *Mintzberg*: Whatever managers do, they have essentially three major roles: interpersonal (figurehead, leader and liaison person); informational (monitor, disseminator and spokes-person); and decisional (entrepreneur, disturbance handler, resource allocator and negotiator). The last group is the most important. Management skills are as important as management ideas and concepts.
- *Ohmae*: Strategic advance comes from planning and strategy, which should be based on: an organization's capability to increase market share/profitability; exploiting any relative superiority; challenging accepted assumptions; and the development of innovations such as new markets or products.
- *Peters*: Company excellence can be guarded by the eight S's – structure, strategy, systems, style of management, skills, corporate strengths, staff and shared values. Managers need to move away from the hierarchical pyramid structure to one that is horizontal, cross-functional and cooperative.
- *Porter*: Also believes an organization's competitive advantage comes from good strategy. All managers should analyse and plan with three factors in mind: the existing rivalry between firms; the threat of new entrants to the market, and substitute products and services; and the bargaining power of suppliers and buyers. He believes that one can understand, predict and measure the competitive advantage of nations.
- *Schein*: The employee and employer have a formal, legal work contract, but also a psycho-logical contract, which includes expectations about how they are treated and encouraged to develop abilities and skills. Assumptions on both sides help form corporate culture. They also develop career anchors, which are the perceptions individuals hold about their organization and which encourage them to remain in it, or leave it.

There are, of course, many other gurus alive and dead. We shall encounter many others of many different nationalities and persuasions, from the Dutchman Hofstede through to the Irishman Handy. In a small but distinctive way, all have made a contribution to the world of organizational behaviour.

A cross-cultural perspective

The rise of many Southeast Asian economies over the past 20 years has led many to speculate on the next century being dominated by the Pacific Rim (despite the crash in the 1990s). This has encouraged many researchers to attempt to understand the niceties of Asian business etiquette and the values underlying it.

Bedi (1991) has listed 25 recommendations for managing day-to-day business relationships in Asia. To some extent these illuminate the values of the society:

- Avoid put-downs: it is very rude to publicly embarrass or humiliate people even (indeed particularly) if not done deliberately.
- Don't expect people to take sides: it is not appropriate to publicly take sides in a heated argument. Reticence to take sides does not therefore imply the rejection of either or both decisions.

- Keep communication channels open: to squash rumours it is better to create an environment in which all relevant people are kept informed and feel able to express their concerns.
- Differentiate between "yes" and "no": what is meant and what is said are not always the same. Various polite formal usages obscure the actual intentions from certain outsiders.
- Don't be alarmed by different odds: many Asians who enjoy gambling often appear rash in their personal betting but remain cautious, prudent and sober when dealing with business issues.
- Don't name-drop to intimidate: it is insulting when name-dropping precedes a presentation of the merits of a product or service.
- Be sensitive to Atlantic crossfire: Asian managers don't understand or enjoy European versus American banter or repartee; they prefer not to take sides.
- Don't fall for the sexist stigma: many Asian customers appear overtly sexist and discriminatory, but this may not be a manifestation of deliberate sexism.
- Keep your fitness fad private: health consciousness is a private matter not to be publicly displayed to score "hero-points".
- Cooperate before competing: most human endeavours demand that one learns to cooperate before competing; hence, it is cooperation that builds teamwork and trust, more than overt competition.
- Don't take courtesy for granted: courtesy is a deep-rooted traditional hospitality that is often at the cost of personal discomfort and should not be taken for granted because of one's position.
- Be careful about community service: make sure you have the time and patience for it; be clear about what it is that you offer; do not be too closely identified with any one organization; and avoid becoming too closely associated with a sectarian organization.
- Don't emphasize your contacts: this tends to emphasize one's influence over one's competence.
- Be discreet about offering domestic advice: the solutions to domestic problems are seen as not being based on common sense or even logic but tradition, face or family pride.
- Avoid expletives: the use of swearing or other foul language in anger or with a not well-known peer is severely frowned upon.
- Don't mix exclusively with Westernized Asians: whereas Westerners feel more comfortable around Asians who speak their language and understand their customs, these Westernized Asians may be deeply mistrusted by those less Westernized.
- Control your anger: a loss of temper is unacceptable, especially to those lower down in the hierarchy, and is not easily forgotten.
- Don't take offence at "fat" remarks: those may be meant as a compliment not an insult. Being large is often seen as being prosperous.
- Don't "prioritize": using various management techniques may be seen to dehumanize relations with associates; it may pay to keep certain things vague.
- Communicate through gifts: gifts are given frequently to smooth human relations and should not ever be seen as a bribe.
- Don't anglicize names: learn, at the very least, to pronounce correctly a person's full name without a lazy anglicization.
- Avoid "boring" subjects: it is easy to be ethnocentric and to talk too extensively about topics that bore your peers.
- Don't be impatient with ambiguity: precise, clear-cut, definitive and direct responses may be desirable in the West but not necessarily in the East.
- Select your speakers carefully: inspirational speakers or those that tell many jokes may be seen as popular in the West but are frequently distrusted in Asia and seen to be trying to cover up something.
- Don't expect perfection: although it is thought of as good to strive for quality, extreme

perfectionists are seen as making people feel inadequate and filling them with fear, rather than inspiration.

Bond (1991) set out four basic beliefs of the Chinese, which are implicit "golden threads" of beliefs that bind the general philosophy together:

- The Chinese believe hierarchies and inequalities are natural, necessary and inevitable. It is better and more efficient to accept inequality than to attempt to impose equality, which leads to chaos.
- The basis of inequality is achievement (through academic means), wealth and, perhaps most importantly, moral example.
- All laws are of necessity rigid, artificial and insensitive to subtle differences and changing circumstances. Judgements made by wise and compassionate people are a better way to regulate the social, personal and political world.
- People have to be interdependent and it is thus crucially important that children are taught skills and values that ensure harmony. Families are the most powerful socializing agent and the most important model for society.

A human resources perspective

Human resources or personnel management is the application of psychological and management science principles in an organization. Traditionally, human resources is seen to have six primary functions:

- Planning, recruitment and selection, and other issues around staffing the organization.
- Training and development of staff at all levels.
- Ascertaining and monitoring all aspects of compensation, namely pay and conditions.
- Issues around safety and health in the workplace.
- Understanding and implementing employee and labour relations.
- Approach research, such as climate/culture surveys, benchmarking other companies, etc.

Just as in other parts of the organization, the human resources function is affected by factors inside and outside the organization, which include changes in the law (e.g. as a function of the European Union), the labour force (people living longer, more migrants), public attitudes to the environment and certain products (petrochemicals), trade union activities (decline, power), stockholder and owner issues (long- versus short-term profits), competition from others, customer demands, and new technology.

One of the major human resources functions is to monitor and improve the quality of working life. Human resources managers need to be constantly aware of all the changes in work psychology and related fields. As Lewin (1951) noted, "there is nothing as practical as good theory".

Howard (1991) has looked at current human resources practice and linked it to organizational issues. Helpfully, he presents a table without jargon, which sets out, in detail, the current concerns of many human resources professionals (reproduced here as Table 1.2).

Human resources or personnel departments are found in nearly all large organizations. Most claim their greatest asset (sometimes liability) is "their people".

All human resources is essentially management of people. Yet all managers are involved in managing people and the management of an organization's human resources is primarily a line or operating management responsibility. The degree to which human resources activities are divided between line or operating managers and the human resources manager and his or her department varies from organization to organization.

In some organizations, a human resources specialist may handle all negotiations as their responsibility, with the human resources manager taking an advisory role, or having no involvement at all. Line managers in some organizations are now starting to compete with human resources specialists to assume responsibility for many traditional human resources activities.

In this sense, human resources people become redundant because their jobs are now taken by

Table 1.2 Work environment changes and human resources practice

Organization responses	Themes of HR practice	Organization development	Human resources training	Individual evaluation
Constant training	Continuous learning	Link organization renewal to continuous learning	Training and re-training; support external development	Select for learning ability; appraise/reward development
Constant innovation	Generating change	Foster climate supporting new ideas; quality improvement programmes	Re-train for new products/services; develop innovativeness	Select for creativity; appraisal/reward risk-taking
Rapid pace of change	Responsiveness to change	Team-building for responsiveness; intergroup problem-solving; conflict resolution	Re-train for new products/services; develop adaptability; resistance to stress	Select and appraise for adaptability, coping
Strategic planning	Coordination of strategy	Team-building for goal clarity and agreement	Gap analyses; help develop plans and tie training to them	Environmental scans and force analyses; tie selection to strategic plans
Flexible structures	Participation	Survey feedback and employee input; autonomous workgroups	Training for empowerment and leadership	Selection for participativeness and leadership
Quality emphasis	Excellence	Quality improvement programmes	Group problem-solving skills for quality improvement programmes	Selection for high work standards
Customer orientation	Service	Team-building to facilitate customer service	Training for customer service	Selection for interpersonal skills
Constituency management	Equitable treatment; flexible HR policies	Foster equitable climate via team building; survey feedback	Training to diversity; basic skills training; gear training to diverse population	Fair selection practices; drug and honesty testing; wide recruiting

Source: Reproduced from Howard (1991: 219–51) with the permission of the Guilford Press.

HR = human resources.

newly empowered and better-educated managers who are taught human resources processes and procedures before or while in the job. Stone (1995) maintains that if human resources specialists are to survive, indeed thrive, they need to obey certain crucial rules:

- The human resources function should always be carried out as close to the operational "sharp end" as feasible.
- The human resources "strategy and policy" function should always be carried out as close to the strategy and policy decision maker as possible.
- The human resources function should never have "line" authority – its only power should be through influence via its know-how, skills and expertise.
- A human resources professional who craves real direct authority should become a line manager and not compromise the real task of the human resources function.
- The best manager of human resources is rarely the head of the human resources department.
- The best manager of human resources is a line manager who is a natural or is well trained.

Human resources professionals must, like all others (marketing, manufacturing, finance), understand the importance of, be sensitive to, and actually help in, achieving bottom-line targets. This may therefore involve down-sizing, instituting "pay for performance" schemes, and attempting to demonstrate the cost-efficiency of training. All human resources departments are, of course, also responsible for:

- *Cost containment*: human resources objectives and activities should *genuinely* focus on cost reduction via reduced headcount and improved expense control. Indeed, human resources departments should themselves model the "lean and mean" department.
- *Customer service*: human resources activities should aim to achieve improved customer service through recruitment and selection, employee training and development, rewards and motivation, and the like; again, the department should have an eye on its own internal and external customers and seek out their feedback regularly.
- *Social responsibility*: human resources objectives should centre on legal compliance and achieving improvements in areas such as equal opportunity, occupational health and safety, and development programmes, while bearing in mind their organization is neither a charity nor uncritical of political correctness.
- *Organizational effectiveness*: human resources should focus on organizational structure, employee motivation, employee innovation, adaptability to change, flexible reward systems, employee relations, and so on.

The old-style personnel manager (often a retired military officer) can evolve into a sophisticated human resources professional. Managed properly, the human resources function should demonstrate to the rest of the organization that rather than a waste of space, it is a significant contributor to company strategy (Stone, 1995).

References

Arnold, J., Robertson, I., & Cooper, C. (1991). *Work psychology*. London: Pitman.
Aronson, E., & Carlsmith, J. (1968). Experimentation in social psychology. In G. Lindsey & E. Aronson (eds.), *Handbook of social psychology* (pp. 1–79). Reading, MA: Addison-Wesley.
Baron, R. (1983). *Behaviour in organizations*. Boston, MA: Allyn & Bacon.
Baron, R., & Greenberg, J. (1990). *Behaviour in organizations*. Boston, MA: Allyn & Bacon.
Bedi, H. 1991. *Understanding the Asian manager*. Hong Kong: Allen & Unwin.

Boehm, V. (1980). Research in the real world – a conceptual model. *Personal Psychology, 33*, 495–503.

Bond, M. (1991). *Beyond the Chinese face*. Hong Kong: Oxford University Press.

Brickman, P. (1980). A social psychology of human concerns. In R. Gilmour & S. Duck (eds.), *The development of social psychology* (pp. 5–25). London: Academic Press.

Campbell, D., & Stanley, J. (1966). *Experimental and quasi-experimental designs for research*. Chicago, IL: Rand-McNally.

Cherrington, D. (1989). *Organizational behaviour: The management of individual and organizational performance*. Boston, MA: Allyn & Bacon.

Cook, M. (1990). *Personnel selection and productivity*. Chichester: Wiley.

Davis-Blake, A., & Preffer, J. (1989). Just a mirage: The search for dispositional effects in organizational research. *Academy of Management Review, 14*, 385–400.

Dipboye, R., Smith, C., & Howell, W. (1994). *Understanding industrial and organizational psychology*. New York: Harcourt Brace.

Eysenck, H. (ed.). (1981). *A model for personality*. Berlin: Springer-Verlag.

Fletcher, G. (1984). Psychology and common sense. *American Psychologist, 39*, 203–213.

Furnham, A. (1983). Social psychology as common sense. *Bulletin of the British Psychological Society, 36*, 105–109.

Furnham, A. (2001). *The 3D manager*. London: Whurr Publishers.

Giddens, A. (1987). *Social theory and modern sociology*. Cambridge: Polity Press.

Hakel, M., Sorker, M., Beek, M., & Moses, J. (1982). *Making it happen: Designing research with implementation in mind*. London: Sage.

Hargreaves, D. (1981). Common-sense models of action. In A. Chapman & D. Jones (eds.), *Models of man* (pp. 215–225). Leicester: British Psychological Society.

Howard, A. (1991). New directions for human resources practice. In D. Bray & Associates (eds.), *Working with organizations and their people* (pp. 219–251). New York: Guilford Press.

Jewell, L. (1985). *Contemporary industrial/organizational psychology*. New York: West.

Kennedy, C. (1991). *Guide to the management gurus*. London: Century Business.

Kenrick, D., & Funder, D. (1988). Profiting from controversy: lessons from the person–situation debate. *American Psychologist, 43*, 23–34.

Kerlinger, F. (1973). *Foundations of behavioural research*. New York: Holt, Rinehart & Winston.

Lacy, A. (1976). *A dictionary of philosophy*. London: Routledge & Kegan Paul.

Lewin, K. (1951). *Field theory in social science*. New York: Harper & Row.

Lowenberg, G., & Conrad, K. (1998). *Current perspective in industrial/organizational psychology*. Boston, MA: Allyn & Bacon.

Marx, M. (1970). *Learning theories*. New York: Macmillan.

Marx, M. (1976). Formal theory. In M. Marx & F. Goodson (eds.), *Theories in contemporary psychology* (pp. 234–260). New York: Macmillan.

Milgram, S. (1974). *Obedience to authority*. London: Tavistock.

Mischel, W., & Mischel, H. (1981). *Children's knowledge of psychological principles*. Unpublished manuscript, Department of Psychology, Stanford University, Stanford, CA.

Morgan, R. (1986). *The image of organizations*. London: Sage.

Muchinsky, P. (1983). *Psychology applied to work*. Homewood, IL: Dorsey.

Newton, T., & Keenan, A. (1988). Is work involvement an attribute of the person or the environment? *Journal of Occupational Behaviour, 4*, 169–178.

Nicholson, N. (2001). *Executive instinct*. New York: Crown.

Orne, M. (1962). On the social psychology of the psychological experiment. *American Psychologist, 17*, 776–783.

Pervin, L. (1984). *Current controversies and issues in personality*. New York: Wiley.

Reicher, S., & Potter, J. (1985). Psychological theory as intergroup perspective. *Human Relations, 38*, 167–189.

Robbins, S. (1991). *Organizational behaviour* (5th edn.). New York: Prentice-Hall.

Robson, C. (2001). *Real world research*. Oxford: Blackwell.

Rosenthal, R. (1966). *Experimenter effects in behavior research*. New York: Appleton-Century-Crofts.

Saal, F., & Knight, P. (1988). *Industrial/organizational psychology: Science & practice*. Pacific Grove, CA: Brooks/Cole.

Schein, E. (1990). Organizational culture. *American Psychologist, 45*, 109–119.

Selltiz, C., Wrightsman, L., & Cook, S. (1959). *Research methods in social relations*. New York: Holt, Rinehart & Winston.

Sigelman, L. (1981). Is ignorance bliss? A reconsideration of the folk wisdom. *Human Relations, 34*, 965–974.

Simon, H., & Newell, A. (1956). Models: Their uses and limitations. In L. White (ed.), *The state of the social sciences* (pp. 334–356). Chicago, IL: University of Chicago Press.

Spector, P. (2003). *Industrial and organizational psychology: Research and practice*. New York: Wiley.

Stone, R. (1995). *Human resource management*. Brisbane, QLD: Wiley.

Stroebe, W. (1980). Process loss in social psychology. In R. Gilmour & S. Duck (eds.), *The development of social psychology* (pp. 181–205). London: Academic Press.

Valentine, E. (1982). *Conceptual issues in psychology*. London: Allen & Unwin.

Weiss, H., & Adler, S. (1984). Personality and organizational behaviour. *Research in Organizational Behaviour, 4*, 1–50.

Wexley, K., & Yukl, G. (1984). *Organizational behaviour and personnel psychology*. New York: Irwin.

Zimbardo, P., Haney, C., Books, W., & Jaffe, P. (1973). Pirandellian prison: The mind is a formidable jailer. *New York Times Magazine*, April, pp. 38–60.

2 The history of organizational psychology and the study of work psychology

Introduction

It is legitimate to pose the questions: Why bother looking at the past? Why study the history of ideas and research in this area? Some may argue that it is a waste of time; others may point to the fact that rarely, if ever, do chemistry books have an historical section on alchemy and, by inference, why should students of work psychology look at the past? Others, as we will see, claim that as history is written by the victors (those whose theories were adopted for whatever reason), it is unreliable and biased, and therefore misleading and better avoided.

A study of the history of work psychology *certainly* tells us where we have been and what we thought (and perhaps where we do not want to go again); it probably gives a sense of where we are now relative to previous ideas; and *possibly* where we are going, though many dispute that. Certainly ideas are not produced in a vacuum: they are all a product of their time and the socio-economic, political and philosophical forces affecting authors.

However, a strong case can be made for knowing the background to the thinking and research in work psychology.

- Many ideas, approaches and methods in organizational and managerial behaviour have not arisen from the pens of ivory-tower thinkers but rather from the responses of practically orientated business men and women who have attempted to manage in the most sensible, enlightened and economically feasible way. To a large extent, they have responded to the social, economic and political conditions they have found themselves in, although some have been proactive and innovative. Inevitably, this means that theory, research and practice in work psychology have reflected the *zeitgeist* of particular circumstances of the times. Current theory and practice may be highly influenced by current economic conditions, philosophical fads and even political movements. In this sense, one may be more able to understand and criticize current research and theorizing if one understands how past conditions have influenced thinking, managing and organizing.
- Although it may be desirable to believe that the history of thinking and research is progressive, with old, weak, inappropriate or simply wrong ideas being rejected, it is more likely that they move in and out of fashion, possibly cyclically. If this is true, and there is good reason to believe that it is, then, with historical insight one may be able to point out much more effectively the strengths and weaknesses of a particular approach. Furthermore, even if the old ideas are "repackaged" or simply

"reheated" so as to be more attractive to current fashion, one may be able to predict how, when and why ideas emerge and fade. In other words, the practice of crystal-ball gazing may be greatly facilitated by having an historical perspective: an economic and historical perspective may greatly facilitate correct trend predictions because one becomes aware which variables influence which.

- An a-historical discipline suffers from the problems of not knowing where ideas come from, their philosophical origin and, perhaps, even some of the implicit assumptions that theories presuppose. Any consideration of the origin of ideas in a discipline gives one a sense of the philosophical school that generated these ideas and how they are related. To a large extent, a historical perspective prevents people "reinventing the wheel".

- Even after a perfunctory acquaintance with work psychology or work psychology history, it becomes apparent that there is not one unchallenged agreed history, but many different debated and contended historical interpretations. Histories can be written from very different perspectives – cultural, gender, specific discipline or power-based – and therefore might offer quite different interpretations. An appreciation of these different perspectives can provide a very useful insight into how different groups have understood and, indeed, understand their current position.

It may be possible to plot and categorize, albeit simply, different historic eras, the business beliefs and values of the time, and the methods of going about management and production. Thus, before the industrial revolution, at least in the West, commercial enterprise was mainly a business of personal fortune seeking. This was followed in international business terms by an *empire-building* colonial rule, possibly exploitative period, up to the end of the First World War. Between the wars a more *protectionist* nationalistic period ensued, followed after the war until the end of the 1960s with *market development* ideas within and between countries. Over the past 25 years, many large companies have ceased even to be international and have become multinational with global interests and concerns.

If the past 200 years are crudely divided into four time periods, one can get some idea of the development or at least change in ideas (see Table 2.1). Certainly, the industrial revolution brought about the most dramatic change in work in history. It provided new sources of power (steam and later electricity), machine automation (that continues to occur) and a whole range of new information and control processes (from clocking in to video surveillance). Electronic-based computer technologies have for 50 years radically transformed the production process and now the service sector in industry.

Thus, in the earliest period, up to and even after the First World War, industrial psychology as it was then called described employees as "factory hands". Early researchers were interested in fatigue and efficiency, and undertook time-and-motion studies to understand better how to design work for maximum profit. This is a very interesting contrast with the work psychologists of today, who are as much concerned with worker well-being and the effect of the organization in the wider society as maximizing profits for management.

Another more simplified system attempts to compare the past with the present. This is less clear as to when the past ended and the present began. It may also be seen as rather naïve, contrasting the past as bad with the present as good. Weisbrod (1995) provides such a table (Table 2.2).

Table 2.1 Changes in value over time

	Profit maximization 1720–1919	Trustee/protectionist 1920–1969	Expansionist/development 1970–1990	Quality of life/meaning 1991–
Values	Primary self-interest	Self- and workers' interest	Enlightened self- and workers' interests	Balance of self-, workers', society and international interests (stakeholders)
Economic values	Profit maximizer, *caveat emptor* (let the buyer beware). Labour is a commodity. Employees are "hands". Managers accountable to owners. Self-interest ultimately benefits all. The pursuit of wealth is fundamental.	Profit satisficer. Do not knowingly cheat customers. Labour has legal rights and obligations. Management accountable also to customers, employees and stockholders. A successful organization is good for society. Money *and* people important. People and profits inseparable.	Profit necessary, *caveat vendor* (let the seller beware). Labour has rights to dignity and meaning at work. Managers accountable to governments as well as stakeholders. A growing large organization benefits all. People and profits equally important.	Profit desirable. Regulate production, advertising and sales. Labour is now people – the most valuable asset. Managers accountable to society, national and international as well as traditional stakeholders. What is good for society at large is good for the organization.
Environmental values	The physical environment determines much business success and failure.	The environment can be mastered, controlled and exploited.	New, rich and untapped environments can be discovered and made to give up their riches.	The environment needs investment and very sensitive management.
Social values	Employees have economic needs to be satisfied. A job is for as long as the organization deems fit. Minority groups are inferior and suitable only for menial jobs. The individual is the unit to manage.	Meeting social needs is also important. A job is for life with the company. Minority groups make an important contribution. *Noblesse oblige.* People have to work in groups and teams.	Organizations hire the whole person. Changing jobs regularly is in the employee's own interest. Minority group members have the same rights as others. People are interdependent on others at work.	Off-the-job activists influence on-the-job effectiveness. Everyone will have career changes and "fallow" periods. Positive discrimination in favour of minority groups. Hiring and rewarding done on a group/team basis.
Technological values	Technology (machinery) must be mastered and adapted to the situation.	Technology can be made ever more efficient to produce and therefore sell more.	Technology can be made to be ergonomically efficient and easy to use; learn and adapt.	People operate technology and their abilities and deficiencies are taken into account both in design and use.

Table 2.2 Characteristics of old and new paradigms of work design

Old paradigm	New paradigm
Technology comes first.	Social and technical systems are optimized together.
People are extensions of machines.	People complement machines.
People are expendable spare parts.	People are resources to be developed.
Tasks are narrow and individual; skills are simple.	Related tasks make an optimum grouping; skills are multiple and broad.
Controls – for example, supervisors, staff, procedures, books – are external.	Individuals are self-controlled; workgroups and departments are self-regulating.
Organization chart has many levels; management style is autocratic.	Organization chart is flat; management is participative.
Atmosphere is competitive and characterized by gamesmanship.	Atmosphere is collaborative and cooperative.
Only the organization's purposes are considered.	Individual and social purposes are considered, as well as the organization's.
Employees are alienated: "It's only a job".	Employees are committed: "It's my job".
Organization is characterized by low risk-taking.	Organization is innovative: new ideas are encouraged.

Source: Reproduced from Weisbrod (1995: 17) with the permission of Elsevier.

It is somewhat simplistic to believe that, at a particular instant in time or over a specific period, the "old paradigm" gave way to the new. Indeed, many organizations today, particularly in developing countries, still operate under the old paradigm. Further ideas and beliefs change slowly – thus, an organization may have new paradigm attitudes to equipment and technology but old paradigm attitudes to people.

Indeed, some modern thinkers tend to be more pessimistic, seeing work design from the 1950s to the 1970s (at least in the West) as better than it is today. There is no doubt that to believe either everything is getting better (naïve optimism) or getting worse (total pessimism) is simplistic. Some features of the work experience are clearly getting better for employer and employee, others not.

Different approaches to historical understanding

It is said that all psychology as well as applied psychology has a long history but a short past, implying that, whereas people (at least since the ancient Greeks) have discussed, debated and described how work should be arranged, it is not until three-quarters of the way through the nineteenth century that the discipline was dignified with academic departments, professors, textbooks and all the other paraphernalia of a recognized discipline. The same is true of work psychology (organizational psychology, or industrial/organizational psychology).

Although it may be argued that Machiavelli, or the founders or critics of the industrial revolution (such as Tawney and Weber), were obviously important management and organizational theorists, their ideas (at least in the case of the former) were much wider (and grander) than simply work psychology, and in the case of the latter tended to be highly specific to issues of their time. It is easy to locate the origins of specific work psychology concepts in Greek philosophy, or nineteenth-century writers. But work psychology research, as opposed to philosophizing, did not begin until the second decade of the twentieth century.

There are many ways of approaching the history of work psychology:

- *The models of man perspective*: Over the years, work psychology researchers and theorists have held different assumptions about people at work. These assumptions have concentrated on different things, such as their motivation (or lack of it), their rationality, their needs, etc. – these "models" have strongly influenced how they have thought about human problems at work. This approach tells us of different approaches at different times, but it is not strictly "historical".
- *The great thinker perspective*: This is perhaps the simplest, "Great Man" style-of-history approach, whereby the past is viewed through the ideas of greater thinkers whose work is considered prototypical, seminal or highly influential. It is an approach that also gives little idea of the development of thinking in a field, and tends to be uncritical and little interested in comparisons. However, understanding how certain individuals thought about the psychology in their day, and how these ideas influenced others, is important.
- *The time-based perspective*: This approach attempts to "carve nature at her joints" by finding the events and dates that marked a change in the thinking or practice of the individuals. For work psychology they usually coincide with major political and economic events, such as world war, recession or hyperinflation, which cause a major shake-up in the way organizations are run. Nearly always, the selected "change-points" are open to debate.
- *The school of thought approach*: This approach sees themes in groups of researchers who develop certain theories, methodologies or approaches to study work psychology. To what extent they are internally consistent is discussed less frequently than how they differ from other schools. Furthermore, they rarely say how strong any school might be on the nature or influence of their followers.
- *The seminal study/research project approach*: Another approach suggests that a programmatic series of studies has influenced the whole area. Perhaps the most famous example is the Hawthorne experiment, which is discussed later. It likes to focus on unique discoveries that altered thinking, at least in a certain area.
- *The textbook content-analysis approach*: This approach argues that early textbooks summarize the topics and theories of the time and are therefore valid ways to understand historical changes. Hence, a content analysis of early textbooks gives a clear insight into historical trends. This is rarely done, and is nearly always restricted to British or US texts published in English. Furthermore, it is far from clear what criteria should be used to select the textbooks. This is a fairly unusual approach and won't be considered in great detail here.
- *A topic-based historical approach*: This approach suggests that it is more meaningful to understand the history of work psychology by focusing on different topics, such as personnel selection and testing reward systems, individually because they themselves have different histories. It is in fact very similar to the previous method and won't be considered separately.

There may be other approaches to looking at the past. Each has a particular lens which is trained largely on the twentieth-century records of the past. Another approach is more socio-political or philosophical. A good example of this is the work of Holloway (1991), who, heavily influenced by the French philosopher Foucault, is eager to understand the history of organizational psychology in its social, political and economic contexts. She is scathing of the disinterested scientist image, believing most work psychology politically suspect:

> In Foucault's conception, power, like knowledge, is never singular or one-way, never homogeneous or monolithic. If machine-pacing, deskilling, piece rates and tight supervision had succeeded in achieving optimal productivity, motivation and job satisfaction would never have seen the light of day. As I have argued, they were a product of the play of different powers at a given time. But even this gives a picture of power which is too simply dichotomous. Amongst workers and amongst employers, the understanding of their interests, the forces imposing upon their actions and the powers and practices available to them, all varied enormously. In addition the state intervened in different ways; for example in Britain during the First World War it initiated the fatigue studies in munitions factories which launched British industrial psychology, at least temporarily, on a welfarist path. Finally psychologists, whether of the "pure" or "applied" variety, have their interests, which feed into the conditions within which particular knowledge emerges. In general, the belief in their own scientific status and neutrality gave them legitimacy and a simple answer to potentially troubling questions of responsibility. These dovetailed nicely with the interests of employers, who wanted their view of the problem resolved and not challenged. They also benefited from the reputation of work psychology as scientific, because it was therefore deemed to be above the politics of industrial conflict. Indeed it appeared to offer them something even better, because it claimed to solve such conflict of interest. Since there is a tendency to understand power as a negative, coercive force, this is important. To say that power is productive is quite separate from making a judgement about the value of its effects, positive or negative. Ultimately the importance of using power-knowledge-practice relations as a central analytical tool is to produce a different knowledge about work psychology. Consistent with this approach, I am not seeking to produce "objective" knowledge but, through a particular reading of history, to undermine that which I regard as the illegitimate power of science to produce a sanitized version of what work psychology is and how it came to be that way. (Holloway, 1991: 10–11)

It should be recognized that there are always two features to taking any perspective or approach. The first is obvious: that any particular perspective gives one a set of concepts or structures by which one can categorize past events. The second is the particular sociopolitical or philosophical assumptions of the author-historian. One can write a history focusing on the hardship of the workers and their heroic, trade union supported, fight for better conditions; or one could write a history of the same period and same events through the eyes of factory owners.

Models of man approach to work psychology

Many observers have pointed out that both researchers and managers hold theories or models as to the nature of human beings – for instance, people are basically trustworthy or altruistic, selfish or conformist. These theories or models supposedly shape how managers or consultants construct theories about, and behave towards, their workers. Furthermore, it is possible to observe that at certain periods of time different models were held.

Perhaps the most celebrated work in this field is that of McGregor (1960), who differentiates between two sets of assumptions that managers have about employees. The first is the traditional view of control which he calls Theory X (Box 2.1). Thus, it is argued, the approach to supervision will be determined to some extent by the view the manager has of human nature. If the manager accepts the assumptions of Theory X, he or she will be work obliged to exercise high levels of control. If, on the other hand, Theory Y is accepted, less control is necessary.

Box 2.1 Theory X and Theory Y

In essence, Theory X assumes:

- Human beings inherently dislike work and will, if possible, avoid it.
- Most people must be controlled and threatened with punishment if they are to work towards organizational goals.
- The average person actually wants to be directed, thereby avoiding responsibility.
- Security is more desirable than achievement.

Theory Y proceeds from a quite different set of assumptions. These are:

- Work is recognized by people as a natural activity.
- Human beings need not be controlled and threatened. They will exercise self-control and self-direction in the pursuit of organizational goals to which they are committed.
- Commitment is associated with rewards for achievement.
- People learn, under the right conditions, to seek as well as accept responsibility.
- Many people in society have creative potential, not just a few gifted individuals.
- Under most organizational conditions the intellectual potential of people is only partially utilized.

Wrightsman (1964) has attempted to systematize the various traditions in philosophical assumptions of human nature. He also attempted to spell out the implicit and explicit assumptions of prominent psychologists and sociologists regarding human nature. Experimental and social psychologists have attempted to specify *empirically* the basic dimensions that underpin the writings of philosophers, theologians, politicians, sociologists and others about the fundamental nature of "human beings". In doing so, they have attempted to spell out the determinants, structure and consequences of various "philosophies of human nature". For instance, Wrightsman (1964) has devised an 84-item scale that measures six basic dimensions of human nature in his *Philosophy of Human Nature Scale*:

- trustworthiness versus untrustworthiness;
- strength of will and rationality versus lack of willpower and irrationality;
- altruism versus selfishness;
- independence versus conformity to group pressures;
- variability versus similarity; and
- complexity versus simplicity.

Two additional dimensions of the philosophies of human nature proposed by Wrightsman (1964) concerned beliefs in the variation that exists among human beings. These two dimensions are: similarity versus variability, and complexity versus simplicity. However, Wrightsman's six-dimension-scale factor analyses into two major variables or subscales: *positive–negative* (strength of will, trust, independence and altruism) and *multiplexity* (variability and complexity), which are by-and-large independent of one another.

Winefield (1984) (following Schein, 1970), who concentrated on models of man particularly in the work psychology literature, has listed four paradigms, or models of man (all human beings):

- *Rational economic man*: This view suggests that man is governed solely by economic incentives and will do anything (and suffer almost intolerable working conditions) simply for financial gain. Workers are conceived as inherently lazy and so financial rewards must be offered as an inducement to get them to work. The theory of rational economic man dominated the early part of this century throughout all Western industrialized nation-states. It was the era of the mass production; of cheap commodities – commodities and artefacts so cheap that for the first time they were within the grasp of the working man.
- *Social man*: The Human Relations Movement, which was very influential from 1940 to 1960, suggested a quite different view of people:

    People may be mere cogs in well oiled industrial machines; they may just be referred to as "hands" and known simply as a name on a clocking-in card, but as living people they inhabit a dynamic and living social world within the factory confines. All workers bring a social world with them into the factory. Once in the factory they create a social world with which they try and fulfil essentially social needs – i.e. these needs are not abandoned when they enter the organization's premises. They want company; they want and create a sense of intimate belongings and they need to give a sense of identity and meaning to their everyday lives. Thus, the era of social man was born. Enlightened managements throughout industrialized nations actively sought to promote social and welfare activities within their workforces: sports facilities; work outings; social clubs; canteen facilities; and washing and bathing facilities. It even resulted in a distinctive style of factory building and industrial architecture; steel and glass factory buildings rose up, bathed in natural light – airy, modern and futuristic-looking. Workplaces became the symbol of the new philosophy of social man. (Winefield, 1984: 26–27)

- *Self-actualizing man*: Again a change in economic conditions with a tremendous surge of growth and expansion in the 1960s appears to have stimulated a change in the model of man. As machines took over the more tedious repetitive tasks, workers and managers began to appreciate that most employees never realized their potential by using their full ability. Indeed, the new view suggested that all people have the need to make full and effective use of our own human resources and endowments: the need to discover new aspects of ourselves, our abilities, our dormant or undiscovered skills, our creative powers. Managers or supervisors were cast in the role of friendly counsellors. In their day-to-day dealings with the workforce they had to understand what was the correct button to press for each worker in their charge. Their role was to try to give authority and freedom to workers within the political limits prescribed, feeling that this was what they wanted, for workers were also seen as self-disciplining. This approach maintained that all workers, irrespective of background, class, education and occupational status, will rise to the challenge when given the opportunity for self-actualization or autonomy in decision.

- *Complex man*: The breakdown in the belief in grand theories, combined with a rise in interest in ergonomics and cognitive psychology, has led to a different view of people. People are seen as essentially variable, changeable animals. Although each person has his or her own hierarchy of needs in his or her life, the actual ordering of the hierarchy will change from time to time and from situation to situation. This variability makes them difficult to predict and understand.

  People's motives are not fixed and immovable, as many of the previous theories assumed. There is a complex interaction between the initial needs of the person, when they enter the organization, and their needs as modified by subsequent organizational experience. For modern complex man there is no one universal model or theory of behaviour that covers all contingencies. Above all, the philosophy of management appears to be eclectic: to be prepared to draw on more than one interpretation, to be alive to individual differences among the workforce.

Cherns (1982) believes that applied psychologists develop and change their model of man as functions of historical contexts that throw up specific problems to be solved (see Table 2.3). In doing so, he proposes that organizational psychologists have in fact moved from a model of man to organizational models. He also notes the consequences of having such models, because they tend to focus on certain issues in the workplace such as selection, motivation, or productivity.

The models of man (in work psychology) approach is not without problems. First, it is not always clear when or why or how these models change – knowing this is crucially important for understanding both the present and the future. Secondly, it is not clear how consensually these beliefs in the models are held. That is, is there widespread consensus on the nature of people at work, or are there at the same time rather different models in operation? Thirdly, are these models quite explicitly conceived or are they much more implicit and rarely spelt out? Indeed, if they are not explicit, how is it determined that they are held? Nevertheless, this approach does offer a useful way of understanding how writers and managers have thought about people at work.

The great thinker perspective

The great thinker perspective remains one of the most popular ways of understanding the history of ideas in work psychology. Allied to this is the early (great) thinker approach or the history of the pioneers. People like the German-trained Munsterberg and Cattell are often mentioned for being the first to write about issues in work psychology. They do not, however, qualify as great thinkers. Essentially, this approach isolates a handful of thinkers whose ideas have been particularly influential for both practice and research in this area. Work psychology textbooks appear to have reached a consensus on who the three most important thinkers were prior to the mid-1930s: a German, Weber; a Frenchman, Fayol; and an American, Taylor. The precise criteria by which these three had been nominated are not entirely clear, but it is certainly true that their ideas have been important. Some of the ideas have been updated and others

Table 2.3 The interactions of context, problem, model and response

Context	Problem	Model	Response
1. Rapid industrialization	Inexperienced workforce	Economic man*	Scientific management
2. Wartime pressure for production	Fatigue	Machine man	Work and environmental design
3. Wartime rapid change in occupation structure	Allocation	Man as peg, task as hole	Testing – fitting man to job
4. Interwar social conflict	"Informal" organization	Emotional man	Human relations
5. Wartime rapid advance in technology	Misfit between man and technology	Man–machine system	Ergonomic design
6. Transition from planned to market economy	Adaptation to changing environment	Organization as open system	Contingency approach
7. Impact of advanced technology on mature systems	Misfit between organization and technology	Organization as sociotechnical system	Job and organization design
8. Educated society	Dissatisfaction with work	Complex man – hierarchy of needs	Job enrichment
9. Challenge to established authority	Industrial conflict	Organization as power system	Industrial democracy

Source: Reprinted from Cherns (1982) with permission of Academic Press.

* No doubt Cherns meant both men and women.

revised so much so that it is possible to stipulate a classic (original) and a contemporary (revised) view. Weber will be concentrated on heavily for three reasons. First, his ideas on the work ethic and bureaucracy were, and are, extremely influential. Secondly, his ideas came from and influenced many disciplines as well as psychology. Thirdly, he took an historical perspective in his day at the turn of the century.

Max Weber

Weber was a polymath, whose training in economics, the law, sociology and other related disciplines enabled him to understand the complexity of organizations. He was the first to think organizationally and how best to design and maintain an efficient and dynamic system. He is well known for his research on two things: the Protestant work ethic and bureaucracy.

The Protestant work ethic

Despite all the argument and research on the Protestant work ethic, there are relatively few clear statements on its actual constituents. Innumerable writers have tried to define or elucidate the components of the Protestant work ethic. Oates (1971: 84) noted:

> The so-called Protestant work ethic can be summarized as follows: a universal taboo is placed on *idleness*, and *industriousness* is considered a religious ideal; *waste*

is a vice, and *frugality* a virtue; *complacency* and *failure* are outlawed, and *ambition* and *success* are taken as sure signs of God's favour; the universal sign of sin is *poverty*, and the crowning sign of God's favour is *wealth*.

Cherrington (1980) listed eight attributes of the Protestant work ethic. The broader meaning of the work ethic typically refers to one or more of the following beliefs:

- People have a normal and religious obligation to fill their lives with heavy physical toil. For some, this means that hard work, effort and drudgery are to be valued for their own sake; physical pleasures and enjoyments are to be shunned; and an ascetic existence of methodological rigour is the only acceptable way to live.
- Men and women are expected to spend long hours at work, with little or no time for personal recreation and leisure.
- A worker should have a dependable attendance record, with low absenteeism and tardiness.
- Workers should be highly productive, and produce a large quantity of goods or service.
- Workers should take pride in their work and do their jobs well.
- Employees should have feelings of commitment and loyalty to their profession, their company and their work group.
- Workers should be achievement-orientated and should constantly strive for promotion and advancement. High-status jobs with prestige and the respect of others are important indicators of a "good" person.
- People should acquire wealth through honest labour and retain it through thrift and wise investments. Frugality is desirable; extravagance and waste should be avoided.

At the centre of the concept of the Protestant work ethic is the idea that the values and beliefs underlying it (morality, control, postponement of gratification, asceticism, hard work) actually lead to economic success on both an individual and a national level. In this sense, the Protestant work ethic can be conceived as a personally held belief system that is predictive of economic success (Furnham, 1990). Economists have attempted to translate or apply Weberian ideas into the language and concepts of today. Ditz (1980), in an interesting essay on the Protestant work ethic and the market economy, has described the work ethic idea of profit making as a calling to "the sacramentalization of acquisition". He explains in lay economic terms how the Protestant work ethic affected the market economy (what Marx called capitalism) over the last few hundred years. Ditz's key concepts were:

- Inputs to productivity – because pessimistic Calvinists were so concerned with scarcity they stressed the need for productive work to bring about surpluses.
- Propensity to save – because maximization of productivity and minimization of consumption were ethically important, saving seemed a most useful solution.
- Risk-taking investments – saving was more acceptable than spending, and investing more acceptable than saving because charging interest was taboo.
- A calculating orientation – effective efficiency means knowledge of and ability in making calculations of input and output, demand and supply, cost, price and profits. Quantitative skills became professionalized.

- Profit making as a calling – profit maximization was the prime objective. The acquisition instinct became a Utopian idea.
- From labour costs to profits – anything that increases net profit is good and anything that lowers it is bad. Labour *per se* is only good when it becomes efficient, cost reducing and effective.
- Encouragement of marketing – marketing helped the consumer consume more effectively and hence the producer produce more efficiently, hence marketing empathy with the consumer.
- Emergence of new elites – the new "would-be-saints" were successful entrepreneurs, captains of industry, elected political leaders, certified men of knowledge and accepted opinion leaders.
- Creation of new democracies – all organizations were turned into meritocratic democracies. Liberty and equality were promoted, as were mobility, democratized social structure, etc.
- Resolution of organized conflict – the Protestant work ethic philosophy was individualistic against government interference, non-conformist and against conflict and militant behaviour. It tended to retreat from conflict and be anti-authoritarian.
- Middle class and mass market – Protestant work ethic endorsers were upward-moving, middle-class oriented and tried to resolve conflicting claims of meritocratic elitism and egalitarianism.
- The manipulation of consumers – promotion of products through advertising, etc. – was given ethical support because self and other material improvement was thought of as morally desirable.

Giddens (1972) has listed five major criticisms of the Protestant work ethic:

1 Weber's understanding of Protestant theology and lay beliefs, particularly Calvinism, Lutheranism and American Puritanism, was erroneous.
2 Similarly, he misunderstood Catholic doctrine, particularly as it differed from Protestantism on economic detail.
3 The data Weber used to support his thesis were limited to mainly Anglo-Saxon material, while other European (German, Dutch, Swiss) data fail to support his hypothesis.
4 Weber's distinction between modern and earlier forms of capitalism was unwarranted because the "spirit of modern" capitalism was apparent in earlier periods.
5 The supposed causal correlation between Puritanism and modern capitalism is unfounded and indeed it may be argued that Puritan ideology and practices were themselves merely epiphenomena of previously established economic changes.

The Weberian Protestant work ethic hypothesis has received a number of reactions that can be classified as follows:

- *Negative*: As an explanation for the rise of capitalism it is descriptively inaccurate, explanatorily tautologous and scientifically meaningless. Calvin was not the parent of capitalism. Marx might have "inverted" Hegel but Weber was wrong to do so to the Marxist ideas about the origin or maintenance of capitalism.
- *Neutral*: Weber's hypothesis, like the proverbial curate's egg, is good in parts but cannot alone account for the origin or maintenance of capitalism in Western

Europe. As an explanatory factor the Protestant work ethic is necessary but not sufficient.

- *Positive*: To identify the Protestant work ethic as a crucial factor in the origin of capitalism was a remarkable piece of scholarship. Though recognizing that other economic, sociological or psychological factors were possibly operating.

Bureaucracy

Weber was interested in power, structure and authority in organizations. A bureaucracy is an organization that displays certain characteristics:

- a division or specialization of labour;
- a well-developed hierarchy;
- a system of procedures and rules by which the rights and duties of employees are defined;
- interpersonal relations based on position rather than personality;
- promotion and selection based on technical competence.

In reality, the ideal bureaucracy is seldom attained and it now has a bad name. Weber described rather than advocated this system, but it now has an Orwellian nightmarish scenario attached to it. The specialization of labour often *inhibits effective communication* among technical specialists and between higher and lower levels of the organization. The procedures and rules sometimes encourage organizational members to *act mechanically* rather than exercising initiative and using their inherent creativity. It acts to disempower people. Incompetence is also present at times, since in real life promotion can be the result of "who one knows" and "how one plays the organizational game" *rather than technical ability*.

Bureaucracies have been criticized specifically for being *inflexible and late* to respond to constant changes. Furthermore, the Peter Principle (people are promoted to their level of incompetence) or the time-serving principle, rather than merit, seem to determine promotability. Conformity to norms, standards and procedures stifles creativity and fully utilizes human resources. Formal control tends to ignore informal networks and discourage personal empowerment. For Schermerhorn, Hunt, & Osborn (1994), there are both advantages and disadvantages in bureaucratization (Table 2.4).

This is not to say that some of the key concepts of bureaucracies are not very important, both in understanding the history of work psychology and structuring organizations today. Five ideas are fundamental to Weber's theory (Schermerhorn *et al.*, 1994).

1. DIVISION OF LABOUR

This means that, rather than an entire job being done by one individual, it is broken down into various component parts, each step being completed by a separate specifically trained individual. Assembly-line production, in which each worker does the same standardized task over and over again, is a prototypical example of division of labour.

The Classical theorists were strong proponents of division of labour. They saw it as a way to increase significantly the economic efficiencies of organizations. Job range and

Table 2.4 The characteristics of Weber's ideal bureaucracy and some associated dysfunctions

Characteristics of Weber's ideal bureaucracy	Associated dysfunctions identified by critics
Labour is specialized, so each person has clear authority and responsibility.	Overspecialization stimulates a divergence of interests, which lead to conflict.
Offices and positions are arranged in a hierarchy of authority.	A very formal hierarchy creates inflexibility in following "official" channels.
Members are selected and promoted on the basis of technical competence.	Bureaucracies become political systems serving an elite corps of managers.
Members have administrative careers and work on a fixed salary.	Conformity to the organization's ways can be detrimental to one's mental health.
Members are subject to rules and controls that are strict and impersonal and are applied universally.	Rules become ends in themselves; rules can only specify minimum requirements.

Source: Reproduced from Schermerhorn et al. (1994: 70) with permission of John Wiley & Sons.

often job depth are therefore reduced by specialization. Efficiency is rated over intrinsic motivation (Robbins, 1991).

Division of labour usually makes efficient use of the diversity of skills that workers hold. In most organizations, some tasks require highly developed skills; others can be performed by the untrained. If all workers were engaged in each step of, say, an organization's manufacturing process, *all* must have the skills necessary to perform both the *most* demanding and the *least* demanding jobs. The result would be that, except when performing the most skilled or highly sophisticated tasks, employees would be working below their skill levels. Since skilled workers are paid more than unskilled workers and their wages tend to reflect their highest level of skill, it represents an inefficient use of organizational resources to pay highly skilled workers to do easy tasks. Furthermore, skills at performing a task successfully increase through repetition. Equally important is the fact that training for specialization is more efficient from the organization's perspective. It is easier and less costly to find and train workers to do specific and repetitive tasks, especially of a highly sophisticated and complex nature. Division of labour increases efficiency and productivity by encouraging the creation of ergonomically sophisticated inventions and machinery. Eight arguments can be made for specialization through divisions of labour:

- *Less skilled workers can be used* because the complex tasks are simplified into smaller jobs, and the workers who do these jobs do not have to be highly trained and are paid less.
- *Selection and training are easier* because the skills required for the specific job are minimal, easier to identify, and training new workers takes less time and is less difficult.
- *Proficiency is gained more quickly* because a specialized task is repetitive, the worker gets more practice and hence becomes an expert rather quickly.
- *There is an increase in efficiency* as workers do not waste time moving from one task to another.
- *There is greater availability of labour* as more potential workers are available because fewer specialized skills are required.

- *The speed at which work is done increases* – more work is done by each worker, so the task gets finished sooner.
- *Concurrent operations are possible* because one worker is not assigned to more than one task, so there is no delay in a second task while he or she completes the first.
- *Specialization increases initial choice*. There is a large variety of tasks to choose from, so the worker can choose, or be assigned, on the basis of his or her preference or particular skill.

The Classical theorists viewed division of labour as a source of increased productivity; because specialization was at the time not widely practised, its introduction almost always generated higher productivity. However, problems such as worker boredom, fatigue, stress, low productivity, poor quality, increased absenteeism and high turnover often outweigh the economic advantages. There is probably an inverse-U relationship between productivity and specialization (that is, too little or too much specialization is associated with low productivity). But the more highly educated the workers, the sooner the optimal period is reached. When employees are given a variety of activities to do, allowed to undertake a complete piece of work, and are brought together into teams, they often achieve higher productivity and satisfaction.

Changing job routines, job enlargement and job enrichment is now thought to be as important as, or more important than, over-specialization. However, experimental studies that have attempted to "compare and contrast" specialization versus enlargement have yielded highly mixed results, although it would appear that more middle-class, highly skilled jobs are best done under enriched conditions and more working-class, less skilled jobs under specialized conditions.

2. UNITY OF COMMAND

The unity of command principle argued that a subordinate should have one and only one superior to whom he or she is directly responsible. In those rare instances when the unity of command principle had to be violated, the Classical viewpoint always explicitly designated that there be a clear separation of activities and a supervisor responsible for each. On this view, there is a clear chain of command.

The unity of command concept was especially logical when organizations were comparatively simple in nature. Under most circumstances, it is still sound advice, and organizations today closely adhere to this principle. Yet there are instances when strict adherence to the unity of command creates a degree of inflexibility that hinders an organization's performance, such as when incompetent superiors block progress. Of course, the question remains as to whether those in the logical and single chain of command are competent both to work and also communicate clearly down the chain.

3. DECENTRALIZATION

Centralization and decentralization refer to the extent to which managers delegate responsibility. *Authority* refers to the rights inherent in a managerial position, acquired from rank or title to give orders and expect the orders to be obeyed. It was to be delegated downward to subordinate managers, giving them both certain rights and certain prescribed limits within which they could operate. Authority in organizations flows downward but it is based on workers' acceptance of it. Authority relates, therefore, to one's position within an organization and ignores the personal character-istics (personality, ability) of the individual manager (Schermerhorn *et al.*, 1994).

When delegating authority, it is important to allocate commensurate *responsibility*. That is, when one is given *rights*, one also assumes a corresponding obligation to perform. To allocate authority without responsibility creates opportunities for abuse, and no-one should be held responsible for what he or she has no authority over. But responsibility cannot be delegated. The Classical view recognized two forms of responsibility: *operating* responsibility and *ultimate* responsibility. Managers pass on operating responsibility, which, in turn, may be passed on further. But there is an aspect of responsibility – its ultimate component – that must be retained. A manager is ulti-mately responsible for the actions of his or her subordinates, to whom the operating responsibility has been passed. Therefore, managers should delegate operating responsibility equal to the delegated authority; however, ultimate responsibility can never be delegated. Hence, when major crises occur, senior managers may be called upon to resign (Schermerhorn *et al.*, 1994).

The Classical theorists also distinguished between two forms of authority relations: line authority and staff authority. *Line authority* is the authority that entitles a man-ager to direct the work of a subordinate. It is the superior–subordinate authority relationship that extends from the top of the organization to the lowest echelon, fol-lowing what is called the *chain of command*. As a link in the chain of command, a manager with line authority has the right to direct the work of subordinates and to make certain decisions without consulting others. As organizations become larger and more complex, managers find that they do not have the time, expertise or resources to do their jobs effectively. Thus, they can create *staff authority* functions to support, assist, advise and in general reduce some of the informational burdens they have (Robbins, 1991).

Early theorists were especially enamoured with authority and they naïvely assumed that the rights inherent in one's formal position in an organization were the sole source of influence. Managers were only minimally dependent on technical specialists. Under such conditions, influence is the same as authority; and the higher a manager's position in the organization, the more influence he or she had. Organizations today have increas-ingly turned to participation, teams and other devices to downplay authoritative superior–subordinate relationships. Managers are increasingly viewing their jobs as liberating and enabling their employees, rather than supervising them. Indeed, we hear now more and more of *empowerment*, which is the delegation of more authority *and* responsibility down the line.

4. SPAN OF CONTROL

How many subordinates can a manager efficiently and effectively lead, manage or control? The *span of control* concept was considered important because, to a large extent, it determined the number of levels and managers an organization has. All things being equal, the wider or larger the span, the more efficient the organization. An example can illustrate the validity of this statement.

Assume that we have two organizations, both of which have approximately 4100 employees. As Table 2.5 illustrates, if one has a uniform span of four and the other a span of eight, the wider span would have two fewer levels and approximately 800 fewer managers. If the average manager made £40,000 a year, the wider span would save

Table 2.5 Necessary levels as a function of different levels of control

Members at each level		
Highest	*Assuming span of 4*	*Assuming span of 8*
1	1	1
2	4	8
3	16	64
4	64	512
5	256	4096
6	1024	
7	4096	
	Workers = 4,096	Workers = 4096
	Managers (levels 1–6) = 1365	Managers (levels 1–4) = 585

£32 million a year in management salaries! In recent years, the pendulum has swung towards creating flat structures with wide spans of control.

5. DEPARTMENTALIZATION

The Classical theorists argued that activities in an organization should be specialized and grouped into departments. Division of labour creates specialists who need coordination, which is facilitated by bringing specialists together in departments under the direction of a manager. Creation of these departments is typically based on the work functions being performed, the product or service being offered, the target customer or client, the geographical territory being covered, or the process being used to turn inputs into outputs.

One of the most popular ways to group activities is by "functions performed" – *functional departmentalization*. A manufacturing manager might organize his or her plant by separating engineering, accounting, manufacturing, personnel and purchasing specialists into common departments. Of course, departmentalization by function can be used in all types of organizations, yet the functions change to reflect the organization's objectives and activities.

If an organization's activities are service- rather than product-related, each service could be autonomously grouped. The assumption underlying *customer departmentalization* is that customers in each department have a common set of problems and needs that can best be met by having specialists for each. Another way to departmentalize is on the basis of geography or territory – *geographical departmentalization*. If an organization's customers are scattered over a large geographical area, then this form of departmentalization is most obvious.

Process departmentalization is another way of categorizing and can be used for processing customers as well as products. Most large organizations continue to use most or all of the departmental groupings. However, customer departmentalization has become increasingly emphasized and rigid departmentalization is being complemented by the use of teams that cross over traditional departmental lines (Robbins, 1991).

The issue of specialization into departments or divisions remains hotly debated. Schermerhorn *et al.* (1994) have set out the advantages and disadvantages of functional specialization (see Table 2.6).

Table 2.6 Major advantages and disadvantages of functional specialization

Advantages	Disadvantages
1. It can yield very clear task assignments that are consistent with an individual's training. 2. Individuals within a department can easily build on one another's knowledge, training and experience. Facing similar problems and having similar training facilitates communication and technical problem-solving. 3. It provides an excellent training ground for new managers, who must translate their academic training into organizational actions. 4. It is easy to explain. Most employees can understand the role of each unit, even though many may not know what individuals in a particular function do.	1. It may reinforce the narrow training of individuals and lead to boring and routine jobs. Communication across technical areas is difficult, and conflict between units may increase. Lines of communication across the organization can become very complex. 2. Complex communication channels can lead to "top management overload". Top management may spend too much time and effort dealing with cross-functional problems. 3. Individuals may look up the organizational hierarchy for direction and reinforcement rather than focus attention on products, services or clients. Guidance is typically sought from functional peers or superiors.

Source: Reproduced from Schermerhorn *et al.* (1994: 381) with permission of John Wiley & Sons.

Concerns with the disadvantages of any form of departmentalization or specialization led theorists to suggest, and organizations to accept, a matrix structure. The matrix departmentalization is an organizational structure that uses multiple authority and support systems. The matrix structure tries to combine the advantages of functional and product designs while minimizing their disadvantages. Every matrix contains three unique sets of relationships: the *top* manager who heads up and balances the dual lines of authority; the *matrix* managers, who share subordinates with functional managers; and the *subordinates*, who report to two different managers. Matrix organization can be very complex and it provides a means of breaking down the barriers between functional and product employees by allowing members from different functional departments to use their skills and abilities on common product problems.

The *advantages* of this approach are fivefold:

- it gives flexibility to managers in assigning people to projects;
- it encourages interdisciplinary cooperation;
- it develops project managers' human, conceptual and administrative skills;
- it often involves and challenges people; and
- it can make specialized knowledge available to all projects.

However, the *disadvantages* include:

- it is often costly to implement;
- it may reward political skill as opposed to managerial skills;
- it can increase the frustration of employees who now receive orders from two bosses; and
- it may lead to more discussion than action.

Weber's contribution to work psychology thinking remains to this day very important. Although bureaucracy is not a pejorative term, some of the ideas that underpin it are fundamentally important in understanding any organization's structure and process.

Henri Fayol

In 1919, Fayol published *Administration industrielle et general* [*General and industrial management*], which argued that all managers (administrators) perform much the same functions: controlling, organizing, planning. Crainer (2000) argued that Fayol's contribution was essentially threefold: he recognized that management issues were *universal* across all organizations; he identified management as a *discipline in its own right*; he believed management could be deferred (by 14 principles, as set out below). Yet although Fayol's ideas have been both robust and enduring, he has been among the most neglected and forgotten of thinkers. Fayol proposed that all operations in business organizations can be classified under six headings:

• technical (production);
• commercial (purchase and sales);
• financial (finding and controlling capital);
• security (protection);
• accounting (balance sheet, costing, records); and
• administrative (planning, organizing, commanding, coordinating and controlling).

He also noted that with regard to administrative operations, managers need to understand that:

• to plan means to study the future and arrange a plan of operations;
• to organize means to build up the material and human organization of the business;
• to command means to make the staff do their work;
• to coordinate means to unite all activities;
• to control means to see that everything is done in accordance with the rules that have been laid down and the instructions given (Duncan, 1978).

Fayol noted that certain functions or operations (technical, commercial, financial, and so on) were accomplished primarily at lower organizational levels, whereas administrative operations were accomplished at the top. Fayol also presented 14 "principles", although he used the term reluctantly and emphasized that they were not rigid or absolute in a scientific sense. Rather, they were guidelines he had often used in his experiences as a business executive. These principles, taken from Fayol's book, are set out below:

• division of work (specialization belongs to the natural order);
• authority and responsibility (responsibility is a corollary of authority);
• discipline (discipline is what leaders make it);
• unity of command (workers cannot bear dual command);
• unity of direction (one head and one plan for a group of activities having the same objective);

- subordination of individual interest to the general interest;
- remuneration (fair, rewarding of effort, reasonable);
- centralization (centralization belongs to the natural order);
- scalar chain (line of authority, gang-plank principles);
- order (a place for everyone and everyone in his place);
- equity (results from a combination of kindliness and justice);
- stability and tenure of personnel (prosperous firms are stable);
- initiative (great source of strength from business); and
- *esprit de corps* (union is strength).

Some have argued that the above are no more than ambiguous and mutually contra-dictory proverbs. Others have argued that these rules of thumb do not promote under-standing of the process of management. Nevertheless, Fayol is remembered for his stress on functions. He made managers question their function(s) and what processes and procedures they had in place to fulfil those functions. It may appear mundane today, but there is no doubt that he was ahead of his time.

Frederick Taylor

Taylor was an American engineer who in 1911 wrote a book called the *Principles of scientific management*. He has been described by Crainer (2000) as "renaissance man with a stopwatch". He was passionate, persistent and creative. A sportsman of talent with an eager eye for fair-play, he was also concerned with order and efficiency. He pointed out three reasons for writing the book, namely:

- to point out, through simple examples, the great loss the country suffers through inefficiency in almost all of its daily acts;
- to try to convince the readers that the cure lies in systematic management rather than in searching for unusual workers to handle affairs; and
- to prove that the best management is a true science based on clearly defined laws, rules and principles, and to show that the principles of scientific management are applicable to all forms of human activities.

Taylor believed in close observation and measurement. He was probably the prototype of the "time-and-motion" expert who hides in a cupboard with a clip board and stop watch. This image of organizational psychologists can be seen from just after the First World War up until the 1970s and is mainly due to Taylor.

Taylor made management scientific, analytic and rigorous. You manage what you measure. But of necessity you need a layer of management doing the measuring which may seem paradoxically unproductive.

He believed that much "commonsensical" management of his day was inefficient and ineffective and in this he was probably correct. He thus articulated what he called principles of scientific management. Essentially, they were:

- To gauge industrial tendencies and the market in order to thereby regularize oper-ations in a manner which will serve the investment, sustain the enterprise as an employing agency, and assure continuous operation and employment.
- To assure the employee not only by continuous operation and employment by

correct gauging of the market, but also to assure by planned and balanced operations a continuous earning opportunity while on the payroll.

- To earn, through a waste-saving management and processing technique, a larger income from a given expenditure of human and material energies, which shall be shared through increased wages and profits by workers and management.
- To make possible a higher standard of living as a result of increased income to workers.
- To assure a happier home and social life to workers through removal, by increase of income, of many of the disagreeable and worrying factors in the overall situation.
- To assure healthy as well as individually and socially agreeable conditions of work.
- To assure the highest opportunity for individual capacity through scientific methods of work analysis and of selection, training, assignment, transfer and promotion of workers.
- To assure by training and instructional foremanship the opportunity for workers to develop new and higher capacities, and eligibility for promotion to higher positions.
- To develop self-confidence and self-respect among workers through opportunity afforded for understanding of one's own works specifically, and of plans and methods of work generally.
- To develop self-expression and self-realization among workers through stimulative influence of an atmosphere of research and valuation, through understanding of plans and methods, and through the freedom of horizontal as well as vertical contacts afforded by functional organization.
- To build character through the proper conduct of work.
- To promote justice through the elimination of discrimination in wage rates and elsewhere.
- To eliminate factors of the environment which are irritating and the causes of friction, and to promote common understandings, tolerances and the spirit of teamwork.

As a result, he advocated such things as:

- time and motion studies to help design jobs more efficiently;
- a differential piece-rate system, so that workers could be incentivized if they exceeded set standards;
- appointing functional foremen to plan, check, record and explain working procedures;
- the standardization of tools, systems and procedures.

Scientific management was strongly influenced by US behaviourism and pragmatism. It was an optimistic, engineering approach to management that asserted that "scientific" principles of the time could be employed in the workplace to make workers both more efficient and happy. It certainly could be demonstrated to work, as productivity can be measured. Indeed, it has been suggested that where measured the productivity of many manual workers increased as much as fifty-fold over the twentieth century.

Scientific management was not without its drawbacks (Duncan, 1978):

- First, scientific management was almost exclusively concerned with the *shop level* and its primary applicability is limited to *production operations*, which are currently less important than other types of organization. As more people become employed in service functions, where work is difficult or impossible to measure in a time-and-motion sense, the applicability of scientific management is reduced.

- The assumptions made by proponents of scientific management concerning the nature of human behaviour are also disputed. The incentive programmes advocated by most of the early writers were built upon the premises that individuals were economically motivated. It was assumed that monetary incentives would induce people to perform at higher levels. Little recognition was given to more latent needs of individuals to be accepted by others and the need for a feeling of achievement. Taylor has been described as a naïve optimist.

- Scientific management has been criticized for holding an excessively rationalistic view of human behaviour. Taylorian man is *Homo economicus* not *Homo psychologicus*. Taylor had an inadequate understanding of the individual incentive to interaction with, and dependence on, the immediate work group. He did attribute "underworking" to group pressures, but misunderstood the way in which these worked. He failed to see that these might just as easily sustain production and morale. He also ignored the psychological needs and capabilities of the workers. The one best way of doing a job was chosen with the mechanistic criteria of speed and output. The imposition of a uniform manner of work can destroy both creativity and innovation; thus, he had too simple an approach to the question of productivity and morale. He sought to sustain both of these exclusively by economic rewards and punishments.

- It has also been argued that Taylor made some fundamental but disputed assumptions about the moral character of human beings, which led him to many of the recommendations he proposed. Taylor appeared to assume that men, both workers and managers, were inherently lazy and that he created an administrative system designed to inhibit their "evil ways". He was less concerned about the individual's loss of freedom than with the material advantages to be gained from the exercise of authority. In this sense, he put efficiency before ethics.

- Finally, scientific management may be said to be more "scientistic" than scientific. Scientism is the application of what is thought of as science, whether it is appropriate or not. It is an attitude that insists that science can solve all problems and that one only needs to apply specific principles in a dispassionate and disinterested way.

- Taylor as an individual has also been attacked because he was egotistical, vindictive and craved personal admiration. Some have suggested that he fraudulently misrepresented important facts in his experiments.

Indeed, Taylor's ideas seem to have been rediscovered, repackaged and relabelled at the end of the 1990s with the idea of "re-engineering the corporation" (Champy & Hammer, 1993). These authors also believed in measuring and identifying key processes to make things more efficient and productive. It was engineering thinking seeing things in terms of machine systems and with "lay offs" as an inevitable consequence.

Other thinkers

It is inevitable that the great thinker approach is selective and partisan. Authors choose and rank order writers that particularly interest them or indeed have been chosen by historians. Apart from Weber, Fayol and Taylor – mentioned above – there are various others who certainly deserve mention. Three are mentioned briefly here, although it is possible to make a good case for many more.

Hugo Munsterberg

Munsterberg studied at Leipzig under Wundt, the home of modern psychology and the father of modern psychology. He then went to Harvard to work with William James, another great early psychologist. He had many interests, one being personnel selection and vocational testing. In an early study he was interested in the causes of railway street car accidents and selecting safe drivers.

Munsterberg was a polyglot interested in many aspects of applied, clinical, educational and economic psychology. He published *Psychology and industrial efficiency* in 1913. His ideas were used extensively in the armies of the First World War.

James Cattell

Cattell was also a student of Wundt. He went from Leipzig to Cambridge to study with Galton and inevitably became very interested in individual differences. His early work on mental testing was to use statistical procedures as opposed to the introspective methodology of the time.

In many ways, he even predated Binet in his belief in the usefulness of public testing programmes. He believed in the use of tests for vocational guidance, diagnosis of work and personal problems, stress, etc. His interest was in both testing ability and personality but mainly the former. This was done through what we now call "brass instrument" technology. His work was boosted by the First World War and the need for putting conscripts in positions best suited to their temperament and ability. Cattell happily bridged the divide between academic psychology and consulting. He edited various academic journals and he also founded a successful consulting company that is still operating today.

In his day, applied psychology embraced clinical, educational and industrial/ organizational psychology. Problems do not come neatly packaged into one area or another.

Kurt Levin

Kurt Levin is thought of as the father of cognitive social psychology, but his ideas have been very influential in work psychology. He was a Jewish German refugee from Nazism and is still widely remembered for his observation that there is nothing as practical as good theory.

From his experiences of the trenches of the First World War, he developed his field theory. He is well known for being the first "interactionist" who proposed the equation $B = f(PE)$: that is, behaviour is the function of the person and the environment. People choose, change and select (work) environments, which, in turn, influence the perceptions and behaviour of people in them.

He was also deeply interested in the psychology of change, proposing processes of unfreezing, changing and then re-freezing behaviour. Many people in business use his "force-field" analysis method. This is essentially a strategic or analytical tool for guiding managers in how to deal with specific issues. It involves four processes: first, specifying where one wants to be (realistic end goal); next, specifying where one is now relative to that goal. Thereafter, the task involves listing the number, strength and power of first the *driving* forces that facilitate movement to the goal but also *restraining* forces.

Levin is also remembered for stressing the importance of people's perceptions of events. He believed that how people perceived or interpreted situations was as important as any evaluation of the actual situation. People make sense of their world and act on those perceptions. Hence he is often thought of as an early attribution theorist.

The great thinker approach to understanding the history of work psychology certainly has its limitations. Who is to be selected to be a great thinker – what is the criterion? Is it that their ideas have stood the test of time and are still influential today, or is it enough that they reshaped work psychology thinking and practice in their own day? Can one qualify as a seminal thinker if all one's ideas have been overturned? Did the thinker have to influence, change or alter work psychology research or the actual behaviour and beliefs of managers; or both? How far back must one go before one can qualify as a great thinker? These are some of the unresolved questions using this approach.

The time-band perspective

The time-band perspective is not unlike the previous two approaches, except it attempts to "cut nature at her joints", not by great thinkers but by time zones. This is often done in descriptive simple histories. Time zones might be the reigns of monarchs (the Victorian, Edwardian, Regency periods); or they may be the two decades between wars (prior to the Second World War); or they may refer to periods that were economically distinct (the Depression, the expansionist 1960s); or they may refer to periods marked out by the particular technology of the time (the computer age). More commonly, the time zones are decades (Gordon, 1993; see Table 2.7).

Note that Gordon (1993) suggests only three perspectives over the whole century. The *structural* period was concerned mainly with the structure of organizations (all Weber's work on bureaucracy), the design of work (Taylor's "scientific management") and management principles (Fayol's maxims). The *behavioural* perspective looked at human relations and group dynamics in the workplace (see Hawthorne study) as well as how managers make decisions and lead. Finally, the *integral* perspective attempted not only to integrate the two (sociotechnical school), but also to understand how the external environment affects all behaviour in the workplace. Three points should be made about this and similar approaches. First, all time-band approaches give a false impression that there were sudden, dramatic and total changes from one approach or paradigm to another, which is clearly wrong. The change from the dominance of one paradigm to that of another is slow, and often two or more approaches co-exist. Secondly, this approach does not explain *why* schools of thought wax and wane. Thirdly, it often presents a very linear view of history, which implies steady progress, whereas in reality some older ideas are never fully abandoned, or indeed those rejected earlier may once again come into fashion and be embraced with new enthusiasm.

Table 2.7 Historical schools of thought and their components (by decade)

School	Decade	Perspective	Description
Organization theory prior to 1900	Before 1900	Structural	Emphasized the division of labour and the importance of machinery to facilitate labour.
Scientific management	1910s	Structural	Described management as a science, with employees having specific but different responsibilities; encouraged the scientific selection, training, and development of workers and the equal division of work between workers and management.
Classical school	1910s	Structural	Listed the duties of a manager as planning, organizing, commanding employees, coordinating activities, and controlling performances; basic principles called for specialization of work, unity of command, scalar chain of command, and coordination of activities.
Bureaucracy	1920s	Structural	Emphasized order, system, rationality, uniformity, and consistency in management; these attributes led to equitable treatment for all employees by management.
Human relations	1920s	Behavioural	Focused on the importance of the attitudes and feelings of workers; informal roles and norms influenced performance.
Classical school revisited	1930s	Structural	Re-emphasis on the Classical principles described above.
Group dynamics	1940s	Behavioural	Encouraged individual participation in decision-making; noted the impact of the workgroup on performance.
Leadership	1950s	Behavioural	Stressed the importance of groups giving both social and task leaders; differentiate between Theory X and Theory Y.
Decision theory	1960s	Behavioural	Suggested that individuals "satisfice" when they make decisions.
Sociotechnical school	1960s	Integrative	Called for considering technology and workgroups when understanding a worksystem.
Systems theory	1960s	Integrative	Represented an organization as an open system with inputs, transformations, output, and feedback; systems strive for equilibrium and experience equifinality.
Environmental theory	1960s	Integrative	Described the existence of mechanistic and organic structures and provided technological analysis of their effectiveness with specific types of environmental conditions and technological types.
Contingency theory	1980s	Integrative	Emphasized the fit between organizational processes and characteristics of the situation; called for fitting the organization's structure to various contingencies.

Source: Reproduced from Gordon (1993) with the permission of Prentice-Hall, Inc.

A retrospective review of the decades of the twentieth century

At the turn of the millennium, Crainer (2000) provided an important and useful dec-ade-by-decade review on the "equivocal" nature of the advances in management think-ing. One theme of his analysis is that each new management idea or practice carried the seeds of its own destruction. The history of management thinking is full of irony and paradox: those dedicated to increasing efficiency and flexibility "succeed" often in doing the opposite. What follows is a summary of his review of the ten decades:

- *1900–1910: Stopwatch science*: This decade saw the introduction of Taylorism engineering and Fayol theorizing. Scientific management meant measuring prod-uctivity, outputs and processes. It also saw an increase in trade unionism as well as the establishment of the Harvard Business School and the award of the first MBAs.
- *1911–1920: Modern times*: This turbulent decade saw the introduction and expan-sion of the Ford Motor plant prototypes of high production factories and assembly plants for years to come. Assembly lines symbolized specialization of labour, ergonomic design, just-in-time techniques and vastly increased efficiency. It allowed for cheaper production and market domination. Crainer (2000) suggests Ford was a "control freak" and noted that "money and power, combined with idiosyncratic and obsessive nature is a heady and at times unbalanced cocktail" (p. 35). The First World War in Europe focused attention on industrial productiv-ity. These ideas about productivity were hungrily imported in Asian countries.
- *1921–1930: Discovering the organization*: It was in this decade that real organiza-tional thinking began. It was when thinkers first thought of organizational charts, of lines of communication and of the development of management processes. It was Alfred Sloan at General Motors who contributed most by creating profes-sional dispassionate, intelligent managers who understood about decision making. He also created a model of both decentralized operations and centralized policy control. He devised business units, brand management and succession planning well before his time. Over time, Sloan's structure became a victim of committee stultification and inflexibility, but provided a useful working model. In this decade, there were many firsts: the first international management congress; the foundation of the Harvard Business Review (1922); the American Management Association and the case study method introduced at the Harvard Business School.
- *1931–1940: Discovering people*: This was the decade influenced by the Hawthorne Studies, which concluded that it was the social processes in informed work groups that had more of an effect on productivity than the physical nature of the work environment. It was only in this decade that managers began to understand the subtlety and complexity of social motivation in the workplace and to realize that workers all needed to be treated fairly and with dignity. Until this time, workers were little understood. In this period, thinkers like Follett talked of team working, responsibility, dealing with confrontation and reciprocal leadership (partnership). Also, as part of the post-depression New Deal in America, the term "industrial democracy" was born, which epitomized the new thinking about workers. In America, the 40-hour week, the minimum wage and the banning of child labour were enacted (1938).
- *1941–1950: Lessons in war*: Wars focus attention with respect both to production and the management of large numbers of people. They are also a catalyst for

inventions, many of which have useful peacetime applications. Furthermore, everyone appreciates that cooperation between management and labour is all the more necessary. The war led to the advent of mass marketing of products like Coca-Cola, Heinz soups, etc. Paradoxically, attempts to reconstruct the deflated and destroyed nations of Germany and Japan led to the establishment of better management practices and techniques than those found in the victorious nations. The Japanese in particular were determined, pragmatic, inventive and paternalistic. In this decade, the first electronic digital computer was introduced and the first Professor of Management post established (Peter Drucker at New York University).

- *1951–1960: Living the dream*: This was, for the West, the decade of plenty: growth, stability and with it loyal, hardworking executives. Schein talked of a psychological contract being an unspoken pact between employer and employee, at least at the management level and was more about stability than ability. It was also a time when the concept of corporate culture came into being. It was also a time when the "theory of marketing" was first propounded and the idea that business should be customer, rather than production, led. At the same time, key thinkers like Maslow, McGregor and Herzberg were writing about work motivation, enlightened management and job enrichment. All lamented the simple-minded, mechanistic, depressing view of the workers held by many in management. In this decade, Hewlett-Packard crafts its own vision statement and Parkinson writes the first "management humour" book.

- *1961–1970: Understanding strategy*: Drucker's ideas began to bite: management by objective; considered risk-taking; devising strategies; integrating teams; having fast informal communication; seeing the business as a whole and its relation to the local economy. There was an interest expressed in the ideas of military strategists (Machiavelli, Von Clausewitz, Sui Tzu). Decision making, gap analysis and planning became important despite the fraudulent assumption that discontinuities could be predicted, that hard data are often very soft and that strategy making can be formalized. Also, for the first time, management was seen as a profession, the chief providers of which were business schools. Managers became information analysts and for the first time were encouraged to think of themselves as a superspecies.

- *1971–1980: Organized paralysis*: "The modern co-operation was a colossus comfortable with its size. Bloated by the concept of synergy, corporations had erected labyrinthian hierarchies. Dusty recesses where little could – or needed to – be done were commonplace" (Crainer, 2000: 143). Various writers like Toffler (*Future shock*, 1991) and Mintzberg (*The nature of managerial work*, 1973) began to challenge complacency and superiority. Americans discovered that Europeans had interesting ideas about self-managed teams and sociotechnical systems. It was the decade when home computers were introduced and where, in America, the mandatory retirement age was raised from 65 to 70.

- *1981–1990: An excellent adventure*: It was in this decade that America and Europe looked to Japan only to find it was American statisticians like Deming who had designed their systems. *Theory Z: How American business can meet the Japanese challenge* by Ouchi (1981) was a bestseller, though it had tried to break stereotypes such as the belief that the Japanese were extremely rational and strategic as opposed to being creative. But it was to become the decade of quality: quality control, quality circles, quality planning. It also became a time of back to basics with ideas about competitive strategy led by Porter and ideas of threats from new competitors and of substitutes, as well as analysing the power of buyers and suppliers. Another guru Peters refocused attention onto employees and customers rather than production and strategy. It was idealistic, optimistic and perfect for the times. It was also a time when management thinkers were involved with ideas of change (Kanter) and leadership (Burns).

- *1991–2000: The new balance of power*: The decade started out with a new buzz word and strategy – re-engineering – which means identifying key processes and making them as efficient as possible. It was all about a radical rethink, starting again, a rejection of the past. It became a synonym for redundancy and downsizing. It focused on process not function. Hence there were many ideas about how "new and improved" organizations should be structured: the shamrock organization, the matrix model. It was a time when people began to think of the role of the chief executive officer. The theories include lean production, lean administration, lean management. At the turn of the century, there was a new model of workers: knowledge workers who had both power and ownership. The new world is not energy, labour or raw material intensive as know-how intensive.

Crainer (2000) concludes that management science is drawn by a quest for ideas, cures and interpretations. Companies like to think of themselves as learning organizations – as adapting when necessary. There is also a concern with ethics and values – of what drives loyalty and motivation. And, finally, there seems to be the unwilling recognition that business life is more about chaos than order; more about uncertainty than certainty.

The school of thought perspective

The school of thought perspective is a fairly common way to "organize" or think about the past and it has much in common with all three approaches mentioned before. Some writers have distinguished between *schools* of thought (or perspectives) and *movements*, or sections within the schools that had particular influence and power at a particular time. However, there are often divisions within schools, so that some writers will separate them and others will not.

The Classical school

The *Classical* (or *structural*) *school* was what the scientific management movement sought to revitalize. Whereas scientific management focused on an organization's technical core, *classical organization* focused on the management of an entire organization. Contributors to Classical organization theory (such as Weber, Fayol and others) were concerned with the *structure* of an organization and with designing processes that would make its operations rational, ordered, predictable, efficient and effective. Classical organization theorists tended to view organizations as giant machines created to achieve goals. They believed in a basic set of universal laws, or principles, that would design and run those "machines" effectively. Although the Classical school of management did not provide a totally unified approach to management, there were many similarities among the views expressed by the major proponents. Classical management was very *prescriptive* in nature: it described how people should manage organizations.

Managers were expected to follow a rational approach and a set of principles to build and operate organizations. Through their work to identify "one best way", systems were developed that led to greater organizational productivity.

Another contribution of the Classical school was their eagerness to pursue scientific enquiry into management and organizational systems. Although the various contributors to the Classical school of management agreed on many issues, there were also a few areas of disagreement. For example, there were differences in thinking about supervision in having only one or possibly many supervisors. Another area of disagreement became evident when managers put the prescriptions from the Classical contributors into practice. Fayol instructed managers to apply his 14 principles *flexibly*, making adjustments to fit each situation. In practice, however, Classical management tended to be closed and rigid. Taylor called for friendly labour–management relations, but the typical Classical approach was often cool, impersonal and adversarial.

The Classical school of management thought has various critics. Many argue that its description of organizational members as rational and economically motivated is incomplete. These critics claim that, when managers ignore the social needs of workers, organizations do not provide adequate motivation and reinforcement programmes. If managers think of organizations as machines rather than social systems, they treat employees as resources to be manipulated for organizational needs. The result has been confrontation between labour and management, as managers direct and control employees, work methods and the pursuit of organizational goals.

A second area of criticism of the Classicists revolves around their attempts to identify universal principles for efficient management. Although many of the Classical principles of management may be appropriate for organizations operating in simple, non-turbulent environments, they are less well suited to conducting business in shifting and multinational "one-world" environments.

The social behavioural school

The *social behavioural school* viewed organizations from social psychological perspectives. The contributors to the social behavioural school were concerned primarily about the welfare of employees. Negative reactions to the "coldness" of scientific management and bureaucratic theory helped ignite the human relations movement as well as the results of the Hawthorne Experiment (see pp. 94–98). Turning from task-orientated styles of management, advocates focused on employees in the belief that satisfied workers would be productive workers. A manager following the guidelines of the human relations movement would be supportive and paternalistic, creating and nurturing cohesive work groups and a psychologically healthy environment for workers. Thus, this social model proposed that increased productivity depended on the extent to which an organization could meet workers' needs for recognition, acceptance and group membership.

Two factors distinguish the behavioural science movement from the Classicists and human relations advocates. First, social scientists stressed the need to conduct systematic and controlled studies of workers and their *attitudes and behaviours*. Secondly, they emphasized that empirical observation of the human side of organizations should take place through *research techniques*, such as field and laboratory experiments. Behavioural scientists considered both the Classicists' rational/economic model and the social model espoused by human relations advocates to be incomplete representations of workers; thus, they presented a model that suggested that employees have a strong need to grow, to develop, and to maintain a high level of self-regard.

Proponents of Classical management theory envisaged increases in organizational control, efficiency and effectiveness as stemming from developments in the technical and mechanical side of an organization, but the behavioural school introduced the importance of personal and social considerations to the management task. It stimulated managers' thinking about employees and the need to design organizations that were more open and flexible. Many of the concepts introduced by the behavioural school of thought are still influential in contemporary organizations. This school also saw the rise of decision theory, which examined how managers made decisions and the role of leadership in groups and organizations as a whole.

Behavioural management thinking has several limitations, however. First, it lacks a good *language* for communicating the importance of its ideas to managers. Psychologists often use jargon that is not easily understood, and many of their theories are highly abstract. Secondly, behavioural scientists have not done well at getting the attention and respect of *key managers* in top positions. As a consequence, many managers still see organizations as mechanical systems, or purely in terms of the financial bottom line. Thirdly, in many ways, behavioural management theorists still assume that there is "one best way" to manage, but some managerial situations may call for the Classical perspective, whereas others require the behavioural perspective. This dilemma is partly addressed by contemporary management theorists.

Contemporary management thought

The past few decades have been marked by the refinement, extension and synthesis of both Classical and behavioural management thinking. *Sociotechnical systems theory*, popular since the late 1960s, tried to counteract the one-sided approach taken by the Classical and behavioural schools by balancing the technical and social-psychological sides of an organization. The perspectives of both Classical and behavioural management were combined and incorporated into several new management models.

One of the contemporary approaches to management perceives an organization as a complete system of related parts. A *system* can be defined as a set of interrelated elements that functions as a unit for a specific purpose. Alas the principle of entropy means that things made of parts tend to fall apart. Systems theorists see organizations as complex networks of interrelated parts that exist in an interdependent relationship with the external environment.

An organization, as a system, is also open and dynamic; that is, it continually receives new energy. This energy may be added in the form of new resources (people, materials and money) or information (concerning strategy, environment and history) from the environment, called *inputs*. The new energy can also alter the *transformation* of the inputs into new *outputs* (Figure 2.1).

When organizations receive new inputs or experience certain transformations, they simultaneously seek stability, balance or *equilibrium*. When organizations become unbalanced or experience disequilibrium, such as when changes in the environment or organizational practices make current resources inadequate, they attempt to return to a steady state, which may mirror or significantly differ from the state of equilibrium. They use information about their outputs, called *feedback* or *exchange*, to modify their inputs or transformations to result in more desirable outcomes and equilibrium.

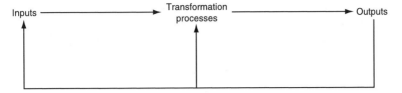

Figure 2.1 The basic systems model.

However, a distinction can, and must, be made between an organic and mechanistic system. An *organic system* is characterized by:

- a flexible structure that can change when confronted with different kinds of task demand;
- loosely defined tasks to be performed by employees;
- consultative-type organizational communications (as opposed to a commanding type of relationship);
- authority that flows more from knowledge centres (individuals, groups or specialized departments) and the nature of relationships than from strict hierarchical positions.

In contrast, a *mechanistic system* of management is characterized by:

- clear definition and relative stability of tasks and responsibility;
- vesting of authority in position and its arrangement according to hierarchical level;
- communications in the form of a downward flow of instructions issued as commands.

Burns & Stalker (1961) argued that organic and mechanistic management systems are appropriate for different kinds of environmental conditions. Dynamic environments, in which uncertainty is high and unique problems and events often arise, require an organic system. The mechanistic system is more compatible with stable environmental conditions.

Table 2.8 Mechanistic and organic management systems

	Mechanistic	*Organic*
Structure	Rigid	Flexible
Tasks	Well-defined, stable, standardized	Dynamic, loosely defined
Change	Resistant	Receptive
Authority source	From hierarchy and position	From knowledge and expertise
Control	Hierarchy	From self and peers
Communication direction	Command-type and downward	Consultative-type, up, down, horizontal, and diagonal
Communication content	Instructions and decisions issued by superiors	Information and advice

Source: Adapted from Burns & Stalker (1961).

According to the *contingency perspective*, the particular methods and techniques that managers should adopt are contingent upon the particular circumstances. Thus, the task for the manager is to identify, understand and explain the critical contingencies in every situation. Thus, they stress the need for diagnostic skills; the ability to identify an appropriate management style and be flexible enough to change styles as the circumstances demand.

Modern theorists have also become very aware of national differences in management and, more particularly, the relative success of some countries compared with others. The Americans in particular have been obsessed by the growing economic power of the Japanese and have, as a result, developed a theory to account for these differences.

In 1981, management professor William Ouchi offered *Theory Z* to integrate the merits of the Japanese (Theory J) and US (Theory A) management styles (Figure 2.2). Theory Z is less a major theory of management than it is a set of organizational and management style characteristics. Theory Z emphasizes terms of employment, decision making, responsibility, evaluation and promotion, control, career paths, and concern for employees.

Theory Z is not a contingency theory of management, because the style of management is universally better than the traditional US approach and prescribes Theory Z as appropriate for almost any management situation. In fact, in many ways, Theory Z reflects a return to the "one best way" thinking of behavioural management theory. In the tradition of behavioural management, Theory Z identifies employees as a key component of organizational productivity and effectiveness. It prescribes how employees "should be" managed, so that organizational efficiency and effectiveness improve. Ouchi's universal management prescriptions call for long-term employment and a concern for employees' total life.

Theory Z is not a complete theory, because it does not explain why certain management practices create an effective organization. Nonetheless, Ouchi's work has again heightened US and European industry's awareness of the variety of management

Theory A (American)	Theory J (Japanese)
Short-term employment	Lifetime employment
Individual decision-making	Collective decision-making
Individual responsibility	Collective responsibility
Rapid evaluation and promotion	Slow evaluation and promotion
Explicit control mechanism	Implicit control mechanisms
Specialized career path	Non-specialized career path
Segmented concern for employee as a person	Holistic concern for employee as a person

Theory Z
(Modified American)
Long-term employment
Collective decision-making
Individual responsibility
Slow evaluation and promotion
Implicit, informal control with explicit, formalized measures
Moderately specialized career paths

Figure 2.2 Theories A, J and Z. Adapted from Oudin & Jaeger (1978).

techniques that may be effective under particular circumstances (Dunham & Pierce, 1989).

Two major contributions have come from the contemporary schools of management thought. First, they have had a *unifying effect*, combining the technical side of organizations that the Classicists examined and the social elements that were the focus of the social psychologist. This strong emphasis on multidimensionality has alerted managers to the independence of organizational subsystems and the importance of integrating them to achieve efficiency and effectiveness. Secondly, the contemporary era has sensitized managers to the fact that *no one set of management principles is appropriate in all situations*. Under some circumstances, the Classical approach is effective. Under other circumstances, the behavioural model is effective. Under still others, managers should integrate and apply ideas from both the Classical and behavioural models. O'Shaughnessy (1966) has provided a helpful chart which contrasts these three approaches (see Figure 2.3).

There are two primary limitations of contemporary management approaches. The first is that each perspective is more complex than the ideas of Classical or behavioural theory, and complexity can make their use more difficult and their adoption less likely. Furthermore, it may be argued that not all are internally consistent. The second

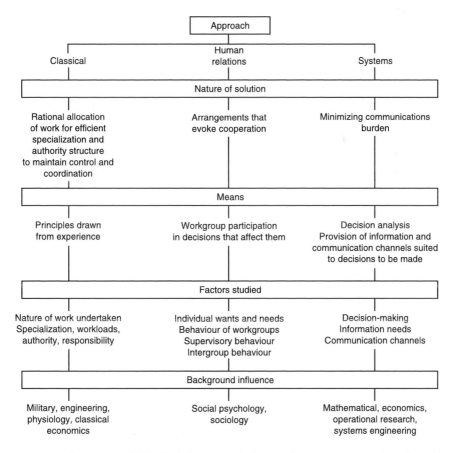

Figure 2.3 Summary of Classical, human relations and systems approaches. Reproduced from O'Shaughnessy (1966) with the permission of Allen & Unwin.

limitation is that few contemporary management perspectives have been thoroughly researched (Dunham & Pierce, 1989).

The seminal study approach

Occasionally, the results of one study may be seminal in the sense that they have a crucial effect on work psychology thought. One particular study is frequently mentioned: the Hawthorne studies. These started with a question about the cost of lighting but produced, for the researchers of the time, an inconclusive, then confusing but then explicable result. The nine-year study was begun in 1924 by the Western Electric Company in association with the US National Academy of Sciences.

A set of studies involving illumination levels were conducted between November 1924 and April 1927. These studies were intended to identify lighting levels that would produce optimal productivity at cheapest cost. It posed a simple question: Would the quality of the lighting in a manual dexterity task affect the speed and quality of production? In the first illumination experiment, however, productivity increased when illumination was increased *and* when it was decreased. Overall, productivity bounced up and down without an apparent direct relationship with illumination level. Although the conditions were systematically changed and the resultant productivity carefully measured, it seemed nothing much reduced productivity.

A second illumination study involved an experimental group, which experienced illumination changes, and a control group for which illumination was held constant. In this experiment, production increased in both groups to an almost equal extent. In yet a third illumination experiment, lighting levels were decreased over time. As a result, productivity levels *increased* for both the experimental and control groups (at least until an extremely low level of illumination was reached). Naturally, these results puzzled the experimenters of the time.

To correct some of the control problems in the lighting study, the Relay Assembly Test Room studies were conducted during 13 periods between 1927 and 1932. The experiments progressed from simply recording output under normal conditions to introducing a group incentive programme, rest periods of varying duration, reducing work weeks, and providing free lunch. Throughout this time, output, morale and attendance rates were shown to increase. It was first thought that relief from monotony, alterations in supervisory styles, and the group incentive programme accounted for the increases. Previously, all employees had worked under conditions such that the overall performance of the group had little effect on individuals. During the experiments, this was changed and individual earnings became closely related to group performance through the group incentive plan. More studies were undertaken to determine exactly how this plan influenced individual performance (Duncan, 1978).

The second Relay Assembly Room and Mica Splitting Test Room experiments had as their goal learning more about the effects of group incentive. Moderate increases in output were noted in these studies, as was an unanticipated resentment from non-experimental groups. Increasingly, the researchers were becoming aware of human attitudes and related behavioural factors. To find out more about these phenomena, between 1928 and 1930 an extensive interviewing programme was conducted among more than 21,000 employees. The interviews made it possible to investigate attitudes about the job, supervisors and working conditions. Finally, in 1931–32, the researchers conducted the Bank Wiring Observation Room studies. In this stage, both *group and informal relations* were recognized as determinants of individual attitudes towards change. Although the experimenters had initially started by looking for physical determinants of productivity, they ended up believing psychological factors were more important.

The researchers found wide differences in the social structure in the work groups they studied. They found work groups' off-work games and activities reflected upon and impacted on their work. They found individuals formed into cliques, which served many psychological functions: protect workers against management; cover for each other; invent and embellish stores and create myths. Apparently well-organized and -managed groups were far from understandable, easily regulated, tightly controlled, well-oiled machines. They were complex, dynamic and permeable groupings that profoundly impacted on working lives. Although the managerial implications of the studies are far-reaching, the value of the Hawthorne studies for researchers and managers lies in their discoveries concerning individuals, individuals in groups, and organizational design. Four conclusions were obvious (Duncan, 1978):

- *Individual differences*. The Hawthorne studies emphasized that individuals are different and that these differences can have a significant impact on managerial behaviour. The interview programme demonstrated the complexity of attitudes, and how overt behaviour may differ from attitudes. Thus, a new wage incentive or vacation policy may be perfectly acceptable to one person and totally rejected by another. Individual differences are systematic, open to investigation and taxonomizable into discrete types or continuous traits.
- *Groups*. After the findings of the Hawthorne researchers were publicized, the importance of group processes was realized. During various stages of the experiments, it became evident that informal groups *not* prescribed by organizations can, and do, exert great influence on individuals. Group pressures can cause individuals to work more or less, to accept or resist change, and to behave in a variety of ways that may differ from their own personal preferences. Further groups outside the organization can directly reflect behaviour in the organization.
- *Individuals in groups*. Formal groups are those required and established by the organization, such as production and sales units. Employees also belong to informal or social groups that are not prescribed by the structure. An established group of individuals who have worked together for a long time may form a social group who eat or pursue leisure activities together. The same is true of "newcomers" or recent employees. Such groups may be quite important in the formation of individual attitudes and in influencing work behaviour.
- *Organizational design*. The implications of the studies for the formal design of organizations have to do with perceiving the organization as a social system. Although the structure of an organization appears very fixed and formal, in reality there is an "organization" that does not show up on the chart. This social organization includes all the social groupings and power alliances that exist in all structures, which include all the friendship groups and political alliances that criss-cross the organization.

The idea of formal and informal groups, as well as organizations, is an interesting and important one, as may be seen as a result of the human relations school. Gray &

Starke (1988) recently attempted an exhaustive *compare* and *contrast* between the two (Table 2.9). Holloway noted:

> The Hawthorne studies combined two radical departures from previous industrial psychology. The first involved a shift from the psycho-physiological model of the worker to a socio-emotional one. The second was a change in method from an experimental one whose object was the body (or the interface between the body and the job), to one whose work object was attitudes as the intervening variable between situation (working conditions) and response (output). Human relations not only made possible the production of different kinds of information for the first time in the workplace, but had a powerful effect on the workers themselves. The Hawthorne interview programme discovered that a sympathetic interview technique (see section 6) could not only elicit new information which was valuable to management, but could itself be instrumental in effecting a change in employees' attitudes. Human relations training was later to be based on this insight. In summary, Hawthorne is where the "sentimental worker" came into being as the object of social science. (Holloway, 1991: 71)

Table 2.9 Comparison of formal and informal organization

Characteristic	Formal organization	Informal organization
1. *Structure*		
A. Origin	Planned	Spontaneous
B. Rationale	Rational	Emotional
C. Characteristics	Stable	Dynamic
2. *Position terminology*	Job	Role
3. *Goals*	Profitability or service to society	Member satisfaction
4. *Influence*		
A. Base	Position	Personality
B. Type	Authority	Power
C. Flow	Top-down	Bottom-up
5. *Control mechanisms*	Threat of firing, demotion	Physical or social sanctions (norms)
6. *Communication*		
A. Channels	Formal channels	Grapevine
B. Networks	Well-defined, follow formal lines	Poorly defined, cut across regular channels
C. Speed	Slow	Fast
D. Accuracy	High	Low
7. *Charting the organization*	Organization chart	Sociogram
8. *Miscellaneous*		
A. Individuals included	All individuals in workgroup	Only those "acceptable"
B. Interpersonal relations	Prescribed by job description	Arise spontaneously
C. Leadership role	Assigned by organization	Result of membership agreement
D. Basis for interaction	Functional duties or position	Personal characteristics, ethnic background, status
E. Basis for attachment	Loyalty	Cohesiveness

Source: Adapted from Gray & Starke (1988: 432).

The Hawthorne researchers have been criticized on various grounds about the conduct of their studies and their analysis of the results. Their basic assumptions about the cooperative or social nature of people and their ability to be satisfied by changes in their environment have been challenged. Furthermore, Mayo and co-researchers have been challenged on ethical grounds. They assumed that "contented" workers were productive workers in much the same way we assume contented cows give more milk (Duncan, 1978).

Perhaps the most serious criticisms made of the Hawthorne studies related to the research methodology employed. Most human relations theory and practice is based upon relatively few observations of some small samples of human beings at work. The Hawthorne researchers may have minimized the effects of economic incentives for no apparent justifiable reason, and elevated supervision and interpersonal relations to a point of primary importance. Some have argued, in effect, that the Hawthorne studies were scientifically worthless. Others have attempted to counter this criticism by claiming that the studies did make a significant contribution by placing monetary incentives in their proper place within the social context. The defenders of the studies maintain that the researchers did not deny the importance of economic incentives but simply rejected them as an independent factor influencing worker performance.

The most frequently rehearsed criticisms of the Hawthorne studies are that:

- *They lack scientific validity and tend towards mysticism*: Human relations writers generally spent little time gathering the data necessary to support this claim. When they did, it was rarely obtained in a systematic manner. For this reason, it projects an aura of mysticism or "armchair philosophizing", which is unacceptable to the modern behavioural scientist.
- *They over-emphasize the group and focus on group decision making*: In human relations writings, the object of concern almost always appears to be the relationship of the individual with the work group, with less concern for the behaviour processes of the individual.
- *They view conflict as fundamentally destructive*: Little concern was given to the positive effects of conflict, such as the stimulation of innovation. Coordination was always the goal.
- *They are evangelistic*: Advocates were insistent upon the value of human relations concepts in solving organizational problems. It has been shown that human relations, like structural thought, is a creed of the "establishment" and supports the pre-eminence of management in organizations.
- *There was no effect*: Some have agreed that a detailed study of the results in fact provides little evidence of any demonstrable effect at all (Knowles, 1958).

Much of the objection to the human relations perspective has been initiated by modern behavioural scientists who are interested in many of the same phenomena. Behavioural scientists are concerned with the systematic analysis of human behaviour and take pride in the objectivity with which they approach their subject and their adherence to the conventional methods of experimental science. They also view their research as interdisciplinary in character and realize that it is often difficult, if not impossible, to understand the sociology of a group separate from the psychology of the individuals comprising it and the anthropology of the culture within which it exists. However, there have been few subsequent studies, of whatever scientific quality, that have had such an influence on work psychology thinking (Duncan, 1978).

Integrating the different perspectives

This history of organizational psychology and work psychology can be approached in different ways through different perspectives. It is important to emphasize that these histories are complementary rather than contradictory.

The history of work psychology can probably be usefully thought of as falling into three categories. From the turn of the twentieth century until the beginning of the Second World War, work psychology was termed "scientific management" or industrial psychology. In this period, workers were thought of as factory hands. Both management and employees were thought of in rational economic terms. The idea that scientific principles could be applied to the world of work (especially management and ergonomics) was new, but the great thinkers of the day – Fayol, Taylor and Weber – all stressed this. They all believed that, by following relatively straightforward explicit principles, organizations could become more efficient. All the writing in this early period emphasized structure, order, logic and rules.

The industrial psychologists of the day certainly saw their job as increasing efficiency. The image of the time-and-motion psychologist hiding in the cupboard spying on workers probably arose at that time. The work psychology researchers and psychologists of the day certainly "took the side of management": they were not interested in occupational fatigue out of compassion for the workers, but rather how to ensure the most cost-efficient production from those workers. Yet it would be unfair to the thinkers and researchers of this first period to argue that they were not concerned with worker welfare. In hindsight it may seem patronizing, but many large companies took a genuine interest in the health and living standards of their workers.

Conscription in the two world wars meant psychologists were very active in selection. When tens of thousands of people are conscripted from all walks of life, it is someone's task to determine whether they would be best suited as pilots or pay-clerks, counter-intelligence experts or cooks. Fitting a person to the job, mental testing and vocational guidance began to emerge at the end of this period.

The second phase in the history of work psychology occurred for various reasons. The seminal Hawthorne studies had a significant effect on researchers and practitioners of the time. The Second World War not only required psychologists to use their expertise in new areas, but at the end of this most destructive of wars the hope for a better world and an end to poverty, inequality and privilege meant the whole idea of work was re-evaluated. There was less emphasis on structure, order and rules, and more on human relations. The social and emotional aspects of work began to be recognized, especially the observations that most people work in groups, which have a powerful influence on their behaviour. The focus of thinking moved from structure and efficiency to how to motivate workers. Attitude surveys were used more frequently to attempt to ascertain what workers thought and wanted. Furthermore, the concept of on-the-job training was then taken more seriously.

For much of the 1950s and 1960s, work psychology psychologists were primarily interested in features of motivation: Why were some people clearly more work-motivated than others? The relationship between motivation and satisfaction, thought earlier to be simple and linear (i.e. satisfied workers are more productive), began to be challenged.

This period is sometimes called the behavioural period, not because researchers were all behaviourists but because they focused less on the formal structure of organizations than on the informal behaviour of people in groups. Leisure activities, attitudes and values, as well as the skills and abilities of individual workers, were thought of as important. Instead of seeing specialization and division of labour as desirable for efficiency, the emphasis was placed on job rotation to reduce monotony and boredom.

At the end of this period (roughly in the 1960s), some attention was being paid to organizational development and change. It was recognized that various attitudes were unhelpful in the workplace, particularly the traditional "us versus them" of management and below. Furthermore, technological changes as well as macroeconomic developments began to show how organizations had to adapt to new working practices. The understanding and adapting to change that began at the end of this period continued into the third phase that we are experiencing today.

The third phase was dominated by rapid technological development. Many of the ideas from the new computer age, such as systems theory, were eagerly applied to organizations. People and organizations were seen as complex, variable and in a state of flux. Whereas engineering concepts dominated in the first phase, and sociological in the second, it was mathematical and economic concepts that were to come to prominence in the third phase. The way in which individuals and groups make and implement decisions was a central theme of the third phase. This led on to looking at the flow of information in organizations and how to make it more efficient.

Leadership style, worker participation, adaptation to change and the culture of organizations were (indeed still are) themes in the third phase. The perceived need for work psychology researchers and psychologists has grown considerably in this phase as they attempt to evaluate, train, measure and change people and new work practices.

It should be emphasized that the ideas of the three phases are not forgotten, ignored or pooh-poohed, but built up. Engineering psychology and ergonomics (ideas from the first phase) are growing apace as the electronic age is upon us. The importance of working groups and teams continues to be emphasized. But it is recognized that we live now in a time of rapid change and it has become part of the focus of work psychology to understand, react to (even prepare for) and adapt to these changes.

Conclusion

This chapter has been concerned with the historical background to the field of work psychology. It was argued that researchers in a discipline who ignore their history run the risk of repeating themselves and not fully understanding the origin of their ideas and research traditions. However, there are quite different ways of understanding the past, some of which were considered in this chapter.

The models of man perspective argues that, at different times, researchers (and managers) have different models (or beliefs) as to how, when and where people work best. These models, which are frequently seen as being rather simplistic and internally consistent, most often concern motivation but also satisfaction.

A quite different method is to select out a few historical figures, usually authors, whose work at one time either greatly influenced or perfectly summarized the beliefs and behaviours of a particular period. What is most debatable is the criteria for their selection and understanding to what extent their ideas remain influential. The time-based perspective is most popular. This attempts to categorize the past hundred years or so in time-bands that reflect the dominance of particular topics or schools of thought. Indeed, this approach is most popular because it attempts to show how, over the course of the twentieth century – and into the twenty-first – different theoretical or methodological paradigms have dominated both academic and popular management writing. One other approach, somewhat akin to the "great man perspective", has been the "great experiment perspective", which selects one particular study to show how it changed thinking or how it illustrates perfectly one methodology.

There is, of course, some similarity between these approaches. Indeed, one would expect their conceptions of the past to overlap, because they are, after all, examining the same phenomenon. However, there is danger in a too simple consensus about the past. It is too easy not to read the original sources and to see everything in too "neat" terms, in particular the internal coherence in schools of thought or the change from one model paradigm to another.

A research perspective

A dozen approaches to management

Management scientists are eclectic: they have and do accept many and varied approaches to understanding management science. Some would argue that this eclecticism is unhealthy and that, where approaches are shown to be quite different, effort should be placed in determining which is right, or at least better. Wenhrich & Koontz (1994) have suggested 12 different approaches (see Table 2.10).

Historians are particularly wary of prognostications about the future, but management scientists are considerably less cautious. One interesting, simple but important area of research is to examine the extent to which predictions come true. For example, Naisbitt (1982) argued that the industrial manufacturing societies of Europe would turn primarily into information societies. This, in turn, would lead to greater changes in business organizations. The following ten changes were hypothesized:

- The best and brightest gravitate towards corporations that foster personal growth.
- The manager's new role is that of coach, teacher and mentor.
- The best people want ownership – psychic and literal – in a company.
- Companies are increasingly contracting or leasing employees for specific purposes and periods of time.
- The top-down management is yielding to a networking, people style of management.
- Intrapreneurship (entrepreneurship within corporation) is revitalizing companies inside out.
- In the new corporation, quality will be paramount.
- Intuition and creativity are challenging the "it's all in the numbers" school of philosophy.
- The large corporations are emulating the personal and productive qualities of small businesses.
- The information economy enables corporations to seek quality-of-life locations over industrial centres.

Table 2.10 A dozen different approaches

Characteristics/contributions	Limitations
Case approach Studies use actual cases. Identifies successes and failures to find general principles	Situations are all different. Weak attempts to identify principles. Limited value for developing management theory. Rarely tested against new cases.
Interpersonal behaviour approach Focus on interpersonal behaviour, human relations, leadership, and motivation. Organizational issues studied through managers' style.	Ignores planning, organizing, and controlling. Underplays organizational forces.
Group behaviour approach Emphasis on behaviour of people in groups. Primarily study of group behaviour patterns. The study of large groups is often called "organizational behaviour".	Often not integrated with management concepts, principles, theory, and techniques. Need for closer integration with organization structure design, staffing, planning, and controlling. Both individual and organizational structure underplayed.
Cooperative social systems approach Concerned with both interpersonal and group behavioural aspects leading to a system of cooperation. Expanded concept includes any cooperative group with a clear purpose.	Too broad a field for the study of management and overlooks many managerial concepts, principles, and techniques. Focuses too narrowly on the cooperative–competition dimension.
Sociotechnical systems approach Technical system has great effect on social system. Focuses on production, office operations, and other areas with close relationships between the technical system and people.	Emphasis only on blue-collar and lower-level office work. Stresses too much technical systems, particularly in jobs where they are less important.
Decision theory approach Focuses on the making of decisions, persons or groups making decisions, and the decision-making process.	There is more to managing than making decisions. The focus is at the same time too narrow and too wide.
Systems approach Recognizes importance of studying inter-relatedness of planning, organizing, and controlling in an organization as well as the many subsystems. Systems have boundaries, but they also interact with the external environment, i.e. organizations are open systems.	Analyses the interrelatedness of systems and subsystems as well as the interactions of organizations with their external environment. Focuses on relations between and neglects processes within.
Mathematical or "management science" approach Managing is seen as mathematical processes, concepts, symbols, and models. Looks at management as a purely logical process, expressed in mathematical symbols and relationships.	Preoccupation with mathematical models. Many aspects in managing cannot be modelled. Weak at the "softer" aspects of management.

Continued

Table 2.10 continued

Characteristics/contributions	Limitations
Contingency or situational approach Managerial practice depends on particular circumstances (i.e. a contingency or a situation). Contingency theory recognizes the influence of given solutions on organizational behaviour patterns.	There is *no* one best way to do things. Difficulty in determining all relevant contingency factors and showing their relationships. Very complex but relative and case-specific.
Managerial roles approach Ten managerial roles were identified and grouped into (1) interpersonal, (2) informational, and (3) decision roles. Focuses on the varied roles managers must have.	Some role activities are not managerial. Activities are evidence of planning, organizing, staffing, leading, and controlling. But some specific managerial activities were left out (e.g. appraising managers). Neglects to examine role of structure.
McKinsey's 7-S framework The seven S's are (1) strategy, (2) structure, (3) systems, (4) style, (5) staff, (6) shared values, (7) skills.	The terms used are not precise and topics are not discussed in length.
Operational approach Draws together concepts, principles, techniques, and knowledge from other fields and managerial approaches. Distinguishes between managerial and non-managerial knowledge. Develops classification system built around the managerial functions of planning, organizing, staffing, leading, and controlling.	Does not, as some authors do, identify "representing" or "coordination" as a separate function. Too eager to taxonomize.

Source: Adapted from Wenhrich & Koontz (1994).

To what extent was he correct? What is more difficult to establish, however, is whether the forecasts came true because of the operation of self-fulfilling prophesies – the idea that managers and individuals read these forecasts and made the changes anticipated, hence fulfilling the prognostication.

Handy (1985) in a book entitled *The future of work*, noted eight major changes in the pattern of work in post-industrialized countries (see Chapter 16):

- A full-employment society was becoming part-employment.
- Manual skills were being replaced by knowledge as the basis of work.
- Industry was declining and services growing.
- Hierarchies and bureaucracies were being replaced by networks and partnerships.
- One-organization careers were being replaced by job mobility and career change.
- The "third stage" of life (post-employment) was becoming more and more important.
- Sex roles at work and at home are no longer rigid.
- Work was shifting southwards, inside countries and between countries.

A study of the past and crystal-ball gazing into the future are no substitute for research in the present. Certainly, researchers need to understand how organizations are managed today; what

managers believe and the current forces that shape work psychology. There is always the important question to ask in each generation: What is it that managers (and workers) actually do, as
opposed to what they say they do?

A cross-cultural perspective

Is organizational success the same in different countries? In their analysis of modern capitalism,
Hampden-Turner & Trompenaars (1993) isolated seven different modes of wealth creation:

- *Making rules and discovering exceptions*: In a search for standards, organizations have to
  create rules, codes, procedures and routine, but they have to be flexible to deal with special
  exceptions and competitive standards. An organization that re-evaluates the standards regularly is one that achieves success.
- *Constructing and deconstructing*: Organizations need to look carefully, regularly and critically at how they are configured, designed and organized. Successful organizations are aware
  of the need periodically to upgrade every prospect of their process.
- *Managing communities of individuals*: If people are the most important resource, organizations have to support (and challenge) them. They need to think simultaneously of the rights,
  obligations and needs of employees, shareholders, customers and the wider society. Given
  that an organization can perform this difficult task, it may be successful, but it cannot expect
  long-term success without it.
- *Internalizing the outside world*: A successful enterprise needs to be alert to changes and
  developments in the outside world (and reject the "not invented here" syndrome) and to
  exploit fully the talent and inspiration of its own workforce.
- *Synchronizing fast processes*: The use (and abuse) of time is clearly related to success.
  Organizations need fast synchronized processes to succeed over their competitors.
- *Choosing among achievers*: Promotion and selection should be based on ability, and rewards
  should be commensurate with contributions. Goals must be set and those who achieve them
  appropriately rewarded. The system should be both fair and seen to be fair.
- *Sponsoring equal opportunities to excel*: Success depends in part on equality of opportunity
  and a fair content. Organizations need to have integrity in helping their employees.

The question remains as to which cultures favour which of the above methods and why.
Terpstra (1978) has listed eight factors upon which cultures differ and which directly affect
internal and international business. They are ever changing and need updating every so often.

1. *Language*	2. *Religion*	3. *Values*
Spoken language	Sacred work objects	Towards:
Written language	Philosophical systems	Time
Official language	Beliefs and norms	Achievement
Linguistic pluralism	Prayer	Work
Language hierarchy	Taboos	Wealth
International languages	Holidays	Change
Mass media	Rituals	Scientific method
Risk-taking		

4. *Law*	5. *Education*	6. *Politics*
Common law	Formal education	Nationalism
Code law	Vocational education	Sovereignty
Foreign law	Primary education	Imperialism
Home country law	Secondary education	Power
Antitrust policy	Higher education	National interests
International law	Literacy level	Ideologies
Regulation	Human resources planning	Political risk

7. *Technology*	8. *Social organizations*
Transportation	Kinship
Energy systems	Social institutions
Tools and objects	Authority structures
Communications	Interest groups
Urbanization	Social mobility
Science	Social stratification
Invention	Status systems

A human resources perspective

Fads and fashions

Despite the fact that management issues change little, like the clothing industry managers are encouraged to pay attention to the latest fashions, which they are assured will solve all problems. They come and go, get rediscovered, forgotten, repackaged, and so on. Most offer quick-fix answers to pressing problems. American business managers frequently identify with these and currently they are:

- *Fads in planning*: One of the fashionable ideas is *strategic alliance*, which means that companies cooperate, as in forming a joint venture, often across national boundaries. Airlines, telecommunications companies and car manufacturers do this.
- *Fads in organizing*: *Corporate culture* refers to the values and beliefs shared by employees and the general patterns of their behaviour. Some believe that if this is planned, designed and controlled correctly, all the ills of the organization will be solved.
- *Fads in staffing*: Organizations have to be staffed by people who are not only competent but also healthy. This requires *wellness* or *fitness* programmes and the management of stress.
- *Paying for performance*: Paying for performance is also currently fashionable. This means measuring the contributions of individuals and rewarding them accordingly, although the problems of measuring performances are often overlooked. Another current popular idea is *demassing*, or down- or right-sizing, which is a euphemism for laying off employees or demoting managers, usually middle managers.
- *Fads in leading*: An *intrapreneur* is a person who acts like an entrepreneur but does so within the organizational environment. Intrapreneurs have been described as "those who take hands-on responsibility for creating innovation of any kind within an organization". Organizations are meant to chase and foster these people.
- *Fads in controlling*: *Quality circles*, widely used in Japan, are seen as a way of improving quality and making US products more competitive. These have been set up all over the place.

Human resources or personnel directors are interested in the application of academic ideas. They face many difficult problems, and popular writers and consultants periodically come up with different solutions. Although many ideas and techniques are important, if not crucial, others are simply dressed up common sense. Hence, management science is very faddish. The list in Table 2.11 is based on that of Rachman & Mescon (1987).

Table 2.11 Five decades of management fads

Decade	Buzzword	Fad
1950s	Computerization	Installing corporate mainframe computers
	Theory Z	Giving people more say in their work so they will produce more
	Quantitative management	Running an organization by the numbers
	Diversification	Countering ups and downs in the business cycle by buying other businesses
	Management by objectives	Setting managerial goals through negotiation
1960s	T-groups	Teaching managers interpersonal sensitivity by putting them in encounter seminars
	Centralization/ decentralization	Letting headquarters make the decisions/letting middle managers make the decisions
	Matrix management	Assigning managers to different groups according to the task
	Conglomeration	Putting various types of businesses under a single corporate umbrella
	Managerial grid	Determining whether a manager's chief concern is people or production
1970s	Zero-based budgeting	Budgeting without reference to the previous year's numbers
	Experience curve	Generating profits by cutting prices, gaining market share and boosting efficiency
	Portfolio management	Ranking businesses as "cash cows", "stars" or "dogs"
1980s	Theory Z	Adopting such techniques as quality circles and job enrichment
	Intrapreneuring	Encouraging managers to create and control entrepreneurial projects within the corporation
	Demassing	Trimming the workforce and demoting managers
	Restructuring	Getting rid of lines of business that aren't performing, often while taking on considerable debt
	Corporate culture	Defining an organization's style in terms of its values, goals, rituals, and heroes
	One-minute management	Balancing praise and criticism of workers in 60-second conferences
	Management by walking around	Leaving the office to visit work stations instead of relying on written reports for information
1990s	TQM manager (total quality management)	Concentrating on producing high quality (no reject) products and services
	Re-engineering	Restructuring the organization from scratch based on an understanding of function
	De-layering/"rightsizing"	Cutting out levels of middle management to produce flatter organizations
	Empowerment	Pushing down responsibility to lower levels in the organization

Source: Adapted from Rachman & Mescon (1987).

References

Burns, T., & Stalker, J. (1961). *The management of innovation*. London: Tavistock.

Champy, J., & Hammer, M. (1993). *Reengineering the corporation*. London: Nicholas Brealey.

Cherns, A. (1982). Culture and values: The reciprocal influence between applied social science and its cultural and historical context. In N. Nicholson & T. Wall (eds.), *The theory and practice of organizational psychology* (pp. 41–63). London: Academic Press.

Cherrington, D. (1980). *The work ethic: Working values and values that work*. New York: Amacom.

Crainer, N. (2000). *The management century: A critical review of 20th century thought and practice*. San Francisco, CA: Jossey-Bass.

Ditz, G. (1980). *The Protestant ethic and the market economy*. *Kyklos, 33*, 623–657.

Duncan, W. (1978). *Essentials of management*. Hinsdale, IL: Dryden Press.

Dunham, R., & Pierce, J. (1989). *Management*. London: Scott, Foresman & Co.

Fayol, H. (1919). *General and industrial management*. London: Pitman.

Furnham, A. (1990). *The Protestant work ethic*. London: Routledge.

Giddens, A. (1972). *Politics and sociology in the thought of Max Weber*. London: Macmillan.

Gordon, J. (1993). *A diagnostic approach to organizational behaviour*. Boston, MA: Allyn & Bacon.

Gray, J., & Starke, F. (1988). *Organizational behaviour: Concepts and applications*. New York: Charles Merrill.

Hampden-Turner, C., & Trompenaars, F. (1993). *The seven cultures of capitalism*. London: Plankus.

Handy, C. (1985). *The future of work*. Oxford: Blackwell.

Holloway, W. (1991). *Work psychological and organizational behaviour*. London: Sage.

Knowles, W. (1958). Human relations in industry: Research and concepts. *California Management Review, 4*, 87–103.

McGregor, D. (1960). *The human side of enterprise*. New York: McGraw-Hill.

Mintzberg, H. (1973). *The nature of managerial work*. New York: Harper & Row.

Munsterberg, H. (1913). *Psychology and industrial efficiency*. New York: Houghton Mifflin.

Naisbitt, J. (1982). *Megatrends: Ten new directions transforming our lives*. New York: Warner.

Oates, W. (1971). *Confessions of a workaholic*. New York: World Publishing.

O'Shaughnessy, J. (1966). *Business organization*. London: George Allen & Unwin.

Ouchi, W. (1981). *Theory 2: How American business can meet the Japanese challenge*. New York: Avon Books.

Oudin, W., & Jaeger, A. (1978). Type 2 organization: Stability in the midst of mobility. *Academy of Management Review, 3*, 3–19.

Rachman, D., & Mescon, M. (1987). *Business today*. New York: Random House.

Robbins, S. (1991). *Organizational behaviour*. New York: Prentice-Hall.

Rosenthal, R. (1966). *Experimenter effects in behaviour research*. New York: Appleton-Century-Crofts.

Schein, E. (1970). *Organizational psychology*. Englewood Cliffs, NJ: Prentice-Hall.

Schermerhorn, J., Hunt, J., & Osborn, R. (1994). *Managing organizational behavior*. New York: Wiley.

Taylor, F. (1911). *Principles of scientific management*. New York: Harper & Brothers.

Terpstra, V. (1978). *The cultural environment of international business*. Cincinnati, OH: Southwestern Publishing.

Toffler, A. (1991). *Future shock*. New York: Bantam Books.

Weisbrod, M. (1995). Participative work design: A personal odyssey. *Organizational Dynamics, 13*, 17–27.

Wenhrich, H., & Koontz, H. (1994). *Management: A global perspective*. New York: McGraw-Hill.

Winefield, I. (1984). *People in business*. London: Heinemann.

Wrightsman, L. (1964). Measurement of philosophies of human nature. *Psychological Reports, 14*, 743–751.

3 Vocational choice, organizational selection and socialization

Introduction

When Churchill stood in the bombed House of Commons during the Second World War he said, "We shape our buildings and afterwards they shape us". By this he implied the two-way direction of causality: we determine the shape of our buildings (for function, among other things) which then determines how we behave in them (quite deliberately). Equally we choose our vocation (job, education, career), but afterwards the job and organization shape us and determine subsequent choices. Often chance factors lead us down job paths that have dramatic consequences for our whole working lives. People act upon the world and often change it and are, in turn, changed by the consequences of their actions. As the proverb puts it, "We make our beds and then we lie in them".

This chapter is about vocational choice, selection and organizational socialization, or how organizations try to mould our beliefs, behaviours and values at work. It concerns the reasons *why* people choose various vocations, the wisdom of those choices and the possibilities of giving them the best possible kind of advice, as to what to do, when and why. Many factors constrain job choices: ability, age, education, as well as social, economic and political factors. Indeed, chance happenings can have a profound effect on vocational choice and satisfaction.

The initial job selection process is a significant issue for school and university leavers. Furthermore, as "jobs for life" end and short contracts become more common, it may be as many as a dozen times during a working life that an individual will seek out a new job, possibly in many varied areas. Once it was thought that vocational guidance was almost exclusively for young leavers. Now there are specialist outplacement and career advisors for middle-aged executives changing jobs in mid-life. Job seekers often need help and guidance in evaluating their own skills, abilities and preferences, as well as evaluating the job market and how to enter and stay in it. Certainly, organizations do (or at least should) invest considerable effort in recruiting, selecting and training employees who will be optimally happy and productive. Employee selection is not an easy business: there are so many variables and factors to consider, not all of which are easy to measure and evaluate. Often "political" issues within an organization mean that there are many constraints on selection that are not particularly relevant to fitting the best person to the job. Selection of the potential employee by the employer (and vice versa) is an important topic in all organizations.

But organizations also play a strong part in shaping individuals. The way they recruit, select, orientate and socialize newcomers can have a powerful and lasting impact on them. Organizations choose employees as much as employees choose organizations. Hence, the *interview* where both groups select each other.

Hogan, Carpenter, Briggs & Hansson (1985) noted that psychologists have been doing "vocational assessments" in industry since just after the start of the twentieth century, whereas academics have been interested in the topic since the 1920s. Over the century the pendulum swung, among different groups (practitioners, academics), from extreme enthusiasm to guarded scepticism about the usefulness of personality tests in industry. Hogan *et al.* have attempted to refute the traditional academic cynicism regarding the utility of personality assessment in occupational selection:

- Classic, well-cited reviews of occupational validity of personality measures are, if considered carefully, much less damaging than typically believed.
- There are too many "personality inventories" that are not equivalent in their theoretical origin, construction or measurement goal – hence the equivocal results, which are relatively easily explained.
- Too many of the personality measures used in occupational settings were devised to detect psychopathology, hence their limited usefulness in selection.

Hogan *et al.* (1985: 24–25) note:

> Key terms are seldom defined; the goals of measurement are often unspecified; the meaning of test scores is rarely examined; and validity issues are often ignored. In the midst of all this confusion, it is a testimonial to the robustness of the enterprise that significant empirical results are ever reported.

Unfortunately, as Hogan *et al.* observe, both applied psychologists and managers tend to think of personality in clinical terms, and hence choose clinical measures. However, they see the importance of organizations doing personality audits, so that sensible training and selection decisions can be made.

Vocational choice and guidance

The fundamental purpose of vocational guidance and counselling is obvious and quite straightforward: it is to help people make appropriate vocational choices and adjustment, and to facilitate the efficient and cost-effective functioning of organizations by the appropriate exploitation of individual assets and abilities. To a large extent, the work on vocational guidance is identical to that of employee selection – except the former takes the perspective of, and is primarily concerned with, the best interests of the employee, whereas the latter is mainly the concern of the employer. Because there are striking individual differences in ability, aptitude, needs, personality and interests, and job differences in the demands they make in terms of personal attributes and skills, people will do better in jobs for which their abilities are suited than in those vocations where their skills are incongruous.

Vocational (occasionally termed "career") psychology focuses on people thinking about careers, preparing for the occupations of their choice and, where appropriate, changing jobs or even leaving the world of paid work for things like "early" retirement. Occupational choice is determined by many factors, including socioeconomic status, ethnicity, gender, intelligence, aptitudes and interests, as well as the community from which people come. Vocational psychologists help people explore their long-range personal and professional goals, look at personal strengths and weaknesses, as well as environmental threats and opportunities to examine salient and suitable career alternatives. Vocational guidance is one of the oldest areas of applied psychology. Super (1983) has reviewed the history of what he calls the *differential psychology applied to occupations* and the *developmental psychology of careers*. He noted the impetus that both world wars gave to the classifying of large numbers of drafted men and assigning them to appropriate military jobs.

Many organizations are becoming aware of the career development of employees. Over time it is quite common for people to be promoted in rank or level (concomitant changes in responsibilities and skills), or move horizontally or laterally (with functional or technical changes). These lead to significant changes, which the individual might or might not be able to cope with.

Arnold (1997) has noted that job changes occur more frequently now and hence people are having to make and remake career decisions more often. People relocate more often and are told that they, rather than the organization, will manage their careers. The following may be of help:

- *Mentoring*: an employee is assigned (or chooses) an older, hopefully wiser employee to guide, assist and support them.
- *Succession planning*: looking at who, when and how people should succeed into jobs.
- *Development centres*: assessment centres used to identify developmental needs.
- *Development through the jobs*: this is essentially old ideas associated with job enrichment and rotation.
- *Career counselling*: helping people to make wise decisions rather than actually giving them advice.

As Dawis (1992) notes, people's interests, values and preferences are stable consequences of various life experiences and are thought of as good indicators of motives. Thus, it is argued that, when combined with abilities, they are good predictors of experience. Hence, a great deal of work has gone into trying to taxonomize the basic interest factors. Dawis derived a table from the work of five scholarly works, which seem to delineate 12 different interest factors (Table 3.1). Certainly, one central feature of occupational psychology is trying to establish reliably the interests of individuals and then recommending jobs that fulfil these interests.

According to Savickas (1995), there are currently four major schisms in vocational psychology:

1   The theory versus practice issue: practitioners claim that academic theories are of little use in the "real world", while academics insist that practice should be informed by research, data gathering and theory.
2   Integration versus separation from other areas of mainstream psychology like developmental, social and personality psychology.
3   Counselling vs. psychotherapy: is career counselling different from or a branch of psychotherapy?
4   Opposition camps with unique constructs which ignore one another.

Table 3.1 Different factors identified in five factor analytic studies

Guildford et al. (1954)	Lorr & Suziedelis (1973)	Rounds & Davis (1979)	Kuder (1977)	Zytowski (1976a)
Mechanical	Mechanical activities	Mechanical activity	Mechanical	Skilled trades
Scientific	Quantitative Science High-status Professional	Science Mathematics Medical Science	Science– mathematics Medical Engineering Dietetics	Mathematic– numeric Medical service
Social welfare	Social welfare activities	Social service Public service	Social welfare	Helping
Aesthetic expression	Art activities	Aesthetics	Artistic Literary Musical	Art
Clerical		Clerical activity	Accounting– clerical	
Business	Sales and business management Leading and directing	Business contact Meeting and directing people	Persuasive Political	Business versus physical science
Outdoor work	Outdoor work Military activity	Nature Military activity	Outdoor Drive	Agriculture Active versus sedentary
Physical drive	Outdoor sports Extroversive– competitive games	Athletics–adventure	Aggressiveness Physical education	
Adventure versus security	Risk and change	Security versus adventure		
	Religious activities	Religion Teaching Domestic arts	Religious Library science Femininity– masculinity	Home-making
Aesthetic appreciation		Aesthetic appreciation Fashionable Appearance		
Cultural conformity Diversion Attention Aggression Thinking Orderliness Sociability Precision	Liberal Non-conformist	Non-conformity		

Source: Modified and reproduced from Dawis (1992) with permission of Consulting Psychologists Press. Copyright 1992 by Davies-Black.

However, there are now more signs of *rapprochement*, convergence and bridging but often through the relativism of postmodern philosophy. Savickas (2001) believes vocational psychology needs to reaffirm research as a core activity and articulate a research agenda. He believes it needs to forge links with related disciplines, bridge the rift between science and practice, and diversify epistemology. Most importantly, it needs to adapt to the new world of working and recommit to the issues of recruitment and training.

Career typology

Once, ability and long service were rewarded by a steady climb up the corporate ladder. The speed and endpoint in the career were defined only by ability and service (and perhaps a bit of politics). Today, the idea of a "job for life" is, for many people, neither possible nor desirable. In many European countries, about one-third to one-half of the workforce are in temporary employment or self-employment. There is now a cohort of young people, aged 30 years and under, who expect and look forward to building up a portfolio of jobs in different companies. They are content to give 5–8 years of loyal and enthusiastic service to a variety of possibly widely different companies so as to increase their experience and competence.

For many people, this new approach to a working life is exciting rather than worrying. It has been estimated that people used to have about 100,000 working hours over a 47-year working life to pursue a career. Now 47 years has shrunk to 30, with many retiring at 50 and thinking of a "second career". Whereas some older people perceive this as a threat, many younger people interpret it as a major opportunity – with change comes growth and opportunity.

Employment has changed and so have careers. The way people approached a career was characterized by many different strategies:

- *Drifters*: appear rather directionless and unambitious. Some seem not to be able to hold down a job for any period of time, but they are flexible and adaptable as they take on new jobs every so often. Drifters are seen by some people to be capricious, fickle or even reckless. More positively, they are adventurous and experimental.
- *Lifers*: are the opposite of drifters – the lifer's first job is their last. Although they might not have chosen their first job judiciously, or with foresight, they settle down for life. Although this may be an excellent strategy if one is in a company on the move, it is more likely to be a trade-off of high risk/gain over security. Furthermore, downsizing and restructuring may leave them not very employable. Lifers are loyal, but they are risk-averse, and liable to be alienated as performance management systems replace seniority-based or service ideologies.
- *Hoppers*: look like snakes-and-ladders experts. They climb short ladders quite fast, perhaps in small companies or departments, but slide down slippery snakes as they change jobs in the search for betterment. They lack the long-term vision of the planner, who has the whole journey mapped out. They may make job move decisions too quickly, based on too few data.
- *Planners*: have clear targets, sometimes over-ambitiously fantasized. They can articulate where they want to be at the big milestones of life (aged 40, 55 or 60). They may even cultivate head-hunters, apply (whimsically) for jobs on a regular

basis, and update their CVs quarterly. Planners are committed to their career development. They understand the modern world of portfolio management.

- *Hobbyists*: are masters of this final strategy. Some are SOBO's – Shoved Out, but Better Off – but many, often in their forties, become concerned with self-development. They echo the observation of a priest, who for years counselled the dying, heard their confessions and their regrets; no-one said that they wished they had spent more time in the office. The hobbyist may take early retirement, turn to consultancy, or simply define quality of life as more important than the rat race. This makes them interesting people, but not always deeply committed to the company's interest. Work is a hobby for these people.

Who exactly is responsible for one's career or, more likely, careers? Three groups have specific responsibilities for an individual's career development. First, the organization itself should provide training and developmental opportunities where possible. Courses, sabbaticals, job shares and shadowing experiences, for instance, all help. They need to provide realistic and up-to-date career information and, where necessary, out-placement services. Indeed, these will become more important in helping people to choose to work for a particular organization.

Managers, too, have responsibilities. They need to provide high-quality and timely feedback on performance so that staff get to appraise themselves realistically. They need to have regular, expectation-managing discussions and support their reports in their action plans. Again, where possible, they need to offer developmental assignments where they can acquire new skills. Honest feedback and opportunities to develop new skills are the best things any manager can do for his or her employees, permanent or temporary.

Of course, individuals must accept responsibility for their own career. They cannot expect to remain passive. Individuals must seek out information on careers within and without the organization; they must initiate talks with their managers about careers and be prepared to invest in assessing their strengths and weaknesses. They need to be prepared to take up development opportunities even if they are outside their particular comfort zone.

The ability to have multiple careers, probably a better way of working than the temporary career, means that people will have to learn new skills and reinvent them-selves. We will all need to be more feedback-seeking and more eager to learn from others. Chosen jobs need to fit ability and values, and a sense of identity. Support and affinity groups, networks and adult learning centres are some of the best sources of help in personal career development. We will all need to learn how to plan and develop our working careers in the future.

Paradoxically, learning from experience seems to be more critical than ever, yet past experience has less relevance to current experience because of the speed of change. In the new world of self-reliant careers, it will be essential for individuals to take an active role in steering their own ship and plotting their own course. Compared with the past, there will need to be a higher degree of learning by oneself, of communicating with others, interdisciplinary work, working in groups and solving personal problems.

Theories in vocational psychology

There is no shortage of theory in vocational psychology, although there is something of a dearth of well designed, conducted and analysed studies to test them. Indeed, there are so many theories in the area it is necessary to group or classify them (Furnham, 1992):

- *Developmental*: These are theories that focus on developmental stages, tasks or phases, typically as aspects of a life-long process. The individual has some measure of control and some freedom of choice; however, environmental factors play a part. Effort is then expended in trying to determine what stage a person has reached and what job is most important for that stage.
- *Needs*: The psychological needs of individuals are considered the paramount determinants. What need-theorists do is try to specify all the salient and relevant needs of both the individual and organization, and show how they can best be fulfilled in different jobs.
- *Psychoanalytical*: Psychoanalytical vocational development theory deals with personality dynamics, using concepts like id, ego and super-ego as well as oral, anal and phallic characteristics. This approach stresses the need for a full dynamic understanding of the individual and how he or she is likely to function in organizations.
- *Sociological*: Theorists in this group consider sociological factors to be major influences. Such factors include the home, school and community as primarily shaping both job choice and fit, which are stressed, rather than personality or ability.
- *Decision making*: This is an emerging approach focusing on the way the individual utilizes information, self-knowledge and perceptions of rewards in making the successive choices involved in career development. However, all theories focus on decisions and state with varying degrees of specificity how decisions are made.
- *Existential*: Comparatively little has been written from this point of view, but there are some indications that it is an area of concern. Much of existential psychology, as it relates to choice and fulfilling potentialities, inevitably touches upon career development.

Vocational psychology has been catholic and eclectic in its reliance on theories from other areas, especially cognitive and moral development, achievement motivation and decision-making skills. Yet it has developed various relatively new themes: the vocational behaviour of women, blacks and linguistic minorities, career development and worker adjustment problems (Fretz & Leong, 1982). The importance of sex differences in occupational choice has received particular attention recently (Hollenbeck, Ilgen, Ostroff, & Vancouver, 1987).

In 2001, a special issue of the *Journal of Vocational Psychology* was devoted to looking both back and forward critically, but realistically, at the field (Betz, 2001; Blustein, 2001). Various contributors tried to list strengths and weaknesses. Tinsley's (2001) suggested strengths were theoretical diversity and research vigour. He listed four weaknesses: much research is done by dabblers in the field rather than those doing systematic and programmatic research; the field is criticized too often by pundits who offer little contribution themselves; others boost a favoured theory, instruments of practice too much; and, finally, vocational psychology has been marginalized to the status of a fringe interest in counselling psychology.

Russell (2001) offered an interesting SWOT analysis of the field:

Strengths:

- The field is large, diverse and interdisciplinary.
- The mission is clear: expand knowledge about vocational choice and adjustment across the life span.
- The field can be distinguished from its competition.
- The field is strong in advancing theories of career choice and adjustment.
- The topic has relevance to adults of all ages.
- Researchers employ a wide variety of method stages.

Weaknesses:

- The mission can become unfocused and fragmented because of interest in such diverse areas.
- The focus often forgets the organizational perspective.
- Researchers do not always draw most efficiently on the up-to-date salient research of other areas.
- Sometimes methodological rigour is poor.

Opportunities:

- Theory building and practical knowledge on career decisions and choices.
- Better guidance given new career opportunities and a more diverse workforce.
- A better understanding of how people adjust to changes at work.
- More insight into how people perceive their career and job transitions.
- Understanding the interface of work, career and family issues.
- How entrepreneurs face new business start-up issues.
- How to reach a wider interdisciplinary audience of academics and practitioners.
- Using different groups and means (i.e. internet) to reach new groups.

Threats:

- Researchers must be willing to learn from theorists in other areas.
- Practitioners must be willing and able to advise individuals and employers.

Because of changes in organizations, careers, technology, education and society at large, it is imperative that vocational psychology "keeps up" with changing times.

Others who have performed a SWOT analysis came to similar conclusions (Subick, 2001). Lent (2001: 220) proposed a new mission statement:

> a) to foster scientific understanding of career choice and development, including issues of occupational preparation, transition, entry, adjustment, satisfaction, health and change or stability; b) to translate career theory and research into practice in the form of developmental, preventive, and remedial services; and c) to train new professionals (and to provide continuing education to more senior professionals) to serve an increasingly diverse clientele consisting of students (of all ages), workers, the unemployed, those undergoing work transition, retirees, and systems (e.g. schools, work organizations, dual-career couples, and families).

Walsh (2001) argues that one of the most important challenges of vocational psychology is keeping up to date with progress in differential psychology (the study of individuals differences). Vondracek (2001), on the other hand, stresses the importance of a developmental perspective in vocational psychology with a full life-span perspective. Hesketh (2001) highlights five important, strategic issues for vocational psychology.

- Understanding the genetic basis of skills (abilities) and how to stretch them if possible.
- Helping people to apply our current knowledge of change transfer of training and adaptive performance.
- Stressing the importance of goal setting and self-efficacy and other metacognitive skills.
- Working at the work/non-work balance and virtual work organizations.
- Trying to better understand the time dimension in vocational psychology.

Many observers, like Fouad (2001), have pointed to vocational psychology's class-bound perception of work. That is, working-class or poor people have had their vocations ignored or marginalized. Vocational psychology seems more a white – rather than blue – collar researched world.

Gottfredson (2001) recommends four strategies for strengthening the future of vocational psychology: (1) not to be confined to examining individuals but to look at the vocational goals of employers, ethnic/cultural groups or the economic system in general; (2) an emphasis on training in measurement theory and methods; (3) to set-up and use a good database; and (4) to find students interested in scientific research.

Recent research has identified differences between the sexes in occupational perceptions and expectations (Bridges, 1988). Kirkcaldy (1988) found, perhaps quite predictably, that females displayed less interest in technical trades and scientific occupations, but more interest in design-orientated and social–educational occupations. Overall, females emerged as less likely to choose task-orientated jobs and more inclined to select creativity expressive occupations, indicating a preference for more permissive, less structured occupations in environments allowing for artistic, emotional and introspective forms of expression.

There has also been a great deal of renewed interest in young people's occupational expectations (Crowley & Shapiro, 1982), although there is nothing new in this (Nelson 1963). Studies have examined pre-school and elementary school children (Tremaine, Schau, & Busch, 1982), secondary school children (Borgen & Young, 1982), as well as university students (Taylor, 1985), and have noted how they change as a function of socioeconomic circumstances.

Schemata theory (the schema or ideas people have about jobs) has been particularly useful in investigating stereotypes of occupations. Levy, Kaler & Schall (1988) asked 110 people to rate 14 occupations along various personality characteristics, including introvert/extravert, feminine/masculine and intelligent/non-intelligent. Two factors emerged – achievements versus helping orientation and high/low educational level – and it appears possible to "plot" people on each dimension. This may be a simple beginning but a useful one in terms of understanding the nature of different jobs (Furnham, 1992).

Kline (1975) has questioned all theories in vocational psychology on the grounds, first, that the theories do not travel across culture and country, and, secondly, that vocational (choice) theories should be part of more general theory relating to all aspects of behaviour.

Recruitment

Research into recruitment processes and procedures is comparatively new. Rynes and Cable (2003) suggest that one has to understand this research in terms of four factors:

1   *The context*: The external job/economic environment but, more importantly, issues around the organization doing the recruiting: location, size, reputation as an employee. The importance of the industry in which the organization operates (e.g. telecommunications, health care, manufacturing), overall familiarity with the organization and its established profitability influence, its image, applicant attraction and ease of recruitment.
2   *Recruitment activities and practices*: Trained, attractive, enthusiastic recruiters can and do have a powerful influence on the perception of the organization. It is not clear if people recruited informally (through personal contacts) survive longer than those recruited formally. Recruitment administrative procedures can signal efficiency and professionalism or, indeed, their opposite. Potential candidates are also influenced by company affirmative action and general selection procedures. Clearly, the advertised pay and benefits are of fundamental importance.
3   *Processes*: High-quality applicants are critical of processes. Companies differ in the time delay between recruitment, decision and hiring, which can have significant effects. Job seekers' social networks often explain their choice of career over and above other factors. Certainly, applicants' pre-interview/screening beliefs about the organization significantly affect their actual performance. Recruiter warmth and interest have powerful consequences on interviewee perceptions.
4   *Outcomes*: This refers to the pre- and post-hire attitudes, behaviours and perceptions of both parties. Further recruitment outcomes inevitably have an impact on those already employed by the organization.

Person–job fit

One of the oldest ideas in psychology is that productivity and satisfaction are directly related to the fit between the characteristics of individuals (ability, personality, temperament) and the demands of the job. Fitting round pegs into round, not square, holes is seen by many as the selector's primary task. A fit is where there is congruence between the norms and values of the organization and those of the person. This concept has both antecedents in selection and socializing processes, and consequences in job-related behaviour. Put more simply, the "fit" idea is that the greater the match between the individual's needs and the environmental attributes, the greater will be the potential for the individual's satisfaction and performance (Furnham, 1992). Rynes and Cable (2003) suggest from their recruitment research that subjective holistic measures of fit produce better predictions than objective, multi-attribute estimates of fit.

Furnham (1987b) provided a simple illustration of this thesis using one famous individual difference (introversion/extraversion) and one dimension of work (whether

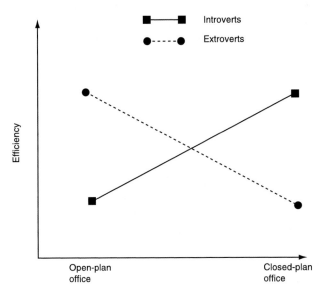

Figure 3.1 Hypothetical relationship between personality and efficiency in two types of office design. Reproduced from Furnham (1987b) with the permission of John Wiley & Sons.

people work in open- or closed-plan offices; see Figure 3.1). Extraverts, with high needs for arousal and stimulation, perform well in an open-plan office with all the excitation of noise, movement and variety, but poorly in closely planned offices that may be relatively deprived of sensory stimulation. The opposite will, of course, be true of introverts, whose high cortical arousal means that they will perform best under conditions of low arousal (that is, closed-plan offices) and less well under the "open-plan" regime. Ignoring individual traits, then, may well obscure these differences. Organizations that attract extraverts (such as the media) may well increase productivity in open-plan offices, whereas those that attract introverts (such as universities) may have to provide places of limited external stimulation to ensure that work is done most efficiently or effectively. Of course, this is not to suggest that other features such as the task itself do not mediate between personality factors and office design, but rather that individual differences should not be ignored.

In a field experiment, Morse (1975) examined the effects of congruence between five personality dimensions and the degree of certainty (routineness and predictability) of clerical and hourly jobs on self-estimates of competence. He measured the personality dimensions: tolerance for ambiguity, attitude towards authority, attitude towards individualism, cognitive complexity, and arousal-seeking tendency. New applicants who clustered at the high end of all or most of these dimensions were assigned to lower-certainty jobs, and those at the lower end were assigned to high-certainty jobs. The rest of the applicants were placed in jobs through the company's regular selection procedure. On the basis of ratings taken shortly after placement and 8 months later, both congruence groups had significantly higher self-ratings of competence than the employees placed in the conventional manner. Furthermore, there were no differences in self-estimates of competence between the two job-congruent groups, even after 8 months. It should be noted, however, that no measure of actual performance was taken, and it is not clear what construct, or set of constructs, self-estimated competence actually refers to. Yet all this seems to suggest the importance of "fit" here between personality traits and the type of job done.

There is no doubt that personality factors are important in influencing performance at work. But it is equally important to take into account environmental/organizational factors and the fit between person and environment. According to Caplan (1983), the theory of person–environment fit distinguishes between two types of fit: *needs*, such as for achievement and values of the person, and the environmental *supplies* and *opportunities* to meet them, which in the employees' terms may be seen as the needs and supplies fit or in the employer's terms as abilities and demands fit (Figure 3.2). The second type of fit distinguishes between objective and subjective person and environment characteristics – the correspondence between objective and subjective P (person) is labelled *accuracy of self-assessment* (or self-awareness), and the correspondence between objective and subjective E (environment) is labelled *contact with reality* (or environmental awareness) (Furnham, 1992).

Furthermore, the exact relationship between *fit* and its opposite, *strain*, is not clear. Caplan (1983) notes three types of relationships:

1   *A U-shape curve*: excesses (too much work) or deficits (too little work) in the environment lead to high levels of strain.
2   *Asymptotic curve*: either an excess of P (but not a deficit) or an excess of E (but not a deficit) can lead to strain.

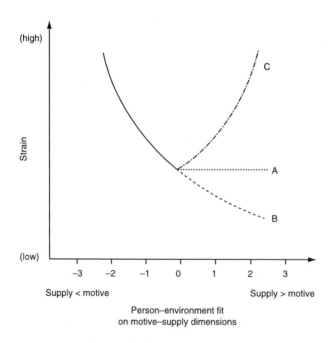

Figure 3.2 Three hypothetical shapes of the relationship between person–environment fit, motive–supply dimensions and strain. Reproduced from Harrison (1978) with the permission of John Wiley & Sons.

3 *Linear effect*: the absolute amount of one PE component (P relative to E) has a
   linear effect on strain.

Chatman (1989) suggests one might develop (and test) specific hypotheses on the
basis of the person–organization fit model. The nine propositions are:

- *Proposition 1*: When a person with discrepant values enters an organization characterized by strong values, the person's values are likely to change if that person is
  open to influence. Furthermore, this person is more likely to behave in accordance
  with the specified norms of the organization.
- *Proposition 2*: When a person with discrepant values enters an organization characterized by strong values, the person's values will not be expected to change if
  the person is not open to influence. This person would be likely to leave the
  organization.
- *Proposition 3*: When a person with discrepant values enters an organization characterized by strong values and he or she scores high on self-efficacy or personal
  control, or when many new members enter at once who share the same values
  with one another, but not with the organization, the values and norms of that
  organization will become more like that of the individual over time.
- *Proposition 4*: In organizations characterized by weak values (low crystallization
  and intensity), a person's values are likely to remain the same; that is, his or her
  values will not change as a function of organizational membership.
- *Proposition 5*: Person–organization fit will be positively related to extra-role (out-
  of-role) behaviour.
- *Proposition 6*: Potential recruits who either initiate spending, or are asked to spend,
  more time with an organization and who are involved in a variety of organizational
  activities (e.g. interviews, phone calls, receptions) before being hired will have
  profiles and/or values similar to those of the firm upon entry.
- *Proposition 7*: The behavioural outcome of high person–organization fit at entry
  will be that the person conforms to the pivotal norms of the organization. Furthermore, changes in individual values will be negatively associated with high
  person–organization fit at entry.
- *Proposition 8*: In organizations that have strong values, a greater variety and
  number of socialization processes, which include such activities as social and
  recreational events, formal training and mentor programmes, will be positively
  associated with person–organization fit and will bring about greater changes in
  individual values, resulting in a closer fit over time.
- *Proposition 9*: During the early stages of organization membership (0–1 year),
  selection experiences will explain more variance in person–organization fit than
  socialization experiences. However, as the recruit becomes "less new" in the organization, the number and type of socialization experiences will explain more
  variance in person–organization fit than person variables will.

On attempting to measure PE fit, the two items (one measuring P and the other E)
are usually commensurate. For instance, in a well-known vocational choice theory,
Holland (1973) has suggested that one can characterize people by their resemblance to
each of the six personality types: realistic, investigative, artistic, social, enterprising and
conventional, which are a product of characteristic interaction among a variety of

cultural and personal influences. As a result of developmental experiences, a person learns at first to prefer some activities to others; later, these activities become strong interests, which lead to a particular group of competencies. When this has occurred, a person's interests and competencies create a particular disposition that leads him or her to perceive, think and act in ways that are more appropriate to some occupations than others. By comparing a person's attributes to those of each model type, one can determine which type he or she resembles most. The three types the person most resembles are placed together in descending order to provide what is termed the person's "personality profile" (see Table 3.2).

There can be little doubt that there is a great deal of support (if fairly modest) for the PE fit theory. Studies have been done on people from widely different occupations (Harrison, 1978), in different countries (Tannenbaum & Kuleck, 1978) and on different age groups (Kahana, Liang, & Felton, 1980). Furthermore, many organizational variables – career change, labour turnover, performance – have been shown to be associated with PE fit (Kasl, 1973). For instance, Caplan, Cobb, French, Harrison & Pinneau (1980) have shown that PE fit (but *not* P *or* E on its own) predicted depression in an occupationally stratified sample of 318 employees from 23 occupations. Similarly, Furnham & Schaeffer (1984) showed that PE fit was positively associated with job satisfaction and negatively with mental illness, and vice versa. Henry (1989) found congruence was related to academic achievement in medical students. Using scores on Holland's inventory, students were classified congruent or incongruent, which was related predictably to overall and science grade point average. As Caplan (1983) concluded, "In general, however, PE fit has explained only an additional 1 per cent to 5 per cent variance in strain. It has, consistently doubled the amount of variance explained" (p. 42). In an attempt to improve the predictive power of PE fit theory, Caplan (1983) has proposed an elaborated cognitive model with the concept of retrospective, non-retrospective and future anticipated fit. He has also noted the importance of the buffering effects of social support on PE strain. These new developments are particularly promising.

There is, then, a wealth of evidence to suggest that a positive fit between a person (their ability, needs, values, etc.) and his or her working environment (its demands, output) leads to satisfaction, good performance, higher mental and physical health. However, as has been noted, one of the major problems of the PE fit literature has been the measurement of P and E. Although researchers have become more and more sophisticated in the identification and measurement of salient, work-related, individual differences, there have been fewer developments in the description, measurement and established consequences of work situations. Researchers have used various psychological theories to test person–job congruence theories (Sims & Veres, 1987a,b).

This need for congruence between a person's interests, preferences and abilities, and the factors inherent in his or her environment, form the basis for a theory of vocational choice proposed by Holland (1973) and continually updated (Holland, 1985), which offers a measure of PE fit. Although a very popular and well researched theory, it does have its critics (Bates, Parker, & McCoy, 1970; Furnham, Toop, Lewis, & Fisher, 1995; Schwartz, Andiappan, & Nelson, 1986).

Smart (1982) showed that vocational-type development is a function of a long series of life-history experiences that extend from individuals' *family backgrounds* through their experiences in *further education*, but that the magnitude, direction and method by which these influences are exerted differ dramatically among the three vocational types (Furnham, 1992).

Table 3.2 Personality types and salient characteristics

	Realistic	Investigative	Artistic	Social	Enterprising	Conventional
Traits	Hardheaded Unassuming Practical Dogmatic Natural Uninsightful	Analytical Intellectual Curious Scholarly Open Broad interests	Open Nonconforming Imaginative Intuitive Sensitive Creative	Agreeable Friendly Understanding Sociable Persuasive Extroverted	Extroverted Dominant Adventurous Enthusiastic Power-seeking Energetic	Conforming Conservative Unimaginative Inhibited Practical-minded Methodical
Life Goals	Inventing apparatus or equipment. Becoming outstanding athlete.	Inventing valuable product. Theoretical contribution to science.	Becoming famous in performing arts. Publishing stories. Original painting. Musical composition.	Helping others. Making sacrifices for others. Competent teacher or therapist.	Being community leader. Expert in finance and commerce. Being well liked and well dressed.	Expert in finance and commerce. Producing a lot of work.
Values	Freedom Intellectual Ambitious Self-controlled Docility	Intellectual Logical Ambitious Wisdom	Equality Imaginative Courageous World of beauty	Equality Self-respect Helpful Forgiving	Freedom Ambitious (–) Forgiving (–) Helpful	(–) Imaginative (–) Forgiving
Identifications	Thomas Edison Admiral Byrd	Madame Curie Charles Darwin	T. S. Eliot Pablo Picasso	Jane Addams Albert Schweitzer	Henry Ford Andrew Carnegie	Bernard Baruch John D. Rockefeller
Aptitudes	Technical	Scientific	Arts	Social & Educational. Leadership & Sales. Interpersonal.	Leadership & Sales. Social & Educational. Business & Clerical. Interpersonal.	Business & Clerical.
Self-Ratings	Mechanical ability	Math ability Research ability	Artistic ability			Clerical ability
Most competent in	Mechanics	Science	Arts	Human Relations	Leadership	Business

Source: Reproduced from Holland (1987: 5) with the permission of Psychological Assessment Resources.

The environments in which people live and work can also be characterized according to their resemblance to six model environments, corresponding to the six personality types above. Because the different types have different interests, competencies and dispositions, they tend to surround themselves with people and situations *congruent* with their interests, capabilities and outlook to the world. People tend to search for environments that will let them exercise their skills and abilities and express their personality; for instance, social types look for social environments in which to work. However, it has been suggested that some environments are more satisfying than others, irrespective of the personality of the person (Mount & Muchinsky, 1978) and that some jobs are simply more desirable than others (Furnham & Koritsas, 1990). Congruent environments provide job satisfaction for individuals because they are among people with tastes and values similar to their own, and where they can perform tasks which they enjoy. Some environments, such as the social or investigative environment, contain people with whom a wide variety of individuals can get along. Mount & Muchinsky's (1978) results suggest that, even if a person's aptitudes would be more congruent with a realistic or investigative environment, they find a social environment interesting enough to obtain satisfaction from it (Furnham, 1992).

Smart (1987) pointed out that Holland's theory suggests that model/fit/congruent environments *reinforce* the characteristic predispositions and attitudes of their corresponding personality types. Based on a sample of more than 2000 graduates traced over the period 1971–1980, he found that graduates educated in investigative environments have higher intellectual self-esteem scores, and those prepared in artistic environments have higher artistic self-esteem scores, when pre- and post-university measures are controlled. And, predictably, it was possible to show that student satisfaction with the programme, staff–student relations and peers was a function of congruence (Smart, 1987).

In addition to the core idea of PE fit, some secondary concepts are proposed which can be used to determine more efficiently the goodness of fit between P and E. Holland (1973) suggests that within a person or environment some pairs of "types" are more closely related than others, and that the relationship within (which yields a measure of *consistency*) and between (which yields a measure of *congruency*) personality types or environments can be ordered according to a hexagonal model (Figure 3.3), in which distances within and between the personality profiles and job codes are inversely proportional to the theoretical relationships between them. These degrees of relatedness or *consistency* are assumed to affect job satisfaction and general well-being. The types are ordered in a particular manner: realistic, investigative, artistic, social, enterprising and conventional (RIASEC). The letters are listed in rank order, so that the type listed first is the type the person most resembles. As a useful and approximate way of showing the degrees of relatedness among the six types, they are arranged at the vertices of a hexagon, such that the closest are most similar. Thus, the *investigative* and *artistic* types are similar and hence closer together, because both are concerned with intellectual pursuits, although in different ways; the investigative type is more methodological and data-orientated, the artistic type more spontaneous. By contrast, the investigative type who is relatively asocial and analytical differs most from the self-confident and persuasive enterprising type. Similarly, the spontaneous, disorderly and creative artistic type contrasts sharply with the self-controlled, conforming and unimaginative conventional type. By inference, intermediate proximities on the hexagon depict

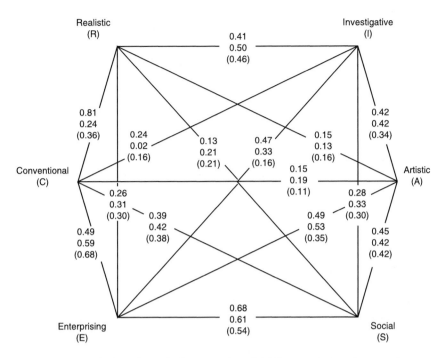

Figure 3.3 Correlations from the hexagonal model. The correlations in parentheses are from Holland's original work; the uppermost correlations are from Furnham & Schaeffer (1984); while the middle correlations are from Furnham & Walsh (1991). Reproduced from Furnham (1992) with the permission of Routledge.

intermediate degrees of psychological similarity, although the correlated results do not totally support that particular shape (Furnham, 1992).

A second concept is *differentiation*, which means that some people and environments are more clearly defined than others; for example, a person or environment may be dominated by a single type (well differentiated) or may resemble many types equally well (undifferentiated). The better the environment or person is differentiated, the more likely the person is to find a congruent job, and the more likely he or she will be to have high job satisfaction and good mental health as a result. Holland (1973) suggests that for inconsistent individuals, with little differentiation, an incongruent environment in which they work can become less stressful as they meet people involved in that environment and adapt to their needs and values.

The third measure is *congruence* or compatibility – that is, how similar a person and job type are (e.g. a realistic type in a realistic environment). This measure is also derived from the hexagon model. Incongruence occurs when an individual of a particular type lives or works in an environment that provides opportunities and rewards foreign to that person's preferences and abilities (e.g. a realistic type in a social environment). Congruence is therefore the best, perhaps the only, measure of PE fit. Strictly speaking, it is only congruence and not consistency or differentiation that measures person–environment fit. Consistency is a characteristic of either a person's profile or an environment, but it says nothing about the relationship between the two; nor does differentiation, which is only a measure of the "peakedness" of a profile. The hexagon model is used in Holland's theory to derive both consistency and congruence but not differentiation. This model is illustrated in Figure 3.3, and includes the correlational results from Holland (1973) and both studies reported by Furnham (Furnham & Schaeffer, 1984; Furnham & Walsh, 1991).

Holland's (1973, 1985) theory has probably attracted more empirical attention than any other theory in the area (Wigington, 1983). Most empirical studies have looked at the relationships between the three measures of PE fit and a specific occupational dependent measure that would be predicted from Holland's model (Raphael & Gorman, 1986). Thus, many studies have looked at the relationships between PE fit and job satisfaction (Furnham & Schaeffer, 1984; Mount & Muchinsky, 1978; Smart, Elton, & McLaughlin, 1986; Wiggins, Lederer, Salkowe, & Rys, 1983). However, a wide variety of other variables has been considered, including mental health (Furnham & Schaeffer, 1984), Protestant work ethic beliefs (Furnham & Koritsas, 1990) and entrepreneurship (Venkatapathy, 1984). Finally, several studies have attempted to correlate other personality systems with that of Holland (Costa, McCrae, & Holland, 1984, Naylor, Care, & Mount, 1986).

Whereas PE fit in this research is seen as the independent variable, the dependent variable (what fit is related to) has varied considerably. Most, but not all, of the studies in this area have yielded modest but significant (and predictable) relationships. It is probably true that these studies have nearly all provided *some* support for Holland's thesis. This is most apparent with respect to job satisfaction. For instance, using different populations in different countries, various studies have yielded similar significant correlations between PE congruence and job satisfaction: Gottfredson (1978), $r = 0.28$ ($N = 112$); Wiggins *et al.* (1983), $r = 0.57$ ($N = 247$); Dore & Meacham (1973), $r = 0.38$ ($N = 54$); Furnham & Schaeffer (1984), $r = 0.37$ ($N = 82$).

Swaney & Prediger (1985) examined the relationship between congruence and job satisfaction for 1688 young adults over a 6-year period. They found a modest but positive significant relationship, as one might expect. Smart *et al.* (1986) confirmed the positive relationship between congruence and satisfaction, but found gender-specific differences with congruence being related to extrinsic job satisfaction in males and overall job satisfaction in females. Heesacker, Elliott & Howe (1988) used two job satisfaction measures in examining the relationship between congruence and satisfaction, and productivity in rural factory workers. One satisfaction measure showed a significant correlation with congruence ($p < 0.03$), and weakly predicted the other ($p < 0.09$). Overall, "social" types were most satisfied, followed by conventional and realistic types and then the lower three types. In accordance with the theory, social, conventional and realistic types were more productive (and satisfied) than the other types, but the types were related to neither absenteeism nor insurance claims. The results did provide strong support for the thesis that congruence is related to increased satisfaction and productivity (Furnham, 1992).

Elton & Smart (1988) also provided modest support for Holland's theory by demonstrating, in a large sample of nearly 2000 young people, that those at the highest level of congruence tended to be less dissatisfied than those at the lowest level of congruence. The theory has been applied to many groups in many countries, including Indian entrepreneurs (Venkatapathy, 1984) and American college-educated working black men and women (Walsh, Bingham, & Sheffey, 1986). The theory has also been applied to leisure activities (Taylor, Kelso, Cox, Alloway, & Matthews, 1979), with modest results.

A number of studies have looked at the correspondence between the Big Five and the

RIASEC model. This is not surprising because of the way personality theorists appear to have reached a consensus on the existence of five orthogonal measures (extraversion, neuroticism, openness-to-experience, agreeableness and conscientiousness). In an early study using the three (not five) factor NEO, Costa *et al.* (1984) asked 350 adult Americans to complete both questionnaires but the results were analysed separately for males and females. Neuroticism correlated weakly with the artistic type in men and negatively with the social type in women. Extroversion was strongly positively correlated with the enterprising type and negatively correlated with the conventional type. Finally, openness was strongly positively correlated with the artistic type and negatively correlated with the conventional type. The results certainly "made sense" though the "Big Five" dimensions did not appear to correlate much with the realistic type. Furthermore, the authors pointed out that one dimension missing from Holland's typology is neuroticism, which is of course directly relevant to occupational behaviour.

De Fruyt and Mervielde (1997) report a similar study to the one above using 934 Flemish-speaking students. However, unlike the above, they analyse their data in terms of the 30 facet scores as well as the total "Big Five" scores. The pattern of correlations showed clearly that few of the Big Five facets (six per trait) were related to the realistic and investigative type, while many were related to the social and enterprising type. Perhaps the clearest results were from the regression, where the five-factor scores were regressed onto each of the six types. The five factors were able to account for 40% of the variance in the *enterprising* types, showing them to be stable, conscientious, extroverts but low on conscientiousness. The five factors accounted for 32% of the variance for *artistic* occupations, although this was primarily due to a very high beta-weight for openness. The third highest *r*-square value (22%) was for *social* occupation, which showed that neurotic, extroverted, agreeable individuals who were open to experience were attracted to this particular type. Thus the authors conclude, as do nearly all other studies in the area, that there is some overlap in the models but that they account for unique variance. Hence they recommend that both instruments are used for educational and vocational counselling.

Costa, McCrae & Kay (1995) have considered how the five-factor NEO personality inventory may be used in career assessment. They suggest that "particular personality traits are likely to develop interests in those vocations that permit the expression of their preferred ways of thinking, feeling and acting" (p. 127). But they do admit that "personality inventories should supplement, rather than replace, vocational interest inventories" (p. 130). They argue for three sorts of data in career assessment: ability, trait and vocational interest data, which makes perfect sense.

They believe, however, that three of the "Big Five" traits (extraversion, openness and agreeableness) are particularly relevant to vocational interests. As for neuroticism, they believe neurotics are "likely to be unhappy in whatever job they have. A different job is unlikely to solve problems that are rooted in the individual's basic emotional make-up" (Costa *et al.*, 1995: 130). Perhaps more importantly, they distinguish between super and primary factors. Thus they point out that two individuals may have two identical conscientiousness scores but that one is high in order and dutifulness (facet level) and modest in competence and achievement striving (also facet levels), while another could have the opposite pattern and that they would be best suited to quite different jobs. They then go on to talk about instruments that can be used to quantify the match between a personal and a specific position. It appears to work by getting job holders/experts to specify how desirable and undesirable the 30 NEO facets are for that particular job. At this stage, however, there is fairly limited evidence for the validity of this instrument.

Studies looking at the overlap between the "Big Five" and the "Holland Six" are fairly consistent. Some dimensions of the "Big Five" (e.g. neuroticism) seem unrelated to the RIASEC types, while some RIASEC types (e.g. conventional) seem unrelated to the "Big Five". Charitably, most reviewers suggest that in actual vocational guidance both measures should be used side by side to account for more of the variance. Yet it remains unclear how one can use the Big Five to calculate measures of congruence which are at the heart of Holland's theory.

Holland's work stands out above nearly all other theories in vocational psychology, which probably accounts for why it has attracted so much attention. From the perspective of the personality theorist, it is a pity that Holland's *six types* have not been "married to" the "Big Five" emerging from recent meta-reviews in personality psychology (see Chapter 4). However, it is possible that one may begin to classify occupations and vocations in terms of the "Big Five", just as Holland has done in terms of his six types, so that both people and jobs are described using the same terminology. When this has been done, and only then, can the potentially very interesting concept of fit be fully investigated.

Furnham (2001) has considered various theoretical, methodological and empirical problems with this research. First, there is the issue of the possible confound of occupational prestige: the idea that some jobs are more glamorous and better paid than others. There are also issues around the cross-cultural application of the theory and measurement to different countries and economic systems.

Expectancy theory and occupational choice

Expectancy theory argues that vocational choice is dependent on what one *values* or wants from a job (money, social status, freedom) and the *expectation* that getting a particular job, or joining a particular vocational group, will actually result. Vroom's (1964) application of expectancy-value theory assumes that the strength of a tendency to act in a certain way depends on the strength of an *expectancy* that the act will be followed by a given consequence (or outcome) and on the *value* or attractiveness of that consequence (or outcome) specifically to the actor. Typically, the two components are seen as combining in a multiplicative manner. This basic formulation has been central, and has proved useful, to many of the major theories of learning, decision making, attitude formulation and motivation (see "Organizational choice", pp. 108–111).

Occupational preference is viewed as a function of attraction (occupational valence, V_j) to an occupation such that:

$$V_j = \sum_{i=1}^{n} (V_i \times I_{ij})$$

where V_j = the value of occupation j, V_i = the value of outcome i, I_{ij} = the cognized instrumentality of occupation j for the attainment of outcome i, and n = the number of outcomes. Occupations which are most instrumental for important rewards and outcomes will naturally have the most positive occupational valence and will be preferred over other occupations.

The second model predicts force towards, or *choice of*, occupations. The force on a person to choose an occupation is seen as a function of the valence of an occupation and that person's expectation that this occupation is attainable. Specifically:

$$F_j = E_j \times V_j$$

where F_j = the force to choose occupation j, E_j = the strength of the expectancy that the choice of occupation j will result in attainment, and V_j = the valence of occupation j. Essentially, the model states that an individual will choose the occupation with the greater F_j or force level.

Several articles have reviewed the empirical research relating to the success of expectancy value theory at predicting occupational preferences and choices (Brooks & Betz, 1990; Wanous, Keen, & Latack, 1983). These reviews have analysed the empirical results from differing perspectives, and the conclusions within and between reviews are predictably equivocal.

Wanous *et al.* (1983) reviewed 16 studies and found the within-person correlation between a valence × instrumentality index and an overall measure of occupational attractiveness to be 0.72. This means that the average "hit rate" is 63.4%. More recently, Brooks & Betz (1990) found that the expectancy × valence interaction accounted for between 12 and 41% of the tendency of introductory psychology students to choose an occupation. A particular concern of reviewers of this literature has been the nature of the analysis used by researchers in the field, and its adequacy in light of the various definitions of motivation. Vroom (1964) proposed that the expectancy-value model be studied in the form of a *within-subjects* framework. Many initial tests of the model used a *between-subjects* analysis, which is thought to contribute to the equivocal results often reported (Zedeck, 1977).

A second inconsistency within the expectancy-value theory literature is with respect to the form of the expectancy model and the relationship of the scores that it yields to effort and behavioural criteria. It remains unclear whether the components of the model should be combined additively or multiplicatively, or whether they should be combined at all.

A recent development in the expectancy-value theory field has been the attempt to apply a decision-modelling approach to examinations of the theory. Behavioural decision theory has been used to study human decision-making procedures.

The paradox of both expectancy valence and decision-modelling approaches is that, although both take individual differences into consideration, they do not take into consideration systematic individual differences. Thus, neither expectancy nor valence is seen to be related to stable, predictable, individual differences. Many measures – such as locus of control, the Protestant work ethic and "need for achievement" – are clearly related to expectations of success or failure (see Chapter 4). Similarly, there are various measures of different teaching and learning styles. Hence, it may be predicted that introverts and extraverts seek jobs that provide opportunities for them to do things both that they like and also that they are good at. Understanding the nature and type of academic/educational tasks preferred by different personality types is therefore highly relevant to vocational psychology.

The Strong vocational interest blank

The Strong test consists of 400 items, to each of which the person taking the test answers "like", "indifferent" or "dislike". The items are concerned with vocations, school subjects, amusements, activities and kinds of people. The test can be scored for more than 40 occupations for men and more than 20 occupations for women. A, B, and C scores are given to each person taking the test for each occupation. The score for a particular occupation is determined by comparing a person's answers with the typical answers made by people actively and successfully engaged in that occupation. An A score means that a person's interests are very similar to those in that field; B, somewhat similar; and C, not at all similar (Furnham, 1992).

Vocational interests are generally set *before* a person enters an occupation and change little thereafter. Strong tested 50 men when they were college freshmen (first-year undergraduate students) and again 20 years later; the median correlation of scores was 0.72. He tested 228 students when they were seniors (final-year undergraduate students) and again 22 years later. The median correlation was even higher: 0.75 (Strong, 1951). Although some people change their interests after entering an occupation, the odds are against it. Furthermore, those who change are more likely to become *less* interested in the occupation, not more interested.

Scores on inventories do predict job success. Ghiselli & Barthol (1953) found 113 studies where scores had been related to success in different occupations: supervisors (n = 52 studies), clerks (n = 22), sales workers (n = 20), skilled workers (n = 8), service workers (n = 6) and protective workers (n = 5). For each of these job categories, there was a low but positive median correlation between scores and success. Although inventories have been used most often to predict supervisory success, the correlations were lowest for this group. Inventories were best in predicting sales success.

The method by which a car-salesman scale was created illustrates the long process of developing a valid inventory. Kennedy (1958) first collected nearly 300 multiple-choice items covering personality, interests and attitudes that he thought might be related to success as a salesman. He then sent the questionnaire to a representative sample of General Motors car dealers throughout the USA, some of whom were selling a high-priced car. At his request, the dealers had several hundred of their salesmen complete the questionnaire. The dealers returned the completed questionnaire, together with a record of the gross earnings of each salesman. The salesmen were divided into a successful and an unsuccessful group on the basis of their earnings. The answers of the two groups to each item were then compared. The 40 items that most sharply differentiated the successful from the unsuccessful were chosen for the final form of the scale. This final form was again sent to the dealers, who had over 700 more of their salesmen complete it. They again returned the completed inventories with records of the earnings of the salesmen. The result was that the scores of the salesmen were significantly related to their earnings (correlation: r = 0.31). The scale worked equally well for salesmen selling the low- and high-priced cars.

Kline (1975), however, has cast doubt on the usefulness of the Strong vocational interest blank (SVIB) for several reasons:

- It seems less applicable outside America.
- Jobs have changed and hence criteria need to be changed.
- The long test performs no better than simply getting a person to tell you their vocational interests.
- People deceive themselves into thinking they have interests when they don't.

The Kuder interest tests

There are various Kuder tests, all of which are very similar to the Strong test. The Kuder General Interest Survey (Kuder, 1970), which is the revised form of the Kuder Preference Record-Vocational and is suitable for 13-year-olds upwards, measures ten interest areas: outdoor, mechanical, computational, scientific, persuasive, artistic, literary, musical, social service and clerical.

There is evidence that the test is valid; for instance, people who were more satisfied/content in their jobs tended to have higher relevant Kuder scores than those who were not. However, Kline (1975: 139) was critical of the test and made four basic objections:

1   There is no evidence that Kuder scores predict better than simple expressed interests or goals.
2   There is evidence that interest dimensions are not those purportedly measured by the Kuder.
3   Ipsative [forced choice] scores can be misleading and need other data for interpretation. They are also worthless for the multivariate statistical analyses necessary for research into interests.
4   Finally, we should stress again that with our concept of interest as merely inferred from voluntary activity it is not surprising that expressed goals and interests are as good predictors as criterion keyed inventories.

Interest level tests continue to be developed and marketed but they remain of limited validity. More importantly, there seems to be very limited theoretical development in the area, which seriously condemns its future.

Personnel selection

Schmitt, Cortina, Ingerick & Wiechmann (2003) distinguish between *can-do* (measured by maximum performance) and *will-do* (measured by typical performance). Can-do is about ability, knowledge, skills and experience, while will-do is about personality and integrity. These two factors influence knowledge, knowing how to do things, what to do and how much energy to invest in the task. These factors in turn influence task proficiency, effort, discipline, teamwork and overall adaptive performance. In turn, this leads to productivity and customer satisfaction as well as negative behaviours such as absenteeism, theft and turnover. The implications of this model are that selection needs to assess:

1   The amount and structure of job knowledge (facts, principles, goals) (sometimes called declarative knowledge).
2   Knowledge and skills to actually perform the task, such as physical ability, self-management and interpersonal processes (sometimes called procedural knowledge).

The above two forms of knowledge are best measured by tests of cognitive ability, perceptual speed, psychomotor abilities and practical intelligence.

3   Motivation, which relates to traits like conscientiousness, achievement motivation, emotional stability and goal orientation.

It is therefore important to measure such things as cognitive ability, physical ability, experience, motivational and non-cognitive traits (i.e. personality) as well as fit by sensitive, cross-culturally fair methods. Most organizations are interested in ensuring high job performance and individual productivity measured by such things as efficiency (ratio of inputs to outputs) and effectiveness (amount and quality of output relative to set standard). But they are also, inevitably, interested in preventing negative or counter-productive behaviour.

Schmitt *et al.* (2003) note various important developments in the area. First, researchers are trying to establish how selection procedures become directly related to organizational performance overall. Second, a closer analysis of why proven valid selection techniques are not adopted while less useful areas are. Third, to examine the strategic significance of selection in how it shapes the organization over time. Fourth, the selection of individuals in the global economy, which means they may need to move country and job frequently. Finally, because of increased outsourcing, organizations have to select those who are chosen to do specific outsourced functions.

Because of its obvious importance, the area of recruitment and selection has attracted a great deal of popular attention (Ryan & Ployhart, 2000). Indeed, there is still probably more writing about the dilemmas and controversies of recruitment and selection in the trade literature (personnel management magazines, business magazines and reports) than in academic journals.

Personnel selection is about the acquisition of human resources. *Recruitment* may be conceived of the activity that generates a pool of applicants who have the desire to be employed by the organization and from whom the most suitable can be selected. *Selection*, on the other hand, occurs when an organization uses one or more methods to assess individuals with a view to making a decision concerning their suitability to join the organization, specifically to perform tasks that may or may not be specified. At different points in time, skilled employees are abundant and at other times rare, hence human resource forecasting and planning can be seen as very important.

There are many ethical and, more importantly, legal constraints on free recruitment, which differ from country to country and time to time. This has become a "hot" topic into which various "minority groups" have demanded research. Table 3.3 shows a summary of research in this area, but it should be recognized that these results may differ from country to country and time to time.

Using tests to select people is fraught with problems. There are two types of selection errors that can lower an organization's success rate. Hiring people who turn out to be

Table 3.3 Summary of adverse impact of five classes of selection test on minorities

	Blacks	*Females*	*Elderly*	*Handicapped*
Intelligence and verbal test	AI	+	ai	?
Work samples	+	NE	NE	NE
Interview	+	AI	ai	ai
Educational requirements	AI	+	ai	?
Physical tests	+	AI	?	AI

NE = No evidence. AI = Established evidence of adverse impact. ai = Some evidence of adverse impact. ? = No proof of adverse impact, but likely to exist, for some tests, or some person. + = Evidence minority does as well or better than majority on this test.

Source: Reproduced from Arvey (1979) with the permission of Addison-Wesley Publishers, Inc.

poor workers is called a *false-positive* error; the opposite is a *false-negative* error. The relationship between false-positive and false-negative errors and good decisions in hiring is shown in Figure 3.4. All organizations have (abundant) evidence of their false-positive decisions but far less about those potentially good employees they never hired.

Two selection paradigms are set out in Figures 3.5 and 3.6. Features that are common to all models include:

- A *job analysis* – that is, a clear understanding of the tasks and functions to be fulfilled.
- A choice of selection *methods* from the number available.
- The choice of, and monitoring of, *actual work-related behaviour* to validate the procedure (for instance, by use of assessment centres).

There are many academic and "how to" books which suggest a series of steps that should be taken. Despite superficially looking very different, they probably have considerable overlap. Compare and contrast Figures 3.5 and 3.6.

		Decision	
		Hire	Reject
Outcome	Good workers	Good decision: accept the best applicant	False-negative
	Poor workers	False-positive	Good decision: reject the worst applicant

Figure 3.4 Selection errors: false-positives and false-negatives.

Job analysis

For many organizations, nearly every aspect of human resource management should start with a job analysis. There are many benefits of such an analysis as illustrated in Figure 3.7. The figure shows that a job analysis is based on both the (written) job description and a detailed behavioural analysis of each specific job. These job analysis data provide valuable information about desirable features of each job holder: minimum professional knowledge, the range of basic skills required and perhaps the ideal traits for someone in that job. These job analyses may be combined section-by-section, department-by-department to develop a human resource plan and strategy for selection, training, appraisal, and so on.

Sackett and Laczo (2003), who prefer the concept "work analysis", believe people have to make eight different decisions and choices before proceeding:

1   *Activity versus attributes*: Activities are work-oriented and focus on tasks or behaviours required to do the job, while attributes are worker-oriented and focus on the ability, skills and knowledge of the worker.

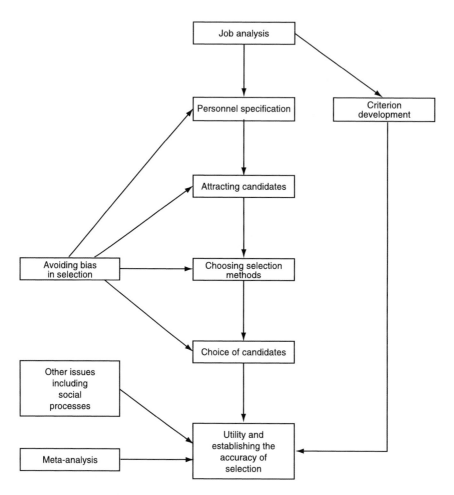

Figure 3.5 The selection paradigm. Reproduced from Smith and Robertson (1989) with the permission of John Wiley & Sons.

2   *General versus specific*: This refers to the level of detail and specificity desired.

3   *Qualitative versus quantitative*: This can be done by using a descriptive narrative format listing activities or attributes or via numeric profiles.

4   *Taxonony-based versus blank slate*: Pre-established job characteristics can be used or else one can start afresh with a blank slate and develop activity-attribute lists for specific jobs or job families.

5   *Observer-based versus informant-based*: This means the work analysis is either done by a trained expert who distils observations into reports or else it is the people in the jobs themselves (incumbents) who list or evaluate activities and attributes.

6   *Knowledge, skills and abilities (KSA) versus KSA plus others*: Nearly all work analyses focus on the triad of knowledge, skills and abilities, but some add other factors such as attitudes, traits and values.

7   *Single job versus job comparison*: One approach is to profile a single job while the other is to compare different jobs within the organization to look at job families.

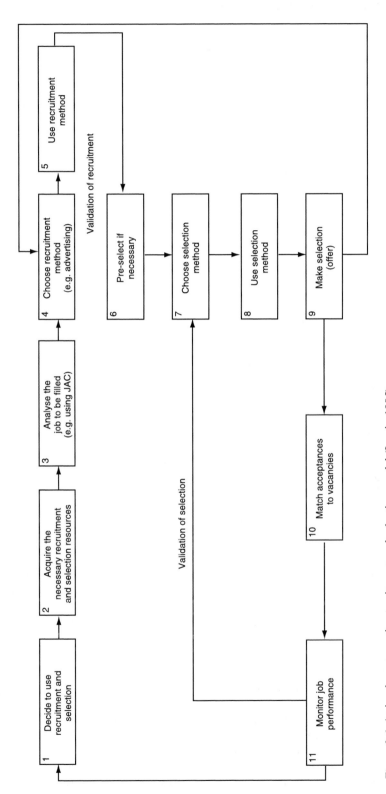

Figure 3.6 A simple systematic recruitment and selection model (Lewis, 1985).

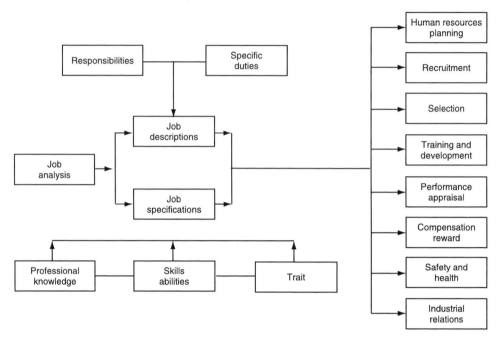

Figure 3.7 How job analysis informs human resources issues.

8   *Descriptive versus prescriptive*: The former describes the job as currently consti-
     tuted, while the latter considers about-to-be-created jobs.

Sackett and Laczo (2003) also describe a model with six component parts: worker
characteristics (abilities, interests, work styles); worker requirements (basic skills,
cross-functioned skills, general knowledge); occupation characteristics (labour market
information, occupation outlook, wages); experience requirements (training, experience, licensing); occupational-specific information (knowledge, skills, tasks, machines/
tools); and occupational requirements (generalized work activities, work context,
organizational context).

They also mention the increasing interest in cognitive task analysis, which looks at
the thought processes that guide behaviour, which is of increasing importance as jobs
become more complex and intellectually challenging. Further strategic job analysis
looks at the skills and abilities required for future jobs so that future skill requirements
can be forecasted.

Various arguments have been proposed for the selection based extensively on job
analysis (Schuler, 1989: 32).

1   Direction of new and relevant dimensions at different levels of abstraction as a
     basis of differentiation between employees and applicants.
2   Determination of relevant dimensions even if not differentiating between actual
     performers. Gains in validity are to be expected when base rates change.
3   Validity of selection based on job analysis should hold longer – i.e. as long as
     job demands are constant – and can be kept under control when demands are

changing. In contrast to the "blind empirical approach", using a given distribution of employees or extreme groups as prominent parts of this population, a job-orientated selection battery can – ideally – be used like a unit construction, exchanging just the elements or dimensions that have varied. (It should be added, however, that we still do not know enough about the interrelationship of different requirements, which could render this ideal an inapt expression of elementarism.)

4   Transparency of the diagnostic process and the personnel decision for the applicant as well as for the people in organizations, thus improving acceptability.

Job analysis refers to one or more procedures designed to collect information about the skills people require to perform jobs effectively. Among the kinds of information sought during job analysis, McCormick (1976) lists the following:

- work activities, including both individual behaviours and job outcomes;
- machines, tools, equipment and work aids used;
- job-related tangibles and intangibles, such as materials processed and knowledge applied, respectively;
- standards of work performance;
- job context;
- personnel requirements, such as education, experience, aptitudes, and so forth.

Ideally, every job in any organization should exist because that job makes a meaningful contribution to the organization's overall goals, whether those goals entail producing a product, providing a service or "maintaining the organization". Job analysis procedures are designed to assess these intended outcomes or job results, as well as the conditions under which those results are obtained. Products and/or services are the output of an organization: they are the end result of the thousands of *tasks* that are performed by its members. Some of these relate directly to the production of the product or the delivery of the service, whereas others relate to the management of the organization. Still other tasks, such as those performed in the personnel department, are support tasks for those who produce the organization's product or service and/or for those who manage.

The tasks that are performed by an individual define his or her specific *position* in the organization. All of the identical or similar positions in an organization make up one *job* in that organization. Groups of jobs that are similar in terms of the demands they make on employees are called *job families*. Positions, jobs and job families are the basic building blocks of an organization's structure, which can be described in an organizational chart ("organogram").

Because job analysis is an activity that requires examining the work people do, it can be confused with other organizational activities that also focus on this work. Job analysis is a process for describing *what is done* in any job, not the best way to do it, or what it is worth to have the job done.

The end product of job analysis is often a *job description*, which is a factual statement of the tasks, responsibilities and working conditions of a particular job. There may also be a *job specification*, which is a statement of the human characteristics needed for the job to be done.

Blum & Naylor (1968) listed nine different techniques for gathering job-analysis information:

- *Questionnaire*, on which workers answer written questions about their jobs.
- *Checklist*, on which workers simply indicate whether or not their jobs include any or all of a list of possible tasks.
- *Individual interviews*, in which workers are presented with oral questions about their jobs.
- *Group interviews*, in which several workers are questioned simultaneously.
- *Diaries*, in which workers are asked to record their daily work activities.
- *Technical conferences*, where "experts" (usually those who supervise the job in question) meet to identify all the aspects of the job.
- *Critical incidents*, in the wake of which workers and/or "experts are asked to describe aspects of the job in question that are crucial either to success or failure".
- *Observation interviews*, in which workers are interviewed at their work stations by the job analyst, who also observes them going about their daily activities.
- *Work participation*, in which the job analyst actually performs the job in question.

The many available methods for job analysis are not strictly comparable, even though they are for the same purpose. They differ in several ways, including the type of information yielded, the time and expense involved, and the level of skill required of the job analyst. For practical purposes, the method chosen will depend to a considerable extent upon the resources available and the purpose for which the job analysis information is obtained. Two popular methods will be described briefly.

A job analysis technique that has been widely used and studied is the *position analysis questionnaire* (PAQ) developed by McCormick, Jeanneret & Mecham (1972). Basically a worker-orientated approach, the PAQ consists of 194 different job elements or statements describing human behaviours that could be demanded by any given job. These job elements are organized into six different categories or divisions:

- information input
- mental processes
- work output
- relationships with other persons
- job context
- other job characteristics

A central question underlies each category and the major subheadings included within each category.

The PAQ is intended to be used as a guide for a highly structured oral interview. That is, the job analyst reads each of the 194 items to the job incumbent, listens carefully to the worker's responses, asks any clarifying questions deemed necessary, and then mentally integrates the information obtained and chooses the appropriate response on the rating scale that applies to each particular item or job element. Depending on the item or question, rating scales may address *extent of use*, with responses ranging from "nominal" or "very infrequently" to "very substantial"; *importance* to the job, ranging from "very minor" to "extreme"; *amount of time*, ranging from "less than one-tenth of the time" to "almost continually"; and *possibility of occurrence*, ranging from "no possibility" to "high". In addition, there are a few statements that require special rating scales or response codes.

The *critical incidents technique*, which focuses on specific behaviours deemed critical or crucial to successful (or unsuccessful) job performance (Flanagan, 1954), is a second approach to job analysis. "Job experts" (usually the job holders or their supervisors) are asked, either individually or in groups, to provide anecdotes or examples of things that they have either done or neglected to do (or witnessed, in the case of supervisors) that had a profound impact on the quality of the work. That is, they are asked to supply critical work-related incidents in salient situations at work. After collecting as many of these as possible, the job analyst typically eliminates redundancies and, usually with the assistance of the job experts, organizes the remaining incidents into meaningful categories or job dimensions. These categories and their associated critical incidents, both good and bad, reflect composites of the essential element of the job being analysed. Robinson (1981) listed the following steps:

1   Convene a panel of experts.
2   Ask the panel to identify the broad, all-encompassing objectives that an ideal job incumbent should meet.
3   Ask the panel to list all of the specific behaviours necessary for meeting each of the broad objectives.
4   From among these, ask the panel to identify "critical tasks" – tasks that are extremely crucial to the job because of their frequency, their importance, or the cost associated with making an error.
5   Determine the extent to which the experts agree to the relative importance of the major dimensions of the job.

There are various sources of error in job analysis. The number of uses to which job analysis information may be put suggests that it is important for this process to be carried out as carefully as possible. The specific kind of error to which job analysis is subject depends somewhat on the method used, but all such error stems from three sources: the database, the interpretation of the information collected, and the environment in which the job analysis is carried out.

The term *database* refers to the number and representativeness of the positions (i.e. jobs) examined in the performance of a job analysis. As a general rule, the smaller the database, the more likely there is to be error in the final job description. A major reason that a small database can lead to error is that the information collected may be biased or incomplete. For example, if only one job incumbent is interviewed, he or she may not perform the full range of duties actually encompassed by the job being analysed and/or may be unwilling or unable to report accurately on job duties. The best protection against such risks is multiple sources of different types of information (this provides evidence of reliability). In short, the larger and more representative the sample of job evaluation (and thus the cost of the exercise), the more certain one can be about the accuracy of the data.

Incomplete or distorted information, whether deliberate or not, is not the exclusive province of job incumbents or other interviewees involved in the process. Interviewers and researchers can also misinterpret the data for a variety of reasons. In addition to making mistakes, there is some evidence that the biases and values of job analysts may creep unnoticed into their work. One study, for example, found a tendency for female job analysts using the PAQ to rate jobs somewhat lower than male analysts describing the same jobs with the same instruments (Arvey, Passino, & Lounsbury, 1977).

The physical and social environments in which the process takes place are the sources of various possible errors in job analysis. These sources include:

- *time pressures* that restrict the database or rush the analyst through the information collecting and/or interpretation;
- *distracting physical environmental conditions*, such as extreme heat, cold or noise;
- *rapidly changing job technology* that can put a job description out of date in a very short time.

A general strategy for dealing with all of the potential sources of error in job analysis is to use multiple sources of information about the job, use more than one analyst if possible, and check and recheck information and results. This is an expensive undertaking and many organizations will lack the resources or the commitment to follow it.

Klinger (1979) has pointed out that traditional job analytic procedures do not specify the *conditions* under which job tasks are performed and the *standards* by which employees doing the job will be evaluated. He suggests an alternative to traditional job description and analysis, which he calls the *results-orientated description*. The major advantage of results-orientated descriptions seems to lie in the explicit link they make between the *task domain* (duties involved) and the *performance domain* (actual work) of the job. For example, it is one thing for a prospective employee to know that he or she must be able to word-process 60 words per minute, but another for the employee to know that this typing will be done on a particular machine in a particular style to an error-free standard in a given time.

Results-orientated description gives the employees clearer statements of expectations and explicitly sets out the standards by which their performance will be evaluated. Their most obvious practical drawback seems to lie in this very specificity, because a results-orientated description must be written for every job position. In addition, results-orientated descriptions would be difficult or impossible to write when groups of employees work cooperatively to accomplish some task, which is often the case.

A second inadequacy of traditional job analysis, which many have noticed, relates to the use of the resulting information for selection and placement. It has been recognized for some time that a successful individual/job/organization match is more than a matter of skills, knowledge and abilities. It also involves a fit between the needs of, or rewards desired by, the individual and those things that the organization and job offer (Wanous, 1977). From a matching perspective, conventional job descriptions and specifications give those involved in selection and placement only half of the information they need. They know what an employee must be able to do for the job, but not what the job can do for the employee.

Job rewards are individually valued outcomes of doing certain work and/or being in a particular work environment. The reward potential of work has often been examined from a motivational perspective. The relatively simpler systematic *description* of the rewards offered by a job and an organization as an addition to a traditional job description is a more recent idea.

It remains crucially important to do a good job analysis. This not only provides very useful hypotheses as to which factors predict occupational behaviour, but perhaps equally important which work-related criteria measures to use as the dependent predicted variable. It is extremely important in any validation work to have salient, robust, important work-related performance measures.

Selection methods

There is a very wide variety of techniques available to select people, from interviews and tests to graphological and astrological assessment. Personal preference and organizational tradition dictate which method is used, rather than more important considerations such as validity, cost, generality and legality. Other criteria may be used, including:

- *Discrimination (differentiation)*: The measurement procedures involved should provide for clear discrimination between candidates. If candidates all obtain relatively similar assessments, selection decisions cannot be made.
- *Fairness/adverse impact*: The measures must not discriminate *unfairly* against members of any specific subgroups of the population.
- *Administrative convenience*: The procedures should be acceptable within the organization and be capable of being implemented effectively within the organization's administrative structure.
- *Cost and development time*: Given the selection decisions (e.g. number of jobs, number of candidates, types of jobs) involved, the costs involved and the time taken to develop adequate procedures need to be balanced with the potential benefits. This is essentially a question of utility.

To a large extent, Table 3.4 illustrates some of the problems involved in choosing a selection instrument. A method that might be ideal on one criterion (validity) is less ideal on another (cost). For the researcher, validity and generality are probably the most important criteria, whereas for the human resources manager it is probably cost and practicality.

However, the above are not the only criteria or considerations, nor are they the only methods used. Some organizations ignore the research literature, which shows graphological analysis to be essentially invalid yet still use it for selection. Yet some methods tend to discriminate more successfully than others. Schmitt (1989) has documented

Table 3.4 Level of validity and subgroup mean differences for various predictors

Predictor	Validity	Subgroup/mean difference
Cognitive ability and special aptitude	Moderate	Moderate
Personality	Low	Small
Interest	Low	?[a]
Physical ability	Moderate-High	Large[b]
Biographical information	Moderate	?
Interviews	Low	Small (?)
Work samples	High	Small
Seniority	Low	Large (?)
Peer evaluations	High	?
Reference checks	Low	?
Academic performance	Low	Moderate (?)
Self-assessments	Moderate	Small
Assessment centres	High	Small

[a] Indicates either a lack of data or inconsistent data.
[b] Mean differences largely between male and female subgroups.

Source: Reproduced from Schmitt (1987) with the permission of John Wiley & Sons.

various predictor methods and the size of differences between subgroups (based on gender, demography, ability, etc.). What is particularly interesting to note about Table 3.4 is that there are no data on some methods, indicating the paucity of good research in this area.

Certainly, the issue of selection methods has generated as much heat as light, but, alas, until relatively recently, no good research in the area. Dipboye, Smith & Howell (1994) have contrasted the "scientific" versus the intuitive approaches to selection (see Figure 3.8). Very few organizations use "scientific" methods, although they claim to do so.

Figure 3.9 shows how one might validate a selection instrument (be it a personality or ability test, or any other measure). Having done and considered the results of a job analysis (Step 1), two things need to be considered: what test to use and which aspect of the job to measure. Thus, for instance, one might choose an extraversion questionnaire for sales persons and select as the criterion (or criteria) either (or both) sales revenue (or profit) or customer responses (Step 2).

Step 3 is to administer the instrument(s) and then measure the performance on the chosen criteria, noting both unusual circumstances that may affect the outcome (such as seasonality) and also the influence of others (in the work team) on the performance criterion (or criteria). Step 4 is to correlate the two or, better still, do some multivariate statistics (regression analysis) to determine which of several characteristics (age, work experience, gender, etc.) other than, but as well as, the factor measured in the selection instrument predict performance. If the relationship is statistically significant and psychologically meaningful, the selection instrument may be used. If not, one has to start again with another instrument (Steps 5 and 6).

Although there is no shortage of tests and instruments to predict occupational behaviour or work performance, the problem is usually finding a good performance

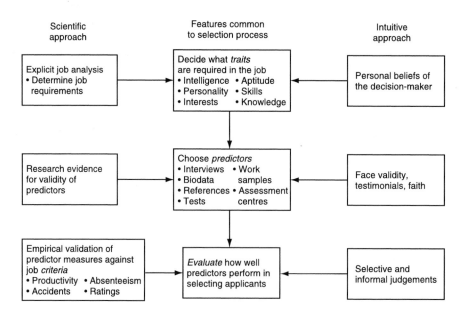

Figure 3.8 A summary of the major components involved in the scientific and intuitive approaches to selection. Reproduced from Dipboye *et al.* (1994) with the permission of Harcourt Brace & Co.

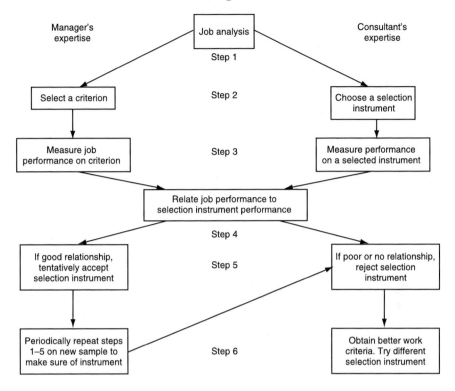

Figure 3.9 Basic selection model.

criterion. Very few organizations keep regular reliable figures on the performance of their employees, such as productivity, absenteeism, and so on. Indeed, it comes as a surprise to most researchers who attempt to validate instruments and help organizations with selection that the latter have little in the way of performance records that they can use.

The cost of selection

Various researchers have tried to calculate the cost of selection itself but also, perhaps more importantly, *return* on selection. The formula was first stated by Brodgen (1950):

$$\text{saving per employee per year} = (r \times \text{SD}_y \times Z) - (C/P)$$

where r = the validity of the selection procedure (expressed as a correlation coefficient), SD = the standard deviation of employee productivity in pounds/dollars, Z = the calibre of recruits (expressed as their standard score on the selection test used), C = the cost of selection per applicant, and P = the proportion of applicants selected. That is, the amount an employer can save, per employee recruited, per year, is:

VALIDITY of the test *times* CALIBRE of recruits *times SD*,

minus

COST of selection *divided by* PROPORTION of applicants selected

Cook (1988: 242–243) provides a worked example:

1   The employer is recruiting in the salary range £20,000 p.a., so *SD* can be estimated – by the 70% "rule of thumb" – at £14,000. (Or SD_y can be measured by *rational estimate* or *superior equivalents* techniques.)
2   The employer is using a test of high level mental ability whose proven validity is 0.45, so $r = 0.45$.
3   The people recruited score on average 1 *SD* above the means for the ability test, so $Z = 1$. This assumes the employer succeeds in recruiting high-calibre people.
4   The employer uses a consultancy, which charges £480 per candidate.
5   Of ten applicants, four are appointed, so *p* is 0.40.

The saving per employee per year is:

$$(0.45 \times £14,000 \times 1) \text{ minus } (£480/0.40) = £6,300 \text{ minus } £1,200 = £5,100$$

Each employee selected is worth over £5,000 a year more to the employer than one recruited at random. The four employees recruited will be worth in all £20,400 more to the employer, *each year*. The larger the organization, the greater the total sum that can be saved by effective selection, hence the estimate given in Chapter 1 of US$18 million [£27 million] for the Philadelphia police force, with 5000 employees. Selection pays off better:

(a) when the calibre of recruits is high;
(b) when employees differ a lot in worth to the organization, i.e. when SD_y is high;
(c) when the selection procedure has high validity.

  Selection pays off less well:

(a) when recruits are uniformly mediocre;
(b) when SD_y is low;
(c) when the selection procedure has low validity.

  Employers should have no difficulty attracting good recruits in periods of high unemployment (unless the pay or conditions are poor). But the third condition – zero validity – is all too likely to apply; many selection methods have zero, or near-zero, validity. But if any of the three terms are zero, their product – the value of selection – is necessarily zero too. Only the right-hand side of the equation – the cost of selection – is never zero.
  In the worked example, even using a fairly expensive selection procedure, the cost per employee selected is only a fifth of the increased value per employee per year, giving the lie to the oft-heard claim that elaborate selection methods, or psychological assessment, aren't worthwhile. In this example, selection pays for itself six times over in the first year. Failure to select the right employee, by contrast, goes on costing the employer money, *year after year*.

Organizational choice

What makes a person choose one organization over another? Expectancy theory (see Chapter 5) has been used to calculate this. Two pieces of information are combined in a unique way to indicate the relative attractiveness of the four organizations: the student's *beliefs* about *outcomes* associated with each one, and the *importance* of each outcome. As shown in Table 3.5, the attractiveness of an organization can be represented as an algebraic formula:

Attractiveness of = Σ Belief about X × Importance of
an organization   each outcome

The *attractiveness* of an organization, often called the *preferred* organization, is an important piece of information, but it is *not sufficient* to indicate the universities to which a student will actually apply. To understand where the student will apply requires information about her *expectancy of being admitted*. At the bottom of Table 3.4, the total attractiveness score for each university is multiplied by the expectancy of admittance to yield *total motivation to apply to each school*:

Total motivation to × Expectancy of being = Attractiveness of
apply to an   admitted to the   the organization
organization   organization

A comparison of the rank orders of attractiveness and of total motivation shows important differences. The Oxbridge university was the most attractive to this student, but she may not even apply to it. According to expectancy theory, the student will certainly apply to the redbrick university, since it is tops in *total* motivation. The "new" university and the Scottish university, although lower in total motivation, will also probably receive the application. Whether or not the student will apply to Oxbridge is *not clear*. That is, no *minimum level* of motivation has been specified in expectancy theory.

If the total motivational score had been zero, expectancy theory predicts that the student will definitely *not* apply. Thus, the theory makes predictions at both extremes. That is, any university with a zero score will not be applied to and the one with the highest score will receive an application. However, expectancy theory does not specify *which* of the universities in between will receive an application.

Expectancy theory also specifies how the student will make her *final choice* after knowing which institutions will accept her. Of course, the final choice depends on which institutions actually accept her. If only one does so, there is no choice to be made. If two or more do so, the choice will be based on the *attractiveness* of each institution. When a person has already been admitted, the expectancy factor is irrelevant. That is, expectancy = 1.0 for all those institutions that accept the student. Therefore, the differences among such institutions are in terms of attractiveness.

Table 3.5 Organizational choice example: How the model operates

Calculating the attractiveness of each college

Type of outcome	Redbrick (technological) university	Oxbridge	"New" university	Scottish university
	Belief × importance = Attractiveness	*Belief × importance = Attractiveness*	*Belief × importance = Attractiveness*	*Belief × importance = Attractiveness*
1. Learn a lot	.8 × 4 = 3.2	.9 × 4 = 3.6	.4 × 4 = 1.6	.8 × 4 = 3.2
2. Low cost	.6 × 2 = 1.2	0 × 2 = 0.0	1.0 × 2 = 2.0	.2 × 2 = 0.4
3. Good job later	.7 × 5 = 3.5	1.0 × 5 = 5.0	.3 × 5 = 1.5	.7 × 5 = 3.5
4. Flexible programme	.7 × 1 = 0.7	.7 × 1 = 0.7	.7 × 1 = 0.7	.7 × 1 = 0.7
5. Desirable location	.4 × 3 = 1.2	.7 × 3 = 2.1	.4 × 3 = 1.2	.9 × 3 = 2.7
Total attractiveness	9.8	11.4	7.0	10.5

Calculating the total amount of motivation to apply to each college

School	Motivational components			
	Total attractiveness of college		*Expectancy of admittance*	*Total motivation*
Redbrick university	9.8	×	.8	=	7.64
Oxbridge	11.4	×	.2	=	2.28
"New" university	7.0	×	1.0	=	7.0
Scottish university	10.5	×	.6	=	6.3

Source: Adapted from Wanous (1992).

Organizational socialization

People choose to apply to specific organizations which select newcomers among applicants, who, in turn, choose from among offers they receive. Once these processes have occurred, most organizations endeavour to make the entry efficient and informative. In a sense, the entry process is that of dual matching between the individual's specific job wants and the capacity of the organization to fulfil them. There is also a match between the individual's capabilities and potential and the requirements of a particular job.

Many individuals enter organizations with inflated and unrealistic expectations and hence initial favourable attitudes towards the job specifically, and the organization in general, decrease the longer the newcomer remains in the job.

The idea of matching, described earlier in this chapter with respect to vocational choice, has been explored in this literature. Wanous (1978) developed the model shown in Figure 3.10, which looks at the way individuals and organizations get matched to each other. The top part of the figure shows how the individual's capabilities are matched to the organization's job requirements and a main consequence of a *mismatch* is the newcomer's job performance. The bottom part of the figure shows the second type of matching, notably between the wanted job outcomes and the capacity of the organization to reinforce those wants.

To some extent, organizational newcomers and the organization itself have quite

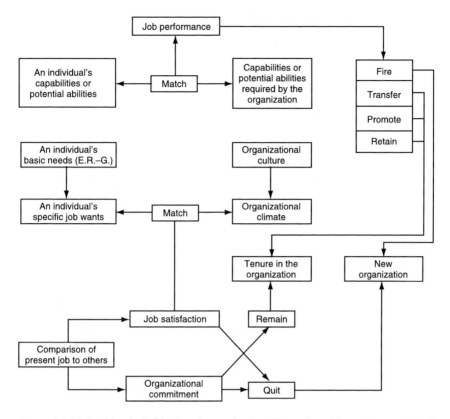

Figure 3.10 Matching individual and organization. Reproduced from Wanous (1978).

different requirements. At each stage – recruitment, selection, orientation and socialization – the organization and individual have somewhat different tasks (Table 3.6).

Many organizations have various rules of thumb that they obey to help in the business of "newcomer orientation". Wanous (1992) specified features that appear to help a great deal, such as:

- Give the person realistic information early on so that appropriate expectations are developed.
- Provide general support and reassurance, particularly at the beginning.
- Recruit models to help show the newcomer what is appropriate.

This sounds very similar to the recommendations of Bandura's self-efficacy theory. Essentially, organizational socialization is how organizations change newcomers. It is concerned specifically with making newcomers conform to the organization and is a process that unfolds over an extended period of time. Its basic objective is to maintain control by ensuring that newcomers share the same norms and values as those already established. Essentially, organizational socialization attempts to teach the newcomer new rules, roles, norms, values and concepts used by the organization. It attempts either overtly to indoctrinate or covertly by subtle pressure to align all members of an organization.

Table 3.6 Individual and organizational issues at four stages of entry

Phase of organizational entry	Whose perspective	
	The newcomer individual	*The organization being entered*
1. Recruitment: The process of mutual attraction	Finding sources of information about job openings Determining the accuracy of information about particular organizations	Finding sources of effective job candidates Attracting candidates with appropriate strategy ("selling vs. realism")
2. Selection: The process of mutual choice	Coping with job interviews and other assessment methods Deciding whether or not to apply Choosing from among job offers	Assessing candidates for future job performance and retention
3. Orientation: The process of initial adjustment	Coping with the stress of entry	Managing both emotional and informational needs of newcomers
4. Socialization: The process of mutual adjustment	Moving through typical stages Detecting one's success	Influencing newcomers by various tactics Using the psychology of persuasion

Source: Reproduced from Wanous (1992) with permission of Addison-Wesley Publishing Company, Inc.

This process takes time and various researchers have tried to describe it. According to Wanous (1992), who reviews four models (Buchanan, 1974; Feldman, 1976a,b; Porter, Lawler, & Hackman, 1975; Schein, 1978) in addition to his own, each is a stage-wise model. All of them, apart from his own, have three stages, rather differently described. Consider the following:

Feldman's (1976a,b) three-stage entry model:

1   *Anticipatory socialization* – "getting in"
    Setting of realistic expectations
    Determining match with the newcomer
2   *Accommodation* – "breaking in"
    Initiation into the job
    Establish interpersonal relationships
    Roles clarified
    Congruence between self and organizational performance appraisal
3   *Role management* – "settling in"
    Degree of fit between life interests outside work and organizational demands
    Resolution of conflicts at the workplace itself
    Diversity due to individual experiences

Schein's (1978) three-stage socialization model:

1   *Entry*
    Search for accurate information
    Creation of false expectations by both parties
    Inaccurate information is basis for job choice

2 *Socialization*
Accept organizational reality
Cope with resistance to change
Congruence between organizational climate and person's needs
Organization's evaluation of newcomer's performance
Cope with either too much ambiguity or too much structure
3 *Mutual acceptance*
Signals of organizational acceptance
Signals of newcomer's acceptance
Commitment to the organization
Commitment to work

Stage 1 for Feldman and Porter *et al.* is equivalent, but for both, Stage 2 is roughly equivalent to Stage 1 in the other models. All models appear to cover the same ground in the first stages but there is clearly more disagreement about the latter stages.

Wanous (1992) has attempted to integrate these into a simple model (Box 3.1). The

---

Box 3.1 Stages in the socialization process

Stage 1: Confronting and accepting organizational reality

  (a) Confirmation/disconfirmation of expectations
  (b) Conflicts between personal job wants and the organizational climates
  (c) Discovering which personal aspects are reinforced, which are not reinforced, and which are punished by the organization.

Stage 2: Achieving role clarity

  (a) Being initiated to the tasks in the new job
  (b) Defining one's interpersonal roles

    (i) with respect to peers
    (ii) with respect to one's boss

  (c) Learning to cope with resistance to change
  (d) Congruence between a newcomer's own evaluation of performance and the organization's evaluation of performance
  (e) Learning how to work within the given degree of structure and ambiguity.

Stage 3: Locating oneself in the organizational context

  (a) Learning which modes of behaviour are congruent with those of the organization
  (b) Resolution of conflicts at work, and between outside interests and work
  (c) Commitment to work and to the organization stimulated by first-year job challenge
  (d) The establishment of an altered self-image, new interpersonal relationships, and the adoption of new values.

Stage 4: Detecting signposts of successful socialization

  (a) Achievement of organizational dependability and commitment
  (b) High satisfaction in general
  (c) Feeling of mutual acceptance
  (d) Job involvement and internal work motivation
  (e) The sending of "signals" between newcomers and the organization to indicate mutual acceptance.

Source: Wanous (1992). Reproduced with the permission of Addison-Wesley Publishing Company, Inc.

first stage refers to the socialization itself and the final stage to the transition from newcomer to insider. The rate at which newcomers proceed through the various stages is primarily determined by the amount of contact between newcomers and insiders, which in turn, leads to:

- establishment, by the newcomer, of a new identity within the organization;
- the acquisition of appropriate role behaviour for the workgroup;
- the development of work skills and abilities;
- adjustment to the workgroup's norms and values;
- making sense of organizational norms, practices and procedures.

Through a variety of means, organizations attempt where appropriate to change the beliefs, feelings, intentions and ultimately the behaviour of their new candidates. Tactics used by organizations can be categorized on six dimensions, depending on whether it is:

- done collectively in an intake group or individually;
- done formally (explicitly, timetabled, costed) or informally;
- done in a specific sequence or simply randomly;
- done on a fixed or variable timetable;
- done by those in a position similar to that of a newcomer or by specialists from human resources;
- done in a way aimed to reinforce the original identity of the newcomer or divest the newcomer of his or her identity (as is often done in the military).

Conclusion

The major cost to most organizations is the salaries of staff. It is both a truism *and* true that people (i.e. staff, employees) are the most valuable asset of any organization. The process of recruitment, selection and socialization of staff is therefore absolutely fundamental for an organization to succeed. Despite considerable progress in the development of valid procedures, many organizations prefer intuitive and often misguided methods to those proven to be valid and reliable.

It is the major purpose of vocational psychology to help guide individuals into jobs best suited to their ability, interests and personality. Given its important applied nature, this topic has attracted much research and theories derived from many different areas of psychology. At the very heart of vocational psychology is the person–job (or person–environment fit) and "fitting the person to the job" is its central concern. The work of Holland, with his hexagonal model by which he describes both individuals and jobs in the same language, has attracted most interest. The central idea is that *congruence* (between the characteristics of the individual and the job) is the best predictor for worker satisfaction.

Another focus of attention has been the expectations and values of those applying for different jobs. Clearly, inappropriate or unfulfillable expectations of things such as pay and conditions inevitably lead to disappointment and possibly poor productivity. Furthermore, employees and employers quite often value different things. This can lead to problems in the evaluation of benefits.

Various tests have been devised to help vocational guidance experts assist job seekers. The business of personnel selection, which itself uses tests, is a very important feature of work psychology. The information the selector or panel obtains and how "accept/ reject" decisions are based upon it has attracted a great deal of attention. A considerable amount of amateurism remains in this extremely important human resources area, as it appears that it is far more difficult to acquire a job than lose one.

Job analysis is usually thought of as the best place to begin to think about selection. Before worrying about the characteristics of the individual, it is thought important to ascertain a comprehensive understanding of the skills, knowledge and abilities required for the job. Although the recruitment period may pre-date the job analysis, it certainly should not occur before the selection procedure and a full "person specification". Various techniques are available to help with job analysis, which, given the rapid increase of technological change, probably have to be regularly updated.

Various methods are used in selection. The aim is always the same: to find the cheapest and most valid measure that differentiates solely in terms of the skills, abilities and knowledge required for the job and not other extraneous variables. Most people have first-hand experience of poor or wrong selection decisions: the appointment of clearly unable and unproductive employees, which are both a cost to their company and a strain on their workmates. The cost of selection can actually be calculated in monetary terms and thus clearly demonstrates the wisdom of investing in selection procedures. Applicants, too, can and do make "calculations" when evaluating the comparative attractiveness of one organization or institution over another.

Once employees are recruited and selected, they need to be socialized into the organization. Various orientation programmes may be considered to help them over the corporate culture shock of the new person. Organizations approach orientation and socialization rather differently, and too many neglect doing it well.

A research perspective

The relationship between the individual and the organization may be described as the psychological contract. This is not a written document, but mutual expectations and satisfaction of needs arising from the people–organization relationship. It involves a process of both giving and receiving by the individual and the organization. The psychological contract covers a range of expectations of rights and privileges, duties and obligations, which do not form part of a formal agreement, but still have an important influence on people's behaviour. That is, the psychological contract is not a legal requirement of the organization (Schein, 1978).

The nature and extent of individuals' expectations vary widely, as do the ability and willingness of the organization to meet them. They may include the idea that the organization shall:

- provide safe, comfortable and hygienic working conditions;
- make every reasonable effort to provide job security;
- attempt to provide challenging and satisfying jobs and reduce alienating aspects of work;
- adopt equitable personnel policies and procedures;
- allow staff genuine participation in decisions that affect them;
- provide reasonable opportunities for personal development and career progression;
- treat members of staff with respect;
- demonstrate an understanding and considerate attitude towards personal problems of staff.

The organization will equally have implicit expectations of its members, for example:

- to accept the values and follow the behavioural norms of the organization;

- to work diligently in pursuit of organizational objectives;
- not to abuse any goodwill shown by management;
- to uphold the image of the organization;
- to be prepared to adjust to changing circumstances;
- to follow rules and regulations, and honour legal contracts.

French, Kast & Rosenzweng (1985) suggest the following list of organizational expectations and requirements:

- Achieving organizational goals that are different from the personal goals of individual members.
- Having sufficient involvement, commitment and initiative from organizational members.
- Requiring individuals to take certain organizational roles.
- Having people perform certain tasks effectively and efficiently.
- Requiring participants to accept authority and to assume responsibilities.
- Achieving the integration and coordination of activities.
- Requiring adherence to policies, rules and procedures.
- Attaining responsiveness to leadership and influence.
- Developing sufficient loyalty to maintain the organization as a social system.

For various reasons, there may be significant differences between the expectations of the organization and the employee. This is because these expectations are not made formal and explicit, as well as there being unrealistic assumptions on the part of both parties. Although it is probably not desirable to make the psychological contract a legal contract, it probably is worth making certain highly significant issues more explicit. It should also be acknowledged that the contract can change and may be most malleable during the early period of employment. Certainly, after industrial unrest or, say, when an employee believes he or she has been unfairly overlooked for promotion, the psychological contract that has been established may undergo a radical revision. A broken contract may lead to people feeling less committed to the organization.

Organizational commitment has been defined by Mowday, Steers & Porter (1979) as "the relative strength of an individual's identification with and involvement in an organization". Griffin & Bateman (1986) believe it has three components:

- a desire to maintain membership in the organization;
- belief in and acceptance of the values and goals of the organization; and
- a willingness to exert effort on behalf of the organization.

Others, such as Allen & Meyer (1990), have distinguished between:

- *Affective commitment:* this essentially concerns the person's emotional attachment to the organization.
- *Continuance commitment:* a person's perception of the costs and risks associated with leaving their current organization.
- *Normative commitment:* a moral dimension, based on a person's felt obligation and responsibility to their employing organization.

Researchers have pointed out that people feel multiple commitments at work – not only to their organization, but also perhaps to their location, department, workgroup or trade union.

There are several distinct theoretical approaches to organizational commitment. One of these, the *behavioural* approach, sees commitment as being created when a person does things publicly, of their own free will, and which would be difficult to retract. If a person freely chooses to join an organization, and subsequently performs other committing acts (e.g. voluntarily working long hours), they will feel more committed to it. Second, there is the exchange approach. Many researchers have tried to identify exactly *which* positive work experiences matter most for organizational commitment. It would appear that factors intrinsic to the job (e.g. challenge, autonomy) are more important in fostering commitment than extrinsic factors (e.g. pay and working conditions). This is especially true for the affective component of commitment (i.e. commitment based on emotional attachment). On the other hand, continuing commitment (i.e. the extent to which leaving would be costly for the person) is more influenced by the person's perception of their past contributions to their organization and their present likely attractiveness (or lack of it) to other employers. There is also some suggestion that commitment is partly a function of the person rather than what happens to them at work; that is, some people are perhaps more prone to feel committed than others. What factors lead to, succeed in sustaining, and break organizational commitment, are indeed "hot" topics of research today.

A cross-cultural perspective

Euro Disney was initially a celebrated disaster. Did it have anything to do with the Americans not being sensitive to cultural differences? When starting businesses, one should be aware of cultural differences: what the customers want and under what working conditions the locals usually work. This is how Robbins (1991: 55) saw the challenges that Euro Disney presented that Disney had never encountered before:

1   In contrast to Americans, the French have little previous exposure to theme parks. The idea of paying just to walk inside the gate is foreign to them.
2   The French reserve one day and only one day a week – Sunday – for family outings. Going out with the family on a Saturday or weekday isn't something they're used to doing.
3   The French vacation *en masse*. In August, everything closes down and everyone goes on holiday. Demand at the theme park is unlikely, therefore, to be as spread out as it is in the USA.
4   The French have long had an aversion to meeting strangers. The idea of being welcomed by strangers with buoyant smiles and a lighthearted greeting is not appreciated.
5   In the USA, 50% of Disney visitors eat fast food at the parks. Most French, however, don't snack. Should Euro Disney have as many eating places as the US parks do? If they do, will they be empty?
6   The French insist on eating lunch at exactly 12:30. How can the restaurants at Euro Disney handle 30,000 or more people, all queuing up for lunch at the same time?
7   The French are impatient. They are not comfortable waiting in long lines. Americans seem to accept waits of half an hour or more for the more popular rides. Will this limit attendance and be the "kiss of death" to the new park?
8   The French adore their dogs. They take them everywhere – inside most French resorts and even fine restaurants. Dogs, however, are and have always been banned from Disney parks.
9   Disney employees wearing badges to identify them by their first names only work well in the USA, where informality is well accepted. Such a practice is an un-French way of doing business.
10 French workers don't like to obey orders. They are not likely to take kindly to management's demands that they do not smoke, chew gum, or converse with their co-workers.

Of course, one can easily accuse Robbins of stereotyping. Remember this is an American "explaining" the failure of a highly successful US organization.

In more reflective mode, Robbins (1991: 62) asks the question: "What are Americans like?". In doing so he identifies nine characteristics:

•   Americans are very *informal*: They don't tend to treat people differently even when there are great differences in age or social standing.

- Americans are *direct*: They don't talk around things. To some foreigners, this may appear as abrupt or even rude behaviour.
- Americans are *competitive*: Some foreigners find Americans assertive and overbearing.
- Americans are *achievers*: They like to keep score, whether at work or at play. They emphasize accomplishments.
- Americans are *independent* and *individualistic*: They place a high value on freedom and believe that individuals can shape and control their own destinies.
- Americans are *questioners*: They ask a lot of questions, even to someone they have just met. Many of these questions may seem pointless ("How ya doing?") or personal ("What kind of work do you do?").
- Americans dislike *silence*: They would rather talk about the weather than deal with silence in a conversation.
- Americans value *punctuality*: They keep appointment calendars and live according to schedules and clocks.
- Americans value *cleanliness*: They often seem obsessed with bathing, eliminating body odours, and wearing clean clothes.

If Robbins is correct, it certainly has important implications for the sort of job the average American prefers, as well as how he or she behaves at selection interviews.

A human resources perspective

What do people look for in a job these days? Yankelovitch (1982) used informative public opinion polls to discern a movement away from valuing economic incentives, organizational loyalty and work-related identity, towards valuing meaningful work, pursuit of leisure, and personal identity and self-fulfilment. Higher productivity seems apparent among younger workers who are employed in jobs that match their values and/or who are supervised by managers who share their values.

It is also interesting to note the similarities between the values held by the "sixties generation" and those reported by Yankelovitch. Consider the similarities between these values and those reported in Box 3.2, which are based on a nationwide sample of managers and human resource professionals. The responding organizational specialists were asked to identify the work-related values they believed to be most important to individuals in the workforce, both now and in the near future. The nine most popular values are listed in Box 3.2. These values are especially important for managers, since they provide an indication of some key concerns of the new workforce. Even though each individual worker places his or her own importance on these values, and even though the USA today has by far the most diverse workforce in its history, this overall characterization is a good place for managers to start when dealing with new and old workers in the new workplace. Whatever their new values they have to be taken into account in the selection interviews. Many myths surround the selection interview.

Much research on the validity and reliability of the interview has yielded the following insights:

- Interviewers make their final decision about an applicant (too) early in the interview session.
- Interviewers are often more influenced by negative information about an applicant than by positive information (when you succeed, no-one remembers; when you fail, no-one forgets).
- Interviewers often have stereotypes of "the ideal successful job applicant", against which actual applicants are compared. Alas, these are not based on good job analysis.
- Interviewers make better (more reliable) decisions when they have better job analysis data.
- Interviewers differ in the ways they interpret pieces of information, and in the ways they use that information to make final decisions about applicants. (There are both good and bad interviewers.)
- Less experienced interviewers tend to be vulnerable to a "contrast effect", whereby an

Box 3.2 The top nine work-related values a sample of organizational specialists believe important for the new workforce.

1. *Recognition for competence and accomplishments* People want to be seen and recognized, both as individuals and teams, for their values, skills, and accomplishments. They want to know that their contribution is appreciated.
2. *Respect and dignity* This value focuses on how people are treated – through the jobs they hold, in response to their ideas, or by virtue of their background. The strong support for this value indicates that most people want to be respected for who they are; they want to be valued.
3. *Personal choice and freedom* People want more opportunity to be free from constraints and decisions made for and about them by authorities. They want to be more autonomous and able to rely more on their own judgement. They wish to have more personal choice in what affects their lives.
4. *Involvement at work* Large portions of the workforce want to be kept informed, included and involved in important decisions at work, particularly as these decisions affect their work and quality of life at work.
5. *Pride in one's work* People want to do a good job and feel a sense of accomplishment. Fulfilment and pride come through quality workmanship.
6. *Lifestyle quality* People pursue many different lifestyles and each person wants his or hers to be of high quality. Work policies and practices have great impact on lifestyle pursuits. The desire for time with family and time for leisure were strongly emphasized.
7. *Financial security* People want to know that they can succeed. They want some security from economic cycles, rampant inflation, or devastating financial situations. This appears to be a new variation on the desire for money – not continual pursuit of money, but enough to feel secure in today's world, enjoy a comfortable lifestyle, and ride out bad times.
8. *Self development* The focus here is on the desire continually to improve, to do more with one's life, to reach one's potential, to learn and grow. There is a strong desire by individuals to take initiative and to use opportunities to further themselves.
9. *Health and wellness* The value reflects the ageing workforce and increased information on wellness. People want to organize life and work in ways that are healthy and contribute to long-term wellness.

Source: Schermerhorn *et al.* (1994). Copyright © John Wiley & Sons Ltd. Reproduced with permission.

"average" applicant will be evaluated inordinately high or low if the person interviewed immediately before was unusually unqualified or unusually qualified, respectively.

- The race and gender of both the interviewer and the applicant often influence the interviewer's decision.
- Interviewers use non-verbal as well as verbal cues in arriving at decisions about applicants, about which they are not always aware.
- Structured interviews are superior to unstructured interviews.
- Panel interviews can improve the reliability and validity of interview data.
- Interview questions should be derived directly from job analyses or from other appropriate job-related information.
- Interviewers are influenced by primacy and recency effects, where information that emerges very early or very late in the interview, respectively, makes a greater impression than information that emerges "in the middle" of the interview. However, it is not clear when primary or recency effects are at work.

- Women are usually evaluated less favourably than equally qualified men, especially if the job in question is a traditionally "masculine" one (such as manager, for example). This may now be changing, even reversing.
- There is little evidence that race is associated with the favourability or unfavourability of interviewers' decisions.
- Applicants' ages play an important role in interviewers' decisions, which generally favour younger applicants.
- Handicapped applicants receive lower hiring recommendations than able-bodied applicants, but the handicapped are typically given credit for higher levels of work motivation.

References

Allen, N., & Meyer, J. (1990). The measurement and antecedents of affective, continuance and normative commitment to the organization. *Journal of Occupational Psychology, 63*, 1–8.

Arnold, J. (1997). The psychology of careers in organizations. In C. Cooper & J. Robertson (Eds.), *International review of industrial and organizational psychology* (pp. 1–37). Chichester: Wiley.

Arvey, R. (1979). *Fairness in selecting employees*. London: Addison-Wesley.

Arvey, R., Passino, E., & Lounsbury, J. (1977). Job analysis results as influenced by sex of incumbent and sex of analyst. *Journal of Applied Psychology, 62*, 411–416.

Bates, G., Parker, H., & McCoy, J. (1970). Vocational rehabilitants, personality and work adjustment: A test for Holland's theory of vocational choice. *Psychological Reports, 26*, 511–516.

Betz, N. (2001). Perspectives on future directions in vocational psychology. *Journal of Vocational Psychology, 59*, 275–283.

Blum, M., & Naylor, J. (1968). *Industrial psychology*. New York: Harper & Row.

Blustein, D. (2001). Extending the reach of vocational psychology. *Journal of Vocational Behaviour, 59*, 171–182.

Borgen, W., & Young, R. (1982). Career perception of children and adolescents. *Journal of Vocational Behaviour, 21*, 37–49.

Bridges, J. (1988). Sex differences in occupational performance expectations. *Psychology of Women Quarterly, 12*, 75–90.

Brodgen, H. (1950). When testing pays off. *Personnel Psychology, 2*, 171–183.

Brooks, L., & Betz, N. (1990). Utility of expectancy theory in predicting occupational choices in college students. *Journal of Counselling Psychology, 37*, 57–64.

Buchanan, B. (1974). Building organizational commitment: The socialization of managers in work organizations. *Administrative Science Quarterly, 19*, 533–546.

Caplan, R. (1983). Person–environment fit: Past, present, and future. In C.L. Cooper (Ed.), *Stress research for the eighties* (pp. 2–33). Chichester: Wiley.

Caplan, R., Cobb, S., French, J., Harrison, R., & Pinneau, S. (1980). *Job demands and worker health*. Ann Arbor, MI: Institute of Social Research.

Chatman, H. (1989). Improving international organizational research: A model of person–organization fit. *Academy of Management Review, 14*, 333–349.

Cook, M. (1988). *Personnel selection and productivity*. Chichester: Wiley.

Cooper, R., & Payne, R. (1978). *Stress at work*. Chichester: Wiley.

Costa, P., McCrae, R., & Holland, J. (1984). Personality and vocational interests in an adult sample. *Journal of Applied Psychology, 69*, 390–400.

Costa, P., McCrae, R., & Kay, G. (1995). Persons, places and personality: Career assessment using the revised NEO personality inventory. *Journal of Career Assessment, 3*, 123–129.

Crowley, J., & Shapiro, D. (1982). Aspirations and expectations of youth in the United States. *Youth and Society, 13*, 391–422.

Dawis, R. (1992). Vocation interests, values and preferences. In M. Dunnette & L. Hough (Eds.), *Handbook of industrial and organizational psychology* (Vol. 2, pp. 833–855). Palo Alto, CA: Consulting Psychologists Press.

De Fruyt, F., & Mervielde, I. (1997). The five-factor model of personality and Holland's RIASEC interest types. *Personality and Individual Differences, 23*, 87–103.

Dipboye, R., Smith, C., & Howell, W. (1994). *Understanding industrial and organizational psychology*. Fort Worth, TX: Harcourt Brace.

Dore, R., & Meacham, M. (1973). Self-concepts and interests related to job satisfaction of managers. *Personnel Psychology, 26*, 49–59.

Elton, C., & Smart, J. (1988). Extrinsic job satisfaction and person–environment congruence. *Journal of Vocational Psychology, 32*, 226–238.

Feldman, D. (1976a). A contingency theory of socialization. *Administration Science Quarterly, 21*, 433–452.

Feldman, D. (1976b). A practical program for employee socialization. *Organizational Dynamics, 4*, 64–80.

Flanagan, J. (1954). The critical incident technique. *Psychological Bulletin, 51*, 327–358.

Fouad, N. (2001). The future of vocational psychology: Aiming high. *Journal of Vocational Behaviour, 59*, 183–191.

French, W., Kast, R., & Rosenzweng, T. (1985). *Understanding human behaviour in organizations*. New York: Harper & Row.

Fretz, B., & Leong, F. (1982). Vocational behaviour and career development, 1981: A review. *Journal of Vocational Behaviour, 21*, 123–163.

Furnham, A. (1987a). Work related beliefs and human values. *Personality and Individual Differences, 8*, 627–637.

Furnham, A. (1987b). The social psychology of working situations. In A. Gale & B. Christie (Eds.), *Psychophysiology and the electronic workplace* (pp. 89–112). Chichester: Wiley.

Furnham, A. (1992). *Personality at work*. London: Routledge.

Furnham, A. (2001). Vocational preference and P–O fit: Reflections on Holland's theory of vocational choice. *Applied Psychology, 50*, 5–29.

Furnham, A., & Koritsas, E. (1990). The Protestant work ethic and vocational preference. *Journal of Organizational Behaviour, 11*, 43–55.

Furnham, A., & Schaeffer, R. (1984). Person–environment fit, job satisfaction and mental health. *Journal of Occupational Psychology, 57*, 295–307.

Furnham, A., Toop, A., Lewis, C., & Fisher, A. (1995). P–E fit and job satisfaction. *Personality and Individual Differences, 19*, 677–690.

Furnham, A., & Walsh, J. (1991). The consequences of person–environment incongruence: Absenteeism, frustration and stress. *Journal of Social Psychology, 131*, 187–204.

Ghiselli, E., & Barthol, R. (1953). The validity of personality inventories in the selecting of employees. *Journal of Applied Psychology, 37*, 18–20.

Gottfredson, G. (2001). Fostering the scientific practice of vocational psychology. *Journal of Vocational Behaviour, 59*, 192–202.

Gottfredson, L. (1978). An analytic description of employment according to race, sex, prestige at Holland's type of work. *Journal of Vocational Psychology, 13*, 210–221.

Griffin, R. S. & Bateman, T. (1986). Job satisfaction and organizational commitment. In C. Cooper & J. Robertson (Eds.), *International review of industrial and organizational psychology* (pp. 157–188). Chichester: Wiley.

Harrison, R. (1978). Person–environment fit and job stress. In C. Cooper & R. Payne (Eds.), *Stress at work* (pp. 175–208). Chichester: Wiley.

Heesacker, M., Elliott, T., & Howe, L. (1988). Does the Holland code predict job satisfaction and productivity in clothing factory workers. *Journal of Counselling Psychology, 35*, 144–148.

Henry, P. (1989). Relationship between academic achievement and measured career interest. *Psychological Reports, 64*, 35–40.

Hesketh, B. (2001). Adapting vocational psychology to cope with change. *Journal of Vocational Behaviour, 59*, 203–212.

Hogan, R., Carpenter, B., Briggs, S., & Hansson, R. (1985). Personality assessment and personnel selection. In H. Bernadin & D. Bownas (Eds.), *Personality assessment in organizations* (pp. 21–52). New York: Praeger.

Holland, J. (1973). *Making vocational choices: A theory of careers.* Englewood Cliffs, NJ: Prentice-Hall.

Holland, J. (1985). *The self-directed search.* Odessa, FL: Psychological Assessment Resources.

Holland, J. (1987). *Manual supplement for the self-directed search.* Odessa, FL: Psychological Assessment Resources.

Hollenbeck, J., Ilgen, D., Ostroff, C., & Vancouver, J. (1987). Sex differences in occupational choice, pay and worth. *Personnel Psychology, 40*, 715–743.

Kahana, E., Liang, J., & Felton, B. (1980). Alternative models of person–environment fit: Prediction of moral in three homes for the aged. *Journal of Gerontology, 35*, 584–595.

Kasl, S. (1973). Mental health and the work environment: An examination of the evidence. *Journal of Occupational Medicine, 15*, 509–518.

Kennedy, R. (1958). *The prediction of achievement and creativity.* New York: Bobbs-Merrill.

Kirkcaldy, B. (1988). Sex and personality differences in occupational interests. *Personality and Individual Differences, 9*, 7–13.

Kline, P. (1975). *The psychology of vocational guidance.* London: Batsford.

Klinger, D. (1979). When the traditional job description is not enough. *Personnel Journal, 58*, 243–248.

Kuder, F. (1970). *General interest survey.* Chicago, IL: Science Research.

Lent, R. (2001). Vocational psychology and career counseling: Inventing the future. *Journal of Vocational Behaviour, 59*, 213–225.

Levy, O., Kaler, S., & Schall, M. (1988). An empirical investigation of role schemeta: Occupations and personality characteristics. *Psychological Reports, 63*, 3–14.

McCormick, E. (1976). Job and task analysis. In M. Dunnette (Ed.), *Handbook of industrial and organizational psychology* (pp. 651–696). Chicago, IL: Rand McNally.

McCormick, E., Jeanneret, P., & Mecham, R. (1972). A study of job characteristics and job dimensions as based on the position analysis questionnaire. *Journal of Applied Psychology, 56*, 347–368.

Morse, J. (1975). Person–job congruence and individual adjustment and development. *Human Relations, 28*, 841–861.

Mount, M., & Muchinsky, P. (1978). Person–environment congruence and employee satisfaction: A test of Holland's theory. *Journal of Vocational Behaviour, 13*, 84–100.

Mowday, R., Steers, R., & Porter, L. (1979). The measurement of organizational commitment. *Journal of Vocational Behaviour, 14*, 224–247.

Naylor, F., Care, E., & Mount, T. (1986). The identification of Holland categories and occupational classification by the VPI and the Strong–Campbell interest inventory. *Australian Journal of Psychology, 38*, 161–167.

Nelson, R. (1963). Knowledge and interests concerning 16 occupations among elementary and secondary school students. *Educational and Psychology Measurement, 23*, 741–754.

Porter, L., Lawler, E., & Hackman, J. (1975). *Behaviour in organizations.* New York: McGraw-Hill.

Raphael, K., & Gorman, B. (1986). College women's Holland-theme congruence: Effects of self-knowledge and subjective occupational structure. *Journal of Counselling Psychology, 33*, 143–147.

Robbins, S. (1991). *Organizational behavior.* Englewood Cliffs, NJ: Prentice-Hall.

Robinson, D. (1981). Content-oriented personnel selection in a small business setting. *Personnel Psychology, 34*, 77–87.

Russell, J. (2001). Vocational psychology: An analysis and directions for the future. *Journal of Vocational Behaviour, 59,* 226–234.

Ryan, A., & Ployhart, R. (2000). Applicants' perceptions of selection procedures and decisions. *Journal of Management, 26,* 565–606.

Rynes, S., & Cable, D. (2003). Recruitment research in the twenty-first century. In W. Borman, D. Ilgen, & E. R. Klinoski (Eds.), *Handbook of psychology* (Vol. 12, pp. 55–76). New York: Wiley.

Sackett, P., & Laczo, R. (2003). Job and work analysis. In W. Borman, D. Ilgen, & E. R. Klinoski (Eds.), *Handbook of psychology* (Vol. 12, pp. 21–38). New York: Wiley.

Savickas, M. (1995). Current theoretical issues in vocational psychology. In W. Walsh and S. Osipow (Eds.), *Handbook of vocational psychology* (pp. 1–31). Hillsdale, NJ: Lawrence Erlbaum Associates.

Savickas, M. (2001). The next decade in vocational psychology: Mission or objective? *Journal of Vocational Behaviour, 59,* 284–290.

Schein, E. (1978). *Career dynamics: Matching individual and organizational needs.* Reading, MA: Addison-Wesley.

Schermerhorn, J., Hunt, J., & Osborn, R. (1994). *Managing organizational behaviour.* New York: Wiley.

Schmitt, N. (1989). Fairness in employment selection. In M. Smith & I. Robertson (Eds.), *Advances in selection and assessment* (pp. 133–153). Chichester: Wiley.

Schmitt, N., Cortina, J., Ingerick, M., & Wiechmann, D. (2003). Personnel selection and employee performance. In W. Borman, D. Ilgen, & E. R. Klinoski (Eds.), *Handbook of psychology* (Vol. 12, pp. 77–105). New York: Wiley.

Schuler, R. (1989). *Personnel and human resource management.* St. Paul, MN: West.

Schwartz, R., Andiappan, P., & Nelson, M. (1986). Reconsidering the support for Holland's congruence-achievement hypothesis. *Journal of Counselling Psychology, 33,* 425–428.

Sims, R., & Veres, J. (1987a). Person–job match: Some alternative models. *International Journal of Management, 4,* 156–165.

Sims, R., & Veres, J. (1987b). A person–job match (congruence) model: Towards improving organizational effectiveness. *International Journal of Management, 4,* 98–104.

Smart, J. (1982). Holland environments as reinforcement systems. *Research in Higher Education, 23,* 279–292.

Smart, J. (1987). Student satisfaction with graduate education. *Journal of College Student Personnel, 5,* 218–222.

Smart, J., Elton, C., & McLaughlin, G. (1986). Person–environment congruence and job satisfaction. *Journal of Vocational Behaviour, 29,* 218–225.

Smith, M., & Robertson, I. (Eds.) (1989). *Advances in selection and assessment.* Chichester: Wiley.

Strong, E. (1951). Interest scores while in college of occupations engaged in 20 years later. *Educational and Psychological Measurement, 11,* 335–348.

Super, D. (1983). Assessment in career guidance: Toward truly developmental counselling. *Personnel and Guidance Journal, 63,* 555–562.

Swaney, K., & Prediger, D. (1985). The relationship between interest–occupation congruence and job satisfaction. *Journal of Vocational Behaviour, 26,* 13–24.

Tannenbaum, A., & Kuleck, W. (1978). The effect on organization members of discrepancy between perceived and preferred rewards implicit in work. *Human Relations, 21,* 809–822.

Taylor, K., Kelso, G., Cox, G., Alloway, W., & Matthews, J. (1979). Applying Holland's vocational categories to leisure activities. *Journal of Occupational Psychology, 52,* 199–207.

Taylor, M. (1985). The roles of occupational knowledge and vocational self-concept crystallization in students' school-to-work transaction. *Journal of Counselling Psychology, 32,* 539–550.

Tinsley, H. (2001). Marginalization of vocational psychology. *Journal of Vocational Behaviour, 59,* 243–251.

Tremaine, L., Schau, C., & Busch, J. (1982). Children's occupational sex-typing. *Sex Roles, 8,* 691–710.

Venkatapathy, R. (1984). Biographical characteristics of first generation and second generation entrepreneurs. *Journal of Small Enterprise Development in Management, 10*, 15–24.

Vondracek, F. (2001). The developmental perspective in vocational psychology. *Journal of Vocational Behaviour, 59*, 252–261.

Vroom, V. (1964). *Work and motivation.* New York: Wiley.

Walsh, W. (2001). The changing nature of the sciences of vocational psychology. *Journal of Vocational Psychology, 59*, 262–274.

Walsh, W., Bingham, R., & Sheffey, M. (1986). Holland's theory and college educated working black men and women. *Journal of Vocational Behaviour, 29*, 194–200.

Wanous, J. (1977). *Organizational entry: Recruitment, selection and socialization of newcomers.* Reading, MA: Addison-Wesley.

Wanous, J. (1978). Realistic job previews: Can a procedure to reduce turnover also influence the relationship between abilities and performance? *Personnel Psychology, 31*, 249–258.

Wanous, J. (1992). *Organizational entry: Recruitment, selection, orientation and socialization of newcomers.* Reading, MA: Addison-Wesley.

Wanous, J., Keen, T., & Latack, J. (1983). Expectancy theory and occupational/organizational choices: A review and test. *Organizational Behaviour and Human Performance, 32*, 66–86.

Wiggins, J., Lederer, D., Salkowe, A., & Rys, G. (1983). Job satisfaction related to tested congruence and differentiation. *Journal of Vocational Behaviour, 23*, 112–121.

Wigington, J. (1983). The applicability of Holland's typology to clients. *Journal of Vocational Behaviour, 23*, 286–293.

Yankelovitch, D. (1982). *New rules: Searching for self-fulfilment in a world turned upside down.* New York: Bantam Books.

Zedeck, S. (1977). An information processing model and approach to the study of motivation. *Organizational Behaviour and Human Performance, 18*, 47–77.

4   Personality and individual differences

Introduction

The history of research into personality and individual difference (ability, biography) predictors of organizational behaviour has been a bit like the search for the Holy Grail: protracted, marked by enthusiastic zealotry, seemingly endless and ultimately unsuccessful. The idea that one might uncover particular personality traits, background experiences or combinations of ability that consistently predict job commitment, motivation and satisfaction (or their opposites) has long attracted work psychologists. It is self-evident that people differ in ability and temperament, and indeed the speed at which they acquire skills; yet it is equally obvious that selection is a difficult and risky business and that these traits cannot totally predict work behaviour. However, there is now impressive, cross-national, meta-analytic results that suggest quite clearly that personality traits are logically, consistently and powerfully related to personality traits (Hogan & Holland, 2003). There is now renewed academic interest in personality and job performance and increasing good evidence that personality traits play a powerful role in determining work-related behaviour (Barrick, Stewart, & Piotrowski, 2002; Hurtz & Donovan, 2000; Witt, Burkes, Barrick, & Mount, 2002). Furthermore, theoretical developments have helped us to understand personality–job performance relations (Hogan & Holland, 2003).

Many questions are pertinent here: Do personality and ability factors relate consistently to occupational behaviour? If not, why not? If yes, which factors (e.g. traits) relate to which behaviours and how? What mechanism or process produces this effect? How much of the variance in occupational behaviour can be accounted for by these individual difference factors alone?

Enthusiasm for the idea that personality and individual differences predict occupational behaviour seems to be *cyclical*. During the 1920s and the 1950s, as well as the 1980s, there was much more enthusiasm for this research and more interest from human resource personnel than at other times. Academic research, and indeed belief in the idea of stable and predictable individual differences, has itself waxed and waned, and periods of naïve optimism have been followed by periods of scepticism, caution, doubt and downright pessimism.

Inevitably, over time, the quality and quantity of research has grown in this area and we are now in a much better position to evaluate the relationships between personality, ability and occupational organizational behaviour. The search for personality correlates and determinants of occupational behaviour (success and failure) has recently received renewed attention (Hough, 2001). Various meta-analyses (where the results of major studies are catalogued and compared) have suggested that there are indeed grounds for optimism regarding the use of personality measures in employee selection (Barrick & Mount, 1991; Barrick *et al.*, 2002; Hough & Furnham, 2003; Judge, Heller, & Mount, 2002; Judge & Ilies, 2002; Judge, Martocchio, & Thoresen, 1997; Salgado, 1997; Tett, Jackson, & Rothstein, 1991). The literature on trait correlates of occupational behaviour is scattered, of highly variable quality, and driven by quite different theoretical models (Furnham, 1991, 1992). Both empirical research and literature reviews have shown that criterion-related validity of (certain) personality constructs is a useful predictor of important, specific job-related criteria. *In other words, personality traits have been shown to (statistically) relate to measured job-performance outcomes.* Thus, Hough, Eaton, Dunnette, Kamp & McCloy (1990) showed that validities in the 0.20s remained stable. Thus, even when people are faking, we find there is evidence that personality tests do predict work behaviour. It would appear that personality tests account for between 15 and 30% of the variance in explaining work behaviour.

Recently, Hogan and Holland (2003) showed that as job performance criteria moved from the general to the specific, so did the estimated true trait validities. They reported .43 for Stability (low Neuroticism), .35 for Extraversion, .34 for Agreeableness, .36 for Conscientiousness and .34 for Openness.

Furnham (1992) has set out what he calls a research model for looking at this area. Figure 4.1 shows a simple model that may help to explain some of the variables that explore the relationship between personality variables and work-related behaviour. One of the features that frustrates any reviewer in this area is the loose use of terminology. Hence, it becomes difficult to specify the basic factors in the model and how they are related, one to another. Figure 4.2 shows five basic factors and how they may relate to occupational behaviour:

- *Ability*: This refers to the extent to which a person can *efficiently* carry out multiple processes in coordination to achieve a specified goal. They extend from relatively simple dextrous, hand–eye coordination tasks to complex intellectual decision processes, and are thus related to intelligence – but distinguished from it. Sometimes abilities are called "competencies", although there is some doubt how (or whether) the two concepts differ.
- *Demographic factors*: This refers to background factors such as sex, age, class and education. Demographic factors usually relate to biographical factors in the life of a particular person (e.g. birth-order, occupation of parents, type of school attended) and are distinguishable from psychographic factors, which refer to beliefs and values.
- *Intelligence*: This refers to the individual's capacity for abstract and critical thinking. Many controversies surround this concept, for instance whether it is uni- or multidimensional, to what extent it is inherited or learnt, and how it should be measured. Despite all the concerns of investigators, few doubt the effect of general intelligence on organizational behaviour.
- *Motivation*: Like intelligence, this is a multidimensional abstract concept that refers to the tendency to attend to some stimuli rather than others, with accompanying emotion, and the drive to cause some actions rather than others. Hence, one talks of the strength of particular motivations, such as the weak need for achievement. The higher the generalized need for achievement, the stronger the motivation for success at work.

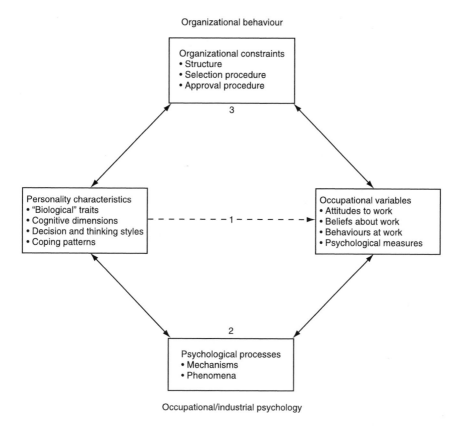

Organizational behaviour

Figure 4.1 A research model for examining the relationship between personality and work. Reproduced from Furnham (1992) with the permission of Routledge.

- *Personality*: This refers to all those fundamental traits or characteristics of the person (or of people generally) that endure over time and that account for consistent patterns of responses to everyday situations. Personality traits supposedly account for the what, why and how of human functioning.

Of course it is possible to criticize this simplistic model. It could be argued, for instance, that ability and intelligence are essentially the same; and that motivation is a function or part of personality. Furthermore, the model takes no account of other people (social norms, corporate culture) or historical or context features.

The model presented in Figure 4.2 is important for four reasons. First, it separates the five features distinguished above. Secondly, the bi-directionality of the arrows suggests that all these factors are *reciprocally* influential. Thirdly, the concept of personality is placed at the centre of the model to suggest its precedence in explanatory terms over the others. Finally, it is suggested that *each* of these factors reciprocally influences occupational behaviour, both on their own and in combination.

Given that there *is* a causal relationship between personality, or, say, ability and occupational behaviour, what patterns are possible?

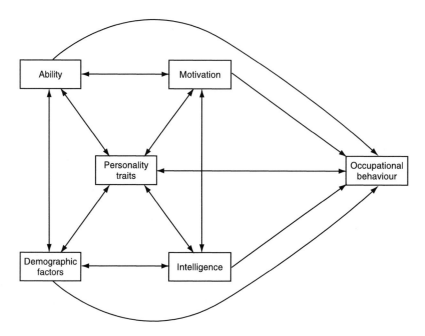

Figure 4.2 Some of the main factors predicting occupational behaviour. Reproduced from
Furnham (1992) with the permission of Routledge.

- *Positively linear*: If the relationship is linear, this implies quite simply that the more
  the ability (or the stronger the trait), the greater the occupational success (the
  stronger the behaviour). Certainly, many practical professionals hold to this very
  simple, somewhat improbable, relationship occurring.
- *Plateauing*: This relationship suggests that once a plateau has been reached, no
  further increase in the ability personality trait has any effect on the organizational
  success of the worker. This makes for a simple "cut-off" point (where the plateau
  begins). Clearly, if this relationship is the correct one, the crucial issue becomes
  where (and why) the plateau begins.
- *Exponential*: This relationship suggests that, beyond certain levels of ability personality, the increase in occupational success-specific behaviour is phenomenal.
  Thus, for instance, very able people achieve substantially and significantly more
  success than do moderately able people.
- *Curvilinear*: The relationship between occupational behaviour and ability personality is curvilinear; it implies that there is an optimal amount of ability to achieve
  occupational success – too much or too little can have equal non-ideal effects.
- *Negatively linear*: It is possible that ability personality may be perfectly negatively
  correlated with success, such that the more ability one has or the more extreme a
  score on a personality trait, the less successful one is occupationally. This may
  indeed be the case in intellectually less demanding jobs.
- *Asymptotic*: This is a negative plateau relationship which indicates that low
  amounts of ability or low personality scores are linked with occupational success,
  but that after a certain point the relationship ends and no further amount of ability
  is linked to occupational success.

- *No relationship*: Here there is no relationship whatsoever between ability personality and occupational success behaviour, presumably being determined by other factors, be they organizational or personal.
- *Ability/personality specific*: If this relationship occurs, it implies that only one particular level of ability is associated with occupational success.
- *Biomodality*: If the relationship is bi-modal, it suggests that two levels of ability – one moderate-to-low, the other moderate-to-high – are the optimal ones for job success. Put another way, two population groups are successful for different reasons.

There are doubtless other possible relationships. There is a vast literature on the correlates of abilities, but very little specifically on the *occupational* correlates of abilities. Perhaps given previous studies in the whole area, the most probable relationship is plateauing, or curvilinear. However, for both, the crucial question remains: At what ability range does performance reach its maximum?

The last decade has seen an explosion of interest and research on how, which and why personality traits predict behaviour at work (De Fruyt & Salgado, 2003). Furthermore, many cross-cultural studies have shown that the relationship between personality and culture seem cross-culturally stable (Nikolaou & Robertson, 2001). Studies have looked at both the positive (job satisfaction and productivity) as well as the negative (absenteeism) side of work behaviour. Thus, Judge *et al.* (1997) showed that sociable, excitement-seeking, gregarious extraverts were more likely to go absent than dutiful, self-disciplined, conscientious employees. Indeed, Ones, Viswesvaran & Schmidt (2003), who reviewed the efficacy of personality-based integrity tests to predict absenteeism, concluded that it was probably better to use these tests in selection to prevent high rates of absenteeism that attempt to deal with it in those already selected.

These studies are clearly becoming ever more sophisticated as they look at the dynamic relationships between traits, states and work variables (Ilies & Judge, 2002). These also discuss the use of personality tests for a select-in versus select-out point of view.

Studies in the area are becoming ever more sophisticated as measures of personality traits and job-performance criteria become more reliable (Smith, Hanges, & Dickson, 2001). Thus Witt *et al.* (2002) showed that some of the "Big Five" traits interact: people high on conscientiousness and agreeableness received better job performance ratings than those high on conscientiousness but low on agreeableness.

Six approaches to personality and individual differences at work

An examination of the highly diverse, dispersed and divergent literature concerning personality at work has highlighted six rather different approaches to the topic (Furnham, 1992).

Classic personality theory

Classic personality theory starts with a theory of personality – usually of a particular trait, such as extraversion, Machiavellism or self-monitoring (see later sections) – and relates empirically assessed measures (as the independent variable) to various work-related behaviours. The personality variable chosen may vary on several dimensions:

- *Single or multiple traits*: A single trait (measuring just one dimension) might be considered – for example, self-monitoring (Snyder, 1974) or locus of control (Rotter, 1966) – or, alternatively, a trait system, bound up in an elaborate theory such as that of Eysenck (1967b) or Cattell (1971a). As we shall see, most personality theorists have tried to discover the basic, fundamental traits (such as the basic elements in the fundamental table) and then measure all of them. It is often the case that multiple traits are used, since single-trait theories are usually not as rich a source of description. Hence, the preference in work psychology for batteries of tests that measure multiple traits (from 5 to 16, although as many as 30) (see pp. 171–188).

- *Cognitive or biological based traits*: Some "traits" or personality dimensions are quite clearly conceived of in cognitive terms – for example, belief systems, such as psychological rather than political conservatism (Wilson, 1973; see Chapter 5) or attributional styles (Brewin, 1988). These cognitive traits refer to the way people perceive the world, or attribute the cause of their own or others' behaviour. On the other hand, some traits, such as extraversion (Eysenck, 1967b) and sensation-seeking (Zuckerman. 1979), are conceived of in biological terms, such that the person's behaviour is a function of physiological, genetic or biochemical differences. The two approaches are equally popular, although some people prefer to research cognitive traits because they believe they are more amenable to changing and "coaching" than biologically based traits.

- *"Normal" and "abnormal" traits*: Some traits are clearly conceived of in terms of abnormal behaviour, such as depression, psychopathy or hypochondriasis. These measure aspects of "abnormal" behaviour, which, although valid and, indeed, at times quite relevant to work-related behaviours, are less useful than "normal" traits, because many working people do not exhibit these traits to any degree. However, this is not true of neuroticism, which is very common. Many of the famous and best established personality tests in psychology (e.g. the MMPI) were initially designed to measure mental illness.

- *Dynamic versus stylistic traits*: This is the distinction made between Freudian and neo-Freudian ideas (such as the oral or anal personality, which supposedly measures deep-seated, possibly unconscious, needs and fears) and stylistic traits that do not presume the same aetiology (in childhood) or processes. To date however, very few Freudian personality tests have been applied to the workplace, save perhaps Kline's (1978) work on the oral and anal personality.

The basic tenet of this "classic personality theory" approach is to measure personality as the independent variable and see how it correlates with some (often rather arbitrarily chosen) work-related behaviour (see Chapter 3).

So far, the approach has been piecemeal and there is very little evidence of a concerted, systematic and programmatic research effort. This means that the evidence for the effect of, say, extraversion on selling has never been clearly replicated and the results from different studies are quite equivocal. There are too many one-off, non-replicated, often unpublished studies to build up a good database.

Sometimes this research has been laboratory-based and hence it frequently has poor ecological validity (i.e. is unrealistic). Few studies have been done relating personality traits to real work psychology, such as appraisal reports (Furnham & Stringfield, 1993). The selection of work-related variables is somewhat random and is based on convenience, because researchers are either unable to get better measures or, indeed, are not sure what to look for. It is difficult to measure individual work-related behaviour reliably, especially in managerial or administrative jobs. The more complex and cognitive the job, usually the more difficult it is to get a representative output measure of productivity.

Essentially, studies such as these are nearly always seen by personality researchers simply as supporting evidence for their ideas, and not as particularly insightful into how the process operates at work. That is, it provides validity evidence for personality theories, not insight into the predictors of organizational behaviour.

Compared with the extensive research on the relationship between personality and, say, learning, mental health or social behaviour, the extant research from classic personality theory on occupational and organizational variables has been disappointing.

Classic occupational psychology/organizational behaviour

Classic occupational psychology/organizational behaviour starts with some work-related variable, be it conceived of at the individual (absenteeism, productivity), group (team output) or organizational (profit) level, and examines its personality correlates. Again, the independent variables may be conceived of, or measured, quite differently:

- *Self-report versus behavioural*: Some variables are measured by questionnaire ratings or interviews, whereas others are measured by actual behaviour such as absenteeism, produce made or sold, or number of promotions. Both self-report and behavioural measures are subject to different forms of systematic error, particularly attribution errors, which often means self-report data make a person appear more variable, and behavioural data make them seem more stable or consistent than they actually are (see Chapter 5).
- *Single versus aggregate measures*: The work-related behaviour may be a single one-off assessment or an aggregate measure made up either from different parts (i.e. combining superior, subordinate, self- and colleague assessments) or measurements conducted over time. Clearly, in terms of reliability and representativeness, aggregate measures are preferable.
- *Within versus between organizations*: Sometimes variables are examined only within an organization, whereas others are compared between organizations. The clear advantage of the latter approach is that one can control for organizational variables which are quite likely to have major effects.

Researchers in this tradition are usually interested in examining personality correlates of specific work behaviours that might help personnel and human resource professionals select, appraise, promote or train individuals. But this research has certain limitations. First, the choice of personality variables has been arbitrary and un-informed. Some personality tests have been favoured mainly because they have been commercially exploited, rather than because they are reliable and valid. Some outdated tests, largely forgotten and condemned by psychometricians, remain a popular choice and hence seriously threaten the nature of the results.

Secondly, statistical analyses have been simple and naïve. As a rule, simple correlations have been computed, rather than partial correlations or more preferably multivariate statistics to prevent type II errors (finding more significant differences than actually occur). Given that both independent and dependent variables are multifactorial, it is essential that sufficiently robust and sensitive multivariate, time-series and log-linear statistics are used to analyse results.

Thirdly, studies in this area are frequently exploratory and are atheoretical rather than based on a sound theory or programmatic research endeavour. As a result, interesting results are rarely followed up and the theoretical implications are rarely exploited. Finally, researchers often ignore possible organizational and societal factors that either directly or indirectly affect the dependent variable. That is, work-related behaviours are rarely solely under the control of the individual and may be moderated by powerful organizational factors which need to be taken into account.

The occupational psychology and organizational behaviour literature studying personality and ability predictors of productivity is growing in quality and quantity (Barrick & Mount, 1991).

The development of a work-specific individual difference measure

A third approach is to develop a personality measure aimed at predicting exclusively a specific work-related behaviour (such as sales revenue) and to use this measure to predict that behaviour. This is not necessarily as tautological as it may at first appear; many of these measures already exist. But they are highly varied and may be:

*   *Narrow versus wide in conceptualization*: The personality measures might attempt to predict a specific (narrow) form of occupational behaviour, such as absenteeism, or a much wider range of occupational behaviours, such as satisfaction or productivity. It is probably true that the former is a much more common approach than the latter (Cook, Hepworth, Wall, & Warr, 1981; Furnham, 1990).
*   *Single versus multiple traits*: The measure (usually a questionnaire) could be multi-dimensional – supposedly assessing many different behaviours/beliefs at work – or unidimensional – assessing just one dimension. However, most measures attempt to assess only one trait, such as the Protestant work ethic (Furnham, 1990).
*   *Self-report versus behaviour*: There is no reason why individual-difference measures need necessarily be self-report based. They could well be biographical, behavioural or physiological. They could be measures of intelligence, assessment centre scores, or even biofeedback results that measure reactions in the central nervous system. All have been used at one time or another to try to predict work-related behaviour.
*   *Attitudinal versus attributional*: Most of these measures are of the self-report kind, but some are attitudinal, systematically examining work-related attitudes and beliefs (Buchholz, 1976), and others are quite specifically concerned with attributional styles (see Chapter 5). Attitudes look at *beliefs* about a particular topic, whereas attributional styles examine characteristic ways in which people see the *causes* of behaviour patterns.

The approach of the development of a work-specific individual difference measure has been taken by those from both personality and occupational psychology traditions. However, there are various self-evident drawbacks. These include the problem that rarely, if ever, do researchers pay much attention to the aetiology or origin of the trait or dimension being measured – Is it the result of experience? Is it genetically linked? Is it related to intelligence? This could be an important feature in understanding developmental features associated with the trait. Secondly, by definition the measures have limited applicability, as they are designed specifically for the workplace and are therefore presumably restricted to it in terms of predictability. Therefore, this is only a disadvantage if one wants to generalize. Thirdly, frequently, but not always, the background theoretical work on the processes, mechanisms and phenomena associated with the trait (which explain how and why the trait determines behaviour) is not done sufficiently well, no doubt because the task is seen primarily as an applied one.

Finally, as mentioned above, there is often a confounding or overlap between the independent and dependent variable, such that it is circular and tautological. Thus, some measures ask a person with whom they communicate at work and then through sociometric analysis proceed to determine their communication patterns. Tautological research is a waste of time.

There is clearly still much scope for this approach to personality at work. The current literature shows sporadic, rather than sustained, effort and some evidence of faddishness regarding the choice of both the independent and dependent variable. Nevertheless, there is some considerable evidence that this approach may prove very fruitful, for example research on work-related attributional style (Furnham, Sadka, & Brewin, 1992).

The concept of "fit" and "misfit" at work

Probably because of its intuitive appeal, this approach has a fairly long history (Pervin, 1967). The idea is quite simple: based on personality and predispositions, some jobs are more suitable for the individual than others. Based on a comparable analysis of both the person and the job, it may be possible to accurately measure the degree of fit (which is desirable) or misfit (undesirable). The work of Holland (see Chapter 3) is most relevant here. Variations on this theme include:

* *Whether the analysis is based more on jobs or individuals*: Clearly, to obtain a measure of fit, both people and jobs need to be analysed and measured; however, the measurement of the one is nearly always based on the concepts/language developed by the other. In most cases, and for obvious reasons, the conceptual language of fit is based on personality or individual differences rather than jobs.
* *Impressionistic versus "geometric"*: A second crucial feature is whether the concept of "fit" is simply subjectively impressionistic or objective, measurable and "geometric". Few would argue that the former approach is the more desirable, but there are certain difficulties associated with the latter approach, notably the complexity of the multidimensional geometric model.
* *Similarity versus complementarity*: There is extensive if somewhat equivocal literature on similarity and attraction between individuals, which offers three hypotheses: similar people are attracted, the attraction of opposites, and the concept of complementarity (which is a mix of the two). Although there is no evidence for the attraction of opposites concept (which, in the context of Pervin's work, becomes the misfit hypothesis), it remains uncertain whether the similarity or complementarity hypothesis is to be supported.

This approach, like the others, is not without its problems. One approach to this area is to devise a limited number of types (of people and/or job) and show their

relationships in some mosaic or pattern. This allows for geometric (Euclidean) calculations. On the other hand, it may be possible to write a formula that expresses fit in the
form of simultaneous equations. The more specific the expression of fit the better.

Secondly, "fit" studies are by definition correlational and not causal; hence it is not
possible to infer directionality such as the idea that misfit *leads to* absenteeism. Also, it
must be assumed that fit gets better over time because people leave (or are fired) from
jobs that don't suit them. On the other hand, jobs do change and it is possible that in a
turbulent environment, with rapidly changing job tasks, very few employees fit their job.
Thirdly, everything in this approach is based on the veridical nature, sensitivity, comprehensiveness and clarity of conceptualization of the variables that make up the fit.
For instance, where these are conceived too vaguely or widely, the resultant fit measures
are practically worthless.

Furnham (2001) pointed out that the concept of fit is far from clear. There is a
person–environment, person–job and person–organization fit as well as supervisor–
subordinate goal and personality fit. There is a difference between objective fit and
subjective fit. There is a fit of supplies (people's interests/preferences and job rewards)
and a demands fit. There is the rather general vocational congruence and a more
specific abilities congruence. Furthermore, fit is dynamic and never static.

These problems notwithstanding, this remains one of the most promising areas of
research because of its predictive power. Predictably, the concept of fit has been
especially popular in such research areas as vocational choice (see Chapter 3) and
"problems" at work (e.g. stress and health). However, the real promise of the fit–misfit
literature lies in predicting motivation and satisfaction at work, an area still currently
neglected.

Longitudinal studies of people in work

It is almost universally recognized that longitudinal research is invaluable in examining
how a multitude of variables (personality, psychographic, demographic) change over
time, relate to one another at different periods, and *predict* behaviour. That is, the
concept of cause is best examined longitudinally. However, it is also widely recognized
that longitudinal research is fiendishly difficult, expensive and problematic. Nevertheless, some studies have examined personality at work over time. Again, studies come in
many different forms:

*   *Short, medium and long time-spans*: It is not always clear what comprises a "longi-
    tudinal" time-span – 1 year, 5 years, 10 years? Studies of less than a couple of years,
    although longitudinal, cannot reveal substantial differences that operate over
    longer periods such as decades. On the other hand, studies carried out over very
    long periods (20 years or more) have difficulties in contacting all of the members of
    the original sample.
*   *Within or between organizations*: Some organizations have sponsored or allowed
    research to be conducted within their (albeit very large) organization. Within-
    organization studies, by definition, seriously restrict the range and type of variable
    that can be examined. On the other hand, between-organization studies (following
    individuals over time) often do not allow for enough comparisons because of a lack
    of control.
*   *Retrospective versus prospective*: Some longitudinal studies are done by archival

research, where past records are compared with current data. Given that reasonable records exist, such studies are robust, useful and sensitive. Alternatively, one can begin a study now and analyse the results at a later date. The latter approach is clearly preferable, because one has more control over what is measured, how and when.

Longitudinal research has problems only if weak or irrelevant data are collected or, of course, if it is discontinued for one reason or another. Scarcity of resources means that good research is often not done. The most common problems are as follows. First, there may be too few participants, or not knowing whether "drop-outs" occur for systematic reasons. Tracing people's behaviour at work over lengthy periods is difficult, but restricting numbers because of costs only limits the generalizability of the research. Secondly, there is the common problem of poor measurement of the variables. Because one is limited to the organization's own records (such as application and assessment forms), or because measurement techniques have substantially improved over the years, early measures may be psychometrically unsound, thus adversely affecting the quality of the results. However, this is not a feature peculiar to longitudinal studies. Thirdly, there is nearly always a restricted range of variables. Studies done on particular individuals (a class of students), or of employees from a particular organization, by definition are restricted and thus may not be reliable. In addition, between-organization variables cannot be considered. Clearly, this is important only if these unmeasured variables are significant; but one can only know this if they are examined.

A few good longitudinal studies of this sort exist, but they too have their limitations and, if we are to understand personality differences at work, it is highly desirable that more research of this sort be done. However, the costs involved, the patience required to carry them out, and researchers' contentment with cross-sectional correlational research, means they are likely to remain a novelty in the area.

Biographical or case-history research

This approach, akin to the "great man" theory of history, examines in detail the life of one individual to see what clues it provides as to which biographical factors predict job success. There are not many examples of this approach, but those that exist do differ on various criteria:

- *Individuals versus groups*: Some approaches consider only the lives of particular individuals, whereas others consider a whole family (a dynasty), or people who have attended a particular institution and done well later in life.
- *Monetary versus "other" success criteria*: It is difficult to decide which criteria of success (or failure) are appropriate to use to select the "successful" people to examine. Often, it is the self-made multimillionaire, the politician or, occasionally, the philanthropist who is chosen.
- *Impressionistic versus scholarly*: Some studies of successful entrepreneurs are in the "bestseller" tradition, in which the "readability" of the story is more important than obtaining or understanding the facts. On the other hand, scholarly biographies are rarely sweepingly interpretative as to how, when and why biographical factors predict occupational success.

The biographical approach is intuitively appealing, and often most interesting to the general public, but it is very uncertain to what extent it can and does inform the issue of personality determinants of work success. Major problems include the obvious fact that only highly successful people are considered. Thus, there is a very serious sampling problem, because there appears to be no theoretical reason why particular people are chosen for analysis. This means that the data available are highly unrepresentative. Secondly, there is almost never a control group. That is, there is no comparable person or group to compare to those studied in detail. It is therefore impossible to understand precisely which factors do or do not relate to occupational success. Finally, atheoretical research means no systematic testing of hypotheses. Rarely, if ever, are biographers led to attempt to seek out particular facts to test hypotheses. Case histories are often considered by empirical researchers as excellent sources of hypotheses that they can test.

Personality testing at work

Personality and ability testing in the workplace is used for both selection and research. Public concerns over testing in recruitment, selection, appraisal and promotion mean that it is a hot topic. There are both advantages and disadvantages to this procedure (Furnham, 1992). Among the main advantages of psychological testing are:

- Tests provide numeric information, which means individuals can more easily be compared on the same criteria. In interviews, different questions are asked of different candidates, and the answers are often forgotten.
- With database records, one can trace a person's development over time. In fact, by going back to test results in a person's file one can actually determine whether, and by how much, the tests were predictive of later success.
- Tests provide explicit and specific results on temperament and ability rather than the ambiguous coded platitudes that are often found in references. A percentage (provided, of course, that it is valid) makes for much clearer thinking about personal characteristics than terms such as "satisfactory", "sufficient" or "high-flyer".
- Tests are fair because they eliminate corruption and favouritism, and stop old-boy, mason or Oxbridge networks self-perpetuating. That is, if a person does not have the ability, or has a "dangerous" profile, they will not be chosen, irrespective of their "other assets".
- Tests are comprehensive in that they cover all the basic dimensions of personality and ability from which other behaviour patterns derive.
- Tests are scientific in that they are empirically based on theoretical foundations; that is, they are reliable, valid and able to discriminate the good from the mediocre and the average from the bad.

Many, often related, objections are made to psychological testing. Among the most common and sensible objections are:

- Many of these tests can be faked; that is, people like to show themselves in a good light and receive a good score so that they may be accepted, but this in a way reflects their real personality (some tests have lie scores to attempt to overcome this).

- Some people do not have sufficient self-insight to report on their own feelings and behaviour; that is, it is not that people lie, but that they cannot, rather than *will not*, give accurate answers about themselves (some tests only look for simple behavioural data to overcome this).
- Tests are unreliable in that all sorts of temporary factors, such as test anxiety, boredom, weariness, a headache and period pains, all lead people to give different answers on different occasions (although this is partly true, it is only a minor factor).
- Most importantly, tests are invalid; they do not measure what they say they are measuring and the test scores do not predict behaviour over time. For many tests, this is indeed the Achilles heel and they are lamentably short of robust proof of their validity.
- They might be able to measure all sorts of dimensions of behaviour, but not the crucial ones to the organization such as trustworthiness and likelihood of absenteeism. Buying personality tests is like having a set menu, and what many managers want is an *à la carte* menu off of which they can select only what they want.
- People have to be sufficiently literate or articulate to do these tests, not to mention sufficiently familiar with North American jargon. Many organizations believe that members of their workforce will not be able to do them properly, that they will take up too much time and might cause needless embarrassment.
- There are no good norms (normative population data), at least for the population they want to test, and comparing them with White North American students can be dangerously misleading.
- The tests are unfair and biased towards WASPs [White Anglo Saxon Protestants]; hence, males tend to do better or get a more attractive profile and therefore get selected. They therefore fly in the face of anti-discriminatory legislation by being meritocratic, which for some is unethical.
- Interpretation of the tests takes skill, insight and experience, and this is either too expensive or not available. In the wrong hands they are dangerous, because profiles are either given inaccurate or too literal interpretations.
- Freedom of information legislation may mean that candidates would be able to see, and hence challenge, either the scores themselves or the interpretation of them. The less objective are the recorded data the better.
- As tests become known, people could buy copies and practise, so that they know the correct or most desirable answers. This occurs extensively with ability and personality testing and, when it does happen, results may have more to do with preparation and practice than a reflection of true ability.

Because the above "objections" or "disadvantages" of tests appear to outweigh the advantages, many organizations have turned to biodata as an alternative. However, it is worth noting that many of the disadvantages apply to biodata also. In this chapter, we look at both the reasons for, and objections to, biodata as a technique.

Trait theories of organizational behaviour

As noted earlier, some trait theories attempt to measure many traits (indeed *all* the major traits), whereas others measure narrow-band or specific traits. Work psychologists have favoured the former because they have sought to describe and measure people at work comprehensively and then determine which traits relate to which occupational behaviours and why. Six measures will be considered. First, we address the two most famous trait theories of the Briton (originally German) Hans Eysenck and the American (originally British) Raymond Cattell. The most widely used, up-to-date, state-of-the-art theory of Costa and McCrae will then be considered, followed by the commercially derived Occupational Personality Questionnaire. Finally, two narrow-band measures used specifically to measure stress and health at work (the A type and the Hardy personality measure) will be considered.

Eysenckian theory: Extraversion, neuroticism and psychoticism

Without doubt, the most sophisticated trait personality theory is that of Hans Eysenck, which has been likened to finding St. Pancras railway terminus (i.e. an elaborate Victorian structure) in the jungle of personality theories. The theory has spawned the Maudsley Personality Inventory (MPI), the Eysenck Personality Inventory (EPI) and the Eysenck Personality Questionnaire (EPQ), the latter of which has been revised. These questionnaires have been subjected to extensive investigation and have proved robust (Helmes, 1989). The theory, which has undergone various changes over time, argues for the psychophysiological basis of personality, and locates three major factors which relate to social behaviour: extraversion, neuroticism and psychoticism. Although the theory has been applied to a wide range of activities, including criminality, sex, smoking, health and learning, less work has been done on the Eysenckian dimension correlates of occupational behaviour. However, over the past 30 years there is evidence not only of the application of Eysenck's theory but its predictive usefulness in the occupational sphere.

Eysenck suggests that there are three fundamental (higher-order) unrelated (orthogonal) traits: extraversion, neuroticism and psychoticism. These traits, which can be measured and described on a continuum, are biologically based and have many behavioural implications. Two traits – extraversion and neuroticism – have however been most investigated at the biological, information-processing and motivational level. Thus findings on extraversion suggest it is substantially biologically inherited; it is explained in terms of cortical arousal and reward sensitivity and that extraverts succeed in high pressure jobs that involve considerable interaction with strangers. They handle overload and stress, have task-focused coping, feelings of self-efficacy and a good sense of well-being. Neuroticism, also substantially biologically based and inherited, is associated with stress vulnerability, sensitivity to punishment and threat avoidance. Neurotics portray highly selective biases in cognitive processes with considerable awareness of danger, cautious decision-making, a generally negative self-concept and often depressed mood and pessimistic outlooks.

A review of the dimension presents an impressive array of findings. Introverts are more sensitive to pain than are extraverts; they become fatigued and bored more easily than do extraverts; excitement interferes with their performance, whereas it enhances the performance of extraverts; and they tend to be more careful but slower than extraverts. The following are some additional differences that have been found:

- Introverts do better in school than extraverts, particularly in more advanced subjects. Also, students withdrawing from college for academic reasons tend to be

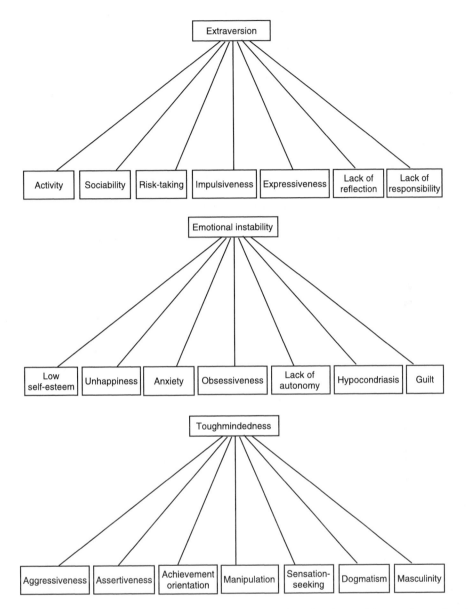

Figure 4.3 Eysenck's three-factor model of personality, showing subfactors. Reproduced from Eysenck & Wilson (1983) with the permission of Penguin Books.

extraverts, whereas those who withdraw for psychiatric reasons tend to be introverts.

- Extraverts prefer vocations involving interactions with other people, whereas introverts tend to prefer more solitary vocations. Extraverts seek diversion from job routine; introverts have less need for novelty.
- Extraverts enjoy explicit sexual and aggressive humour, whereas introverts prefer more intellectual forms of humour, such as puns and subtle jokes.

- Extraverts are more active sexually, in terms of frequency and different partners, than introverts are.
- Extraverts are more suggestible than introverts.

Introverts are more easily aroused by events and more easily learn social prohibitions than extraverts. As a result, introverts are more restrained and inhibited. There is also some evidence that introverts are more influenced by punishments in learning, whereas extraverts are more influenced by rewards. It is hypothesized that individual differences along this dimension have both hereditary and environmental origins. Indeed, several studies of identical and fraternal twins suggest that heredity plays a major part in accounting for differences between individuals in their scores on this dimension.

Extraverts are more likely than introverts to prefer occupations that involve social contact. There is, therefore, a danger that introverted workers may become over-aroused if their jobs involve considerable extra organizational contact and a relative absence of routine. Blunt (1978) argued that introverted managers would thus tend to choose positions involving relatively routine duties (finance, production or technical managers), whereas extraverted managers would be more likely to select jobs in sales, marketing or transport. The results were broadly as hypothesized, except that transport managers were less extraverted and production managers more extraverted than predicted. Eysenck (1967a) collected EPI data on 1,504 businessmen. His results are shown in Table 4.1.

On the E scale (a measure of extraversion), the business groups are relatively introverted, but significantly different between themselves, with the finance, R&D and consultants groups being the most introverted, and those belonging to more than one group being the most extraverted. Eysenck (1967a: 250) noted:

> Successful businessmen are on the whole stable introverts; they are stable regardless of what type of work they do within business, but their degree of extroversion may

Table 4.1 Personality scores of businessmen in different areas of business

	N	Neuroticism		Extraversion		Lie scale	
		Mean	SD	Mean	SD	Mean	SD
General management	165	7.04	4.03	11.13	3.58	2.80	2.12
Production	135	6.90	3.77	11.05	3.72	3.08	1.69
Research & development	574	7.42	4.05	9.98	3.88	2.76	1.49
Finance	132	7.53	4.49	10.12	3.40	2.93	1.97
Sales	168	7.04	3.64	11.33	3.98	2.93	1.92
Personnel	88	7.11	4.04	11.34	4.36	2.95	1.72
Consultancy	218	7.32	3.93	10.09	3.93	2.91	1.66
More than one of above	24	7.70	5.16	11.91	3.26	2.66	1.49
Total	1,504						
Standardized data							
Normal population	2,000	9.06	4.78	12.07	4.37	–	–
Salesmen	37	8.38	4.72	13.63	3.76	–	–
Professional	23	7.95	5.11	11.40	4.91	–	–
Normal population	651	–	–	–	–	2.26	1.57

Source: Eysenck (1967a).

be related to type of work. The data are probably reasonably reliable because relatively few respondents failed to answer, and because scores on the lie scale did not indicate any market tendency to "fake good". The results suggest that the EPI may have some modest role to play in furthering research into the personality patterns of persons engaged in business and industry.

The notion that introverted workers are better able to handle routine work activities than extraverted ones was investigated by Cooper & Payne (1967) in a study carried out in the packing department of a tobacco factory where the work was repetitive and light. Job adjustment, as assessed by two supervisors, was negatively related to extraversion, and those workers who left the job in the 12 months after testing were significantly more extraverted than those who remained. Neuroticism was also implicated, being related to poor job adjustment and to frequency of non-permitted absence.

The use of both conditioning and arousal theory is evident in the thinking of Cooper & Payne (1967):

- Because extraverts condition poorly and introverts readily, extraverts are less able to tolerate tasks of a routine nature, since inhibition accumulates and inhibits sustained task performance.
- Because extraverts are under-aroused, they seek arousal and do not function as well as introverts with a minimal or moderate sensory variation input.

Various studies have found extraverts to be *bored* by monotonous tasks and hence do them poorly (Kim, 1980). Others have shown how personality is related to *training*, with introverts often doing better than extraverts (Organ, 1975; Wankowski, 1973; Wilson, Tunstall, & Eysenck, 1972). Personality may also affect mood, which can affect job performance (Bishop & Jean-Renaud, 1976; Christie & Venables, 1973).

Morgenstern, Hodgson & Law (1974) demonstrated that introverted individuals function less efficiently in the presence of distractions, whereas extraverts show improvement in the presence of distractions. They concluded:

> It would seem that the extraverted subjects do not merely prefer to be in the company of others, but that their work efficiency actually improves in the face of distractions, while the solitary preference of the introverts are reflected in their reduced efficiency of work when distracted. Paying heed to such preferences, as measured by the Eysenck Personality Inventory, is therefore not only a method of increasing contentment at work by means of personnel selection, but should also result in improved efficiency of output. (Morgenstern *et al.*, 1974: 220)

Can personality traits predict success at highly complex tasks? Jessup & Jessup (1971) tested would-be pilots with the Eysenck Personality Inventory early in their course and discovered that the subsequent failure rate varied considerably as a function of personality. Specifically, 60% of the neurotic introverts failed, against 37% of the neurotic extraverts, 32% of the stable extraverts and only 14% of the stable introverts. Thus, high levels of neuroticism had a much greater adverse effect on introverts than on extraverts. Jessup and Jessup note that they expect the introverted cadet to learn better, both in the aircraft and lecture room, than extraverts. They concluded:

> The comparative failure of the specifically neurotic introvert may be tentatively explained as follows. High arousal in the visceral system is associated with high N [neuroticism]; high cortical arousal with low E [extroversion]. Given that there is an optimal level of arousal for learning to fly and that this is a particularly stressful experience, it seems likely that the neurotic introvert will be aroused beyond the optimum; the learning of the stable introvert on the other hand profits from cortical arousal with suffering from additional visceral arousal. (Jessup & Jessup, 1971: 120)

Similar findings were reported by Bartram & Dale (1982), who found a tendency for successful pilots to be more stable and more extraverted than those who failed flying training. They had data on over 600 pilots from the Army Air Corps and the Royal Air Force. The consistent finding that neuroticism is negatively related to flying success makes intuitive sense. Flying can obviously be stressful, with a single mistake proving fatal. In such circumstances, pilots who are especially susceptible to stress are likely to perform less well than those who are more stable.

Looking at more common jobs, Kirton & Mulligan (1973) found attitudes towards organizational change to be related to a combination of neuroticism and extroversion among 258 managers from eight companies with at least 1,000 employees each. Individuals scoring high on both neuroticism and extraversion, and individuals scoring low on both scales (neurotic extraverts and stable introverts), had more positive attitudes towards change in managerial practices in general, more positive attitudes towards specific, innovative appraisal schemes or promotional policies being introduced, and the least amount of discontent with the institution and with superiors.

Turnbull (1976) found that among more than 100 male college students involved in a summer of selling books, neither EPI extraversion scores alone nor in combination with other personality scales predicted sales success. Sales success was determined on the basis of total wholesale business and a sales index indicating the amount of business per call made. In the global studies presented earlier, the sales vocations were only weakly related to extraversion. Turnbull noted a wide range of scores on the extraversion/introversion dimension among the individuals applying for the job and no personality differences between those who completed the summer of sales and those who dropped out. It was found as predicted that extraversion scores increased from the beginning to the end of the summer as a result of the summer of sales experience, an increase that was equal for more successful and less successful salesmen.

Sterns, Alexander, Barrett & Dambrot (1983) found extraverts preferred jobs with greater cognitive task demands, pace of task demands, cognitive closure, extrinsic rewards and intrinsic rewards. Neuroticism, on the other hand, was negatively related to each of the above preferences except for extrinsic rewards. Extraverts were less satisfied than introverts with the clerical work itself, supervision and co-workers. The participants were non-managerial civil service clerical employees in a job that would suit stable introverts more than extraverts.

Recent studies have looked at the relationship between personality and job satisfaction. Furnham, Forde & Ferrari (1999a) looked at the relationships among the three Eysenckian superfactors (Extraversion, Neuroticism and Lie) and 21 primary factors and various work motivations grouped under Herzberg, Mausner & Snydeman's (1959) two-factor model. According to Herzberg and co-workers' theory, individuals have two major needs: (1) *hygiene needs*, which are influenced by the physical and psychological conditions in which they work; and (2) *motivator needs*, which Herzberg *et al.* described as being very similar to the higher-order needs in Maslow's (1954) hierarchy factors (or dissatisfiers). These include supervision, interpersonal relations, physical working conditions, salary, company policies and administrative practices, benefits and job security.

Motivator needs are fulfilled by what Hertzberg *et al.* (1959) labelled *motivator factors* or *satisfiers*: achievement, recognition, the work itself, responsibility and advancement. Motivator factors are concerned with the nature of the work itself, the consequences of work, and those facets of the job that satisfy an individual's need for self-actualization (i.e. self-fulfilment) in his or her work, and it is only from the performance of the task that individuals can enjoy the rewards that will reinforce their aspirations.

Furnham *et al.* (1999a) demonstrated that nearly one-third of the variance in hygiene factors could be accounted for by neuroticism, whereas one-fifth of the variance in motivator factors could be accounted for by extraversion:

> If there are systematic differences in the work-related factors different people seek out and value, it would be well for managers to pay attention to trait variables in selection to ensure a better P–E fit. Equally, if extraverts seek out recognition, reward, and responsibility more than introverts, it may be useful for managers to introduce different performance management schemes for different groups of workers. If it is true that extraverts value – and are presumably motivated and satisfied by – Herzbergian motivator factors, it would benefit organizations and managers to attempt to provide these facets. Thus job rotation and empowerment should be motivating for the extraverts as well as the practice of instituting performance appraisal and public reward schemes. On the other hand, neurotics are likely to become demotivated and job dissatisfied. (Furnham *et al.*, 1999a: 1042)

It should be pointed out, however, that Furnham, Petrides, Jackson & Cottr (2002) were unable to fully replicate these results and it seemed to them that personality trait variables account for less of the variance in job satisfaction than previously thought.

The Eysenckian trait dimensions have also been found to predict "negative" occupational variables. There has been some interest in the relevance of personality to performance under rather monotonous conditions. It might be predicted that under-aroused extraverts would find it more difficult than introverts to maintain performance over time. Extraverts showed a greater deterioration than introverts in driving performance over a four-hour period (Fagerström & Lisper, 1977). However, their performance improved more than that of introverts when someone talked to them or the car radio was turned on.

Shaw & Sichel (1970) compared the personality characteristics of accident-prone and safe South African bus drivers. Most of the accident-prone drivers were neurotic extraverts, whereas the safe drivers were predominantly stable introverts. As might have been expected, it is the impulsiveness component of extraversion rather than the sociability component that is more closely related to poor driving and accident proneness (Loo, 1979) (see Chapter 8).

Eysenck & Eysenck (1985: 329) concluded:

> In sum, it appears that preferences for different kinds of occupation and occupational success are both determined to some extent by personality. The research to date mostly suffers from the disadvantage that job characteristics are discussed in

an *ad hoc* fashion. A major dimension along which jobs can be ordered is the extent to which the behaviour of and individual doing that job is constrained by external factors. For example, a car worker on an assembly line has minimal control over his work activities, whereas a university lecturer has greater control. It seems likely that personality will be a more consequential determinant of job satisfaction and success when severe constraints exist. It may be coincidence that two of the occupations wherein personality has been found to be relevant (flying and driving) both involve considerable constraints. In other words, the fit of a worker to his job is especially important when the worker has little scope for tailoring the work environment to his needs.

All trait theorists have acknowledged the importance of the two fundamental traits of extraversion and neuroticism. Eysenck's theory and test have been very successfully employed by researchers to examine the relationship between these traits and work-related behaviours. Being under-aroused and stimulus-hungry, extraverts become bored and make errors. They trade off speed for accuracy, with the opposite being true for introverts. Neurotics tend to become anxious and hypochondriacal, and are hence unreliable and somewhat unpredictable. As we shall see, the research of Costa & McCrae (1985) in the USA has picked up and extended the pioneering work of Eysenck.

Cattell's 16PF

Perhaps the most famous of all personality tests applied to industrial, organizational and occupational settings is Cattell's (1971a) 16PF, first published over 40 years ago. For Cattell, the test has several advantages: it is unusually *comprehensive* in its coverage of personality dimensions; it is based on the *functional* measurement of previously located natural personality structures; the measurements are relatable to an *organiza-tioned* and *integrated* body of practice and theoretical knowledge in clinical education and industrial psychology.

The test measures 16 dimensions of personality (and 6–9 second-order factors) which are supposedly independent and identifiable, and reliably and validly measurable. The psychometric properties of the scale are well documented, as is the problem of deception (people faking on it). The test has been around so long, is very shrewdly and aggressively marketed in a variety of countries, and Cattell himself has been such an active researcher and zealous advocate of the test, that it has attracted incredible attention. For instance, if one consults the handbook printed 25 years ago (Cattell, Eber, & Tatsuoka, 1970), one finds incredible evidence of the application of the test. These data are in fact divided into two sections. The first concerns available specification equations against criteria: various weights are given (per personality dimension), derived from multiple regressions, to specific measurable job-success criteria. Policemen to school counsellors are considered.

For example, consider the following, where the letters (A, B, C, etc.) refer to one or other of the 16 traits and the numbers (.44, −.11, etc.) to the weighting of each:

Salesmen: Retail. Two studies, the larger by Industrial Psychology, Inc., have related actual sales volume in comparable situations (retail bakery route salesmen, soft-drink salesmen) with the following average equation:

Salesmanship $=.44A - .11B + .11C - .22E + .11F - .11G + .22H - .33L - .11M + .11N + .11O + .44Q_3 + .22Q_3 - .22Q_4 + 1.87$.
[Group mean = 5.56]

In this case, even the smaller weights have been retained because the sign was the same in the two studies. It will be clear from this, as from some other instances, that the popular stereotypes and impressions on which occupational selections are still often based can be erroneous. Thus, dominance, E+, is actually not effective in face-to-face selling, and the view of the successful salesman as an "extravert" has to be modified. For although gains are shown through exviant deviations (the temperament source traits of A, F, and H), self-sufficiency, Q_2, is actually oppositely weighted to the extravert direction; i.e. the inviant endowment is required.

Salesmen: Wholesale. On wholesale (grain) salesmen, personality has similarly been correlated with *actual sales income*, resulting in the following equation:

Wholesale Sales Success $=.21A + .10B + .10C + .10E + .21F + .10G - .10L - .31M + .21N - .31Q_2 + .21Q_3 - .21Q_4 + 3.80$.
[Group mean = 5.09]

It will be noted that intelligence shifts to a positive effect here, autism (M) is more of a drawback than it was in the retail field, and so on, but otherwise there is a "family similarity" between the two types of sales activity. (Cattell *et al.*, 1970: 166–167)

Secondly, equations are derived and cross-validated on samples. Occupations as varied as accountants to athletes, military cadets to musicians, and sales personnel to social workers, are considered. For example, in the case of executives and industrial supervisors, Cattell *et al.* (1970: 199) noted:

Perhaps the classing together of several types of executives has smoothed out some special characteristics that will later be found; but at present, except for high warmth, intelligence, and independence, the profile diverges little from that of "the man in the street". However, the characteristics are in the direction that psychological analysis would suggest, namely, a high tolerance of people in affectothymia (A+), toughness in Factor H, shrewdness in N, some self-development in (Q3+), and a marked willingness to try new ideas and new methods (Q1).

At the second order the executives are not high in cortertia (QIII) as one might expect, and the chief characteristics are some independence and exvia.

The pattern for the supermarket personnel is one of interpersonal warmth (A+), as might be expected, but it is clearly not a sales pattern, nor even an exviant (extraverted) one. A glance at the second-order anxiety component (C□, O□, Q4+, L+) shows an appreciably raised anxiety level, and one wonders about the degree to which the personal tensions and detailed cares of the manager's position have produced this, or the degree to which a position of this kind simply tolerates performance by quite anxious persons. The sober desurgency (F□) seems consistent with individual difference variables selected for examination. Although there is general consensus about the dependent variable that is considered (i.e. job satisfaction; minor psychiatric morbidity; blood pressure), there seems to be theoretical consensus as to what type of individual difference variable to consider. However, one variable that has been examined extensively and to the relative neglect of nearly all others has been the "Type A" behaviour pattern.

Costa and McCrae's "Big Five"

The direct inheritor of the Eysenckian and Cattellian traditions are the Americans Costa & McCrae, whose work in the 1980s and 1990s revived the world of personality theory and testing. Working within the psychometric trait tradition, they settled on three and then five dimensions of personality. Now called the "five-factor approach" (FFA) or "five-factor model" (FFM), there is now broad agreement on the approach/ model, including those who adopt the lexical approach – that is, those who look at natural language and the relationship between everyday terms for personality traits (Goldberg, 1992). Indeed, there is an active psycho-lexical tradition in personality theory which attempts to "recover" the basic dimensions of personality through analysis of natural language. Researchers have found impressive evidence, across various different languages, of the emergence of similar factors which are analogous to the "Big Five". What they have not done, however, is to look at the association between personality traits and work outcomes. There are vigorous critiques of the FFM, but these have not reduced its popularity among personality researchers (Block, 1995; Eysenck, 1992).

Costa & McCrae (1985) argue that there are five basic unrelated dimensions of personality (Table 4.2). Much debate has concerned how clear these factors are. Table 4.3 spells out the five dimensions in greater detail, through using different methods.

A second body of research has been to compare the NEO-PI as the questionnaire is called, with other measures. A third, perhaps most important topic of applied research has been to examine the validity of the measure – that is, to examine what the test scores predict. The test has been applied to all sorts of worlds. Consider Table 4.4, which shows the clinical applications of the five measures. Table 4.4 may help a clinical psychologist think about how patients with different personalities present their problems, the sort of problems they are likely to have, and some of the treatment decisions that need to be made.

However, it is in the world of work that organizational behaviour researchers have become most interested in the FFM. It has proved a robust and reliable measure. For instance, Piedmont & Weinstein (1994) related the NEO-PI factor scores with four supervisor ratings: adaptive capacity, task orientation, interpersonal relations and overall rating. They found that, whereas the correlation between conscientiousness and all four ratings was significantly positive and between extraversion it was so with three out of the four (not the overall rating), neither Openness to experience nor Agreeableness was related to either rating.

Yet, what is clear from this literature is that, whereas some personality dimensions are good predictors of job proficiency, not all are. This is for at least three reasons. *First*, quite logically, different traits relate to different behaviours and, if a trait is unrelated to a particular occupational behaviour, it is unlikely that the two are correlated. Thus, neuroticism seems related only to "negative" behaviour at work, such as absenteeism, but not such things as productivity. This was the point made so clearly by Robertson & Kinder (1993). They showed that if there were good theoretical reasons to suppose certain specific traits (from a large battery) were related to specific measurable work outcome variables, the validity coefficients were around .20 but could rise to .30.

Table 4.2 The big five traits

High	Average	Low
1. *Neuroticism*		
Sensitive, emotional, and prone to experience feelings that are upsetting.	Generally calm and able to deal with stress, but you sometimes experience feelings of guilt, anger or sadness.	Secure, hardy and generally relaxed, even under stressful conditions.
2. *Extraversion*		
Extraverted, outgoing, active and high-spirited. You prefer to be around people most of the time.	Moderate in activity and enthusiasm. You enjoy the company of others but you also value privacy.	Introverted, reserved and serious. You prefer to be alone or with a few close friends.
3. *Openness to experience*		
Open to new experiences. You have broad interests and are very imaginative.	Practical but willing to consider new ways of doing things. You seek a balance between the old and the new.	Down-to-earth, practical, traditional and pretty much set in your ways.
4. *Agreeableness*		
Compassionate, good-natured and eager to cooperate and avoid conflict.	Generally warm, trusting and agreeable, but you can sometimes be stubborn and competitive.	Hard-headed, sceptical, proud and competitive. You tend to express your anger directly.
5. *Conscientiousness*		
Conscientious and well organized. You have high standards and always strive to achieve your goals.	Dependable and moderately well organized. You generally have clear goals but are able to set your work aside.	Easy-going, not very well organized, and sometimes careless. You prefer not to make plans.

Source: Adapted from Costa & McCrae (1987).

Secondly, not all personality measures were equally sound psychometrically. *Thirdly*, and perhaps most importantly, the most common reason for the poor correlation between personality and occupational behaviour is because of the weak measurement of the latter. Measures of occupational behaviour, including training and selection criteria, have problems often because the measures are badly skewed, not aggregated, or unreliable. Where efforts are made to obtain reliable and valid measures of job performance, the results suggest the utility of personality tests as predictors of job performance. Because of the poor reliability of individual measures, most researchers recommend that a battery of tests be used.

It would not be difficult to underestimate the popularity of the FFM and the quantity of research that is emerging of relevance to the work psychologist. The traits of extraversion and conscientiousness seem very important, particularly if the job involves people contact. Neuroticism, or "negative affectivity", as it is sometimes called, is also a useful negative predictor of work success.

In the last 10 years, personality measures have been reborn in industrial and organizational psychology and much research has focused on the personality–performance relationship. In particular, organizational psychology rediscovered the utility of personality measures in selection contexts. There were three main reasons for this. *First*, other than an interview (and application form and references), the selection method of choice for organizational psychology was a cognitive test. However, cognitive ability

Table 4.3 Examples of adjectives, Q-sort items and questionnaire scales defining the five factors

Factor		Factor definers		
Name	Number	Adjectives[a]	Q-sort items[b]	Scales[c]
Extraversion (E)	I	Active Assertive Energetic Enthusiastic Outgoing Talkative	Talkative Skilled in play, humour Rapid personal tempo Facially, gesturally expressive Behave assertively Gregarious	Warmth Gregariousness Assertiveness Activity Excitement-seeking Positive emotions
Agreeableness (A)	II	Appreciative Forgiving Generous Kind Sympathetic Trusting	Not critical, sceptical Behaves in giving way Sympathetic, considerate Arouses liking Warm, compassionate Basically trustful	Trust Straightforwardness Altruism Compliance Modesty Tender-mindedness
Conscientiousness (C)	III	Efficient Organized Planning ability Reliable Responsible Thorough	Dependable, responsible Productive Able to delay gratification Not self-indulgent Behave ethically Has high aspirational level	Competence Order Dutifulness Achievement Self-discipline Deliberation
Neuroticism (N)	IV	Anxious Self-pitying Tense Touchy Unstable Worrying	Thin-skinned Brittle ego defences Self-defeating Basically anxious Concerned with adequacy Fluctuating moods	Anxiety Hostility Depression Self-consciousness Impulsiveness Vulnerability
Openness (O)	V	Artistic Curious Imaginative Insightful Original Wide interests	Wide range of interests Introspective Unusual thought processes Values intellectual matters Judges in unconventional terms Aesthetically reactive	Fantasy Aesthetics Feelings Actions Ideas Values

[a] Checklist items defining the factor in a study of 280 men and women rated by ten psychologists serving as observers during an assessment weekend at the Institute of Personality Assessment and Research.
[b] California Q-set items from self-sorts by 403 men and women in the Baltimore Longitudinal Study of Aging.
[c] NEO Personality Inventory N, E, and O facet scales and preliminary A and C facet scales from self-reports by 214 adult men and women.

Source: Reproduced from McCrae & John (1992) with the permission of Blackwell.

Table 4.4 Treatment characteristics associated with standing on the five factors

Factor and pole	Clinical presentation	Key problems	Treatment opportunities	Treatment pitfalls
1. Neuroticism				
High	A variety of painful feelings.	Full gamut of neurotic misery.	Psychological pain motivates compliance.	Existence likely to remain uncomfortable; high N cannot be interpreted away.
Low	Emotional blandness, especially if also low E.	Situational problems.	Wants and can benefit from advice and values classification.	Emotional blandness may be misunderstood as defensiveness.
2. Extraversion				
High	Needs to talk; needs people.	Excitable; if also high N, unstable mood, interpersonal conflict.	Comfortable with less structured approaches; optimistic and energetic.	Talkativeness can blunt treatment focus.
Low	Reluctant to talk. Can feel overwhelmed by people.	Somber. If also high N, depression, withdrawal, apathy.	Comfortable with structured approaches.	Lacks enthusiasm for interaction with therapist.
3. Openness				
High	Likes variety, novelty; curious.	Problems vary, but conceptualized in abstract, imaginative terms.	Prefers imaginative approaches.	Excessive curiosity can scatter resources.
Low	Discomfort and perplexity in reaction to novel experiences.	Problems vary, but conceptualized in conventional, concrete terms.	Responds well to practical approaches. Education, support, behaviour therapy.	Rigidity and lack of curiosity can be misunderstood as resistance.
4. Agreeableness				
High	Genuinely compassionate and generous; sees the sweet side of life.	Easily exploited, naïve, gullible; if high N, over-sensitive to criticism.	Treatment alliance easily formed.	Accepts interpretations uncritically. Needs to please therapist interferes with disclosure of transference.
Low	Wants to be admired, to be "somebody".	Sees bitter side of life. Unpopular, overly competitive; lacks social support. Envious, suspicious, holds grudges.	Assertiveness and clear thinking about self-interest facilitate problem-solving.	Hostility, scepticism towards therapist; difficult to form treatment alliance.
5. Conscientiousness				
High	Loves accomplishment.	Overwork.	Works hard to benefit from treatment. Willing to tolerate discomfort and frustration.	(Possibly none.)
Low	Loves leisure.	Low achievement, impulsivity, half-hearted problem-solving.	(Possibly none.)	Unlikely to do homework; likely to reject interventions that require hard work or toleration of discomfort.

Source: Reproduced from Miller (1991) with the permission of Lawrence Erlbaum Associates, Inc.

tests almost always result in an adverse impact for certain "protected classes" of employees. Meta-analytic evidence suggests that most personality variables have significantly less of an adverse impact on the protected classes than cognitive ability variables do (Hough, 2001). Secondly, research has provided general agreement on the taxonomy of personality variables, enabling psychologists to organize the literature on personality and job performance. Exploration of personality performance relationships within, rather than across, personality constructs revealed statistically and practically significant relationships where they had not been revealed before (Hough, 2001). Thirdly, meta-analytic reviews by Barrick & Mount (1991) and by Tett *et al.* (1991) provided further evidence that personality measures were more valid than generally believed.

The multidimensional conceptualizations of job performance have also been critically important in highlighting the relevance of personality and measurement variables for predicting job performance (Campbell, McCloy, Oppler, & Sager, 1993). It is now evident that personality variables correlate differently with different job performance constructs (Judge & Ilies, 2002; Judge *et al.*, 2002). Another factor that has prompted the rebirth of personality variables in organizational psychology is the fact that more than half of the developed economies are considered service economies. This growth in both the service and sales sector has affected how organizational psychologists define and measure job performance (Hough & Schneider, 1996) and has highlighted the importance of investigating the link between personality and job performance.

It has now been recognized that part of the reason for the decline of personality variables in psychology, particularly organizational psychology, was because no well-accepted taxonomy existed for classifying personality traits (Barrick & Mount, 1991). Taxonomies are critically important to the advancement of science, as they facilitate the organization and accumulation of knowledge, hypothesis generation, efficient communication among scientists, and retrieval of information (Fleishman & Quaintance, 1984). Thus it is recent personality taxonomies which have provided the organizing principles that have enabled researchers to establish relationships between personality constructs and job-related criteria (Hough & Schneider, 1996), and which have highlighted the importance of investigating the link between personality and job performance.

In general, the taxonomies used are based upon measures of normal and adult personality. The initial purpose in the construction of these was the accurate description of individual differences in personality, thus providing a broad description of personality that could be used in a whole range of settings (Ones & Viswesvaran, 2000). An example of the inventories relevant to this study is the "five-factor model" (FFM). However, it has been argued that the taxonomy the organizational psychologists use makes a difference to the outcome of the analysis. Conclusions about the usefulness of personality and the nature of the personality–performance relationship depend upon the taxonomy used. Many respected personality psychologists believe that the FFM is an adequate taxonomy for organizational psychology (Costa & McCrae, 1995; Digman, 1990; Goldberg, 1990). Indeed, the FFM has been shown to be useful as an organizing taxonomy for organizational research (Barrick & Mount, 1991; Ones, Schmidt, & Viswesvaran, 1993). However, some scepticism about the adequacy of the FFM has been raised (Block, 1995; Hough, 1992).

Research clearly suggests that personality variables correlate differently with different job performance constructs (Day & Silverman, 1989; Hough, 1996). Current research on the relation between personality and job performance has involved the integration of personality measures with the FFM. This method was used in various reviews of criterion validity (Barrick & Mount, 1991; Tett *et al.*, 1991).

Barrick & Mount (1991) conducted a large-scale meta-analysis of 117 validity studies and a total sample that ranged from 14,236 people for Openness to Experience to 19,721 for Conscientiousness. Performance measures within these groups were classi-fied into three broad criteria: job proficiency, training proficiency and personnel data. Barrick & Mount (1991) reported that Conscientiousness was consistently found to be a valid predictor for all five occupational groups and for all performance criteria. However, the other four personality factors only generalize their validity for some occupations and some criteria. Extraversion was observed to be a valid predictor (across the criterion types) for two occupations, managers and sales. Emotional Stabil-ity was a valid predictor for police; Agreeableness was a valid predictor for police and managers; while Openness to Experience was found to predict the training proficiency criterion relatively well, as did Emotional Stability and Agreeableness. Similarly, Open-ness to Experience was not found to be a valid predictor of job proficiency or personnel data. In a follow-up study, Mount & Barrick (1995) found that overall validity of Conscientiousness has been underestimated and that the overall score and both of its dimensions (dependability and achievement) predicted specific performance criteria better than global criteria (e.g. overall rating of job performance).

Tett *et al.* (1991) used only confirmatory studies – that is, studies based on hypothesis testing or on personality-orientated job analysis. Mean validities derived from con-firmatory studies were considerably higher than those derived from exploratory studies. These results generally supported those reported by Barrick & Mount (1991), but are distinctly more positive for the predictive validity of traits. In essence, Tett *et al.* (1991) found that *all* personality dimensions were valid predictors of job performance. How-ever, Extraversion and Conscientiousness had lower validity coefficients, whereas Neuroticism, Openness to Experience, and Agreeableness had higher validities than had been previously shown.

A third review of the relationship between personality measures and performance criteria was conducted by Hough *et al.* (1990), who examined the relationship of nine personality dimensions and a range of performance criteria, specific to military set-tings. Their results indicate that Adjustment (Emotional Stability) and Dependability (Conscientiousness) were valid predictors for the two most used performance criteria – training and job proficiency – and that the "Big Five" are predictors of training criteria. Thus, the findings of Hough *et al.* (1990) were partly convergent with those of Barrick & Mount (1991) but also provided evidence of some divergence. Further research by Hough (1992) suggests that each of the nine personality constructs correlates with important job and life criteria and that each of the nine constructs has a different pattern of relationships with that criterion. On the basis of Hough's data, it has been suggested that Barrick & Mount overemphasised the broad dimensions of Conscien-tiousness at the expense of other useful personality traits (Furnham, 2001). The fact that other personality variables are not correlated with all occupational categories or criterion types does not necessarily mean that they are unimportant. Different jobs make different demands on employees and may contribute to a pattern of job-dependent validity coefficients (Furnham, 2001).

In a further European contribution to the debate, Salgado (1997) undertook a meta-analytic review that differed from previously in that it only included studies conducted in the European Community. Salgado (1997) found that the overall validity of personality constructs is small, excepting Emotional Stability (Neuroticism) and Conscientiousness even when effects of measurement error in predictors and criteria and range restrictions have been corrected. In this respect, the results show great similarity to those of Barrick & Mount (1991) and Hough *et al.* (1990). Again, concurrent with Barrick & Mount (1991) and Hough *et al.* (1990), but partially divergent from Tett *et al.* (1991), Conscientiousness showed the highest estimated true validity, which could be generalized for all occupations and criteria. A third finding of Salgado (1997) was that the estimated true validity for Emotional Stability was comparable to that for Conscientiousness. Moreover, as with Conscientiousness, Emotional Stability could be generalized across jobs and criteria. This finding is contrary to Barrick & Mount (1991) but is consistent with Hough *et al.* (1990). Openness to Experience was found to be a valid predictor for training proficiency, thus consistent with Barrick & Mount (1991) and Hough *et al.* (1990). Other results support the suggestion that individuals with high scores in Openness to Experience may be those who are most likely to benefit from training programmes (Dollinger & Orf, 1991). A positive correlation was found between Extraversion and two occupations in which interpersonal characteristics were likely to be important, in line with the results of Barrick & Mount (1991) and Hough *et al.* (1990). However, contrary to Barrick & Mount (1991), Extraversion did not seem to be a valid predictor for training proficiency (Salgado, 1997). Finally, the results for Agreeableness suggest that this factor may be relevant to predicting training performance. This is consistent with Barrick & Mount (1991) and Hough *et al.* (1990).

Saville & Holdsworth's Occupational Personality Questionnaire

Sometimes commercial organizations, rather than academic researchers, devise personality measures to be sold as diagnostic instruments. One such organization, which has expanded greatly over the past 20 years all around the world, is Saville & Holdsworth Ltd (SHL, 1984), which claims several advantages for its Occupational Personality Questionnaire (OPQ). It is said to be based on a conceptual model providing comprehensive coverage of personality, and to be psychometrically sound. It is also designed to be easily used in occupational contexts.

The most comprehensive versions of the OPQ measure 30 scales derived from a conceptual model based on existing personality inventories, repertory grid studies and criteria for occupational success, with an additional social desirability scale. The scales are grouped into three categories, associated with relationships with people, thinking style, and feelings and emotions, respectively (see Table 4.5). The OPQ manual presents data showing that the 30 "concept model" scales have generally satisfactory internal consistency and test–retest reliability.

Two major issues have exercised researchers, rather than the consultants who distribute the test widely. The first is whether the underlying dimensions of this measure (relating, thinking, feeling) are indeed independent of one another. In two studies, Matthews, Stanton, Graham & Brinelow (1990) found that test constructors "understated" the degree of intercorrelation of the 31 concepts. In a later study, Matthews & Stanton (1994) found that the dimensions measured by the OPQ are in fact fairly similar to the "Big Five" model discussed earlier (see Table 4.6). They suggest that further work may be necessary to establish conclusively that the "Big Five" is the strongest model in psychometric terms. The thrust of much prior work on the "Big Five" has been to show that a three-factor model fails to capture important broad

Table 4.5 Descriptive statistics for the OPQ
concept scales

Scale	Mean	SD
Relating		
Persuasive	36.2	5.6
Controlling	36.6	7.0
Independent	33.9	4.6
Outgoing	34.3	7.6
Affiliative	38.9	5.1
Socially confident	33.5	7.9
Modest	28.5	6.1
Democratic	33.1	5.6
Caring	37.6	4.9
Thinking		
Practical	34.4	7.1
Data rational	29.8	8.2
Artistic	36.4	7.6
Behavioural	37.8	4.2
Traditional	28.1	4.9
Change orientated	38.0	5.0
Conceptual	31.7	5.3
Innovative	35.2	7.3
Forward planning	32.5	5.3
Detail-conscious	32.0	6.9
Conscientious	34.4	7.1
Feeling		
Relaxed	31.9	6.3
Worrying	30.6	5.4
Tough minded	26.6	7.7
Emotional control	31.6	7.1
Optimistic	37.2	5.5
Critical	34.1	4.3
Active	34.2	6.1
Competitive	27.4	7.0
Achieving	29.9	6.4
Decisive	30.4	5.1
Socially desirable	24.3	4.8

Source: Reproduced from Matthews *et al.* (1990) with the
permission of Elsevier Science.

elements of personality. Proponents of the "Big Five" have perhaps paid insufficient
attention to the possibility that five factors may be too *few*. The hypothesis that openness may be split into cognitive and non-cognitive elements may also merit further
work. However, it was not supported in the OPQ data perhaps because the questionnaire does not include scales directly related to self-rated intelligence.

A second, perhaps more important, line of research is the validity of the OPQ – does
it really predict occupational behaviour? Robertson & Kinder (1993) carried out a
meta-analysis of 21 different populations who had all completed the OPQ. They
showed that, if specific hypotheses were tested, there was strong evidence of the
criterion-related validity of the OPQ. They noted that personality variables seem
most important where the work performance is associated with creativity, analysis,
management of others, energy and communication.

Table 4.6 Comparison of six-factor OPQ dimensions with alternative models

Eysenck (1991)	Extraversion		Neuroticism		Psychoticism*	
Six-factor solution	Extraversion	Activity	Openness	Neuroticism	Conscience	Agreeableness*
SHL (1984) Pentagon model	Extraversion	Vigorous	Abstract	Emotional stability*	Methodical	–
Hough (1992)	Affiliation	Achievement, potency	Intellectance	Adjustment*	Dependability	Agreeableness*
Matthews & Oddy (1993)	Surgency	Achievement, strivings	Intellectance, autonomy	Emotional stability*	Orderliness	Affection*
Zuckerman et al. (1991)	Sociability	Activity	–	N-anxiety	Psychopathy and related traits*	Aggression-hostility

* Dimension is reversed in polarity with respect to other dimensions in the same column.

Source: Reproduced from Matthews & Stanton (1994) with the permission of Elsevier Science.

Although the amount of empirical research on the OPQ is much less than that on the EPQ, the 16PF or the NEO-PI mentioned earlier, it is growing. The advantage it has over the other questionnaires is not so much its theoretical basis or psychometric properties, but the database of thousands and thousands of working people around the world who have completed it.

The concepts of style and preference

The concept of style in psychology can be traced back 70 years. It is probably true that the concept of *cognitive* style preceded others like learning style. The concept of style is particularly attractive, more so than trait. Applied psychologists in educational, clinical and work settings have embraced the concept and this has led in turn to a profusion of concepts and measures.

Messick (1976) listed 19 cognitive style variables alone. Messick (1994) has argued that human activity displays both *substance* (content/level or performance) and *style* (manner/form or performance), though as we shall see is more a distinction between ability and style, than traits and style.

The idea of style is for many people intuitively appealing. Style appears to imply choice, preference and therefore change. One can *choose* a learning style, *adopt* a cognitive style and *moderate* an attributional style. It is much easier and more natural to change style than personality, let alone ability. It may therefore particularly appeal to optimists or those in the training and development business to use this sort of language. The traditional view of styles is that they are stable dispositions to behave in a certain way (Baron, 1985). According to Baron, this does not mean that individuals always behave in the same way: "Styles, like other traits, may be somewhat situation specific" (p. 380). Baron uses the example that although each person has a modal style of walking, people will walk faster when in a hurry or swing their arms more when in a carefree mood. This property of styles is shared by learning styles and cognitive styles.

Inherent in the notion of style, whether it is learning style, cognitive style or walking style, is that, despite some variability, individuals tend to exhibit consistent patterns of behaviour across situations and over time. However, they can choose to change those styles and learn other forms of behaviour.

Yet many personality and cognitive theorists and psychometricians have given up on stylistic concepts and measures. The field is therefore fragmented, idiosyncratic and egocentric. Confusion remains about the two major style concepts: cognitive style and learning style. Cognitive styles determine the amount and organization of information available to the individual at the moment. It mediates the influence of personality tests and motivation and intellectual functioning. However, different "style" researchers have used very different concepts.

Cognitive styles have three distinct research origins: (1) *perceptual* factors – speed and strength of closure; (2) *ego adaptation* – maintaining harmony and equilibrium of feelings/impulses; and (3) *developing cognitive systems* – Gestaltism. Compared with cognitive styles, *learning styles* are both broader and more focused; include cognitive, affective, sociological and physiological preferences *specifically in relation to the learning situation*; are stable but innate or learned; and tend to confound ability with style.

Messick (1976) explained that cognitive styles "have their roots in the study of perception and thus have had close ties since their inception with the laboratory and the clinical psychologists ... have tended to utilise measures derived from laboratory apparatus or clinical tools" (p. 10). It is not surprising, therefore, that cognitive style instruments are generally projective and are assessed in terms of accuracy and correctness of performance. In contrast, most learning style instruments have been designed for easy administration in a classroom context by teachers. They are generally self-report inventories that measure typical or usual ways of behaviour and preferences. The concept of preference is an important one in learning style measurement. While style refers to the processes a learner is likely to use, preference refers to the choices a learner makes. The notion that people choose one learning situation or condition over another is termed learning preference. Thus, learning styles instruments are not measuring the accuracy of correctness of responses but merely gathering information on how a student "likes", "tends" or "prefers" to learn. Learning styles instruments do, in fact, measure preferences.

Learning style is the composite of characteristic cognitive, affective and physiological factors that serve as relatively stable indicators of how a learner perceives, interacts with and responds to the learning environment. It is demonstrated by the pattern of behaviour and performance by which an individual approaches educational experiences. Messick (1984) defines cognitive styles as "characteristic self-consistencies in information processing that develop in congenial ways around the underlying personality trends" (p. 61). According to Messick (1976: 5):

> They are conceptualised as stable attitudes, preferences, or habitual strategies determining a person's typical modes of perceiving, remembering, thinking, and problem solving. As such, their influence extends to almost all human activities that implicate cognition, including social and interpersonal functioning.

It has always been easier to distinguish ability from style, than personality from style (Messick, 1984; Tiedemann, 1989):

1   Ability questions refer to *how much* and *what*; style questions refer to *how*. Ability refers to what kind of information is being processed, by what operation, in what form and how efficiently. Style refers to the manner or mode of cognition.

2   Ability implies *maximal* performance; style implies *typical* propensities. Ability is measured in terms of accuracy, correctness and speed of response, whereas style emphasizes the predominant or customary processing model.

3   Abilities are *unipolar*; style is *bipolar*. Ability levels range from none to a great deal, whereas styles usually have two different poles with quite different implications for cognitive functioning.

4   Abilities are *value directional*; styles are *value differentiated*. Usually, having more of an ability is considered better than having less, whereas supposed stylistic extreme poles have adaptive value but in different circumstances.

5   Abilities are often *domain specific*; styles cut across domains. Abilities are often specific to various domains (e.g. verbal, numerical, or spatial areas), whereas styles often serve as high-level heuristics.

6   Abilities are *enabling* variables because they facilitate task performance; styles are *organizing* and controlling variables. Abilities dictate level of performance, whereas styles contribute to the selection, combination and sequencing of both topic and process.

The difference between traits and styles is, however, much less clear. Studies in the area suggest correlations between established traits (i.e. Extraversion/Neuroticism) and well measured styles (i.e. learning styles) to be in the $r = .20$ to $r = .40$ range (Furnham, 1992, 1996). Indeed, most styles are measured and thought about in trait-like terms (Furnham & Steele, 1993). Several researchers have attempted to integrate personality traits and style theory. However, as Messick (1994) notes, these efforts do not fulfil the aspiration of style theorists, who believe that styles embrace personality *and* cognition. It is, of course, a moot point to argue that trait theorists themselves do not take cognisance of cognitive variables.

Furnham (1995) has pointed out a number of unsatisfactory answered problems for the issue of style:

1   *Aetiology of a cognitive/teaching style.* The question arises as to the origin of styles: are they biologically based, the result of early learning, neither, or both? This is a fundamental question that must be answered to avoid tautology. Aetiology determines how much a style may be changed.

2   *Variance accounted for.* Even if styles exist and determine in part the learning that takes place in social behaviour, few would argue that they are the only – or even the most important – factor that determines learning. The question then needs to be asked whether the amount of variance accounted for by this factor is so small as to be trivial, or, indeed, a major and central feature. Do styles have incremental validity over ability, personality or value measures?

3   *The nature of style as a variable.* If cognitive/learning style is a moderator variable between intelligence, personality and performance, the precise nature of this relationship needs to be spelt out. Indeed, it is necessary to list all relevant variables that relate to learning and specify how they interact.

4   *The process underlying style.* So far, a great deal of the research in this field has

been descriptive and taxonomic, aimed at identifying various styles and their consequences. Less work has gone into describing the mechanism or process by which the style operates.

Furnham (1995: 411) concludes:

> A pessimist might argue that despite fifty years of research into cognitive/learning style, we still know precious little if the above questions have not been answered or even attempted. An optimist, though, might be impressed by the research effort that has gone into this topic, by the proliferation of ideas, and by the evidence already accumulated. Nevertheless, pessimists sound more profound that optimists, and hence most recent reviewers in the field tend to be highly critical of developments in this area.

Similarly, Messick (1994: 131) notes: "The literature of cognitive and learning styles is peppered with unstable and inconsistent findings, whereas style theory seems either value in glossing over inconsistencies or confused in stressing differentiated features selectively".

Sternberg & Grigorenko (1997) remain in favour of the style concept. They argue that thinking style is a subset of cognitive style, which itself is a subset of style (a distinctive/characteristic method/manner of acting/performing). They provide three explanations for why psychologists would be interested in cognitive styles, none of which has anything to do with predictive validity or parsimonious explanations. The first is that style bridges the concept of cognition and personality, though they overlook the extensive work on the relationship between cognitive processing and personality traits (especially Neuroticism) (Furnham & Cheng, 1996). Next, cognitive style added to measures of ability improves the predictability of school behaviour, yet very little evidence is brought to bear supporting this assertion. Third, cognitive styles help explain occupational choice and performance. Yet again, any reviewer of this literature may be equally impressed by the poor predictive power of cognitive styles in the workplace (Furnham, 1992, 1994).

Sternberg & Grigorenko (1997: 703) set out five criteria for the evaluation of theories of style:

1 *Theoretical specification*: the positing of a reasonably complete, well-specified and internally consistent theory of styles that make connection with extant psychological theory.
2 *Internal validity*: a demonstration by factor analysis or some other method of inter-analysis that the underlying structure of the item or subset is as predicted by the theory.
3 *Convergent external validity*: a demonstration that the measures of styles correlate with other measures with which, in theory, they should correlate.
4 *Discriminant external validity*: a demonstration that the measures of styles do not correlate with other measures with which, in theory, they should not correlate.
5 *Heuristic generativity*: the extent to which the theory has spawned, and continues to spawn, psychological research and ideally, practical application.

They argue:

> We believe that styles have a great deal of promise for the future. First, they have provided and continue to provide a much-needed interface between research on cognition and personality. Second, unlike some psychological constructs, they have lent themselves to operationalisation and direct empirical tests. Third, they show promise for helping psychologists understand some of the variation in school and job performance that cannot be accounted for by individual differences in abilities. For example they predict school performance significantly and add to the prediction provided by ability tests. Finally, they can truly tell something about environments as well as individuals' interactions with these environments, as shown by the fact that correlations of styles with performance that are significantly positive in one environment are significantly negative in another environment. (Sternberg & Grigorenko, 1997: 710)

Suffice it to say that the concept of style in psychological theory and measurement remains problematic. Indeed, it could be argued that because style affects many forms of social behaviour – particularly in applied settings like work and leisure – certain behaviours in the testing situation may themselves be indices of style. That is, how people complete tests, be they behavioural or self-report, may be a good individual difference measure.

The Type A behaviour pattern

The Type A behaviour pattern was conceived nearly 25 years ago when it was found that the coronary patients being studied behaved similarly in many ways: they were extremely competitive, high-achieving, aggressive, hasty, impatient and restless. They were characterized by explosive speech patterns, tenseness of facial muscles, and appeared to be under pressure of time and the challenge of responsibility. These individuals were described as having a Type A personality, as opposed to the more relaxed Type B, possessed by those with a low risk of coronary heart disease. Type A individuals are often deeply involved in and committed to their work, so that other aspects of their lives are relatively neglected.

The original Type A researchers, Friedman & Rosenman (1974), identified the following Type A characteristics:

* Possessing the habit of explosively accentuating various key words in ordinary speech without real need and tending to utter the last few words of sentences far more rapidly than the opening words. This reflects underlying aggression or hostility, and mirrors one's underlying impatience with spending even the time required for one's own (Type A) speech.
* Always moving, walking and eating rapidly.
* Feeling or revealing to others an impatience with the rate at which most events take place. Often finishing the sentences of others.
* Often attempting to do two or more things at the same time, such as thinking about an irrelevant subject when listening to someone else speak. This "polyphasic" activity is one of the most common traits of Type A individuals.

- Finding it always difficult to refrain from talking about or turning any conversation to themes that have personal interest. At times when this manoeuvre fails, pretending to listen but really remaining preoccupied with these personal thoughts.
- Almost always feeling vaguely guilty when attempting to relax or do nothing for even just a few hours.
- No longer noticing the more interesting or beautiful things encountered during the day.
- Not having any time to spare, because they are so preoccupied with getting things worth having.
- Attempting to schedule more and more in less and less time. Making fewer allowances for unforeseen events that might disrupt the schedule. Also, having a chronic sense of time urgency – a core aspect of Type A personality.
- Having aggressive, hostile feelings to all Type A individuals.
- Resorting to certain characteristic gestures or nervous tics, such as clenching fists, or banging a hand upon a table for emphasis.
- Becoming increasingly committed to translating and evaluating personal activities and the activities of others in terms of numbers.

Rosenman & Friedman (1974) also outline the following characteristics of a Type B personality:

- Being completely free of all the habits and exhibiting none of the traits of the Type A personality.
- Never suffering from time urgency and impatience.
- Harbouring no free-floating hostility and feeling no need to impress others with one's achievements or accomplishments unless the situation demands.
- Playing in order to find relaxation and fun, not to demonstrate achievement at any cost.
- Being able to work without agitation and to relax without guilt.

Over the years, the literature on this behaviour pattern has exploded and there are many relatively sophisticated models describing the personal, social and cultural antecedents of the Type A pattern, through to the environmental, organizational and personal consequences, as well as potentially important moderating effects (Price, 1982).

Recent research on the Type A behaviour pattern has demonstrated that Type A individuals are more aggressive, more neurotic, more extraverted and more anxious, as well as in greater need for control than Type B individuals (Furnham, 1990). Many studies have shown that Type A individuals have feelings of insecurity and self-doubt and feel depressed or anxious about their self-worth (Price, 1982). Furnham, Borovoy & Henley (1986) reported two studies looking at the differences in self-perceptions of Type As and Bs. In the first, Type As rated themselves significantly higher on various *negative* traits (complaining, conceited, cruel, dominating, selfish and unkind) and lower on *positive* traits (patient, reasonable, tolerant and unselfish). This was replicated in a second study, in which Type As, compared with Type Bs, believed themselves to be more ambitious, cold, complaining, conceited, cruel, dishonest, dominating, enthusiastic, gloomy, insincere, jealous, malicious, impatient and selfish. Furnham *et al.* argue that high levels of Type A behaviours are associated with a tendency to process information about the self in a fashion that attempts to bolster self-esteem. They note:

Thus, while Type A may have lower self-esteem, and rate themselves more highly on negative traits and less so on positive traits compared to Type Bs, they remember more positive traits about themselves. This "information processing strategy" is an attempt to deny the recognized personal limitations and bolster self-esteem. Whereas neurotics, when presented with both negative and positive information about self, selectively process self-deprecatory rather than self-appreciatory information, A types do the reverse – that is, to a greater extent than most normal subjects. (Furnham *et al.*, 1986: 371)

Despite the extensive work done on the Type A measure, relatively little research has looked at the behaviour of Type As at work. However, various speculations have been made. Price (1982) sees the workplace as the key environmental factor influencing Type A behaviour. She argues that by modelling or imitating hard-driving, competitive, aggressive behaviour of successful people at work, men in particular learn to be Type A. Certain other factors, common in the (American) workplace, lead to (or at least reward) this behaviour pattern. They include:

- peer pressure to work overtime, compete for prizes, and so on;
- being outcome- or product-orientated, which confuses the quality/quantity of work with worth;
- job overload to meet high, often unrealistic, performance standards;
- setting deadlines that reflect chronic time urgency;
- crisis generation as a consequence of time management problems.

In short, the workplace for men rewards Type A behaviour, which leads to considerable personal stress. The Type A person is a workaholic with an exaggerated success ethic. Various people have undertaken empirical work in this field (Begley & Boyd, 1985).

Mettlin (1976) looked at 943 white-collar, middle-class males in New York from five different work settings: the administrative staff and professional staff of a state health agency, supervisory personnel from a public service organization, officers from industrial and trade unions, faculty at a major private university, and administrative officers of a large banking corporation. They found that not only were the Type A behaviour patterns significantly related to status as measured by rank, level of occupational prestige and income, they were also found to be significantly related to rapid career achievement as indicated by rank and income related to age.

In a review of various studies, Chesney & Rosenman (1980) bore out the connection between Type A personality and high occupational status. They found that "Type As tended to describe their jobs as having more responsibility, longer hours and heavier workloads than do Type Bs. Despite these factors, Type As in general did not report more job dissatisfaction, anxiety, or depression than do Type Bs" (p. 208). Chusmir & Hood (1988) found as predicted that in both working men and women, Type A behaviour patterns were significantly linked to need for achievement, autonomy and power, as well as job commitment, but not job satisfaction.

Whereas some studies showed Type A behaviour is associated positively with productivity and negatively with satisfaction, others have failed to find any relationship (Matteson, Ivancevich, & Smith, 1984). However, Bluen, Barling & Burns (1990) found that, after partialling out various possibly salient biographical factors, and impatience and irritability, Type A did predict policies sold and job satisfaction in insurance salesmen.

The results of various studies lead one to derive fairly plausible and testable hypotheses:

* Type As are more sensitive, and hence responsive, to rewards (Blumenthal, McKee, Haney, & Williams, 1980).
* Because Type As are hurried and time urgent, they will work faster but with more errors than Type B workers (Price, 1982).
* Type As tend to be aggressive and interpersonally hostile, which makes them difficult to handle, unpredictable and touchy (Hooker, Blumenthal, & Siegler, 1987).
* Type As set unrealistically high performance standards of themselves, and others, and hence frequently do not attain them (Ward & Eisler, 1987).
* Type As work harder, suffer more stress and ignore minor ailments (influenza), but when they do become ill they suffer major illnesses (Price, 1982).
* Type As tend to be more committed to, and perform better at, organizational goals (Price, 1982).

These and many other related hypotheses could be tested, all of which suggest that being Type A is a mixed blessing in an organizational setting. It certainly suggests that Type As are more likely to experience stress and more likely to generate it in others.

Despite lack of agreement about the aetiology, components and psychological processes associated with the Type A behaviour pattern, it does appear that researchers have identified a personality variable, or more likely a cluster of variables, that predict not only stress at work but also outside it. For instance, Howard, Cunningham & Rechnitzer (1986) found that whether a particular job characteristic (such as role ambiguity) is stressful depends on whether the person is Type A or B, and that intrinsic job satisfaction has the potential to moderate these effects. Generally, Type As "fit" unambiguous environments and find ambiguous environments stressful, whereas the opposite is true for Type Bs.

The "hardy personality"

Although the Type A/Type B distinction may provide many clues as to stress-prone personality characteristics, many believe the theory is not adequate to explain why some people suffer ill health as a result of high stress. Kobasa (1979) developed the "hardy personality" concept and measure to explain the connection between stress and health. The theory states that, among persons facing significant work stressors, those high in hardiness will be significantly less likely to fall ill, either mentally or physically, than those who lack hardiness or who display alienation, powerlessness and threat in face of change. The key attribute – hardiness – is defined as a personality cognitive or attributional style that expresses commitment, control and challenge. *Commitment* is the ability to believe in the truth and importance of who one is and what one is doing and, thereby, the tendency to involve oneself fully in the many situations of life, including work, family, interpersonal relationships and social institutions. *Control* is defined as the tendency to believe and act as if one can influence the course of events. Persons with control seek explanations for why something is happening with emphasis on their own responsibility and not in terms of other actions or fate. This is, of course, internal locus of control: the belief that one is personally in control of one's destiny. The third aspect of the hardy personality, *challenge*, is based on the individual's belief that change, rather than stability, is the normative mode of life. Thus, with regard to "challenge", an individual looks for stimulation, change and opportunities with an openness of mind and willingness to experiment.

Kobasa (1979) suggests that hardiness leads to a type of coping. Keeping specific stressors in perspective, hardy individuals' basic sense of purpose in life allows them to ground events in an understandable and varied life-course. Knowing that one has the resources with which to respond to stressors, hardy individuals' underlying sense of control allows them to appreciate a well-exercised coping repertoire. Viewing stressors as potential opportunities for change and as challenges enables hardy individuals to see even undesirable events in terms of possibility rather than threat. Kobasa found evidence to support her theory, namely that executives with high stress but low illness were more hardy and showed stronger commitment to self, and vigorousness towards the environment.

Thus, whereas the Type A literature focused on individuals prone to stress, the hardiness concept focused on individuals who cope well with stress. A problem for the Type A literature is that it focuses more on the causes of stress rather than how people cope with it. There are many other personality theories and models that claim to measure traits that predict behaviour. Indeed, there is an enormous, diffuse literature on this topic.

The biodata method

It seems self-evident to the lay person that, from a personal point of view, the past predicts the future. That is, the most useful predictor of a person's behaviour at work is his or her personal history – his or her biographical facts.

Over 80 years ago, Goldsmith (1922) devised an ingenious new solution to an old problem: selecting people who could endure selling life insurance. He took 50 good, 50 poor and 50 average salesmen from a larger sample of 502, and analysed their *application forms*. Age, marital status, education, (current) occupation, previous experience (of selling insurance), membership of clubs, whether candidate was applying for full- or part-time selling, whether the candidate him/herself had life insurance, and whether (not what) candidates replied to the question "What amount of insurance are you confident of placing each month?" – collectively distinguished good from average and average from bad. Goldsmith scored the various variables as shown in Table 4.7: the higher the positive score, the more predictive of success.

Goldsmith turned the conventional application form into what was called a *weighted application blank* (WAB). The WAB works on the principle that "the best predictor of future behaviour is the past behaviour", and the easiest way of measuring past behaviour is what the applicant writes on his or her application form. The principle is familiar to anyone with motor insurance, and is the basis of the actuarial profession. Goldsmith (1922: 155) concluded:

> The study of these 502 blanks has, therefore, indicated that for a life insurance company, the score on the personal history blank bears a positive relationship to

Table 4.7 Early biodata scoring scheme: the weighted application blank

Age		Marital status		Service	
18–20	−2	Married	+1	Full time	+2
21–22	−1	Single	−1	Part time	−2
23–24	0	*Occupation*		*Insurance*	
25–27	+1	Social	+1	Carried	+1
28–29	+2	Unsocial	−1	Not carried	−1
30–40	+3	*Experience*			
41–50	+1	Previous life insurance experience			+1
51–60	0	*Confidence*			
Over 60	−1	Replies to question: "What amount			
Education		of insurance are you confident			
8 years	+1	of placing each month"			+1
10 years	+2	Does not reply			−1
12 years	+3				
16 years	+2				

Source: Goldsmith (1922).

the applicant's future success, and that on this blank a lower critical score may be set, below which it would not be worth while to license an applicant.

By the end of the 1930s, the WAB technique was well developed; ready-made tables had been drawn up from WAB construction. Furthermore, various studies continued to be done in this area.

Mosel (1952) found 12 personal data items that distinguished between high and low department-store sales figures. These factors included age, education, height, weight, marital status and dwelling. In the 1950s, the US Green Giant Co. found that its seasonal pea- and corn-canners often inexplicably left within a few days of starting work, causing the company great inconvenience and expense. Dunnette & Maetzold (1955: 308) devised a WAB to reduce turnover:

the typically stable Green Giant production worker lives (locally), has a telephone, is married and has no children, is not a veteran (not an ex-serviceman), is either young (under 25) or old (over 55), weighs more than 150 pounds but less than 175, has obtained more than ten years' education, has worked for Green Giant, will be available for work until the end of summer, and prefers field work to inside work.

The WAB was used only for male applicants; female employees didn't present a turnover problem. It proved successful for many years, so validating the use of WABs in selection.

This profile retained its predictive validity over three successive years, and into three other Green Giant canning factories, but it didn't work for non-seasonal cannery workers. Scott & Johnson (1967) found *permanent* workers' turnover was predicted by a regression equation:

Tenure = 0.30 (age) + 8.82 (sex) − 0.69 (miles from plant) + 5.29 (type of residence) + 2.66 (children) + 1.08 (years on last job) − 1.99

where female =1; male = 0; live with parents, or in a room (bedsit) = 0; live in own home = 1.

Permanent cannery workers who stay the course had family and domestic responsibilities (and tended to be women), whereas the profile for seasonal workers identifies young college students, or semi-retired people, both wanting a short-term job. Buel (1964) showed the WAB to have both concurrent and predictive validity with regard to voluntary female clerical turnover. Similarly, Scott & Johnson (1967) found the WAB to be useful for selecting unskilled employees. They found that females who lived close to the plant and those with family responsibility (married, older, several dependents) were more likely to become long-term employees.

Walther (1961) tried to identify predictors of success and failure at foreign service clerical jobs. Employees filled out a 68-item biodata-type questionnaire and were later categorized as above and below average. The questionnaire items seemed to fall into various clusters, most of which showed significant differences. The results appeared to indicate that above-average employees preferred to work closely with supervisors; were sensitive to their wishes; disliked routine and liked variety; wanted to do things well and worked best when set a particular target or standard; were sociable and enjoyed working with people; had a tendency to placate, avoid, divert or ignore aggressive behaviour; and preferred activities involving the influencing of others through social relationships. Interestingly, the measure seemed as good at predicting success as failure. That is, differences on the various dimensions – please authority, social isolation, social leadership – seemed to discriminate closely between success and failure.

In a more robust and comprehensive study, Baehr & Williams (1968) examined 210 salesmen and 16 district managers on 15 personal background dimensions, including parental success and adjustment, general health, and financial responsibility. The criterion variable was multifaceted and intercorrelated, and consisted of such things as performance ratings, sales rank, and so on. Upper- and lower-rated salesmen differed on the three criteria, especially financial responsibility (Table 4.8).

WAB construction is mindlessly empirical in the eyes of its critics: "The procedure is raw empiricism in the extreme, the 'score' is the most heterogeneous value imaginable, representing a highly complex and usually unravelled network of information". It doesn't matter why an item differentiates successful from unsuccessful estate agents, only that it does. WABs have been used successfully to test job turnover, oil company executive success, military promotability, and much more.

The classic WAB is supposedly invisible and unfakeable. It is invisible because the applicant expects to complete an application "blank" and it is unfakeable because most of the items *could* be verified independently, if the employer could afford the time and the expense (some can: it's called "positive vetting"). The classical WAB has tended to be supplanted since the 1960s by "biodata", or biographical inventories, or life-history data. Biodata use a questionnaire format with multiple-choice answers.

Biodata have been used successfully to predict success with sales/research engineers, oil industry research scientists, pharmaceutical industry researchers, bus drivers, "custodial officers" and police officers. Biodata are used for professional, clerical, sales, skilled and unskilled labour. They have been shown to work with similar success in different countries. Biodata were used most frequently for selecting sales staff, least often for managerial occupations. But they have been used to predict many occupational behaviours with many different groups. Smith, Albright, Glennon & Owens (1961) found research competence and creativity could be predicted from biodata.

Cascio (1976) used biographical data from both minority and majority group members to predict job turnover. Nevo (1976) used biographical data to predict success for

Table 4.8 Significance of the differences between mean personal-history factor scores for the upper-rated and lower-rated salesmen on the paired-comparison performance indices

| | Upper-rated salesmen | | Lower-rated salesmen | | |
| | (n = 72) | | (n = 52) | | t |
Personal-history factor	M	SD	M	SD	
School achievement	1.96	1.52	2.19	1.65	0.82
Higher educational achievement	4.59	1.68	4.69	1.90	1.30
Drive	4.13	2.04	4.15	1.90	0.00
Leadership and group participation	2.90	1.66	2.44	1.78	1.48
Financial responsibility	5.54	1.43	4.11	1.79	4.92***
Early family responsibility	8.63	1.98	7.31	2.63	3.17**
Parental family adjustment	6.47	2.25	6.79	2.06	0.80
Stability	6.01	1.68	5.08	2.56	2.46*
School activities	3.32	1.88	3.08	1.76	0.73
Professional successful parents	3.79	1.46	3.60	1.55	0.73
Educational–vocational consistency	1.42	0.95	1.25	0.99	0.95
Vocational decisiveness	2.22	1.35	2.14	1.12	0.39
Vocational satisfaction	5.69	1.81	5.67	1.72	0.00
Selling experience	6.25	1.39	5.92	1.44	1.27
General health	3.42	1.15	3.27	1.11	0.71

t = t-test of statistical significance. *$P < 0.05$, ** $P < 0.01$, ***$P < 0.001$.

Source: Reproduced from Baehr & Williams (1968) with the permission of the American Psychological Association.

both men and women in the Israeli Army. Using only 13 biographical variables and military values as the criteria, they found various significant correlates: father's educational and occupational level, mother's age, intensity of athletic activities, and sound attitudes in high school. Keinan, Friedland, Yitzhaky & Moran (1981) used biodata successfully to predict motion sickness in seamen. They found that a combination of biographical data and optokinetic tests explained 40% of the variance in performance. More recently, biodata were shown to be effective in predicting accidents (Hansen, 1989).

Most modern researchers use a mixture of classic WAB and biodata. They are also generally much more reticent about item content, so it is often unclear how much of each they include. The success of the classic WAB depends on the general public never suspecting application forms have any but the usual bureaucratic purpose. Essentially, biodata permit "the respondent to describe himself in terms of demographic, experimental or attitudinal variables presumed or demonstrated to be related to personality structure, personal adjustment or success in social, educational or occupational pursuits" (Eberhardt & Muchinsky, 1982: 82).

A distinction can be made between "hard" items and "soft" items. The former represent historical and verifiable information about an individual, whereas the latter are of a more abstract nature and cover value judgements, aspirations, motivations, attitudes and expectations. Although soft biodata may be open to distortion and could lead individuals to "fictionalize" their past lives, they may be useful to tap into success-related constructs not readily measured by hard items (such as "assertiveness" in the first of the above examples). Some studies use both hard and soft data. For instance,

Metcalfe (1987) used only five biographical factors: sex, age, education, marital and family status, as well as soft "data".

Various attempts have been made to develop standardized biographical question-naires. For instance, Owens (1976) and Owens & Schoenfeldt (1979) developed a bio-graphical questionnaire that appeared to have a stable factor structure (Eberhardt & Muchinsky, 1982). The 13 factors that emerged are interesting in their own right:

- *Warmth of parental relationship* (e.g. warm relationship with parents: affection, praise and attention given by parents).
- *Academic achievement* (e.g. competitive in academic situations, parents satisfied with grades, high academic standing).
- *Social extraversion* (e.g. directed group activities, held leadership positions, effective in social situations, dated more frequently).
- *Athletic interest* (e.g. frequent participation in athletic events, excellent perform-ance in athletic activities).
- *Intellectualism* (e.g. regularly read literary, business or scientific magazines; watched educational and cultural TV shows).
- *Aggressiveness/independence* (e.g. enjoyed discussion courses, tried to get others to see their point of view, regarded as radical, said what they felt).
- *Socioeconomic status* (e.g. high parental educational level, above average family income, high parental occupational level).
- *Parental control versus freedom* (e.g. parents more strict, critical and punitive; parents allowed less freedom and tended to nag or push for better achievement).
- *Social desirability* (e.g. wished to become more socially acceptable, "took things out" on friends and parents, suffered "attacks of conscience").
- *Scientific interest* (e.g. enjoyed science and lab courses and found them quite easy, worked with scientific apparatus outside class).
- *Positive academic attitude* (e.g. liked school and teachers, enjoyed courses more while doing more homework, teachers aroused interests).
- *Religious activity* (e.g. active in church, religious or charitable organizations, went to church more often, had stronger religious beliefs, attended summer camp).
- *Sibling friction* (e.g. felt more friction and competition towards siblings, argued or fought with siblings, more younger brothers and sisters).

Modified versions of this scale have been used successfully to predict success in real estate agencies (Mitchell & Klimoski, 1982). More unusual perhaps, Niener & Owens (1982) showed that two biographical questionnaires correlated highly and positively 7 years apart. Lautenschlager & Schaffer (1987) showed that Owens' questionnaire revealed components that were stable over time (for men and women) and across geo-graphical locations.

What is the difference between biodata and personality tests? There are essentially three, according to Cook (1988):

- Biodata questions allow a definite answer, whereas personality questions often do not. Most biodata questions could be answered by someone who knows the respondent well.
- Personality inventory questions are carefully phrased, to elicit a rapid, unthinking reply, whereas biodata items often sound quite clumsy in their desire to specify

precisely the information they want. For instance, with regard to personal appearance, as compared with the appearance of my friends, I think that:

(a) Most of my friends have a better appearance.
(b) I am equal to most of them in appearance.
(c) I am better than most of them in appearance.
(d) I don't feel strongly one way or the other.

In a personality inventory this would read more like: "I am fairly happy about the way I look – TRUE/FALSE".

- Personality inventories have fixed keys, whereas biodata items are re-keyed for each selection task. Personality questions lose their validity faster than biographical questions.

Reilly & Chao (1982) reviewed various alternatives to ability tests for predicting a variety of criteria and found that the mean validities for biodata ranged from .32 against job tenure to .46 against productivity. Validities for clerical or sales occupations were also higher than those for military or non-specific non-managerial occupations. Their overall conclusion was that "of the alternative reviewed, only biodata and peer evaluation have evidence of validity equal to that of tests" (p. 59).

Schmitt, Gooding, Noe & Kirsch (1984) reviewed research published between 1964 and 1982. The weighted average of 99 validity coefficients was $r = .24$, definitely poorer than assessment centres, work samples and peer ratings, but definitely better than personality inventories. Biodata were used to predict Performance ratings ($r = .32$), Turnover ($r = .21$), Achievement/grades ($r = .23$), Status change ($r = .33$), Wages ($r = .53$) and Productivity ($r = .20$). The high correlation with wages, based on seven samples and 1544 individuals, is unexplained.

Hunter & Hunter (1984) reviewed biodata research using validity generalization analysis to arrive at a single estimate of biodata validity, based on pooled samples of 4000–10,000 people, for four criteria: Supervisor ratings ($r = .37$), Promotion ($r = .26$), Training success ($r = .30$) and Tenure ($r = .26$). Generalizable validity implies that certain biographical pointers have fairly general predictive validity. Early WAB research occasionally gave some very contradictory results. Owning one's own home is generally a "good sign", but *it* wasn't for shop saleswomen, the most efficient of whom lived in boarding houses.

Are there any biographical pointers that have fairly general predictive validity? Cook (1988: 92–93) lists three:

- *Experience*: Experience has very moderate predictive validity for supervisor ratings, but zero validity for training grades (Hunter & Hunter, 1984). Arvey, McGowen & Hogan (1981) reviewed half a dozen studies and concluded that there was little evidence that experience predicted productivity. General experience, in supervising people or selling, had no predictive validity. Research on air traffic controllers found experience was used only when it was directly and specifically relevant; having used a radio or flown an aircraft does not predict efficiency as an air traffic controller, but experience of instrument flying does.
- *Seniority*: How long the person has been employed is often used to decide who is promoted: "Buggins's turn". Trade unions, in the UK and the USA, often insist it

should be the sole criterion. Seniority almost always plays a large part in deciding who is "released" when the workforce has to be reduced: "last in, first out". There is no reason to expect seniority to be related to efficiency, and there hasn't been much research on the link, though Gordon & Fitzgibbons (1982) found seniority to be quite unrelated to efficiency in female sewing machine operators. Many would argue that the relationship between seniority and work productivity is in fact curvilinear (as a curve on a graph, it would be an inverse U).

- *Age*: Hunter & Hunter (1984) reviewed over 500 validity coefficients, and found age alone to have zero validity as a predictor, whether the criterion was supervisor rating or training grade. Age does predict job turnover; younger employees are more likely to leave. Age can distort WAB/biodata scoring; older men tend to have dependants, higher living expenses and to belong to more organizations than do younger men, so a WAB using age-related items for individuals with diverse ages could give misleading results.

Rothstein, Schmidt, Erwin, Owens & Sparks (1990) looked at the cross-validation of biodata using 11,000 first-line supervisors in 790 organizations. Their results showed that, contrary to popular belief, biodata validities are intrinsically specific to particular organizations:

> In summary, this research has shown that the validity of a well developed auto-biographical questionnaire instrument generalizes across a major job family: first-line supervision. All biodata items were based on a review of information about the job. Each item was based on a rationale or hypothesis as to its applicability to the candidate population; no item was keyed unless the relationship could be explained in psychological terms and the item showed validity across different organizations. All developmental samples were large, and the stability of all relationships was determined through later replications in multiple organizations. The findings of this study indicate that the validity of this instrument is temporally stable as well as generalizable. The findings also provide evidence against the hypothesis that the validity of biodata stems from measurement of knowledge and skills acquired on the job. Finally, the results of this study constitute additional evidence against the general hypothesis of situational specificity of validities; the findings disconfirm this hypothesis in an important noncognitive domain. This is significant because it has been hypothesized that situational specificity can be expected to be greater in noncognitive than in cognitive domains. (Rothstein *et al.*, 1990: 183)

Other attempts to use biodata in selection have been made by Russell (1990) and Szymanski & Churchill (1990).

Recent biodata studies have also proved successful. McDaniel (1989) noted that various organizations required (US) government-issued security clearance, but that the application of background investigation information in personnel screening differs in various ways from biodata:

- Biodata screen applicants from a diverse set of occupations, whereas screening is used for people in positions of trust.
- Biodata are usually restricted to pencil-and-paper methodology, while screening uses interviews, references and other methods.

- Biodata are usually concerned with identifying occupational capability, whereas screening is concerned mainly with behavioural reliability, integrity and personal adjustment.

More recently, Smernou & Lautenschlager (1991) gave nearly 2000 students a 389 autobiographical data form and the Maudsley Personality Inventory, which measures neuroticism and extraversion. They then did a cluster analysis on the autobiographical inventory, and related the clusters to the two personality variables. The clusters associated with neuroticism contained information about perceived parental expectations and evaluations, mode of disciplinary control, parental functions, adjustment modes, psychological needs and social maturity. Physical health, academic performance and attitudes, work and leisure time interests were also identified. With regard to extraversion, various clusters resulted, dealing with parental training, standards and socialization practices, intimate behaviours, socioeconomic indicators and relations with important others. Behavioural antecedents of extraversion were found to be reliance on people, extensive participation in diverse activities, leadership tendencies, self-reliance, inquisitiveness and interests in many subjects. Feelings of self-satisfaction and good health were present in the lives of many extraverts.

The fact that biological clusters and factors are related to personality dimensions should be no surprise. The question remains, apart from psychometric questions of reliability, which is the most efficient, effective, sensitive and non-feedback means of gathering data about people to be used to predict occupational success and failure?

In general, the evidence suggests the "shelf life" of biodata is between 3 and 5 years. However, it should be noted that the majority of the studies to have reported considerable shrinkage have used job turnover as the criterion. Turnover is more readily affected by labour-market conditions than performance measures and, where the latter are used, the outlook may not be as bleak.

Savage (1990) has listed seven conditions for the successful use of biodata:

- The criteria for job success or acceptability must be *decided* clearly. Any method of selection can only be as good as the criteria which it aims to measure. Where something is designed specifically to measure specific criteria in a certain organizational situation, like a biodata form, the need to establish criteria carefully is greatly enhanced. A purely empirical approach necessitates asking a very large number of people a very large number of questions purely for research purposes – a situation that is rarely feasible in the UK – particularly in private sector organizations.
- The likely candidates for the job should be of broadly similar age and background. There seems to be very little experience of using biodata forms when candidates come from widely different backgrounds and ages.
- Success or failure in the job must be based on individual differences. If success or failure in the job are linked to items such as track record or specific job experience, or simply turning up for work, then a methodology such as biodata, which is geared to deciphering individual differences between applicants, is unlikely to be very successful.
- There must be strong commitment from the company to the idea of using the biodata forms. The introduction of a biodata form will have a considerable effect on the way recruitment is administered. There are also likely to be queries and may even be some complaints. If everyone is not committed to the idea, these problems

can assume overwhelming proportions and result in the biodata experiment being curtailed or cancelled.

- People must be aware of what constitutes "success" in using biodata. The predictive power of "classical" biodata forms is measured in purely statistical terms. The results tend to show themselves in terms of a percentage increase in successful candidates over a period of time. It is still possible in any individual case for the biodata prediction to be totally wrong. Unless people understand the nature of the statistical proofs of its success, they may become disillusioned and may focus in on one or two apparently glaring anomalies. This undermines the whole credibility of the process.
- The application blank must be in a format acceptable to candidates. Graduate trainees in particular have tended to become very wary of the use of biodata forms. They take exception to the multiple-choice format and can voice their disapproval to career services and other students. At a time when young people are in short supply, this may cause some employers to be concerned that potentially good applicants may be deterred from applying. However, it is worth pointing out that this does not appear to apply to all applicants, only to certain groupings.
- Suitable methods must be found to make the scoring of the biodata quick, accurate and administratively easy. Some of the early biodata forms were hand-scored. This is so appallingly laborious that it takes some very marked increases in accuracy to convince anyone that it is worthwhile.

Despite the fact that there is no grand theory underlying the biodata method, it has a long and interesting history. It represents a serious empirical attempt to examine the "commonsensical" relationship between an individual's personal history (biography) and their behaviour at work.

Intelligence at work

There is a "large and compelling literature" showing that intelligence is a good predictor of both job performance and training proficiency at work (Drasgow, 2003). Extensive meta-analytic reviews have shown that intelligence is a good predictor of job performance, particularly in complex jobs. Although debated, researchers suggest the correlation between intelligence and job performance is around $r = .50$ (Schmidt & Hunter, 1998). The central question is what other factors like personality or social/ emotional intelligence (sometimes called "social skills") account for the rest of the variance. But referring to "g" or general intelligence, Drasgow (2003) is forced to conclude: "for understanding performance in the workplace, and especially task performance and training performance, g is the key . . . g accounts for an overwhelming proportion of the explained variance when predicting training and job performance" (p. 126).

In a careful review of their own work and that of others, as well as criticisms of it, Ree & Carretta (1999) concluded thus: "Occupational performance begins with learning the knowledge and skills required for the job and continues into on-the-job performance and beyond. We and other investigators have demonstrated that g predicts training performance, job performance, lifetime productivity, and finally, early mortality" (p. 179).

But there are very different approaches to intelligence. Sternberg (1990) identified seven academic metaphors of intelligence, their central questions and typical theorists

Box 4.1 What are the advantages and disadvantages of biodata?

Advantages

- *Objectivity*   The same questions are asked of everyone who completes the form, and the answers given are assessed in a consistent way. In this sense a biodata questionnaire is probably a fairer means of selection than more conventional procedures. It is also possible to monitor candidates' responses to individual questions and eliminate items that show evidence of discrimination against some social groups.
- *Cost*   Although there may be fairly extensive R&D costs, once criteria are known, biodata are very cheap. Biodata forms can be developed in multiple-choice formats which are amenable to machine scoring or direct entry to a computer terminal. Thus, processing large numbers of applicants can become a routine clerical activity, freeing valuable personnel professionals' or line-managers' time.
- *"Checkability"*   It is possible, in theory at any rate, to check up on the answers of the respondents. This fact may reduce faking.
- *Validity*   Nearly all the studies have shown that biodata are a valid and reliable way of selecting individuals. Certainly, the results look as if biodata are better than interviews and personality questionnaires, and as good as ability tests.
- *Self-presentation*   Most people prefer, and expect, to be asked about their biographies rather than their personalities. For many, biodata are more preferable and acceptable than personality tests.

Disadvantages

- *Homogeneity versus heterogeneity*   If many biographical items are used in selection, the organization inevitably becomes more homogeneous, which has both advantages and disadvantages. Heterogeneity may occur across divisions (with different criteria) but not within them.
- *Cloning the past*   Biodata work on the idea that past behaviour predicts current performance, but if current criteria are very unstable (say in a rapidly changing market) one is perpetually out of date. Biodata may be best in stable organizations and environments.
- *Faking*   Biodata has been shown to be fakeable. Goldstein (1971) checked information given by applicants for a nursing aide post with what previous employers said. Half the sample overestimated how long they had worked for their previous employer. Overstating previous salary and describing part-time work as full-time were also common. More seriously, a quarter gave reasons for leaving their previous job with which the employer did not agree, and no fewer than 17 per cent gave as their previous employer someone who had never heard of them.
- *Fairness in the law*   If biodata items show major biographical correlates such as sex, race, religion and age, one may want to select or reject particular individuals, which is illegal. Items such as age, sex, and marital status may in fact be challenged by the courts if such items are included in inventories for the purpose of personnel selection. In that event, whatever gains in predictive power are to be derived through the inclusion of these items must be weighed against the possible expenses of legal defence.
- *Discovering the selection criteria can be useful in itself*   Many organizations have never really examined their selection in detail. The criteria have just grown up over time or reflect the personal preferences of recruiters. The process of diagnosing clear selection criteria in advance of setting up a biodata system will have considerable benefits for the whole of the selection process.

Box 4.1 (continued)

- *Minorities can't easily be identified and treated fairly*   In setting up a biodata form, the link between the information on the form and suitability for the job needs to be established. This in itself tends to ensure that any other elements are excluded from the selection process. In addition, the research necessary to set up the form can provide the basis for setting up and monitoring an equal opportunities programme. Biodata forms, especially when computer-scored, are completely blind to incidental items such as a person's name, which might indicate ethnic background.
- *Biodata do not travel well*   The same criteria do not have the same predictability across jobs, organizations, countries or time periods. Because criteria have to be established every time, the development of biodata can be expensive.
- *A-theoretical*   The major disadvantage of biodata being entirely empirical and non-theoretical is that one can never know which of a myriad of biographical factors to choose from. Because there is no theory, one cannot explain *which* features predict occupational success and *why*.
- *Time-consuming*   In a *predictive* design, the questionnaire is intended to be used for applicants, hence it is developed using data from applicants. The disadvantage is that it is a very time-consuming process. For example, it might take at least 12 months to obtain reliable, meaningful job-related data on new employees. If an organization does not have a regular intake of new staff, there could be two or three years' delay between sending the draft biodata form to applicants and obtaining a sample of employees large enough to warrant further development work.
- *Shrinkage over time*   Biodata scoring keys do not appear to hold up indefinitely. There is evidence that the validity of biodata shrinks over time, and periodic re-validation and re-weighting may be necessary.

Source: Based on Gunter *et al.* (1993).

taking this position. He argued that specific models or metaphors generate specific questions about intelligence which theories and research seek to address. Scientists may be unaware of these metaphors, which can both limit but also expand views on intelligence. The metaphors are:

1   *Geographic*, which seeks to map the mind and understand the structure of intelligence.
2   *Computational*, which seeks to understand information-processing programmes and processes underlying intelligence.
3   *Biological*, which attempts to understand how the anatomy, physiology and chemistry of the brain and central nervous system account for intelligence thought through hemispheric localization and neural transmission.
4   *Epistemological*, which attempts to answer the fundamental question of what are the structures of the mind though which all knowledge and mental processes are organized.
5   *Anthropological*, which asks what form intelligence takes as a cultural invention and may be comparative and relativistic.
6   *Sociological*, which examines how social pressures (mediated learning experiences) in development are internalized.
7   *Systems*, which is concerned with how we understand the mind as a system which cross cuts metaphors.

According to Sternberg (1990), researchers in the controversial field of intelligence tend either to be *lumpers* or *splitters*. The former emphasizes that people who tend to do well on one sort of IQ test do well on practically all others. Lumpers talk of general intelligence (g) and see the IQ score (derived, of course, from a good test) as being highly predictive of educational, business and life success. Splitters, on the other hand, tend to be more impressed by different types of intelligences. They note that while being equally bright, some (arts) students are good at words while others (science students) are good at numbers. Splitters have, of course, made very different distinctions. Gardner (1983), for example, talks of seven multiple intelligences, though few researchers in the field recognize these as intelligences:

- *Verbal* or linguistic intelligence (the ability to use words).
- *Logical* or mathematical intelligence (the ability to reason logically, solve number problems).
- *Spatial* intelligence (the ability to find your way around the environment and form mental images).
- *Musical* intelligence (the ability to perceive and create pitch and rhythm).
- *Body-kinetic* intelligence (the ability to carry out motor movement; for example, being a surgeon or a dancer).
- *Interpersonal* intelligence (the ability to understand other people).
- *Intrapersonal* intelligence (the ability to understand oneself and develop a sense of one's own identity).

Another distinction to be been made is that between *fluid* and *crystallized* intelligence (Cattell, 1971b). The analogy is to water – fluid water can take any shape, whereas ice crystals are rigid. Fluid intelligence is effectively the power of reasoning and the processing of information. It includes the ability to perceive relationships, deal with unfamiliar problems and gain new types of knowledge. Crystallized intelligence, on the other hand, consists of acquired skills and specific knowledge in a person's experience. Crystallized intelligence thus includes the skills of an accountant or lawyer, as well as mechanic or salesperson.

Fluid intelligence peaks before 20 and remains constant, with some decline in later years. Crystallized intelligence, on the other hand, continues to increase as long as the person remains active. Thus, a schoolchild is quicker than an old-age pensioner at solving a problem that is unfamiliar to both of them, but even the most average older person will excel at solving problems in his or her previous area of occupational specialization.

In some cases, people try to solve problems by thinking about them in familiar terms – that is, by using crystallized intelligence. Most intelligence tests use both types of intelligence, though there is a clear preference for fluid intelligence tests. Thus, consider the following:

a) Underline which of these numbers does not belong with the others:
   625, 361, 256, 193, 144
b) Underline which of the following towns is the odd one out:
   Oslo, London, New York, Cairo, Bombay, Caracas, Madrid

The former is a measure of fluid, the latter of crystallized, intelligence.

These two types of intelligence are highly correlated, although they are conceptually different. Usually what you have learned (crystallized intelligence) is determined by how well you learn (fluid intelligence). Other factors, like personality, do play a part – introverts like to read, study and learn, while equally bright extroverts like to socialize, have fun and experiment. Introverts who like learning thus often do better at tests of crystallized intelligence. And, self-evidently, motivation is important – a highly motivated adult will learn more efficiently and effectively than an adult less interested in learning. Thus, one good reason to have a measure of crystallized ability is that a tendency to work hard is a good measure of scholastic and business success – and hard work results in better scores in tests of crystallized ability. Another reason is that even short vocabulary tests provide very reliable scores.

With changing technology, the value of crystallized intelligence may be dropping. Crystallized intelligence comes with age and experience. It is a repository of knowledge. But, if that knowledge can be cheaply, accurately and efficiently stored and accessed by computers, by highly fluid intelligence "Young Turks", whence the usefulness of the years of experience? Sceptics might argue that computers could also assist in fluid intelligence problems, thus making that sort of intelligence equally less valuable. Yet, in the business world, it seems to be less and less the case.

Furnham (2001) has argued that it is business CEOs' fluid intelligence, personality and motivation that appear to be the key to success. In a different age, when education came through the apprenticeship system, the value of crystallized intelligence was particularly great. It still is in some sectors. Being a wine-buff, an antiques expert or a skilled musician means long hours devoted to accumulating wisdom.

In the cut and thrust of a quick-changing business, crystallized intelligence is of less use, save, of course, a good memory for how things did not work out in the past. Tomorrow belongs to the quick-witted, agile, fluid thinkers and less to the salty old stalactites and stalagmites, who cling to the cave walls gradually getting bigger.

What is, however, very clear is that despite problems that need to be overcome like potential litigation over test bias, organization psychology can add a great deal by carefully assessing employer and employee intelligence.

The publication of a highly controversial book on intelligence (*The Bell Curve*, Hernstein & Murray, 1994) and passionate although not necessarily well-informed debate led over 50 of the world's experts on intelligence to write to the *Wall Street Journal* on 15 December 1994. Their 25 point summary is an excellent and clear statement on what psychologists think about intelligence:

The Meaning and Measurement of Intelligence

1   Intelligence is a very general mental capability that, among other things, involves the ability to reason, plan, solve problems, think abstractly, comprehend complex ideas, learn quickly and learn from experience. It is not merely book learning, a narrow academic skill, or descriptive of test-taking smarts. Rather, it reflects a broader and deeper capability for comprehending our surroundings – "catching on", "making sense" of things, or "figuring out" what to do.

2   Intelligence, so defined, can be measured, and intelligence tests measure it well. They are among the most accurate (in technical terms, reliable and valid) of all psychological tests and assessments. They do not measure creativity, character,

personality or other important differences among individuals, nor are they intended to.

3 While there are different types of intelligence tests, they all measure the same intelligence. Some use words or numbers and require specific cultural knowledge (such as vocabulary). Others do not, and instead use shapes or designs and require knowledge of only simple, universal concepts (many/few, open/closed, up/down).

4 The spread of people along the IQ continuum, from low to high, can be represented well by the bell curve (in statistical jargon, the "normal curve"). Most people cluster around the average (IQ 100). Few are either very bright or very dull. About 3% of Americans score above IQ 130 (often considered the threshold for "giftedness"), with about the same percentage below IQ 70 (IQ 70–75 often being considered the threshold for mental retardation).

5 Intelligence tests are not culturally biased against African-American or other native-born, English-speaking people in the USA. Rather, IQ scores predict equally accurately for all such Americans, regardless of race and social class. Individuals who do not understand English well can be given either a non-verbal test or one in their native language.

6 The brain processes underlying intelligence are still little understood. Current research looks, for example, at speed of neural transmission, glucose (energy) uptake and electrical activity of the brain.

Group Differences

7 Members of all racial-ethnic groups can be found at every IQ level. The bell curves of different groups overlap considerably, but groups often differ in where their members tend to cluster along the IQ line. The bell curves for some groups (Jews and East Asians) are centred somewhat higher than for whites in general. Other groups (blacks and Hispanics) are centred somewhat lower than non-Hispanic whites.

8 The bell curve for whites is centred roughly around IQ 100; the bell curve for American blacks roughly around IQ 85; and those for different subgroups of Hispanics roughly mid way between those for whites and blacks. The evidence is less definitive for exactly where above IQ 100 the bell curves for Jews and Asians are centred.

Practical Importance

9 IQ is strongly related, probably more so than any other single measurable human trait, to many important educational, occupational, economic and social outcomes. Its relation to the welfare and performance of individuals is very strong in some arenas in life (education, military training), moderate but robust in others (social competence), and modest but consistent in others (law-abidingness). Whatever IQ tests measure, it is of great practical and social importance.

10 A high IQ is an advantage in life because virtually all activities require some reasoning and decision making. Conversely, a low IQ is often a disadvantage, especially in disorganized environments. Of course, a high IQ no more guarantees success than a low IQ guarantees failure in life. There are many exceptions, but the odds for success in our society greatly favour individuals with higher IQs.

11 The practical advantages of having a higher IQ increase as life settings become

more complex (novel, ambiguous, changing, unpredictable or multifaceted). For example, a high IQ is generally necessary to perform well in highly complex or fluid jobs (the professions, management); it is a considerable advantage in moderately complex jobs (crafts, clerical and police work); but it provides less advantage in settings that require only routine decision making or simple problem solving (unskilled work).

12   Differences in intelligence certainly are not the only factor affecting performance in education, training and highly complex jobs (no-one claims they are), but intelligence is often the most important. When individuals have already been selected for high (or low) intelligence and so do not differ as much in IQ, as in graduate school (or special education), other influences on performance loom larger in comparison.

13   Certain personality traits, special talents, aptitudes, physical capabilities, experience and the like are important (sometimes essential) for successful performance in many jobs, but they have narrower (or unknown) applicability or "transferability" across tasks and settings compared with general intelligence. Some scholars choose to refer to these other human traits as other "intelligences".

Source and Stability of Within-Group Differences

14   Individuals differ in intelligence due to differences in both their environments and genetic heritage. Heritability estimates range from .4 to .8 (on a scale from 0 to 1), most thereby indicating that genetics plays a bigger role than does environment in creating IQ differences among individuals. (Heritability is the squared correlation of phenotype with genotype.) If all environments were to become equal for everyone, heritability would rise to 100% because nearly all remaining differences in IQ would necessarily be genetic in origin.

15   Members of the same family also tend to differ substantially in intelligence (by an average of about 12 IQ points) for both genetic and environmental reasons. They differ genetically because biological brothers and sisters share exactly half their genes with each parent and, on average, only half with each other. They also differ in IQ because they experience different environments within the same family.

16   That IQ may be highly heritable does not mean that it is not affected by the environment. Individuals are not born with fixed, unchangeable levels of intelligence (no-one claims they are). IQs do gradually stabilize during childhood, however, and generally change little thereafter.

17   Although the environment is important in creating IQ differences, we do not know yet how to manipulate it to raise low IQs permanently. Whether recent attempts show promise is still a matter of considerable scientific debate.

18   Genetically caused differences are not irremediable (consider diabetes, poor vision and phenylketonuria), nor are environmentally caused ones necessarily remediable (consider injuries, poisons, severe neglect and some diseases). Both may be preventable to some extent.

Source and Stability of Between-Group Differences

19   There is no persuasive evidence that the IQ bell curves for different racial–ethnic groups are converging. Surveys in some years show that gaps in academic achievement have narrowed a bit for some races, ages, school subjects and skill levels, but this picture seems too mixed to reflect a general shift in IQ levels themselves.

20 Racial–ethnic differences in IQ bell curves are essentially the same when youngsters leave high school as when they enter first grade. However, because bright youngsters learn faster than slow learners, these same IQ differences lead to growing disparities in amount learned as youngsters progress from grades one to twelve. As large national surveys in the USA continue to show, black 17-year-olds perform, on average, more like white 13-year-olds in reading, maths and science, with Hispanics in between.

21 The reasons that blacks differ among themselves in intelligence appear to be basically the same as those for why whites (or Asians or Hispanics) differ among themselves. Both environment and genetic heredity are involved.

22 There is no definitive answer to why IQ bell curves differ across racial–ethnic groups. The reasons for these IQ differences between groups may be markedly different from the reasons why individuals differ among themselves within any particular group (whites or blacks or Asians). In fact, it is wrong to assume, as many do, that the reason why some individuals in a population have high IQs but others have low IQs must be the same reason why some populations contain more such high (or low) IQ individuals than others. Most experts believe that environment is important in pushing the bell curves apart, but that genetics could be involved too.

23 Racial–ethnic differences are somewhat smaller but still substantial for individuals from the same socioeconomic backgrounds. To illustrate, black students from prosperous families tend to score higher in IQ than blacks from poor families, but they score no higher, on average, than whites from poor families.

24 Almost all Americans who identify themselves as black have white ancestors – the white admixture is about 20%, on average – and many self-designated whites, Hispanics and others likewise have mixed ancestry. Because research on intelligence relies on self-classification into distinct racial categories, as does most other social science research, its findings likewise relate to some unclear mixture of social and biological distinctions among groups (no-one claims otherwise).

Implications for Social Policy

25 The research findings neither dictate nor preclude any particular social policy, because they can never determine our goals. They can, however, help us estimate the likely success and side-effects of pursuing those goals via different means.

Self-esteem at work

Since the work of Korman (1970), the concept of self-esteem at work as a motivating variable has attracted some attention. The idea is relatively simple: people with self-confidence outperform those without confidence. For instance, Terborg, Richardson & Pritchard (1980) found that self-esteem was highly correlated with effort and the quality and quantity of output. Ellis & Taylor (1983) found that self-esteem was related to the job search process, including the sources individuals used to find jobs, interview evaluations received from organizational recruiters, satisfaction with job search, number of offers received, and acceptance of a job before graduation. Hollenbeck & Whitener (1988) illustrated their point that personality traits can and do predict occupational behaviour by focusing specifically on self-esteem. They argued, following various theoretical tenets, that with ability held constant, self-esteem is related to work motivation and performance only in those situations characterized by high job involvement. They then reviewed various studies that confirm their thesis.

However, there are other, more general studies on self-esteem and employee behaviour. Sullivan (1989) has reviewed the area and suggested that two paradigms govern all self theories – self as active agent, and self as self-concept – and that all theories of motivation can be subsumed. The self as agent relates to many other psychological theories, such as need, balance, equity and expectancy theory, whereas the self as process involves various other theories such as self-reinforcement, self-schema and self-efficacy. Sullivan argued that different motivation theories are predictive for the initiation, direction, intensity, persistence and termination of work behaviour – so rejecting the possibility of a grand theory. Equally, however, he saw self-theories as essential to explanation and prediction of work-related behaviour.

Brockner (1988) argued that employees bring to their work different levels of self-esteem, which correlate with how they act, feel and think while on the job. Everyone needs to feel good about themselves, and much of what we do and believe is concerned with enhancing, preserving and restoring our self-esteem. Brockner notes that, compared with workers with low self-esteem, those with high self-esteem are:

- more apt to work harder in response to negative feedback;
- less likely to imitate the managerial style of their supervisors;
- less likely to perform deferentially as a function of the supportiveness of their workgroup;
- less negatively affected by chronic stressors, such as role ambiguity and conflict, and acute stressors, such as stress and lay-offs;
- more likely to be productive in quality circles.

Brockner recognizes that self-esteem may be both global and specific, and that there is a whole range of related concepts, such as self-confidence and self-assurance. His review of the literature is both comprehensive and fascinating. For instance, self-esteem has been shown to be related to occupational choice. Those high in self-esteem believe that their career is likely to satisfy their desires and that they possess more of the ability in order to succeed than those low in self-esteem. Because people act and think in ways consistent with their self-esteem, those with more self-esteem are more ambitious. Furthermore, the way they search for jobs is likely to be more successful.

People low in self-esteem are usually more susceptible to influence by organizational events than their high self-esteem counterparts. This is because self-esteem is:

- related to social comparisons and uncertainty concerning the correctness of one's beliefs and behaviours;
- related to a greater need for social approval and dependency upon others to provide positive evaluations;
- related to susceptibility to the influence of negative feedback (i.e. more upset by negative comments).

Brockner (1988: 77) notes:

> To illustrate how the cognitions may interrelate and provide further evidence on the plasticity hypothesis, consider the effect of success versus failure feedback on the

subsequent performance of low and high SEs [self-esteems]. Several studies have shown that individuals generally perform better following success than failure. Why might this be so, and especially for low SEs?

1   Expectancies. The effect of the success–failure variable may be to alter workers' expectations for their performance at a subsequent task, such that they approach it far more optimistically following success than failure.
2   Attentional Focus. It is possible that failure induces self-focused attention (whereas success may elicit task-focused attention). Thus, following failure, workers may be more self-focused than subsequent to success, accounting for better performance in the latter than the former condition.
3   Goal Setting. Related to attentional focus above, it is possible that success causes individuals to focus on the task in ways that facilitate performance. For example, prior success may "psychologically free up" the worker to think about strategies for effective performance, which is believed to be one of the mediators of goal-setting effects (Locker *et al.* 1981). Said differently, failure and its resultant self-focused attention probably interferes with workers' abilities to set goals or contemplate strategies to achieve goals.
4   Attribution. It may not merely be the outcome, but rather the attribution for that outcome, that influences subsequent performance. Thus, failure coupled with pessimistic attributions for the failure may cause workers to perform worse than following success.

Any or all of these cognitive mechanisms could mediate the impact of feedback on subsequent performance. Moreover, the plasticity of hypothesis posits that such performance-relevant cognitions are more manipulable among low than high SEs, suggesting that success versus failure feedback may have a greater effect on the subsequent performance of the former than the latter group.

Research findings tend to support the original theory, namely that workers low in self-esteem tend to be more affected by all sorts of organization stimuli, including peer-group interactions, evaluation feedback, socialization practices, leadership behaviours, and so on. More importantly, perhaps, self-esteem has been seen to moderate between such things as lay-offs and performance.

Why personality traits may not predict behaviour at work

The use of personality tests and psychometric testing remains a keenly debated topic (Roberston, 1998; Warr, 1997). Some are concerned specifically with test validity (Barrett, 1998; Warr, 1997) and others with the trends of use of tests in business. Roberston (1998) has argued that European data provide clear evidence that personality is logically, consistently and powerfully related to work behaviours. However, for practitioners he has specific advice: the unfocused (i.e. unthought-out) use of tests is not likely to be of value; only psychometrically valid instruments should be used; candidates do "fake good" in selection assessment testing; personality factors interact and hence one needs to look at the overall profile of individuals; work-related behaviour is determined by both person(ality) and situational (contextual) factors; personality data have clear diagnostic value; but personality data alone are insufficient for most human resource decisions. Few academic researchers would disagree with this. However, how, when and why human resources professionals use tests is quite a different matter. It is dictated much more by comparing policy, the belief of senior managers and the money available for selection and recruitment, rather than on scientific and psychometric criteria.

Most observers believe that personality traits are correlates, indicators or predictors of social behaviour in the workplace or elsewhere. But it is equally true that the diverse and patchy literature is highly equivocal about that relationship, with as many studies indicating a statistically significant relationship as not. Where a theoretically meaningful and statistically significant relationship is found, researchers usually rejoice. But what does one do with no significant findings? Why do personality traits *not* predict occupational behaviour?

The following explanations are not mutually exclusive or rank ordered, but they may explain non-significant findings between measured personality traits and assessed work output (Furnham, 1992):

- There are problems with the theoretical formulation of personality in the first place, in that the personality theory or system has been poorly or inaccurately conceived. Quite simply, the theory is wrong.
- The measurement of the personality trait is poor for a variety of reasons:

    - It measures a single trait which is actually multidimensional and should be measured as such.
    - The measure has poor reliabilities (e.g. Cronbach's alpha, which is a measure of the internal coherence of questionnaires) or is not a valid measure of what is being tested.

- Various systematic errors involved with self-report, such as attributional errors or dissimulators, render the scores meaningless.
- Although the personality measures and theory are satisfactory, there is no reason to suppose that the trait(s) selected actually predict the occupational behaviour specified. That is, the dependent variable (sales figures, appraisal reports) is quite simply, and for good theoretical reasons, not related to the independent variable (e.g. extraversion).
- The measurement of the occupational behaviour (e.g. absenteeism, productivity) is poor for several reasons:

    - Only one or very few measures have been taken, so threatening the reliability of the measure (i.e. no good aggregate measure is used).
    - The occupational behaviour measure is subject to systematic error, whether it is derived by observation, test data or self-report.

- The occupational behaviour is shaped and constrained by other factors more powerful than personality traits. That is, although there is a coherent and consistent relationship between personality and occupational behaviour, other factors such as union agreements, unalterable working conditions and incentive schemes (usually the lack of) suppress or diminish the relationship that actually exists.
- Personality is a moderator variable rather than a direct predictor of occupational behaviour, and thus its force depends on a wide range of other variables (such as social class, intelligence and organizational structure) being present.
- Sampling problems have "washed" out or suppressed the relationship. For example, because of self-selection or rigorous recruitment to many jobs, people

in them are too homogeneous in terms of their personality to show strong findings.
- For practical reasons, it is impossible to sample the occupational behaviour unconstrained by other factors, hence the range is limited and related to other factors.
- Through resignation, sacking and self-selection, people with particular traits inappropriate to a job producing a specific occupational behaviour actually leave, thus reducing the possibility of finding an effect.

Both individuals and organizations change over time; possibly the latter more often and radically than the former. Furthermore, there are different types of fit: person–organization, needs–supplies, demands–abilities (Cable & De Rue, 2002). However, most organizations have to manage change to grow and to develop. This means that any "fit" between an individual and the job he or she does is able to change. Furnham (2001) has argued that four dynamic forces come into play:

1   People *choose* their job and working environments. Personal occupational choice is based on a number of things, such as pay, location, job security and training. It is also a function of personality traits, attitudes and values. This choice is always a matter of balancing various factors that may be implicit or explicit. The organization also makes a choice in the selection process and may well have a number of quite specific criteria like size (minimum height), fitness (not wearing spectacles), skills (literacy, numeracy) or demography (sex, age, education). These criteria might change radically so that one selection cohort may differ radically from another. Furthermore, employees' values and needs may change, making them eager for different things and very responsive to development opportunities. Equally they may deeply resent an organization breaking its implicit contracts and try to change them, which is a protracted and painful experience.
2   People *adapt* to the job they are in. They adapt aspects of their working style to the requisites of the job often quite soon after they start a job. Most organizations attempt through primary socialization (induction, mentoring, training) to mould individual behaviour into the then currently acceptable pattern of work behaviour. They try to adapt workers to the job they are in by specifying the times of day they are required to work, the pace of work, responsiveness to colleagues and customers. Some adaptations are relatively easy, others very difficult because they represent a style of work that may be fairly incompatible with traits. Thus if extraverts trade off accuracy for speed to increase arousal and introverts the precise opposite, it may be very difficult for an extravert to adapt to, say, the requirements of a proof-reader, while introverts may have great difficulty being an auctioneer.
3   People *change* various aspects of the job. Individuals change their physical social environment and personalize many aspects of their working lives. They arrange their personal working space given identical offices or equipment. These changes may be to facilitate better or different working styles or may be little more than an impression management exercise. The less technical, team-based or computerized the work, the more scope people have to change the job to suit their needs, traits and values. Workers can negotiate, earn or unilaterally change the way in which they do the job, which may or may not affect their outputs and that of their colleagues.

4   Jobs themselves *evolve* with new technology, markets and global requirements. Many aspects of a job may change while a person is still in it. Increased automation, the different needs of clients or a change in the market may mean the job has to change.

Butcher also outlined eight factors that influence (often adversely) the validity of psychological assessment in industrial settings:

a.   Invalid response patterns may occur as a result of an individual's fear that management will use the test results against him or her.
b.   The attitudes of local labour organizations may affect the psychological evaluation. The union may actively protest the evaluation, encourage assessments beneficial to the employee, take a more positive, neutral, or negative position, any of which might affect the validity of the evaluation through psychological assessment methods.
c.   For example, it may wish to eliminate candidates for promotion who may not remain in the position long. Factors other than personality variables, such as better pay elsewhere or unpleasant working conditions, may be more powerful determinants of job tenure.
d.   The psychological tests selected should be the most valid available measures of the attributes in question.
e.   Management may have been "oversold" on psychological techniques, and may expect easy categorical answers to complex or unanswerable questions.
f.   The assessment questions may be inappropriate. I was once asked whether it would be possible to use psychological tests to detect the sexual preference of male candidates who would be applying for positions as airline stewards. The managers wanted to reject homosexuals, who, they believed, would "harass the male customers." Clearly, this is an inappropriate (and in many jurisdictions, unlawful) use of personality assessment.
g.   Some aspects of the evaluation may be unwarranted violation of the individual's right to privacy. There must be valid psychological reasons for having the particular information sought in making the assessment.
h.   The report or the recommendations from the assessment must be used properly. (Butcher, 1985: 280–281)

Conclusion

There is no doubt that individual differences (personality traits, ability beliefs or attributions) have an important role in determining behaviour at work. The following questions remain: *Which* of these individual factors are most important? *How* do these factors relate to behaviour at work (i.e. what is the nature of the process)? *What* is the nature of the interaction between these factors? There have been many different approaches to examining the role of individual differences at work, each with its particular limitations, but most research has resulted from the application of established personality theories to the world of work. Less work has been done on ability measures, but there has been a long and continuous interest in biographical correlates of work.

Review studies performed over the past 10 years, which have considered the results of a vast amount of research in the area, show that personality traits (particularly the "Big

Five") do significantly predict a fairly wide range of behaviours in the workplace. The strength of the relationship suggests between 10 and 40% of the variance can be accounted for in terms of these traits alone. However, none dispute that other factors such as ability, as well as organizational constraints and method, inevitably affect performance.

Many people assume that the relationship between personality/ability and performance is linear – more ability, better performance; but it is equally possible that other relationships endure, such as a plateau (once a particular score has been reached, there is no further improvement in performance) or indeed an inverse U (very low *and* very high scores are associated with low performance).

There are many different approaches to this research area. Some personality theorists have dabbled with organizational behavioural variables, and some work psychologists have (in a rather amateurish way) examined how personality traits affect work behaviour. Others have tried to develop a work-personality measure, and those particularly interested in vocational choice have examined the concepts of fit between the ability, style and needs of the person and the task-requirements of the job. The best studies have examined people over time to determine how personality traits and abilities, measured early on in a career, predict organizational behaviour as much as 20 years later.

Personality and ability tests are useful in selection, but there are clearly arguments for and against. There are certainly many to choose from. The theories and measures of Eysenck, Cattell and Costa & McCrae are among the best in the area. Each has associated with it a wealth of studies validating the measure with organizational data. Certainly, the theories are overlapping and the results replicative. All acknowledge the importance of traits such as extraversion, neuroticism and conscientiousness in predicting work behaviour.

There are other theories and measures that are more specific, in conceptualization and predictive usefulness. These, such as the Type A and the Hardy personalities, have proved very useful in predicting susceptibility to work stress.

There is also a long and historical research tradition that favours examining a person's biography rather than their personality. Because it is argued that past experiences are both powerful learning and shaping phenomena, and because the past is the best predictor of the future, researchers have attempted to isolate which specific biographical experiences (number of schools attended, experience in the military, age of first marriage or first mortgage) are indicators of work success or failure. The atheoretical nature of this work, together with the possibility that it is highly discriminatory, means it has drawn strong criticism, but it certainly has its advocates.

Another individual difference factor thought to be particularly important is self-esteem. There is now ample and accumulating evidence to suggest that self-confidence is self-fulfilling and that those with high self-esteem tend to be healthier, happier and more productive at work. Much of the current research, however, has documented the importance of intelligence in predicting many work outcomes.

As we get to know more about the biological and genetic basis of personality, there is increasing evidence that personality is related to job variables thought previously to be almost entirely a function of the environment. Thus, for instance, it seems that personality variables which have known heritabilities are strong predictors of job satisfaction. This led Ilies and Judge (2003) to publish a paper entitled "On the heritability of job satisfaction".

Finally, although personality theorists are eager to demonstrate the importance of individual differences in the workplace, there are many good reasons why so much of the research literature demonstrates so few clear relationships between personality and work-related behaviour.

A research perspective

Personality and distraction at work

Many people work in noisy environments – call centres, shops, open-planned offices, factories, etc. Although fewer people in Europe now work in manufacturing, more work in the service sector, which is often a very distracting environment. There are many visual and verbal distractions, which are often uncontrollable. Yet psychologists have been interested in using such things as music in the workplace to improve productivity. Playing music in the workplace is a tradition dating back to at least the turn of the century, when music was used primarily in an attempt to relieve tedium and boredom. Early research into the effects of music in the workplace suggested that "easy listening" (which was sometimes termed "industrial music") was most appropriate for routine activities, as it helped to relieve tension and boredom associated with these types of tasks. Smith (1961) found evidence for this in the attitudes of key-punch operators listening to music during break periods between complex mental activities. It was shown that attitudes to the music were universally positive; all operators wanted the music to be a permanent feature in their office and 90% said they were happier when the music was playing. However, the music had no significant effect on task performance.

There have been inconsistencies in the results of studies looking into the effects of music on task performance, as opposed to perception. In a review of research in this area, Uhlbrock (1961) noted that most factory workers preferred to work where music was played rather than where it was not played; however, not all workers liked music while they worked, with between 1 and 10% being annoyed by it. Furthermore, music can have adverse effects on the output of individual employees (Furnham & Bradley, 1997).

Early studies focused specifically on how background stimulation affected the nature of the task. Others have focused on the nature of the distraction. Furnham and Allass (1999) studied the effects of complex and simple music, as rated on factors such as tempo, repetition, melodic complexity and instrumental layering, and noted that there was no significant effect of musical complexity on performance. However, in a similar vein, Kiger (1989) found that scores in a reading comprehension test were significantly higher in a "low information-load music" condition than either a silent condition or a "high information-load music" condition, where "information load" was measured by tonal range, repetition and rhythmic complexity.

Other studies have focused on individual differences and the interaction of personality and environmental factors. Eysenck's (1967b) theory of personality holds individual variation in cortical arousal as its central issue. Eysenck argued that introverted individuals have a lower optimum cortical arousal level than extraverted individuals, whose optimum arousal level is high. Introverts and extraverts differ in the amount of externally derived stimulation that they require to reach their optimum point of arousal. Due to their lower neurological threshold of arousal, introverts do not need as much external stimulation to reach their optimum level of functioning and so are satisfied at much lower intensities of stimulation. If they are subjected to stimulation which pushes them over their optimum functioning threshold, introverts experience an inhibition of excitation and become aversive to the over-stimulating environment; their performance on a task will deteriorate. Those individuals classified as extraverts need more external stimulation to reach their optimum functioning level and this encourages them actively to seek out stimulation in the environment. Introverts are significantly more likely to choose to study in a quiet area of the library away from noise and activity, whereas extraverts consciously seek out busier study areas which provide the opportunity for social interaction.

Furthermore, introverts and extraverts have been shown to differ in their habits when it comes to studying to music, with extraverts choosing to listen to music while studying on more occasions than introverts (Furnham & Bradley, 1997), and extraverts reporting studying twice as often (50% of the time) as introverts (25% of the time) in the presence of music (Daoussis & McKelvie, 1986).

Furnham, Gunter and Peterson (1994) examined the distracting effects of television on cognitive processing. Both extraverts and introverts performed better in silence, but the extraverts performed better than the introverts in the presence of television distraction. This result was attributed to the television drawing on cognitive resources required for the reading comprehension.

Morgenstern *et al.* (1974) found that extraverts tended to perform better in the presence of a distracter than in silence, whereas introverts functioned less efficiently in its presence. Participants were required to attend to, and remember, specific words from a list read to them, either in silence or while being distracted by German or English words, or distortions of these. The detrimental effects of distraction on short-term memory varied as a function of extraversion, where the most extraverted participants remembered more words when distractions were present than when in silence. The most introverted individuals, however, remembered fewer words while being distracted.

Other studies have looked at music as the distracter. Furnham and Bradley (1997) found that, in the presence of pop music songs separated by a male voice, scores on a reading comprehension test and scores on a delayed recall short-term memory test were significantly reduced for introverts and significantly increased for extraverts. In an investigation into the effects of complex and simple music (as rated on factors such as instrumental layering and tonal complexity) compared with silence, Furnham and Allass (1999) found that there was a marked (yet non-significant) trend for the performance of introverts to deteriorate with music, and for this performance to deteriorate further as the complexity of the music increased. Extraverts, on the other hand, showed improvement in performance as the complexity of the music increased, with the most superior performance being seen in the complex music condition. These studies provide support for Eysenck's theory of personality. However, Furnham, Trew and Sneade (1999b) did not find significant interactions, although the trend was in the predicted direction.

These, and related findings, led Furnham (2001) to state that it is important to remember that personality variables act not only as main effects, but often more powerfully in *interaction* with other variables. Three quite distinct types of variables can be distinguished: *individual difference* variables (e.g. abilities, beliefs, traits and values); *situational variables* (e.g. corporate culture, group norms, physical context); and *work-outcome* or *task-related* variables (e.g. productivity, satisfaction, supervisor ratings, absenteeism). The early literature focused on person × situation interactions but often did not take sufficient cognisance of the possibility of a three-way interaction.

A cross-cultural perspective

The expatriate manager

There are many reasons why organizations of all sorts and sizes are thinking about sending managers abroad. These include:

- An increase in world trade, and multinational and global organizations.
- The globalization of market competition, more international mergers and acquisitions, and joint ventures, which have increased the need for coordination of international activities.

- Managers themselves and human resources professionals see international assignments as excellent opportunities for personal growth and promotion.

There are various reasons for individuals volunteering and organizations justifying sending people on international assignments.

There is, of course, a cost to some managers and their families, namely culture shock. But as Furnham & Bochner (1986) have pointed out, compared with many others business people are less likely to experience adverse effects. They list eight possible reasons for this:

- Business people are usually posted elsewhere for a set, specific and relatively short period of time. Hence, they may see their move as relatively temporary and not requiring much adaptation and change.
- Businessmen and businesswomen are posted abroad for a specific purpose, usually to deal with particular technical and managerial problems. This is not to say that the problems are simple – indeed, they are often complex and highly intractable – but rather that their problems are confined to work. They do not, as a rule, have to worry about transportation, accommodation and other domestic problems. Students and migrants, on the other hand, often have a great many personal and logistical problems in addition to any difficulties they might face at college or work.
- Business people have strong sponsorship. Many are given financial incentives for working abroad and often their lifestyle overseas is an improvement on what they have left behind. Furthermore, the sponsorship may not only be financial, but may include social and political benefits that increase rather than decrease a person's social standing, political power and influence in the new society.
- A tour abroad often increases opportunities for advancement on return. Whereas this may be true of students, it is less certain for them. Indeed, many business people travel specifically to enhance their chances for promotion. Hence, any hardships on the trip may be seen as a small price to pay for the rewards to be gained later.
- In contrast to students (and some migrants), business people tend to be older and are usually more mature. Although the literature is equivocal on this point, it is generally the case that older, more experienced people cope better with the problems of international removals.
- Businesses often provide accommodation enclaves, "old-hand" guides and a social-support network that insulate the foreigner against the initial difficulties and surprises of relocation. However, the long-term benefits associated with these "ghettos" are debatable.
- Because businesses are primarily interested in the work their employees do, the employees' time is carefully structured and scheduled. This, as unemployment researchers have shown, is directly related to a reduction in mental illness.
- The social relationships both inside and outside the workplace are probably more likely to be on an equal footing for business people than for students. Such equal-status peer-group interaction probably goes some way in accounting for the relatively better adjustment of business people than that of students, whose social relationships are more often asymmetrical with respect to status. There are, therefore, practical reasons why business travel is not as stressful as students' sojourning or migration.

A human resources perspective

Selecting high-flyers

There is a great deal of interest in the early identification of high-flyers at work – that is, people with executive potential who may excite. In one of the few studies in the area, Spreitzer, McCall and Mahoney (1997) identified empirically 14 dimensions classified under two headings:

Scale	Sample item
	End-state competency dimensions
1. Sensitive to cultural differences	When working with people from others cultures, works hard to understand their perspectives
2. Business knowledge	Has a solid understanding of our products and services
3. Courage to take a stand	Is willing to take a stand on issues
4. Brings out the best in people	Has a special talent for dealing with people
5. Acts with integrity	Can be depended on to tell the truth regardless of circumstances
6. Is insightful	Is good at identifying the most important part of a complex problem or issue
7. Is committed to success	Clearly demonstrates commitment to seeing the organization succeed
8. Takes risks	Takes personal as well as business risks
	Learning–oriented dimensions
9. Uses feedback	Has changed as a result of feedback
10. Is culturally adventurous	Enjoys the challenge of working in countries other than his or her own
11. Seeks opportunities to learn	Takes advantages of opportunities to do new things
12. Is open to criticism	Appears brittle – as if criticism might cause him or her to break
13. Seeks feedback	Pursues feedback even when others are reluctant to give it
14. Is flexible	Doesn't get so invested in things that he or she cannot change when something doesn't work

High-flyers, however, do fail and derail. Furnham (2003) identified the Icarus syndrome associated with derailment. The war for talent continues. The illusive high-flyers appear in short supply. Is the pool of these highly competent, creative, motivated, entrepreneurial, committed, innovative, stress-resistant people drying up? The problem is not only where to find these "wunder-kinds" but also how to manage them. "Creative" high-flyers are paradoxically delicate creatures who need careful nurturance. A common problem with high-flyers is that they fly too high too soon. Indeed, they are prone to the Icarus syndrome.

Icarus was the son of the inventor Daedulus in the Greek myth. Both got locked up by the Cretan King Minos, but to escape the talented and inventive Daedulus made them both wings of feathers and wax. The wise father told his son the only "design fault" was that the wings might melt if he flew too close to the sun. Clearly the physics of the ancient Greek storytellers was not too good, as the higher one flies the cooler (not the hotter) it gets. But Icarus ignored the good advice of his wise father, flew too high and due to melting of his wings crashed into the sea and drowned.

It is not clear from the myth precisely why he disobeyed his father. Was he a sensation-seeker prone to accidents and did it out of boredom? Was he a disobedient child who liked to rebel? Was he simply "cocking-a-snoop" at King Minos and beguiled by his own hubris? Was he a narcissist having passed out top of the self-esteem class of life? We do not know. Indeed, it is the function both of myths and case studies that they allow for multiple interpretations. But the modern derailed high-flyer bears a canny resemblance to Icarus. But how and why are they chosen? What did the assessors miss? Or was the problem in the way they were managed?

It was probably a self-esteem problem or, to use another good Greek word (and legend), narcissism. Narcissism is malignant self-love; over-bearing self-confidence; inexplicably high self-esteem. The problem for the high-flyer is this: you probably need a great deal of self-esteem to get the job, but you need to lose some of it while on the job.

The manifestation of too much, as well as too little, self-esteem can be both a cause and a consequence of management failure. The Americans have long believed in the power and importance of self-esteem, which partly explains their self-confidence and assertiveness. It is often surprising to see young people in particular of very average ability look so manifestly confident. They appear all to have passed "Assertiveness 101" but failed "Charm 101", telling you openly and frankly about their beliefs, problems, wishes and values, as if they deserve automatic respect or are fascinating on the topic. They express little interest in others, believing they are intrinsically interesting, important and love-worthy.

The self-esteem industry believes that all sorts of nasty consequences follow low self-esteem: failure at school, delinquency, unemployment, crime, depression, and so on. And yet we rather like the self-effacing compared with the arrogant.

Of course, one should clearly distinguish between the genuine and the fake article. There are those who are genuinely humble and meek, believing that their ability and contribution are somehow pretty average, even unworthy. The trouble with humility is that one can easily be abused by those with hubris, and be trodden upon. There is, however, deep within Anglo-Saxon culture a respect for the amateur, self-effacing person who with sheer talent wins through. It's the story of the hare and the tortoise, David and Goliath, and the victory of the humble and the meek, who shall inherit the earth. Part of the appeal of the film *Chariots of Fire* depicted just an alliance.

But people with low self-esteem seldom get into positions of power. Low self-esteem prevents risk-taking, bold decision-making, opportunism and openness to excitement and challenges, which are the stuff of success in business. We all need enough self-respect for healthy day-to-day functioning. We need to be sufficiently interested in, and confident about, ourselves to function well in the cut and thrust of business life.

It is those with seeming limitless self-esteem and concomitant hubris that are the real problem. But extreme narcissists are a hazard and not that uncommon among our captains of industry. They are often people completely preoccupied with being superior, unique or special. They shamelessly exaggerate their talents and indulge in addictively boastful and pretentious self-aggrandisement. They are often mildly amusing but narcissists often possess extremely vindictive characteristics.

The psychological interpretation of unnaturally high levels of narcissism is essentially compensatory. Many business narcissists believe they have been fundamentally wronged in the past and that they are "owed". Their feelings of internal insecurity can be satisfied by regular adulation, affirmation and recognition. They yearn for a strong positive self-image to combat their real feeling of helplessness and low self-esteem.

One of the most frequently observed characteristics of the narcissist is capriciousness – inconsistent, erratic, unpredictable behaviour. Naturally, most psychologists see the origins of narcissistic behaviour in early childhood: the inconsistent parent (care-giver) who was attentive to all outward, public signs of achievement and success, but blind to and ignorant of (or worse, disapproving of) the child's personal feelings. Perhaps, then, we should blame Daedulus for Icarus's plight!

This inconsistency often leads to the young adult being confused and never developing a clear sense of who they are or establishing a coherent value system. They are "not comfortable in their own skin". This can and does result in a lifelong compensatory quest for full self-regard and self-assertion. The wells of the origin of the problem are both deep and murky, and the passions they engender appear remorseless.

The narcissist is quite plainly dysfunctional. He or she fails to understand or appreciate others, be they colleagues, subordinates or clients. They often see people as sort of possessions whose major function is as an accessory to their pursuit of fame and glory. People at work are used to reflect in their glory. Do any of our current or past great business figures spring to mind at this point?

Personal and work relationships for narcissists are particularly interesting. If the narcissist's "other half" is prepared to offer continual, unconditional, even escalatory admiration, all is well. But they have to direct all their efforts, all the time, to minister to the needs of their master to overcome the inner emptiness and worthlessness he or she is experiencing. Naturally, narcissists search them out because they are rare, probably equally dysfunctional, people labelled appropriately as "complementary narcissists". They are comple(i)mentary in both senses of the word.

Many high-flyers, like Icarus, are narcissists. Indeed, they find that their narcissism serves them well. They appear confident and give others confidence. What happens to high-flyers is this: their strengths are noticed and they are fast-streamed. Whichever part of the organization they work in they tend to excel. If they are in marketing, they tend to be ideas and action men; resourceful and imaginative. If they are in finance, they tend to be brilliant not only with figures but strategic planning. They love number tumbling and "modelling the future".

But they tend to be forgiven in their faults, which are overlooked. The fact that high-flying marketing executives are undisciplined, inconsistent, poor at paperwork and egocentric is ignored and downplayed. They can be unrealistic, impractical and spend-thrift. Similarly, analytic strategists may be prone to analysis paralysis; unable to influence others and prone to building up large departments of like-minded types almost like a university department.

High-flyers like Icarus zoom ahead with company blessing. But their flaws, the wax wings, get noticed too late. That for which they are famous soon becomes that for which they become infamous. Known for their integrity, they can suddenly be seen as rigid, intolerant zealots. Known for their people skills, they can be labelled soft, indecisive, too tolerant of poor performance.

Alas, the very characteristics which helped one climb the greasy ladder to the top leads to the downfall. Irony? Poetic justice? No . . . just bad selection and management. And one wonders why Icarus was locked up in the first place.

References

Arvey, R., McGowen, S., & Hogan, D. (1981). *The use of experience requirements in selecting employees*. Unpublished paper, Department of Psychology, University of Georgia, Athens, GA.

Baehr, M., & Williams, G. (1968). Underlying dimensions of personal background data and their relationship to occupational classification. *Journal of Applied Psychology, 51*, 481–490.

Baron, J. (1985). What kinds of intelligence components are fundamental? In J. W. Segal, S. F. Chipman, R. Glaser (Eds.), *Thinking and learning skills, Vol. 2: Research and open questions* (pp. 365–390). London: Lawrence Erlbaum Associates.

Barrick, M., & Mount, M. (1991). The "Big 5" personality dimensions and job performance: A meta-analysis. *Personnel Psychology, 44*, 1–25.

Barrick, M., Stewart, G., & Piotrowski, M. (2002). Personality and job performance. *Journal of Applied Psychology, 87*, 43–51.

Bartram, D., & Dale, H. (1982). The Eysenck personality inventory as a selection test for military pilots. *Journal of Occupational Psychology, 55*, 287–296.

Begley, T., & Boyd, D. (1985). The relationship of the Jenkins Activity Survey to Type A behaviour among business executives. *Journal of Vocational Behaviour, 27*, 316–328.

Bishop, D., & Jean-Renaud, G. (1976). End-of-day mood on work and leisure days in relation to extroversion, neuroticism, and amount of change in daily activities. *Canadian Journal of Behavioural Science, 8*, 388–400.

Block, J. (1995). A contrarian view of the five-factor approach to personality description. *Psychological Bulletin, 117*, 187–215.

Bluen, S., Barling, J., & Burns, W. (1990). Predicting sales performance, job satisfaction, and depression using the achievement striving and impatient–irritability dimensions of Type A behaviour. *Journal of Applied Psychology, 75*, 212–216.

Blumenthal, J., McKee, D., Haney, T., & Williams, R. (1980). Task incentives, Type A behaviour pattern, and verbal problem solving performance. *Journal of Applied Social Psychology, 10*, 101–114.

Blunt, P. (1978). Personality characteristics of a group of White South African managers. *International Journal of Psychology, 13*, 139–146.

Brewin, C. (1988). *Cognitive foundations of clinical psychology*. London: Lawrence Erlbaum Associates.

Brockner, J. (1988). *Self-esteem at work: Research, theory and practice*. Lexington, MA: Lexington Books.

Buchholz, R. (1976). Measurement of beliefs. *Human Relations, 29*, 1177–1188.

Buel, W. (1964). Voluntary female clerical turnover: The concurrent and predictive validity of a weighted application blank. *Journal of Applied Psychology, 48*, 180–182.

Butcher, J. (1985). Personality assessment in industry: Theoretical issues and illustrations. In H. Bernardin & D. Bownas (Eds.), *Personality assessment in organizations* (pp. 277–309). New York: Praeger.

Cable, D., & De Rue, D. (2002). The convergent and discriminant validity of subjective fit perceptions. *Journal of Applied Psychology, 87*, 875–884.

Campbell, J., McCloy, R., Oppler, S., & Sager, L. (1993). A theory of performance. In N. Schmitt & W. Borman (Eds.), *Personnel selection in organizations* (pp. 35–70). San Francisco, CA: Jossey-Bass.

Cascio, W. (1976). Turnover biographical data, and fair employment practice. *Journal of Applied Psychology, 61*, 576–580.

Cattell, R. (1971a). *The scientific analysis of personality*. Harmondsworth: Penguin.

Cattell, R. (1971b). *Abilities: Their structure, growth and action*. New York: Houghton-Mifflin.

Cattell, R., Eber, H., & Tatsuoka, M. (1970). *Handbook for the 16PF questionnaire*. Champaign, IL: IPAT.

Chesney, M., & Rosenman, R. (1980). Type A behaviour in the work setting. In C. Cooper & R. Payne (Eds.), *Current concerns in occupational stress* (pp. 187–212). Chichester: Wiley.

Christie, M., & Venables, P. (1973). Mood changes in reaction to age, EPI scores, time and day. *British Journal of Social and Clinical Psychology, 12*, 61–72.

Chusmir, L., & Hood, J. (1988). Predictive characteristics of Type A behaviour among working men and women. *Journal of Applied Social Psychology, 18*, 688–698.

Cook, J., Hepworth, S., Wall, T. & Warr, P. (1981). *The experience of work*. London: Academic Press.

Cook, M. (1988). *Personnel selection and productivity*. Chichester: Wiley.

Cooper, R., & Payne, R. (1967). Extroversion and some aspects of work behaviour. *Personnel Psychology, 20*, 45–47.

Costa, P. T., & McCrae, R. R. (1985). *The NEO personality inventory*. Odessa, FL: Psychological Assessment Resources.

Costa, P. T., & McCrae, R. R. (1987). *Your NEO summary*. Odessa, FL: Psychological Assessment Resources.

Costa, P. T., & McCrae, R. R. (1995). Solid ground in the wetlands of personality: A reply to Block. *Psychological Bulletin, 117*, 216–220.

Daoussis, L., & McKelvie, S. (1986). Musical preferences and effects of music on a reading comprehension test for extraverts and introverts. *Perceptual and Motor Skills, 62*, 283–289.

Day, D. V., & Silverman, S. B. (1989). Personality and job performance: Evidence of incremental validity. *Personnel Psychology, 42*, 25–36.

De Fruyt, F., & Salgado, J. (2003). Applied personality psychology: Lessons learned from the IWO field. *European Journal of Personality, 17*, 123–131.

Digman, J. (1990). Personality structure: Emergence of the five-factor model. *Annual Review of Psychology, 41*, 417–440.

Dollinger, S. J., & Orf, L. A. (1991). Personality and performance in "personality": Conscientiousness and openness. *Journal of Research in Personality, 25*, 276–284.

Drasgow, F. (2003). Intelligence and the workplace. In W. Borman, D. Ilgen, & R. Klemoski (Eds.), *Handbook of psychology* (Vol. 12, pp. 107–130). New York: Wiley.

Dunnette, S., & Maetzold, S. (1955). Use of a weighted application blank in hiring seasonal employees. *Journal of Applied Psychology, 39*, 308–310.

Eberhardt, B., & Muchinsky, P. (1982). An empirical investigation of the factor stability of Owen's biographical questionnaire. *Journal of Applied Psychology, 67*, 130–145.

Ellis, R., & Taylor, M. (1983). Role of self-esteem within the job search process. *Journal of Applied Psychology, 68*, 632–640.

Eysenck, H. (1967a). Personality patterns in various groups of businessmen. *Occupational Psychology, 41*, 249–250.

Eysenck, H. (1967b). *The biological basis of personality*. Springfield, IL: Thomas.

Eysenck, H. (1992). Four ways, five factors are *not* basic. *Personality and Individual Differences, 13*, 667–674.

Eysenck, H., & Eysenck, M. (1985). *Personality and individual differences: A natural science approach*. London: Plenum Press.

Eysenck, H., & Wilson, G. (1983). *Know your own personality*. Harmondsworth: Penguin.

Fagerström, K., & Lisper, H. (1977). Effects of listening to car radio, experience and personality of driver on subsidiary reaction time and heart rate in a long term driving task. In R. Machie (Ed.), *Vigilance* (pp. 81–97). New York: Plenum Press.

Fleishman, E., & Quaintance, M. (1984). *Taxonomies of human performance*. Orlando, FL: Academic Press.

Friedman, M., & Rosenman, R. (1974). *Type A behaviour and your heart*. New York: Knopf.

Furnham, A. (1990). *The Protestant work ethic*. London: Routledge.

Furnham, A. (1991). Personality and occupational success: 16PF correlates of cabin crew performance. *Personality and Individual Differences, 12*, 87–90.

Furnham, A. (1992). Personality and learning style: A study of three instruments. *Personality and Individual Differences, 13*, 429–430.

Furnham, A. (1994). *Personality at work*. London: Routledge.

Furnham, A. (1995). The relationship of personality and intelligence to cognitive learning styles and achievement. In O. Saklofske & M. Zeidner (Eds.), International handbook of personality and intelligence (pp. 397–413). New York: Plenum Press.

Furnham, A. (1996). The FIRO-B, the learning style questionnaire, and the five-factor model. *Journal of Social Behaviour and Personality, 11*, 285–299.

Furnham, A. (2001). Vocational preference and P–O fit. *Applied Psychology, 50*, 5–29.

Furnham, A. (2003). *The incomplete manager*. London: Whurr Publishers.

Furnham, A., Allass, K. (1999). The influence of musical distraction on the cognitive performance of extraverts and introverts. *European Journal of Personality, 13*, 27–38.

Furnham, A., & Bochner, S. (1986). *Culture shock*. London: Routledge.

Furnham, A., Borovoy, A., & Henley, S. (1986). Type A behaviour pattern: The recall of positive personality and self-evaluation. *British Journal of Medical Psychology, 59*, 365–374.

Furnham, A., & Bradley, A. (1997). Music while you work: The differential distraction of background music on the cognitive test performance of introverts and extraverts. *Applied Cognitive Psychology, 11*, 445–455.

Furnham, A., & Cheng, H. (1996). Psychiatric symptomology on the recall of positive and negative personality information. *Behaviour Research and Therapy, 34*, 731–733.

Furnham, A., Forde, L., & Ferrari, K. (1999a). Personality and work motivation. *Personality and Individual Differences, 26*, 1035–1043.

Furnham, A., Gunter, B., & Peterson, E. (1994). Television distraction and the performance of introverts and extraverts. *Applied Cognitive Psychology, 8*, 705–711.

Furnham, A., Petrides, K., Jackson, C., & Cottr, T. (2002). Do personality factors predict job satisfaction. *Personality and Individual Differences, 33*, 1325–1342.

Furnham, A., Sadka, V., & Brewin, C. (1992). The development of an occupational attribution style questionnaire. *Journal of Occupational Behaviour, 13*, 27–39.

Furnham, A., & Steele, H. (1993). Measuring locus of control. *British Journal of Psychology, 84*, 443–479.

Furnham, A., & Stringfield, P. (1993). Personality and occupational behaviour. *Human Relations, 46*, 827–848.

Furnham, A., Trew, K., & Sneade, I. (1999b). The distracting effects of vocal and instrumental music on the cognitive test performance of introverts and extraverts. *Personality and Individual Differences, 27*, 381–393.

Gardner, H. (1983). *Frames of mind*. New York: Basic Books.

Goldberg, L. R. (1990). An alternative "description of personality": The Big-Five factor structure. *Journal of Personality and Social Psychology, 59*, 1216–1229.

Goldberg, L. (1992). The development of markers for the big-five factor structure. *Psychological Assessment, 4*, 26–42.

Goldsmith, D. (1922). The use of the personal history blank as a salesmanship test. *Journal of Applied Psychology, 6*, 149–155.

Goldstein, I. (1971). The applications blank: How honest are the responses? *Journal of Applied Psychology, 55*, 491–492.

Gordon, F., & Fitzgibbons, W. (1982). Empirical test of the validity of seniority as a factor in staffing decisions. *Journal of Applied Psychology, 67*, 311–319.

Gunter, B., Furnham, A., & Drakeley, R. (1993). *Biodata*. London: Methuen.

Hansen, C. (1989). A causal model of the relationship among accidents, biodata, personality, and cognitive factors. *Journal of Applied Psychology, 74*, 81–90.

Helmes, E. (1989). Evaluating the internal structure of the Eysenck personality questionnaire: Objective criteria. *Multivariate Behavioural Research, 24*, 353–364.

Hernstein, R., & Murray, C. (1994). *The bell curve*. New York: Free Press.

Herzberg, F., Mausner, B., & Snyderman, B. (1959). *The motive to work*. New York: Wiley.

Hogan, J., & Holland, B. (2003). Using theory to evaluate personality and job-performance relations. *Journal of Applied Psychology, 88*, 100–112.

Hollenbeck, J., & Whitener, E. (1988). Reclaiming personality traits for personnel selection: Self-esteem as an illustrative case. *Journal of Management, 14*, 81–91.

Hooker, K., Blumenthal, J., & Siegler, I. (1987). Relationship between motivation and hostility among Type A and Type B middle-aged men. *Journal of Research and Personality, 21*, 103–113.

Hough, L. M. (1992). The "Big Five" personality variable construct confusion: Description versus prediction. *Human Performance, 5*, 139–155.

Hough, L. M. (1996). Personality at work: Issues and evidence. In M. D. Hakel (Ed.), *Beyond multiple choice: Evaluating alternatives to traditional testing for selection* (pp. 52–65). Hillsdale, NJ: Lawrence Erlbaum Associates.

Hough, L. M. (2001). I owe its advance to personality. In B. Roberts & R. Hogan (Eds.), *Personality psychology in the work-place* (pp. 19–49). Washington, DC: American Psychological Association.

Hough, L. M., Eaton, N. L., Dunnette, M. D., Kamp, J. D., & McCloy, R. A. (1990). Criterion-related validities of personality constructs and the effects of response distortion on these validities. *Journal of Applied Psychology, 75*, 581–595.

Hough, L. M., & Furnham, A. (2003). Use of personality variables in work settings. In W. Borman, O. Ilgen, & R. Klimoski (Eds.), *Handbook of psychology* (Vol.12, pp.131–169). New York: Wiley.

Hough, L. M., & Schneider, R. J. (1996). Personality trait, taxonomies, and applications in organizations. In K. R. Murphy (Ed.), *Individual differences and behavior in organizations* (pp. 31–88). San Francisco, CA: Jossey-Bass.

Howard, J., Cunningham, D., & Rechnitzer, P. (1986). Role ambiguity, Type A behaviour, and job satisfaction. *Journal of Applied Psychology, 71*, 95–101.

Hunter, J., & Hunter, R. (1984). Validity and utility of alternative predictors of job performance. *Psychological Bulletin, 96*, 72–98.

Hurtz, G., & Donovan, J. (2000). Personality and job performance. *Journal of Applied Psychology, 85*, 869–879.

Ilies, R., & Judge, T. (2002). Understanding the dynamic relationships among personality, mood and job satisfaction. *Organizational Behaviour and Human Decision Processes, 89*, 1119–1139.

Ilies, R., & Judge, T. (2003). On the heredability of job satisfaction. *Journal of Applied Psychology, 88*, 750–759.

Jessup, G., & Jessup, H. (1971). Validity of the Eysenck personality inventory in pilot selection. *Occupational Psychology, 45*, 111–123.

John, O. (1989). Towards a taxonomy of personality descriptors. In D. Buss & N. Canter (Eds.), *Personality psychology: Recent trends and emerging directions* (pp. 261–271). New York: Springer.

Judge, T., Heller, D., & Mount, M. (2002). Five-factor model of personality and employee absence. *Journal of Applied Psychology, 87*, 530–541.

Judge, T., & Ilies, R. (2002). Relationship of personality to performance motivation. *Journal of Applied Psychology, 87*, 797–807.

Judge, T., Martocchio, J., & Thoresen, C. (1997). Five-factor model of personality and employee absence. *Journal of Applied Psychology, 82*, 745–755.

Kanfer, R., Warberg, C., & Kantrowitz, R. (2001). Job search and employment. *Journal of Applied Psychology, 88*, 750–759.

Keinan, G., Friedland, N., Yitzhaky, J., & Moran, A. (1981). Biographical, physiological, and personality variables as predictors of performance under sickness-inducing motion. *Journal of Applied Psychology, 66*, 233–241.

Kiger, D. M. (1989). Effects of music information load on a reading comprehension task. *Perceptual and Motor Skills, 69*, 531–543.

Kim, J. (1980). Relationships of personality to perceptual and behavioural responses in stimulating and non-stimulating tasks. *Academy of Management Journal, 23*, 307–319.

Kirton, M., & Mulligan, G. (1973). Correlates of managers' attitudes toward change. *Journal of Applied Psychology, 58*, 101–107.

Kline, P. (1978). *OOQ and OPQ personality tests*. Windsor: NFER.

Kobasa, S. (1979). Stressful life events, personality, health: An enquiry into hardiness. *Journal of Personality and Social Psychology, 37*, 1–11.

Korman, A. (1970). Toward a hypothesis of work behaviour. *Journal of Applied Psychology, 54*, 31–41.

Lautenschlager, G., & Schaffer, G. (1987). Re-examining the components and stability of Owen's biographical questionnaire. *Journal of Applied Psychology, 72*, 149–152.

Loo, R. (1979). Role of primary personality factors in the perception of traffic signs and driver violations and accidents. *Accident Analysis and Prevention, 11*, 125–127.

Maslow, A. (1954). *Motivation and personality*. New York: Harper.

Matteson, M., Ivancevich, J., & Smith, S. (1984). Relation of Type A behaviour to performance and satisfaction among sales personnel. *Journal of Vocational Behaviour, 25*, 203–214.

Matthews, G., & Oddy, K. (1993). Recovery of major personality dimensions from trait objective data. *Personality and Individual Differences, 15*, 419–431.

Matthews, G., & Stanton, N. (1994). Item and scale factor analysis of the Occupational Personality Questionnaire. *Personality and Individual Differences, 16*, 733–743.

Matthews, G., Stanton, N., Graham, N., & Brinelow, C. (1990). A factor analysis of the scales of the occupational personality questionnaire. *Personality and Individual Differences, 11*, 591–596.

McCrae, R., & John, O. (1992). An introduction to the five-factor model and its applications. *Journal of Personality, 60*, 175–215.

McDaniel, M. (1989). Biographical constructs for predicting employee suitability. *Journal of Applied Psychology, 74*, 964–970.

Messick, S. (Ed.) (1976). *Individuality and learning*. San Francisco, CA: Jossey-Bass.

Messick, S. (1984). The nature of cognitive styles: Problems and promise in educational practice. *Educational Psychologist, 19*, 59–74.

Messick, S. (1994). The matter of style: Manifestations of personality in cognition, learning and teaching. *Educational Psychologist, 29*, 121–136.

Metcalfe, B. (1987). Male and female managers: An analysis of biographical and self-concept data. *Work and Stress, 1*, 207–219.

Mettlin, C. (1976). Occupational careers and the prevention of coronary prone behaviour. *Social Science and Medicine, 10*, 367–372.

Miller, T. (1991). The psychotherapeutic utility of the five-factor model of personality. *Journal of Personality Assessment, 57*, 415–433.

Mitchell, T., & Klimoski, R. (1982). Is it rational to be empirical? A test of methods for scoring biographical data. *Journal of Applied Psychology, 67*, 411–458.

Morgenstern, F., Hodgson, R., & Law, L. (1974). Work efficiency and personality: A comparison of introverted and extroverted subjects exposed to conditions of distraction and distortion of stimulus in a learning task. *Ergometrics, 17*, 211–220.

Mosel, J. (1952). Prediction of department stores sales performance from personal data. *Journal of Applied Psychology, 36*, 8–10.

Mount, M., & Barrick, M. (1995). The big five personality dimensions. *Research in Personnel and Human Resources Management, 13*, 153–200.

Nevo, B. (1976). Using biographical information to predict success of men and women in the army. *Journal of Applied Psychology, 61*, 106–108.

Niener, A., & Owens, W. (1982). Relationships between two sets of biodata with 7 years' separation. *Journal of Applied Psychology, 67*, 146–150.

Nikolaou, I., & Robertson, I. (2001). The Five-Factor model of personality and work behaviour in Greece. *European Journal of Work and Organizational Psychology, 10*, 161–186.

Ones, D. S., & Viswesvaran, C. (2000). Personality at work: Criterion-focused occupational personality scales (COPS) used in personnel selection. In B. W. Roberts & R. Hogan (Eds.), *Applied personality psychology: The intersection of personality and I/O psychology* (pp. 63–92). Washington, DC: American Psychological Association.

Ones, D. S., Viswesvaran, C., & Schmidt, F. L. (1993). Comprehensive meta-analysis of integrity test validities. *Journal of Applied Psychology Monograph, 78*, 679–703.

Ones, D. S., Viswesvaran, C., & Schmidt, F. L. (2003). Personality and absenteeism: A meta-analysis of integrity tests. *European Journal of Personality, 17*, 19–38.

Organ, D. (1975). Extroversion, locus of control, and individual differences in conditionability in organizations. *Journal of Applied Psychology, 60*, 401–404.

Owens, D., & Schoenfeldt, L. (1979). Toward a classification of persons. *Journal of Applied Psychology, 64*, 569–607.

Owens, W. (1976). Background data. In M. Dunnette (Ed.), *Handbook of industrial and organizational psychology* (pp. 609–646). Chicago, IL: Rand-McNally.

Pervin, L. (1967). *Personality: Theory and research*. New York: Wiley.

Piedmont, R., & Weinstein, H. (1994). Predicting supervisor ratings of job performance using the NEO personality inventory. *Journal of Psychology, 128*, 255–265.

Price, V. (1982). *Type A behaviour pattern: A model for research and practice*. London: Academic Press.

Ree, M., & Carretta, T. (1999). Lack of ability is not always the problem. *Journal of Business and Psychology, 14*, 165–178.

Reilly, R., & Chao, G. (1982). Validity and fairness of some alternative selection procedures. *Personality Psychology, 35*, 1–61.

Robertson, I. (1998). Personality and organizational behaviour. *Selection and Development Review, 14*, 11–15.

Robertson, I., & Kinder, A. (1993). Personality and job competency. *Journal of Occupational and Organizational Psychology, 66*, 225–244.

Rosenman, R., & Friedman, M. (1974). Neurogenic factors in pathogenesis of coronary heart disease. *Medical Clinics of North America, 58*, 269–279.

Rothstein, H., Schmidt, F., Erwin, F., Owens, W., & Sparks, C. (1990). Biographical data in employment selection: Can validities be made generalizable. *Journal of Applied Psychology, 75*, 175–184.

Rotter, J. (1966). Generalized expectancies for internal versus external control of reinforcement. *Psychological Monographs, 80*, 609.

Russell, C. (1990). Selecting top corporate leaders: An example of biographical information. *Journal of Management, 16*, 73–86.

Salgado, J. (1997). The five factor model of personality and job performance in the European Community. *Journal of Applied Psychology, 82*, 30–43.

Schmidt, F., & Hunter, J. (1990). The validity and utility of selection methods in personnel psychology. *Psychological Bulletin, 124*, 262–274.

Schmitt, N., Gooding, R., Noe, R., & Kirsch, M. (1984). Meta-analysis of validity studies published between 1964 and 1986 and the investigation of study characteristics. *Personnel Psychology, 27*, 407–422.

Scott, R., & Johnson, R. (1967). Use of the weighted application blank in selecting unskilled employees. *Journal of Applied Psychology, 51*, 393–395.

Shaw, L., & Sichel, H. (1970). *Accident proneness*. Oxford: Pergamon Press.

SHL (1984). *Occupational personality questionnaire*. Esher, UK: Saville & Holdsworth Ltd.

Smernou, L., & Lautenschlager, G. (1991). Autobiographical antecedents and correlates of neuroticism and extroverts. *Personality and Individual Differences, 12*, 49–53.

Smith, D., Hanges, P., & Dickson, M. (2001). Personnel selection and the five factor model. *Journal of Applied Psychology, 86*, 304–315.

Smith, W. (1961). Effects of industrial music in a work situation requiring complex mental activity. *Psychological Reports, 8*, 159–162.

Smith, W., Albright, L., Glennon, J., & Owens, W. (1961). The prediction of research competence and creativity from personal history. *Journal of Applied Psychology, 45*, 59–62.

Snyder, M. (1974). Self-monitoring of expressive behaviour. *Journal of Personality and Social Psychology, 30*, 526–537.

Spreitzer, G., McCall, W., & Mahoney, J. (1997). Early identification of international executive potential. *Journal of Applied Psychology, 82*, 6–29.

Sternberg, R. (1990). *Metaphors of mind*. Cambridge: Cambridge University Press.

Sternberg, R., & Grigorenko, E. (1997). Are cognitive styles still in style? *American Psychologist, 52*, 700–712.

Sterns, L., Alexander, R., Barrett, G., & Dambrot, F. (1983). The relationship of extroversion and neuroticism with job preference and job satisfaction for clerical employees. *Journal of Occupational Psychology, 56*, 145–155.

Sullivan, J. (1989). Self-theories and employee motivation. *Journal of Management, 15*, 345–363.

Szymanski, D., & Churchill, G. (1990). Client evaluation cues: A comparison of successful and unsuccessful sales people. *Journal of Marketing Research, 27*, 163–174.

Terborg, J., Richardson, P., & Pritchard, R. (1980). Person–situation effects in the prediction of performance: An investigation of ability, self-esteem, and reward contingencies. *Journal of Applied Psychology, 65*, 574–583.

Tett, R., Jackson, D., & Rothstein, M. (1991). Personality measures as predictors of job performance: A meta-analytic review. *Personnel Psychology, 44*, 703–725.

Tiedemann, J. (1989). Measures of cognitive style: A critical review. *Educational Psychologist, 24*, 261–275.

Turnbull, A. (1976). Selling and the salesman: Prediction of success and personality change. *Psychological Reports, 38*, 1175–1180.

Uhlbrock, R. (1961). Music on the job: Its influence on workers' morale and production. *Personnel Psychology, 14*, 9–38.

Walther, R. (1961). Self-description as a predictor of success or failure in foreign service clerical jobs. *Journal of Applied Psychology, 45*, 16–21.

Wankowski, J. (1973). *Temperament, motivation and academic achievement.* Unpublished report, Department of Psychology, University of Birmingham.

Ward, C., & Eisler, R. (1987). Type A behaviour, achievement striving, and a dysfunctional self-evaluation system. *Journal of Personality and Social Psychology, 53*, 318–326.

Warr, P. (1997). The varying validity of personality scales. *Selection and Development Review, 13*, 3–7.

Wilson, G. (1973). *The psychology of conservatism.* London: Academic Press.

Wilson, G., Tunstall, O., & Eysenck, H. (1972). Measurement of motivation in predicting industrial performance: A study of apprentice gas fitters. *Occupational Psychology, 46*, 15–24.

Witt, L., Burkes, L., Barrick, M., & Mount, M. (2002). The interactive effects of conscientiousness and agreeableness on job performance. *Journal of Applied Psychology, 87*, 164–169.

Zuckerman, M. (1979). *Sensation seeking: Beyond the optimal level of arousal.* London: Wiley.

5 Work-related attitudes, values and perceptions

Introduction

Because work is such an important part of people's lives, they quite naturally have strong, complex and diverse attitudes to it. However, attitudes to (and indeed behaviour at) work may be shaped by strongly held social values and beliefs. Everyone has certain implicit and explicit values that reflect their unique upbringing, their education and the wider culture within which they live. Some of their values are overtly materialistic, others completely spiritual. These values about freedom, equality and altruism are very relevant in the workplace. For instance, they are partly responsible for where people choose to work. We often hear of people boycotting organizations and products that are associated with specific values antithetical to their own. They would clearly never work for these organizations. Many people seek out organizations whose values (expressed in their mission statement, or whose reputation is known) fit their own. Some take the role of "whistle-blower" against their own organization when they see things done that conflict with their values (Furnham & Taylor, 2004).

Values are related to belief systems; that is, values are groups of beliefs about a particular object or process. Thus, people may have a fairly elaborate gender belief system about such issues as discrimination against women, biological differences between the sexes, attitudes to homosexuals and lesbians, and the problem associated with people of one gender working in a job commonly associated with the opposite gender (a man as midwife, a woman as soldier). These belief systems are, in turn, related to highly specific attitudes to issues at work. Attitudes to pay and to absenteeism may be part of a reward belief system shaped by values about equity.

This chapter first examines various beliefs systems that have been identified by psychologists over the years and discusses how these relate to the world of work. Many are overlapping and positively correlated with each other (Furnham, 1990). Secondly, the issue of social perception will be discussed. People are frequently required to make social judgements about others in the process of selection, appraisal or promotion. Various factors conspire to influence the processes by which these judgements are made, and these issues are discussed.

Do work attitudes predict behaviour at work?

Most people interested in social attitudes are interested in predicting and changing behaviour, and for many there is the naïve assumption that attitudes predict behaviour. That is, if we can measure a person's attitude to the French, a political party's creed, or strawberry jam, then we can accurately infer their behaviour with respect to French people, that person's voting habits, or their purchasing and consumption of strawberry jam. Unfortunately, as many people have found, *overall attitudes are fairly poor predictors of subsequent behaviour*.

There are several reasons for this. Consider first the *level of specificity* at which we usually measure attitudes and behaviour. Often, attitudes are measured at a very general *abstract* level and behaviour at a highly *specific* level. The more the two are in alignment, the better the one predicts the other. To predict a particular work-related behaviour, one needs to measure specific related attitudes to that behaviour. Secondly, consider the problem of *single versus multiple act* measurement. If people are interested in attitudes to women, it is better to look at a series of possible behaviours associated with them. Attitudes are much better predictors when a series of behaviours (multiple acts) is taken into account. "One-shot" measures of behaviour are often unreliable and do not give us much information about the relationships between attitudes and behaviour. One needs to aggregate observed or recorded behaviour to make certain the measure is robust and reliable before attempting to see if it is logically related to any particular attitude pattern. Thirdly, *situational* factors may strongly influence attitudes as well as behaviours. Where situational pressures are strong, such as at the scene of an accident or in a religious building, people of widely different attitudes may act in a similar way. Thus, external factors may constrain behaviour and reduce or even change the relationship between attitudes and behaviour. Fourthly, it is possible that a given behaviour might relate to a *range of attitudes*. For instance, imagine we are interested in predicting how likely people are in general to help in accidents, and specifically how likely to help a Black child knocked over by a motorcyclist. A person might be unfavourably disposed to Black people, very positive about children, and very strongly against motorcyclists. It is difficult to know which of these attitudes would best predict behaviour.

Other factors, too, mediate between attitudes and behaviour, many of which are known and appear to have a systematic relationship. Thus, rather than despair, it may be possible to show a strong relationship depending on how one measures both attitudes and behaviour. For instance, Ajzen & Fishbein (1980) have concluded from their extensive research that "A person's attitude has a consistently strong relation with his or her behaviour when it is directed at the same target and when it involves the same action" (p. 912). Work attitudes *can* predict work behaviour when both are appropriately measured and relevant confounding factors are taken into consideration.

Where do particular attitudes come from and how are they maintained? How is it that some people are in favour of nuclear disarmament, others against it, and still others do not seem to have an opinion either way? Are these attitudes a result of personality characteristics (authoritarian personalities tend to be against nuclear disarmament); upbringing, education or social class (working-class, less well educated people are less likely to approve of disarmament); exposure to or choice of media (readers of tabloid newspapers are more likely to be against disarmament than those of quality newspapers); or some other factor? Three important issues mean that the answer to this question (as with the others) is complex. First, factors that lead to the *adoption* of an attitude often differ from those that *maintain* it. (We know, for instance, that *social* factors are important in determining when and why certain young people begin to smoke, but that *personality* factors are much more important in explaining why they continue.) Secondly, each set or group of attitudes may be maintained by different factors. Thus, personality factors may relate to racial attitudes, whereas social-class factors relate to attitudes towards health. Thirdly, these different factors are themselves interrelated and confounded, and hence are difficult to tease apart.

In fact, most of the particular belief systems identified try to explain the aetiology of the belief system, although not all explain its relevance to work. It is worth considering some of these, if nothing else, to explore how they might relate to organizational behaviour.

The theories of reasoned action and planned behaviour

The theories of reasoned action and planned behaviour continue to attract attention in social psychology and represent two of the most pervasive social cognition models to date. They are believed to describe how, when and why attitudes predict behaviour and what one needs to measure to understand that process. Indeed, a survey by Fishbein & Ajzen (1993) identified more than 250 empirical investigations explicitly based on the two theories, and over recent years there has been a further increase in the application of these theories to a range of behaviours.

The theory of reasoned action (TRA: Ajzen & Fishbein, 1980; Fishbein & Ajzen, 1975) is a widely used model for explaining human behaviour and is depicted in Figure 5.1. The TRA contends that the immediate determinant of behaviour is the intention to perform it. Intentions represent conscious plans or decisions to exert effort to perform the behaviour and the stronger the intention to perform the behaviour, the more likely should be its performance.

Intentions, in turn, are determined by two conceptually independent components – attitudes and subjective norms. Attitudes are conceptualized as overall positive or negative evaluations of the behaviour, and in this instance refer to attitudes towards using homeopathy. Attitudes, in turn, are assumed to be a function of an individual's salient behavioural beliefs about the consequences of performing the behaviour. An individual who believes that a particular behaviour will lead to a positive outcome will hold a favourable attitude to that behaviour, whereas an individual who believes that the behaviour will lead to a negative outcome will hold an unfavourable attitude. Based on expectancy-value conceptualizations, attitudes are also based on the evaluation of these beliefs. Hence, attitudes are the multiplicative combination of behavioural beliefs and the evaluation of these beliefs. This can be expressed algebraically by the following equation:

$$B = \sum_{i=1}^{i=I} b_i \cdot e_i \tag{1}$$

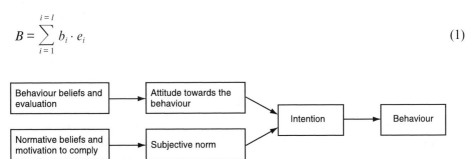

Figure 5.1 Schematic representation of the theory of reasoned action. Adapted from Ajzen & Fishbein (1980).

where b_i is the belief that performing the behaviour, B, leads to a particular consequence i (i.e. the subjective probability that the behaviour has a consequence i); e_i is the evaluation of consequence i; and l is the number of salient consequences.

The second determinant of intention is a social factor termed *subjective norms*. Subjective norms refer to the perceived pressure from significant others to perform or not perform the behaviour, and in this instance refers to perceived pressure to either use or not use homeopathy. Subjective norms, in turn, are assumed to be a function of normative beliefs. Normative beliefs are an individual's perceptions of whether salient others' (individuals or groups whose beliefs about an individual's behaviour are important to them) think they should or should not engage in the behaviour. Subjective norms are also determined by the individual's motivation to comply with that referent's expectation. Hence, subjective norms are the multiplicative combination of normative beliefs and the motivation to comply. This can be expressed algebraically by the following equation:

$$SN = \sum_{j=1}^{j=m} nb_j \cdot mc_j \qquad (2)$$

where SN is the subjective norm; nb_j is the normative belief (i.e. subjective probability) that referent j thinks that the individual should perform the behaviour; mc_j is the motivation to comply with referent j; and m is the number of salient referents.

There is empirical support for the TRA, which has been employed as a theoretical framework to predict intention and behaviour in a range of behaviours. Table 5.1

Table 5.1 Recent applications of the TRA to a range of behaviours

Study	n	Behaviour	Outcome
Arvola, Laehteenmaeki & Tuorila (1999)	92	Purchasing unfamiliar and familiar cheeses	The results supported the TRA for the intention to purchase familiar cheese, with attitudes and subjective norms predicting intentions. The model was not as useful in predicting intention to purchase unfamiliar cheese.
Moore, Barling & Hood (1998)	257	Testicular and breast self-examination	The TRA was strongly supported by the results, with intentions to perform self-examination being predicted by attitudes and subjective norms. Intentions, in turn, predicted behaviour.
Sneed & Morisky (1998)	1,394	Condom use among Filipino sex workers	The results strongly supported the TRA. Attitudes and subjective norms predicted intention to use a condom. Intention, in turn, predicted behaviour.
Vincent, Peplau & Hill (1998)	105	Women's career behaviour	Support was provided for the TRA. Women's gender role attitudes and their perceptions of significant others' preferences predicted their career intention. Intentions, in turn, predicted career behaviour 14 years later.

presents some recent applications of the TRA, with a brief description of the outcomes. The table shows that the components of the TRA significantly contribute to the prediction of intention and behaviour across a range of behaviours. Intentions to engage in the behaviours were well predicted by the combination of attitude towards the behaviour and subjective norm. Intentions, in turn, predicted behaviour.

The performance of the TRA has been assessed in two meta-analyses. In a widely cited meta-analysis based on 87 studies that employed the TRA, Sheppard, Hartwick & Warshaw (1988) reported a mean multiple R of .66 for predicting intention from attitude and subjective norm, and a mean R of .53 for predicting behaviour from intention. Van den Putte (1993) has provided a more recent and extensive meta-analysis based on 113 studies, and reported a mean multiple R of .68 for predicting intention from attitude and subjective norm, and a mean R of .62 for predicting behaviour from intention. Such findings confirm that the TRA has significantly enhanced the ability to predict intentions and behaviour on the basis of attitudes and subjective norms, as compared with the average correlations between attitudes and behaviour of .15 reported by Wicker (1969).

However, Ajzen (1988) himself conceded, "The theory of reasoned action was developed explicitly to deal with purely volitional behaviours" (p. 127) and acknowledges that the enactment of behaviour is not always *under complete volitional control*, in that there may be internal obstacles (e.g. skills, ability, knowledge) or external obstacles (e.g. time, money, opportunity) that may limit performance. To accommodate such factors, Ajzen (1991) included a third conceptually independent component in the model, termed "perceived behavioural control", which resulted in the formulation of the theory of planned behaviour (TPB) (see Figure 5.2). Perceived behavioural control (PBC) is a measure of the amount of control the individual has over the behaviour in question.

As seen from Figure 5.2, the PBC component can have both a direct impact on behaviour and an indirect impact through behavioural intention. The proposed relationship between PBC and behaviour is based upon two rationales. First, holding intention constant, the enactment of a behaviour will increase as PBC increases. Secondly, PBC will influence behaviour directly to the extent that perceived control reflects actual control.

In addition, levels of PBC should also influence behavioural intentions, in that if an individual perceives that he or she has little control over the performance of a behaviour, their motivation to do so is likely to be weak. Perceived behavioural control works in parallel with attitudes and subjective norms as determinants of intentions;

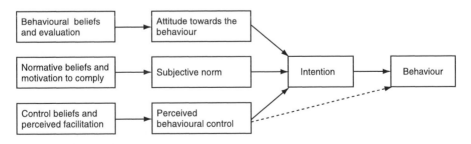

Figure 5.2 Schematic representation of the theory of planned behaviour. Adapted from Ajzen (1991).

thus, a stronger intention to enact a behaviour is therefore dependent upon positive attitudes, perceived social acquiescence and perceived ease of behavioural performance.

Just as behavioural beliefs and normative beliefs are assumed to influence attitudes and subjective norms respectively, control beliefs are assumed to influence PBC. Control beliefs are judgements about whether one has access to the necessary resources and opportunities to perform the behaviour, and include both internal control factors (e.g. skills) and external control factors (e.g. opportunities). Perceived behavioural control is also determined by the perceived power of the control belief to facilitate or inhibit performance of the behaviour. Hence, PBC is the multiplicative combination of control beliefs and the perceived power of the control belief. This can be expressed algebraically by the following equation:

$$PBC = \sum_{k=1}^{k=n} c_k \cdot p_k \tag{3}$$

where *PBC* is perceived behavioural control; c_k is the control belief (i.e. subjective probability that the individual has control over factor k); p_k is the perceived facilitating or inhibiting power of factor k in performing the behaviour; and n is the number of control factors.

There is considerable empirical support for the TPB, which has been employed as a theoretical framework to predict intention and behaviour in a range of health- and non-health-related behaviours. Table 5.2 presents some recent applications of the TPB to non-health-related behaviours, with a brief description of the outcomes. The table clearly shows that the addition of the PBC component improved the predictive

Table 5.2 Recent applications of the TPB to a range of non-health related behaviours

Study	n	Behaviour	Outcome
Ajzen & Driver (1991)	146	Leisure participation	The PBC component contributed significantly to the prediction of intention and behaviour.
Evans & Norman (1998)[a]	210	Understanding pedestrians' road-crossing decisions	The PBC component emerged as the strongest predictor of intentions, suggesting that perceptions of control have an important role in road safety behaviour.
Parker *et al.* (1992)[a]	881	Intention to commit various driving violations	The addition of the PBC component improved the predictive performance of the original TRA model. In particular, PBC was the dominant predictor of intention, in the case of speeding and drink-driving.
Roberts & Smith (1998)	188	Attitudes and behaviour of children towards peers with disabilities	Attitudes and PBC were significant predictors of intention. In turn, intentions moderately predicted actual behaviour, while PBC was not a significant predictor of behaviour.

[a] = The prediction of intention only.

performance of the original TRA model. In each study, PBC significantly contributed to intention, and in two studies was the dominant predictor of intention, suggesting the predictive utility of this component.

Ajzen (1991) reviewed a number of studies that confirmed the effects of PBC on both intentions and behaviour. The studies included a diverse range of behaviours, including getting an "A" in a college course, participation in elections and voting, and playing video games. The multiple correlations predicting behaviour from intentions ranged from .20 to .78 (mean .51) and in most studies the prediction of behaviour improved with the addition of the PCB component. In line with the TPB, the strength of this effect varied as a function of perceived control over the behaviour, with PBC being most useful as a predictor of behaviours lower in volitional control. Furthermore, the addition of PBC improved the prediction of intention (mean $R = .71$) and was found to be a significant predictor of intention in all the studies reviewed, suggesting that this component is both a reliable and significant independent predictor of intention across a range of behaviours.

Madden, Ellen & Ajzen (1992) compared the TRA and TPB across a range of 10 behaviours. The behaviours differed with respect to controllability, with behaviours such as renting a video and taking vitamins being regarded as relatively easy to control, and behaviours such as sleeping and shopping being regarded as more difficult to control. The addition of PBC led to an average increase in the multiple correlation of .21. The inclusion of PBC also led to an improvement in the model's performance in the prediction of behaviour by an average of .16. Furthermore, evidence supported Ajzen's contention that PBC will be a useful predictor of behaviours lower in volitional control.

Godin and Kok (1996) conducted a meta-analysis of studies performed between 1985 and 1996 that applied the TPB to a wide range of health-related behaviours. The results suggested that the theory is a useful predictor in a number of health-related behaviours. The averaged R^2 for intention and behaviour was .41 and .34, respectively. In general, attitudes and PBC significantly contributed to the prediction of intention, whereas subjective norms contributed to the prediction of intention less often, suggesting social influence is less important than attitudes and PBC in health-related behaviours. Intention remained the dominant predictor of behaviour; however, PBC contributed significantly in half of the studies. The exception was for addictive behaviours (e.g. smoking) and clinical screening behaviour (e.g. cancer screening), where PBC played a stronger role than intention. Such behaviours are likely to be influenced not only by personal motivation but other factors such as addiction, easy access to health services and availability of resources.

Although there is extensive empirical support for the TPB, the PBC component has attracted criticism. In particular, there is a lack of conceptual clarity concerning the notion of PBC (Terry, 1993; Terry & O'Leary, 1995). Ajzen (1985, 1988; Ajzen & Madden, 1986) conceptualized PBC as not only an estimate of the extent to which an individual has control over performing a behaviour, but also the individual's appraisal of their ability to perform that behaviour. The implication is that Ajzen proposed two processes of control, theoretically distinguishable from one another. The first, related to perceived controllability over behaviour (cf. Rotter's, 1966, locus of control), refers to judgements regarding control over external barriers. The second, related to Bandura's (1982) self-efficacy beliefs, refers to perceived levels of internal control. Indeed, Bandura (1982) has argued that "locus of control and self-efficacy bear little or no relation to each other" (p. 124). Furthermore, it cannot be assumed that there will be a correspondence between an individual's perception of the extent to which external barriers may impede the performance of a behaviour and their judgement that the behaviour will be easy to perform. For example, an individual may perceive few external barriers to performing a behaviour, yet may lack confidence in their ability to so.

Indeed, there is a growing body of empirical evidence to support this theoretical distinction. Moreover, studies have included a diverse array of behaviours (e.g. food choice, exercise, cannabis/alcohol use, academic achievement), suggesting the distinction between PBC and self-efficacy is robust. In addition to the theoretical distinction, the two variables may have a differential influence on behavioural intentions and actual behaviour. According to Bandura (1982), self-efficacy influences behaviour primarily via its effects on motivation (or intention) to perform a behaviour, not on behaviour itself.

While there is empirical support for the influence of self-efficacy and PBC on intention, the relationship between self-efficacy, PCB and behaviour is not consistent. Ajzen (1991) states that "The theory of planned behaviour is, in principle, open to the inclusion of additional predictors if it can be shown that they capture a significant proportion of the variance in intention or behaviour after the theory's current variables have been taken into account" (p. 199). Similarly, in a comprehensive review of the TPB, Conner and Armitage (1998) examined both empirical and theoretical evidence supporting the addition of six variables in the theory (including the distinction between self-efficacy and PBC).

While the PBC and self-efficacy components have received much empirical support, the influence of past behaviour on current behaviour as an additional variable within the theory has also attracted considerable attention. It is argued that many health behaviours are determined not by the social cognitive variables described in the TRA/TPB, but rather by one's previous health-related behaviour (Sutton, 1994). This argument is based on the findings of a number of studies showing past behaviour to be the best predictor of future behaviour.

However, Ajzen (1991) argues that the inability of the TRA to account for the influence of past behaviour on subsequent behaviour might be attributed to the absence of the perceived control component. Ajzen proposes that the effect of past behaviour is primarily mediated by the perceived behavioural control component, which is consistent with Bandura's (1982) claim that past behaviour provides important information about an individual's sense of control. Hence, when perceived control is taken into account, past behaviour should no longer contribute to the prediction of intention and behaviour.

Figure 5.3 is a schematic representation of the complex relationship between the components of the theory of reasoned action, the theory of planned behaviour and the additional contribution of past behaviour to intentions and actual behaviour. *The "bottom line" is that attitudes (alone) are poor predictors of behaviour at work.* However, if various other beliefs are measured (such as those shown in Figure 5.3) plus past behaviour, it is quite possible to be reasonably good at predicting behaviour in the workplace.

Do attitudes predict behaviour at work, such as absenteeism, measured productivity or accidents? The two theories outlined above would suggest they do, but only under certain circumstances and in conjunction with the measurement of other variables. Thus, in addition to attitudes, one needs to consider, and measure, subjective norms or beliefs about how others in the organization behave; personal beliefs about self-efficacy;

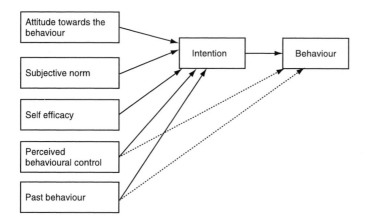

Figure 5.3 Schematic representation of the proposed relationship between the TRA and extended TPB variables.

the extent to which the individual believes he or she has personal control over the behaviour; as well as their history of this specific behaviour in the past. Next, one has to measure, as accurately as possible, their actual behavioural intentions. Once these factors have been carefully measured and considered, it becomes possible to show when, where, why and how attitudes do predict behaviour at work.

Work-related belief systems

Over the years, different researchers have isolated various beliefs or belief systems which they have attempted to describe and measure. Others have concentrated on needs rather than beliefs. Many of these have been shown to relate directly to the world of work (Furnham, 1990).

Achievement motivation

Psychological work on need for achievement or achievement motivation can be traced back to the personality theorist Murray (1938), who included achievement as one of his 20 basic needs. Achievement motivation was defined thus:

> The desire to accomplish something difficult. To master, manipulate, or organize physical objects, human beings, or ideas. To do this as rapidly and independently as possible. To excel oneself. To rival and surpass others. (p. 26)

These needs were seen to be largely unconscious, dispositional tendencies, general in nature and not specifically linked to situations and which tend to be stable over time. Since the Second World War, there has been a considerable growth of interest in achievement motivation, led by Atkinson (1964) and McClelland (1961), who attempted to predict the economic achievement of societies from the achievement needs of its individual members.

There are various quite different models, theories and hypothesized processes about the nature of achievement motivation. Although there is still a considerable amount of conjecture, as well as equivocal findings, it is probably the case that there is some agreement as to the nature of individuals high and low in achievement motivation. The following are said to be the characteristics of people high in need for achievement (nAch). They:

- exercise some control over the means of production and produce more than they consume;
- set moderately difficult goals for themselves;
- try to maximize likelihood of achievement satisfaction;
- want concrete and regular feedback on how well they are doing;
- like assuming personal responsibility for problems;
- show high initiative and exploratory behaviour in their environment;
- continually research the environment for opportunities of all sorts;
- regard growth and expansion as the most direct signs of success;
- strive continually to improve (the Japanese *kaizen* concept).

There are many measures of need for achievement, such as the scale devised by Lynn (1969) and shown in Box 5.1.

Achievement theorists have emphasized the importance of parental expectation, early upbringing and education in trying to explain why some people are clearly much more motivated to succeed at work than others. A major problem with this variable is that it is easy to fake. This problem is so acute in relation to measures of achievement orientation that researchers have had to resort to projective techniques such as the thematic apperception test (TAT), which requires people to tell stories about pictures presented to them, the content of which is analysed later for achievement themes. This is considered a better device because it is less fakeable and because it supposedly taps "unconscious" achievement needs more accurately.

Despite these problems, researchers have shown consistently that this belief system

---

Box 5.1 A short need for achievement questionnaire

Please circle either the "yes" or "no" against each answer. Please be sure to answer each question and decide one way or another even if it is hard to make a decision.

1. Do you find it easy to relax completely when you are on holiday?   Yes   No
2. Do you feel annoyed when people are not punctual for appointments?   Yes   No
3. Do you dislike seeing things wasted?   Yes   No
4. Do you like getting drunk?   Yes   No
5. Do you find it easy to forget about your work outside normal working
   hours?   Yes   No
6. Would you prefer to work with a congenial but incompetent partner, rather
   than with a difficult but highly competent one?   Yes   No
7. Does inefficiency make you angry?   Yes   No
8. Have you always worked hard in order to be among the best in your own
   line?   Yes   No

Scoring. Score 1 mark for "yes" answers to questions 2, 3, 7, 8. Score 1 mark for "no" answers to questions 1, 4, 5, 6.

Source: Reproduced from Lynn (1969) with the permission of the British Psychological Society.

predicts qualitatively and quantitatively work-related behaviour. It is related to drive, ambition, conscientiousness at work and is fairly predictive (together with other factors, such as intelligence) of being in the "fast track" at work.

Authoritarianism

The concept of authoritarianism arose when investigators asked the following question in the immediate post-Nazi period: "Do extremely prejudiced people have unique personality characteristics?" Based on interviews with specific people, these investigators believed they had found an overall system of values and beliefs, which they called authoritarianism (Adorno, Frenkel-Brunswick, Levison, & Sanford, 1950).

This personality dimension is made up of various parts (see below). Authoritarians are described in psychoanalytic terminology as having a weak ego. This is reflected in the concepts of superstition, stereotyping and projectivity (projecting onto others things one does not like about oneself). Considerable research on this topic has provided a picture of a person who is generally conservative in political and social attitudes, deferential to authority, and prone to be offended by deviation from the conventional moral orders. They tend to be hard-driving, non-caring bosses who prefer the stick to the carrot to motivate others. They like working in regimented, structured organizations such as the army, police and fire service, and seek out order, stability and control.

Authoritarians have been shown to avoid situations that involve ambiguity and are reluctant to believe that "good people" possess both good and bad attributes. However, they often appear less interested in political affairs, participate less in political and community activities, and tend to prefer strong leaders. There are several measures of authoritarianism. The best known (and hence most widely used) is the California F Scale (Adorno *et al.*, 1950), which attempts to measure prejudice, rigid thinking, and so on. Participants are requested to respond on a 7-point Likert scale (ranging from "strongly agree" to "strongly disagree") to 29 items that attempt to measure various aspects of authoritarianism, including:

- *Conventionalism*: rigid adherence to conventional middle-class values ("Obedience and respect for authority are the most important virtues that children should learn").
- *Authoritarian submission*: uncritical acceptance of authority ("Young people sometimes get rebellious ideas, but as they grow up they ought to get over them and settle down").
- *Authoritarian aggression*: a tendency to condemn anyone who violates conventional norms ("A person who has bad manners, bad habits and is of poor breeding can hardly expect to get along with decent people").
- *Anti-intraception*: rejection of weakness or sentimentality ("The businessman and the manufacturer are much more important to society than the artist and professor").
- *Superstition and stereotyping*: a belief in mystical determinants of action, and rigid, categorical thinking ("Some day it will probably be shown that astrology can explain a lot of things").
- *Power and toughness*: preoccupation with dominance over others ("No weakness or difficulty can hold us back if we have strong enough willpower").

- *Destructiveness and cynicism*: a generalized feeling of hostility and anger ("Human nature being what it is, there will always be war and conflict").
- *Projectivity*: a tendency to project inner emotions and impulses outwards ("Most people don't realize how much our lives are controlled by plots hatched in secret places").
- *Sex*: an exaggerated concern for proper sexual conduct ("Homosexuals are hardly better than criminals and ought to be punished").

The California F Scale is set out in Box 5.2. The more you agree with each statement, the more authoritarian you are.

As ever, criticisms have been made of this measure and there are now more up-to-date and psychometrically valid questionnaires measuring authoritarianism. Results from studies appear to suggest that authoritarianism is a good predictor of type of occupation chosen and experiences of equity at work. Authoritarians like traditional, bureaucratic organizations where rank and power determine interpersonal relations. They are often powerfully against anti-discrimination legislation (i.e. positive discrimination) and fiercely opposed to change if they have been in an organization for some time.

Beliefs about work

Some researchers have attempted quite specifically to look at work-related beliefs. The first published account of the "beliefs about work" questionnaire was provided by Buchholz (1976). The measure contains five indices:

- *The work ethic*: the belief that work is good in itself, offers dignity to a person and that success is a result of personal effort.
- *The organization belief system*: the view that work takes on meaning only as it affects the organization and contributes to one's position at work.
- *Marxist-related beliefs*: the opinion that work is fundamental to human fulfillment, but as currently organized represents exploitation of the worker and consequent alienation.
- *The humanistic belief system*: the view that individual growth and development in the job is more important than the output.
- *The leisure ethic*: regards work as a means to personal fulfilment, through its provision of the means to pursue leisure activities.

Buchholz (1978) looked at the relationship between age, sex, race, education and job status with work beliefs and values in the general population. Whereas humanistic work beliefs did not differentiate between people of different backgrounds, Marxist-related beliefs did. Individuals who were younger rather than older, female rather than male, poorly rather than better educated, Black rather than White, and workers rather than management, tended to support "Marxist ideas". The work ethic was related only to age (young people showed a stronger work ethic orientation than older people), whereas the leisure ethic was related to occupation (top management indicated that they liked their work and were not willing to accept leisure as a substitute for the benefit of work). Buchholz concluded that, in general, the work ethic is not held very strongly but that no other belief system emerges as being clearly preferable to it. Dickson &

Box 5.2 The California F scale*

1. Sex crimes, such as rape and attacks on children, deserve more than mere imprisonment; such criminals ought to be publicly whipped, or worse.
2. What youth needs most is strict discipline, rugged determination and the will to work and fight for family and country.
3. There is hardly anything lower than a person who does not feel a great love, gratitude and respect for his parents.
4. Every person should have complete faith in some supernatural power whose decision he obeys without question.
5. Young people sometimes get rebellious ideas, but as they grow up they ought to get over them and settle down.
6. Obedience and respect for authority are the most important virtues children should learn.
7. Homosexuals are hardly better than criminals and ought to be severely punished.
8. Nowadays when so many different kinds of people move around and mix together so much, a person has to protect himself especially carefully against catching an infection or disease from them.
9. People can be divided into two distinct classes: the weak and the strong.
10. No sane, normal, decent person could ever think of hurting a close friend or relative.
11. Some day it will probably be shown that astrology can explain a lot of things.
12. Nowadays more and more people are prying into matters that should remain personal and private.
13. If people would talk less and work more, everybody would be better off.
14. An insult to our honour should always be punished.
15. Most of our social problems would be solved if we could somehow get rid of the immoral, crooked and feeble-minded people.
16. When a person has a problem or worry, it is best for him not to think about it, but to keep busy with more cheerful things.
17. Science has its place, but there are many important things that can never possibly be understood by the human mind.
18. The wild sex life of the old Greeks and Romans was tame compared to some of the goings-on in this country, even in places where people might least expect it.
19. Human nature being what it is, there will always be war and conflict.
20. The true US way of life is disappearing so fast that force may be necessary to preserve it.
21. What this country needs most, more than law and political programmes, is a few courageous, tireless, devoted leaders in whom the people can put their faith.
22. No weakness or difficulty can hold us back if we have enough willpower.
23. Familiarity breeds contempt.
24. Some people are born with an urge to jump from high places.
25. Most people don't realize how much our lives are controlled by plots hatched in secret places.
26. A person who has bad manners, habits and breeding can hardly expect to get along with decent people.
27. Nobody ever learned anything really important except through suffering.
28. Wars and social trouble may someday be ended by an earthquake or flood that will destroy the whole world.
29. The businessman and the manufacturer are much more important to society than the artist and the professor.

* Abridgement of "F-Scale Clusters: Forms 45 and 40" in Adorno *et al.* (1950: 255–257).

Buchholz (1977) compared these same work beliefs among three working groups in Scotland and the USA. Overall, the Marxist-related and leisure belief systems most differentiated the workers from the two cultures. They also examined the effects of company size, occupation, age, education and religion on work belief and found much the same as Buchholz (1978).

The questionnaire devised to measure these belief systems comprises 45 items, each with five response alternatives ranging from "strongly disagree" to "strongly agree" (Box 5.3). Because this measure has the advantage of being sphere-specific, in the sense that it tries to measure different, unrelated work beliefs, it has been shown to be fairly predictive of the behaviours of managers. Certainly, work ethic beliefs are positively – and Marxist-related beliefs negatively – related to personal satisfaction and productivity (Furnham, 1990, 1992). These two systems are opposed on many issues, such as pay, promotion and how people are managed. The measure is also related to how people manage others, as well as more general social and political beliefs.

Beliefs in a just world

The "beliefs in a just world" pattern was identified over 25 years ago and concentrates on the tendency of people to blame victims of misfortunes for their own fate (Lerner, 1980). The essence of this hypothesis or theory was succinctly summarized by Lerner & Miller (1978: 1030–1031):

> Individuals have a need to believe that they live in a world where people generally get what they deserve. The belief that the world is just enables the individual to confront his physical and social environment as though they were stable and orderly. Without such a belief it would be difficult for the individual to commit himself to the pursuit of long range goals or even to the socially regulated behaviour of day-to-day life. Since the belief that the world is just serves such an important adaptive function for the individual, people are very reluctant to give up this belief, and they can be greatly troubled if they encounter evidence that suggests that the world is not really just or orderly after all.

Considerable laboratory evidence has accumulated to support the concept, most of which attempts to explain how and when victims are blamed for their fate, how these beliefs arise, and their consequences.

Rubin & Peplau (1973, 1975) devised a self-report inventory to measure the attitudinal continuity between the total acceptance and rejection of the notion that the world is a just place. Half the items suggest that the world is a just place where good deeds are rewarded (e.g. item 11: "By and large people deserve what they get"), and half refer to an unjust world where good deeds are no more likely to be rewarded than bad deeds (e.g. item 4: "Careful drivers are just as likely to get hurt in traffic accidents as careless ones").

Many studies have used this scale to examine further the relationship between "just world" and other beliefs and behaviours (Furnham & Procter, 1989). The measure is not without its difficulties. For instance, Furnham & Procter considered the validity of the unidimensionality of the concept of a just world. They suggested that there might well be three worlds: *a just* world where people get what they deserve (the good and virtuous are rewarded and the bad punished); an *unjust* world where the opposite

Box 5.3 Beliefs about work questionnaire

Work ethic
1. By working hard a person can overcome every obstacle that life presents.
4. One must avoid dependence on other persons wherever possible.
6. A man can learn better on the job by striking out boldly on his own than he can by following the advice of others.
7. Only those who depend on themselves get ahead in life.
11. One should work like a slave at everything one undertakes until one is satisfied with the results.
30. One should live one's own life independent of others as much as possible.
39. To be superior a man must stand alone.

Organizational belief system
3. Better decisions are made in a group than by individuals.
9. One's contribution to the group is the most important thing about one's work.
10. One should take an active part in all group affairs.
18. It is best to have a job as part of an organization where all work together even if you don't get individual credit.
22. Working with a group is better than working alone.
25. Survival of the group is very important in an organization.
31. The group is the most important entity in any organization.
41. Work is a means to foster group interests.
42. Conformity is necessary for an organization to survive.

Marxist-related beliefs
2. Management does not understand the needs of the worker.
13. Workers should be represented on the board of directors of companies.
15. Factories would be run better if workers had more of a say in management.
26. The most important work in America is done by the labouring classes.
27. The working classes should have more say in running society.
28. Wealthy people carry their fair share of the burdens of life in this country (R).
29. The rich do not make much of a contribution to society.
34. The work of the labouring classes is exploited by the rich for their own benefit.
36. Workers should be more active in making decisions about products, financing, and capital investment.
44. The free enterprise system mainly benefits the rich and powerful.
45. Workers get their fair share of the economic rewards of society (R).

Humanistic belief system
8. Work can be made satisfying.
14. The workplace can be humanized.
17. Work can be made interesting rather than boring.
19. Work can be a means of self-expression.
24. Work can be organized to allow for human fulfilment.
32. The job should be a source of new experiences.
33. Work should enable one to learn new things.
37. Work should allow for the use of human capabilities.
38. One's job should give one a chance to try out new ideas.
40. Work can be made meaningful.

Leisure ethic
5. Increased leisure time is bad for society (R).
12. The less hours one spends working and the more leisure time available the better.

Box 5.3 continued

16. Success means having ample time to pursue leisure activities.
20. The present trend towards a shorter work week is to be encouraged.
21. Leisure time activities are more interesting than work.
23. Work takes too much of our time, leaving little time to relax.
35. More leisure time is good for people.
43. The trend towards more leisure is not a good thing (R).

Responses
(R) Reverse the scoring
Strongly disagree; Mildly disagree; Neither agree nor disagree; Mildly agree;
Strongly agree; scored 1 to 5 respectively

Source: Reproduced from Buchholz (1976) with the permission of Plenum Publishing Corporation.

---

occurs (the good go unrewarded and may even be punished, but the wicked win out in the end); and a *random* or *a-just* world where neither occurs consistently, in that some good deeds are rewarded, others are ignored, and still others are punished. Furthermore, it is possible that people believe that some aspects of their life are just (e.g. interpersonal relations) and others unjust or a-just (sociopolitical happenings).

Nevertheless, the "belief in a just world" measure has been shown to correlate significantly with demographic variables such as age, income and religion, but also such personality factors as attitudes to authority, conservatism and locus of control. People with strong needs to believe in a just world find it difficult to deal with others' misfortune, such as illness. Hence, they may be particularly unsympathetic to colleagues who are absent with a serious illness, because they find it difficult to accept the idea that some illnesses and diseases strike people at random.

In a recent review, Furnham (2003: 812) noted:

> two distinct research interests have emerged over the past decade. The first has been concerned with devising better and sensitive measures of the BJW [belief in a just world]. All four self-report measures devised prior to 1991 attempted to provide an overall BJW score. Since then all measures have attempted to measure particular facets of BJW beliefs. This has meant making various distinctions between for instance imminent vs ultimate justice or hope for, vs ability to promote, a just world. What most of these latter studies have been able to show is that these different, but related beliefs are systematically associated with different dependent variables.

The second major development has been to view the "belief in a just world" as a *healthy* coping mechanism rather than being the manifestation of anti-social beliefs and prejudice (Dalbert, 2001). There has been a subtle movement from focusing on victim derogation to positive coping. Recent studies have portrayed BJW beliefs as a personal resource or coping strategy, which buffers against stress and enhances achievement behaviour. For the first time, BJW beliefs have been seen as an indicator of mental health and planning. This does not contradict the more extensive literature on BJW and victim derogation. Rather, it helps to explain why people are so eager to maintain their beliefs, which may be their major coping strategy. Belief in a just world is clearly functional for the individual. One important issue for future research is how BJW relates to other coping strategies and which are favoured by health individuals who have low BJW beliefs. Again the focus is on how BJW relates to personal experiences rather than that of others.

Rubin & Peplau's (1975) "belief in a just world" scale is shown in Box 5.4. Beliefs about justice are no doubt related to such factors as pay and reward, satisfaction at work, as well as views about equity. All issues concerning distribution and procedural justice at work are, no doubt, related to "just world" beliefs, as well as sensitivity to all issues to do with "fairness" in the workplace.

Conservatism

A concept closely linked with authoritarianism is that of conservatism. Wilson (1973: 3) has claimed that conservatism is

> a general factor, underlying the entire field of social attitudes much the same as intelligence, is conceived as a general factor which partly determines abilities in different areas.

Wilson's theoretical stance to the conservative attitudes syndrome is that it is intimately

---

Box 5.4 Belief in a just world

Please read the following statements and then indicate the extent to which you agree with each.

1. I've found that a person rarely deserves the reputation he has.
2. Basically, the world is a just place.*
3. People who get "lucky breaks" have usually earned their good fortune.*
4. Careful drivers are just as likely to get hurt in traffic accidents as careless ones.
5. It is a common occurrence for a guilty person to get off free in British courts.
6. Students almost always deserve the grades/marks they receive in school.*
7. Men who keep in shape have little chance of suffering a heart attack.*
8. The political candidate who sticks up for his principles rarely gets elected.
9. It is rare for an innocent man to be wrongly sent to jail.*
10. In professional sport, many fouls and infractions never get called by the referee.
11. By and large, people deserve what they get.*
12. When parents punish their children, it is almost always for good reasons.*
13. Good deeds often go unnoticed and unrewarded.
14. Although evil men may hold political power for a while, in the general course of history good wins out.*
15. In almost any business or profession, people who do their jobs well rise to the top.*
16. British parents tend to overlook the things most to be admired in their children.
17. It is often impossible for a person to receive a fair trial in British courts.
18. People who meet with misfortune have often brought it on themselves.*
19. Crime doesn't pay.*
20. Many people suffer through absolutely no fault of their own.

* "Just world" items, which are reversed and added to unjust world (unmarked) items.

Source: Reproduced from Rubin & Peplau (1975) with the permission of Blackwell Publishers.

related to genetic and environmental factors that determine feelings of insecurity and inferiority. The common basis for all of the various components of the syndrome is assumed to be a "generalized susceptibility to experience threat or anxiety in the face of uncertainty" (p. 263). The conservative individual tends to avoid both stimulus and response uncertainty, and this avoidance is reflected in the attitudes that are expressed verbally as well in other aspects of behaviour. Wilson assumes that conservative beliefs:

> serve a defensive function. They arise as a means of simplifying, ordering, control-ling, and rendering more secure, both the *external* world (through perceptual pro-cesses, stimulus preferences, etc.) and the *internal* world (needs, feelings, desires, etc.). Order is imposed upon inner needs and feelings by subjugating them to rigid and simplistic external codes of conduct (rules, laws, morals, duties, obligations, etc.), thus reducing conflict and averting the anxiety that would accompany aware-ness of the freedom to choose among alternative modes of action. (Wilson, 1973: 261–264)

Wilson provides a "model" (see Figure 5.4) for this psychological process.

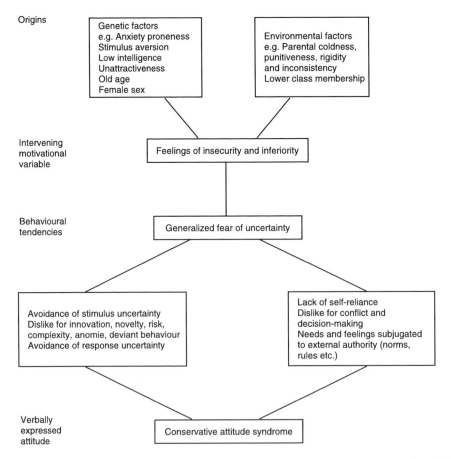

Figure 5.4 A theory of the psychological antecedents of conservatism. Reproduced from Wilson (1973) with the permission of Academic Press.

There has been considerable interest in this variable. For instance, Feather (1979) demonstrated that conservative people tend to emphasize values such as security, cleanliness, obedience, politeness and salvation, which are concerned with attachment to rules, authority and ego defences, while devaluing equality, freedom, love and pleasure, as well as open-minded, intellectual and imaginative modes of thought. He also found, as have many others, that older people tend to be more conservative than younger people, and females slightly more conservative than males.

Conservative people tend to be risk-averse and hence not very entrepreneurial. By definition they resent change and prefer to work in hierarchical organizations. One instrument, the "catch-phrase" conservatism questionnaire of Wilson & Patterson (1968), is given in Box 5.5.

Perceived control

The perceived control personality variable or dimension relates to beliefs about internal versus external control of reinforcement (i.e. the cause of behavioural outcomes). It assumes that individuals develop a general expectancy regarding their ability to control

---

Box 5.5 "Catch-phrase" conservatism questionnaire

Which of the following do you favour or believe in?
(Circle "Yes" or "No". If absolutely uncertain, circle "?". There are no right or wrong answers; do not discuss; just give your first reaction. Answer all items.)

1. Death penalty	Yes ? No		26. Computer music	Yes ? No
2. Evolution theory	Yes ? No		27. Chastity	Yes ? No
3. School uniforms	Yes ? No		28. Fluoridation	Yes ? No
4. Striptease shows	Yes ? No		29. Royalty	Yes ? No
5. Sabbath observance	Yes ? No		30. Women judges	Yes ? No
6. Beatniks	Yes ? No		31. Conventional clothes	Yes ? No
7. Patriotism	Yes ? No		32. Teenage drivers	Yes ? No
8. Modern art	Yes ? No		33. Apartheid	Yes ? No
9. Self-denial	Yes ? No		34. Nudist camps	Yes ? No
10. Working mothers	Yes ? No		35. Church authority	Yes ? No
11. Horoscopes	Yes ? No		36. Disarmament	Yes ? No
12. Birth control	Yes ? No		37. Censorship	Yes ? No
13. Military drill	Yes ? No		38. White lies	Yes ? No
14. Co-education	Yes ? No		39. Birching	Yes ? No
15. Divine law	Yes ? No		40. Mixed marriage	Yes ? No
16. Socialism	Yes ? No		41. Strict rules	Yes ? No
17. White superiority	Yes ? No		42. Jazz	Yes ? No
18. Cousin marriage	Yes ? No		43. Straitjackets	Yes ? No
19. Moral training	Yes ? No		44. Casual living	Yes ? No
20. Suicide	Yes ? No		45. Learning Latin	Yes ? No
21. Chaperones	Yes ? No		46. Divorce	Yes ? No
22. Legalized abortion	Yes ? No		47. Inborn conscience	Yes ? No
23. Empire-building	Yes ? No		48. Coloured immigration	Yes ? No
24. Student pranks	Yes ? No		49. Bible truth	Yes ? No
25. Licensing laws	Yes ? No		50. Pyjama parties	Yes ? No

Score 2 for Yes; 1 for ?; 0 for No for odd numbers; Score 2 for Yes; 1 for ?; 2 for No for even numbers.

Source: Reproduced from Wilson & Patterson (1968).

their lives. People who believe that the events that occur in their lives are the result of their *own* behaviour and/or ability, personality and effort are said to have the *expectancy of internal control*, whereas people who believe that events in their lives are a function of luck, chance, fate, God(s), powerful others or powers *beyond their control*, comprehension or manipulation are said to have an *expectancy of external control*. It is one of the most widely analysed individual difference dimensions in the whole of psychology. Indeed, various scales exist which purport to measure this general dimension, as well as scales designed to tap beliefs in specific settings, such as health, educational, political and religious settings. In each instance, locus of control has been significantly, consistently and predictably related to beliefs and behaviours – nearly always indicating the psychologically adaptive features associated with inner locus of control. Locus of control is related to desire for control, conceived of as a trait reflecting the extent to which individuals are generally motivated to control the events in their lives. People with high desire for control tend to have internal control, to have higher aspirations, to be more persistent and respond more to challenge, and to see themselves as the source of their success (Burger, 1985).

The concept of locus of control has been applied to *behaviour in organizations*. In a review paper, Spector (1982) noted that locus of control is related to motivation, effort, performance, satisfaction, perception of the job, compliance with authority and supervisory style, as well as an important moderating factor between incentives and motivation, satisfaction and turnover. For instance, "internals" tend to prefer piece-rate systems, whereas "externals" tend to be more satisfied with direct supervision, to comply more with the demands of coercive supervisors, and to be more compliant with social demands than internals. Spector concluded that much more organizational theory may be applicable to internals. Similar studies on employment, unemployment and labour market discrimination have demonstrated different levels of internality and externality as a function of work experience. Indeed, Hammar & Vardi (1981) found that in organizational settings that encouraged personal initiative in career development (personnel policies and promotion practices), internals played a more active role than externals in their career progress. However, in settings that did not reinforce self-initiative, locus of control had little effect on career self-management and job experience. Hammar & Vardi noted the existence of a feedback loop from career experience to locus of control, such that favourable experiences increase tendencies towards internal control, which, in turn, increases a person's initiative in self-development with future favourable outcomes. Similarly, Lawler (1971) found that the more people are orientated towards internal control, the more they will feel that their performance will lead to desired outcomes, and the more they are orientated to external control, the less likely they are to have high performance-to-outcome expectancy.

In a large study of nearly 3000 employed people, Andrisani & Nestle (1976) examined the influence of internal/external control on success in the world of work. Locus of control was significantly related to occupational attainment, hourly earnings, job satisfaction, annual earnings and perceived financial progress:

> More specifically, the cross-sectional data suggest that internals are in the better and higher status occupations, earn more money, and tend to be more highly satisfied in their work than comparable externals. The longitudinal data further suggest that internals experience more favourable employment circumstances than

their external counterparts, namely greater earning and job satisfaction. (Andrisani & Nestle, 1976: 160)

Franz (1980) looked at the effect of work (labour market experience) upon the internal locus of control of a large group of young Americans. He found, as predicted, that increases in hourly earnings, additional labour market experience, and more years of formal schooling increase feelings of internal control. However, public sector employment was associated with increasing external locus of control as a result of bureaucratic structures tending to restrict opportunities for developing abilities. More recently, some studies have related locus of control beliefs to economic crisis (Chebat & Filiatrault, 1986), whereas others have attempted to develop a measure specifically of economic locus of control, which was demonstrated to be related to the Protestant work ethic (Furnham, 1986).

Studies since the mid-1960s have revealed refreshingly unequivocal results supporting the fact that instrumentalism (internal locus of control) is a cause and consequence of success, and fatalism is a cause and consequence of failure. Results show the following:

- *Motivation*: Instrumentalists are more likely to believe that their efforts will result in good performance, and they exhibit stronger belief in their own competence.
- *Job performance*: Instrumentalists perform better because of their greater effort, seeking of more information in complex task situations, and exhibit greater personal career effectiveness.
- *Job satisfaction*: Instrumentalists should be more satisfied than fatalists (externals) (generally, as well as in the job) partly because of their success.
- *Leadership*: Instrumentalists prefer participative approaches from their supervisors, rely more on personal persuasion with their subordinates, and seem more task-orientated and less socially orientated.
- *Job perception*: Instrumentalists perceive more personal control over their environment, request more feedback on the job and perceive less role strain.
- *Turnover*: Highly job-satisfied instrumentalists exhibit the same rate of turnover (presumably low) as fatalists, whereas highly job-dissatisfied instrumentalists exhibit more turnover than fatalists.

Spector (1988) devised a very simple locus of control measure, reproduced here as Box 5.6. This simple measure has been shown to be closely related to work motivation and satisfaction (Furnham & Drakeley, 1993). Certainly, there is now ample evidence that high, although not extremely high, internal scores are good predictors of occupational success.

The Protestant work ethic

The concept of the Protestant work ethic (PWE) was devised by the German sociologist Max Weber (1905), who saw it as a partial explanation for the origin of capitalism. People who believe in the Protestant work ethic tend to be achievement- and success-orientated, stress the need for efficacy and practicality, tend to be anti-leisure, and are conservative and conscious about wasting time, energy and money (see Chapter 2).

It has been argued that PWE-believing parents socialize their children by rewarding them for success, independent rational behaviour and postponement of gratification.

Box 5.6 Work locus of control

1. A job is what you make of it.	T	F
2. In most jobs, people can pretty much accomplish whatever they set out to accomplish.	T	F
3. If you know what you want out of a job, you can find a job that gives it to you.	T	F
4. If employees are unhappy with a decision made by their boss, they should do something about it.	T	F
5. Getting the job you want is mostly a matter of luck.	T	F
6. Making money is primarily a matter of good fortune.	T	F
7. Most people are capable of doing their jobs well if they make the effort.	T	F
8. In order to get a really good job, you need to have family members or friends in high places.	T	F
9. Promotions are usually a matter of good fortune.	T	F
10. When it comes to landing a really good job, who you know is more important than what you know.	T	F
11. Promotions are given to employees who perform well on the job.	T	F
12. To make a lot of money you have to know the right people.	T	F
13. It takes a lot of luck to be an outstanding employee in most jobs.	T	F
14. People who perform their jobs well generally get rewarded for it.	T	F
15. Most employees have more influence on their supervisors than they think they do.	T	F
16. The main difference between people who make much money and people who make a little money is luck.	T	F

Score: 1–4 (T)   5–6 (F)   7 (T)   8–10 (F)
         11 (T)   12–13 (F)   14–15 (T)   16 (F)

Low scores indicate high on fatalism; high scores indicate high in instrumentalism.

Source: Reproduced from Spector (1988) with the permission of The British Psychological Society.

They therefore become economically successful, thus explaining the relationship between the Protestant work ethic and economic growth.

Experimental studies on the Protestant work ethic, reviewed by Furnham (1990), have shown believers to be competitive, very eager to have equitable rather than equal rewards, have a tendency towards workaholism, and are able to tolerate tedious jobs. Protestant work ethic beliefs have also been shown to be good predictors of leisure-time and retirement activity, as well as vocational preference and the saving of money.

Although many commentators believe the Protestant work ethic is in terminal decline, there is evidence that it is alive and well, although transformed in character. Box 5.7 shows the scale devised by Mirels & Garrett (1971), the scale that is most frequently used to measure PWE beliefs. Responses are made on a 7-point Likert scale where 1 = "I disagree strongly" and 7 = "I agree strongly". High scores indicate high PWE beliefs; three items have reversed scoring (R).

Research on the work ethic is alive and well. Evidence of this comes from Miller, Woehr & Hudspeth (2002), who recently developed a new (and improved) multi-dimensional Work Ethic Profile. This 65-item questionnaire measures seven conceptually and empirically distinct facets of the work ethic, including such things as self-reliance, delay of gratification and attitudes to wasted time. They argue that this measure is not only conceptually grounded in the original Weberian construct, but is appropriate for use *today* and across different religions.

Box 5.7 Protestant work ethic

1. Most people spend too much time in unprofitable amusements.
2. Our society would have fewer problems if people had less leisure time.
3. Money acquired easily (e.g. through gambling or speculation) is usually spent unwisely.
4. There are few satisfactions equal to the realization that one has done one's best at a job.
5. The most difficult college courses usually turn out to be the most rewarding.
6. Most people who don't succeed in life are just plain lazy.
7. The self-made man is likely to be more ethical than the man born to wealth.
8. I often feel I would be more successful if I sacrificed certain pleasures.
9. People should have more leisure time to spend in relaxation (R).
10. Any man who is able and willing to work hard has a good chance of succeeding.
11. People who fail at a job have usually not tried hard enough.
12. Life would have very little meaning if we never had to suffer.
13. Hard work offers little guarantee of success (R).
14. The credit card is a ticket to careless spending.
15. Life would be more meaningful if we had more leisure time (R).
16. The man who can approach an unpleasant task with enthusiasm is the man who gets ahead.
17. If one works hard enough one is likely to make a good life for oneself.
18. I feel uneasy when there is little work to do.
19. A distaste for hard work usually reflects a weakness of character.

Source: Reproduced from Mirels & Garrett (1971) with the permission of the American Psychological Association. Reprinted with permission.

Workaholism

Oates (1971) claimed to have invented the neologism "workaholic", meaning the addiction to work and the compulsion or the uncontrollable need to work incessantly. But unlike other forms of addiction, which are held in contempt, workaholism is frequently lauded, praised, expected and even demanded. According to Oates (1971), signs of this "syndrome" include boasting about the hours of work, invidious comparisons between self and others on the amount of work achieved, an inability to refuse requests for work, and general competitiveness:

> The workaholic's way of life is considered in America to be one and the same time (a) a religious virtue, (b) a form of patriotism, (c) the way to win friends and influence people, (d) the way to be healthy and wise. Therefore, the workaholic, plagued though he be, is unlikely to change. Why? Because he is a sort of paragon of virtue. He is the one chosen as "the most likely to succeed". (Oates, 1971: 12)

As is customary with populist expositions of psychological variables, a taxonomy is provided by Oates, who listed *five types of workaholic*:

- *Dyed-in-the-wool*: Such a workaholic has five major characteristics – high standards of professionalism, vigorous intolerance of incompetence, overcommitment to institutions and organizations, and considerable talent with marketable skills.

- *Converted*: A person who has given up the above but may behave like a workaholic on occasions for the rewards of money or prestige.
- *Situational*: Workaholism not for psychological or prestige reasons but necessity within an organization.
- *Pseudo-workaholic*: Someone who may look on occasions like a workaholic but has none of the commitment and dedication of a true dyed-in-the-wool character.
- *Escapist as workaholic*: Someone who remains in the office simply to avoid going home or taking part in social relationships.

Finally, Oates (1971) considered the religion of the workaholic. He argues that they are worried by the future with its meaninglessness and hopelessness. Workaholics tend to be unforgiving, lacking in a sense of irony and humour, as well as of wonder and awe. Once the negative factors are renounced, a workaholic experiences a much better quality of life.

It has been suggested that people become helplessly addicted to work, just as some become addicted to drugs. They are prepared to forsake everything in their desire to work. Is this a latter-day manifestation of the Protestant work ethic? Machlowitz (1980) has defined workaholics as people whose desire to work long and hard is intrinsic and whose work habits always exceed the prescriptions of the job they do and the expectations of the people with whom, or for whom, they work. Machlowitz quotes Galbraith on the first page of her book, who noted that "No ethic is as ethical as the work ethic". Throughout her book, she assumes that the workaholic is the embodiment of the Protestant work ethic. According to Machlowitz, all true workaholics share six *traits*, some more paradoxical than stereotypic. Workaholics:

- are intense, energetic, competitive and driven;
- have strong self-doubts;
- prefer labour to leisure;
- can – and do – work any time and anywhere;
- make the most of their time;
- blur the distinctions between business and pleasure.

All workaholics have these traits, but may be subdivided into four distinct types:

- *Dedicated*: These are quintessentially the single-minded, one-dimensional workaholics frequently described by lay-people and journalists. They shun leisure and are often humourless and brusque.
- *Integrated*: These individuals integrate outside features into their work. Thus, although work is "everything", it does sometimes include extracurricular interests.
- *Diffuse*: Such people have many interests, connections and pursuits, which are far more scattered than those of the integrated workaholic. Furthermore, they may change jobs fairly frequently in pursuit of their ends.
- *Intense*: This type of workaholic approaches leisure (frequently competitive sport) with the same passion, pace and intensity as work. They become as preoccupied with leisure as with work.

Machlowitz (1980: 41–42) notes:

> Seeing paternal love as contingent on achievement instead of unconditional surely spurs progress, but it may also be the source of self-doubts ... success is self-perpetuating, but the promise of failure is even more propelling and compelling.

The reasons why workaholics shun vacations and time off are that they have never had a good experience of holidays, either because they have expected too much or chose the wrong type. As their jobs are their passion, they do not feel that they need to get away from it all. Traditional forms of recreation seem like a waste of time and are incomprehensible to them; the preparation for, and anxiety that precedes taking, a holiday are more trouble than they are worth, and workaholics are afraid they would lose complete control of their jobs if they took a holiday. However, workaholics do report being remarkably satisfied and content with their lives. Machlowitz (1980) found little difference between workaholic men's and women's sources of joy and frustration. These were fourfold: in his or her home life, the workaholic felt free of the responsibility for supervising or performing household duties; their job offered them autonomy, control and variety; the job needed the workaholic's "particular" skills and working styles; the workaholic felt healthy and fit for work. Although they never appear to feel successful, many non-frustrated workaholics do report happiness.

Machlowitz (1980) offers some advice for workaholics, maximizing the pleasures and minimizing the pressures of that particular lifestyle:

- find the job that fits – that exercises one's skills and abilities;
- find the place that fits – that provides the most convivial environment;
- find the pace that fits – that allows one to work at the most desirable speed;
- create challenges in your work – to deal with pressures effectively;
- diversify each day – because of short attention spans;
- make sure that every day is different – to improve levels of stimulation;
- use your time; don't let it use you – establish your own circadian rhythm and plan your day around it;
- don't deliberate excessively on decisions that don't warrant the attention;
- let others do things for you – learn how to delegate;
- work alone or hire other workaholics – to prevent intolerance and impatience with others;
- become a mentor, teacher, guide and counsellor to others;
- make sure you make time for what matters to you – such as your family, leisure pursuits;
- get professional help – if you have a job, home or health crisis as a function of your life.

Box 5.8 shows Machlowitz's workaholism questionnaire.

Competitiveness

Competitiveness is both an economic and a psychological concept. It is often thought of favourably in the former discipline but unfavourably in the latter. As a psychological variable, it may be defined as the motive to be better than others or the desire to win in

---

Box 5.8 Machlowitz's workaholism questionnaire

1. Do you get up early, no matter how late you go to bed?	Yes	No
2. If you are eating lunch alone, do you read or work while you are eating?	Yes	No
3. Do you make daily lists of things?	Yes	No
4. Do you find it difficult to "do nothing"?	Yes	No
5. Are you energetic and competitive?	Yes	No
6. Do you work weekends and holidays?	Yes	No
7. Can you work any time and anywhere?	Yes	No
8. Do you find vacations "hard to take"?	Yes	No
9. Do you dread retirement?	Yes	No
10. Do you really enjoy your work?	Yes	No

Source: Adapted from Machlowitz (1978).

---

interpersonal situations. Clearly, it plays an important role in personal and organizational life and may be indispensable to sporting and entrepreneurial success. This has led to the development of such measures as Houston, Farsee & Du's (1992) competitive index. Each question is answered on a "true/false" basis and is an instrument worth exploring in the work setting:

Item
I get satisfaction from competing with others
It's not usually important to me to be the best
Competition destroys friendships
Games that have no clear-cut winner are boring
I am a competitive individual
I will do almost anything to avoid an argument
I try to avoid competing with others
I would like to be on a debating team
I often remain quiet rather than risk hurting another person's feelings
I find competitive situations unpleasant
I try to avoid competing with others
In general, I will go along with the group rather than create conflict
I don't like competing against other people
I don't like games that are winner-take-all
I dread competing against other people
I enjoy competing against an opponent
When I play a game I like to keep score
I often try to outperform others
I like competition
I don't enjoy challenging others even when I think they are wrong.

In an important study, Lynn (1991) showed that of eight belief factors, the best predictor of a country's wealth is the competitive attitudes of its young people. This finding supports that of other researchers in both disciplines. Lynn concludes:

If it is granted that economic growth is desirable and that competition as a means of achieving economic growth is also desirable, the question needs to be considered, whether it would be possible to increase the competitiveness of young people as a means of enhancing economic growth. The psychological principles that would be employed to achieve this objective are reasonably clear. Values, attitudes and behaviour are developed by rewarding them or, in more technical psychological terminology, through the administration of positive reinforcements. Many parents use this principle to encourage competitiveness in their children, as when they give praise or presents when their children do well in school or in games. Many teachers also use this method when they award grades or marks for good work, and prizes or trophies for success in sports. Parents and teachers already have a broad but amateurish understanding of how competitiveness is developed.

To increase the level of competitiveness in young people would require a more systematic application of these psychological principles and a close examination of societies like those of the Pacific Rim to analyse how their high levels of competitiveness are achieved. The problem of how to deal with losers in the competitiveness process would also need to be addressed to mitigate the damaging effects of alienation and low self-esteem that inevitably accompany failure in competitive endeavour. The way to surmount this problem is through the application of the principle that *everyone can be good at something*. The principle is not strictly true, but it has enough truth to be useful for dealing with this problem. At present schools place great emphasis on verbal learning and ability and give little attention to the development of visuo-spatial abilities which are employed in engineering, design, building and the craft skills. Many adolescents who lack strong verbal ability do poorly in schools and become alienated, but they have strong visuo-spatial abilities which could be developed and which would allow them to succeed in fields where those with strong verbal abilities are unable to compete. There are still other areas where those with modest academic abilities can achieve success, such as music, art and sport. This is the way to overcome the problem of the alienation of losers to which critics of competition have rightly pointed. (Lynn, 1996: 107–108)

Furnham, Kirkcaldy & Lynn (1996) found low competitiveness to be linked to national wealth, but argued that competitiveness may peak and then decline once a country reaches a certain level or standard of wealth.

Social values and work

Researchers on the topic of social values have conceived of them as a system of beliefs concerned with such issues as competence and morality, and which are derived in large part from societal demands. These value systems are organized summaries of experience that capture the focal, abstracted qualities of past encounters, have an "oughtness" (specifying prescribed and proscribed behaviours) quality about them, and which function as criteria or a framework against which present experience can be tested. Also, it is argued that these act as general motives.

A value is the enduring belief that a specific instrumental mode of conduct and/or a terminal end state of existence is preferable. Once a value is internalized, it consciously or unconsciously becomes a *standard criterion* for guiding action: for developing and *maintaining attitudes* towards relevant objects and situations, for justifying one's own and others' actions and attitudes, for *morally judging* self and others, and for comparing oneself with others.

Research by Feather (1975) and others has demonstrated that these value systems are systematically linked to culture of origin, religion, chosen university discipline, political persuasion, generations within a family, age, sex, personality and educational background. These values in time may determine vocational choice and occupational behaviour. Feather has argued that social attitudes precede values, which emerge as abstractions from personal experience of one's own and others' behaviour. These values in time become organized into coherent *value systems*, which serve as frames of reference that guide beliefs and behaviour in many situations, such as work. Feather has argued that values, attitudes and attributions are linked into a cognitive–affective (thinking–feeling) system. Thus, people's explanations of unemployment are "linked to other beliefs, attitudes and values within a system in ways that give meaning and consistency to the events that occur" (p. 805). Thus, it may be expected that there are coherent and predictable links between one's general value system and specific work-related beliefs.

What are the things people want and consider important in their lives? Recent research by Schwartz (1992) and his collaborators showed that people's values can be organized into ten types. They are:

- benevolence – active protection of others' welfare;
- universalism – equality and justice;
- self-direction – independence in thought and action;
- stimulation – excitement;
- hedonism – sensuous and emotional gratification;
- achievement – personal success through competence;
- power – status and respect;
- security – safety and harmony of self and social groups;
- conformity – restraint of actions and impulses likely to harm others or violate norms;
- tradition.

These value types can be graphically represented as ten slices of a pie (Hui, 1992) (see Figure 5.5). The types that are adjacent to each other (in terms of the ranks they are given) are more likely to be compatible with each other. Interpersonal conflicts may result when people working closely with each other share neither the same nor adjacent personal values.

Personal values can be reflected in the values at work, which may be categorized into two facets. The first facet is whether the work value concerns an *outcome* of work (e.g. recognition, pay) or a *resource* that one shares merely by being associated with the work organization (e.g. working conditions, company reputation). The second facet categorizes work outcomes into *instrumental* (e.g. benefits), *affective* (e.g. relationship with co-workers) and *cognitive* (e.g. achievement, contribution to society). Some values are associated with the work ethic – achievement and hard working – whereas others are related to interpersonal relationships at work (Hui, 1992).

Employees who score highly on these work values focus on the *content* of their work. They are intrinsically motivated, achievement-orientated and hardworking, strive to

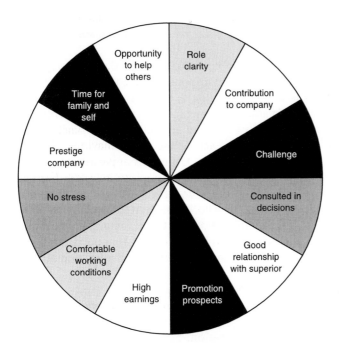

Figure 5.5 A circumflex model of work values. Reproduced from Hui (1992) with the per-mission of Addison-Wesley-Longman China Limited.

move upwards and seek challenges. They usually have completed higher education, occupy senior positions in organizations and tend to be higher in organizational commitment.

Other values are associated with the *context* of work: high salary, job security, pleasant physical working environment and many fringe benefits. These are related to a greater extent to a person's basic survival needs than are the content-orientated values. People who have strong context-orientated, and thus extrinsic, work values ascribe much importance to social status, comfort, salary and benefits. They view work not as an end in itself, but as a means to attain other, more desirable ends. It is quite possible that a fairly large proportion of workers in developing countries are context-orientated, as they strive to better the livelihood of themselves and their families: work is primarily a chance for them to move up the social ladder. Employees who hold these values are often lower in organizational commitment than other employees (Hui, 1992).

A person's values can be assessed by means of self-report questionnaires. Rokeach's (1973) value survey is one of the most widely known instruments. Respondents are required to rank, in order, 18 terminal values and 18 instrumental values. The *terminal values* are "desirable end-states of existence", such as salvation, peace of mind, true friendship and world peace. The *instrumental values* are "desirable modes of conduct", such as being ambitious, clean, honest and loving. These modes of conduct are instru-mental to attaining the desired end-state. Some researchers have made modifications to the response format of Rokeach's value survey (see Schwartz, 1992). Others have added to, or changed, the list of values presented to the person.

Rokeach's value survey was not developed for measuring work values. However, another instrument – the value survey module (Hui, 1992) – can be used for this purpose. Respondents indicate on each of 18 items how important that item is for them. Before reading on, you may want to complete the value survey module and score your responses on it (see Box 5.9).

The self-report questionnaire approach has its flaws. One problem is that the researcher using it often obtains highly skewed responses. Some people may respond by saying that almost everything is important to them, because most of the items to be rated are socially desirable ones. An alternative method that tries to solve this problem is the *ipsative* (forced choice between two or more alternatives) approach: instead of asking people simply how much they *value* each of the items, they are instructed to choose between two items or to rank order a list. Using this approach, we can see, as Schwartz noted, that work values can be arranged around a circle (see Figure 5.5). Some work values are incompatible with each other, whereas others can be held at the same time. Research indicates that people who consider it important to "have an opportunity for high earnings", for example, also want to "have good physical working conditions". However, these same people would not consider it important to "make a real contribution to the success of the company", an item on the other side of the circle (Hui, 1992: 70–71).

Although there is still no agreement about the definitive list of values, or how they are measured, it does appear that they tap into very fundamental aspects of a person's beliefs. Values are particularly related to workers' perceptions of justice and other moral issues. They also relate to work motivation. So far, this chapter has discussed nine individual difference factors that relate to work. This list is far from comprehensive, but it is illustrative. Some have been conceived of as personality traits, others as belief systems, and still others as behaviour patterns. They have nearly all been applied to the world of work rather than arising out of research in this area. Furthermore, many have been shown to be intercorrelated. More importantly, many have been shown to be predictors of choice of work, as well as behaviour at work. Of course, there are many other factors that predict behaviour at work (see Chapters 3 and 4), but it should be remembered that these should be considered among the more important factors. Many of these variables may vary as a function of time and experience. Indeed, just as they may, in part, determine organizational behaviour, so the experience of work might well modify them.

Perceiving others at work

Most people at work are often required to evaluate others: in the process of selection, appraisal, teamwork and meetings, they formulate opinions about their peers, sub-ordinates and supervisors. How these perceptions are formed, and how they relate to organizational behaviour, are critical questions for the manager. In social psychology there is an extensive and highly relevant literature on *person perception* and *decision-making*, which will be considered briefly.

Person perception

Person perception is concerned with the manner in which people perceive the personal characteristics of others, in particular their ability, mood, motivation and personality. Various non-verbal cues – such as posture, gesture, body movement, facial expression, direction of gaze, tone of voice, rate, amount and fluency of speech, orientation and

Box 5.9 Value survey module

Think of an ideal job, disregarding your present job. In choosing an ideal job, how important would it be to you to have the following? Please circle a number.

1 – of utmost importance
2 – very important
3 – of moderate importance
4 – of little importance
5 – of very little or no importance

1. Have sufficient time left for your personal or family life	1	2	3	4	5
2. Have challenging tasks to do, from which you can get a personal sense of accomplishment	1	2	3	4	5
3. Have little tension and stress on the job	1	2	3	4	5
4. Have good physical working conditions (good ventilation and lighting, adequate work space, etc.)	1	2	3	4	5
5. Have a good working relationship with your direct superior	1	2	3	4	5
6. Have security of employment	1	2	3	4	5
7. Have considerable freedom to adopt your own approach to the job	1	2	3	4	5
8. Work with people who cooperate well with one another	1	2	3	4	5
9. Be consulted by your direct superior in his decisions	1	2	3	4	5
10. Make a real contribution to the success of your company or organization	1	2	3	4	5
11. Have an opportunity for high earnings	1	2	3	4	5
12. Serve your country	1	2	3	4	5
13. Live in an area desirable to you and your family	1	2	3	4	5
14. Have an opportunity for advancement to higher-level jobs	1	2	3	4	5
15. Have an element of variety and adventure in the job	1	2	3	4	5
16. Work in a prestigious, successful company or organization	1	2	3	4	5
17. Have an opportunity for helping other people	1	2	3	4	5
18. Work in a well defined job situation where the requirements are clear	1	2	3	4	5

Scoring guide

Origins of the VSM: The composition of the VSM is based on research among 116,000
respondents. This research is described in Hofstede (1984).

Respondents: The purpose of the scores is to locate groups of respondents on the four
dimensions (one of which is individualism). The four dimensions were developed for
describing national cultures. For obtaining acceptably reliable scores, groups of respondents should not be smaller than 20.

Individualism index: In the original study, the mean scores of 14 "work goals" questions
were first standardized, then factor-analysed, and factor scores on the two resulting factors
were transformed into the individualism and masculinity indices. This procedure cannot
be followed for the present VSM, because it contains only 10 of the 14 original goal
questions. However, with the help of regression analysis, an approximation has been
developed for the computation of the indices. The computation of the individualism index
(IDV) uses the mean scores on questions 1, 4, 8 and 13 of the questionnaire you completed
above. If we call these $\times 1$, $\times 4$, $\times 8$ and 13, the formula becomes IDV $= 76 \times 4 - 43 \times 1 + 30 \times 8 - 27 \times 13 - 29$.

Source: Reproduced from Hui (1992) with the permission of Addison Wesley Longman China Ltd.

distance – are perceived in the course of social interaction and they influence the interpretations placed on other people's behaviour. What people do in the process of selection is to *seek out*, and *attend to*, many not equally salient pieces of information about individuals, to integrate that information into a coherent whole, and then make judgements between individuals. However, because of the complexity of this topic in certain circumstances, such as those described below, misinterpretations, errors and systematic biases are likely to arise.

Implicit personality

Implicit personality theory is a set of concepts and assumptions used to describe, compare and understand people. We all have our own idiosyncratic, non-explicit (thus implicit) theories of personality. Implicit personality theories differ among individuals, and the differences are greatest between people of different cultures. In attributing characteristics to others, people form clear judgements about stable characteristics (e.g. enduring characteristics such as age, beliefs, ability, manner and personality traits) but also form dynamic perceptual judgements of characteristics that change, such as moods, emotions and motives.

For instance, the boxer Muhammed Ali has made explicit his implicit theory of personality, which is based on fruit. The theory depends on the hardness/softness of the inside and outside of fruit. This allows for four types of fruit (Figure 5.6). The boxer confessed to being a "grape" (in his view the most desirable of the various fruit) but usually letting the public see only his "walnut" personality. Although this charming theory based on the observable and unobservable aspects of human behaviour is appealing, it may be rather simplistic and could lead to over-hasty categorization.

Perhaps one of the areas where lay theories are best observed is at work. Managers frequently hold strong beliefs based on personal implicit theories. As a result, many "theories" in occupational psychology reflect this bias. McGregor (1960) has argued that managers have two basic theories (called X and Y) about the personality of employees which lead them to exercise high levels of control (if a follower of theory X) or less control (if a follower of theory Y). Followers of theory X are pessimists: they believe people don't like work, avoid it, have little ambition, try to avoid responsibility and therefore need firm direction, control and coercion. Theory Y followers are more optimistic, believing that under the right conditions people not only work hard and show commitment but seek both responsibility and challenge.

		Outside	
		Hard	Soft
Inside	Hard	Pomegranate	Prune
	Soft	Walnut	Grape

Figure 5.6 Muhammed Ali's personality theory, based on fruit.

Logical errors

Implicit personality theory leads people to form hypotheses or assumptions about what traits or abilities go together in a person (people who like computers are shy; Germans are all hardworking; people who speak more than one language are socially very skilful). Usually intuitively, they use this interpretation to form an extensive and consistent view of other people when faced with incomplete information. This is often referred to as the logical error, the assumption being that certain traits are always found together.

A famous experiment was conducted to test this principle in which students on a psychology course were given descriptions of a guest speaker before he addressed the class (Asch, 1946). He was described to one-half of the class as "warm" and to the other half as "cold". The lecturer then entered the class and led a discussion for about 20 minutes. When he left the classroom, the students were asked to describe him. The students who were told that he was going to be "cold" were more likely to attribute to him traits such as self-centredness, unsociability, humourlessness and ruthlessness than were the students who were told he was "warm". The students who thought of the lecturer as "warm" were also more likely to interact with him during the discussion. Thus, changes in person perception can arise from varying even minor cues or stimuli, leading to a totally altered view of the person perceived.

Another study concerned the contents of a person's supermarket basket. Again only one item differed between two full baskets (instant coffee versus coffee beans for grinding), but observers formed quite different perceptions of the shopper. Occasionally very minor factual details on an applicant's curriculum vitae can induce the same logical errors.

Halo effect

The "halo effect" occurs when people perceive others in terms of the concepts of good and bad; *all* good qualities are possessed by the former and all bad qualities by the latter (also called the horns effect, being the opposite of the halo effect). Given an adverse explicit evaluation at a particular stage of his or her career, a person may find that, later, when his or her performance has improved, the evaluation bears the scars of the earlier assessment. It is said that when you make a serious error at work, no-one forgets, but that if you score a significant success, no-one remembers. Similarly, in an interview, if an interviewer perceives in the interviewee a desirable attribute similar to one of their own, the interviewer may make a favourable overall assessment. The reverse would be true when a deficiency is identified at an earlier stage. Hence, attractive people are rated favourably on many other unrelated dimensions (e.g. intelligence, word-processing skills, moral behaviour) and vice versa. There is evidence to suggest that our perceptions of people are markedly influenced by our initial good/bad evaluations of them. It has been suggested that our overall attitudes towards others can to a large extent be determined by our evaluations of them along three dimensions:

- activity (active versus passive);
- strength or potency (strong versus weak);
- evaluative (good versus bad).

Halo effects occur essentially when information is not appropriately weighted (McKenna 1987: 142).

Stereotyping

This well-known short-hand error is connected with the tendency to label people with traits or qualities that typically belong to a reference group. For example, one may consider a Scot to be mean or thrifty, a Jew to be a shrewd business person, or an African to be musical or sports-talented. Therefore, we attribute to a member of the race in question the characteristics of the stereotype. Biased perception arises when people rely on the stereotyped image and ignore critical information concerning the individual. Stereotyping does not necessarily result only in the creation of negative impressions; they can also be positive. It has been argued that many stereotypes contain the "kernel-of-truth" in them which is embellished, over-employed, and so on.

Assumed similarity

Assumed similarity is the tendency to see others as having characteristics more like our own than is really the case. Many people are inclined to project their own emotional or motivational state onto others. They also believe that others have personalities like their own, particularly if they are friendly with them. People who are asked to predict the behaviour of others usually tend to make predictions more like their own behaviour than like the behaviour of the person whom they observe. That is, they attribute to others the motives and emotions that they possess but may feel uncomfortable about.

Some of the pitfalls in person perception have been identified here, and there are some situations in business when employees make unrealistic generalizations about the personal characteristics of those with whom they come into contact with (McKenna, 1987: 144).

Attribution theory

Attribution theories suggest that as people observe another's behaviour, they try to establish whether it was caused by internal or external forces. They are concerned with how people attribute success and failure for their own and others' behaviour, and the emotional and behavioural consequences of those attributions. When something is internally caused, it is seen as being under the personal control of the individual; if it is externally caused, it is the result of situational demands that confront the individual.

This can be illustrated by the use of a simple example. An employee is late for work; this may be because of sleeping in because of a late-night party the previous night, or because he or she was caught up in a traffic queue that was the result of a road accident. If the former were the case, it would be an internal attribution; if the latter were the case, it would be an external attribution. It is, of course, possible to have both (McKenna, 1987).

The actor–observer difference suggests that, as observers of social behaviour, people assume that often *other* people's behaviour is *internally* controlled but, when considering their own behaviour, they exaggerate the extent to which their *own* behaviour is *externally* determined. The tendency to take greater account of the situation in explaining our own behaviour and less account of the situation in explaining other people's behaviour is sometimes called *fundamental attribution error*. In appraising the performance of an employee in an organization, effort or ability is often referred to when explaining performance with reference to internal factors. But when performance is explained with reference to external factors, often luck or the difficulty of the job is mentioned. Obviously, the attitudes of the appraiser to the person being appraised will have an influence on the final outcome.

People seem to take into consideration various aspects of the behaviour of others that they observe before coming to a conclusion:

- *Distinctiveness*: This refers to how different the behaviour being observed is from other related behaviour. Is it unusual, distinctive, peculiar or not? For example, if an employee's attendance record is exemplary, and this is reinforced by an overall satisfactory performance at work, a recent bout of prolonged absenteeism could be considered unusual. Therefore, in these circumstances the observer attaches an external attribution to this behaviour (i.e. the absenteeism is outside the control of the employee). If, however, the absenteeism fits into a general pattern, and is not unique, an internal attribution will be attached to the behaviour in question (i.e. the employee is personally responsible for his or her behaviour).
- *Consensus*: If everyone who is faced by a similar set of circumstances reacts in the same way, that behaviour shows consensus. For example, a particular employee's late arrival at work is observed; when the observer establishes that all those who took the same route to work as the particular employee were also late, possibly because of delays attributable to bad weather, the conditions necessary for consensus arise. If consensus is high, one is likely to attach an external attribution to the particular employee's lateness. However, if the other employees who travelled the same route arrived at work on time, the consensus factor would be absent and an internal interpretation could be attributed to the particular employee's lateness (i.e. it was his or her fault).
- *Consistency*: The observer of a person's behaviour always takes consistency (over time) into account. For example, if an employee comes in late to work regularly over a 6-month period, his or her behaviour is consistent. This could be contrasted with an example of an employee arriving late on the odd occasion and being rather unpredictable and inconsistent. The more consistent the behaviour, the more likely the observer is inclined to attribute the behaviour in question to internal causes, and vice versa.

The above considerations focus on judging actions in a situational context. An attribution perspective is important because the way an observer perceives and makes sense of an action or behaviour will influence his or her response and provide a foundation for predicting future events. Attributions have powerful decisional consequences. There is a danger in prematurely attributing causation to particular actions or behaviour, because it may end up over-simplifying reality. There is no substitute for judiciously collecting information, weighing it carefully and considering all the alternatives, before deciding on a cause. Being aware of systematic and widespread attribution errors can help prevent them from occurring (McKenna, 1987: 145–146).

Decision-making

Psychologists have appeared to rejoice in revealing the mistakes of intuitive judgement or the inaccuracies in lay theories. There is a long list of errors, fallacies and biases of ordinary people. These include being insufficiently sensitive or mindful of: the *sample size* in interpreting statistics or generalizations (small sample sizes give results difficult to replicate); the *reliability* of information used to support or refute an argument; the *accuracy* of information retrieved from *memory* with all its attendant biases and failures; the relevance of paying attention to *base-rate* frequencies (i.e. the distribution of behaviour for most people on a particular issue); the necessity of testing *disconfirming information* (rather than only asking for information likely to confirm theories); and so on.

In each case, psychologists have demonstrated that people make erroneous assumptions or incorrect calculations in dealing with statistical manipulations. Although people probably do not have statistical theories, they do appear to have ideas about order, randomness, and so on, which dictate their statistical behaviour. For instance, many lay people feel threatened by randomness and lack of control, and hence operate as if the former did not occur and they, therefore, were able to experience some kind of control over events (Furnham, 1988).

The authors to have contributed most to the understanding of lay statistical inferences are Kahneman & Tversky (1982). Their work has been heavily criticized, but remains the most important in the area. In looking at people's probabilistic predictions, they specified various heuristics or problem-solving techniques that people use, as well as the systematic biases associated with them. The three most important were representativeness, availability, and adjustment and anchoring.

Representativeness

In judging whether people are representative of a class or group, people often ignore several factors that should influence their probability judgements (e.g. if we know someone is shy, withdrawn and unhelpful, neat and tidy with a need for order and structure, this person seems suited to being a librarian). These include:

- *Prior probabilities*: Base-rate frequencies of the absolute number of people in any category must be taken into account before judging their representativeness of that group or category (i.e. how many librarians have the characteristics of our applicant?).
- *Sample size*: Results drawn from small samples are seen to be equally, and sometimes even more, accurate as results drawn from larger samples, which is incorrect (i.e. the larger the sample, the more accurate the probabilities).
- *Misconceptions of chance*: People inappropriately expect that a sequence of events generated by a random process represents the essential characteristics of that process, even when the sequence is short. (Therefore, people overestimate the replicability of findings based on small populations.)
- *Insensitivity to predictability*: People appear to be insensitive to the reliability of the evidence upon which they make their predictions and do not know the rule that the higher the predictability, the wider the range of predictable values. (That is, if the evidence is unreliable, all outcomes are equally possible.)

- *Illusion of validity*: The more supposedly representative a sample or item is, the more confidence people will have in the validity of their judgement, even when they are aware of the many factors that limit accuracy. (For example, people still conduct interviews despite repeated demonstrations of their weaknesses.)
- *Misconceptions of regression*: People do not develop correct intuitions about this phenomenon when it is bound to occur or they invent a spurious causal explanation for it. Essentially, the phenomenon is incompatible with the belief that the predicted outcome should be maximally representative of the input, and hence that the value of the outcome variable should be as extreme as the value of the input variable.

Availability

This refers to the fact that, when people judge the frequency or probability of an event, they bring to mind available instances or occurrences of that event which they themselves have experienced. Availability problems lead to predictable biases:

- *Retrievability (recall) of instances*: Where instances are easily retrieved from memory, they appear more numerous than those events, of equal frequency, whose instances are less retrievable. Similarly, more recent or more salient events' frequencies are overestimated compared with less recent and less salient occurrences (i.e. the more easily something is remembered, for whatever reason, the more validity it acquires).
- *Effectiveness of search set*: The ease of search for information, based on a set of strategies, leads to errors in judgement because items more easily retrieved are thought of as being more frequent.
- *Imaginability*: The extent to which the problem can be imagined influences judgements: the more easily salient issues can be imagined, the more their effects will be overemphasized and vice versa. Thus, the more abstract and/or unimaginable a phenomenon, the less weight is given to it in various judgements.
- *Illusory correlation*: This judgement of how frequently two events co-occur is often based on the strength of the associated bond between them – when this is strong, people conclude that the events have been paired, even though they have not. Thus, people might overestimate the association between physical features (e.g. prominent ears) and delinquency, despite the fact that there is *no* evidence of this association.

Adjustment and anchoring

A mistake in the initial value or starting point often leads to computational errors. Three particular problems frequently occur:

- *Insufficient adjustment*: This occurs when calculations are based on initial figures which anchor the answers and are never sufficiently adjusted thereafter, even when the first "guess" was badly wrong.
- *Biases in evaluation of conjunctive and disjunctive events*: People often tend to overestimate the probability of conjunctive events (e.g. drawing a red marble, with replacement, seven times in succession from a bag containing 90% red marbles) and

underestimate the probability of disjunctive events (e.g. drawing a red marble once in seven times from a bag containing 10% red marbles). This is because the overall probability of conjunctive events is lower than the probability of each elementary single event, whereas the overall probability of a disjunctive event is higher than the probability of each elementary event.

- *The assessment of subjective probability distributions*: Individuals tend to state overly narrow confidence intervals which reflect more certainty than is justified by their knowledge about the assessed qualities.

Tversky & Kahneman (1974) found that the cognitive biases resulting from the reliance on heuristics are found among lay people *and* experts. Surprisingly, what they found was not that people use these heuristics, but rather that they fail to learn rules such as "regression to the mean" even when they (both experts *and* lay people) have been exposed to this phenomenon often (i.e. that the children of very tall parents often are not as tall as either, being more "average" in height). Their work has attracted considerable research, mainly confirmatory.

Kahneman & Tversky (1982) have argued that there are many reasons for the study of errors in statistical reasoning: they expose our intellectual limitations; they reveal the psychological processes that govern judgement and inference; they map which principles are intuitive or counter-intuitive. For them, intuitive judgements are those reached by an informal or unstructured mode of thinking, those that are compatible with our lay view of the world, and those that we apply to the procedure of our normal conduct. They argue that one should distinguish between errors of comprehension and errors of application because, although people may understand a particular statistical law, they may not recognize when it should be applied.

To help people distinguish scientific logic from poor logic, Marks and Kammann (1980) have developed maxims in an attempt to prevent lay people from being fooled by bogus "psychic phenomena". There 10 rules are as follows:

- *If-what-then-what* – make the theorist be specific by asking what the theory predicts.
- *Disprovability* – ask the theorist what piece of evidence would be required to disprove his or her theory.
- *Burden of proof* – it is for the theorist to prove or substantiate his or her belief in the theory, rather than your disbelief.
- *Alternative thinking* – it is possible that other phenomena (i.e. mediating variables) explain the theorist's evidence, just as well as the phenomena he or she cites.
- *Missing negative cases* – very often, negative cases (those that "disprove" a theory) are omitted, so making the data look stronger. These need to be sought out.
- *Personal observation* – subjective validations are not sufficient unless accompanied by detailed recorded observations.
- *Testimonials* – personal experience is poor evidence because often people are not fully aware of forces acting upon them or their real needs and motives.
- *Sources* – it is worth examining the credibility of the source of a theory, i.e. where it is published, debated, etc., as these sources are frequently dubious.
- *Emotional commitment* – the more a person is ego-involved in a theory, the less rationally and sceptically it may be assessed.

- *Ad hominem technique* – "First a believer may hold certain authorities to be infallible, and quote their opinions as evidence. Second, he may try to place contrary believers into a category of bad people and thus reject their arguments out of hand. Third, he may turn against you, accusing you of bad motives or stupidity. All of these arguments are fallacious, and it is not only important to recognise them, but also not to use them. The object is to learn, not to win" (Marks & Kammann, 1980: 226).

Conclusion

Managers and employees bring to their work pre-established beliefs, attitudes and values that their organization might reinforce or attempt to change. Many of these belief and value systems are good predictors of work-related behaviour. The judgements and decisions made by people at work are subject to modification by the workplace itself. Furthermore, how managers gather information and make judgements is a topic of considerable importance, particularly given all the data on the errors they make.

It is naïve and dangerous to presume that the simple expression of attitudes reflects how a person will or does behave. Equally, to assume that you can change behaviour by changing attitudes is largely mistaken. To measure attitudes by interview or questionnaire, believing that they will predict behaviour, is fraught with problems, although it is possible if certain specific steps are followed. Substantial developments in the theories of planned action and planned behaviour have, however, meant that we are now in a much better position to understand when work-related attitudes predict work-related behaviour.

We all have beliefs about achievement, authority, justice, control and the importance of work. These attitudes sometimes form into fairly complex and coherent belief systems that are central to the way individuals see their world. This chapter has looked at nine of the many different "topics" that fit into the area of work-related attitudes. Over the years, researchers from many different traditions have developed theories and measures of these different belief systems, attempting to explain how and why they are held by different people and (most importantly) their behavioural consequences. Many of these attitudinal systems have been "tested" in the workplace and found to be predictive. These belief systems appear to relate to almost all aspects of behaviour at work: how employees select their potential employer, how they behave at interview, how quickly they adapt to and get socialized by the organization, their job satisfaction and productivity, their job history of promotion, and why and when they leave the organization.

Other researchers have focused more particularly on the values of employees, rather than their attitudes. Various research groups have attempted to devise questionnaires that measure the fundamental values of all peoples and show how these values relate to their attitudes, beliefs and behaviours. More managers are beginning to recognize that fundamental values strongly influence the work behaviour of employees.

Finally, this chapter looked at the issues associated with how selectors and managers form impressions of others and the common problems encountered in the way they collect and assess personal information. Brief mention was also made of some of the well-known processes and biases involved in the attribution of the causes of work-related behaviour. Special attention was paid to some of the many frequently occurring errors and biases made by decision-makers in the workplace.

A research perspective

What are the beliefs and values of leaders? How does one perceive this all-important role in the organization? Mintzberg's (1975) study of chief executive officers suggested a different way of looking at leadership. In an excellent piece of writing, he distinguished between folklore and fact concerning management work:

- *Folklore*: Managers are reflective systematic planners.
  Fact: Managers work at an unrelenting pace; their activities are characterized by brevity, variety and discontinuity, and most of them dislike reflection.
- *Folklore*: Effective managers have no regular duties to perform.
  Fact: Managers have many ritualistic, ceremonial and negotiation duties.
- *Folklore*: Managers need and use management information system aggregated data.
  Fact: Managers favour the oral medium.
- *Folklore*: Management is (becoming) a science and a profession.
  Fact: Much still depends on the intuition and personal judgement of managers.

Mintzberg observed that managerial work encompasses ten roles. Almost all roles include activities that could be construed as leadership – influencing others towards a particular goal. In addition, most of these roles can apply to non-managerial positions as well as managerial ones. The role approach resembles the behavioural and trait perspectives, because all three call for specific types of behaviour independent of the situation; however, the role approach is more compatible with the situation approach and has been shown to be more valid than either the behavioural or trait perspective.

- *Figurehead*: The manager, acting as a symbol or representative of the organization, performs diverse ceremonial duties. By attending Chamber of Commerce meetings, heading the local charity drive, or representing the chairman of the firm at an awards banquet, a manager performs the figurehead role.
- *Leader*: The manager, interacting with subordinates, motivates and develops them. The supervisor who conducts quarterly performance interviews or selects training opportunities for his or her subordinates performs this role. This role emphasizes the socio-emotional and people-orientated side of leadership. Although it may include some task activities, these are more often incorporated into the decisional roles, described below.
- *Liaison*: The manager establishes a network of contacts to gather information for the organization. Belonging to professional associations or meeting over lunch with peers in other organizations helps the manager perform the liaison role.
- *Monitor*: The manager gathers information from the environment inside and outside the organization. The manager may attend meetings with his or her subordinates, scan company publications, or participate in company-wide committees as a way of performing this role.
- *Disseminator*: The manager transmits both factual and attitudinal information to subordinates. Managers may conduct staff meetings, send memoranda to their staff, or meet informally with them on a one-to-one basis to discuss current and future projects.
- *Spokesperson*: The manager provides information to people outside the organization about its performance and policies. The manager who oversees preparation of the annual report, prepares advertising copy, or speaks at community and professional meetings fulfils this role.
- *Entrepreneur*: The manager designs and initiates change in the organization. The supervisor who redesigns the job of subordinates, introduces flexible working hours, or brings new technology to the job performs this role.
- *Disturbance handler*: The manager deals with problems that arise when organizational operations break down. A person who finds a new supplier for an out-of-stock part on short

notice, who replaces unexpectedly absent employees, or who deals with machine breakdowns performs this role.

- *Resource allocator*: The manager controls the allocation of people, money, materials and time by scheduling his or her own time, programming subordinates' work efforts, and authorizing all significant decisions. Preparation of the budget is a major aspect of this role.
- *Negotiator*: The manager participates in negotiation activities. A manager who hires a new employee may negotiate work assignments or compensation with that person.

Given the importance and number of roles a manager has to perform, it is important to know a manager's role preference; the prescribed and proscribed role preferences of his or her company, and the perceived regularity of changing and maintaining roles, as well as difficulties associated with each.

An interesting research question concerns whether leaders with rather different role preferences have different work-related beliefs and attitudes. Do their attitudes help them become or stay leaders? Which roles do the best leaders excel at most?

A cross-cultural perspective

A Muslim perspective

For Muslims, like other "people of the book", religious life and economic life are inextricably entwined. Islamic law is a moral and legal code which should apply to all business. Westwood has considered how this growing religion affects business and organizational life:

- Muslims may interpret the power of Allah so as to feel that their own effort and initiative is irrelevant. Some have linked this "fatalism" with a low work and achievement orientation, and so slower material and economic development. There are problems with this argument, but certainly a belief in pre-destination and an external cause for one's actions would make a difference to how human behaviour and its outcomes are viewed, and to motivation, effort and achievement.
- In Islam, business cannot be separated from the religious realm, and the laws of Islam apply to business as to every other sphere of life. The question of usury and interest (*riba*) earning has been a problem in modern Islam. Traditionally, the lending of money to earn interest was prohibited. Today, this is more often interpreted in terms of not earning an unreasonable amount of interest. But even as recently as 1976, the Finance Minister of Kuwait strongly criticized the charging of interest as contrary to Islam.
- In terms of performance appraisal, the West has developed objective impersonal systems which focus on specific aspects of performance. For the Islamic manager, it is difficult to see a person impersonally and to evaluate a set of separate, objective performance outcomes or characteristics. He is led to consider the employee as a whole person. This will include an overall evaluation of whether the person is "good" and a proper Muslim. The same would apply to promotion criteria and decisions, where general evaluations, as indicated above, together with loyalty and seniority, may be more important than job performance criteria.
- The Islamic tradition of consultation for consensus building is also seen by some commentators to be part of the organizational expectations and management style of Islamic businesses.
- Western bureaucratic traditions of high specialization, clear division of labour, and impersonality are not so apparent in an Islamic context. There is much more reliance upon personal relationships, trust, and a sense of the organization as a community – perhaps reflecting the strength of the Islamic community ideal. Much of this would be true for most Southeast Asian cultures.
- It has been argued that Muslims have a past-orientation. This, together with the belief in

pre-destination and fatalism, tends to mean that planning, including career planning, is a neglected or underemphasized activity. It may even be viewed as ungodly, since it pre-empts the will of Allah. Change itself is viewed with suspicion and a preference shown for the status quo. Change may be viewed as unnecessary, a threat, or in the hands of God. Such values would also make a difference to how job security would be viewed.

- The *Quran* instructs people to honour and fulfil their obligations. Hence, violation of an agreement or contract would not only have legal but also moral implications; it would be a sin. Contracts are often not, then, in writing; a Muslim would expect another Muslim to fulfil the spirit of a verbal agreement. (Westwood, 1992: 57–58)

    With mass migration in the latter half of the twentieth century, the Muslim populations of most European and North American countries have grown phenomenally. Furthermore, since the Second World War the oil-rich Muslim countries of the Middle East have been able to exhort considerable economic and political influence over the whole business world. The globalization of the world market means that Muslims, Christians, Buddhists, Hindus, Jews and others are having to do business with each other more often. Powerful monotheistic religions (Christianity, Islam, Judaism) influence very considerably the values and behaviour of their adherents and how they prefer to do business. An appreciation of these different beliefs may help cross-cultural business contact significantly.

    Islamic psychologists like Ali (1988, 1992) have tried to "translate" Western Christian ideas for use in Arabic countries. Thus he tried to define the Islamic work ethic thus:

> Work is an obligatory activity and a virtue in light of the needs of man and the necessity to establish equilibrium in one's individual and social life. Work enables man to be independent and is a source of self-respect, satisfaction, and fulfillment. Success and progress on the job depend on hard work and commitment to one's job. Commitment to work also involves a desire to improve the community and societal welfare. Society would have fewer problems if each persona were committed to his work and avoided unethical methods of wealth accumulation. Creative work and cooperation are not only a source of happiness but are considered noble deeds too. (Ali, 1988: 577)

He later found in a study of 117 Saudi Arabian managers that they were all highly committed to the Islamic work ethic (IWE). He concludes:

> Contrary to the myth-absence of the IWE, the results reaffirm a strong commitment to hard work and to the value of working in one's life. Indeed, the Islamic emphasis on constant struggle in working for the actualization of ideals and on justice and generosity in the workplace as necessary conditions for society's welfare positions Islam as a leading force advocating productive but humanistic approaches to organized work. (Ali, 1992: 516–517).

A human resources perspective

Pilfering and theft

Mars (1984), who studied pilfering and cheating at work, believed that at least some of it represented a way of "hitting out at the boss, the company, the system or the state". He classified different types of job cheats at work along two dimensions.

    The first of the two dimensions he labelled *grid*. Strong grid jobs limited the workers' autonomy by closely defining the tasks to be performed and the jobholders' performance expectations. Weak grid jobs gave their occupants a high degree of autonomy, allowing them to organize their work how they wished. The second dimension was *group*. This related to which workers were free from, or subject to, group controls. In a strong group occupation, the worker was under the control of fellow workers who could exert and impose their views on him, whereas weak group jobs gave the individual freedom from such pressure. Mars classified occupational groups into four categories, which he called *hawks, wolves, vultures* and *donkeys*:

- *Hawks (weak grid, weak group)*: These are individualistic entrepreneurs, innovative professionals and small businessmen. However, this category also includes fairground buskers, taxi owner-drivers and wheeler-dealer "Mr Fixits". The people involved all possess a high degree of autonomy from group control and job definition, meaning that they can bend the rules to suit themselves. They are not high taxpayers!
- *Wolves (strong grid, strong group)*: Employees in these occupations operate in "wolf packs". They pilfer according to agreed rules and through a well-defined division of labour. Like a wolf pack, they possess a group hierarchical structure, with a leader who gives orders, and informal rules that control the behaviour of members through sanctions. Gangs of dockers, teams of miners, refuse collection gangs and airline crews fall into this category.
- *Vultures (weak grid, strong group)*: Vultures operate on their own when they are stealing, but they need the support of a group in order to do so. They characteristically have jobs that involve much moving around, and where successful performance depends, to some extent, on an individual's flair and ability. The effect is that rules might be relaxed. Many forms of selling jobs come into this category. Hence, travelling salesmen, waiters and driver-deliverers operate vulture fiddles. Some even boast of their behaviour.
- *Donkeys (strong grid, weak group)*: Donkeys are people who are constrained by their jobs and are isolated from other workers. Transport workers, machine-minders and supermarket cashiers are all in donkey occupations. Donkeys can either be very powerful or very powerless: they are powerless if they passively accept the constraints placed upon them, but they can exert power through rejecting such constraints, breaking the rules and thus causing temporary disruptions (Huczynski & Buchanan, 1991: 554–555).

When there is a lack of fit between a person's job and their cosmology (ideas, values, attitudes appropriate to them), people react in various ways. They could resign (withdrawing mentally from this personal conflict); they could experience a nervous breakdown; or they could experience a sense of alienation. Such alienation in the organization is often manifest in above-average absenteeism, employee turnover, sabotage and fiddling. Thus, fiddling represents only one of a number of possible responses by an individual to a situation of work alienation. Furthermore, the fiddles of donkeys are not fired primarily by the desire for monetary gain. Instead, the organizing and operating of the fiddles provide these workers with some degree of individuality and an element of creativity which is missing from their jobs.

Human resources investigations are more and more concerned with "office crime". They need to understand how and why these crimes are committed before people can be caught.

References

Adorno, T., Frenkel-Brunswick, E., Levison, D., & Sanford, N. (1950). *The authoritarian personality*. New York: Harper.

Ajzen, I. (1985). From intentions to action: A theory of planned behaviours. In J. Kuhl & J. Beckmann (Eds.), *Action control: From cognition to behaviour* (pp. 11–39). Heidelberg: Springer-Verlag.

Ajzen, I. (1988). *Attitudes, personality and behaviour*. Milton Keynes: Open University Press.

Ajzen, I. (1991). The theory of planned behaviour. *Organizational Behaviour and Human Decision Processes, 50*, 179–211.

Ajzen, I., & Driver, B. L. (1991). Prediction of leisure participation from behavioural, normative and control beliefs: An application of the theory of planned behaviour. *Leisure Sciences, 13,* 185–204.

Ajzen, I., & Fishbein, M. (1980). *Understanding attitudes and predicting social behaviour.* Englewood Cliffs, NJ: Prentice-Hall.

Ajzen, I., & Madden, T. (1986). Prediction of goal-directed behaviours. *Journal of Experimental Social Psychology, 22,* 453–474.

Ali, A. (1988). Scaling an Islamic work ethic. *Journal of Social Psychology, 124,* 575–583.

Ali, A. (1992). Islamic work ethic in Arabia. *Journal of Social Psychology, 126,* 507–519.

Andrisani, P., & Nestle, G. (1976). Internal/external control as contributor to, and outcome of, work experience. *Journal of Applied Psychology, 61,* 156–163.

Arvola, A., Laehteenmaeki, L., & Tuorila, H. (1999). Predicting the intent to purchase unfamiliar and familiar cheeses: The effects of attitudes, expected liking and food neophobia. *Appetite, 32,* 113–126

Asch, S. (1946). Forming impressions of personality. *Journal of Abnormal and Social Psychology, 41,* 258–290.

Atkinson, J. (1964). *Motives in fantasy, action and society.* Princeton, NJ: Van Nostrand.

Bandura, A. (1982). Self-efficacy mechanism in human agency. *American Psychologist, 37,* 122–147.

Buchholz, R. (1976). Measurement of beliefs. *Human Relations, 29,* 1177–1188.

Buchholz, R. (1978). An empirical study of contemporary beliefs about work in American society. *Journal of Applied Psychology, 63,* 219–221.

Burger, J. (1985). Desire for control and achievement related behaviours. *Journal of Personality and Social Psychology, 48,* 1520–1533.

Chebat, J.-C., & Filiatrault, P. (1986). Locus of control and attitudes toward the economic crisis. *Journal of Psychology, 126,* 559–561.

Conner, M., & Armitage, C. J. (1998). Extending the Theory of Planned Behaviour: A review and avenues for further research. *Journal of Applied Social Psychology, 28,* 1429–1464.

Dalbert, C. (2001). *The justice motive as a personal resource.* New York: Plenum Press.

Dickson, J., & Buchholz, R. (1977). Management and belief about work in Scotland and the USA. *Journal of Management Studies, 14,* 80–101.

Evans, D., & Norman, P. (1998). Understanding pedestrians' road crossing decisions: An application of the theory of planned behaviour. *Health Education Research, 13,* 481–489.

Feather, N. (1975). *Values in education and society.* New York: Free Press.

Feather, N. (1979). Value correlates of conservatism. *Journal of Personality and Social Psychology, 37,* 1617–1630.

Feather, N. (1985). Attitudes, values and attributions: Explanations of unemployment. *Journal of Personality and Social Psychology, 48,* 876–889.

Fishbein, M., & Ajzen, I. (1975). *Belief, attitude, intention, and behaviour.* New York: Wiley.

Fishbein, M., & Ajzen, I. (1993). Research based on theories of reasoned action and planned behaviour. Unpublished manuscript, University of Massachusetts at Amhurst.

Franz, R. (1980). The effect of early labour market experience upon internal/external locus of control among male workers. *Journal of Youth and Adolescence, 9,* 202–210.

Furnham, A. (1986). Economic locus of control. *Human Relations, 39,* 29–43.

Furnham, A. (1988). *Lay theories.* Oxford: Pergamon Press.

Furnham, A. (1990). *The Protestant work ethic.* London: Routledge.

Furnham, A. (1992). *Personality at work.* London: Routledge.

Furnham, A. (2003). Belief in a just world: Research progress over the past decade. *Personality and Individual Differences, 34,* 795–811.

Furnham, A., & Drakeley, R. (1993). Work locus of control and perceived organizational climate. *European Work and Organizational Psychologist, 3,* 1–9.

Furnham, A., Kirkcaldy, B., & Lynn, R. (1996). Attitudinal correlates of national wealth. *Personality and Individual Differences, 21,* 345–353.

Furnham, A., & Procter, E. (1989). Belief in a just world: Review and critique of the individual difference literature. *British Journal of Social Psychology, 28*, 365–384.

Furnham, A., & Taylor, J. (2004). *The dark side of behaviour at work*. London: Palegrave Macmillan.

Godin, G., & Kok, G. (1996). The theory of planned behaviour: A review of its applications to health-related behaviours. *American Journal of Health Promotion, 11*, 87–98.

Hammar, T., & Vardi, Y. (1981). Locus of control and career self-management among non-supervisory employees in industrial settings. *Journal of Vocational Behaviour, 18*, 13–29.

Hofstede, G. (1984). *Cultures consequences*. Beverly Hills, CA: Sage.

Houston, J., Farsee, D., & Du, T. (1992). Assessing competitiveness: A validation study of the competitiveness index. *Personality and Individual Differences, 13*, 1153–1156.

Huczynski, A., & Buchanan, D. (1991). *Organizational behaviour*. London: Prentice-Hall.

Hui, H. (1992). Values and attitudes. In R. Westwood (Ed.), *Organizational behaviour* (pp. 63–90). Hong Kong: Longman.

Kahneman, D., & Tversky, A. (1982). Variants of uncertainty. *Cognition, 11*, 143–157.

Lawler, E. (1971). *Pay and organizational effectiveness: A psychological review*. New York: McGraw-Hill.

Lerner, M. (1980). *The belief in a just world: A fundamental delusion*. New York: Plenum Press.

Lerner, M., & Miller, D. (1978). Just world research and the attribution process: Looking back and ahead. *Psychological Bulletin, 85*, 1030–1050.

Lynn, R. (1969). An achievement motivation questionnaire. *British Journal of Psychology, 60*, 526–534.

Lynn, R. (1991). *The secret of the miracle economy*. London: SAU.

Machlowitz, M. (1978). *Workaholics: Living with them, working with them*. New York: Mentor.

Machlowitz, M. (1980). *Workaholics*. New York: Mentor.

Madden, T. J., Ellen, P. S., & Ajzen, I. (1992). A comparison of the theory of planned behaviour and the theory of reasoned action. *Personality and Social Psychology Bulletin, 18*, 3–9.

Marks, D., & Kammann, R. (1980). *The psychology of the psychic*. Buffalo, NY: Prometheus Books.

Mars, G. (1984). *Cheats at work: An anthropology of workplace crime*. London: Allen & Unwin.

McClelland, D. (1961). *The achieving society*. New York: Free Press.

McGregor, D. (1960). *The human side of enterprise*. New York: McGraw-Hill.

McKenna, E. (1987). *Psychology in business*. London: Lawrence Erlbaum Associates.

McKenna, E. (1994). *Business psychology and organizational behaviour*. Hove, UK: Lawrence Erlbaum Associates.

Miller, M., Woehr, D., & Hudspeth, N. (2002). The meaning and measurement of work ethic. *Journal of Vocational Behaviour, 60*, 451–489.

Mintzberg, H. (1975). *The nature of managerial work*. New York: Harper & Row.

Mirels, H., & Garrett, J. (1971). The Protestant ethic as a personality variable. *Journal of Consulting and Clinical Psychology, 36*, 40–44.

Moore, S. M., Barling, N. R., & Hood, B. (1998). Predicting testicular and breast self-examination behaviour: A test of the theory of reasoned action. *Behaviour-Change, 15*, 41–49.

Murray, H. (1938). *Exploration in personality*. New York: Oxford University Press.

Oates, W. (1971). *Confessions of a workaholic*. New York: World.

Parker, D., Manstead, A., Stradling, S., Reason, J., & Baxter, J. (1992). Intention to commit driving violations. *Journal of Applied Psychology, 77*, 97–101.

Roberts, C., & Smith, P. (1998). Additudes and behaviour of children towards peers with disabilities. *International Journal of Disability, Development and Education, 46*, 35–50.

Rokeach, M. (1973). *The nature of human values*. New York: Free Press.

Rotter, J. (1966). Generalized expectancies for internal and external control of reinforcement. *Psychological monographs, 80*, 1–28.

Rubin, Z., & Peplau, L. (1973). Belief in a just world and reactions to another's lot. *Journal of Social Issues, 21*, 73–93.

Rubin, Z., & Peplau, L. (1975). Who believes in a just world? *Journal of Social Issues, 31*, 65–90.

Schwartz, S. (1992). Universals in the content and structure of value: Theoretical advances and empirical tests in 20 countries. In M. Zanna (Ed.), *Advances in experimental social psychology* (pp. 1–65). New York: Academic Press.

Sheppard, B. H., Hartwick, J., & Warshaw, P. R. (1988). The theory of reasoned action: A meta-analysis of past research with recommendations for modifications and future research. *Journal of Consumer Research, 15*, 325–339.

Sneed, C. D., & Morisky, D. E. (1998). Applying the Theory of Reasoned Action to condom use among sex workers. *Social Behaviour and Personality, 26*, 317–327.

Spector, P. (1982). Behaviour in organizations as a function of employees' locus of control. *Psychological Bulletin, 91*, 482–497.

Spector, P. (1988). Development of the work locus of control scale. *Journal of Occupational Psychology, 61*, 335–340.

Sutton, S. (1994). The past predicts the future. In D. Rutter & L. Quine (Eds.), Social psychology and health (pp. 71–88). Aldershot, UK: Avebury.

Terry, D. J. (1993). Self-efficacy expectancies and the theory of reasoned action. In D. J. Terry, C. Galllois, & M. McCamish (Eds.), *The theory of reasoned action: Its application to AIDS-preventive behaviour* (pp. 34–50). Oxford: Pergamon Press.

Terry, D. J., & O'Leary, J. E. (1995). The theory of planned behaviour: The effects of perceived behavioural control and self-efficacy. *British Journal of Social Psychology, 34*, 199–220.

Tversky, A., & Kahneman, D. (1974). Judgment under uncertainty: Heuristics and biases. *Science, 185*, 1124–1131.

Van den Putte, B. (1993). On the theory of reasoned action. Unpublished doctoral dissertation, University of Amsterdam, Amsterdam.

Vincent, P. C., Peplau, L. A., & Hill, C. T. (1998). A longitudinal application of the theory of reasoned action to women's career behaviour. *Journal of Applied Social Psychology, 28*, 761–778.

Weber, M. (1905). Die protestantische Ethik und der "Geist" des Kapitalismus. *Archiv für Sozialwissenschaft und Socialpolilik, 20*, 1–54.

Westwood, R. (1992). *Organizational behaviour: Southeast Asian perspectives.* Hong Kong: Longman.

Wicker, A. W. (1969). Attitudes versus actions: The relationship of verbal and overt behavioural responses to attitude objects. *Journal of Social Issues, 25*, 41–48.

Wilson, G. (1973). *The psychology of conservatism.* London: Academic Press.

Wilson, G., & Patterson, J. (1968). A new measure of conservatism. *British Journal of Social and Clinical Psychology, 7*, 264–268.

6   Work motivation and satisfaction

Introduction

One of the oldest, and most difficult, topics in psychology is the fundamental problem of why people are motivated to do anything at all, and if they do something, why that and not something else. Managers and researchers talk of goals, incentives, needs, reinforcers and rewards, and it is clear that there are many definitional problems. The question is why people choose, or not to choose, to do something, how much effort they put into it, and how persistent they are in trying to achieve it. The issue is really twofold: the nature of the driving force (where it comes from; what are its properties) and the direction and maintenance of the drive (what effects does it have on individual behaviour). As Greenberg and Baron (2003) note, motivation and job performance are not synonymous; motivation is multi-faceted, people are motivated by more than just money. These problems have intrigued and fascinated psychologists and managers of all persuasions for a very long time. Indeed, there are so many approaches and theories in this area that most reviewers have attempted to classify or taxonomize them into groups, such as need reduction theories, expectancy value theories and mastery/growth theories.

Motivation is a hypothetical construct which refers to a set of multiple internal processes with multiple consequential behaviours. It is goal directed. Motivational processes result from certain things about the individual: ability (job knowledge), dispositions (stable traits), beliefs and values, and affective mood state. These are also related to an individual's skills. However, motivation is also closely related to job context: the nature of the task/job, the physical environment, implicit and explicit rewards (reinforcements), social norms and the wider corporate culture. These factors also relate to how easy or hard it is to do the job. Thus individual factors and job context together determine motivational processes that affect a person's effort, persistence, attention and task strategy. Thus motivational processes lead to intentions that result in behaviour, but these are highly dynamic and change over time (Mitchell & Daniels, 2003).

This chapter looks at various different theories of work motivation. They can be divided up or categorized in different ways. Foster (2000) divided them into *content* theories concerned with *why* people work and *process* theories concerned with *what* factors determine an individual's persistent or willingness at work. He notes that academics and practitioners evaluate these theories in different ways: academics ask the question "*what* is the evidence in support of the theory?", whereas practitioners ask "*how* can it be successfully implemented in their world?" However, the recommendations to raise and sustain motivation look alarmingly common-sensical: reinforce performance, create supportive social environments, have clear attainable work goals, provide enough resources to do the job, and make sure there is a fit between the employee's and employer's motives and values.

For Westwood motivation, as a concept, has certain specific features:

- Motivation is an internal state experienced by the individual. Whilst external factors, including other people, can affect a person's motivational state, it develops within the individual and is unique to that individual.
- The individual *experiences* a motivational state in a way that gives rise to a desire, intention or pressure to act.
- Motivation has an element of choice, intention, or willingness. That is, the individual experiencing a state of arousal (externally or internally generated), responds by choosing to act in a way and at a level of intensity that *they* determine.
- Action and performance are a function, at least in part, of motivation. It is therefore important to predict and understand actions and performance.
- Motivation is multifaceted. It is a complex process with several elements and the possibility of multiple determinants, options, and outcomes.
- Individuals differ in terms of their motivational state and the factors that affect it.
- Furthermore, the motivational state of an individual is variable; it is different across time and across situations. (Westwood, 1992: 288)

According to Berry (1998), two things in the nineteenth century set ideas about motivation on a new track. First, Darwinism and with it the growth of evolutionary ideas. Second, experimental physiology with its emphasis on experimentation. It was believed – and indeed still is by many – that we can study human motivation in the same way as we study animal motivation, and that the latter may indeed inform the former.

There is recognition that there is a difference between the *ability* to act and the *willingness* to act and exert some effort. Most people, including academic theorists, have a relatively simple view, which suggests that a person's ability and motivation in interaction lead to performance and that feedback (i.e. reward) affects both ability (in the form of new learning) and motivation (to increase or decrease performance).

For practitioners, the issue is how to increase motivation. Popular interventionist attempts include pay incentive schemes (performance-related pay), job redesign, increased job participation through quality circles, and old-fashioned token economies. Most managers have heard of *virtuous* and *vicious* cycles and seek after the former, sometimes called high-performance cycles. The idea is that employees give of their best if they are committed to their work goals, which are stretching but attainable; they get feedback which suggests they are succeeding and indeed they believe they can succeed. The aim is organizational commitment and optimal performance. Commitment is about accepting the goals and values of the organization, a willingness to work hard for the organization, and a desire to remain affiliated and loyal to it.

Most people believe that job satisfaction is not only strongly correlated with job productivity but that it actually causes productivity. Yet there is very little evidence for the happy-productive worker hypothesis. This led Fisher (2003) to try to determine why this occurs. She believes that people mistakenly generalize from their own experience of feeling happier (more satisfied) when they believe they are performing better than usual. Not only is it unclear whether performance leads to satisfaction or the other way around, but also that this might occur only for very short-term, highly specific incidents.

Another approach is that of Warr (1985), who looked at what he called and listed "reason for action as a synonym for motivation or drive":

- *Intrinsic desirability of an immediate outcome*, which may be conceived as hedonically satisfying, optimally arousing or deliciously complex. Of course, people can be motivated to prevent an outcome, just as much as achieve it.
- *Intrinsic desirability of consequential outcomes*, in the sense that the value of a particular action is, in part, measured by the desirability of the events that flow from it.
- *Social comparison* between what people have, and what they want, and how they compare to other people as a motivator because assessment of satisfaction depends on how satisfied others appear to be with them.
- *Social pressures* from others (advertisers, models, pressure groups) to move a particular way or seek certain rewards.
- *Trends in aspiration levels* may change through, for instance, the process of adaptation: as research become familiar and more easily attained, people adapt to them and seek out further rewards.
- *Perceived probability of success* is important because if it is high people will be motivated to "work" for it, whereas if it is low it will be much less motivating.
- *Habits* should not be discounted because regular routines and attribution styles affect both the intensity and content of wants and actions.
- *Other wants and actions*, such as the desire to fulfil self-esteem needs, may be a powerful motivator.
- *The structure of action*, in the sense that the way in which behaviours are organized, in time, may be very motivating or very hard work.

There may well be other reasons for action, but this list is a good start. Note that this is a fairly simple commonsensical list of motivations that does not posit complex, intrapsychic forces that unconsciously drive a person. Many people find psychoanalytic and neo-Freudian theory attractive, because it is dynamic, complex and powerful, in contrast to trait theories, which appear static and weak. Nevertheless, the amount and type of evidence offered in favour of many Freudian ideas is so weak that the case for this perspective must remain "not proven".

The motivation to do something can be internal or external: it can come from the inside or the outside. Internal motivation can be conscious, thoughtful, proactive or pre-conscious, less rational, emotional (hot) or determined by genes and dispositions (cool). External motivation relates both to task and social factors.

Most recent good research in this area has found a complex interaction between personality, ability, motivation, productivity and job satisfaction (Steel-Johnson, Beauregard, Hoover, & Schmidt, 2000). Thus Lee, Sheldon & Turban (2003) proposed a model which suggests that personality factors influence the way a person sets work goals, which in turn influences their mental focus and goal level aspirations, which in turn predicts their job productivity and enjoyment. Similarly, Tett and Burnett (2003) argued that personality traits interact with work situational factors (i.e. job demands, distracters, constraints, releasers and facilitators) to influence a person's work behaviour and motivation and hence productivity.

The motivation to work

There are various self-evident reasons why people work: work provides a source of income, a source of activity and stimulation, a source of social contacts, a means of structuring time, and a source of self-fulfilment and self-actualization. Nearly everyone chooses to work because of the explicit and implicit rewards that it brings. However, people experience different amounts and types of motivation to work.

The debate about the power of money to motivate is very old, extremely controversial and quite naturally unresolved. Those who believe money is at best a weak motivator point to surveys where money is placed low on the list of the most desirable features of a job (after security, opportunities for advancement, recognition, etc.). Those who believe in the power of money point to the way those people such as salesmen, on almost exclusively performance-related pay, work extremely efficiently and effectively. However, it is generally agreed that:

- Money is a good motivator for those who need or value it enough. This is not a tautology, although it may seem to be. People differ enormously in how much they value the symbolism, power and value of money. The greater the need, the greater the motivational power.
- Money is most effective when it has noticeable effects. Large, lump-sum increases make people feel materially better off, and able to buy "luxuries".
- Money motivates when it is actually, and is seen to be, rewarding performance. If people see a simple but direct relationship between input (hard work) and output (money), they feel able to control and predict their income. This is true of those individuals or groups who work in gain-sharing programmes (e.g. worker cooperatives), which allow them to benefit financially from any productivity gains they achieve.

One topic that never goes away is the ability of money to motivate the average worker. Middle managers believe money is the most powerful motivator. Paradoxically, it is nearly always those who do not have it in their power to motivate with money who believe this to be the case. In contrast, those who have control of the purse strings may not regard money as very relevant.

If money *is* a powerful motivator or satisfier at work, why has research consistently shown that there is no relationship between wealth and happiness? There are four good reasons why this should be so:

- *Adaptation*: Although there is evidence to suggest that people feel "happier" after a pay rise, windfall or lottery win, one soon adapts to this and the effect wears off rapidly.
- *Comparison*: People define themselves as wealthy by comparison with others. However, upon moving into more up-market circles, they find there is always someone else who is wealthier.
- *Alternatives*: According to economists, the declining marginal utility of money means that as one has more of the stuff, other things such as freedom and true friendship appear much more valuable.
- *Worry*: Increased income is associated with a shifting of concern from money issues to the more uncontrollable elements of life (such as self-development), perhaps because money is associated with a sense of control over one's fate.

The power of money as a motivator is short-lived. Furthermore, it has less of an effect the more comfortable people are. Albert Camus, the author, was right when he said it was a kind of spiritual snobbery to believe people could be happy without money. But given or earning a modest amount, the value of other work-benefits becomes greater.

There are various economic and psychological theories of work motivation. Several points can be made about (psychological) theories in general. First, few if any of the theories were developed to account specifically for *work*-motivation. Nearly all of them are general motivation theories applied to the world of work and supposedly applicable to all individuals. Secondly, nearly all the theories have received, at best, limited empirical and often equivocal support for their propositions. Indeed, there seems to be almost no relationship between a theory's popularity and its empirical support. Most, it seems, have at least a descriptive if not explanatory value. Thirdly, it is probably true to say that the theories are neither overlapping nor contradictory, given the diversity of their epistemological origins, although they may be contradictory on specific issues. Fourthly, there are various ways to classify or categorize theories which help one to understand the background to the theories.

Compensation, money and pay

Every job has an inducement/incentive and, one hopes, an alignment between inputs (amount of work) and outputs (e.g. pay). This wage–work bargain is in fact both a legal and a psychological contract, which is often very poorly defined.

Organizations determine pay by various methods, including historical precedents, wage surveys and job evaluations (using points). They have to benchmark themselves against the competition so as to meet or exceed the market rate. It is believed that monetary rewards are better at improving performance than goal-setting (management by objectives) or job-enrichment strategies.

Nearly everyone is paid – in money – for work. But organizations differ widely in how money is related to performance. The question of central interest to the organizational psychologist is the power of money as a motivator, which works in several ways:

1 *Piece work*: Here workers are paid according to how much they produce. This can only be judged when workers are doing fairly repetitive work, where the units of work can be counted.
2 *Group piece work*: Here the work of a group is used as the basis for pay, which is divided out between the group members.
3 *Monthly productivity bonus*: Here there is a guaranteed weekly wage, plus a bonus based on the output of the department as a whole.
4 *Measured day work*: This is similar to (3) except that the bonus depends on meeting some agreed rate or standard of work.
5 *Merit ratings*: For managers, clerical workers and others it is not possible to measure the units of work done. Instead, their bonus or increments are based on merit ratings made by other managers.
6 *Monthly productivity bonus*: Managers receive a bonus based on the productivity of their departments.
7 *Profit-sharing and co-partnership*: There is a guaranteed weekly wage, together with an annual or twice-yearly bonus for all based on the firm's profits.

8   *Other kinds of bonus*: These include a bonus for suggestions which are made and used, as well as competitions for making the most sales, finding the most new customers, not being absent, etc.
9   *Use of other benefits*: Employees can be offered other rewards, such as medical insurance or care of dependants.

The money – whether in cash or deposited electronically in a bank account – that employees receive in exchange for working in an organization is tied up with other fringe benefits (insurance, sick leave, holiday, pensions), and these are difficult to separate. If money-pay itself satisfies a variety of important and fundamental needs of employees, it is a good motivator to the extent that good job performance is necessary to obtain it. If employees' needs are complex and not clearly related to income, or if the quality or quantity of work performance is not directly related to reward, it serves as a much weaker motivator.

A topic of considerable interest is the issue of performance-related pay – that is, linking pay with performance. Piece work and related methods are used most for skilled manual work. There have been many studies of rates of work when there is payment by results.

For managerial and support staff, merit-pay plans can be based on appraisals done by managers, supervisors, peers, subordinates and customers. Wage incentives are often applied to sales, and over 85% of firms use them for some of their staff. They are even used for professors. Managers may have a bonus based on the performance of their section. But, for many employees, productivity is more difficult to measure, so incentives are based on appraisals and merit ratings. The great advantage of these schemes is that they are very flexible and many aspects of work performance can be rewarded, including stress tolerance, delegation, initiative, oral expression or anything else. As Johns (1991) notes, overall the evidence suggests that managers like these systems and that there is a clear, measurable reward between performance and (monetary) reward. Yet problems with introducing fair systems and ensuring that raters of performance are both fair and differentiating, means many organizations severely curtail the amount of merit pay. Hence seniority and job level account for much more variance in performance pay than actual job performance.

A major problem with performance-related pay systems is that ratings of performance tend to drift to the centre. Feeling unable to deal with conflict or anxiety between people in a team, managers overrate poor performers and underrate better performers, so undermining the fundamental principles of the system. Also, as has been pointed out, merit increases are too small to be effective. Paradoxically, in difficult economic times, when higher motivation and effort are required, the size of merit pay awards tends to be slashed.

The secrecy that surrounds merit pay means many employees have no way of comparing their salary with others, and thus cannot see the benefits (or not) of an equitably administered system. If working well, an open system that shows the amount of merit pay separate from other increases (i.e. cost-of-living) is most effective. This is partly the case because many managers overestimate the pay of their peers and subordinates, and underestimate the pay of their superiors. These tendencies reduce satisfaction with pay and the perceived link between performance and rewards.

There are different types of performance-related pay (PRP) systems, depending on who is included (to what levels), how performance is measured (objective counts, subjective ratings or a combination) and which incentives are used (money, shares, etc.). The aim of such systems is straightforward: good performers should be motivated to continue to work hard because they see the connection between job performance and (merit-pay) reward. Equally, poor performers should be motivated to "try harder" to achieve some reward.

For some organizations, the experiment with PRP has not been a success. Sold as a panacea for multiple ills, it has sometimes backfired to leave a previously dissatisfied staff even more embittered and alienated. There are various reasons for the failure of PRP systems. *First*, there is frequently a poorly perceived connection between pay and performance. Many employees have inflated ideas about their performance levels, which translate into unrealistic expectations about rewards. When thwarted, employees complain, and it is they who want the system thrown out. Often the percentage of performance-based pay is too low, relative to base pay. That is, if a cautious organization starts off with too little money in the pot, it may be impossible to discriminate between good and poor performance, so threatening the credibility of the whole system.

Secondly, for many jobs, the lack of objective, relevant, countable results requires an over-reliance on performance ratings. These are very susceptible to systematic bias – leniency, halo, etc. – which render them neither reliable nor valid.

A *third* major cause of failure is resistance from managers and unions. The former, on whom the system depends, may resist these changes because they are forced to be explicit, to confront poor performance and tangibly to reward the behaviourally more successful. Unions always resist equity- rather than equality-based systems because the latter render the notion of collective bargaining redundant.

Fourthly, many PRP plans fail because the performance measure(s) rewarded are not related to the aggregated performance objectives of the organization as a whole – that is, to those aspects of the performance which are most important to the organization. Also, the organization must ensure that workers are capable of improving their performance. If higher pay is to drive higher performance, workers must believe in (and be capable of) performance improvements.

However, PRP plans can work very well indeed, providing various steps are taken. First, a bonus system should be used in which merit (PRP) pay is not tied to a percentage of base salary but is an allocation from the corporate coffers. Next, the band should be made wide while keeping the amount involved the same: say 0–20% for lower-paid employees and 0–40% for higher-paid employees. Performance appraisal must be taken seriously by making management raters accountable for their appraisals; they need training, including how to rate behaviour (accurately and fairly) at work. Lawler (1981) has provided an excellent summary of the consequences of merit-pay systems (Table 6.1).

For many workers, job security is regarded as more important than level of wages, and this is particularly true of unskilled, lower-paid workers and those with a family history of unskilled work. Having a secure job is not only important for the family, it is also a status symbol. Worry about job insecurity increased in the 1990s as the result of many jobs being taken over by computers. This is a major problem with the contemporary work scene; the big companies in Japan have succeeded in offering job security to their staff, but the losses are then taken by the subsidiary firms. And wage incentives affect whether or not people will work at all. In the past this was a choice between work and a life of leisure for some; today, it is a choice between work and social security. However, there are definite limitations to the effects of money on work.

Table 6.1 Effectiveness of merit-pay and bonus-incentive systems in achieving various desired effects

Type of compensation plan	Performance measure used	Desired effects			
		Tying pay to performance	Minimizing negative side-effects	Encouraging cooperation	Gaining acceptance
Merit-pay systems					
For individuals	Productivity	Good	Very good	Very poor	Good
	Cost-effectiveness	Fair	Very good	Very poor	Good
	Ratings by supervisors	Fair	Very good	Very poor	Fair
For groups	Productivity	Fair	Very good	Poor	Good
	Cost-effectiveness	Fair	Very good	Poor	Good
	Ratings by superiors	Poor	Very good	Poor	Fair
For organization as a whole	Productivity	Poor	Very good	Fair	Good
	Cost-effectiveness	Poor	Very good	Poor	Good
Bonus systems					
For individuals	Productivity	Very good	Fair	Very poor	Poor
	Cost-effectiveness	Good	Good	Very poor	Poor
	Ratings by superiors	Good	Good	Very poor	Poor
For groups	Productivity	Good	Very good	Fair	Fair
	Cost-effectiveness	Fair	Very good	Fair	Fair
	Ratings by superiors	Fair	Very good	Fair	Fair
For organization as a whole	Productivity	Fair	Very good	Fair	Good
	Cost-effectiveness	Fair	Very good	Fair	Fair
	Profit	Poor	Very good	Fair	Fair

Personality and motivation

Over the last decade or so, research and reviews have once again stressed the importance of personality traits as primary factors in determining job motivation and then
performance. For example, Barrick, Stewart & Piotrowski (2002) looked at personality
and motivation in American sales representatives. They measured three aspects of
motivation: accomplishment striving (task orientation), status striving (attempts to get
power/dominance at work) and communion striving (get on with others at work). They
found conscientiousness predicted accomplishment striving and extraversion predicted
status striving but that only the latter predicted actual job performance. They argue that
personality traits are *distal* variables and motivational patterns are *proximal* variables,
which relate directly to work productivity. Hence their relevance, albeit one stage
removed from personality variables. For instance, Kanfer and Ackerman (2000) showed
personality, but not intelligence, to be related to work motivation. They also found
some age and gender correlates of work motivation, but concluded that personality
variables are strongly and logically related to work motivation.

Two meta-anlayses are particularly important. Judge and Ilies (2002) reviewed 65
studies of the relationship between personality and job performance motivation. They
looked at three types of motivation: goal setting, expectancy and self-efficacy. Goal
setting was predicted by three factors, which indicated that stable (i.e. non-neurotic),
agreeable and conscientious individuals set themselves higher goals. Expectancy motivation was most closely predicted by two factors indicating that stable, conscientious
individuals had higher expectancy motivation. Finally, self-efficacy motivation was
predicted by two factors showing that stable extraverts (the "sanguine" type) had higher
self-efficacy motivation.

They performed some regressions, which showed the following: Personality traits
accounted for between a third (for expectancy motivation) and two-thirds (for goal
setting motivation) of the variance. The two factors that seemed most consistent were
Neuroticism and Conscientiousness. The overall pattern appeared to indicate
that stable, conscientious, disagreeable, extraverts had the highest levels of overall
motivation. They concluded thus:

> The validity of Neuroticism and Conscientiousness should not be surprising in that
> these two Big Five traits are the most important correlates of job performance. If
> personality affects performance mostly through motivation, and Neuroticism and
> Conscientiousness are the best predictors of performance, then it would almost
> have to be the case that these two traits best predict performance motivation. One
> might wonder why Neuroticism tended to be a stronger correlate of performance
> motivation given that Conscientiousness is a stronger correlate of job performance.
> A plausible explanation is that whereas Neuroticism primarily influences perform-
> ance through motivation, Conscientiousness influences performance in other ways.
> For example, Conscientious individuals are likely to be orderly and decisive which
> may give these individuals an edge in many jobs. (Kanfer & Ackerman, 2000:
> 803)

In a related study, Judge, Heller & Mount (2002) looked at the relationship between
the "Big Five" personality traits and job satisfaction in over 150 studies. Their results
were clear: Neuroticism was the strongest correlate of job satisfaction, followed very

closely by Conscientiousness and then Extraversion. These results came as no surprise and confirmed the findings on happiness, namely that stable extraverts are disposition-ally happy at work and play. Judge *et al.* concluded thus:

> Drawing from the tripartite (cognitive, affective, and behavioral) categorization of attitudes, the Big Five traits may influence job satisfaction through each of these processes. Cognitively, these traits may influence how individuals interpret charac-teristics of their jobs, as is the case when individuals with positive core self-evaluations interpret intrinsic job characteristics more positively, even controlling for actual job complexity. Affectively, these traits might influence job satisfaction through their effect on mood or mood at work. Finally, behaviourally, employees who are Emotionally stable, Extraverted and Conscientious may be happier at work because they are more likely to achieve satisfying results at work. Part of this effect may operate through job performance, such that Conscientious employees perform better and are more satisfied with their jobs because of the intrinsic and extrinsic rewards that high performance provides. In part, it may operate through situation selections, such that Extraverted employees are more likely to spend time in situations that make people happy, such as in social interactions. Given the links between personality and job performance, and personality and job satisfaction presented herein, perhaps the time has come for a framework that takes the link-ages among personality, job performance, and job satisfaction into account. Such models may involve more proximal predictors, such as integrity, which is related to the five-factor model. (Judge *et al.*, 2002: 536)

Need theories

Need theories are based on the simple idea that work-related behaviours are directed to satisfying certain needs. Depending on the type and quality of that need, people will strive in, and outside, work to satisfy them.

Maslow's theory

Without doubt the best known theory is that of Maslow (1954). It as if people who have been given only one lecture on psychology in their entire lives have had it dedicated to Maslow's theory.

Maslow supposed that people have five types of needs that are activated in a *hier-archical* manner, and are then aroused in a specific order such that a lower-order need must be satisfied before the next higher-order need is activated. Once a need is met, the next highest need in the hierarchy is triggered, and so forth. The five needs are as follows:

- *Physiological needs* are the lowest-order, most basic needs and refer to satisfying fundamental biological drives such as the need for food, air, water and shelter. To satisfy these positive needs, organizations must provide employees with a salary that allows them to afford adequate living conditions (e.g. food and shelter). Employees need sufficient rest breaks to allow them to meet their psychological needs. Organizations may provide exercise and physical fitness facilities for their employees, because providing such facilities may also be recognized as an attempt to help employees remain healthy by gratifying their physiological needs. It is only in rare or exceptional circumstances (war, natural disaster, disease, epidemic) that organizations would find their employees "stuck" at this level. However, many organizations in Third World developing countries might find their employees struggling to satisfy these more primitive needs, simply because of the relative poverty of the country.

- *Safety needs* are activated only after physiological needs are met. Safety needs refer to needs for a secure, predictable, habitable, non-threatening environment, free from threats of either physical or psychological harm. Organizations may provide employees with life and health insurance plans, opportunities for savings, pensions, safety equipment and secure contracts that enable work to be performed without fear of harm. Similarly, jobs that provide life-long tenure and no-lay-off agreements enhance psychological security. Individuals are of course threatened (or feel threatened) by a wide range of factors and it is not clear whether organizations should attempt to distinguish between real and imagined, serious or highly unlikely, threats to security (Furnham, 1992).

- *Social needs* are activated *after* both physiological and safety needs. They refer to the need to be affiliative – to have friends, to be liked, included and accepted by other people. Friends, relations and work colleagues help meet social needs, and organizations may encourage participation in social events, such as office parties, sports days and competitions, which provide an opportunity for meeting these needs. Many organizations spend vast sums of money on facilities for out-of-work hours activities for their staff, so that people in the same organization, but different sections or departments, may meet, chat and affiliate. Social needs are especially likely to be aroused under conditions in which "organizational uncertainty" exists, such as the possibility of a merger, closure or the now common "right sizing". Under such conditions, employees may be likely to seek their co-workers' company to gather information about what's going on, and how best to combine their efforts to deal with the problem.

Taken together, the above three needs – physiological, safety and social needs – are known as *deficiency needs*. Maslow believed that, without having these met, an individual will fail to develop into a healthy person, both physically and psychologically. The next two higher-order needs are known as *growth needs* and their gratification is said to help people grow and develop to their fullest potential.

- *Esteem needs* refer to a person's desire to develop self-respect and to gain the approval of others. The desires to achieve success, have personal prestige and be recognized by others all fall into this category. Companies may have awards, prizes or banquets to recognize distinguished achievements. Printing articles in company newsletters describing an employee's success, assigning private parking spaces and posting signs identifying the "employee of the month" are all examples of things that can be done to satisfy esteem. The inflation of job titles could also be seen as an organizational attempt to boost employees' self-esteem. Cultural and subcultural factors determine which sort of reward actually contributes to self-esteem. These policies are most popular in low-paid service industries or in sales forces where people have limited contact with peers. Most people in most organizations, it seems, have difficulty satisfying this need level.

- *Self-actualization needs* refer to the need for self-fulfilment – the desire to become all that one is capable of becoming, developing one's potential and fully realizing one's abilities. By working at their maximum creative potential, employees who are self-actualized can be extremely valuable assets to their organizations. Individuals who have become self-actualized supposedly work at their peak, and represent the most effective use of an organization's human resources. The definition of self-actualization is by no means clear, hence it becomes very difficult to operationalize, measure and test. Few jobs provide total, free and open scope for employees to achieve total self-fulfilment (Furnham, 1992).

Maslow conceived of the dynamic forces of behaviour as *deprivation* and *gratification*. *Deprivation*, or lack of satisfaction with respect to a particular need, leads to its dominance and the person's behaviour is entirely devoted to satisfying that need. However, once satisfied or gratified, it will recede in importance and the next highest level will be stimulated or activated. Thus, beginning with the lowest level, the entire process involves deprivation leading to dominance, gratification and activation of the next level.

Maslow provided key points to his theory (Westwood, 1992: 293):

- *The deficit principle*: If a need is not satisfied, it generates tension and a drive to act. A satisfied need does not motivate.
- *The prepotency principle*: Note that the needs are arranged in hierarchy. Some needs are more important and vital than others and need to be satisfied before others can serve as motivators.
- *The progression principle*: The prepotency of needs follows up the hierarchy. That is, physiological needs must be met first, followed by safety needs, then by social needs, and so on.
- *The need structure is open-ended*: The topmost need, self-actualization, implies striving to attain one's perceived potential. But as we grow and develop, our conception of our potential also shifts and so full self-actualization remains a potential, something to continue to strive for but which is never fully attained. This is a necessary mechanism, otherwise people may satisfy all their needs and no longer be motivated to act.

The fact that the theory is all embracing has attracted a great deal of attention. It has also been enthusiastically applied to the world of work. Predictably, perhaps, the research has been highly critical. Few have been able to find evidence of the five- (or two-) tier system (Mitchell & Mowdgill, 1976), and there is precious little evidence that needs are activated in the same order. It is not certain how, when or why the gratification of one stimulates or activates the next highest category. But it does seem that some of the ideas are most useful: individuals clearly have different needs, which relate to work behaviours. Organizations as a whole may be classified in terms of the needs that they satisfy (Furnham, 1992).

Berry (1998: 240) noted:

> Given that Maslow's need-hierarchy theory has received so little support, how do we explain the interest it captured in industry? There are at least three ways to explain this. For one thing, Maslow's terms have been publicized to an extent that they are incorporated in our everyday language. Self-actualization is now a word in

the dictionary. Secondly, Maslow's ideas have a humanistic appeal, and they make sense to us. The theory treats humans sympathetically and appeals to managers because it explains why some supposed work incentives may not operate as such. The theory says that employees are not simply interested in higher pay. There are other satisfactions at work, such as personal respect. Third, theories that have sweeping implications for work motivation provide a way for managers to make group interventions. Perspectives have been more readily adopted by management than individual-oriented theories of motivation because of the type of changes managers are able to make. They must do things that affect large numbers of people rather than single individuals. Theories like Maslow's suggest ways in which they can.

Alderfer's ERG theory

Alderfer's ERG theory is much simpler than Maslow's theory, in that Alderfer specifies that there are only *three* types of needs, but that they are not necessarily activated in any specific order. Furthermore, according to this theory any need may be activated at any time.

The three needs specified by ERG theory are Existence, Relatedness and Growth. *Existence* needs correspond to Maslow's physiological and safety needs; *relatedness* needs correspond to the need for meaningful social relationships; *growth* needs correspond to the esteem and self-actualization needs.

ERG theory is much less constraining than Maslow's needs hierarchy theory. Its advantage is that it fits better with research evidence, suggesting that, although basic categories of need do exist, they are not exactly as specified by Maslow. Despite the fact that need theorists are not in complete agreement about the exact number of needs that exist and the relationships between them, they do agree that satisfying human needs is an important part of motivating behaviour on the job. All argue that many aspects of work-related behaviour are attempts to satisfy these basic needs.

The theory has not attracted as much attention as Maslow's theory, but seems a reasonable modification of it. However, like Maslow's theory, it is rather difficult to test (Furnham, 1992).

Murray's needs and presses

Murray (1938) believed that motivation represents the central issue in personality theory and argued that people are motivated by the desire to satisfy tension-provoking drives (called *needs*). He defined need as a force in the "brain region", which energizes and organizes perceptions, thoughts and actions, thereby transforming an existing unsatisfying situation in the direction of a particular goal. Murray expanded the list of biological ("viscerogenic") needs to include hunger, thirst, sex, oxygen deprivation, the elimination of bodily wastes, and the avoidance of painful external conditions (such as harm, heat and cold). He also posited the existence of mental ("psychogenic") needs, which are derived from the viscerogenic ones. Murray eventually settled on a list of 20 identifiable and presumably distinct needs (Table 6.2).

Ascertaining an individual's needs is not an easy task. Some needs are inhibited or repressed because of their unacceptable nature, rather than overt and readily observable. A need may focus upon one specific goal or it may be so diffuse as to permit

Table 6.2 Murray's original taxonomy of needs

Need	Description	Representative questionnaire item	Accompanying emotion(s)
n Abasement	To submit passively to external force; to accept blame, surrender, admit inferiority or error	"My friends think I am too humble."	Resignation, shame, guilt
n Achievement	To accomplish something difficult; to master, manipulate, surpass others	"I set difficult goals for myself which I attempt to reach."	Ambition, zest
n Affiliation	To draw near and enjoyably cooperate or reciprocate with liked others; to win their affection, loyalty	"I become very attached to my friends."	Affection, love, trust
n Aggression	To overcome opposition forcefully to fight, revenge an injury, oppose or attack others	"I treat a domineering person as rudely as he treats me."	Anger, rage, jealousy, revenge
n Autonomy	To get free of confinement or restraint; to resist coercion, be independent	"I go my own way regardless of the opinion of others."	Anger due to restraint; independence
n Counteraction	To master or make up for a failure by restriving; to overcome weakness	"To me a difficulty is just a spur to greater effort."	Shame after failure, determination to overcome
n Defendance	To defend oneself against assault, criticism, blame; to vindicate the ego	"I can usually find plenty of reasons to explain my failures."	Guilt, inferiority
n Deference	To admire and support a superior; to praise, be subordinate, conform	"I often find myself imitating or agreeing with somebody I consider superior."	Respect, admiration
n Dominance	To control one's human environment; to influence, persuade, command others	"I usually influence others more than they influence me."	Confidence
n Exhibition	To make an impression, be seen and heard; to excite, amaze, fascinate, shock others	"I am apt to show off in some way if I get a chance."	Vanity, exuberance
n Harm avoidance	To avoid pain, physical injury, illness, and death; to escape danger, take precautions.	"I am afraid of physical pain."	Anxiety
n Infavoidance	To avoid humiliation; to quit or avoid embarrassing situations, refrain from acting because of the fear of failure	"I often shrink from a situation because of my sensitiveness to criticism and ridicule."	Inferiority, anxiety, shame
n Nurturance	To give sympathy and gratify the needs of someone helpless; to console, support others	"I am easily moved by the misfortunes of other people."	Pity, compassion, tenderness
n Order	To put things in order; to achieve neatness, organization, cleanliness	"I organize my daily activities so that there is little confusion."	Disgust at disorder
n Play	To act funny without further purpose; to like to laugh, make jokes	"I cultivate an easygoing, humorous attitude toward life."	Jolliness
n Rejection	To separate oneself from disliked others; to exclude, expel, snub others	"I get annoyed when some fool takes up my time."	Scorn, disgust, indifference

n Sentience	To seek and enjoy sensuous impressions	"I search for sensations which shall at once be new and delightful."	Sensuousness
n Sex	To form and further an erotic relationship; to have sexual intercourse	"I spend a great deal of time thinking about sexual matters."	Erotic excitement, lust, love
n Succorance	To have one's needs gratified by someone sympathetic; to be nursed, supported, protected, consoled	"I feel lonely and homesick when I am in a strange place."	Helplessness, insecurity
n Understanding	To ask or answer general questions. An interest in theory, analysing events, logic, reason	"I think that *reason* is the best guide in solving the problems of life."	A liking for thinking

Source: Ewen (1980).

satisfaction by many different objects in the environment; or an activity may provide its own pleasures, rather than being directed towards a particular goal. Furthermore, *needs often operate in combination*: one may assist another, as when a person actively persuades a group to complete a challenging task (n Dominance subsidiary to n Achievement), argues passionately for freedom (n Dominance subsidiary to n Autonomy), or rules others through the use of force and punishment (n Aggression subsidiary to n Dominance). Alternatively, they may "fuse" into a more equally weighted composite. Thus, an individual may humbly serve a domineering master (n Defence fused with n Abasement) or become a prize-fighter (n Aggression fused with n Exhibition). Needs may also *conflict* with one another (e.g. n Affiliation with n Dominance) and can be triggered by external as well as internal stimuli, so personality cannot be studied in isolation from environmental forces.

> At every moment, an organism is within an environment which largely determines its behaviour . . . (usually) in the guise of a *threat of harm* or *promise of benefit* . . . The *press* of an object is what it can *do to the subject* or *for the subject* – the power it has to affect the wellbeing of the subject in one way or another. (Murray, 1938: 39–41)

Thus, *press* refers to those aspects of the environment that facilitate or obstruct a person's efforts to reach or avoid a given goal.

Murray distinguished between an individual's interpretation of external events ("beta press") and reality as defined by objective inquiry ("alpha press"). In addition, a single need–press interaction is referred to as a *thema*. For example, if a person is rejected by someone else and responds in kind, the thema would consist of p Rejection (the environment event) causing Rejection (the need evoked). Alternatively, p Rejection might lead to (say) n Abasement or n Aggression; or the thema might be initiated by a need, as when an excessive n Affiliation causes inappropriate behaviour that provokes disdain and p Rejection. Or other people may actually be favourably disposed towards oneself (p Affiliation, alpha press), but be misperceived as hostile and threatening (p Aggression, beta press) (Furnham, 1992: 133).

The number of people that have been strongly influenced by Murray's theory is testament to its worth. Compared with Maslow's theory, Murray has many more needs (enabling one to be diagnostically much more specific) that are not hierarchically arranged. However, these needs are only categorizing tools or labels, because they do not help to understand when, why or how a need will be activated, expressed or satisfied. Descriptively and taxonomically the system devised by Murray has immense appeal, but its explanatory value is limited.

Murray was overly fond of neologisms, and his taxonomy has been criticized as making too many finicky distinctions, whereas other important details remain unclear (e.g. how psychogenic needs are derived from viscerogenic ones). Perhaps the major criticism of Murray's work is the failure to provide robust empirical evidence of the distinct nature of the 20 needs. Clearly, multivariate tests need to be employed to examine the structure of these needs, which are likely to be interrelated (Furnham, 1992).

Jahoda's latent needs theory

Based on her work on the unemployed dating from the 1930s, Jahoda (1982) has developed a theory based on the idea that what produces psychological distress in the unemployed is the deprivation of the latent, as opposed to explicit, functions of work. These include:

- *Work structures time*: Work structures the day, the week and even longer periods. The loss of a time structure can be very disorientating. Feather & Bond (1983) compared the structure and purposeful activity among employed and unemployed university graduates. They found, as predicted, that the unemployed were less organized and less purposeful in their use of time, and reported more depressive symptoms than the employed. A predictable pattern of work, with well-planned "rhythms", is what most people seek.

- *Work provides regularly shared experiences*: Regular contact with non-nuclear family members provides an important source of social interaction. There is a vast literature on social-skills deficits that suggests that social isolation is related to disturbed mental states. There is now a growing interest in the social support hypothesis, which suggests that social support from family and friends buffers the major causes of stress and increases coping ability, so reducing illness. If one's primary source of friends and contacts is work colleagues, then the benefits of social support are denied precisely when they are most needed. There is also a wealth of studies in organizational psychology that suggest that one of the most frequently cited sources of job satisfaction is contact with other people.

- *Work provides experience of creativity, mastery, and a sense of purpose*: Both the organization and the product of work imply the interdependence of human beings. Take away some sense of relying on others, and them on you, and the unemployed are left with a sense of uselessness. Work, even not particularly satisfying work, gives some sense of mastery or achievement. Creative activities stimulate people and provide a sense of satisfaction. A person's contribution to producing goods or providing services forges a link between the individual and the society of which he or she is a part. Work roles are not the only roles that offer the individual the opportunity of being useful and contributing to the community but, without doubt, for the majority they are the most central roles and consequently people deprived of the opportunity to work often feel useless and report that they lack a sense of purpose. However, many critics would not agree with the points made here.

- *Work is a source of personal status and identity*: A person's job is an important indicator of personal status in society – hence the often amusing debates over job titles, such as "sanitary engineer" for street cleaner. Furthermore, it is not only to employed people that jobs give a certain status, but also to their families. The employed person therefore is a link between two important social systems – family and home. Unemployed people have lost their employment status and hence identity. Not unnaturally, there is a marked drop in self-esteem during unemployment.

- *Work is a source of activity*: All work involves some expenditure of physical or mental effort. Whereas too much activity may induce fatigue and stress, too little activity results in boredom and restlessness, particularly among extraverts. People seek to maximize the amount of activity that suits them by choosing particular jobs or tasks that fulfil their needs. The unemployed, however, are not provided with this possibility and have to provide stimulation consistently to keep them active (Furnham, 1992).

Jahoda's "deprivation theory" has had its critics. Fryer (1986) offered three kinds of criticism:

- *Pragmatic* – the theory is very difficult to test.
- *Methodological* – one cannot be sure which of, or how, the deprivations are caused by unemployment; people *not* deprived do not necessarily enjoy, appreciate or acknowledge this state.
- *Empirical* – the theory does not take into account changes over time and undivided difference in reaction.

In a sense, Jahoda (1982) argued that people are *deprived*, whereas Fryer (1986) argued that institutions *impose* things on people (such as stigma). Furthermore, whereas the former underplayed individual choice and personal control, the latter tended to underplay social identity and interdependence of people at work.

Jahoda's theory is essentially that work provides people with both explicit and implicit, obvious and latent sources of satisfaction. Studies on unemployment have made apparent some of the less obvious needs that work fulfils. Although Jahoda's (1982) theory is not easy to test in its entirety, it has stimulated both research and theorizing. For instance, Warr (1987) developed a vitamin theory that suggested that work provides nine specific beneficial "opportunities". The theory is that job factors are like vitamins that can be grouped into two types. First, there are those (C and E) that improve health but, once the required dosage has been achieved, increasing amounts have no positive or negative effect. Secondly, there are those (A and D) that act much the same except that at high dosages they have a negative effect on health – the relationship is therefore curvilinear between these vitamins and health.

Table 6.3 shows that Warr has a clear concept of fit, whereby certain personality types or those with specific need profiles would presumably seek out and respond to jobs that offered more of these characteristics. To some extent these are tautological, yet the concept is important: to the extent that certain jobs fulfil specific needs, it is likely that those with these needs will be satisfied in them. Presumably this relationship is curvilinear rather than linear, so one may use the concept of the optimal fulfilment of needs.

All need theories imply that organizations can motivate employees by fulfilling needs. Table 6.4 lists some examples. The theories differ on the needs they focus on. They do not explain why individuals have different needs but all assume that people are motivated to fulfil specific needs in (and out of) the workplace. The implication for managers is that they ascertain the individual and group needs of their staff and try to find imaginative (and presumably cost-sensitive) ways of fulfilling them.

Equity theories

Equity theory, borrowed by psychologists from economics (Adams, 1965), views motivation from the perspective of the comparisons people make among themselves. It is part of exchange theory, which has clear applications to organizational behaviour. It proposes that employees are motivated to maintain fair or "equitable" relationships among

Table 6.3 Possible matching characteristics for each environmental category

Category		Possible matching characteristics
1.	Opportunity for control (AD)	High growth-need strength (ES) High desire for personal control High need for independence (ES) Low authoritarianism (ES) Low neuroticism High relevant ability
2.	Opportunity for skill use (AD)	High growth-need strength (ES) High desire to use/extend skills (ES) Relevant skills which are unused Low neuroticism
3. (a)	Externally generated goals: Level of demands (AD)	High growth-need strength (ES) High desire for high workload (ES) Type B behaviour High need for achievement Low neuroticism High relevant ability (ES)
3. (b)	Externally generated goals: Task identity (AD)	High growth-need strength (ES) High desire for task identity
4.	Variety (AD)	High growth-need strength (ES) High desire for variety (ES)
5. (a)	Environmental clarity: Feedback (AD)	High growth-need strength High desire for feedback
5. (b)	Environmental clarity: Role clarity (AD)	High need for clarity/intolerance of ambiguity (ES) External control beliefs (ES?) Low need for achievement (ES?)
6.	Availability of money (CE)	High desire for money
7.	Physical security (CE)	High desire for physical security
8.	Opportunity for interpersonal contact (AD)	High sociability Lack of contact in other environments High desire for social support
9.	Valued social position (CE)	High desire for social esteem

ES = empirical support is available for a significant person–situation interaction in respect of job satisfaction. AD = vitamins that at high levels reduce mental health. CE = vitamins that at high levels do not cause decrement.

Source: Reproduced from Warr (1987) with the permission of Oxford University Press.

themselves and to change those relationships that are unfair or "inequitable". Equity theory is concerned with people's motivation to escape the negative feelings that result from being, or feeling that, they are treated unfairly in their jobs once they have engaged in the process of *social comparison*. Some have argued that the theory is too individualistic.

Equity theory suggests that people make social comparisons between themselves and others with respect to two variables – *outcomes* (benefits, rewards) and *inputs* (effort, ability). *Outcomes* refer to the things workers believe they and others get out of their jobs, including pay, fringe benefits and prestige. *Inputs* refer to the contribution employees believe they and others make to their jobs, including the amount of time worked, the amount of effort expended, the number of units produced, and the qualifications brought to the job. Equity theory is concerned with outcomes and inputs as they are *perceived* by the people involved, *not* necessarily as they actually are, although

Table 6.4 Ways of satisfying individual needs in the work situation

Need	Organizational conditions
Physiological	Pay
	Mandatory breakfast or lunch programmes
	Company housing or health benefits
Safety	Company benefits plans
Security	Pensions
	Life-long employment plans
	Insurance schemes
Belongingness	Coffee breaks
Relatedness	Sports teams and other extracurricular activities
	Work teams
Esteem	Autonomy on the job
	Responsibility
	Pay (as symbol of status) and job title
	Prestige office location and furnishings
Achievement	Job challenge and skill usage
Competence	Pay
Power	Leadership positions
	Authority
Self-actualization	Challenge
Growth	Autonomy, educational opportunities

that in itself is often very difficult to measure. Not surprisingly, therefore, workers may disagree about what constitutes equity and inequity in the job. Equity is therefore a subjective, not objective, experience, which makes it more susceptible to being influenced by personality factors (Furnham, 1992: 139).

Employees compare themselves to others. Essentially they have four choices:

- *Self-inside*: An employee's comparison to the experiences of others in a different position inside his or her current organization.
- *Self-outside*: An employee's comparison to the experiences of others in a situation or position outside his or her current organization.
- *Other-inside*: Compare another individual or group of individuals inside the employee's organization.
- *Other-outside*: Compare another individual or group of individuals outside the employee's organization.

Equity theory states that people compare their outcomes and inputs to those of others in the form of a ratio. Specifically, they compare the ratio of their own outcomes and inputs to the ratio of other people's outcomes and inputs, which can result in any of three states: *overpayment, underpayment* or *equitable payment*:

- *Overpayment inequity* occurs when someone's outcome–input ratio is *greater than* the corresponding ratio of another person with whom that person compares himself or herself. People who are overpaid are supposed to feel *guilty*. There are relatively few people in this position.
- *Underpayment inequity* occurs when someone's outcome–input ratio is *less than* the corresponding ratio of another with whom that person compares himself or her-

self. People who are underpaid are supposed to feel *angry*. Many people feel under-
benefited.
* *Equitable payment* occurs when someone's outcome–input ratio is *equal to* the
corresponding ratio of another person with whom that person compares himself or
herself. People who are equitably paid are supposed to feel *satisfied*.

According to equity theory, people are motivated to escape these negative emotional
states of anger and guilt. Equity theory admits two major ways of resolving inequitable
states. *Behavioural* reactions to equity represent things people can do to change their
existing inputs and outcomes, such as working more or less hard (to increase or
decrease inputs) or stealing time and goods (to increase outputs). In addition to
behavioural reactions to underpayment inequity, there are also some likely *psychological* reactions. Given that many people feel uncomfortable stealing (goods or time)
from their employers (to increase outputs) or would be unwilling to restrict their productivity or to ask for a salary increase (to increase inputs), they may resort to resolving
the inequity by changing the way they think about their situation. Because equity
theory deals with perceptions of fairness or unfairness, it is reasonable to expect that
inequitable states may be redressed effectively by merely *thinking* about the circumstances differently. For example, an underpaid person may attempt to *rationalize* that
another's inputs are really higher than his or her own, thereby convincing himself or
herself that the other's higher outcomes are justified (Furnham, 1992).

There are various reactions to inequity: people can respond to overpayment
and underpayment (i.e. being under-benefited) inequities in behavioural and/or
psychological ways (i.e. being over-benefited), which help change the perceived *inequities* into a state of perceived *equity*. Table 6.5 shows the four "classic" reactions to
inequity.

Another way of seeing this is to point out that people have six possible reactions to
perceived inequality:

* change their inputs (e.g. exert less effort)

Table 6.5 Reactions to inequity

	Type of reaction	
Type of inequity	*Behavioural*	*Psychological*
Overpayment inequity (Guilt) O > I	Increase your inputs (work harder) or lower your outcomes (work through a paid vacation, take no salary)	Convince yourself that your outcomes are deserved based on your inputs (rationalize that you work harder, better, smarter than equivalent others and so you deserve more pay)
Underpayment inequity (Anger) I > O	Lower your inputs (reduce effort) or raise your outcomes (get pay increase, steal time by absenteeism)	Convince yourself that others' inputs are really higher than your own (rationalize that the comparison worker is really more qualified or a better worker, and so deserves higher outcomes)

Source: Adapted from Greenberg & Baron (1995) with the permission of Prentice-Hall, Inc.

- change their outcome (e.g. individuals paid on a piece rate basis can increase their pay by producing more "widgets" of lower quality);
- distort perceptions of self (e.g. "I used to think I worked at an average pace; now I realize that I work a lot harder than everyone else");
- distort percepts of others (e.g. "Her job isn't as easy and desirable as I previously thought it was");
- choose a different referent (e.g. "I may not make as much as my brother, but I'm doing a lot better than my next-door neighbour");
- leave the field (e.g. quit the job, take early retirement).

An analogous set of behavioural and psychological reactions can be identified for overpayment inequity. Specifically, a salaried employee who feels overpaid may raise his or her inputs by working harder, or for longer hours or more productively. Similarly, employees who lower their own outcomes by not taking advantage of company-provided fringe benefits may be seen as redressing an overpayment inequity. Overpaid persons may readily convince themselves psychologically that they are really worth their higher outcomes by virtue of their superior inputs. People who receive substantial pay raises may not feel distressed about it because they rationalize that the increase is warranted on the basis of their superior inputs, and therefore does not constitute an inequity. Robbins (1991: 213) argues that:

The theory establishes four propositions relating to equitable pay:

1   *Given payment by time, over-rewarded employees will produce more than will equitably paid employees.* Hourly and salaried employees will generate high quantity or quality of production in order to increase the input side of the ratio and bring about equity.
2   *Given payment by quantity of production, over-rewarded employees will produce fewer, but higher-quality units, than will equitably paid employees.* Individuals paid on a piece-rate basis will increase their effort to achieve equity, which can result in greater quality or quantity. However, increases in quantity will only increase inequity since every unit produced results in further overpayment. Therefore, effort is directed towards increasing quality rather than increasing quantity.
3   *Given payment by time, under-rewarded employees will produce less or poorer quality of output.* Effort will be decreased, which will bring about lower productivity or poorer-quality output than equitably paid subjects.
4   *Given payment by quantity of production, under-rewarded employees will produce many low-quality units in comparison with equitably paid employees.* Employees on piece-rate pay plans can bring about equity because trading off quality of output for quantity will result in an increase in rewards with little or no increase in contributions.

Because of its emphasis on justice and fairness, equity theory is closely related to concepts of organizational justice, which is usually broken down into three areas: *distributive* justice, which is about how (when and why) rewards are distributed; *procedural* justice, which is about the particular ideas and procedures used to determine rewards; and *interactional* justice, which focuses on treatment received from others. According to Greenberg and Baron (2003), the following are simple organizational justice based motivational tips for managers: avoid under-payment; avoid over-payment; give people a voice in decisions affecting them, and explain outcomes thoroughly and sensitively.

Research has generally supported the theory's claim that people will respond to overpayment and underpayment inequities in the ways just described. For instance, Pritchard, Dunnette & Jorgensen (1972) hired male clerical workers to work part time over a two-week period and manipulated the equity or inequity of the payment their employees received. *Overpaid* employees were told that the pay they received was higher than that of others doing the same work. *Underpaid* employees were told their pay was lower than that of others doing the same work. *Equitably paid* employees were told the pay they received was equal to that of others doing the same work. People who were overpaid were more productive than those who were equitably paid, and people who were underpaid were less productive than those who were equitably paid. Moreover, both overpaid and underpaid employees reported being more dissatisfied with their jobs than those who were equitably paid.

In two field experiments, Greenberg (1986, 1990) obtained results that were consistent with the theoretical predictions of equity theory. In one study, insurance company employees were temporarily and randomly assigned to the offices of co-workers who were considered to be of equal status, higher status or lower status. Some employees remained in their own offices (the control group). Compared with employees who were transferred to offices with equal-status co-workers, those who were assigned to offices with higher-status co-workers raised their performance, and those who were assigned to offices with lower-status co-workers lowered their performance (as measured by number of life insurance applications).

In another study, thefts among employees in manufacturing plants were examined during a period in which pay was temporarily reduced by 15%. Because two large contracts were lost, the host company temporarily reduced its payroll across the board for the two plants. In plant 1, the president met with all employees and explained the causes of the pay cut and its duration (10 weeks). Plant 2 had only a short meeting with employees. The amount of the cut was announced, but no other information or explanation was offered. No pay cuts were made in plant 3, and it was used as a control group. Both the plants in which pay was reduced had significantly higher theft rates than the control plant did. However, plant 1 had a significantly lower theft rate than plant 2. Employees in plant 2 experienced the highest degree of perceived inequity: "Workers whose pay reduction was adequately explained to them did not express heightened payment inequity while their pay was reduced" (Greenberg, 1990: 565).

As one might expect, equity theory has its problems: how to deal with the concept of negative inputs; the point at which equity becomes inequity; and the belief that people prefer and value equity over equality. Nevertheless, the theory has stimulated an enormous literature, which partially addresses itself to the issue of motivation. In essence, then, the theory predicts that people are motivated to achieve subjectively perceived equity. The management implications are twofold: (1) that comparative pay and benefits between different groups, sections and levels in an organization are a major source of motivation or demotivation; (2) employees need to feel they are fairly dealt with – that they and their colleagues are rewarded equitably for their efforts.

Value theories

Researchers on the topic of social values have conceived of them as a system of beliefs concerned with such issues as competence and morality and which are derived in large part from societal demands. These value systems are organized summaries of experience that can act as general motives (see Chapter 5).

Research by Feather (1985) and others has demonstrated that these value systems are systematically linked to culture of origin, religion, chosen university discipline, political persuasion, generation within a family, age, sex, personality and educational background. Feather has argued that social attitudes precede values which emerge as abstractions from personal experience of one's own and others' behaviour. These values become organized into coherent value systems in time, which serve as frames of reference that guide beliefs and behaviour in many situations, such as work. He has argued that values, attitudes and attributions are linked into a cognitive–affective system. Thus, people's explanations of unemployment are "linked to other beliefs, attitudes and values within a system in ways that give meaning and consistency to the events that occur" (Feather, 1985: 885). Thus, it may be expected that there are coherent and predictable links between one's general value system and specific work-related beliefs (Furnham, 1992: 142).

Furnham (1987) found that Protestant work ethic beliefs, as measured by two different scales, were associated with values such as *security, cleanliness, obedience* and *politeness*, and negatively associated with values such as *equality, harmony, love, broadmindedness, imaginativeness* and being *intellectual*. He also found that work-involvement beliefs were associated with values such as *sense of accomplishment, security, social recognition, ambitiousness, responsibility* and *self-control*, and negatively associated with values such as a *comfortable life, pleasure, imaginativeness* and being *loving*. On the other hand, it was demonstrated that Marxist work-related beliefs were positively associated with values such as *equality, peace, inner harmony, love* and *forgiving*, and negatively associated with a *sense of accomplishment, salvation, ambition, obedience, politeness* and *responsibility*. Similarly, the leisure ethic was shown to be associated with values such as a *comfortable life, happiness, pleasure, imaginativeness* and *independence*, and negatively associated with a *sense of accomplishment, salvation, ambitiousness, capability, obedience* and *politeness*. The basic idea of value theory is that people seek out jobs that fulfil their values. Values relate to a wide variety of features at work: how one is rewarded, how one responds to authority, how proud one is in the organization. Organizations also have values, which can be seen in their mission statements, although cynics point out that what a company says it values and how it acts are often very different.

Locke's value theory

A comparative theory of job satisfaction is the value theory developed by Locke (1976). Rather than focusing on needs, Locke argued that job satisfaction may be more closely related to whether or not work provides people with what they *want, desire* or *value*. Workers examine what their jobs provide in terms of, for example, pay, working conditions and promotion opportunities, and then compare those perceptions to what they value or find important in a job. To the extent that the two match, job satisfaction results (Figure 6.1).

Figure 6.1 An illustration of Locke's theory of goal-setting. Reproduced from Mulkis (1989).

There is a difference between Locke's theory and that of need theories such as Maslow's, partly because the latter are not specific and do not consider the need for money. It would be unlikely that money could be identified as a *need* for these workers, in the way that either Maslow (1954) or Murray (1938) defined needs. However, it is easy to believe that most workers would *value* more money than they are currently receiving.

An implication of Locke's (1976) theory is that, although knowing the importance or value that a worker attaches to a particular outcome does not *by itself* predict how satisfied the worker will be, importance should predict the *range* of potential worker attitudes. Some workers attach a high value to the level of their pay; to them, money is one of the major outcomes associated with working, perhaps the most important. Consequently, variations in pay will be strongly related to their satisfaction. Other workers, once they are making enough money to satisfy their basic needs, are not as concerned with how much they make. Variations in the pay of these workers will not have much effect, either positive or negative, on satisfaction. Thus, value theory states that the more important a job-related factor is to workers, the greater its potential effect on their satisfaction.

Whereas there is some evidence consistent with Locke's value theory (Mobley & Locke, 1970), there has been limited empirical research on this approach. Nevertheless, the concept of values is an important addition to the satisfaction literature and it can be easily interpreted in terms of other studies, such as that of Rokeach (1973). Need theories imply that the satisfaction of all workers depends on the fulfilment of a few basic needs. This, in turn, implies that satisfaction can be achieved through a limited number of strategies designed to address whichever of these needs are unfulfilled for a particular worker. Worker values, on the other hand, introduce another dimension. Even though outcomes such as pay, fringe benefits and working conditions are the same for two workers, and even though these outcomes may provide equivalent levels of need fulfilment, the workers' satisfaction will differ to the extent that their values differ. This approach is more consistent with the ways in which people actually react to their jobs. People choose and change their jobs on the basis of these principles or values. Landy (1985) pointed out that value theory is theoretically consistent with more general models of emotion, which state that emotional responses such as attitudes are triggered by a general state of physiological *and* psychological arousal. Landy noted that valued outcomes are more likely than non-valued outcomes to lead to arousal, and thereby have implications for satisfaction.

The managerial implication of value theories is to examine the values of employees more closely, but also the values the organization implicitly or explicitly supports, as demonstrated by how it operates. Just as a fit between personal and organizational goals may be felt to be motivating, so a misfit is often deeply demotivating.

Reinforcement theories

These theories, and there are many, specify how a history of past benefits (or punishments), or reinforcements, modify behaviour so that future benefits will be secured. Most are "black box" theories interested in *stimulus–response* associations, but not what goes on in between.

The direct application of behavioural modification principles to the work situation claims to provide procedures by which human performance can be shaped and altered. At the centre of *behaviour modification* is the concept of reinforcement contingency: the rate of performance will increase when valued outcomes (reinforcers) are made contingent on the performance. It makes no difference to the theory what the person needs, expects, values or wants, although these factors may impact on the differential power or effect of each reward (and punishment). It is sufficient merely to establish the reinforcement contingency or relationship to effect a behavioural change. Individual differences of various sorts dictate what are and what are not reinforcements. The argument is that people perform certain work-related acts that are subject to reinforcement (or punishment and extinction) contingencies. People work with a certain degree of effectiveness, and when a particular behaviour results in a reward (there is a reinforcement contingency between, say, payment and work efficiency), performance improves. Learning theorists assert that all behaviour is shaped and sustained through the action of contingent reinforcement; work-related behaviours are simply special examples of this more universal phenomenon. Behaviour modification has not met with universal approval, either as a theory of work behaviour or as an ethically acceptable approach to work management (behaviour modification may severely restrict a worker's freedom of choice) (Furnham, 1992).

A second type of reinforcement theory is the *social learning theory*. Whereas need theory attributes work solely to the person (internal motives), and behaviour modification theory explains work in terms of the action of the environment (contingent reinforcement), social learning theory emphasizes *both* the person and the environment. The individual (who has unique traits, cognitions, perceptions, attitudes and emotions) and the environment (which provides reinforcement) combine to affect performance. It is not enough to say merely that a person works because he or she is reinforced, one needs to take the person's cognitions, attitudes or emotions into account as well. For example, people learn work performance through copying the behaviour of others as a consequence of the reinforcers they are perceived to obtain, not simply through a series of discrete trial-and-error experiences. Because cognitive processes appear to mediate behaviour, the way people experience and perceive reinforcers is affected by feelings, images and thoughts, as is the way they perform.

Some managers self-evidently use social learning theory in the workplace. Some of the strategies have been directed at changing the environmental stimuli that set the occasion for rewarded behaviour, whereas others have manipulated the consequences of behaviour in such things as performance appraisal schemes.

There are some fairly general rules of reinforcement that are applied by all managers.

- *Do not reward all people the same*: Pay, praise, responsibility and other reinforcements should be distributed *fairly* to all employees, according to relevant sensitive and measured performance criteria (not sex or marital status, for instance). Reward must be linked to personal input.
- *Appreciate that failure to respond can have reinforcing consequences*: Withdrawing reinforcement (ignoring performance) causes a behaviour to cease, as does the act of not applying reinforcement in the first place.
- *Tell people what they must do to receive reinforcement*: Workers should know whether to concentrate on quality, quantity or something else.
- *Tell a person what he or she is doing wrong and find out why it is happening*: Organizations should institute performance evaluation systems that include regular and comprehensive feedback to help change behaviour.
- *Do not punish someone in front of others*: In using punishment, individuals should attempt to reduce dysfunctional secondary consequences associated with it. By keeping punishment private, the need for workers to "save face" with their co-workers or subordinates, which may cause them to act in ways detrimental to the organization's goals, is reduced.
- *Make the consequences appropriate for the behaviour*: Reinforcements, such as praise, bonuses, promotions and demotions, should fit the type of behaviour being reinforced.

There has long been a debate about the usefulness or otherwise of punishment as a strategy. Problems such as resentment and sabotage may accompany a manager's use of punishment. It is also wise to remember that:

- *Although a behaviour may be suppressed as a result of punishment, it may not be permanently abolished*: For example, an employee may be reprimanded for taking unauthorized breaks. The behaviour may stop, but only when the supervisor is visible. As soon as the threat of punishment is removed from the situation (when the manager is no longer present), the employee may continue to take or even increase breaks.
- *The person who administers punishment may end up being viewed negatively by others*: A manager who frequently punishes subordinates may find that he or she has an unpleasant effect on the work unit, even when not administering punishment, because the manager has become so associated with punishment.
- *Punishment may be offset by positive reinforcement received from another source*: A worker may be reinforced by peers at the same time that punishment is being received from the manager. Sometimes, the positive value of such peer support may be strong enough to cause the individual to put up with the punishment, and the undesirable behaviour continues.

Reinforcement and learning theories are among the oldest in psychology. Advocates emphasize that punishment (negative reinforcement) is usually not effective, since it suppresses rather than eliminates undesirable responses. They also noted that the more quickly reinforcement is given after the response, the more effective it becomes. The principles and procedures of learning theory are quite simple (Table 6.6).

Finally, when complex responses are desired, *shaping* is sometimes useful. This

Table 6.6 Motivational techniques from learning theory

Procedure	Operationalization	Behavioural effect
Positive reinforcement	Manager compliments employee when work is completed on time	Increases desired behaviour
Negative reinforcement	Manager writes a warning each time work is handed in late	Increases desired behaviour
Punishment	Manager increases employee workload each time work is handed in late	Decreases desired behaviour
Extinction	Manager ignores the employee when work is handed in late	Decreases undesired behaviour

Source: Adapted from Huczynski & Buchanan (1991).

involves positively reinforcing responses that are part of the more complex one until the desired response is obtained.

Jablonsky & De Vries (1972) have suggested the following guidelines for applying operant conditioning as a motivating technique:

- Avoid using punishment as a primary means of obtaining desired performance.
- Positively reinforce desired behaviour and ignore undesired behaviour if possible.
- Minimize the time-lag between response and reinforcement.
- Apply positive reinforcement frequently on a variable ratio schedule (see Chapter 9).
- Determine the response level of each individual and use shaping to obtain final complex response.
- Determine environmental factors that are considered positive and negative by the individual.
- Specify desired behaviour in operational terms.

Reinforcement theories have led to the development of what is called behavioural contingency management (Lufthans & Kreitner, 1974: 144). This approach is described below:

1   *Identify performance-related events*: The first step consists of identifying the specific behaviours that contribute to effective performance. These behaviours must be observable and countable. For example, if the performance problem is late reports, the behavioural events could refer to the number of reports submitted by a specified date.
2   *Measure the frequency of response*: Before trying to change a behaviour, a baseline measure of its frequency must be established. Sometimes a behaviour believed to be problematic turns out to have a low frequency, and the manager realizes that the behaviour is not really a problem after all. In measuring the frequency of a response, all responses can be counted if they are infrequent, such as absenteeism and tardiness. If the responses are frequent, however, only samples of behaviour need to be counted, such as the number of correct strokes of a data entry operator during a five-minute sample every two hours.

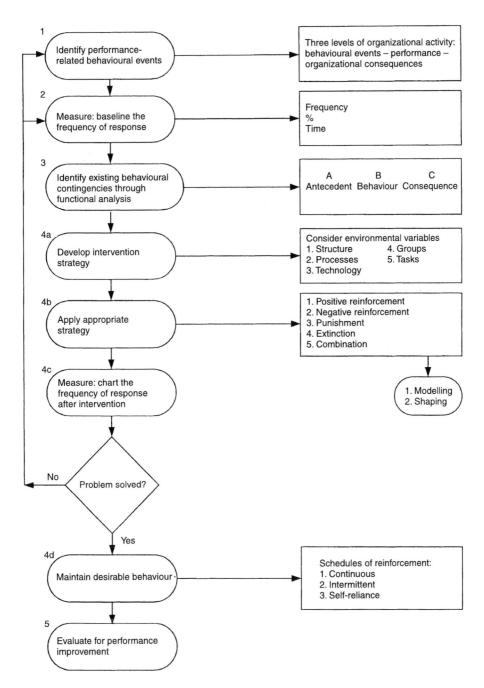

Figure 6.2 Behavioural contingency management. Reproduced from Lufthans & Kreitner (1974) with the permission of the American Management Association.

3   *Identify existing contingencies through a functional analysis*: A functional analysis refers to an examination of the antecedents and consequences of behaviour. The antecedents consist of environmental conditions surrounding the behaviour and any actions that occurred immediately prior to the behaviour. The consequences consist of all the outcomes associated with the behaviour, both positive and negative. Since human behaviour is so complex, identifying all the antecedents and consequences is extremely difficult.

4   *Intervention strategies*: The first three steps provide a foundation for altering behaviours by changing the reinforcement contingencies. The success of organizational behaviour modification depends on selecting and implementing an appropriate intervention strategy. The basic strategies were described earlier: reinforcement, punishment, escape, avoidance and extinction contingencies, or a combination of these. The goal of the intervention is to change the frequency of the identified behaviour. Once the strategy is applied, the results are monitored and charted.

5   *Evaluate*: The final step of behavioural contingency management is to evaluate whether the changes in behaviour resulted in performance improvement and contributed to desirable organizational consequences. Behavioural contingency management is supposed to be directed towards performance improvement and bottom line results. Several successful applications of organizational behaviour modification have been reported in various organizations, including industry, government and the military.

Being very practically orientated, it is clear what managers should do to motivate their staff if they are followers of learning theory. Sensitively, subtly and discretely applied, it works well, but sophisticated workforces are sometimes hostile to it.

Expectancy theories

Expectancy theory asserts that people are motivated to work when they expect they will be able to achieve and obtain the things they want from their jobs. Expectancy theory characterizes people as rational, logical and cognitive beings, who think about what they have to do to be rewarded and how much the reward means to them before they perform their jobs.

Expectancy theory specifies that motivation is the result of *three* different types of beliefs/cognitions that people have. These are known as:

- *expectancy* – the belief that one's effort will result in performance;
- *instrumentality* – the belief that one's performance will be rewarded;
- *valence* – the perceived value of the rewards to the recipient.

An employee may believe that a great deal of effort will result in getting much accomplished, whereas others believe there are other occasions in which hard work will have little effect on how much gets done. For example, an employee operating a faulty piece of equipment may have a very low *expectancy* that his or her efforts will lead to high levels of performance, and hence probably would not continue to exert much effort.

It is also possible that even if an employee works hard and performs at a high level, motivation may falter if that performance is not suitably rewarded by the organization

– that is, if the performance was not perceived as *instrumental* in bringing about the rewards. So, for example, a worker who is extremely productive may be poorly motivated to perform if he or she has already reached the top level of pay given by the company. If behaviour is not explicitly or implicitly rewarded, people are unlikely to repeat it.

Even if employees receive rewards based on their performance, they may be poorly motivated if those so-called "rewards" have a low *valence* to them. Someone who doesn't care about the rewards offered by the organization would not be motivated to attempt to attain them. It thus behoves an organization to determine what rewards its employees value, because rewards of low valence will not affect motivation. To a large extent, personality factors determine valence – the value of rewards (Furnham, 1992).

Expectancy theory posits that motivation is a multiplicative function of all three components. This means that higher levels of motivation will result when valence, instrumentality and expectancy are all high, rather than when they are all low. The multiplicative assumption of the theory therefore implies that, if any one of the components is zero, then the overall level of motivation will be zero. Thus, even if an employee believes that her effort will result in performance that will result in reward, motivation may be zero if the valence of the reward she expects to receive is zero (Figure 6.3).

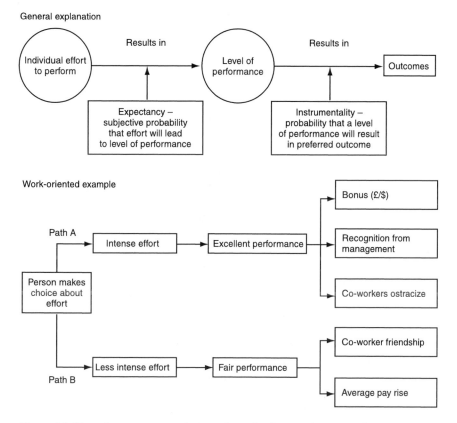

Figure 6.3 How the expectancy theory of motivation works. Reproduced from Donnelly *et al.* (1987) with the permission of McGraw-Hill.

The specific way in which the components are formally related involves two equations. First, the valence of outcome *j* (the attractiveness of that particular outcome) is a function of the valence times instrumentality summed over all the alternative outcomes. This may be represented algebraically as:

$$V_j = f \sum_{1}^{N} V_k I_{jk}$$

where *f* is a constant; V_j is the valence of outcome *j*; I_{jk} is the perceived instrumentality for achieving *j* with outcome *k*; V_k is the valence of outcome *k*; and *N* is the number of outcomes. Instrumentality, according to Vroom (1964), varies from −1 (outcome *k* never leads to the attainment of outcome *j*) to +1 (outcome *k* is perceived as always leading to outcome *j*). The classic situation to which this equation has been applied is workers' satisfaction. Satisfaction with a job (outcome *j*) is related to how instrumental that job is at achieving certain other outcomes such as salary (outcome *k*) and the valence of attractiveness of those outcomes (V_k).

The second equation involved in the theory deals with a person's motivation to perform. Vroom (1964) notes that the force acting on a person is the sum of products of the values of the outcomes and the strength of the expectancies that the behaviour will result in the outcome:

$$F_i = \sum_{1}^{N} E_{jk} V_j$$

where F_i is the motivational force to perform act *j*; E_{jk} is the expectancy that act *j* will be followed by outcome *k*; V_j is the valence of outcome *j*; and *N* is the number of outcomes. This equation has been used to predict choice of occupation, duration of work, and effort. For example, it has been shown that the stronger the attractiveness of a certain outcome, and the more people believe that their jobs are instrumental in achieving that outcome, the stronger the person will be motivated to work.

Expectancy theory assumes that *motivation* is not equivalent to job performance, but is only one of several determinants. In particular, the theory assumes that *personality*, *skills* and *abilities* also contribute to a person's job performance. Some people are better suited to do their jobs than others by virtue of the unique characteristics and special skills or abilities they bring to their jobs.

Expectancy theory suggests that job performance will be influenced by people's *role perceptions*: what they believe is expected of them. Poor performance results not necessarily from poor motivation, but from misunderstandings about the role one is expected to play in the organization.

Expectancy theory also recognizes the role of *opportunities to carry out one's job*. It is possible that even the best employees will function at low levels if their opportunities are limited. Even the most highly motivated salesperson will perform poorly if opportunities are restricted – that is, if the available inventory is very low (as is sometimes the case among certain popular cars), or if the customers are unable to afford the product (as is sometimes the case among salespersons whose territories are heavily populated by unemployed persons) (Furnham, 1992: 150).

Motivation, together with a person's skills, personality traits, abilities, role perceptions and opportunities, also combine to influence job performance. Thus, it is important to recognize that expectancy theory quite realistically views motivation as just one of several determinants of job performance. Over the years, the basic ideas have changed. Porter & Lawler (1968) adapted and expanded the theory (Figure 6.4). According to their model, job performance is a multiple combination of abilities and skills, effort and role perceptions. If individuals have clear role perceptions, if they possess the necessary skills and abilities, and if they are motivated to exert sufficient effort, the model suggests that they will perform well. Abilities and skills refer to both physical and psychological characteristics, such as finger dexterity, mental ability and the proficiency people have developed from experience or training.

Role perceptions refer to the clarity of the job description and to whether individuals know how to direct their efforts towards effectively completing the task. Those who have clear perceptions of their role responsibilities apply their efforts where they will count, and perform the correct behaviours. Those who have incorrect role perceptions tend to spend much of their time in unproductive efforts that do not contribute to effective job performance.

According to the model, performance produces extrinsic and intrinsic outcomes. The relationship between performance and rewards is not direct, but the relationship for intrinsic rewards tends to be more direct than for extrinsic rewards. Whether the job performance will produce intrinsic outcomes is primarily determined by the design of the job and the values of the worker, whereas the relationship between extrinsic outcomes and satisfaction depends on the equity perception of the employee.

Lawler (1973) later developed what was called the "facet model". The facet model is highly cognitive in nature and it reflects the view that people respond to their *perceptions* of reality more directly than to reality itself. As with Adams's (1965) equity theory, the facet model states that the only desirable or satisfying condition is one in which the input–output comparison process indicates equality, when perceptions of

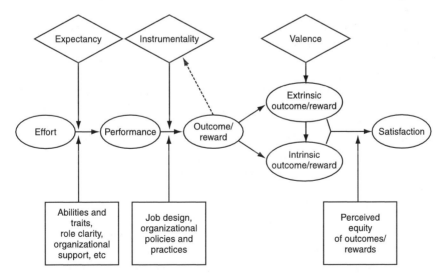

Figure 6.4 Porter and Lawler's expanded expectancy model. Adapted from Porter & Lawler (1968).

what should be received balance perceptions of what is actually received. If workers feel that they are receiving *less* than is due, dissatisfaction with the job results; if workers perceive that they are receiving *more* than is deserved, uncomfortable feelings of inequity, and possibly guilt, ensue. The notion of feeling overpaid or overcompensated is the most controversial aspect of the equity theory of motivation, and it remains a problem of Lawler's (1973) satisfaction theory. One way to reduce the supposed guilt that results from overpayment is to work harder, so increasing input.

Research on Lawler's model has been limited and somewhat inconclusive. Wanous & Lawler (1972) examined satisfaction with 23 different job facets, using several measures of satisfaction. One of the measures, as specified by the facet satisfaction model, was the difference between the current level of the facet and the level that the worker believed *should* be associated with her job. They found that overall job satisfaction ratings could be predicted from this different score, as suggested by the theory. However, the same data were later re-analysed by Wall & Payne (1973), who found that perceptions of the level of outcomes received predicted overall satisfaction best, with those workers who perceived greater outcomes being more satisfied. Furthermore, what the workers thought they *should* receive did not improve the prediction of satisfaction. Wall and Payne therefore argued that the type of difference score suggested by Lawler's model is inherently flawed because their measure of equity was wrong.

Another problem is that the facet model assumes that people use rational cognitive processes, carefully weighing their own, as well as others', inputs and outcomes, and basing their attitudes on the logical comparative conclusions derived from those comparisons. There are good reasons to suggest that many people are *not* this rational. Furthermore, it is not at all clear, even if people do compare inputs and outcomes, that this comparison is as simple as Lawler's (1973) model suggests. Weiner (1980) showed that job satisfaction can be predicted more accurately if the difference between what you actually receive and what you think you should receive is computed as a percentage of what you actually receive (satisfaction = [actual – desired]/actual), rather than as a simple difference (satisfaction = actual – desired).

Expectancy theory has generated a good deal of research and has been successfully applied to understanding behaviour in many different organizational settings. However, although some specific aspects of the theory have been supported (particularly the impact of expectancy and instrumentality on motivation), others have not (such as the contribution of valence to motivation, and the assumption that expectancy, instrumentality and valence are multiplied). Despite mixed support, expectancy theory has been a dominant approach to the field of organizational motivation, in part because of the theory's important implications for organizational practice. It offers simple but specific ideas as to how to motivate individuals (Table 6.7). Lowenberg and Conrad (1998) have noted that the theory attempts to predict individual choices, not the motivation of groups. It is a *within* not *between* individual theory.

One important recommendation is to *clarify people's expectancies that their effort will lead to performance*. Motivation may be enhanced by training employees to do their jobs more efficiently, thereby achieving higher levels of achievement for their efforts. It may also be possible to enhance effort–performance expectancies by following employees' own suggestions about ways of changing their jobs. To the extent that employees are aware of the problems in their jobs that interfere with their work, attempting to alleviate these problems may help them perform more efficiently. Where possible, therefore, a manager should *make the desired performance level attainable*. It is

Table 6.7 Suggestions from expectancy theory as to how to motivate

Recommendation	Corresponding practice
Clarify the expectation that working hard will improve job performance.	Design jobs so as to make the desired performance more attainable.
Clearly link valued rewards to the job performance needed to attain them.	Institute *pay-for-performance* plan, paying for meritorious work.
Administer rewards that have a high positive valence to workers.	Use a *cafeteria-style benefit plan*, allowing workers to select the fringe benefits they most value.

important to make it clear to people what is expected of them *and* to make it possible for them to attain that particular level.

A second practical suggestion from expectancy theory is to *link valued rewards to performance clearly*. Managers should therefore attempt to enhance their subordinates' beliefs about instrumentality – that is, make it clear to them exactly what job behaviours will lead to what rewards. Furthermore, the introduction of sensitive and fair performance-related pay systems enhances this. Expectancy theory specifies that it would be effective. Performance increases can result from carefully implemented merit systems (management–performance systems).

One obvious practical suggestion from expectancy theory is to *administer rewards that have positive valence to employees*. The reward must be valued by employees for it to have potential as a motivator. It is a mistake to assume that all employees care about having the same rewards made available to them by their companies. Values are in part personality dependent. Some might recognize the incentive value of a pay rise, whereas others might prefer additional vacation days, improved insurance benefits, day-care facilities for children, free health insurance, a motor car or an impressive job title. With this in mind, more companies are instituting cafeteria-style benefit plans: incentive systems through which the employees select their fringe benefits from a menu of available alternatives. The success of these plans suggests that making highly salient rewards available to employees may be an effective motivational technique (Furnham, 1992: 151).

Arnold, Robertson & Cooper (1991: 176) argue that, if expectancy theory is correct, it has important implications for managers wishing to ensure that employees are motivated to perform their work duties:

They would need to ensure that all three of the following conditions were satisfied:

1   Employees perceived that they possessed the necessary skills to do their jobs at least adequately (expectancy).
2   Employees perceived that if they performed their jobs well, or at least adequately, they would be rewarded (instrumentality).
3   Employees found the rewards offered for successful job performance attractive (valence).

But they note that the theory has not done especially well when evaluated in research. The following points can be made:

- Research studies that have not measured expectancy, or have combined it with instrumentality, have accounted for effort and/or performance better than studies that assessed expectancy and instrumentality separately.
- People often add the components rather than multiplying them.
- The theory does not work where any of the outcomes have negative valence (i.e. are viewed as being undesirable).
- The theory works better where the outcome measure is objective performance, or self-reported effort and performance, rather than effort or performance reported by another person.
- The theory works best where the person is choosing between not less than ten and not more than 15 outcomes.
- Self-report measures of valence, instrumentality and expectancy have often been poorly constructed.
- Most research has compared different people with each other, rather than comparing different outcomes for the same person. The latter would enable a better test of VIE theory (Arnold *et al.*, 1992: 178).

But reviewers of the theory remain unequivocal. Compare Schwab, Olian-Gottlieb & Heneman (1979: 146):

> there is a nagging suspicion that expectancy theory over-intellectualizes the cognitive processes people go through when choosing alternative actions (at least insofar as choosing a level of performance or effort is concerned). The results of the present review are consistent with this suspicion.

Landy (1985: 336–337) notes:

> The cognitive nature of the approach does a good job of capturing the essence of energy expenditure ... A manager can understand and apply the principles embodied in each of the components of the model. Instrumentalities make sense. The manager can use this principle to lay out clearly for subordinates the relationships among outcomes (e.g. promotions yield salary increases, four unexcused absences result in a suspension of one day). Similarly, the manager can affect effort–reward probabilities by systematically rewarding good performance.

Arnold *et al.* (1991) note how little attention the theory pays to explaining *why* an individual values or does not value particular outcomes: no concepts of need are invoked to address this question. The theory proposes that people should ask someone how much they value something, but not bother about *why* they value it. This is another illustration of the theory's concentration on process, not content.

Mitchell and Daniels (2003) believe expectancy theory is better at predicting outcomes within, rather than between, individuals. Furthermore, it generates less research than it used to because of researchers' concentration on other theories like goal setting, self-efficacy and self-regulation.

Job facet theory and quality of working life

The quality of working life movement of the 1960s and 1970s argued that jobs could be redesigned to make them intrinsically satisfying and thus motivating. Hackman & Oldham (1980) proposed that the motivating potential of any job is not simply an additive function of the five job dimensions (Figure 6.5), but rather a multiplication function:

$$\text{MPS} = \left(\frac{\text{skill variety} + \text{task identity} + \text{task significance}}{3} \right) \times \text{autonomy} \times \text{feedback}$$

where MPS = the motivating potential score.

The theory suggests that there are three critical psychological states that are relevant to the world of work (Figure 6.5). They are:

- *Experienced meaningfulness*: Job holders must feel that the work has personal meaning and be worthwhile according to their system of values.
- *Experienced responsibility*: Job holders must feel that they are responsible for work processes and outcomes.
- *Knowledge of results*: Job holders need to be given information, on a regular basis, about whether or not their job performance is leading to appropriate and satisfactory results.

Psychological states are affected by the nature of the job and five core job dimensions. Three of these affect the meaningfulness of the job:

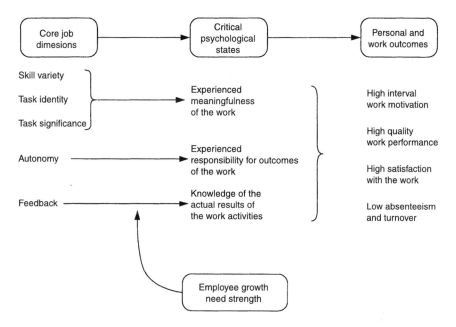

Figure 6.5 The job characteristics model of work motivation. Reproduced from Hackman and Oldham (1980) with the permission of Addison-Wesley.

- *Skill variety* – whether the job requires the use of a range of job skills and offers a variety of tasks to perform.
- *Task identity* – whether the job holder is able to complete a "whole" and identifiable piece of work.
- *Task significance* – whether the job is perceived to have an impact upon others and their lives in the organization and/or in general.

Each of these is necessary for the work to be experienced as meaningful. The fourth and fifth dimensions are related to experienced responsibility and knowledge of results, respectively:

- *Autonomy* – the degree of freedom, independence and discretion job holders may exercise in their work; to be personally responsible for job process and outcome.
- *Feedback* – the extent to which the work process itself offers direct and frequent feedback about the effectiveness of performance.

When core job dimensions are positively present, they impact on the critical psychological states and lead to positive outcomes such as increased motivation, higher-quality performance and work satisfaction, and lower absenteeism and labour turnover. The extent to which the relationships hold depends upon the strength of the individual's growth need (Westwood, 1992: 227).

A job with a high MPS should have more motivating potential than a job with a lower score. From inspecting the formula, it is the case that autonomy and feedback are the most important factors in the MPS because, if either is zero, the MPS is zero. However, skill, variety, task identity and/or task significance can be zero or low and the MPS could still be reasonably high if autonomy or feedback is high.

The result of the facet theory model was to focus on designing motivating jobs. The *sociotechnical systems* perspective points to the need to consider both the technical and social aspects of work in designing a work process. *Autonomous workgroups* combine sociotechnical systems perspectives with group-based job enrichment design. Where a whole or major part of the production process is allocated to a work team who are then given significant autonomy to conduct the work process in a manner they determine, satisfaction results. As far as possible, how these targets are achieved is left to the group. They may establish their own schedules, decide on break-times, allocate work to different members of the group, rotate workers within the group, have responsibility for ordering resources, do their own maintenance and quality control checks, decide on new appointments, and even decide on reward allocations. The Volvo car company designed and built an entire plant around sociotechnical systems perspectives and autonomous working groups. They broke away from the mass-assembly line principles of car manufacturing begun by Ford (Westwood, 1992: 228).

The motivation implications of this theory for the manager are to consider whether it is possible to redesign jobs so as to empower workers and provide them with more interesting, significant and meaningful work. However, some jobs are virtually impossible to redesign. Furthermore, some people do not want more meaning and responsibility in their jobs: they are happy with what they have adapted to.

Attributional style

Attributional style is a personality characteristic that was first introduced by Abramson, Seliman & Teasdale (1978) and further elaborated by others (Peterson *et al.*, 1982). According to the reformulated learned helplessness model of depression (Abramson *et al.*, 1978), individuals vulnerable to depression differ from the non-vulnerable in the causal judgements they habitually make for the good and bad events in their lives. Abramson *et al.* speculated that a "depressive attributional style" is characterized by the tendency to view aversive or negative events as caused by *internal* factors (in contrast to external factors, such as the environment or the actions of others); by factors that are *stable* (rather than unstable or temporary); and by factors that exert *global* influence across many domains in one's life (rather than specific or narrow influence in only a few situations). This style inevitably affects work motivation.

Seligman and his colleagues developed the Attributional Style Questionnaire (ASQ; Peterson *et al.*, 1982). The questionnaire presents people with 12 different hypothetical situations, half of which are interpersonal or affiliative in nature and half of which are achievement related, to allow for the possibility that attributional style for affiliative events is different from attributional style for achievement events, as well as to build cross-situational generality. Within each class of situations there are three positive and three negative outcomes. Respondents are required to imagine themselves in the situations described, write down one major cause of the outcome, and then rate the cause on separate 7-point scales for the three attributional dimensions of internality, stability and globality, as well as the degree of importance of the situation. The ASQ has been mainly employed in studies of depression, although the causal relationship between attributions and depression is still unclear (Furnham, 1992: 161).

Despite the documented importance of attributions in achievement motivation (Weiner, 1986), little attention has been paid to the role of attributional style in occupational settings. One exception is the work of Seligman & Schulman (1986). Based on a sample of 94 experienced life insurance sales agents who, in the nature of their job, repeatedly encounter failure, rejection and indifference from prospective clients, Seligman and Schulman examined whether explanatory style predicts work productivity and quitting. They found, as predicted, that individuals who habitually *explained failure with internal, stable and global causes* initiated fewer sales attempts, were less persistent, produced less, and quit more frequently than those with a more optimistic explanatory style. The results showed that agents who had an *optimistic explanatory* style on the ASQ sold 37% more insurance in their first two years of service than those with a pessimistic style. Agents in the top decile sold 88% more insurance than those in the bottom decile. In a prospective one-year study of 103 newly hired agents, individuals who had an optimistic explanatory style when hired remained in their job twice as long and sold more insurance than agents with a pessimistic explanatory style.

The theoretical significance of these findings is that they support the reformulation's claim that a dysfunctional explanatory style predisposes to poor motivation and performance, and poor performance is then triggered by failure in those individuals with the predisposing style. The interaction of the two components increases the likelihood of helplessness deficits, here operationalized by quitting and poor productivity. These results suggest that an unhealthy explanatory style predicts performance deficits in a work setting, beyond the clinical syndrome of depression, wherein it has most often been tested.

Furnham, Sadka & Brewin (1990) devised a new measure of attributional style, the Occupational Attributional Style Questionnaire (OASQ), which assesses how a person makes causal attributions for specifically occupational outcomes. The measure consists of ten items that present brief descriptions of hypothetical situations that are commonly experienced by, or particularly relevant to, employed individuals. Five of the hypothetical events describe positive outcomes and five describe negative outcomes (see Box 6.1). For each hypothetical event, respondents are asked to vividly imagine themselves in the situation, and to write down the single most likely cause of the event. They then rate this cause on nine separate 7-point scales labelled internality, stability, externality, chance, personal control, colleague control, foreseeability and importance. A British study showed that the attributional correlates of salary were most consistent and explicable: high salaries were positively correlated with internal personal control and importance judgements, but negatively correlated with external, chance and *superior* control attributions. Dimensions of the scale correlated strongly with job satisfaction and motivation. The pattern of correlations is strongest for the positive events, rather than the negative ones. Eight of the nine attributions for positive events were correlated with job satisfaction in the predicted direction. That is, job satisfaction was associated with internal, personal control and foreseeable attributions but negatively associated with unstable, specific, external, chance and superior control attributions. Very much the same pattern emerged for intrinsic job motivation – although it is probably worth pointing out that the correlations were somewhat higher.

Attributions for positive events in particular (and to a lesser extent with positive and negative combined) were correlated with social class, salary, job satisfaction and intrinsic motivation. These attributions were what Seligman & Schulman (1986) called the optimistic versus pessimistic explanatory style for bad events. They found that an optimistic attributional style for both good and bad events predicted survival and productivity in the job of sales agents, just as the same style predicted salary, satisfaction and motivation in this study.

Contrary to the predictions of learned helplessness theory, attributions for positive events were uniquely linked to job attitudes and salary. Similar findings have been reported by Brewin & Shapiro (1984), who found that responsibility for positive

---

Box 6.1 The hypothetical events used in this study

Positive outcomes
Imagine that you apply for promotion and get it.
Imagine that you solve a major problem that has occurred at work.
Imagine that you very successfully lead a group project with a positive outcome.
Imagine that you are voted the most popular boss in your section.
Imagine that you are given a special performance reward at work.

Negative outcomes
Imagine that you are turned down at a job interview.
Imagine that your boss always acts aggressively towards you.
Imagine that you can't get all the work done others expect of you.
Imagine that you give an important talk in front of your colleagues and they react negatively.
Imagine that you are given a poor annual report by a superior.

outcomes, but not negative outcomes, was linked to academic achievement. In contrast, it is attributions for negative outcomes, rather than positive outcomes, that are most strongly associated with depression. Further research is necessary to explain these discrepancies. However, to find an individual difference variable with such widespread predictive power is relatively rare in psychology (Furnham, 1990).

Of course, correlational results do not show the direction of causality or rule out the probability of bi-directionality. Just as an optimistic attributional style may lead to success and satisfaction, so success may enhance, maintain or change attributional style. The literature in this field suggests that a mutual reciprocal causal model is probably in operation (Furnham, 1992: 164).

The emerging attribution style literature has important motivational implications for managers. Clearly, workers with optimistic attribution styles are more self-motivated and more productive. Although it is possible to re-educate people with less adaptive attributional styles, it is naturally easier to select people with that style. Managers need to ascertain how their staff explain both success and failure, and then to encourage the whole workgroup to adopt the optimistic attribution style.

Comparison and integration of the different theories

Both the manager and the student tend to be overwhelmed by the number of different theories of motivation. As a consequence, reviewers have either tried to compare and contrast them (or some of them) or to provide an integrated theory (see Figure 6.6).

Schermerhorn, Hunt & Osborn (1991: 178) compared what are called content (as opposed to process) theories thus:

1 *How many different individual needs are there?* Research has not yet defined the complete list of work-related individual needs. Each of the needs we have discussed above has been found to be especially useful by various experts. As a manager, you can use these needs as a starting point for understanding the many different needs that people may bring with them to the work setting.

2 *Can one work outcome satisfy more than one need?* Yes, some work outcomes or

Maslow		Aldefer		McClelland		Herzberg
Need hierarchy		ERG theory		Acquired needs theory		Two-factor theory
Self-actualization				Need for achievement		Motivators satisfiers
				Need for power		
Self-esteem						
		Relatedness		Need for affiliation		Hygiene dissatisfiers
Social						
Safety and security						
		Existence				
Physiological						

Figure 6.6 Comparison of content motivation theories.

rewards can satisfy or block more than one need. Pay is a good example. Pay is a source of performance feedback for the high need achiever. Pay can also be a source of security as well as a way of satisfying physiological and social needs.

3   *Is there a hierarchy of needs?* Research evidence fails to support the existence of a precise five-step hierarchy of needs as postulated by Maslow. Rather, the evidence seems to suggest that needs operate in a more flexible hierarchy, such as that utilized in ERG theory. Further, it appears useful to distinguish between lower-order and higher-order needs in terms of motivational properties.

4   *How important are the various needs?* A person's frame of reference appears to influence the importance he or she will place on particular needs. In turn, societal culture tends to influence this frame of reference.

5   *What is the manager's responsibility, as defined by the content theories?* Although their details vary, each content theory generally suggests that the manager is responsible for creating a work environment within which individual subordinates can find opportunities to satisfy their important needs. To the extent that some needs are acquired, the manager's responsibility may also include acquainting subordinates with the value of needs to which the work setting can positively respond.

Various researchers have also attempted to integrate or amalgamate all or most of the theories discussed above. Katzell & Thompson (1990) believe the above theories are not wrong but incomplete. They constructed an integrative model of attitudes, motivation and performance that identifies equity theory, need theory (personal dispositions), VIE (valence instrumentality and expectancy) theory, goal-setting theory and behavioural theory (reinforcement) (Figure 6.7). Katzell and Thompson's model is broader than this review of the major motivation theories, because it contains such

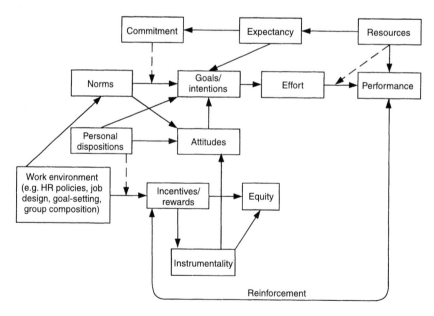

Figure 6.7 Integrative model of work attitudes, motivation and performance. Reproduced from Katzell & Thompson (1990) with the permission of Lawrence Erlbaum Associates, Inc.

constructs as norms, attitudes and the work environment. The constructs in the model are read from left to right. The solid lines between constructs in the model indicate a causal relationship between them. For example, the work environment determines incentives and rewards, such as pay and promotions. A dotted line indicates a moderating relationship. For example, the relationship between the work environment and incentives and rewards is affected by workers' personal traits and needs. Incentives and rewards also influence perceived equity and instrumentality, or the link between performance and outcomes. In addition, incentives and rewards have a reciprocal association with job attitudes, such as job satisfaction, whereas job attitudes, in turn, affect perceptions of incentives and rewards. After accounting for the causal and moderating effects of other constructs, the model assumes that performance feeds back to incentives and rewards, which serve as reinforcement for future performance.

Katzell tested the integrative model using data from 350 workers in three organizations and generally found support for the relations hypothesized by the model. This model provides a framework for organizational development interventions. For example, according to the model, if the incentives and rewards system in an organization is improved in the eyes of the employees, their attitudes, perceived equity and instrumentalities should first show the effects of the change. Specifically, if the intervention is effective, employee attitudes should improve, and perceived equity and instrumentalities should increase.

Effective management must combine theories of motivation

Others have also attempted to combine, integrate or amalgamate the major theories, partly because none has been more than moderately successful at predicting worker performance. Clearly, what is required is a dynamic multifaceted theory, which can take into account the number of variables that together affect the activation, direction and persistence of work behaviour.

Porter & Lawler (1968) provide a good illustration of how components of several motivation theories can be combined to provide a broader perspective than any single theory (see Figure 6.8). The Porter–Lawler model was developed as an expanded version of expectancy theory. The model has nine parts. Here valences (1) and expectancies (2) combine to produce effort (3). Consistent with Vroom's (1964) description of expectancy processes, effort does not determine performance directly, but rather combines with ability and other worker characteristics (4) and the workers' perception of what is expected on the job (5) to produce performance (6). Performance can result in intrinsic and/or extrinsic rewards (7a; 7b), the levels of which may have implications for future expectancies. Consistent with equity theory, the rewards received are compared with a standard representing what the worker believes is fair (8). This comparison can have positive or negative effects on job satisfaction (9), which in turn has implications for the valence of rewards available in the future. Note the similarity of Figures 6.4 and 6.8.

The theory has clear implications: people expect input will be proportional to output and that the more difficult the perceived demands, the higher the perceived rewards.

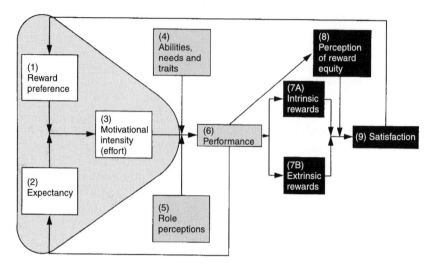

Figure 6.8 An integrative motivational model. Adapted from Porter & Lawler (1968).

Motivation-enhancing techniques

Management science is notoriously faddish, and hence theories and associated tech-niques move in and out of favour. For a short while they enjoy unparalleled popularity and are adopted by certain organizations. Disillusionment inevitably follows unrealistic – indeed naïve – expectations, and the techniques are dropped and replaced by others. One reason (out of many) why the technique does not work might be because the role of individual differences is ignored. Consider the following two techniques.

Goal-setting

It is supposed that if an organization (or a departmental/section head) sets *difficult but attainable* goals within the capacity of employees, workers will strive harder to achieve them. It is suggested that, if the workers are *involved* in the goal-setting process, it will encourage ownership of the set standards. Further psychological, even formal, *con-tracts* are encouraged, so that agreed goals are able to be referred to. A final crucial component refers to the frequency, quality and veridicality of the feedback received by employees on how their performance is matching up to the planned goal. No doubt the quality, quantity and difficulty of attaining the goal will be influenced by individual preferences and perceptions.

   Goal-setting is the process of developing, negotiating and formalizing the targets or objectives that an employee is required to attain. These task goals are important because of their linkage with task performance. Locke's (1984) research, and that of others, provides considerable support for his predictions that:

- *Difficult goals are more likely to lead to higher performance than are less difficult ones*: However, if the goals are seen as too difficult or impossible, the relationship with performance no longer holds. For example, you are likely to sell more if you have a goal of six cars a month than if you have a goal of two. However, if your goal is 40 a month, which is impossible, your performance very likely will be lower than with a goal of six.

- *Specific goals are more likely to lead to higher performance than are no goals or vague or very general ones (such as "do your best")*: For example, setting a goal of selling six cars a month is more specific and should lead to more performance than a simple "try as hard as you can".
- *Task feedback, or knowledge of results, is likely to motivate people towards higher performance by encouraging the setting of higher-performance goals*: Feedback lets people know where they stand and if they are on or off course in their performance.
- *Goals are more likely to lead to higher performance when people have the abilities and the feelings of self-efficacy required to accomplish them*: The person must actually be competent to accomplish the goals and feel confident in those abilities.
- *Goals are more likely to motivate people towards higher performance when they are generally accepted and there is considerable commitment to them*: One way of obtaining commitment is by participating in the goal-setting process and having "ownership" of the goals. Goals assigned by someone else can be equally effective, if assigners are authority figures, and the assignment implies that the subordinate can actually reach the goal. Assigned goals are often challenging and help define the standards people use to attain self-satisfaction with their performance. According to Locke & Latham (1990), assigned goals only lead to poor performance when they are inadequately explained.

Berry (1998: 255) notes:

> Goal-setting theory can be applied in the work setting. In fact, goal setting is inherent in many organizations' procedures for employee performance review. Employees undergo evaluation, are given feedback, and goals for improvement are set. In spite of the common use of goal setting for such motivational purposes, there has been little study of these field applications, and most research evaluating the theory's predictions has been done in the laboratory.

Job enlargement and enrichment

The idea behind the technique of job enlargement and enrichment is to expand the content of a job (by increasing task number and variety) while also encouraging employees to perform at a higher level. Thus, simultaneously, it is possible to increase job responsibility and control, as well as task variety and level. This approach stresses various specific principles: combine jobs to enable workers to perform an entire job; form natural work units to allow workers to be identified with their work; establish client relationships to allow service and product providers to meet recipients and clients; load jobs vertically to allow greater responsibility and control at work; and open feedback channels to give workers knowledge of their results.

An enriched job has eight important characteristics according to Herzberg and colleagues (see pp. 333–337):

- *Direct feedback*: A worker should get immediate knowledge of the results he or she is achieving. This evaluation of performance can be built into the job (by electronic monitoring, say, in a call centre) or provided by a supervisor.

- *Client relationships*: An employee with an enriched job has a client or customer to serve, whether that client is inside or outside the organization. The canteen worker and CEO chauffeur have enriched jobs.
- *New learning*: An enriched job allows its incumbent to feel that he or she is psychologically advancing. In contrast, an impoverished job allows for no new learning.
- *Scheduling*: Employees should have the freedom to schedule some part of their own work, such as deciding when to tackle which assignment.
- *Unique experience*: An enriched job has some unique qualities or features, such as custodial assistants having the opportunity to report on building damage to management.
- *Control over resources*: Groups of workers should have their own mini-budgets and be responsible for their own costs (i.e. profit centres). Or the individual workers might be authorized to order as many supplies as needed to get the job done (such as the purchase of diskettes for a microcomputer).
- *Direct communication authority*: An enriched job allows the worker to communicate directly with other people who use his or her output, such as a quality-control technician handling customer complaints about quality.
- *Personal accountability*: A good job makes workers accountable for their results. In this way, they can accept congratulations for a job well done and blame for a job done poorly.

Over the last decade, there has been a great deal written about empowerment: a concept that remains rather fuzzy. At its simplest level it refers to leaders sharing power (and therefore responsibility) with their staff. It refers to increasing workers' autonomy, discretion and freedom at work: the choice – how, when and where to work. Some jobs permit empowerment, others do not. The person working on a highly regulated and automotized assembly line quite simply has few options.

Work-related locus of control

The locus of control concept has been effectively and enthusiastically applied to occupational behaviour (see Chapter 5). It is one area in which an individual difference variable has been extensively and systematically examined in relation to work motivation. This is not surprising, given that locus of control is similar to many expectancy theories in occupational psychology. Several studies in the 1970s illustrated this point: Lawler (1971) found that, among managers, internals are more likely to feel performance leads to outcome, and externals are less likely to have performance-to-outcome expectancy; while Broedling (1975) found a predicted significant relationship between locus of control and the well-known expectancy model constructs of valence, valence × instrumentality, and superiors' ratings of effort and performance. Similarly, Szilagyi & Sims (1975) found that internals perceive stronger performance-to-reward *and* effort-to-performance expectancies than externals across various occupational levels.

Some studies have been longitudinal in their approach. Andrisani & Nestel (1976) related locus of control to a range of occupational variables in 2972 respondents studied cross-sectionally and longitudinally. Regression analysis showed that internal locus of control beliefs were significantly related to occupational attainment, hourly earnings, job satisfaction, annual earnings and perceived financial progress. The longitudinal analysis showed that changes in occupational attainment, annual earnings and dropping out of the labour force were related to locus of control beliefs. The authors noted:

> These findings ... suggest that internal/external expectancies both affect one's behavior toward the environment and are affected by one's environment ... It suggests that opportunities for success and success itself are effective means for raising initiative to succeed, and that the somewhat more external outlook of those at the lower end of the socio-economic spectrum may reflect unfulfilled expectancies of success, rather than – or as well as – a lack of initiative. (Andrisani & Nestel, 1976: 162–163)

In another longitudinal study of 976 young men, Franz (1980) found internal control was associated with race (being White), years of formal schooling, weeks worked and hourly wages (higher). He argued that locus of control and work experience are reciprocal elements, such that labour market success affects locus of control beliefs, which in turn affect work-related behaviour. Based on a large sample of 2857, Becker & Krzystofiak (1982) examined the effect of labour market discrimination (over a two-year period) on subsequent locus of control beliefs. They found, for instance, that perceptions of employment discrimination influenced the level of externality among Blacks, over and above their racial status. The results provide powerful evidence for the fact that work experiences (labour market discrimination) can powerfully affect locus of control. Vecchio (1981) also used a large population of 1131 full-time male US workers to demonstrate that belief in external control was significantly related to overall job satisfaction: Black workers believed more in external determinants of success, and locus of control did not moderate the relationship between job quality and satisfaction. However, these results must be treated with caution, as both locus of control and job satisfaction were measured by single-item self-report measures.

Hammer & Vardi (1981) tested several hypotheses regarding the effect of locus of control on work-related behaviour. They believed that in organizational settings that facilitate career self-management, internals more than externals will exert more effort towards attaining the jobs they want, will use more specific strategies to attain preferred jobs, will initiate more job moves, will experience more upward mobility, and will perceive mobility as contingent upon personal factors such as skills and competence, experience and performance, rather than seniority or sponsorship. Most of the hypotheses were confirmed and the authors were sensitive to the reciprocal causation:

> There is a feedback loop from career experience to locus of control, where favourable experiences increase tendencies toward internal control, which in turn increases the employee's initiative in self-development with future favourable outcomes. Unfavourable experiences increase the tendencies toward external control which reduces a person's willingness to take an active part in career management ... One might consider the role which locus of control plays in career self-management as similar to the role of need achievement in successful job performance. If the need is present but is allowed to lay dormant by an unstimulating, non-challenging environment, it will benefit neither the employee nor the organization. (Hammer & Vardi, 1981: 27)

In addition to large-scale surveys, there have been several smaller-scale studies with a variety of participants (Richards, 1983). For instance, Brownell (1982) used business school students and middle managers in a laboratory simulation. He found that internally orientated individuals performed best in conditions of high participation, whereas externally orientated individuals performed best in conditions of low participation. He argued that his results are consistent with the hypothesis that performance is the result of the interaction between locus of control and source of control in a particular situation. Payne (1987) reported the results of a study in which locus of control correlated significantly with four of five "objective" success measures of R&D professionals.

Miller, Kets de Vries & Toulouse (1982), on the other hand, used top executives and actual business behaviour to show that locus of control is directly related to strategy-making. Locus of control was powerfully correlated with many strategic variables, but shown to be mediated by the organization's structure and the business environment. In attempting to interpret their findings, the authors note:

> Though these congruencies appear to be very significant, some doubt remains as to the causal network that induces them. Some might argue that the locus of control of the chief executive influences his strategy-making behaviour, and that this in turn has an impact on structure and environment. For example, internals may perceive "constraints" in the environment as loose and malleable; they turn competitors' challenges into opportunities for innovation. Externals may see their environments as having many rigid boundaries that cannot be violated. The result in the first case is an innovative, proactive, risk-embracing strategy, and, in consequence, a more sensitized differentiated structure capable of operating in a more dynamic and heterogeneous environment. The result in the second case is a conservative strategy and a more monolithic and closed structure that is confined to operating in a stable, undifferentiated environment. The data here are most consistent with these conjectures. (Miller *et al.*, 1982: 250)

But a different causal network might be at work. There might be a selection or a developmental activity performed by structure and environment that influences chief executives' locus of control. Perhaps externals are selected by, and thrive in, untechnocratized, monolithic structures facing stable environments, and internals are chosen by and rise to the top of more open and differentiated structures in more dynamic and heterogeneous environments. This may even be a "training" influence whereby stable environments push personality in an external direction and dynamic ones do the opposite. These hypotheses are cast into doubt but are by no means entirely ruled out by the findings presented here. Further longitudinal research would be useful in helping to establish the most important one.

The idea that locus of control is a moderator variable has been noted by many subsequent authors. For instance, in a study of nurses, Blau (1987) found that locus of control moderated the relationship between withdrawal cognitions (thinking of quitting, intention to search) and job turnover. Internals showed significantly stronger, negative relationships than externals between these satisfaction facets and withdrawal cognitions and turnover. Similarly, Storms & Spector (1987) examined job frustration in 160 community mental health workers and found that externals were more likely to respond to frustration with counter-productive behaviour (sabotage, aggression, withdrawal) than persons with an internal locus of control (Furnham, 1992: 155).

In an extensive review, O'Brien (1984) tabulated and criticized the literature on the relationship between locus of control beliefs and work (as well as unemployment, retirement and leisure). He examined internal/external determinants of occupational choice and career planning. He drew three conclusions on the basis of this:

1 Internals are more likely than externals to choose jobs that have higher skill requirements and provide greater personal autonomy. However, this appears to apply to choices of ideal occupations. When internals and externals are asked about their actual or realistic choices, they display few differences. Actual choices are probably constrained by situational factors, such as social pressures and accessibility of various jobs. It is possible that actual job choices are determined jointly by locus of control and situational factors, but further research is needed for this to be demonstrated.

2 Internals sometimes report more effort than do externals in career planning. It appears that the extent of the difference between internals and externals is determined by the degree to which their organizational environment encourages and provides opportunities for career development. Evidence suggests that internals are more likely to report greater career planning than externals if they are in organizations where career advancement is possible and the criteria for advancement are related to personal motivation and skill. Further research is needed before this hypothesis can be considered to have been supported.

3 Nearly all research studies use self-reports as measures of occupational choice and planning. Hence the results may not extend to objective choices and objectively measured planning behaviour. Another qualification that needs to be made is that results from various studies may differ because of the use of different locus of control scales. The score of different scales is not necessarily unsound, but interpretations are difficult when no information is provided about the degree of correspondence between revised scales and one or more commonly used locus of control scales. (O'Brien, 1984: 14–15)

Results seem to indicate that internals perform better than externals "on the job" and obtain jobs with higher skill utilization and occupational status. According to O'Brien (1984), three possible explanations could be put forward to account for this:

- internals show great job mobility as a function of their career planning and choice;
- internals obtain better jobs because of greater effort, work motivation and therefore promotion;
- internals are promoted because they choose task behaviours that approximate more closely the behaviours required for optimal job performance.

In attempting to provide an answer to the above, O'Brien tabulated various salient studies but found equivocal results. However, he lists four possible explanations for the different results from various studies:

1 *Situation factors*: In some studies, the performance of internals and externals could have been affected systematically by differences in their situations. In addition, the failure of some studies to measure situational factors precluded estimation of locus of control–situational interactions.

2   *Valence differences*: Many studies did not establish that the value or attractiveness of performance outcomes was equivalent for internals and externals.
3   *Ability*: Some studies found that significant differences between internals and externals disappeared when ability was controlled for. Hence studies that failed to measure ability might be interpreted as showing different ability distributions among internals and externals.
4   *Use of performance ratings*: Although ratings are more often associated significantly with objective performances when both types of performance measures are used, the degree of correspondence is often low.

Despite these difficulties of interpretation, some generalizations are possible. Locus of control accounts for a small percentage of the variance in performance measures (the direct effect is generally less than 10%). When interaction between locus of control and structure is estimated, the percentage of variance accounted for is increased. Internals tend to be rated by supervisors as higher on performance than externals. However, the results do not allow one to infer actual performance differences, as the ratings could be because of an interaction between the public presentation of internals and externals with raters' stereotypes of the better-performing employee. The results could also be attributable to systematic differences in the abilities of internals and externals and in the job structures in which they are found.

O'Brien (1984) is critical of studies that interpret findings that individuals with external locus of control report higher levels of stress. He believes locus of control might play a part in distorting responses to stress questions and that most studies fail to measure objective stress factors, the objective degree of structure in jobs, or the behaviour of internals and externals *subsequent* to the onset of stressors.

Locus of control is an important *moderator* variable, which, together with biographical and job facet variables, determines work-related behaviour. It is also a reciprocal variable in that it determines *and* is determined by work-related behaviour. Unfortunately, many extant studies prevent clear interpretations.

Spector (1986) performed a meta-analysis of locus of control studies. He found that high levels of perceived (internal) control were associated with high levels of job satisfaction (overall and individual facets), commitment, involvement, performance and motivation, as well as lower levels of physical symptoms, emotional distress, role stress, absenteeism, intent to leave and actual turnover. Correlates ranged from .2 to .5, suggesting that between 5 and 25% of the variance in occupational behaviour can be accounted for by the locus of control variable. There is no doubt, therefore, that the locus of control variable accounts for an important and significant amount of individual difference variance with regard to work motivation and productivity.

The work on locus of control is important because it illustrates many important complicating features of single-measure predictors of motivation. First, as researchers point out, the relationship is not perfectly linear; secondly, there are many feedback loops showing how the consequences of certain behaviour affects locus-of-control beliefs; and, thirdly, that locus of control is possibly one of many moderator variables that influence motivation.

Measuring job motivation and involvement

There are major problems in measuring job motivation. Asking people is problematic, both because some people find it very difficult to report their motives accurately, even if they want to (they simply don't have sufficient insight into themselves), and because there are strong pressures put on people to give socially desirable, rather than truthful, answers (i.e. they lie). It is equally difficult to infer motivation from actual behaviour because, although it is true that efficient performance is a function of hard work, it may be impaired by a range of other activities, such as the group norm of production, machine breakdown or the non-delivery of crucial items.

Traditionally, the measure of job motivation falls into two categories (Cook, Hepworth, Wall, & Warr, 1981). The first is to complete fairly straightforward, brief, face-valid measures of motivation or involvement. However, it is not always clear why certain items that look like personality trait items are included. The second expectancy theory approach attempts a context-free, non-specific measure of expectancies (that effort will lead to the goal being achieved) and *valence* (the idea that the value of the goal is high).

Lodahl & Kejner's (1965) Job Involvement Questionnaire is used extensively with research in the area. It is described in Box 6.2. Another simple measure is Warr, Cook & Wall's (1979) Intrinsic Motivation Questionnaire (Box 6.3).

Box 6.2 Job involvement questionnaire.

Items

1. I'll do overtime to finish a job, even if I'm not paid for it
2. You can measure a person pretty well by how good a job he does
3. The major satisfaction in my life comes from my job
4. For me, mornings at work really fly by
5. I usually show up for work a little early, to get things ready
6. The most important things that happen to me involve my work
7. Sometimes I lay awake at night thinking ahead to the next day's work
8. I'm really a perfectionist about my work
9. I feel depressed when I fail at something connected with my job
10. I have other activities more important than my work (R)
11. I live, eat and breathe my job
12. I would probably keep working even if I didn't need the money
13. Quite often I feel like staying home from work instead of coming in (R)
14. To me, my work is only a small part of who I am (R)
15. I am very much involved personally in my work
16. I avoid taking on extra duties and responsibilities in my work (R)
17. I used to be more ambitious about my work than I am now (R)
18. Most things in life are more important than work (R)
19. I used to care more about my work, but now other things are more important to me (R)
20. Sometimes I'd like to kick myself for the mistakes I make in my work

Responses
Strongly agree; Agree; Disagree; Strongly disagree; scored 1 to 4 respectively.
(R) items are reversed before scoring 1 = 4, 2 = 3, 3 = 2, 4 = 1.

Source: Reproduced from Lodahl & Kejner (1965) with the permission of the American Psychological Association.

Box 6.3 Intrinsic motivation questionnaire

Items

1. I feel a sense of personal satisfaction when I do this job well
2. My opinion of myself goes down when I do this job badly
3. I take pride in doing my job as well as I can
4. I feel unhappy when my work is not up to my usual standard
5. I like to look back on the day's work with a sense of a job well done
6. I try to think of ways of doing my job effectively

Responses

No, I strongly disagree; No, I disagree quite a lot; No, I disagree just a little; I'm not sure about this; Yes, I agree just a little; Yes, I agree quite a lot; Yes, I strongly agree; scored 1 to 7 respectively.

Source: Warr *et al.* (1979).

Furnham (1993) has developed the Expectancy–Value Questionnaire. This approach suggests that people are most motivated at work when they have realistic expectations of the outcome or benefits at work *and* of the value they place on them. People with inappropriate expectancies become disappointed, frustrated and demotivated. Too high and too unrealistic expectations are frequently associated with turnover and poor productivity. The more accurate people are at predicting what rewards the job provides, the better. Secondly, and equally important, people value rewards at work differently. For some, "flexitime" is more important than salary; for others, security is rated much more highly than career opportunity. Employees naturally respond much more positively to the rewards and outcomes they value.

Expectancy–value theory therefore measures what people expect from a job and how much they value that aspect of it (value = how important the item is to you; expectancy = how will you expect the job to provide the item). Motivation is a function of the multiplication of expectancy and value. The 24-item questionnaire set out below is filled out twice, first to evaluate to what extent individuals expect to find these factors in the job and how much they individually value them. A score is obtained for each item.

$$(A)\ \frac{\text{Value} - \text{expectancy}}{\text{Expectancy}} \qquad (B)\ \frac{\text{Value} - \text{expectancy}}{\text{Value}}$$

A high *positive* means high value but low expectancy (i.e. they value a facet of the job but don't expect to get it), whereas a high *negative* score means high expectancy but low value (i.e. they expect something on the job but do not value it highly). The difference between equations (a) and (b) is that in the former the disparity is seen as a function of the expectancy, whereas the latter is a function of the value. The closer the score is to zero, the more expectancy and value are in alignment. The various items are:

1   Achievement in work
2   Advancement; chances for promotion
3   Benefits, vacation, sick leave, pensions, insurance, etc.

4 Company image; to be employed by a company for which you are proud to work
5 Contribution to society
6 Convenient hours of work
7 Co-workers; fellow workers who are pleasant and agreeable
8 Esteem; that you are valued as a person
9 Feedback concerning the results of your work
10 Independence in work
11 Influence in the organization
12 Influence in the workplace
13 Job interest; to do work which is interesting to you
14 Job security; permanent job
15 Job status
16 Meaningful, interesting work
17 Opportunity for personal growth and development
18 Opportunity to meet people and interact with them
19 Pay; the amount of money you receive
20 Recognition for doing a good job
21 Responsibility
22 Supervisor, a fair and considerate boss
23 Use of ability and knowledge in your work
24 Work conditions; comfortable and clean

These items are rated on a 6-point scale (high to low value and expectation).

Measuring job motivation, involvement and commitment is not very problematic in terms of theory. The major problem is that people either dissimulate their answers (usually lie about how motivated they are to get the job, and how demotivated they are on the job) or are not able to report on their motivational patterns accurately. Motivation is complex and many workers are unable to articulate what features of their job are motivating or not.

Work satisfaction

Are some personality types more likely to be job-satisfied than others, regardless of the job? What sort of people are most satisfied in what sorts of jobs? Are job-satisfied individuals more productive than less satisfied individuals? Is job satisfaction a consequence, rather than a cause, of productivity at work? These are some important questions one may wish to ask of the literature on job satisfaction. A central question concerns the relationship between job (work) and general life satisfaction. Data point to a close correlation between the two, suggesting that trait happiness or subjective well-being determine both satisfactions and that there is a unity between life and labour (Tait, Youtz-Padgett, & Baldwin, 1989).

Job satisfaction is important because of its association with positive (productivity, pro-social) and negative (absenteeism, theft, turnover) behaviours. Because of the importance of these outcomes, the topic is regularly assessed.

It is self-evident that there should be major individual differences in job satisfaction, and that different people in the same job experience different sources and amounts of satisfaction, and two people doing quite different jobs may experience comparable levels of satisfaction. However, *the* most important question is whether personality (and other individual differences) is a *main factor* or *interacts* with the job to produce job satisfaction. Thus, we have the following possible equation:

$$JS = f(P \times J \times PJF \times E)$$

where JS = job satisfaction, P = personality, J = job characteristics, PJF = person–job fit and E = error. There are two possible main effects: personality and job.

- If it can be shown that some personality types are more satisfied (or dissatisfied) irrespective of the nature of the job, presumably the main effect of personality accounts for a good deal of the variance.
- If it can be shown that some jobs cause their incumbents to be more satisfied (or dissatisfied) irrespective of the personality (skills, abilities, etc.) of the incumbents, the main effect of job probably accounts for a good deal of the variance.
- If it can be shown that a particular fit (or misfit) between a person (personality) and the job (demands) causes particular sources of satisfaction or dissatisfaction, the interaction between person and job is presumably the major source of the variance.

Unfortunately, the equation is made somewhat more complicated by the fact that job satisfaction is, itself, multidimensional. Depending on the particular theorist one reads or the measures that one adopts, there may be as many as ten different, but inevitably related, dimensions of job satisfaction, for example, with working conditions, co-workers and reward structure. Hence, one might find after extensive empirical evidence the following sorts of hypothetical equations (where P is a measure of personality/ability traits, J is an index of the job, and PJF is the fit measure between the two):

$$JS \text{ (working conditions)} = 4.86P + 1.35J + 2.41PJF + 2.14$$

$$JS \text{ (co-workers)} = 10.21P + 0.86J + 1.11PJF + 6.81$$

$$JS \text{ (reward structure)} = 3.11P + 9.87J + 2.23PJF + 1.33$$

The attraction of these sorts of equations is great; however, they can never be as simple as this. Both personality and jobs are multidimensional and the multiplication of the two means that there could be extremely awkward equations that are simply not cost-effective to calculate. Nevertheless, the idea is a good one, although there will no doubt be considerable debate as to whether the P or J factor accounts for most of the variance (Furnham, 1992: 198).

Shultz and Shultz (1998) have reviewed nine personal characteristics associated with job satisfaction:

1   *Age*: Job satisfaction increases with age possibly because age brings increased confidence, competence, self-esteem and responsibility.
2   *Gender*: The results are inconsistent but may point to men being more satisfied possibly because they tend to be paid more and have more opportunities for promotion.
3   *Race*: Whites appear more satisfied than Blacks, who are often confined to lower-level, more poorly paid jobs with fewer opportunities for advancement.

4   *Cognitive ability*: There is no consistent finding, as highly intelligent people may be in insufficiently challenging, tedious jobs, while less able people cannot cope with the intellectual demands placed on them. Education is negatively correlated with satisfaction possibly because of unfulfilled expectations.
5   *Job experience*: There is evidence of a trend: new workers tend to be most satisfied with the stimulation, challenge and opportunities. This levels off and even declines but picks up again in middle age.
6   *Use of skills*: People like to use their skills and abilities to perform high-quality work. The more they can do so, the happier they are.
7   *Job congruence*: Self-evidently the better the match between an individual's temperament and abilities and the demands of the job, the happier they tend to be.
8   *Personality*: Stability (*vs* Neuroticism), internal (*vs* external), locus of control and committed (*vs* alienated) individuals express more job satisfaction.
9   *Occupational level*: Seniority is associated with satisfaction.

There are clear positive and negative output variables associated with satisfaction and dissatisfaction. Presumably job performance is a clear correlate of satisfaction but what remains debatable is what causes what. There are, however, also many negative correlates of dissatisfaction, including absenteeism, turnover and theft.

Theories of the causes of job satisfaction

Despite the variety of variables suggested as having major, minor or moderating effects on job satisfaction, it is possible to divide these factors into three distinct groups:

*   *Organizational policies and procedures*: These concern such things as the reward system (the perceived equity of pay and promotions), supervision and decision-making practices, and perceived quality of supervision. Inevitably, each and all of these can affect job satisfaction.
*   *Specific aspects of the job*, such as overall workload, skill, variety, autonomy, feedback and the physical nature of the work environment. These must have an important effect.
*   *Personal characteristics*, such as self-esteem, ability to tolerate stress and general life satisfaction, help determine job satisfaction.

Surveys consistently indicate that 80–90% of people are relatively happy at work. However, it is clear that, although job satisfaction is generally high, this is not true of all work settings and jobs, nor is it true of all socioeconomic and ethnic groups. Given that sociological and organizational factors obviously contribute to job satisfaction, the question must remain as to the personality factors associated with those who claim either to be highly job-satisfied or not at all job-satisfied. Consider, for example, Table 6.8, which looks at how to increase job satisfaction. Locke (1984) identified eight factors of work and appropriate strategies, but rarely considered the important moderating role of personality factors. Hence, with few exceptions, the proposed solutions are focused on organizational rather than individual differences (Furnham, 1992: 199).

Although it is important to list and taxonomize factors that influence job satisfaction, what must follow is a description of the process whereby individuals in particular jobs experience quite different levels of job satisfaction.

Table 6.8 Major job values and ways to implement them

Job aspect	Job value	Wider value or need	Ways to implement
Work	Personal interest	Pleasure	Recruiting, selection, placement, job enrichment, goal-setting, participation in decision-making
	Importance		
	Chance to use skills	Growth	
	Responsibility		
	Autonomy	Self-esteem	
	Variety		
	Achievement, progress		
	Feedback		
	Clarity		
	Harmony		
	Participation		
	Pressure		
	Fatigue avoidance	Physical well-being	Design of workplace
Pay and benefits	Fairness	Justice, need satisfaction	Job analysis; wage surveys; objective work measurement or performance ratings; high pay and benefits; incentive plans
	Job security		Manpower planning
Promotions	Fairness	Justice, visibility, growth	Promotions on merit
Recognition	Recognition	Justice, visibility	Praise and credit for work and effort
Working conditions	Resources	Helps to get work done	Provide resources
	Hours	Helps get off-the-job values	Flexitime, four-day week
	Shift work (−)	Interferes with home life, health	Compensation (through pay, time off)
	Safe physical conditions	Health, well-being	Remove hazards, safety programmes
	Privacy	Facilitates concentration; privacy	Closed office design
Co-workers/ subordinates	Similarity	Friendship	Recruiting, selection, placement
	Competence, cooperation	Helps get work done	Same as above, plus training
Management/ supervision	Respect	Self-esteem	Being honest with employees; concerned with their wants
	Trust		Consistent honesty
	Two-way communication		Listening to employees
	Provide above values	See above	Participation, influence
Unions	Pay	See above	Higher pay, benefits

Source: Reproduced from Locke (1984) with the permission of John Wiley & Sons.

Job satisfaction and life satisfaction

Are people who are generally happy and satisfied with life also happy at work (and vice versa). Does life satisfaction lead to job satisfaction, or vice versa, as the work–life lobby would have us believe. There are essentially three models that look at this relationship:

- *Spill over*: job and work experience influence one another.
- *Segmentation*: the two spheres are pretty separate.
- *Compensation*: people seek to compensate for an unhappy experience in the other sphere (i.e. those in a dissatisfying job seek a rich, happy, fulfilled private life.

Research supports most clearly the spill over model. The correlation between an individual's work and life satisfaction is in the region of $r = .40$ to $r = .50$. The idea is that life satisfaction affects job satisfaction and vice versa – that is, the relationship is reciprocal. There are as a result various "explanations" for this.

First, because work is such a fundamentally important feature of life, people who enjoy their jobs will report greater satisfaction in their lives. Second, basic differences in personality predispose people to be satisfied with all aspects of their life – work and out-of-work existences. The data suggest both are true. Heller, Judge & Watson (2002) found personality factors predicted satisfaction with both work and life; but that the two were related to each other. They noted:

> Similar to researchers, practitioners need to understand that job satisfaction is not simply a function of the job or of organizational characteristics, but rather reflects more broadly enduring individual differences in personality, affectivity, values and preferences. At a surface level, this could be interpreted by practitioners to mean that organizations need not invest resources in enhancing employees' jobs, because their satisfaction with their jobs will be considerably constrained by their enduring personality characteristics. We do not support this view; whereas personality can place broad limits on the levels of satisfaction experienced by employees, improving work conditions still can increase their job satisfaction by influencing how they feel, think or act on the job. We also believe it would be premature to use personality traits such as core self-evaluations in selection procedures; more predictive validity and economic utility data are needed before such a selection process can be seriously considered. In essence, we think our findings suggest that employers need to "know" their employees better – in terms of their personalities, temperament, and other characteristic tendencies. This may help employers create better training, motivational and compensation systems that are more finely tuned to their employees' characteristics. (Heller *et al.*, 2002: 839)

Herzberg's two-factor theory

Herzberg, Mausner, Petersen & Capwell (1957) reviewed the early satisfaction research literature, and found no relationships between job satisfaction and work performance. They concluded that there *were* systematic relationships between workers' attitudes and their behaviour, but that these relationships had gone unnoticed because researchers had confused job satisfaction and job *dissatisfaction*. According to Herzberg *et al.*, job satisfaction depends upon a certain set of conditions, whereas job dissatisfaction is the result of an entirely different set of conditions. Thus, although it is possible to think of satisfaction and dissatisfaction as two extremes on a single continuum, they are determined by different factors. Hence, it may be more helpful to think of two factors (Figure 6.9).

Herzberg, Mausner & Snyderman (1959) examined the relationship between satisfaction and performance, and formalized a theory based on their results. According to the

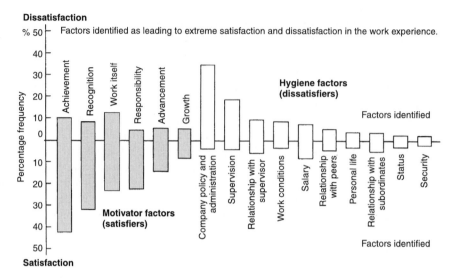

Figure 6.9 Herzberg's two-factor theory. Adapted from Westwood (1992).

theory, people have two major types of needs. The first of these Herzberg called *hygiene needs*, which are influenced by the physical and psychological conditions in which people work. Herzberg called the second set of needs *motivator needs*, and described them as being very similar to the higher-order needs in Maslow's (1954) need hierarchy theory. Herzberg *et al.* (1959) claimed that these two types of needs were satisfied by different types of outcomes or rewards. Hygiene needs were said to be satisfied by the level of certain conditions called *hygiene factors* or *dissatisfiers*. The factors that Herzberg found to be related to hygiene needs are: supervision, interpersonal relations, physical working conditions, salary, company policies and administrative practices, benefits and job security. These factors are all concerned with the *context* or *environment* in which the job has to be performed. When these factors are unfavourable, then job dissatisfaction is the result. Conversely, when hygiene factors are positive, such as when workers perceive that their pay is fair and that their working conditions are good, barriers to job satisfaction are removed. However, the fulfilment of hygiene needs cannot by itself result in job satisfaction, only in the *reduction* or elimination of *dissatisfaction*. Herzberg compared hygiene factors to modern water- and air-pollution controls: although such controls do not cure any diseases, they serve to *prevent* the outbreak of disease. In the same way, he and his colleagues believed that hygiene factors did not cause satisfaction, but that they could prevent dissatisfaction.

Unlike hygiene needs, motivator needs are fulfilled by what Herzberg *et al.* (1959) called *motivator factors* or *satisfiers*. They identified the following motivator factors: achievement, recognition, work itself, responsibility and advancement. Whereas *hygiene* factors are related to the *context* of work, *motivator* factors are concerned with the *nature* of the work itself and the consequences of work. According to the theory, the factors that lead to job satisfaction are those that satisfy an individual's need for self-actualization (self-fulfilment) in their work, and it is only from the performance of the task that individuals can enjoy the rewards that will reinforce their aspirations. Compared with hygiene factors, which result in a "neutral state" (neither satisfied nor dissatisfied) when present, positive motivator factors result in job satisfaction. When recognition, responsibility and other motivators are absent from a job, however, the result will not be dissatisfaction, as with the absence of hygiene factors, but rather the same neutral state associated with the *presence* of hygiene factors (Furnham, 1992: 202).

Attractive though the theory is, it has received little empirical support. Researchers since the 1970s who have tried to replicate Herzberg's findings have shown that both factors can lead to either satisfaction or dissatisfaction. Furthermore, the theory says nothing about individual differences, so that some people may be strongly in favour of job enrichment and others strongly against it. Indeed, modern writers believe the theory should be laid to rest (Judge, Bono, & Locke, 2000). This is no doubt attributable to the fact that various methodological errors were introduced into the early theory-testing work. These included the real possibility that all the results could be put down to classic attribution errors, such that personal failure is attributed externally (to hygiene factors) and success internally (to motivation factors). Secondly, the theory-testing work was nearly all done on white-collar workers (accountants and engineers), who are hardly representative of the working population. Essentially, five objections are frequently made:

- *Selective bias and defensive behaviour*: Responses to critical incident questions may "selectively recall" situational factors and project failures to external factors.
- *Method dependency*: When there are variations in methodology (questionnaires, interviews or behavioural observations), different results are obtained. This suggests that results are as dependent on how information is gathered as on what that information is.
- *Assumption about the nature and measurement of satisfaction*: There appears to be substantial evidence questioning the dual-factor argument that hygiene factors lead only to dissatisfaction when absent and motivators are only capable of providing satisfaction.
- *Individual variations*: The evidence points to questions of how well the theory applies to people in different categories based on gender, socioeconomic status, culture, age, and so on.
- *Organizational differences*: Effects of the two-factor theory vary with the climate of the organization within which it is implemented.

Despite serious doubts about the validity of the theory, researchers were very eager to implement one key implication of the theory, namely job enrichment.

The idea that repetitive and boring jobs cause employees' production to fall below potential and for them to feel dissatisfied was suggested in the 1930s by human relations researchers, who introduced such regimes as *rotating* workers among a variety of jobs and *enlarging* individual tasks to enable workers to identify more closely with a total product, thereby increasing their pride in craftsmanship. Herzberg *et al.* recommend *job enrichment* (and by implication job satisfaction), defined as an attempt by management to design tasks in such a way as to build in the opportunity for personal achievement, recognition, challenge and individual growth. It provides workers with more responsibility and autonomy in carrying out a complete task, and with timely feedback on their performance (Furnham, 1992: 203–204).

In summary, job enrichment consists of the following measures:

- removing controls from a job while retaining accountability – motivate by responsibility;

- increasing the accountability of the individual for his own work – motivate by responsibility and recognition;
- giving each person a complete and natural module of work – motivate by achievement;
- granting job freedom for a person's own work – motivate by responsibility, achievement and recognition;
- making timely reports on performance available to the worker instead of to the supervisor – motivate by recognition;
- introducing new tasks not previously performed – motivate by growth and learning;
- assigning specific tasks so the employee can develop expertise in performing them – motivate by responsibility, achievement and recognition.

Studies on the efficacy and cost-effectiveness of job enlargement and job enrichment have led to equivocal results (Foster, 2000). Various problems have also been noted in implementing the two-factor theory. Some are characteristic of all efforts to change, whereas others are unique to alterations in motivational programmes:

- *Education*: Many managers simply do not understand or approve of job enrichment.
- *Ideology*: Division of labour or specialization and control are a part of the way jobs have traditionally been performed.
- *Organization*: Job enrichment is a long-term investment, whereas organizational controls demand immediate returns. Since job enrichment often requires that jobs be redesigned, vested interests cause resentment when a task is taken from one organizational unit and placed in another.
- *Management*: Managers often fear loss of control over operations, knowing that knowledge is power.
- *Technology*: Technology dictates the design of many jobs and leaves little flexibility for redesigning them.
- *Employees*: Some employees do not wish to perform enriched jobs. Indeed, they are threatened by these steps.
- *Implementation*: Implementors often become overly enthusiastic and unrealistic in what can or should be done.
- *Diagnosis*: Job enrichment has become almost a fad, and many attempts have not been preceded by adequate diagnosis of the problems.
- *Uniqueness of setting*: Some say a particular organization is unique and such a programme would not work in a specific setting.
- *Nothing new*: This is the contention that job enrichment is "nothing new" for a particular firm: all the jobs are meaningful (Duncan, 1978: 141–142).

In short, there are certain problems associated with job enrichment. First, cost–benefit data pertaining to job enrichment are not often reported. Cost–benefit analysis is often expensive to implement, and the benefits are sometimes questionable. Secondly, situational factors specifically supporting job enrichment often have not been system-atically assessed. Thirdly, many reports of the success of job enrichment have been evangelical in nature – that is, authors overstate the benefits and understate the prob-lems. There are few reported failures in the literature, possibly because of such bragging.

Finally, evaluations of job enrichment programmes have too often not been conducted rigorously using the scientific method appropriately to judge their effectiveness accurately.

There is always a trade-off between enrichment and task specialization. *Job simplification* usually means greater specialization and efficiency but lower intrinsic rewards, and enrichment means less specialization and greater intrinsic satisfaction.

Reif & Luthans (1972), who made the following observations, suggested that the two-factor theory be used selectively as a motivational technique since:

- Some workers are alienated by the middle-class values inherent in job enrichment rather than by the job itself. Contentment on the job is not necessarily related to satisfaction, since many people are perfectly capable of finding satisfaction outside the work environment.
- Some people do not view improved job design and meaningful work as an adequate compensation for the alteration of existing patterns of social interaction which sometimes ensues.
- Enrichment may have negative effects because some workers feel inadequate and fear failure.

Two major implications for the study of individual determinants of job satisfaction stem from the work of Herzberg and the celebrated two-factor theory. The first is that, although certain personality traits are positively associated with job satisfaction, they have no impact on dissatisfaction. That is, different traits can and do (in appropriate conditions) determine dissatisfaction but not satisfaction. Thus, for instance, extraversion and internal locus of control might relate to satisfaction and neuroticism to dissatisfaction. The idea that different trait dimensions operate on satisfaction and dissatisfaction differently is a testable thesis derived directly from Herzberg. The second implication of this work refers to the personality characteristics of people who either shun or yearn for job enrichment. Various hypotheses could be entertained and then tested: people with internal locus of control favour enrichment (and respond to it) more than those with external locus of control; extraverts seek out job enrichment more than introverts; ability is positively correlated with attitudes to job enrichment, and so on.

Some have argued that most industrial and organizational psychology has been designed by and tested on middle-class white-collar workers and hence shows a bias in that regard. That may well be true. It could also be true that, because of volunteer effects, participants in job satisfaction studies have been predominantly from some personality groups (i.e. extraverts), which may well have biased the results (Furnham, 1992: 204–205).

Donnelly, Gibson & Ivancevich (1987) have done an excellent compare-and-contrast exercise with the theories of Maslow and Herzberg, as shown in Figure 6.10.

Social learning theory

Social learning approaches to job satisfaction and attitudes are similar to Lawler's (1973) facet model, in that attitudes are seen to be determined in part by an examination of the behaviour of other workers. Instead of comparing inputs and outcomes, however, social learning theory claims workers use other people as sources of information for selecting appropriate attitudes and behaviours. Workers' attitudes, at least in part, are copied, reflected or modelled from the attitudes of co-workers. Specifically, by

1. Similarities

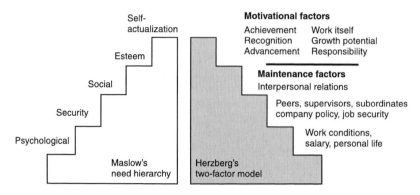

2. Differences

Comparing Maslow's and Herzberg's theories.

Topic	Maslow's need hierarchy	Herzberg's two-factor theory
1. Relevance	People in society in all types of jobs and in retirement.	Most relevant to white-collar workers and professional employees.
2. Impact of needs on behaviour	All needs can motivate behaviour.	Only some intrinsic needs serve as motivators.
3. Role of financial rewards	Financial reward can motivate.	Financial reward is not a key motivator.
4. Perspective	Applies to all people and their lives.	Is work centred.
5. Type of theory	Descriptive (what is).	Perspective (what should be).

Figure 6.10 Comparison of the theories of Maslow and of Herzberg. Reproduced from Donnelly *et al.* (1987) with the permission of McGraw-Hill, Inc.

observing co-workers, workers infer their attitudes towards the organization, the job as a whole and specific job facets. People perceive certain co-workers, usually those with similar jobs and interests, or those who are believed to be successful or powerful, as being appropriate *models*, and base their own attitudes on what they believe theirs to be. Thus, the theory maintains that a worker's job satisfaction is not determined internally, but externally.

Several studies conducted by Weiss have examined the social learning of work attitudes, of which job satisfaction could be seen as one. Weiss & Shaw (1979) studied the effects of models' evaluative comments on the task satisfaction of individuals who watched an instructional videotape, on which could be seen the hands of a "trainee" who was assembling a simple electric circuit, while the voice of the "trainer" explained the steps involved in the task. The participants could also hear, in the background, the voice of the trainee and another person. In some conditions, the trainee made positive comments about the task, whereas in others he made negative comments. Weiss and Shaw found that participants who overheard the positive comments had more favourable attitudes after performing the task than did those who overheard the negative comments. Precisely how long these positive attitudes last is not known, nor are the causes of the various individual differences that were observed.

Weiss (1978) also found that the modelling of work values was influenced by supervisors' behaviour; there was great similarity between the values of workers and supervisors when the supervisors demonstrated consideration towards their subordinates. He also discovered that workers who were low in self-esteem, or who had relatively negative perceptions of their own abilities and worthiness, modelled the values of successful and competent supervisors more strongly than did high self-esteem subordinates. Weiss suggested that high self-esteem people may have greater confidence in their own judgments, and therefore feel less of a need to rely on cues provided by others.

Social learning appears to be a means by which people develop attitudes, not only in work settings but also in other social situations. However, not everyone is equally likely to model the behaviour of others, nor is everyone equally likely to serve as a model. Consequently, social learning is apt to be a better explanation for job satisfaction and other attitudes in certain situations, and for certain people than for others. Essentially, social learning theory traditionally sees individual differences as error variance. However, there is no reason to deny that there are individual differences in the extent to which people are likely to be influenced by the ideas, beliefs and behaviours of those around them. Personality differences are not incompatible with social factors operating (Furnham, 1992: 210–211).

Measuring job satisfaction

It is possible to measure job satisfaction in various ways: by standard questionnaire, group or individual interviews, exit interviews as well as overt behaviours. Questionnaire measures of job satisfaction are of two kinds: general (overall) and specific. The former simply attempt to ascertain general overall satisfaction with the "total package" that is the job. There are many questionnaires that attempt to do this, dating back over 50 years. There are also dimensions or facet-specific measures which attempt to assess satisfaction with quite different features of the job, such that one is able to ascertain precise measures of different things such as satisfaction with pay, supervisory style, physical conditions, and so on.

The Brayfield & Rothe (1951) index is a frequently used measure, aptly titled the "overall job satisfaction" measure (Box 6.4). Another example of this approach is the extensively used Minnesota Satisfaction Questionnaire (Weiss, Davis, England, Lofquist, 1967). The scale purports to measure intrinsic (I) and extrinsic (E) motivation in different areas but yields an overall satisfaction score (Box 6.5).

An example of the multifaceted test can be found in the much more complex "index of organizational reactions" devised by Smith (1976). This scale yields scores on various satisfaction scales such as supervision, nature of work, amount of work, working conditions, co-workers, pay, the future of the organization, and overall job satisfaction (Box 6.6).

Current issues

Judge and Church note a strange lack of direct interest by practitioners in the concept of job satisfaction:

> One might expect the notion of job satisfaction to be in the forefront of employers' minds. Interestingly enough, however, the extent to which organizations have

Box 6.4 Overall job satisfaction questionnaire

Items

1. My job is like a hobby to me
2. My job is usually interesting enough to keep me from getting bored
3. It seems that my friends are more interested in their jobs (R)
4. I consider my job rather unpleasant (R)
5. I enjoy my work more than my leisure time
6. I am often bored with my job (R)
7. I feel fairly well satisfied with my present job
8. Most of the time I have to force myself to go to work (R)
9. I am satisfied with my job for the time being
10. I feel that my job is no more interesting than others I could get (R)
11. I definitely dislike my work (R)
12. I feel that I am happier in my work than most other people
13. Most days I am enthusiastic about my work
14. Each day of work seems like it will never end (R)
15. I like my job better than the average worker does
16. My job is pretty uninteresting (R)
17. I find real enjoyment in my work
18. I am disappointed I ever took this job (R)

Responses: Strongly agree: Agree; Undecided; Disagree; Strongly disagree; scored 5 to 1 respectively. (R) reverse items.

Source: Brayfield & Rothe (1951).

adopted the term and institutionalized intervention based on job satisfaction related theory and research is considerably more mixed. Job satisfaction, for example, is rarely included as part of an organization's key values, basic beliefs, core competencies or guiding principles, nor is the topic given much direct exposure in popular business books. Rather, the idea of having satisfied employees is more likely to be considered some form of outcome or end-state, which occurs as a result of adherence to some more proactively typically action oriented set of factors, behaviours or set of interventions.

Generally speaking, attention to job satisfaction related issues seems to range anywhere from complete repression of the term to fully integrated measurement and evaluation tools, such as annual organization culture surveys, multi-rater feedback methodologies or the Balanced Scorecard approach. Even in those organizations where job satisfaction issues are addressed directly through formal institutional systems and policies, the conceptualization tends to be more outcome-oriented, such as morale, commitment or even turnover. Thus, while these areas are entirely different psychological constructs in the literature, managers and practitioners often use the terms interchangeably when working with and responding to these types of issues. This blurring of the construct itself and intermittent level of implementation raises some important issues for researchers and theorists working in the area of job satisfaction, as well as for the practitioners who must work within and manage such complex boundaries. (Judge & Church, 2000: 176–177)

Box 6.5 Minnesota satisfaction questionnaire

Items

In my present job, this is how I feel about:

1. Being able to keep busy all the time (activity, I)
2. The chance to work alone on the job (independence, I)
3. The chance to do different things from time to time (variety, I)
4. The chance to be "somebody" in the community (social status, I)
5. The way my boss handles his men (supervision – human relations, E)
6. The competence of my supervisor in making decisions (supervision – technical, E)
7. Being able to do things that don't go against my conscience (moral values, I)
8. The way my job provides for steady employment (security, I)
9. The chance to do things for other people (social service, I)
10. The chance to tell people what to do (authority, I)
11. The chance to do something that makes use of my abilities (ability utilization, I)
12. The way company policies are put into practice (company policies and practices, E)
13. My pay and the amount of work I do (compensation, E)
14. The chances for advancement on this job (advancement, E)
15. The freedom to use my own judgement (responsibility, I)
16. The chance to try my own methods of doing the job (creativity, I)
17. The working conditions (working conditions, E)
18. The way my co-workers get along with each other (co-workers, I)
19. The praise I get for doing a good job (recognition, E)
20. The feeling of accomplishment I get from the job (achievement, I)

Responses: Very dissatisfied; Dissatisfied; I can't decide whether I am satisfied or not; Satisfied; Very satisfied; scored 1 to 5 respectively.

Source: Reproduced from Weiss *et al.* (1967).

Conclusion

For the reviewer of organizational behaviour theories of job motivation and satisfaction, there is alas considerable frustration, not because the theories are not insightful or true, but rather that they all seem to focus on only part of the truth. Hence, some theorists, such as Porter & Lawler (1968), have attempted to integrate all theories into a grand model which takes account of the different features.

There are many criteria for evaluating theories – such as elegance, parsimony, coherence – but perhaps the most important and fundamental is validity. However, it is the validity of theories – that is, the extent to which they have predictive power – which is important. Robbins (1991) listed six major motivation theory groups and then attempted to assess their power to predict productivity, satisfaction turnover and satisfaction:

- *Need theories*: At least four theories which focused on needs: Maslow's hierarchy, motivation-hygiene, ERG, and the three-needs theories. Their power lies mainly in explaining and predicting job satisfaction.
- *Task characteristics theories*: The job characteristics model addresses many types of work behaviour. Individuals with a high growth need – which probably includes an

Box 6.6 Index of organizational reactions

Items and responses
Supervision

1. Do you ever have the feeling you would be better off working under different supervision? (*Rate overall supervision*)
   I almost always feel this way; I often feel this way; I sometimes feel this way; I seldom feel this way; I never feel this way; scored 1 to 5 respectively.
2. How do you feel about the supervision you receive? (*Rate overall supervision*)
   I am extremely satisfied; I am well satisfied; I am only moderately satisfied; I am somewhat dissatisfied; I am very dissatisfied; scored 5 to 1 respectively.
3. How does the way you are treated by those who supervise you influence your overall attitude towards your job? (*Rate overall supervision*)
   It has a very unfavourable influence; it has a slightly unfavourable influence; it has no real effect; it has a favourable influence; it has a very favourable influence; scored 1 to 5 respectively.
4. How much do the efforts of those who supervise you add to the success of your organization? (*Rate overall supervision*)
   A very great deal; quite a bit; only a little; very little; almost nothing; scored 1 to 5 respectively.
5. The people who supervise me have: (*Rate overall supervision*)
   Many more good traits than bad ones; more good traits than bad ones; about the same number of good traits as bad ones; more bad traits than good ones; many more bad traits than good ones; scored 5 to 1 respectively.
6. The supervision I receive is the kind that: (*Rate overall supervision*)
   Greatly *discourages* me from giving extra effort; tends to *discourage* me from giving extra effort; has little influence on me; *encourages* me to give extra effort; greatly *encourages* me to give extra effort; scored 1 to 5 respectively.

Company identification

7. There is something about working for this organization that:
   Greatly *encourages* me to do my best; definitely *encourages* me to do my best; only slightly *encourages* me to do my best; tends to *discourage* me from doing my best; definitely *discourages* me from doing my best; scored 5 to 1 respectively.
8. From my experience, I feel this organization probably treats its employees:
   Poorly; somewhat poorly; fairly well; quite well; extremely well; scored 1 to 5 respectively.
9. How does working for this organization influence your overall attitude towards your job?
   It has a very unfavourable influence; it has an unfavourable influence; it has no influence one way or the other; it has a favourable influence; it has a very favourable influence; scored 1 to 5 respectively.
10. How do you describe this organization as a company to work for?
    Couldn't be much better; very good; fairly good; just another place to work; poor; scored 1 to 5 respectively.
11. I think this organization, as a company, considers employee welfare:
    Much less important than sales and profits; less important than sales and profits; about as important as sales and profits; more important than sales and profits; much more important than sales and profits; scored 1 to 5 respectively.

Box 6.6 continued

Items and responses
Kind of work

12. Work like mine:
    Discourages me from doing my best; tends to *discourage* me from doing my best;
    makes little difference; slightly *encourages* me to do my best; greatly *encourages* me to
    do my best; scored 1 to 5 respectively.
13. How often when you finish a day's work do you feel you've accomplished something
    really worthwhile?
    All of the time; most of the time; about half of the time; less than half of the time;
    rarely; scored 5 to 1 respectively.
14. How does the kind of work you do influence your overall attitude towards your
    job?
    It has a very unfavourable influence; it has a slightly unfavourable influence; it has no
    influence one way or the other; it has a fairly favourable influence; it has a very
    favourable influence; scored 1 to 5 respectively.
15. How many of the things you do on your job do you enjoy?
    Nearly all; more than half; about half; less than half; almost none; scored 5 to 1
    respectively.
16. How much of the work you do stirs up real enthusiasm on your part?
    Nearly all of it; more than half of it; about half of it; less than half of it; almost none
    of it; scored 5 to 1 respectively.
17. How do you feel about the kind of work you do?
    Don't like it, would prefer some other kind of work; it's OK, there's other work I like
    better; I like it, but there is other work I like as much; I like it very much; it's exactly the
    kind of work I like best; scored 1 to 5 respectively.

Amount of work

18. I feel my workload is:
    Never too heavy; seldom too heavy; sometimes too heavy; often too heavy; almost
    always too heavy; scored 5 to 1 respectively.
19. How does the amount of work you're expected to do influence the way you do your
    job?
    It never allows me to do a good job; it seldom allows me to do a good job; it has no
    effect on how I do my job; it usually allows me to do a good job; it always allows me to
    do a good job; scored 1 to 5 respectively.
20. How does the amount of work you're expected to do influence your overall attitude
    towards your job?
    It has a very favourable influence; it has a favourable influence; it has no influence one
    way or the other; it has an unfavourable influence; it has a very unfavourable influence;
    scored 5 to 1 respectively.
21. How do you feel about the amount of work you're expected to do?
    Very dissatisfied; somewhat dissatisfied; neither satisfied nor dissatisfied; somewhat
    satisfied; very satisfied; scored 1 to 5 respectively.

Co-workers

22. How do you generally feel about the employees you work with?
    They are the best group I could ask for; I like them a great deal; I like them fairly well; I
    have no feelings one way or the other; I don't particularly care for them; scored 5 to 1
    respectively.

Box 6.6 continued

Items and responses
Co-workers cont'd

23. How is your overall attitude towards your job influenced by the people you work with?
    It is very favourably influenced; it is favourably influenced; it is not influenced one way or the other; it is unfavourably influenced; it is very unfavourably influenced; scored 5 to 1 respectively.

24. The example my fellow employees set:
    Greatly *discourages* me from working hard; somewhat *discourages* me from working hard; has little effect on me; somewhat *encourages* me to work hard; greatly *encourages* me to work hard; scored 1 to 5 respectively.

25. How much does the way co-workers handle their jobs add to the success of the organization?
    It adds almost nothing; it adds very little; it adds only a little; it adds quite a bit; it adds a very great deal; scored 1 to 5 respectively.

26. In this organization there is:
    A very great deal of friction; quite a lot of friction; some friction; little friction; almost no friction; scored 1 to 5 respectively.

Physical work conditions

27. How much pride can you take in the appearance of your workplace?
    A very great deal; quite a bit; some; little; very little; scored 5 to 1 respectively.

28. How do you feel about your physical working conditions?
    Extremely satisfied; well satisfied; only moderately satisfied; somewhat dissatisfied; very dissatisfied; scored 5 to 1 respectively.

29. How do your physical working conditions influence your overall attitude towards your job?
    They have a very unfavourable influence; they have a slightly unfavourable influence; they have no influence one way or the other; they have a favourable influence; they have a very favourable influence; scored 1 to 5 respectively.

30. The physical working conditions make working here:
    Very unpleasant; unpleasant; neither pleasant nor unpleasant; pleasant; very pleasant; scored 1 to 5 respectively.

31. For the work I do, my working conditions are:
    Very poor; relatively poor; neither good nor poor; reasonably good; very good; scored 1 to 5 respectively.

32. How do your physical working conditions affect the way you do your job?
    They help me a great deal; they help me a little; they make little difference; they tend to make it difficult; they make it very difficult; scored 5 to 1 respectively.

Financial rewards

33. For the job I do, I feel the amount of money I make is:
    Extremely good; good; neither good nor poor; fairly poor; very poor; scored 5 to 1 respectively.

34. To what extent are your needs satisfied by the pay and benefits you receive?
    Almost none of my needs are satisfied; very few of my needs are satisfied; a few of my needs are satisfied; many of my needs are satisfied; almost all of my needs are satisfied; scored 1 to 5 respectively.

35. Considering what it costs to live in this area, my pay is:
    Very inadequate; inadequate; barely adequate; adequate; more than adequate; scored 1 to 5 respectively.

Box 6.6 continued

Items and responses
Financial rewards cont'd
36. Does the way pay is handled around here make it worthwhile for a person to work especially hard?
    It definitely *encourages* hard work; it tends to *encourage* hard work; it makes little difference; it tends to *discourage* hard work; it definitely *discourages* hard work; scored 5 to 1 respectively.
37. How does the amount of money you now make influence your overall attitude towards your job?
    It has a very favourable influence; it has a fairly favourable influence; it has no influence one way or the other; it has a slightly unfavourable influence; it has a very unfavourable influence; scored 5 to 1 respectively.

Career future

38. How do you feel about your future with this organization?
    I am very worried about it; I am somewhat worried about it; I have mixed feelings about it; I feel good about it; I feel very good about it; scored 1 to 5 respectively.
39. How do your feelings about your future with the company influence your overall attitude towards your job?
    They have a very favourable influence; they have a favourable influence; they have no influence one way or the other; they have a slightly unfavourable influence; they have a very unfavourable influence; scored 5 to 1 respectively.
40. The way my future looks to me now:
    Hard work seems very worthwhile; hard work seems fairly worthwhile; hard work seems worthwhile; hard work hardly seems worthwhile; hard work seems almost worthless; scored 5 to 1 respectively.
41. Do you feel you are getting ahead in the company?
    I'm making a great deal of progress; I'm making some progress; I'm not sure; I'm making very little progress; I'm making no progress; scored 5 to 1 respectively.
42. How secure are you in your present job?
    I feel very uneasy about it; I feel fairly uneasy about it; I feel somewhat uneasy about it; I feel fairly sure of it; I feel very sure of it; scored 1 to 5 respectively.

Source: Smith (1976).

increasingly larger proportion of the workforce today than in past generations because of increasing educational levels and technical job requirements – will be both high performers and satisfied when their jobs offer skill variety, task identity and significance, autonomy, and feedback.

- *Goal-setting theory*: It is established clear and difficult goals lead to higher levels of employee productivity. This evidence leads us to conclude that goal-setting theory provides one of the more powerful explanations of this dependent variable. The theory does not address absenteeism, turnover or satisfaction.
- *Reinforcement theory*: This theory has a substantial record for predicting factors such as quality and quantity of work, persistence of effort, absenteeism, tardiness and accident rates. It does not consider in any detail employee satisfaction or the decision to quit.

- *Equity theory*: Equity theory deals with all four outcome criteria set out above. However, it is strongest when predicting absence and turnover behaviours and weak when predicting differences in employee productivity.
- *Expectancy theory*: It has proven to offer a relatively powerful explanation of employee productivity, absenteeism and turnover. But expectancy theory assumes that employees have few constraints on their decision discretion, which acts to restrict its applicability.

For major decisions, such as accepting or resigning from a job, expectancy theory works well, because people are more prone to take the time to consider the costs and benefits of all the alternatives carefully. But expectancy theory is *not* a very good explanation for more typical types of work behaviour, especially for individuals in lower-level jobs, because such jobs come with considerable limitations imposed by work methods, supervisors and company policies. Thus, in explaining employee productivity, expectancy theory's power increases where the jobs being performed are more complex and higher in the organization, where discretion is greater.

Table 6.9 attempts a numerical comparison of the six theories. These theories have implications for how to manage people. Various techniques have arisen, such as job enrichment, which stem from specific theories. Yet more recently, various concepts such as locus of control and attribution style, which originated outside organizational psychology, have been very successfully applied to understanding work motivation, productivity and satisfaction.

Table 6.9 Power of motivation theories[a]

Theories						
Variable	*Need*	*Task characteristics*	*Goal-setting*	*Reinforce-ment*	*Equity*	*Expectancy*
Productivity	3[b]	3[c]	5	3	3	4[d]
Absenteeism	2	3		4	4	4
Turnover		3			4	5
Satisfaction		4			2	

[a] Theories are rated on a scale of 1 to 5, 5 being highest.
[b] Applies to individuals with a high need to achieve.
[c] Applies to individuals with a high need for growth.
[d] Limited value in jobs where employees have little discretionary choice.

Source: Reproduced from Landy & Becker (1987) with the permission of JAI Press..

A research perspective

Nearly 30 years ago, two US educationalists (Rosenthal & Jacobson, 1968) demonstrated a well known but often ignored fact. They compared the performance of equivalent pupils under two groups of teachers: those who had been led to believe their students were slow learners, and those who believed their children were of superior ability and capacity. Pupils in the latter group learned faster. Children whose teachers expected them to succeed did better in all tests compared with those whose teachers had lower expectations of them. The expectations of the pupils themselves were important, but often these were a direct function of the teacher's expectations.

Careful studies of how expectations were communicated and affected performance showed several processes in operation. When their expectations were high, the teachers tended to teach qualitatively and quantitatively more new or novel material. They tended to pay closer attention to, give more clues to, and allow longer responses from those whom they believed to be bright. The teachers also initiated and engaged in more interactions with high- than with low-expectation students. Teachers tend to praise high-expectation students more, and proportionally more per correct response, whereas low-expectation students are criticized more, and proportionally more per incorrect response.

In short, different expectations lead to different treatments, which lead to different performances. The results of the research indicate quite clearly that:

- What managers expect of their subordinates and the treatment they are given largely determines performance and career progress.
- A unique characteristic of superior managers is their ability to create high-performance expectations which subordinates fulfil.
- Less effective managers fail to develop similar expectations and, as a consequence, the productivity of their subordinates suffers.
- Subordinates, more often than not, appear to do what they believe they are expected to do.

A good illustration concerns the manager of a US insurance company. He had observed that outstanding insurance companies grew faster than average or poor ones, and that new insurance agents performed better in outstanding companies than in average or poor ones, regardless of their sales aptitude. He decided to group his superior agents in one unit to stimulate their performance and to provide a challenging environment in which to introduce new salespeople.

Accordingly, the manager assigned his six best agents to work with his best assistant manager, an equal number of average producers to work with an average assistant manager, and the remaining low producers to work with the least able manager. He then asked the superior group to produce two-thirds of the premium volume achieved by the entire agency the previous year. Although the productivity of the "super staff" improved dramatically, the productivity of those in the lowest unit actually declined and the attrition among them increased. The performance of the superior agents rose to meet their manager's expectations, whereas those of the weaker ones declined lamentably.

When salespeople are treated by their managers as talented, they try to live up to that image and do what they know superior salespeople are expected to do. But when the salespeople with poor productivity records are treated by their managers as having "little chance" of success, this negative expectation also becomes a managerial self-fulfilling prophecy. Less successful salespersons have great difficulty maintaining their self-image and self-esteem. In response to low managerial expectations, they typically attempt to prevent additional damage to their egos by avoiding situations that might lead to greater failure. They either reduce the number of sales calls they make or avoid trying to "close" sales when they might result in further painful rejection, or both. Low expectations and damaged egos lead them to behave in a manner that increases the probability of failure, thereby fulfilling their manager's prophecy.

How do managers develop the art of high expectations? The answer, in part, seems to be that superior managers have greater confidence than other managers in their *own* ability to develop the talents of their subordinates. Contrary to what might be assumed, the high expectations of superior managers are based primarily on what they think about themselves – about their own ability to select, train and motivate their subordinates. What managers believe about themselves subtly influences what they believe about their subordinates, what they expect of them and how they treat them. If they have confidence in their own ability to develop and stimulate them to high levels of performance, they will expect much of them and will treat them with confidence that their expectations will be met. But if they have doubts about their own ability to stimulate their staff, they will expect less of them and will treat them with less confidence.

Put another way, the superior manager's record of success and confidence in their own ability lends credibility to their high expectations. As a consequence, their subordinates accept these expectations as realistic and try hard to achieve them. This important process merits further research, particularly as to how and when expectations arise in the first place and why they change.

A cross-cultural perspective

Management scientists in Southeast Asia have offered their unique perspective on motivation. Westwood (1992) has reviewed two writers who have made interesting contributions. Hsu (1971) identified three basic needs: *sociability, security* and *status,* which he argued are satisfied through *interpersonal interaction.* That is, basic needs and motivation are essentially *social* phenomena. He states that "the Chinese conception of man . . . is based on the individual's transactions with his fellow human beings" (Hsu, 1971: 277). The Western view of personhood and personality as an individual, independent entity is contrasted with an Asian relational, social view. The focus is not on individual factors but on social behaviour and the relation between an individual, his or her actions, and the "interpersonal standards of the society and culture". The satisfaction of basic needs depends on being able to bring behaviour into line with such *social norms* and *expectations.* The force to act is dependent upon the presence of socially sanctioned outcomes and of social recognition for having behaved in a socially acceptable fashion.

> There are important behavioural consequences of such an orientation. *People are strongly concerned about social expectations and relations.* They worry about the opinion of others and tend to conform to social norms and strive not to cause offence to others. A key motivating force is the *avoidance of social disapproval* and being *socially shunned.* This leads to behaviours designed to protect "face", to give a good impression to others, to maintain social harmony, and to achieve social acceptance. People will strive to avoid punishment, embarrassment, conflict, rejection, ridicule, and retaliation in a social setting. (Yang, 1981: 161)

"This is a significant rethinking of motivation that avoids the overemphasis on the independently operating individual of many Western theories, which seem to describe motivation and behaviour in a social vacuum. Yang links the 'social-orientation' to many clearly observed and researched aspects of traditional Chinese behaviour patterns. You should recognize that this concept is linked to traditional Chinese cultural values (and, indeed, to Confucianism), and Yang accepts that more 'modern' Chinese may be operating out of a different framework". (Westwood, 1992: 300)

A human resources perspective

Minzberg (1975) is famous in part for his paper showing what managers actually do, as opposed to what they say or believe they do. He agreed that any manager's effectiveness is significantly influenced by his or her insight into what he or she does at work. To assist in this problem, he suggested managers ask the questions in Box 6.7.

Box 6.7 Self-study questions for managers

1. Where do I get my information, and how? Can I make greater use of my contacts to get information? Can other people do some of my scanning for me? In what areas is my knowledge weakest, and how can I get others to provide me with the information I need? Do I have powerful enough mental models of those things I must understand within the organization and in its environment?

Box 6.7 continued

2. What information do I disseminate in my organization? How important is it that my subordinates get my information? Do I keep too much information to myself because dissemination of it is time-consuming or inconvenient? How can I get more information to others so they can make better decisions?

3. Do I balance information collecting with action taking? Do I tend to act before information is in? Or do I wait so long for all the information that opportunities pass me by and I become a bottleneck in my organization?

4. What pace of change am I asking my organization to tolerate? Is this change balanced so that our operations are neither excessively static nor overly disrupted? Have we sufficiently analysed the impact of this change on the future of our organization?

5. Am I sufficiently well informed to pass judgement on the proposals that my subordinates make? Is it possible to leave final authorization for more of the proposals with subordinates? Do we have problems of coordination because subordinates in fact now make too many of these decisions independently?

6. What is my vision of direction for this organisation? Are these plans primarily in my own mind in loose form? Should I make them explicit in order to guide the decisions of others in the organization better? Or do I need the flexibility to change them at will?

7. How do my subordinates react to my managerial style? Am I sufficiently sensitive to the powerful influence my actions have on them? Do I fully understand their reactions to my actions? Do I find an appropriate balance between encouragement and pressure? Do I stifle their initiative?

8. What kind of external relationships do I maintain, and how? Do I spend too much of my time maintaining these relationships? Are there certain types of people whom I should get to know better?

9. Is there any system to my time scheduling, or am I just reacting to the pressure of the moment? Do I find the appropriate mix of activities, or do I tend to concentrate on one particular function or one type of problem because I find it interesting? Am I more efficient with particular kinds of work at special times of the day or week? Does my schedule reflect this? Can someone else (in addition to my secretary) take responsibility for much of my scheduling and do it more systematically?

10. Do I overwork? What effect does my workload have on my efficiency? Should I force myself to take breaks or reduce the pace of my activity?

11. Am I too superficial in what I do? Can I really shift moods as quickly and frequently as my work patterns require? Should I attempt to decrease the amount of fragmentation and interruption in my work?

12. Do I orientate myself too much towards current, tangible activities? Am I a slave to the action and excitement of my work, so that I am no longer able to concentrate on issues? Do key problems receive the attention they deserve? Should I spend more time reading and probing deeply into certain issues? Could I be more reflective? Should I be?

13. Do I use the different media appropriately? Do I know how to make the most of written communication? Do I rely excessively on face-to-face communication, thereby putting all but a few of my subordinates at an informational disadvantage? Do I schedule enough of my meetings on a regular basis? Do I spend enough time touring my organization to observe activity at first hand? Am I too detached from the heart of my organization's activities, seeing things only in an abstract way?

14. How do I blend my personal rights and duties? Do my obligations consume all my time? How can I free myself sufficiently from obligations to ensure that I am taking this organization where I want it to go? How can I turn my obligations to my advantage?

Source: Reproduced from Minzberg (1975) with the permission of the President and Fellows of Harvard College.

References

Abramson, L., Seligman, M., & Teasdale, J. (1978). Learned helplessness in humans: critique and reformulation. *Journal of Abnormal Psychology, 87*, 32–48.

Adams, J. (1965). Inequity in social exchange. In L. Berkowitz (Ed.), *Advances in experimental social psychology* (Vol. 2, pp. 267–299). New York: Academic Press.

Andrisani, P., & Nestel, G. (1976). Internal/external control as contributor to and outcome of work experience. *Journal of Applied Psychology, 61*, 156–165.

Arnold, J., Robertson, I., & Cooper, C. (1991). *Work psychology: Understanding human behaviour in the workplace*. London: Pitman.

Barrick, M., Stewart, G., & Piotrowski, M. (2002). Personality and job performance. *Journal of Applied Psychology, 87*, 43–51.

Becker, B., & Krzystofiak, F. (1982). The influence of labour market discrimination on locus of control. *Journal of Vocational Behaviour, 21*, 60–70.

Berry, L. (1998). *Psychology at work*. New York: McGraw-Hill.

Blau, G. (1987). Locus of control as a potential moderator of the turnover process. *Journal of Occupational Psychology, 60*, 21–29.

Brayfield, A., & Rothe, H. (1951). An index of job satisfaction. *Journal of Applied Psychology, 35*, 307–311.

Brewin, C., & Shapiro, D. (1984). Beyond locus of control: attribution of responsibility for positive and negative outcomes. *British Journal of Psychology, 15*, 43–50.

Broedling, L. (1975). Relationship of internal/external control to work motivation and performance in an expectancy model. *Journal of Applied Psychology, 60*, 65–70.

Brownell, P. (1982). The effects of personality–situation congruence in a managerial context. *Journal of Personality and Social Psychology, 42*, 753–763.

Cook, J., Hepworth, S., Wall, T., & Warr, P. (1981). *The experience of work*. London: Academic Press.

Donnelly, J., Gibson, J., & Ivancevich, J. (1987). *Fundamentals of management*. Homewood, IL: Irwin (BPI).

Duncan, W. (1978). *Essentials of management* (2nd edn.). Hillsdale, IL: Dryden.

Ewen, R. (1980). *An introduction to theories of personality*. New York: Academic Press.

Feather, N. (1985). Attitudes, values and attributions: Explanations of unemployment. *Journal of Personality and Social Psychology, 48*, 876–889.

Feather, N., & Bond, M. (1983). Time structure and purposeful activity among employed and unemployed university graduates. *Journal of Occupational Psychology, 56*, 241–254.

Fisher, C. (2003). Why do lay people believe satisfaction and performance are correlated. *Journal of Organizational Behaviour, 24*, 1–25.

Foster, J. (2000). Motivation in the workplace. In N. Chmiel (Ed.), *Introduction to work and organizational psychology* (pp. 302–326). Oxford: Blackwell.

Franz, R. (1980). Internal/external locus of control and labour market performance. *Psychology: Quarterly Journal of Human Behaviour, 17*, 23–29.

Fryer, D. (1986). Employment deprivation and personal agency during unemployment. *Social Behaviour, 1*, 3–23.

Furnham, A. (1987). The social psychology of working situations. In A. Gale & B. Christie (Eds.), *Psychophysiology and the electronic workplace* (pp. 89–111). Chichester: Wiley.

Furnham, A. (1990). *The Protestant work ethic*. London: Routledge.

Furnham, A. (1992). *Personality at work*. London: Routledge.

Furnham, A. (1993). *Expectations about work*. Unpublished manuscript, University College London.

Furnham, A., Sadka, V., & Brewin, C. (1990). The development of an occupational attribution style questionnaire. *Journal of Organizational Behaviour, 13*, 27–39.

Greenberg, J. (1986). Equity and workplace status: A field experiment. *Journal of Applied Psychology, 73*, 606–613.

Greenberg, J. (1990). Employee theft as a reaction to underpayment inequity. *Journal of Applied Psychology, 75*, 561–568.

Greenberg, J., & Baron, R. (1995). *Behaviour in organizations* (6th edn.). Boston, MA: Allyn & Bacon.

Greenberg, J., & Baron, R. (2003). *Behaviour in organizations*. New York: Prentice-Hall.

Hackman, J., & Oldham, G. (1980). *Work redesign*. Reading, MA: Addison-Wesley.

Hammer, T., & Vardi, Y. (1981). Locus of control and career self-management among non-supervisory employees in industrial settings. *Journal of Vocational Behaviour, 18*, 13–29.

Heller, D., Judge, T., & Watson, D. (2002). The confounding role of personality and trait affectivity in the relationship between job and life satisfaction. *Journal of Organizational Behaviour, 23*, 815–825.

Herzberg, F., Mausner, B., Petersen, O., & Capwell, D. (1957). *Job attitudes: Review of research and opinion*. Pittsburgh, PA: Psychological Services of Pittsburgh.

Herzberg, F., Mausner, B., & Snyderman, B. (1959). *The motivation to work*. New York: Wiley.

Hsu, F. (1971). Psychological homeostasis and Zen: Conceptual tools for advancing psychological anthropology. *American Anthropologist, 73*, 274–278.

Huczynski, A., & Buchanan, D. (1991). *Organizational behaviour*. New York: Prentice-Hall.

Jablonsky, S., & De Vries, D. (1972). Operant conditioning principles extrapolated to the theory of management. *Organizational Behaviour and Human Performance, 14*, 340–358.

Jahoda, M. (1982). *Employment and unemployment: A social-psychological analysis*. Cambridge: Cambridge University Press.

Johns, E. (1991). *Organizational behavior*. New York: HarperCollins.

Judge, T., Bono, J., & Locke, E. (2000). Personality and job satisfaction. *Journal of Applied Psychology, 85*, 237–249.

Judge, T., & Church, A. (2000). Job satisfaction: Research and practice. In C. Cooper & E. Locke (Eds.), *Industrial and organizational psychology* (pp. 167–198). Oxford: Blackwell.

Judge, T., Heller, D., & Mount, M. (2002). Five-factor model of personality and job satisfaction: A meta-analysis. *Journal of Applied Psychology, 87*, 530–541.

Judge, T., & Ilies, R. (2002). Relationship of personality to performance motivation: A meta-analytic review. *Journal of Applied Psychology, 87*, 797–807.

Kanfer, R., & Ackerman, P. (2000). Individual differences in work motivation. *Applied Psychology, 49*, 470–482.

Katzell, R., & Thompson, D. (1990). An integrative model of work attitudes, motivation and performance. *Human Performance, 3*, 63–85.

Landy, F. (1985). *Psychology of work behaviour*. Pacific Grove, CA: Brooks/Cole.

Landy, F. J., & Becker, W. S. (1987). Motivation theory reconsidered. In L. L. Cummings & B. M. Staw (Eds.), *Research in organizational behaviour* (Vol. 9, pp. 1–31). Greenwich, CT: JAI Press.

Lawler, E. (1971). *Pay and organizational effectiveness: A psychological view*. New York: McGraw-Hill.

Lawler, E. (1973). *Motivation in work organization*. Monterey, CA: Brooks/Cole.

Lawler, E. (1981). *Pay and organization development*. Reading, MA: Addison-Wesley.

Lee, F., Sheldon, K., & Turban, D. (2003). Personality and goal-striving process. *Journal of Applied Psychology, 88*, 256–265.

Locke, E. (1976). The nature and causes of job satisfaction. In M. Dunnette (ed.), *Handbook of industrial and organizational psychology* (pp. 1297–1349). Chicago, IL: Rand-McNally.

Locke, E. (1984). Job satisfaction. In M. Gruneberg & T. Wall (Eds.), *Social psychology and organizational behaviour* (pp. 93–117). Chichester, UK: Wiley.

Locke, E., & Latham, G. (1990). Work motivation and satisfaction. *Current Directions in Psychological Science, 1*, 240–246.

Lodahl, T., & Kejner, M. (1965). The definition and measurement of job involvement. *Journal of Applied Psychology, 49*, 24–33.

Lowenberg, G., & Conrad, K. (1998). *Current perspectives in industrial/organizational psychology.* Boston, MA: Allyn & Bacon.

Lufthans, F., & Kreitner, R. (1974). Behavioural contingency management. Personnel, July–August, pp. 63–85.

Maslow, A. (1954). *Motivation personality.* New York: Harper & Row.

Miller, D., Kets de Vries, D., & Toulouse, J.-M. (1982). Top executive locus of control and its relationship to strategy-making, structure and environment. *Academy of Management Journal, 25*, 237–253.

Minzberg, H. (1975). The manager's job: Folklore and fact. *Harvard Business Review, 53*, 100–110.

Mitchell, T., & Daniels, D. (2003). Motivation. In W. Norman, D. Ilgen, & R. Klimoski (Eds.), *Handbook of psychology* (Vol. 12, pp. 225–253). New York: Wiley.

Mitchell, V., & Mowdgill, P. (1976). Measurement of Maslow's need hierarchy. *Organizational Behaviour and Human Performance, 16*, 334–349.

Mobley, W., & Locke, E. (1970). The relationship of value importance to satisfaction. *Organizational Behaviour and Human Performance, 5*, 463–483.

Mulkis, L. (1989). *Management and organizational behaviour.* London: Pitman.

Murray, H. (1938). *Explorations in personality.* New York: Oxford University Press.

O'Brien, G. (1984). Locus of control, work and retirement. In H. Lefcourt (Ed.), *Research with the locus of control construct* (Vol. 3, pp. 7–72). New York: Academic Press.

Payne, R. (1987). Individual differences and performance among R & O personnel. *R & O Management, 17*, 153–161.

Peterson, C., Semmel, A., Von Baeyer, C., Abramson, L., Metalsky, G., & Seligman, M. (1982). The attributional style questionnaire. *Cognitive Research and Therapy, 6*, 281–300.

Porter, L., & Lawler, E. (1968). *Managerial attitudes and performance.* Homewood, IL: Dorsey.

Pritchard, R., Dunnette, M., & Jorgensen, D. (1972). Effects of perceptions of equity and inequity on worker performance and satisfaction. *Journal of Applied Psychology, 57*, 75–94.

Reif, W., & Luthans, F. (1972). Does job enrichment really pay off? *California Management Review, 14*, 30–37.

Richards, J. (1983). Validity of locus of control and self-esteem measures in a national longitudinal study. *Educational and Psychological Measurements, 43*, 897–905.

Robbins, S. (1991). *Organizational behaviour.* Englewood Cliffs, NJ: Prentice-Hall.

Rokeach, M. (1973). *The nature of human values.* New York: Free Press.

Rosenthal, R., & Jacobson, L. (1968). *Pygmalion in the classroom.* New York: Holt, Rinehart & Winston.

Schermerhorn, J., Hunt, J., & Osborn, R. (1991). *Managing organizational behaviour.* New York: Wiley.

Schwab, D., Olian-Gottlieb, J., & Heneman, H. (1979). Between-subjects expectancy theory research: A statistical review of studies predicting effort and performance. *Psychological Bulletin, 86*, 139–147.

Seligman, T. M., & Schulman, P. (1986). Explanatory style as a predictor of productivity and quitting among life insurance sales agents. *Journal of Personality and Social Psychology, 50*, 832–838.

Shultz, D., & Shultz, S. (1998). *Psychology and work today.* Englewood Cliffs, NJ: Prentice-Hall.

Smith, F. (1976). Index of organizational reaction (IOR). *JSAS Catalogue of Selected Documents in Psychology, 6*(54), 1265.

Spector, P. (1986). Perceived control by employees: A meta-analysis of studies concerning autonomy and participation at work. *Human Relations, 11*, 1005–1016.

Steel-Johnson, D., Beauregard, R., Hoover, P., & Schmidt, A. (2000). Goal orientation and task demand effects on motivation, affect and performance. *Journal of Applied Psychology, 85*, 724–738.

Storms, P., & Spector, P. (1987). Relationships of organizational frustration with reported behavioural reactions: The moderating effects of locus of control. *Journal of Occupational Behaviour, 60*, 2–9.

Szilagi, A., & Sims, H. (1975). Locus of control and expectations across multiple occupational levels. *Journal of Applied Psychology, 60*, 638–640.

Tait, M., Youtz-Padgett, M., & Baldwin, T. (1989). Job and life satisfaction. *Journal of Applied Psychology, 74*, 502–507.

Tett, R., & Burnett, D. (2003). A personality trait-based interactionist model of job performance. *Journal of Applied Psychology, 88*, 500–517.

Vecchio, R. (1981). Workers' beliefs in internal versus external determinants of success. *Journal of Social Psychology, 114*, 199–207.

Vroom, V. (1964). *Work and motivation*. New York: Wiley.

Wall, T., & Payne, R. (1973). Are deficiency scores deficient? *Journal of Applied Psychology, 58*, 322–326.

Wanous, J., & Lawler, E. (1972). Measurement and meaning of job satisfaction. *Journal of Applied Psychology, 56*, 95–105.

Warr, P. (1985). Twelve questions about unemployment and health. In B. Roberts, R. Finnegan, & D. Gallie (Eds.), *New approaches to economic life* (pp. 387–399). Manchester: Manchester University Press.

Warr, P. (1987). *Work, unemployment and mental health*. Oxford: Oxford University Press.

Warr, P., Cook, J., & Wall, T. (1979). Scales for the measurement of some work attitudes and aspects of psychological wellbeing. *Journal of Occupational Psychology, 52*, 129–148.

Weiner, B. (1986). *Motivation*. New York: Holt, Rinehart & Winston.

Weiner, N. (1980). Determinants and behavioural consequences of pay satisfaction: A comparison of two models. *Personnel Psychology, 33*, 741–757.

Weiss, H. (1978). Social learning of work values in organization. *Journal of Applied Psychology, 63*, 711–718.

Weiss, H., Davis, R., England, G., & Lofquist, L. (1967). *Manual for the Minnesota satisfaction questionnaire*. Minneapolis, MN: Industrial Relations Centre, University of Minnesota.

Weiss, H., & Shaw, J. (1979). Social influences on judgements about tasks. *Organizational Behaviour and Human Performance, 24*, 126–140.

Westwood, R. (1992). *Organizational behaviour: South East Asian perspective*. Hong Kong: Longman.

Yang, K. (1981). Social orientation and individual modernity among Chinese students in Taiwan. *Journal of Social Psychology, 113*, 159–170.

7   Stress at work

Introduction

All jobs are potentially stressful, although the stresses vary widely. Some jobs are incredibly boring, involving machine monitoring or property guarding, and others are over-stimulating and physically demanding, leading to exhaustion. Stress is certainly pervasive. In a recent study of the 147 million workers in the European Union, 30% complained of backache, 28% of stress, 20% of fatigue, 17% of muscular pains and 13% of headaches (Paoli, 1997). There is certainly nothing new about either the acuity or chronicity of work stress, except perhaps the rapid rise in the number of people claiming to be stressed. Due to the popularity of the idea, and thanks to saturated media coverage, most people have learned to recognize classic symptoms: changes in eating, drinking, smoking patterns; irritability and moodiness; absent-mindedness, tiredness and exhaustion; anxiety and depression; negativism and susceptibility to illness.

The word "stress" is derived from the Latin word *stringere*, which means "to draw tight" (Cox, 1978). It is such an overused and elusive term that many have agreed it should be completely abandoned. Many definitions exist: some believe stress can and should be *subjectively* defined; others feel one needs an *objective* definition. Some researchers believe a *global* definition is appropriate; others emphasize that stress is *multidimensional*. Until the eighteenth century, it colloquially implied hardship, adversity or affliction. It was later used by physicists to describe a force exerted upon an object, so that resultant changes in volume, shape and size were called "strains". Hence, "stresses and strains".

Sometimes a concept becomes so oversized and extended it becomes meaningless. That happened to "alienation" for sociology and "neurosis" for psychiatry. Is the same true for stress? It has been seen as a confounding, dependent, epiphenomenal, independent, intervening and moderating variable. Briner (1999) has put forward a good case for abandoning the concept in favour of "feeling/emotions at work". He notes quite correctly that stress is both stimulus and response. It is, at one and the same time, thought of as cause and consequence, trait and coping style, biological phenomenon and disrupter of performance. Because of this terminal confusion, the research is often bad. Even more provocatively, Briner (1999) believes that stress is a modern myth because the better the research, the more the evidence for the relationship between work stress and personal reactions evaporates.

In the nineteenth century, the pursuit and maintenance of a constant internal state was seen as the essence of "free and independent life" (Cox, 1978). Research sought to identify those adaptive changes responsible for steady-state maintenance. This motiv-ation towards equilibrium was called "homeostasis", from the Greek words *homoios* meaning "similar", and *stasis* meaning "state". Stress was considered to be a threat to homeostasis ("a rocking of the boat"), but this usage of the term was subject to change and imprecision.

Yet lots of questions remain and are often discussed in the popular press. Is work stress primarily a function of the person or the job? That is, does it arise because some are (neurotically) vulnerable to stress whereas others are hardy and resistant? These days most people speak as if stress is imposed on them by work condition, yet in earlier times people spoke about "having nerves", implying nervous dispositions. Other ques-tions include: Is there the possibility that moderate amounts of stress may be good for one? Should people be taught coping skills to overcome inevitable work stress? And because there is a stress industry committed to finding work stress, is it frequently misdiagnosed? Perhaps it is not an accident that *The little book of stress* was written by Candappa (1998) in response to the very popular *The little book of calm* (Wilson, 1966). On the cover of the humorous stress book we read, "Calm is for wimps, Get Real, Get Stressed" and "Learn to love stress and remember, worrying is just meditation for realists". It gives various pieces of advice: recognize your limitations and ignore them, but tell other people what theirs are.

The vacillation between trying to understand stress as a *stimulus* and/or as a *response* laid the foundations for subsequent models of stress, which are broadly conceived as environmental, medical and personal. Cox (1978) identified three distinctive models, namely response-based, stimulus-based and interactive. *Response-based* models con-ceived of stress as a dependent variable – that is, a response or reaction to a stressor such as danger or overwork. *Stimulus-based* models considered stress as an environ-mental variable (such as excessive noise, cold or tasks to be completed in a short period of time), whereas *interactive models* attempted to incorporate both response and stimulus elements, as well as possible intervening factors such as personality differences.

One of the main advocates of the response-based approach, which is perhaps the most popular, is Selye (1956), whose ideas dominated the work on stress for many years. For him stress is the lowest common denominator in a person's reaction to every conceivable kind of stress or exposure, challenge and demand. Selye noted that injec-tions of bovine ovarian extracts into rats resulted in a triad of morphological changes, namely adrenocortical *enlargement*, gastrointestinal *ulceration* and thymicolymphatic *shrinkage*. He also observed that the injection of any other foreign extracts led to the same responses, as did exposure to cold, heat, X-rays, pain, forced exercise, and so on. He concluded that the triad was a "non-specific" response, since it occurred regardless of the precise nature of the stimulus. He thus used the term "general adaptation syn-drome" to describe this response pattern, and three temporal phases were subsequently isolated: (1) an *initial alarm reaction*, (2) quickly yielding to a stage of *resistance*, and (3) culmination in *exhaustion* if coping efforts were unsuccessful. Selye identified what he called "diseases of adaptation", which arise indirectly as the organism or person struggles to cope with the initial stressor. According to this model, a homeostatically disruptive agent induces a call for adaptation in some unspecified way.

By the mid-1950s, Selye seems to have settled on the response-based definition of stress as "the sum of all non-specific changes caused by function or damage". This was later reworded to "the non-specific response of the body to any demand made upon it", rendering it even more inclusive.

Critics of Selye's model concentrated primarily on the non-specificity of the hypothesis. Many have claimed that conventional laboratory situations, designed for the study of physical stressors, are likely to elicit accompanying emotional responses such as discomfort or even pain. Selye suggested that it may be this, as much as the physical stressor itself, to which the individual responds. A second problem with Selye's model was his admitted inability to locate the "first mediators" of the stress response – that is, the path through which the same responses could be triggered, regardless of the nature of the stressor. For instance, the first mediator may simply be the psychological apparatus involved in emotional arousal, which he believed accompanied exposure to noxious stimuli. This would place the hypothesized first mediator at an integratively higher, more complex, psychological level than the blood or neutral systems that Selye had conjectured. In this sense, later work focused on the individual's perceptual and affective (emotional) response to stress, rather than simply on physiological reactions.

The widely accepted view in the 1950s, when Selye was developing his response-based definition, conceived of stress as an environmental characteristic exerting its effects upon the individual. Stress was seen as an independent variable, as something that happens to, as opposed to being caused by, an individual. Stressful situations were identifiable through lack of control, over- or under-stimulation of the senses, isolation, and so on. The main problems with this approach lay in the difficulty of quantifying the level of stress in a given situation, together with the extent to which individuals differed in their appraisals of threat and stress.

From these competing models emerged the interactionist perspective, where stress was seen to occur when a subset of *environmental* demands coincided with a subset of *individual* susceptibility characteristics. Transactional, homeostatic and balance models are all included in this category, but most were non-interactive (Figure 7.1). As well as incorporating both stimulus and response elements, the interactive model focused in particular on the appraisal mechanisms through which a situation was labelled

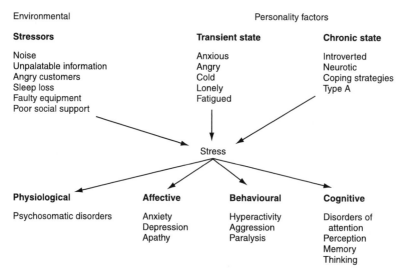

Figure 7.1 A non-interactive model. Note how personal and environmental factors are seen to be independent of each other and that cognitive appraisal of the situation *and* coping strategies are not considered.

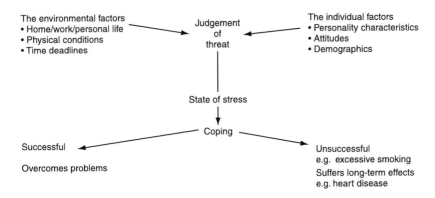

Figure 7.2 The stress process. Reproduced from Cooper *et al.* (1988) with the permission of Penguin Books.

"stressful" (Figure 7.2). The focus on appraisal is essentially a psychological perspective, which suggests that certain characteristics associated with the individual (perhaps as a result of previous experiences) lead them to perceive some events or environmental factors as more threatening than others. Essentially, these models try to specify all the salient environmental stressors that may lead to stress as well as salient characteristics of the individuals; but more importantly how and which interact to cause stress.

Among the first to promote the interactionist perspective was Lazarus (1966). Central to his stress model was the concept of threat, which was regarded as an imagined or anticipated future deprivation of something one values. Furthermore, threat usually relates to the "self", and the maintenance and enhancement of the self is believed to be a fundamental human motive. He refers to cognitive processes as "appraisal" processes, which include attention, perception and evaluation. Primary appraisal, which consists of processes involved in threat perception, is distinguished from secondary appraisal, which is related to coping with and reducing threat.

Factors in both the environment and the person interact to determine both primary and secondary appraisal. Physical elements such as objective danger, imminence and ambiguity of cues increase the potential for primary threat perception, as do motivational characteristics and belief systems within the individual. Secondary appraisal is governed by the interaction between situational constraints and coping dispositions, and general beliefs about the environment and one's resources. Lazarus's (1966) theoretical formulation, with its emphasis on individual differences in threat appraisal, has proved to be highly durable. It is, quite clearly, a psychological model of stress.

A variation of the interactive model was described by Cox & Mackay (1979) (Figure 7.2). The central element concerned the dynamic relationship between four aspects of the individual and the environment. The environment imposes demands and constraints on the one hand, yet provides supports on the other. The individual possesses both values and needs (demands) as well as coping resources. Cognitive appraisal of demands and resources is continuous, and a perceived imbalance between the two leads to the subjective experience of stress as well as to coping attempts aimed at restoring homeostasis. Such coping attempts may become manifest through a variety of different outlets such as cognitive reappraisal, physiological responsivity and behavioural activity. What is not made clear, however, is the point at which responsivity should be labelled "stressful", a criticism that may be levelled at interactive models generally.

Another variation of the interactive model was proposed by Cooper & Marshall (1976) to describe workplace stress. Six potential sources of work stress were identified, including factors intrinsic to the job, role-related factors and interpersonal relationships at work. These impinged to some extent upon each individual and could hypothetically lead to any of a variety of symptoms of occupational ill health (e.g. job dissatisfaction, depressive moods or cardiovascular disease).

Some features are common to each interactive model. Whether explicit or implicit, the context in which each model is presented concerns adaptiveness and homeostasis. Furthermore, each model fundamentally suggests that environmental stimuli (external stressors), individual differences (particularly with respect to cognitive appraisal thereof) and various outcome measures (stress reactions) must all be considered simultaneously. As such, these models attempt to isolate the parameters associated with stress research. However, what they gain in breadth they tend to lose in depth. In other words, the focus on "what" variables need to be included takes place at the expense of "how" (i.e. the mechanisms) stress actually occurs.

Figure 7.2 presents an interactive model which suggests that stress arises only when certain individual factors (age and stage, personality, even mood) lead the person to see certain circumstances (workload, change in boss) to be threatening. Thus, neurotics, who are prone to anxiety, nearly always report having more qualitative and quantitative stress than stable individuals. Once threatened, every person has coping mechanisms, some adaptive and successful, others less so. The application of a healthy coping mechanism to the perception and reality of stress leads to its reduction, but having unsuccessful coping mechanisms can actually exacerbate the problem, turning an acute problem into a chronic one.

This notion of a mismatch between demands and resources is central to the majority of stress conceptualizations. McGrath's (1976: 1352) much quoted definition, like that of Lazarus (1966), focuses on perceptual factors in the individual:

> A potential for stress exists when an environmental situation is perceived as presenting a demand which threatens to exceed the person's capabilities and resources for meeting it, under conditions where s/he expects a substantial differential in the rewards and costs for meeting the demand versus not meeting it.

In many ways, this definition incorporates what most theorists see as the main ingredients in stress, namely subjective appraisal of a demanding environment, a realization that demands may outstrip resources, and that the consequences of not coping are important. In the absence of a universally agreed definition of stress, the widely accepted protocol of describing environmental factors as "stressors", individual responses as "strains", and the vast gamut of mediating activity in the form of cognitive processing and personality dispositions as "intervening variables" can usefully be adopted.

Theories and models in stress research

To many observers, research on stress was more empirical than theoretical. There were few good comprehensive theories; however, famine has been replaced by a time of plenty with the development of control, cybernetic, ethological, facet, fit and imbalance theories for stress at work (Cooper, 1998). These will be described very briefly to indicate what they focus on and how they differ.

Control theory (Spector, 1998)

The model emphasizes a person's generalized locus of control (or perceived self-efficacy) and actual environmental control, which together determine *perceived* control. Perceived control at work acts as a direct and moderator variable. It directly predicts stress and strains: high perceived control, low stress and vice versa. It also mediates between an environmental stressor (objective or subjective) and stress:

> Perceived control is posited to moderate the relation between environmental and perceived job stressor. Specifically, when control is high, the strength of relation between environmental and perceived stressor should be low. The individual is not likely to interpret the condition/situation as a job stressor and will not exhibit an emotional reaction. Conversely, when perceived control is low, the relation between environmental and perceived job stressor will be strong. An individual is likely to interpret the condition/situation as being a job stressor and will exhibit an emotion reaction. Note that the control must be over the specific job stressor itself. More general control is not going to have an effect unless it is perceived to be effective against the job stressor. Being able to determine one's work schedule is not going to reduce the perceived job stressor of being fired. Having two attractive job offers in hand will greatly reduce the impact, however. (Spector, 1998: 157)

The implications of the model are fairly obvious and they are to increase a person's perceptions of control both through environmental and psychological interventions:

> Perhaps the most important implication of the present model is that control can reduce the effect of environmental job stressors. Control must be over the job stressor itself, as merely increasing control in general will often make matters worse. The individual who finds a situation to be a job stressor will likely benefit from being given more control over particular aspects that are perceived as job stressors. For example, if an individual finds the amount of work is difficult to handle, being given control over work assignments and work pace will be helpful. Being given the opportunity to participate in organizational decisions could be counterproductive because it produces yet another demand that increases workload . . .
>
> There are many organizational techniques that might potentially enhance perceived control. Job redesign has as one objective increasing control and responsibility over tasks. Autonomous work groups allow more control than traditional working arrangements. Survey feedback is intended to give input to employees over issues that concern them. Team building could be used for much the same objective by allowing discussions of work problems . . .
>
> Another more specific intervention that is directly targeted to control over job stressors would be to train supervisors to conduct special problem-solving sessions with subordinates. Supervisors would help subordinates identify their job stressors, and implement strategies designed to enhance perceived control

over those situations. This can be done by having meetings during which work problems are discussed and solutions to those problems developed. (Spector, 1998: 164)

Cybernetic theories (Cummings & Cooper, 1998; Edwards, 1998)

Cybernetics is about feedback and homoeostatis. People seek out and get information on their performance which affects their steady state and efforts to stabilize it. People have a preferred state and an actual state of being and a comparison or gap process. Their aim is to adjust the one to the other through feedback, which may be accurate or not, likely or not, salient or not. They are required to use adjustment processes (task-related, psychological coping strategies) to achieve this.

> From a cybernetic perspective, assessing stresses and threats in the workplace requires information about employees' preferred and actual working conditions, so a comparison can be made between the two. The greater the discrepancy between the preferred and the actual, the greater the likelihood of experienced strain. Moreover, because not all strains require equal attention, information is needed about the relative importance of working conditions for employees' well-being. Stress interventions would have the greatest effect by focusing on the most import-ant working conditions showing the greatest discrepancy between the preferred and the actual. (Cummings & Cooper, 1998: 117)

Edwards has a more complex cybernetic model:

> The direct effect of discrepancies on coping indicates that the person may attempt to avoid or reduce stress before well-being is damaged. The indirect effect of dis-crepancies on coping through well-being signifies that coping may occur after well-being has been damaged ... The effects of discrepancies on well-being and coping are moderated by importance and duration. Importance intensifies the effects of discrepancies on well-being and coping. Likewise, the effects of discrep-ancies on well-being and coping are intensified by duration, such that well-being and coping are influenced more by those discrepancies upon which the person focuses his or her attention. Importance and duration are affected by discrepancy size, such that larger discrepancies are considered more significant and draw more attention. Importance also affects duration, with greater attention devoted to discrepancies considered more consequential to the person's overall well-being. (Edwards, 1998: 129)

Edwards (1998) also notes criticisms of cybernetic models of behaviour:

- This approach cannot explain, predict or describe the conscious, self-motivated behaviour of people at work.
- The sole purpose of the system is to reduce discrepancy which may be done cynically by lowering standards.
- They are reactive (to feedback) and do not consider proactive forethoughts and goals.
- They are deductive, not inductive.

Naturally, these criticisms are refuted:

> Edwards cybernetic theory views stress, coping, and well-being as critical elements of a negative feedback loop. Stress refers to a discrepancy between perceptions and desires, and the effects of this discrepancy intensify as its importance and duration increase. Stress damages well-being and stimulates coping, which signifies efforts to improve well-being either directly or by altering the determinants and moderators of stress. These basic feedback processes are embedded in a hierarchy of feedback loops, in which loops at a higher level activate loops at lower levels and efforts to resolve discrepancies at lower levels help resolve discrepancies at higher levels. Thus, this theory depicts the dynamic, ongoing process by which people appraise the environment as stressful or benign and attempt to alter or adapt to the environment to reduce stress and improve well-being. (Edwards, 1998: 131)

Over the past 30 years or so, three specific models have tended to dominate and guide researchers' interests. They are the social-environment model, the person–environment fit model and various job demand control/support models.

Social-environment model (Michigan model)

This early model was an attempt to categorize and describe the main groups of variables that causally interact to produce stress. The model started with the *organizational* and social *environment* – that is, features of the organization that could influence stress. Thus the history, profitability, size, structure and workforce of the organization are all factors that can lead to psychological stressors such as conflict and overload. Thus potential stressors include having too much or too little to do, and being unclear as to where responsibility lies. Stressors in turn lead to *strains* according to the model, which are the particular behavioural, emotional and physical reactions of the individual strains lead directly to stress. However, this four-factor linear path is moderated by two factors: individual difference factors associated with the individual (e.g. cognitive abilities, coping styles, personality traits, general physical health) as well as their social relationships at work. Thus if workers under strain have good social support groups and health facilities, their strains might not lead to stress.

This relatively simple model was sufficient to provoke researchers in the 1960s and 1970s to begin to undertake empirical research in the area. However, it soon became apparent that while the model had heuristic value, it was essentially too simple to explain the complex aetiology of stress. This, in turn, led to the development of the next major model in the area.

Person–environment fit model

This model was developed by a number of researchers but summarized by Caplan (1983). According to Caplan, the theory of person–environment (PE) fit distinguishes between two types of fit: the *needs* (such as for achievement) and *values* of the person, and the environmental *supplies* and *opportunities* to meet them, which in the employee's terms may be seen as the needs and supplies fit or in the employer's terms as the abilities and demands fit. The second type of fit distinguishes between objective and subjective person and environment characteristics – the correspondence between objective and subjective P is labelled *accuracy of self-assessment* (or self-awareness), while the correspondence between objective and subjective E is labelled *contact with reality* (or environmental awareness). Objective misfit is a square peg in a round hole: the abilities and temperament of the individual do not match the demands of the job. Subjective misfit is about perceptions and it is these that are usually assessed in research. They effectively involve how the worker perceives him or herself and the job environment and requirements.

Furthermore, the exact relationship between fit and its opposite – strain – is not clear. Caplan (1983) noted three types of relationships:

- *A U-shape curve*: excesses (too much work) or deficits (too little work) in the environment lead to high levels of strain.
- *Asymptotic curve*: either an excess of P (but not a deficit) or an excess of E (but not a deficit) can lead to strain.
- *Linear effect*: the absolute amount of one PE component (P relative to E) has a linear effect on strain.

There is a great deal of support – if fairly modest – for the PE fit theory. Studies have been done on people from vastly different occupations, from different age groups and in different countries. Furthermore, many dependent variables, including career change, labour turnover, performance and motivation, have been shown to be associated with PE fit (Kasl, 1973). For instance, Caplan, Cobb, French, Harrison & Phinneau (1980) have shown that PE fit (but not P or E on its own) predicted depression in an occupationally stratified sample of 318 employees from 23 occupations. Similarly, Furnham and Schaeffer (1984) showed PE fit was positively associated with mental health and vice versa. As Caplan (1983) concluded: "In general, however, PE fit has explained only an additional 1% to 5% variance in strain. It has, however, consistently doubled the amount of variance explained" (p. 42).

In an attempt to improve the predictive power of PE fit theory, Caplan (1983) has proposed an elaborated cognitive model and the concept of retrospective/non-retrospective and future/anticipated fit. He has also noted the importance of the buffering effects of social support on PE strain.

Demand-control model

Based essentially on the work of Karasek and colleagues (Karasek & Theorell, 1990), this model stated originally that the combination (additive or multiplicative) of excessive psychological demands on a person *and* the lack of decision latitude (control) directly leads to the development of cardiovascular disease. Again these (demand and control) can be defined objectively and subjectively. It certainly is clear that there is more decision latitude between jobs than demands. Both factors are complex and multifactorial and not always easy to measure. However, the results have certainly tended to confirm the original hypotheses and lead to a focus on worker control over the way they worked.

Effort–reward imbalance theory (Siegrist, 1996)

This theory focuses on the degree to which individuals are rewarded for their efforts. When a high degree of effort is not rewarded by an equitably high degree of reward, emotional tensions arise and illness risk increases. Effort in this model is the individual's response to the demands made upon him or her and can be divided into *extrinsic* effort, which refers to the individual's efforts to cope with external demands, and *intrinsic* effort, which corresponds to the individual's own drive to fulfil his or her expectations. According to the theory, the development of intrinsic effort follows a long-term track in the individual. Young employees without extensive work experience and with a high degree of "vigour" are saddled with ever more commitments, which lead to an increasing number of conflicts. If the individual is unable to decrease the number of commitments, "immersion" will be the result in the old employee – with feelings of frustration and irritation. A high level of psychological demands as part of the culture in a company may make the intrinsic efforts become internalized. Reward is a composite measure of monetary rewards, esteem and social control. Composite measures of effort–reward imbalance are based upon calculations of the ratio or the difference between scores for effort and reward, respectively. There are clear overlaps with equity theory in this model.

After a fairly long period of research not guided by much theory, the area of organizational stress has seen considerable model building and theoretical development, which can be seen in Cooper's (1998) edited volume on the topic.

Occupational stress

The job of managers becomes ever more complicated as the nature of work and society in general becomes more complicated and sophisticated. Many people look at the salaries and benefits of middle, but particularly senior, managers with envy. But the rewards are high often because the costs are high. There are inevitably "downsides", difficulties or drawbacks of business leadership and management, specifically chronic (over long periods of time) or acute (extreme amounts) occupational stress.

In most management jobs, leaders are both supported and challenged. They are supported by peers, subordinates and superiors, who also challenge them to work harder and "smarter". Thus, it is possible to think of the average manager in terms of support and challenge thus:

- *Much support, little challenge*: Managers in this role are in the fortunate position of good technical and social support, but the fact they are under-challenged probably means that they underperform. They may be stressed by boredom and monotony.
- *Much support, much challenge*: This combination tends to get the most out of managers as they are challenged by superiors, subordinates, shareholders and customers to "work smarter" but are given the appropriate support to succeed.
- *Little support, much challenge*: This unfortunate, but very common, situation is a major cause of stress for any manager because he or she is challenged to work consistently hard but only offered minimal emotional, informational (feedback) and physical (equipment) support.
- *Little support, little challenge*: Managers in some bureaucracies lead a quiet and unstressed life because they are neither challenged nor supported, which usually means neither they nor their organization benefits. They belong to the "psychologically quit but physically stay" employee.

Box 7.1 Cooper's work stress questionnaire.

Could you please circle the number that best reflects the degree to which the particular statement is a source of stress for you at work.

	No stress at all		Stress		A great deal of stress	
Work overload	0	1	2	3	4	5
Work underload	0	1	2	3	4	5
Time pressure and deadlines	0	1	2	3	4	5
The amount of travel required by my work	0	1	2	3	4	5
Long working hours	0	1	2	3	4	5
Taking my work home	0	1	2	3	4	5
Lack of power and influence	0	1	2	3	4	5
Attending meetings	0	1	2	3	4	5
My beliefs conflicting with those of the organization	0	1	2	3	4	5
Keeping up with new technology	0	1	2	3	4	5
Threat of job loss	0	1	2	3	4	5
Competition for promotion	0	1	2	3	4	5
Having to move with my job in order to progress my career	0	1	2	3	4	5
Doing a job beyond the level of my competence	0	1	2	3	4	5
Doing a job below the level of my competence	0	1	2	3	4	5
Inadequately trained subordinates	0	1	2	3	4	5
Interpersonal relations	0	1	2	3	4	5
Hiring and firing personnel	0	1	2	3	4	5
Unsympathetic boss	0	1	2	3	4	5
Incompetent boss	0	1	2	3	4	5
Performance-related compensation	0	1	2	3	4	5
Unrealistic objectives	0	1	2	3	4	5
Dealing with conservative groups	0	1	2	3	4	5
Dealing with shareholders	0	1	2	3	4	5
Dealing with unions	0	1	2	3	4	5
My spouse's attitude towards my career	0	1	2	3	4	5
Demands of work on my relationship with my family	0	1	2	3	4	5
Demands of work on my private life	0	1	2	3	4	5
My relationship with my colleagues	0	1	2	3	4	5
My relationship with my subordinates	0	1	2	3	4	5
Making mistakes	0	1	2	3	4	5
Feeling undervalued	0	1	2	3	4	5
Promotion prospects	0	1	2	3	4	5
Rate of pay	0	1	2	3	4	5
Managing people	0	1	2	3	4	5
Office politics	0	1	2	3	4	5
Lack of consultation and communication in my organization	0	1	2	3	4	5

(The higher the totalled score, the greater the occupational stress)

Source: Cooper *et al.* (1988). Reproduced with the permission of Penguin Books.

Most research has concentrated specifically on the stressed manager whose work and home life provide an excess of challenge over support. A good indication of the typical and common causes of stress can be found in the questionnaire in Box 7.1. Clearly, the higher your score, the higher your stress. But, as we can see, stress is multidimensional, having different, clearly definable and unique factors.

The causes of stress

We have noted that there are both internal-to-the-person and external-in-the-environment causes of stress. These will be considered separately. However, three points need to be made about these lists of causes. First, these lists are not usually rank-ordered, because the importance of each stressor differs from job to job and from time to time. However, for most individuals these stressors are not equal; in fact, they may not exist at all for some managers. Secondly, many of these stressors are related, so that although they are listed independently of one another, it is highly likely that they are fairly closely interrelated. Thirdly, it is likely that these lists are not fully comprehensive in that there are probably factors – unique to certain jobs – that are not on the list. Nevertheless, they provide a beginning to understanding the problem.

Work-related causes of stress

- *Occupational demands intrinsic to the job.* Some jobs are quite simply more stressful than others. Various studies have shown that certain features associated with particular jobs are stressful. For example, the greater the extent to which the job requires (a) making decisions, (b) constant monitoring of machines or materials, (c) repeated exchange of information with others, (d) unpleasant physical conditions, and (e) performing unstructured rather than structured tasks, the more stressful the job tends to be. Thus, the jobs listed in Table 7.1 tend to be most stressful. Cooper, Cooper & Eaker (1988) have mentioned other stressful features intrinsic to a job. Again we have a series of lists with all the drawbacks that that implies (Table 7.2).

Table 7.1 Examples of stressful jobs

High-stress jobs because of danger, extreme pressure, or having responsibility without control	*High-stress jobs because of "occupational risk" of depression serious enough to require therapy*
Air traffic controller	Air traffic controller
Customer complaints	Actor
Department worker	Clergyman/Priest
Inner-city high school teacher	Computer programmer
Journalist	Dentist
Junior doctor	Government worker
Police officer	Lawyer
Prison officer	Management consultant
Social worker	Middle manager
Taxi driver	Psychiatrist
Therapist	Police officer
	Politician
	Teacher

Table 7.2 Sources of role stress at work

Role ambiguity	Role conflict
Lack of clarity about scope and responsibility of job	Conflicting job demands
Lack of clarity of objectives for role	Requirements to perform tasks disliked or outside job specification
Inadequate information about work role	Physiological strain
Low job satisfaction	Low job satisfaction
Job-related threats to mental and physical health	Job-related tension
Physiological strain	
Higher job-related tension	
Intentions to leave job	
Lower self-confidence	
Life dissatisfaction	
Low motivation to work	
Depression	
Greater futility	
Lower self-esteem	

Source: Cooper *et al.* (1988).

- *Role conflict: stress resulting from conflicting demands.* For many executives, it is important that they engage in role juggling – rapidly switching from one role and one type of activity to another (from boss to friend, teacher to partner, law enforcer to father confessor). This is common among working mothers but also human resource directors. The adverse effects of role conflict are less pronounced in work settings characterized by friendliness and social support than in work settings where such conditions are lacking.
- *Role ambiguity: stress resulting from uncertainty.* This can occur when managers are uncertain about several matters relating to their jobs, such as the scope of their responsibilities, what is expected of them, and how to divide their time between various duties. Sometimes, ambiguity results from not having clear job descriptions, goals or specified responsibilities, but often it is attributable to changes occurring in the organization or the marketplace at large. It is thus fairly common. Figure 7.3 shows the typical features of role ambiguity and conflict as well as the many negative outcomes of this type of stress.
- *Over- and underload stress from having too little or too much to do.* Work overload can be both quantitative and qualitative. Quantitative overload stress occurs when managers are asked to do more work, in a limited period, than they are able to do. Qualitative overload stress occurs when managers believe they lack the required skills, ability or resources to perform a given job. Similarly, stress is related to both types of underload. Quantitative underload leads to boredom that occurs when employees have too little work to do, and qualitative underload occurs when boring, routine, repetitive jobs are associated with chronic lack of mental stimulation.
- *Responsibility for others: stress resulting from a heavy burden.* Most managers are (or should be) responsible for their subordinates: they have to motivate them, reward and punish them, communicate and listen to them, and so on. Considerable stress is often experienced by managers when confronting the human costs of organizational policies and decisions: listening to endless complaints, mediating disputes, promoting cooperation and exercising leadership.

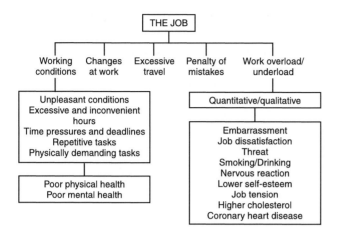

Figure 7.3 Characteristics of the potentially stressful job. Reproduced from Cooper *et al.* (1988) with the permission of Penguin Books.

- *Lack of social support: stress from being socially isolated or ignored.* Having friends and supporters in times of difficulty helps managers see stressful events as less threatening and more controllable than if they had little or no support. They can provide emotional, financial and information support at different times. Friends and supporters can also often suggest useful strategies for dealing with the sources of stress. In addition, they can also help reduce the negative feelings that often accompany exposure to stressful events. Social support is of course also quantitative and qualitative. Usually it is better to sacrifice quantity for quality, although ideally one would have both in liberal amounts to prevent stress.
- *Lack of participation in decisions: stress from helplessness and alienation.* Many middle managers are or feel they are the victims of decisions made at a higher level, over which they have no control. The major cause is that managers are neither allowed to witness nor to contribute to important business decisions that affect their jobs.

The last three points all concern relationships at work, which may include problems with superiors, colleague and subordinates as well as customers and shareholders (Table 7.3).

Table 7.3 Stressful relationships at work

Superiors	Colleagues	Subordinates
Lack of consideration	Isolation	Requirements for participation
Job pressure	Rivalry	Mismatch of formal/actual powers
	Political pressure	Conflict of participation versus higher
	Lack of support in difficult	production
	situations	Resentment of loss of status
		Refusal of subordinates to cooperate

Source: Cooper *et al.* (1988).

- *Poor performance appraisal: stress from little, none or obviously biased feedback*. At least two types of stress result from problems with performance appraisals. The first is not receiving any appraisals and hence not knowing how one is (or should be) doing (above, below, or average). The second is being given negative feedback without being told how to improve one's performance. Unless an organization has a good, well thought through performance appraisal system, employees can suffer great stress.

- *Working conditions: stress from poor working conditions*. Some jobs have, inevitably, to be performed in difficult and unpleasant working conditions such as extremes of temperature (heat or cold), loud noise, crowding, poor lighting, or with old and inefficient machinery. Unpleasant features such as noise are at their most stressful when they are unpredictable, uncontrollable and excessive. The best example is road construction engineers with drills digging up the road. Very stressful for them, it is equally unpleasant for those in close proximity who cannot control, reduce or predict when the noise occurs. Managers in manufacturing, engineering and the building trades often suffer from this source of stress.

- *Organizational change: stress that comes from adaptation*. As the speed, type and amount of organizational change occurs, so does the stress, particularly that experienced by middle managers. Shifts in company policy, reorganizations, mergers and acquisitions, delayering – all lead to uncertainty and with it stress. In addition to this, the structure and climate of a changed organization, or an organization that requires change, may itself be a major cause of stress.

- *Career development: stress from being stuck at the same level or beneath the "glass ceiling"*. Most organizations at least hold out the *carrot* of career development based on a mixture of performance and seniority. As a result, managers build up expectations about their career development. Having these realistic (or unrealistic) expectations thwarted is indeed a source of stress and frustration.

- *Home–work interface: stress that results from having two jobs*. Although probably more common among females than males, stress often results from conflicts over time and loyalties between the many demands of the home and work. Since managers experience severe conflict between home and work demands, with neither being tolerant of the other or supportive, the obvious result is stress.

As noted earlier, this list is not rank-ordered or exhaustive; nor are all the factors unrelated. However, they are among the most common in developed and industrialized countries.

Individual/personality causes of stress

Do some employees carry their own stress with them? Are neurotics more sensitive to all (even minor) stresses than stable individuals? Although working and home conditions do affect managerial stress, it may equally be true that stress is influenced by personal factors such as personality traits, attributional styles, coping mechanisms and intelligence. There are various individual difference factors that appear to make people prone to stress. Once again the list is neither exhaustive, nor does it consider problems that are unrelated.

Neuroticism and stability: the anxious worriers

There is a fairly consistent body of literature which suggests that people with "negative effect", namely those with a mix of anxiety, irritability, neuroticism and self-depreciation, tend to be less productive, less job satisfied and more prone to absentee-ism (Furnham, 1992). Neurotics tend to dwell on their mistakes, disappointments and shortcomings, and to focus more on the negative aspects of the world in general. They seem more prone to experiencing stress and less able to cope with it. Furthermore, most know they are neurotic but are powerless to do anything about it. Neuroticism is often associated with high absenteeism and low morale among workers.

Locus of control: the instrumentalist and the fatalist

This personality variable or dimension relates to beliefs about internal versus external control of reinforcement – that is, the cause of behavioural outcomes. It assumes that individuals develop a general expectancy regarding their ability to control their lives. People who believe that the events that occur in their lives are the result of their own behaviour and/or ability, personality and effort are said to have the *expectancy of internal control*, whereas those who believe events in their lives to be a function of luck, chance, fate (God(s), powerful others or powers *beyond their* control), comprehension or manipulation are said to have an *expectancy of external control*. Managers with internal locus of control tend to see threatening events at work as less stressful and they cope with it better than managers with external locus of control. Locus of control is related to *desire for control*, conceived of as a trait reflecting the extent to which indi-viduals are generally motivated to control the events in their lives. People with high desire for control tend to have internal control, to have higher aspirations, to be more persistent and respond more to challenge, and to see themselves as the source of their success (Burger, 1985).

More recently, the locus of control concept has been applied to *behaviour in organizations*. Spector (1982), in a review paper, noted that locus of control is related to motivation, effort, performance, satisfaction, perception of the job, compliance with authority and supervisory style, as well as being an important moderator between incentives and motivation, satisfaction and turnover. For instance, internals tend to prefer piece-rate systems, whereas externals tend to be more satisfied with direct supervision, to comply more with demands of coercive supervisors, and to be more compliant with social demands than internals (see Chapter 4).

Type A behaviour: the competitive, frantic manager

Over 25 years ago, psychiatrists became interested in whether heart attack patients shared any psychological traits. Through various studies they did indeed find a pattern, labelled the Type A pattern, which was initially characterized by excessive and com-petitive drive and an enhanced sense of time urgency. From the start, however, this behaviour pattern was seen to be multidimensional, having many components such as an intense sustained desire to achieve, an eagerness to compete, persistent drive for recognition, a continuous involvement in deadline activities, an habitual propensity to accelerate mental and physical functions, and consistent alertness. Considerable research has identified other traits associated with this syndrome. It is suggested that this behaviour is learnt. Price (1982) has suggested that this behaviour pattern is learned in open, competitive economies, where upward mobility is possible, success is thought to be a function of individual effort, and progress is best defined in terms of material or tangible achievements and related states. Among the social and cultural antecedents of the Type A behaviour pattern are the education system, urbanization and socio-economic factors.

Coping strategies: the poor coper

As Figure 7.2 illustrates, whether people suffer from stress or not is largely dependent on their coping strategies. Hence, psychologists have spent considerable effort in describing and categorizing different strategies, some of which are thought to be "successful" and adaptive, and others not. These strategies are stress-specific concepts, hence they tend to be better predictors of occupational stress than broadband stress concepts.

One distinction made by Folkman & Lazarus (1980) was between *problem*-focused coping (aimed at problem-solving or doing something to alter the source of stress) and *emotion*-focused coping (aimed at reducing or managing the emotional distress that is associated with, or cued by, a particular set of circumstances). Others have pointed out that this distinction is too simple. Thus, Carver, Scherer & Weintraub (1989) distinguished between the two types of coping as follows: some emotion-focused responses involve denial, others involve positive reinterpretation of events, and still others involve the seeking out of social support. Similarly, problem-focused coping can potentially involve several distinct activities, such as planning, taking direct action, seeking assistance, screening out particular activities, and sometimes stopping acting for an extended period. This list details both adaptive and non-adaptive coping strategies mentioned by Carver *et al.* Hence, researchers have concentrated on multidimensional instruments to measure coping (Endler & Parker, 1990).

Many studies have shown how coping styles and behaviours mediate between various variables. Thus, using a six-dimensional coping questionnaire, Parker & Brown (1982) demonstrated how some behaviours reduced and others exacerbated the relationships between life events and depression. Similarly, Patterson & McCubblin (1987) noted how 12 coping strategies in adolescents were clearly related to substance use and abuse.

The 15 strategies outlined by Carver *et al.* (1989) are:

1 Positive reinterpretation and growth
2 Active coping
3 Planning
4 Seeking social support for emotional problems
5 Seeking social support for instrumental problems
6 Suppression of competing activities
7 Religion
8 Acceptance
9 Mental disengagement
10 Focus on/venting emotion
11 Behavioural disengagement
12 Denial
13 Restraint coping

14   Alcohol use
15   Humour

It is argued that, for various reasons, individuals tend to adopt and habitually use a few of these coping patterns, which may or may not be successful. However, it does appear that people can be taught or trained to relinquish less successful coping strategies and adopt others.

Optimism: a buffer against stress

One personal factor that seems to play an important role in determining resistance to stress is the familiar dimension of *optimism/pessimism*. Optimists are hopeful in their outlook on life, interpret a wide range of situations in a positive light, and tend to expect favourable outcomes and results. Pessimists, by contrast, interpret many situations negatively, and expect unfavourable outcomes and results. The results of recent studies indicate that optimists are much more stress-resistant than pessimists. For example, optimists are much less likely than pessimists to report physical illness and symptoms during highly stressful periods such as final exams (Seligman & Schulman, 1986) (see Chapter 5).

Optimists and pessimists adopt sharply contrasting tactics for coping with stress. Optimists concentrate on *problem-focused coping* – making and enacting specific plans for dealing with sources of stress. In addition, they seek *social support* – the advice and help of friends and others – and refrain from engaging in other activities until current problems are solved and stress is reduced. Pessimists tend to adopt rather different strategies, such as giving up in their efforts to reach goals with which stress is interfering, and denying that the stressful events have even occurred. Furthermore, they have different attributional styles: the optimist attributes success internally and failure externally, and vice versa. Indeed, that is how optimism and pessimism are both measured and maintained.

Hardiness: viewing stress as a challenge

Another individual difference factor that seems to distinguish stress-resistant people from those who are more susceptible to its harmful effects is *hardiness* (Kobasa, 1979). This term refers to a cluster of characteristics rather than just one. Hardy people appear to differ from others in three respects. They show higher levels of: *commitment* – deeper involvement in their jobs and other life activities; *control* – the belief that they can, in fact, influence important events in their lives and the outcomes they experience; and *challenge* – they perceive change as a challenge and an opportunity to grow rather than as a threat to their security.

Together, these characteristics tend to arm hardy persons with high resistance to stress. People classified as high in hardiness report better health than those low in hardiness, even when they encounter major stressful life changes. Hardiness is a useful concept for understanding the impact of stress. However, recent evidence suggests that commitment and a sense of control are the most important components of hardiness. Thus, further research into this personal dimension and its role in resistance to stress should focus primarily on these aspects.

There may well be other individual differences which are highly predictive of stress, but the ones mentioned above have attracted most research attention (Greenberg & Baron, 1994). Furthermore, these different dimensions are, no doubt, intercorrelated.

The consequences of stress

The consequences of work stress are felt by individuals, their families, the organizations they work for and the economy as a whole. Indeed, it is even possible through absentee-ism and performance-related measures to calculate the effects of stress. It runs into many hundreds of billions of dollars, pounds and marks.

For the individual, the effects of work stress classically occur in three areas, although there may be strong individual differences (see Box 7.2). Attempts to "manage" (control and reduce) stress essentially happen at two levels. First, some organizations focus on individual employees, trying to help them learn better techniques to prevent or reduce their personal stress levels. Secondly, others focus on the job or the organization as a whole in attempting to reduce stress.

Personal approaches

Lifestyle (diet and exercise) change

A healthy mind (psyche) is supposedly found in a healthy body. Hence, organizations attempt to help people through better living. This includes a better diet (less salt, fat, sugar) and the reduction or elimination of alcohol, tobacco and other "recreational" drugs. They do this via their canteen arrangements as well as through legislation (no-smoking buildings). Others install expensive fitness centres with regular programmes for employees. Certainly, there are enough research findings that demonstrate physically

---

Box 7.2 Common symptoms of stress

Physiological symptoms

- A noticeable decline in physical appearance
- Chronic fatigue and tiredness
- Frequent infections, especially respiratory infections
- Health complaints, such as headaches, backaches, stomach and skin problems
- Signs of depression, change in weight or eating habits

Emotional symptoms

- Boredom or apathy: lack of affect and hopelessness
- Cynicism and resentfulness
- Depressed appearance, sad expressions, slumped posture
- Expressions of anxiety, frustration, tearfulness

Behavioural symptoms

- Absenteeism, accidents
- Increase in alcohol or caffeine consumption; increased smoking
- Obsessive exercising
- Irrational: quick to fly off the handle
- Reduced productivity; inability to concentrate or complete a task

fit people suffer less physical stress from physical stressors, although the relationship between psychological stressors, fitness and stress is less clear.

Relaxation and meditation

A rather more Eastern or mental approach to stress is to teach potentially stressed workers how to meditate and relax. The former involves clearing one's head of external thoughts and concentrating on inner stillness. Relaxation techniques can be physical, involving such things as stretching, deep breathing and even laughing. People tend to select techniques they feel are most suitable for them, although they may not be.

Cognitive self-therapy

Sports psychologists as well as clinicians have shown how effective certain cognitive or thinking strategies are. Most emphasize the way we conceive a stressor can be very maladaptive but can be changed. Thus, people are often asked to describe stressors and think about them in different terms. Thus, stressful becomes challenging, impossible becomes possible. Often, emphasis is placed on making people feel that stressors are temporary and controllable, not stable and eternal. People who have tendencies to perfectionism often need this type of therapy.

Behaviour therapy

This approach attempts to overcome stress by focusing on behaviours that reduce it. Just as people who are socially phobic or have panic attacks can be taught ways to overcome that very specific type of stress, so all people can be taught "little tricks" that help them overcome the stress. Certainly, one focus is on out-of-work activities such as leisure and vacations. The impact of the personal life on the working life should not be underestimated.

Organizational approaches

Changes in organization structure/function

The way the organization is structured may be a cause of stress, but indeed changing it can cause stress. Right-sizing, re-engineering and reprocessing have changed many organizations for the better, because they are flatter and more decentralized. Learning new procedures and worrying about security may increase stress, but the hope for many managers is that productivity will increase and stress will decrease as a function of the changes.

Job redesign

Jobs can be enlarged, enriched, divided, shared and redefined. Some are too large for one person, others too small. As processes and technology have changed, some jobs have not, and current holders are often under various stresses. Few organizations consider carefully the issue of job redesign as a major stress reducer.

Reviews of the stress management or alleviation literature appear to indicate the following:

- Stress management at work is usually narrowly defined to focus on the individual worker as the target for change. Interventions aimed at modifying stress aspects of the work environment, especially organizational structure and job redesign, are rare.
- Programmes are mostly preventive and they seek to improve worker awareness and recognition of stress. The label *stress management* is thus misleading, because neither workers nor organizations with apparent stress problems are singled out.
- Programmes are usually offered to workers in white-collar occupations, although this may be changing. Training typically includes education and some type of relaxation exercise, and may additionally include meditation, biofeedback or a cognition-focused technique.
- Programmes have been generic in nature, not targeting specific work stressors or stress symptoms.
- Few studies compare the relative effectiveness of different training techniques. Thus, although doing something appears to be better than doing nothing, the specific techniques used may not matter much.
- Evaluations have been based on individual-orientated measures (e.g. anxiety) that have been assessed over short post-training periods. In other words, the effects may not be very general and may not last long.
- Stress management has been associated with significant reductions in anxiety, depression, somatic complaints, sleep disturbances, muscle tension, blood pressure and urinary balance.
- The changes observed immediately after training have not always been maintained in follow-up evaluations.

Essentially the "cost" of stress for the individual is usually in terms of health, whereas for the organization it is usually in terms of performance. Hence, one finds the phenomenon of *job burnout*, which is characterized by a state of emotional exhaustion, a depersonalization of others in the workplace, and feelings of (with evidence for) low personal accomplishment.

Coping with stress also occurs at the level of the individual and the organization. Individuals may elect to use behaviour modification, career counselling, relaxation training or attendance at fitness or "wellness" programmes to relieve their stress. Also, organizations sometimes attempt to diagnose and then cure some of the major structural or process causes of stress by improving the physical work environment, job redesign, structural reorganization, introducing management by objectives and ensuring greater levels of employee participation, particularly in planning changes that affect them most.

Do organizational stress-reducing techniques work? Cooper & Sadri (1991) compared a group receiving stress counselling and a matched group who did not. Whereas they found no change in job satisfaction or organizational commitment, they did find the counselled group showed a decline in absenteeism, anxiety and depression, and an increase in self-esteem.

Organizations often believe the cost of stress to them is such that it is worth investing in both preventive and interventionist policies. They may provide sport facilities, employ dieticians to provide advice on canteen meals, or provide counselling courses. Furthermore, stress-prone individuals are now being more carefully considered in selection decisions.

National differences in working habits, workplace legislation and social security systems naturally lead to differences in the amount of stress experienced by workers. Do national or corporate cultures lead employees to be differentially sensitive to stress? It is quite possible, indeed likely, but there are so many possibly confounding variables and so little good evidence. However, it is quite possible to speculate and derive testable hypotheses. Using Hofstede's (1984) dimensions, consider the following:

- High power distance cultures demand obedience and rule following. Stress may be associated with deviation from the rules and procedures, as well as initiating changes. There is unlikely to be role ambiguity in these cultures or socially prescribed ways of dealing with stress.
- Feminine cultures associated with caring and nurturing can be stressful because of the ever-present danger of hurting or offending others. Masculine cultures can be aggressive, explosive and tactless, and may feature physical punishments and verbal put-downs. Certainly, feminine cultures stress cooperation and consensus, whereas masculine cultures prefer rugged individualism.

It is perhaps because different cultures have quite different ways of defining and dealing with success and failure in the workplace that one may well expect major differences in the experience of stress.

Health and safety at work

Many groups are concerned with health and safety at work. Pre-eminent among these are ergonomists, who are primarily concerned with man–machine interaction, the design or work tasks and environments. With a good understanding of anatomy, physiology and psychology, ergonomists are concerned with everything from designing ways to help people lift heavy loads to concerns with fatigue, boredom and monotony.

Classic textbooks on ergonomics have chapters on shift-work, eating habits and vision as well as environmental factors like lighting, noise, vibration and colour at work (Kroemer & Grandjean, 1999). These are often categorized under certain areas like posture and movement, information and operation, environmental factors and job tasks. More recently, cognitive ergonomists have become interested in human–computer interaction so that design can promote productivity and satisfaction. Ideally, ergonomists have an input into all aspects of job design so that they can maximize the productivity and satisfaction of workers at all levels. Equally, their task is to minimize stress of all types, particularly physical, but increasingly psychological, stress.

The modern workplace is probably much more complex than and equally as dangerous as that of two to three generations ago. Certainly the cognitive rather than the physical/manual demands on people have changed with technology. Both accidents and stress at work are often the result of human error, where a combination of three factors can lead to catastrophic consequences: individual misjudgement, design faults and organizational culture. People have lapses and make mistakes particularly under stress, which can lead to serious chronic and acute health consequences both for themselves and others.

Chmiel (2000) lists three classic violations of safety procedures. Workers do not comply with explicit safety procedures because:

1   They do not perceive any risks doing so. Self-protective behaviour is a function of *risk perception*. If people's perception of the threat to themselves and things they value are different from the organization's viewpoint, they are unlikely to follow safety guidelines.
2   *Attitudes to safety*. People have complicated, multidimensional attitudes to work-safety. Some are deeply sceptical, others do not believe in individual responsibility, while others have very strange beliefs about the arrangements in place to protect their safety. These attitudes reflect their safety behaviour at work.
3   *Personality*. People certainly are differentially accident-prone. Impulsive, easily distracted, less intelligent people seem more prone to accidents.

As a result, organizations try to follow good safety practices by having good, accurate accident *reporting*, putting into place regular *safety programmes* and, in general, trying to establish a *climate of safety*.

Some jobs and industries are inevitably hazardous: aviation, chemicals, mining. In these industries, attempts are made both to train individuals well as well as to design environments that take account of human fallibility.

The psychology of absenteeism

It is very difficult to come up with really accurate national or business figures on absenteeism. There are essentially three reasons for this. The *first* is that many companies do not collect absenteeism data – they have no systems to do it, or the issue is too sensitive from both a management and union perspective. The *second* reason is that although an organization may indeed collect these data regularly and accurately, it is quite simply too ashamed to publish or publicize them. The *third* reason is that there are too many definitions in the accident literature to be able to agree on how to collect the data. Some distinguish between authorized/certified versus unauthorized/uncertified absence, contractual versus non-contractual absence, sickness (injury)/medical versus non-sickness, non-injury/personal absence, and so on. In other words, simple aggregated statistics are deeply misleading because they include different types of absenteeism.

There are abundant data on the sort of factors known to be related to levels of absenteeism. At the level of the *individual* worker, obvious factors include general health and resistance to illness, work-induced fatigue and shift-work, but also non-work-induced fatigue (such as child care) and preferred hobbies (that sap energy or are dangerous).

Inevitably, *environmental* factors have an impact on absenteeism. Ambient flu and viruses are important, as are fluctuations in atmospheric conditions. Jobs with well-known stresses like uncontrollable and excessive noise, powerful unpleasant odours and bright lights also affect illness behaviour.

Certainly, *administrative* factors relate closely to all aspects of absenteeism, particularly the index of absence used, the administrative categories used for the attribution of absence and the level of aggregation of absence data – particularly whether it is by the day, the week, the work group, the shift, the plant and so on.

But we do know – despite various scare stories – that absenteeism still has a relatively low base rate. It is not that common a problem, except in very specific sectors at particular periods of time. We also know that people underestimate their own absentee records but tend to inflate views about the absence of others. Self-evidently, managers and employees hold different standards about how much absenteeism is acceptable. Indeed, the very meaning of absence varies considerably among different groups. For some people, it is a form of legitimate extra pay to compensate for perceived poor pay, extra stress or reduced holidays. For others, it is a way of getting even with colleagues who seem to take excessive time off work. Certainly, supervisors' behaviours, values and modelling are crucial in shaping the attendance patterns of individual workers. Organizations themselves differ in how they measure and react to absenteeism.

It is difficult to assess the real cost of absence from work. It is true to say that there are various *stakeholders* in company absenteeism. For the *individual* worker, absenteeism can affect income and job security, as well as reputation, which is related to job security. Equally, failing to go absent (with legitimate sick leave) may have both acute and chronic effects on employees' personal health.

The *work group* itself has a considerable stake in absenteeism, particularly with respect to morale. People in work groups are very sensitive to equity – the ratio of inputs to outputs. If a group member takes excessive and perceived inappropriate absences without some equitable cost to that individual (reduced wages, increased workload when present, reduced holidays), other group members are often affected. They may take revenge by going absent themselves, so lowering the productivity of the group as a whole.

Inevitably the *organization* as a whole has a serious stake in absenteeism. It is not difficult to see how both acute and chronic levels of absenteeism affect profit, staffing, customer relations and company reputation, all of which affect the share price. How organizations plan for dealing with unforeseen absences is indeed a fascinating index of their adaptability.

The *unions* are stakeholders in absenteeism. They negotiate over the causes and cures of problems and see it as a major topic to dispute.

Every *worker's family* has a stake in absenteeism. Pressures at work, particularly with regard to retaining the job in times of poor job security, could lead to ill-health that affects the whole family. Equally, pressures in the home can be a direct cause of absenteeism. Parental absenteeism patterns also provide a powerful model for young children and may influence either their readiness or reluctance to go absent. It has even been suggested that school truancy and phobia are clearly related to parental absence from work.

Also, *society as a whole* has a stake in absenteeism. Social values determine the value of work and leisure, illness and health, loyalty to family and employer. Albeit a crude measure of a society's health and happiness, absenteeism figures in the former Eastern bloc countries, though rarely reported, were certainly an amazing index of the inefficiency of socialism.

The most recent academic literature on absenteeism has tended to use the term "organizational withdraw" to refer to both turnover and absence. However, it is mainly seen as a form of lack of commitment to the organization. Greenberg and Baron (1994) have distinguished between *continuance* commitment (the desire to remain working for the organization), *affective* commitment (identification with the values and goals of the organization) and *normative* commitment (feeling obliged to stay because of pressure from stress). Companies attempt to increase commitment by job enrichment, aligning company and employee interests, and careful selection. However, as Sonnentag and Frese (2003) have shown, while stress has been shown to be clearly related to lowered commitment, turnover intentions and behaviour, it has not been shown unequivocally to be related to stress. It is possible that stress is one factor but only under certain conditions, like when people do not feel their efforts are being properly rewarded.

So, what causes absenteeism? There are a bewildering number of explanations and theories. They are not contradictory but complementary, each emphasizing a different cause. But perhaps they indicate best of all the complexity of the issue. Johns (1997) lists nine models:

1   *Process and decision models*. This approach suggests that absence is the result of many factors, especially personal attitudes to attendance, perceived control over personal behaviour and personal moral obligation to the organization. This approach stresses that individuals make calculated and rational decisions to go absent.

2   *Withdrawal models*. The argument here is that job satisfaction is the best predictor of absenteeism but more related to frequency than overall days lost. Commitment is less important but includes the extent to which people believe the organization is committed to them. People go absent or withdraw as a reaction to unhappiness with their work.

3   *Demographic models*. These list all related factors that predict frequent absenteeism. Age is important but may not be linear (U-shaped), in that older and younger people are absent more. Gender is important but the results are equivocal. Women are usually more often absent, due primarily to child care, but gender is confounded by many other factors (status, income). There is evidence of gender-absence cultures such that when stressed men go on strike and women go absent.

4   *Medical models*. Sickness is the major cause of illness and is usually linked to smoking and drinking (quantity and chronicity), psychological illness (particularly neurosis) and pain. The extent to which lifestyle that is modifiable causes illness which leads to absence is most often debated.

5   *Stress models*. Stress causes absence and comes from many sources – the job (intrinsic and extrinsic factors), the home life, the personality of the individual. But it could be that those who are more absent exhibit less stress due to recuperative activities. In other words, absence relieves stress – the question is what is the optimum amount?

6   *Social and cultural models*. Department, unit, climate or "cultural" factors have a powerful influence on absenteeism. Normative perceptions are very important – thus the simple rating of peer absence (how much absence colleagues take) is the best predictor of own frequency of illness. People are sensitive to levels of acceptable absence and culturally acceptable explanations/excuses for their absence.

7   *Conflict models*. These suggest that absenteeism is the manifestation of the unorganized conflict between management and labour (as opposed to strikes, which are usually organized). Absence is an index or a metric of industrial relations.

8   *Deviance models*. Absenteeism is deviant because of the negative consequences for organizational effectiveness and the violation of legal and psychological contracts. It can be seen as a product of negative traits: malingering, disloyalty and laziness.

Those who take this perspective maintain that (all) job absence is a sign of wickedness.

9   *Economic models*. These are rational economic explanations for absenteeism. Absenteeism and attendance are products of labour supply. As wage rates increase it is more attractive to sell leisure for work, but as income increases people need time for consumatory purposes. Absenteeism is prone in cash-rich, time-poor workers.

Absenteeism is a complex problem with multiple, interlinked causes that are only partly controllable by managers in companies. Like a lot of business problems, there is no simple solution. But a good start is to begin to measure it reliably to get a better idea of the precise nature of the problem in one's own organization.

Accident proneness

What is an accident? When does an accident become deliberate and hence blameable? When is an accident really an accident? Does stress cause accidents? A number of definitions exist but all contain concepts which can be distilled into three main points, the more of which are present, the more likely the event will be called "an accident". An accident has a low degree of:

- expectedness – nobody expects it to happen.
- avoidability – is it avoidable.
- intention to cause the accident – no one intended it to happen.

Thus accidents are unfortunate, unpredictable, unavoidable and unintentional inter-actions with the environment.

It is important area of research primarily because of costs to the accident victims, their families, employers and society at large. There are also various myths, such as the idea that people are motivated to have an accident so that they can take time off work. There is little or no evidence that people do this, consciously or unconsciously. Accidents frequently occur because the job demands more of the employee than can be given. They occur because people are not fully trained, they have memory lapses or they are under stress. We know many basic facts about accidents:

- We know that fatigue is often a major factor in accidents.
- We know a very frequent cause is "human error/incorrect beliefs or actions". This is said to be a major causative factor in up to 45% of incidents in nuclear power plants, 60% of aircraft accidents, 80% of marine accidents, 90% of road traffic accidents. People get tired and bored; they take short cuts and ignore safety instructions; they misread dials or do not follow guidelines for medicine use. Consider how many aeroplane travellers ignore safety instructions. Note the number of people on construction sites not wearing their prescribed equipment. Also consider how bored security people get.
- We know that jobs most associated with accidents are more varied, less repetitive, less preplanned and more mobile, which require the assimilation of more complex information. The more uncontrolled and unpredictable the working environment, the greater the demands it places on the person's information-processing capacity

and the more he or she is at risk. Thus those features of task design which make
working life more satisfying may also make it less safe.

- Accidents often occur when people confront issues and problems for the first time.
  And they have to make decisions quickly based on a lot of complex information.
  Routine jobs don't take too much effort to learn and master. But complex jobs
  requiring quick responses do. That is why pilots, for example, are carefully selected
  and trained. A disturbing paradox arises: more satisfying jobs are often more
  accident-prone jobs.

British statistics in the early 1990s showed that around 500 people are killed each year
in accidents at work, compared with 5000 or more fatal accidents on the road and
another 5000 in the home. These figures suggest that work is relatively safe. Work is
more organized and better regulated than domestic activities or driving.

However, less than 40% of the population is exposed to the risks of work, and the
working population does not include those people who are most at risk – the very
young, the very old and the infirm. Most people work during the relatively safe daylight
hours and when they are more or less fully alert; and people are more likely to be at risk
because of the influence of drink and drugs away from the working environment.
Taking these factors into account, work is surprisingly dangerous.

Some facts, published by the Health and Safety Executive (1997), are enlightening:

- In 1995, British trade unions secured £304 million for workplace injuries.
- Recent careful case studies in fairly typical organizations showed that one spent
  37% of annualized profits on accident compensation; while another lost 5% of its
  running costs directly to accidents.
- In all, 8% of accidents at work were judged to have the potential for serious
  consequences, such as fatalities, multiple injury or catastrophic loss.
- While accident insurance covers injury, ill-health and damage, there are many
  important, accountable costs such as legal costs, production delays, overtime
  working, fines, the use of temporary labour, and so on.
- Figures for the 1990s show that 1.1 million people per year in Britain sustained a
  workplace injury.
- 30 million days were lost annually on average, costing about £700 million.
- The overall cost of work accidents and work-related ill-health was estimated to be
  between £4000 and £9000 per event.
- It was even suggested that 1.75–2.75% of the country's gross domestic product is
  spent on issues relating to accidents.

Although some employers believe that complying with health and safety legislation is
a cost and a drain on their budget, there is evidence that the reverse is true. *Accident
costs exceed prevention costs.* Prevention costs include: safety materials and hardware,
clothing and equipment, guards, communication and publicity campaigns, training
time and maintenance, ongoing inspection and auditing effort, coordination and decision-making time, and support staff costs. But it remains difficult to persuade some
employers to adopt safety procedures.

There are two principal ways of looking at the accident problem (Pheasant, 1991):

- *Theory A*: Accidents are caused by unsafe behaviour (and some people are more prone to behave more unsafely than others). Accidents may therefore be prevented by changing the ways in which people behave. This is the concern primarily of personality and social psychology. This theory focuses on individuals.
- *Theory B*: Accidents are caused by unsafe systems of work. Accidents can therefore be prevented by redesigning the working system. This is the approach taken by cognitive psychologists and ergonomists. This theory focuses on systems.

Accidents are a function of different things at work, including the physical work environment, the safety culture and everybody's commitment to it, as well as individuals' general health and ability and desire to follow safety procedures (Oliver, Cheyne, Tomas, & Cox, 2002).

As might be expected, older people have fewer accidents. Job-related experience seems to be most relevant to accident rate, although the effects of number of years in industry and of number of hours worked on a specific task (where the job involves a number of tasks) can also be demonstrated.

The relationship of physical and anthropometric differences to accident susceptibility has also been shown in many specific tasks. For example, the following physical attributes will tend to increase accident-proneness:

- Colour blindness, when colour distinction is important in the task. There are certain jobs, for example being a pilot, from which colour-blind individuals are excluded.
- Extremes of height and reach. Very tall people bump into things, whereas very short people may not have the required reach. Size is also related to strength.
- Slimness of arms, wrists or fingers (which could slip through safety gates and so on). Hence, there are issues regarding the use of certain equipment by children.
- Epilepsy, where fits may be unpredictable and uncontrollable.

Some people do have a lot of accidents: the clumsy child; the forgetful adult; the poorly coordinated teenager. This concept of the *accident-prone person* originated when it was discovered that a small percentage of the population had a high percentage of accidents. Obviously, it is not true that some individuals are more prone than others to all types of accidents; nor are *all* (or even most) accidents sustained by a small, fixed group of people. But *people drive as they live* – that is, there are consistencies of behaviour (in response to particular stimuli) which suggest that they may be related to accidents.

Studies from First World War munitions factories showed that a small number of people were involved in a disproportionately large share of accidents. Researchers asked why. Was this due to physical or psychological characteristics; specific to a job or more general; a permanent or transient effect; due to greater risk exposure; because having one accident may increase the likelihood of having another; due to biases in reporting?

There is little evidence of the relationship between accidents and intelligence. People with defective vision are found to be accident-prone in some (but not all) working situations. Accident-prone people perform significantly less well in a complex experimental task involving undivided attention. Interestingly, accident-free steelworkers tended to be more popular than accident repeaters (that is, more extrovert and outgoing). Those *actively* involved in accidents have higher absenteeism rates than those *passively* involved or not involved. Not surprisingly, accident-prone individuals also take more risks and think the work is less dangerous.

By chance alone, a small number of individuals would be involved in many accidents. The theory of accident proneness is based on identifying *individuals* who have certain characteristics. The theory would have validity if the same individuals repeatedly had large numbers of accidents. Some people do fall into this category, but we do not need a theory of accident proneness to identify them. For instance, alcoholism and drug addiction are valid predictors of accidents, and so we can reduce accidents by identifying and treating these conditions. However, on the basis of *group* data, it is fruitless to attempt to identify high-accident *individuals* without any other information.

Are accident-prone people more likely to have particular types of accidents rather than others? It is important to distinguish between personality *traits* and mood *states*. The former are stable over time (for example, neuroticism, extroversion) whereas the latter are transient. We know that psychological states (not personality traits) do affect accidents. For instance:

- Influenza can result in a 50% impairment in a reaction-time test.
- Being over the UK alcohol limit by 5% results in slower reactions and bad judgement.
- A typical worker feels "low and miserable" for 20% of the time: 50% of accidents occur during these periods of negative mood.
- Drivers and pilots have more accidents when going through major life events (for example, divorce).
- Women are more accident-prone before and during menstruation, both for active and passive accident involvement.

A number of studies have examined the relationship between personality (particularly extroversion and neuroticism) and accidents (particularly car accidents). Despite various methodological difficulties and differences, the results are fairly consistent (Furnham & Saipe, 1993).

Booysen and Erasmus (1989) reviewed personality factors associated with accident risk. No fewer than 43 traits (many of them related) were examined regarding their relationship to accidents. In a conceptual factor analysis, the authors suggested that two factors were relevant: recklessness (extroversion, domineering, aggressive, sensation-seeking) and anxiety-depressive. They then administered a personality questionnaire to nearly 200 bus drivers who were divided into three groups depending on their previous involvement in accidents and the seriousness of accidents that they had been involved in. Four factors – dominance, carefreeness, emotional sensitivity and shrewdness – were relevant. People involved in more accidents were more dominant (aggressive) and more carefree (extravert), more neurotic and less shrewd.

Hansen (1989) studied 362 chemical industry workers and hypothesized that traits of social maladjustment, various aspects of neurosis, cognitive ability, employee age and actual job experience would have independent causal effects on accidents. A *social maladjustment* scale was constructed, which along with a measure of (*neurotic*) *distractibility* was clearly linked to accidents. Both scales, though correlated, demonstrated independent causal relationships to accidents, suggesting two major factors at work. Hansen believed that the central question for psychologists should be changed from

"What personality or cognitive trait is related to accidents?" to "What is the strength of the causal impact that trait anxiety has on accidents?"

Extroverts seek excitement and stimulation whereas introverts try to avoid it. The former put the car radio on to improve concentration; the latter turn it off. Extroverts like variety, novelty and change more than introverts. They take more risks because they need stimulation. The long, straight road is tedium for the extrovert, a joy for the introvert. Being a quality controller, a security guard or a lighthouse keeper is hell for the extrovert. So, when they are bored they do things to liven up their world – and this leads to accidents (see Chapter 4).

The problem is even worse if the extrovert is rather emotionally unstable and prone to moodiness. Extroverts take risks, act impulsively and drive badly to increase excitement; neurotics react badly and erratically under stress and can easily have their attention distracted. This is why pilots are deliberately selected to be stable introverts not unstable extroverts.

Since extroverts are assumed to be less socialized than introverts, it is reasonable to assume that they should be less bound by the prescribed rules of society regarding motor vehicle operation. Therefore, they have more traffic accidents and violations than introverts. In short, they are more likely to ignore warning signals and legal requirements.

Not surprisingly, it is those types who love thrills and hate boredom that have accidents and get speeding fines. They can be found – young or old – queuing for dangerous rides at amusement parks and playing fast, aggressive video games. The need for constant new sensation is the factor that makes them so susceptible to accidents. They take needless risks, partake in dangerous sports and are, quite simply, an insurance nightmare. In fact, not only do sensation seekers find it more difficult to get life insurance, given their hobbies and history, they choose not to buy it!

There is sufficient evidence that personality variables do relate to all sorts of accidents in all sorts of populations. Aggressive, impulsive, neurotic and fatalistic traits appear in particular to be associated with accidents. They account for about 10% of the variance, which is certainly not to be dismissed. The *two independent, unrelated factors* that are the best predictors of accidents are extroversion/sensation-seeking/A-type behaviour and neuroticism/anxiety/instability. Thus, the following are related to accident proneness:

- *Stimulus seeking*. The more people like variety and change, prefer people to things, get bored easily, and trade speed for accuracy, the more they are likely to do things (drive fast, ignore warnings, try untried new activities) that lead to accidents.
- *Emotional instability*. The more moody, pessimistic and unhappy people are, the more likely they are to become self-absorbed or jittery and "take their eye off the ball", which may lead to accidents.
- If they are *young, male* and *not very well educated*, as well as stimulus seeking and emotionally unstable, they really are likely to be accident-prone.

However, there are a great number of methodological shortcomings of research in this area which prevent the questions of the relationship between personality and accidents being fairly reviewed. These include the following:

- Accident reporting is erratic, biased, inconsistent and done for legal purposes only.

Any investigation of industrial (or domestic) accidents is crucially dependent on the quality (and quantity) of accident reporting. Reporting systems might fulfil organizational, medical and legal needs but frequently not those of the ergonomist or the industrial psychologist. Hence, they are investigated as events rather than as processes, as most measures do not provide measures of exposure.

- Retrospective studies cannot discriminate between the stress that caused the accident and the stress produced by its occurrence. There is a tremendous shortage of good longitudinal studies in the area.
- The confounding of dependent and independent variables by such practices as explaining causality by *post hoc* discrimination between accident and non-accident groups.
- The "lumping" together of all sorts of accidents as if all accidents were the same. Clearly, one needs a good taxonomy of accidents to make prediction clear. Thus, driving accidents may be seen to be quite different from household accidents, and accidents at work different from accidents at leisure.
- Although there is agreement as to what personality variables are important in accident research, there is less agreement about which measures to use. Alas, this means that because different measures are used, comparisons cannot be made; hence, the corpus of knowledge arising is only at the rather vague conceptual stage.

Conclusion

Stress is the mental and physical condition that results from a perceived threat or demand that cannot be dealt with readily. A *stressor* is the external or internal force that brings about the stress. *Strain* is the adverse effect of stress on an individual. Burnout is a state of exhaustion stemming from long-term stress. In short, stressor + stress + strain = "burnout".

Stress has a variety of behavioural, cognitive and physiological symptoms or consequences. The physiological symptoms link to the fight-or-flight response when faced with a stressor. Psychological symptoms include fear, anxiety, emotional disorder, and defensive attitudes and behaviour. Major job-related behavioural symptoms of stress include problems with concentration and judgement, sickness, absenteeism and lack of cooperation. Men tend to have *more* stress symptoms than women, but women have a greater *incidence* of minor symptoms, although this may be confounded with the type of jobs they do. An optimal (not necessarily minimum) amount of stress exists for most people and most tasks. Whether people experience stress usually depends upon their cognitive evaluation of the situation *and* their perceived coping skills.

Some people are more susceptible to the adverse consequences of job pressures than others because of some factor within their personality. Two such factors that predispose people to job stress are Type A behaviour (impatience and hostility) and a belief that life is controlled by external forces (external locus of control). Other factors include optimism and hardiness.

Sources of stress in one's personal life include daily hassles; disappointments with private life, hobbies, interests and sports; physical and mental health problems; financial problems; school-related problems; terrifying experiences; and any sort of significant life change. The major sources of stress in work life include: role conflict (having to choose between competing demands or expectations); role ambiguity; role overload or underload (having too much or too little to do); lack of social support;

alienation from decision-making; the home–work interface; job insecurity and unemployment.

Job burnout is a condition of emotional, mental and physical exhaustion, along with cynicism towards work in response to long-term job stressors. Three major signs or stages indicate the presence of burnout: emotional exhaustion, depersonalizing relationships and low personal accomplishments. Burnout can be managed in ways similar to managing stress. One important specific strategy both to prevent and to overcome burnout is to develop realistic expectations.

Methods of stress management under an individual's control vary from highly specific techniques to general strategies that reflect a lifestyle. The individual methods of stress management described here are: identify personal stress signals, eliminate or modify the stressor, build a support network, get physical exercise, practise everyday methods of relaxation, and practise the relaxation response. Organizational methods of reducing and preventing stress include reducing stressful conditions, practising participative decision-making, providing emotional support to employees, participating in "wellness" programmes and employee assistance programmes (professional counselling for stressed employees). Figure 7.4 attempts to capture the main variables in this area.

Health and safety at work, absenteeism and accidents have all been implicated as correlates and consequence of stress. Accidents and absenteeism cost industry a great deal of money and organizations are understandably eager to first understand and then reduce the incidences of these problems. It is recognized that they are nearly always a consequence of complex individual difference, social and organizational factors, which suggests that simple intervention strategies are unlikely to be successful.

A research perspective

Mentors: a source of social support to the new employee

In many fields, young and inexperienced individuals learn from older, more experienced employees. Thus, in medicine and law, interns learn much from established physicians and attorneys; and in science, graduate students acquire a broad range of knowledge and skills from established researchers under whose guidance they work. The same process of *mentorship* operates in business settings. Young and relatively inexperienced employees often report that they have learned a great deal from a mentor – an older and more experienced employee who advises, counsels and otherwise enhances their personal development. The stress of induction is considerably reduced.

Research on the nature of such relationships suggests that mentors do many things for their protégés. The mentor is not the boss, nor is he or she trying to teach something specific. Mentors provide much-needed emotional support and confidence during the stressful early learning experiences. They advance a protégé's career by nominating him or her for promotions, and by providing opportunities for the protégé to demonstrate his or her competence. They suggest useful strategies for achieving work objectives that protégés may not generate themselves. They bring protégés to the attention of top management, a necessary first step for advancement. They also protect protégés from the repercussion of errors, and help them avoid situations that may be risky for their careers.

Of course, the potential gains are offset by possible risks or hazards. Protégés who hitch their wagon to a falling rather than a rising star may find their own careers in danger when their mentors suffer setbacks. Indeed, in some cases they may find themselves without a job if a purge follows defeat in a political struggle. In addition, not all the advice they supply is helpful. There is

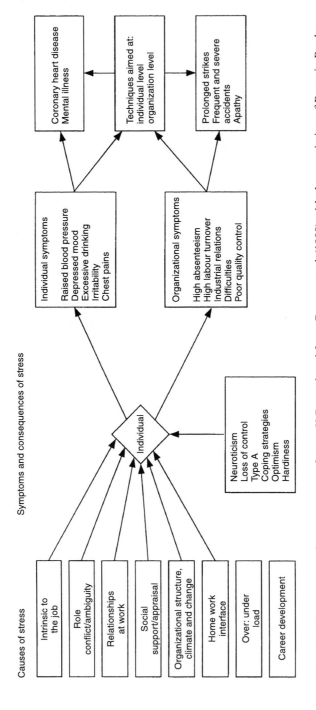

Causes of stress

Symptoms and consequences of stress

Intrinsic to the job

Role conflict/ambiguity

Relationships at work

Social support/appraisal

Organizational structure, climate and change

Home work interface

Over: under load

Career development

Individual

Neuroticism
Loss of control
Type A
Coping strategies
Optimism
Hardiness

Individual symptoms

Raised blood pressure
Depressed mood
Excessive drinking
Irritability
Chest pains

Organizational symptoms

High absenteeism
High labour turnover
Industrial relations
Difficulties
Poor quality control

Coronary heart disease
Mental illness

Techniques aimed at:
individual level
organization level

Prolonged strikes
Frequent and severe accidents
Apathy

Figure 7.4 Symptoms and consequences of stress.?? Reproduced from Cooper *et al.* (1988) with the permission of Penguin Books.

furthermore always the danger that protégés will become so dependent upon their mentors that their development as self-reliant individuals able to accept authority and responsibility is slowed.

Mentors themselves are not totally selfless benefactors who never want anything in return. On the contrary, they expect several things from protégés. First, they expect their protégés to turn in hard work and effort on assigned tasks. Secondly, they expect them to be loyal supporters within the organization; after all, they are now members of the mentor's team. Thirdly, mentors may gain recognition from others in the company for helping nurture young talent, and can bask in the reflected glory of any success gained by their protégés. Finally, they may reap psychological benefits from feeling needed, and from a sense of accomplishment in helping the younger generation.

How do mentors select or get assigned their protégés? Existing evidence suggests that they may begin by noticing and being impressed by a young employee's initial performance, or find interacting with them easy and pleasant. This may be because mentor and protégé share similar attitudes and backgrounds, or because protégés are socially skilled and clearly transmit their desire for an experienced tutor. In still other cases, would-be protégés approach potential mentors and actively ask for help or attempt to initiate a relationship in other ways.

Most human relationships develop over time, and mentorship is no exception to this general rule. In fact, most mentor–protégé relationships seem to pass through several distinct phases. The first, known as *initiation*, occurs once the relationship begins and assumes importance for both parties. The second phase, known as *cultivation*, may last two to five years. During this time, the bond between mentor and protégé deepens, and the young individual may make rapid career strides because of the skilled assistance he or she is receiving. The third stage, *separation*, begins when the protégé feels it is time to assert independence and strike out on his or her own, or when there is some externally produced change in the role relationships (e.g. the protégé is promoted; the mentor is transferred). Separation can also occur if the mentor feels unable to continue providing support and guidance to the protégé (e.g. if the mentor is experiencing physical illness or psychological problems). This phase can be quite stressful in cases where the mentor resents the protégé's growing independence, or in instances where the protégé feels that the mentor has withdrawn support and guidance prematurely. If separation is successful, the relationship may enter a final stage termed *redefinition*. Here, both individuals perceive their bond primarily as one of friendship. They come to treat one another as equals, and the role of mentor and protégé may fade away completely. However, the mentor may continue to take pride in the accomplishment of the former protégé, whereas the latter may continue to feel a debt of gratitude towards the former mentor.

Recent evidence suggests that some of the early claims for the powerful benefits of mentorship were probably overstated. Nevertheless, having an experienced, powerful mentor does seem helpful in many situations, and gives at least some young people an important edge. Unfortunately, this conclusion has unsettling implications for women, who often have less access to suitable mentors than men do. Several factors contribute to this state of affairs. First, there are simply fewer senior female executives available to serve as mentors to young female employees. Secondly, women have fewer interactions with people in positions of power in many organizations. As a result, they are less plugged into informal networks, and less likely to obtain a mentor. Thirdly, women are becoming more visible in many organizations. This may cause at least some potential mentors to feel reluctant to adopt this role; after all, if a female protégé is unsuccessful, her failure will receive more attention and reflect on the mentor to a greater extent than might be the case with a male protégé. Fourthly, many potential male mentors are reluctant to adopt this role because of concern over misinterpretation of the relationship. They realize that their interest in and concern for a younger female employee may well be misinterpreted by others, and this may pose a danger to their own careers. Kram (1986) has noted the career and psychological functions of mentoring which may be used much more as a stress reducer for both parties (Box 7.3).

Box 7.3 Mentoring functions

Career functions

Sponsorship
Opening doors. Having connections that will support the junior's career advancement.

Coaching
Teaching "the ropes". Giving relevant positive and negative feedback to improve the junior's performance and potential.

Protection
Providing support in different situations. Taking responsibility for mistakes that were outside the junior's control.

Exposure
Creating opportunities for the junior to demonstrate competence where it counts. Taking the junior to important meetings that will enhance his or her visibility.

Challenging work
Delegating assignments and skills in order to stimulate growth and preparation to move ahead.

Psychological functions

Role modelling
Demonstrating valued behaviour, attitudes and/or skills that aid the junior in achieving competence, confidence, and a clear professional identity.

Counselling
Providing a helpful and confidential forum for exploring personal and professional dilemmas. Excellent listening, trust, and rapport that enable both individuals to address central developmental concerns.

Acceptance and confirmation
Providing continuing support, respect, and admiration, which strengthens self-confidence and self-image. Regularly reinforcing both as highly valued people and contributors to the organization.

Friendship
Mutual caring and intimacy that extends beyond the requirements of daily work tasks. Sharing of experiences outside the immediate work setting.

Source: Reproduced from Kram (1986) with the permission of Jossey-Bass Publishers, Inc.

A cross-cultural perspective

Easternization

The growth (and recent collapse) of the Pacific Rim countries such as Japan, Korea, Hong Kong, Taiwan and Thailand has meant an increasing interest in sociocultural differences in management. Applied researchers in the above countries have spent much time trying to understand the role of national culture in managing for productivity in a foreign environment. The misunderstandings associated with working with people from diverse backgrounds can be very stressful.

Komin (1995) examined business in Thailand by looking at history, the evolution of the family business, the social system and interpersonal networks. He sought to describe a Thai perspective on managerial practices, such as pace and process, negotiation, communication, the work ethic, job satisfaction, conflict management and leadership styles. In doing so, he contrasted Western and Thai values, which any business person working in Thailand should consult. It also offers an insight into the possible causes of both stress and misunderstanding for a Westerner working in Thailand (Table 7.4).

Naturally a table such as this is drawn up to show differences, not similarities. However, it provides for the Western manager in Thailand, or indeed the Thai manager in the West, an explicit checklist of differences that can easily lead to misunderstanding, distress and mistrust. Indeed, for all multinational workers it may be useful to have such a table.

Some stress can lead to very dramatic results. Perhaps the most puzzling is the "sudden death" syndrome found particularly among Japanese executives. Some say hard work never killed anyone, but that is not true in Japan! There have been various responses to sudden or premature deaths among Japanese, Koreans and other Pacific Rim workers. Various hypotheses

Table 7.4 A comparison of Western and Thai management values

Management function	Western values	Underlying Thai values
Communication	Direct, to the point Open and frank Assertive Direct to the person Face to face On paper	Indirect, subtle Soft Politeness/good manners Vocal/tonal qualities Avoid overstepping hierarchy/status Third-party intervention Person to person
Problem-solving	Linear, rational approach Facts and figures Straightforward Short-term task orientated	Holistic approach Person- and situation-orientated Long-term orientated
Conflict handling	Directness/issue orientated Short-term Confrontation/get it out in the open Logic, facts Competition Task/result, short-term	Indirectness/widespread Personalization/long-term Avoidance/compromise Feeling/people Collaboration Relationships, long-term
Leadership	Position power based Skills/competencies Assertive spokesperson Self ahead of others "Cut & dried", work-orientated Achievement-orientated Combative Participative decision making	Informal power/influence Total character Unaggressive and humble Superior "pull", subordinate "push" and colleague "support" "Trust" and relationship Seniority-maturity Consensus seeking Accepted, admired/have *bararmee* Limited participation with regard to person/situation
Motivating	Money/promotion Self-actualization Task orientation Individual achievement Future-based Individualism Materialism	Money/promotion and have *nam jai*, *kreng jai* and *hai kiat* Relationship orientated Individual/family orientated Spiritual fulfilment Relatively collectivistic Success, social status, rapport with family, friends, and associates

Source: Komin (1995).

have been proposed to explain the high proportion of Japanese chief executive officers dying prematurely:

- *Over-identification with the employer and/or job*: Most Japanese managers work for one firm for their entire careers, and have an extremely close personal identification with the fate of that organization.
- *Perfectionism*: Japanese culture fosters perfectionism, to the point that managers may feel the need to rise to impossible standards. Japanese business persons complain about the constant strain of needing to please everyone, in both their professional and personal lives.

- *Workaholic lifestyle*: Most Japanese executives have relatively little time for family life and tend to restrict socializing at night to business purposes.
- *Competitive business culture*: Japanese executives work in a highly competitive business culture which places them under constant pressure.
- *Poor dietary habits*: Evening business functions offer the temptation to consume high-calorie, high-cholesterol hors d'oeuvres and alcoholic drinks and then skip dinner. Also, there is a tendency to "grab a quick bite" while working late instead of eating a balanced meal, or relying on candy or caffeine for energy.

Clearly, these five factors are the recipe for ill health in all cultures.

A human resources perspective

Burnout

Burnout is simply the outcome of physical, psychological and emotional exhaustion. But this exhaustion may be symptomatic of being alienated from one's work.

There are many varied, paradoxical and indeed mutually contradictory causes of burnout. Boredom, the opposite of a heavy workload, may cause it. Poor communication between supervisors, peers, subordinates and clients is a common cause. Poor or inequitable rewards may be another reason. Too much responsibility with too little support is also found to contribute to it. Having to acquire new and specialized skills too frequently to do quite different, important but meaningless tasks is yet another cause.

Classic causes and consequences of burnout are the following well-established facets of alienation:

- meaninglessness – the idea that there is no purpose, inherent worth or meaning in day-to-day work;
- estrangement from the goals of the organization – assigning personally low value to those things the organization values highly;
- powerlessness – the expectancy that, whatever one does, it will not relate to success or happiness.

What are the symptoms of burnout? First, victims of burnout complain about physical exhaustion. They have low energy and feel tired much of the time. They report many symptoms of physical strain, such as frequent headaches, nausea, poor sleep and changes in eating habits. Secondly, they experience emotional exhaustion. Depression, feelings of helplessness and feelings of being trapped in one's job are all part of the syndrome. Thirdly, people suffering from burnout often demonstrate a pattern of mental or attitudinal exhaustion, often known as depersonalization. They become cynical about others, tend to treat them as objects rather than as people, and hold extremely negative attitudes towards their organization. In addition, they tend to derogate themselves, their jobs, their managers and even life in general. Finally, they often report feelings of low personal accomplishment.

People suffering from burnout conclude that they have not been able to accomplish much in the past, and assume that they probably will not succeed in the future. Burnout can be defined as a syndrome of emotional, physical and mental exhaustion, coupled with feelings of low self-esteem or low self-efficacy, resulting from prolonged exposure to intense stress. Not much fun really.

Certainly, some employees may feign burnout for ulterior motives; others try to hide it. But the genuinely burnt out cannot and do not give of their best. Some jobs aim to burn out their holders. Consultancy firms are notorious for not hiring anyone over 40 because they cannot take the strain of the high commitment of time and energy.

Box 7.4 Symptoms of burnout

The major signs that burnout is occurring fall into three categories: physical condition, behavioural changes, and work performance.

Physical condition	*Behavioural changes*	*Work performance*
Headache	Increased irritability	Reduced efficiency (more
Sleeplessness	Changing moods	time spent working, but
Weight loss	Reduced tolerance for	with less productivity)
Gastrointestinal	frustration	Dampened initiative
disturbances	Increased suspiciousness of	Diminished interest in
Exhaustion and fatigue	others	working
Fidgetiness	Greater willingness to take	Reduced capacity to
Frequent colds/flu	extreme risks	perform effectively under
	Overuse of alcohol and	stress
	tranquillizers	Increased rigidity of
		thought (closed thinking,
		inflexible)

Box 7.5 Are you burnt out?

If your total score is over 40 you are at, or near, burnout.
Add odd number questions to obtain your score on emotional exhaustion.
Add even number questions to obtain your score on depersonalization.

Answer each question in terms of frequency	*Never*	*Once or twice*	*About once a week*	*A few times a week*	*Every day*
1. I feel that my work drains me emotionally.	1	2	3	4	5
2. I seem to treat clients and colleagues like objects.	1	2	3	4	5
3. I feel exhausted and fatigued at the beginning of the day.	1	2	3	4	5
4. I have definitely become more callous and devious at work.	1	2	3	4	5
5. I feel I am working harder than others at work.	1	2	3	4	5
6. I think the job is hardening me emotionally.	1	2	3	4	5
7. Working with people (clients, colleagues) is a real strain.	1	2	3	4	5
8. I don't care what happens to this company and those working for it.	1	2	3	4	5
9. I feel pretty much at the end of my tether.	1	2	3	4	5
10. I believe many colleagues blame me for their problems.	1	2	3	4	5

References

Booysen, A., & Erasmus, J. (1989). Die verband tussen enkde personlik-heidfactore en belsings risiks. *South African Journal of Psychology, 19*, 144–152.

Briner, R. (1999). Feeling and smiling: An overview of what we currently know about emotion in the workplace. *The Psychologist, 12*, 16–19.

Burger, J. (1985). Desire for control and achievement related behaviours. *Journal of Personality and Social Psychology, 46*, 1520–1533.

Candappa, R. (1998). *The little book of stress*. London: Ebury Press.

Caplan, R. (1983). Person–environment fit: Past, present and future. In C. L. Cooper (Ed.), *Stress research: Issues for the eighties* (pp. 35–78). Chichester, UK: Wiley.

Caplan, R., Cobb, S., French, J., Harrison, R., & Phinneau, S. (1980). *Job demands and worker health*. Ann Arbor, MI: Institute for Social Research.

Carver, C., Scherer, M., & Weintraub, J. (1989). Assessing coping strategies: A theoretical based approach. *Journal of Personality and Social Psychology, 56*, 267–283.

Chmiel, N. (2000). Safety at work. In N. Chmiel (Ed.), *Introduction to work and organizational psychology* (pp. 255–273). Oxford: Blackwell.

Cooper, C. (Ed.) (1998). *Theory of organizational stress*. Buckingham: Open University Press.

Cooper, C., Cooper, R., & Eaker, L. (1988). *Living with stress*. Harmondsworth, UK: Penguin.

Cooper, C., & Marshall, J. (1976). *Understanding executive stress*. London: Macmillan.

Cooper, C., & Sadri, G. (1991). The impact of stress counselling at work. *Journal of Social Behaviour and Personality, 6*, 411–423.

Cox, T. (1978). *Stress*. London: Macmillan.

Cox, T., & Mackay, C. (1979). The impact of repetitive work. In R. Sell & P. Shipley (Eds.), *Satisfaction in job design* (pp. 24–37). London: Taylor & Francis.

Cummings, T., & Cooper, C. (1998). A cybernetic theory of organizational stress. In C. Cooper (Ed.), Theories of organizational stress (pp. 101–120). Buckingham: Open University Press.

Edwards, J. (1998). Cybernetic theory of stress, coping and well-being. In C. Cooper (Ed). *Theories of Organizational Stress* (pp. 122–152). Buckingham: Open University Press.

Endler, N., & Parker, J. (1990). Multidimensional assessment of coping. *Journal of Personality and Social Psychology, 58*, 844–854.

Folkman, S., & Lazarus, R. (1980). An analysis of coping in a middle aged community sample. *Journal of Health and Social Psychology*, 21, 219–239.

Furnham, A. (1992). *Personality at work*. London: Routledge.

Furnham, A., & Saipe, J. (1993). Personality correlates of convicted drivers. *Personality and Individual Differences, 14*, 329–336.

Furnham, A., & Schaeffer, R. (1984). Person–environment fit, job satisfaction and mental health. *Journal of Occupational Psychology, 57*, 295–307.

Greenberg, G., & Baron, R. (1994). *Behavior in organizations*. Boston, MA: Allyn & Bacon.

Hansen, C. (1989). A causal model of the relationship among accidents, biodata, personality and cognitive factors. *Journal of Applied Psychology, 74*, 81–90.

Health and Safety Executive (1997). *The costs of accidents at work*. Norwich: HMSO.

Hofstede, G. (1984). *Culture's consequences*. Beverly Hills, CA: Sage.

Johns, G. (1997). Contemporary research on absence from work: Correlated causes and consequences. *International Review of Industrial and Organizational Psychology, 12*, 114–166.

Karasek, R., & Theorell, T. (1990). *Healthy work*. New York: Basic Books.

Kasl, S. (1973). Mental health and the work environment: An examination of the evidence. *Journal of Occupational Medicine, 15*, 509–518.

Kobasa, S. (1979). Stressful life events, personality, health: An enquiry into hardiness. *Journal of Personality and Social Psychology, 37*, 114–128.

Komin, S. (1995). Sociocultural influences in management for productivity in Thailand. In K. Hway (Ed.), *Easternization: Sociocultural impact on productivity* (pp. 81–97). Tokyo: APO.

Kram, K. (1986). Mentoring in the workplace. In D. Hall & Associates (Eds.), *Career development in organizations* (pp. 179–199). San Francisco, CA: Jossey-Bass.

Kroemer, K., & Grandjean, E. (1999). *Fitting the task to the human.* Abingdon, UK: Taylor & Francis.

Lazarus, R. (1966). *Psychological stress and coping processes.* New York: McGraw-Hill.

McGrath, J. (1976). Stress and behaviour in organizations. In M. Dunnette (Ed.), *Handbook of industrial and organizational psychology* (pp. 1351–1396). Chicago, IL: Rand-McNally.

Oliver, A., Cheyne., Tomas, J., & Cos, S. (2002). The effects of organizational and individual factors on occupational accidents. *Journal of Occupational and Organizational Psychology, 75,* 473–488.

Paoli, P. (1997). *Second European survey on the work environment, 1995.* Dublin: European Foundation for the Improvement of Living and Working Conditions.

Parker, E., & Brown, L. (1982). Coping behaviours that mediate between life events and depression. *Archives of General Psychiatry, 39,* 1386–1392.

Patterson, J., & McCubblin, H. (1987). Adolescent coping style and behaviours. *Journal of Adolescence, 12,* 163–186.

Pheasant, S. (1991). *Ergonomics, work and health.* London: Macmillan.

Price, V. (1982). *Type A behaviour pattern.* London: Academic Press.

Seligman, M., & Schulman, P. (1986). Explanatory style as a predictor of productivity and quitting among life insurance agents. *Journal of Personality and Social Psychology, 48,* 832–840.

Selye, H. (1956). *The stress of life.* New York: McGraw-Hill.

Siegrist, J. (1996). Adverse health effects of high-effort/low reward conditions. *Journal of Occupational Health and Psychology, 1,* 27–41.

Sonnentag, S., & Frese, M. (2003). Stress in organizations. In W. Borman, D. Ilgen, & R. Klimosk (Eds.), *Handbook of psychology* (Vol. 12, pp. 454–491). New York: Wiley.

Spector, P. (1982). Behaviour in organizations as a function of locus of control. *Psychological Bulletin, 91,* 482–497.

Spector, P. (1998). A control theory of the job stress process. In C. Cooper (Ed.), *Theories of organizational stress* (pp. 153–165). Buckingham: Open University Press.

Wilson, P. (1996). *The little book of calm.* Harmondsworth, UK: Penguin.

8　Cooperation, power and ethical behaviour in organizations

Introduction

What are the costs of working with, versus against, others within the organization? Is competition (rather than cooperation) within an organization healthy, with all the subsequent departmental or sectional rivalry? How should one foster cooperation in an organization? How does the power and influence process in organizations promote or inhibit cooperation? What sort of power is most effective in organizations? Are "office politics" inevitable and manageable or deeply undesirable but uncontrollable? And what are the ethical implications of organizational behaviour? Should business men and women follow a particular ethical code and, if so, which one and why? This chapter will concern itself with all these issues.

Social and biological psychologists have long discussed the issue of pro-social or altruistic behaviour – how, whether, why it occurs. Although most researchers and writers believe in the benefits of altruism, it is far from clear how it can be fostered, particularly in large and complex organizations. How can one ensure employees help and support each other so that all gain?

Which types of organizations foster altruism, which cooperation and which competition? The answer to this question is probably best understood in terms of the process of cooperation and competition. Most people at work are neither *independent* (unless they work alone) or *dependent* (on one or a few others) but *interdependent*. They work in teams, groups and sections that may be characterized by cooperation, helpfulness and mutual support. Equally, they are as likely to be indifferent or aggressive to other sections of the organization, even being in open conflict with them. Whereas some people have pointed out that competition can raise standards (and reduce costs) *within* the organization, others feel that the potential negative costs of competition are far too great, leading to conflict, resentment and even destructive behaviour.

Cooperation involves mutual assistance or coordination between two or more persons or work teams. It may occur when two or more persons or groups work together to progress towards shared goals, but it works on different levels for different periods of time. For instance, can there be cooperation when people share the same means to different ends, as in negotiation? The answer is yes, temporarily and at a higher level. The occurrence of true cooperation in work settings is affected by several factors relating to individuals (e.g. strong tendencies towards reciprocity, communication, personal orientations and preferences). It is also affected by several organizational factors (e.g. reward systems, interdependence among employees). Indeed, cooperative individuals may seek out cooperative organizations in which to work. *Competition* develops when one individual, group or organization achieves gains at another's expense (i.e. one side's gain is the other side's loss). Cooperation has been described as "win–win", while competition has been described as "win–lose".

There are those who argue that competitiveness is a requirement of economic growth and progress. Lynn (1991) showed that the level of competitiveness among young people in a society is directly related to economic growth:

> The tough minded tradition regards competition as a positive good and the engine of progress in general as well as of economic growth. This tradition is rooted in both biology and in social science. In biology it is expressed in Charles Darwin's theory of evolution which states that it is through competition between individuals and species that evolutionary progress has taken place. Less efficient and capable individuals and species have been progressively eliminated and have become extinct, leaving increasingly efficient and capable individuals and species as the survivors. Without competition human beings would never have evolved. Human beings are the supremely successful competitors in the evolutionary struggle and have done so well that we have achieved mastery over the world and all other species, except for our greatest enemy, the bacteria who still remain to be conquered . . .
>
> It is not only biology which identifies competition as the mechanism through which progress is achieved: the same theory holds in the social sciences. It was first set out systematically in 1776 by Adam Smith in *The Wealth of Nations*. Smith argued that every man working to further his own advantage, in competition with others doing similar work, is the process through which a society grows prosperous. Does the baker sell bread through motives of altruism to further the public good, Smith asked? Of course not. The baker sells bread to make money for himself and his family. And by doing this, and by being allowed to make money, the baker's selfish motives allow the public to buy cheap bread and promote public well-being. If the baker is not permitted to sell bread at a profit to himself, he will not sell bread at all. Anyone who doubts this should pay a visit to Moscow and see for themselves. (Lynn, 1991: 106–107).

Some of the most interesting experiments in social psychology involve studying cooperation and competition. The most famous is the Prisoner's Dilemma Game: Two prisoners have the choice of confessing or not confessing. If they trust and support each other by not confessing, each receives a light sentence; if they both confess, they receive relatively heavy sentences; and if one confesses and the other does not, the former is released and the latter gets a very heavy sentence. The dilemma is that if one has complete trust in the other, he would do best by being untrustworthy himself and confessing.

The dilemma is that mutual competitiveness never pays. In a more realistic study, Deutsch and Krauss (1960) asked people to imagine that they were running a trucking company (either the Acme Company or the Bolt Company) and had to get a truck from one point to another as quickly as possible. The two trucks were not in competition; they had different starting points and different destinations. However, the faster route for both converged to a one-lane road, and the two trucks had to go in opposite directions. The only way both could use the road was for one of them to wait until the other had passed through. If either truck entered the road, the other could not use it; if they both entered the road, neither of them could move until one had backed up. Also, each company had a gate across the direct route that could be raised by pressing a button. If the gate was raised, it prevented the road from being used.

Each truck was provided with an alternative route that did not conflict with the other, but was much longer. Taking the alternative route was guaranteed to lose points, whereas taking the direct route would gain points. The players were told that their goal was to earn as many points as possible for the company. Nothing was said about earning more points than the other player. It was clear that the optimal strategy was to cooperate by alternating using the one-lane road. They could both use the direct route, and one would be delayed only a few seconds while the other was getting through. Despite this, there was little cooperation between the players. Instead of allowing each other to use the road, they raised their gates, and both players ended up losing points.

Conflict is a process that begins when one person or group perceives that another person or group takes action inconsistent with the perceiver's interests. Conflict situations involve concern with one's own outcomes, and concerns with others' outcomes. Contrasting styles or approaches to resolving the conflict occur, such as competing, collaborating, avoiding, accommodating and compromising, which will be discussed later.

Modern theories of conflict emphasize that it is a process and it involves the perceptions, thoughts, feelings and intentions of all participants. *Organizational conflict* stems from both organization-based and interpersonal factors. The first category includes competition over scarce resources, ambiguity over responsibility or jurisdiction, interdependence, reward systems that pit people or units against one another, and power differentials. The second category includes attributional errors, faulty communication, and personal characteristics or traits. It is the interaction of particular people with special values in a unique organizational context that leads to processes of influence that may be either cooperative or conflictual in nature.

Although conflict often exerts negative effects on organizations, interfering with communication and morale, it sometimes produces positive outcomes. These include bringing problems out into the open, enhanced understanding of each other's positions among adversaries, increased consideration of new ideas, better decisions and increased organizational commitment.

A key task with respect to conflict is managing its occurrence, deriving the benefits of conflict while minimizing its harmful effects – and *not* eliminating it entirely. It is naïve to see all conflict as bad, and all problems at work as being solvable. *Bargaining* or *negotiation* is the most common procedure for resolving organizational conflicts. Many factors influence the course and outcomes of bargaining, including specific tactics used by participants, their perceptions of each other's interests and priorities, and their overall approach to bargaining – "win–lose" or "win–win". Third-party interventions such as *mediation* and *arbitration* can also prove helpful in resolving conflicts. Another approach involves the induction of *superordinate goals* – ones shared by both sides. Conflicts can also be resolved through *escalative intervention* – actions that temporarily intensify current conflicts to resolve them more effectively. To minimize interpersonal conflict between people of different racial and ethnic groups, some companies have attempted to *manage diversity*, such as by bringing together people from different groups and allowing them to have successful work experiences together.

There are alternatives to cooperation and conflict, such as compromise or accommodation or, indeed, avoidance of each other or other parties. Often it is organizational culture, situational factors and immediate goods that determine whether conflict or cooperation will occur.

Cooperation in organizations

Cooperation is a basic form of coordination of activities. It occurs when two or more persons or groups work together and help each other, usually to achieve some shared goals. Whether cooperation occurs "naturally" is much disputed. Indeed, whether it is even desirable is not entirely clear. Cooperation ideally yields positive outcomes for all participants because the final significant goal could only be achieved (qualitatively and quantitatively) through cooperation. Furthermore, participants should obtain an equitable share of the outcome depending on how the reward system is structured. There are both individual and organizational determinants and correlates of cooperation at work. Various factors appear to encourage it, including the following.

- *The reciprocity norm*. Reciprocity is at its most basic level "tit-for-tat". It represents the tendency to behave towards others exactly as they have acted towards you. This is a very primitive norm and it is therefore fairly consistent across organizations, cultures and individuals. It is in many ways a highly effective strategy for behaviour, as many experimental games have shown. Note, however, that competition (and aggression) can be reciprocated just as easily as cooperativeness.

  The norm of cooperative reciprocity is usually self-sustaining, and individuals (managers, leaders) can fairly easily start it off. Soon after reciprocity occurs, it usually yields obvious and noted benefits and therefore the process is sustained. But it can very easily peter out or become diluted.

  However, there is a consistent and major force that acts against this, namely self-serving attribution bias. For the cooperative reciprocity factor to operate, a person must judge the effort and motivation of another and then match it reciprocally. An individual needs to attribute the cooperative behaviour to various possible causes. If one judges others' cooperative effort as *lower* than it is, and one's own as *higher*, it is natural to undermatch their lack of cooperation. If this misperception is endemic, it is a sure recipe for disaster because a genuinely meant helpful response is misperceived, and punishment and competition may result. What some organizations try to do is to make explicit an *internal economy* of costs and benefits, even explicitly in terms of points. Thus, asking for certain help costs so many points, whereas giving another type of help earns one a certain number of points. Making explicit the worth of different types of cooperative help can assist in reducing subjective bias. Furthermore, by creating an internal economy, the organization can attempt to encourage various forms of cooperation at particular times.

- *Communicative propinquity*. Studies of personal friendship have demonstrated that propinquity (physical closeness) leads to communication, which in turn leads to liking, trust and enhanced cooperation. Studies of personal friendship have clearly demonstrated this, but it is not clear whether this always occurs in organizational settings. People who work in close physical proximity tend to like and trust each other more than those who come into contact less frequently. Often, simply frequent contact and an open exchange of views may convince all parties that working together is the best strategy, which in turn leads to better communication. Thus, if people are required to meet frequently, under non-threatening conditions, it is quite likely that friendship groups will arise, which leads to cooperation. Working on split sites or in different buildings reduces propinquity and may in due course reduce cooperation.

- *Personal beliefs and attitudes.* Some of the belief systems addressed in Chapter 4 are associated with competition and some with cooperation. Thus, people with conservative, work-ethic and just-world beliefs tend to favour competition over cooperation. They favour the operation of the free market over interventionism, of equity over equality, of meritocracy rather than reverse discrimination. Although some authoritarian individuals may express both aggression and prejudicial beliefs, the fact that some attitudes and belief systems stress the virtues of (open, fair) competition over cooperation does not imply that they are unreasonable, hostile or do not have the real goals of the organization at heart. However, it is the personal values that individuals hold and that organizations espouse that predicts most directly whether cooperation will be fostered.

- *Reward systems.* Every organization has an explicit reward policy that may ultimately lead to cooperative or competitive behaviours. Individual performance-related pay or bonus schemes may ultimately lead individuals to fight over scarce resources rather than cooperate. Team-based performance may, on the other hand, increase within-team cooperation but threaten between-team help. Win–lose situations inevitably encourage competition. Many Western organizations currently give their employees mixed signals. They stress team-based cooperation, but reward individuals uniquely, even when certain forms of individualism benefit the person and not the team. A major source of conflict in organizations is the perception of equity in organizational input and output (see Chapter 5).

- *Job description and organizational structure.* The way jobs are described and how they function within organizations may, through the deliberate structuring of team interdependence, rather than dependence or independence, foster cooperation. Thus, if individuals are required to work with others on simple but natural tasks, it is probably that this structural interdependence leads to beneficial teamwork and cooperation. There are of course different types of interdependence:

  - *pooled* interdependence, where groups rely on one another and in some sense belong to the same parent group;
  - *sequential* interdependence, where the operation of one individual or group proceeds or follows another, as on an assembly line;
  - *reciprocal* interdependence, where the operation of each party proceeds and acts as a prerequisite for the functioning of the other.

  Furthermore, inter-organizational cooperation can also be sought and fostered. Organizations can join together in cartels to increase their output, improve market share, or more sinisterly control the market. Having an external enemy, as Bismarck found, can be a great spur for individuals to club together and help one another. New patterns of trade, technological advances and governmental regulations can create precisely the new playing field that leads competitors to become cooperators; hence, the beginning of mergers and the formation of consortia.

- *Group homogeneity.* Homogeneous as opposed to heterogeneous or diverse groups appear to experience less conflict. Given similarity in culture, class and education, members of the group see things in the same way and respond in a similar fashion.

They often shave similar values and have similar ideas about justice, equity and equality. Groups can be homogenous in terms of age, education and gender, all of which usually helps cooperation in the long run. However, most workforces are becoming more diverse, which can, in the short term, lead to conflict.

Precisely how, when and why inter-organizational cooperation occurs is usually a function of the organizations involved (large corporations, small groups) *and* the environmental conditions that encourage that coordination. Argyle (1991) argues that individuals may be cooperative in different ways: cooperating towards achieving greater material rewards, cooperating in communal relationships, or simply coordinating one's activities. He notes that all work cooperation is often essential because some tasks are simply too large for one person, such as dealing with large objects or heavy loads; some tasks require division of labour, between individuals who have specialized skills for different parts of the job; working in groups means that people can help and instruct one another; and it provides company – that is, social satisfaction: the benefits of cooperation at work are not confined to material rewards.

For Argyle (1991), cooperation does not occur by chance. It occurs because people have affiliative needs (for friendship), because there are both explicit and implicit incentives for cooperation, and because decision-making is qualitatively better and more likely to be carried out if shared. Cooperation is usually ensured by a judicious mix of specified organizational rules and individual skills. But perhaps the three central questions are: What characterizes cooperative groups? Are cooperative groups more effective? What are the benefits to the individual? If a group is not cooperative, it does not necessarily mean that it is competitive. Some groups have clear behavioural norms that prescribe cooperation and proscribe both competition and/or indifference to one another by working alone.

What characterizes cooperative groups? Argyle (1991) lists five clearly observable factors:

- mutual help – the regularity, genuineness and relevance of freely offered mutual help;
- division of labour – people are allowed, or even encouraged, to do what they are best at and/or like doing most;
- interpersonal attraction – people are more attracted to each other and the group;
- commitment – commitment and loyalty to the group, measurable by turnover and voluntary help;
- internalized motivation to be helpful – that is, certain characteristics of individuals.

Other factors that may be important are the history of the group (how it was originally formed and group members selected), who the group competitors are, how members of the group are rewarded, and the relative value of staying with the group. Most group members are able quite sensitively and accurately to label their own groups as competitive, neutral/indifferent or cooperative. But clearly, group dynamics mean that groups can change, and they do so very quickly. Crises can nurture cooperation and success indifference. However, it may be considerably more difficult to change a feuding group into a genuinely cooperative group.

Are cooperative groups more effective? This is perhaps the most crucial question for the applied psychologist, and the answer naturally has various caveats. Certainly, the results seem to suggest that cooperative groups, compared with competitive groups, seem to do better. Argyle (1991) offers five explanations:

- *Motivation*: The reverse prediction might be made that individual competition would arouse greater motivation because individual efforts and their rewards are more closely related. Deutsch (1949) found no evidence for any difference in motivation; there was a non-significant trend for cooperative groups to be more motivated, perhaps because of pressure from other members of the group. However, the effects of cooperative motivation were greater in smaller groups, as would be expected.
- *Coordination*: Deutsch found that observers rated the cooperative group members as working together and coordinating more. It is found that larger groups do less well, *per capita*, at tug-of-war pulling and similar tasks, partly because of coordination losses, i.e. not all pulling at the same time and social loafing.
- *Help*: In cooperative groups there is more helping, in competitive groups more interference. Cooperative group members see that their rewards depend partly on the activities of the others, and feel some responsibility for others' performance, and a positive attitude towards it. The behaviour of self and others are seen as interchangeable.
- *Communication*: There is more communication in cooperative groups, fewer communication difficulties, and less trouble in understanding the others. Cooperative group members are more likely to accept the ideas and suggestions of others. There is more social influence in cooperative groups.
- *Division of labour*: However, there is *less* homogeneity and greater division of labour in cooperative groups, with individuals specializing on what they do best. In problem-solving groups it is often possible to divide up the work in this way, and to take advantage of each member's expertise. (Argyle 1991: 127–128)

Styles or patterns of communication frequently encourage or discourage co-operation. It seems that cooperativeness and competitiveness have different origins. *Cooperation* usually results when employers:

- use descriptive, as opposed to evaluative, speech: they present feelings and perceptions that do not imply that the others need to change;
- take a problem orientation, rather than trying to control others: this implies a desire to collaborate in exploring a mutual problem rather than trying to alter colleagues or subordinates;
- are spontaneous and honest, rather than appearing to use a "strategy", which involves ambiguous and multiple motivations: they do not appear to be concealing their true aims;
- convey empathy for the feelings of their employees, rather than appearing unconcerned or neutral about the listener's welfare: they give reassurance that they are identifying with the listener's problem, rather than denying the legitimacy of the problems;
- indicate that they feel equal, rather than superior, to the employee: they suggest that they will enter a shared relationship, not simply dominate their interaction;
- communicate that they will experiment with their own behaviour and ideas, rather

than be dogmatic about them: they do not give the impression that they know all the answers and do not need help from anyone.

Competition results when communication conveys a "we–they" attitude or a "win–lose" attitude. A we–they attitude polarizes the interacting groups by establishing a communication barrier between them. The following usually characterize the win–lose attitude: defining conflict as win–lose; pursuing only one's own goals; understanding one's own needs, but publicly disguising them; aggrandizing one's own power; using threats to get submission; over-emphasizing one's own needs, goals and position; adopting an attitude of exploiting the other whenever possible; emphasizing only differences in positions and superiority of one's own position; isolating the other person or group. The issue of whether cooperation or competition is healthy in organizations remains contentious. The question nearly always becomes ideological, with free-marketeers providing impressive data showing the benefits of competition, and protectionists trying to point out all the drawbacks of competitiveness.

Ideology is a set of instrumental and philosophical beliefs that help people identify threats and opportunities in project work and which provide guidelines for appropriate action (Hosking & Morley, 1991). To that extent, it may be argued that much decision-making, indeed all research, is imbued with ideology. The idea that researchers have no values or presuppositions that may colour both their research and interpretation of their findings is a myth. Most strive for some sort of "objective" disinterested interpretation of their data in the cause of science, but they rarely achieve this. Management is not value-free and in that sense is ideologically influenced. What is important is how coherent and explicit the ideology is, and whether all major decisions are made by referring back to ideological "first principles".

Conflict in organizations

Conflict, disagreements and opposition have always existed between individuals, groups and organizations. There can be conflict over ideas and values, over emotions and over policy. Conflict can operate at the individual level (between specific individuals), between groups (sections, teams, departments) and between whole organizations and institutions. Conflict is often about organizational factors, such as interdependency, rewards, ambiguity of roles, reward and change. As a consequence, there are different views about it. Thus, the *traditionalists* viewed it negatively – as something that was destructive, irrational and therefore should be avoided. The *human relations* school latterly believed conflict inevitable and even at times beneficial to a group's performance. The *interactionist* view is that conflict should not only be tolerated but encouraged because a harmonious cooperative tranquil group is too likely to become apathetic, lazy and unresponsive to innovation. Different schools hold quite different views on conflict:

- *Pluralist school.* Pluralists see intra- and inter-organizational conflict as inevitable, occasionally even desirable, because it assists evolutionary change. Conflict represents a mechanism by which issues are confronted and solutions found between various groups serving their own interests. One has thesis, antithesis and synthesis. Often, compromise solutions occur to ensure mutual survival. Conflict is stimulating and beneficial because it challenges the apathetic, non-response-to-change groups. Pluralists argue that an optimal level of conflict can be generated, which is useful, self-critical and viable. Indeed, pluralists argue that conflict often brings about necessary change, increases cohesiveness and improves organizational effectiveness. It is the engine of change.

- *Radical and Marxist school*. This "revolutionary" view sees organizations in one of the theatres of war, fighting as one side in the class war. The view emphasizes the disparity of power between the owners of the means of production (managers) and the workers. Thus, organizational conflict is about professional values, limited resources, career progress, special privileges, and so on. Conflict is used to justify and legitimize power differences.

Essentially, conflict occurs when:

- mutually exclusive goals or values exist, or are perceived to exist by the groups involved;
- interaction is characterized by behaviour designed to defeat, reduce or suppress the opponent, or to gain a mutually designated victory;
- the groups face each other with mutually opposing actions and counter-actions;
- each group attempts to create a relatively favoured position *vis-à-vis* the other; or
- there is a long, and remembered history of conflicts.

   Conflicts take many forms and follow a fairly clear escalatory pattern. *Latent* conflict refers to the time when the conditions for conflict exist. Groups may compete for scarce resources, strive for autonomy and have different goals. *Perceived* conflict refers to occasions when group members intellectually or cognitively know that conflict exists. If one group misunderstands another group's position, for example, perceived conflict may exist. *Felt* conflict occurs when one or more of the parties feel aggressive or anxious. Here the conflict becomes personalized to the individuals or groups involved. *Manifest* conflict refers to observable behaviour designed to frustrate another's attempts to pursue his or her goals. Both open aggression and withdrawal of support illustrate manifest conflict. At this stage, conflict should be resolved. *Conflict aftermath* refers to the situation after conflict is resolved or suppressed. It describes the resulting relationship between the parties in conflict.

   It is important to be able to distinguish between *functional* and *dysfunctional* conflict, yet this distinction is neither precise nor clear. It can, of course, always be distinguished in terms of its consequences. If conflict leads to improvements in goal attainment, it can be seen as functional; if not, dysfunctional. However, this cannot help one judge *a priori* whether conflict will be beneficial or not.

The conflict process

The conflict process can be thought of as progressing through four identifiable stages: potential opposition, realization, behaviour and outcomes, although there are inevitably feedback loops in this simple model (Figure 8.1).

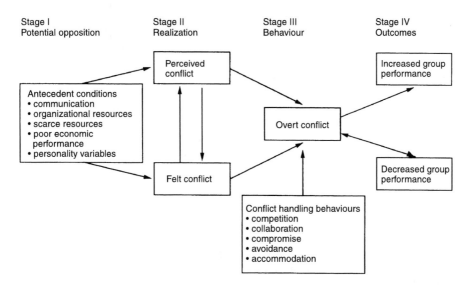

Figure 8.1 The conflict process. Reproduced from Robbins (1991) with the permission of Prentice-Hall, Inc.

Stage I: potential opposition

The first step in the conflict process is the presence of conditions that create opportunities for conflict to arise. They *need not* lead directly to conflict, but one of these conditions or factors is necessary if conflict is to arise. That is, these are necessary but not sufficient. These factors may concern such things as communication patterns, organizational structure and personal values, as well as scarcity of resources, threats of redundancy and takeover, as well as a history of conflict.

*   *Communication.* Various problems arise from semantic difficulties, misunderstandings and "noise" in the communication channels. Individuals and groups may have different objectives, goals, values and ideologies that have not been accurately communicated. Poor communication is certainly not the source of *all* conflicts, although there is considerable evidence to suggest that problems in the communication process act to retard collaboration and stimulate misunderstanding. Certainly, a breakdown in communications is both a cause *and* consequence of inter and intra-organizational conflict.
*   *Structure.* Structure refers to the formal interrelationship of the organization, such as size, degree of specialization, and standardization in the tasks assigned to group members; heterogeneity of members; leadership styles; reward systems; and the degree of dependence between groups (see Chapter 15). Thus, a change in leadership style from democratic to autocratic, or from even-handed to partisan, may lead to intra-organizational between-group conflict. Sometimes it can be fairly easily guessed, by looking at a company's formal organizational chart, where and why conflict occurs. Organizational structure can also relate to organizational space and specialization, which act as forces to stimulate conflict. The larger the group, department or section and the more specialized its activities, the greater the

likelihood of conflict with others. The potential for conflict tends to be greatest where group members have few skills, a long investment in their company and feel threatened.

An open style of leadership and too much reliance on participation may also stimulate conflict. Participation and conflict are often highly related, paradoxically because participation encourages the promotion of real or imagined differences. The suppression of participation does not necessarily reduce underlying conflict if it exists, but neither necessarily does open participation in decision-making. Reward systems, too, are found to create conflict when one member's gain is at another's expense. Finally, if a group is dependent on another group (in contrast to the two being mutually independent), or if the interdependence allows one group to gain at another's expense, opposing forces are stimulated.

- *Individual difference variables.* The evidence indicates that certain personality types – for example, individuals who are highly authoritarian, dogmatic and who demonstrate low self-esteem – lead to potential conflict (see Chapters 4 and 5). Furthermore, those with differing value systems – for instance, those who value equality over equity in the distribution of rewards – are likely to clash (Furnham, 1994). However, one should be careful not to confuse conflict and cooperation between persons and/or between groups. Although it may be true that some individuals are driven, through personality or ideological factors, to promote harmony or its opposite, there is a major difference between individual conflict and group conflict (see Chapter 10).

The potential for real, bitter and self-defeating conflict is present in many organizations. The competition over scarce resources, the homogeneity of groups with quite different perspectives and the corporate culture of internal competitiveness, all may lead to conflict.

Stage II: realization and personalization

If the conditions cited in Stage I generate frustration, then the potential for explicit opposition becomes realized in the second stage. The antecedent conditions can lead to conflict only when one or more of the parties are affected by, and cognisant of, the conflict. However, because a conflict is perceived does not necessarily mean that it is personalized. People may be aware that they and a co-worker are in disagreement, yet it may not make them tense or anxious and it may not even influence work behaviour towards the co-worker. It is at the level where conflict is felt, when individuals become emotionally involved, that parties experience anxiety, tension or hostility that is the essence of conflict. Conflict is relatively easy to see because it is "affective".

Stage III: behaviour

At this stage, people engage in action that frustrates (or attempts to frustrate) the attainment of another's goals. This action must be intended – that is, there must be a known effort to undermine another. The conflict is out in the open, observable. Overt conflict covers a full range of behaviours, from subtle, indirect and highly controlled forms of interference, to direct, aggressive, violent and uncontrolled struggle. This behaviour may range from disruptive behaviour in committees to Luddism and even arson. This conflict behaviour may remain at a low level for a long period of time or may suddenly escalate.

Stage III is also where most conflict-handling behaviours are initiated. Once the conflict is overt, the parties will usually develop a method for dealing with the conflict lest it escalates. This does not exclude conflict-handling behaviours from being initiated in Stage II, but in most cases these techniques for reducing the frustration are used not as preventive measures but only when the conflict has become observable.

Using two dimensions – *cooperativeness* (the extent to which one party attempts to satisfy the other party's concerns) and *assertiveness* (the extent to which one party attempts to satisfy his or her own concerns) – five conflict-handling orientations can be identified: *competition* (assertive and uncooperative), *collaboration* (assertive and cooperative), *avoidance* (unassertive and uncooperative), *accommodation* (unassertive and cooperative) and *compromise* (midway on both assertiveness and cooperativeness dimensions) (Thomas, 1976; see Figure 8.2).

- *Competition*: When one party seeks to achieve certain goals, regardless of the impact on the parties to the conflict, he or she competes to dominate. These win–lose struggles often utilize the formal authority of a mutual superior as the dominant force, and the conflicting parties will each use his or her own power base to resolve a victory in his or her favour. It may be highly acrimonious and last for long periods of time, although this may be very costly for organizations and they frequently resort to other solutions (such as buying their competitors).
- *Collaboration*: Collaboration occurs when each of the parties in conflict really desires to satisfy fully the concerns of all parties, to cooperate and to search for a mutually beneficial outcome. The behaviour of the parties is aimed at solving the problem and at clarifying the differences rather than accommodating various points of view. The participants usually consider the full range of alternatives; the

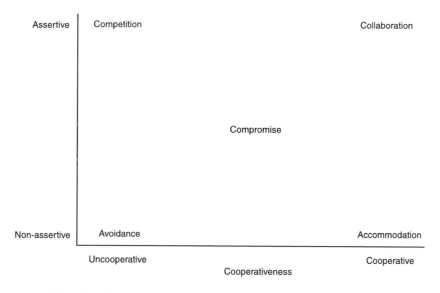

Figure 8.2 Dimensions of conflict-handling orientations. Reproduced from Thomas (1976) with the permission of John Wiley & Sons.

similarities and differences in viewpoint become more clearly focused; and the causes or differences become outwardly evident. Collaboration is often thought of as a win–win approach to resolving conflicts, although not everyone would agree with this.

- *Avoidance*: One party to the conflict may recognize that a conflict exists but may react by withdrawing, or by suppressing the conflict. The result is indifference or the desire to evade overt demonstration of a disagreement. The parties may prefer physical separation and maintain a territory that is distinct from the others. If withdrawal is not possible or desired, the parties may deny their differences. When group members are required to interact because of the interdependence of their tasks, suppression is a more probable outcome than withdrawal. Sometimes companies split as a way of avoiding conflict.
- *Accommodation*: When the parties seek to appease their opponents, they may be willing to place their opponents' interests above their own. To maintain the relationship, one party is willing to be self-sacrificing or accommodating. This should not necessarily be seen as a sign of weakness. It should also not always be taken at face value.
- *Compromise*: When each party to the conflict must give up something, sharing occurs, resulting in a compromise where there is no clear winner or loser. Thus, there is a rationing of the object of the conflict or, where the object is not divisible, one rewards the other by yielding something of a substitute value. In negotiations, compromise is usually required to reach a settlement and agree upon a labour contract (Thomas, 1976).

This two-dimensional picture of conflict handling based on assertiveness and cooperation is clearly a useful way to categorize various ways of handling conflict. However, it is not the only way to describe or categorize different responses to conflict, nor has it received detailed empirical support. Although models such as this provide a very promising start, they should not be seen as anything more than simple taxonomies. For instance, there may be many different types of collaboration, some nearer compromise and some nearer accommodation. Similarly, rather than have cooperativeness as a dimension and competitiveness as an orientation, it may be interesting to reverse the two and see what new pattern arises.

Stage IV: outcomes

Overt conflict behaviour and attempts at successful conflict-handling result in specific consequences. As Figure 8.1 demonstrates, they may be functional in that the conflict has resulted in an improvement in the group's performance. Conversely, group performance may be hindered and the outcome then would be dysfunctional. Properly managed, moderate amounts of conflict can be beneficial to the organization. The benefits of functional conflict include:

- emergence of talented individuals;
- need satisfaction for particular individuals;
- innovation and change to solve the problem;
- relief of boredom;
- uncovering of new ways of understanding issues;
- re-establishment of harmonious relations.

Too much or too intense conflict can be harmful to individuals and organizations. The consequences of dysfunctional conflict include:

- massive waste of time;
- demonstrations of self-interest;
- emotional and physical damage to people;
- diversion of efforts away from production goals;
- high financial and emotional costs;
- excessive fatigue to individuals and groups.

Conflict can increase group performance, not where there is open or violent aggression, but there are instances where it is possible to imagine how low or moderate levels of conflict could improve the effectiveness of a group. Further conflict is constructive when it improves the quality (and quantity) of decisions, stimulates creativity and innovation, encourages interest and curiosity among group members, provides the medium through which problems can be aired and tensions released, and fosters an environment in favour of self-evaluation and change. The evidence suggests that conflict can improve the quality of decision-making by allowing *all* views, particularly the ones that are unusual or held by a minority, to be weighed in important decisions. Conflict can be an antidote for "group think" (see Chapter 10). It does not allow the group to "rubber stamp" decisions that may be based on weak assumptions or inadequate consideration of relevant alternatives. Conflict challenges the *status quo* and therefore furthers the creation of new ideas, promotes reassessment of group goals and activities, and increases the probability that the group will respond to change.

Yet uncontrolled opposition breeds discontent, which acts to dissolve common ties, and eventually leads to destruction of the group. Dysfunctional varieties of conflict can reduce group effectiveness: retarding of communication, reductions in group cohesiveness, and subordination of group goals to the primacy of infighting among members. At the extreme, conflict can bring group functioning to a halt and potentially threaten the group's survival. Poor customer relations and rumour-making are common organizational symptoms to dysfunction conflict.

The secret, of course, is to maintain conflict at a type and level, such that it leads to functional as opposed to dysfunctional outcomes. In this sense, healthy, fun-orientated competitiveness may be the positive side of conflict that organizations should strive to achieve. Indeed, some organizations attempt extracurricular competitiveness by having sporting or other contests aimed at awakening the competitive spirit of the employees.

Loss of equilibrium within a group may occur because of a variety of behaviours that lead to communication blockages and distortions and thence to conflict. Some of these behaviours are more often destructive than constructive. They include:

- *Restricting information*: A member of the group implies he or she knows the answer to a group problem, but is not telling. Often, employees believe erroneously that crucial information affecting them is actually hidden from them. Although this may not be true, it certainly can lead to serious problems if it does occur.
- *Dissimulation*: Deliberate distortion of the facts to preserve a position in the group. There are of course many sorts of lies, including white lies, bare-faced lies and partial lies.

- *Pairing and dividing*: Pairing involves breaking into subgroups rather than solving the conflict as a group coalition – that is, giving different groups different information so that none has a full picture.
- *Put-downs (and open rudeness)*: The put-down of others, through verbal or physical aggression, may maintain the structure of the group. Self-put-downs may get sympathy and diffuse the opposition – the "poor me" game. Put-downs are often seen in the nicknames groups have for themselves and each other.
- *Fights*: Win–lose conflicts (verbal and economic rather than physical) which are difficult to resolve.
- *Flights* Running away, sometimes actually leaving the group. More frequently, "sulking" behaviour and withdrawal.
- *Making (white, random, but always distracting) noise*: Speaking to be heard rather than to contribute; filling silences without content.
- *Suppressing emotions*: Rather than letting the emotional blockages out, the person demands logic, rationality. This is unfortunate, as much of the blockage is emotional and *should* be expressed.
- *Changing the topic*: Changing the focus from one topic to another, or from one person to another.

There are many other variations on these tactics. People learn to use the tactics which work for them. Hence, the person who uses the sulk response will continue to use it because it has been successful in the past. These behaviours may be both a cause and a consequence of conflict.

Figure 8.3 illustrates the curvilinear or optimal theory of conflict idea. Too little conflict (competition) and organizations may become self-satisfied and complacent. Too much competition, with all the energy and emotion dedicated to "fighting", may mean that the overall productivity and performance of the organization decline. Not everyone would agree with this model, some preferring to see the relationship between conflict and performance as linear. Although the optimal level hypothesis is appealing, it does not inform us how the optimal level is attained or sustained. Nor does it specify whether this optimum is the same within various groups or organizations, or differs over time as a function of external factors.

Causes of conflict

Conflict may prevent members from "seeing", understanding or even tackling the task at hand (i.e. the major goal of the organization). It can dislocate the entire group and produce polarizations, factions and mutually distrusting groups. In certain instances, extreme interpersonal and inter-unit conflict may subvert the appropriate objectives in favour of less relevant subgoals, and lead people to use defensive and blocking behaviour in their group. Often, the major problem, observable to an outsider, is that conflict stimulates a win–lose situation, where reason is secondary to emotion and the ultimate loser is the organization as a whole.

There are many reasons why conflicts develop in, and among, workgroups, as well as between individuals. Some of the more important reasons relate to problems of communication, basic differences in values and influence processes, and a lack of shared perceptions and attitudes. As organizations grow larger, horizontal (lateral) and vertical specializations become necessary and effective communication becomes more

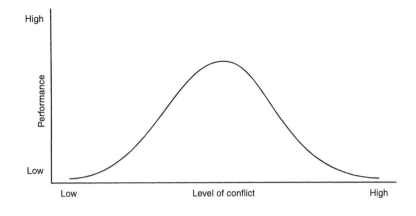

Situation	Level of conflict	Type of conflict	Unit's internal characteristics	Unit performance outcome
A	Low or none	Dysfunctional	Apathetic Stagnant Non-responsive to change Lack of new ideas	Low
B	Optimal	Functional	Viable Self-critical Innovative	High
C	High	Dysfunctional	Disruptive Chaotic Uncooperative	Low

Figure 8.3 Conflict and unit performance. Reproduced from Robbins (1991) with the permission of Prentice-Hall, Inc.

difficult. With more units at every organization level, the differences in the goals and interests among groups are accentuated. Even if organizations are delayered and remain flat, the fact that unit size increases so much means intra- rather than inter-unit communication becomes the problem. As a result, the members of one group will tend to have incorrect attitudes about, and perceptions of, the mission and proper functions of other groups.

   Typical organizational causes of conflict include:

- *Mutually dependent tasks*: When two groups depend on each other to achieve their goals, they may try harder to cooperate. However, if their efforts fail, the conflict can be more intense because of the unwanted dependency.
- *Imbalance in task dependency*: When group A is dependent on group B, but B is not dependent on A, conflict may result.
- *Criteria of performance*: When one group is responsible for only one aspect of an entire process, conflict frequently occurs. For example, production departments may prefer to produce at the same rate all year to avoid seasonal lay-offs. Inventory control, on the other hand, may prefer irregular rates of output based on demand,

so as to minimize inventory carrying costs. The needs of one group may be dramatically opposed to those of another.

- *Environmental variations*: When different units in the same organization use different procedures to deal with different environments, conflict is likely. Radical procedural differences between the two groups that have different customers can cause resentment and loss of morale.
- *Resource dependency*: When two groups depend on the same resources, such as space and equipment, conflicts will probably occur unless priorities are carefully specified. Generally speaking, the more fixed the resources in terms of size, and the more the parties compete for them, the more intense will be the conflict.
- *Special training*: When groups from different disciplines meet – marketing, accounting, engineering – one often finds stereotyping, misunderstanding and conflict because of the use of jargon and the tendency to perceive problems from one point of view.

Structural solutions

To improve inter-group and inter-organizational relations, greater integration or collaboration among groups must occur. Structural strategies and solutions can effectively increase integration. They differ from *process* strategies in that they call for a change in the organization's formal reporting relationships – its structure – rather than a change in individuals' interpersonal behaviour. Structural strategies may require adding at least one of the following formal managerial mechanisms to the problem situation:

- *Hierarchy*: Providing a common superior who is arbitrator, peacemaker, and still eager to coordinate the work of two interacting groups.
- *Plans*: Blueprints to direct the activities of interacting groups while minimizing their interaction; having fewer meetings while getting on with the job is essentially the aim. By using plans, even the integration of geographically distant groups can be effective. The use of common or superordinate goals can have an influence similar to plans; they can refocus the efforts of conflicting groups and can re-arrange group boundaries.
- *Linking roles*: Individuals in informal positions to act as conduits between interacting groups, to improve communication by resolving issues lower in the hierarchy; this is the same as the first solution, but at a lower level, and informally as opposed to formally.
- *Task forces*: Specially convened groups of representatives from all parties to work on problems faced by the interacting groups. Task forces integrate perspectives and defuse conflict by presenting the ideas of their group to the others' representatives. They are mediators and advocates of the organization as a whole.
- *Integrating roles or units*: Analogous to the informal linking role, a permanent coordinating individual or group of people to act as an interface between interacting groups. A project or product manager, for example, coordinates the decisions of such interdependent groups as sales representatives, R&D engineers and the production line.
- *Matrix organization*: A popular organizational design, integrating both functional departments and project groups through a dual authority and reporting system.

This idea goes in and out of fashion, and immense conflict can be caused by attempting to change a non-matrix organization into a matrix organization.

Each of these solutions attempts to be organizational and structural rather than process-orientated. That is, rather than focusing on interpersonal or inter-group relations and process, this approach focuses on the explicit structure of the organization, often seen in the organization chart. Some theorists believe that structure influences process, so this is the phenomenon to concentrate on. Others believe that influence and the political processes that are at the heart of conflict are not closely linked to structure and may be manipulated directly to solve problems.

Conflict management

Organizational conflict may be manifested in argument, competition, non-cooperation and even deliberate sabotage. As previously noted, arguments and competition may be beneficial (and not require management) because:

- arguments may be a didactic method of teaching and airing different views, as long as they are not trite, circular and destructive;
- competition sets and raises standards and may "sort" successful from less successful contributors;
- competition stimulates, focuses and channels energies in the best direction. People become more task-centred, loyal to and identify with their particular group.

But for competition to be productive within or between groups, at least three conditions have to be met. First, it has to be perceived as genuinely open, which in fact yields a paradox: open competition leads to healthy collaborative competition, but, without collaborative attitudes to begin with, it is unlikely to occur. Secondly, there need to be explicit, fair and adequate rules and procedures for dealing with competition. Thirdly, the outcomes of competition (success and failure) must result from, and therefore be under the control of, the participants and not rely on chance.

In essence, then, conflict is the simultaneous arousal of two or more incompatible motives or demands. It may also be considered as a process in which one or both sides in a dispute (individuals, workgroups or organizations) intentionally interfere in the efforts of the other side, or at least benchmarks them to achieve an objective. People in conflict usually experience tension, anxiety and frustration. Individuals with high frustration tolerance generally use effective coping methods to deal with frustration, including compensation (finding a substitute goal for the one that is blocked). On the other hand, people with low frustration tolerance usually respond to frustration with anger, verbal and physical aggression, or counterproductive defensive behaviour.

Process consultants are sometimes called into organizations to reduce (even eliminate) conflict. Nearly always psychotherapeutically trained, they believe, along with psychoanalysts, that much of the conflict is symbolic of deeper issues. Through a wide variety of techniques, including focus groups, they aim to surface and make more explicit the causes of conflict and the pain they are causing. They are often interesting, because many of the causes specified are counter-intuitive and not what management expects. The process consultant's intervention is nearly always cathartic in the sense that they encourage the discharge of pent-up feelings, so much so that most parties feel better afterwards, although it is unclear how long that lasts.

Power and influence in organizations

Power is the potential to influence others: it is the capacity to have a desired attitudinal or behavioural effect on others. It stems from two sources: *personal* and *positional*. Individuals have power based on their abilities, expertise and knowledge. Some have *charismatic power* based on their magnetic and alluring personality. Others have *expert power* because of their knowledge. When people defer, or continually refer, to others before behaving, this is called *referent power*. But jobs offer positional power which is the influence that comes with the office. Thus they have *legitimate power* in their authorization to do certain things. Most have the power to reward or punish (known as *coercive power*). Most people in business have *informational power*: to spread without, leak or distort information.

One of the most popular concepts of the last decade has been *empowerment*. This is essentially the process that attempts to give employees more autonomy at work. Power is given to the workers: workgroups are encouraged to find their own solutions to problems and to work in ways they feel beneficial and productive. Managers set targets: empowered workgroups find ways of achieving them. While there are many stories of success, there are also incidences of rejection and failure. Some managers do not like relinquishing power and control, while some workers do not like the accountability and responsibility that is inevitably part of the process.

Both individuals and groups have power (Greenberg & Baron, 2003). That group power can be a function of various things. For instance, power is a function of the *control of resources*. The more important and desirable the resources (space, technology, budgets) a group has, the more power it wields. Groups also have *strategic power*: they occupy a central position/role in decision making; they appear indispensable; and they influence higher level decisions.

Power in organizations is not always easy to discuss or research. Power, politics and influence are all closely associated with each other. Managers attempt to influence their staff via many techniques and they themselves are the targets of influence from their superiors. Their power may be positional power that comes with the office or personal power that comes with their charm, persuasibility and expertise. Those who have power deny that they do; many people seek it but pretend not to; and those who have achieved it are secretive about their methods. As Hosking & Morley (1991) point out, power is not a fixed structural characteristic or the property of any one individual or group. Power is produced in some relationships and not others. People have quite different power bases, depending on their particular resources (money, information, allies) *and* how much they are valued by others.

Where does power come from? What bestows power on an individual, group or organization? Early researchers were interested in categorizing the bases and sources of power (French & Raven, 1959). They talked about *reward* and *coercive* power (the ability to mobilize positive or negatively valued outcomes), *legitimate* power (which is determined by the culture values in particular contexts), *referent* power (the power of an individual or group to achieve conformity to group norms), *expert* power (which is usually informational power) and *position* power (which comes from a manager's position in a particular network of relationships). The *bases* of power refer to what the holder has that gives the individual or group its knowledge or the power to reward or punish. The *sources* of power refer to where the holder derives the power base, such as personality or position.

Essentially, the greater A's dependency on B, the greater power the latter has over the former. Dependency is inversely proportional to alternative sources of supply – if everyone is educated, education gives you no special advantage or power. Power over others, or their dependency on you, is a function of three aspects of control:

- *Importance*: The thing(s) one controls must be seen as important. Thus, because people and organizations do not like uncertainty, individuals who reduce it have power. Thus, during industrial unrest, the human resources negotiators have increased power.
- *Scarcity*: Any reserve that is plentiful is cheap. Because knowledge is power, it explains why certain groups refuse to share or pass on their knowledge.
- *Non-substitutability*: The source of power is unique and cannot be replaced by something else.

Although power involves the formal capacity of the *control* of "others" in the organization, influence may be defined as an attempt to *persuade* another to behave as desired. Influence may be regarded as a form of control, if it is successful.

Kipnis, Schmitt, Swaffer-Smith & Wilkinson (1984) asked managers the sort of strategies they used often, and they found a range of identifiable strategies. Different strategies require different resources and have different consequences (Hosking & Morley, 1991). First, there is *push and pull*: this involves the threat of force, the withdrawal of resources and other coercive measures. Blocking support, using sanctions such as loss of promotion and perks, and assertiveness, such as setting deadlines and enforcing rules, all come under push strategies. These strategies are more acceptable in some corporate cultures than others. Secondly, *persuasion*: this is the use of argument, evidence and facts to bargain or reason with others. Whereas most managers like to believe this is the most preferred strategy, there is no evidence that it is. Thirdly, *preventive*: these are really non-decision-making strategies aimed at keeping people out of the decision-making process. Finally, *preparatory*: these are coalition-building strategies aimed at securing the help and support of others.

Yukl & Fable (1993) have identified eight major tactics of social influence, outlined in Table 8.1 and ranked in terms of frequency of use. A notable feature of this taxonomy of influence techniques is that there is little differentiation in the tactics used by peers, subordinates or bosses.

Estimating the choice of tactic to be used is influenced by the context of the situation and the characteristics of the person one is trying to influence. It has, for example, been noted that upward appeals and integration were used more frequently when the boss was perceived as highly authoritarian, whereas rational persuasion was used more frequently when the boss was perceived as highly participative. Clearly, many factors are involved in determining which and when particular social influence tactics are chosen. These include the culture and history of the organization, the ability and personality of those attempting to influence as well as those being influenced, and the particular circumstances requiring that the influence takes place.

Power has also been categorized into various subunits identified by French & Raven (1959). Yukl (1981) reviewed 11 field studies that compared the effectiveness of the

Table 8.1 Tactics of social influence

Rank	Tactic	Description
1.	Consultation	Asking for participation in decision-making or planning a change.
2.	Rational persuasion	Using logical arguments and facts to persuade another that desired result will occur.
3.	Inspiration aspects	Arousing enthusiasm by appealing to one's values and ideals.
4.	Ingratiation	Getting someone to do what you want by putting him/her into a good mood or getting him/her to like you.
5.	Coalition	Persuading by seeking the assistance of others or by noting the support of others.
6.	Pressure	Seeking compliance by using demands, threats or intimidation.
7.	Upward appeals	Noting that the influence request is approved by higher management.
8.	Exchange	Promising some benefit in exchange for complying with a request.

Source: Reproduced from Yukl & Fable (1993) with the permission of the American Psychological Association.

French & Raven power categories, and concluded that referent and expert power were more commonly associated with positive results. He also presented a list of recommended strategies for the effective use of other power bases as well. A brief summary is provided in Box 8.1.

Yukl and Fable have since compacted these power bases into two underlying dimensions – position and personal power. Under these two dimensions are additional power bases as illustrated in Figure 8.4. The bases should not be thought of as mutually exclusive – often they are used together, with some bases more compatible together than others (e.g. expert and legitimate power). Yukl & Fable (1993) have recently investigated the differences in choice of tactics to use with subordinates, peers and superiors (directional differences), and which tactics are used. They also looked at tactic

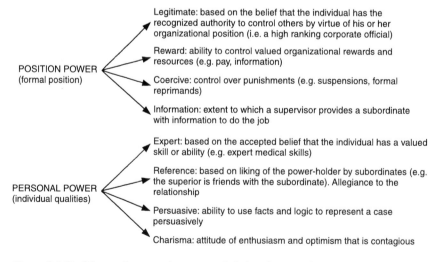

Figure 8.4 Position and personal power and their subcategories.

Box 8.1 Recommended strategies for the effective use of power

Expert power
1. *Promote an image of expertise:* Make sure that people are aware of your special skills and training. Avoid projects with a low probability of success, especially when starting out.
2. *Maintain credibility:* Avoid careless statements. Do not lie to subordinates.
3. *Act confident and decisive in a crisis:* Never express doubts or appear confused.
4. *Keep informed:* Technical knowledge is the basis for expert power.
5. *Recognize subordinate concerns:* Expertise that is irrelevant to the needs of the workers will not be effective.
6. *Avoid threatening the self-esteem of subordinates:* Do not use expertise to make subordinates feel ignorant.

Legitimate power
1. *Make polite requests:* Do not emphasize status differences by being rude.
2. *Make requests in a confident tone:* Enthusiasm implies that the request is important.
3. *Make clear requests and check for comprehension:* If subordinates don't understand what is requested, all the legitimate power in the world won't help.
4. *Make sure that requests appear legitimate:* The supervisor's authority to make a request should be clear.
5. *Explain the reason for the request:* Do not assume that the logic for a decision is obvious.
6. *Follow the proper channels:* Do not rely upon subordinates to implement your orders.
7. *Exercise authority regularly:* Frequent requests enhance legitimacy.
8. *Insist on compliance and check to verify it:* Non-compliance will undermine authority.
9. *Be responsive to subordinate concerns:* Understand the reasons for non-compliance.

Reward power
1. *Be sure compliance can be verified:* Rewards cannot be administered if compliance cannot be checked.
2. *Be sure the request is feasible:* Subordinates will not comply if the request seems impossible.
3. *Be sure the incentive is attractive:* A reward is not a reward unless the subordinate desires it.
4. *Be sure that the leader is a credible source of the reward:* Subordinates must believe that the leader can deliver the reward.
5. *Be sure that the request is proper and ethical:* Rewards should not be perceived as bribes.

Coercive power
1. *Inform subordinates about rules and penalties for violations:* It is unfair to punish workers who are unaware of the rules.
2. *Administer discipline consistently and promptly:* Failure to act can encourage further disobedience.
3. *Provide sufficient warning before resorting to punishment:* Indicate what is expected and give subordinates a chance to learn from their mistakes.
4. *Get the facts before using reprimands or punishment:* Wrongful punishment will undermine respect for the manager's authority.
5. *Stay calm and avoid appearing hostile:* Managers who lose their tempers risk making the problem worse.
6. *Maintain credibility:* Follow through with punishments, but do not threaten to use punishment beyond your authority.
7. *Use appropriate punishment:* Actions should be consistent with policy and rules, as well as with the severity of the infraction.
8. *Administer warnings and punishments in private:* Embarrassing a subordinate in public could lead to resentment and retaliation.

Source: Adapted from Yukl (1981: 47–58). with the permission of Prentice-Hall, Inc.

Box 8.2 Summary of Yukl & Fable's results

1. The majority of influence attempts consist of weak forms of rational persuasion. Although used more frequently in upward influence attempts, rational persuasion was also used frequently in downward and lateral directions.
2. Ingratiation techniques and personal appeals are used more frequently in initial influence attempts with exchange, whereas legitimating tactics were used more in immediate follow-up attempts. Ingratiation was used most frequently in initial influence attempts with subordinates or peers, often in combination with another tactic.
3. Coalition and pressure tactics appear to be used most often in delayed follow-up attempts.
4. Inspirational tactics are employed most frequently with subordinates, usually in combination with another tactic such as rational persuasion, consultation or ingratiation.
5. Consultation was used most frequently with subordinates or peers and usually combined with another tactic such as rational persuasion, inspirational appeals or ingratiation.
6. Personal appeals are used most often in initial influence attempts with peers.
7. Exchange is used most often in immediate follow-up attempts with subordinates and peers.
8. A legitimate tactic is most often used with immediate follow-up, typically with rational persuasion or pressure, with coalition being most often used as a follow-up with the target most frequently being a peer or superior.

combinations and differences in the choice of tactics for successive influence attempts made with the same target person (sequencing differences).

The underlying assumption is that most managers will prefer to use tactics that are: socially acceptable and feasible in terms of the agent's position and personal power in relation to the target; not costly in terms of time, effort, loss of resources, or alienation of the target; and likely to be effective for a particular objective – given the anticipated level of resistance of the target. Some tactics are easier to use in a particular direction, because the agent's authority and position power are greater in that direction or because their use is consistent with role expectations. A summary of the patterns of results found by Yukl and Fable is presented in Box 8.2.

It should be borne in mind that these are generalizations from a single study – one should not ignore the fact that the process of influence is a dynamic one and it is seldom an isolated episode but part of an evolving and reciprocal relationship. The situation is further complicated by the fact that individuals in an organization may wield different types of power (e.g. a new manager will lack the expert power of a longstanding secretary, yet will have the whip hand in terms of position power). In such a case, it would be unwise for the manager to use coercive tactics. Effective managers have been shown to be the ones that use appropriate tactics in appropriate situations.

Organizational politics

Organizational politics may be categorized as actions not officially sanctioned by an organization undertaken to influence others and to meet one's personal goals. They are often seen as immoral, devious and counter-productive. Political action may occur under the following conditions:

- Where uncertainty exists (e.g. where should resources be used?). That is, where there are no clear explicit rules as to how to behave.
- Where important decisions have to be made that involve large amounts of scarce resources.
- Where organizational units have conflicting interests, and no open and agreed way of resolving these interests.
- Where organizational units have approximately equal power. However, it may well be that power involves the exploitation of symmetries. Indeed, power politics applies when one party has all the power and does not need to use other tactics.

McKenna (2000) lists nine organizational factors that cause "political behaviour": ambiguous goals, changes in organizational structure, scarce resources, changes in technology and the business environment, too many non-programmed decisions, low trust, role ambiguity, unclear performance evaluation and a win–lose organizational attitude.

Mintzberg (1983) has categorized various political games that may occur under such circumstances. These are outlined in Table 8.2. However, to call these games might lead to misinterpretations. Political processes are not a game; they are serious activities of networking, negotiation and influence, pursued by all managers.

Wolfe (1988) has maintained that typical managerial values are inculcated in such a way as to undermine integrity. He has identified the following ways of thinking, which have become common practice in some organizations:

- *Bottom-line mentality*: the belief that a financial success is the only thing worthy of consideration. Short-term solutions, which are immediately financially sound, are therefore promoted at the expense of later problems. Such thinking engenders the unrealistic belief that everything may be reduced to money.
- *Exploitative mentality*: using people in a way that promotes stereotypes and undermines empathy and compassion; the sacrifice of concern for others in favour of one's own immediate interests.

Table 8.2 Mintzberg's categorization of political games

Games	Typical major levels	Purpose
Authority games		
Insurgency	Lower-level managers	To resist formal authority.
Counterinsurgency	Upper-level managers	To counter resistance to formal authority.
Power base games		
Sponsorship	Any subordinate	To enhance base of power with superiors.
Alliance	Line managers	To enhance base of power with subordinates.
Empire building	Line managers	To enhance base of power with subordinates.
Rivalry games		
Line versus staff	Line managers and staff personnel	To defeat each other in the quest for power.
Rival camps	Any groups at the same level	To defeat each other in the quest for power.
Change games		
Whistle blowing	Low-level managers	To seize control over the organization.

Source: Reproduced from Mintzberg (1983) with the permission of Prentice-Hall, Inc.

- *Spin doctor mentality*: the belief that anything is right if the public can be made to believe that it is right.

From the point of view of efficiency and economy, these values are rarely beneficial to the organization and may lead to excessive political behaviour. Often, a new attitude to management and influence is required – one that relies on the mutual benefits of all concerned, that decentralizes authority and allows all individuals in the system a greater degree of autonomy, opportunity for growth and the expression of individual skills.

McKenna (2000) has listed common techniques or tactics to promote political interests in the organization. They are:

- Control information: in effect, restrict it to certain parties.
- Control lines of communication: put in place gatekeepers to restrict access.
- Use outside experts: consultants may seem neutral but are paid and directed by management and "do their bidding".
- Control the agenda: ensure only certain things are discussed.
- Game playing: leaking information, getting friends only to give feedback, etc.
- Image building: have "spin doctors" to project the desirable image.
- Building coalitions: befriend powerful others or start small "cells" with specific aims.
- Controlling decision parameters: this is pre-decision work, trying to influence the decision before it happens.
- Eliminate a political rival: paradoxically by getting them promoted out of harms way.
- Security: a more powerful job for oneself.

Greenberg & Baron (2003) assert that personal characteristics of individual managers (ambition, machiavellism, popularity) and organizational factors (ambiguous roles and goals, scarce resources, centralization and complexity) lead to political tactics. These include trying to control information, building powerful coalitions, associating with powerful others and attracting others. They recommend four suggestions for combating organizational politics: clarifying job expectations, open the communications process, be a good role model, and confront those being inefficient, unethical or irresponsible.

Political process is an inevitable part of organizational life. Hosking & Morley (1991) argue that people at work differ in their opportunity to influence others and processes, so are different in the way they can, and do, protect and promote their interests. These influence-processes certainly make collective action possible and may help or hinder productivity. The processes of networking, negotiation, influence and exchange are often called office politics. Through understanding the nature of power, some managers are clearly more successful than others at promoting their particular projects. However, political skill depends on context: the personality of individuals, their understanding of relationships and how the organization accepts the use of particular strategies.

Office politics are a function of both individual employees and the culture or context of the organization. Some corporate cultures sanction and indeed promote certain types of political processes. Political processes occur simply because organizations as a whole do not have unitary goals. Partisan interests lead to influence and political processes. A plurality of interests means that certain groups become committed to particular ideas, values or outcomes, which they seek to implement or promote by particular processes.

Hosking & Morley (1991) maintain that political issues can openly be understood in the wider context if one appreciates several factors:

- The values of individuals and organizations: "The processes of political decision-making are processes in which persons and groups more or less collectively create and mobilize value to achieve influence" (p. 127). This can often be seen in mission statements.
- The extent to which, and in what ways, the change constitutes an "issue" to all parties concerned.

They believe that organizational politics have focused too much on political structures and not political processes. However, other approaches have looked at political behaviour within organizations. Farrell & Peterson (1982) stress that there are three dimensions in which to describe this organizational, political behaviour:

- *Internal/external dimension*: external factors include the media, competitive (collaborative) organizations, legal bodies, etc.; internal approaches include exchange of favours, blocking votes, etc.
- *Vertical/lateral* dimension: this refers to whether the political process is aimed at supervisors or subordinates (vertically) or to groups of similar status and level (laterally).
- *Legitimate/illegitimate* dimension: this suggests that legitimate means follow authority structures and sanction procedures, whereas illegitimate ones do not.

Hosking & Morley (1991) are strongly against the last dimension. They argue that organizing is intrinsically political. The way managers build, maintain, mobilize and exploit relationships, deal with power and focus openly on certain activities but not others is clearly political, and clearly what everyone needs to do. All negotiation, influence and networking is therefore political activity. They believe that to understand organizational politics in its widest form, one needs to shift attention from structures and formal authority to relational processes and social influences. Others believe the more negative features of political behaviour can be dealt with by more open communication, senior managers setting good examples, giving clear targets and feedback on them, attempting to eliminate coalitions and cliques, and by confronting those who play political games.

Group power

It is important to recognize that power is not exclusive to individuals; organizational politics and power relationships may also occur in groups and subunits. Companies often rely on different units to control different aspects of the same business – finance, human resource management, market research. The amount of dependence between units and the relative importance of each will dictate the proportional power of each group. Two models have been developed to explain how certain groups come to acquire different levels of power:

- *The resource dependency model: controlling critical resources.* An organization may be described as a complex set of subunits constantly exchanging resources with each other (i.e. money, personnel, equipment); hence there is a degree of dependency between the units. Each form and degree of the dependency may be said to represent a form of power over the other unit. Therefore, units with more resources and more vital resources carry heavier weight in terms of power. This imbalance will lead to resource asymmetries. Similarly, the more one unit depends on another, the less power it has. Two factors will influence which unit will come to control the most important resources: the period within which the company was formed (i.e. what elements were most important at the beginning of the formation of the company) and the background characteristics of the entrepreneur starting the company (i.e. the particular product or service that the organization provides as dictated by the entrepreneur will in part determine where the heaviest weight will come in terms of resource allocation).

- *The strategic contingencies model: power through dependence.* To the extent that a department is able to control the relative power of various organizational subunits by virtue of its actions, it is said to have control over strategic contingencies. Lawrence & Lersch (1967) found that power was distributed in different departments in different industries – in successful firms, strategic contingencies were controlled by the departments that were most important for organizational success. For instance, in the food-processing industry where it was critical for new products to be developed and sold, successful firms had strategic contingencies controlled by R&D departments. The factors that give subunits control over such contingencies are outlined in Figure 8.5.

Fiorelli (1988) investigated power within workgroups and noted how some misuses of power may be disruptive to interdisciplinary groups, retarding work productivity. The study setting was a 142-bed urban rehabilitation hospital. Fiorelli found that professional expertise (e.g. group expert power) was not significantly related to participation. Hence, many workgroups labelled "interdisciplinary teams" may be functioning more like "multidisciplinary teams", without the synergy, commonality of purpose and common problem-solving one would associate with the former approach. Moreover,

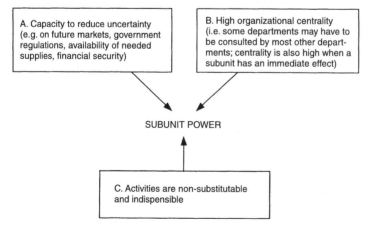

Figure 8.5 Factors determining control in subunits.

some treatment decisions were also overwhelmingly influenced by one discipline, highlighted by the fact that power within the teams was not evenly distributed. This is likely to be an ineffective process, in that skills within parts of the group may be being neglected to the detriment of decision-making procedures.

It is evident, then, that autocratic decision-making is not an efficient mode of operation when a group is striving towards a "shared approach" to problem-solving. Hence, influence techniques should be limited to rational persuasion rather than legitimate power, since productivity was positively related to democratic decision-making. The other power-type positively related to team productivity was expert power and reward, and coercive power had detrimental effects, raising some concern for interdisciplinary groups motivated by rewards and punishments. Meaningful participation is obviously better than the traditional "stick" or "carrot" approach. Thus, although the traditional approach to management has been autocratic, investigators now realize the value and efficiency of empowerment techniques that are designed to increase participation, autonomy and self-management.

Under decentralized empowerment management schemes, workers are typically organized into teams on the basis of relatively complete task functions (assigning tasks, solving quality problems and selecting, training and counselling fellow team members). Some of the most successful companies have adopted the empowerment system to good effect – General Motors, Procter & Gamble, Tektronix and General Electric. Such companies boast higher productivity, better attendance, less turnover, and improvements in both product quality and the quality of work for employees.

For such decentralized companies to be self-perpetuating, one must be clear of the most effective techniques and attitudes towards influencing and empowering new employees. This seeming total lack of structure may be endemic to most managers and, indeed, may be too radical a change to accommodate too quickly. However, even in more traditional organizations, changing attitudes towards management from control, order and compliance to actions that enable individuals to contribute more fully, productively and with less alienation, is worthy of some close consideration.

Because of differences in the way that different individuals will perceive the same behaviour, the appropriateness of the influencing technique is likely to be problematic, unless one is able to understand what is important to the person to be influenced. Different writers therefore suggest the following maxims to increase the efficaciousness of the exchange and hence the successfulness of the process of influence:

- Think about the person to be influenced as a potential ally, not an adversary; the goal is to find areas of mutual benefit and develop trusting, sustainable relationships.
- Know the world of the potential ally, including the pressures as well as the person's needs and goals – a prerequisite for an understanding of the ally is an understanding of his or her context. Many factors can adumbrate this perception, such as the frustration of meeting resistance (i.e. the desire to influence may be so strong that inappropriate strategies may be repeated, resulting in increased belligerence on the part of the target). Similarly, there is often a tendency to stereotype individuals who are not compliant with one's personal desires. Such stereotypes usually conceal more than they reveal. Stereotypes are often formed through the perceiver's lack of ability to appreciate the organizational forces acting on the target (and not just his or her personality). Resistance may not be down to personality or

inflexibility but to factors such as daily time demands, the amount of contact that the person has with customers, suppliers and other outsiders, the organization's information flow (or lack of it), the style of the potential ally's boss, the beliefs and assumptions held by that person's co-workers, and so forth. Although manipulating these factors may be beyond the ability of the influencer, an understanding of them will aid in the framing of the request.

- Be aware of key goals and available resources that may be valued by the potential ally. Influencers often underestimate the range of currencies available to them (most frequently lower-level employees who are not open to the range of possible currencies that they possess).
- Understand the exchange transaction itself so that win–win outcomes are achieved. Reciprocal transactions and mutual gain should be viewed as the target for the influencer, in terms of both increasing the probability of the effectiveness of the influence strategy to be employed and setting the scene for future successful transactions. Secondly, although it may be anathema to admit to being incorrect (particularly from a manager's point of view), a stubborn clinging to an ineffective idea, transaction or influence strategy can be damaging to both short- and long-term patterns of organizational relationships. Although plans often build their own momentum and are illustrative of clear focus, one should not find oneself in a position of irrational commitment through personal bias. Similarly, one should be cognizant of the law of diminishing returns through overuse of previously successful influencing strategies. Just because one strategy may be successful with one target, it may not be successful with another, or even over time with the same target – it is intuitively obvious that a broader repertoire of strategies is likely to increase the influencing power of the individual.

One should view the relationship between parties as being important, both in terms of the immediate effect of the successfulness of the transaction and in terms of establishing trust for the future.

The central tenet in the area of influence and power was that hierarchical relationships based on coercive and compliant management-dominant relationships are unnecessarily restrictive, inefficient and are inhibitors of workers' creativity, involvement and motivation. Thus, influence tactics that highlight reciprocity and are founded on a mutual benefits system among peers, subordinates and managers are likely to inculcate a greater degree of autonomy, personal investment in the company and higher levels of motivation.

Business ethics

Business ethics is primarily about people at work resolving conflicting interests between different parties, such as customers, directors, employees, investors and suppliers. It is usually concerned with applying tests of fairness and integrity, which is essentially about rights, duties and a shared sense of moral values. Ethics are relative judgements: business ethics is a journey rather than a destination.

Two questions appear to dominate at the moment. First, why is business ethics so high on the business agenda? The answer seems to be the numerous headline financial scandals and the fact that consumers and investors appear to be losing trust in business people. People in business understand the importance and value of "reputational risk", which many see as higher than credit, market or operational risk. The second question – easy to ask, but difficult to answer – is do "ethical organizations" do better (make more money, are more stable) than a-ethical or non-ethical organizations? The data are weak and difficult to obtain and the vested interest in the answer too high. But there is research in support of the basic contention (Barnett & Schubert, 2002).

However, many do not fully understand that the application of business ethics is not just about the application of rules and being "legal". Indeed, it may be argued that excessive regulation and compliance undermines ethics because it stops people thinking for themselves. You cannot impose integrity. Ethics is what one thinks about before acting, not acting itself. For some (e.g. Barnett & Schubert, 2002), ethics is about a covenantal relationship between stakeholders that is based on mutual commitment and shared valued. It is a pledge to uphold mutual principles and ways of working. Furthermore, it imbues the whole organizational climate and culture.

Ideas about the concepts of corporate responsibility and business ethics have changed considerably over the last hundred years. The Depression, the Second World War, the consumer movements in the 1960s and the renewal of aggressive capitalism in the 1980s all influenced what individual workers and managers believed to be the social role, if any, of their organizations. There is now a considerable literature on business ethics. Thus there are concerns and learned papers on human resource ethics (Greenwood, 2002), marketing ethics (Brinkman, 2002) and the ethics associated with performance management systems (Kerssens-van Drongelen & Fisscher, 2003). New developments in science have led to new dilemmas, such as the ethics of genetic testing in the workplace (MacDonald & Williams-Jones, 2002).

For some, the concept of *caveat emptor* (let the buyer beware) was enough. It was, so many believed, the duty of companies to serve their shareholders, employees and customers by maximizing profits and staying within the law. But, over the past decade or so, for a variety of reasons, businessmen, academics and writers have been considering in more detail the relationship and responsibility between companies and society. As a result, the subdiscipline of business ethics has arisen. Its remit includes the following:

- Should a company place the interests of its shareholders before that of its employees or of the environment?
- Should a company be responsible for all the social consequences of its operations?
- When is regulation necessary, when excessive and when counter-productive?
- What does a corporation "owe" its employees?
- To what extent should an organization be accountable for its products?
- Is there an ethical difference between tax avoidance and tax evasion?
- Is the only social responsibility of business to maximize profits?

Brinkman (2002) argues that there are at least four distinguishable approaches to professional ethics. First, there is the *moral conflict* approach, which sees ethics as primarily a way to analyse, handle and prevent conflict by addressing or introducing a moral dimension to decision-making. The second is the *professional code* approach, which sees professional ethics as essentially a question of developing and implementing rule sets of desirable behaviour. The third is the *professional role morality* approach, which focuses on conflicting rights and duties between multiple parties at work. Finally, there is the *moral climate* approach, which stresses the collective conscience of the organization and the predominant ideology with respect to ethical behaviours. It is recognized that these approaches are indeed linked and that organizations will employ more than one at a time.

Researchers have tried to find universal moral standards which they may be able to use to develop robust international corporate codes of ethics. Schwartz (2002) believes it is possible to identify six universal moral standards: trustworthiness, respect, responsibility, fairness, caring and citizenship. Thus it is argued that it is possible to develop specific principles:

- be honest to stakeholders;
- stick to values despite financial loss;
- fulfil commitments;
- avoid conflicts of interest;
- respect the rights of others;
- take responsibility for actions;
- treat stakeholders fairly;
- avoid unnecessary harm;
- act benevolently;
- obey the law;
- protect the environment.

Similarly, others have attempted to develop ethical questionnaires for use not only in research, but also in applied settings (Shanahan & Hyman, 2003).

A radical alternative to the emphasis placed on business ethics was proposed by Friedman (1980). He argued that businesses should concentrate on producing goods and services efficiently and legally, in open and free competition and without deception and fraud, and that socio-ethical problems should be left to concerned individuals and government agencies. Indeed, as Hannafey (2003) has demonstrated, entrepreneurs face uniquely complex moral problems. Others argue that organizations and the business community do have some responsibility to act in what they see to be the interests of society and to pursue and advocate ethical positions.

The idea of corporate social responsibility goes back a long way. At the end of the nineteenth century, Carnegie in the USA, and Rowntree and Cadbury in the UK, took the idea of paternalistic responsibility for the workers and the immediate neighbourhood very seriously. Their ideas were based, in large part, on two principles:

- The *charity* principle – the need to assist the less fortunate, such as the elderly, handicapped, sick and unemployed (the deserving poor).
- The *stewardship* principle – the need for business organizations to act as caretakers of the land and people and to hold these in trust for the benefit of society.

To a certain extent, this constituted no more than the application of the old *noblesse oblige* maxim. By the middle of the twentieth century, these "ethical" principles were under attack by many critics of various persuasions, who argued the principles:

- were simply a capitalist smokescreen, hiding owners' profit and greed;
- simply reduce market efficiency;
- have only marginal impact and should be facilitated by other means;
- are quite simply too impractical, costly and ultimately unworkable;

- neither indicate the appropriate magnitude of social concern, nor have to weigh social against other responsibilities.

In the USA, criticisms of the ethics of social responsibility led to the development of corporate responsiveness. This is the idea that, if companies learn of a salient social problem, they should act upon it, and even be proactive rather than reactive. This idea was popular for some time but itself came under criticism. The major criticism was that this approach did not explain which values social responsiveness should try to encourage. That is, the ethical values and principles that dictated what a company should respond to were never fully explicated. This "new" principle did not specify how to effectively manage a conflict of values. Hence, the interest in business ethics, which may be defined as "the study of people's rights and duties at work and of the rules that are applied in business decisions".

Business ethics and practices are often culturally specific: what is thought of as desirable or acceptable in one culture may not be so in another. In an excellent comparative paper, Palazzo (2002) contrasted American and German business ethics. By examining basic assumption differences between the cultures based on religion and beliefs, Palazzo showed why people in the two countries have such different attitudes to ethics. Thus Americans from a dissenting Protestant tradition are individualistic, with a "doing" orientation and believe in pragmatic truth, whereas Germans from a Feudal Catholic or Lutherian tradition are collectivistic and believe in idealistic truth.

Business ethics questions apply at very different levels:

- At the *societal* level, questions concern the ethics of dealing with certain countries, the desirability of capitalism versus socialism, the role of government in the marketplace. At this level, the discourse is about societies and principles.
- At the *stakeholder* level, questions concern the employees, suppliers, customers, shareholders and those related to them. Ethical questions here are about the company's obligation to these various groups.
- At the *company policy* level, the questions concern all the company's rules and regulations, the ethical implications of lay-offs, perks, work rules, motivation, leadership, payment schemes, and so on.
- At the *personal* level, the ethical questions are about how people in the organization should and do behave towards each other.

Business ethics are concerned with values, rights, duties and rules. To a large extent, companies are interested in the definition and application of rules covering such things as keeping promises and mutual respect for persons and property. Many organizations even try to enshrine their ethics in the company mission statement.

Despite very clear attempts to spell out the principles by which the company or organization should operate, the problem of *relativism* remains – the problem that because we cannot decide on matters of right and wrong in a completely rational way, there will always be disagreement between different positions. Because all ethical decisions are personal, some argue that each individual has to work out their own moral code, which they have no right to impose on others. From this point of view, we cannot challenge the ethics of others, so long as they are sincerely held.

A more common and worrying argument is that of cultural relativism – that ethical codes and procedures are unique to particular cultures, societies and groups. Hence,

Box 8.3 Arguments for and against the social involvement of business

Arguments for social involvement of business
- Public needs have changed, leading to changed expectations. Business, it is suggested, received its charter from society and consequently has to respond to the needs of society.
- The creation of a better social environment benefits both society and business. Society gains through better neighbourhoods and employment opportunities; business benefits from a better community, since the community is the source of its workforce and the consumer of its products and services.
- Social involvement discourages additional government regulation and intervention. The result is greater freedom and more flexibility in decision-making for business.
- Business has a great deal of power that, it is reasoned, should be accompanied by an equal amount of responsibility.
- Modern society is an interdependent system, and the internal activities of the enterprise have an impact on the external environment.
- Social involvement may be in the interests of stockholders.
- Problems can become profits. Items that may once have been considered waste (e.g. empty soft-drink cans) can be profitably used again.
- Social involvement creates a favourable public image. Thus, a firm may attract customers, employees and investors.
- Business should try to solve the problems that other institutions have not been able to solve. After all, business has a history of coming up with novel ideas.
- Business has the resources. Specifically, business should use its talented managers and specialists, as well as its capital resources, to solve some of society's problems.
- It is better to prevent social problems through business involvement than to cure them. It may be easier to help the hard-core unemployed than to cope with social unrest.

Arguments against social involvement of business
- The primary task of business is to maximize profit by focusing strictly on economic activities. Social involvement could reduce economic efficiency.
- In the final analysis, society must pay for the social involvement of business through higher prices. Social involvement would create excessive costs for business, which cannot commit its resources to social action.
- Social involvement can create a weakened international balance of payments situation. The cost of social programs, the reasoning goes, would have to be added to the price of the product. Thus, US companies selling in international markets would be at a disadvantage when competing with companies in other countries that do not have these social costs to bear.
- Business has enough power, and additional social involvement would further increase its power and influence.
- Business people lack the social skills to deal with the problems of society. Their training and experience is with economic matters, and their skills may not be pertinent to social problems.
- There is a lack of accountability of business to society. Unless accountability can be established, business should not get involved.
- There is not complete support for involvement in social actions. Consequently, disagreements among groups with different viewpoints will cause friction.

Source: Reproduced from Weihrich & Koontz (1993) with the permission of the McGraw Hill Companies.

we must understand and accept other cultures but not judge them. Here, local customs and codes dictate behaviour, not one's own moral principles. However, this position also neglects to understand that most cultures and groups are themselves diverse and it may be only the beliefs and principles of the dominant minority that we observe.

Relativism prevents moral decisions from being resolved. Clearly, ethical principles can be adapted for certain situations or groups. Where ethical principles and codes come into conflict, issues need to be resolved, perhaps by appealing to a new higher-order principle.

Many large organizations provide ethical guidelines for their members. Although these change from time to time, country to country and sector to sector, there is often considerable overlap. The following ten points are reproduced with the permission of the American Psychological Association (1981):

- *Responsibility*: Psychologists are expected to maintain the highest professional standards, to take responsibility for the consequences of their acts, and to ensure that their services are used appropriately.
- *Competence*: Psychologists keep abreast of current scientific and professional information, and recognize the limitations of their competence and their techniques. They provide only those services for which their training and experience qualify them.
- *Moral and legal standards*: While recognizing the personal nature of such standards, psychologists are expected to be sensitive to community standards and to the possible impact of their behaviors on the public's trust in psychologists and on psychologists' ability to fulfill their professional responsibilities.
- *Public statements*: Announcements or advertisements by psychologists should serve to assist the public in making informed judgments and choices. Professional qualifications and affiliations must be accurately described, and the limits and uncertainties associated with one's service should be specified.
- *Confidentiality*: Psychologists should never reveal information about people obtained in the course of their work; only with the consent of the person involved or that person's legal representative, except in those *very unusual* circumstances when failure to do so would result in an obvious danger to that person or to others.
- *Welfare of the consumer*: Consumers of psychologists' services should be fully informed as to the purpose and nature of procedures, be they evaluative, educational, therapeutic, or training-orientated in design. Psychologists acknowledge that clients, students, or participants in research procedures have complete freedom of choice with respect to their participation or withdrawal.
- *Professional relationships*: Psychologists respect the needs, special competencies, and obligations of their colleagues in psychology and other professions, as well as the prerogatives and obligations of the institutions and organizations with which they are associated.
- *Assessment techniques*: Psychologists promote clients' welfare and best interests when developing and using psychological assessment techniques by guarding against the misuse of results, by maintaining appropriate test security, and by respecting the client's right to know the results, the interpretations, and the bases for any conclusions or recommendations.
- *Research with human participants*: Psychologists respect the dignity and welfare of

their research participants, as well as federal and state regulations and professional standards governing the conduct of research with human beings.

* *Care and use of animals*: Psychologists ensure the welfare of animals used for research purposes, and treat them humanely. They recognize that, laws and regulations notwithstanding, an animal's immediate protection is determined by the researcher's conscience and standards. [This is the only one of the ten principles that is not immediately applicable to the work of industrial and organizational psychologists.]

Conclusion

Neither cooperation nor conflict is inevitable in organizations, and both occur frequently and naturally. Although some believe cooperation is much better in the long term and is not likely to occur without considerable help, others believe competitiveness (sometimes seen as conflict) helps to raise effort and improve standards. One should not believe that having strong sectional or group interests with organizations is a bad thing, or that politics is necessarily a "dirty word" in organizations.

Cooperation occurs for various reasons between individuals and groups within an organization. The reciprocity norm, physical closeness, similarity in beliefs and values, the reward system that favours it and the structure of the organization – all promote cooperation. Although it is fairly easy to describe behaviours that both lead to, and result from, cooperation, it is probably fair to say that the jury is still out on whether it is better to forsake competitiveness for cooperation lest concern that the former (of necessity) leads to destructive conflict. It is probably the case that competitiveness works better in certain jobs (sales versus R&D), certain groups (young males versus mature females) and certain sectors (finance versus government) to increase productivity qualitatively and quantitatively.

Conflict appears to develop over several identical stages, from a sense of opposition to overt behavioural conflict, which may have various consequences. Naturally, organizations (and the individuals) have clear preferences for the way in which they choose to deal with the conflict. This may be to maintain, foster and even encourage open competitive conflict or its opposite, to avoid any manifestations of it, possibly by keeping feuding parties as far apart as possible.

Many observers agree that the presence or absence of conflict and competition is most dysfunctional when at extremes: a complete absence of conflict is probably unhealthy, just as high levels can be very destructive. Conflict has to be managed.

Conflict is often about power and influence and the way the former is manifested in organizations. Many employees complain about office politics and the way it reduces both morale and productivity. Managers have many possible ways of influencing their employees, from explicit commands to subtle suggestions. Their preference, and the effectiveness of the various methods, depends much on the sort of power they have, such as expert, "legitimate" or reward power.

Organizational politics are often described in the language of games, although, of course, they are deadly serious, with very important consequences. Politics often occur with competing groups within the organization. Here, sporting analogies are common, because it is often through competition and conflict that teams get better.

Issues of competition and conflict within and between organizations inevitably lead to discussions of business ethics and ethical/moral decisions, which organizations have to consider with respect to their clients, customers, staff and society at large. Many professional organizations have their own moral and ethical guidelines, but much conflict remains within this area. At the one extreme are those who believe business is not, and should not be, engaged in social involvement, while at the other there are those who believe it is fundamental to all human concerns.

A research perspective

Harassment and bullying at work

People in positions of power can abuse or misuse that power. They may over use punishment because they believe it an effective way to change behaviour. Using a harsh or punitive style can lead people to feel intimidated and targeted at work.

Harassment occurs in many guises and for many reasons. Perhaps the best known type of power abuse is currently called sexual harassment. It involves unwanted advances, requests, contact and communication with possible attendant punishment for non-compliance. The essence of harassment is four-fold: it is unwanted; it can adversely affect a person's employment; it actually interferes with a person's job performance; and it creates a hostile and intimidating work environment.

Harassment often leads to lawsuits, and it is only then that companies act. However, it is recognized that harassment is in the eye of the beholder. Various attributions of intent and motivation are made by both parties (accuser and accused), often based on flimsy evidence.

The word "harassment" has replaced an older concept, namely "bullying". Furnham (2004) has noted that bullying is widespread. Bullying at work is any form of behaviour (verbal, written or physical) designed to coerce, frighten or threaten staff – either as individuals or as part of a group. Usually bullying is unprovoked, continuous and aggressive. It is essentially an abuse of power.

Bullying can be verbal (name-calling, teasing, malicious-rumour-spreading) or physical (hitting, slapping, damaging belongings), but company rules, political correctness and threats of serious retribution have driven it underground. It is often always indirect: non-verbal, "forgetful" (ignoring/not including others), implicative. Occasional arguments and disagreements are not bullying behaviour. Nor necessarily is raising one's voice an example of bullying.

Some workers report frequent bullying by their managers, even out of the workplace. Senior managers are often the last to find out as bullying is easily disguised and well hidden. Therefore, senior managers underestimate or deny it. Furthermore, bullied workers are often reluctant to report it. They fear retribution from the powerful bully who may ensure they get the sack, or even worse.

There is evidence of the enduring effects of bullying on work performance. Bullied workers have lower self-confidence and self-esteem. Their concentration goes down and their absenteeism goes up. They produce less and are conspicuously unhappy, often as a direct result of the bullying/harassing experience.

Persistently bullied or harassed workers are socially isolated from the workgroup. They may originally be victimized because they are different: in terms of education, race, shape, track-record, career path, age, gender, ability. Usually the workgroup colludes with the "bullying" manager. Bullies rarely operate alone, although they may do so. Work teams assist, instigate and reinforce the bully by acts of omission and commission. Only a minority help the victim.

Bullying is complex, dynamic and widespread. Frequently, it is deeply embedded in the organizational culture despite the protestations of senior managers. The cause and manifestations of bullying need to be understood at four levels:

1   *The bullies themselves.* They can usually be characterized by three things. They are lacking in

social skills. They can be passive-aggressive, or simply aggressive, but rarely assertive. They have almost no emotional intelligence and poor coping skills. The problem is this: they do not know how to charm, persuade or influence, so they resort to intimidation. They force others to obey them by fear and threat because they cannot conduct themselves in any other way.

2   *The workgroup*. Studies have shown the existence of group attitudes – pro-victim or pro-bullying – which have a powerful influence on the bullies. If the bullying boss is allowed to get away with it, it is almost always due to the acquiescence of the workgroup. They stand by, silent witnesses. The more the group is divided into informal cliques and gangs, the more they are likely to ignore bullying of an out-group member, or even support it. Divide and conquer leads to bullying.

3   *The organization*. The organization as a whole may, in effect, be a culture for bullies to thrive. The real, as opposed to, espoused attitudes, beliefs and behaviours of senior managers is important. Certainly, official policies and practices on bullying, discipline and equal opportunities do play a part. However, what is official, human-resource-generated policy and what happens in reality are poles apart. The informal banter behind closed doors in directors' meetings, or the men's room repartee, are better clues to the true nature of the organization.

4   *Wider society*. All organizations are embedded in the wider society. Media images of the bully often portray them as sad, mad or bad. Some cultures see them as inevitable, others as able to eradicate them. Public opinion can easily be mobilized over court cases where bullies are given either very light or very heavy punishments. Few organizations have any sort of data on the topic: how often workers report being bullied; for how long; by whom; in what way; where and when. It is not clear how victims feel, or what actions they think are realistically appropriate to prevent it. Some organizations see data-gathering as a waste of time. They believe a very small minority of "supposed victims" are demanding ridiculous bureaucratic regulations because they don't like their manager who quite rightly tells them off periodically. Others see it as an imperative to understand and cope with the problem. They don't believe it is necessary to do good "bullying audits" to provide the necessary evidence to legitimize the allocation of resources to deal with a problem which inevitably leads to reduced productivity.

It is important that all levels are consulted in an organization in order to develop guidelines specifying both what is meant by bullying and what should be done about it. Policies handed down from "on high" are much less successful. Peer-led approaches can also help with "buddying the bully", to use a current American expression. But one also needs to help those frustrated and unskilled managers who, for one reason or another, can't motivate their staff. Bullies are found as much in boardrooms as playgrounds. They make the life of their staff and peers a misery and they nearly always lead to reduced productivity. That fact alone should be enough to warrant doing something about it.

A cross-cultural perspective

Confucian ideas in management

Westwood (1992) has looked at how Confucian ideas have influenced management. Confucianism is a Chinese social philosophy and set of moral guidelines. Its influence upon the Chinese persists, despite the range of circumstances that the various Chinese communities in the region have found themselves in (see Box 8.4).

Harmony is the central principle of Confucianism. This calls for moderation in all things and the maintenance of equilibrium: pursuing the *middle way*. Individuals are to exercise self-control, not allow their passions to get out of control, and to restrain appetites and desires. The pursuit of

Box 8.4 Confucian-based values and some implications for managerial and organizational behaviour

Cultural values/orientations	Implications for managerial/organizational behaviour
Harmony	• A social goal covering all organizational relationships.
	• Managers are required to ensure a harmonious atmosphere.
	• Avoidance of open conflict.
	• Harmony preferred as an "end" – even over optimal business decisions.
Jen	• Paternalist/moral leadership.
	• High relationship orientation.
Li (norms of propriety)	• An implicit normative system of order. Less need for formalized and externalized means of control.
	• Managerial decisions regarding employees often judged against moral, rather than technical or rationalistic, criteria.
	• Leader's position legitimized by perceived conformance to *Li* and other virtues.
Collectivism	• Strong in-group/out-group identification.
	• Western managerial approaches built on individualism (e.g. MBO, performance evaluation and appraisal) may not be appropriate or effective.
	• Subordination of individual interests to the collective interest.
Familism	• Achievement is for the collective, and usually the family, not the individual.
	• Family-owned and managed enterprises preferred and a paradigm.
	• Maintenance and perpetuation of family interests provide a basic business rationale.
	• Organizations ordered on a family model led by a "family" head.
Reciprocity	• Leader–subordinate relationships built on view of reciprocal mutual obligation.
	• An implicit rule governing social relationships at work.
	• Less need for formal contracts to bind people to obligations.

Source: Reproduced from Westwood (1992: 54–5) with the permission of Addison Wesley Longman China Ltd.

the key virtues – righteousness, wisdom, fidelity, filial piety, propriety – helps people to maintain inner harmony and at the same time enhance harmoniousness in social relations.

Confucianism also places great value on *education* and *self-development*. A "gentleman" should be well versed in the scholarly classics and be broadly knowledgeable. Under Confucianism, a proper inner state is reflected in proper social behaviour, and collectively this gives rise to a properly ordered social system and state.

Social harmony was accomplished partly by this externalization of inner qualities, but also by a set of more explicit social values, including:

• *Jen*: loosely, human-heartedness in which the person can only be considered fully human when he or she takes proper account of others and acts towards them as he or she would want to be acted towards.

• *Li*: rules of propriety or proper behaviour. Not explicit rules as such, but the cultivation of an awareness of what is appropriate in any given situation. It serves to structure social relationships and to maintain order in hierarchical structures.

The chief collective in the Chinese case is *family*, the extended family and kinship groups. Individuals will put the interests of the family above their own and above any wider interests, even of the state. Family relationships are strong, persistent and tightly structured, with roles clearly defined and implicit rules for appropriate behaviour. A key value/rule in family relationships is *filial piety* (i.e. the virtue of respecting and obeying one's father).

Chinese culture is described as *relationship-centred*, with relationships founded upon principles of virtuous behaviour and *Jen*, which gives a moral quality to behaviour and to the nature of relationships. Redding (1990) suggests that Chinese society has relied upon these implicit moral relationships for maintaining order, rather than upon order through jurisdiction. One implicit rule governing relationships is *reciprocity*.

The notion of *guanxi*, which refers to the status of intensity of a continuing relationship between two parties, is also important. People are very conscious of this and will seek to develop *guanxi* to build up the relationship, intensify the bonds and build on reciprocations. In particular relationships, the quality of *guanxi* governs how one should behave within it and, again, there are implicit rules governing the behaviour.

Chinese culture has been described as a "shame" culture. In a collectivist and relationship-centred culture in which Confucian social norms are emphasized, behaviour is judged according to conformity to those norms and relationship obligations. If a person behaves badly, he or she breaks those norms and is judged socially. The person will be aware that he or she has acted improperly and will feel shame.

The key relationships are identified in Confucianism in the *Wu Lun*: the firm hierarchical relationships between prince and minister, father and son, husband and wife, older brother and younger brother, friend and friend. These are unequal relationships but with reciprocal obligations and duties. The dominant party must be shown respect and obedience, but at the same time must offer care and protection to the subordinate party. They also represent clear role positions, and role occupants must behave according to their role positions as guided by *li* and other prescribed "rules".

Hierarchical structures with uneven power distributions spread beyond family and are prevalent in most social structures, including organizations. The respect for authority also transcends the child–parent relationship and becomes a generalized value. It is difficult to challenge anyone with authority, and to do so would cause loss of "face" and shame (Westwood, 1992: 53).

Although, given the above, Chinese society appears highly structured and organized, with clear statuses, hierarchies and rules of behaviour, it remains relationship-centred. Despite the structural arrangements, what really matters are *personal relationships*. In Chinese organizations, managers manage through personal contacts and relationships. It is the quality of the relationships between people that matters and determines what happens, not aspects of a formal and impersonal system.

These values naturally lead to a particular type of business. Redding & Wong (1986: 276–278) summarize the typical Chinese family business in the following way:

- Centralization of the power of decision-making, usually to a single dominant owner-manager, entrepreneur, founder, or father figure.
- Small in scale as a basic tendency (and even when larger-scale exceptions do occur, they tend to remain highly centralized).
- A low level of specialization, with fewer and less detailed job specifications, less breaking up of the organization into specialized departments, fewer people responsible for a spread of activities across various fields.
- Less standardization of activities and thus fewer routine procedures.
- A relative lack of ancillary departments such as research and development, labour relations,

public relations, market research, and a tendency instead for all employees to deal with the main product or service of the company.
- A strong overlap between ownership and control, the private family business being vastly predominant.

This form of organizational structuring is not merely a function of size or other typical contingency factors. The structural configuration has developed because it meets the cultural requirements of organization members.

A human resources perspective

How can human resources specialists help companies take part in more "socially responsible" activities. In personnel, specialists are concerned about selecting (and not putting off) good people and maintaining the image of the company. It is imperative, many believe, to have social action programmes that show the organization is concerned about the environment, the community and the wider society. The sorts of issues that these programmes consider include:

- *Do not debate only objectives and neglect means*: Self-evidently, a business must make profits if it is to survive in the existing system. However, no firm can expect profitability in the midst of social tension, strife or boycotts. Thus, business and social critics both have defensible arguments.
- *Top management commitment*: Commitment to the social action programmes by top management is essential. Employees can be expected to get involved only when they see that people at the top are really serious.
- *Financial figures cannot tell the whole story*: Social involvement cannot be measured only in money. When social action pays off, it is likely to do so only over the long run. However, this should not put off organizations attempting to evaluate programmes.
- *Forget the institutionalization approach*: In spite of attempts to organize for social commitment, attempts to develop formal organizational units to engage in social action restrict the firm's ability to adapt to changing problems.
- *Credibility is essential*: Organizations and communities must cooperate and communicate if social programmes are to succeed.
- *Involve employees*: Employees should be encouraged to become individually involved in such things as neighbourhood tutoring programmes for the disadvantaged and similar activities.
- *Directors should be involved*: Since directors represent owner interests, they must be committed to social action. Boards of directors might even be expanded to provide representation of non-owner groups such as consumers and other stakeholders.
- *Seed money and advice are helpful*: Minority-owned businesses and other targeted help-groups can be greatly assisted by these forms of direct involvement.
- *Put social action in the mainstream of running the business*: Social action needs to be greatly assisted by these forms of direct involvement.
- *Safety reassurance*: Organizations should make it apparent that they are concerned about, and have action plans set in place, in anticipation of potential accidents.

References

American Psychological Association (1981). Ethical principles of psychologists. *American Psychologist, 36*, 630–633.

Argyle, M. (1991). *Cooperation*. London: Routledge.

Barnett, T., & Schubert, E. (2002). Perceptions of the ethical work climate and covenantal relationship. *Journal of Business Ethics, 36*, 279–290.

Brinkman, J. (2002). Business and marketing ethics as professional ethics. *Journal of Business Ethics, 41*, 159–177.

Deutsch, M. (1949). A theory of cooperation and competition. *Human Relations, 2*, 129–139.

Deutsch, M., & Krauss, R. (1960). The effect of threat on interpersonal bargaining. *Journal of Abnormal and Social Psychology, 61*, 181–189.

Evered, P., & Selman, J. (1992). Coaching and the art of management. *Organizational Dynamics, 6*, 16–32.

Farrell, D., & Peterson, J. (1982). Patterns of political behaviour in organizations. *Academy of Management Review, 7*, 403–412.

Fiorelli, J. (1988). Power and workgroups: Team members' perspectives. *Human Relations, 41*, 1–12.

French, J., & Raven, B. (1959). The basis of social power. In D. Cartwright (Ed.), *Studies in social power* (pp. 150–167). Ann Arbor, MI: University of Michigan Press.

Friedman, M. (1980). *Free to choose*. Harmondsworth, UK: Penguin.

Furnham, A. (1994). *Personality at work*. London: Routledge.

Furnham, A. (2004). *Myths and management*. London: Palegrave Macmillan.

Greenberg, J., & Baron, R. (2003). *Behaviour in organizations*. New York: Prentice-Hall.

Greenwood, M. (2002). Ethics and HRM. *Journal of Business Ethics, 36*, 261–278.

Hannafey, F. (2003). Entrepreneurship and ethics. *Journal of Business Ethics, 46*, 99–110.

Hosking, D.-M., & Morley, I. (1991). *A social psychology of organizing*. Hemel Hempstead, UK: Wheatsheaf.

Kerssens-van Drongelen, I., & Fisscher, O. (2003). Ethical dilemmas in performance management. *Journal of Business Ethics, 45*, 51–63.

Kipnis, D., Schmitt, S., Swaffer-Smith, C., & Wilkinson, I. (1984). Patterns of managerial influence. *Organizational Dynamics, 4*, 58–67.

Lawrence, P., & Lersch, W. (1967). *Organization and environment*. Cambridge, MA: Harvard University Press.

Lynn, R. (1991). *The secret of the miracle economy*. London: SAU.

MacDonald, C., & Williams-Jones, B. (2002). Ethics and genetics. *Journal of Business Ethics, 35*, 235–241.

McKenna, E. (2000). *Business psychology and organizational behaviour*. Hove, UK: Psychology Press.

Mintzberg, H. (1983). *Power in and around organizations*. Englewood Cliffs, NJ: Prentice-Hall.

Palazzo, B. (2002). US-American and German business ethics. *Journal of Business Ethics, 41*, 195–216.

Redding, S. (1990). *The spirit of Chinese capitalism*. Berlin: W. de Gruyter.

Redding, S., & Wong, G. (1986). The psychology of Chinese organizational behaviour. In M. Bond (Ed.), *The psychology of the Chinese people* (pp. 267–275). Hong Kong: Oxford University Press.

Robbins, S. (1991). *Organizational behaviour* (5th edn.). Englewood Cliffs, NJ: Prentice-Hall.

Schwartz, M. (2002). A code of ethics for corporate Code of Ethics. *Journal of Business Ethics, 41*, 27–43.

Shanahan, M., Hyman, M. (2003). The development of a virtue ethics scale. *Journal of Business Ethics, 42*, 197–208.

Thomas, K. (1976). Conflict and conflict management. In M. D. Dunnette (Ed.), *Handbook of industrial and organizational psychology* (pp. 889–935). Chichester, UK: Wiley.

Weihrich, H., & Koontz, H. (1993). *Management: A global perspective*. New York: McGraw-Hill.

Westwood, R. (1992). *Organizational behaviour*. London: Longman.

Wolfe, D. (1988). Is there integrity in the bottom line: Managing obstacles to executive integrity. In S. Srivastava (Ed.), *Executive integrity* (pp. 140–171). San Francisco, CA: Jossey-Bass.

Yukl, G. (1981). *Leadership in organizations*. Englewood Cliffs, NJ: Prentice-Hall.

Yukl, G., & Fable, C. (1993). Influence tactics in upward, downward, and lateral influence attempts. *Journal of Applied Psychology, 75*, 132–140.

9 Learning and training at work

Introduction

Few people begin a job fully trained. Furthermore, with changes in technology, promotion to higher management levels, job rotation and enrichment, nearly everyone needs to regularly learn new skills, acquire new information and understand different processes. As a consequence, all organizations should educate and train staff to raise their level of performance. This may be achieved by providing new and relevant knowledge and information, by teaching new skills, or by changing attitudes, values and motives.

The purpose of training is to enhance skill and knowledge: productivity and satisfaction. It is necessary when new systems, equipment or concepts are introduced into a company. It differentiates the way in which people work but should provide a standardization of approach. Good training can and should provide a focus for aligning the workforce with the company strategy. It can also ensure that workforce skill levels are up to national or industry standards. Good training can be a powerful individual motivator and a good catalyst for change. Finally, it may be an arena for providing a link between the individual and the company's values. But training is more than acquiring knowledge and skills. It is about learning in general, which can lead to cognitive, affective and behavioural changes. That is, there are multiple outcomes of training, each of which needs to be understood and assessed.

Porteous (1997) has argued that training is aimed at developing and improving three things:

- *Knowledge*: technical information needed to perform adequately in the job.
- *Skills*: psychological and motor processes necessary to perform the job.
- *Abilities*: cognitive factors that represent capabilities.

As an index of the growth of training, he notes that at any one time a quarter of all Europeans are in some sort of education. It has been shown that about half of all employees in large companies report having had some training in the previous year, a quarter of whom said it was off-the-job training. It is argued that training is cost-effective because it leads to competitive advantage, increased effectiveness and a more adaptable workforce. This, however, remains difficult to prove.

It is possible to analyse the whole training process in terms of quite different components, as suggested by Schultz & Schultz (1998):

1   *The objectives of training programmes*: whether these are based on a sensible and objective needs assessment and organizational analysis.

2   *The training staff*: their qualifications, enthusiasm and training style.
3   *The pre-training environment*: the company's explicit and implicit attitudes to training (pro versus anti).
4   *The pre-training attributes of the trainees*: their abilities, expectation, motivation and job involvement, as well as their locus of control and self-efficacy beliefs.
5   *The psychological factors in learning*: active versus passive; whole versus part; massed versus distributed; the amount and type of feedback and reinforcement.
6   *Training methods*: on the job, in a simulated workplace, apprenticeship, programmed instruction, computer-assisted instruction; job rotation; business games, case studies, role-playing.
7   *Evaluation methods*: how programmes are evaluated.

Workers appear to be better educated than ever before. Most believe that more education and better qualifications mean better prospects. Consequently, more people spend longer in higher education before starting work and may sponsor their own part-time education while at work.

Whole sections and divisions receive training, as well as individuals. Topics vary enormously: from creativity to computer literacy and from team-building to time management. Training is popular, partly because it is seen as a reward for good performance. Many senior managers believe that training helps sustain a flexible and adaptive workforce. It is seen as a powerful management tool, to support planned and desired development. In theory, what an organization does is: (1) conduct a proper training needs assessment; (2) based on the results of that assessment, set certain training objectives; (3) then design and deliver the training; and (4) evaluate how successful it has been.

Kraiger (2003) has defined training and development as "systematic" processes initiated by (or at the direction of) the organization that result in relatively permanent changes in the knowledge, skills or attitudes of organizational members. He argues that one can see training as a form of instruction, learning or organizational change.

Those interested in training research have addressed the thorny issue of attempting to assess (and model) training effectiveness. Noe & Colquitt (2002) have argued that training effectiveness is determined by a range of complex and interlinked variables. First, training is determined by various factors that operate before *and* during training. Second, pre-training influences work on the organizational, social, team and individual levels. The model states that three individual factors are important: *age, personality* (anxiety, conscientiousness, goal orientation) and *job* (career attitudes). Training motivation is a function of these things as well as valence (relevance) of training. Furthermore, trainability refers to the person's actual skills and abilities. The model can be used to differentiate:

1   *Readiness for training*: the ability to learn the material and see how the training is relevant and free from anxieties (fears about the training).
2   *Motivation to learn*: this is a function of prior success in motivation programmes and influences attendance, exertion and application of skills after the programme.
3   *Mastery orientation*: this concerns the trainee's desire to learn, acquire skills and knowledge, make mistakes, etc.

Training courses come in many shapes and sizes. Most jobs require *technical knowledge* training, which may be done on the job, via simulated teaching or through traditional classroom instruction. There is now more emphasis on what one may call *human relations* training or management skills training. All sorts of training may occur, using such things as in-basket training (learning how to deal with the letters, memoranda, telephone calls, faxes and e-mails supposedly accumulated in the in-tray of a hypothetical executive), role-playing (not acting, but playing the role of a particular executive), management games (complex, often computer-based, scenarios usually representing conflict or opportunity situations), sensitivity training (a process- rather than content-orientated programme that attempts to raise awareness) and team training (where the focus is often team integration, interdependence). Training is used to improve various capabilities, basic learning, intellectual skills, cognitive strategies, motor skills and even attitudes.

Organizations provide training, education and development. *Training* is normally thought of as being skills-based. Skills are specific and usually easy to measure. *Education* refers to "in-house" or outside courses such as MBAs, which some companies subsidize for specific groups (often fast-trackers or those whose services they wish to retain). *Development*, on the other hand, is usually individual-based and a long-term investment dedicated to trying to get the best out of an individual.

Managers at all levels *and* those reporting to them are the target of training. Training appears to be more and more important in the framework of career planning and business innovations. Training is often one response to competition. Bernardin & Russell (1993) have shown training responses to six major change forces (Table 9.1).

Training is often specifically the way to induce and sustain organizational change. It is hoped that training transfer is good – that is, that training will transfer from the course and the classroom to the work-bench and work environment. Indeed, *transfer of training* probably remains the most important topic in this whole area. Organizations have wisely considered how post-training interventions and organizational support can help justify the money spent on training. Indeed, there is now talk of the learning organization, which (by definition) is one that has an enhanced capacity to adapt, change, grow or learn. Organizations in fast-moving technical areas only survive and prosper by being really good at continuous learning; by having systems that create, capture and share knowledge and that really encourage experimentation and flexibility.

What is the difference between teaching (educating) and training? One may compare the *education* of students versus the *training* of managers (although, of course, the former may be trained and the latter educated) (see Table 9.2). The differences lie in the *spirit* and ultimate *aim* of the two enterprises. The one aim is to teach, the other to train. In academic courses, students are taught theory, first principles and abstract understanding. Their teachers are concerned that they understand the background and the theory behind what they are learning. The learning is often abstract, without any obvious purpose except to deepen understanding of processes, procedures and principles (Furnham, 1992).

But management training in a particular topic is nearly always practical and concrete. Value-for-money demands the speedy acquisition of skill. Background details, historical origins and theoretical models are rapidly jettisoned in favour of practical understanding and hands-on skills. "Training effectiveness" is defined as the speed and cost by which employees acquire relevant skills, not the extent to which they understand theoretical concepts.

Table 9.1 Major forces affecting organizations and their implications for training

Forces	Training implications
Increased global and domestic competition	Greater need for competitive strategies. Employees need to be skilled in the technical aspects of their jobs. Managers need to be trained in management techniques that maximize employee productivity.
Rapid changes in technology and computerization	Employees need to be trained to have higher technological skills (e.g. computers, engineering) and to be able to adapt to changes in operations, job design and workflow.
Changes in the workforce	The workforce is increasingly being made up of more minorities, women, people with disabilities, older workers and better-educated people who value self-development and personal growth. Managers need to be able to relate to issues facing diverse employees and to work in a cooperative manner with employees. They also need to ensure that employees are capable of participating more in organizational decisions.
Greater demands on management time	Managers need to be trained to be able to make quick and accurate decisions.
Widespread mergers, acquisitions and divestitures	Long-term training plans are needed which are linked to corporate business plans and strategies.
Occupational obsolescence and the emergence of new occupations	Greater changes in occupations (because of the changing nature of the economy, the shift from manufacturing to service industries, and the impact of research, development and new technology) require flexible training policies to prevent lower productivity and increased turnover.

Source: Reproduced from Bernardin & Russell (1993) with the permission of McGraw-Hill.

Table 9.2 A contrast between teaching and training

Teaching students	Training managers
Philosophy Theoretical/abstract	Practical/concrete
Aim Understanding	Doing
Context Context–independence	Context-specific
Time-frame Long-term, unlimited	Short-term, immediate
Resources Self-initiated	Provided
Tone Criticism/sceptical	Enthusiasm/zealous
Medium Verbal/processes	Diagrammatic/models
Values Content	Style

Education versus training

Education and training are not the same. Training tends to be specific and tries to minimize individual differences and ways of doing things, whereas education is more general and celebrates individual differences. Both are continuous processes, though not seen as such by many.

Educating students, even those on applied courses, remains context-independent in the sense that they are rarely taught for a specific organization or purpose. Doctors, dentists, accountants and lawyers are taught their subjects with the knowledge that they may take their skills and practise in a multitude of contexts. Hence, abstract concepts are more useful because they generalize better. But management training, particularly if it is organizationally sponsored, is highly *context-specific*. Adults are trained in the "house" (or organization-specific) style, using the unique house concepts and language. It is frequently a source of pride to organizations that training is so context-specific: senior managers believe it provides a source of unity, is highly efficient and the extent to which it can be applied elsewhere is irrelevant. There are only a few general training courses where learning and skills are meant to be applied in diverse contexts. Hence, education travels better than training.

The time-frames of education and training are very different. Academic educators tend to take a longer view of things. They resist being rushed, know relatively few deadlines, and tend to be (erroneously) very tolerant of students who fail to complete their work on time. They argue that great work takes time; ideas have to mature. This stands in sharp contrast to the time-obsessed trainer, who believes that managers live in flux and the world is a capricious ever-changing place. Hence, the shelf-lives of ideas and methods are short, and training must be for the here and now. Trainers use topical examples, are conscious of fashion, and like to boast about being up-to-date, state-of-the-art users of both ideas and technology. Students in education are then expected to be disciplined, inner-directed and self-initiated. Facilities and resources such as libraries and computers are provided, but students are expected to be enterprising self-starters who seek out more or better resources. Management trainees expect and receive all the materials they need for the topic, because time is short, and it is considered the job of the trainers to compile. Sophisticated and up-to-date technology is available for the trained, not the taught.

Academics are cautious, critical, sceptical (even cynical) people. Many are intellectually phlegmatic, muted in their enthusiasm. They take a long time to be convinced of things and are trained to be questioning and doubting. Students are taught literary criticism; managers are taught literary appreciation. Trainers, on the other hand, are rewarded for, and reward themselves for, high levels of enthusiasm and certainty. Their models, the "gurus", know the answers, are certain about the solution, believe in the theory. They persuade by personal conviction, much like an evangelist. Indeed, training is evangelical: it is often made out to be fun, and its benefits are praised.

Teaching students is a verbal process. That is not to say that diagrammatic models, formulae and charts are not used, but rather they are more frequently used to summarize and illustrate. Academics try to understand the process or mechanism which may, or may not, be easily open to illustration. But the medium, like the message, is verbal and abstract, too complex and subtle for easily comprehensible transparencies.

Trainers, on the other hand, are often reliant on elaborate, often multi-coloured transparencies. They love "models", which are pretty pictures that "illustrate" their point. How and why things are categorized or boxed in a particular way is rarely spelt out. Pictures are used to simplify, categorize, make easily memorable, and often contain cartoons and other jokes. Sometimes amusing terms are used to facilitate memorization.

Academic lectures may contain excellent content but are often delivered in a dry, unappealing, lecturing style. A lecture has been described as a process whereby the notes of the lecturer become the notes of the students – without passing through the minds of either! A monotonous delivery with no pacing or contrasts in style is frequently the lot of the undergraduate: competent, sometimes brilliant, content spoilt by unsophisticated delivery and presentation style. Management trainers, on the other hand, always demonstrate a polished, modern, sophisticated style. Powerpoint presentations, videos, even role-plays are carefully prepared, and there is variety, amusing stories and a good pace. But frequently the content or substance suffers at the hands of the performance. Trainers prefer easy access to ideas, whereas teachers prefer the comprehensiveness of the course coverage.

Some will no doubt object strongly to this compare-and-contrast exercise, claiming how mislabelled they have been. Often, when a distinction is made, one pole or type is more attractive than the other, and neither side will happily accept what they see as a slur on their educational activities. Nevertheless, it does illustrate major differences between teaching and training.

Adult learners require different sorts of teaching and training than students. They tend to have *higher self-esteem* and be more critical. They need to be more involved in the planning and evaluation of training. Of course, they bring *more experience* to the training than do young people, which may help them integrate knowledge much more easily. Recognizing the value of time more readily, adults in training have a greater *readiness to learn* than students. Finally, whereas many young people see education as the accumulation of education for future use, adults tend to think of it as learning a way to be more effective in problem-solving today.

The learning organization

The idea, now very popular, of a learning organization is essentially one that has the *enhanced* capacity to adapt, change, grow and learn. Many organizations recognize that they work in a global, competitive, knowledge-intensive, rapidly changing and technologically innovative economy. So organizations need to accept and plan for continuous updating of knowledge and techniques; they need to encourage flexibility and innovation and they need to encourage a learning culture. They do these by various means:

• Sharing knowledge more widely throughout the company.
• Publishing in- and out-house directories of employee expertise.
• Hiring and employing a chief information officer.
• Encouraging and financing employee sabbaticals to acquire expertise.
• Providing good, helpful and accessible on-line resources.

Companies encourage self-directed learning and also job experts as trainers (not specialist trainers).

Management literacy

The word "literacy" has clearly been hijacked. It used to have a simple and clear meaning which referred to the ability to read. But now we have *computer literacy* and *media literacy*. Governments want people to be *economically literate* so that they can make wise decisions about their future and take responsibility for lives. Social psychiatrists now talk about *psychiatric literacy*. What they mean is the ability of the general public to recognize mental illness in general. Can people spot a panic attack of a phobic or the delusional state of a schizophrenic? Do they see the manic phase of a bi-polar sufferer as "normal" or not? Can they differentiate a narcissistic personality disorder and paranoid psychosis?

But what about *management literacy*? Most managers need to be literate in four areas. First, they need sufficient knowledge of their speciality. Lawyers need to know about the law, engineers about engineering, marketers about marketing, and human resources managers about human behaviours at work. Second, they all need basic financial competence. Hence the popularity of courses called "Finance for non-financial managers". *Financial literacy* is necessary in all jobs, the more so the higher one flies. Understanding cash flow, balance sheets, pricing and labour costs becomes significant. Third, managers need to understand their business, the peculiarities of their sector, product and clients. Though there may be some important similarity across sectors, such that managing an airline may be little different from managing a shipping company, and managing a clothing retailer not that different from managing a food retailer, there are numerous business peculiarities one needs to fully understand: the supply chain, the demography of clients, market share, and so on.

But there is a fourth and often overlooked literacy. It may be called *people literacy* or *psychological literacy*. It is about understanding oneself and others. The popularity of the rather muddled concept of emotional intelligence attests to the importance of the idea. *Management literacy* can and should be taught.

General learning principles

Learning from reading is aided more by time spent recalling what has been read than by re-reading. Individuals remember new information that confirms their previous attitudes better than they remember new information that does not confirm their previous attitudes. What is learned is more likely to be available for use if it is learned in a situation much like that in which it is to be used, and immediately preceding the time when it is needed.

Behaviour that is rewarded (reinforced) is more likely to recur. To be most effective, this reinforcement must follow immediately and be connected to the desired behaviour. Mere repetition, without reinforcement for learning, is an ineffective approach to learning.

The sense of satisfaction that stems from achievement is the type of reward that has considerable transfer value to other situations requiring learning. The value of any external reward depends partly on who dispenses the reward. If the reward giver is highly respected, an extrinsic reward may be of great value. Learners progress in an area of learning only as far as they need to in order to achieve their purposes, and thus these need to be established. Individuals are more likely to be enthusiastic about a learning situation if they themselves have participated in the planning aspects of the sessions.

Autocratic leaders have been found to make members more dependent on the leader and to generate some resentment among those included in the group. Discipline that is too strict tends to be associated with greater conformity, anxiety, shyness and acquiescence.

Many people in learning or training situations experience criticism, failure and discouragement, such that their self-confidence, aspirations and sense of worth are damaged, which needs to be addressed. People who have met with little success and continual failure are clearly not apt to be in the mood to learn. Early recognizable success is therefore important.

Individuals tend to think best and learn fastest whenever they encounter an obstacle or intellectual challenge that is of interest to them. Additionally, the best way to help people form a general concept is to explain the abstract concept, followed by many and varied everyday examples.

The following checklist of ten items can often serve to enhance the training process. Decisions are typically required in connection with each, and the difficulty is that, too often, facts and data are lacking that would determine the best manner of organizing the training course. This would simply indicate that research on the training process is as necessary as training itself.

However, a good start involves consideration of the following items (Blum & Naylor, 1968: 250):

1 Motivation is not only a desirable but often also a necessary accompaniment of learning.
2 The number of units or lessons to teach most effectively must be a considered judgement; too often it is arbitrarily and artificially set.
3 The amount to be learned in any one unit must be planned. For optimal learning, the unit should not be too large and complex or too simple.
4 Any training is practically never comprehensive or exhaustive. The amount to be learned has to be related to the desired job performance. For example, a person doesn't need to know how a motor operates to drive a car.
5 The task to be performed should be demonstrated.
6 The demonstration must be immediately followed by the doing on the part of the learner.
7 A discussion-and-question session should follow the doing, to clear up any misconceptions on the part of the learner between the explanation of why and the demonstration of how.
8 Ample and adequate practice opportunity should be encouraged. Some learners tend to overestimate their performance, and erroneously and prematurely believe that the task has really been learned.
9 Observable progress during practice goes a long way towards encouraging a sufficient amount of practice. Plotting the learning curve wherever practical is to be encouraged.
10 A summary and review of the entire learning process should be made by the learner, with the teacher available for last-minute pointers and for establishing that the task has been learned according to performance that meets the criterion or standard.

Theories of learning

Psychologists have developed various theories to explain how, when and why people learn. Many of these theories are based on specific principles:

- *Goal-setting*: people learn best when they have clear goals that are difficult enough to challenge rather than discourage them.
- *Reinforcement*: people learn best when given prompt, continuous and positive reward for having learned new skills.
- *Feedback*: learning is virtually impossible without clear and accurate feedback on results.
- *Modelling*: people can learn efficiently and effectively by copying others who have the required skills.
- *Distributed practice*: most people prefer to learn complex tasks at various "sittings", rather than on one occasion.
- *Whole versus part*: for many complex tasks, people prefer and do better with part learning (each part separately) rather than whole training (the complete entity).
- *Transfer of learning*: the more similar the place, tools and conditions of learning to the circumstances under which the learnt behaviour is to be exercised, the better the transfer of learning.

Many people talk of *learning curves*, which are characterized by a rapid increase in the earlier learning period and a tapering off towards the end of the process. This has been established for nearly a hundred years, although its shape depends on what is being taught and how. The principles of learning have been investigated by applied psychologists for many years (Blum & Naylor, 1968). Hence, many subtle distinctions have been made. For example, take knowledge of results or feedback, which is important both for its information and reinforcing characteristics. Many types have been described:

- *Extrinsic versus intrinsic*: a pilot receives intrinsic feedback about the path of the plane from bodily cues, but extrinsic feedback from the flight-deck instruments.
- *Primary versus secondary*: a competitive archer receives primary feedback from seeing the arrow in (or not in) the target board, but secondary feedback from the facial expression of the instructor.
- *Augmented versus summary*: augmented feedback is immediate and concurrent with behaviour; summary occurs at a later point – it is both delayed and global.
- *Specific versus general*: this is self-evident.

Interestingly, results suggest that learning is facilitated by increased precision in feedback *up to a point*: too much feedback overloads and can cause a decrease in performance. Learning takes place in many ways in the organization: through association, rewards and punishments, and by observation. These will be discussed in turn.

Classical conditioning: learning by association

This simple type of learning was described by Pavlov at the beginning of the twentieth century. Pavlov observed that a certain stimulus (the *unconditioned stimulus*), such as food, would elicit a naturally occurring reflexive response (the *unconditioned response*), such as salivation. Over time, if that unconditioned stimulus was paired with another, neutral stimulus (the *conditioned stimulus*), such as a bell, that stimulus would come to elicit a response similar to the naturally occurring unconditioned response (the *conditional response*) – in this case, salivation. This process of classical conditioning takes advantage of the natural tendency for some stimuli to elicit some responses automatically (reflexively). By repeatedly pairing an unconditioned stimulus with another, neutral one, that previously neutral stimulus eventually brings about the same response as the original stimulus. In fact, as the conditioning occurs, people respond to the conditioned stimulus because they develop the expectation that it will be followed by the unconditioned stimulus. Equally, once this pairing stops, the behaviour will be extinguished.

The process of classical conditioning can explain a variety of organizational behaviours. For example, workers who have witnessed dangerous industrial accidents after certain warning alarms have sounded may be expected to experience fear the next time those lights begin to flash. An employee praised by their boss while standing in front of a new employee, means when they see that new employee they will associate him or her with the praise received, and will probably feel good once again. People tend to like, and to evaluate highly, co-workers associated with praise and vice versa (Greenberg & Baron, 1994).

Although classical conditioning explains some types of learning in organizations, its usefulness is limited. It deals only with behaviours that are *reflexive* in nature; that is, they are involuntary and they occur automatically.

Operant conditioning: learning through rewards and punishments

Operant conditioning (also known as instrumental conditioning) is based on the simple fact that behaviour usually produces consequences. If our actions have pleasant effects, then we will be more likely to repeat them in the future, but if actions have unpleasant effects, they are less likely to be repeated. This phenomenon, known as the *law of effect*, is fundamental to operant conditioning and the work of B. F. Skinner (1957). There is some evidence that negative reinforcement (even something as mild as verbal condemnation) has more immediate and powerful consequences than positive reinforcement.

Employees learn to engage in behaviours that have positive results and actions that are pleasurable. The process by which people learn to perform acts leading to desirable outcomes is known as *positive reinforcement*. Whatever response led to the occurrence of these positive events is likely to occur again, thus strengthening the response. For a reward to serve as a positive reinforcer, it must be made *contingent* on the specific behaviour sought. An employee may be rewarded for his or her good attendance by receipt of a monetary bonus. But that bonus is a positive reinforcer only when it is clearly tied to the desired behaviour. Employees who do not perceive a link between the good attendance record and the reward will not be necessarily reinforced for their good attendance. They must see contingency.

On the other hand, employees also learn to perform acts because they permit them to *avoid* undesirable consequences. Unpleasant events, such as reprimands, rejection, firing, demotion and termination, are some of the consequences faced for certain actions in the workplace. The process by which people learn to perform acts leading to the avoidance of such undesirable consequences is known as *negative reinforcement*, or

Table 9.3 Contingencies of reinforcement: a summary

The four reinforcement contingencies may be defined in terms of the presentation or withdrawal of a pleasant or unpleasant stimulus. Positively or negatively reinforced behaviours are strengthened; punished or extinguished behaviours are weakened.

Stimulus presented or withdrawn	Desirability of stimulus	Name of contingency	Strength of response	Example
Presented	Pleasant	Positive reinforcement	Increases	Praise from a supervisor encourages continuing the praised behaviour
	Unpleasant	Punishment	Decreases	Criticism from a supervisor discourages enacting the punishment behaviour
Withdrawn	Pleasant	Extinction	Decreases	Failing to praise a helpful act reduces the odds of helping in the future
	Unpleasant	Negative reinforcement	Increases	Future criticism is avoided by doing whatever the supervisor wants

Source: Adapted from Greenberg & Baron (1992).

avoidance. Whatever response led to the termination of these undesirable events is likely to occur again, thus strengthening the response (Greenberg & Baron, 1994).

However, the connection between a behaviour and its consequences is not always strengthened; it may be weakened by punishment. Punishment involves presenting an undesirable or aversive consequence in response to an unwanted behaviour. A behaviour accompanied by an undesirable outcome is less likely to occur again if the person eventually learns that the negative consequences are contingent on the behaviour. Punishment is not the same as negative reinforcement. Whereas negative reinforcement removes an aversive stimulus, thereby increasing the strength of the response that led to its removal, punishment applies an aversive stimulus, thereby decreasing the strength of the response that led to its presentation.

The link between a behaviour and its consequences may also be weakened via the process of *extinction*. When a response that was once rewarded is no longer rewarded, it tends to weaken; it will gradually die out, or be *extinguished*. Ignoring requests and behaviour is probably the most common way of extinguishing it. Many people hope that, by simply ignoring something, it might go away. Indeed, sometimes it does, because it was extinguished.

The various relationships between a person's behaviour and the consequences resulting from that behaviour – *positive reinforcement, negative reinforcement, punishment,* and *extinction* – are known collectively as *contingencies of reinforcement*. The four contingencies are summarized in Table 9.3.

Observational learning: learning by modelling others

This occurs when one person acquires new information or behaviours *vicariously* (but sometimes purposefully) by observing what happens to others. The person whose behaviour is imitated is usually called the *model*. But for this sort of learning to occur, the learner must pay careful *attention* to the model. Learning will be most effective when models get the attention of others. Second, workers must have good *retention* (memory) of the model's actions. The person learning to do the job must be able to develop some verbal description or mental image of the model's actions in order to remember them. If the learner can imagine himself or herself behaving just as the model did – a process known as *symbolic rehearsal* – then learning will be facilitated. Third, there must be some *behavioural reproduction* (practice) of the model's behaviour. Unless workers are capable of doing just what the model does, they do not have any hope of being able to learn observationally from the model. The ability to reproduce many observed behaviours may initially be limited, but can improve with practice. Finally, workers must have some *motivation* to learn from the model (Table 9.4).

In observational learning, the learning process is controlled by the learners themselves. On-the-job, observational learning occurs both formally and informally. Observational learning is a key part of many formal job instruction training programmes. Given a chance to observe experts doing their jobs, followed by an opportunity to practise the desired skills, and given feedback on their work, workers tend to be very effectively trained. Observational learning also occurs in a very informal and casual manner. Workers who experience the norms and traditions of their organizations, and who subsequently incorporate these into their own behaviour, have also learned through observation. Observational learning is responsible, in part, for the ways new employees are socialized into their organizations (i.e. how they "learn the ropes") and how they come to appreciate their organization's traditions and ways of doing things (i.e. its culture). It is the old apprenticeship system. How can one use some of the above theories to maintain and reward good performance among employees?

A *reinforcer* is any event (i.e. a pay rise, praise) that increases the probability of the behaviour preceding it. For example, praising an employee for superb performance on a special project positively reinforces the employee's good work.

Although rewards may help reinforce desirable behaviour, rewarding employees for everything they do that may be worthy of reward is not always practical (or, as we will see, advisable). Rewarding every desired response is called *continuous reinforcement*. Unlike an animal learning to perform a trick, people on the job are rarely reinforced continuously. Organizational rewards tend to be administered following *partial* (or

Table 9.4 Behaviour modelling: theory and practice

Vicarious learning process	Behaviour modelling practice
Attention	Use senior figures in organization to indicate salient learning points and introduce material.
Retention	Show trainees a realistic but simple version of a model displaying an example of desirable behaviour. Support this with specific learning points.
Motoric reproduction	Provide trainees with an opportunity to practise and develop mastery of the material (usually involves role-play of realistic work experiences).
Motivation	Ensure that trainees receive or anticipate positive reinforcement contingent on target behaviours.

Source: Arnold, Robertson & Cooper (1991).

intermittent) *reinforcement* schedules – that is, rewards are administered intermittently, with some desired responses reinforced and some not.

Four varieties of partial reinforcement schedules have direct application to organizations (Luthans & Kreitner, 1985).

- *Fixed interval schedules* are those in which reinforcement is administered the first time the desired behaviour occurs after a specific amount of time has passed. For example, the practice of issuing monetary payments each Friday at 3.00 pm or receiving pay rises once a year on the anniversary date of hiring are good examples of fixed interval schedules. In both instances, the rewards are administered on a regular, fixed basis. Fixed interval schedules are not especially effective in maintaining desired job performance, although they are widely used. They encourage time-serving rather than quality work, because they focus on how much time is spent, not what is done in that time. However, for historical reasons they remain very popular.
- *Variable interval schedules* are those in which a variable amount of time (usually based on some average amount) must elapse between the administration of reinforcements. For example, an auditor who pays surprise visits to the various branch offices on an average of every eight weeks (e.g. visits may be six weeks apart one time, and ten weeks apart another) to check their books is using a variable interval schedule. Because the employee cannot tell exactly when they will be rewarded, they will tend to perform well for a relatively long period. They may slack off after they have been reinforced, but they cannot stay that way for long because they don't know how long they will have to wait until they are reinforced again. This is the semi-random inspection idea, which works fairly well.
- *Fixed ratio schedules* are those in which reinforcement is administered the first time the desired behaviour occurs after a specific number of such actions have been performed. Any type of *piecework pay system* constitutes a fixed ratio schedule of reinforcement. Immediately after receiving the reinforcement, work may slacken off, but it will then pick up again as workers approach the next performance level at which the reinforcement is administered. This rather primitive system is really successful only when the output can be easily and openly measured. It is too difficult to implement for "higher level jobs".
- *Variable ratio schedules* are those in which a variable number of desired responses (based on some average amount) must elapse between the administration of reinforcements. The classic example of the effectiveness of variable ratio schedules is playing slot machines. Since these machines pay off after a variable number of plays, the gambler can never tell whether the next pull of the handle will hit the jackpot. It is this lack of knowledge about what will happen that makes the variable ratio schedule so effective in maintaining performance. The salesman or woman is also on a variable ratio schedule. Although they try very hard to make their sales more predictable, selling is often a matter of keeping at it, knowing that every so often one makes a major sale. Managers may also reward their support staff on this schedule to ensure optimal performance. Thus, they may give them occasional presents of significant worth, but they cannot predict when.

How can an organization develop a programme to maintain and reward productive and efficient behaviour? To be effective, programmes must follow certain steps in their development. The first step is to *specify the desired behaviours*. For example, instead of saying it is important to improve customer service, it would be better to say that your employees must answer your customers' enquiries more quickly, or reduce complaints.

The second step is to *conduct a baseline audit*, which involves determining the rate at which the desirable (i.e. pinpointed) behaviour already occurs. This is necessary to identify the baseline rate of desirable behaviours, so that any changes in these behaviours resulting from the reinforcement can be identified. Third, *define a criterion standard*, such as what constitutes the level of performance desired from your employees. Fourth, *choose a reinforcer*. What will be the consequence of performing the desired behaviour? The reinforcer should be something that supervisors can deliver in a timely fashion immediately after the desired behaviour. Fifth, it is essential to *selectively reward desired behaviours that approximate to the criterion standard*. The process of selectively reinforcing behaviours approaching the goal is known as *shaping*. The idea is similar to that in sculpture. That is, reinforcement or reward is given most often and most clearly when the desired behaviour reaches the set standard.

Finally, after the desired goal has been attained, it is important to *re-evaluate the programme periodically*. Is the goal behaviour still performed? Are the rewards still working? To expect some changes in these events over time is not unusual. As a result, it is important to audit the behaviour in question. Without careful monitoring, the behaviours trainees worked so hard to develop may change.

Punishing and disciplining undesirable behaviour

Discipline is the systematic administration of punishment. Punishment is the process through which an undesirable outcome follows the performance of an unwanted behaviour, thereby attempting to reduce the strength of that behaviour. An unpleasant stimulus is not by itself a punishment; an unpleasant stimulus may be considered a punishment only when it suppresses an unwanted behaviour. Research on punishment suggests it works best under the following conditions (Greenberg & Baron, 1994: 76–77):

- *Deliver punishment immediately after the undesired response occurs*: When the undesirable consequence is delivered immediately after the undesirable behaviour occurs, people are more likely to make the connection between the two events. The undesirable consequence will serve as a punishment, thereby reducing the probability of the unwanted behaviour. The more time that separates the undesirable behaviour and its consequence, the weaker the association between them will be.
- *Punish moderately – nothing too severe or too slight*: Punishment that is too weak (e.g. non-verbal, to show disapproval when someone makes an error) is unlikely to work, because employees may easily become accustomed to the mildly undesirable consequences. On the other hand, punishment that is too intense (e.g. immediate dismissal) is unlikely to work, because other employees are likely to reject it as unfair and inhumane, and may resign.
- *Punish the undesirable action, not the person*: Effective punishment is impersonal. It should not be treated as an act of revenge or a chance to vent frustrations. When discipline is handled impersonally, the punished person is less likely to feel humiliated and, as a result, the administrator is less likely to be the victim of revenge. To punish impersonally, managers must focus their remarks on the employee's behaviour instead of his or her personality.

- *Use punishment consistently with all employees*: Punishment is most effective when administered according to a continuous reinforcement schedule. *Every* undesired response should be punished every time it occurs. Consistency is also important in punishing all employees. Everyone who commits the same infraction should be punished the same way by any of the managers in charge. Fairness demands that managers show no favouritism.

- *Clearly communicate the reasons for the punishment given*: Making clear exactly what behaviours lead to what disciplinary actions greatly facilitates the effectiveness of punishment. Clearly communicated explanations can only help strengthen the connection between the behaviour and its consequences. Communicating information about poor performance is often done in a disciplinary interview.

  In a disciplinary interview, the manager should refer to any past disciplinary interviews that have occurred, identify exactly what problem was noted, and seek an explanation from the employee. This may be followed by a warning, which should be carefully tied to specific performance problems, and a written record should be made of this agreement. It is helpful to explain that the rule is being enforced fairly – namely, that all others who have broken the same rule are punished the same way. Finally, one should seek a commitment from the employee and a follow-up meeting should be scheduled in which the same problematic behaviour, if any, will be reassessed.

- *Be careful not to follow punishment with non-contingent awards*: One should never inadvertently reward unwanted behaviour, otherwise the effect of the punishment may be greatly diminished. Such an action sends the wrong message to the other employees. For punishment to be most effective, a supervisor must not inadvertently reward undesirable behaviours.

Current trends in training

Large organizations still have comparatively large training budgets. They buy-in, or have in-house, training departments, centres, even country castles, to run training courses for their staff. Courses cover all sorts of topics: induction to the organization, specific job-related or people skills (assertiveness, negotiation), and culture-change developmental workshops aimed at middle or senior managers. Training is affected by many factors: during economic downturns, training budgets look easy targets for cuts; product and technical innovations mean training has to respond to different needs; demographic changes among employees and customers can render certain programmes redundant.

There are some noticeable trends in management and business training in the new millennium. The boom of the 1990s, with its inevitable heroes and fads, has given way to a new caution. Different themes have begun to emerge, which are likely to endure. Kraiger (2003) has highlighted four new methods:

1 *Computer-based training*: This is thought to be flexible, widely available and cheap, though there remains no good evidence that it is cheaper or better than instructor-led traditional training. It can capitalize on programme customization and learner control.

2 *Team training*: This contrasts task-work and team-work skills and is about such things as team coordination training and resource management training. Part of

this is cross-training, which attempts to provide exposure to, and practice with, other team-mates' tasks, roles and responsibilities to increase understanding. Another theme is guided team self-correction, which is essentially learning to become self-managing.

3   *Cross-cultural training*: This involves the skills of being sensitive and flexible with regard to cultural differences in an increasingly diverse workforce.

4   *Corporate training*: Through corporate universities, distance learning and special-ized executive courses, organizations attempt to have tight control over the cur-riculum and values in training.

Although not *all* are apparent in *all* organizations, at least seven themes are apparent (Furnham & Gunter, 1994):

- *Learning not training*: Training is about acquiring specific skills; learning is more concerned with general principles. Training is for the here and now; it is company-specific; it is highly practical even pragmatic. Learning has less immediate application, but is designed to be more useful in various contexts. Companies have preferred training because it is believed to be more cost-effective. Many firms do not believe it is their task to provide a rather general university-based education; that, they have argued, is a luxury that managers can buy for themselves, but more and more companies see the benefit in well-educated managers (the intelligent general-ist). Because there is nothing as practical as good theory, they send their people off to acquire MBAs, or on longer developmental courses. The opportunity for learn-ing (as opposed to training) may actually help staff retention in these firms and may even encourage better applicants. Some companies approach business schools to teach their own client-derived syllabus, taught and approved by the university.

- *Less provincial, chauvinistic, ethnocentric perspective*: We now have a global market, an international workforce and multinational products. Management has had to take this into consideration. Cosy "we/they" stories, case histories from local com-panies, and a homogeneous workforce are a thing of the past. All managers need to take a larger perspective – not just pan-European, but the global market; hence, the focus on cultural differences, and comprehensive briefings on how other companies in other countries do things. All managers are being encouraged to be multilingual and comfortable in cross-cultural communication.

- *Competency-led training*: Despite the vagueness of the concept of competency, many organizations have been forced to think exactly which competencies (skills, abilities, traits) they require of their managers. Having done this, they are usually much more focused on the kind of training they need. In the past, trainers provided what *they* thought appropriate, or more prosaically what they could offer. Now they are being required to integrate the training programme into the company's overall competence-led training or human resource strategy. Courses that do not fit may be jettisoned, and others have to be created to meet the needs of the proposed strategy. In this sense, training follows strategy, although competencies are often defined so vaguely that the trainers can easily adapt what they have to satisfy their clients in the board room.

- *Team-building rather than leadership*: Nearly everyone works in groups, and busi-ness sense is, we are told, dependent not on individuals but on teams. It really is true that a chain is only as strong as its weakest link. Heterogeneous teams do best:

those with overall ability but whose members each had different skills, preferences and approaches that *complemented* each other. Just as people may have to be trained to become leaders, they may also have to be trained to be followers. Training programmes now focus on how to build, sustain and manage a team; how to assess your favourite and most comfortable role when operating a team; how to select individuals with a team in mind; and how to be a better team member.

- *Virtual-reality training*: Trainers have always worried about the generalizability of training; that is, whether what you learn on courses in comfortable hotels or cosy training centres is actually applied, let alone remembered, in the real work setting. The more realistic or similar the training environment to the work environment, the less, by definition, is there a problem of generalization. Think how much airlines spend on simulators! Trainers, too, are now considering training *in situ* – on the shop floor, in the executive office, or in the sales room. Although this may cause some inconvenience or might even actually be dangerous to customers or equipment, it is thought worth it. Shadowing (or observing someone "on the job") is becoming more popular and is supposedly a useful teaching aid.

- *Using managers as trainers*: It is not only because of the expense of staffing a permanent training department, or calling in consultants, that there is a trend for managers to become trainers themselves. People rightly expect that, in some circumstances, managers can act as trainers, because they are the ones with the most relevant knowledge. Most managers do not have the time and skill to become explicit trainers rather than simply people to be imitated, but they can do a very useful job. Some organizations have attempted to redefine job titles to reflect this. Hence, supervisors become coaches, and managers the support staff!

- *Using subordinate feedback*: Most managers are used to being appraised by their superiors and occasionally by their peers. Trainers, on the other hand, are used to being rated by their course attendees. Because it is your subordinates who know you best, and have to live with the consequences of your particular style, it is arguably they who provide the most useful feedback to managers on how to improve their management skills. Many organizations are even considering using subordinate ratings, not only as useful feedback techniques in training, but also a possible source of data for staff appraisals. More and more trainers are now using upward or "bottom-up" feedback rather than the traditional downward appraisal. Hence, subordinates appraise superiors, not the other way around.

Outdoor training

What is the philosophy of outdoor training? To a large extent, the answer depends on what traditional classroom or on-the-job-training does not do. Essentially, there are three good arguments:

- *Experimental versus theoretical learning*: Since the 1960s when sensitivity groups thrived, many trainers have pointed out that *real* learning occurs when people are put into difficult, novel, problematic situations. People have to be shocked out of their complacency to learn about themselves and others properly. In trainer jargon, "unfreezing" needs to take place before real learning occurs. Learning occurs while people deal with these novel situations: not before with the study of elaborate theories or abstract ideas, and not afterwards with bland briefing. The philosophy of outdoor training is that people learn most about themselves, their teams and their limitations by *doing*.

- *Emotions not ideas*: Most training courses are about ideas, concepts, skills, models. They involve brain work and traditional classroom activities. But, as outdoor trainers tell you, management in a tough world is about *self-confidence* and *courage*. Most training aims at the head but not the heart. People who have been on an outdoor training course will tell you immediately about the whole gamut of emotions they experience: pure blind fear, incredible fury and anger, maudlin depression and self-doubt, and unexpected tension-releasing humour. A major aim of outdoor training is to teach people that, when pushed to the limit of their ability, they *can do it*. The great Victorian virtues of self-reliance, fortitude and even stoicism can be, and need to be, learned by a successful manager. This does not take place with the cold learning experience of the classroom but the white-hot experience of physical danger. Outdoor training is unashamedly about emotional learning.

- *Team membership and leadership*: There are plenty of leadership courses but not too many on follower-ship. Anglo-Americans come from an individualistic culture, not a collective one: teamwork does not come easily or naturally. Hence, it is more attractive to be the leader, because in that role you can more easily impose your individualistic style and preferences on others. Learning to sail a yacht in choppy seas, or cross a gorge via a pulley, sling and ropes, requires real cooperation. Teams in the bush need to be *inter*dependent: you need them and they need you. You cannot survive on your own. And at times, the leader needs to be a follower, and vice versa.

All people need to learn how to be an effective member of a team – to exploit personal assets, use expertise, and to draw out the abilities and skills of others. This is rarely learned in intellectual problem-solving in the classroom, making paper-models or being videotaped. The real team involvement in these situations is pretty minor, but that is definitely not the case on some outdoor courses. Not all outdoor training provides all the benefits; rather than gaining self-confidence, some people can and do experience nothing but self-doubt. They can return broken, not built up, but others, discovering new-found strengths and abilities, pack up and go to other organizations, believing they would do better there.

Another change occurs in the greater use of more varied techniques for training, particularly on-the-job and computer-based training. Bernardin & Russell (1993) provide a very helpful and fairly exhaustive list of currently used techniques (Table 9.5).

One way to conceptualize different training methods has been suggested by Corder (1990). He first distinguishes what one is trying to teach and divides it crudely into the tangible (specific skills) and intangible (ideas, concepts). Next, he distinguishes between two types of teaching approach in terms of their aims and processes (not level of difficulty): these are labelled "hard" and "soft". A hard approach aims to have trainees supply correct answers and demonstrate specific skills; a soft approach aims to promote more general proficiency (Table 9.6).

The tangible/hard quadrant is the traditional world of skills training. Whereas tangible/soft is more concerned with raising awareness, intangible/soft is the most vague and may involve such things as the examination of the strategies of entrepreneurs, and how to lead focus groups.

Table 9.5 Experimental training methods

Uses	Benefits	Limitations
On-job training		
Learning job skills	Good transfer.	Depends on the trainer's skills and willingness.
Apprenticeship training	Limited trainer costs.	May be costly because of lost production and mistakes.
Job rotation	High trainee motivation since training is relevant.	May have frequent interruptions due to job demands. Often is haphazardly done. Trainees may learn bad habits.
Computer-based training		
Gaining new knowledge	Self-paced.	Costly.
Drill and practice	Standardization of training over time.	Trainees may fear using computers.
Individual training	Feedback given. Good retention.	Limited opportunities for trainee interaction. Less useful for training interpersonal skills.
Equipment simulators		
To reproduce real-world conditions	Effective learning and transfer.	Costly to develop.
For physical and cognitive skills	Can practise most of the job skills.	Sickness can occur.
For team training		Requires good fidelity.
Games and simulations		
Decision-making skills	Resembles the job tasks.	Highly competitive.
Management training	Provides feedback.	Time-consuming.
Interpersonal skills	Presents realistic challenges.	May stifle creativity.
Case study analysis		
Decision-making skills	Decision-making practice.	Must be updated.
Analytical skills	Real-world training.	Criticized as being unable to teach general management skills.
Communication skills	Active learning.	Trainers often dominate discussions.
To illustrate diversity of solutions	Good for developing problem-solving skills.	
Role-play		
For changing attitudes	Gain experience of other roles.	Initial resistance of trainees.
To practise skills	Active learning.	Trainees do not take it seriously.
To analyse interpersonal problems	Close to reality.	
Behaviour modelling		
To teach interpersonal skills	Allows practice.	Time-consuming.
To teach cognitive skills	Provides feedback. Retention is improved.	May be costly to develop.
Sensitivity training		
To enhance self-awareness	Can improve self-concept.	May be threatening.
To allow trainees to see how others see them	Can reduce prejudice.	May have limited generalizability to job situations.
To improve insights into differences	Can change interpersonal behaviours.	

Source: Reproduced from Bernardin & Russell (1993) with the permission of McGraw-Hill.

Table 9.6 Soft and hard teaching tangible and intangible subjects

	Tangible subject	*Intangible subject*
(A) Teaching grid		
Hard teaching	Getting people to acquire specific knowledge and master particular techniques: rules, memorizing complex worked examples, hands-on/mastery	Translating intuition and judgement into a transmittable form: guidelines presented as rules, samples of "good work", "what" more than "how"
Soft teaching	Giving people a basic appreciation and understanding: overview, awareness, concepts, simple examples, demonstrations	Helping people to learn to think for themselves: analytical skills, what questions to ask, self-awareness, discovery learning
(B) Training examples		
Hard teaching	Critical path analysis Constructing spreadsheets Evaluating financial ratios Calculating staff bonuses	Tips for effective writing Caring for customers Rules for public speaking "Excellent" companies
Soft teaching	The phasing out of CFCs The paperless office Cost-consciousness Company induction	Outdoor leadership tasks Group dynamics workshops Life planning/biographies Shadowing entrepreneurs
(C) Management education		
Hard teaching	Providing expert theoretical knowledge and advanced technical and analytical tools	Providing critical keynote conceptual frameworks Mapping competing theoretical perspectives, noting the partiality of each
Soft teaching	Designing and managing learning within sophisticated experimental and simulated operating environments	Facilitating a community of reflex enquiry Encouraging the sharing and collective sense-making of personal experiences

Source: Reprinted from Snell & Jones (1994) with the permission of Sage Publications.

Corder (1990) acknowledged that, by necessity, much management training falls into the intangible/soft quadrant, because in many cases simple encapsulation would not do justice to the issues, processes and contextual peculiarities under consideration. Snell & James (1994) note that there has been a spate of in-company training initiatives within the intangible/hard quadrant (such as corporate culture-change programmes, time management and customer-care skills).

Snell & James (1994) have attempted to describe management training in terms of the quadrants. Thus, tangible/hard is very much the traditional classroom teaching, and intangible/hard is more case-study based and less specific. Intangible/soft is the vaguest of all and it attempts to provide a safe learning environment to experiment with various ideas.

Table 9.7 Cost–benefit (yield) analysis for continuing medical education

	Time cost high	*Time cost low*
Narrow benefit	Reading most articles in medical journals or attending most postgraduate lectures	Reading review articles or attending update lectures
Broad benefit	Attending Balint training	Video-based skills

Source: Reprinted from Pendleton (1995).

How does one use training most effectively to keep highly skilled professionals up to date. Consider the problem of training general practitioners or physicians through what is often called *continuing medical education*. The speed of development in medicine means regular update training sessions are required. But what is the most effective and efficient method to ensure doctors are trained in the latest methods? Pendleton (1995) offers a cost–benefit analysis of the issue (Table 9.7).

Pendleton (1995) argues that maximum yield is defined here as having a low cost in terms of time and broad benefit or impact on practice. Video-based skills training makes a difference on every consultation after it has been taken, and requires just three days – a sound investment – and it has been extremely well received. Large numbers have taken part; it is now a feature of most vocational training schemes in general medical practice. Balint training is a form of psychotherapeutically based reflection on practice in peer groups with a leader. It has a broad effect on practice but the training typically lasts for many years. Its yield, being broad but slow, would be classified as medium. Similarly, medium yield would describe attendance at update lectures or reading review articles in journals. But, since the absolute time involved in this activity is low compared with Balint training, more people take part in it.

The lowest yield of all is that which is associated with the most common media for continuing medical education, journal articles and postgraduate lectures, which are usually so narrow in their focus that it takes a great deal of time and effort to cover significant areas of a doctor's work. Thus, not surprisingly, continuing medical education is poorly attended and most journals are poorly read. This is not a failure of motivation on the part of the doctors, but a failure of insight on the part of the providers of continuing medical education. They have based their activity on the traditional academic aims, media and methods, when their audience is professional. They have also omitted the cost–benefit analysis of their work as perceived by their potential audience. Any choice of training method needs a careful cost–benefit analysis.

Developing a training strategy

What stages does one go through in developing a training strategy and programme. Lambert (1993) has identified a sensible self-explanatory step-by-step flow chart of the necessary steps (Figure 9.1).

Certainly, one sadly neglected element of training is a thorough, regular review of training needs. This review or analysis is usually focused on two fundamental questions: Is there a problem in level or type of individual performance? And can training be of any value in correcting the problem?

Training needs analysis must precede decisions about methods of training. Various

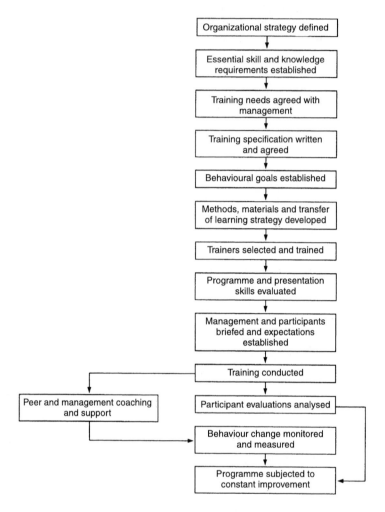

Figure 9.1 Training design and development. Reproduced from Lambert (1993) with the permission of Pitman Press.

checklists are available that can be used to identify training needs in a unit, although some doubt always remains about the extent to which training would solve (in the past) the problem. Too much and too little training can cause problems: the former is too great an expense for the training itself; the latter is too great an expense as a result of poor productivity, errors, wastage and accidents.

Training needs can be considered at the *organization* level, the *individual* skills level or through a careful *task* analysis, which looks at individual units of behaviour that are broken down into specific operations in an hierarchical fashion. The latter is usually best done for skilled physical tasks, rather than cognitive tasks.

Once training needs have been established, training methods should be considered. Although it is true that certain trainers favour certain methods, not because of their proven efficacy so much as out of personal preference, it is difficult to find clear evidence pointing to the use of one technique over others. Popular techniques include case studies, role-playing, business games, job rotation, shadowing and "understudy assignments", as well as on-the-job training. Some organizations believe the best way to learn is through traditional apprenticeship models, others that intensive early instruction is best, and some that simulations are a very cost-effective way of learning.

Essential principles of training

Participation

For training to be effective, trainees must be actively involved, performing the desired skills.

People learn more quickly – and tend to retain their learned skills – when they actively participate in learning. The principle of participation applies to learning cognitive skills, just as it does to learning motor skills.

Repetition

The fact that learning is facilitated by repeating the desired behaviours is well established. Practice is more effective when spread out over time than when all done at the same time. When practice periods are too long, learning can suffer from fatigue, whereas learning a little at a time allows the material to sink in. The question of exactly how long one should practise and how long one should rest depends on many factors, such as the nature of the task and the ability of the person performing it.

Transfer of training

For training to be most effective, what is learned during training must be applied to the job. In fact, the more closely a training programme matches the demands of the job, the more effective the training will be (Baldwin & Ford, 1988). By using sophisticated computer-based techniques to simulate real flight conditions carefully, airline pilot trainees can learn what it is like to manipulate their craft safely, without actually risking their lives and expensive equipment. Naturally, training that is any less elaborate in the degree to which it simulates the actual work environment is less effective (e.g. a home computer flight-simulation game).

Porteous (1997) has argued that transfer of training is improved if five steps are put in place:

1 *Overlearning of skills*: All skills should be practised until completely proficient.
2 *Principles*: Workers should fully understand *why* something is done or works not merely *how* to do it.
3 *Realistic simulations*: Training is best done with real equipment, real customers and in real situations.
4 *Adaptation*: Training should include an ambiguous, tricky or unusual situation so that trainees find their own solutions outside regular procedures.
5 *Monitoring*: Newly trained staff will require monitoring and updating, showing when and whether they are practising new skills.

The success of transfer from the training to the work setting depends on various things. For instance, successful transfer is a function of:

- *Time*: the amount of positive transfer decreases as a function of time.
- *Task similarity*: having to learn a new response to an "old" stimulus leads to negative transfer.
- *Amount of initial learning*: the more (and better) the learning on the initial task, the better the transfer.
- *Task difficulty*: there is greater transfer from a difficult task to an easier task than vice versa.
- *Knowledge of results*: feedback affects performance but not learning.

Noe & Colquitt (2002) recently provided a useful list of characteristics of effective training:

- Trainees understand the objectives, purpose and intended outcomes of the training programme.
- The training content is meaningful and relevant to job experiences (i.e. examples, exercises, assignments, etc., are based on job relevant information).
- Trainees are provided with learning aids to help them learn, organize and recall training content (i.e. diagrams, models and advanced organizers).
- Trainees have the opportunity to practise in a relatively safe environment.
- Trainees receive feedback on their learning from trainers, observers, peers or the task itself.
- Trainees have the opportunity to observe and interact with other trainees.
- The training programme is efficiently coordinated and arranged.

Feedback

No learning of any type can be effective without feedback – knowledge of one's actions. Feedback provides information on the effectiveness of one's training.

Motivating trainees

Patrick (2000) has pointed out that one of the most important yet fundamental features of training – namely, the motivation to volunteer and learn – is neglected. Various strategies include:

- Make sure the training material is interesting, thereby arousing curiosity and hence attention.
- Make sure it is relevant to the current or future job and organizational needs.
- Ensure trainee confidence through early success, which also increases personal expectancy of success.
- Ensure the outcomes of the training are positive.

The motivation to learn is a function of four things: the individual's work attitudes (involvement, commitment), their locus of control (expectancies of self-efficacy), their relation to the process of evaluation and environmental culture.

Learning styles

Do people have different strategies of, preferences for, or styles of learning? This may have important implications for the way in which they are trained. Much research has examined differences between extraverts and introverts. Eysenck (1981: 203–204) summarized the findings as follows. In spite of the relatively small volume of research on the effects of introversion/extraversion on learning and memory, there appear to be some fairly robust findings. Some of the more important of these have been discussed earlier and will now be listed:

- Reward enhances the performance of extraverts more than introverts, whereas punishment impairs the performance of introverts more than extraverts.
- Introverts are more susceptible than extraverts to distraction.
- Introverts are more affected than extraverts by response competition.
- Introverts take longer than extraverts to retrieve information from long-term or permanent storage, especially non-dominant information.
- Introverts have higher response criteria than extraverts.
- Extraverts show better retention-test performance than introverts at short retention intervals, but the opposite happens at long retention intervals.

Although it is probably premature to attempt any theoretical integration of these various findings, it is nevertheless tempting to argue that introverts are characteristically better motivated on performance tasks than extraverts, with the consequence that their normal expenditure of effort and utilization of working memory capacity is closer to the maximum. Since introverts, as it were, start from a high motivation baseline, it follows that they are less able than extraverts to utilize extra processing resources to handle increasing processing demands (e.g. from distracting stimulation, from response competition or from difficult retrieval tasks).

Eysenck (1978) listed six practical applications for personality variables to learning situations:

- *Selection*: advice based on personality traits as to fit.
- *Streaming and task-setting*: streaming pupils/students by personality or setting them different tasks.
- *Re-education*: intervention in learning difficulties based on the understanding of traits.
- *Ascertainment*: monitoring of personality development over time to anticipate problems.
- *Training*: the education of teachers in differential psychology.
- *Research* that takes the role of individual differences seriously.

As a basis for identifying different learning styles, several psychologists have attempted to describe the overall learning process. The theory that has received most attention in the management literature is that of Kolb (1976, 1984). His model combines the two bi-polar dimensions of cognitive growth: the active–reflective dimension and the abstract–concrete dimension. The first ranges from direct participation to detached observation, and the second ranges from dealing with tangible objects to dealing with theoretical concepts. Kolb defined a four-stage cycle of learning: it begins with the acquisition of concrete experience, which gives way to reflective observation on that experience. The theory-building or abstract conceptualization then occurs, which is then put to the test through active experimentation. The cycle thus recommences, since the experimentation itself yields new concrete experiences.

Each stage of the cycle requires different abilities, and the learner must decide which ones to apply in any situation. Individuals tend to be more skilled in some abilities than others, and are thus inclined to favour a particular learning style. Kolb classified learning styles according to a four-fold taxonomy based on the two cognitive dimensions:

- *divergers* reflect on specific experiences from various different perspectives;
- *assimilators* develop a theoretical framework on the basis of that reflection;
- *convergers* test the theory in practice;
- *accommodators* use the results of that testing as a basis for new learning.

In Kolb's model, individuals prefer to gather information either through concrete experience or abstract conceptualization, and they prefer to process that information either through reflective observation or active experimentation. Concrete experience includes affective learning skills, while reflective observation involves perceptual learning skills. Four learning-style categories are possible, based upon how a person combines preferences in gathering and processing information. Accommodators combine concrete experience and active experimentation; divergers combine concrete experience and reflective observation; assimilators combine reflective observation and abstract conceptualization; and convergers combine abstract conceptualization and active experimentation. The identified strengths of divergers are described as their imaginative abilities and understanding of people, whereas their weaknesses are found in their inability to make decisions or being paralysed by alternatives. Assimilators are said to be orientated towards building theoretical models and using inductive reasoning. A weakness of this style may occur with the lack of practical applications generated from theory. Convergers use deductive reasoning and prefer the application of ideas; convergers are also relatively unemotional and would rather work with things than with people. Making decisions too quickly and solving the wrong problem have been identified as weaknesses of convergers. The accommodator is quick to involve himself in new situations in a trial-and-error manner – risk-taking. Research by Kolb (1984) clearly links style to choice of higher education course and career. He found that individuals with certain cognitive styles gravitate towards higher education courses that reinforce those styles (e.g. business reinforces active, receptive styles; mathematics reinforces reflective, perceptive styles). Moreover, he discovered that cognitive styles also affect managerial behaviour. For example, managers who held high-risk, high-pressure jobs in the trust department of a bank tended to be active and receptive. Managers in low-risk, low-discretion jobs tended to be reflective and perceptive. Similarly, receptive managers tended to rely on information from other people in their investment decisions, whereas perceptives relied on analytically orientated printed material.

Thus, individuals who emphasize a systematic strategy do best in courses that take an orderly, step-by-step approach to the subject, courses in which what is learned builds on, and follows directly from, what was learned earlier (e.g. mathematics). Intuitive individuals seem to do best in courses requiring creativity and the generation of ideas. Learning activities in which the student must rely on a personal sense of what is appropriate (e.g. sculpturing) are likely to be preferred by these individuals. Individuals who are strongest in active strategies probably tend to do best in courses that emphasize experimentation and action. Trying out the information in a practical setting is an attractive way of learning, and examinations in which demonstration or application is required may be easiest for these individuals. Individuals who emphasize reflective strategies, on the other hand, do best in courses dealing with abstract ideas and theoretical models. Pondering meanings and implications of information is valued learning activity for these individuals, and examinations are easiest that allow for a thoughtful presentation of ideas. There are several questionnaires that measure what are called preferred learning styles (Furnham, 1992; Kolb, 1976). Indeed, although slightly different in terms of their terminology and questionnaires, there is undoubtedly overlap between them. Box 9.1 provides a description of Honey & Mumford's (1982) four types.

The preferred learning style of an individual and the preferred teaching style of a trainer, training department or organization clearly form a "fit". It is naturally expected that the better the fit, the more efficient and effective the training.

Training needs

For an organization to decide on its training needs, methods and procedures, an audit needs to be carried out. Training should begin with a training needs assessment, followed by a training design with highly specific behavioural outcomes and objectives. The training/learning tasks are derived from, and are a function of, the behavioural objectives. Berry (1998) argued that the training needs assessment should enable the trainer to decide on various fundamental factors: the number of practice sessions required, the length and intensity of those sessions, and the nature of the content (i.e. task practised as a whole, or subtasks). The analysis should also indicate salient individual differences among the trainees, such as their abilities, knowledge and motivation. Needs assessments can be used to identify topics and trainees for special attention. Goldstein (1986) argued that training needs assessment has three facets:

- *Organizational analysis*: *Where* and *what* is the training and development needed in the organization? What is the cost–benefit ratio? Where is training most likely to be successful in the organization? It may consist of climate indexes, management requests, customer survey data or exit interviews.
- *Job/task analysis*: A variety of methods may be used to determine the skills or competences required to perform at every task. Once the skills, tasks and jobs have been carefully specified, they may be trained. Analysis may be based on job descriptions, work samples or performance data.
- *Person analysis*: This involves both the needs of individuals and groups. This may come from appraisal, interviews, questionnaires, tests, diaries or assessment centres. Training should ideally start with a careful needs assessment and end with careful and rigorous evaluation.

Once these analyses have been done, training objectives may be set and methods/techniques can be considered. These are varied and quite different in cost efficacy and popularity:

- *Lecture*: the chalk-and-talk approach is still popular despite, or perhaps because of, the passivity of participants.

Box 9.1 Honey & Mumford's four learning types

Activitists

Activists involve themselves fully and without bias in new experiences. They enjoy the "here and now" and are happy to be dominated by immediate experiences. They are open-minded, not sceptical, and this tends to make them enthusiastic about anything new. Their philosophy is "I'll try anything once". They rush in where angels fear to tread. They tend to throw caution to the wind. Their days are filled with activity. They revel in short-term crisis fire-fighting. They tackle problems by brainstorming. As soon as the excitement from one activity has died down, they are busy looking for the next. They tend to thrive on the challenge of new experiences, but are bored with implementation and long-term consolidation. They are gregarious people, constantly involving themselves with others but, in doing so, they hog the limelight. They are the life and soul of the party. They seek to centre all activities around themselves. According to Honey & Mumford (1982), having this learning style means various strengths and weaknesses.

Strengths: Flexible and open-minded; happy to have a go; happy to be exposed to new situations; optimistic about anything new and therefore unlikely to resist change.

Weaknesses: Tendency to take the immediately obvious action without thinking; often take unnecessary risks; tendency to do too much themselves and hog the limelight; rush into action without sufficient preparation; get bored with implementation/consolidation.

Reflectors

Reflectors like to stand back to ponder experiences and observe them from many different perspectives. They collect data, both first-hand and from others, and prefer to chew thoroughly before coming to any conclusions. The thorough collection and analysis of data about experiences and events are what counts, so they tend to postpone reaching definitive conclusions for as long as possible. Their philosophy is to be cautious, to leave no stone unturned: "Look before you leap", "Sleep on it". They are thoughtful people who like to consider all possible angles and implications before making a move. They prefer to take a back seat in meetings and discussions. They enjoy observing other people in action. They listen to others and get the drift of the discussion before making their own points. They tend to adopt a low profile and have a slightly distant, tolerant, unruffled air about them. When they act, it is a part of a wide picture which includes the past as well as the present and others' observations as well as their own.

Strengths: Careful; thorough and methodical; thoughtful; good at listening to others and assimilating information; rarely jump to conclusions.

Weaknesses: Tendency to hold back from direct participation; slow to make up their minds and reach a decision; tendency to be too cautious, and not take enough risks; not assertive – they aren't particularly forthcoming and have no "small talk".

Theorists

Theorists adapt and integrate observations into complex but logically sound theories. They think problems through in a vertical, step-by-step logical way. They assimilate disparate facts into coherent theories. They tend to be perfectionists who won't rest easy until things are tidy and fit into their rational schemes. They like to analyse and synthesize. They are keen on basic assumptions, principles, theories, models and systems thinking. Their philosophy prizes rationality and logic. "If it's logical, it's good". Questions they frequently ask include: "Does it make sense?" "How does this fit with that?" "What are the basic assumptions?" They tend to be detached, analytical and dedicated to rational objectivity rather than anything subjective or ambiguous. Their approach to problems is consistently logical, which is their "mental set" and they rigidly reject anything that doesn't fit with it. They prefer to maximize certainty and feel uncomfortable with subjective judgements, lateral thinking and anything flippant.

Box 9.1 continued

> *Strengths*: Logical "vertical" thinkers; rational and objective; good at asking probing questions; disciplined approach.
>
> *Weaknesses*: Restricted in lateral thinking; low tolerance for uncertainty, disorder and ambiguity; intolerance of anything subjective or intuitive; full of "should, ought and must".
>
> **Pragmatists**
> Pragmatists are keen on trying out new ideas, theories and techniques to see if they work in practice. They positively search out new ideas and take the first opportunity to experiment with applications. They are the sort of people who return from management courses brimming with new ideas that they want to try out in practice. They don't like "beating about the bush" and tend to be impatient with ruminating and open-ended discussions. They are essentially practical, down-to-earth people who like making practical decisions and solving problems. They respond to problems and opportunities "as a challenge". The philosophy is: "There is always a better way" and "If it works it's good".
>
> *Strengths*: Keen to test things out in practice, practical, down to earth, realistic, business-like, gets straight to the point; technique-orientated.
>
> *Weaknesses*: Tendency to reject anything without an obvious application; not very interested in theory or basic principles; tendency to seize on the first expedient solution to a problem; impatient with waffle; task-orientated, not people-orientated.

- *Audio-visuals/films*: like the above, they are popular, expensive and often not very effective in the development of skills.
- *Simulators*: depending on the skills, these can be very expensive, but essential (e.g. flight deck).
- *Conferences*: although this may help with morale and modifying attitudes, they are not good ways to teach specific skills.
- *Laboratory training*: given the appropriate "staff–student ratio" on training sequences, this can be very efficient.
- *Case method*: this method is useful for the cognitive analysis of "real" problems to demonstrate that problems/issues have multiple causes and effects.
- *Role-playing*: this can be similar to any of the above methods and may be best for teaching interpersonal skills.
- *Business games*: these provide practice in decision-making and experience in interacting with others where feedback and the dynamic quality of the game are intrinsically motivating.
- *Programmed instruction/self-instruction*: this pre-dates computers, but is essentially a "home pack" of exercises that teaches skills.
- *Computer-assisted instruction*: now very popular, these are interaction exercises that supposedly teach skills at the pace of the learner in an interesting and enjoyable way.

The above list is not exhaustive, nor are the methods unrelated. A central question for any practitioner is the efficacy (and cost) of the various methods.

Kraiger has noted various and important but unanswered questions about traditional needs assessments:

Are all three levels of analysis necessary, and under what conditions is a subset of these analyses acceptable? In what order should these be carried out? Traditionally, organizational analyses are recommended prior to job and task analyses, but could organizational decision makers make better decisions about commitment to training if they understand what tasks are to be trained or exactly what the performance deficiencies are? How much convergence is there among different constituents (e.g. decision makers, managers, and employees) with respect to problem identification, and what methods are optimal for resolving differences in discrepancies among sources?

Regarding organizational analysis, should the same processes and sources used to identify training resources be used to assess climate for transfer? What are useful ways for assessing and building commitment to training through organizational analysis? How do prior experiences with training affect perceptions of the utility of training solutions identified during training? (Kraiger, 2003: 184).

Measuring the effectiveness of training

The evaluation of training is usually based on several models. The most traditional model is the standard *before-and-after* design. In the ideal situation, two groups (minimally) are required. Both are measured at time A and it is hoped there is no difference between them in terms of demographic variables (age, sex, years of service, seniority) or their skills or abilities. One group, the *experimental* group, is then trained and is measured at time B. The *control* group receives no training (or possibly a placebo) and is also measured at time B. Training can be said to succeed if there is a statistically significant and meaningful difference at time B with the experimental group performing better.

The *after-only* model is often used more out of need than choice. It has the advantage of overcoming the pre-test sensitizing effect that can lead to superficial change in the above model, but there is always a problem of *spontaneous remission*. This refers to changes (for the better or worse) that happen irrespective of the training programme.

The third, and perhaps most commonly used, criterion is to use either retention (i.e. measurement of skills over time) or to measure some *organizationally relevant* variable that the training was meant to address. In other words, training was designed for a specific purpose, then the organizational effects are monitored. This also usually takes the form of monitoring, not trainee knowledge or skill but gross organizational outcome variables (absenteeism, turnover, profits) over time. Evaluating the short- and long-term efficacy is very important in business. All organizations want a good return on investment, and seeing training as an investment rather than a cost requires providing evidence that it changes behaviour and thus productivity.

Does coaching work?

The popularity of executive coaching has taken many by surprise. Clearly, it has fulfilled some important need. Just as the rich and powerful once needed a personal therapist both as a trophy and as an adviser, so managers now appear to have the need for an executive coach and their very expensive conversation.

What is the evidence that coaching works? Is there absence of evidence or evidence of absence? The answer appears to be that there is no good, scientific evidence that coaching does what it says it does – delivers its impressive promises.

The question of course is how to answer the question. One clue may be in how scientists try to ask a very similar question, namely "Does alternative medicine work?" Scientific evaluations have a "gold standard" to evaluate the claims – randomized controlled trials. Better still, they are "blind" trials. There are essentially three features to this method, *all* of which are important to determine whether coaching works: randomization, the use of a control group and the concept of blinding.

Randomization means that people (read patients or managers) are randomly consigned to different therapists, coaches or to the control group. Why is randomization important? The answer is that it controls for the volunteer effect. We know that all sorts of factors in the doctor–patient, coach–manager relationship can affect outcome. It may be the age, education or physical good looks of either party that affects outcome, rather than the process itself.

If coaching works should it work for all managers? And it should work for all (trained) coaches who follow the process. If it only works for certain types of people with certain coaches, then we need to know why and whether some specific factor (other than the coaching process) is having an effect.

A manager has to be (randomly) assigned to their coach. Neither party likes this much, but that is too bad. We know that some psychologists have a selection interview to decide whether both parties feel they "can do business with each other". The scientific question is why the treatment only works for certain combinations of giver and receiver. If it does, this needs to be in the small (or indeed big) print.

The second feature of the scientific approach is the concept of a *control group* or indeed *control groups*. What this means is that some managers are allotted to a real management coach. Another group may be allotted to a physical coach or another manager. There are essentially two types of control groups: one in which the patient manager does nothing at all and sees if the coach experience is better than nothing; the other is where the manager does some other activity quite different from the coaching.

Control groups tell the evaluator whether changes in the managers' performance would have happened anyway, naturally over time. It's called in the business "spontaneous remission". The body (perhaps the mind) heals itself. Nothing needs to be done for this to happen. Time heals. But it could be that what is having the beneficial effect is simply talking to someone else (about anything) or getting out of the office or being made to feel important. Control groups really tell us about the process itself.

The third component is called *blinding*, ideally double-blinding. In medicine, this means neither the doctor/nurse nor the patients know whether they are getting the (real) drug or a sugar pill. The reason is that patient and doctor knowledge powerfully influences the outcome via the placebo effect.

With therapy you can't "blind" the parties involved. However, you can blind the assessor, in the sense that the person does not know what treatment the patient/manager has had. So after 6 months, say, of "something" (executive coaching, exercise, nothing) the subordinates of the managers in the trial are required to rate them on their performance. Better still, some hard behavioural data are used to see which group changes most – and in what direction. Managers' self-reports may be produced, but they may be completely delusional.

Does coaching work? Maybe. How do you know? Find, say, 100 managers. Send, randomly, 33 to a real manager coach, 33 to a physical training instructor and 33 to listen to music for two hours every 3 weeks for 6 months. After this time, measure the managers' performance, self-esteem, satisfaction and the like. Best of all, ask the managers' staff to measure the managers (upward measurement) without them knowing whether they were in the coaching, physical training or music group.

If, and only if, the coached manager has statistically different and better evaluations than the other groups can we really say coaching works for everybody. If not, the questions of, for whom, when and how coaching works, if it can be demonstrated to work at all, will have only just begun to be addressed.

Pitfalls of training

There are many reasons why training fails. Lambert (1993: 244) supplies 18 reasons, many of which occur all too frequently:

- Inaccurate or incomplete needs identification. That is, the need for training of a particular type was misdiagnosed in the first place.
- Failure to predetermine outcomes relevant to business needs of the organization. Unless one sets out a realistic and specific goal or outcome of training, it is very difficult to know if it has succeeded or failed.
- Lack of objectives, or objectives expressed as "will be able to" rather than "will". There is a difference between can do and will do, often ignored by evaluators.
- Training seen by management and participants as having little or no relationship to real life. It is seen as a break and an alternative to work, rather than as a means to improve.
- Excessive dependence by trainers on theory and chalk-and-talk training sessions. This method is least effective for the learning of specific skills.
- Trainers untrained or under-trained. It is far too easy to call yourself a trainer with little personal training in the skills required. Some courses have "train-the-trainer" sessions, but these are all too rare.
- Training programmes too short to enable deep learning to take place or skills to be practised. The longer and more spaced out the programme, the more participants learn and the more that is retained.
- Use of inappropriate resources and training methods which have to be considered beforehand, particularly the fit between the trainer and the trainee's style.
- Trainer self-indulgence, leading to all sessions being fun sessions, rather than actual learning experiences.
- Failure to pre-position the participants in terms of the company's expectation(s) of them after training. This means having a realistic expectation, per person, of what they should know, or should be able to do after the training.
- Failure to de-brief participants effectively after training, particularly as how best to practise and thus retain the skills they have acquired.
- Dependence on dated and invalid research to justify approaches. This is a very common problem.
- Excessive use of "good intentions" and "flavour of the month training", rather than those known to be effective.
- Training limited to lower levels of the organization, because it is cheaper and easier to deliver and evaluate.
- Inability of top management team to "walk like they talk"; that is, managers do not model what trainers instruct.
- Use of training to meet social, ideological or political ends, either of trainers or

senior management. That is, training is not really about skill acquisition but more about, for instance, a fight between various departments.

- Failure to relate to bottom-line performance. This means that training takes place without any consideration of its effect on productivity or profitability.
- Training design developed to accentuate enjoyable experiences and games rather than the transfer of learning to the workplace.

Does training work? What should be measured and what can be measured to determine whether training of any sort has worked. There are at least four common methods of doing this, as follows (Kirkpatrick, 1976).

Did participants like the programme?

The questionnaire or "happy sheet" is the most common method of evaluating training. The participant is more likely to be objective on a written questionnaire that guarantees anonymity than in a face-to-face interview. To be useful, a questionnaire should follow several criteria:

- Word questions carefully. Pre-test all questions by administering them to a group other than the group that will be evaluated.
- Measure only one aspect of the training at a time.
- Make the responses to each item on the questionnaire mutually exclusive and exhaustive.
- Leave room for additional written comments.

These measurements are valuable for analysing positive and negative feedback on, or directly after, the programme. But they cannot say how much a participant has learnt or the skills they have acquired. They are also very sensitive to rating errors (see Chapter 5).

Did participants learn the skills?

A job or task simulation is an excellent way of validating training results. An alternative is to have the participants watch each other. For example, in role plays, which are appropriate if verbal skills are being taught, one person can play the supervisor, another the employee, and a third can observe the skill being measured. To ensure that skills are measured accurately, standardized procedures and forms must be used. Skills must be measured both before and after training. It is also important to measure observable behaviour, not inferences about behaviour.

Did participants use the skills on the job?

This validation attempts to prove actual skill use. To ensure that on-the-job improvements derive from training rather than from external factors, set up a control group of people within the organization who have not had training. The following guidelines tend to achieve accurate test results:

- To ensure consistency, use the same or a proven equivalent instrument (e.g. questionnaire) before and after training.

- To obtain objective measures, managers, subordinates and a random cross-section of all subordinates need to be selected for training.
- Measurements for the control and training groups must be made simultaneously to minimize the chances of measuring changes that occur over time and in the work environment.
- Pre-training measurements 30–90 days in advance need to be made. People sometimes behave in an "unnatural" manner if they know they are scheduled for a training programme. Equally, post-training measurements should be done 30–90 days after the programme.
- Confidentiality must be maintained, as subordinates may be worried about the repercussions of poor ratings.
- The assessment instrument must be valid and deliver consistent results.
- Measurement must be done only on what is actually taught and measure *all* the skills taught, not just a few.

Did the programme affect the bottom line?

This validation demands observable, quantifiable, tangible and verifiable facts that show specific profit or performance results. Although hard data are preferable, soft data can be used if they can be verified. In other words, a statement that department efficiency increased by 5% is an acceptable measure of success, but only if it can be proven by a source outside the group or department. A control group is difficult to use in validation because of the wide range of internal and external variables that affect bottom-line performance other than the training itself. If it is difficult to match the control group's and training group's functions and experience through random selection, match pairs of supervisors and then assign them randomly to the training or control group.

If it is not possible to create a control group, one can compare results to an earlier period. For example, you might compare production rates for the October before and after training. But you must examine carefully all external factors that might have affected the results. Although these results are not a rigorous level-4 validation, they are useful. Lambert (1993: 238–239) has suggested that training works best if it is double smart (Box 9.2).

Finally, Kirkpatrick (1976) proposed four basic questions essential in the business of training evaluation. These are shown in Table 9.8, together with possible answers to what might be measured and various data sources. However, Kraiger (2003) has pointed out some recent critiques of Kirkpatrick's approach. They are critical for four reasons. First, it is theoretical and outdated based on an old-fashioned behavioural rather than modern cognitive approach. Second, there are unsubstantiated assumptions about the relationship between outcomes (i.e. people cannot learn if they don't like the programme). Third, it treats both trainee reactions and learning itself as if they were unidimensional, whereas we know that this is not the case. Fourth, evaluation has different purposes: decision-making, feedback and marketing. Thus what is measured must fit the purpose.

Conclusion

People are selected on the basis of their skills and abilities. Yet they also have to be trained throughout their working lives to retain skills and acquire new ones. Global

Box 9.2 The conditions under which training works best

S *Specific* in that they should define and demand observable behaviours.
Significant in that they make a valid contribution to the desired culture, vision, mission and goals of the organization.

M *Measurable* in that they are applied over time consistently and constantly in all appropriate situations.
Meaningful in that they are congruent with the values and proper expectations of the individuals who must make them work.

A *Achievable* by the participants with effective training and other support.
Attainable within the organizational, economic, legislative and social climates as it exists.

R *Realistic* in that adequate time is designed into the programme for sufficient threat-free practice by all.
Reward-driven within the existing or emergence culture, so that desired behaviours will be reinforced in activity.

T *Timely* so that they meet the credible present and future needs of the organization.
Team-orientated* so that everyday support is seen as appropriate.

* Where the skills are to be applied uniquely and in isolation by participants, a somewhat different but equally valid approach to implementation, based on planned self-reward, is required. This research addresses the more common situation where participants can and must exercise the same skills together.

Source: Reprinted from Lambert (1993) with the permission of Pitman Press.

competition, technological change, differences in the workforce, and mergers and acquisitions, all are reasons why organizations invest in training their staff. Some see training as important for the acquisition of highly specific skills. Others believe in educating their staff through long, fairly general and very expensive courses. Equally, some organizations are eager to develop their more senior staff so that they realize their potential.

The psychology of learning is a well-established area of study dating back to the founders of the discipline. The ideas of classical and operant conditioning have been known since the beginning of the century, although observational and instructional learning is how most people learn at work. Learning theory is clearly about the most effective reinforcement or reward schedules that are meant to maintain desirable behaviour. It is both sad and surprising that so few managers have taken the time to understand learning theory and its implications.

The costs and importance of training makes it a "hot" topic among many managers. Different fads often appear and disappear. Current fads include the use of outdoor training, of "virtual reality" training, and more use of managers themselves as trainers. The number and type of training methods are legion and they may be categorized in various ways, such as hard/soft, specific/general, and so on. Certainly, considerable thought needs to be given to a cost–benefit analysis of various training methods in order to choose the best for a particular purpose.

Most organizations need, but few have, a good training strategy that extends from a careful analysis of the training required to a careful evaluation of the efficacy of the training done. One of the issues relating to the strategy is establishing the learning style preferences of the individual. It seems that we are able to specify certain unique learning styles and infer how individuals like to acquire knowledge. Learning might mean

Table 9.8 Four critical training questions

What we want to know	What to look at / What might be measured	Alternative data / Measurement dimensions	Source of data	Gathering methodology
I. *Are the trainees happy? If not, why not?*	Trainee reaction during workshop	Relevance / Threat / Ease of learning	Trainees' comments / Questions about exercises	Observation / Interview / Questionnaire
a. Concepts not relevant				
b. Workshop design	Trainee reaction after workshop	Perceived "worth" or relevance – learning energy	"Approach behaviour" / "Approach behaviour" to project. Questions about project, concepts	Observation / Interview / Questionnaire
c. Trainees not properly positioned				
II. *Do the materials teach the concepts? If not, why not?*	Trainee performance during workshop	Understanding / Application	Learning time / Performance on exercises / Presentations	Observation / Document review
a. Workshop structure	Trainee performance at end of workshop	Understanding / Application / Facility / Articulation	Action plan for project / Use of tools on exercises / Presentation	Observation / Document review / Interview / Questionnaire
b. Lessons				
– Presentation				
– Exercise				
– Trainers				
III. *Are the concepts used? If not, why not?*	Performance improvement projects*	Analysis / Action plan / Results	Discussions / Documentation / Actual results	Observation / Interview / Document review / Questionnaire
a. Concepts				
– Not relevant				
– Too complex	Problem-solving technique	Questions asked / Action proposed / Action taken	Discussion / Documentation / Results	Observation / Interview / Document review / Questionnaire
– Too sophisticated/simple				
b. Inadequate tools				
c. Environment not supportive	On-going management approach*	Dissemination effort / Language / People management process	Discussions / Meetings / Documentation	Observation / Interview / Document review / Questionnaire
d. Skills/concepts not required yet				
IV. *Does application of the concepts positively affect the organization? If not, why not?*	Problem-solving*	Problem identification / Analysis / Action / Results	Discussions / Documentation / Results	Interview / Document review / Questionnaire
	Problem prediction and prevention*	Potential problem identification / Analysis / Action	Discussion / Documentation / Results	Interview / Document review / Questionnaire
	Performance measures*	Output measures	Performance data / Diagnostic measures	Document review

* Specific to a particular workshop.

Source: Reproduced from Kirkpatrick (1976) with the permission of McGraw-Hill.

the acquisition of certain behaviour patterns and the extinction of others. Managers need to be careful in their use of punishment lest it have the opposite effect or particularly undesirable consequences.

The most difficult issue for many companies is measuring the effectiveness of training. There are many ways of doing so, ranging from simple participant feedback to examining some specific output variable (such as productivity) some time after training. It remains very difficult, but it is extremely important, to attempt to evaluate whether training works, by a variety of methods and using specific criteria.

A research perspective

Training transfer and generalization

Does management training work? Although it may be shown to work in the training room, it is much less clear if those being trained use their newly acquired skills and insights in their actual place of work.

The transfer of learning (or training) is the process by which the effects of training learnt in one situation transfer into others. If transfer was not possible, there would be little justification for formal education; every element of knowledge, skill and capacity would have to be taught separately. This would effectively damn many training programmes. But there are at least five types of transfer:

- *Lateral transfer*: Lateral transfer involves performance at the same level of complexity as the initial learning, but in a different context. In other words, it refers to the ability to complete new learnt tasks at work as well as in the training room.
- *Sequential transfer*: Sequential transfer occurs when trainees build on a learning foundation. A skill learned today may have some relationship to a fact or idea learned tomorrow. For example, keyboard skills transfer to many tasks.
- *Vertical transfer*: Vertical transfer occurs when learning at one level (e.g. comprehending statistical facts) facilitates that at another (e.g. the solution of mathematical problems). It amounts to a transfer from the simpler components of a task to the more complex ones.
- *Positive transfer*: When training or performance in one task can be transformed to another, positive transfer occurs. Positive transfer manifests itself in the following situations: learning Mandarin may aid the learning of Cantonese; and mastering the skill of word-processing results in the positive transfer of understanding spreadsheets.
- *Negative transfer*: Negative transfer is said to occur when previous learning in a particular task hinders learning in another task. Errors may arise in a factory when an employee with experience of driving one particular model of a fork-lift truck drives another model. The pedals for braking, reversing and accelerating can differ in position from one model to the next.

Transfer is important in evaluating the cost of training: the more transferable, the more cost-efficient. Related to the concept of transfer is the concept of generalizability. There are various types of generalizability – from the training room to the factory floor, from one highly specific skill to others, and over time. Most training programmes evaluate training immediately after it has ended, rather than, say, 6 months later. Of course, the extent to which information and skills have been retained is dependent on many factors, apart from the course itself. The way the organization rewards skills acquisition and allows opportunity for practice is obviously important.

For the researcher the problem is: (1) to identify the factors that maximize or minimize skill transfer and generalization; (2) to understand the process by which this occurs; and (3) to offer advice to maximize effective generalization.

A cross-cultural perspective

A cross-cultural study of management development

Sparrow (personal communication 1995) contrasted the attitudes to management development of companies in different countries.

USA
- Management is considered something separate, definable, generalizable, teachable.
- The climate is of expansion, oversupply of space, undersupply of resources and time.
- Drive, entrepreneurialism, versatility, adaptability and opportunism are favoured.
- Empirical thinking, numerical skills, personal experience (not society's codified wisdom) are valued.
- Man-management skills, social and political skills, and leadership are considered important.
- Training and thinking focuses on basic character: personality and behaviour are thought to underlie most skills.
- Trial period of 5–7 years before being assessed for management.
- Vertical moves through functional hierarchies – career anchor jobs are usual.
- Formal assessment of general management potential through assessment centres, etc.
- Mobility within internal labour market; skills believed transferable.
- 80/20 internal/external resourcing rule.
- High potential elites of around 10% of management population.
- Age 40 make or break for advancement.

France
- Only 13% take part in dual in-/out-house training courses.
- Strong central government control over education curriculum (school and university).
- Companies spend 1.5% of payroll on training by law.
- Mainly in-company training, company-specific contingencies, no more than needed for the job.
- Training does not improve external mobility for most managers.
- Little training for manual workers; resources biased towards off-the-job management training.
- Elite political model: tall hierarchy, intricate careers, patronage, mobility.
- Legally defined "cadres": 5 years' study at Grande Ecoles after Baccalaureat.
- Preparatory test for Grandes Ecoles final selection.
- Headquarters in Paris.
- *Pantouflage* – movement from civil service to private industry.
- Management is a position from which it is legitimate to hold authority.
- Management is an intellectual task, not interpersonally demanding educated cleverness.
- Advertisements for managerial jobs stress reasoning ability, analysis, synthesis, evaluation, articulation.

Germany
- Sophisticated system of vocational education and training.
- Dual system of school/company experience.
- Triple stakeholders in training: company, trade unions, government.
- School leavers selected for company programmes.
- Broad competencies values: managers and manual workers have common exposure.

- Low supervision mentality, greater control of quality (i.e. supervision is found in early stages in any process).
- Blurred divisions between supervisors, technical staff, manual workers.
- Employees rotate through two or more jobs usually.
- Promotion dependent on starting qualifications, nature of work, access to training.
- Management development function neither company-specific nor strategic.
- No MBA educational philosophy.
- Job grades have more validity than skills or competencies.
- Two-year part-time course for managers who are "late age" graduates.
- Highest proportion of PhDs in the world in management.
- Functional career model – move in same sector, contiguous functions.
- Managers must manage something – select on functional and technical knowledge.
- Career development coincides with increased skill specialization.

Japan
- Tradition which links education level with business success.
- Education is seen as a means of self-improvement.
- Senior members required to "take care of" younger members.
- Propensity to learn anything of value to the group (i.e. share learned information) and knowledge for perceived corporate good.
- Exclusive "outside shunning" corporate culture – stronger internal bonding.
- Planning and organization of development activities over long term and on grand scale with other Japanese participants.

A human resources perspective

Knowledge management

Taxi drivers in London "do the knowledge". They have knowledge colleges that help them effectively remember the entire London A to Z. This prodigious task takes 2–3 years and actually results, so cognitive neuroscience brain imaging has shown, in parts of the brain growing and being more active.

You can spot students of "the knowledge" on Sunday morning on mopeds with clip boards. It is a form of rote learning. They have to remember names, places and routes. Dozens of roads have the same name in London differing only by post code. And routes on the map give no indication about one-way streets, long-term diversions, traffic-calming devices (designed mainly to infuriate). So it becomes experimental as well as applied learning.

Very little in business involves rote learning. Even in the most technical of jobs, rote learning is unusual. And the higher one goes in organizations, the more strategic and less technical one gets. So now we are told not that people are our greatest asset, but that knowledge is. And that may be in many heads even if they do not know it.

So now we have knowledge managers. But what is knowledge management? It has been defined many ways. However, the following is a pretty reasonable and sufficient definition: "The systematic process of finding, selecting, organizing, distilling and presenting information in a way that improves an employee's comprehension in a specific area of interest".

Knowledge management helps an organization to gain insight and understanding from its own experience. Specific knowledge management activities help focus the organization on acquiring, storing and utilizing knowledge for such things as problem-solving, dynamic learning, strategic planning and decision-making. It also protects intellectual assets from decay, adds to firm intelligence and provides increased flexibility.

But the actual, crypto, quasi and even real intellectuals have been wading around in this murky pool. The first thing they do is make distinctions. The first is between data information and knowledge, which is pretty self-evident. But as scepticals have wisely noted:

- A collection of data is not information.
- A collection of information is not knowledge.
- A collection of knowledge is not wisdom.
- A collection of wisdom is not truth.

Then there is the difference between different types of knowledge. Consider the following three:

- *Tacit knowledge*: represented by individual or group experience and expertise, is implicit: used for sense-making, problem-solving and the gaining of perspective, and is personal: held within us and rarely documented.
- *Explicit knowledge*: based on policies, procedures, instructions, standards and results, readily communicated, often through written documentation, and provides a record of "organizational or institutional memory".
- *Cultural knowledge*: the basis for what we deem to be fair and trustworthy, an underlying comprehension of how we treat new truths and situations, and is often tied to an organization's vision, mission and overall philosophy.

Davenport & Prusak (1998) set out the 10 principles of knowledge management:

1 Knowledge management is expensive (but so is stupidity!)
2 Effective management of knowledge requires hybrid solutions of people and technology.
3 Knowledge management is highly political.
4 Knowledge management requires knowledge managers.
5 Knowledge management benefits more from maps than models, more from markets than hierarchies.
6 The sharing and use of knowledge are often unnatural acts.
7 Knowledge management means improving knowledge work processes.
8 Knowledge access is only the beginning.
9 Knowledge management never ends.
10 Knowledge management requires a knowledge contract.

But does that help at all? Perhaps the first and most fundamental questions to ask is as follows: "Why don't people (in the same organization) share information?" There are, of course, many answers. But perhaps the most common reasons are:

- *Power*: Knowledge is power; expensively obtained; destabilizing if simply "given away". The keeper of the files is the great controller. Professionalism is about acquiring specialist knowledge . . . and with it money, power and influence. Hence the powerful resistance not to give it away.
- *Salience*: Even if prepared to share, do people know what knowledge to share, when, where, why and with whom? What is useful? Will they understand it? Will it go out of date?
- *Culture/climate*: The corporate culture (or immediate climate) does not support or facilitate many forms of participation, or sharing. Despite their vision, mission, values and statements, many organizations are deeply protective of their secrets. We know the story of the people who know the Coca Cola recipe. They are probably more likely to be the norm than the exception.
- *Time*: Busy people simply don't have the time to share in areas where knowledge is changing fast.
- *Language*: Specialist knowledge is associated with complex jargon that even "native speakers" (i.e. specialists) don't know they are using and becoming impenetrably incomprehensible. Obfuscation through acronym is the end to knowledge management's discussion.

- *Benefits*: There appear only to be costs but no benefits of the sharing process. It appears entirely to be a one-way street benefiting the organization. In this world of portfolio management and short-term contracts, it may be that holding onto one's specialist knowledge is the only way to ensure re-employment.

  So what are the problems and issues for knowledge management?

- *Knowledge acquisition*. Where and how to acquire the knowledge most efficiently. This applies to both the individual and the organization.
- *Knowledge prioritization*. How to decide what is the most important knowledge and that what is relatively trivial. This may change dramatically over time.
- *Knowledge categorization*. How best to group and sort this knowledge into meaningful categories. This presents an enormous problem with retrieval as all personal computer owners' know.
- *Knowledge storage*. Where and how to store knowledge cheaply, efficiently and reliably so that it is easily and efficiently retrievable.
- *Knowledge creation*. How to use principles of synergy to create "new" knowledge. This is like getting the knowledge to work for you and is far from straightforward.
- *Knowledge exploitation*. How best to use the knowledge that we have so extensively and expensively collected. In many ways, this is the hardest bit. It is most fundamental to the whole knowledge management exercise but is far from clear. The web means more and more people can easily access all sorts of facts – some of them even true. A more mobile, better educated workforce is less loyal and in small groups more flexible.

Getting to exploit the knowledge of their staff is nothing new. We may have knowledge managers whose task it supposedly is to do this, but what evidence is there that they succeed. Paradoxically, isn't it the one area in which practical knowledge and know-how is pretty sparse in knowledge management.

References

Arnold, J., Robertson, I., & Cooper, C. (1991). *Work psychology*. London: Pitman.

Baldwin, T., & Ford, J. (1988). Transfer of training: A review and directions for further research. *Personnel Psychology, 41*, 63–105.

Bernardin, H., & Russell, J. (1993). *Human research management: An experiential approach*. New York: McGraw-Hill.

Berry, L. (1998). *Psychology at work*. New York: McGraw-Hill.

Blum, M., & Naylor, J. (1968). *Industrial psychology*. New York: Harper.

Corder, C. (1990). *Teaching hard, training soft*. Aldershot, UK: Gower.

Davenport, T., & Prusak, L. (1998). *Working knowledge: How organizations manage what they know*. Boston, MA: Harvard Business School Press.

Eysenck, H. (1978). The development of personality and its relation to learning. In S. Murray-Smith (Ed.), *Melbourne studies in education* (pp. 134–181). Melbourne, VIC: Melbourne University Press.

Eysenck, M. (1981). Learning, memory and personality. In J. Eysenck (Ed.), *A model of personality* (pp. 169–209). Berlin: Springer.

Furnham, A. (1992). *Personality at work*. London: Routledge.

Furnham, A., & Gunter, B. (1994). *Business watching*. London: ABRA Press.

Goldstein, I. (1986). *Training in organizations*. Monterey, CA: Brooks/Cole.

Greenberg, J., & Baron, R. (1992). *Behavior in organizations*. Boston, MA: Allyn & Bacon.

Honey, P., & Mumford, A. (1982). *The manual of learning styles*. Maidenhead, UK: Honey Press.

Kirkpatrick, D. (1976). Evaluation of training. In R. Craig & L. Bittel (Eds.), *Training and development handbook* (pp. 261–270). New York: McGraw-Hill.

Kolb, D. (1976). *Learning style inventory: Technical manual*. Boston, MA: McBer.

Kolb, D. (1984). *Experimental learning*. Englewood Cliffs, NJ: Prentice-Hall.

Kraiger, K. (2003). Perspectives on training and development. In W. Borman, D. Ilgen, & R. Klimoski (Eds.), *Handbook of psychology* (Vol 12, pp. 171–192). New York: Wiley.

Lambert, T. (1993). *Key management tools*. London: Pitman.

Luthans, S. F., & Kreitner, R. (1985). *Organizational behaviour and beyond*. Glenview, IL: Scott, Foresman.

Noe, R., & Colquitt, J. (2002). Planning for training impact: Principles of training effectiveness. In K. Kraiger (Ed.), *Creating, implementing and maintaining effective training and development*. (pp. 53–79). San Francisco, CA: Jossey-Bass.

Patrick, J. (2000). Training. In N. Chmiel (Ed.), *Introduction to work and organizational psychology* (pp. 100–123). Oxford: Blackwell.

Pendleton, D. (1995). Putting practice into psychology. In P. Collett & A. Furnham (Eds.), *Social psychology at work* (pp. 225–235). London: Routledge.

Porteous, M. (1997). *Occupational psychology*. London: Prentice-Hall.

Schultz, D., & Schultz, S. (1998). *Psychology and work today*. Upper Saddle River, NJ: Prentice-Hall.

Skinner, B. F. (1957). *Contingencies of reinforcement*. New York: Appleton-Century.

Snell, R., & James, K. (1994). Beyond the tangible in management education and development. *Management Learning, 25*, 319–340.

10 Group dynamics

Introduction

Very few people work alone: the artist in the studio, the writer in the study, the crafts-man at the bench, all are the exception rather than the rule. Indeed, solitary confine-ment is often thought of as a major source of torture. Not only do most people work with others, but they do so quite specifically in groups, sections, teams or departments. Furthermore, many workers will tell you that the group processes and dynamics in the team, which they may refer to as morale or team spirit, is often a major determinant of the efficacy of that team's work. Workers are part *dependent*, part *independent* and part *interdependent* on others. Some who work on production lines are utterly dependent on others, whereas others work in offices where the interdependence is less crucial. Work teams, it is argued, increase efficiency. They also lead to innovation because of the cross-fertilization of ideas. They can improve learning because they can integrate and link information that individuals cannot.

Humans are social animals. They seek out the company of others and even the most primitive sort of work in hunter-gatherer societies is essentially cooperative and col-laborative. People choose to become members of groups for a variety of different reasons (Table 10.1).

If people work in groups or teams, it becomes crucially important to understand how they operate, how and why intra- and inter-group cooperation and competition occur, and their organizational consequences. Group dynamics refers to the psychological processes that occur in groups. We shall concentrate on how these psychological pro-cesses directly affect the work product or outcome of the group, and how that outcome influences the group dynamics.

Table 10.1 Why people join groups

Security	Groups provide safety in numbers, protection against a common enemy
Mutual benefits (goal achievement)	By joining together, group members can work to ensure attainment of shared goals and benefits
Need to be social	Groups satisfy the basic need to be with others, to be stimulated by human companionship
Self-esteem	Membership in certain groups provides people with opportunities to feel good about their accomplishments and to identify with others from the same group
Mutual self-interest	Banding together, people can share their mutual interests (such as hobbies)

In all modern organizations, employees are formally grouped into different units, such as sections, departments and centres. Also, during breaks at work and in after-work activities, they form into informal friendship groups based on common interests. The social relationships that occur in these formal and informal groups can have a significant effect on the way people work together and ultimately the quality and quantity of their work output. However, it would be naïve and misleading to suggest that group dynamics are the major determinant of work output: this was the fallacy perpetuated by the Human Relations School (see Chapter 3). The ability and training of employees, their personal motivation, the quality of their equipment and the appeal of their product, as well as the corporate culture and climate, all play a role alongside group dynamics in determining productivity. Yet a workgroup can be a powerful source of support or frustration to individual workers. Furthermore, membership of that group brings with it an identity that may be both positive and negative.

People in teams have to be aware of the task they are performing, other people and themselves. Efficient group functioning takes effort and skill, which can "eat into" productivity time. The concept of *process loss* refers to the effort expended on social group dynamics that should or could be used on task accomplishment (Spector, 2003). Obviously, the easier the group relations, the more effort can be devoted to doing the job itself. Essentially, process losses are due to coordination problems (problems of integration) and motivational processes (problems of social loafing in teams) (Unsworth & West, 2000).

Various factors determine the effectiveness of a group, measured by such things as output, group continuity and morale. They include the primary *task* of the group (challenge, complexity), the *composition* and *structure* of the group (size, diversity), *managerial support* (via training, rewards) and the group dynamics, which are analogous to the group processes.

What is a group?

Essentially, a group is made up of persons (more than two, which is a dyad) who *communicate regularly, share goals* and interact with each other *over time*, so building up affective (or emotional) bonds. Groups have four defining characteristics:

- They are composed of more than two people involved in social interaction, who must be able to influence each other's beliefs and behaviours.
- They share common goals on certain issues – agreed goals, objectives and targets. Goal-sharing is an achievement of any group as much as defining characteristic.
- They have a relatively stable structure – rules and roles that endure over time and across different social situations.
- They openly perceive and recognize themselves as being a (stable) group.

All teams are groups but not all groups are teams. Groups can work without one another: teams cannot.

Thus, we have command groups, task groups, interest groups and friendship groups, all of which have some of the above characteristics. According to Cordery (2002), at work teams can be divided into four types:

- *work teams*, attempting to achieve specific tasks;

- *parallel teams*, which operate alongside formal organizations;
- *project teams*, created for a specific purpose over a specific time;
- *management teams*, whose task it is to run the business.

Groups mobilize powerful forces that need to be managed, as they can be both constructive and destructive. Indeed, the very essence of being a manager is doing things well with or through other people. Like Likert (1961), one could argue that:

- workgroups are important sources of individuals' social need satisfaction;
- groups in organizations that fulfil this psychological function are also more productive;
- management's task is therefore to create effective workgroups by developing "supportive relationships";
- an effective organizational structure consists of democratic/participative workgroups, each linked to the organization as a whole through overlapping memberships;
- coordination is achieved by individuals who carry out "linking functions".

There are a few "universals" with respect to groups: features that seem to be true of all groups. First, small groups do *exist* and must be dealt with by managers. Second, group formation is *inevitable*. When individuals come into contact with one another, various types of definable groups emerge. In organizations, the "old timers" might form a social unit with other long-term employees, and "newcomers" might tend to interact closely among themselves. Third, all groups *mobilize powerful forces* that affect individuals. History is full of seemingly inconsequential individuals who, when placed in command of a group, have influenced the course of human development. Fourth, group behaviour has both *good and bad consequences*. A group can be effective in stimulating certain aspects of individual behaviour. They may also inhibit performance, as when a group of workers puts pressure on a "rate buster" for producing above the standards set by the membership. Finally, understanding group dynamics can increase the chances of obtaining *desirable consequences* from group interaction. When managers understand the group dynamics in organizations, they can use the group more effectively to accomplish the goals of the organization and of the individual employees.

There are many issues facing the new workgroup. These have to be solved by the group. This takes place explicitly and implicitly over time. Furthermore, groups can change the way in which they do some of these things, but the way each group solves these problems makes it unique.

- *Climate*: How close, friendly, casual should group interaction be? Should the group be intimate or simply associative?
- *Participation*: How much and what type of participation should occur? This refers to the quality and quantity of group members' interactions with each other.
- *Goal comprehension*: How much of the goals of the group need to be understood by each member and how crucial is it that all members are committed to them?
- *Communication*: What channels are preferred and how is the group networked? Do they prefer face-to-face contact rather than a fax? Are they all regular e-mailers? Do they all have open access to each other?
- *Conflict-handling*: How are conflicts and disagreements handled? What systems and

rules have developed for preventing and solving conflict? Indeed, whether conflict is encouraged or discouraged at all.

- *Decision-making*: How are decisions made and by whom (e.g. democracy and secret vote, senior managers by show-of-hands) (see Chapters 11)?
- *Performance evaluation*: How are members to be appraised? What are the criteria? Is it formal or informal? What is the regularity of appraisal and who does it? For what purpose is it primarily done (i.e. salary increase, promotion)?
- *Division of labour*: How are tasks assigned and subgroups formed? Are members put into sub-departments on the basis of their skills, demography or interests?
- *Leadership*: How are leaders elected and what are their functions? How do team heads get elected and what do they have to do to stay in office?
- *Process monitoring*: How are internal and task processes monitored and checked, and how is feedback provided? Who takes the soundings regarding group morale?

Sundstrom, De Meuse & Futrell (1990) argue that the effectiveness of working groups or teams is dependent on three sorts of factors. First, *organizational context*, which refers to the corporate culture, the technology, the mission clarity, the autonomy of the group, the type of feedback and rewards, the opportunities for training, and the physical environment of the organization. Second, it depends on *boundaries*: how the group or team is differentiated from others and how the group is integrated with other groups in the organization. Thirdly, effectiveness is dependent on *group development*: the interpersonal processes, norms, roles and overall cohesion. Clearly, there must be other factors as well, such as simply knowing how to perform the task. Sundstrom *et al.* were also able to distinguish four distinct types of working groups in a simple typology. Groups at work, they argue, come in a vast range of types, each with different functions, aims and ambitions:

- *Active/involvement*: These are committees, review panels, quality circles and advisory councils, which have generalists and whose group life-span is short. They do not have to synchronize with other groups and their output is typically decisions, proposals and recommendations.
- *Production/service*: These may be assembly or mining teams, or manufacturing/ flight attendant crews. They have a variable membership and usually have to be synchronized with suppliers and customers. Their output is often assemblies, components, service and repairs.
- *Project/development*: These include research, planning and development teams and task forces. Usually, members are experts in these groups and are neither integrated nor synchronized with the activities of the rest of the organization. Their output is plans, presentations and reports.
- *Active/negotiation*: These are often sports and entertainment groups, as well as surgery and cockpit crews. They are exclusive experts closely synchronized with the rest of the organization. Their output varies from concerts to medical operations.

This may be a useful typology for categorizing workgroups, but such typologies do not tell us much about the group dynamics within any specific workgroup.

Group development

How do groups form and develop over time? Why do they change? Why do some groups evolve and change continually while others remain "caught-in-time"? And why do some groups suddenly collapse? Tuckman (1965) believed that groups usually go through a particular stage-wise sequence before reaching a mature and effective stage. This concept suffers all the problems of all stage-wise theories, such as not clarifying *how long* each stage lasts, what determines the *change* from one to another, whether the sequence is always linear, whether one can skip a stage, and so on. Nevertheless, the idea has become very popular, partly because it allows group participants to understand the process through which their group is going. It is thought to be useful in predicting group development (Hellriegel, Slocum, & Woodman, 1992).

Forming   In the forming stage, members focus their efforts on defining goals and developing procedures for performing their task. Group development in this stage involves getting acquainted, and understanding leadership and other member roles. In this stage, individual members might:

- keep feelings to themselves until they know the situation;
- act more securely than they actually feel about how the team functions;
- experience confusion and uncertainty about what is expected of them;
- be reserved and polite, at least superficially, certainly not hostile to others;
- try to size up the personal benefits relative to the personal costs of being involved in the group or team.

At this stage, they are concerned with "sniffing" out and around other group members to see if they are going to stay in the group and how they are going to get involved.

Storming   Conflicts often emerge over task behaviours, the relative priorities of goals, who is to be responsible for what, and the task-related guidance and direction of the leader. Competition over the leadership role and conflict over goals are dominant themes at this stage. Some members may withdraw or try to isolate themselves from the emotional tension generated. It is believed that the group cannot effectively evolve into the third stage if the leader and members go to either extreme. Suppressing conflict may create bitterness and resentment, which will last long after members attempt to express their differences and emotions. Withdrawal by key members can cause the group to fail more quickly at this stage. Some groups genuinely have little to "storm" about, but others suppress this stage, which can cause problems at a later date.

Norming   Task-orientated behaviours in the norming stage usually evolve into the sharing of information, acceptance of different opinions, and positive attempts to reach mutually agreeable (or compromise) decisions on the group's goals. The group sets the rules by which it will operate, and emotions often focus on empathy, concern and the positive expressions of feelings, leading to group cohesion. Cooperation within the group is a dominant theme, while a sense of shared responsibility for the group develops. However, it is both noticeable and surprising that different groups under very similar circumstances find very different solutions to their psychological processes, and hence develop spectacularly different behavioural norms.

Performing   During the performing stage, the group shows how effectively and efficiently it can perform its task. It is the stage characterized by interdependence and problem-solving. The roles of individual members are usually accepted and understood. The members usually understand when they should work independently and when they should help each other. Groups differ after the performing stage: some continue to learn and develop from their experiences, and new inputs improve their efficiency and effectiveness. Other groups – especially those that developed norms not fully supportive of efficiency and effectiveness – may perform only at the level needed for their survival. A minimally adequate level of performance may be caused by excessive self-orientated behaviours by group members, the development of norms that inhibit task effectiveness and efficiency, poor group leadership, or other factors.

Adjourning   The adjourning stage involves the termination of task behaviours and disengagement from relations-orientated behaviours. Some groups, such as a project team created to investigate and report on a specific problem within 6 months, have a well-defined point of adjournment. This stage has also been called the "mourning" stage, as it is not unusual for groups that have disintegrated to leave members feeling sad and nostalgic.

To create functional and effective working teams, it may be useful to consider how people behave naturally. Thus, Hackman (1987) suggests that there needs to be four stages in creating workteams. This adjourning or mourning stage should be considered by people setting up formal, task-orientated workgroups:

1   "Pre-work", considering the group's goals, the authority it might need; indeed, more importantly, even whether it needs to exist at all.
2   Create performance conditions, specifically the equipment, material and personnel.
3   Form and build the team by making clear who is, and who is not, in the group, agreeing on expected behaviour, tasks, roles, and so on.
4   Providing continuing assistance by eliminating group problems, replenishing material and replacing people who leave.

Stages 1 to 3 can be done "on paper" in the planning stage. Yet, as all managers discover, however well formulated, some teams or groups do not function well because the "dynamics", which are more difficult to plan, can be destructive. In lay terms, "the chemistry" of individual personalities is a powerful force in any group. Groups develop and change over time. The cycle described by Tuckman (1965) may repeat itself when new members arrive or old ones leave. Because of these developmental changes, few groups are totally stable and easily predictable.

However, Herriot and Pemberton (1995) are very critical of the stage-wise theory *myth*. They note:

> The Seven Stages of Team myth derives from the same historical period and the same assumptions. Why does a sequence of developmental stages have to be passed through before the team can tackle its task? Because learning about how to operate together has to happen before real work can start. Or rather, more precisely, because we have to "work hard at our relationships" before we can start the task. This myth was supported by a widely quoted rhyming mnemonic – forming, storming, norming and performing – still the staple fare provided by many trainers and consultants.

Yet here again, the evidence fails to support the myth. In organizational settings, teams don't spend a lot of time on process. On the contrary, they usually leap rapidly (perhaps too rapidly) into the task they think they have been given. Then they have alternate periods of getting on with their work and changing the way they do it. It's hardly surprising that there is no fixed sequence or pattern. After all, there is a tremendous variety in the nature of the tasks they undertake – resolving problems, devising strategy, achieving a tactical objective, reporting on feasibility, planning and restructuring, running a campaign. Tasks differ in ambiguity and familiarity: imagining a new service or product that people might be persuaded to buy is a much more ambiguous task than designing an improved model of an automobile. Different tasks require different ways of working. (Herriot & Pemberton, 1995: 193)

Their argument is that team tasks determine processes which determine team roles. *Overall, the context determines both tasks and processes.* Therefore, team roles are a consequence of other more important things. However, Herriot & Pemberton do acknowledge that there are time-related events in the life of a team that are important:

Some processes may be very important at particular points in the time span of tasks. For example:

- Issues and ideas are going to be crucial near the beginning of the strategy-making task.
- Managing boundaries will be important at the end of a problem-solving task when the solution has to be sold to the problem's owners.
- Keeping motivation and momentum going will prevent a campaign from sagging in the middle.
- Constant evaluation of progress will ensure that the tactical objective is adhered to.
- Evaluation of progress and outcome is essential for the universal task of learning, which cannot occur unless activity is reflected upon. (Herriot & Pemberton, 1995: 197)

Formal and informal groups

Most workgroups have certain common characteristics:

- a *formal structure*;
- they are *task-orientated*;
- they tend to be *permanent (ish)*;
- their activities (should) contribute *directly* to the organization's collective purpose;
- they are *consciously* and formally organized by someone for a reason.

Formal groups are explicitly constituted by organizational decision-makers to accomplish a specific task. They are found in several senses: they exist formally, they have formal rights and obligations to follow and, quite often, their behaviour is fairly formatted and constrained. Formal group leaders are appointed, and the group's structure, rules and procedures are often codified. Historical patterns of behaviour are often based on ideas about the division of labour constituting formal groups. People then *fill* an established role and are required to behave within the constraints of set, formal rules. Roles have titles, job descriptions and contracts. The formal groups can be seen in the organization's chart (or "organigram").

On the other hand, *informal* groups evolve naturally and spontaneously. They develop through a variety of forces and may contain people from various sections and levels who may have something in common that forms them into an informal group. These may be common beliefs (religious), common leisure activities (sports), common fears or aspirations, or a common energy. This may be formal members of some outside workgroup such as the Rotarians, the Masons or the Round Tablers. To some extent, they may be considered to be cliques – that is, people of the same rank in the same department (horizontal), of different ranks (vertical), or sundry employees with some other specific factor in common. They function to support friendship, mutual help and confirmation of specific beliefs and ideologies.

Formal and informal groups can, in fact, be subdivided further into subgroups. Thus, Greenberg & Baron (1992) suggest formal groups can be divided into:

- *command* groups, which are determined by organizational structure and rule (standing committees or boards);
- *task* groups, determined by individuals with particular expertise (*ad hoc* groups or commissions).

On the other hand, informal groups can be divided into:

- *interest* groups, the members of which come together because they share a common interest. These voluntary groups may be concerned with union representation, pollution, the cases of particular workers, or issues outside the organization itself;
- *friendship* groups, which exist quite specifically to satisfy social needs.

The formal and informal groups are never totally separate. The composition, structure and operation of informal groups will in part be determined by the formal arrangements that exist in the company. These provide the context within which social relationships are established and can take place. Such formal constraints can include physical layout, work shifts, numbers of staff employed and the type of technology used. All informal groups arise out of a combination of formal factors and human needs. The nature of the formal organization is based on the choices made by senior company managers.

Organizations meet only a small range of the individual's needs. The informal organization emerges to fulfil those needs neglected or ignored by the formal system. It differs from the formal system by being more casual in terms of its composition of its members and nature of their interaction. To identify different informal groups, one does not look at the workflow or the organization chart, but at who interacts with whom, and what friendships exist between individuals. The following is one way of distinguishing between formal and informal groups on relevant criteria.

One should read Table 10.2 (indeed all figures and tables) critically. For instance, the Control Mechanisms specified above consider only negative or punishment methods, some fairly extreme. Groups control members by promise of reward and not just threat of punishment.

Table 10.2 Informal and formal groups

		Informal group	*Formal group*
A.	*Structure*		
	(a) Origin	Spontaneous	Planned
	(b) Rationale	Emotional	Rationale
	(c) Characteristics	Dynamic	Stable
B.	*Position terminology*	Role	Job
C.	*Goals*	Member satisfaction	Profitability or service to society
D.	*Influence*		
	(a) Base	Personality	Position
	(b) Type	Power	Authority
	(c) Flow	Bottom-up	Top-down
E.	*Control mechanisms*	Physical or social sanction (norms)	Threat of firing or demotion
F.	*Communication*		
	(a) Channels	Grapevine	Formal channels
	(b) Networks	Poorly defined, cut across regular channels	Well-defined, follows formal lines
G.	*Charting*	Sociogram	Organization chart
H.	*Miscellaneous*		
	(a) Individuals included	Only those "acceptable"	All individuals in workgroup
	(b) Interpersonal relations	Arise spontaneously	Prescribed by job description
	(c) Leadership role	Result of the membership	Assigned by organization
	(d) Basis for interaction	Personal characteristics status	Functional duties or position
	(e) Basis for attachment	Cohesiveness	Loyalty

Source: Adapted from Gray & Starke (1984: 412).

Group characteristics

There are various characteristics of groups which are the major variables for under-standing workgroup dynamics. These may be seen as dimensions or categories that allow one first to describe and then to understand group dynamics.

Group size

The membership of groups usually ranges from three to about twelve people. Downsizing or "rightsizing" in many organizations means that formal workgroups are becoming larger. People in groups of more than twelve members find mutual interaction difficult and tend to split into separate groups of seven or eight. The following are some effects of the size of a group (divided into small, medium and large) on nine different group factors.

There is a considerable literature on the consequences of group size. For instance, as size increases (beyond an optimum of seven to nine people), the (verbal) *participation* of each member decreases. Indeed, inhibitions regarding participation increase among many members as the group size increases. Size is also related to *satisfaction* and, once again, beyond a group of seven to nine members, size leads to lower satisfaction, partly because of slower communication and partly because, as size grows, more different viewpoints have to be considered. Most importantly, what about size and *performance*? For *additive* tasks (e.g. moving heavy equipment) the potential performance is increased, but for *disjunctive* tasks (e.g. detecting an error in a program), where performance depends on the best member, it also increases because of the increased probability of having good members. But just as there is "potential" performance increase, there is also the likelihood of process loss associated with social loafing. In conjunction tasks (e.g. assembling the work), group performance is determined by the performance of the weakest member. As Steiner (1976) noted, for additive and disjunctive tasks, larger groups might perform best (up to seven to nine members), but at increasing costs to the efficiency of individual members, whereas performance on conjunctive tasks decreases as group size increases.

Table 10.3 is inevitably a simplification and may even seem arbitrary to some. Yet it does highlight some of the more typical effects the sheer size of the group has on its dynamics. Clearly, the size of the group is highly relevant to how it operates and ultimately performs. The most interesting question is, of course, the *optimal size* of a group given a specific task.

Cohesiveness

Cohesiveness is the glue that holds groups together. Group cohesiveness is determined by certain factors such as *contact*; cohesiveness is often simply a function of propin-

Table 10.3 Some possible effects of size on groups

Category/dimension	Group size		
	2–7 members	*8–12 members*	*13–16 members*
Leadership			
1. Demands on leader	Low	Moderate	High
2. Differences between leaders and members	Low	Low to moderate	Moderate to high
3. Direction by leader	Low	Low to moderate	Moderate to high
Members			
4. Tolerance of direction from leader	Low to high	Moderate to high	High
5. Domination of group interaction by a few members	Low	Moderate to high	High
6. Inhibition in participants by ordinary members	Low	Moderate	High
Group process			
7. Formalization of rules and procedures	Low	Low to moderate	Moderate to high
8. Time required for reaching judgement decisions	Low to moderate	Moderate	Moderate to high
9. Tendency for sub-groups to form within group	Low	Moderate to high	High

Source: Hellriegel *et al.* (1992).

quity (the fact that groups are in close physical proximity). Because of physical constraints (distance, walls, buildings, floors, storeys), people may find it difficult to interact with each other. Time spent together and the type (severity) of initiation, as well as length of induction into the group, clearly relate to cohesiveness. It is quite clearly more difficult to be part of a cohesive group where interpersonal contact is minimized. A second factor is *interdependence*; groups tend to be more cohesive where it is necessary to work together and pool their resources to achieve their goals. The "we-ness" of cohesiveness is often dependent on interdependence (neither dependence nor independence). Similarly, biography and ideology are important: the more homogeneous the group in terms of the individual member attitudes, beliefs and values, the more cohesive it is likely to become. Similarity leads to attraction, but the relationship may be curvilinear to the extent that being too homogeneous or heterogeneous in beliefs leads equally to low cohesiveness in the long-term group size. Thirdly, *kinship* is important; in some cultures, kinship is an automatic unqualified criterion of cohesiveness. Whereas in the West it may be considered nepotistic to employ relations, this is not always the case in the East, where blood relations are the first chosen, in part to ensure group cohesion and loyalty.

Other factors influencing cohesiveness include threat and competition, success, similarity of members, size, and the toughness of initiation (Johns, 1992). Usually, the consequences of cohesiveness include more participation in group affairs, greater conformity and often (but not always) greater success. Highly cohesive groups tend to be more or less productive than less cohesive groups (because of the greater distribution or variance of productivity of the latter).

Sayles & Strauss (1966) report four main kinds of workgroups in a car factory, cohesiveness being one of the key variables that distinguishes them:

- *Apathetic groups*: low cohesion and no clear leadership, no strong grievances but low output; found among people doing jobs with low pay and skills, for example on long assembly lines.
- *Erratic groups*: cohesive with centralized leadership, which may swing suddenly towards violent pro-union or pro-management activity; seem to have deep-seated grievances; found among people doing identical jobs.
- *Strategic groups*: highly cohesive, high union activity and continuous pressure about grievances; found among highly skilled and paid workers doing individual jobs.
- *Conservative groups*: moderately cohesive, few grievances, high output; found among people in highest status jobs.

If they have a sufficiently cooperative attitude, cohesive groups are more productive, especially at tasks requiring cooperation, presumably because coordination over the joint task is more easily accomplished. This categorization illustrates nicely how this one variable – that is, group cohesiveness – can be used to categorize or describe quite different groups in the same organization.

There are both positive and negative causes of cohesiveness (Greenberg & Baron, 1992). Cohesiveness is an important moderate variable that has both clear causes *and* consequences. Thus, long, difficult or severe group initiation, the perception of an external threat to the group, and much time spent together, may lead to positive outcome (more participation, higher morale, less absenteeism). However, a history of success may paradoxically lead to greater cohesiveness but negative outcomes, because of group complacency.

Roles

Group roles are the set of behaviours expected of an employee who occupies a particular position in the organization. They imply that everyone in the team has a specific function or purpose. These behaviours are wide-ranging; they include work duties as well as extracurricular duties. Often, the role expectations are communicated by formal, written job specifications, rules and regulations. Spector (2003) has differentiated between *formal* roles, which are related to job descriptions, and *informal* roles, which arise from group interaction experiences.

Naturally, the way roles are communicated can lead to role conflict and ambiguity. Roles are also culture-specific. For instance, Leung (1992) argues that roles are less well-defined in South East Asia. Things at work seem defined on verbal communication rather than explicit shared statements, which can prove particularly difficult for Westerners.

There are various different features of roles. Role *identity* is the attitude and behaviour consistent with a particular role. Identity might be in flux or very stable; it may be very clear or rather vague. Role *perception* is how the role holder and the group members see the role. Role *expectations* are how people believe one *should* act in a given set of circumstances. To a large extent, role stereotypes are role expectations concentrated into generalized categories. Role *ambiguity* exists when job goals and methods are unclear. Role *conflict* occurs when there are differences in role expectations which may be contradicted. There is a large literature dealing with task- and relationship-orientated roles. Some of the earlier and most important work was done by Bales (1950), who, by observing how groups characteristically behaved, described the common roles members adopt. Bales argued that all group interaction could be broadly categorized into two types: socio-emotional and task-orientated. Indeed, one finds in many groups a leader (captain) and deputy (vice-captain) – one focusing on task, the other morale.

Hoffman (1979) has argued that managers tend to adopt one of three problem-solving roles – task-orientated, relations-orientated, self-orientated – which may be further subdivided (Hellriegel *et al.*, 1992: 323–324).

Task-orientated role

The task-orientated role of members facilitates and coordinates decision-making tasks:

- *Initiators* offer new ideas or modified ways of considering group problems or goals, as well as suggesting solutions to group difficulties, including new group procedures or a new group organization.
- *Information seekers* try to clarify suggestions and to obtain authoritative information and pertinent facts.
- *Information givers* offer facts or generalizations that are authoritative or relate experiences that are pertinent to the group problem.
- *Coordinators* clarify relationships among ideas and suggestions, pull ideas and suggestions together and coordinate members' activities.

- *Evaluators* assess the group's functioning; they may evaluate or question the practicality, logic, facts or suggestions of other members.

Relations-orientated role

The relations-orientated role of members builds group-centred tasks, sentiments and viewpoints:

- *Encouragers* praise, agree with and accept the ideas of others; they indicate warmth and solidarity towards other members.
- *Harmonizers* mediate intragroup conflicts and relieve tension.
- *Gatekeepers* encourage the participation of others by saying such things as "Let's hear from you Alison", "Why not limit the length of contributions so we can all react to the problem" and "John, do you agree?"
- *Standard setters* express standards for the group to achieve or apply in evaluating the quality of group processes, raise questions about group goals and assess group movement in light of these goals.
- *Followers* go along passively and serve as friendly members.
- *Group observers* tend to stay out of the group process and give feedback on the group as if they were detached evaluators.

Self-orientated role

The self-orientated role focuses only on members' individual needs, possibly at the expense of the group:

- *Blockers* are negative, stubborn and unreasoningly resistant; for example, they may try repeatedly to bring back an issue that the group considered carefully and intentionally rejected.
- *Recognition seekers* try to call attention to themselves; they may boast, report on personal achievements, and in unusual ways struggle to avoid being placed in an inferior position.
- *Dominators* try to assert authority by manipulating the group or certain individuals in the group; they may use flattery or assertion of their superior status or right to attention; and they may interrupt the contributions of others.
- *Avoiders* maintain distance from others; these passive resisters try to remain insulated from interaction.

There are several ways of categorizing work roles, as we shall see later in this chapter. There is clearly overlap between the various systems, but the existence of so many attests to the many roles that workgroup members take up.

Norms

Norms are the unspoken, unwritten rules that guide individual group members' behaviour. Norms can be both *prescriptive* – dictating behaviours that *should* occur – and *proscriptive* – dictating behaviours that *should not* occur. Break the norms and one is punished. Spector (2003) suggested a pattern – first inform, then scold, then punish and, finally, ostracize those who deliberately flout the rules. Norms develop for all sorts of reasons: *through precedent* – because people tend to repeat models they have seen and follow behaviour patterns, they tend to establish clear habitual patterns (sitting in the same place, doing things in the same order). Or they develop *through a carry-over from the situation* – because of codified professional standards of conduct (i.e. running committees). Many group members bring a pattern of behaviour with them which they repeat. Norms also develop through explicit orders and suggestions – newcomers get socialized into "how things are around here". *Critical events* also lead to norm development – the way crises or unusual situations were handled in the past are remembered and successful behaviours are repeated and unsuccessful solutions avoided. Norms serve to make behaviour consistent, stable and predictable. Shared beliefs and values lead to shared attitudes, which are closely related to the development of norms. There are norms about dress, loyalty, reward allocation and performance.

Porter, Lawler & Hackman (1975) suggest that norms have three salient characteristics. First, they are primarily concerned with observable behaviours, and less with thoughts and feelings. A punctuality norm is concerned with the time that people show up for work, and less about how people should feel about starting work at that particular time. Naturally, people have clear ideas and feelings about norms and inevitably struggle to change them occasionally. Second, norms develop only for behaviours that are important to the group. Only behaviours that affect the survival and proper functioning of the group and the well-being of the members will lead to the development of norms. Norms are interpretation schemes grounded in the membership of groups. Third, norms usually specify a range of acceptable behaviours rather than a single behaviour. The norm may specify that staff should be in the office by 9.15 a.m., but someone who shows up at 9.20 a.m. does not usually create much negative feeling among group members. On the other hand, if a staff member is late by one hour, it is possible that this behaviour will lead to a serious reprimand from management.

Norms are associated with the internal working of the group, but to the outsider it is only the group's external image that is visible. The outsider recognizes private language, technical slang and in-jokes as peculiar to a particular group. Similarly, the distinctive way in which members of the group dress conveys that group's identity. Often, group members are not aware of the fact that they are conforming to the norms. Put simply, group members see more differences between themselves than outsiders (McKenna, 1994).

Norms apply to the quantity and quality of output, production practices, the manner in which individuals relate to each other, the appropriate dress to wear and when, demonstrations of loyalty to the organization, times when it is important to look busy even if the workload is light, who to socialize with at work and outside work, and conventions with regard to the allocation of resources. Some norms are beneficial from the organization's point of view when they help to maintain the quality of output. Yet other norms are considered by the organization to be counter-productive, for example norms supportive of restrictive practices.

According to Chell (1987) and summarized by McKenna (1994: 300–301):

- the majority of group members generally find the group norms acceptable;
- only the significant aspects of group life are covered by them;
- group behaviour, rather than the thoughts and feelings of members, is the focal point of attention;

- members of the group accept them to varying degrees;
- there is variation with regard to the degree of toleration members will accept when it comes to deviations from the norm;
- the process of managing the group is facilitated by them;
- they develop slowly and change slowly;
- conformity to norms can be a function of a person's status within the group (e.g. this is conspicuous when some members, normally of high status, are given latitude to deviate from the norm);
- there is usually an accepted set of rewards and punishment associated with compliance or non-compliance with certain norms.

But, if norms demand conformity, there are problems if:

- the personal goals of the individual and those of the organization are in conflict;
- the individual does not feel a sense of pride from belonging to the group;
- the individual seems to be more preoccupied with achieving his or her own ends, rather than those of the group;
- the individual is not recognized as a fully fledged group member because of occupying a peripheral position within the group;
- the individual considers the price of conformity to be too high; for example, the person could harm his or her career as a result of compliance;
- the individual refuses to conform, because the effort by the group to force compliance appears to be unconvincing, or on this occasion the group's judgement is perceived to be unsound.

Feldman (1987) argued that four main purposes can be served by norms. First, norms express the central values of the group and, in so doing, can inspire members and project to others the nature of the group. Second, norms simplify and make more predictable the behaviour expected of group members, so that members' behaviour can be anticipated. This can smooth the functioning of the group. Third, norms assist the group in avoiding embarrassing situations when, for example, members may avoid discussing certain issues likely to hurt the feelings of a particular member. Finally, norms help the group to survive. This could arise when the group rejects deviant behaviour that poses a threat to its existence. However, a successful group that does not feel threatened may be more tolerant of deviant behaviour (McKenna, 1994).

What are the specific conditions that encourage the enforcements of specific norms? Groups do not establish norms for every conceivable situation, but form and enforce them with respect to behaviours that they believe to be particularly important. Group norms are most likely to be enforced if they:

- *Aid in group survival and the provision of benefits*: A group might develop a norm not to discuss individual salaries with members of other groups in the organization to avoid calling attention to pay inequities in its favour.
- *Simplify or make predictable the behaviour expected of group members*: A group may develop a norm that results in some highly predictable way of behaving: split the bill evenly, take turns "picking up the tab", or individually pay for what each ordered (equality, turn-taking or equity solutions).

- *Help the group to avoid embarrassing interpersonal problems*: Groups might develop norms about not discussing religious, moral or political issues, or about not getting together socially in members' homes (so that differences in taste or income do not become too obvious).
- *Express the central values or goals of the group and clarify what is distinctive about the group's identity*: This may refer to dress or speech codes, or preferred and sanctioned leisure activities.

Not all long-standing members of a group are aware of the implicit group norms they follow and obey. However, newcomers are acutely aware of the dictates that strong norms afford.

Status

Individual members and groups as a whole have particular prestige accorded to them. Relative social position or rank given to members is the essence of status. It is the group's evaluation of a member. As we have seen before, this can be divided into *formal* status, which may include job title, uniform, specific benefits (car parking space, size of office, class of travel tickets, etc.), and *informal* status, whereby certain groups, say older employees, those with special skills or those with special needs, are accorded status. Status is functional: it reinforces roles, provides stability and a sense of identification by reminding the group of its values. But status is neither fixed, nor tangible. A famous example was reported by Whyte (1948). Observing the interaction between waitresses (considered to be of lower status) and chefs (considered to be of higher status), Whyte found that conflicts emerged when the waitresses passed their orders directly to the chefs. The chefs resented the initiation of such action from the lower-status waitresses. Then, after an "order wheel" was installed, the waitresses simply attached their orders to it, thereby allowing the chefs to take the orders whenever they were ready. Higher-status individuals no longer had to respond to the actions of lower-status individuals, eliminating considerable conflict. Such findings are typical of the tendency for people of higher status to expect to influence others, rather than to be influenced by them (Figure 10.1).

Status affects communication: from form of address to the preferred target of communication. High-status group members are the targets/recipients of communication but have a disproportionate opportunity to respond. They are also perceived to be more knowledgeable, although all they may possess is self-confidence and assertiveness.

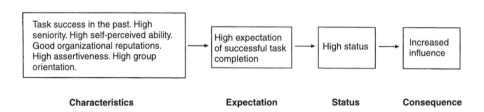

Characteristics   Expectation   Status   Consequence

Figure 10.1 The causes and consequences of status.

Communication structure

Groups are structured in different ways. Most groups have a clear explicit (and implicit) structure. They also have an affective or "liking" structure, which, by use of sociometric methods, can reveal friendly groups, popular and unpopular people, and "isolates". There are various simple methods that may be used to determine the affective or liking structure of the group. Ask each member who they like most (or least) and plot the "affective links" between all members. This can be done by asking about your most and least preferred co-worker (see Chapter 12).

More interesting, perhaps, is the communication structure of a group. This shows who in small groups can and does communicate with whom both "officially and unofficially". Channels of communication are often set up to be used, which reflects the structure. These structures differ widely, as Figure 10.2 illustrates. They are, of course, easier to illustrate with small groups of five to seven members, such as portrayed in Figure 10.2, but the principle may be applied to larger groups.

As ever, there are often trade-offs between speed and accuracy and involvement in tasks. In short, centralized networks (e.g. the wheel) are superior on simple tasks, and decentralized networks (circle, completely connected) seem superior at complex tasks. "Wheels" are preferred by organizations that like to have a headquarters totally in charge. They can communicate with "out-stations" who cannot communicate with each other, hence perhaps resulting in low overall satisfaction of group members. On the other hand, "circles" are more democratic, but they can be very slow. Given enough time, all networks become pretty equivalent, except where the organization or group struggles constantly to maintain a rigid structure.

The wheel clearly shows the leader of the group. Unfortunately, the lack of opportunity for communication for the other group members leads to low levels of member satisfaction. Only the leader is really satisfied in this pattern. And even the leader's satisfaction may be short-lived if the group is working on a complex task, since the wheel pattern is associated with low performance on such tasks. However, the

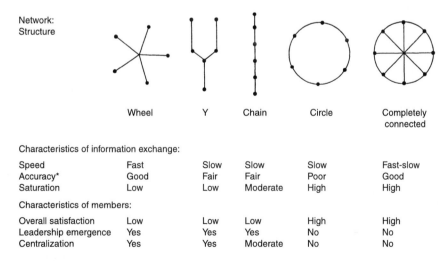

Network: Structure	Wheel	Y	Chain	Circle	Completely connected
Characteristics of information exchange:					
Speed	Fast	Slow	Slow	Slow	Fast-slow
Accuracy*	Good	Fair	Fair	Poor	Good
Saturation	Low	Low	Moderate	High	High
Characteristics of members:					
Overall satisfaction	Low	Low	Low	High	High
Leadership emergence	Yes	Yes	Yes	No	No
Centralization	Yes	Yes	Moderate	No	No

Figure 10.2 Communication patterns in groups. Reproduced from Bavelas (1950) with the permission of the Acoustical Society of America.

pattern can be very effective on simple tasks if group members accept the leader's authority. The Y pattern is very similar to the wheel.

The *chain* pattern of communications results when group members communicate only with certain people in the group, but everyone is somehow connected with someone else in the group. In this pattern, it is not clear who the leader is. There may be two or more leaders. Member satisfaction tends to be better than in the wheel pattern, but not as high as in some of the other patterns. In terms of performance, chain patterns tend to work moderately well for both simple and complex problems. The greatest drawback facing groups with chain patterns is a lack of coordinated effort. The groups do not function like a team, and leadership is weak. The *circle* pattern is quite similar to the chain pattern; the only difference is that the two end-people are now connected with each other. With the *all-channel pattern*, everyone in the group can talk to everyone else, and over time they do. The result is that leadership is unclear, because it is shared by all members.

This type of interaction is essential for dealing with complex tasks. On the other hand, if the task is simple, the performance of a group using the all-channel pattern will be only moderate, primarily because it will take longer than it would with the wheel pattern. Since time is such a valuable resource, it might be better to use the wheel pattern for solving simple tasks, unless the intent is to develop people for long-term effectiveness.

The characteristics of an effective workgroup

McGregor (1960), famous for his Theory X and Theory Y, drew up a list that may prove an interesting comparison. The following are, according to him, crucial characteristics of effective work teams:

1   The "atmosphere" tends to be informal, comfortable, relaxed. There are no obvious tensions. It is a working atmosphere in which people are involved and interested. There are no signs of boredom.
2   There is much discussion in which virtually everyone participates, but it remains pertinent to the task of the group. If the discussion gets off the subject, someone will bring it back in short order.
3   The task or the objective of the group is well understood and accepted by the members. There will have been free discussion of the objective at some point, until it was formulated in such a way that the members of the group could commit themselves to it.
4   The members listen to each other! The discussion does not have the quality of jumping from one idea to another unrelated one. Every idea is given a hearing. People do not appear to be afraid of being foolish by putting forth a creative thought, even if it seems fairly extreme.
5   There is disagreement. The group is comfortable with this and shows no signs of having to avoid conflict or to keep everything on the plane of sweetness and light. Disagreements are not suppressed or overridden by premature group action. The reasons are carefully examined, and the group seeks to resolve them rather than to dominate the dissenter. On the other hand, there is no "tyranny of the minority". Individuals who disagree do not appear to be trying to dominate the group or to express hostility. Their disagreement is an expression of genuine difference of

opinion and they expect a hearing in order that a solution may be found. Sometimes there are basic disagreements which cannot be resolved. The group finds it possible to live with them, accepting them but not permitting them to block its efforts. Under some conditions, action will be deferred to permit further study of an issue between the members. On other occasions, where the disagreement cannot be resolved and action is necessary, it will be taken but with open caution and recognition that the action may be subject to later reconsideration.

6   Most decisions are reached by a kind of consensus in which it is clear that everyone is in general agreement and willing to go along. However, there is little tendency for individuals who oppose the action to keep their opposition private and thus let an apparent consensus mask real disagreement. Formal voting is at a minimum; the group does not accept a simple majority as a proper basis for action.

7   Criticism is frequent, frank and relatively comfortable. There is little evidence of personal attack, either openly or in a hidden fashion. The criticism has a constructive flavour in that it is orientated towards removing an obstacle that faces the group and prevents it from getting the job done.

8   People are free in expressing their feelings as well as their ideas, both on the problem and on the group's operation. There is little pussy-footing, there are few "hidden agendas". Everyone appears to know quite well how everyone else feels about any matter under discussion.

9   When action is taken, clear assignments are made and accepted.

10   The chairman of the group does not dominate it, nor on the contrary does the group defer unduly to him or her. In fact, as one observes the activity, it is clear that the leadership shifts from time to time, depending on the circumstances. Different members, because of their knowledge or experience, are in a position at various times to act as "resources" for the group. The members utilize them in this fashion and they occupy leadership roles while they are thus being used. There is little evidence of a struggle for power as the group operates. The issue is not who controls, but how to get the job done.

11   The group is self-conscious about its own operations. Frequently, it will stop to examine how well it is doing or what may be interfering with its operation. The problem may be a matter or procedure, or it may be an individual whose behavior is interfering with the accomplishment of the group's objectives. Whatever it is, it gets open discussion until a solution is found. (Reproduced from McGregor (1960: 232–35) with the permission of McGraw–Hill.)

McGregor's observations may well be culture- or sector-specific; that is, although they apply well to US industry, they are not as relevant to, say, modern Japan. Furthermore, these observations may not be particularly apt for groups in crisis.

To a large extent, effectiveness is determined by a combination of factors that need to fit together and constantly adapt to each other (Randolph & Blackburn, 1989). These include *task/technology*, which partly determines the type of people (ability, traits) who would best fit in the group. Task variables such as skill variety, autonomy and feedback in part dictate the *individuals'* personalities, perceptions, abilities and motivations. *Group size and composition* must relate both to the individuals and the task. Thus, complex group tasks usually require larger, more heterogeneous and able groups than do simple tasks. The *physical layout* and environment are fundamentally important. Technology, personal preference and group size each in turn affect – and are affected by

– the physical ergonomic layout of the organizations. Finally, the *organizational system* of procedures, rewards and policies relates to all of the variables.

The fundamental point is that there needs to be a fit between these variables that is inevitably dynamic. Although misfit is nearly always linked with group ineffectiveness and inefficiency, fit alone is not sufficient for guaranteed effectiveness. It is necessary but not sufficient.

Teamwork

After extensive work in the area, West and colleagues have developed a practical and tested model of how teams work (Unsworth & West, 2000). It is based on a three-fold factor model whereby team inputs affect both processes and outputs. According to the model, there are four crucial facets to the Input Factor:

- *The task*, which can be described along various dimensions like autonomy, feed-back, identity, significance or variety. The simple, but fundamental, question is the nature of the tasks the team is expected and required to perform.
- *Team composition*, which is the mix of individuals in the team. A central, political and research question concerns whether it is better to maximize heterogeneity (or diversity), in terms of age, ethnicity and education, or homogeneity. The results of studies are contradictory, which reflects reality. That is, there are both advantages and drawbacks of diversity. Advantages include innovation and creativity; disadvantages include conflict, turnover and imbalance in team contribution.
- *Organizational context*, which includes organizational climate, office politics, intrigue and competitiveness; environmental uncertainty; the technical assistance available; and the rules about rewards for the team. Intra-team effectiveness is a function of inter-team and context factors, which can have a profound effect on all aspects of team functioning.
- *Cultural context* refers to those value differences that influence work (see Chapter 15). Attitudes towards ambiguity and time are both a function of culture. However, it is perhaps the individualism–collectivism aspect of culture that is most relevant to teamwork. Teamworking is much more natural in collectivist cultures.

A central question for many employers is how to form, maintain and develop teams at work. There are issues of team composition, team building and team training. This may also involve building and reviewing team visions.

According to the model, there are five facets of the Process Factor that are import-ant. These are:

- *Leadership* is both transactional and transformational (see Chapter 12); leaders inspire, motivate, challenge and help individuals. Their task is to emphasize com-mitment, purpose and loyalty. They are there to describe an ideal future, to chal-lenge standards, to bring about synergy and enthusiasm and to encourage others. This does not mean the idea of self-managed teams is not a good one. There can be many benefits to autonomous work groups: decision-making is faster and more open, individuals learn more, and the self-efficacy of individuals is increased.
- *Communication* is always important. Two facets are highlighted: (1) the usual medium of communication (i.e. email, face-to-face, teleconferencing) and (2) who and how they facilitate communication.

- *Decision making*, which refers to all the processes described in Chapter 11; namely, how solutions are identified, how optimal solutions are evaluated and chosen, and how solutions are implemented. It also includes how dissent is handled.
- *Cohesiveness*, which refers to the degree of attraction and liking between team members. Cohesive groups help one another more. Cohesion is both a cause and consequence of team success.
- *Team climate* refers to the atmosphere in a team which relates to feelings of ambiguity, conflict and tension. Orientation to the task, mutual support, attitudes to safety and a shared vision are all parts of team climate.

Inevitably, there are other, but similar, models of team effectiveness. Cordery (2002) provides a similar input–process–output model but chooses to highlight slightly different factors. Thus the input factors are job design (with special reference to team autonomy), work meaning (impact on others, and self-beliefs about potency), interdependence (task versus outcome), team composition (demographic and team role hetero- or homogeneity), team context (resources, feedback, recognition), team processes (decision-making, motivation). Cordery notes than input–process–output models assume that effectiveness is best described and explored by input and process factors. However, the model is imprecise and therefore hard to test. It is not clear whether some of the input variables direct outcomes directly and what are the nature and number of feedback loops. In short, the model is too abstract and therefore to some extent not very practical.

Group diversity

Are diverse groups – measured in terms of culture, gender, experience, and so on – more or less efficient than homogeneous groups? Certainly, it requires greater managerial skill to lead culturally diverse groups. It is important to recognize and celebrate differences explicitly. It is also important to have a superordinate goal or vision to establish a goal that transcends individual differences. Clearly, power relationships (dominance) by different group members must be handled sensitively, and power should be distributed by ability and motivation, rather than ethnicity. Mutual respect needs to be fostered and, like all teams, regular, accurate and constructive feedback needs to be given.

Adler (1991: 141) believes:

> For effective functioning, multicultural teams must (1) use their diversity to generate multiple perspectives, problem definitions, ideas, action alternatives, and solutions, (2) learn to achieve consensus (agree on specific decisions and directions, despite the diversity), and (3) balance the simultaneous needs for creativity (divergence) with those of cohesion (convergence). If teams fail to generate many ideas, they become no more effective than individuals working alone. If teams fail to achieve consensus, their diversity paralyzes them. If teams fail to balance creativity and cohesion, they become awkwardly inefficient structures having little value to the organization.

Overall, it would appear that diverse groups have both obvious advantages and disadvantages (Box 10.1). Such lists of advantages and disadvantages are often found in

Box 10.1 Advantages and disadvantages of cultural diversity in groups

Advantages	*Disadvantages*
Culturally synergistic advantages Organization benefits from multiculturalism	Disadvantage attributable to cultural diversity: organizational costs attributable to multiculturalism
Expanding meanings Multiple perspectives Greater openness to new ideas Multiple interpretations Expanding alternatives Increasing creativity Increasing flexibility Increasing problem-solving skills	Diversity increases Ambiguity Complexity Confusion Difficulty converging meanings Miscommunication Hard to reach a single agreement Difficulty converging actions Hard to agree on specific actions
Culture-specific advantages: benefits in working with a particular country or culture	Culture-specific disadvantages: costs in working with a particular country or culture
Better understanding of foreign employees	Overgeneralizing Organization policies Organization practices Organization procedures Ethnocentrism
Ability to work more effectively with particular foreign clients	
Ability to market more effectively to specific foreign customers Increased understanding of political, social, legal, economic and cultural environment of foreign countries	

Source: Reproduced from Adler (1991: 80) with the permission of PWS-Kent Publishing Co., a division of Wadsworth, Inc.

management writings, and may be seen as an attempt to avoid being prescriptive. Some would argue that to be outstanding, you cannot be risk-averse, and you may have to take a strongly unpopular position while controlling various possible negative consequences. There is no simple answer for all groups. Furthermore, group dynamics mean that each has to sort out many processes simultaneously.

For Hosking & Morley (1991), to realize the potential of any group there needs to be a "total design". Crucially, all facets of the business should interact with the activities of the core design. There must be sufficient diversity of expertise among group members, who all need to have a clear idea about their particular task and their place within the group. Equally, groups need norms and standard operating procedures that facilitate active open-minded thinking. All groups need to be fully networked with the rest of the organization. Moreover, diverse group members need to take a variety of primary roles, or at least certain procedures should be put in place to take over those roles. Finally, the leaders of groups, especially diverse groups, need to take special responsibility for ensuring that the group process is healthy.

How do groups influence the performance of tasks? Steiner (1976) argued that this question could only be answered once one was able to classify the tasks that groups do.

On the basis of some specific questions, he was able to classify tasks into nine different types (Table 10.4).

The first question is, can the task be broken down into subcomponents (i.e. Is it divisible?) or is that inappropriate (i.e. Is it unitary?). For unitary tasks, group cooperation may be impractical, whereas for divisible tasks the division of labour may be very desirable. The second question is which is more important, quantity or quality. A maximizing task is one that requires speed and quantity, which may be better done in groups, whereas an optimizing task stresses a qualitatively preferred outcome. The *third* question relates to how the individual inputs are related to the group product, and this yields five different possible answers (additive, compensatory, disjunctive, conjunctive and discretionary). Every task can be thus classified through these three questions. Some assembly jobs are divisible, maximizing (preferably optimizing) and conjunctive, whereas some problem-solving tasks are often unitary, optimizing and disjunctive. Furthermore, this model is testable.

On many simple additive tasks, group productivity amounts to group potential minus two other factors. These are motivational losses, such as social "loafing", which is the tendency to let others do the work (the "free-rider" effect), and coordination losses, where not all members of the group necessarily "pull together" or at the same time. In compensatory tasks, the group product is the average of individual judgements, but individuals' personality and repetition may mean that particular poor judgements outweigh good ones. In disjunctive tasks, groups can correct errors and reject incorrect suggestions, but in this situation the group is only successful if the group members possess the necessary resources to solve the problem, actually propose the best solution, and correct/best solutions elicit more support than incorrect solutions.

In Steiner's task classification, it is possible to ascertain the performance of groups working on different tasks. Here the focus is not on the nature or preferred roles of the group members, or indeed on particular group processes, but on the type of task that the group is trying to complete. Steiner's work has probably not attracted the attention it deserves. He suggests many testable hypotheses about when to attempt to work in groups and when not to (Table 10.5).

Individuals, teams and occupational success

Most big and small organizations are essentially networks of small work groups/teams that have to coordinate their efforts. Because this is thought to be crucial for business success, various techniques have been used to attempt to help intra- and intergroup functioning. Spector (2003) lists three: *self-managed or autonomous* teams that manage themselves; *quality circles* that meet to help resolve problems around quality and efficiency; and *team-building*, which focuses on interpersonal issues, which in turn helps team functioning in the long run.

Most major decisions in business organizations are made by teams. Team-building is considered an essential part of occupational behaviour, as teams open up a wider range of experience and abilities. The team concept seeks to reduce worker alienation in highly regimented work settings. When group members learn all the tasks performed by their team, they can rotate from job to job. The teams can also make their own operating decisions. Camaraderie and the opportunity to participate, in turn, build loyalty and pride of workmanship. Work teams create the potential for improved quality and productivity, while making for more rewarding jobs for the team members.

Table 10.4 A summary of Steiner's typology of tasks

Question	Answer	Type	Examples
Can the task be broken down into subcomponents, or is division of the task inappropriate?	Subtasks can be identified	Divisible	Playing a football game, building a house, preparing a six-course meal.
	No subtasks exist	Unitary	Pulling on a rope, reading a book, solving a mathematical problem.
Which is more important: quantity produced or quality of performance?	Quantity	Maximizing	Generating many ideas, lifting the greatest weight, scoring the most runs.
	Quality	Optimizing	Generating the best idea, getting the right answer, solving a mathematics problem.
How are individual inputs related to the group's product?	Individual inputs are added together	Additive	Pulling a rope, stuffing envelopes, shovelling snow
	Group product is average of individual judgements	Compensatory	Averaging individuals' estimates of the number of beans in a jar, weight of an object, room temperature.
	Group selects product from pool of individual members' judgements	Disjunctive	Questions involving yes/no, either/or answers, such as mathematics problems, puzzles and choices between options.
	All group members contribute to the product	Conjunctive	Climbing a mountain, eating a meal, relay races, soldiers marching in file.
	Groups can decide how individual inputs relate to group products	Discretionary	Deciding to shovel snow together, opting to vote on the best answer to a mathematical problem, letting leader answer question.

Source: Steiner (1976).

Table 10.5 Performance of groups working on various types of tasks

Task	Group productivity	Description
Additive	Better than best	Group outperforms the best individual member.
Compensatory	Better than most	Group outperforms a substantial number of group members.
Disjunctive (eureka)	Equate to the best	Group performance matches the performance of the best member.
Disjunctive (non-eureka)	Less than the best	Group performance can match that of the best member, but often falls short.
Conjunctive (unitary)	Equal to the worst	Group performance matches the performance of the worst member.
Conjunctive (divisible with matching)	Better than the worst	If subtasks are properly matched to ability of members, group performance can reach high levels.

Source: Steiner (1976).

There is considerable literature on whether teams produce qualitatively and quantitatively better ideas and solutions than individuals working apart. Essentially, two factors are important in determining whether "too many cooks spoil the broth" or "many hands make light work": the nature of the task (structured versus creative) and the ability of the individuals (high versus low) (see Chapter 11). Whatever the research results show, most senior management occurs in teams, and many managers see themselves akin to sports captains (or coaches) who select, train and lead teams (to win the game).

There is a surprising paucity of psychological and sociological studies that focus on individual difference reactions or role preferences in teams. This is reflected by the fact that few measures exist to determine team-role behaviour. Very few tests attempt to ascertain how people characteristically behave in work teams. Personality tests supposedly measure behaviours in a wide variety of settings (both in and out of teams), whereas occupational-based measures often ignore the social dimensions of work-related behaviour. Being aware that just as the right mix of people (in terms of ability, preferences and predispositions) creates efficient, effective and contented teams, the opposite (the wrong mix) can have potentially disastrous results, managers have long attempted to design or develop optimal teams in terms of the composition of members (Furnham, 1992).

There is considerable literature on the creation of teams, the way in which they function, and the consequences of their make-up. Most of the work in this field is proscriptive and prescriptive, based on various case studies (Handy, 1985). However, there is little empirical evidence to support the various theories in this area. There are at least two major problems that have contributed to this relatively sorry state of affairs. The first is the extreme difficulty in measuring salient, ecologically valid and reliable team-dependent outcome variables to establish some criterion of team success. Unless one has a reasonable measure of team performance, it is difficult to discover how the individual difference factors in a team differ. Second, and perhaps equally importantly, is the lack of psychometrically valid measures of how people behave in teams. Although there are innumerable measures of personality, coping and attributional styles, there are very few measures that explicitly set out to examine how people behave in work teams (Furnham, 1992).

In the UK, the Belbin Team-Role Self-Perception Inventory (BTRSPI) is used extensively in applied settings, especially selecting, counselling and developing management teams (Hogg, 1990), but has received comparatively little psychometric assessment or validation. Indeed, it has been subjected to extensive investigation and criticism (Dulewicz, 1995; Furnham, Steele, & Pendleton, 1993; Senior, 1997).

For well over a decade, Belbin (1981) attempted to answer the fundamental question of why some business teams (that is, groups playing a week long MBA-type "business game") were successful and others were not. He contended that there are five criteria for an effective team:

1   Each member contributes to achieving objectives by performing a functional role (professional/technical knowledge) and a team role.
2   An optimal balance in both functional and team roles is needed, depending on the team's goals and tasks.
3   Team effectiveness depends on the extent to which members correctly recognize and adjust to the relative strengths within the team (available expertise and team roles).
4   Personality and mental abilities fit members for some team roles and limit their ability to play others.
5   A team can deploy its technical resources to best advantage only when it has the range and balance of team roles to ensure sufficient teamwork.

Belbin's research led him to conclude that people adopt roles in teams and that there are particular roles adopted (or indeed not adopted) in a team. The "theory" is rich on description and taxonomization.

Belbin's measure, however, is not the only one that attempts to assess team-role behaviour. McCann & Margerison (1989) have also developed a team-role measure that also has eight types: explorer–promoter, assessor–developer, thruster–organizer, concluder–producer, checker–inspector, upholder–maintainer, reporter–advisor and creator–innovator. This measure appears to be heavily influenced by the Jungian theories developed in the Myers–Briggs test (Myers & McCauley, 1985). It not only has norms but also evidence of internal reliability and concurrent validity; however, there appears to be little or no evidence of the factorial structure of the measure (to confirm the classification or taxonomic scheme), or any evidence of the predictive or constructive validity of the test. Importantly and ironically, it provides no evidence that any one mix of "team types" is any more efficient than any other.

Belbin's (1981) self-perception inventory (BSPI) first appeared in his popular book *Management teams*. It outlines the "theory" that suggests eight quite distinct team-role types. In later editions, he changed various names (i.e. chairman to coordinator; company worker to implementer) and introduced a new role called "specialist". Although norms based on a very limited number of people (78 in all) were provided, little evidence of the psychometric properties of the test were offered. Thus, we know little of the test's reliability (test–retest, split-half, internal), validity (concurrent, content, predictive, construct) or its dimensionability. The BSPI questionnaire is unusual and problematic for several reasons. First, it is an ipsative (forced-choice) test, where participants are required to read seven hypothetical situations, and then rate either eight (version 1) or ten (version 2) behaviour statements relating to that situation and "distribute a total of ten points among the sentences which you think most accurately describe your behaviour". It means, in effect, that questionnaire completers have to choose between options, not give their preferences. Thus, because you are asked to choose between options, it is not clear whether people choose between too strongly liked or strongly disliked items. Thus, imagine you were asked to compare cheeses. Person A is a cheese lover and has difficulty choosing between Cheddar and Brie, Cheshire and Camembert because she loves them all. Person B is a cheese loather and faced with the same forced choice in pairs finds it equally difficult. It is curious that A and B could have precisely the same score, although one hates and the other loves cheese. Johnson, Wood & Blinkhorn (1988: 154) pointed out five uncontroversial drawbacks of such ipsative tests:

- They cannot be used for comparing individuals on a scale by scale basis.
- Correlations among ipsative scales cannot legitimately be factor analysed in the usual way.
- Reliabilities of ipsative tests overestimate, sometimes severely, the actual reliability of the scales; in fact, the whole idea of error is problematical.
- For the same reason, other validates of ipsative tests overestimate their utility.
- Means, standard deviations and correlations derived from ipsative test scales are not independent and cannot be interpreted and further utilized in the usual way.

Johnson *et al.* are highly critical of ipsative tests in general, particularly those used in occupational settings.

A second problem of the BSPI concerns the way in which the questions are asked. Both versions are arranged such that, for each of the seven sections, respondents are required to specify their typical behaviour. Thus, for instance, one reads: "When involved in a project with other people . . ." or: "I gain satisfaction in a job because . . .". These situations are vague, inconsistent and do nothing to let the respondent know about crucial aspects of the nature of the group or team that they are involved with. This could easily lead to poor reliability (Argyle, Furnham, & Graham, 1981).

A third problem concerns the fact that the measure is entirely a-theoretical. As he explained in his book, Belbin (1981) used standard psychometrically validated measures such as the 16PF and Eysenck Personality Inventory (EPI), but developed his typology not by theoretically deductive but observational and inductive means (see Chapter 4). A major problem with this approach lies in the fact that previously well-documented and theoretically important traits, such as neuroticism, tend to be over-looked. Frequently, poorly psychometrized tests marketed for human resource training might appear to neglect "negative" personality traits such as neuroticism (Furnham, 1992).

After finding little support for Belbin's theory, Broucek and Randall (1996: 404) noted:

> it is understandable that little support has been given to team role theory in the academic literature. Nevertheless Belbin's work has attracted considerable support among trainers and consultants. Perhaps that is because the group roles themselves have more than intuitive appeal.

It is both puzzling and annoying to academics to find that both consultants and clients seem uninterested and disinterested in validating theories and measures upon which they often make enormously important decisions. Even more perplexing is the fact that once measures have been shown to be seriously wanting, it has little or no effect on the popular use and retention of the measure.

Herriot and Pemberton (1995) have attacked "team theories", which they call myths. They believe work tasks determine processes, not the other way around. The organizational context sets the tasks the team has to tackle and this also impacts on the work processes. Roles, which are almost epiphenomenal, are simply the different parts people play in helping along the process. Different processes require different roles.

The problem lies in distinguishing "real teams" from experimental teams. Real teams have a well known set of characteristics: shared leadership roles, collective work products, discussion, decisions, and so on. Experimental teams such as those set up to "play" business games and those used for studies are different. It may be that they come to focus on their individual roles and personalities precisely because they are "unreal", whereas real groups would get on with the task. In other words, the emphasis on roles is misplaced and primarily a methodological artefact.

Personality variables have typically accounted for between 5 and 10% of the variance in work-related outcomes. These findings are not counter-intuitive: bright, hard-working people in teams improve performance, but this study highlights the relevance of the interpersonally oriented traits (agreeableness, extraversion, neuroticism) which influence social cohesiveness.

Barrick, Stewart, Neubert & Mount (1998) noted that American research of group-member personality on team outcomes has been very artificial because the research has seen laboratory studies using creativity as the performance criterion. "Relatively little has been done to understand the relationship of personality to the performance of actual work teams completing production tasks that are additive" (p.380). In their study of over fifty working teams, they found brighter teams and those higher on agreeableness, conscientiousness and extraversion received high ratings for team performance.

However, recently there have been some important studies on the personality traits of team members and their effects. Neuman, Wagner & Christiansen (1999) assessed over 300 retail assistants in 82 teams and gave each team a "Big Five" score dependent on the *average* score and their *variability*. These scores were correlated with two outcome measures – namely, ratings of customer service and task completion. Their results showed the team's average team member scores on conscientiousness, agreeableness and openness predicted performance, while variability in extraversion and neuroticism predicted performance. It was the two major factors of extraversion and neuroticism that best predicted team variability.

These recent studies certainly indicate the relevance of personality traits to teamwork performance. These studies highlight two important things. First, team trait-profile variability or heterogeneity is clearly an important factor. Second, that whereas some traits have an obvious direct effect on outcome, others have more moderately or mediating effects such that they influence outcomes. Stable extraverted teams were more likely to experience positive intragroup interactions that led to greater social cohesion and thence a greater capability to maintain itself.

Despite the lack of psychometric evidence for his test, Belbin (1981) has made some interesting findings that require replication. Excellent teams tend to have the following characteristics, which can be described in terms of the team members' roles in the team:

- The leader should have attributes similar to the "chairman" type profile, described above. He or she should be a patient but commanding figure who generates trust and who knows how to use the spread of abilities in the team effectively.

- Excellent teams often include a person who generates creative and original solutions to problems (a plant).
- There should be a spread of mental abilities. If everyone in the team is *very* bright, then the team will spend most of its time arguing and won't agree on any effective solutions to problems.

Teams that excel have a wide spread of abilities, which include, in particular, one completer (to finish the work) and one company worker (to organize the team). A winning team often contains people with a wider spread of team roles than other less successful groups.

Another mark of excellent teams is that the team members often have team roles to which they are most suited; they perform a role that best fits their personal characteristics and abilities. In less successful teams, this may not be the case; people may be given a role just because they have done it before, and no account is taken of how well they performed in that role previously.

An excellent team can sense its own faults and do something about them by *compensating* for its team-role weaknesses. One way in which it can compensate is by allocating appropriate members of the team to cover the missing role. The greater the spread of abilities in the team, the easier it is to do this. An excellent team is also sensitive to competition for particular roles, because where such a situation exists there may be a "personality clash". Two team members may work against each other and may have a damaging effect on the team's overall performance. Being aware of this possibility, the team can work out how the role could be shared or, alternatively, how to allocate one person to another role (Furnham, 1992).

Table 10.6 shows a description of the eight roles that Belbin feels people play in teams, along with their consequences. Some people may be happy in some of these roles, others comfortable in only one. Central to Belbin's theory is that successful teams have all the roles covered (i.e. are heterogeneous), whereas less successful teams have members who do not choose to fulfil particular roles (i.e. are homogeneous). It is this central point that is the focus of most research in this promising area.

Benefits and drawbacks of working in groups

Social psychologists are concerned how the actual or imaginary presence of others influences the individual's attitude, behaviours and emotions. As such, they have been fascinated by what happens when human beings work together. Working together is a double-edged sword in that it can facilitate productivity but also inhibit it. Social psychologists have observed and described processes directly relevant to working in groups. Two (only) will be discussed.

Social facilitation

In one of the first psychology experiments ever published, Triplett (1898) found that competitive cyclists were much faster when they raced against other cyclists, as opposed to the clock. Being a good experimentalist, he took his observations back into the laboratory and replicated them with a quite different task – children turning a fishing

Table 10.6 A description of the eight "key team roles"

Type	Symbol	Typical features	Positive qualities	Allowable weaknesses	Observed contributions
1. *Team leaders* a. Chairman	CH	Calm, self-confident, controlled	A capacity for treating and welcoming all potential contributors on their merits without prejudice – a strong sense of objectives	No more than ordinary in terms of intellect, creative ability	1. Clarifying the goals, objectives. 2. Selecting the problems on which decisions have to be made, and establishing their priorities. 3. Helping establish roles, responsibilities and work boundaries within group. 4. Summing up the feelings and achievements of the group, and articulating group verdicts.
b. Shaper	S	Highly strung, outgoing, dynamic	Drive and a readiness to challenge inertia, ineffectiveness, complacency	Proneness to provocation, irritation and impatience	1. Shaping roles, boundaries, responsibilities, tasks and objectives. 2. Seeking to find pattern in group discussion. 3. Pushing the group towards agreement on policy and action towards making decisions.
2. *Creative thinkers* a. Plant	PL	Individualistic, serious-minded, unorthodox	Genius, imagination, intellect, knowledge	Up in the clouds, inclined to disregard practical details or protocol	1. Advancing proposals. 2. Making criticisms that lead up counter-suggestions. 3. Offering new insights on lines of action already agreed.
b. Monitor evaluator	ME	Sober, unemotional	Judgement, discretion, hard-headedness	Lack inspiration or the ability to motivate others	1. Analysing problems and situations. 2. Interpreting complex written material and clarifying obscurities. 3. Assessing the judgements and contributions of others.

Source: Adapted from Belbin (1981).

3. Negotiators

a. Resource investigator	RI	Extroverted, enthusiastic, curious, communicative	A capacity for contacting people and exploring anything new. An ability to respond to challenge	Liable to lose interest once the initial fascination has passed	1. Introducing ideas and development of external origin. 2. Contacting other individuals or groups of own volition. 3. Engaging in negation-type activities.
b. Teamworker	TW	Socially orientated, rather mild	An ability to respond to people and to situations and to promote team spirit	Indecisiveness at moments of crisis	1. Emphasizing the need for task completion, meeting targets and schedules and generally promoting a sense of urgency. 2. Looking for and spotting errors, omissions and oversights. 3. Galvanizing others into activity.

4. Company workers

a. Company workers	CW	Conservative, dutiful, predictable	Organizing ability, practical commonsense, hard-working, self-discipline	Lack of flexibility, unresponsiveness to unproven ideas	1. Transforming talk and ideas into practical steps. 2. Considering what is feasible. 3. Trimming suggestions to make them fit into agreed plans and established systems.
b. Completer finisher	CF	Painstaking, orderly, conscientious, anxious	A capacity for follow-through. Perfectionism	A tendency to worry about small things. A reluctance to "let go"	1. Giving personal support and help to others. 2. Building on to or seconding a member's ideas and suggestions. 3. Drawing the reticent into discussion. 4. Taking steps to avert or overcome disruption of the team.

reel as fast as possible. Early studies confirmed that both the presence of co-actors *and/or* an audience improved performance. This process was called "social facilitation". However, some researchers working in the area found precisely the opposite effect – that is, social inhibition in the presence of others.

The solution to these equivocal results was found by Zajonc (1965), who argued that social facilitation was caused by heightened arousal, which leads people to perform that dominant response more quickly and accurately. If they are performing a well-learned (well practised) act, this dominant response is more likely to be correct; if not (and the person is a bit of a novice), the dominant response is more likely to be incorrect. Put another way, performance on easy "automatically" done tasks is improved by the presence of others, whereas performance on difficult, cognitively controlled tasks is often inhibited and rendered less effective.

One can therefore predict that being watched at a task you are good at improves your performance. In fact, there are other reasons that may increase arousal:

- *Evaluation apprehension* (see Chapter 2): Evaluation apprehension is fear caused by being evaluated by others, particularly experts. Henchy & Glass (1968) assigned individuals to one of four conditions: "alone", "experts together" (i.e. task performance in the presence of two others, explicitly introduced as experts), "non-experts together" (i.e. task performance in the presence of two non-experts) and "alone recorded" (in which the participant performed the tasks alone, but was filed for later evaluation by experts). As predicted, facilitation of dominant (well-learned) responses only occurred in the expert-together and in the alone-recorded conditions, whereas task performance in the non-expert-together condition was similar to that in the alone condition. These results demonstrate that some concern for being evaluated is necessary for the enhanced display of dominant responses.
- *Distraction conflict*: Distraction conflict is caused by the conflict of paying attention to both the task and the other people watching. This naturally reduces effectiveness at the task and depresses performance.

Some people have argued that simply being with others increases synergy. This may well be true, but, as this research shows, it does not necessarily improve the performance of individual members. Yet organizational groups have to exist because it is not feasible for individuals to do the job on their own. Tasks require specialists from different parts of the firm.

Social "loafing"

When people work together on additive tasks (shovelling snow, filling election envelopes, etc.), they work less efficiently than they would if they performed the task alone. This was observed 50 years ago by Ringlemann, who found that, when asked to pull on a rope, individuals pulled an average 63 kg of force, but when put together in tug-of-war teams this dropped to 53 kg per person. Again this observation has been taken back into the laboratory and replicated using a quite different task (Latane, Williams, & Harkins, 1979).

This process may be attributable to the social impact of any group being equally divided among its members. Thus, the larger the group, the less the impact on each member. Responsibility is diffused and each member feels less responsible for (literally) "pulling their weight". This may be partly because group members feel their contribution is less necessary.

Given that social loafing is a problem, Baron & Greenberg (1992) suggested ways of overcoming it:

- *Make workers identifiable*: By pointing out individuals' contribution to their group's performance, people would be unlikely to get away with taking a free ride.
- *Make work more involving*: Jobs that are involving are not likely to induce social loafing; the fact that they are so interesting keeps people performing at a high level.
- *Reward individuals for their contributions to their group*: Instead of being rewarded only for individual contributions, employees should be rewarded for helping others, for enhancing their group's overall performance.
- *Threaten punishment*: People who believe they will be punished for failing to maintain performance standards will refrain from loafing and will attempt to meet those standards.

The benefits of group work may be seen as a simple equation:

Group outcome = group potential (ability × motivation) – process losses + process gains

The potential process gains commonly observed in groups are:

- *Social facilitation*: The mere presence of other members can have an energizing effect in some circumstances.
- *Increased knowledge, ability and effort*: Groups can invariably bring more information to a task than any one individual can: "Many hands make light work". More energy can by definition be devoted to a task by a group than by any single individual.
- *Diversity of views*: The diversity of opinions and approaches can serve as a valuable resource for a group. One member's deficiencies may be balanced by others' strengths.
- *Group pressures to conform to norms*: Once a group arrives at a decision, the pressures of a group on individuals can be a powerful force in implementing solutions.

Unfortunately, each of the above potential advantages can serve as a source of process loss:

- *Social interference and loafing*: The mere presence of others can lead to anxiety and thus detract from performance, particularly on complex tasks. Group members tend to exert less effort when their individual products are not identifiable. So-called "social loafing" has been observed across a wide variety of tasks.
- *Failure to use available knowledge and abilities*: Groups often assign weights to individual contributions within the group on the basis of perceived rather than actual expertise. For example, some research has revealed that the amount of time that members spent talking was a stronger predictor of how much they influenced final group decision than was actual expertise.
- *Diversity of views can lead to conflict*: Groups can fall into win–lose competition

in which members fight to win arguments rather than work to achieve group goals.

- *"Group-think"*: Groups can pressure their members into an unthinking conformity. High-level decision-making groups in the government and military could fall prey to "group-think", which is a mode of thinking that people engage in when they are deeply involved in a cohesive ingroup, when the members' striving for unanimity overrides their motivation to appraise alternative courses of action realistically (see Chapter 11).

Intergroup behaviour

Intergroup relations refer to the relationships *between* groups, whereas intragroup relations are concerned with the relationships *within* a group. Intergroup relations can be categorized by patterns of cooperation, competition or conflict. Some writers believe conflict is inevitable, others that it is not. It is certainly common and is not always totally undesirable. Furthermore, there is often as much intergroup conflict within organizations as between them.

It was argued earlier in this chapter and in Chapter 8 that people join groups for many reasons. People join, stay and leave groups, in part because of the social identity associated with being a member of that group. We think of ourselves partly in terms of the group to which we belong: "I am part of the senior marketing group"; "I am a chartered accountant"; "I am a research scientist working in R&D". Inevitably, people seek out groups that enhance their prestige. As a group's prestige changes, so do people eager to join it or leave it. The fate of one's company can therefore affect one's identity. The shares plunge; a scandal erupts; the product is thought dangerous or unhealthy. Because I am part of that company I take on, in part, its aura.

Hence, people spend a lot of effort in joining or trying to join groups that enhance their identity. Equally, they attempt to hide or disguise their membership of groups that are thought of as less favourable. One way of doing this in business is rebranding or renaming. Typists become secretaries become personal assistants; staff department becomes personnel becomes human resources. The motive to have a positive group-derived social identity is a powerful driver both in work and outside work.

Where groups are helpful, cooperative and mutually supportive, they are often of little interest to business psychologists. However, when they are in conflict, they exercise the problem-solving abilities of managers and researchers alike. It is common to talk about working in "silos". The marketing department works in its area/building, as do human resources, finance, and so on. They know, like and trust each other but are less certain about members of the same organization but from different groups. There is no one organizational culture but many. There can also be unhelpful intergroup (team, department) rivalry, distrust and competition. This can be very bad for the organization as a whole.

Groups can have powerful effects on their members. Intergroup conflict has been viewed by some as divisive and dysfunctional, because it acts against the accomplishment of organizational goals. Others have seen it as being beneficial to productivity and progress. The major causes of conflict include:

- *Mutually dependent tasks*: Where two or more groups do not perceive each other to be equitable in terms of effort or contribution, they may experience intense conflict precisely because of their dependence.

- *Imbalance in task dependency*: This occurs when one group is dependent on another but the latter is not, in turn, dependent on the former.
- *Criteria of performance*: Differences in the speed, quantity, quality or consistency of performance between two groups can lead to considerable conflict.
- *Environmental variations*: Where different groups deal with different customers, regions or processes, they may perceive others as having unfair advantages.
- *Resource dependency*: Conflict is commonly seen regarding the use of shared resources.
- *History of conflict*: This may lead to entrenched attitudes and a long history of competition.
- *Pathological or ambitious leaders*: They may deliberately encourage conflict for their own ends.

There are various solutions to the problem of group conflict. These include the *domination* of one group's views, preferences and practices over the other; *compromise*, where both give up something to achieve peace; and *integration*, when a new way of performing a task is discovered. Finding superordinate goals for conflicting groups is often a very good way of overcoming problems, at least in the short term.

Tajfel (1978) suggested that it is important to distinguish between interpersonal and intergroup behaviour and theories: addressing problems at the one level might not easily be extrapolated to explain phenomena at the other. Interpersonal behaviour means acting as an individual with some idiosyncratic characteristics and a unique set of personal relationships with others; intergroup behaviour, on the other hand, means acting as a group member. In the first case, the various social categories one belongs to are less important than the constellation of individual and interpersonal dynamics. In the second case, the reverse is true; who one is as a person is much less important than the uniform worn, the language spoken, the speciality used or the jargon acquired.

What Tajfel proposed was that social interactions can be depicted as falling some-where along a continuum defined by the two extremes of interpersonal and intergroup behaviour. It could be a function almost entirely of an individual's attitude, beliefs, values, personality or pathology. Or it could be entirely a function of the obvious or less obvious membership of a group. Where it falls depends on three factors, the first of which is the clarity with which different social categories can be identified. Where social divisions such as Black and White, man and woman, are clearly discernible, this will tend to locate the behaviour towards the intergroup end. Where the category differences are less salient, the behaviour is more likely to be interpersonal. The second factor is the extent to which the behaviour or attitude within each group is variable or uniform. Interpersonal behaviour will show the normal range of individual differences; when groups are salient, people's behaviour becomes much more similar. The third factor is how far one person's treatment of, or attitude towards, others is idiosyncratic or uni-form and predictable. In our interpersonal dealings, we supposedly negotiate a variety of ways of responding to those we know; intergroup encounters, on the other hand, tend to be marked by stereotyped perceptions and behaviours (Brown, 1996: 388)

The area of intergroup conflict, categorization and prejudice has a long history in psychology (Brown, 1996; LeBon, 1985; Tajfel, 1978; Zimbardo, 1969). However, British

Table 10.7 The interpersonal–group continuum

Factors	Interpersonal	Group
Presence of two or more social categories	Obscured or not relevant	Clearly visible and salient
Uniformity or behaviour and attitudes within one group	Low	High
Stereotyped or uniform treatment of other group members	Low	High

Source: Reproduced from Brown (1996) with the permission of Blackwell Publishers.

Table 10.8 Response to a negative social identity

	Individual strategy	*Collective strategies*
Aim	Change one's personal standing in society	Change standing of one's group in society.
Method	Leave the group, e.g. accountants attempting to "pass" as actuaries	(1) Restrict comparisons to other subordinate groups, e.g. concern by workers over wage differences; neglect of worker–employer disparities. (2) Change the dimensions of comparison, e.g. stress job security over pay. (3) Direct confrontation with dominant group, e.g. demands for minimum wage or pay review bodies.
Possible outcomes	Some individuals may benefit, but many unable to; position of groups unchanged	(1) Some changes may occur among subordinate groups; major status differences between groups unchanged. (2) May create climate for change if new dimensions achieve social recognition. (3) May lead to change if society is unstable and dominant group's position is under challenge from other directions.

Source: Reproduced from Brown (1996) with the permission of Blackwell Publishers.

social psychologists have made it their speciality and have described fundamental intergroup processes that occur in many groups.

As Brown (1997) has noted, the fundamental process of prejudice and a cornerstone of all intergroup theories is *categorization*, which is essentially the business of differentiating between "us" and "them". Social categories simplify and order. However, a second very important and well-known process occurs thereafter, which is to *minimize within-group differences*. People perceive and think about those within the group they have categorized differently. This can then easily lead to discrimination. This is known as the perceived intragroup homogeneity effect. What is most frequently observed is perceived outgroup homogeneity, expressed in the "they are all the same" philosophy. We are different; they are the same. There are lots of amusing British jokes about this phenomenon: "I am Oxford, You are Cambridge . . . they are the London School of Economics".

People at work talk about those working in silos. They mean that different groups or functions are kept apart, often physically. Furthermore, the organizational chart may encourage people to categorize: between the values, behaviours and personality of those in marking versus engineering, accounts/finance versus human resources. Hence the beginning of stereotyping and distrust. However, research on crossed categorization suggests that if you mix people, the distrust decreases. This may be only slight and very dependent on which categories are crossed. Brown (1997) has summarizes well the psychological issues associated with the problem of categorization:

1   A fundamental aspect of human cognition is people's need and ability to categorize the world. This arises because of the enormous amount and complexity of information with which we have to deal. This is as true of the social world as it is of the physical world. Associated with this simplification function of categorization are a number of biases and other outcomes which have important implications for understanding prejudice and how it can be reduced.
2   One direct outcome of categorization is a cognitive accentuation of differences between categories and a diminution of the difference within categories. These differentiation and assimilation processes have been shown to affect intergroup perceptions, attitudes, and behavioural discrimination.
3   When two or more systems of categorization operate simultaneously the effect can be to reduce the biases associated with any one of the categorizations in isolation. This is most evident in laboratory settings. In naturalistic contexts often one categorization will dominate over the other(s).
4   Once a given categorization comes into play differences within groups are attenuated. This is usually not a symmetrical process – some groups may be seen as more homogenous than others. Often the outgroup is seen as more homogenous although in certain intergroup contexts – particularly those involving minorities – and along value discussions central to a group's identity, the reverse is observed.
5   The adoption of a particular categorization in a given situation depends upon the ease of its cognitive accessibility to the person concerned and the degree of fit between that category system and the actual differences and similarities between people in that situation. Factors affecting accessibility and fit include the person's needs, goals and habitual dispositions, and features of the stimuli such as visibility, proximity and interdependence.
6   Some have claimed that categorical differences are a less important basis for prejudice than perceived differences in beliefs. This claim is only tenable in those situations where group memberships are not psychologically salient. Otherwise the evidence shows that categorization factors are more important than interpersonal difference in belief. A more limited role for belief dissimilarity at the intergroup level is, however, possible. (Brown, 1997: 78–79)

According to researchers in the area, categorization occurs before stereotyping. It is essentially the perception that most, if not all, members of some category share various attributes. Thus we find all people in marketing are shallow, optimistic extraverts, while people in finance are grey bean-counters with no sense of fun. These intra-organizational stereotypes can be about other departments; about groups, senior or junior to oneself; or indeed about customers, clients or competitors.

When people join groups they are often "socialized into" stereotypes. That is, they not only bring with them their personal experiences but learn to acquire the group's values and ways of perceiving the world.

Stereotypes simplify rather than clarify. They are dangerous for many reasons, perhaps most because of the consequences they have on everyday thinking. Stereotypes encourage the assumption that there is a strong relationship between group membership and some belief or behaviour: this can be very dangerous or misleading in all parts of business. In marketing and human resources in particular, people in business need to be aware of both homogeneity and heterogeneity. It is important to break down groups to see variability as much as similarity.

A second problem associated with stereotypes is that they can easily distort thinking. There is a wealth of experimental evidence that stereotypes are hypotheses in search of confirmatory information (Brown, 1997). That is, stereotypes affect data-gathering and judgement. It makes people less disinterested, more involved and more biased. This can lead to poor judgement about people. It can, of course, also lead to making an illegal decision with regard to the law, especially in relation to recruitment, selection, discipline and firing.

Given that categorization and stereotyping are inevitable, the question for the organizational psychologist is how to reduce it. The answer, of course, is contact between members of different groups. Brown (1997) and Hewstone & Brown (1986) have noted that contact should be under very specific conditions:

- The organization should provide clear, unequivocal support for the contact.
- Group contact should be sufficiently close, frequent and of appropriate duration to allow members really to get to know each other.
- Ideally people should be of equal status (i.e. rank, position) within the organization.
- The contact activities should be cooperative rather than competitive.

Anyone at work is probably a member of several groups. Group membership has powerful social and individual effects. Simply being a member of a group means one "takes on" the characteristics of that group, certainly in the eyes of others. Group choice is not always a matter of choice – physical characteristics cannot easily be changed. Being aware of the dangers *within* the organization – intergroup hostility, rivalry, distrust and poor cooperation – has led many in business to try to reduce stereotyping with beneficial effects for the company as a whole.

Women at work

Women have always taken part in paid work but their numbers have increased dramatically over the past 100 years, particularly in developed countries. Around 1900 less than a fifth of women worked in the West, but by the turn of the twentieth-first century over two-thirds of women of working age were in paid employment. Often wars, economic growth and changing attitudes are powerful incentives to increase the number of women in the workforce.

As a consequence, researchers have become interested in such topics as sex-segregation in female- and male-oriented jobs. It is still true that women tend to have different occupations and career choices than men and they tend to work with each other. However, the last quarter of a century has seen many changes; for example, male-dominated jobs have become either "gender-integrated" or "female-dominated" because jobs were growing and there were not enough men or they had fewer attractions for men. This literature on differences between the sexes in relation to career choice and development is called *horizontal* segregation.

A much "hotter" topic has been called *vertical* segregation, which is about differences between men and women in senior, middle and junior positions. For many years there was discussion about the "glass ceiling", whereby various barriers were put in place to prevent women rising to senior positions. Porteous (1997) has argued that three explanations are offered to account for the glass ceiling effect: the belief that men and women have innately different capabilities; prejudice and stereotyping of senior managers and shareholders; and power and politics in most organizational cultures. The question of whether men and women are indeed similar or different in their abilities and or preferences remains a very hotly debated issue. Males are thought of as assertive, ambitious and self-reliant, while females are thought of as empathic, caring and sensitive. Often both managers and observers believe when women succeed it is due to luck, discrimination or favouritism, while male success is more likely to be attributed to ability.

Many senior female managers claim to feel trapped. When they are assertive they are accused of being aggressive or pushy. Despite there being little data on the actual ability of men and women managers, women are thought of as better in situations that require cooperation, while men are better thought of in situations that require direction and control.

The under-representation of women in higher-level management jobs has various consequences: lack of role models and mentors; a reduced senior informal social network; and increased performance pressures.

Diversity and discrimination at work

At the heart of a great deal of conflict is difference: differences of opinions, values, creeds and beliefs. It is often said that a homogenous workgroup is easier to manage and more productive in certain circumstances than a heterogeneous workgroup.

However, the workplace in most Western industrial countries is becoming very obviously more heterogeneous or diverse. This has occurred through increased third migration as well as legislation that prohibits any form of discrimination on the basis of sex, age, disability, religion, sexual orientation, and so on. Most organizations are proud to claim that they are equal opportunity employers, meaning that they support non-discrimination, which inevitably leads to diversity.

Despite this, people from a wide variety of minority groups report discrimination. The gender gap, however, probably receives the most attention. Differences may be visible/invisible, historical/current, possibly job relevant/definitely irrelevant. Thus as Lawthorn (2000) notes, diversity can occur around factors like marital status, education, political affiliation, geographic origins, state of health and size.

Many people feel uncomfortable with the ideas and philosophy of diversity, which they see as an imported ideology that does not understand business issues. They see diversity (doing, being, thinking different) as a possible threat to efficient functioning. They believe people in the organization should assimilate the dominant (corporate and national) culture norms to facilitate communication. They believe that equal treatment means the same treatment for all. Furthermore, they resist what they see to be the need to change individuals rather than change the culture/values of the organization. Managers often recruit in their own image, which inevitably leads to homogeneity. However, what senior managers want to know is, is there a good business case? That is, does a heterogeneous, diverse organization outperform a homogeneous organization? Reviewers suggest the data are equivocal (Lawthorn, 2000).

Many Western governments have put into place legislation which attempts to remove what is seen to be unfair and prejudicial discrimination. One observable feature of this is that CVs contain no information about the applicant's age, religion, birthplace, race or marital status. Furthermore, interviewers can no longer call for photographs or question applicants about their criminal record or even to ask which clubs and societies they belong to.

Several issues are important here:

- *Adverse impact*: This refers to the ratio of people selected to those that applied from minority groups. Thus if only 60% of black applicants are selected compared with 85% of whites, this is referred to as adverse impact.
- *Reverse discrimination*: To increase the numbers of discriminated against groups (blacks, women, disabled people), some organizations have differential cut-off points, such that either people are appointed more on their demography than their ability or else certain groups are given preferential treatment. This may include giving extra points (IQ) to certain groups.
- *Targets of Discrimination*: These include: (1) older workers – those over 55 but more so those over 65; (2) workers with disabilities, be they sensory (vision, hearing), motor (wheelchair-bound) or cognitive (learning, speech); (3) women – not only in terms of hiring, firing and promotion, but also comparable pay for jobs of equivalent skills; (4) sexual orientation – gay men and lesbian women; (5) physical attractiveness – looks and fatness.

Affirmative action programmes remain deeply controversial. Some believe that they have had disappointing results because they may have changed hiring but have had no effect on promotion or retention. Both those who are seen to be "winners" and "losers" of the preferential treatment may oppose it because of their implication that people are chosen who are unqualified, unsuitable or second rate.

There are, as a result, psychologically tested, fair employment practices. Some have advocated race-norming, which is a method of boosting test scores for minority group job applicants to "equalize" their hiring rates. Another approach is banding, which groups people from different groups into bands (e.g. accept, consider, reject) but based on different scores. There are also important issues for ensuring that disabled people are able to complete tests fairly. Consider how to administer a blind person an IQ test.

Conclusion

Most people work in groups or teams, which make up departments or sections. Understanding group processes can help considerably in managing teams. Groups such as committees, quality circles, task groups and expert panels are frequently convened to perform certain tasks. Typically, groups follow a pattern in their development, called forming, norming, storming, performing and mourning. Usually, employees are members of two somewhat distinct but overlapping groups: formal groups that are explicit and imposed, as well as informal groups that form for all sorts of reasons. Although their dynamics may be much the same, their structure, goals, influence and communication channels are probably quite different.

It is possible to describe and differentiate all (work) groups by quite different characteristics: size, cohesiveness, roles, norms, status, communication structure, and so on. What most managers want to know is what are the defining characteristics of an effective workgroup? Although different writers have come up with impressive lists of these criteria, it is far from certain as to whether they are all true for all groups. Most of these listed characteristics are commonsensical, whereas there are often examples of unlikely groups or teams that perform spectacularly well.

Given the increasing multicultural and heterogeneous nature of all cultures and workforces, a question of current interest is whether group diversity is advantageous or disadvantageous. As in so many other aspects of work, this apparently simple question has no easy answer. Homogeneous groups have certain advantages over heterogeneous groups, particularly in the short term. Most of the research on diversity has concentrated on gender or racial diversity, yet recent work has suggested that the *roles* that group members need to fill are most relevant to the diversity issue. The research shows that working groups need team leaders, creative thinkers, negotiators and company workers. If a team is homogeneous in the sense that all group members want to adopt certain roles (monitor–evaluator, completer–finisher) but avoid others (resource investigator), the research suggests that it would not perform well, at least compared with other groups that were heterogeneous and had all the team roles covered.

The social psychological literature has attempted to answer the very fundamental but crucially important question concerning the benefits and drawbacks of working in groups at all. Groups do provide synergy, but this in and of itself can have contradictory effects. Working with or watched by others on a task that has been well mastered probably improves performance, whereas the presence of colleagues or observers on less well mastered skills may inhibit performance. Equally, many people use the opportunity of "groupwork" to avoid doing much at all – namely, social loafing. In fact, to avoid this too common problem in committees and other workgroups, some organizations deliberately set out rules that lessen the behaviour of social loafing.

Finally, although most business psychologists focus on intragroup behaviour, it is equally important to focus on intergroup behaviour. It is obvious from every organizational chart that large companies have many different groups, on the same and different levels, which may be encouraged to cooperate or compete for scarce resources. The study of intergroup behaviour suggests that certain situations are likely to lead to group conflict. The extent to which individual behaviour is determined by individual personality characteristics or group factors depends largely on group members. Furthermore, groups appear to have fairly strong forces to discriminate in favour of ingroup members and against outgroup members. Yet it is because groups bestow an identity on individuals by dint of their membership that they can have such an impact on individuals.

A research perspective

Reducing intergroup conflict

When departments or sections within an organization clash, any manager hopes to reduce conflict. For nearly 50 years, psychologists have been investigating the contact hypothesis, which in its earliest form posited simply that association with persons from a disliked group leads to the growth of liking and respect for that group. But even Allport (1979), in his classic statement, acknowledged that "the case is not so simple" (p. 261) and he accepted that contact could increase conflict, as well as reduce it. Allport emphasized the "nature of contact" and saw that its effect would depend on the kinds of people and situations involved. Perhaps his greatest contribution at this early stage was the provision of a taxonomy of relevant factors (see Box 10.2), which, today, almost 30 years later, is just as striking and useful as it was then (ibid.: 262–263).

On the basis of this taxonomy, Allport grouped together studies done in a wide variety of settings and was able to summarize the effects of particular types of contact. He concluded that the outcomes of contact would be favourable when participants were of equal status, pursuing common goals and backed by social and institutional support (Allport, 1979).

Others have also addressed this issue. Cook (1978) predicts that less derogatory outgroup attitudes will result when individuals have personal contact with members of a group they dislike, but under the following five conditions:

- Participants from the two groups have equal status within the confines of the contact situation.
- The characteristics of outgroup members with whom interaction takes place disconfirm the prevailing group stereotype.
- The contact situation encourages, or perhaps necessarily requires, cooperation in the achievement of a joint goal.
- The contact situation has high "acquaintance potential" (i.e. it enables individuals to get to know each other as individuals, rather than as stereotypical outgroup members).
- The social norms within and surrounding the contact situation favour "group equality" and "egalitarian intergroup association".

Perhaps the best-known work in this area is that of Amir (1976), who was particularly interested in reducing racism. The crux of Amir's painstaking assessment can be seen in his summary of favourable conditions that tend to reduce prejudice and unfavourable conditions that tend to strengthen prejudice. The favourable conditions were:

- Where there is equal status contact between members of various ethnic groups.
- When the contact is between members of a majority and *higher* status members of a minority group.
- When an "authority" and/or the social climate are in favour of, and promote, the intergroup contact.
- When the contact is of an intimate rather than a casual nature.
- When the ethnic intergroup contact is pleasant or rewarding.
- When the members of *both* groups in the particular contact situation interact in functionally important activities or develop common goals or superordinate goals that are more important than the individual goal of *each* of the groups.

The unfavourable conditions were:

- When the contact situation results in competition between the groups.
- When the contact is unpleasant, involuntary, tension-laden.
- When the prestige or status of one group is lowered as a result of the contact situation.
- When members of a group, or the group as a whole, are in a state of frustration.
- When the groups in contact have moral or ethical standards which are objectionable to each other.
- In the case of contact between a majority and a minority group, when the members of the minority group are of lower status, or are lower in any relevant characteristic, than the members of the majority group.

Box 10.2 Dimensions of contact

Quantitative aspects of contact
- (a) Frequency
- (b) Duration
- (c) Number of persons involved
- (d) Variety

Status aspects of contact
- (a) Minority member has inferior status
- (b) Minority member has equal status
- (c) Minority member has superior status
- (d) Not only may the individuals encountered vary thus in status; but the group as a whole may have relatively high status (e.g. Jews) or relatively low status (e.g. Negroes)

Role aspects of contact
- (a) Is the relationship one of competitive or cooperative activity?
- (b) Is there a superordinate or subordinate role relation involved; e.g. master–servant, employer–employee, teacher–pupil?

Social atmosphere surrounding the contact
- (a) Is segregation prevalent, or is its egalitarianism expected?
- (b) Is the contact voluntary or involuntary?
- (c) Is the contact "real" or "artificial"?
- (d) Is the contact perceived in terms of intergroup relations or not perceived as such?
- (e) Is the contact regarded as "typical" or as "exceptional"?
- (f) Is the contact regarded as important and intimate, or as trivial and transient?

Personality of the individual experiencing the contact
- (a) Is his initial prejudice level high, low, medium?
- (b) Is his prejudice of a surface, conforming type, or is it deeply rooted in his character structure?
- (c) Has he basic security in his own life, or is he fearful and suspicious?
- (d) What is his previous experience with the group in question, and what is the strength of his present stereotypes?
- (e) What are his age and general education level?
- (f) Many other personality factors may influence the effect of contact.

Areas of contact
- (a) Casual
- (b) Residential
- (c) Occupational
- (d) Recreational
- (e) Religious
- (f) Civic and fraternal
- (g) Political
- (h) Goodwill intergroup activities

Source: Allport (1979).

However, Hewstone & Brown (1986) believe contact is not enough. They believe the contact hypothesis assumes that prejudice is caused by ignorance, which is not always necessarily true. Furthermore, the discovery of great similarity that supposedly follows contact is also not necessarily true. They also believe that the contact hypothesis does not distinguish between the contact between group members at an interpersonal versus intergroup level. They argue that, in addition to contact, two groups need superordinate, shared goals, real motives to cooperate (rather than compete), and ways of grouping or classifying people that cut across the old in-/out-group categories.

The role of conflict between specialist, functional groups or teams within any organization can have a serious long-term effect on both morale and productivity. Many senior managers spend considerable amounts of time and effort attempting to reduce conflict, prejudice and destructive competition, while increasing cooperation. The above research suggests some useful ideas to test out.

A cross-cultural perspective

Many observers have noted how the collectivism of many Eastern countries impacts quite differently on work-related group processes compared with the individualism in the West. Thus, in contrast to Westerners, many Asians make special efforts to join groups whose membership they greatly value. They appear to sacrifice their self-interest to the group much more than their Western counterparts would. Furthermore, they make clear distinctions between ingroup members who they respect and outgroup members to whom they may be apathetic or hostile. The following are typical characteristics of Asian groups, which may be compared with workgroup practices in Europe:

- *Kinship*: Familiarism and nepotism is common in Asia, and often outlawed in the West. It has been estimated in Korea that about 30% of companies have family members as executives. For many Asians, the family provides security and support. The preference for kin in key positions is based on the belief that they are more trustworthy, committed and loyal. Hence, cohesiveness is usually higher in Asian groups.
- *Adherence to group norms*: Asian groups expect, demand and extract closer adherence to group norms. Group members tend to be highly sensitive to implicit and explicit cues that may jeopardize their relationships with others. Compared with the West, there is much less tolerance for deviants, who fear being ostracized from the group.
- *Less well defined roles*: Compared with the West, job specifications and duties are often much less clearly defined. Oral communications seem to play a more important role in day-to-day work. The lesser degree of specialization and standardization certainly encourages flexibility but may encourage conflict. Inevitably, role ambiguity is more common in Eastern than Western workgroups.
- *Stress on harmony*: South East Asians seem to spend more time on socio-emotional activities (such as a shared lunch) than Westerners. Because it is very important for all individuals to get along with each other, group solidarity is a goal in and of itself. Hence, it becomes more important to share in more socio-emotional than task-orientated activities.

A human resources perspective

One model of groups that has endured has become known as the Tavistock model, developed by Bion (1961), a British psychologist. It has various premises.

When the aggregate becomes a group, the group behaves as a system – an entity that in some respects is greater than the sum of its parts – and the primary task of the group is *survival*. Although this task is often disguised, group survival becomes a latent motivation for all group members. It provides the framework for the exploration of group behaviour. Appreciating the group as a whole requires a perceptual shift on the part of the observer, a blurring of individual separateness, and a readiness to see the collective interactions generated by group members. In gestalt terms, the group is focal and individuals are background.

The group-as-a-whole approach can be summarized as follows:

- The primary task of any group is what it must do to survive.
- The group has a life of its own arising out of the fantasies and projections of its members.
- The group uses its members in the service of its primary task.
- The behaviour of any group member at any moment is the expression of his or her own needs, history and behavioural patterns *and* the needs, history and behavioural patterns of the group.
- Whatever the group is doing or talking about, the group is always talking about itself, reflecting itself.
- Understanding the process of the group provides members with heightened awareness and the ability to make previously unavailable choices about their identities and functions in a group setting.

According to Bion (1961), like dreams, groups have a manifest overt aspect and a latent covert aspect. The manifest aspect is the *workgroup*, whose members consciously pursue an agreed objective and work towards the completion of a task. Although group members have hidden agendas, they rely on internal and external controls to prevent these hidden agendas from emerging and interfering with the group task. They pool their rational thinking and combine their skills to solve problems and make decisions.

Groups do not always function rationally or productively, and individual members are not necessarily aware of the internal and external controls they rely on to maintain the boundary between their announced intentions and their hidden agendas. The combined hidden agendas of group members constitute the latent aspect of group life, the *basic assumption* group. In contrast to the rational group, this group consists of unconscious wishes, fears, defences, fantasies, impulses and projections. The workgroup is focused away from itself, towards the task; the basic assumption group is focused inwards, towards fantasy and a more primitive reality. Tension always exists between the two; it is balanced by various behavioural and psychological structures, including individual defence systems, ground rules, expectations and group norms.

On the basic assumption level of functioning, the group behaves *as if* a certain assumption is true and valid and *as if* certain behaviours are vital to the group's survival. "Basic" refers to the survival motivation of the group; "assumption" underscores the fact that the survival motivation is based not on fact or reality but on the collective projections of the group members. Bion (1961) identifies three distinct types of basic assumptions: dependency, fight/flight and pairing. Turquet (1974) added a fourth one: one-ness.

Dependency
The essential aim of this level of group functioning is to attain security and protection from one individual, either the designated leader or a member who assumes that role. The group behaves as if it is stupid, incompetent or psychotic, in the hope that it will be rescued from its impotency by a powerful God-like leader who will instruct and direct towards task completion. When the leader fails to meet these impossible demands, the group members express their disappointment and hostility in a variety of ways. The dependency function often serves as a lure for a charismatic leader who exerts authority through powerful personal characteristics.

Fight/flight
In this mode of functioning, the group perceives its survival as being dependent on either fighting (active aggression, scapegoating, physical attack) or fleeing from the task (withdrawal, passivity, avoidance, ruminating on past history). Anyone who mobilizes the aggressive forces of the group

is granted leadership, but the persistent bickering, in-fighting, and competition make most leadership efforts short-lived. In flight functioning, leadership is usually bestowed on an individual who minimizes the importance of the task and facilitates the group movement away from the here and now.

Pairing

Pairing phenomena include bonding between two individuals who express warmth and affection leading to intimacy and closeness. Such pairs often provide mutual intellectual support to the extent that other members become inactive. The pair need not be a man and a woman. When the group assumes this mode of functioning, it perceives that its survival is contingent on reproduction; that is, in some magic way, a "Messiah" will be born to save the group and help it complete its task.

Oneness

Described by Turquet (1974: 357), this level of functioning occurs "when members seek to join in a powerful union, to surrender self for passive participation, and thereby to feel existence, well-being and wholeness". The group commits itself to a "movement" – a cause outside itself – as a way of survival. Leaders who offer a philosophy of life or methods to achieve higher levels of consciousness become attractive to the group in this type of basic assumption functioning.

The basic assumption life of any group is never exhausted, nor is it imperative for a group to rid itself of its basic assumption characteristics. In fact, as Bion perceived society, certain institutions capitalize on our collective basic assumption strivings and provide structures and vehicles to channel these strong primitive feelings. Hence, the Church attempts to satisfy dependency needs; the military and industry employ fight/flight motivation; and the aristocracy and the political system – with their emphasis on breeding and succession – build on basic assumption pairing. The interest in mysticism and cosmic consciousness seems to be an expression of basic assumption one-ness.

The Tavistock method can be applied in many different group situations. Primarily intended to teach group dynamics and increase the awareness of group phenomena, the method is formally applied in *group relations conferences*, events that are characterized by a clear statement of objectives, specific staff roles, and a perverse all-encompassing application of the group-as-a-whole theoretical approach.

The aims of such conferences tend to be to examine the ways in which authority is vested in leaders by others, to study the factors involved as they happen, to establish the covert processes that operate in and among groups, and to study the problems encountered in the exercise of authority. There is no attempt to prescribe specifically what anyone shall learn. Participants are provided with experience-based group opportunities to study their behaviour as it happens, and conference events allow consultation with at least one staff member to facilitate that task.

Consultants consult only to a group, not to individual members, and only within the time boundaries prescribed. The consultant's role is often the subject of much consternation among members, which is deliberate, in the interests of assisting members to pursue the task of the event in which they are involved. The consultant does not engage in social amenities, advice-giving or nurturing, but performs his or her task by providing interventions for the group's consideration and reporting his or her observations back to the group. Thus, the consultant confronts the group by drawing attention to group behaviour. This is done by means of description, process observation, thematic development and other interventions, some of which are designed to shock the group into awareness of what is happening. Participants typically experience some pain as they explore issues of authority, responsibility, boundaries (of input, roles, tasks and time), projection, organizational structure and large-group phenomena.

Group members inevitably project onto the staff their fantasies, fears and doubts about authority and power. Exploration of these projections can yield significant advances in learning, but the role of consultant is difficult. Strict adherence to it is a hallmark of the Tavistock method.

References

Adler, N. (1991). *International dimensions of organizational behaviour*. Boston, MA: PWS Kent.

Allport, G. (1979). *The nature of prejudice*. Reading, MA: Addison-Wesley.

Amir, Y. (1976). The role of intergroup contact in changes of prejudice and ethnic relations. In P. Katz (Ed.), *Toward the elimination of racism* (pp. 245–308). New York: Pergamon.

Argyle, M., Furnham, A., & Graham, J. (1981). *Social situations*. Cambridge: Cambridge University Press.

Bales, R. (1950). *Interaction process analysis: A method for the study of small groups*. Reading, MA: Addison-Wesley.

Barrick, M., Stewart, G., Neubert, M., & Mount, M. (1998). Relating member ability and personality to work-team processes and team effectiveness. *Journal of Applied Psychology, 83*, 377–391.

Bavelas, A. (1950). Communication patterns in task-oriented groups. *Journal of the Acoustical Society of America, 22*, 725–730.

Belbin, M. (1981). *Management teams*. London: Heinemann.

Bion, W. (1961). *Experiences in groups*. New York: Basic Books.

Broucek, W., & Randall, G. (1996). An assessment of the construct validity of the Belbin Self-Perception Inventory and Observer's Assessment from the perspective of the five-factor model. *Journal of Occupational and Organizational Psychology, 69*, 389–405.

Brown, R. (1996). Intergroup relations. In M. Hewstone, W. Stroebe, J.-P. Codel, & G. Stephenson (Eds.), *Introduction to social psychology* (2nd edn., pp. 361–410). Oxford: Blackwell.

Brown, R. (1997). *Prejudice: It's social psychology*. Oxford: Blackwell.

Chell, E. (1987). *The psychology of behaviour in organizations*. London: Macmillan.

Cook, M. (1978). *Perceiving others: The psychology of interpersonal perception*. London: Methuen.

Cordery, J. (2002). Team working. In P. Warr (Ed.), *Psychology at work* (pp. 346–350). Harmondsworth, UK: Penguin.

Dulewicz, V. (1995). A validation of Belbin's team roles from 16PF and OPQ using bosses' ratings of competence. *Journal of Occupational and Organizational Psychology, 68*, 81–99.

Feldman, D. (1987). The development and enforcement of group norms. *Academy of Management Review, 9*, 47–53.

Furnham, A. (1992). *Personality at work*. London: Routledge.

Furnham, A., Steele, H., & Pendleton, D. (1993). A psychometric assessment of the Belbin Team-Role Self-Perception Inventory. *Journal of Occupational and Organizational Psychology, 66*, 245–257.

Gray, J., & Starke, F. (1984). *Organizational behaviour: Concepts and applications*. Columbus, OH: Charles E. Merrill.

Greenberg, J., & Baron, R. (1992). *Behaviour in organizations*. Boston, MA: Allyn & Bacon.

Hackman, J. (1987). Group influences on individuals in organization. In M. Dunnette (Ed.), *Handbook of individual/organizational psychology* (pp. 455 Brown, 1996; 525). Palo Alto, CA: Consulting Psychologists Press.

Handy, C. (1985). *Understanding organizations*. Harmondsworth, UK: Penguin.

Hellriegel, D., Slocum, J., & Woodman, R. (1992). *Organizational behaviour* (6th edn.). St Paul, MN: West Publishing Co.

Henchy, T., & Glass, D. (1968). Evaluation apprehension and the social facilitation of dominant and subordinate responses. *Journal of Personality and Social Psychology, 10*, 446–454.

Herriot, P., & Pemberton, C. (1995). *Competitive advantage through diversity*. London: Sage.

Hewstone, M., & Brown, R. (Eds.) (1986). *Contact and conflict in intergroup encounters*. Oxford: Basil Blackwell.

Hoffman, L. (1979). Applying experimental research on group problem-solving to organizations. *Journal of Applied Behavioural Science, 15*, 375–391.

Hogg, C. (1990). Team-building. *Personnel management: fact sheet #34.*

Hosking, D. M., & Morley, I. (1991). *A social psychology of organizing.* London: Harvester.

Johns, G. (1992). *Organizational behaviour: Understanding life at work.* New York: HarperCollins.

Johnson, C., Wood, R., & Blinkhorn, S. (1988). Spariouser and spuriouser: The use of ipsative personality tests. *Journal of Occupational Psychology, 61*, 153–161.

Latane, B., Williams, K., & Harkins, S. (1979). Many hands make light work: The causes and consequences of social loafing. *Journal of Personality and Social Psychology, 39*, 822–832.

Lawthorn, R. (2000). Against all odds: managing diversity. In N. Chmiel (Ed.), *Introduction to work and organizational psychology: A European perspective* (pp. 387–406). Oxford: Blackwell.

LeBon, G. (1985). *Psychologie des foules.* Paris: Alcan.

Leung, K. (1992). Groups and social relationships. In R. Westwood (Ed.), *Organizational behaviour: South East Asia perspectives* (pp. 243–264). Hong Kong: Longman.

Likert, R. (1961). *New patterns of management.* New York: McGraw-Hill.

McCann, R., & Margerison, C. (1989). Managing high-performing teams. *Training and Development Journal, 11*, 53–60.

McGregor, D. (1960). *The human side of enterprise.* New York: McGraw-Hill.

McKenna, E. (1994). *Business psychology and organizational behaviour.* Hove, UK: Lawrence Erlbaum Associates.

Myers, J., & McCauley, M. (1985). *Manual: A guide to the development and use of the Myers–Briggs type indicator.* Palo Alto, CA: Consulting Psychologists Press.

Neuman, G., Wagner, S., & Christiansen, N. (1999). The relationship between work-team personality composition and the job performance of teams. *Group and Organizational Management, 24*, 28–45.

Porteous, M. (1997). *Occupational psychology.* London: Prentice-Hall.

Porter, L., Lawler, E., & Hackman, J. (1975). *Behaviour in organizations.* New York: McGraw-Hill.

Randolph, W., & Blackburn, R. (1989). *Managing organizational behaviour.* Boston, MA: Irwin.

Sayles, L., & Strauss, G. (1966). *Human behaviour in organizations.* Englewood Cliffs, NJ: Prentice-Hall.

Senior, B. (1997). Team roles and team performance: Is there "really" a link? *Journal of Occupational and Organizational Psychology, 70*, 241–258.

Spector, P. (2003). *Industrial and organizational psychology.* Chichester, UK: Wiley.

Steiner, I. (1976). Task-performing groups. In J. Thibaut, J. Spence, & R. Carson (Eds.), *Contemporary topics in social psychology* (pp. 393–421). New York: General Learning Press.

Sundstrom, E., De Meuse, K., & Futrell, D. (1990). Work teams: Applications and effectiveness. *American Psychologist, 45*, 120–133.

Tajfel, H. (1978). *Differentiation between social groups.* London: Academic Press.

Triplett, N. (1898). The dynamogenic factor in pace making and competition. *American Journal of Psychology, 9*, 507–533.

Tuckman, B. (1965). Development sequences in small groups. *Psychological Bulletin, 63*, 384–399.

Turquet, P. (1974). Leadership: The individual and the group. In E. Gibbard, J. Hartman, & R. Mann (Eds.), *The analysis of groups* (pp. 75–91). San Francisco, CA: Jossey–Bass.

Unsworth, K., & West, M. (2000). Teams: The challenges of co-operative work. In N. Chmiel (Ed.), *Introduction to work and organizational psychology* (pp. 327–346). Oxford: Blackwell.

Whyte, W. (1948). *Human relations in the restaurant industry.* New York: McGraw-Hill.

Zajonc, R. (1965). Social facilitation. *Science, 149*, 269–274.

Zimbardo, P. (1969). The human choice: Individualism, reason and order versus de-individualism, impulse and chaos. In W. Arnold & D. Levine (Eds.), *Nebraska symposium on motivation* (Vol. 17, pp. 237–307). Lincoln, NB: University of Nebraska Press.

11 Decision-making

Introduction

Decision-making is arguably the most important of all managerial activities. It is the most common activity and most crucial role of senior managers. It is about how managers process information. Essentially, decision-making is concerned with the processing of generating options and then choosing among them. Decisions in organizations can be divided into various groups, and each decision has various phases. For instance:

- *operational decisions*: usually with short-term effects and of a routine nature;
- *tactical decisions*: usually with medium-term effects and of a non-routine nature but not going so far as to review the organization's goals;
- *strategic decisions*: usually with long-term effects and concerning the organization's goals.

Decision-making is particularly interesting because it brings together so many different strands of psychology: cognitive, personality and social.

Research on decision-making is concerned with very specific issues, such as how people infer information from data, how personal preferences affect decision-making and the deciding process itself. As Connolly and Ordonez (2004) note, this area is both *descriptive* and *prescriptive*: it seeks to ascertain what people actually do and what they should do in the decision-making process. They note that decision-making is at the heart of so much in work psychology: personnel selection and placement, strategic and resource planning, appraisal and assessment. People in business all want to make better decisions. Most of the decisions senior managers have to make are complex. These decisions are often made in groups. They often have very serious consequences.

For all sorts of reasons, people think in automatic ways that lead to poorer judgements (Hastie & Dawes, 2001). In essence, people are frequently not rational. Hastie and Dawes (2001) note that a rational choice can be defined as one that meets four criteria:

1 It is based on the decision-maker's current assets. Assets include not only money, but physiological state, psychological capacities, social relationships and feelings.
2 It is based on the possible consequences of the choice.
3 When these consequences are uncertain, their likelihood is evaluated according to the basic rules of probability theory.
4 It is a choice that is adaptive within the constraints of those probabilities and the

values or satisfactions associated with each of the possible consequences of the choice.

Don't we make all our decisions like that? Decidedly not! Hastie & Dawes note that two things drive research in this area: what makes a good decision and what makes a decision difficult.

Research in the area tends to break down into various sections (Plous, 1993). The first is how decisions are influenced by selective perception, biases in memory, pressures to be consistent and the very context in which we make the decision. A person's ability, experience and motivation have a powerful influence on how they see things. Second, cognitive dissonance has shown how people feel pressured to be consistent in their beliefs and behaviours. Third, there is a wealth of studies suggesting that our memory of events is very select. Finally, there are well-known context affects, including the contrast affect, the primacy-recency affect, and the horns and halos affect, which suggest the context in which decisions are made profoundly shape them.

Cognitive psychologists appear to rejoice in demonstrating how many errors and biases we all make when we think we are being perfectly rational. For instance, there is a great deal of work on how important decisions are often a function of how a problem is worded. In this sense, decisions have "plasticity" (Plous, 1993). Polsters, politicians and pundits soon learn that the simple wording of a question significantly influences the answers that clever, reasonable people give to them. Plous (1993: 76) notes:

> Before relying on results from survey research and other studies of judgement and decision-making, it is important to consider how people's answers would have changed as a function of factors such as:
>
> - The order in which the questions were presented.
> - The context in which the questions appeared.
> - Whether the question format was open or closed.
> - Whether the questions were filtered.
> - Whether the questions contained catch phrases.
> - The range of suggested response alternatives.
> - The order in which response alternatives were presented.
> - Whether middle categories were provided.
> - Whether problems were framed in terms of gains or losses.

There are many well-researched "traps" that people fall into when making business decisions. These include *over-confidence* in personal ability to make the right choice. It occurs when judgements are difficult and can have disastrous consequences. Another is *self-fulfilling prophecies*, which is seeking (only) confirmatory evidence that self-perpetuates beliefs.

Often decision-makers have problems over time. They go for momentary gratification, downplaying the long-term consequences. Sometimes the negative consequences of behaviour are not understood or foreseen. Others fall into *investment* or *sunk cost traps*, where prior expenditure of time, money or effort leads people to make bad decisions.

Many business case studies are about the wise and foolish decisions individuals and companies made in branding products, innovation, restructuring, and so on.

Decision-making is about risk assessment and the weighing up of probabilities. It is about how individuals, groups and self-regulating teams come to decide on patterns of action. Most decisions involve trade-offs.

To compromise is to trade off one thing for another. Much of business is about designing the optimal trade-off of different qualities or values. For all businesses, the three most quoted trade-off issues are *quality, speed* and *cost*. Imagine that you want to commission a piece of work. It may be the manufacturing of a product, a staff survey, the evaluation of a management process, or the purchase of a new IT system. Trading off means not getting the maximum amount of all three, but trading off one against the others. You can usually have two of the three, but not all three together. Consider the organizations and managers who typically trade off one of the three:

Good and cheap, but not so fast

This is where speed is traded off for quality and price. In this sense, quality can be cost-effective, but at the price of speed. If one is prepared to wait for people to work at their own speed, or when their erratic timetable allows, they may do the job well (even relatively cheaply), but it does drag on. Amateurs, part-timers and enthusiasts often perform tasks with total commitment and with relatively little reward, but they cannot be rushed. Some organizations believe that quality is worth the wait. They may even argue that there is no alternative (the thing cannot be rushed), or, indeed, that time spent is an index of quality. Research and development scientists, academics, writers and so on believe that they can come up with the goods only if they are not hurried.

Good and fast, but not cheap

This is where price is traded off for speed and quality. If you want high-quality work with a very short lead time, you must be prepared to pay for it. In a sense, this is the concept of overtime. You can get sophisticated professionals (lawyers, doctors, engineers) to work through the night to provide excellent results, but you need to be prepared to pay for it. High flyers working to a tight delivery date command high salaries. There is always a cost, which is money. Some businesses are used to frenetic output. They believe things have to be "right first time" and on time – and they are prepared to pay for it. Money can buy hard work, commitment and quality.

Fast and cheap, but not good

This is where quality is traded off for speed and price. This is the cheap and cheerful, "pile them high and sell them cheap" end of the market. The fast-food industry does not pretend to offer fine dining. It provides cheap food served immediately. Naturally, organizations and individuals that trade off this way do not neglect quality; they merely set a lower standard. One can buy products and hire people at highly competitive prices, but most people rightly suspect that just as there is no such thing as a free lunch, there are very rarely any real bargains. At the end of the day, one gets what one pays for. And if it is really cheap and quickly done, it is rarely very good.

Some organizations have departments of strategic planning which are dedicated to helping senior managers make better decisions. Other organizations believe better decisions are made if particular processes are followed (Simon, 1976; Zander, 1982). More recently, there has been increasing interest in decision-making by computer and expert systems. We can now build computerized chess programs that can beat Grand Masters. Given the number of human errors we constantly find in decision-making, and accepting that computers excel at logical deductions following simple and robust algorithms, it is quite possible that many mundane, but also many high-order, decisions can be better made with computer assistance. The sheer speed and accuracy with which computers are able to process large amounts of data means that many managers are now dependent on computer analysis for their decision-making. There are individual, corporate and national differences in decision-making style. But there are also universal phenomena: many decisions have to be made in a short time-span with various constraints.

Most decision-making involves going through a series of specific steps (Greenberg & Baron, 2003). First, the issue, problem or topic needs to be carefully *identified and delineated*. This step sounds simple but is often overlooked, only to cause significant problems later on. Indeed, when outside experts or consultants are called in, their first task is often to redefine the nature of the problem requiring a solution. A problem may be identified in terms of the preferred solution or in terms of its symptoms. This phase may also be characterized by an extensive information search. The next step is to *define the objective* or *outcomes* of the decision – that is, what people are trying to achieve. Again, this step is obvious but often glossed over, only to cause problems later. Third, it becomes crucial to decide *how to make the decision* – that is, by what method, with what support, given specific information, and so on. Most groups do not consider that they need to decide how to decide; they merely adapt the policy that they used in the past.

A fourth step is to *generate alternative solutions* to the problem. This step involves alternative development, evaluation and choice. One needs to think about all alternatives, know the ultimate value of each and the probability that each will work. The logical fifth step is to *evaluate those solutions*. Once evaluated, *one choice (or combination of choices) needs to be made*, which constitutes the decision. Of course, this needs to be implemented correctly and efficiently and the *follow-up or consequences analysed*. The eight steps shown in Box 11.1 are usually required, although frequently some are skipped, often with dire consequences.

This eight-step model is prescriptive rather than descriptive. In other words, it is recommended that decision-makers use the model as a checklist. This linear model is inevitably simplistic: not every step requires a similar amount of time or effort, and it may be necessary to go back and repeat a step at a later date. Nevertheless, it provides both the researcher and the decision-maker with a heuristic model by which they can evaluate a decision process.

The prescriptive or normative approach focuses on the best way to make decisions. In doing so, the aim is to develop a set of procedures, techniques or processes that optimize accurate and efficient decisions. The descriptive approach (also known as the behavioural decision-making approach) attempts to show how people (managers) actually make decisions. Whereas the former approach often strives for rationality, the latter shows how irrational decision-makers are. Rational-choice models of decision-making aim to choose alternatives that maximize measurable gains, attain personal goals, and seem logical and systematic. However, most research shows the "bounded" rationality of decision-makers.

There are many practical reasons why decision-making is far from ideal. Often the

---

Box 11.1 Sample diagnostic questions for the eight-step decision-making process

Phase 1	Situational analysis	What are the key elements of the situation? What constraints affect the situation? What resources are available?
Phase 2	Objective setting	Is the problem stated clearly? Do group members understand what they will work on? By what criteria will decision-making be judged?
Phase 3	Choosing decision methods	How will we generate alternatives? Who will be involved and at what stage?
Phase 4	Search for alternatives	Are those individuals most involved in the problem also involved in the decision-making? Has complete information been sought? Are information holders involved in the decision-making? Is a diversity of means used to generate ideas? Are all ideas encouraged, regardless of their content?
Phase 5	Evaluation of alternatives	Are criteria for assessment clearly specified and understood by group members? Are differences of opinion included in the evaluation? Are some alternatives pilot-tested?
Phase 6	Making the decision	Are group members clear that selection is occurring? Are action plans made to fit with the decision? Are group members committed to the decision?
Phase 7	Evaluation of the decision	Are responsibilities for data collection, analysis, and reporting clearly assigned? Does a comprehensive evaluation plan exist? Does an evaluation schedule exist?
Phase 8	Consequences analysis	Was the implementation of the decision clear and effective? What aspects/features of the decision worked best? How does this experience affect how the group will continue to make decisions?

Source: Adapted from Gordon (1993).

---

information available is limited and possibly biased. Decisions have to be made very speedily. A rather limited number of decision options are on offer and it is difficult to compare them because of the inability to quantify the decisions. Where no alternative or even combination of alternatives is viable, the decision-maker may simply defer the decision or more likely change the objectives.

One aspect of decision-making that is overlooked is the issue of negotiation. Often negotiations have to occur before, during and after decision-making. Negotiation takes skill: to build up and maintain social relationships, represent one's group but also strike a hard bargain. There are cultural differences in bargaining that also need to be considered.

Decisions can be classified into various types. Many are routine, with considerable guidance available on how and what to do, given company policy and past history. These may be considered well structured, and so organizations have a programme to deal with them. Other decisions have to be more creative because they are made about phenomena that are new or where there is a limited amount of data or experience to go on. These may be considered ill-structured or unique. The former are sometimes called *programmed* (everyday, routine, lower level) and the latter *non-programmed* (unusually creative, higher level). In day-to-day decision-making, the idealized list in Box 11.1 is rarely adhered to: often, certain steps are missed or skipped over in a very perfunctory way. Many managers are "action-orientated", preferring doing from thinking, and hence may not spend sufficient time on such crucial issues as the generation and evaluation of feasible alternatives (phases 4 and 5).

Furthermore, many managers do not distinguish sufficiently between everyday programmed decisions concerned with *doing things right* and unusual, unprogrammed decision about *doing the right thing*. The more senior the manager, the more doing the right thing is more important than doing things right. Naturally, the more senior the manager, the more he or she is confronted with ill-structured, non-programmed decisions. Indeed, some people say that is what senior managers are paid for: to make good, but difficult, decisions.

From Table 11.1 it is quite apparent that one can make a distinction between the usual and regular and the unusual and irregular decisions (Baron & Greenberg, 1990). In one sense, the everyday programmed decisions become so routine that they are not perceived to be decisions at all. It is only the unusual, non-programmed issues about which most managers believe decisions are warranted. This may be unwise, particularly if programmed decisions are not thoroughly and regularly re-evaluated in the light of new developments, technology or competitor practices. In the short term, to programme and routinize a decision may be highly efficient, but could in the longer term lead to serious incompetence, because of the mindless application of an old and less

Table 11.1 Programmed versus non-programmed decisions

Question	Type of decision	
	Everyday programmed decisions *Doing things right*	*Unusual non-programmed decisions* *Doing the right things*
1. What type of tasks are involved?	Routine	Creative
2. How much reliance is there on organizational policies?	Considerable guidance from past decisions	No guidance from past decisions
3. Typically, who makes the decisions?	Lower-level workers Supervisors	Upper-level supervisors Managers
4. Speed of decisions	Fast	Slow
5. Risk associated with decisions	Low	High

Source: Adapted from Baron & Greenberg (1990).

efficient decision to a new problem. In this sense, "computerizing" decision-making may be paradoxically inefficient unless it is regularly reviewed and updated.

Another way of looking at decisions is to consider how much *risk* is involved. Some decisions are "stabs in the dark", because they are based on limited information. Others are less risky because, given that we have reliable information, it is not too difficult to anticipate the outcome. Alas, the perception of risk is often confused with the cost or importance of the decision as much as with the actual risks involved.

A variety of conditions can increase the likelihood of incorrect problem recognition and formulation, and hence decision-making. These conditions include:

- *Others define the problem*: When asked to help solve a problem that someone else has defined, most people take that problem as the "given" and work within the constraints of the problem statement. The more authority or power that the problem-giver wields, the more likely is the solver intimidated into accepting, without question, the statement of the problem. Problems need to be owned and carefully defined.
- *A quick solution is desired*: If a decision is needed quickly, the amount of time spent in formulating or reformulating a problem is likely to be cut short. Although there is no particular merit in spending long periods of time on solving problems, too much haste can result in mistakes.
- *A low-quality solution is acceptable*: People attach a lower priority to some problems than others. When this is the case, less time is likely to be spent formulating and solving the problem than if a high-quality solution were critical. The accuracy and robustness of the solution are rarely specified.
- *The problem appears familiar*: If a problem seems similar to one experienced recently, people are naturally more likely to apply a ready-made solution than to question the "real" need(s). This can lead to a quick solution or a fix.
- *Emotions are high*: Stressful or emotional conditions may lead to an abbreviated search for a satisfactory statement of the problem. Anger and anxiety easily cloud good judgement.
- *No prior experience in challenging problem definitions*: Defining a problem and its solution statement requires training and practice. Managers unaccustomed to challenging or reformulating a problem statement are unlikely to do so effectively.
- *The problem is complex*: When a situation involves many variables, and the variables are hard to identify and/or measure, the problem is harder to formulate and solve.

Personal decision style

Do different individuals prefer to make decisions in different ways? It is perfectly apparent to most individuals that on a day-to-day basis people make decisions in very different ways. These differ on a wide variety of dimensions, some of which are related to one another:

1 *Fast versus slow*: some can and do make decision rapidly, whereas others like to ponder.
2 *Risk versus risk-averse*: some seem unconcerned with risk, but for others risk appears to freeze them.

3   *Empirical versus intuitive*: some like to gather data and make actuarial, probabilistic decisions with statistical support; others work more on gut feel.
4   *Rule following versus rule breaking*: some like to follow rules, theories and past behaviours, while others rejoice in thinking "outside-the box" and being innovative.
5   *People versus things*: some managers find it easy to make decisions about things (machinery, branding), others about people (employees, customers).
6   Individual versus group: some managers like to make decisions on their own with minimal consultation; others like to consult widely.

There are a number of these dimensions and researchers have not been slow in trying to devise questionnaire which attempt to characterize an individual's personal style. Thus we have different typologies, such as Directive, Analytic, Conceptual or Behavioural. Others have talked about left- versus right-brain decision-making or the difference between adaptors and innovators. Thurholm (2004) recently looked at the psychological correlates of four well-known styles:

- a *rational* style characterized by comprehensive search for information, inventory of alternatives and logical evaluation of alternatives;
- an *intuitive* style characterized by attention to details in the flow of information, rather than systematic search for, and processing of, information, and a tendency to rely on premonitions and feelings;
- a *dependent* style characterized by a search for advice and guidance from others before making important decisions;
- an *avoidant* style characterized by attempts to avoid decision-making whenever possible.

Based on various other studies, Furnham (1999) devised the measure shown in Box 11.2, which gives four scores. The *painstaking* style is that of the obsessional prone to analysis paralysis. Gathering the facts and being clear about their implications is a good thing but they can easily go too far. The painstaking decision-making has problems with uncertainty. They have low tolerance for ambiguity, which is pretty tough given how ambiguous and unclear the world is. The *buck-passing* style means that, fearful of the consequences, and in particular the possibility that one may have to be accountable and responsible for bad decisions, it is easier to leave it up to someone else – select committee, experts, consultants, even politicians – whom one can blame if anything goes wrong. *Procrastinating* is perhaps the most common of all the sins in decision-making. The *hypervigilant* are the most neurotic of the decision-making world. They are the victims of irritable bowel syndrome, migraine and other side-effects of business decision-making.

Furnham (1999) has also described various professional types that relate directly to their decision-making preferences and style based on two dimensions. Some professionals (accountants, architects, doctors) are technically sophisticated problem-solvers who have little idea or notion of a client/customer and their needs. Others believe their expertise is primarily dependent on the understanding and appropriate application of complex rules and procedures.

In some large businesses and consultancies, these professionals may be crudely divided into client-facing versus backroom boys (or girls). They gravitate to a comfortable

Box 11.2 Consider your own style:

	SA	A	D	AD
1. I like to evaluate all alternatives	4	3	2	1
2. To be honest, I don't make decisions until I have to	4	3	2	1
3. I admit to wasting time on trivialities before making a decision	4	3	2	1
4. I feel pessimistic about ever making good business	4	3	2	1
5. I collect considerable data before decision-making	4	3	2	1
6. I prefer leaving most business decisions to others	4	3	2	1
7. I often delay acting on decisions after I have made them	4	3	2	1
8. I always feel immensely pressured when making important decisions	4	3	2	1
9. I must be clear about my objectives before choosing what to decide	4	3	2	1
10. I often fear the responsibility that goes with decision-making	4	3	2	1
11. I put off thinking about deciding as long as I can	4	3	2	1
12. I constantly worry about what can go wrong when decision-making	4	3	2	1
13. I like weighing evidence for and against extensively	4	3	2	1
14. I prefer that experts rather than I make most business decisions	4	3	2	1
15. I have been known to miss many decision-making deadlines	4	3	2	1
16. I spend much effort after a decision trying to convince myself that I was right	4	3	2	1

A = Agree; D = Disagree; SA = Strongly Agree; SD = Strongly Disagree

Painstaking: add together	1, 5, 9, 13
Buck-passing: add together	2, 6, 10, 14
Procrastinating: add together	3, 7, 11, 15
Hypervigilant: add together	4, 8, 12, 16

niche that reflects personal preferences and predilections. Indeed, it may be possible to classify them into four broad groups:

1 *The adviser:* Advisers are client-centred. They are genuinely interested in, care about and listen to clients. They see themselves as specialist professionals, not academic experts. They know that problems are not standard and tend to be flexible in how to apply the rules and policies. Clients like these professionals. They tend to "think aloud" for clients, giving them various options to choose from. They believe that the client should choose/decide based on the best advice they give. Advisers are usually extrovert, curious and a bit maverick. Many are distrusted because they get on so well with clients. Often colleagues are jealous of them, as they are asked for by name more than others.

2 *The technical specialist:* Technical specialists pride themselves on knowing their area well. They have a mental library of odd cases, interesting exceptions and unique problems, yet still believe most problems are of a particular type. They are good at diagnosis, but once done, attempt to apply rule-bound standard solutions. They solve many problems well – quickly, efficiently and correctly. Although odd cases amaze them, they can be a little inflexible in applying unique solutions. They certainly come across as able, workmanlike and efficient. Crisp, down-to-earth

types, they may be a little insensitive to client needs. They are not always tolerant of clients who cannot explain or describe what they want to know.

3   *The counsellor:* Counsellors enjoy client work and try to see problems from their point of view. They tend to understand that problems are not neatly the province of one professional or another; accountancy issues have legal implications. They know the rules and procedures, but are not unduly hampered by them. They get involved and can read people well. They are different from advisers, predominantly in their ability to think outside the box, offering unusual rule-bending solutions. They are good judges of others' characters and have a very loyal following.

4   *The expert:* Experts are academic – they know a lot, think clearly, have independent ideas. Client problems for them are an intellectual challenge. Once the client has explained the problem to the best of their ability, the expert gets to work, creating new frameworks, ever on the lookout for loopholes. The client's problem becomes their problem, but the client's feelings, anxieties and so on are soon forgotten. Expertise comes from the depth of knowledge and knowing how to apply it. They can become intrigued by problems that completely obsess them. People are not their thing – problem-solving excites them most.

These four types are derived from two factors. The first is whether the professional is client- or problem-centred. The client-centred adviser and counsellor enjoy client contact, build strong relationships and measure their success by client happiness. The problem-centred are more interpersonal and happy when they solve the problem elegantly. The specialist and the expert sell their expertise and their ability to come up with a clever answer.

The other dimension is about creativity, rule breaking and dependency. The adviser and the specialist work within their professional expertise. They concentrate on getting the information salient to their framework. They try to apply their knowledge to the problem. Counsellors and experts tend to be more lateral and less ego- and ergocentric. They are curious, observant and like to look for patterns. They are not scared to go beyond their remit.

How "rational" are human beings?

Most people like to believe they are rational, logical human beings about to make good decisions. The meaning of rationality is certainly unclear. Simon (1976) set out six different facets of rationality, including objective and subjective. Objectively, rationality involves choosing the option that yields the highest measured gains. Subjectively, it may be defined by the maximal attainment of personal goals. It can even be considered to be a process: if the decision-making process is systematic and logical, one could see the decision as rational.

Although people strive for rationality, the sheer complexity of many business problems means the gathering, interpretation and analysis of the problem is neither as systematic nor as thorough as rational-choice models require or suppose. Thus, psychologists have talked about "bounded rationality" through which one can hope for a *satisficing* (or good enough) rather than an optimal decision. This principle usually reduces the complexity of the task. Indeed, the bounded rationality model of decision-making, with managers identifying only minimum requirements that alternative decisions might meet, is probably the best descriptive model, although there will always be exceptions.

Certainly, there may be cultural differences in the use of the bounded rationality model (Leung, 1992). Thus, some Western cultures (particularly the USA) are problem-solving orientated, whereas others (Eastern) are situation-accepting. Western cultures favour information- (fact-) gathering and analysis; some non-Western cultures place greater store on intuition. Again, many Westerners are taught, and are fairly experienced in, probabilistic thinking, whereas some non-Westerners prefer to see the world either in terms of total certainty or total uncertainty.

Tosi & Mero (2003) have written about the *garbage can* model or *organized anarchy* model of decision-making. This inverts the rule about problems requiring solutions but sees organizational decisions that search for a problem. When big organizations have many overlapping departments, task forces and committees with vague and overlapping responsibilities, there are too many people making decisions. Decision-makers have different goals and needs but cannot be involved in all decisions. Some try to influence others but often groups, like individuals, have competing priorities. Thus the same problem may be perceived quite differently by individuals who work against one another.

Rational decision-making shows how decisions should be made, not how they are made. Case studies, even those with experts, show people to follow the bounded rationality model much more closely than the perfect rationality model. Johns (1992) has contrasted the two approaches. Thus, the perfect rationality model sees problem identification as accurate, easy and straightforward, and the bounded rationality model sees it as problematic – issues are ignored or downplayed, people jump too quickly to solutions, and there is attention to symptoms and not causes. Equally, the search for data in the perfect rationality model is fast, but in the bounded rationality model it is slow, costly, patchy and often insufficient. The perfect rationality model of decision evaluation states that the ultimate value of each is known, as is the probability, and the criterion of choice is based heavily on economic gain. The bounded rationality model stresses the potential ignorance or miscalculation of values and probabilities, and political and egocentric factors entering into the criterion of choice.

There is evidence to suggest that people are as much rationalizing as rational. Psychologists have appeared to rejoice in revealing the mistakes of intuitive judgement or the inaccuracies in managers' everyday decision-making. There is a long list of errors, fallacies and biases of many managers. These include being insufficiently sensitive or mindful of *sample size* in interpreting statistics or generalization; the *reliability* of information used to support or refute an argument; the *accuracy* of information retrieved from *memory*, with all its attendant biases and failures; the relevance of paying attention to *base-rate* frequencies; the *need to test disconfirming information*, and so on.

In each case, psychologists have demonstrated that lay people make erroneous assumptions or incorrect calculations in dealing with statistical manipulations. Although managers probably do not have statistical theories, they do appear to have ideas about order, randomness, and so on, which dictate their statistical behaviour. For instance, many lay people feel threatened by randomness and lack of control, and hence operate as if the former did not occur and they, therefore, were able to experience some kind of control over events.

Without doubt, the authors who have contributed most to the understanding of lay statistical inferences are Kahneman & Tversky, with their work in the 1970s and 1980s. In looking at people's probabilistic predictions, they specified various heuristic rules (three in particular) that people use, as well as systematic biases associated with them (see Chapter 5).

Tversky & Kahneman (1973) argue that these cognitive biases, resulting from the reliance on heuristics, are found among lay people and experts. What they find surprising is not that people use heuristics but rather that they fail to learn rules such as "regressions to the mean" even when they (both expert and lay people) have been exposed to this phenomenon so often. Their work has attracted considerable research (mainly confirmatory).

Kahneman & Tversky (1982) have argued that there are many good reasons for the study of errors in statistical reasoning: they expose our intellectual limitations; they reveal the psychological processes that govern judgement and inference; they map which principles are intuitive or counter-intuitive. For them, intuitive judgements are those reached by an informal or unstructured mode of thinking, those that are compatible with our lay view of the world, and those that we apply in the procedure of our normal conduct. They argue that one should distinguish between errors of comprehension and errors of application, because, although people may understand a particular statistical law, they may not recognize when it should be applied.

Table 11.2 lists some sources of error and bias commonly found among lay people, specifically those relating to the acquisition, output and feedback of information on judgements (Furnham, 1988).

With the belief that people can reason accurately in statistical terms about familiar kinds of events that they encounter on a daily basis, so long as they are also able to code them clearly, Kunda & Nisbet (1985) set out to study people's statistical reasoning. They point out that inferring the probability that one will enjoy a film, given that a close friend likes it, involves the processing of different statistical information (base rate of generally liking films, degree of co-variation, aggregation principle).

However, there is considerable evidence that supports the hypothesis that people make consistent errors about such things as the consistency of the behaviour of others. Also, not understanding the aggregation principle properly, lay people do not realize that predictability of social behaviour on single occasions (items, situations) is often very low. In a series of seven studies, Kunda & Nisbet (1985) set out to demonstrate their point. For instance, they showed that:

- People do not appreciate the aggregation principle (the rule that the magnitude of a correlation increases with the number of units of evidence on which it is based), in that they think total to total correlations no greater than item to item correlations. Thus, two groups of people are more likely to agree than are two individuals, because observations at the group level are more stable than at the individual level; that is, reflect the true score and less error.
- People tend to overestimate the agreement between any two individuals, but underestimate the agreement between any two groups of individuals.
- Even if experts do understand the aggregation principle in the abstract, they are unable to apply it to important real-world evaluations.
- Both lay and expert subjects were more accurate about correlations that obtain for abilities than those that obtain for traits.

Table 11.2 Common sources of error in decision-making

	Bias/source of bias	Description	Example
1. Acquisition of information	Availability	Ease with which specific instances can be recalled from memory affects judgements of frequency.	Frequency of well-publicized events is overestimated (e.g. deaths attributable to homicide, cancer); frequency of less well-publicized events is underestimated (e.g. deaths attributable to asthma and diabetes).
		Chance "availability" of particular "cues" in the immediate environment affects judgement.	Problem-solving can be hindered/facilitated by cues perceived by chance in a particular setting (hints set up cognitive "direction").
	Selective perception	People structure problems on the basis of their own experience.	The same problem can be seen by a marketing manager as a marketing problem, a financial problem by a finance manager, etc.
		Anticipation of what one expects to see biases what one does see.	Identifications of incongruent objects – e.g. playing cards with red spades – are either inaccurately reported or cause discomfort.
		People seek information consistent with their own views/hypotheses.	Interviewers seek information about candidates consistent with first impressions rather than information that could refute those impressions.
		People downplay or disregard conflicting evidence.	In forming impressions, people will underweigh information that does not yield to a consistent profile.
	Frequency	Cue used to judge strength of predictive relationships is observed relative frequency rather than observed relative frequency. Information on "non-occurrences" of an event is unavailable and ignored.	When considering relative performance (of, say, two persons), the absolute number of successes is given greater weight than the relative number of successes to successes and failures (i.e. the denominator is ignored). *Note:* the number of failures is frequently unavailable.
	Concrete information (ignoring base rate or prior information)	Concrete information (i.e. vivid or based on experience/incidents) dominates abstract information (e.g. summaries, statistical base rates, etc.).	When purchasing a car, the positive or negative experience of a single person you know is liable to weigh more heavily in judgements than available and more valid information (e.g. in consumer reports).
	Illusory correlation	Belief that two variables co-vary when in fact they do not. (Possibly related to "Frequency" above.)	Selection of an inappropriate variable to make a prediction.
	Data interpretation	Order effects (primacy/recency).	Sometimes the first items in a sequential presentation assume undue importance (primacy), sometimes the last items (recency).
		Mode of presentation.	Sequential versus intact data displays can affect what people are able to access. Contrast, for example, complete listed unit-price shopping *vs* own sequential information search.

Continued

Table 11.2 continued

	Bias/source of bias	Description	Example
	Data presentation	Mixture of types of information, e.g. qualitative and quantitative logical data displays.	Concentration on quantitative data, exclusion of qualitative data, or vice versa. Apparently complete "logical" data displays can blind people to critical omissions.
		Context effects on perceived variability.	Assessments of variability of, say, a series of numbers, is affected by the absolute size (e.g. mean level) of the numbers.
2. Output	Question format	The way a person is required or chooses to make a judgement can affect the outcome.	Preferences for risky prospects have been found to be inconsistent with the prices which people are willing to pay.
	Scale effects	The scale on which responses are recorded can affect responses.	Estimate of probabilities can vary when estimated directly on a scale from zero to one, or when "odds" or even "long-odds" are used.
	Wishful thinking	People's preferences for outcomes of events affect their assessment of the events.	People sometimes assess the probability of outcomes they desire more highly than their state of knowledge justifies.
	Illusion of control	Activity concerning an uncertain outcome can itself induce in a person feelings of control over the uncertain event.	Activities such as planning, or even the making of forecasts, can induce feelings of control over the uncertain future.
3. Feedback	Outcome-irrelevant learning structure	Outcomes observed yield inaccurate or incomplete information concerning predictive relationships. This can lead, *inter alia*, to unrealistic confidence in one's own judgement.	In personnel selection you can learn how good your judgement is concerning candidates selected, but you usually have no information concerning subsequent performance of rejected candidates.
	Misperceptions of chance fluctuations (e.g. gambler's fallacy)	Observation of an unexpected number of similar chance outcomes leads to the expectation that the probability of the appearance of an event not recently seen increases.	So-called "gambler's fallacy" – after observing, say, nine successive reds in roulette, people tend to believe that black is more likely on the next throw.
	Success/failure attributions	Tendency to attribute success to one's skill, and failure to chance.	Successes in one's job, e.g. making a difficult sale, are attributed to one's skill; failures to "bad luck".
	Logical fallacies in recall	Inability to recall details of an event leads to "logical" reconstruction which can be inaccurate.	Eye-witness testimony being very fallible.
	Hindsight bias	In retrospect, people are not "surprised" about what has happened in the past. They can easily find plausible explanations.	Being more confident of post-hoc explanations than predictions.

Source: Furnham (1988).

Recognition of the aggregation principle seems to be well developed only in domains where people are able to detect co-variations at more than one level. The recognition of the role of chance in producing events, and the realization that the co-variations at one level of aggregation are far from perfect, do not suffice to prompt recognition of the aggregation principle. Even when subjects accurately perceive item to item correlations to be very low, they do not use the aggregation principle to extrapolate to total correlations unless they have also had the opportunity to perceive that the total to total correlations are high. Accurate co-variation detection in a given domain, at more than one level of aggregation, may be required if the rule is to be induced in that domain.

Thus, ironically, people are probably able to apply the aggregation principle best for domains for which they already have had substantial opportunity to observe co-variation. They are unable to benefit from its use in domains where it would be most beneficial – domains where they are familiar with co-variation at only one level of aggregation or at no level. As a consequence, people make very serious errors when assessing co-variation in such domains. When they are familiar only with co-variation at the item to item level, as in several of the domains we examined, they tend to underestimate co-variation grossly at the total to total level. It seems likely that when they are familiar only with co-variation at the total to total level they would tend to grossly overestimate co-variation at the item to item level. And when they have no familiarity with a domain, they seem sure to make at least one of these errors. (Kunda & Nisbet, 1985: 41)

Thus, for people to be good decision-makers they need to be familiar with the data they are using to be able to code them; and to know whether the data that they are correlating are drawn from distributions of the same kinds of events. But they need also to understand such crucial factors as probability, as well as the difference between cause and correlation. Many decision-makers have to make higher-order decisions based on the information (decisions) brought to them by advisers (experts, subordinates, etc.). Clearly, one salient feature of a good decision-maker is choosing, briefing and training competent advisers.

Managers are also notoriously inaccurate at making probabilistic judgements, despite often being very confident in them, even in the face of contrary evidence (Einhorn & Hogarth, 1978; Kahneman & Tversky, 1973). Experiments using all sorts of materials have come up with very much the same answers. For instance, Blackmore & Troscianko (1985) looked at lay people's beliefs in the paranormal and they divided them into sheep (believers) and goats (non-believers). Using a variety of tasks (including coin-tossing), they found, as predicted, that goats were better than sheep at tasks involving judgements about probabilities. Also, sheep had the illusion of control because they did not understand the random nature of the task and thought they could exercise some control over the outcome. The results of this study seem to suggest that people's beliefs in paranormal phenomena are intricately linked to this (mis)understanding of simple statistical rules.

At the heart of much scientific and lay thinking is the notion of cause, which is not the same as correlation. A correlation between A and B may exist because A causes B, B causes A, A and B show reciprocal causative effects, or A and B are both caused by C. Many lay people infer cause from correlation and it is often difficult for scientists themselves to avoid this trap. The concept of correlation can be traced back almost exactly 100 years to Galton, who noted that two things co-relate when the variation for the one is accomplished on the average by more or less variation of the other, and in the same direction. In an intriguing study, Valsiner (1985) found that only 13 out of 95 individuals demonstrated an adequate understanding of the correlation coefficient and that some individuals shift their interpretation from the population level analysis, where they belong, to the individual level. Valsiner argued that lay people tend to operate at first in terms of quantitatively heterogeneous classes where a correlational coefficient is calculated, but then switch their thinking to the qualitatively homogeneous view as they interpret it. In other words, correlational data based on inter-individual variability of specimens within a class are translated into knowledge that is believed to be applicable to individual cases.

Given the above findings, there appears to be little doubt about the fact the average manager is not potentially a very competent psychometrician. But it is quite possible to educate people about statistics. Fong, Krantz & Nisbet (1986) demonstrated that people reason statistically by using (often incorrect) abstract rules, but that by directly manipulating these rules (through education) their reasoning about a wide variety of content domains can be affected. They note:

> It seems to us that courses in statistics and probability theory concentrate almost entirely on calculus while often ignoring its common-sense roots . . . If introductory statistics courses were to incorporate examples of how statistical principles such as the law of large numbers can be applied to judgements in everyday life, we have no doubt that such courses would have a more far-reaching effect on the extent to which people think statistically about the world. (Fong *et al.*, 1986: 281–282)

A good deal of work has gone into the law of large and small numbers, which basically states that larger samples are more representative of the population from which they are drawn than are smaller samples (Furnham, 1988).

Most senior managers have to be numerate. Furthermore, they often have to commission research using statistics and to understand the results. Research into this field suggests that they frequently make errors.

Other reviewers have listed well-known imperfections in individual decision-making. Greenberg & Baron (2003) note three framing effects:

- *Risky choice framing effect*: this is the tendency to avoid risks when situations are presented in a way that emphasizes potential gains, but to take risks when situations are presented in a way that emphasizes potential losses.
- *Attribute framing effect*: this is the tendency to evaluate a characteristic more positively when presented in positive as opposed to negative terms.
- *Goal framing effect*: this is the tendency to be more strongly persuaded by information that is framed in negative rather than positive terms.

They also list other common biases:

- *Implicit favourites*: a bias towards a preferred option before all options have been considered.
- *Hindsight*: the tendency to perceive outcomes as more inevitable after rather than before they occur.

- *Person sensitivity*: the tendency to give too little credit to others when things are going poorly and too much credit when things are going well.
- *Escalation of commitment*: the tendency to continue to support previously unsuccessful courses of action.

Behavioural economics and money decisions

The lessons from behavioural economics have been successfully used following recent academic work on decision-making. There are now many books and pamphlets designed to try to help people make better money decisions.

Hilton (1998) set out the Eight Deadly Sins of Investing:

1 *Confirmation bias:* Only looking for information and news that is in favour of your ideas. This often goes with false consensus bias, which is the tendency to overestimate the number of people who share your preference.
2 *Optimism bias*: Believing that you are above average and that misfortune is more likely to befall others. Although this can be psychologically healthy, it is potentially very dangerous in decision-making.
3 *Illusion of control*: Overestimation of the control you have over economic affairs, thinking that you can always influence the outcome. Indeed, it is one of the great frustrations of business life that some things are completely out of one's control.
4 *Overconfidence in prediction*: Believing that your prognostication of the future is the best one. In one famous study, refuse collectors were better than finance ministers. Often, as people get older their confidence increases but their accuracy at predicting economic conditions does not.
5 *Risk and regret aversion*: Either being too cautious to invest or too risky to get out. The latter is an anticipated fear of losses and can lead to excessive conservatism.
6 *Mental rigidity*: The psychology of over- or under-reaction in financial markets. People react insufficiently to information that disconfirms prevailing market opinion.
7 *Group-think*: Responding to conformist pressure to think like others.
8 *Memory distortion*: Selective forgetting and memory for past experience in the financial world.

In their intriguingly entitled book *Why smart people make big money mistakes – and how to correct them*, Belsky & Gilovic (1999) go through cognitive heuristics in everyday language in an attempt to warn people about the dangers and difficulties of them. The first is *mental accounting*, which originates from the belief that not all money is equal depending on where it comes from (gambling win, tax rebate, salary cheque). Furthermore, people may be cautious with big amounts and reckless with smaller amounts that soon add up. Belsky & Gilovic list five warning signs:

You may be prone to mental accounting if . . .

- You don't think you're a reckless spender, but you have trouble saving.
- You have savings in the bank *and* revolving balances on your credit cards.
- You're more likely to splurge with a tax refund than with savings.
- You seem to spend more when you use credit cards than when you use cash.

- Most of your retirement savings are in fixed-income or other conservative investments.

(Belsky & Gilovic, 1999: 45)

The second issue concerns the well-known *loss aversion and sunk cost fallacy* problem. Belsky & Gilovic recommend people need to test their personal threshold for loss, they need to diversify, focus on the big picture and forget the past. They even recommend reframing losses as gains. They state:

You might be a victim of loss aversion or the sunk cost fallacy if:

- You make important spending decisions based on how much you've already spent.
- You generally prefer bonds over stocks.
- You tend to sell winning investments more readily than losing ones.
- You're seriously tempted to take money out of the stock market when prices fall.

(Belsky & Gilovic, 1999: 69)

The third investment decision issue concerns *status quo bias and the endowment effect*. Belsky & Gilovic recommend that people should not forget that deciding not to decide is a decision. Further, that all decisions have opportunity costs. They note:

You might suffer from decision paralysis if:

- You have a hard time choosing among investment options.
- You don't contribute to retirement plans at work.
- You tend to beat yourself up when your decisions turn out poorly.
- You frequently buy things that offer "trial periods" – but infrequently take advantage and return them.
- You delay making investment or spending decisions.

(Belsky & Gilovic, 1999: 100)

The next issue is essentially about *understanding and using probabilities correctly*. Belsky & Gilovic warn investors not to be impressed by short-term success, to accept the role of chance in investment decisions, and so on.

Another issue concerns the well-established *anchoring or confirmation* bias problem. Their warnings for these are:

You may be prone to the confirmation bias or anchoring if:

- You're especially confident about your ability to negotiate and bargain.
- You make spending and investment decisions without much research.
- You're especially loyal to certain brands for the wrong reasons.
- You find it hard to sell investments for less than you paid.
- You rely on sellers to set a price rather than assessing the value yourself.

(Belsky & Gilovic, 1999: 146)

They call over-confidence the *ego-trap* and warn investors – know thyself and seek second opinion. Here they note seven warning signals:

Overconfidence may cost you money if:

- You make large spending decisions without much research.
- You take heart from winning investments but "explain away" poor ones.
- You think you are "beating the market" consistently.
- You make frequent trades, especially with a discount or on-line brokerage.
- You think selling your home without a broker is smart and easy.
- You don't know the rate of return on your investments.
- You believe that investing in what you know is a guarantee of success.

(Belsky & Gilovic, 1999: 170)

The final problem is following *conformity* or relying too much on the behaviour of others. Again their warning signals explain the issues clearly in everyday language:

You may be prone to following the herd if:

- You make investment decisions frequently.
- You invest in "hot" stocks or other popular investments.
- You sell investments because they're suddenly out of favour, not because your opinion of them has changed.
- You're likely to buy when stock prices are rising and sell when they are falling.
- You make spending and investment decisions based solely on the opinions of friends, colleagues, or financial advisers.
- Your spending decisions are heavily influenced by which products, restaurants, or vacation spots are "in".

(Belsky & Gilovic, 1999: 192)

Finally, Belsky & Gilovic note some simple but profound principles derived from behavioural economics and which profoundly influence decision-making. Every dollar (pound, euro) spent is the same whatever its origin. Losses seem to hurt people more than gains please them. Past mistakes should not lead to more being made. Beware paying attention to small things and beware following the trend.

Individual versus group decision-making

Many decisions are made in groups, teams, panels or committees. This is usually thought of as beneficial in terms of quality (groups are more vigilant and they generate and evaluate more and better ideas) and decision acceptance. They supposedly bring a greater range of knowledge and information, generate more alternatives, and have a better comprehension of the problem. Bringing people together can increase the amount of knowledge needed to make good decisions; there may be a *pooling of resources*. A related benefit is that in decision-making groups there can be a *specialization of labour*. It becomes possible for individuals to do only those tasks at which they are best suited, thereby also improving the potential quality of the group's efforts. Another benefit is that group decisions are likely to enjoy *greater acceptance than individual decisions*. People involved in making decisions may be expected to understand those decisions better and be more committed to carrying them out than decisions made for them by someone else.

However, there are also some problems associated with using decision-making groups. There are conformity pressures, and powerful individuals can dominate. One self-evident problem is that groups are likely to *waste time*. Another potential problem is that disagreement over important matters may *breed ill-will* and group conflict. Constructive disagreement is not necessarily bad, and can actually lead to better group outcomes. However, lack of agreement can cause bad feelings to develop between group members. Groups are sometimes ineffective because of members' *intimidation by group leaders*. A group composed of several "yes-men" (or "women") trying to please a dominant leader tends to discourage open and honest discussion of solutions. Group decisions lead to risky recommendations.

It is relatively simple to determine whether individuals or groups make the "best" decisions. One should here make a distinction between two types of context: between groups and individuals, a group (of any size) versus an individual, or a group of *n* working as one group versus *n* individuals working alone with their data pooled. As we shall see, in the first case groups usually do better at all tasks, but in the latter case nominal groups (groups in name only) usually outperform real groups. Research in this area points to two important factors: the nature of the task *and* the competence of individuals. *Tasks* can be divided into well-structured and poorly structured. Those that are *well-structured* have a definite, clear right or wrong answer; we find these in arithmetic, maths, physics, and so on (e.g. calculate the amount of carpeting necessary for the room you are currently in). Other tasks are *poorly structured* in the sense that they do not have a single correct answer but a best or most interesting answer. Poetry, advertising, art and literature output and decisions are of this type (e.g. decide on the best colour for the walls and ceiling for the room you are currently in). The research in this area has yielded consistent answers. *Groups do better on well-structured tasks, although they take longer.* Webber (1974) asked individuals to work either individually or in groups of five on several well-structured problems. Comparisons between groups and individuals were made with respect to accuracy (the number of problems solved correctly) and speed (the time it took to solve the problems). It was found that the average accuracy of groups of five persons working together was greater than the average accuracy of five individuals working alone. However, it was also found that groups were substantially slower than individuals in reaching solutions.

A laboratory study by Bouchard, Barsaloux & Drauden (1974) compared the effectiveness of individuals and brainstorming groups working on creative problems. Specifically, the participants were given 35 minutes to consider the consequences of everyone suddenly going blind. Comparisons were made of the number of solutions generated by groups of four or seven people and a like number of individuals working on the same problem alone. Individuals were far more productive than groups (Baron & Greenberg, 1990).

However, a second crucial feature is the *ability* of the decision-makers. For the benefits of group decision-making to be realized, it is essential that the group members have the necessary knowledge and skills to contribute to the group's task. In short, for there to be a beneficial effect of pooling resources, there has to be something to pool. In other words, two heads may be better than one, but only when there is something in each of those heads. The quality of decision is, as one would expect, in part determined by ability.

This idea has been supported by Laughlin & Johnson (1966), who studied lone individuals and pairs working on several well-structured word problems. On the basis of their performance on similar tasks performed one week before the experiment,

Table 11.3 Comparison of individual and group decision-making

Factor	Individual	Group
Type of problem or task	When creativity or efficiency is desired	When diverse knowledge and skills are required
Acceptance of decision	When acceptance is not important	When acceptance by group members is valued
Quality of the solution	When "best member" can be identified	When several group members can improve the solution
Characteristics of individuals	When individuals cannot collaborate	When group members have experience of working together
Climate of the decision-making	When the climate is competitive	When the climate is supportive of group problem-solving
Amount of time available	When relatively little time is available	When relatively more time is available

Source: Reproduced from Gordon (1991: 253) with the permission of Prentice-Hall, Inc.

participants were classified according to their ability on the task. During the experiment, they performed the task either alone or in pairs of varying ability. It was found that two people of high ability working together performed better than any one person working alone. However, when two persons of low ability were paired, no such improvement occurred. These results suggest that "pooling of ignorance" does not help at all.

The comparative efficiency and effectiveness of individual versus group decision-making has naturally attracted much research. Several crucial factors appear to help make up one's mind as to whether to use individuals or groups (Table 11.3). The results have clear implications. For logical structured problems, choose able people and put them in groups. For less well-structured problems, choose those acknowledged to be creative and make them work alone, pooling the output of some of these individuals.

Brainstorming

Brainstorming is thought to be best suited to finding lists of alternative solutions to problems. It is assumed that the technical details of *how* to achieve and implement these alternatives can be worked out at a later stage. Brainstorming was developed for use in creating advertising campaigns. It is now put to such diverse uses as thinking of new products, making recommendations for new employee benefits, finding ways of raising money for a cause, and searching for new ways to lay out the workgroups in a government agency. Brainstorming is not well suited to arriving at complex solutions to problems or working out the details of a plan (e.g. how to arrange the equipment in an office).

Rules for brainstorming

To conduct an effective brainstorming session, the following rules are usually adhered to:

- The size of the group should be about five to seven people. If there are too few people, not enough suggestions are generated. If too many people participate, the session becomes uncontrolled.
- No criticism is allowed. All suggestions should be welcome, and it is particularly important not to use derisive laughter or disapproving non-verbal behaviour.
- Freewheeling is encouraged. The more outlandish (even impractical, off-the-wall) the idea, the better. It is always easier to moderate an idea than to dream it up.
- Quantity and variety are very important. The more ideas put forth, the more likely there is to be a breakthrough idea. The aim is to generate a long list of ideas.
- Combinations and improvements are encouraged. Building *on the ideas of others*, including combining them, is very productive. "Hitch-hiking" and "piggy-backing" are essential parts of cooperation in brainstorming.
- Notes must be taken during the sessions, either manually or with an electronic recording device. One person serves as "recording secretary".
- The alternatives generated during the first part of the session should later be edited for duplication and categorization. At some point, the best ideas can be set aside for possible implementation.
- The session should not be over-structured by following any of the preceding seven rules too rigidly. Brainstorming is a spontaneous small-group process and is meant to be fun.

Brainstorming was first claimed to be an effective method of group problem-solving by Osborn (1957), who argued that this technique increases the quality and quantity of ideas generated by group members. Osborn stated that by engaging in brainstorming, "the average person can think up twice as many ideas when working with a group than when working alone" (Diehl & Stroebe, 1987).

Taylor, Berry & Block (1958) were the first to reject the claim. They found that nominal groups (which are made up of individuals who "brainstormed alone" and then had their non-redundant ideas combined) outperformed interacting groups of the same number. This finding has been consistently replicated and the research has significantly advanced during the past three decades. The most influential initial work was carried out in the 1970s by Bouchard and his colleagues. They manipulated such things as group size and the balance between male and female members, and even modified the brainstorming procedure itself, in order to understand what in fact determined the problem-solving effectiveness of groups and individuals (Bouchard, 1972). The work conducted during the 1980s and 1990s tried to determine *why* individuals performed better than groups (Paulus & Dzindolet, 1993). Over the past few years, the theories and models proposed have been used together with advanced computer technology to develop electronic brainstorming systems. The most recent research illustrates their effectiveness in overcoming problems such as criticism, *production blocking, social loafing* and *evaluation apprehension* (Gallupe, Cooper, Grise, & Bastianutti, 1994).

Brainstorming experiments usually involve unstructured, open-ended, "creative" tasks. The tasks traditionally used range from the "thumbs problem" (whereby the benefits and difficulties of growing an extra thumb on each hand are assessed) to the "blind world problem" (which involves thinking up the consequences if suddenly everyone went blind). The methodological diversity of these experiments makes it very hard to compare one study with another. Attempts have been made to find a universal index of performance called the creative production percentage (CPP = group/

individual output × 100) (Thornberg, 1991). Also, most studies have involved four-person groups, but studies investigating dyads, as well as much larger groups, do exist. The four-person groups reviewed, which were conducted between 1958 and 1981, have a CPP of 25 to 125. Although the majority have a CPP of around 60–70, the extreme values could be accounted for by methodological differences, such as variations in the task requirements, differences in quality measurements (e.g. some studies assess quality as the average quality but others rate total quality and differences in time allowance and brainstorming instructions).

Bouchard & Hare (1970) investigated group size and compared groups of five, seven and nine members with equivalent nominal groups. Previous experiments had never gone above four-person groups, yet Osborn had suggested that the optimal size of brainstorming groups was between seven and ten. Bouchard & Hare's prediction that the growth curve of nominal groups would level off and be overtaken by that of the real groups was not confirmed. Instead, they found that there was a nominal group effect up to groups of nine persons.

Considerable research has been directed at answering the question: "Why are real groups repeatedly less productive than the same number of individuals working alone?" Diehl & Stroebe (1987) identified three potential group effects: social loafing, evaluation apprehension and production blocking. Working in groups has traditionally been seen to have potentially two opposing effects, that of social loafing and that of social facilitation. *Social loafing* is defined as when interacting group members (with pooled outputs) exert less effort than similar participants working alone. Depending on the task, however, findings from social facilitation studies have shown that individually identifiable participants' performances will be greater than the output of others working alone on tasks. To explain the latter phenomenon, investigators have argued along the lines of a "presence theory" and an "evaluation theory". The former theory argues that the mere presence of others leads to an increased motivation to perform, whereas the latter theory argues that the presence of others becomes associated with evaluation and/or competition, along with other things, which again will increase the motivation to perform. Social loafing studies have tended to identify a "group verses individual effect" rather than an "evaluation effect"; that is, in traditional brainstorming sessions, some individuals can easily loaf, contributing very little.

Williams, Harken & Latane (1981) demonstrated that identifiability of individual output was an important factor involved in evaluation. However, Harkins & Jackson (1985) tested this notion using brainstorming techniques and found that identifiability was a factor involved in evaluation, but only when this output evaluation took place as a result of competition with co-workers.

Kerr & Bruun (1983) claimed that social loafing depended heavily on task features: whether the task was disjunctive (where only the best answers counted) or additive (where outputs were summed). They claimed that dispensability (and hence the likelihood to loaf) matters less with additive tasks than disjunctive tasks. The possibility of redundancy may in fact promote dispensability. Social loafing could be deemed responsible for only a small proportion of productivity loss, and other processes must be contributing. This may be a consequence of the nature of brainstorming, which requires little effort, as opposed to physical tasks, where loafing may account for more loss (Diehl & Stroebe, 1987).

A second possible interpretation which has been offered to account for real group productivity is *evaluation apprehension*. Many individuals refrain from expressing their views in various social settings, such as the classroom or the boardroom, because they are uncertain as to how they are going to be received. This notion of "the unpleasant experience of negative evaluation from other group members" has been investigated as a plausible cause of productivity loss in brainstorming groups; but the results have been somewhat contradictory. Colaros & Anderson (1969) concluded that productivity was lowest in the condition which aimed to produce the highest amount of evaluation apprehension. This finding differed from that of Maginn & Harris (1980), who found that individual productivity in the presence of observers was not significantly different from that of individuals working without observers. However, the methodology of the two experiments was dissimilar in that the former experiment induced evaluation apprehension by deceiving the participants with respect to the number of experts who were present in the group, whereas the latter experiment manipulated evaluation apprehension by telling the participants that three external judges were observing them. Furthermore, the latter experiment examined only individuals working alone and tried to lower productivity (to that of real groups) with apprehension, whereas the former experiment dealt with real groups and tried to illustrate an increase in productivity in the "no-expert" condition. The lack of support found in this area indicates that a more powerful cause of productivity loss exists.

Production blocking is the notion that, because only one individual can speak at a given time in a group, this prohibits the other group members from airing their ideas when they occur to them. This waiting time can cause them to forget (due to the limitation of the short-term memory) or consider the idea to be less original or relevant with respect to the presently viewed idea. This contradicts the original claim that brainstorming allows individuals to express their ideas, which in turn stimulates other members. Traditionally, brainstorming has adopted "equal person-hour" methodology. This allows members of real groups of size n to have only one nth of the amount of speaking time of the equivalent nominal group members. By varying nominal group members' time allowance, so that it was comparable to real group members' assumed time allowance, Diehl & Stroebe (1987) tested whether this procedural explanation of the blocking effect was valid. Two experiments which tried to manipulate time allowance or even speaking-time allowance failed to yield a reduction in the productivity gap between real and nominal groups.

New computer-aided techniques to "unblock brainstorms" have only recently been constructed and tested (Gallupe *et al.*, 1994). This new technique, called "electronic brainstorming", aims to overcome the problems of social loafing, evaluation apprehension and production blocking. Electronic brainstorming involves group members sitting at computer terminals and typing in their ideas, but also having full access to the other group members' ideas as they are produced. It aims to integrate the two important and advantageous features of nominal and real group brainstorming, namely being able to generate ideas freely and also being able to share ideas respectfully. Ideas on the screen have not been found to be distracting, which was found to be the case with traditional brainstorming (Gallupe *et al.*, 1994). Simultaneous contributions lessen the potential effect of blocking and the anonymous nature of the technique alleviates evaluation apprehension. In Gallupe and co-workers' original and pioneering study comparing electronic with non-electronic brainstorming, they found that electronic brainstorming four-person groups outperformed the four-person traditional (verbal) brainstorming groups and failed to find a difference between nominal and interacting groups using the electronic technique. In electronic brainstorming groups, performance increased with group size, which contrasts with non-electronic brainstorming groups, which failed to produce performance increments with an increase in group size. Electronic brainstorming was not advantageous when only two people were involved (and thus anonymity and production blocking was at its lowest); however, as group size and therefore anonymity and production blocking increased, the true potential of this new technique was exhibited. Per-person productivity and average per-person output of ideas tended to remain stable with an increase in group size (unlike non-electronic brainstorming, where a fall was noted). This was attributed to the fact that production blocking remained at a constant low level throughout different electronic brainstorming sessions. Lastly, satisfaction is greater with electronic brainstorming groups and it increases with group size, in contrast with non-electronic brainstorming.

Thus, the very features that mean brainstorming does not work can be overcome using computer networks. Social loafing is less likely to occur because individuals may be concerned that the ideas they key in are logged and counted. Evaluation apprehension does not occur because the source of the ideas is anonymous. Production blocking does not occur because participants can access and attend to others' ideas when it suits them.

There are various things individual managers can do to improve their decision-making. Greenberg and Baron (2003) suggest four ways of avoiding errors:

1   *Reducing hypervigilance*: decision makers with a sense of anxiety frantically search for quick, effective solutions. Decision-makers often need reassurance and support.
2   *Reducing unconflicted adherence*: the tendency to stick with an early decision rather than looking at the downsides or more impartially the alternatives.
3   *Reducing unconflicted change*: the opposite of the above, namely to change one's mind quickly.
4   *Reducing defensive avoidance*: a form of procrastination and the disowning of responsibility.

Greenberg & Baron also note the importance of making ethical decisions by asking the decision-maker to consider some salient questions, such as: Does it violate various "shall not's"? Will anyone get hurt? Would it embarrass you to have the decision made public? How would you feel if it were done to you? What are your gut feelings about the project? Another three suggestions are given by Plous (1993: 143–144):

Maintain Accurate Records.
By keeping track of how frequently particular events have occurred in the past, it is possible to minimize primacy and recency effects, availability biases, and other distortions that can arise from the serial presentation of information.

Beware of Wishful Thinking.
In many cases, the probability of desirable events is overestimated and the probability of undesirable events is underestimated (although there are obviously exceptions to this rule, such as cases in which the availability of a feared outcome inflates probability estimates). One of the best ways to protect against wishful thinking is to ask uninvolved (but informed) third parties for independent assessments.

Break Compound Events into Simple Events.
If compound events are made up of statistically independent simple events (i.e. those whose outcomes are unrelated), a useful strategy is to estimate outcome probabilities for each simple event alone. Then, if the compound event is conjunctive, multiply these probabilities together.

Research in this area is particularly fascinating because so many of the results are counter-intuitive. What the findings seem to show is that brainstorming is most often used when it is least effective. It is odd that advertising agencies and design departments are so reliant on brainstorming techniques, when all the scientific literature suggests it is not the best strategy. It is possible that brainstorming groups function to fulfil other needs in the organization, which may or may not compensate for the resultant loss of creativity. Furthermore, fundamental processes at work in brainstorming groups appear to mitigate against good decisions being made or really creative answers being found.

Techniques to improve decision-making

Electronic meetings

Because of the expensiveness (and danger) of international travel and the expansion of the internet, it is more common to have electronic decision-making meetings. These can be held in the same room or building or indeed right round the world. Attenders sit in front of their PC on which they type their answers, comments or votes. As with all other meetings, there is a chair-person, objectives and an agenda.

The input is shared (entered and put on screen) and can be anonymous. It is stored so that accurate detailed minutes can be produced. Weatherall & Nunamaker (1996) argue that there are eight benefits of electronic meetings:

1   They are shorter: information is immediately shared and frequent voting focuses the discussion.
2   Time-scales are reduced because you can have larger meetings with more people on more sites and immediate recording of all transactions.
3   More and better ideas are produced because of anonymity, more open discussion and the constant voting helps to prioritize ideas.
4   Meetings can easily be arranged, timetabled and attended. People only need access to a linked PC.
5   Electronic recording ensures better documentation.
6   Greater commitment often ensues because electronic displays and recordings ensure better feelings of the democratic process.
7   Action taking can be immediate because voting and minutes are instantly produced.
8   Money is saved because of the reduction of travel and secretarial time.

They note:

> Electronic Meetings are ideal for exchanging information and opinions on any subject. The chairperson and facilitator are free to set up any questions or

statements they wish in order to initiate and focus discussion. Questions can be changed or added quickly and easily. Anonymity is usually helpful but can be switched off or limited if required.

Large and small Electronic Meetings can be effective. Meetings can be *same* or *different time, same* or *different place*.

Input is often summarized into categories or key issues without losing any of the comments.

Using Electronic Meetings to gather feedback from customers or employees is a very simple technique for getting outstanding results. The participants have only to type in their input, read others peoples' input and discuss.

An *exchange of information and opinions* can take as little as five minutes of one session of an Electronic Meeting or, if the subject is important enough, can occupy an entire meeting. (Weatherall & Nunamaker, 1996: 110)

All organizations, particularly those involved in product development, are eager for new, different, creative solutions. One possible solution to this problem is to search for and select people known to be creative, in the hope both that their creativity will remain stable (or increase) and that it is relevant to the issues and problems of the organization. Because of problems associated with the measurement of creativity and the unreliability of selection interviews, this method is often used but frequently unsuccessful. However, organizations do attempt to stimulate creativity by certain methods, which include the following:

Lateral thinking

Lateral and vertical thinking were contrasted by de Bono (1985), the latter being supposedly a logical step-by-step activity. It can be characterized as in Table 11.4.

Table 11.4 Characteristics of lateral versus vertical thinking

Lateral thinking	Vertical thinking
Tries to find new ways for looking at things; is concerned with change and movement.	Tries to find absolutes for judging relationships: is concerned with stability.
Avoids looking for what is "right" or "wrong"; tries to find what is different.	Seeks a "yes" or "no" justification for each step; tries to find what is "right".
Analyses ideas to determine how they might be used to generate new ideas.	Analyses ideas to determine why they do not work and need to be rejected.
Attempts to introduce discontinuity by making "illogical" (free association) jumps from one step to another.	Seeks continuity by logically proceeding from one step to another.
Welcomes chance intrusions of information to use in generating new ideas; considers the irrelevant.	Selectively chooses what to consider for generating ideas; rejects any information not considered to be relevant.
Progresses by avoiding the obvious.	Progresses using established patterns; considers the obvious.

Source: Based on de Bono (1970, 1985).

Various techniques recommended by de Bono include:

- *reverse* – turning the idea around, upside down, inside out, its opposite;
- *cross-fertilization* – asking experts from other fields how to solve the problem;
- *analogies* – finding metaphors or analogies for the working of a process;
- *random word stimulation* – the application of randomly chosen words (rust, hard, sweet) to organizational issues to find links.

De Bono's ideas are popular but there is still little empirical evidence that they work. As a guide for certain strategies to increase innovation they appear adequate, and although they may be necessary, there is little evidence that they are sufficient.

Devil's advocate

This well-known didactic technique is designed not to kill new ideas but to stimulate greater activity in answering criticism. The devil's advocate presents a public objective critique which creative groups are challenged to rebut. It is assumed that having to defend assumptions and explicitly argue for what may be implicit helps individuals or groups come to better decisions or "unblock" barriers. The devil's advocacy technique is similar in process, but has some distinct differences. The steps are as follows:

1   Divide the group in half.
2   One subgroup prepares a set of recommendations for solving the problem and builds an argument for them.
3   This subgroup represents its recommendations to the second subgroup.
4   The second subgroup critiques the recommendations, trying to uncover everything wrong with them.
5   The critique is presented to the first subgroup, which then revises its recommendations to try to satisfy the criticisms.
6   Steps 3–5 are repeated until both groups are satisfied with the recommendations.
7   Final recommendations are recorded in writing.

Expert system

The use of artificial intelligence means that computers can be programmed to devise many alternatives, given that certain parameters are fed in. Expert systems come in very varied packages. Yet the rapidly increasing sophistication of computer technology means they have considerable flexibility and power to generate data. For example, consider the rapid rise in expert chess computers. Clearly, for numerical (or spatial) data the role of expert systems must be on the increase.

Most organizations seek to be innovative, partly for their own sake, but partly to develop the best methods and practices by which to operate. Managers seek both *product* and *process* organization. Innovation is quite simply the application of new inventions, be they new goods and services, or better ways of doing things. However, there is little good research that attempts to evaluate these methods. As a result, many businesses tend to be faddish in favouring one method over another.

The process usually involves several steps: having the original idea; trying it out through systematic or pragmatic experimentation; and costings and feasibility determination, which seek to look at the cost–benefit analysis and final application. Just as there are innovative pro-change individuals, so innovative organizations have special characteristics. These include the culture, strategy, structure and staff that seek out, welcome and implement innovation.

In innovative organizations, *staffing* is handled with a clear commitment to innovation. Managers in highly innovative organizations pay special attention to filling critical *innovation roles*. They make sure that the following roles in particular are always filled with highly talented people:

- *idea generators* – the creative source of new, practical and relevant insight;
- *information gatekeepers* – continuously scan the environment for new knowledge; they are resource investigators;
- *product champions* – adopt new ideas and push for their implementation; they have to be persistent and courageous;
- *project managers* – organize and manage technical support for innovations;
- *leaders* – challenge and support others to keep up the quest for continuous innovation.

Equally, one can find characteristics of organizations that resist innovation:

- *vested interests* – individuals and groups think they are more important than the organization as a whole and that change isn't necessary;
- *short time horizons* – short-term results are emphasized over investments for long-term gains; no investment in the future;
- *overly rational thinking* – an emphasis on systems and routines drives out opportunities for innovation;
- *poor incentives* – reward systems support the "safety" of past routines and discourage risk-taking;
- *excessive bureaucracy* – an emphasis on rules and efficiency slows and frustrates creative people;
- *change orientation* – the importance not only of adapting to change but of leading it means that many organizations are rightly becoming interested in fostering innovation and sustaining it.

Searching for methods and techniques to provide innovative answers and make better decisions is a never-ending quest. Alas, the empirical evaluation of these techniques is difficult and usually occurs long after they have been introduced to the organization.

Group-think

When groups develop a very cohesive, internally consistent set of roles and norms, they sometimes become concerned about not disrupting the group's decisions. Group morale, happiness and contentment are more salient than the task (decision-making) that the group has been forced to undertake. *Group-think* (Janis, 1972) is the term given to the pressure that highly cohesive groups exert on their members for uniform and acceptable decisions that actually reduces their capacity to make effective decisions (Table 11.5).

The concept of group-think was proposed as an attempt to explain the ineffective decisions made by US government officials, which led to such fiascos as the Bay of Pigs

Table 11.5 The warning signals of group-think

Symptom	Description
Illusion of invulnerability	Ignoring obvious danger signals, being overly optimistic and taking extreme risks.
Collective rationalization	Discrediting or ignoring warning signals that run contrary to group-thinking.
Unquestioned morality	Believing that the group's position is ethical and moral and that all others are inherently evil.
Excessive negative stereotyping	Viewing the opposing side as being too negative to warrant serious consideration.
Strong conformity pressure	Discouraging the expression of dissenting opinions under the threat of expulsion for disloyalty.
Self-censorship of dissenting ideas	Withholding dissenting ideas and counter-arguments, keeping them to oneself.
Illusion of unanimity	Sharing the false belief that everyone in the group agrees with its judgements.
Self-appointed mindguards	Protecting the group from negative, threatening information.

Source: Reproduced from Greenberg & Baron (1995) with the permission of Prentice-Hall, Inc.

invasion in Cuba, the successful Japanese attack on Pearl Harbor, and the Vietnam War. Analyses of these cases have revealed that, in each case, the President's advisers discouraged the making of more effective decisions. Members of very cohesive groups may have more faith in their group's decisions than any idea they may have personally. As a result, they may suspend their own critical thinking in favour of conforming to the group. When group members become tremendously loyal to each other, they may ignore information from other sources if it challenges the group's decisions. The result of this process is that the group's decisions may be completely uninformed, irrational or even immoral (Baron & Greenberg, 1990).

Some of the potential consequences of group-think include:

- Fewer alternatives are considered when solving problems; preferred accepted solutions are implemented.
- Outside experts are seldom used; indeed, outsiders are distrusted.
- Re-examination of a rejected alternative is unlikely.
- Facts that do not support the group are ignored, or their accuracy challenged.
- Risks are ignored or glossed over; indeed, risk is seldom assessed.

Fortunately, managers can take steps to reduce the likelihood of group-think. Furthermore, they can also reduce the effects of group-think once it occurs. Reducing group-think, however, is much more difficult than preventing it in the first place, because groups engaging in group-think seldom realize that they are doing so. To prevent or reduce the effects of group-think, managers can:

- encourage each member of the group to evaluate his or her own and others' ideas openly and critically;
- ask influential members to adopt an initial external (even critical) stance on solutions (even leave the group for set periods);
- discuss plans with disinterested outsiders to obtain reactions;

- use expert advisers to redesign the decision-making process;
- assign a devil's advocate role to one or more group members to challenge ideas;
- explore alternative scenarios for possible external reactions;
- use subgroups (select committees) to develop alternative solutions;
- meet to reconsider decisions prior to implementation.

Given that group-think is potentially dangerous, organizations often choose to implement decisions that avoid it. Baron & Greenberg (1990) advocate the following:

- *Promote open inquiry*: Group-think arises in response to group members' reluctance to "rock the boat". Group leaders should encourage group members to be sceptical of all solutions and to avoid reaching premature agreements. It helps to play the role of the "devil's advocate" – to find fault intentionally with a proposed solution – so that all its shortcomings are considered. The idea is that decisions that were successful in the past may not be successful in the future.
- *Use subgroups*: Split the group. Because the decisions made by one group may be the result of group-think, basing decisions on the recommendations of two or more groups trying to solve the same problem is a useful check. If the groups disagree, a spirited discussion of their differences is likely to raise important issues. However, if the groups agree, it seems they are less likely all to be victims of group-think. With such a strategy there is always the risk that it might cause friction and reduce cohesion, but the ultimate benefit for decision-making probably makes it worthwhile.
- *Admit shortcomings*: When group-think occurs, group members feel confident that they are doing the right thing, which discourages people from considering contrary information. However, if group members acknowledge some of the flaws and limitations of their decisions, they may be more open to corrective influences. Thus, asking others to point out their misgivings and hesitations about a group's decision may avoid the illusion of perfection that contributes to group-think. Groups must be encouraged to believe that doubt, not certainty, is always acceptable.
- *Hold "second-chance" meetings*: Before implementing any decision, it may be a good idea to hold a second-chance meeting in which group members are asked to express any doubts and to propose any new ideas they may have. As people get tired of working on problems, they may hastily reach agreement on a solution. A second-chance meeting can be useful to see if the solution still seems as good after "sleeping on it".

Not all groups are susceptible to group-think. But to promote successful group decision-making, Zander (1982) suggests the practical manager follow various points. Those which seem most sensible are detailed below:

- State the problem clearly, indicating its significance and what is expected of the group when faced with solving it.
- Break a complex problem into separate parts, and make decisions affecting each part.
- Focus discussion on the key issues and, when all avenues are explored, put a stop to analysis, and call for a vote, if necessary, when the time is right.

- Assist members to cope with other people's ideas, and then ask them to substantiate the correctness of their own ideas.
- Before making a final decision, encourage members to consider any adverse repercussions likely to flow from a given solution.
- Be suspicious of unanimous decisions, particularly those arrived at quickly, and avoid them.
- Make sure that those who are charged with the implementation of a group's decision understand exactly what they are expected to do.
- Avoid wide differences in status among members, or alternatively help members recognize these differences and explore ways of reducing their inhibitions with respect to "status" in the group.
- Prepare procedures in advance to deal with urgent or crisis decisions.
- Protect the group from damaging effects of external criticism, but at the same time let the group benefit from critical ideas or observations of a constructive nature that are likely to improve the quality of its deliberations.
- Encourage members to evaluate the skills residing in the group and find ways of improving them.

It is clear that, based on the warnings provided by different writers and consultants, there are dangers pertaining to group-think on boards, committees and in task groups.

Group polarization when taking risky decisions

Do groups tend to encourage compromise and safe and cautious decisions or the opposite, namely risky decisions. Counter-intuitively, it would appear that groups tend to encourage risk; that is, compared to the decisions of individuals, groups appear to shift decisions to extremes. Consider the following:

> Mr A, an engineer who is married and has one child, has been working for a large manufacturing corporation since graduating from university five years ago. He is assured of a life-time job with a modest, although adequate, salary and liberal pension benefits upon retirement. On the other hand, it is very unlikely that his salary will increase much before he retires. While attending a conference, Mr A is offered a job with a small, newly founded company, which has a highly uncertain future. The new job would pay more to start and would offer the possibility of a share in the ownership if the company survived the competition of the larger firms.

Imagine that you are advising Mr A. Listed below are several probabilities or odds of the new company proving financially sound. Please check the lowest probability that you would consider acceptable to make it worthwhile for Mr A to take the new job:

- The chances are 1 in 10 that the company will prove financially sound.
- The chances are 3 in 10 that the company will prove financially sound.
- The chances are 5 in 10 that the company will prove financially sound.
- The chances are 7 in 10 that the company will prove financially sound.
- The chances are 9 in 10 that the company will prove financially sound.
- Please check here if you think Mr A should not take the new job no matter what the probabilities.

In tasks such as the above, individuals are more cautious than groups (Stoner, 1961). Thus, if four individuals recommended that the riskier course of action be taken if the odds of success are 30%, a group composed of these same individuals might recommend that the riskier course of action be taken if the odds of success are lower, say 10%. Because of this shift in the direction of riskiness by groups compared with individuals, the phenomenon became known as the *risky shift*.

However, some groups tend to make more cautious or conservative decisions if the prevailing norm swings them that way. Why do groups shift to risk or caution? Often, group discussion generates ideas and arguments novel to individuals. These new data provide excellent justification for individuals' initial tendencies towards either risk or conservatism. Thus, group discussion provides more and often better reasons for one's initial decision (to risk or caution), thereby exaggerating it. Group members also like to "bill themselves" as first among equals – that is, similar to, but better than, the group. One such way of doing this is to upstage others in a discussion favouring the more extreme of the preferred and group-accepted decisions. Also, with the diffusion of responsibility in groups, it is easier to be more extreme because individual responsibility is lessened.

Lamm & Myers (1978) have found that jury members who believe a defendant is innocent or guilty before deliberation tend to be even more certain of these convictions *after* joint discussions. Apparently, the risky shift is part of a more general tendency for group members to shift their individual views in a more extreme direction, a phenomenon known as *group polarization*. The group polarization effect refers to the tendency for group members to shift their views about a given issue to ones that are more extreme in the same direction as the views they held initially. In effect, group polarization means that, if a person is initially in favour of a specific decision/plan, they will be more in favour of it *after* group discussion, whereas those against the decision at the beginning will be more opposed to it after group discussion. Thus, one can have shift to caution as much as shift to risk. Often, the prevailing norms of the culture determine which way groups will go (towards caution or risk). Thus, if the culture prescribes being adventurous with regard to business but cautious and risk-averse with regards to safety, decision groups will increase risky business decisions but be highly cautious on safety decisions.

Groups polarize for two reasons:

- *Social comparison*: People compare themselves with others and endorse strong cultural values to gain approval. Thus, they would *shift to caution* over issues of child protection, environmental pollution, and so on, but *shift to risk* over personal issues such as job changes.
- *Persuasive information*: It is possible that discussions yield useful information that appears to accumulate in favour of one side.

It is important to distinguish between *individual* and *group* polarization. It is common to find group polarization because of informational effects or because of the application of a majority rule, but not individual polarization. Clearly, the effects of risky/caution shift and group polarization have important implications for organizational decision-making.

Group polarization effects are indeed real; they may cause a group to become either more conservative or more risky, depending on the initial opinions of the majority of group members. When emphasis is placed on reaching a consensus, group members are more likely to shift their positions. Moreover, polarization is more likely to occur during active group discussions, although it should be pointed out that it does not always, of necessity, occur.

Conclusion

The survival and growth of an organization depends on timely, accurate and optimal decisions in all aspects of its operation, from selection to software purchasing. The pricing of products, the purchase of equipment, and the outsourcing of departments are difficult and important decisions that have to be made every day by managers at many different levels.

Various models of decision-making have been proposed. Some are prescriptive (how to do it), others proscriptive (how not to do it) and some simply descriptive (it is often done). A simple but important linear prescriptive model suggests that good decision-making goes through different steps or phases (usually in a prescribed order). All too frequently, as noted by descriptive studies, certain steps are ignored or passed over too quickly. These include spending time on choosing a method to make decisions, as well as generating a sufficiently long and diverse list of reasonable alternative decisions.

Many decisions in organizations are programmed in both the computational and organizational sense because they are relatively routine. It is the higher-order, "doing the right thing" type of decision that of necessity exercises the efforts of senior managers most.

It is relatively easy to list, with hindsight, particular conditions that appear to lead to poor decision-making. Problem complexity, powerful emotions and time pressure are all factors that have been shown both in case studies and in experimental work to lead to poor decision-making. However, it cannot be assumed that if these particular conditions do not apply (i.e. no time pressure) that decisions would be better. Much depends on who makes the decision and the strategy that they employ.

An issue of central interest to decision-making researchers is how "rational" human beings are. Decision-making is about the collecting and processing of information. Psychologists have spent years studying particular cognitive processes, such as attention to, selection of, integration of and recall of information, which are of direct relevance to decision theorists. Most Westerners appear to operate in terms of bounded rationality, being satisfied with an adequate rather than an optimal decision. There is considerable evidence from cognitive psychologists of the bias most individuals experience in the acquisition and processing of information.

For all sorts of reasons, including the diffusion of responsibility and an attempt to achieve better decisions, most business decisions are made not by individuals but in groups. Although the drawbacks of this approach are acknowledged (takes longer, encourages conformity, causes ill feeling), the benefits are seen to outweigh the disadvantages (greater synergy, possibility of specialization, acceptance of decision). The results show that, when comparing the combined ideas of pooled individuals with the output of a group, "too many cooks spoil the broth", particularly with respect to unstructured problems. Groups outperform individuals on logical tasks, particularly when members are bright.

Notwithstanding these complications, research on group judgement and decision-making suggests the following tentative conclusions:

- Many individual heuristics and biases appear to operate with equal force in groups.
- Group discussion often amplifies preexisting tendencies.
- Groups usually perform somewhat better than average individuals, particularly if an appointed leader encourages all group members to express an opinion.
- The best member of a group often outperforms the group (a fact that can sometimes be exploited by using the dictator decision technique).
- Brainstorming is most effective when conducted by several people independently, rather than in a group session. (Plous, 1993: 214)

The evidence on brainstorming is counter-intuitive for many. It shows that, by following the rules of brainstorming, groups tend to be less creative than a nominal group of individuals working alone. Three major reasons have been posited to account for this: social loafing, evaluation apprehension and production blocking. More recently, computer-assisted electronic brainstorming appears to have overcome these problems.

Organizations live in a competitive world and seek in the main to be original. Hence, they look for methods (such as lateral thinking) or systems (such as expert systems) that promise more creative solutions and better judgements. However, there is little systematic evidence to suggest that many of these systems deliver what they promise.

Some groups, especially those that are highly cohesive, homogeneous and have a history of success, may suffer from group-think, which can lead them to make very poor decisions. As a consequence, various writers have attempted to list techniques that may be used to reduce the likelihood of group-think occurring.

Finally, when presented with decisions that may involve risk, the literature seems to suggest that groups polarize their decisions – that is, they tend to go to extremes, unlike individuals, whose decisions are not dramatically polarized.

A research perspective

One of the most important decisions most managers have to make concerns the decisions and judgements (often specific ratings) made at performance appraisals, because they are subject to certain biases and errors. Indeed, these "errors" or "biases" occur in nearly all instances where ratings are made; for instance, when market researchers rate campaigns, when selectors rate candidates, and when managers rate performances. These are particularly sensitive to many systematic errors:

- *Central tendency*: Providing a rating of average, or around the midpoint, for all qualities. Since many employees do perform somewhere around an average, it is an easily rationalized escape from making a valid appraisal.
- *Contrast error*: Results when a rater measures a person against other employees he or she has recently rated, or relative to the average performance of other members in the work unit, rather than in comparison with established performance criteria. If the previous individual received an undeserved higher or lower rating because the other rated workers were working at a lower or higher than expected level, or if the recently rated others were rated incorrectly and the rating error can be attributed to the errors or to a lack of knowledge of performance criteria, the actual rate may be beneficial or harmful, but not accurate.
- *Different from me*: Giving a rating lower than deserved because the person has qualities or characteristics dissimilar to the rater (or similar to those held in low esteem).
- *Halo effect*: Rating an employee excellent in one quality (punctuality), which in turn influences the rater to give that employee a similar rating or a higher than deserved rating on

other qualities (motivation). Thus, attractive people are seen as good workers irrespective of their true performance. Related to this is the logic error, where a rater confuses one performance dimension with another and then incorrectly rates the dimension because of the misunderstanding.

- *Horn effect*: Rating a person unsatisfactory in one quality, which in turn influences the rater to give that person a similar rating or a lower than deserved rating on other qualities.
- *Initial impression*: Rating based on first impressions; failing to recognize most consistently demonstrated behaviours during the entire appraisal period.
- *Latest behaviour*: Rating influenced by the most recent behaviour; failing to recognize the most commonly demonstrated behaviours during the entire appraisal period.
- *Lenient or generous rating*: Rating consistently higher than the expected norm or average; being overly loose in rating performance qualities. This is probably the most common form of rating error. A major reason for this error is the avoidance of conflict.
- *Performance dimension order*: Two or more dimensions on a *performance* instrument follow each other and both describe or relate to a similar quality. The rater rates the first dimension accurately and then rates the second dimension similarly to the first because of their proximity. If the dimensions had been arranged in a significantly different order, the ratings might have been different.
- *Same as me*: Giving the ratee a rating higher than deserved because the person has qualities or characteristics similar to those of the rater (or similar to those held in high esteem).
- *Spillover effect*: Allowing past performance appraisal to influence current ratings unjustly. Past performance ratings, good or bad, result in a similar rating for the current period, although demonstrated behaviour does not deserve the rating, good or bad.
- *Status effect*: Overrating employees in higher-level jobs held in high esteem and underrating employees in lower-level jobs or jobs held in low esteem.
- *Strict rating*: Rating consistently lower than the normal or average; being constantly overly harsh in rating performance qualities.

A cultural perspective

Cultural variations in decision-making

There are national and organizational differences in the way groups go about making decisions. Culture determines what is seen as a problem, how facts are gathered and how decisions are made (Table 11.6).

The cultural impacts on international management are reflected by these basic beliefs and behaviours of the people. Some specific examples where the culture of a society can directly affect management approaches are as follows:

- *Centralized versus decentralized decision-making*: In some cultures, all important organizational decisions are made by top managers; in others, these decisions are diffused throughout the organization, and middle- and lower-level managers actively participate in, and make, key decisions.
- *Safety versus risk*: In some cultures, organizational decision-makers tend to be risk-averse and have great difficulty with conditions of uncertainty. In other societies, risk-taking is encouraged, and decision-making under uncertainty is common.
- *Individual versus group rewards*: In some cultures, employees who do outstanding work are given individual rewards in the form of bonuses and commissions. Other cultural norms require group rewards, and individual rewards are frowned upon.
- *Informal versus formal procedures*: In some cultures, much is accomplished through informal means, whereas in others formal procedures are set forth and followed rigidly.
- *High versus low organizational loyalty*: In some cultures, people identify very strongly with

Table 11.6 The cultural contingencies of decision-making

Five steps in decision-making	Cultural variations	
1. Problem recognition	*Problem-solving.* Situation should be changed.	*Situation acceptance.* Some situations should be accepted rather than changed.
2. Information search	*Gathering facts.*	*Gathering ideas and possibilities.*
3. Construction of alternatives	*New, future-orientated alternatives.* Adults can learn and change.	*Past-, present- and future-orientated alternatives.* Adults cannot change substantially.
4. Choice	*Individual decision-making.* Decision-making responsibility is delegated. Decisions are made quickly. Decision rule: Is it true or false?	*Group decision-making.* Only senior management makes decisions. Decisions are made slowly. Decision rule: Is it good or bad?
5. Implementation	*Slow.* Managed from top. Responsibility of one person.	*Fast.* Involves participation of all levels. Responsibility of group.

Source: Adler (1986).

their organization or employer, whereas in others people identify with their occupational group.

- *Cooperation versus competition*: Some cultures encourage cooperation between their people; others encourage – even prefer – competition.
- *Short-term versus long-term horizons*: Some cultures prefer to focus most heavily on short-term time horizons, such as short-range goals of profit and efficiency, whereas others are more interested in long-range goals, such as market share and technological development.
- *Stability versus innovation*: The culture of some nations encourages stability and resistance to change; other cultures put high value on innovation and change.

Adler (1986) set about describing, through the use of opposites, different styles. Although the above is rather simplistic, erroneously implying there are only two highly differentiated cultural styles, it is true that cultural beliefs and practice do influence how business decisions are made.

There is a further interesting cultural variant in decision-making, ethical behaviour. The ideas of honest communication, fair treatment and competition, respect for the law, corporate social responsibility and responsibility to the organization over the individual do not travel well. One culture's business ethics are not necessarily those of another. The explicit and implicit code of ethics that businesses follow in decision-making is often very varied. A few guidelines may help one identify cultural differences in business ethics decision-making. First, identify all stakeholders that will be affected by the decision. Next, specify in detail the cost and benefits of each outcome. Consider also the moral expectations, professional norms and codes that surround such decisions. Look at the past history of decision-making and the ethical position frequently adopted by the company in previous years.

A human resources perspective

Most decision-making is done in groups for the reasons described. An organization might like to decide which techniques it prefers for which problem. The following are the most common (Robbins, 1991: 339–340).

Brainstorming

Brainstorming is an idea-generation process that specifically encourages any and all alternatives, while withholding any criticism of those alternatives. It is meant to overcome pressures for conformity in the interacting group that inhibit the development of creative alternatives. However, brainstorming is merely a process for generating ideas and, as we have seen, it can be mis-applied. It is best when used for structured decisions, and then only with talented people. The next two techniques go further by offering ways in which it is possible to arrive at a preferred solution.

Nominal group technique

The nominal group technique is a group decision method in which individual members meet face to face to pool their judgements in a systematic but independent fashion. This particular technique attempts to limit discussion or interpersonal communication during the decision-making process, hence the term *nominal*. Group members are all physically present, as in a traditional committee meeting, but members operate independently. Specifically, a problem is presented and then the following steps are followed:

1   Members meet as a group, but before any discussion takes place, each member independently writes down his or her ideas on the problem.
2   This silent period is followed by each member presenting one idea to the group. Each member takes his or her turn, going around the table, presenting a single idea until all ideas have been presented and recorded (typically on a flip chart or chalkboard). No discussion takes place until all ideas have been recorded.
3   The group now discusses the ideas for clarity and evaluates them.
4   Each group member silently and independently rank-orders the ideas. The final decision is made based on the idea with the highest aggregate ranking.

The chief advantage of the nominal group technique is that it permits the group to meet formally but does not restrict independent thinking, as does the interacting group.

Delphi technique

The Delphi technique is a group decision method in which individual members, acting separately, pool their judgements in a systematic and independent fashion. This is a more complex and time-consuming alternative. It is similar to the nominal group technique, except that it does not require the physical presence of the group's members. In fact, the Delphi technique never allows group members to meet face to face. The following steps characterize the Delphi technique:

1   The problem is identified and members are asked to provide potential solutions through a series of carefully designed questionnaires.
2   Each member anonymously and independently completes the first questionnaire.
3   Results of the first questionnaire are compiled at a central location, transcribed and reproduced.
4   Each member receives a copy of the results.
5   After viewing the results, members are again asked for their solutions. The results typically trigger new solutions or cause changes in the original position.
6   Steps 4 and 5 are repeated as often as necessary until consensus is reached.

Like the nominal group technique, the Delphi technique insulates group members from the undue influence of others. Because it does not require the physical presence of the participants, the Delphi technique can be used for decision-making among geographically scattered groups.

Table 11.7 Evaluating group effectiveness

Effective criteria	Type of group			
	Interacting	*Brainstorming*	*Nominal*	*Delphi*
Number of ideas	Low	Moderate	High	High
Quality of ideas	Low	Moderate	High	High
Social pressure	High	Low	Moderate	Low
Time/money costs	Moderate	Low	Low	High
Task orientation	Low	High	High	High
Potential for interpersonal conflict	High	Low	Moderate	Low
Feelings of accomplishment	High to low	High	High	Moderate
Commitment to solution	High	Not applicable	Moderate	Low
Builds group cohesiveness	High	High	Moderate	Low

Source: Reproduced from Murningham (1981: 61) with the permission of American Management Association International, New York.

The Delphi technique has its limitations. Because the method is extremely time-consuming, it is often not applicable when a speedy decision is required. Additionally, the method may not develop the rich array of alternatives that the interacting or nominal group techniques do. The ideas that might surface from the heat of face-to-face interaction may never arise.

Various techniques have been made to compare these techniques against "named" face-to-face, normally interacting groups. Table 11.7 is a fairly comprehensive comparison.

Stepladder technique

This method adds new members to a group who have already discussed the problem at hand. Thus two people begin: they work independently on the problem before coming together to discuss their ideas and come up with an agreed solution. While this is happening, a third person also considers the problem and presents his or her ideas to the dyad *after* they have discussed the issues. The triad then discusses, revisits the problem and re-evaluates their decision. Then a fourth, fifth … person is added. Each time the group with the new person works together at finding a solution. The rationale, according to Greenberg and Baron (2003), is that through this specific procedure the latest group member will not be influenced by the group, which is required to consider a constant influx of new ideas.

Focus groups

This technique is used widely in marketing. A group of customers, users or consumers is identified (often based on certain characteristics) and brought together to provide feedback on products, services, and so on. It is much like a customer survey, but the respondents are not selected at random. One pitfall of this method is that people may not be totally honest in their answers (e.g. they may say that they travel frequently to Europe because they wish they did or they want to be seen as sophisticated). Recent studies indicate that focus-group responses tend to be more reliable if the respondents are rewarded in some way (a nominal payment or gift), because they then feel a responsibility to respond honestly.

The dialectical enquiry

This method was developed for complex, strategic decisions and it can encourage intense, heated debate:

1   Divide the group in half or thirds.

2   One subgroup prepares in writing a recommended solution, with assumptions and key data.
3   The other subgroup(s) develops plausible assumptions to criticize the first subgroup's ideas. This subgroup also prepares a set of recommendations.
4   Both subgroups present their arguments to each other, orally and in writing. The groups debate in an atmosphere of goodwill.
5   Agreement is then reached on which assumptions survived, and recommendations are developed based on these assumptions.
6   Final recommendations are recorded in writing and signed by all.

It is easy to see that this technique can often yield very heated discussion and debate.

References

Adler, N. (1986). *International dimensions of organizational behaviour*. Boston, MA: PWS Kent.

Baron, R., & Greenberg, J. (1990). *Behavior in organizations*. Boston, MA: Allyn & Bacon.

Belsky, G., & Gilovich, T. (1999). *Why smart people make big money mistakes – and how to correct them*. New York: Simon & Schuster.

Blackmore, S., & Troscianko, T. (1985). Belief in the paranormal. *British Journal of Psychology, 16*, 459–468.

Bouchard, T. (1972). A comparison of two group brainstorming procedures. *Journal of Applied Psychology, 59*, 418–421.

Bouchard, T., & Hare, M. (1970). Size performance, and potential in brainstorming groups. *Journal of Applied Psychology, 54*, 51–55.

Bouchard, T., Barsaloux, J., & Drauden, G. (1974). Brainstorming procedure, group size and sex as determinants of the problem-solving effectiveness of groups and individuals. *Journal of Applied Psychology, 59*, 135–138.

Colaros, P., & Anderson, L. (1969). Effect of perceived expertness upon creativity of members of brainstorming groups. *Journal of Applied Psychology, 53*, 1159–1163.

Connolly, T., & Ordonez, L. (2004). Judgement and decision-making. In W. Norman, D. Ilgen, & R. Klimoski (Eds.), *Handbook of psychology* (Vol. 12, pp. 493–517). New York: Wiley.

de Bono, E. (1970). *Lateral thinking: Creativity step by step*. New York: Harper & Row.

de Bono, E. (1985). *Six thinking hats*. Boston, MA: Little, Brown.

Diehl, M., & Stroebe, W. (1987). Productivity loss in brainstorming groups: Toward a solution of a riddle. *Journal of Personality and Social Psychology, 53*, 497–509.

Einhorn, H., & Hogarth, R. (1978). Confidence in judgement: Persistence of the illusion of validity. *Psychological Review, 85*, 395–416.

Fong, E., Krantz, D., & Nisbet, R. (1986). The effects of statistical training on thinking about everyday problems. *Cognitive Psychology, 18*, 140–152.

Furnham, A. (1988). *Lay theories*. Oxford: Pergamon Press.

Furnham, A. (1999). *The hopeless, hapless and helpless manager*. London: Whurr Publishers.

Gallupe, R., Cooper, W., Grise, M. L., & Bastianutti, L. (1994). Blocking electronic brainstorms. *Journal of Applied Psychology, 79*, 77–80.

Gordon, R. (1993). *A diagnostic approach to organizational behaviour*. Boston, MA: Allyn & Bacon.

Greenberg, J., & Baron, R. (2003). *Behavior in organizations*. New York: Prentice-Hall.

Harkins, S., & Jackson, J. (1985). The role of evaluation in eliminating social loafing. *Personality and Social Psychology Bulletin, 11*, 457–465.

Hastie, R., & Dawes, R. (2001). Rational Choice in an Uncertain World. London: Sage.

Hilton, D. (1998). *Psychology and the City*. London: Centre for the Study of Financial Innovation.

Janis, I. (1972). *Victims of group-think*. Boston, MA: Houghton-Mifflin.

Johns, E. (1992). *Organizational behaviour*. New York: HarperCollins.

Kahneman, D., & Tversky, A. (1973). On the psychology of prediction. *Psychological Review, 80*, 237–251.

Kahneman, D., & Tversky, A. (1982). Variants of uncertainty. *Cognition, 11*, 143–157.

Kerr, N., & Bruun, S. (1983). Dispensability of members' efforts and group motivation losses: Free rider effects. *Journal of Personality and Social Psychology, 44*, 78–94.

Kunda, Z., & Nisbet, R. (1985). *The psychometrics of everyday life*. Paper presented at the British Psychological Society Annual Conference, Swansea.

Lamm, H., & Myers, D. (1978). Group-induced polarization of attitudes and behaviour. In L. Berkowitz (Ed.), *Advances in experimental social psychology* (pp. 145–195). New York: Academic Press.

Laughlin, P., & Johnson, H. (1966). Group and individual performance on a complementary task as a function of the initial ability level. *Journal of Experimental Psychology, 2*, 407–414.

Leung, K. (1992). Decision-making. In R. Westwood (Ed.), *Organizational behaviour: South East Asian perspectives* (pp. 343–361). Hong Kong: Longman.

Maginn, B., & Harris, R. (1980). Effects of antiquated evaluation on individual transforming performance. *Journal of Applied Psychology, 65*, 219–225.

Murningham, J. (1981). Group decision-making: What strategies should you use? *Management Review*, February, pp. 61–71.

Osborn, A. (1957). *Applied imagination*. New York: Scribner.

Paulus, P., & Dzindolet, M. (1993). Social influence processes in group brainstorming. *Journal of Personality and Social Psychology, 64*, 575–586.

Plous, S. (1993). *The psychology of judgement and decision-making*. New York: McGraw-Hill.

Robbins, S. (1991). *Organizational behaviour*. New York: Prentice-Hall.

Simon, H. (1976). *Administrative behavior*. New York: Free Press.

Stoner, J. (1961). *A comparison of individual and group decisions involving risk*. MSc thesis, Sloan School of Industrial Management, MIT, Cambridge, MA.

Taylor, D., Berry, P., & Block, C. (1958). Does group participation when using brainstorming facilitate or inhibit creative thinking. *Administration Science Quarterly, 3*, 23–47.

Thornberg, T. (1991). Group size and member diversity influence on creative performance. *Journal of Creative Behaviour, 25*, 324–333.

Thurnholm, P. (2004). Decision-making style: habit, style or both. *Personality and Individual Differences, 36*, 931–944.

Tosi, H., & Mero, N. (2003). *The fundamentals of organizational behaviour*. Oxford: Blackwell.

Tversky, A., & Kahneman, D. (1973). Availability: A heuristic for judging frequency and probability. *Cognitive Psychology, 5*, 207–232.

Valsiner, J. (1985). Common sense and psychological theories: The historical nature of logical necessity. *Scandinavian Journal of Psychology, 26*, 97–109.

Weatherall, A., & Nunamaker, J. (1996). *Introduction to electronic meetings*. Chandlers Ford: EMS.

Webber, R. (1974). The relationship of group performance to the age of members in homogeneous groups. *Academy of Management Journal, 17*, 570–574.

Williams, K., Harken, S., & Latane, B. (1981). Indentifiability as a deterrent to social loafing: Two cheering experiments. *Journal of Personality and Social Psychology, 40*, 303–311.

Zander, A. (1982). *Motives and goals in groups*. New York: Academic Press.

12 Leadership

Introduction

The topic of leadership is one of the oldest areas of research in the social sciences, yet one of the most problematic. Novelists, historians and journalists have always been interested in what makes a great (and a failed) leader: what are their unique character-istics and strengths; allowable weaknesses and peculiar foibles; and, most intriguing, what makes them fall from grace? Do special circumstances (crises) "throw up" certain types of leaders who are only suitable in that situation? Are most leaders in business the victims of the Peter principle (promoted until their level of incompetence is reached)? Is succession planning for leaders really viable, given that circumstances change so often?

Ten years ago, Hogan, Curphy & Hogan (1994) in an excellent review considered what we know about leadership under eight headings: What is leadership? Does leader-ship matter? How are leaders chosen? How should leaders be evaluated? Why do we choose so many flawed leaders? How to forecast leadership? Why do leaders fail? How do leaders build teams? Later, they (Hogan, Curphy, & Hogan, 2001) summarized their conclusions thus: The fundamental task of leadership is to build and maintain a high performing team, a team that wins, that beats its competition. A person's performance as a leader should be evaluated in terms of the performance of his team, and not in terms of how much his boss likes him. Leadership is directly related to organizational effectiveness – an effective organization is composed of high performing teams. Effec-tive leaders are seen as honest/trustworthy, decisive and able to make good decisions, competent at the business, and visionary – having a sense of direction and purpose. There are a large number of bad managers in every organization, and their staff know who they are, even when the bosses don't. The fewer bad managers in an organization, the more effective it will be.

House (1998) provides eight slightly different definitions of leadership based on his reading of the literature. Themes in these definitions include directing group activities; initiating/maintaining expectations and interaction; influence, through communica-tions to goal achievement; providing a shared vision, creating opportunities and building confidence; inducing followers to act; create social order; giving purpose to collective effort; a catalytic force that empowers others. House (1998) notes how recent definitions have increasing emphasis on values and ideology.

As we shall see, thinking about leadership has moved through various themes or paradigms: trait theory (1930–1950s), where leadership was the leader; the behavioural school (1960s), where leadership styles were described; and contingency theory

(1970–1990s), which focused on leader–follower relations. As Spector (2003) has noted, questions have changed from "Who will make a good leader" to "What do good leaders do" to "Under a given condition, who will be a good leader and what behaviour is likely to be effective" to "How does the interaction between subordinate and supervisor affect the subordinate behaviour?"

In contrast to many students, many executives believe leadership quality/ability is something you have or haven't got: it is rarely trainable and relatively fixed. But few can agree on what the "something" is. Cynics have pointed out that there are almost as many definitions of leadership as there are persons who have attempted to define the concept. Speculators and researchers disagree on how leaders are identified; how they can, should and do influence followers; and which situational factors influence leader behaviour. Most definitions agree that leadership is an influence process. For what they are worth, definitions suggest leadership is the art of getting others to do (and want to do) something you believe should be (must be) done. It is about interpersonal influence, goal-setting and communication. Leaders of all sorts and at all levels need to be person-centred, supportive, democratic and flexible. They also need strategic vision.

What has exercised the passion of many is trying to make distinctions between leaders and managers: are they qualitatively different or mutually distinct? Some argue they differ fundamentally in how they think, work and influence others (Zaleznik, 1977). The essential difference between leaders and managers is that while managers perform a rational, analytic, intellectual function, leaders inspire by vision, values, confidence and determination. Kotter (1987) argues that whereas leadership is about coping with change, management is about coping with complexity. More memorably, Bennis (1989) suggested that managers do things right, whereas leaders do the right thing. Most now agree that managers have to do two things: carry on traditional management functions (planning, budgeting, staffing) and assume prescribed roles (figurehead, information disseminator, negotiator). Leaders, on the other hand, challenge the *status quo*, communicate a new vision, direction and strategy, and motivate and inspire others. Thus, it is usually agreed that leaders and managers are not mutually exclusive but they are distinct, although it is quite possible for people to be both or neither.

Psychologists and management scientists have long been interested in the emergence, functions, traits, styles, abilities and weaknesses of leaders. Indeed, one reason for the diversity and differences in theories in this area lies in the fact that researchers have concentrated on different facets or features of leaders and leadership. Equally, different leaders have in particular been investigated: among the most popular are business, political and military leaders. Some are elected, some self-appointed; some are spectacularly skilful, others almost complete failures. Yet the obvious problem of finding some commonality over the definition of what a leader is, or does, makes comparative analysis across leaders highly problematic. Various definitions have been proposed, including "those members of the group who (most) influence the activities of the group" (Krech, Crutchfield, & Ballachey, 1962) and "the person who comes closest to realizing the norm and values of the group" (Homans, 1950). Essentially, leadership is the process of influencing the behaviour of individuals or groups towards the achievement of organizational goals. Hosking & Morley (1991: 240) believe leadership is "a more or less skilful process of organizing achieved through negotiation, to achieve acceptable influence over the description and handling of issues within and between groups". Of course, it has always been acknowledged that all members of a group are to some extent leaders. Leadership is situation-specific and qualitative. Also, because leadership acts are nearly always interpersonal, leaders are influenced by their followers and vice versa. It is the continuity and consistency of leadership that is important.

Some attempts to understand leaders have focused on what sort of *power* they wield. French & Raven (1960) distinguished between coercive (power to punish), reward (power to reward), legitimate (positional power), expert (special skill or knowledge power) and referent (the power of a follower's identification) power. Leaders need different types of power, which must be acknowledged as legitimate. Another way of looking at power is to consider the type of power that different management styles are associated with (Muczyk & Reimann, 1987). Thus, one has the directive democrat (high on direction and high on participation), the permission democrat (low on direction, high on participation), the directive autocrat (high on direction, low on participation) and the permissive autocrat (low on direction, low on participation). Avolio, Sosik, Jung & Berson (2003) believe it is important to distinguish between moral and immoral leadership. Moral leadership is epitomized by pro-social leaders who are empathic, focused on building collective missions, considerate, self-sacrificing and trustworthy. In contrast, immoral leadership is generally dominating, exploitive, fear-inducing, manipulative as well as self-aggrandizing and self-centred.

Most theories have focused on the *leader* and the *traits* of successful leaders. Work psychologists have attempted to describe these factors; practitioners have been interested from the point of view of selection and training. Another focus has been on the *led* rather than the leader or the whole topic of "followership". Social psychologists have focused on a different factor, namely the *influence process*. Thus, different methods of influence have been described, such as coercion, manipulation, authority and persuasion. More recently, the context or *situation* has been the focus of researchers who have attempted to taxonomize the salient situation factors that influence leadership. A final area of interest is in what characteristics lead to someone becoming or *emerging* as a leader, while others focus on the behaviours of successful *effective* leaders.

Hosking & Morley (1991) have argued that the social science literature on leadership is divided very noticeably between focusing on the leader as a *person* rather than on the process or *context* of leadership. Focusing on the person often ignores the subtle and complex ways in which contextual or organizational factors support or frustrate the development and expression of particular personalities. There must be reciprocal influence between the style of the leader and the culture of the organization. Focusing on the context or organization often sees leadership from a "managerialist perspective" of roles, structures, goals and so on, which ignore the cognitive and political uniqueness of the people who hold those roles:

> The study of leadership often has come down to the study of leaders, who they are, what they do, and with whom. "Who they are" means managers possessing personal characteristics which set them apart from their context. "What they do" is reduced to behaviours or activities, and "with whom" reduces to "contacts", classified and understood in terms of formal status (subordinate, lateral and the like). The social aspects of a leader's context often are reduced to a number, "variety" and status (peer, subordinate, and the like) of their "contacts" . . . What is

important about the treatment of behaviour or activity is that it is viewed as an input, made by a leader to a context. (Hosking & Morley, 1991: 244–245)

These different topics, related though they are, have led to different questions being asked (Muchinsky, 1990; see Table 12.1).

Over the past decade, various writers have proposed a totally new philosophy or style of leadership. Schermerhorn, Hunt & Osborn (1994: 517) have summarized these ideas (see Table 12.2). However, as they point out, some important and fundamental questions remain regarding these new ideas, such as whether some of these functions are always needed and desirable, and whether (if they want to) people can be trained in these new methods. Also, many fads and fashions remain in the leadership literature. For instance, it is assumed that leaders have functions, such as to challenge (motivate, direct) and to support (encourage, help), and that in many organizations the latter has been neglected. Hence, some radical organizations have replaced the title "manager"

Table 12.1 The six major areas of investigation: in the study of leadership

Topic	Research focus	Research questions
Power that comes with the role	Influence tactics; use of power. Role requirements.	How does organizational history and structure effect leader's power?
The leaders themselves	Personality traits; cognitive ability.	What most differentiates effective versus ineffective leaders?
Those who are led	Group dynamics.	What types of subordinates desire what type of leadership?
Influence process	The range and type of influence attempts.	When are leaders susceptible to influence?
The situation and setting of leadership	Situation effects on leader behaviour; Physical, social and political.	How does the environment modify leader behaviour?
How do leaders emerge?	Group dynamics and history.	How do leaders become recognized and stay in position?

Source: Based on Muchinsky (1990).

Table 12.2 Themes in the new leadership literature

Less emphasis needed on	Greater emphasis needed on
Planning	Vision/mission
Allocating responsibility	Infusing vision
Controlling and problem-solving	Motivating and inspiring
Creating routine and equilibrium	Creating change and innovation
Power retention	Empowerment of others
Creating compliance	Creating commitment
Emphasizing contractual obligations	Stimulating extra effort
Leader detachment and rationality	Leader interest in others and intuition
Reactive environmental approach	Proactive environmental approach

Source: Reproduced from Schermerhorn *et al.* (1994) with the permission of John Wiley & Sons.

with "coach", to emphasize what they see to be the most crucial role of a leader: to train, support, encourage and give constant feedback to their subordinates, much as a coach does to sports players. For many managers, this is a fashion they hope will soon disappear.

Shackleton and Wale (2000) pose the obvious question: are leaders really necessary? That is, do we romanticize leadership and over-emphasize its importance? Certainly, leaders can be neutralized to having little effect because of the characteristics of their followers, the task they are trying to achieve or the nature of the organization.

The current emphasis on teams means that it is quite possible that different leadership styles are required at different levels, or in different domains, of the organization. At the lower or production levels, more traditional "command and control" management may be appropriate, whereas at higher levels, more team-based leadership may be appropriate.

Avolio *et al.* (2003) point out that despite all the interest in – and money spent on – leadership, choice and development, we still know very little about the area. However, they do note some major trends and future directions. These include an interest in strategic leadership, e-leadership, collective leadership and leadership developments. Researchers have begun to ask the important and difficult questions about how, when and why leadership does (and does not) effect fundamental change in individuals, groups and organizations. Leaders give meaning to their followers: they create their realities and how they do this is recognized as important. Indeed, it has been suggested that leadership is essentially in the eye of the beholder: it is a process perceived by others and then labelled "leadership".

A historical review of approaches to leadership

Centuries ago, most leaders were born: kings, knights and barons inherited their role. As various talented, assertive or corrupt people assumed leadership roles, it was assumed there may be physical differences that set them apart: the Roman nose, the strong jaw, the firm handshake.

Since the nineteenth century, social scientists have tended to approach leadership in rather different ways. Although one approach has largely "given way" to the one following it, there have always been researchers who have carried on researching within a rather unpopular and unfashionable framework, because they were either behind or ahead of the times. Because these very different approaches have given birth to specific theories and ideas about the nature of leadership, they are reviewed here.

It is possible to classify the major leadership theories into three groups. Leadership *trait* theory assumes that there are distinctive physical and psychological characteristics that account for leadership effectiveness. *Behavioural* leadership theory assumes that there are distinctive styles that effective leaders continually use: these may be variously classified (i.e. autocratic, democratic, laissez-faire) or based on grids/models that specify dimensions such as task- versus person-orientated. *Situational* (or contingency) leadership theories assume that leadership style varies from situation to situation.

The trait approach

This was characterized by the *great person approach* to leadership. Three questions guided the research efforts of the trait theorists before the Second World War:

- Could specific traits of great leaders be identified?
- Was it possible to select people for leadership positions by identifying those who possess the appropriate traits?
- Could someone learn the trait that characterizes an effective leader?

It was assumed that a finite set of individual traits – age, height, social status, fluency of speech, self-confidence, need for achievement, interpersonal skills, attractiveness, and so on – distinguished leaders from non-leaders and successful leaders from unsuccessful leaders (Stogdill, 1948). The sorts of traits more frequently investigated have been grouped under different headings: physical characteristics (height, energy), social background (education, social status), intellectual ability (intelligence quotient, verbal fluency), personality (self-confidence, stress tolerance), task orientation (achievement need) and social skills (personal competence, tact).

Over the years, a considerable amount of effort went into identifying traits associated with successful leaders (Box 12.1). Note that these traits include personality traits, cognitive abilities, interpersonal styles and ability factors. For the psychologist used to distinguishing between various types of individual differences, the list looks very jumbled; indeed, rather arbitrary.

For more than 40 years, there have been attempts to look at personality traits associated with good leadership and management success in particular (Furnham, 1994; Ghiselli, 1963). Ghiselli believed that individual intelligence is itself a good predictor of management success within a specific range. He divided traits into three categories: of *great* importance (supervisory ability, occupational achievement, intelligence, self-actualization, self-assurance and decisiveness); of *moderate* importance (lack of need for security, affinity with the working class, lack of need for financial reward, maturity); and of *little* importance (masculinity/femininity).

Box 12.1 Personality traits and other features associated with leaders

Traits expected to characterize good leaders

Pleasant appearance	Intelligence
Good grooming	Self-confidence
Moderate weight	Interpersonal sensitivity
Adaptability	Tactfulness
Alertness	Persuasiveness
Assertiveness	Fluency
Cooperativeness	Creativity
Ambition	Dependability
Aggressiveness	Judgement
Enthusiasm	Achievement orientation
Persistence	Extraversion
Stress tolerance	Integrity
Responsibility	

Source: Derived from lists provided by Yukl (1980).

Table 12.3 What people want in their leaders, colleagues and subordinates

	Boss Mean	Colleague Mean	Subordinate Mean	Rank			
				USA*	B	C	S
Ambitious	66.16	59.09	70.60	16	14	18	7
Broadminded	77.66	70.30	72.48	7	5	6	6
Caring	61.21	59.19	53.17	13	18	14	19
Competent	81.08	79.83	82.58	2	2	3	3
Cooperative	70.84	82.75	80.22	14	11	2	4
Courageous	71.23	60.43	59.84	12	10	12	16
Dependable	74.66	78.67	82.75	10	7	4	2
Determined	70.45	68.14	76.70	17	12	8	5
Fair-minded	79.34	67.62	63.22	6	4	9	13
Forward-looking	80.99	59.76	56.80	3	3	9	13
Honest	84.89	84.88	84.83	1	1	1	1
Imaginative	63.73	62.46	65.73	9	16	14	11
Independent	60.93	59.93	63.04	20	20	15	14
Inspiring	77.51	65.62	60.49	4	6	11	15
Intelligent	74.03	69.90	69.79	5	9	7	8
Loyal	60.95	60.23	66.85	19	19	13	9
Mature	64.59	52.30	47.55	15	15	20	20
Self-controlled	61.34	57.06	58.72	18	17	19	17
Straightforward	69.66	67.48	65.16	8	13	10	10
Supportive	74.56	72.52	63.80	11	8	5	12

Notes: Rank order of most characteristics to have in one's boss (B), subordinate (S), colleague (C).
* Data from Kouzes and Posner's original American study.

Traits, of course, are not totally independent of each other. First, Ghiselli (1963) argued that intelligence and self-actualization are important for success, yet the concept of power over others is not very important. He argued that the supervisory ability trait basically refers to the ability to use planning, organizing and control to direct subordinates, which is clearly relevant in all leadership.

Certainly, it is difficult to imagine anyone being a successful leader without having such traits as vigour, persistence, originality, self-confidence, stress tolerance (hardiness), an ability to influence, a capacity to structure tasks and a willingness to take responsibility for the consequences of one's actions.

In an interesting and unique study of military leaders, Dixon (1976) adopted a trait approach. He argued that authoritarianism (see Chapter 5) accounted for the military mistakes that occurred again and again. The most important of these were: a tendency to underestimate the capabilities of the enemy relative to one's own; an inability to admit mistakes, which motivates attempts to blame others, and makes it difficult to learn from experience; a fundamental conservatism, which inhibits change and ignores technical advances; a failure adequately to use reconnaissance; a tendency to discount warning signals, which indicate that things are going wrong; passivity and procrastination; a failure to take the initiative and exploit advantages gained; and, finally, a predisposition to use frontal assaults, often against the enemy's main line of defence. His argument is that the dynamics of authoritarianism – concern with power and toughness, fear of failure, resistance to change – are sufficient to explain most military fiascos. Indeed, as Hosking & Morley (1991: 16) note, "there is evidence to support the view that some of the most pervasive and dysfunctional aspects of behaviour in organizations may be a direct result of pathological elements in the personalities of top managers". That is, some leaders are attracted to organizations, and they to them, that promise to gratify certain neurotic needs.

A rather different trait approach is that of Kouzes and Posner (1988), who asked American managers to rank-order 20 positive traits they would like to see in their leader. Furnham (2002b) replicated this study but asked his British participants to rate these as desirable in a boss, a colleague and a subordinate (Table 12.3). The rank-order of traits chosen by the 2615 North American managers studied by Kouzes and Posner (1988) shows strong similarities to the UK data. The top three and bottom five were identical. The greatest differences were between caring, determined and straightforward. The paired comparisons between the three positions (boss, colleague, subordinate) showed some very interesting differences. There were, however, consistent differences in others like dependable and inspiring.

In total, 11 of the 20 ratings comparing boss and colleague were significant. For all but two, the mean rating of the boss was higher. Thus participants felt, compared to a colleague, it was important that the boss was more ambitious, broadminded, courageous, fair-minded, forward-looking, inspiring, intelligent, mature and self-controlled, while they felt the colleague should be more cooperative and dependable.

Not surprisingly, the different scores between ratings of boss and colleague showed more stark differences. The participants believed that, compared to their subordinate, a boss should be significantly less ambitious, more broadminded, more caring, less cooperative, more courageous, and less dependable, less determined, more fair-minded, more forward looking, more independent, more inspiring, less intelligent, more loyal, more self-controlled, more straightforward and more supportive.

Of the comparisons between colleague and subordinate, 11 yielded significant differences. Participants felt subordinates should score lower than colleagues on caring, fair-minded, inspiring, mature, straightforward and supportive, but higher on ambitious, competent, dependable, determined and loyal.

Locke (1997) has identified (from personal observation and reading) various "traits" of leaders under quite specific headings:

A. Cognitive ability and modes of thinking

1. *Reality focus*: they are not susceptible to evasions, rationalizations and delusions but face the actual and often grim reality.
2. *Honesty*: this applies to the assessment of the market, judgements about the attractiveness of own products and capabilities of employees, and how to deal with suppliers, lenders and customers.
3. *Independence and self-confidence*: being confident to break new ground, think "outside the box" and "borrow" the best ideas from others.
4. *Active mind*: continually searching for new ideas and solutions. It takes constant thought to undertake constant realistic improvements.
5. *Competence and ability*: in a sense, this is simply intelligence – to make valid generalizations from data, to grasp causal connections and to see actionable principles from overwhelmingly complex data.
6. *Vision*: a detailed innovative, long-term plan for the future of company products and services.

B. Motivation, values and actions

1. *Egoistic passion for the work*: a sort of intrinsically motivated workaholism. The passion is a source of energy.
2. *Commitment to action*: this means doing after thinking, getting-on-with-it.
3. *Ambition*: personal drive and desire to achieve expertise and a level of responsibility.
4. *Effort and tenacity*: being hard-working and resilient; and not easily discouraged by failure.

C. Attitude towards employees

1. *Respect for ability:* hiring and developing people with drive, talent and the right attitude.
2. *Commitment to justice*: rewarding people appropriately.

Locke (1997) argued that the dozen traits are, in themselves, not sufficient for business success. But he has argued that these traits are timeless and universal, and do not only apply to successful Americans in the twentieth century. However, he ducks the question as to where these traits come from and whether they are changeable or not. He does raise and answer two central questions:

> Would quantitative analysis support 12 distinct traits, or could they be grouped into a smaller number without loss of important information? My prediction is that they can be combined into a smaller number ... Do the traits operate independently (e.g. in additive fashion) or are there interactions between them? I have one prediction here: I think dishonesty negates all a person's other virtues in that it divorces a person from reality in principle ... A complicating factor, however, is that people are not always consistent in their honest and dishonesty. (Locke, 1997: 92)

Locke (1997) does, however, make a particularly interesting point: he notes that not all successful leaders have been recognized or admired for what they have done. Indeed, many have been reviled and despised, mainly for sociopolitical reasons.

   However, it has been recognized that, although statistically significant, many of the effects that were attributed to certain leader traits were quite small and of limited practical value. It has also been noted that, even though certain traits increase the likelihood that a leader will be effective, they do not guarantee effectiveness. Trait theory also ignores the roles of subordinates. The research in this tradition is inconsistent and non-replicable. The list of traits simply grows over time, leading to confusion, disputes and little insight into why leadership traits operate as they do. The trait approach identifies people in leadership roles after they have been seen to be successful. It is unclear, therefore, whether these traits make the leader or whether the leadership role shapes the traits. The trait approach may also be thought of as a fundamental attribution error – that is, explaining the behaviour (success or failure) almost exclusively in terms of the internal traits and motives of leaders, while ignoring or underplaying organizational, social and economic factors that clearly play a large part. Lay people remain trait theorists when it comes to explaining leadership, which means that this school of thought is still alive and well. Indeed, it can be observed today in those business managers who have replaced the term "trait" with "competency" and who believe a particular combination or profile of competencies predicts leadership success. Yet at all levels, the trait approach is never more than descriptive because very rarely do the trait theorists explain how, when and why the traits they stipulate are necessary and sufficient for the leadership process to be successful. They also do not stipulate how much of a trait or ability one needs, or, indeed, what occurs if that ability is missing.

The re-emergence of the trait approach

Over the past 20 years, there has been a strong re-emergence of interest in the personality of leaders. This has occurred because of advances in the taxonomization and measurement of personality (see Chapter 4), and also because of better data on leadership. Various meta-analyses have been done that have clear implications for the selection of leaders.

For example, Hogan *et al.* (1994) showed a clear relationship between leadership and (1) extraversion (dominance, sociability, surgency), (2) stability (emotional control, self-confidence, positive mood), (3) agreeableness (cooperativeness, diplomacy) and (4) conscientiousness (integrity, responsibility).

Judge and Bono (2000) looked at 14 samples of leaders in 200 organizations to determine which of the Big Five traits predicted transformational leadership. They hypothesized that extraversion, openness and agreeableness would be positively related, and neuroticism negatively related, to ratings of transformational leadership behaviours. Their hypotheses were partially confirmed: Extraversion and Agreeableness were related, but Neuroticism and Conscientiousness were unrelated, to leadership.

Judge, Bono, Ilies & Gerhardt (2002) reviewed the extant literature on personality and leadership. Ten writers, mainly from the 1990s, listed what they thought to be the essential traits of effective or emergent leaders. Judge *et al.* noted considerable overlap, such that most writers listed such things as self-confidence, adjustment, sociability and integrity, but that others like persistence and masculinity were unique to specific reviewers. However, in their meta-analysis they considered the possible linkages between personality and leadership. As hypothesized, they found that Neuroticism was negatively correlated, and that Extraversion, Openness and Conscientiousness were positively correlated, with both leadership emergence and effectiveness. Their results provide strong support for the personality approach to leadership once the traits are organized according to the five-factor model. Extraversion was the most consistent correlate because of the assertiveness, dominance and sociability of extraverts. However, they accept the point that the research does not always explain why these traits are related to leadership:

> Is Neuroticism negatively related to leadership because neurotic individuals are less likely to attempt leadership, because they are less inspirational, or because they have lower expectations of themselves or others? Similarly, extraversion may be related to leadership because extraverts talk more, and talking is strongly related to emergent leadership. Alternatively, it may be that individuals implicitly expect leaders to be extraverted. Implicit views of leaders include aspects of both sociability ("outgoing") and assertiveness ("aggressive," "forceful"), or extraverts could be better leaders due to their expressive nature or the contagion of their positive

emotionality. Open individuals may be better leaders because they are more creative and are divergent thinkers, because they are risk takers, or because their tendencies for esoteric thinking and fantasy make them more likely to be visionary leaders. Agreeableness may be weakly correlated with leadership because it is both a hindrance (agreeable individuals tend to be passive and compliant) and a help (agreeable individuals are likeable and empathetic) to leaders. Finally, is Conscientiousness related to leadership because conscientious individuals have integrity and engender trust because they excel at process aspects of leadership, such as setting goals, or because they are more likely to have initiative and persist in the face of obstacles? Our study cannot address these process oriented issues, but future research should attempt to explain the linkages between the Big Five traits and leadership. (Judge *et al.*, 2002: 774)

The behavioural approach

After the Second World War, researchers tended to focus on leaders' observable behaviour rather than traits. The increasing interest in behaviourism encouraged researchers to focus on the external observable behaviours of leaders, good and bad. Perhaps the best-known distinctions arising from this school were the authoritarian, democratic and *laissez-faire* models of leadership, which are prototypical descriptors of the behavioural styles of most leaders (Table 12.4). It was argued that what leaders

Table 12.4 A distinction between three styles of leadership

Three basic leadership styles

Authoritarian	Democratic	Laissez-faire
All determination of policy by the leader.	All policies a matter of group discussion and decision, encouraged and assisted by the leader.	Complete freedom for group or individual decisions, with a minimum of leader participation.
Techniques and activity steps dictated by the authority, one at a time so that future steps were always uncertain to a large degree.	Activity perspective gained during discussion period. General steps to group goal sketched, and when technical advice was needed, the leader suggested two or more alternative procedures from which choice could be made.	Various materials supplied by the leader, who made it clear that information would be supplied when requested and took no other part in work discussion.
The leader usually dictated the particular work task and work companion of each member.	The members were free to work with whom ever they chose, and the division of tasks was left up to the group.	Complete non-participation of the leader.
The leader tended to be "personal" in the praise and criticism of the work of each member; remained aloof from active group participation.	The leader was "objective" or "fact-minded" in praise and criticism and tried to be a regular group member in spirit without doing too much of the work.	Infrequent spontaneous comments on member activities unless questioned and no attempt to appraise or regulate the course of events.

Source: French *et al.* (1985).

actually did (rather than the abilities and traits they had) would unlock the mystery of leadership. The approach involves three steps: (1) observe leader behaviour, (2) categorize it and (3) determine which behaviours are most (and by implication least) effective.

Research groups at major US universities began to identify and categorize rather different factors. Thus, Fleishman & Harris (1962) identified two major unrelated sets of leader behaviours: consideration and initiating structure. *Consideration* is the "relationship-orientated" behaviour of a leader. It is instrumental in creating and maintaining good relationships with subordinates. Consideration means being supportive and friendly, representing subordinates' interests, communicating openly with subordinates, recognizing subordinates, respecting their ideas and sharing concern for their feelings. It refers to the socio-emotional people-focused aspect of leadership. *Initiating structure* involves "task-orientated" leader behaviours, which are instrumental in the efficient use of resources to attain organizational goals. Initiating structure includes scheduling work, deciding what is to be done (and how and when to do it), providing direction to subordinates, planning, coordinating, problem-solving, maintaining standards of performance, and encouraging the use of uniform procedures.

After the importance of consideration and initiating structure behaviours was first identified, many leaders believed that they had to behave one way or the other. If they initiated structure and were primarily task-orientated, they could not be considerate, and vice versa. Of course, this was spurious, because leaders have been found to be both high and low on both dimensions simultaneously. Thus, one could conceive of four types depending on this twofold dimensional classification: *directing* (high structure, low consideration), *coaching* (high structure, high consideration), *supporting* (low structure, high consideration) and *delegating* (low structure, low consideration). Randolph & Blackburn (1989) believed that managers need to ask themselves four specific questions in a set order to establish the best leadership style in a given set of circumstances:

1   What is the nature of the task to be performed? (directing)
2   Do the subordinates have the ability and motivation to perform the task? (delegating)
3   What characteristics of the leader might influence his or her ability to use the chosen leadership style? (supporting)
4   Does the nature of the leader's context influence his or her ability to use the chosen leadership style? (coaching)

Randolph & Blackburn (1989) believed that managers need to ask two questions about tasks and subordinate characteristics to determine the ability and motivation of subordinates. To apply the model, managers would first analyse the task structure and variability and its intrinsic motivation. To determine the fit between task and employees, managers would then analyse the subordinates' ability and willingness to take responsibility, their task-relevant education or experience, their need for achievement, their present need structure, and their desire for control. From this analysis, managers could determine where on the ability and motivation continuum to place their employees.

Managers could select the appropriate style of leadership for the situation. Next, the model calls for an analysis of leader and context characteristics (using two more questions) to see if the chosen style can be implemented. The leader characteristics of relations with subordinates, experience/knowledge, power needs, and personal power bases will influence a leader's analysis of the situation. In addition, the context characteristics of the position power of the leader, the style of previous people in the leader's position, the style of other leaders around the manager, and organizational norms of operation will act to constrain the leadership of choices available to the manager. These additional aspects can influence the choice of appropriate leadership style for a given situation. (Randolph & Blackburn, 1989: 364)

Several questionnaires were developed to assess the content of leader behaviour as reflected by these two factors. The first, the leader behaviour description questionnaire (LBDQ), could be completed by a subordinate who described how his or her leader behaved in various situations. A second questionnaire, the leader opinion questionnaire (LOQ), was meant to be completed by a supervisor/leader and it deals with questions on ideal methods of supervision. One early research study attempted to compare supervisors having different consideration and initiating-structure scores with various performance measures (Fleishman, Harris, & Burtt, 1955). The first measure was obtained from proficiency ratings made by plant management. Other criterion measures were unexcused absenteeism, accidents, formally filed grievances and employee turnover. Indexes for each of these measures were computed for each foreman's workgroup for an 11-month period.

Supervisors who worked in production divisions were compared with supervisors in non-production divisions on consideration scores, initiating-structure scores and proficiency ratings. In the production divisions, the supervisors who were rated by their superiors as most proficient scored high on structure and low on consideration. In the non-production divisions, the relationships were reversed. After comparing the leadership scores and proficiency ratings, the researchers compared leadership scores to the other performance measures: unexcused absenteeism, accidents, formally filed grievances and employee turnover. It was determined that high structure and low consideration were related to more absenteeism, accidents, grievances and turnover. That is, being high on task-orientation and low on socio-emotional leadership tends to lead to signs of organizational distress and poor productivity.

Likert (1961) also identified two types of leader behaviour: *job-centred behaviours* were devoted to supervisory functions, such as planning, scheduling, coordinating work activities, and providing the resources needed for task performance; *employee-centred behaviours* included consideration and support for subordinates. These dimensions of behaviour, of course, correspond closely to the dimensions of initiating structure and consideration identified by Fleishman *et al.* (1955). Likert suggested that the type of leadership style significantly influences various performance criteria. Criteria such as productivity, absenteeism, attitudes, turnover and defective units (quality control) were found to be more favourable from an organizational standpoint when employee-centred or general supervision was utilized. The choice, it was argued, was of the either/or variety – that is, management can be categorized and practised as employee-centred or job-centred. Likert's recommendation was to develop employee-centred managers whenever possible. Cynics would say that psychologists, particularly those from the Human Relations school (see Chapter 2), would be socio-emotional orientated and that this soft but "cuddly" approach would, over time, lead to poor productivity.

The work of Blake & Mouton (1985) probably most clearly epitomizes the behavioural approach. Their ideas, similar to those above, were based on two unrelated

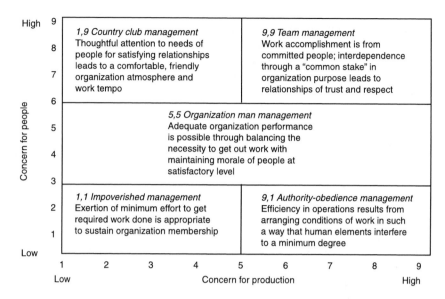

Figure 12.1 Blake & Mouton's grid. Reproduced from Blake, Mouton, Barnes & Greiner (1964) with the permission of the President and Fellows of Harvard College.

dimensions, which yielded what became to be known as the managerial grid (Figure 12.1). The first dimension, *concern for production*, involves an emphasis on output, cost-effectiveness and, where appropriate, a concern for profits. *Concern for people* involves promoting friendships, helping subordinates with work, and paying attention to issues of importance to employees. As their managerial grid shows, any combination of these two leader behaviours is possible. The combinations produce five distinct styles of leadership:

- *Country club (1,9)*: A country club leader emphasizes concern for people but devotes little time and energy to production.
- *Impoverished (1,1)*: An impoverished leader shows little concern for both people and production.
- *Organization person management (5,5)*: This leader demonstrates a moderate concern for both people and production.
- *Authority-obedience (9,1)*: An authority-obedience leader shows a low concern for people but has a strong production orientation.
- *Team (9,9)*: A team leader, also commonly referred to as a 9,9 leader, simultaneously shows a strong regard for employees and a strong production orientation.

Blake & Mouton believed that the team leader (9,9) style is universally the most effective. Furthermore, they claim that experienced managers prefer the team style of leadership in many different sets of circumstances. The fact that the 9,9 style may be preferred, however, does not mean that it necessarily is effective. Although the managerial grid is appealing and well structured, research evidence suggests that there is no universally effective style of leadership (9,9 or otherwise). That is, such good research evidence as exists is equivocal; it suggests that there is no universal truth as to the best style of leaders. In certain circumstances, the country club leaders would be effective, whereas in a different set of circumstances the authority-obedience leader may be just what is required.

The behavioural approach to leadership was a significant advance over the trait approach. Effective leadership became transformed into what leaders *do* as opposed to what they *are*. Thus, there was an increased emphasis on training leaders to be more effective. Observable managerial behaviours are far less ambiguous and more visible than traits. It is far more useful to describe a leader as one who "never gives subordinates a chance to express their feelings" than to say the leader is "highly dominant". Indeed, interest in the behavioural approach coincided with the rise of behaviourism in psychology. However, the behavioural approach fell into the trap of all neat-and-simple typological classifications. First, the groupings or categories tend to be rather simple; not all observed leader behaviour fits neatly into them. Second, competing typologies exist and it is not clear which is correct or most useful. Third, although the typologies are a useful descriptive beginning, they tell us little about the full leadership process, or which style is most effective in which circumstances and why.

The situation or contingent approach

The major premise of this third approach is that the abilities, qualities and skills required by a leader are determined to a large extent by the demands of the situation (context: historical, economic, political) in which he or she is to function as the leader. Just as the trait approach is completely internally focused, so the situational approach is externally focused. Naturally, the focus of this approach was the identification and description of situational characteristics and then specification of the appropriate match of leader abilities or behaviours.

Fiedler's (1967) contingency model, which is a good example of this approach, attempted to identify optimal matches between leaders and situations. Fiedler measured traits by asking leaders about their least preferred co-worker (LPC). Leaders described the person with whom they least wanted to work along several dimensions, such as pleasant/unpleasant, friendly/unfriendly, cold/warm, open/closed, untrustworthy/trustworthy, kind/unkind and sincere/insincere, which reflects a leader's underlying disposition towards others.

Fiedler found that leaders with high LPC scores are *relationship-orientated*. They tend to evaluate their least-preferred co-worker in fairly favourable terms. These individuals need to develop and maintain close interpersonal relationships. Task accomplishment is a secondary need to this type of leader and it becomes important only after the need for relationships is reasonably well satisfied. In contrast, leaders with low LPC scores tend to evaluate fairly negatively the individuals with whom they would least like to work. They are *task-orientated* rather than relationship-orientated. Only when tasks are accomplished in an effective and efficient manner are low LPC leaders likely to work on establishing good social and interpersonal relations.

Some situations supposedly favour certain leaders more than others do. Situational favourableness is the extent to which a leader has control and influence and, therefore, feels that he or she can determine the outcomes of a group interaction. Three factors supposedly determine how favourable a situation is to a leader:

- *Leader–member relations* is the strongest determinant of situation favourability. This relationship reflects the leader's degree of acceptance by the group and the members' level of loyalty to the leader. Group members' support, an ability to work well together, loyalty and dependability are some of the attributes that enhance situational favourableness for a leader.
- *Task structure* is the second most important determinant of situation favourability. A highly structured task provides a detailed, unambiguous goal, and this structure clarifies how to achieve this goal. Situational favourableness rises as the amount of task structure increases.
- *Position power* refers to a leader's direct ability to influence subordinates. Position power may include legitimate, reward, co-service, expert, resource and referent power.

The situation is most favourable for a leader when the relationship between the leader and group members is good, when the task is highly structured, and the leader's position power is strong (Cell 1 in Figure 12.2). The least favourable situation for a leader exists when the relationship between the leader and group members is poor, the task is unstructured, and the leader's position power is weak (Cell 8 in Figure 12.2). The types of leader behaviour needed to achieve high levels of group performance under favourable conditions are not the same as the types of behaviour needed to achieve group performance under unfavourable conditions. Fiedler argued that appropriate leader behaviour can be obtained by choosing a leader with a LPC score that matches the situation.

Given the way in which the theory is clearly specified, it is readily testable. Fiedler's theory characterized leaders through reference to attitudes of personality traits (least preferred co-worker), but explained the effectiveness of leaders through reference to their behaviours. Fiedler assumed quite reasonably that leaders with a certain trait (high or low LPC) will behave in a particular fashion. Fiedler's theory is considered by

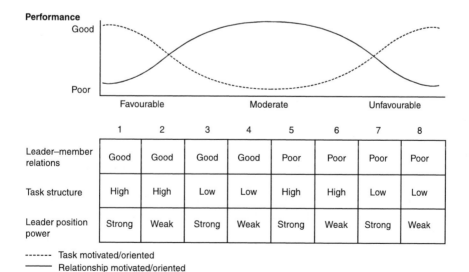

	Favourable			Moderate			Unfavourable	
	1	2	3	4	5	6	7	8
Leader–member relations	Good	Good	Good	Good	Poor	Poor	Poor	Poor
Task structure	High	High	Low	Low	High	High	Low	Low
Leader position power	Strong	Weak	Strong	Weak	Strong	Weak	Strong	Weak

------- Task motivated/oriented
——— Relationship motivated/oriented

Figure 12.2 Fiedler's contingency model leader–situation matches.

many to be a "black box" theory of leadership, because it describes the elements that enter a "box" (attitudes towards others) and shows the product that leaves the box (leader effectiveness). What is unclear, however, is the process inside the box, which transformed the original components into the final product. In the case of Fiedler's theory, what is missing is the explanation of *how* attitudes determine effectiveness through behaviour.

Most of the problems with Fiedler's theory are to do with the LPC measure. It is unclear what construct this scale really measures. Evans & Dermer (1974) believed the scale more readily measures dogmatism than cognitive complexity. Shiflett (1973) questioned the adequacy of the cut-off point, which supposedly separates high from low LPC scores. That is, when you divide a continuous variable (LPC scores) into two groups (high and low), you must have a highly sensitive scale that permits such a split to occur. Although Fiedler's theory addresses only high and low LPC scores, some researchers have trichotomized LPC scores into high, middle and low. Kennedy (1982) found that middle LPC leaders were generally superior to both high and low LPC leaders in situations described by the model. He also found middle LPC leader performance to be largely independent of the situation factors that affect the perform-ance of high and low LPC leaders. The theory has, it seems, been let down by the measure.

Fiedler's theory has contributed a great deal to the field of leadership research. It has pointed research in new directions. Some researchers have proposed additional factors that contribute to situational favourability. Others modified the LPC scale, and yet other studies proposed new approaches to classifying situations. But the theory has been a catalyst for leadership researchers, who now believe leader effectiveness is a contingent phenomenon. Ultimately, the efficacy of the theory depends not only on the sensitivity and robustness of the rather simplistic LPC measure but also on whether the three-dimensional features associated with situational favourability are the most salient.

Another situational approach has been that of House & Mitchell (1974), who con-ceived of *path–goal theory*. According to path–goal theory, different kinds of leadership are appropriate for different kinds of situations. This stresses yet again the familiar concept of fit (between leader and situation). Self-evidently, if a leader is supervising experienced employees who work on a highly structured assembly line, the leader does not need to spend much time telling the workers how to do their jobs; they already know how to. Leader behaviours must also match the characteristics of those being led. The leadership style that motivates employees with strong needs for autonomy, for example, is different from the style necessary to motivate and satisfy employees with weaker needs for autonomy.

The challenge facing leaders is thus twofold: they must analyse situations and iden-tify the most appropriate leadership style, and they must develop the capacity to be flexible enough to use different leadership styles as appropriate. The extent to which leadership behaviour matches situational factors will determine the level of subordinate motivation, satisfaction and performance. House & Mitchell (1974) identified four leadership styles (see Table 12.5):

- *Directive*: the leader directs, and there is no subordinate participation in decision-making.
- *Supportive*: the leader is friendly and is interested in subordinates as people.

Table 12.5 Effective leadership styles under different conditions

Sample situational characteristics	Leadership styles			
	Directive	*Supportive*	*Achievement*	*Participative*
Task				
Structured	No	Yes	Yes	Yes
Unstructured	Yes	No	Yes	No
Clear goals	No	Yes	No	Yes
Ambiguous goals	Yes	No	Yes	No
Subordinates				
Skilled in task	No	Yes	Yes	Yes
Unskilled in task	Yes	No	Yes	No
High achievement needs	No	No	Yes	No
High social needs	No	Yes	No	Yes
Formal authority				
Extensive	No	Yes	Yes	Yes
Limited	Yes	Yes	Yes	Yes
Workgroup				
Strong social network	Yes	No	Yes	Yes
Experienced in collaboration	No	No	No	Yes
Organizational culture				
Supports participation	No	No	No	Yes
Achievement-orientated	No	No	Yes	No

Source: Reproduced from Gordon (1993) with the permission of Prentice-Hall, Inc.

- *Participative*: the leader asks for, receives and uses suggestions from subordinates to make decisions.
- *Achievement-orientated*: the leader sets challenging goals for subordinates and shows confidence that they can achieve the goals.

The path–goal theory, unlike Fiedler's theory, suggests that these four styles are used by the same leader in different situations (House & Mitchell, 1974).

Path–goal theory is fairly similar to Holland's (1973) theory of vocational preference (see pp. 119–126). Both are fit models and both attempt to define very few style variables that can account for both person and situation variables. Certainly, the "commonsensical" nature of this theory makes it look attractive, but the rather simplistic styles mean that it is unlikely to account for all the many variations in leadership styles observed.

Gordon (1993) has attempted a description of situations in which each type of leadership style is likely to result in positive, desirable outcomes (Table 12.5). What is most helpful about tables such as this is that, if one can describe the characteristics of the situation requiring leadership, one may be able to predict which style is likely to be most effective. However, it remains important to collect empirical evidence to support Table 12.5.

The important key in this theory is the way the leader affects the "paths" between subordinate behaviour and goals. In a sense, the leader is the coach who charts out realistic paths for the team. The leader can affect the paths by:

- recognizing and stimulating subordinates' needs for rewards over which the leader has some control;
- rewarding goal achievement;
- supporting subordinates' efforts to achieve the goal;
- helping reduce frustrating barriers to achieving goals;
- increasing the opportunities for personal satisfaction for subordinates.

Basically, the leader attempts to help the subordinate find the best path, to set challenging goals, and to remove stressful barriers along the way.

Since the path–goal theory was proposed, there have been a few studies testing its assumptions. House & Mitchell (1974) stress that the type of leadership needed to enhance organizational effectiveness is contingent on the situation in which a leader is placed. A leader may, therefore, be effective in one situation but quite ineffective in another. Whereas Fiedler (1967) argues that a leader's trait (LPC) determines whether leader and situation produce a healthy match, House & Mitchell focus on the observable behaviour of the leader. Also, whereas Fiedler feels that the situation must fit the leader, House & Mitchell believe that healthy leader–situation matches can be obtained either by matching the situation to the leader or by modifying the behaviour of the leader to fit the situation.

A third influential situational–leadership theory is offered by Vroom & Yetton (1973):

> Their theory attempts to identify the appropriate leadership style for a given set of circumstances or situations. Five leadership styles are suggested by the Vroom & Yetton theory:
>
> A-I   The leader solves the problems or reaches a decision using available information.
>
> A-II The leader obtains the information from followers, then decides on the solution to the problem. The leader may or may not inform followers what the problem is in acquiring information from them. The role of followers is to supply information.
>
> C-I   The leader shares the problem with subordinates individually, getting their ideas and suggestions without bringing them together as a group. The leader makes the decisions, which may or may not reflect followers' influence.
>
> C-II The leader shares problems with subordinates as a group, obtaining their ideas and suggestions. The leader then makes a decision that may or may not reflect followers' influence.
>
> G-II The leader shares a problem with followers as a group. Together the group generates and evaluates alternatives and attempts to reach consensus on a solution. The leader acts as a chairperson. The solution that has the support of the entire group is accepted and implemented.

The letters in the code identify the leadership practice: A stands for autocratic, C stands for consultative, and G stands for group. The appropriate style of leadership (A-I; A-II; C-I; C-II; G-II) depends on seven attributes of the problem situation. The attributes, along with diagnostic questions, are shown in [Table 12.6]. The leader, if interested in, say, the importance of the quality of a decision (the first problem attribute), could ask

Table 12.6 Problem attributes and diagnostic questions developed by Vroom & Yetton

Problem attributes	Diagnostic questions
A	The importance of the quality of the decision.	Is there a quality requirement such that one solution is likely to be more rational than others?
B	The extent to which the leader possesses sufficient information/expertise to make a high-quality decision.	Do I have sufficient information to make a high-quality decision?
C	The extent to which the problem is structured.	Is the problem structured?
D	The extent to which acceptance or commitment on the part of subordinates is critical to the effective implementation of the decision.	Is acceptance of my decision by subordinates critical to effective implementation?
E	The probability that the leader's autocratic decision will receive acceptance by subordinates.	If I were to make the decision by myself, is it reasonably certain that it would be accepted by my subordinates?
F	The extent to which the subordinates are motivated to attain the organizational goals which are represented in the objectives explicit in the statement of the problem.	Do subordinates share the organizational goals to be obtained in solving the problem?
G	The extent to which subordinates are likely to be in conflict over preferred solutions.	Is conflict among subordinates likely to affect the preferred solution?

Source: Reproduced from Donnelly *et al.* (1987) with the permission of Irwin (BPI), a member of the McGraw-Hill Companies.

himself or herself the diagnostic question: "Is there a quality requirement such that one solution is more likely to be rational than another?" (Donnelly, Gibson, & Ivancevich, 1987: 394–395)

Vroom & Jago (1988) then proposed some key features of problem situations that leaders should consider:

- *Quality requirements*: how important is it that a good decision is made?
- *Commitment requirement*: how important is it that subordinates feel committed to the decision?
- *Leader information*: does the leader have enough information to make a high-quality decision?
- *Problem structure*: is it clear what the current situation is, what one wants to achieve, and what alternative paths to the goal are available?
- *Commitment probability*: if the leader alone made the decision, would the subordinates feel committed to the decision?
- *Goal congruence*: do subordinates share the organization's goals in solving this problem?
- *Subordinate conflict*: is conflict likely among subordinates concerning which solution is best?
- *Subordinate information*: do subordinates have enough information to make a good decision?
- *Time constraint*: is time too short to involve subordinates in decision-making?

- *Geographical dispersion*: would it be too expensive to bring together geographically dispersed subordinates?

Vroom & Jago (1988) believe two further factors are relevant: the importance to the leader of minimizing decision time and of maximizing opportunities for subordinate development.

Arnold, Robertson & Cooper (1995: 297) have noted that in Vroom & Yetton's (1973) original model, the first seven questions required only a "yes" or "no" answer for any given decision situation. According to the answer, a path was traced through a decision tree, and the optimal leader style (or styles) was specified. In many cases, more than one style was considered optimal. Vroom & Jago's (1988) model increased the number of questions to reflect more aspects of the situation, and also required responses to most questions to be made on a 5-point scale rather than a simple "yes" or "no". Furthermore, by using some mathematical formulae, the one best style for any given decision problem can be specified.

The revised model is more complex and supposedly more sensitive to situational differences. Computer software has been developed that allows people to input their answers to the questions listed above, and then to calculate an overall "suitability score" for each possible style. However, there are general rules of thumb governing the use of the leader styles. First, where subordinates' commitment is important, more participative styles are better. Second, where the leader needs more information, A-I should be avoided. Third, where subordinates do not share organizational goals, G-II should be avoided. Finally, where both problem structure and leader information are low, C-II and G-II tend to be best. However, it should be apparent that, in some cases, other factors such as time constraints or staff development needs can override these rules of thumb (Arnold *et al.*, 1995: 297).

Vroom & Yetton's original model has received some research support (Crouch & Yetton, 1987). However, the skill with which leaders put their style into action was at least as important as choosing a style deemed to be appropriate in the first place (Tjosvold, 1986). Vroom & Jago's new model has yet to receive the same examination, but looks promising.

Vroom & Yetton's approach is important for several reasons. First, it is widely respected among researchers in leadership behaviour. Second, the authors believe that leaders have the ability to vary their styles to fit the situation. This point is critical to acceptance of situational approaches to leadership. A third reason is that they believe that people can be developed into more effective leaders. Donnelly *et al.* (1987: 397) have compared and contrasted these theories (Table 12.7).

Yukl (1980) also provided a summary of how leaders are (or should be) influenced by the situation in which they find themselves. His conclusions were effectively sixfold, few of which are counter-intuitive:

- The lower managers are in the hierarchy, the less likely they are to use participative leadership and the more likely they are to focus on technical matters and to monitor subordinate performance.
- Managers of production functions will be more autocratic and less participative than sales or staff managers. The most participative are likely to be managers of staff specialists such as lawyers, personnel and engineers.

Table 12.7 Comparing three situational theories

Points of comparison	Contingency theory (Fiedler)	Path–goal theory (House)	Vroom & Yetton theory
1. Theme	No best style. Leader success determined by the interaction of environment and leader personality variables.	Most successful leaders are those who increase subordinate motivation by charting out and clarifying paths to effective performance.	Successful leadership style varies with the situation. Leader can learn how to recognize the requirements of the situation and how to fit style to meet these requirements.
2. Leadership styles (range of choices)	Autocratic or democratic.	Instrumental to achievement.	Autocratic to participative.
3. Research base (number of supportive studies)	Large, in many settings: military, educational, industrial. Some contradictory results.	Moderate to low, generally supportive.	Low but increasing, generally supportive.
4. Application value for managers	Moderate to low: leaders can't generally be trained.	Moderate.	High: leaders can be trained.

Source: Reproduced from Donnelly *et al.* (1987) with the permission of Irwin (BPI), a member of the McGraw-Hill Companies.

- Leaders are more directive and less participative as the task becomes more structured. This occurs because directive and autocratic behaviour is easier to exercise on tasks for which one knows the answers. On more complex and less structured tasks (e.g. creative), leaders will need to depend more on subordinates to determine the best way to perform the work.
- Leaders are less participative and more autocratic as the number of their followers increases. With increased size of the group, leaders are also less likely to show consideration or support for followers.
- As the stress of the situation increases (time constraints, hostile environment), the leader becomes more directive and task-orientated and less considerate.
- As subordinate performance and competence decline, leaders are more likely to react with increasingly close, directive, punishing and structuring behaviour, and less consideration and participation.

Aditya, House & Kerr (2000) pointed out other contingency theories. One was Hersey & Blanchard's (1982) *situational leadership theory*, which is based on the maturity of the leader–follower relationship. Thus leaders have to move from a letting to a selling to a participating to a delegating style depending on their relationship. Another salient theory is Fiedler's *cognitive resource theory*, which stresses the interaction between leadership traits and situational factors. Under high stress conditions, intelligence is negatively and experience is positively related to performance, whereas the opposite is true under low stress conditions.

Transformational, charismatic and visionary leadership

The fourth and most recent trend centres around the notion of the *transformational* leader (Bass, 1985; Conger, 1989; Titchy & Devanna, 1986), which is contrasted with the *transactional* leader. Transactional leaders assume that they can only achieve leadership and get subordinates to follow what they want by offering some sort of exchange. Subordinates will follow a leader if he or she is able to offer something to them that they value or need. Leadership is therefore a transaction whereby subordinates submit to the requests of the leader and follow his or her demands in return for something. Transformational leaders, on the other hand, supposedly use charisma to energize and motivate people to perform beyond their original expectations. They do this by:

- raising their awareness about certain key outcomes or processes;
- getting them to place team or organizational goals and interests above their own;
- having them adjust their need levels so that they have a stronger drive for responsibility, challenge and personal growth (Bass, 1985).

What distinguishes exceptional or exemplary transformational leaders? Various researchers have attempted to pinpoint specific features by studying those leaders they have identified as superior, although it is not clear how this is specified or measured. If, by definition, leadership is situation-specific, or a function of interaction between situational variables, it would appear that any identification of particular individual leader characteristics may be unreliable. If, however, the level of abstraction of description is very high, different studies may be superficially similar. Consider the following.

Kouzes & Posner (1988) have identified specific attitudes and behaviours that outstanding leaders have in common. Exemplary leaders share the following five *behavioural practices* and ten *commitments*:

- Exemplary leaders *challenge the process*. They are pioneers; they seek out new opportunities and are willing to change the *status quo*. They innovate, experiment and explore ways to improve their organizations. Such leaders view mistakes as learning experiences and are prepared to meet any challenges that confront them. Challenging the process requires two leader commitments: to search for opportunities and to experiment and take risks.
- Exemplary leaders *inspire a shared vision*. They look towards and beyond the horizon. They envisage the future with a positive and hopeful outlook. Exemplary leaders are expressive; their genuine natures and communication skills attract followers. They show others how mutual interest can be met through commitment to a common purpose. Inspiring a shared vision requires leaders to commit to envisioning the future and enlisting the support of others.
- Exemplary leaders *enable others to act*. They instill followers with spirit-nurturing relationships based on mutual trust. Exemplary leaders stress collaborative goals. They actively involve others in planning and permit others to make their own decisions. These leaders make sure that their followers feel strong and capable. Enabling others to act requires two leader commitments: fostering collaboration and strengthening others.
- Exemplary leaders *model the way*. They are clear about their values and beliefs. Exemplary leaders keep people and projects on course by consistently behaving

according to these values and by modelling the behaviour that they expect from others. They plan thoroughly and divide projects into achievable steps, thus creating opportunities for small wins. Through their focus on key priorities, such leaders make it easier for others to achieve goals. To model the way requires leaders to commit to setting an example and to planning small wins.

- Exemplary leaders *encourage the heart*. They encourage people to persist in their efforts by recognizing accomplishments and contributions to the organization's vision. They let others know that their efforts are appreciated and they express pride in their team's accomplishments. Exemplary leaders find ways to celebrate achievements. They nurture team spirit, which enables people to sustain continued efforts. Encouraging the heart requires leaders to be committed to recognizing contributions and celebrating accomplishments.

Kinlaw (1989) identified six characteristics of "superior" leaders:

- *Establishing a vision*. Superior leaders create expectations for significant and lasting achievements. They give meaning to work by associating even menial tasks with valued goals.
- *Stimulating people to gain new competencies*. Superior leaders stimulate people to stretch their minds and their skills. They freely share their own expertise and keep people in touch with new resources.
- *Helping people to overcome obstacles*. Superior leaders help others to overcome obstacles. They help others to find the courage and strength to persevere in the face of even the greatest difficulties.
- *Helping people to overcome failure*. Superior leaders help people to cope with failure and disappointment. They are quick to offer new opportunities to people who have failed.
- *Leading by example*. Superior leaders are models of integrity and hard work. They set the highest expectations for themselves and others.
- *Including others in their success*. Superior leaders are quick to share the limelight with others. People associated with superior leaders feel as successful as the leaders.

Furnham (2000a) emphasized the role of courage in leaders. He differentiated between three types of courage: the *interpersonal courage* that is displayed when doing such things as confronting under-performers; the *courage to fail* by taking well-calculated risks in doing something new and innovative; and *moral courage* to assert and do that which is right, ethically, morally and legally.

Bass, Avolio, Jung & Benson (2003) noted the essential features of transformational leadership:

> *Idealised influence*: These leaders are admired, respected, and trusted. Followers identify with and want to emulate their leaders. Among the things the leader does to earn credit with followers is to consider followers' needs over his or her own needs. The leader shares risks with followers and is consistent in conduct with underlying ethics, principles, and values.

> *Inspirational motivation*: Leaders behave in ways that motivate those around them by providing meaning and challenge to their followers' work. Individual and team spirit is aroused. Enthusiasm and optimism are displayed. The leader encourages

followers to envision attractive future states, which they can ultimately envision for themselves.

Intellectual stimulation: Leaders stimulate their followers' effort to be innovative and creative by questioning assumptions, reframing problems, and approaching old situations in new ways. There is no ridicule or public criticism of individual members' mistakes. New ideas and creative solutions to problems are solicited from followers, who are included in the process of addressing problems and finding solutions.

Individualised consideration: Leaders pay attention to each individual's need for achievement and growth by acting as a coach or mentor. Followers are developed to successively higher levels of potential. New learning opportunities are created along with a supportive climate in which to grow. Individual differences in terms of needs and desires are recognized. (Bass *et al.*, 2003: 208).

Bass *et al.* (2003) found that both transformational and transactional leadership styles predicted military unit performance. Kirk, Shamir & Chen (2003) tried to resolve an interesting paradox in the transformational leadership literature – that this leadership style leads to both dependence on the leader as well as independence (growth and empowerment). They were able to resolve the conflict by stating that two mediating variables predict different outcomes. The more the leader encourages personal identification with the follower, the more likely dependence, but the more likely he or she encourages social identification with the work group, the more independence is likely to result.

The work on charismatic, inspirational and transformational leadership represents a step in the direction of taking these concepts out of the realm of the mystical and into a form that can be used to improve organizational leadership. In theory, training programmes can teach charismatic skills, which include instruction in modelling (the use of exemplary behaviour), appearance, body language and verbal skills (with an emphasis on rhetoric), metaphors, analogies and para-language (word intent). Leaders can be taught how to express confidence in subordinates, the use of participative leadership, ways of providing autonomy from bureaucratic restraints, and goal-setting techniques. To teach managers how to envision and to be more inspirational, exercises often require executives to talk about how they expect to spend their day at some future date, say five years hence, or what they expect their organization to look like at some future date. They may even be asked to write a paper about how they see or hope to influence their organization's future. Whether training can actually allow an organization to develop its own charismatic, inspirational or transformational leaders is open to question. Some, because of their individual characteristics (personality, ability), simply cannot effectively adopt these styles. There is also a danger of manufacturing actors who lack values, vision and ideas, but can "manipulate" followers.

Still others have focused on managerial expectations. Livingstone (1989) asserted that leaders who have confidence in their ability to develop followers to high levels of performance will expect much of those followers and will treat them in a manner which displays confidence that their expectations will be met. On the other hand, managers who have doubts about their ability to stimulate employees will expect less of their employees and will treat them in a manner that reveals this lack of confidence.

Hence, those who follow the Pygmalian effect theory (or the concept of self-fulfilling prophecies) in management stress the following five points:

- Leaders should have belief in their ability to develop the potential of their followers, to provide the appropriate amounts of direction and support that the followers need to be successful.
- Leaders should be able to establish and communicate goals that are challenging, realistic and attainable. Goals that are neither too easy nor too difficult are optimally motivating.
- Leaders should have positive assumptions about the potential of others – an ability to see them as winners. Such leaders are not discouraged by current appearances.
- Leaders should have a commitment to excellence and a genuine, intense enthusiasm for what they do. Positive involvement, commitment and intensity are contagious.
- Leaders should focus on the human aspect of the task as well as on procedures, conceptual frameworks and technology. The human aspect is the one that leads to improvement.

More recently, Conger & Kanungo (1987) distinguished between ordinary and charismatic leaders. They did so by specifying ten dimensions and then describing how the two types of leaders differ (Table 12.8).

Interesting and richly descriptive although this approach is, it explains neither the aetiology (where the differences come from) nor the process (how behaviours lead to consequences) of these two types. Historically this may be seen as a mixture of the trait and behavioural approaches with some of their limitations. Although this attempt to differentiate between "good" and "bad" leaders is descriptively useful and interesting, it does not tell us how many there are of this type, or much about the average leader.

New approaches to leadership

Because this area of research is of intense interest to both theoreticians and practitioners, new theories of leadership are constantly developed. These are not always radical new theories as such, but tend to focus on rather different aspects. Muchinsky (1990) has nominated three new theories:

- *Cognitive-resource utilization theory*, which stresses that leaders have two sources of competence, namely prior experience and intelligence. Typically, when stressed, leaders rely on the former rather than the latter and hence they under-utilize their cognitive resources. The theory stresses under what situational conditions it is more efficient to rely on experience versus intelligence. It also naturally assumes that both are crucially important. However, they are likely to be related, as the latter (intelligence) may dictate the quality, quantity and memorability of the former.
- *Implicit leadership theory*, which is fairly radical because it assumes that leadership is almost entirely "in the eye of the beholder", that is, constructed. Thus, what is good, effective and efficient in a leader is determined not by an objective measure but rather by perceptions and expectations of followers. Here, concepts such as reputation count more than objective and measurable outcomes. In this sense, leaders cannot be selected or trained, but only "made" by others.

Table 12.8 Behavioural characteristics of charismatic and non-charismatic leaders

	Non-charismatic leaders	*Charismatic leaders*
Relation to *status quo*	Essentially agrees with *status quo* and strives to maintain it.	Essentially opposed to *status quo* and strives to change it.
Future goal	Goal not too discrepant from *status quo.*	Idealized vision which is highly discrepant from *status quo.*
Likeableness	Shared perspective makes him or her likeable.	Shared perspective and idealized vision makes him or her a likeable and honourable hero worthy of identification and imitation.
Trustworthiness	Disinterested advocacy in persuasion attempts.	Disinterested advocacy by incurring great personal risk and cost.
Expertise	Expert in using available means to achieve goals within framework of the existing order.	Expert in using unconventional means to transcend the existing order.
Behaviour	Conventional, conforming to existing norms.	Unconventional or counter-normative.
Environmental	Low need for environmental sensitivity to maintain *status quo.*	High need for environmental sensitivity for changing the *status quo.*
Articulation	Weak articulation of goals and motivation to lead.	Strong articulation of future vision and motivation to lead.
Power base	Position power and personal power (based on reward, expertise and liking for a friend who is a similar other).	Personal power (based on expertise, respect and admiration for a unique hero).
Leader–follower relationship	Egalitarian, consensus-seeking, or directive. Nudges or orders people to share his or her views.	Elitist, entrepreneur and exemplary. Transforms people to share the radical changes advocated.

Source: Modified from Conger & Kanungo (1987: 641).

- *Substitute theory* is even more radical, because it suggests that various other factors can substitute for leaders. If leaders supply guidance, recognition and support, it could well be that these may be found in other solutions such as egalitarian work-teams, the members of which together perform this function. Sometimes the structure of the job or the technology provides all the self-leadership that is necessary.

Other contemporary theories nominated by Aditya *et al.* (2000) include:

- *Leader-member exchange theory*: a theory that is based on the idea that some followers become trusted members of an "in-group", with the concomitant respect and latitude, while others remain "out-group" members who are treated quite differently.
- *Neo-charismatic theories*: theories that focus on how extraordinary leaders achieve outstanding results through follower motivation, commitment, loyalty and respect. These charismatic leaders have powerfully attractive visions of the future and an ability to mobilize the emotions of their followers.

- *Value-based leadership*: this stresses that under uncertain and ambiguous situations, self-confident leaders who are apparently motivated by strong values do well.

Finally, Spector (2003) has considered the limited research on gender and leadership. A question that needs to be asked is why women are usually under-represented in high-level leadership positions in most organizations. Various concepts like the glass ceiling have been mentioned, as well as differences in men's and women's abilities, attitudes and career preparation approaches. There is also evidence of subtle stereotyping, which shows that men are more likely to be seen to have the characteristics necessary for good leadership. There is, however, some evidence that the natural leadership styles of men and women are rather different. Men tend to be more autocratic and less democratic than women. However, it is recognized that leadership style may be powerfully shaped by corporate cultures as well the demands of the particular leadership task and situation.

There will always be new theories in this area, some more serious than others. Some simply re-package ideas and concepts in more up-to-date language. Others, influenced by philosophical or sociopolitical trends (e.g. postmodernism), will try to interpret what has been written through the lens of this new trend. Still others will come up with some genuinely new, interesting and important theories that will provide insights and testable hypotheses. However, the very generality and complexity of the concept makes the whole process very difficult to capture in powerful, parsimonious theories.

Followership and mutual influence

Various studies have attempted to examine, from the follower perspective, which characteristics they most admire in their leaders. Perhaps the best-known study is that of Kouzes & Posner (1988), which found a clear rank-ordering. Employees were simply asked to rank-order, from the list of 20 traits, those that they would most admire in their possible manager/leader (Table 12.3). Although it is not surprising that the top five came where they did, many people express surprise about the last five. Note that less than a quarter of the managers rated ambition and loyalty as unimportant. Indeed, it is an important development to attempt to understand leadership through the experiences and behaviour of followers.

Dirks and Ferrin (2002) proposed a theoretical framework to examine the burgeoning concept of trust in leadership. They argued that trust in leaders (measured both affectively and cognitively) is determined by the leaders' actions and practices, attributes of the follower and the length of their relationship. However, this trust leads systematically to some very important outcomes, such as job performance and satisfaction, commitment, satisfaction with the leader, and the quality and quantity of exchange between the two.

Followers or subordinates have a crucial role to play in the whole leadership business. Leadership is merely the case of a two-way influence process. To some extent, subordinates "manage upwards" just as they are "managed downwards" by the leadership. Furthermore, every leader is him or herself managed by another and both a leader and a follower at the same time. Ideally, there is a comfortable "fit" between leaders and followers.

There is often tension between leaders and followers, and the latter have to resolve some fundamental dilemmas or conflicts, such as the following:

- *Alliance versus competition*: to view the leader as a trustworthy ally or as a competitor to be beaten
- *Clarifying expectations versus second-guessing*: to seek unambiguous explanations of what the leader wants or to risk misinterpretation about orders and expectations
- *Initiative versus dependence*: to suggest and promote ways to achieve the organization's goals and enhance one's own development or to wait for the leader to take the initiative
- *Competence versus inferiority*: to feel capable in one's work, given one's experience and training, or to feel inept and out of step with one's colleagues
- *Differentiation versus identification*: to feel very different from the leader in terms of skills, aspirations, values and professional concerns, or to identify with the leader as someone to emulate
- *Relating personality versus relating impersonally*: to view the leader as a fellow human, facing similar problems in managing family and career, and in developing friendships, or to view the leader's world as different and distant, and thus to relate to him or her on a utilitarian basis only
- *Mutual concern versus self-interest*: to keep the leader's welfare and development seriously in mind or to be totally preoccupied with one's own success
- *Integrity versus denial*: to accept the relationship with its limitations or to reject or misrepresent it.

To some extent, leadership–followership could be seen as a dimension rather than a distinction. Indeed, Tannenbaum & Schmidt (1958) suggested a scale from autocratic to participative leadership (see Figure 12.3).

De Cremer and van Knippenberg (2002) asked the important question: "How do leaders promote cooperation [among their followers]?" They isolated two crucial factors that they tested in three experimental studies. The first was *procedural fairness*, which they argue promoted respect and belongingness, and the second was *charismatic leadership*, which increases motivation. Their studies showed both factors were important and engender cooperation because they appeal to the relational concerns of their followers.

Sceptics may be tempted to pose the seemingly heretical question, "Does leadership matter?" That is, how important is the quality and type of leadership to group morale, organizational success or profitability? Does one need a special kind of influence for organizational success? Naturally, leaders are needed when organizations do not have rules or policies for each contingency, or when decisions have to be made about change. Yet all leaders only have limited latitude for their actions.

In many organizations, selection, promotion and succession policies regarding who achieves leadership positions lead to considerable homogeneity in styles and values. More importantly, a leader's performance is often strongly affected by external factors beyond his or her control. Some organizational factors neutralize leadership in the sense that they reduce the possibilities for influence. Equally, some organizations prefer substitutes for leadership through such concepts as self-managed teams.

Kerr & Jermier (1978) have attempted to specify certain circumstances that neutralize leaders. Where the subordinates or followers are able, experienced, knowledgeable, professional and indifferent to rewards, it is difficult to see what roles leaders could play. Equally, if this is clear, routine, intrinsically satisfying and provides its own feedback, the role of leaders is naturally reduced. Finally, if the organization has inflexible rules

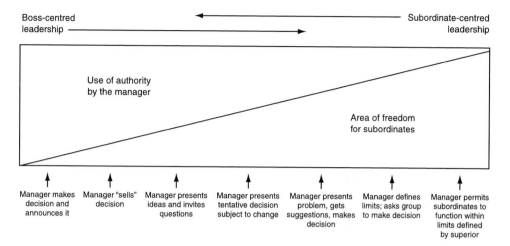

Boss-centred leadership — — — — Subordinate-centred leadership

Use of authority by the manager

Area of freedom for subordinates

| Manager makes decision and announces it | Manager "sells" decision | Manager presents ideas and invites questions | Manager presents tentative decision subject to change | Manager presents problem, gets suggestions, makes decision | Manager defines limits; asks group to make decision | Manager permits subordinates to function within limits defined by superior |

Figure 12.3 Leadership–behaviour continuum. Reproduced from Tannenbaum & Schmidt (1958) with the permission of the President and Fellows of Harvard College.

and procedures, or groups are very cohesive, or there is a significant geographical distance between leader and followers, leaders wield less power and influence.

Although organizational leadership is important, it may be that its influence can be overestimated.

Networking, negotiating and enabling

Hosking & Morley (1991) have argued persuasively that, in relation to leadership, indeed the whole of "management science", theories of the person and theories of the organization are kept artificially separate. They believe they must be combined and illustrate this by examining three leadership practices, as follows.

Networking

Networking is the process of building relationships within and between groups. It is necessary for leaders to understand the challenges they face and how to discriminate between important and less important information. Networking is the building of organizational intelligence, which requires relationships in which people are willing to be reasonably open and honest. Networking helps leaders and managers gather information for agenda-setting and implementation. Leaders are managers of meaning, and the sifting, interpretation and combination of information is crucial. In this sense, the quality of the network (in terms of the type and nature of information supplied) is more important than its size.

Networking can be formal and informal, in work and outside of work. Because it helps leaders to understand different points of view, respect differences and understand issues, it is fundamental to the skilful leadership process. Networkers give as well as receive; they influence and promote their views and perspectives.

Negotiation

For some, negotiation is the essence of leadership itself. This is seen in a much wider context than in terms of simple industrial relations and bargaining. Rather, it is seen as the process leaders must go through with their followers in negotiating a shared view of what is important. Leaders need to reduce ambiguity, clarify communications and negotiate a shared commitment to group goals. Negotiation is dialogue and the exercise of acceptable influence.

Enabling

For leaders to support a culture of productivity, they need to encourage and enable others. They have to develop a strong cooperative context where differences are respected and individuals are developed and empowered. It is an ultimate aim of the enabling process that followers turn into leaders. People need to be taught to think for themselves and about the work and the needs of the organization. Each needs to develop a realistic appraisal of their potential and that of the workgroup and organization. For leaders, enabling means knowing the group and its issues, as well as establishing norms that support actively open-minded thinking. It also means that leaders need to handle the anxieties and dilemmas of group life.

The word "enabling" is nearly synonymous with the new term "empowerment", which is viewed as something leaders do by changing or transforming the motives and goals of followers. Leaders supposedly enable people to help themselves and take responsibility for their own learning. The aim is to move away from the culture of dependency. Yet Hosking & Morley (1991: 259) insist that enabling is an organizational process concerned with the interdependence of social relationships:

> Enabling is about helping others to help themselves with respect to their own relational setting. It is about enabling others in relation to their own valuation and projects, and not with respect to the goals of a leader. Talk of power equalization is just another version of managerialism unless participants are helped to construct the valuational basis of their activities and relationships.

Emerging issues and areas

Avolio *et al.* (2003) have identified important (but often long-standing) issues for future theory and research. The first is the old *born/made* distinction because of its implications for the efficacy, indeed possibility, of leadership development and training. The issue is can leaders be developed (i.e. through self-awareness) or leadership taught. The fad for 360° feedback systems suggests people still believe leader development is necessary, desirable and hopefully cost-effective. The question remains as to the best way to train good leaders.

A second big area is to examine *leadership across cultures*: how different cultures, values and practices moderate or mediate the relationship between leaders and followers. The question here is how and by what process different cultures define leadership differently and their varied expectations of the role of leaders.

Third, because of changes in advanced information technology, there is an emerging interest in *e-leadership*, which is about how leaders utilize technology to maximize the speed of information processing, communication and decision-making. Avolio *et al.* conclude:

> In sum, now where hierarchies are less clear, more leaders will likely emerge without position power. How leaders acquire, utilise, distribute, and replenish their influence and power is even more interesting today, given the seismic shift in organizations, the workforce, and the environmental context. How followers will play a role in the leadership dynamic may represent one of the most significant and important frontiers for research in the future. It is also likely that there will be far fewer followers and more leaders needing to figure out how to share leadership. Shared leadership also represents a new frontier for leadership researchers, especially shared leadership across time, distance, organizations, and cultures in the form of virtual teams. (Avolio *et al.*, 2003: 298)

Conclusion

Leadership is one of the most extensively investigated processes, yet there remains considerable controversy about how to define, investigate or conceptualize it. Some debates have been about the difference between leaders and managers, and others about the person or context of leadership. Various areas of investigation were specified, as were new themes in this literature.

This chapter looks at the major four approaches to leadership historically. The *trait* approach attempted to identify those characteristics of individual leaders that made them successful. Despite considerable efforts, ranging from detailed biographical studies to extensive (even exhaustive) psychological research, there remains no clear unambiguous evidence that certain traits, abilities or attitudes are good predictors of leadership in all circumstances.

The *behavioural* approach attempted to categorize leadership styles or types, of which the best known is the three-category authoritarian, democratic and *laissez-faire* model. By specifying various unrelated dimensions of leadership behaviour, it is possible for researchers to come up with various styles: traditionally four based on high/ low scores on two dimensions. Although these typologies are immediately recognizable, they are often insufficient to capture the full range of leadership styles adopted by people and they do not explain the process of leadership.

The *situational* approach has attracted most attention. By specifying situational or task factors (usually two or three), it is possible to examine leadership strategies in a range of different situations. The basic idea underlying this approach is that different situations call for different styles of leadership; hence it is seen as the first job of researchers in this area to categorize or taxonomize situations in terms of leadership styles required. Situational theories have been most popular over the past 20–30 years and some exist that stress rather different features of the situation. There is equivocal support for all of these in studies that have attempted to compare and contrast them for their explanatory power or veridicality. However, it is possible to compare and contrast them, and the three most popular are compared on four criteria, including the application value for managers.

The fourth approach has been to concentrate on exceptional leaders, sometimes called transformational or *charismatic*. Once again, different researchers have come up with different lists of practices (behaviours) that appear to be associated with these, although there is considerable overlap, even if the languages seem rather different. Although it is relatively straightforward to distinguish between charismatic and non-charismatic leaders, it is clearly much less easy to specify the aetiology (origin) or particular process that charismatic leaders use.

There are inevitably various "new" approaches to leadership, although it is not difficult to slot them into the above fourfold grouping. Perhaps one of the more interesting approaches is to examine what followers or subordinates most value in a leader.

The more recent managerial and work psychology literature has investigated very specific leadership practices, such as networking, negotiating, and enabling or empowering. These are fundamental leadership practices, but the way they are described has important implications for all leadership theory.

A research perspective

The competencies of leadership

What particular attributes does one need for a leadership position? Human resource specialists now prefer the term "competency". The popularity of the concept of competency is usually attributed to Richard Boyatzis's (1982) book, *The competent manager*. The concept of competency seemed to offer a fresh start by getting away from the muddle of traits versus motives. It also seemed to offer a neutral term that looked at work-related performance.

In his book, Boyatzis lists 19 different competencies and describes a programme of research conducted in a variety of different private and public sector organizations to discover competencies related to managerial effectiveness. The competencies included motives, traits, skills, self-image and knowledge. One method of identifying competencies was the "behavioural event interview" (similar to the critical incident technique). Unlike the usual critical incident study, incidents were obtained in interviews with managers pre-selected on the basis of effectiveness ratings. This sample included 253 managers at all levels of management, some rated low, some rated medium and some rated high in effectiveness. Incidents were classed into competency categories, with traits and skills being inferred from an analysis of behaviour in relation to the manager's intentions and the situation. The analysis of variance found nine competencies with a significant trend, such that the mean competency score was highest for effective managers and lowest for ineffective managers. These nine competencies were as follows:

- *Efficiency orientation*: Demonstrating concern for task objectives, higher inner work standards, and high achievement motivation, by behaviour such as setting challenging but realistic goals and deadlines, developing specific action plans, determining ways to overcome obstacles, organizing the work efficiently, and emphasizing performance when talking to others.
- *Concern with impact*: Demonstrating high need for power and concern for power symbols, by behaviour such as acting assertively, attempting to influence others, seeking high status positions, and expressing concern about the reputation of the organization's products and services.
- *Proactivity*: Demonstrating a strong belief in self-efficacy and internal locus of control, by behaviour such as initiating action rather than waiting for things to happen, taking steps to circumvent obstacles, seeking information from a variety of sources, and accepting responsibility for success or failure.
- *Self-confidence*: Demonstrating belief in one's own ideas and ability, by behaviour such as taking decisive action rather than hesitating or vacillating, and making proposals in a firm, unhesitant manner, with appropriate poise, bearing and gestures.
- *Oral presentation*: Ability to use symbolic, verbal and non-verbal behaviour and visual aids to make clear and convincing presentations to others.

- *Conceptualization*: Ability to identify patterns or relationships in information and events (inductive reasoning), and to convey the meaning by developing a concept, model or theme, or by using appropriate metaphor and analogy; also the ability to develop creative solutions and new insights into problems.
- *Diagnostic use of concepts*: Deductive reasoning, using a concept or model to interpret events, analyse situations, distinguish between relevant and irrelevant information, and deter deviations from plans.
- *Use of socialized power*: Ability to develop networks and coalitions, gain cooperation from others, resolve conflicts in a constructive manner, and use role modelling to influence others.
- *Managing group process*: Ability to manage group processes to build member identification and team spirit, by behaviour such as creating symbols of group identity, emphasizing common interests and need for collaboration and providing public recognition of member contributions.

In summary, competencies were inferred from descriptions of effective and ineffective behaviour, based on incidents distinguishing between more effective and less effective managers. The competencies included motives, personality traits, cognitive skills and interpersonal skills. In general, the findings are remarkably similar to those from earlier trait studies using different research methods. Boyatzis did not undertake any formal analysis of the competencies needed by human resource managers. However, he does refer to functional differences between manufacturing, marketing and personnel. The sample size for personnel was very small ($n = 38$), and limited performance data are reported. Of Boyatzis's 19 competencies, 10 show some relationship with performance. Yukl (1980) provides definitions of the nine he found to show a significant trend (see the list above). The tenth is:

- *Perceptual objectivity*: Demonstrating objectivity, not being limited in view by excessive subjectivity or personal bias, prejudices or perspectives, able to view an event from multiple perspectives simultaneously, able to distance oneself emotionally and to minimize personal projection.

Boyatzis sought criterion evidence at three levels (his invention):

- *Skill*: criterion data were drawn from the behavioural event interview, which is a variant of the critical incident technique. It is an "unusual" criterion measure. The interviews were conducted with three performance groups of poor, average and superior.
- *Trait/motive*: criterion data were drawn from a McBer-developed test, Picture Story Exercise, which is a variant on Murray's Thematic Apperception Test. Kolb's Learning Style Inventory was also used.
- *Social role*: the criterion data were a brainstormed list of characteristics that were used together with Primoff's Job Element Form to determine the extent to which the element distinguished between the three performance levels.

Only skill-level data are reported and those are only descriptive of function differences, not of performance differences by function. Many investigators have attempted to devise a definitive list of skills or competencies. Research in this field is very limited, but Ulrich, Brockbank & Yeung (1989: 34) reviewed the available literature and made some very useful points. They believe that human resource competencies at the highest level can be described as compromising three overlapping, higher-order sets:

- *Knowledge of the business world*: that is, understanding the financial, strategic and technological capabilities of the organization.

- *Delivery of traditional human resource practices*: the delivery of those practices usually associated with the human resource function.
- *Management of change processes*: the extent to which the human resource function is able to increase an organization's ability to change through creating meaning, problem-solving, innovation, transformation and role influence.

As part of their research, Ulrich *et al.* (1989) identified:

- 10 knowledge of business activities related to competencies;
- 21 human resource practices under six headings: staffing, development, performance appraisal, reward, communication and organizational design;
- 30 practices that relate to the management of change.

Thus, in total, they identified 67 behaviours under the 34 supracompetency areas, based on their research using 91 companies and 10,000 individuals. Their research led them to several important conclusions. First, human resource practices and competencies vary by industry. Industry conditions set the *criteria* for the ways that human resource practices should be delivered. Second, the most competent human resource professionals work in businesses that deliver *both* operational and strategic human resource practices. This may be because they have to be flexible and adaptable. Finally, the more successful human resource professionals are those who tend to concentrate on the business, rather than on an employee-advocate role.

This research warrants replication.

A cross-cultural perspective

Westwood & Chan (1993: 123) present a Southeast Asian perspective on leadership:

> Leadership is an imported construct from the West. In Western cultures with a high value on individualism, the urge to stand out as a leader among a group becomes a natural and widely accepted notion. Southeast Asian societies are more collectivist, and there are other cultural values that push superior–subordinate relationships more towards a type of relationship that is better described as headship. The typical categories of leadership style and behaviours that we find in the Western tradition may not be applicable. Indeed, the rather simple dimensions and categories used in the West, such as concern for people, concern for production, or democratic, autocratic, *laissez-faire*, may not be subtle or rich enough to portray the complexities of styles and behaviours exhibited by the Southeast Asian manager/leader.

They began with the distinction between leadership and headship. Headship has been described as being imposed on the followers, whereas leadership is accorded by the followers to the leader. Under headship, the person who is head has achieved that status through some means outside of the leader–led relationship (e.g. inheritance) and has a perceived right to "head" the group and to determine what the group does. A "leader" must exhibit qualities or behaviours that followers find credible, useful and appropriate, and which enable the conferring of leadership upon the leader. Further distinctions can be made:

- Headship is maintained through an organized system and not by fellow group members' spontaneous recognition of the individual's contribution to group progress.
- The group is chosen by head persons in line with their interests and is not internally determined by the group itself.
- In headship, there is little or no sense of shared feeling or joint action in pursuit of the given goal.

- In headship, there is a wide social gap between the group members and the head, who strives to maintain the social distance.
- The leader's authority is spontaneously accorded by fellow group members and particularly by followers. The authority of the head derives from some extra-group power which he has over the members of the group, who cannot meaningfully be called followers.

Westwood & Chan (1993) suggest that this description of headship is closer to the reality of the superior–subordinate relationships in many organizational contexts in Southeast Asia than Western notions of leadership style and behaviour. This is especially true for the large number of family-based, owner-managed enterprises. The owner-manager comes close to the notion of headship outlined above, although we might need to qualify some of the statements, especially the third. In the West, people who show themselves as capable of leadership or as possessing certain skills and qualities are made into leaders.

They present a sophisticated model with two basic requirements. One requirement is for order and compliance. To lead/head others, there needs to be some form of established order that structures the relationship between the leader/head and others. There must be some basis upon which the group will accept the leader/head and comply with his or her intentions. This is true of leadership situations anywhere. Second, there is a requirement for social harmony, even in the face of inequality in relationships. Southeast Asian culture stresses the importance of social harmony as a dominant and pervasive value. This applies as much, if not more so, to relations in a leadership situation.

Westwood & Chan (1993: 141) conclude:

> In the Southeast Asian case, there are two basic requirements in any leadership/headship situation: requirements for order and compliance and requirements for harmony. Requirements for order and compliance are met through traditional cultural values that support and legitimate natural hierarchies, acceptance of and defence to authority, and role conformity. Together this value system allows a leader to adopt an apparently autocratic style. But this is only half the story. The requirements for harmony are strong and pervasive throughout Southeast Asia, and leaders and managers must also work to maintain that. Superior–subordinate relations may be unequal but they are also characterized by mutual obligation and reciprocation. The leader must display "proper" behaviour, be considerate and human hearted, respect the "face" and dignity of the subordinate, and lead through moral character.
>
> The model for leadership is the father: strong and clear power but with a genuine and expected obligation to take care of the subordinate. The best description of the style of leadership that follows from the interrelationship of the two elements is paternalism. Paternalism gives rise to some specific orientations and behaviours and to certain leadership strategies and tactics that were discussed earlier in the chapter.
>
> Finally, we considered whether the more recent leadership approaches from the West, contingency theories, and transformational leadership models had any applicability in Southeast Asia. Although there are some loose affinities, neither approach really matches with the subtleties and complexities of leadership in the Southeast Asian context.

A human resources perspective

Leaders that derail

Many people remark that, when reading psychiatric manuals or diagnostic criteria, they often feel they recognize themselves or others. They may well be right. Consider the following, which is taken from a very well respected psychiatric manual. (DSM-IV-TR: published by the American Psychiatric Association). The APA consider the personality disorders. Personality disorders are not due to physiology and trauma, though they are often immune to treatment. It should be noted that the diagnostic criteria applied to these "disorders" are very strict – psychiatrists need clear, objective evidence that nearly all the behaviours specified under each type are there.

The personality disorders provide a good start for understanding a managerial madness. In this sense, some managers are genuinely mad – at least in the psychotic sense – and this accounts for their failure.

There are very important points to be made when looking at these personality disorders. It helps to explain why some organizations seem to select mad managers. Many of the predominant characteristics of the personality orders are, in moderation, often desirable in business. Narcissistic managers have plenty of self-esteem and can inspire confidence. The obsessive-compulsiveness of that disorder can be ideal for businesses that require careful checking or monitoring. Too little or too much of these traits can cause derailment.

Hogan and Hogan (2001) took the personality disorders, translated them into everyday language and described how they measured the "dark side" of the personality. His thesis is that there are both positive (strengths) and negative (shortcomings) facets of each of these disorders (Table 12.9). A limited amount of each can be a strength. However, too much is clearly a weakness. McCall (1999) had a similar idea, noting that competencies can have a darker side (Table 12.10).

The idea, then, is that any human characteristic – normal or pathological – can, in excess, be a weakness. There is no linear relationship between these characteristics and success or failure.

Table 12.9 Strengths and shortcomings of our derailment factors

Factor	Strengths	Shortcomings
1. Excitable	Empathy and concern	Emotional explosiveness
2. Sceptical	Social and political insight	Excessive suspicion
3. Cautious	Evaluates risks appropriately	Indecisiveness and risk-aversion
4. Reserved	Emotionally unflappable	Insensitive and poor communicator
5. Leisurely	Good social skills	Passive aggression
6. Bold	Courage and energy	Overbearing and manipulative
7. Mischievous	Unafraid of risk	Reckless and deceitful
8. Colourful	Celebrations and entertainment	Impulsive and distractible
9. Imaginative	Creativity and vision	Bad ideas
10. Diligent	Hard work and high standards	Micromanagement
11. Dutiful	Corporate citizenship	Indecisiveness

Table 12.10 Competencies and their dark side

Competency	Potential dark side
Team player	Not a risk taken, indecisiveness, lacks independent judgement
Customer-focused	Can't create breakthroughs, can't control costs, unrealistic, too conservative
Biased towards action	Reckless, dictatorial
Analytic thinker	Analysis paralysis, afraid to act, inclined to create large staffs
Has integrity	Holier than thou attitude, rigid, imposes personal standards on others, zealots
Innovative	Unrealistic, impractical, wastes time and money
Has global vision	Misses local markets, over-extended, unfocused
Good with people	Soft, can't make tough decisions, too easy on people

Most managers believe that one cannot get enough of some characteristics, such as intelligence, integrity and innovativeness, and they are sought out by selectors. They then become puzzled when their star managers derail.

Consider four of these disorders and how they are manifest at work:

Paranoid personality disorder

Distrust and suspicion of others at work. The motives of all sorts of colleagues and bosses are interpreted as malevolent, all the time. The "enemy" is both without and within.

1   They suspect without much evidence that others are exploiting, harming or deceiving them about almost everything, both at work and at home.
2   They are preoccupied with unjustified doubts about the loyalty or trustworthiness of sub-ordinates, customers, bosses, shareholders and so on, on both big and small matters.
3   They are reluctant to confide in others (peers at work) because of the fear that the information will be used against them, kept on file or used to sack them. They may even be wary of using email.
4   They read hidden or threatening meanings into most benign remarks or events from emails to coffee-room gossip, and they remember them. They are hypersensitive to criticism.
5   They persistently bear grudges against all sorts of people going back many years and can remember even the smallest slight.
6   They perceive attacks on their character or reputation that others don't see and are quick to react angrily or to counter-attack. They seem hyper-alert and sensitive.
7   They have recurrent suspicions, without justification, regarding fidelity of their sexual or business partners and can be pretty obsessed with sex.

Schizoid personality disorder

Here, managers seem detached from social relationships. They often have a restricted range of expression of emotions in interpersonal settings. They seem more emotionally flat rather than necessarily. They are thought of as "cold fish", unresponsive and desperately low in EQ (emotional intelligence quotient)

1   They neither desire nor enjoy close relationships at work, including being part of a family. They are never team players and hate the idea of being so.
2   They almost always choose solitary activities, feeling uncomfortable even at an informal gathering.
3   They have little, if any, interest in having sexual contact with others – perhaps not a bad thing at work.
4   They take pleasure in few, if any, activities. They seem joyless, passionless, emotionless.
5   They lack close friends or confidantes other than first-degree relatives. They are isolates at work but apparently not unhappy with their friendlessness.
6   They appear indifferent to the praise or criticism of others. Absolutely nothings seems to get them going.
7   They show emotional coldness, detachment, or flattened emotionality. The ultimate cold fish.

Histrionic personality disorder

These managers have excessive emotionality and attention seeking. They are the "drama queens" of the business world.

1   Most are uncomfortable in situations in which they are not the centre of attention and try always to be so. They delight in making a drama out of a crisis.

2   Their interaction with others is often characterized by inappropriate sexually seductive or provocative behaviour. Needless to say, this causes more of a reaction in women than men.

3   They display rapidly shifting and shallow expression of emotions. They are difficult to read.

4   Most use physical appearance (clothes) to draw attention to self but this may include body piercing or tattooing. They certainly get a reputation in the office for their "unique apparel".

5   Many have a style of speech that is excessively impressionistic and lacking in detail.

6   They always exhibit self-dramatization, theatricality and exaggerated expression of emotion – usually negative. Even the dullest topic is imbued with drama.

7   They are easily influenced by others or circumstances – and therefore both unpredictable and persuadable.

8   Many consider relationships to be more intimate than they actually are. Being rather dramatic, they feel humdrum working relationships more intensely than others.

Narcissistic personality disorder

This manager is marked by grandiosity (in fantasy or behaviour), need for admiration, and lack of empathy. Self-centred, selfish, egotistical: they are everywhere in business – alas.

1   They have a grandiose sense of self-importance (e.g. exaggerated achievements and talents, expectation to be recognized as superior without commensurate achievements).

2   Most are preoccupied with fantasies of unlimited success, power, brilliance and money.

3   They believe that they are "special" and unique and can only be understood by, or should associate with, other special or high-status people (or institutions). They may try to "buy" themselves into exclusive circles.

4   They always require excessive admiration and respect from everyone at work.

5   Bizarrely, often they have a sense of entitlement, i.e. unreasonable expectations of especially favourable treatment or automatic compliance with their manifest needs.

6   Worse, they take advantage of others to achieve their own ends, which makes them terrible managers.

7   They lack empathy. All are unwilling to recognize or identify with the feelings and needs of others. They have desperately low EQ.

8   Curiously, they are often envious of others and believe that others are envious of them.

9   They show arrogant, haughty behaviours or attitudes all the time and everywhere at work (and home). At times this can be pretty amusing but is mostly simply frustrating.

Managers, initially thought of as high flyers, can easily fail and derail. This is partly because their weaknesses are overlooked but paradoxically because of the extreme nature of their strengths. Thus self-confidence becomes narcissism. Few organizations when selecting managers are concerned with "selecting out" those with problems like the well-established personality disorders. These dark side variables may initially serve leaders well but in the end often account for their derailment.

References

Aditya, R., House, R., & Kerr, S. (2000). Theory and practice of leadership. In C. Cooper & E. Locke (Eds.), *Industrial and organizational psychology* (pp. 131–165). Oxford: Blackwell.

Arnold, J., Robertson, I., & Cooper, C. (1995). *Work psychology: Understanding human behaviour in the workplace*. London: Pitman.

Avolio, B., Sosik, J., Jung, D., & Berson, Y. (2003). Leadership models, methods and applications. In W. Borman, D. Ilgen, & R. Klimoski, (Eds.), *Handbook of psychology* (Vol. 12, pp. 277–307). New York: Wiley.

Bass, B. (1985). *Leadership and performance beyond expectation*. New York: Free Press.

Bass, D., Avolio, B., Jung, O., & Benson, Y. (2003). Predicting unit performance by assessing transformational and transitional leadership, *Journal of Applied Psychology, 88*, 207–218.

Bennis, W. (1989). *On becoming a leader*. Menlo Park, CA: Addison-Wesley.

Blake, R., & Mouton, J. (1985). *The managerial grid*. Houston, TX: Gulf.

Blake, R., Mouton, J., Barnes, L., & Greiner, L. (1964). Breakthrough in organization development. *Harvard Business Review*, November/December, p. 136.

Boyatzis, R. (1982). *The competent manager*. Chichester, UK: Wiley.

Conger, J. (1989). *The charismatic leader*. San Francisco, CA: Jossey-Bass.

Conger, A., & Kanungo, R. (1987). Toward a behavioural theory of charismatic leadership in organizational settings. *Academy of Management Review, 12*, 641–657.

Crouch, A., & Yetton, P. (1987). Manager behavior, leadership style, and subordinate performance. *Organizational Behavior and Human Decision Processes, 39*, 384–396.

De Cremer, D., & van Knippenberg, D. (2002). How do leaders promote co-operation? *Journal of Applied Psychology, 87*, 858–866.

Dirks, K., & Ferrin, D. (2002). Trust in leadership. *Journal of Applied Psychology, 87*, 611–628.

Dixon, N. (1976). *On the psychology of military incompetence*. London: Jonathan Cape.

Donnelly, J., Gibson, J., & Ivancevich, J. (1987). *Fundamentals of management* (6th edn.). Homewood, IL: BPI Irwin.

Evans, M., & Dermer, J. (1974). What does the least co-worker scale really measure? *Journal of Applied Psychology, 59*, 202–206.

Fiedler, F. (1967). *A theory of leadership effectiveness*. New York: McGraw-Hill.

Fleishman, E., & Harris, E. (1962). Patterns of leadership behaviour related to employee grievances and turnover. *Personnel Psychology, 15*, 43–56.

Fleishman, E., Harris, E., & Burtt, R. (1955). *Leadership and supervision in industry*. Columbus, OH: Ohio State University Press.

French, J., & Raven B. (1960). The bases of social power. In D. Cartwright & A. Zander (Eds.), *Group dynamics* (pp. 607–623). Ann Arbor, MI: University of Michigan Press.

French, W., Kast, F., & Rosenberg, J. (1985). *Understanding human behaviour in organizations*. New York: Harper & Row.

Furnham, A. (1994). *Personality at work*. London: Routledge.

Furnham, A. (2002a). Managers as change agents. *Journal of Change Management, 3*, 21–29.

Furnham, A. (2002b). Rating a boss, a colleague and a subordinate. *Journal of Management Psychology, 17*, 655–671.

Ghiselli, E. (1963). Management talent. *American Psychologist, 18*, 631–641.

Ghiselli, E. (1971). *Explorations in management talent*. Santa Monica, CA: Goodyear.

Gordon, G. (1993). *A diagnostic approach to organizational behaviour*. Boston, MA: Allyn & Bacon.

Hersey, P., & Blanchard, K. (1982). *Management of organizational behavior*. Englewood Cliffs, NJ: Prentice-Hall.

Hogan, R., Curphy, G., & Hogan, J. (1994). What we know about leadership. *American Psychologist, 49*, 493–504.

Hogan, R., Curphy, G., & Hogan, J. (2001). Assessing leadership: A view from the dark side. *International Journal of Selection and Assessment, 9*, 40–51.

Hogan, R., & Hogan, J. (2001). Assessing leadership: A view from the dark side. *Journal of Selection and Assessment, 9*, 40–51.

Holland, J. (1973). *Making vocational choices: A theory of careers.* Englewood Cliffs, NJ: Prentice-Hall.

Homans, G. (1950). *The human group.* London: Routledge & Kegan Paul.

Hosking, D.-M., & Morley, I. (1991). *A social psychology of organizing.* London: Harvester Wheatsheaf.

House, R. (1998). Leadership. In N. Nicholson (Ed.), *Encyclopedic dictionary of organizational behaviour* (pp. 284–288). Oxford: Blackwell.

House, R., & Mitchell, T. (1974). Path–goal theory of leadership. *Journal of Contemporary Business, 3*, 81–99.

Judge, T., & Bono, J. (2000). Five factor model of personality and transformational leadership. *Journal of Applied Psychology, 85*, 751–765.

Judge, T., Bono, J., Ilies, R., & Gerhardt, M. (2002). Personality and leadership: A qualitative and quantitative review. *Journal of Applied Psychology, 87*, 765–780.

Kennedy, J. (1982). Middle LPC leaders and the contingency model of leader effectiveness. *Organizational Behavior and Human Performance, 30*, 1–14.

Kerr, S., & Jermier, J. (1978). Substitutes for leadership: Their meaning and measurement. *Organizational Behavior and Human Performance, 22*, 378–394.

Kinlaw, D. (1989). *Coaching for commitment.* San Diego, CA: University Associates.

Kirk, R., Shamir, B., & Chen, W. (2003). The two faces of transformation leadership. *Journal of Applied Psychology, 88*, 246–255.

Kotter, J. (1987). *The leadership factor.* New York: McGraw-Hill.

Kouzes, J., & Posner, B. (1988). *The leadership challenge.* San Francisco, CA: Jossey-Bass.

Krech, D., Crutchfield, R., & Ballachey, E. (1962). *Individual in society.* New York: McGraw-Hill.

Likert, R. (1961). *New patterns in management.* New York: McGraw-Hill.

Livingstone, J. (1989). *High expectations in management.* New York: Sterling Institute Press.

Locke, E. (1997). Primemovers: The traits of great business leaders. In C. Cooper & S. Jackson (Eds.), *Creating tomorrow's organization* (pp. 75–96). Chichester, UK: Wiley.

McCall, M. (1999). *High flyers.* Cambridge, MA: Harvard University Press.

Muchinsky, P. (1990). *Psychology applied to work.* New York: Brooks/Cole.

Muczyk, C. J., & Reimann, B. (1987). The case for directive leadership. *Academy of Management Executive, 1*, 304–318.

Randolph, W., & Blackburn, R. (1989). *Managing organizational behaviour.* Boston, MA: Irwin.

Schermerhorn, J., Hunt, J., & Osborn, R. (1994). *Managing organizational behavior.* New York: Wiley.

Shackleton, V., & Wale, R. (2000). Leadership and management. In N. Chmiel (Ed.), *Introduction to work and organizational psychology* (pp. 277–301). Oxford: Blackwell.

Shiflett, S. (1973). The contingency model of leadership effectiveness. *Behavioral Science, 18*, 429–440.

Spector, P. (2003). *Industrial and organizational psychology.* Chichester, UK: Wiley.

Stogdill, R. (1948). Personal factors associated with leadership: A review of the literature. *Journal of Psychology, 25*, 35–71.

Tannenbaum, R., & Schmidt, W. (1958). How to choose a leadership pattern. *Harvard Business Review, 36*, 95–101.

Titchy, N., & Devanna, M. (1986). *The transformational leader.* New York: Wiley.

Tjosvold, D. (1986). *Working together to get things done.* Lexington, MA: D. C. Heath.

Ulrich, D., Brockbank, W., & Yeung, A. (1989). Beyond belief: A benchmark for human resources. *Human Resource Management, 28*, 311–335.

Vroom, V., & Jago, A. (1978). On the validity of the Vroom–Yetton model. *Journal of Applied Psychology, 63*, 151–162.

Vroom, V., & Jago, A. (1988). *The new leadership: Managing participation in organizations.* Englewood Cliffs, NJ: Prentice-Hall.

Vroom, V., & Yetton, P. (1973). *Leadership and decision-making.* Pittsburgh, PA: University of Pittsburgh Press.

Westwood, R., & Chan, D. (1993). Headership and leadership. In R. Westwood (Ed.), *Organizational behaviour: Southeast Asian perspectives* (pp. 118–140). Hong Kong: Longman.

Yukl, E. (1980). *Leadership in organizations.* New York: Wiley.

Zaleznik, A. (1977). Managers and leaders: Are they different. *Harvard Business Review*, 55, 31–57.

13 Culture at work

Introduction

Cross-cultural psychology looks at the comparative effects of (national, ethnic, corporate) culture on human behaviour and thought processes. It focuses on how socio-cultural factors (social, economic, historical, ideological) shape and influence human behaviour. It is an interesting, important and difficult area to research. No society or culture is homogeneous. Cultures are dynamic, inconsistent and multifaceted. They are therefore difficult to categorize and compare. Furthermore, the processes by which culture influences an individual's or group's behaviour are far from clear.

Most organizational psychology research emerges from Western, developed, capitalist societies. In addition, it is published in English language research journals. Some people in business, perhaps naively, assume that organizational behaviour is universal. That is, that what motivates people at work; what causes them stress; how best to appraise, develop and reward workers; and when, why and how to develop teams; is essentially the same in all countries. Universalists believe (and hope) that what "works" in Alaska also works in Zambia; that managerial practices that are effective in Japan will work just as well in Jena and Johannesburg; and that things like individuals' achievement motivation and sense of fairness and justice do not alter from society to society.

Others, often learning through experience, come to recognize that many aspects of business are culture-specific. These include how rewards are allocated (e.g. via the principle of equality or equity); the acceptability of showing favouritism to certain groups (like relatives) and what sort of leadership is desirable. Culture affects how people negotiate, how they try to resolve conflicts and how they like to make decisions.

No-one living in Eastern or Western Europe since the end of the Second World War has not been affected by attempts at European integration. Legal, fiscal and economic factors have been important in bringing together nation-states that have fought each other for hundreds of years.

But how united or "unitable" is Europe? Should we celebrate things we have in common or rejoice in our differences. Psychological studies of European differences have pointed up a number of subtle differences that can lead to confusion as well as contempt at work. Collett (1994) considered a number of these. Let us consider here just one relating to *time and punctuality*: some countries are *time-bound* (Germany, Britain, Switzerland and Scandinavia), whereas others are *time-blind* (Spain, Portugal, Greece). Time-bound societies emphasize schedules, deadlines, time waste, timekeeping, a fast pace of life. Time-blind societies are more relaxed and casual about time.

Hence what is late in one society is not necessarily so in another. As societies become more time-bound, they have a more competitive attitude to time, and so "fast" is better. Hence fast-living, fast-eating, fast-tempo, manic-type work behaviour emphasizing "catching up" and not being "left behind". Time-bound societies see time as linear, time-blind as cyclical. Time-bound societies centre work around clocks, schedules, delivery dates, agendas, deadlines. This can make for serious misunderstandings at work.

Collett (1994) points out various other time-related distinctions that relate to the world of work. The first is the time-blind culture's ability to distinguish between sacred and profane time. The former is for eating, family, sleeping. Profane time is used for everything else. Hence in Spain, meetings can easily be interrupted: it is not dedicated solely to the meeting. There is also the distinction between *mono-* and *poly*-chronic time. Time-bound societies are monochronic – they do one thing at a time. Time-blind are polychromic, happily ignoring appointments, schedules, deadlines and tolerating inter-ruptions. Third, there is the issue of *time-orientation*: past, present and future. Thus the British are thought to be interested more in the distant and recent past and therefore do not invest so much in the future, whereas the Germans have a longer view of the future investing in basic research, education and training.

The understanding and use of time is crucial in business. Not only does it lead to how, when, where and why work is done, but people with conflicting ideas and theories may have very different conceptions and expectations. This can lead to misunderstand-ings and animosity.

A topic of considerable importance and debate is the issue of *corruption in business*. Furnham (2003) notes the fundamental differences between the way different people in and from different organizations do business. The trouble with the concept of corrup-tion is that one person's expediency is another's misbehaviour. "I am expeditious; he is opportunistic; they are corrupt", the saying may go. The two issues that are most talked about in business are bribery and nepotism. Business arrogance and illegal profit-taking are also widely discussed. The line between sponsoring a fact-finding mission, being given a present, taken out to lunch and accepting a bribe is a thin one. Clearly in some countries (see below) and for some jobs (procurement) the temptations are high and the custom normal.

Nepotism is the appointment of people to positions based on family relationships rather than ability. There are other corrupt methods in business such as mafia-type threats for money. More sophisticated methods involve accountancy half-truths and other methods of fiddling the books. There may be three sources of corruptions: the country, the organization and the person. Every year, various organizations publish a corruption index that reflects the degree to which corruption is perceived to exist among public officials and politicians. The best organizations use polls. Table 13.1 lists the top 15 and bottom 15 countries on the 2001 index published on the web at //www.transparency.org/cpi/2001/cpi2001.html. The list goes from least to most corrupt.

Multinationals that operate all around the world are familiar with the problems of corruption. Corruption is subtle and leads to massive inefficiency. Everyone gets sucked into it. It is perhaps no accident that there is a correlation between corruption and gross national produce; the richer the country, the less corruption.

But within countries, there is some evidence of corruption varying from one organ-ization to another for all sorts of historical, social and economic reasons, and some organizations are deeply corrupt. There is widespread nepotism, bribery, "fiddling of

Table 13.1 The 2001 Corruption Perceptions Index

	Rank	Country	Score	Surveys used
Top 15	1	Finland	9.9	7
	2	Denmark	9.5	7
	3	New Zealand	9.4	7
	4	Iceland	9.2	6
	5	Singapore	9.2	12
	6	Sweden	9.0	8
	7	Canada	8.9	8
	8	Netherlands	8.8	7
	9	Luxembourg	8.7	6
	10	Norway	8.6	7
	11	Australia	8.5	9
	12	Switzerland	8.4	7
	13	United Kingdom	8.3	9
	14	Hong Kong	7.9	11
	15	Austria	7.8	7
Bottom 15	77	Cote D'Ivoire	2.4	3
		Nicaragua	2.4	3
	79	Ecuador	2.3	6
		Pakistan	2.3	3
		Russia	2.3	10
	82	Tanzania	2.2	3
	83	Ukraine	2.1	6
	84	Azerbaijan	2.0	3
		Bolivia	2.0	5
		Cameroon	2.0	3
		Kenya	2.0	4
	88	Indonesia	1.9	12
		Uganda	1.9	3
	90	Nigeria	1.0	4
	91	Bangladesh	0.4	3

the books", theft, and so on. The public suspects that organizations in certain sectors are less than honest and they may well be right. Curiously, recent revelations suggest that in Europe public corporations are more corrupt than private corporations, whereas in America the reverse is true.

Whence national differences?

Most researchers interested in industrial/organizational psychology and applied psychology soon become aware of various national differences in both scientific and applied practice (Furnham, 2004). These differences are not usually about how good research is done (at least within the empiricist tradition) but about different methodological emphases, fashions and business concerns. It is apparent that particular psychological instruments (ability, personality tests) are used extensively in one country but in few others. Equally, sociopolitical, economic and legal issues mean that whereas it is impossible (or at least unwise) to collect certain organizational information (absenteeism, appraisal, productivity reports) in one country, it is easily available in a second.

There are national differences in what is the preferred outcome or dependent measure used to validate the instrument. Thus in America, organizations have long collected supervisor evaluations on staff, together with other ratings, such as self-ratings, direct reports (subordinate ratings) and peer ratings of work performance. This has meant the multi-rater (360°) feedback literature has been dominated by Americans, though there are signs that the Europeans are now taking an interest. However, this requires organizations to try to obtain reliable, multi-dimensional ratings on employees, which can prove "politically" difficult.

It is also apparent that some issues, and the academic literature which accompanies them, is nation-specific. For instance, the concern with integrity testing (honesty, integrity, conscientiousness, dependability, trustworthiness, reliability) appears almost exclusively to be an American obsession. On the other hand, the Europeans have been very concerned with employment status.

It is unclear why integrity testing is so much more popular in America, because it is unlikely that the incidence of workplace deviance is very different between Europe and America. Cook (1998) has suggested that honesty tests have become popular in America since 1988 when the general use of the polygraph was restricted. Furthermore, he suggests that the implementation of fair employment law has meant that some American organizations have stopped using tests that measure such things as conscientiousness, which give reasonable indexes of honesty, integrity and morality. Hence they have felt the need to use specific tests to measure this phenomenon. It is often local employment law that affects selection procedures and which, in turn, some years later, influences academic interests. Also, high-profile litigation cases have a sudden and dramatic influence on companies, often dissuading them from using particular tests.

Within Europe it is possible to see various clear patterns (Furnham, 2004). Because of dictatorships in Portugal and Spain until the 1970s, their psychology was more cut off from that of many other countries. The French insistence on the use of their own language meant they integrated very slowly into European psychology. The Belgians and Scandinavians have their national journals in English, and the Dutch use English language textbooks. A north/south divide exists in Europe, with the British, Dutch, Germans and Scandinavians being North American-oriented, while many psychologists of other nationalities – French, Italian, Portuguese and Spanish – have a more inward-looking focus. However, it is possible that those countries that resist European integration (Britain, Norway, Switzerland) may in time be different in their approach to human resources issues than those big (France, Germany and Italy) and small (Belgium, The Netherlands, Ireland) countries that embrace it so warmly. However, increased academic contact, together with the hegemony of both the English language and American psychology, have meant that over time national preferences and differences in this area have been decreasing. This is, at least for those in the Anglo-Saxon empiricist tradition, good news for research.

There are various sociopolitical and demographic factors that lead to growing national differences and similarities (Furnham, 2004). The first is *legal*. In Europe, European legislation has and will have a homogenizing effect on such things as selection, as well as more general policies and practices. Thus in 1989, the European Commission published a Preliminary Draft Community Charter of Fundamental Social Rights (COM(89)248), which all member states will be invited to ratify. The twelve proposals concern rights relating to:

1   Freedom of movement.

2   Equitable wages.
3   Improved living and working conditions.
4   Social protection.
5   Freedom of association and collective bargaining.
6   Vocational training.
7   Equal treatment of men and women at work.
8   Information, consultation and worker participation.
9   Health protection and safety at work.
10 Minimum working age and adequate training for adolescents.
11 Adequate income and social protection for the elderly.
12 Integration for the disabled into working life.

It is not difficult to see how such legislation creates standardized conditions and leads organizations in different countries to adopt similar practices. Europe hopes to be harmonized and hence there is much talk of the "Euromanager". Managerial attitudes and behaviours are a function of various both within- and between-company and -national systems – assessment, compensation, recruitment and selection.

A second homogenizing factor in Europe is similar *demographics*. All of the larger countries of Europe are showing a dramatic decline in birth rates. Hence organizations have turned more to immigrants from ethnic groups as well as to older and married women. All this has impacted on issues like sex and race discrimination; language and general skills training and upgrading; the introduction of flexible working hours and crèche facilities.

A third factor is *pan-European political movements* like the Green Party, which stresses the relevance of environmental issues, which in turn impact on working conditions as well as how products are produced and marketed. Strong political alliances in the European Parliament encourage trends that have an impact across the continent.

As well as quasi-political and legal bodies, various pan-European networks of psychologists have emerged to share resource and perspectives. The European Network of Organizational and Work Psychologists (ENOP) has produced a model for a European curriculum in work and organizational psychology, designed to serve as a common frame of reference for the training of work and organizational psychologists. The curriculum was produced through discussion with interested parties, including the European Association of Work and Organizational Psychology (EAWOP).

The globalization of many forces – including the academic – means that, in the end, most academics end up being oriented towards America. Those who speak English as their first language (nearly all parts of the old British Empire and new Commonwealth) or as a second unofficial language probably get the message and take the lead from America fastest. It is also true that many researchers are eager to import American theories, tests and methodologies. It is not so much that American academics are aggressive exporters as their European colleagues appear to be enthusiastic importers. What this means in effect is that over time national differences are likely to decrease, though no doubt special legal or economic circumstances will lead to special interests.

Europeans, probably more so than outsiders, are highly conscious of their differences rather than similarities. With many different languages, histories and economies, it is no accident that organizational practices are so different. These inevitably impact on how organizations are structured and run, and more important for work psychologists, on what individual differences are measured, when and why. The use of tests in selection provides an excellent example.

Various studies have focused on national difference in selection processes. Smith & Abrahamson (1992) looked at 10 studies done in European countries to compare their method of selection. The authors concluded, after calculating correlations, that the results indicated far more similarities than differences. The much higher use of graphology in France and references in Britain are the only factors that seem to stand out.

A more robust survey covered 12 Western European countries (Dany & Torchy, 1994). For Cook, this indicates various interesting features:

- The French favour graphology but no other country does.
- Application forms are widely used everywhere except The Netherlands.
- Reference are widely used everywhere, but are less popular in Spain, Portugal and The Netherlands.
- Psychometric testing is most popular in Spain and Portugal, and least popular in West Germany and Turkey.
- Aptitude testing is most popular in Spain and The Netherlands, and least popular in West Germany and Turkey.
- Assessment centres are not used much, but are most popular in Spain and Portugal. (Cook, 1998: 23)

Cook further speculates:

> What the USA does today, Britain does tomorrow. "Today" and "tomorrow" are years apart – but how many? Suppose Britain is 20–30 years "behind" the USA. The future in Britain will see mental ability tests being used very widely in all organizations at all levels. The future will see personality tests used quite widely at supervisory level and above, and WABs used quite widely below. The future will see the demise of the unstructured interview and the free-form reference and a proliferation of rating systems.
>
> But the future could turn out quite differently. In one important respect Britain is only 10 years "behind" the USA – equal employment legislation. British personnel managers might now be belatedly adopting methods the law will shortly force them to abandon. By 2002 mental ability tests could be virtually outlawed, personality tests suspect, and biographical method unthinkable. Selectors might be forced back onto the classic trip, or forced out of business all together. (Cook, 1998: 25)

Over half the companies in Finland, Spain and Portugal use psychometric tests in selection, whereas under a third use them in Germany, France, The Netherlands and Turkey. This may reflect either scepticism or legal restraints on the part of the latter countries. Certainly the use of tests in general (personality and aptitude) appears to be similar, though far fewer countries use assessment centres because of costs.

Corporate culture

As well as national culture there is also the powerful force called corporate culture. There are some research preoccupations and themes of organizational thought that have come together to influence the development of the concept of corporate culture.

For over a decade, this originally anthropological concept has been considered, debated and discussed by researchers, business gurus, newspaper and magazine writers, and line managers.

For the past 20 years in management circles, corporate culture has been "flavour of the month". Books, articles and papers appearing on this topic have been numerous and it is now widely adopted in both professional and academic circles. It has been used to predict and explain a great variety of behaviours in organizations, both successful and unsuccessful, and many large and small organizations have attempted what they call culture change programmes. At present, it remains actively discussed and analysed in industrial/work psychology circles and equally debated in board meetings. It has taken a long time for some managers and management scientists to realize that "soft" human resource issues may play such an important part in any organization's success (or failure).

However, it should not be thought that the application of this anthropological concept to management is particularly new, as references to it date back at least 30 years. Work psychologists have tended to use related terms, such as climate, values, norms and beliefs, rather than culture. However, factors such as the influence of sociology and anthropology on management science, and the comparative rise of Far Eastern organizations, have meant that concepts such as culture have been seen to be a part-explanation for success, and hence for why "culture" is such a popular topic now. Smircich & Calas (1987) provide three explanations for the popularity of the concept. First, there are shifts in the perspective of business managers realizing that national and corporate culture may be more important than strategy in determining organizational efficiency. Second, there have been shifts in organizational and communication theory to a "softer", more radical approach that conceptualizes organizations as socially constructed, investigates the symbolic nature of management and looks at the unique use of language within organizations. Third, there have also been shifts in the human sciences from a positivistic explanation to a constructivist understanding that emphasizes the importance of subjective perception of employees (Furnham & Gunter, 1993).

How is it that so many individuals within an organization share basic attitudes, behaviour patterns, expectations and values? In other words, how does a culture form and how is it maintained? What is the origin of corporate culture? Corporate culture is based on the needs of individuals to reduce uncertainty and to have some reference to guide their actions. This uncertainty-reducing need is resolved by the evolution of behaviour standards (do's and don'ts) and norms of perceiving events.

First, organizational culture may be traced, at least in part, to the *founders of the company* or those who strongly shaped it in the recent past. These individuals often possess dynamic personalities, strong values and a clear vision of how the organization should be. Since they are on the scene first, and/or play a key role in hiring initial staff, their attitudes and values are readily transmitted to new employees. The result is that these views become the accepted ones in the organization, and persist as long as the founders are on the scene, or even longer. Given the length of time over which cultures become established, the reasons why people do things may well be forgotten, yet they perpetuate the values and philosophies of founders.

Second, organizational culture often develops out of, or is changed by, an *organization's experience with external exigencies*. Every organization must find a niche and an image for itself in its sector and in the marketplace. As it struggles to do so, it may find that some values and practices work better for it than others – for example, one organization may gradually acquire a deep, shared commitment to high quality, and another company may find that selling products of moderate quality, but at low prices, works best for it. The result: a dominant value centring around price leadership takes shape. Hence, the pressure to change culture to "fit" the external environment is constant, particularly in turbulent times. Indeed, it is because the business environment changes more rapidly than the corporate culture that many managers see culture as a factor in business success.

Third, culture develops from the *need to maintain effective working relationships* among organization members. Depending on the nature of its business, and the characteristics of the person it must employ, different expectations and values may develop. Thus, if a company needs rapid and open communication between its employees, and informal working relationships, an open expression of views will probably come to be valued within it. In contrast, very different values and styles of communication may develop in other organizations working in other industries with different types of personnel. Just as groups go through a well-known sequence in their development, remembered as forming, storming, norming and performing, so do corporate cultures. Indeed, it is the development of behavioural norms that is at the very heart of culture.

For Schein (1990), culture is created through two main factors. First, there is norm formation around critical incidents, particularly where mistakes have occurred; that is, the lessons learnt from important corporate events (often crises) are crucially important factors in the formation (or change) of culture. Second, there is identification with leaders and what leaders pay attention to, measure and control; how leaders react to critical incidents and organizational crises; deliberate role modelling and coaching; operational criteria for the allocation of rewards and status; operational criteria for recruitment selection, promotion retirement and excommunication. The role of unique visionary leaders cannot be understated. Understanding the factors that lead to the establishment of corporate culture is important because they also serve to highlight the factors that need to be concentrated on when changing that culture.

The problem of definition

Culture is a core concept in many of the social sciences. After an exhaustive historical examination of the relevant literature, Kroeber & Kluckhohn (1952: 181) provide one of the most complete definitions of culture:

> Culture consists of patterns, explicit and implicit, of and for behaviour acquired and transmitted by *symbols*, constituting the distinctive achievement of human groups, including their embodiment in *artefacts*; the essential core of culture consists of traditional (i.e. historically derived and selected) ideas and especially their attached *values*; culture systems may, on the one hand, be considered as products of action, on the other as conditioning elements of further action.

This definition is well rehearsed, but others have attempted to produce a clearer and more comprehensive definition. Eldridge & Crombie (1974: 89–90) wrote:

> Culture is a characteristic of all organizations through which, at the same time, their individuality and uniqueness is expressed. The culture of an organization

refers to the unique configuration of norms, values, beliefs, ways of behaving and so on that characterize the manner in which groups and individuals combine to get things done. The distinctiveness of a particular organization is intimately bound up with its history and the character-building effects of past decisions and past leaders. It is manifested in the folkways, mores, and the ideology to which members defer, as well as in the strategic choices made by the organization as a whole. The individuality or cultural distinctiveness of an organization is attained through the more or less constant exercise of choice, in all sections and levels . . . The character of organizational choice is one of the major manifestations of organizational culture.

Eldridge & Crombie (1974) drew attention to three dimensions of culture: depth or vertical dimension; breadth or lateral coordination of the contributing parts; and the progression dimension, which refers to coordination through time. They elaborated as follows:

The depth dimension is exemplified in the formulation and adoption of policies, programmes, procedures and practices that represent the basic values and strategic commitments of the organization as a whole – the inducement of behaviour at the "surface", in the day-to-day organization functioning. (Eldridge & Crombie, 1974: 96)

The construct of culture has caused much confusion. Although there are multiple definitions, they tend to be vague and overly general. This confusion is exacerbated by the various disciplines interested in this topic (anthropology, sociology, psychology), which, although increasing the number of definitions, does not necessarily increase clarity. Hence, occupational psychologists and work psychologists could be accused of "muddying the waters" rather than clarifying the concept (Furnham & Gunter, 1993).

Although it may be seen as a somewhat pointless etymological exercise, it is worthwhile considering how various researchers and reviewers have understood the concept of organizational or corporate culture. There have been several ways of arriving at a useful, clear, working definition. Some have attempted to specify the *dimensions* of culture (Hampden-Turner, 1990; Schein, 1990); others have concentrated on the other *functions* of corporate culture (Graves, 1986; Williams, Dobson, & Walters, 1989); others have made a serious effort to *taxonomize* culture (Deal & Kennedy, 1982); and of course there have been a host of attempts simply to *define* it succinctly (Bowers & Seashore, 1966; Gonzalez, 1987).

There is no shortage of definitions for corporate culture. Consider:

. . . a historical, transmitted pattern of meanings embodied in symbols, a system of inherited conception expressed in and developed by their knowledge about attitudes towards life . . . Culture is the fabric of meaning in terms of which human beings interpret their experience and guide their actions. (Geertz, 1973: 78)

Culture is the best way we do things around here. (Bowers & Seashore, 1966: 97)

Culture is a system of informal rules that spells out how people are to behave most of the time. (Deal & Kennedy, 1982: 11)

Culture can now be defined as (a) a pattern of basic assumptions, (b) invented, discovered, or developed by a given group, (c) as it learns to cope with its problems of external adaptation and internal integration, (d) that has worked well enough to be considered valid and, therefore (e) is to be taught to new members as the (f) correct way to perceive, think and feel in relation to those problems. (Schein, 1990: 110)

According to Schneider (1987), culture involves underlying assumptions about both the world and human nature. These assumptions include views of the relationship with nature and of human relationships. The relationship with nature reflects several dimensions: control over the environment, activity versus passivity or doing versus being, attitudes towards uncertainty, notions of time, attitudes towards change, and what determines "truth". Views about the nature of human relationships include: the importance of task versus relationships, the importance of hierarchy, the importance of individual versus group. For example, some cultures, often Western, view man as the master of Nature, which can be harnessed and exploited to suit man's needs; time, change and uncertainty can be actively managed. "Truth" is determined by facts and measurement. Other cultures, often Eastern, view man as subservient to, or in harmony with, Nature. Time, change and uncertainty are accepted as given. "Truth" is determined by spiritual and philosophical principles. This attitude is often referred to as "fatalistic" or "adaptive".

Assumptions regarding the nature of human relationships are also different. The importance of relationships over task, of the hierarchy and of the individual versus the group is clearly different, not only between the East and West, but also within Western cultures. In Eastern cultures, for example, importance is placed on relationships over task, on the hierarchy and on the group or collective. By contrast, in Western cultures, the focus is more on task and on the individual, and the hierarchy is considered to be of less importance. However, there is variance between the USA and Europe, as well as within Europe (east and west). Indeed, there may also be important corporate culture differences within different sectors of the economy.

Sackmann (1990) has expanded on the perspective of organizational culture as a variable or concept. She argues that the use of culture as a variable is based on three major assumptions:

- Culture is *one* of several organizational variables.
- This variable "culture" consists of a finite and patterned set of components, which are visible and manifest in artefacts as well as collective behaviour and, in fact, cultures *are* these artefacts.
- Culture serves several functions that contribute to the success of organizations.

Organizations have, or develop in addition to other products, the product "culture", which is itself composed of subproducts such as artefacts, symbols and collective verbal and non-verbal behaviour. Other products include "myths, sagas, language systems, metaphors, symbols, ceremonies, rituals, value systems and behaviour norms" (Shrivastava, 1985: 103). More concrete and recognizable examples of artefacts are the logo of a firm, the architecture of buildings, existing technologies and machinery or tools, the interior design and the use of a work setting, documents and products, the organization chart, the typical and expected clothing of employees, and existing status symbols such as company cars, reserved parking or furniture. Verbal examples can be seen in language in general and speeches, jargon, humour, stories, sagas, legends and myths in particular. Non-verbal behaviours include interpersonal behaviours such as the typical way of approaching each other (e.g. shaking hands), gestures and dress codes – as well as existing forms and functions of rites, rituals and ceremonies, such as personal birthday wishes from the boss, congratulations and awards for long tenure, the Friday afternoon after-work drinks, celebrations of company anniversaries, or the Christmas party.

These components together form the product of culture, whose major importance is seen in its attributed functions. It is assumed that culture serves predominantly two functions which contribute to organizational success or prevent it. First is internal integration and coordination culture, which represents the "social glue" and generates a "we-feeling", thus counteracting processes of differentiation or separateness, which are an unavoidable part of organizational life. Second, organizational culture offers a shared system of meanings, which is the basis for communication and mutual understanding. If these two functions are not fulfilled in a satisfactory way, culture may significantly reduce the efficiency of an organization (Furnham & Gunter, 1993).

Most emphasis is placed on the integration function of culture, the consistency among its subcomponents and the general consensus about acceptance of these subcomponents. As a result, cultures can be evaluated and designated "good" or "bad". A "good" culture is consistent in its components and shared among organizational members; it makes the organization unique, thus differentiating it from other organizations. Such a culture is created primarily by an organization's leader(s) and/or founder(s), who can also influence, imprint or change this culture; that is, they can control it. However, what is most crucial in any culture is the relationship between the corporate culture and the company strategy and goals.

Dimensions, factors and other distinctions

Another way to understand corporate culture is to make various distinctions, or spell out the factors or dimensions underlying the culture. For instance, Schein (1990) has listed seven dimensions of organizational culture. Schein argues that these seven dimensions provide the basis for an interview that can reveal some of the more hidden, implicit facets of corporate culture (see Table 13.2). This list is potentially useful, not only because it provides possible markers for the measurement of corporate culture, but also it attempts to anchor dimensions in clearly stated opposites.

According to Deal & Kennedy (1982), corporate culture has several specific elements: a widely shared philosophy in the business environment and *shared values*, such as "The consumer is important; things don't just happen, you have to make them; we want to make employee interests our own"; *specific rites and rituals*; and a primary (but informal) *means of communication*. In their highly popular and readable book, they offer, most helpfully and insightfully, examples of how these elements or markers can be seen in the various cultures they describe.

The model developed by Schein (1985) helps to organize the pieces of the cultural puzzle. According to Schein's model, culture is represented at three levels: behaviours and artefacts; beliefs and values; underlying assumptions. These levels are arranged according to their visibility, such that behaviour and artefacts are the easiest to observe, and the underlying assumptions need to be inferred. While behaviour and artefacts may be observable and beliefs and values can be articulated, their meaning may not be readily comprehensible. To understand what the behaviour or beliefs actually mean to the participants/employees, the underlying assumptions have to be brought to the

Table 13.2 Dimensions of corporate culture

Dimension	Questions to be answered
1. The organization's relation to its environment.	"Does the organization perceive itself to be dominant, submissive, harmonizing, searching out a niche?"
2. The nature of human activity.	"Is the 'correct' way for humans to behave to be dominant/ proactive, harmonizing, or passive/fatalistic?"
3. The nature of reality/truth.	"How do we define what is true and what is not true; and how is truth ultimately determined both in the physical and social world?"
4. The nature of time.	"What is our basic orientation in terms of past, present, and future, and what kinds of time units are most relevant for the conduct of daily life?"
5. The nature of human nature.	"Are humans basically good, neutral or evil, and is human nature perfectible or fixed?"
6. The nature of human relationships.	"What is the 'correct' way for people to relate to each other, to distribute power and affection? Is life competitive or cooperative? Is this the best way to organize society on the basis of individualism or groupism? Is the best authority system autocratic/paternalistic or collegial/ participative?"
7. Homogeneity versus diversity.	"Is the group better off if it is highly diverse or if it is highly homogeneous, and should individuals in a group be encouraged to innovate?"

Source: Reproduced from Stein (1985) with the permission of Jossey-Bass Inc.

surface or made manifest, which is most difficult as this level of culture is considered to be taken for granted and thus out of awareness.

Schein (1990) has noted that any definable group with a shared history can have a culture and that within an organization there can therefore be many subcultures. If the organization as a whole has had shared experiences, there will also be a total organizational culture. Within any given unit, the tendency for integration and consistency will be assumed to be present, but it is perfectly possible for co-existing units of a larger system to have cultures that are independent of, and even in conflict with, each other.

> The strength and degree of internal consistency of a culture are, therefore, a function of the stability of the group, the length of time the group has existed, the intensity of the group's experiences of learning, the mechanisms by which the learning has taken place (i.e. positive reinforcement or avoidance conditioning), and the strength and clarity of the assumptions held by the founders and leaders of the group. (Schein, 1990: 11)

Essentially, all these attempts to define and describe organizational culture have led to a position where certain agreements and disagreements are acknowledged (Furnham & Gunter, 1993: 75–76) (see Box 13.1). Inevitably, there remains more disagreement than agreement. This is not necessarily a bad thing, as disagreement frequently encourages people to seek for answers to academic and applied problems.

The issue of the definitive list of dimensions of corporate culture has not, and will not, be resolved. Although there remains much overlap between different lists and concepts, as yet no consensus remains.

Box 13.1 Assumptions about corporate culture

Agreement over the concept of culture
- It is difficult to define (even a pointless exercise).
- It is multidimensional with many different components at different levels.
- It is not particularly dynamic and ever changing (being relatively stable over short periods of time).
- It leads to significant misunderstandings (that are unexpected) when cultures meet.
- Culture shock or moving into a different corporate culture is real, painful and debilitating.
- It represents a group solution to certain problems which may be adaptive or maladaptive; positively or negatively related to productivity.
- It takes time to establish, and therefore change, a corporate "culture".
- It is, in many senses, intangible but has numerous observable artefacts.
- It is clearly linked to implicit beliefs and values underlying behavioural norms.

Disagreement
- What are the exact components/facets of corporate culture: i.e., what makes something part of corporate culture and what not part of culture.
- How to categorize/dimensionalize culture: what typology to use; which dimension to apply; what terminology we should use.
- How national, ethnic, corporate, departmental, gender (etc.) cultures overlap, interact, and influence each other.
- How, when, or why corporate culture can be changed.
- Whether to celebrate corporate departmental culture differences or work to eliminate them.
- Whether it is possible to bridge already established departmental or corporate cultures.
- How organizational corporate culture differs from organizational climate.
- Who estimates a culture and when and how does it form.
- Whether some cultures are adaptive and others maladaptive: what is the healthiest, most optimal, or desirable culture.
- How corporate culture relates to organizational success or failure: that is, whether and how.

Source: Reproduced from Furnham & Gunter (1993) with the permission of Routledge.

Classifying and categorizing culture

To compare and contrast, evaluate and predict, it is clearly important that one is first able to classify or taxonomize organizational cultures. Categorization is the beginning of science; what follows this all-important stage is an understanding of the processes and mechanisms that account for the origin and maintenance of culture. Various attempts have been made at this "natural history" task. First, however, it is perhaps important to try to understand the advantages and disadvantages of the quest as a whole (Furnham & Gunter, 1993: 77–78) (Box 13.2).

There are various different ways to classify culture according to geographical, economic, historical, religious, linguistic, political or other criteria. There are various studies to show that national and organizational cultures are interlinked. This in itself is not surprising; indeed, common sense would predict it. However, because of the very different methodologies and approaches, there is not yet any standard taxonomy of the stages within an organization and the extent to which they affect each other. Without

Box 13.2 Advantages and disadvantages of classification systems for corporate culture

Advantages
- One is able to compare and contrast cultures so as to be able to predict (and control) areas of misunderstandings/friction before they occur.
- Empirical data of groups, clusters or types may yield counter-intuitive findings that simple guesswork would not show. In other words, there may be good reasons why two superficially similar types do not "fit" together.
- It may be useful to prepare a behavioural culture atlas for a traveller from one organization to another. Only a scheme or category system could facilitate this.
- Theories of classification can be tested by gathered empirical data. In this sense, they can be discarded, revised, or maintained.
- It helps people become aware of their own culture and how it differs from others. It serves to make the implicit explicit and help the whole audit process.
- It specifies the areas of training that becomes necessary for the culture traveller within and across organizations and culture. Like the periodic table for the chemist or the map for the explorer, a typology of culture allows more interesting and important work to be done.

Disadvantages
- Classification systems are only as good as the evidence/data upon which they are based and these are frequently poor: hence the taxonomies are weak, commonsensical or wrong.
- Different statistical techniques yield different dimensions and is not certain which is most useful. There is no agreement upon a particular way of treating the data, yet each reveals a rather different problem.
- Very "broad-brush" approaches (that offer a small number of distinguishable types) can be insensitive, missing out on the really interesting and important subtle differences. In fact, they may be dangerous, giving the illusion of knowledge which is often incomplete or incorrect.
- Classifying culture does not tell you either the consequences of differences or similarities or how to fix them. This knowledge may be implied but it is not necessarily provided.

Source: Reproduced from Furnham & Gunter (1993) with the permission of Routledge.

doubt, however, Hofstede's work has attracted most recent interest and critical acclaim. It was his aim to describe national culture as parsimoniously as possible, by extracting the most fundamental underlying dimension.

From his extensive database collected throughout IBM, Hofstede (1980) developed four "dimensions" of culture – power distance, uncertainty avoidance, individualism and masculine/feminine – against which he was then able to plot 40 different nationalities. His study showed that within one multinational organizational culture, there can be marked differences based on national norms. Using Hofstede's dimensions, various researchers have tried to select and carry out culturally sensitive interventions in overseas organizational development.

Hofstede's dimensions are as follows:

- *Power distance*: The extent to which the less powerful members of institutions and organizations accept that power is distributed *unequally*.
- *Masculinity/femininity*: A situation in which the dominant values in masculine

society are success, money and things, or in feminine society, caring for others and the quality of life.

- *Uncertainty avoidance*: The extent to which people feel threatened by ambiguous situations, and have created beliefs and institutions that try to avoid these.
- *Individualism/collectivism*: This reflects the belief that people are supposed to look after themselves and their immediate family, or that people belong to in-groups or collectives, which are supposed to look after them in exchange for loyalty.

Hill (2001) reviewed the factors that lead to the amusing if puzzling differences between the big and small nations of Europe. He characterizes the British as senti-mental, the French as inquisitive individualists, the Germans as methodical mystics, the Spanish as egocentric egalitarians, the Italians as artless aesthetes, the Belgians as open-minded opportunists, the Dutch as democratic dogmatists, the Greeks as intelli-gent improvisers, and so on. He interprets Hofstede's four dimensions for Europe thus:

1) *Individualism* can be correlated to a large extent with national wealth. Understand-ably the northern European countries lie at the "individualistic" end of the scale with, perhaps surprisingly, Austria and, not so surprisingly at the time, Spain trailing behind and Portugal even further to the back of the pack.
2) *Power distance*, which means the extent to which a society accepts the fact that power in organizations is unevenly distributed, is small in the northern European countries of Scandinavia, the UK and Germany (also rather surprisingly Austria) and relatively large in France, Belgium, Italy, Spain, Portugal and Greece. Fortu-nately the extreme attitude quoted in the section on the Belgians, namely "the boss is on holiday and no decisions are taken in his absence", is hardly true any longer of Belgian, German, French or other Continental industries, although there are still some examples around.
3) *Uncertainty avoidance*, the extent to which a society feels threatened by unsure and ambiguous situations and consequently searches for statutory structures; is weak-est in Denmark, Sweden, Austria, Switzerland and Finland, as well as in the Large Power Distance countries of the Mediterranean. As Hofstede points out, it is no coincidence that the Germans have a law in their constitution to cope with the eventuality that none of the other laws work.
4) *Masculinity versus femininity*, which represents opposing poles in social attitudes (showing off, "performing", achieving, "big is beautiful" versus putting personal relationships, respect for quality of life etc, before money), rates the German-speaking countries as relatively "masculine" and The Netherlands and Scandinavia as "feminine". The record in the case of the Mediterranean countries is mixed: Italy and Greece turn out to be very "masculine" while Spain, contrary to the macho folklore, proves to be "feminine". (Hill, 2001: 289)

More importantly, these national characteristics can be applied to organizations. Thus, all organizations can be described in terms of their score on four corporate culture dimensions.

There are, of course, many ways of diagnosing or describing corporate culture. One approach is to contrast the outsiders' and insiders' perspective. Thus, from the *outside*, an observer could note:

- the physical setting – inside and outside buildings (the buildings, style, logo);
- what the company says about itself – press releases, adverts, etc.;
- the way the company greets strangers (formal/informal, relaxed/busy, elegant/nondescript) and inducts new people;
- the history of the company: stories about why the company is a success, what kind of people it attracts, the nature of an average day;
- how people spend their time, both while at work and how they choose to interact after work.

From the *inside* it may be equally possible to highlight features of corporate culture by:

- understanding the career path progression of employees;
- noting how long people stay in middle-management jobs;
- examining the content of what is being discussed or written about in meetings, memos, etc.;
- examining anecdotes and stories that pass through the cultural network.

It should be pointed out that this insider/outsider approach describes culture only according to the visible elements of culture. Naturally, there have been many attempts to classify and codify culture. Interestingly, nearly all these attempts have resulted in the description of four types (Handy, 1980).

According to Deal & Kennedy (1982), quite distinct types are identifiable (Box 13.3). This fourfold classification was one of the first in the area and has attracted considerable interest if not research. It was the work of consultants who, by moving from one client company to another on a regular basis, were easily able to observe aspects of the corporate culture that the employees do not see. Those who underplay the role of corporate culture in day-to-day working habits need only change their job or company to be persuaded of the effect of corporate culture. There are, however, various other ways of classifying corporate culture: Williams *et al.* (1989) (see Box 13.4) and Graves (1986) (see Box 13.5). Like all other authors in this area, Graves offers no evidence for the categories or explains how he came to choose his particular categorizing system.

However, comparing four different classificatory systems (Table 13.4) shows striking similarities. Of course, this table does not include theorists who argue that corporate culture is not definable in terms of simple dimensions.

The fact that four different research groups, working independently, have come up with such similar groupings/categories does suggest a certain degree of reliability in their observations. To this extent this work is a promising start. But it does not explain how such cultures arise or how they change or do not change. Implied in many observations, especially those of Deal & Kennedy (1982), is that different sectors of the economy often share similar corporate cultures, but it remains unclear as to whether these cultures are healthy and adaptive or not. The danger with taxonomic descriptions, as psychologists found with personality theories, is that they are often just tautological. Thus, an extravert is seen as someone outgoing, sociable and impulsive; and social impulsives are called extraverts. But we need to know the process that explains why some people become or are extraverts and others introverts, and the "mechanism" that determines the behaviour. This is precisely the challenge for corporate culture theorists: having so well described and categorized cultures, they need now to explain the origin

Table 13.3 Dimensions of corporate culture

Low	High
The power distance dimension (POW) (Australia, Israel, Denmark, Sweden, Norway)	(Philippines, Mexico, Venezuela, India, Brazil)
• Less centralization • Flatter organization pyramids • Smaller wage differentials • Structure in which manual and clerical workers are valued equally to white-collar jobs	• Greater centralization • Tall organization pyramids • More supervisory personnel • Structure in which white-collar jobs are valued more than blue-collar jobs
The masculine/femininity dimensions (MAS) (Sweden, Denmark, Thailand, Finland, Yugoslavia)	(Japan, Australia, Venezuela, Italy, Mexico)
• Sex roles are minimized • Organizations do not interfere with people's private lives • More women in more qualified jobs • Soft, yielding, intuitive skills are rewarded • Social, not only material, rewards are valued	• Sex roles are clearly differentiated • Organizations may interfere to protect their interests • Fewer women are in qualified jobs • Aggression, competition, and justice are rewarded • Work is valued as a central life interest
The individualism/collectivism dimension (IND) (Venezuela, Colombia, Taiwan, Mexico, Greece)	(USA, Australia, Great Britain, Canada, The Netherlands)
• Organization as "family" • Organization defends employee interests • Practices are based on loyalty, sense of duty, and group participation	• Organization is more impersonal • Employees defend their own self-interest • Practices encourage individual initiative
The uncertainty avoidance dimension (UNC) (Denmark, Sweden, Great Britain, USA, India)	(Greece, Portugal, Japan, Peru, France)
• Less structuring of activities • Fewer written rules • More generalists • Variability • Greater willingness to take risks • Less ritualistic behaviour	• More structuring of activities • More written rules • More specialists • Standardization • Less willingness to take risks • More ritualistic behaviour

Source: Adapted from Hofstede (1981).

Box 13.3 Deal & Kennedy's taxonomy of corporate culture

1. *Tough-guy macho culture*
• A world of risk-taking individualists, eager for immediate feedback.
• Frequently construction, management consultancy, venture-capital, media, publishing, sports (High Risk Quick Return).
• High risk, high gain philosophies abound.
• Heroes are survivors who win high stakes.

Box 13.3 continued

- The chance-like nature of success in this world means many superstitious, "comfort blanket" rituals exist.
- Very short-term oriented.
- Unlikely to learn from failures, setback.
- The culture fosters immaturity and distrust of colleagues.

2. *Work hard–play hard culture*
- The culture encourages people to maintain a high level of relatively low-risk activity.
- Frequently real-estate, computer companies, automotive distributors, door-to-door sale operations.
- Success comes with persistence, so this is most rewarded.
- Client/customer centred, aimed at meeting a need and filling it.
- Heroes are friendly, carousing, super-sales people.
- Rites and rituals revolve around energetic games and contests, meetings.
- The action-oriented culture is ideal for people who thrive on quick tangible feedback.
- But quality is sacrificed for quantity.
- There may also be lack of thoughtfulness and attention.
- They can get fooled by success because of little long-term planning.
- High energy enthusiasts drift into cynicism when the quick-fix existence loses its meaning.
- The culture requires great respect and cultivates young people.

3. *Bet your company culture*
- The culture is a high-risk, slow feedback existence with less pressure but "slow-drip water torture".
- Frequently banks, mining companies, large-system business, architectural firms, computer-design companies, actuarial insurance companies.
- They are often ponderous, deliberate companies where good ideas are given a proper chance to show success.
- Decisions are slow, consultative but top-down.
- Heroes can cope with long-term ambiguity, respect authority and technical competence and rely upon it.
- These organizations move with awesome slowness.
- These cultures are vulnerable to short-term fluctuations and cash-flow problems.

4. *Process culture*
- This is the classic bureaucracy – a world of little feedback where it is difficult to concentrate on outcome, so people concentrate on process.
- Frequently government, local government, utilities, some banks and insurance companies, heavily regulated industries.
- It is characterized by excessive memos where people try to "cover their ass" by cc-ing others.
- Protectiveness and caution are natural responses to the absence of feedback.
- Heroes are orderly, punctual, attend to detail.
- Sport/play is important – which sport, how often, who with.
- Special language and jargon abound.
- Greeting rituals may be peculiar to this company.
- Co-worker rituals – tough guys score points off each other; workers/players drink together, betters mentor each other; process people discuss memos.

Source: Reproduced from Furnham and Gunter (1993) with the permission of Routledge.

Box 13.4 Williams, Dobson, & Walters' taxonomy of culture

Power, role, task and people cultures

1. *Power orientation*: power-orientated organizations attempt to dominate their environment and those who are powerful within the organization strive to maintain absolute control over subordinates. They buy and sell organizations and people as commodities, in apparent disregard of human values and general welfare. They are competitive and have voracious appetites for growth. Within the organization, the law of the jungle often seems to prevail among executives as they struggle for personal advantage.

2. *Role orientation*: such organizations would more typically be described as a bureaucracy. There is an emphasis upon legality, legitimacy and responsibility. Conflict is regulated by rules and procedures. Rights and privileges are defined and adhered to. There is a strong emphasis upon hierarchy and status. Predictability of behaviour is high and stability and respectability are often valued as much as competence.

3. *Task orientation*: in such organizations' structures, functions and activities are all evaluated in terms of their contributions to organizational goals. Nothing is allowed to get in the way of task accomplishment. If individuals do not have the skills or technical knowledge to perform a task, they are retrained or replaced. Authority is based upon appropriate knowledge and competence. Emphasis is placed on a rapid and flexible organization. Collaboration is sought if this promotes goal achievement. Task and project groups are common.

4. *People orientation*: this type of organization exists primarily to serve the needs of its members. Authority may be assigned on the basis of task competence, but this practice is kept to a minimum. Instead, individuals are expected to influence each other through example and helpfulness. Consensus methods of decision-making are preferred. And roles are assigned on the basis of personal preference and the need for learning growth.

Source: Reproduced from Williams *et al.* (1989) with the permission of the Institute of Personnel and Development.

(aetiology) and process (mechanism) by which these cultures arise and perpetuate themselves.

The major impact of corporate culture on organizations

Clearly, corporate culture generates strong but subtle pressures to think and act in a particular way. Thus, if an organization's culture stresses such values as service to customers, participative decision-making and a paternalistic attitude towards employees, individuals within the company will usually tend to adopt or at least express these values in their own behaviour. If, in contrast, an organization's culture involves maximizing output, centralized decision-making and "going by the book", individuals' actions will often reflect these attitudes and values.

Corporate culture also relates to performance, although many argue there is no compelling evidence for a clear direct link between culture and performance. One view is that, to influence performance, organizational culture must be strong (basic aspects of the culture are strongly accepted by most employees), and must also possess certain key traits (e.g. humanistic values, concern about quality, innovativeness of products).

But according to Baron & Greenberg (1992), there are three reasons why this relationship is far from clear. First, much of the research on this issue has erroneously assumed that organizations possess a single, unitary culture. Therefore, the findings

Box 13.5 Graves's taxonomy of culture

1. *Barbarian*
- Anti-bureaucratic, ego-driven, rejects procedures and formality.
- Warriors (workers) are workaholics, mavericks, pop-star individualists.
- Leadership is charismatic and groups are unstable.
- There is an atmosphere of perpetual ferment.
- Members share the experience of thrill of the switchback, the euphoria of high life and the bitterness of despair.
- Character types are "fixers" in strong battle, truculent in defeat and contemptuous of a settled life.

2. *Monarchical*
- Contempt for formalization and bureaucracy and planning, yet loyalty and doggedness are highly praised.
- Heavily dependent on the skills of the leader.
- In this culture, succession can be a serious problem.
- Promotion comes from within and the quality of leadership is variable.

3. *Presidential*
- There is, in the democratic culture, the elected leader who embodies the needs and aspirations of all the people in the organization.
- The leader is sustained by subordinates who know his term is short and his influence limited.
- The leader needs to give clear messages to prevent people drifting into subgroups.
- Bad cultures of this type tend to be reactive rather than proactive, living off internal momentum.

4. *Pharaonic*
- A culture with a passion for order, status and ritual.
- The culture is changeless but shadowy, healthy but false.
- Individualism is accepted but the pre-eminence of the system is maintained.

Source: Adapted from Graves (1986) with the permission of Pinter.

reported may apply only to some groups of employees (often top management in the companies studied). Second, serious questions remain about the measures of cultural strength (qualitative and quantitative) used in these projects. Different researchers have adopted different definitions; thus it is not clear that the same variable was being assessed in all cases. Third, none of the studies conducted to date have included appropriate comparison groups. To demonstrate that possession of certain types of culture contributes to corporate success, it is necessary to show that such cultures are indeed characteristic of highly productive organizations, but not of less successful ones. To date, no clear data have been presented on this issue. It is perhaps surprising given all the interest in corporate culture, that we still have no very good evidence of the sort of impact corporate culture has on such fundamental processes as motivation, morale or productivity.

One learns something about corporate culture through the process of organizational socialization. What employees learn about, and how they learn about the history of the organization and the reputation of the leaders, says much about corporate culture. An

Table 13.4 Comparisons of corporate culture taxonomies

1. *Tough guy culture* Risk taking Individualistic	1. *Power culture* Entrepreneurial Ability values	1. *Barbarian* Ego-driven Workaholic	1. *Power-oriented* Competitive Responsibility to personality rather than expertise
2. *Work/play hard* Persistent Sociable	2. *Achievement* Personal Intrinsic Motivation	2. *Presidential* Democratic Hierarchical	2. *People-oriented* Consensual Rejects management control
3. *Bet your company* Ponderous Unpressurized	3. *Support culture* Mutuality Trust	3. *Monarchical* Loyalty Doggedness	3. *Task-oriented* Competency Dynamic
4. *Process culture* Bureaucratic Protective	4. *Role culture* Order Dependable	4. *Pharaonic* Ritualized Changeless	4. *Role-oriented* Legality Legitimacy Pure bureaucracy

Source: Reproduced from Furnham and Gunter (1993) with the permission of Routledge.

organization develops or builds a culture which afterwards shapes how people "learn the ropes" or "speak the language" in that organization. They do so through organizational socialization, which is the process through which individuals are transformed from outsiders into participating, effective members of organizations (see Chapter 3).

For Schein (1990), it is more interesting to understand how culture is *preserved* through socialization; that is, the way newcomers are encouraged to think and feel in the way prescribed by companies. For him, there are seven dimensions along which organizational culture socialization processes vary:

- *Group versus individual*: the extent to which the organization processes recruits in batches, as in boot camps, or individually, as in professional offices. This may be partly associated with the size of the organization (larger organizations favour batches).
- *Formal versus informal*: the extent to which the process is institutionalized and formalized, as in set training programmes, handled informally through apprenticeships, individual coaching by the immediate superior, or the like (larger usually means more formal).
- *Self-destructive and reconstructing versus self-enhancing*: the extent to which the process destroys aspects of the self and replaces them, as in boot camps, or enhances aspects of the self, as in professional development programmes. Clearly, few organizations attempt the dramatic strategy of the Army, but some do attempt a fairly radical change policy, whereby the induction process attempts to shake individuals into a new approach.
- *Serial versus random*: the extent to which role models or mentors are provided, as in apprenticeship or monitoring programmes, or are deliberately withheld, as in sink-or-swim kinds of initiations in which the recruit is expected to figure out his or her own solutions.
- *Sequential versus disjunctive*: the extent to which the process consists of guiding the

recruit through a series of discrete steps and roles versus being open-ended and never letting the recruit predict what organizational role will come next. Few organizations presumably aim to be disjunctive, but it can occur by chance.

- *Fixed versus variable*: the extent to which stages of the training process have fixed timetables for each stage, as in military academies or rotational training programmes, or are open-ended, as in typical promotional systems where one is not advanced to the next stage until one is "ready". The latter is of course more demanding and may be part of a secondary selection procedure.
- *Tournament versus contest*: the extent to which each stage is an "elimination tournament" in which one is out of the organization if one fails, or a "contest" in which one builds up a track record batting average.

The clearest way to examine the effect of culture on an organization, however, is to examine what occurs when two cultures collide in a merger. When two (or more) organizations combine after a merger or acquisition, the implicit features of their two cultures may become all too painfully apparent. Employees are required to explain and question why they perform certain processes in a particular way and not in the preferred manner of the other organization. Usually the corporate culture of the most powerful or economically successful company dominates. Research by Laurent (1983) shows that senior to middle-level executives of different nationalities have differing preferences of organizational structure. The statement that Laurent found had the most variance was: "it is important for a manager to have at hand precise answers to most of the questions that his subordinates may raise about their work". The results ranged from 10% agreement for Swedish managers to 66% agreement for Italian managers. If these are typical responses, then there are clear indications about the kind of organizational culture and structure each nationality would prefer. The Italian end of the spectrum would probably assume a more hierarchical structure, with less room for flexibility and delegation than the Swedish. There are many case studies illustrating what happens when two corporate cultures collide. The world of mergers and acquisitions is one where the collision of culture is common.

The issues that Schneider (1987) sees as leading to a possible clash between national and corporate culture include:

Planning and staffing

- Should planning be formal versus informal, short- versus long-term, explicit versus implicit?
- Is planning irreligious (i.e. no-one but God can know the future)?
- Can we control or shape the future (the fundamental part of strategic planning)?

Career management

- Can people be evaluated, measured and assessed fairly, dispassionately and comprehensively?
- Does the past predict the future? Is *what* you know more important than who you are and who you know?
- Can skills be matched to jobs, the latter being unchanging and clearly specifiable? Also, are some skills more valued than others (arts versus science; specialist versus generalist)?

- Should one expect geographic mobility of the workforce? Is relocation acceptable and desirable?
- Is promotion always desirable and a criterion of success?

Appraisal and compensation

- Is objectivity in appraisal and performance-related pay possible and important?
- Is work-related feedback important? Does it ignore the problem of "face saving" common in the Far East?
- Can appraisal feedback be used for correction and change of individual behaviour? Is the assumption that individuals have actual control over their outcomes?
- Does management by objectives have various unstated assumptions (goals can be set, measured, negotiated) that may be challenged?
- Does tying performance to reward ignore the contribution of groups?
- Do incentives for some break the egalitarian spirit of communities or groups?

In other words, where cultural values clash, all sorts of extremely important issues surface, some of them fundamental to the national culture.

Evan (1978), in an attempt to ascertain the impact of culture on organizations, was highly critical of the current literature. Hence, he set out a six-point programme for future research:

> First, a multinational or, better still, a multicultural research team is necessary to eliminate as many unconscious cultural assumptions and biases as possible on the part of the researchers themselves. *Secondly*, a multidisciplinary team is essential in order to measure how much of the variance in the structure and performance of organizational systems is attributable to cultural variables as compared with other variables such as psychological, structural, inter-organizational, and economic. *Thirdly*, one of the principal problems confronting a research team would be to adapt or construct a research instrument, such as those mentioned above, that will tap cultural variables with a high level of reliability and validity. *Fourthly*, the research instruments measuring cultural variables would be used on a representative sample of the population of a society and a representative sample of the members of one or more organizations in order to measure "societal culture" as well as "organizational subculture". *Fifthly*, in designing sample surveys, at least two modes of cross-societal comparisons would be used: intra-systemic comparisons (that is, matching domestic or national firms with those of foreign subsidiaries), distinguishing wholly owned subsidiaries from joint ventures, and controlling for various structural and industrial characteristics; and intra-organizational comparisons, that is, subsidiaries of the same company and of comparable size, function, and technology in different societies. *Sixthly*, in addition to sample surveys, at least two other complementary research methods would be desirable – laboratory and field experiments – in order to test major causal hypotheses; and supported by sample surveys to test the impact of cultural values on organizational behaviour and organizational system performance. (Evan, 1978: 107–109)

Cultural dimensions and international management

In an approach not dissimilar to Hofstede (1980), Trompenaars (1993, 1997) describes and contrasts seven dimensions of culture. He also offers tips on doing business with those at opposite extremes of each dimension; how to behave when managed by people from that particular culture and how to reconcile the two.

- *Universalism versus particularism*: For universalists, all rules (at work and in society) apply equally to everybody. The focus is on rules, contracts and trustworthiness. Universalists argue for a rational, professional, impersonal, legislation approach to work. They like consistency, uniformity and open, formal ways of business operations. In contrast, particularists put friendship and relationships first. They are prepared to override contracts for friendship and emphasize relationship-building and maintenance. They build networks, do deals privately and believe all cases have to be judged on their particular and specific merits.
- *Individualism versus communitarianism*: Individualistic cultures stress personal decision-making, freedom and responsibility. They like pay-for-performance, management-by-objective, key result area methods. They follow their own career path and easily and happily leave organizations. High flyers are heroes. In contrast, communitarian cultures work in small groups that provide help and protection. They take longer to take joint decisions and are sensitive to morale, cohesiveness and teamwork. They do not stress individual success but instead the role of superordinate goals. They prefer group loyalty with little job turnover and mobility.
- *Specific versus diffuse*: A specific orientation refers to the desire to contact others for very specific purposes. Thus people are direct, definitive, precise and emphasize principles. In business they aim to meet objectives, follow clear, precise, detailed instructions, reduce conflict, and keep business and private lives separate. A diffuse orientation refers to relationships that are indirect, ambiguous, tactful, evasive. People are seen as a whole. Businesses stress continuous evolution and it is acknowledged that private and business issues overlap. Accepting vagueness and ambiguity allows, it is believed, for subtle, personality interpretations that benefit all.
- *Neutral versus affective*: Neutral cultures do not do emotions. They admire cool, self-possessed, stoical, unemotional behaviour. They shun expressive, enthusiastic behaviour, which is seen as childish or lacking in control. They choose to avoid hot topics and admire those with sangfroid. Affective cultures spontaneously express their emotions and feel it appropriate to show how they feel. They express positive and negative emotions easily, effusively, vehemently and without inhibition. They can appear enthusiastic, vital and animated, even histrionic.
- *Achievement versus ascription*: Achievement cultures see individual performance (alone) as the basis of authority, rank and power. Skill, knowledge and technical expertise are the sole criteria to be judged. Ascriptive cultures ascribe organizational status on the basis of affluence, age, sex or familiar relationships. Titles, seniority and experience are the major bases of power and respect.
- *Past and present versus future time orientation*: Past- and present oriented cultures look back or focus on contemporary impact and style. History and traditions are important and plans are rarely executed. Future-oriented cultures have serious plans and aspirations. They talk about prospects, potentials and have a great interest in the future. They look for opportunities and tend to be optimistic.

- *Internal versus external*: Internal cultures stress personal control and fear being "out of control". The economic and physical environment is seen to be controllable, mastered, dominated. Conflict and resistance is healthy and shows determination. Internals like clear, tangible goals with concomitant rewards. External cultures are more fatalistic: they see luck, chance and change as powerful and real factors in business success. They stress harmony and expect shifts, cycles and changes, and so value flexibility and compromise. They tend to be more patient, polite and persistent.

Gooderham and Nordhang (2004) have suggested various lessons may be drawn from the work of Trompenaars:

- Universalism vs particularism. Companies from universalist cultures negotiating with a potential joint venture partner in China must recognize that relationships matter and take time to develop. They form the basis of the trust that is necessary in order to do business. In a particularist culture, contracts are only a rough guideline or approximation.
- Individualism vs Communitarianism. Companies from individualistic cultures such as the USA will face difficulties in introducing methods of individual incentives such as pay-for-performance and individual assessment in subsidiaries in communitarian cultures such as Germany or Japan.
- Neutral vs emotional. Multinational teams consisting of individuals from highly neutral and highly affective cultures need careful management and considerable inter-cultural understanding. Otherwise, the affective persons will view the neutral persons as ice-cold, and the affective persons will be viewed out of control by the neutrals.
- Specific vs diffuse. Managers from specific cultures such as Denmark are much more prone to criticize subordinates directly and openly without regarding their criticism as a personal matter. In the context of a subsidiary in a diffuse culture such as Russian, this may constitute an unacceptable loss of face.
- Achievement vs ascription. Sending a young manager to run a subsidiary in an ascriptive culture such as India will involve difficulty. Likewise promoting younger people within the subsidiary on the basis of their performance. (Gooderham & Nordhang, 2004: 144)

Assessing and measuring corporate culture

Many different instruments attempt to measure corporate cultures. An indication of their usefulness may be obtained by examining studies that have used them. Xenikou & Furnham (1996) examined the psychometric properties of four of the measures of corporate culture. They found the *organizational culture inventory* to be most robust. The inventory was not designed to sample domains of interpersonal and task-related styles that might be promoted by an organization, or exhaustively to tap the variety of socially derived cognitions that constitute culture. Instead, it is intended to enable respondents to clarify their own experiences of their organization's culture with respect to these specific styles, to compare their perceptions to the aggregated perceptions of co-workers, and to understand how their own thinking styles might be affected by organizational norms.

The twelve types are set out below (Cooke & Lafferty, 1989):

- A *humanistic–helpful culture* characterizes organizations managed in a participative and person-centred way. Members are expected to be supportive, constructive and open to influence in their dealings with one another. (Helping others to grow and develop; taking time with people.)
- An *affiliative culture* characterizes organizations that place a high priority on constructive interpersonal relationships. Members are expected to be friendly, open and sensitive to the satisfaction of their workgroup. (Dealing with others in a friendly way; sharing feelings and thoughts.)
- An *approval culture* describes organizations in which conflicts are avoided and interpersonal relationships are pleasant – at least superficially. Members feel that they should agree with, gain the approval of and be liked by others. (Making sure people accept you; "going along" with others.)
- A *conventional culture* is descriptive of organizations that are conservative, traditional and bureaucratically controlled. Members are expected to conform, follow the rules and make a good impression. (Always following policies and practices; fitting into "the mould".)
- A *dependent culture* is descriptive of organizations that are hierarchically controlled and non-participative. Centralized decision-making in such organizations leads members to do only what they are told and to clear decisions with superiors. (Pleasing those in positions of authority; doing what is expected.)
- An *avoidance culture* characterizes organizations that fail to reward success but nevertheless punish mistakes. This negative reward system leads members to shift responsibilities to others and to avoid any possibility of being blamed for a mistake. (Waiting for others to act first; taking few chances.)
- An *oppositional culture* describes organizations in which confrontation prevails and negativism is rewarded. Members gain status and influence by being critical, and thus are reinforced to oppose the ideas of others and to make safe (but ineffectual) decisions. (Pointing out flaws; being hard to impress.)
- A *power culture* is descriptive of non-participative organizations structured on the basis of the authority inherent in members' positions. Members believe they will be rewarded for taking charge, controlling subordinates and, at the same time, being responsive to the demands of superiors. (Building upon one's power base; motivating others in any way necessary.)
- A *competitive culture* is one in which winning is valued and members are rewarded for outperforming one another. People in such organizations operate in a "win–lose" framework and believe they must work against (rather than with) their peers to be noticed. (Turning the job into a contest; never appearing to lose.)
- A *competence/perfectionistic culture* characterizes organizations in which perfectionism, persistence and hard work are valued. Members feel they must avoid all mistakes, keep track of everything, and work long hours to attain narrowly defined objectives. (Doing things perfectly; keeping on top of everything.)
- An *achievement culture* characterizes organizations that do things well and value members who set and accomplish their own goals. Members of these organizations set challenging but realistic goals, establish plans to reach these goals, and pursue them with enthusiasm. (Pursuing a standard of excellence; openly showing enthusiasm.)

- A *self-actualization culture* characterizes organizations that value creativity, quality over quantity, and both task accomplishment and individual growth. Members of these organizations are encouraged to gain enjoyment from their work, develop themselves, and take on new and interesting activities. (Thinking in unique and independent ways; doing even simple tasks well.)

These cultures were in turn grouped into three categories: Types 1–4 were described as *satisfactory*, 5–8 as *security* and 9–12 as *dependent* cultures.

Research by Cooke & Rousseau (1988) indicates that organizations characterized by chief executives as being excellent or ideal (i.e. for implementing successful organizational strategies) take the form of satisfaction-orientated cultures. Security-orientated cultures use organizational sanctions to promote particular behaviour patterns and often are more behaviour-inhibiting (e.g. risk-avoiding), in contrast to satisfaction cultures, which tend to be behaviour-amplifying (e.g. risk-seeking). Cooke & Rousseau found that the security-orientated styles fall into two empirical factors: people/security and task/security. *People/security* characterizes beliefs focusing on control in interpersonal relations and includes the following four dimensions:

- *Approval*: conflict is avoided and interpersonal relationships are superficially pleasant. Members believe they agree with, gain the approval of and are liked by others.
- *Conventional*: conservative, traditional and bureaucratically controlled. Members believe they must conform, follow the rules and make a good impression.
- *Dependent*: hierarchically controlled and non-participative. Decision-making is centralized and members believe they must do as they are told and clear all decisions with superiors.
- *Avoidance*: the emphasis is on punishment of mistakes and not rewards for success. Negative reward systems lead to shifting responsibilities to others and avoiding any possibility of being blamed for a mistake.

Task/security characterizes beliefs focusing on control in task-related activities:

- *Oppositional*: confrontation prevails and negativism is rewarded. Members gain status and influence by being critical and opposing the ideas of others.
- *Power*: descriptive of non-participative organizations structured on the basis of hierarchy and position authority. Members are rewarded for taking charge, controlling subordinates and being responsive to their own superiors.
- *Competitive*: winning is valued and members are rewarded for outperforming one another. Members operate in a win–lose framework and believe they must work against (rather than with) peers to be noticed.
- *Perfectionistic*: perfectionism, persistence and hard work are valued. Members believe they must avoid all mistakes, keep track of every detail, and work long hours to attain narrowly defined objectives.

Using this measure, Cooke & Rousseau (1988) showed clear evidence of agreement within the organizations, significant differences across organizations, and that sub-culture differences occur across hierarchy levels. They were able to draw up the profile of an excellent organization, one with security-orientated norms and an "ideal" culture profile. This scored high on satisfaction styles and low on people and task/security styles.

In another study, Rousseau (1990) showed that certain cultural norms were related to actual performance on the job as well as employees' perceptions of role clarity, role conflict, overall satisfaction and propensity to stay in the organization. Earlier, Rousseau (1988) examined security-orientated cultures in great detail and found that these "high reliability" organizations have strong norms that support hierarchical referral, avoid conflict and tend to be behaviour-inhibiting and associated with employee dissatisfaction and role conflict. The fact that the organizational culture inventory is easy to use, has proven psychometric qualities and is frequently used in research means that it may prove a most useful tool to answer some of the fundamental questions concerning corporate culture.

The corporate culture concept is with us for some time to come. Although it will no doubt lose its popular appeal as it is replaced by yet another "solution" to all management problems, it has uncovered enough of a hornet's nest among academics from different disciplines and epistemological perspectives to fuel argument and research for many years to come. Just as there is no shortage of definitions of culture, so there has been a sudden increase in measures that attempt to ascertain corporate culture. Certainly, the majority of these new measures tap into similar dimensions, but it remains unclear as to whether they are able to describe all of the many features of culture in all companies.

Corporate climate

A related concept much used by researchers is that of corporate climate. Administrators and managers are well aware that the actual atmospheric climate (i.e. the weather) can, and does, greatly affect organizations. Many organizations have been either partially or totally destroyed by unfortunate climatic disturbances such as floods, hurricanes and tornadoes. Organizational climate also affects an organization and can be potentially just as devastating to its survival as atmospheric climate. However, the two climates do not affect the same resources of the organization. Whereas atmospheric climate acts primarily upon the physical resources of the organization, organizational climate acts upon the human resources (the personnel) of the organization.

Organizational psychologists have become increasingly interested in organizational climate because of the significant relationships exhibited between this construct, job satisfaction and job performance. In fact, the concept of organizational climate is now well established in the management literature: it has been around for over 30 years and well over a dozen reviews have appeared of research in this field. An organization's climate can be manifest through appropriate corporate audits which collate the individual views of an organization's employees to produce a perceptual profile of the organization. As interest in organizational climate has grown, several definitions have appeared in the literature over the past few years, which are discussed later (Furnham & Gunter, 1993: 112).

One view of organizational climate sees it as a feature of the organization that people, regardless of where they work, experience daily. It is not as subtle or as endearing as culture, but more akin to morale. Furthermore, this type of "psychological" climate has just as vital an impact on individuals in the workplace as does the atmospheric climate in respect of people's general moods and activity. In fact, organizational

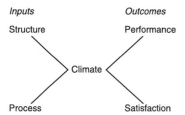

Figure 13.1 Climate as a moderator variable.

climate may prove to be one of the primary causes of *job satisfaction* and *job perform-ance* in organizations. According to some writers, it is a moderator variable between the structure and process in an organization and major employee outputs (Figure 13.1). In essence, this implies that the structure of the organization and the daily procedures and processes influence and establish a climate, which, in turn, affects performance and employee satisfaction. But, as we shall see, this is a contested view.

The creation of a healthy, motivating organizational climate is mainly the result of leadership behaviour and style. The internal climate of an organization encompasses the nature of the organization's communications networks, reward systems, leadership style, goal-setting techniques and other factors. In asking about an organization's cli-mate, we are really asking how effective that organization is in mobilizing its human resources. Climate is the focus of a complex set of forces within an organization that impinge upon those who work in it. A knowledge of climate variables enables manage-ment to harness those forces towards the accomplishment of organization goals.

Essentially, corporate climate can be seen as *part* of corporate culture, although the difference between the two is not clear. There tends to be less disagreement on the concept of climate than that of culture, because climate was originally part of the field of organizational and occupational psychology. Because the concept of culture came from the field of anthropology, psychologists have spent much more effort trying to define it.

In fact, there has been considerable debate as to the differences between organ-izational culture and climate (Ashkanasy, Wilderom, & Peterson, 2001). Culture researchers have been interested in the evolution and stability of organizational social systems over time, while climate researchers have been more interested in the impact of systems on individuals and groups. Culture researchers look at the underlying assump-tions, values and meaning, while climate researchers look more at "surface" factors that are more easily observable. According to Denison:

> Culture refers to the deep structure of organizations, which is rooted in the values, beliefs, and assumptions held by organizational members. Meaning is established through socialization to a variety of identity groups that converge in the workplace. Interaction reproduces a symbolic world that gives culture both a great stability and a certain precarious and fragile nature rooted in the dependence of the system on individual cognition and action. Climate, in contrast, portrays organizational environments as being rooted in the organization's value system, but tends to present these social environments in relatively static terms, describing them in terms of a fixed (and broadly applicable) set of dimensions. Thus, climate is often considered as relatively temporary, subject to direct control, and largely limited to

those aspects of the social environment that are consciously perceived by organizational members. (Denison, 1996: 624)

Culture, Denison argues, takes on a historical perspective and is rooted in sociology and anthropology, while climate takes an historical snapshot and is rooted in psychology:

> On the surface, the distinction between organizational climate and organizational culture may appear to be quite clear: Climate refers to a situation and its link to thoughts, feelings, and behaviours of organizational members. Thus, it is temporal, subjective, and often subject to direct manipulation by people with power and influence. Culture, in contrast, refers to an evolved context (within which a situation may be embedded). Thus, it is rooted in history, collectively held, and sufficiently complex to resist many attempts at direct manipulation. The two perspectives have generated distinct theories, methods, and epistemologies as well as a distinct set of findings, failings, and future agendas. However, at a deeper level, when one begins to compare the individual studies that make up these two literatures, these seemingly clear distinctions begin to disappear. Over time, the underlying similarity of the two research topics has led a number of culture researchers to apply the quantitative, comparative and Lewinian approaches associated with climate research, whereas several climate researchers have studied the evolution of social contexts from a social constructionist point of view that makes it difficult to distinguish from culture research. Despite these points of convergence, however, considerable effort is still devoted to the maintenance of a narrow orthodoxy within each literature that makes it difficult, if not impossible, to build on some of the obvious points of integration. (Denison, 1996: 644–645)

As early as 1960, Gellerman saw the climate as the "personality" of organizations. He listed five steps for analysing the character of a company: (1) identify the people in the organization whose attitudes count; (2) study these individuals and determine their goals, tactics and blind spots; (3) analyse the economic challenges facing the company in terms of policy decisions; (4) review the company history, giving particular attention to the careers of its leaders; and (5) integrate the total picture with the aim of extracting common denominators instead of adding up all the parts to create a sum.

Rousseau (1988) has provided a useful chronology of climate definitions that enables one to compare and contrast different conceptions (Table 13.5). She notes:

> The lack of boundaries differentiating what climate is from what it is not is troublesome – and may in fact be "suppressing" research on climate by causing researchers to focus on either specific perceptions of context exclusively (eschewing any mention of the climate concept as in the case of motivation and leadership research) or to reject its relevance to the study of organization.
>
> Nonetheless, climate, as a concept, clearly does have specific boundaries that differentiate it from both other characteristics and other perceptions. Two consistent defining attributes of climate persist through its various conceptualizations: it is a perception and it is descriptive. Perceptions are sensations or realizations experienced by an individual. Descriptions are a person's reports of these sensations. Whether individual differences or situational factors explain large or minute

Table 13.5 Climate definition chronology

Forehand & Gilmer (1964)	Characteristics that (1) distinguish one organization from another, (2) endure over time, and (3) influence the behaviour of people in organizations. The personality of the organization.
Findlater & Margulies (1969)	Perceived organizational properties intervening between organizational characteristics and behaviour.
Campbell *et al.* (1970)	A set of attitudes and expectancies describing the organization's static characteristics, and behaviour–outcome and outcome–outcome contingencies.
Schneider & Hall (1972)	Individual perceptions of their organizations affected by characteristics of the organization and the individual.
James & Jones (1974)	Psychologically meaningful cognitive representations of the situation; perceptions.
Schneider (1975)	Perceptions or interpretations of meaning which help individuals make sense of the world and know how to behave.
Payne *et al.* (1976)	Consensus of individuals' descriptions of the organization.
James *et al.* (1978)	Sum of members' perceptions about the organization.
Litwin & Stringer (1978)	A psychological process intervening between organizational characteristics and behaviour.
Joyce & Slocum (1979)	Climates are (1) perceptual, (2) psychological, (3) abstract, (4) descriptive, (5) not evaluative, and (6) not actions.
James & Sell (1981)	Individuals' cognitive representation of proximal environments . . . expressed in terms of psychological meaning and significance to the individual . . . an attribute of the individual, which is learned, historical and resistant to change.
Schneider & Reichers (1983)	An assessed molar perception or an inference researchers make based on more particular perceptions.
Glick (1985)	("Organizational Climate") A generic term for a broad class of organizational, rather than psychological, variables that describe the context for individuals' actions.

Source: Reproduced from Rousseau (1988) with the permission of John Wiley & Sons.

amounts of variance in these descriptions varies from one notion of climate to the next, and is more an empirical than a definitional one . . .

It is in the distinctions between different types of *beliefs* where the nature and operation of climate can perhaps be best understood. Beliefs are the result of an individual's attempt to make sense of a set of stimuli, a situation, or patterns of interactions between people. There are cognitions, the result of information processing, but beliefs are more than perceptions *per se* (such as sights and sounds). In a sense, perceptions are simply informational cues that are registered or received. Beliefs are the result of active cognitive processing . . . Initiated by perceptions, beliefs result from the interpretation and organization of perceptions into an understanding of the relationship between objects, properties and/or ideas. Self-report measures of molar constructs such as climate involve interpretation. (Rousseau, 1988: 142)

An important but related issue is the amount of consensus within an organization concerning the perceived climate. Pace & Stern (1958) suggested a two-thirds agreement, but Guion (1973) has argued that it should be 90% for the concept of climate to be invoked. Payne (1990) has argued that the concept of organizational climate is invalid, because people in different parts of the organization have radically different perceptions of the organization (hence, the perception is not shared) and that, where perceptions are consensually shared only in small groups, they are not representative of the climate of the whole organization. Thus, for Payne (1990), it is possible to have departmental but not organizational climates.

This conceptual muddle has become worse with the introduction of the concept of corporate or organizational culture (Schein, 1990). However, there are as many, if not more, problems associated with the concept of corporate culture as there are with corporate climate. One way to circumvent, rather than overcome, the conceptual issues is to talk of *employee perceptions* rather than of culture or climate. Naturally, employee perceptions differ within an organization as a function of seniority, department, and so forth, and those perceptions influence, and are influenced by, organizational behaviours. But because the term climate has been used in the past, it is used again here to examine the current literature.

The second major theoretical problem concerns the effect of climate (or employee perception) on organizational behaviour. Climate may be conceived of as an *independent, dependent, moderator* or *epiphenomenal* variable. If climate is conceived of as an independent variable, as for instance in the work of Campbell, Dunnette, Lawler & Weick (1970), it is assumed that organizational climate itself directly influences (causes) various work outcomes, which can be both positive (e.g. productivity, satisfaction and motivation) and negative (e.g. absenteeism, turnover and accidents). Others have considered climate as a dependent, outcome variable – that is, the result, and not the cause, of organizational structure and processes. In this sense, climate may be a useful index of an organization's health, but not a causal factor of it. A third, and perhaps more common, approach has been to see climate as a moderator variable, in that climate may be the indirect link between two organizational outcomes. Thus, climate may be the moderator variable between job satisfaction and productivity. Various (untested but heuristically satisfying) models consider climate as one of several powerful moderator variables (Litwin & Stringer, 1968). Finally, some researchers believe that climate is epiphenomenal, neither a direct cause nor an effect variable, but one that emerges in some form in all organizations, but having no influence on the organization itself. Few take this view: certainly, if it were true, climate would not be worth investigating.

There are many models that use the concept of climate (Bonoma & Zaltman, 1981; Litwin & Stringer, 1968), but very few specify the exact relationship between climate and other organizational processes or products. Few theorists or researchers have acknowledged that climate may be *both* an independent and dependent (cause and consequence) variable simultaneously. Few studies have tested any longitudinal path analytic models to determine which major factors influence climate and which are influenced by it. Yet this would seem to be a potentially important and relevant theoretical and empirical avenue to pursue (Furnham & Gunter, 1993: 118–120).

The causes and consequences of climate

The antecedents of climate can, in principle, be specified, measured and delineated. Indeed, various "models" (discussed later) have been developed to explain which of various factors interact to "produce" climate and how they do so. There are many ways to categorize these factors:

- *external forces*: economic, market, political, social, technological;
- *organizational history*: the culture, values and behaviour patterns of the organization;
- *management*: the organizational structure and leadership pattern.

Two kinds of influence of climate on individuals may be distinguished. First, there is *direct influence* that affects all or almost all members of the company or some subunit of it. The second kind of effect is termed *interactive influence*, which exists when a climate has a certain effect upon the behaviour of some people, a different effect on others, and possibly no effect at all on still others.

Certain behaviours never occur in some organizations (for cultural reasons), because the stimuli that would elicit them are never presented. Organizations themselves place constraints on people through rules and regulations, routine practices, instructions, taboos and explicit injunctions. It is not uncommon for the ambitious person to find him or herself in a climate that puts restraints upon freedom, thus narrowing alternatives of action. Out of it develop ways of behaving, ways of working, ways of loafing, ways of cooperating and ways of resisting. Newcomers to an established subculture may rebuke the current job-holders as being cynical about the system, apparently unaware that there is good reason to be cynical. They may find to their embarrassment that hasty evaluation of people and established practices can backfire.

How do management programmes affect organizational climate? Moxnes & Eilertsen (1991) note that few researchers have examined the influence of training on organizational variables such as climate. They argue that, just as climate variables facilitate and disrupt various training initiatives, so programmes can affect overall climate. Using a 51-item questionnaire, they measured ten dimensions of climate, including enthusiasm and communication about personal problems. First, they examined all employees who had and had not taken part in the training programme, but found few significant differences. Then, looking at two different years' results, it seemed management training had a small but specific effect on organizational climate. Curiously, participants in training programmes had a more negative perception of their work climate than non-participants on seven or eight of the ten climate indices. The authors offer three different explanations for these findings: the data reflect real changes in the working environment; the managers became more aware that the climate was bad, and the scores thus reflect changes in participants' perceptions of organizational environment without any "real" change; participants used words ("conflict", "trouble", "criticism") in new and positive ways having reconceptualized their environment.

> By giving supervisors a sense of dissatisfaction with their own performance and opening their eyes to the prevailing conflicts in their divisions, they should, according to change theory, become more motivated to perform well. (Moxnes & Eilersten, 1991: 400)

This paradoxical case has important implications for studies on climate, because it points to three things:

- Training programmes can and do affect organizational climate, which no doubt affects enthusiasm for training programmes.

- Programmes that emphasize increased awareness may increase dissatisfaction and negative perceptions, which may, or may not, have strong motivating effects.
- Climate is relatively sensitive to training programmes.

Various researchers in the fields of human resources and organizational psychology have attempted to describe the effects or consequences of organizational climate. For instance, Gordon & Cummins (1979) argued that considerable research has shown that various "climate" issues are clearly related to company profit. They listed thirteen:

1 The organization has clear goals.
2 The organization has defined plans to meet its goals.
3 The planning system is formal.
4 Planning is comprehensive.
5 Information for decision-making is available.
6 Information for decision-making is used.
7 Good lateral communications exist.
8 Overall communications are good.
9 Units understand each other's objectives.
10 Clear measures of managerial performance exist.
11 Managers are clear about the results expected of them.
12 Benefits are competitive.
13 Compensation is related to performance.

Thus, they assert, with some supporting evidence, that, if these structural and climatic features occur in an organization, it is likely to be profitable.

There is no shortage of models or theories explaining, or at least describing, how climate is both the cause and consequence of critical organizational factors. As we shall see, there is little agreement between these models, and even less empirical evidence to support them.

Organizational climate is depicted here as having an influence on *all* aspects of the organization. The manager is involved in all stages in Figure 13.2, from the person, through the process, to the outcome. Managerial effectiveness, which is the ability to manage the organizational climate, will have a direct effect on all stages of these processes within the organization. Note, however, that the direction of nearly all the errors is "one way", suggesting unidirectional causality. Also, from this model, it is not clear what causes or maintains the particular climate.

Researchers have been particularly interested in the behavioural and attitudinal correlates of organizational climate. Field & Abelson (1982) provide a clear model (Figure 13.2). Three aspects of this model are of particular importance. First, there is the multiplicity of influences on individuals' perceptions of climate. Managerial behaviour may be the most significant means by which these influences are communicated to individual employees, but it is still only one determinant of climate perceptions. The second aspect of the model in Figure 13.2 that merits attention is the moderating effect of the workgroup, the task and the personality of the individual employee on perceptions of climate. Finally, individual characteristics modify responses to perceived climate in a similar fashion (Furnham & Gunter, 1993: 128).

As shown at the foot of the model in Figure 13.2, the three responses to a work situation generally believed to be influenced by organizational climate are motivation,

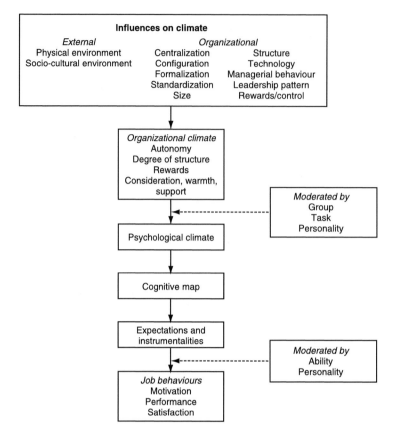

Figure 13.2 The causes and consequences of climate. Reproduced from Field & Abelson (1982) with the permission of Plenum Publishing Corporation.

performance and reported job satisfaction. Of these three, the relationship between climate and job satisfaction has received the most attention. Note, however, that this model has few feedback loops, and it does not explain whether organizational climate is shared or stable.

Perhaps the best known and most influential model of the role of organizational climate in business performance is the Burke–Litwin model (Figure 13.3). This model suggests that external social, political, economic and market forces shape or determine not only who becomes leader, but the style of leadership in any organization. As well as developing the organization's mission and strategy and influencing its culture, leaders sanction, promote and prescribe a host of management practices that determine how things are done in the organization. These management practices relate to the structures and systems in the organization, which are formal explicit structures that support particular practices. It is these practices that determine the work unit climate. Note that it is "work unit" climate and not organizational climate that is the focus of attention here. It is assumed that, because some management practices might not be inherent or consistent throughout the organization, it will be work unit climates, which are dependent on them, that are influenced, rather than some managerial organization-wide climate. The work unit climate, in turn, affects the motivation of all members of that

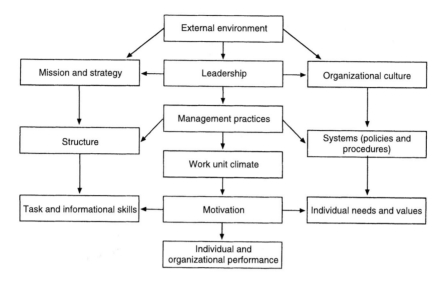

Figure 13.3 The Burke–Litwin model of individual and organizational performance. Reproduced from Litwin & Stringer (1968) with the permission of Harvard University Press.

unit, which relates logically to its output, be it personal motivation or production. Thus, through its operations at different levels, climate can be a central facet of organizational functioning.

Although it is not clear precisely how one would test this model (although Lisrel or standard path analysis offer analytical possibilities), it does indicate clearly what one needs to change to alter the climate. And from the model it is not clear how climate leads to changes in performance. Certainly, the research that has been done to date suggests that the most direct path is down the centre of the model, yet note that not all the "boxes" are connected (and therefore presumably do not influence each other) and that the direction of influence is one way.

Despite the appeal of many of these models, they have certain drawbacks. First, they cannot all be correct, because they do not concur with one another. Some scholars see climate as a moderating factor strongly determined by environmental and structural factors, whereas others see it as all pervasive. Rarely is climate precisely defined and explained, and it is possible that researchers are using the term in quite different ways. Second, few of these models have received any empirical support (Furnham & Gunter, 1993: 128–132).

Measuring climate

There are many ways of measuring organizational climate. The first is *categorical*, which attempts to classify organizations into pre-existing theoretical types. The second is *dimensional*, which attempts to classify organizations on a set of pre-established dimensions which are thought to capture or fully describe the organizational climate. A third less well used method is to obtain archival data or other objective evidence to generate an aggregate index of an organizational climate. Miceli & Near (1985) used this method to look at organizational climate factors associated with "whistle-blowing".

The categorical approach has not been very popular or successful. Examples of this approach can be seen in the work of Ginsberg (1978), who described three basic climates (inception, post-entrepreneurial and bureaucratic), and Halpin & Croft (1962), who believed climates could be categorized as open, autonomous, controlled, familiar, paternal or closed. Although this approach has attracted a certain amount of research, it has limitations: a lack of fine discriminability, inappropriate categories and, most importantly, the idea that organizational climates are multidimensional and should be measured on various salient, albeit related, dimensions.

Early attempts to measure organizational climate tried to generate taxonomies of self-perceived climate, usually through factor-analytic methods. Campbell *et al.* (1970) reviewed four investigations of the structure of managerial climate (Kahn, Wolfe, Quinn, Snoek, & Rosenthal, 1964; Litwin & Stringer, 1968; Schneider & Bartlett, 1968; Taguiri, 1968), and found four dimensions common to these studies. These were individual autonomy, degree of structure imposed on the position, reward orientation, and consideration, warmth and support. Although other dimensions were found in these studies, Campbell *et al.* were a little concerned about the small number of dimensions uncovered. They stated:

> Even though the sets required of the respondents were different, perhaps the content of the stimuli (items) were very similar across the four studies. Also, the relatively small number of factors which were found implies that a great deal of environmental variation remains to be uncovered. (Campbell *et al.*, 1870: 394)

Some dimensional organizational climate measures exist. Litwin & Stringer's (1968) 50-item organizational climate questionnaire (form B) is designed to measure nine characteristics reflecting the organizational emphasis on structure, responsibility, reward, risk, warmth, support, standards, conflict and identity. There are many others, including those of House & Rizzo (1972), Payne & Mansfield (1973), Jones & James (1979) and Zohar (1980).

However, to prevent there being as many climate questionnaires as there were climate surveys conducted, Koys & De Cotiis (1991) undertook a content analysis of dozens of studies; their results are shown in Table 13.6. This provided them with the evidence and material to construct their own eight-dimensional scale.

Evans (1968) proposed a "system" model for organizational climate, which allowed him to formulate some interesting, and testable, hypotheses. He lists six:

1   The climate of an organization tends to be perpetuated from one generation of members to another unless the structure of the inputs and outputs and intra-organizational processes are changed along with the feedback effects. This hypothesis, if true, in effect cautions against the inclination to solve an organizational climate problem by recruiting a new executive. He is not likely to succeed unless he is sufficiently knowledgeable, powerful and charismatic as to alter the inputs, the intra-organizational processes, the outputs and the feedback effects.

2   Inertial forces maintaining organizational climate tend to increase with the size of an organization. As the size of an organization increases, differentiation increases

Table 13.6 Psychological climate dimensions

Summary dimension	Dimension label as found in the literature	Summary dimension	Dimension label as found in the literature
Autonomy	Autonomy Closeness of supervision (reversed) Individual responsibility Leader's initiation of structure (reversed)	Support	Support Leader's consideration Leader work facilitation Leader's psychological distance Hierarchical influence Management awareness
Cohesion	Cohesiveness Conflict (reversed) Esprit Peer relations Status polarization (reversed) Universalism Workgroup cooperation, friendliness, and warmth Sociability	Recognition	Recognition and feedback Opportunities for growth and advancement Reward–punishment relationship Rewards
Trust	Intimacy versus aloofness Leader trust Management insensitivity (reversed) Managerial trust Openness	Fairness	Fairness and objectivity of the reward system Promotion clarity Policy clarity Policy clarity and efficiency of structure Altruism Egalitarianism
Pressure	Job pressure Role overload, role conflict, role ambiguity Time-span orientation Achievement emphasis Job standards Measuring of results Production emphasis	Innovation	Innovation Organizational flexibility Impulsive Security versus risk Challenge and risk Future orientation

Source: Reproduced from Koys & De Cotiis (1991) with the permission of Plenum Publishing Corporation.

both in relation to the number and type of statuses and number and type of subunits. Accompanying an increase in status and functional differentiation is an increase in the scope of problems of role socialization, role performance and inter-subunit coordination. In the face of mounting problems associated with an increase in size, the difficulties of deliberately modifying the internal organizational climate are correspondingly greater.

3   If the organizational climate as perceived by members of the focal organization is more favourable than the climate as perceived by members of organizations comprising the organization-set, there will be less innovation because of a reduced motivation to change. Conversely, if the climate as perceived by members of the focal organization is less favourable than the climate as perceived by members of organizations comprising the organization-set, there will be greater innovation.

4   Organizational climate is more susceptible to deliberate efforts to modify it when there is a weak consensus regarding it. As between *internal* and *external*

organizational climate, it is probably easier to alter the former than the latter because of the greater control that the focal organization can exercise over its members than over the members of organizations comprising its organization-set.

5   As differences in subunit climates of an organization increase, there is a tendency for greater conflict to arise over proposals for innovation and for a discrepancy to occur in the rate of technical and administrative innovations – that is, for the degree of "organizational lag" to increase.

6   Technical innovations, because they are manifested in the products or services of an organization, are more likely to generate faster changes in the external organizational climate than administrative innovation. (Evans, 1968: 120–121)

Conclusion

Corporate culture is a subtle but pervasive force. Just as various forces (economic, political, religious and ethnic) shape national culture, so various environmental and historical forces influence corporate culture. There are well-established cross-cultural differences in the perception of time, interpersonal space preferred and language used. Organizational culture can be strong or weak depending on the cohesiveness, size and value consensus in the organization. A strong culture is not necessarily a good culture and it may be resistant to change.

Corporate culture permits and encourages the shared meanings in every organization. It can be seen in the rites, rituals, myths, legends, symbols, language and artefacts of that culture. Furthermore, it functions to give members an organizational identity, it facilitates collective commitment, it promotes social system stability, and it partly shapes the behaviour of all employees by helping them make sense of their surroundings. For many business people, an adaptable, healthy organizational culture can provide a competitive advantage. Hence, some managers try to develop a specific culture by developing a sense of history, creating a sense of oneness and membership, and increasing exchange among members.

Corporate culture has proved very difficult to define with any precision. One way of describing it has been to specify particular dimensions or, indeed, types of corporate culture. The dimensional versus categorical approaches have different advantages and disadvantages, although neither says much about how the corporate culture works or functions. Yet both provide a way for organizations to describe their own culture, both as it exists *and* how they wish it to exist.

Apart from the work on definitions, descriptions and taxonomies, the question of central interest remains the impact of the corporate culture on such things as productivity, morale and procedures.

The concept of corporate climate has proved in some ways just as elusive for work psychologists, although it has been around for considerably longer. Again, there are definitional differences and rather different ways of measuring climate. However, there are some fairly sophisticated and widely used models of corporate culture that place it as a central variable relating to both motivation and productivity.

A research perspective

Organizational justice

Organizational justice is people's (manager and employee) perceptions of fairness in an organization's policies, pay systems and practices. The concept of justice and how justice is meted out in any organization must be fundamental to that organization's corporate culture. Recently, research on this important topic has increased considerably. The psychological literature tends to be *descriptive* (focusing on perceptions and reactions), whereas the moral philosophy writings are more *prescriptive* (specifying what should be done).

Questions of justice and fairness occur whenever decisions have to be made about the allocation of resources, whatever they are in a particular business. Concern about the outcomes of justice decisions is called *distributive* justice. However, there are also questions about how fair decisions are made and the procedures each organization has in place to make those decisions. Concern about fairness policies is called *procedural* justice.

Distributive justice

Research in distributive justice goes back 35 years to Homans (1950), who was interested in the "rules of social exchange". He argued that rewards should be proportionate to costs, and that net rewards should be proportionate to investments. Most current research focuses on employees' perceptions of the fairness of the outcomes (both rewards and punishments) they receive. Results show clearly that fairness perceptions are based on relative judgements – that is, comparisons with salient others. That is, how happy one is with fairness decisions (such as decisions about pay) is dependent on the perceptions or knowledge of others' pay. It is not the absolute amount of reward people focus on but their relative reward compared with that of salient others.

The question is who one compares oneself to, on what criterion of one's job, and for how long. It seems that most employees are able to distinguish between unfavourable outcomes (not as good as one hoped) and unfair outcomes. Clearly, employees react much more strongly and angrily to unfair than they do to unfavourable outcomes. There may be various cultural factors that relate to distributive justice; that is, in collective cultures, equality may be seen as more fair than equity decisions, whereas the reverse is true of individualistic cultures.

Procedural justice

Procedural justice concerns the means rather than the ends of social justice decisions. As predicted, employees are more likely to accept organizational decisions on such things as smoking bans, parental leave policies, pay and even disciplinary actions if they believe the decisions are based on fair procedures.

The evaluation of procedural justice issues depends on both the environmental context within which the interaction occurs and the treatment of individuals. There are all sorts of factors built into a justice procedure that are crucial. They include:

* adequate notice for all interested parties to prepare;
* a fair hearing in terms of giving all parties a fair chance to make their case;
* a perception that all judgements are made upon good evidence rather than on intuition;
* evidence of two-way (bilateral) communication;
* the ability and opportunity to refute supposed evidence;
* consistency of judgement over multiple cases.

Although there are, or should be, general context-independent criteria of fairness, there are always special cases. All employees are very concerned with interactional justice, which is the quality of interpersonal treatment they receive at the hands of decision-makers. Two features are important here: social sensitivity, or the extent to which people believe that they have been treated with dignity and respect, and informational justification, or the extent to which people believe they have adequate information about the procedures affecting them (Cropanzo & Greenberg, 1997). Quite simply, procedures matter because a good system can lead people to take a long-term view, becoming tolerant of short-term economic losses for long-term advantage.

Research has demonstrated many practical applications or consequences of organizational justice. Using fair procedures enhances employees' acceptance of institutional authorities. Furthermore, staffing procedures (perceptions of fairness of selection devices) can have pernicious consequences if thought unfair.

A cross-cultural perspective

Deming's do's and don'ts

After the Second World War, the American statistician and engineer Edwards Deming was asked by the Japanese to help them improve their quality control in manufacturing. Although he believed that every organization needs to adapt his advice to suit their own purposes, he continually repeated his fourteen points (do's) and seven diseases (don'ts). Nearly 30 years after his first work, he was "discovered" by his fellow Americans and lauded for the work he did. Faced with Japanese excellence in production and quality, the Americans began to re-import his ideas. Deming's philosophy does not fit with many "commonsensical" ideas; for instance, he is against performance-related pay. Furthermore, his philosophy leads to special types of corporate culture. Although the Japanese manufacturing sector took happily to his ideas and thrived on them, the question remains as to the cross-cultural applicability of this philosophy. Essentially, Deming's philosophy is as follows:

The fourteen points
1   *Create constancy of purpose for improvement of product and service*: Deming suggests a radical new definition of a company's role. Rather than making money, it is to stay in business and provide jobs through innovation, research, constant improvement and maintenance.
2   *Adapt the new philosophy*: In many countries, people are too tolerant of poor workmanship and sullen service. They need a new religion in which mistakes and negativism are unacceptable.
3   *Case dependence on mass inspection*: Many firms typically inspect a product as it comes off the line or at major stages; defective products are either thrown out or reworked; both are unnecessarily expensive. In effect, a company is paying workers to make defects and then to correct them. Quality comes not from inspection but from improvement of the process. With instruction, workers can be enlisted in this improvement.
4   *End the practice of awarding business on price tag alone*: Purchasing departments customarily operate on orders to seek the lowest-priced vendor. Frequently, this leads to supplies of low quality. Instead, they should seek the best quality and work to achieve it with a single supplier for any one item in a long-term relationship.
5   *Improve constantly and forever the system of production and service*: Improvement is not a one-time effort. Management is obligated to look continually for ways to reduce waste and improve quality.
6   *Institute training*: Too often, workers have learned their job from another worker who has never been trained properly. They are forced to follow unintelligible instructions. They can't do their jobs because no-one tells them how.
7   *Institute leadership*: The job of a supervisor is not to tell people what to do or to punish them, but to lead. Leading consists of helping people do a better job and of learning by objective methods who is in need of individual help.
8   *Drive out fear*: Many employees are afraid to ask questions or to take a position, even when

they do not understand what the job is or what is right or wrong. People will continue to do things the wrong way, or not to do them at all. The economic loss from fear is appalling. It is necessary for better quality and productivity that people feel secure.

9   *Break down barriers between staff areas*: Often, staff areas – departments, units, whatever – compete with each other or have goals that conflict. They do not work as a team so they can solve or foresee problems. Worse, one department's goals may cause trouble for another.

10   *Eliminate slogans, exhortations and targets for the workforce*: These never helped anybody do a good job. Let people introduce their own slogans.

11   *Eliminate numerical quotas*: Quotas take account only of numbers, not quality or methods. They are usually a guarantee of inefficiency and high cost. A person, to hold a job, meets quota at any cost, without regard to damage to the company.

12   *Remove barriers to pride in workmanship*: People are eager to do a good job and are distressed when they can't. Too often, misguided supervisors, faulty equipment and defective materials stand in the way. These barriers must be removed.

13   *Institute a vigorous programme of education and retraining*: Both management and the work-force will have to be educated in the new methods, including teamwork and statistical techniques.

14   *Take action to accomplish the transformation*: It will take a special top management team with a plan of action to carry out the quality mission. Workers can't do it on their own, and neither can managers. A critical mass of people in the company must understand the four-teen points, the seven deadly diseases and the obstacles.

The seven deadly diseases

1   *Lack of constancy of purpose*: A company that is without constancy of purpose has no long-range plans for staying in business. Management is insecure, and so are employees.

2   *Emphasis on short-term profits*: Looking to increase the quarterly dividend undermines qual-ity and productivity.

3   *Evaluation by performance, merit rating, or annual review of performance*: The effects of these are devastating – teamwork is destroyed, rivalry is nurtured. Performance ratings build fear and leave people bitter, despondent and beaten. They also encourage mobility of management.

4   *Mobility of management*: Job-hopping managers never understand the companies they work for and are never there long enough to follow through on long-term changes that are neces-sary for quality and productivity.

5   *Running a company on visible figures alone*: The most important figures are unknown and unknowable – the multiplier effect of a happy customer, for example.
    [Diseases 6 and 7 are relevant only in the USA.]

6   *Excessive medical costs.*

7   *Excessive costs of warranty, fuelled by lawyers that work on contingency fees.*

A human resources perspective

Why do a climate audit?

There are many sound reasons for an organization to audit its climate. But audits are performed by people, and people are expensive. Before deciding to embark on any audit, an organization needs to know the justification for committing manpower, time and effort to pursuing it (Furn-ham & Gunter, 1993: 12–16):

*   *To separate fact from opinion*: Audit provides factual information on how a company is perceived by its employees. Audits yield quantifiable data grounded in the views of the

workforce, and thus go far beyond vague "gut feeling" beliefs of managers who may not always be in touch with staff opinions.

- *To obtain unbiased management information*: Since a climate audit systematically analyses "objective" evidence (albeit about subjective perceptions) and presents facts rather than value judgements, it corrects preconceived ideas about the status of a company's management systems and procedures, and false ideas about whether or not the various parts of the company are working in a manner consistent with the policies and objectives delegated from the board of directors.
- *To know factually if the company is at risk*: A human resources audit provides vital feedback to management as to whether the organization is meeting its legal and contractual obligations. This reduces the possibility of customer complaints and expensive legal suits.
- *To identify areas of opportunity*: An audit analyses evidence concerning the effectiveness of the organization and its structure: it can identify the circumstances under which resources and time are utilized effectively. By specifically concentrating on how people spend their time, utilize space, machinery and technology and so on, waste of various forms can be examined.
- *To improve communications and motivation*: Since the audit report reaches top management, it can promote communication between the lowest and the highest levels within the company. It enables employees at all levels to suggest improved methods of operation.
- *To improve insight into recruitment and selection*: By selecting (or rejecting) people with specific preferences, values and potentialities, it is possible both to maintain and to change a culture. Audits can demonstrate the homo- or heterogeneity of a department or organization as a whole.
- *To assist with the assessment of training company staff*: A human resources audit can provide useful information about training for the personnel who participate. These audits provide information on who has been trained on what, their reactions to courses, and any perceived further training needs.
- *A bottom-up view of the organization*: Communication generally flows down an organization more freely and regularly than it flows up. Hence, senior managers do not always have their fingers on the pulse of working life among the rank and file. A climate audit can provide a very useful and important feedback mechanism to senior management.
- *Audits can be used for evaluation*: If an audit is done before a major change programme is put into place and again at some point afterwards, the effectiveness of the programme as a whole can be established. Thus, a before-and-after measure of its success can be gained through the use of a human resources audit.
- *Audits show potential fit and misfit in mergers and acquisitions*: By comparing two companies before a merger or an acquisition, it may be possible to predict the level of difficulty that each may have in adjusting to the other. By auditing similar aspects of the different organizations involved, the nature, extent and implications of their unique characteristics can be examined.
- *Audits make good economic sense*: Making decisions based on little, poor or no information is highly risky. The probability that an audit will provide a good return is increased if it is well prepared, salient issues are correctly analysed, and the resultant data properly interpreted. Audits provide a safe, anonymous means for both unhappy and satisfied employees to express their opinions about all aspects of the organization.
- *Audits are part of the management measurement trend*: In all aspects of management, there is an increasing trend towards using empirical measurement. Climate audits are part of this sensible movement towards a more scientific approach to management and fact-gathering. Financial audits have been done by accountants for decades. Human resources audits are now also emerging as respectable corporate procedures, providing a professional approach to the evaluation and measurement of organization problems.
- *Peer pressure to do audits is already widespread*: Pressure from competitors who already

conduct human resources audits has provided a stimulus to many organizations to do the same. In addition, chief executives these days often expect answers to human resources questions that only audits can provide.

- *Audits may help ensure survival*: Those organizations that do not audit their human resources regularly may miss out on crucial signs of much needed internal adjustments. Audits can help diagnose a latent problem long before it becomes impossible to deal with.

References

Ashkanasy, N., Wilderom, C., & Peterson, M. (Eds.) (2001). *Handbook of organizational culture and climate*. New York: Sage.

Bonoma, T., & Zaltman, G. (1981). *Psychology for management*. Boston, MA: PWS Kent.

Bowers, D., & Seashore, S. (1966). Predicting organizational effectiveness with a four-factor theory of leadership. *Administrative Science Quarterly, 11*, 238–263.

Campbell, J., Dunnette, M., Lawler, E., & Weick, K. (1970). *Managerial behaviour, performance and effectiveness*. New York: McGraw-Hill.

Collett, P. (1994). *Foreign bodies*. London: Simon & Schuster.

Cook, M. (1998). *Personnel selection*. Chichester, UK: Wiley.

Cooke, R., & Lafferty, J. (1989). *Organizational culture inventory*. Plymouth, MI: Human Synergistic.

Cooke, R., & Rousseau, D. (1988). Behavioural norms and expectations: A quantitative approach to the assessment of organizational culture. *Group and Organizational Studies, 13*, 245–273.

Cropanzo, R., & Greenberg, J. (1997). Progress in organizational justice. In C. Cooper & I. Robertson (Eds.), *International review of industrial and organizational psychology* (pp. 317–332). New York: John Wiley.

Dany, F., & Torchy, V. (1994). Recruitment and selection in Europe. In C. Brewster & H. Hegewisch (Eds.), *Policy and practice in European human resource management* (pp. 68–88). London: Routledge.

Deal, T., & Kennedy, A. (1982). *Corporate cultures*. Reading, MA: Addison-Wesley.

Denison, D. (1996). What is the difference between organizational culture and organizational climate. *Academy of Management Review, 21*, 619–654.

Eldridge, J., & Crombie, A. (1974). *A sociology of organizations*. London: Allen & Unwin.

Evan, R. (1978). Measuring the impact of culture on organizations. *International Studies of Management and Organizations, 2*, 91–113.

Evans, W. (1968). A systems model of organizational climate. In R. Taguiri & G. Litwin (Eds.), *Organizational climate: Explorations of a concept* (pp. 107–124). Cambridge, MA: Harvard University Press.

Field, R., & Abelson, M. (1982). Climate: A reconceptualization and proposed model. *Human Relations, 35*, 181–201.

Furnham, A. (2003). *Mad, sad and bad management*. Cirencester, UK: Management Books 2000.

Furnham, A. (2004). A European perspective on personality assessment in organizations. In B. Schneider and D. Smith (Eds.) *Personality and Organization* (pp. 25–57). Mahwah, NJ: Lawrence Erlbaum Associates.

Furnham, A., & Gunter, B. (1993). *Corporate assessment*. London: Routledge.

Geertz, C. (1973). *The interpretation of culture*. New York: Basic Books.

Gellerman, S. (1960). The company personality. *Management Review, 48*, 69–76.

Ginsberg, L. (1978). Strategic planning for work climate modification. *Amacon, 10*, 2.

Gonzalez, R. (1987). *Corporate cultures modification: A guide for managers*. Manila: National Books.

Gooderham, R., & Nordhang, O. (Eds.) (2004). *International management: Cross-boundary challenges*. Oxford: Blackwell.

Gordon, G., & Cummins, W. (1979). *Managing management climate*. New York: D. C. Heath.

Graves, D. (1986). *Corporate culture – diagnosis and change: Auditing and changing the culture of organizations*. London: Pinter.

Greenberg, J., & Baron, R. A. (1990). *Behaviour in organizations*, 3rd edn. Boston, MA: Allyn & Bacon.

Guion, R. (1973). A note on organizational climate. *Organizational Behaviour and Human Performance, 9*, 120–125.

Halpin, A., & Croft, D. (1962). *The organizational climate of schools*. Chicago, IL: University of Chicago Press.

Hampden-Turner, C. (1990). *Corporate culture: From vicious to virtuous circles*. London: Hutchinson.

Handy, C. (1980). *Understanding organizations*. Harmondsworth, UK: Penguin.

Hill, R. (2001). *We Europeans*. Brussels: Europublication.

Hofstede, G. (1980). *Culture's consequences*. Beverly Hills, CA: Sage.

Homans, G. (1950). *The human group*. London: Routledge & Kegan Paul.

House, R., & Rizzo, R. (1972). Toward the measure of organizational practices: Scale development and validation. *Journal of Applied Psychology, 56*, 388–396.

Jones, A., & James, L. (1979). Psychological climate: Dimensions and relationships of individual and aggregated work environment perception. *Organizational Behaviour and Human Performance, 23*, 201–250.

Kahn, R., Wolfe, D., Quinn, R., Snoek, J., & Rosenthal, R. (1964). *Organizational stress: Studies in role conflict and ambiguity*. New York: Wiley.

Koys, D., & De Cotiis, T. (1991). Inductive measures of psychological climate. *Human Relations, 44*, 265–285.

Kroeber, A., & Kluckholm, C. (1952). Culture: A critical review of concepts and definitions. *Peabody Museum of American Archaeology and Ethnology, 47*, 1–60.

Laurent, A. (1983). The culture diversity of Western conceptions of management. *International Studies of Management and Organization, 8*, 75–96.

Litwin, G., & Stringer, R. (1968). *Motivation and organizational climate*. Cambridge, MA: Harvard University Press.

Miceli, M., & Near, J. (1985). Characteristics of organizational climate and perceived wrongdoing associated with whistle-blowing decisions. *Personnel Psychology, 38*, 525–544.

Moxnes, P., & Eilertsen, D. (1991). The influence of management training upon organizational climate: An exploratory study. *Journal of Organizational Behaviour, 12*, 399–411.

Pace, C., & Stern, G. (1958). An approach to the measurement of the psychological characteristics of college environment. *Journal of Educational Psychology, 49*, 269–277.

Payne, R. (1990). Madness in our method: A comment on Jackofsky & Slocum's paper "A longitudinal study of climate". *Journal of Organizational Behaviour, 11*, 77–80.

Payne, R., & Mansfield, B. (1973). Relationship of perceptions of organizational climate to organizational structure, context, and hierarchical radical positions. *Administrative Science Quarterly, 18*, 515–526.

Rousseau, D. (1988). The construction of climate in organizational research. In L. C. Cooper & I. Robertson (Eds.), *International review of industrial and organizational psychology* (pp. 139–158). Chichester, UK: Wiley.

Rousseau, D. (1990). Normative beliefs in fund-raising organizations: Links to organizational performance and individual responses. *Group and Organizational Studies, 4*, 123–141.

Sackmann, S. (1990). Managing organizational culture: The juggle between possibilities and dreams. In A. Anderson (Ed.), *Communication yearbook* (Vol. 13, pp. 114–148). Los Angeles, CA: Sage.

Schein, E. (1985). *Organizational culture and leadership*. San Francisco, CA: Jossey-Bass.

Schein, E. (1990). Organizational culture. *American Psychologist, 45*, 109–119.

Schneider, B. (1987). *National vs corporate culture: Implication for human resource management.* Paper presented to the International Personnel & Human Resource Management Conference, Singapore.

Schneider, B., & Bartlett, C. (1968). Individual differences and organizational climate. *Personnel Psychology, 21*, 323–333.

Shrivastava, P. (1985). Integrating strategy formulation with organizational culture. *Journal of Business Strategy, 7*, 103–111.

Smircich, L., & Calas, M. (1987). Organizational culture: A critical assessment. In K. Roberts & L. Porter (Eds.), *Handbook of organizational commitment* (pp. 228–263). Beverly Hills, CA: Sage.

Smith, M., & Abrahamson, M. (1992). Patterns of selection in six countries. *The Psychologist, 5*, 205–207.

Taguiri, R. (1968). The concept of organizational climate. In R. Taguiri & G. Litwin (Eds.), *Organizational climate: Explorations of a concept* (pp. 11–32). Cambridge, MA: Harvard University Press.

Trompenaars, F. (1993). *Riding the waves of culture.* London: Nicholas Brealey.

Trompenaars, F. (1997). *The better business guide to international management.* Amsterdam: United Nations.

Williams, A., Dobson, P., & Walters, M. (1989). *Changing culture: New organizational approaches.* London: Institute of Personnel Management.

Xenikou, A., & Furnham, A. (1996). A correlational and factor analytic study of different measures of corporate culture. *Human Relations, 49*, 349–371.

Zohar, D. (1980). Safety climate in industrial organizations: Theoretical and applied implications. *Journal of Applied Psychology, 65*, 96–102.

14 Organizational structure, change and development

Introduction

This chapter is about organizations as a whole: their formal structure, how they change and how they develop over time. Most observers believe that the beginning of the twenty-first century is a time of great change with respect to how we structure and grow organizations. What will happen to low-tech jobs in the high-tech revolution? What will organizations look like in 20 years? Speculations on the future of organizations are many and varied, although there do appear to be some common threads (see Chapter 16). Two themes seem consistent. The first is that organizations are getting *flatter*: this means there are fewer levels, less hierarchy. The second is that businesses are trying to integrate their functions better to achieve "joined-up" processes that reduce waste and help competitiveness.

Toffler, a famous futurologist, has also considered the future of work in what he calls the third wave. Rather optimistically, he sees the new worker as independent, resourceful, flexible and skilful. He distinguishes between seven types of employment: structural, trade-related, technological, frictional, normal, informational and natrogenic (policy decisions), the first of which is most important. He believes the concept of a (steady) job is an anachronistic part of the old second wave. Current crises at work are part of the inevitable process of restructuring (i.e. downsizing and re-engineering). The tone of his vision can best be shown by the following quote:

> In the Second Wave industries, you're getting layoffs and wage cuts, deferred benefits, tighter and tighter pressures on the worker. In Third Wave industries, the talk is all about employee participation in decision-making; about job enlargement and enrichment, instead of fractionalization; about flexi-time instead of rigid hours; about cafeteria-style fringe benefits which give employees a choice, rather than a *fait accompli*; about how to encourage creativity rather than blind obedience. (Toffler, 1984: 22)

Inevitably, if these futurologists are even in part correct, we must expect the organization of the future to be quite unlike the organization of the past in terms not only of its size, purpose, structure and function, but its very rationale for existence (see Chapter 16).

There are many forces for organizational change, which, according to Robbins (1991), include:

- Rapid changes in *technology*, nearly always associated with the microchip revolution, robots, virtual reality, and so on. Rapid product obsolescence must occur.
- *Economic shocks* associated with such things as oil crises, the stock market crash and sudden inflation characteristic of the age of discontinuity.
- *Social trends* associated with demographic trends and social attitudes, towards relationships, possessions, and so on.
- *Global political* changes, such as the fall of communism, the end of apartheid and the associated knock-on effects on multinationals.
- Economic *competition* from new and different sources.

The general economy, the habits of customers, the stability of supplies, the enthusiasm of competitors and some sociopolitical forces, can all lead to significant change in business life. But perhaps the most important is, inevitably, rapid and profound changes in technology, as well as concerns with resource dependency (Johns, 1991). Technology has changed not only production but communication and led to sudden, dramatic globalization of products, markets and the workforce.

Change is predictable: perhaps the only constant. Senior (2000) distinguishes quite simply between situations that are hard and soft:

Hard situations or difficulties:

- tend to be smaller scale;
- originate internally;
- are less serious in their implications;
- can be considered in relative isolation from their organizational context;
- have clear priorities as to what might need to be done;
- generally have quantifiable objectives and performance indicators;
- have a systems/technical orientation;
- generally involve relatively few people;
- have facts which are known and which can contribute to the solution;
- have agreement by the people involved on what constitutes the problem;
- tend to have solutions of which the type at least is known;
- have known timescales;
- are "bounded" in that they can be considered separately from the wider organizational context and have minimal interactions with the environment.

Soft situations or messes

- tend to be larger scale;
- originate externally;
- have serious and worrying implications for all concerned;
- are an interrelated complex of problems which cannot be separated from their context;
- have many people of different persuasions and attitudes involved in the problem;
- have subjective and at best semi-quantifiable objectives;
- not everything is known and it is not clear what needs to be known;
- have little agreement on what constitutes the problem let alone what might be possible solutions;

- have usually been around for some time and will not be solved quickly, if at all, bringing about an improvement may be all that can be hoped for;
- fuzzy timescales;
- are "unbounded" in that they spread throughout the organization and, sometimes, beyond.

(Senior, 2000: 351–352)

Strobel (1997) has argued that weak change forces imply proactive change, moderate change forces require reactive change and strong change forces demand rapid change. Those more closed to change react by a change in leadership, organizational tinkering or downsizing/restructuring. Those more open to change try process re-engineering and restructuring middle management to give them more autonomy. Those most open to change are more experimental and radical. Strobel concludes:

> Different situations demand different change recipes. But all change paths go through three broad phases: unfreezing the organization, making change happen, and following up and preparing for the next one. It is useful to distinguish between the different levels of "change-force" intensity. Weak change forces are difficult to discern and require skill in communications and in identifying the value creating idea – but there is time for experimentation. Moderate change forces are those which have started to affect performance but do not threaten survival: getting people's attention is easier and multi-disciplinary teams should be employed.
>
> Those organizations with high resistance have very few "change agents" and require a radical approach to break the dominant culture. The process should start with resistors at the top, can benefit from headstrong leadership (though can equally end in a disastrous ego trip), and requires some form of reorganization. In organizations that can be opened to change, management has to help the change agents, and top down experimentation is desirable. In organizations that are already open to change, there is usually little risk in leaving the resistors until last. Bottom up experimentation and goal cascading should be possible. (Strobel, 1997: 543)

The business environment is becoming more uncertain because of simultaneous increases in complexity of operation and the increased rate of change. Many prognosticators believe that organizations will become "virtual corporations" characterized by small, dynamic, temporary networked alliances. The new organization will electronically network all sorts of groups aiming to provide excellent services as they are needed. It is uncertain whether these new "organizations" will improve the quality of working life, which can be defined in terms of such things as participation, trust, reward and responsiveness. Inevitably, rapid changes in technology have impacted on the shape and functioning of organizations. Some organizations have seen developments in, and a miniaturization of, technology, but because they are in the mechanistic, mass-production, integrated business remain relatively slow to change. Intensive, organic, non-routine businesses are not so reliant on technology as a driver of change.

One new idea is *just-in-time technology*, which attempts to reduce warehouse stocks. With fewer stocks workers have to be more flexible, multi-skilled and quick to react. Technology has destroyed old jobs and created new ones. Many jobs have become automated. Many corporate giants have been split up to attempt to create more adaptive, flexible, creative, customer-sensitive businesses. Most organizations aim for that perfect combination of lean production and high-performance structures and processes that minimizes cost and maximizes revenue. Hence the vogue for business process re-engineering which attempted to redesign processes that cut across functions and departments, that pushed decision-making down organizations and that maximized the use of information technology. It aimed at quick response production.

For the work psychologist, huge and rapid changes mean a knowledge explosion, product obsolescence and new patterns of working, environmental changes associated with greater competition, more sophisticated consumer demand, changes in the availability of certain resources, and national and international political changes. No organization can resist these changes. What is clearly desirable is adaptable and adaptive organizations, and flexible employees and management.

Change can be both continuous and discontinuous. It can be minor fine-tuning change or major dramatic change. It is usually aimed at making organizational processes, structures and strategy more profitable, streamlined and adaptive.

Looking critically at the adaptiveness of the organizational structure as a strategic response to environment, uncertainty is now much more common. Restructuring by downsizing the original structure or adopting a different (e.g. matrix) structure are common forms of strategic response to the increasing uncertainty. According to Johns (1991), there are many other forms of strategic response. These include *vertical integration* (attempting to take formal control of all sources of supply and distribution), *mergers and acquisitions* (by acquiring competitors, increasing economies of scale or by diversifying to reduce resource dependence on a particular segment of the environment), *strategic alliances* (which are active cooperative relationships between legally separate organizations, including competitors, suppliers, customers or even trade unions) and *interlocking directorates* (when people serve as directors on more than one management board and bring their knowledge and expertise to both).

The speed of development and spread of advanced information technology is for many organizations *the* issue to consider. Because technology usually means more highly automated systems and greater possibilities of integration among specialities, it has important implications for organizational structure and job design. Although usually flatter organizations are most appropriate, sometimes the new technology suggests greater centralization and sometimes decentralization. Unit and process technologies perform best, it would appear, under more organic structures, whereas mass-production functions perform best under more mechanistic structures. In short, the less routine technologies and the more interdependent technologies call for more organic structures (Johns, 1991). Telecommuting and the "portable office" are some of the changes resulting from advanced information technology, which generates, aggregates, stores, modifies and transmits information with ever increasing efficiency.

It is possible to list, weight and then predict the result when forces for change meet those in favour of stability (Peters, 1987) (Table 14.1). As a result, there are many different metaphors for change, some emphasizing natural transition and growth, others "whitewater" rapids. Peters argues that one should not believe the phrase "If it ain't broke, don't fix it", because it can always be improved. Peters believed that there are major differences in business functions (Table 14.2).

Some argue that speculating about the future is idle and pointless. It is far better to try to influence the future by what one does in the present. This involves designing an efficient organizational structure.

Table 14.1 Forces for and against change

Forces for change	Forces resisting change
Internal forces	*Individual resistance*
1. New technology	1. Fear of the unknown
2. Changing work values	2. New learning required
3. Creation of new knowledge	3. Disruption of stable friendships
4. Product obsolescence	4. Distrust of management
5. Desire for leisure and alternative work schedules	
Environmental forces	*Organizational resistance*
1. Competition	1. Threat to the power structure
2. Changes in consumer demands	2. Inertia in organizational structure
3. Resource availability	3. System relationships
4. Social and political change	4. Sunk costs and vested interests
5. International changes/globalization	

Source: Adapted from Cherrington (1989).

Table 14.2 Changes in basic business functions

Function	Old emphasis	New emphasis
Manufacturing	Capital and automation more important than people; volume, low cost and efficiency more important than quality and responsiveness	Short production runs; fast product changeover; people, quality and responsiveness most important
Marketing	Mass markets; mass advertising; lengthy market tests	Fragmented markets; lengthy market creation; small-scale market testing; speed
Financial control	Centralized; specialized staff review proposals, set policy	Decentralized; financial specialists members of business teams; high spending authority at local level
Management information	Centralized information control; information hoarded for sake of "consistency"	Decentralized data processing; personal computer proliferation; multiple databases permitted
Research and development	Centralized: emphasis on large projects; cleverness more important than reliability and serviceability; innovation limited to new products and services	All activities/functions hotbeds for innovation; not limited to new products and services; emphasis on "portfolio" of small projects; speed

Source: Reproduced from Hellriegel, Slocum & Woodman (1992) with permission of West Publishing.

The uptake of innovation

Individuals and organizations differ in the speed (and willingness) to take-up innovation. Rogers (1983), who has written extensively on the topic, identified five typical (personal) characterizations of people that could easily be applied to organizations.

The first are the *innovators*. These are individuals who are always seeking to try out new ideas or equipment. They come in many shapes or forms: the eccentric, genius inventor, childlike adults who enjoy the electronic toys of their youth, socially inadequate technophiles who prefer computers to people. They may scour the pages of specialist magazines for new equipment or may even try building it themselves. They had CDs, computers, microwaves and faxes long before most people even knew what they were. They prefer to surf the Internet rather than play in the surf. Some can be innovation junkies who go for anything new and different regardless of its quality, usefulness or design. Others like to improve on current ideas and techniques.

Next come the *early adopters*. These people take little or no persuasion and are among the first of the population to take on the innovation. They are at the beginning of the steep climb of the S-curve. All they have to be told is that there is new equipment that is faster, smarter or more elegant than theirs and they want it. Early adopters are ideal types for the advertiser because one mention of the product is sufficient to spur them to buy.

As the diffusion of innovation occurs and the new phenomenon becomes recognized, the *early majority* begin to take an interest. They need to be sold the idea, persuaded to buy. A little sceptical and a little cautious, the early majority are good candidates to adopt innovation but need some convincing. This is the midpoint on the diffusion curve and includes the bulk of the population. The product or the idea appears in the media and in shops more widely than before and the new "thing" seems to be everywhere.

The *late majority* need the hard sell. Scepticism turns to cynicism when they are faced with an innovation, and they frequently demand that its benefits are proved to them. They may have bought some new idea or product that proved to be pretty useless or cumbersome, and they have not forgotten it. Some argue that the later one adopts the innovation, the cheaper it is and the more reliable. The pocket calculator is one example among many, and this also persuades the late majority to be cautious – perhaps rather too cautious for the advertiser.

Finally, at the top of the curve is the *laggard*. Like innovators, laggards come in very different forms but share a common reaction to innovation. There is the technophobe, terrified of anything not simple and mechanical. They share a fear of, and hostility to, innovation. For employers and legislators, the only way to make them comply is to change the rules. You have to ban or physically remove old equipment or make laws (for instance, about seat belts or gas appliances) to achieve compliance. There are few easy ways to persuade laggards, and advertising of product benefits is a waste of time for this group.

The problem of the diffusion of innovation for the manufacturer is threefold. First, they have to segment their market and be able to identify the demographic, geographic and psychographic correlates of the five different types mentioned above. Next, they have either to change their marketing strategy as the population moves up the S-curve or target it quite specifically to the different groups. But the third problem is the greatest of all: what to do when even the laggards have adopted the innovation? The only solution is to find a new product, a new idea, a new approach and start all over again.

Teleworking

Furnham (2000) noted that the data on the expansion of the electronic collage may be unreliable, but everything indicates that it is rapidly expanding. A recent American study showed that 62% of companies encouraged telecommuting in 1996, up from 40% in 1994 (Mineham, 1996). In late 1997, more than 10 million Americans telecommuted and nearly 70% of 500 companies employed telecommuters. European data are less reliable, but a similar growth pattern indicates that the virtual workplace is a reality now. *Investors in People* commissioned a British study, which showed that 73% of companies responding had "arrangements in place for teleworking" (Cascio, 2000).

The idealized picture of the home-based teleworker was the handsome executive dressed in designer tracksuit in a state-of-the-art IT office composed of blonde wood, shiny chrome and sleek computers. The office would be attached to a beautiful home in a rural idyll. Reduced commuting would help the greener and cleaner environment. And the happy teleworker had ultimate flexibility. They could structure all the work around their personal commitments – children, aged parents, animals, and so on. The Internet, with email, the fax machine and the new generation of computers, we were told, would be the superior new medium of communication. We could all work in our preferred space, at our preferred time of day, in comfortable clothes and free from petty and trivial interruptions.

One study on telecommuters found that they reported being 40% more productive while working away from the office, mainly because they have fewer distractions. Another study conducted by telecoms giant AT&T found that telecommuters were so happy that one said they would look for another job if they were forced back into the old office (Cascio, 1998; Holland & Hogan, 1998).

Even more impressive, people could be members of virtual teams without ever meeting but have total access to one another. The advantages include:

- teleworking eliminates lack of access to experts – everyone is on-line, all the time;
- intercontinental teams can be formed – proximity is not an issue;
- consultants can be hired and do not need to charge travel, lodgings and downtime;
- one can hire the best people in the world to join the network at negligible cost;
- people can easily be part of different teams at the same time;
- because everything is online, swift responses to any event, including demands of the market, are possible.

Organizations were tempted to support this strategy, which claimed to encourage work in the non-traditional workplace. They were told that teleworking led to space savings, reduced absenteeism, greater retention, and therefore increased employee satisfaction leading to increased productivity. Indeed, teleworkers may even become independent of pension plans and so on, and essentially become self-employed.

The cost of all the IT equipment which had to be regularly updated seemed to be forgotten in the calculations. Some managers expressed their doubts (Hewlett-Packard teleworkers have to pay for their own equipment). Tele-employees were difficult to monitor. Were they at work? Were they producing anything? Some suspected that it was no more than a type of paid child care. Was company family-friendliness going too far? Surely teleworking was really only for those who did not need close supervision, regular feedback and who could be trusted. Telecommuting really makes sense only with the right job, the right person, the right reason and the right boss. Not all employees had such a suitable alternative location for teleworking – the quiet, spacious "spare bedroom".

Other important issues seemed to go unanswered. How frequently should boss and teleworker be in touch? Who is responsible for maintaining and insuring business equipment? What are the conditions of work? What are their measurable outputs of work? What do customers think of teleworkers? And, more importantly, what are the psychological needs of certain individuals that are not satisfied in the satellite telecottage? After all, office gossip and political games in the office are fun. People are a source of stimulation. Also, getting out of the house can, in itself, be liberating.

Many people find teleworking alienating. Electronic communication is too cold, too impersonal. We are social animals built for social interactions, skilled at reading non-verbal cues, happy to be in contact groups.

An organized job gives one a sense of identity and loyalty. One study found that teleworkers gradually lost their identification with an interest in their organization, and vice versa. Out of sight, out of mind (Furnham, 2000; Ramsower, 1985). Teleworkers can become forgotten telecolonial people. Teleworking is certainly not for everyone. Extraverts find that they get bored because they miss out on the daily contact. The ambitious discover that they are left out of the public–corporate loop. The extremely conscientious feel cheated because their boss cannot observe how genuinely hard they are working. And the brightest and best leave the organization because, as teleworkers, they are seen as cheap labour – the long-term consequences could be disastrous.

Organizational charts

Organizational structure is closely related to strategy. Organizational structure is concerned with how the work of the organization is divided and assigned/coordinated to various individuals, groups and departments. The structure of the organization clarifies certain issues for all staff: "What am I supposed to do?", "Who do I report to?" and "Who do I go to if I have a problem?" Structure is the way a company is put together. It is about the allocation of responsibilities, the designation of formal reporting channels, and the systems and mechanisms that underlie the effective coordination of effort (Randolph & Blackburn, 1989). It was Weber (see Chapter 2) who set out some fundamental principles with respect to organizational structure like chain of command, unity of command and division of labour.

Organizational structure is about the vertical and horizontal divisions and coordination of labour. The *vertical* division is about autonomy, control and communication. Modern thinking about de-layering and "rightsizing" is linked to delegation and enabling (empowering) (see Chapter 12), which means flatter organizations with fewer vertical levels. The *horizontal* division of labour is concerned with job design, differentiation and departmentalization. As well as horizontal and vertical differentiation, organizations often have spatial differentiation, which is the extent to which the locations of an organization's facilities and personnel are geographically dispersed.

Organizations rely on a structure, made implicit in a chart, to ensure the efficient coordination of activities. But there may also be specific liaison personnel, task forces or integrators whose job it is specifically to improve organizational coordination. Every organization can be evaluated in terms of its structural variables, such as complexity, formalization and centralization. Considerable controversy remains about whether structure affects process or vice versa; or, indeed, how structure impacts on productivity. Certainly the way an organization is formally structured has a systematic and powerful effect on various measurable output variables, like productivity. As such, it affects various different processes, including:

- allocating tasks and responsibilities to individuals (e.g. how much choice they have about how they work);
- specifying and defining jobs with descriptions and key result area targets;

- designing the formal reporting relationships throughout the organization;
- deciding on the number of levels in the hierarchy (tall versus flat);
- deciding on the span of control of each supervisor and manager.

One concept of relevance here is that of *formalization* or the extent to which jobs are standardized. Highly formalized jobs mean there is little latitude in what is to be done, how, when or where. The more formal the job, the more explicit the job descriptions, the more rules and clearly defined procedures, and the easier it is to structure groups. Usually, professional jobs are low on formalization and unskilled jobs are high on formalization, but there are exceptions. Structure involves assigning authority, responsibility and accountability, which are defined thus (Johns, 1992):

- *Authority* is a form of power that orders the actions of others through commands that are effective because those who are commanded regard the commands as legitimate.
- *Responsibility* is an obligation placed on a person who occupies a certain position.
- *Accountability* is the subordinate's acceptance of a given task to perform because he or she is a member of the organization. It requires that person to report on his or her discharge of responsibilities.

Organizations are layered, and within the hierarchical structure there are usually three broad interrelated levels: technical, managerial and external. The dimensions of structure can be identified in various ways, but are usually taken to include the grouping of activities, the responsibilities of individuals, levels of hierarchical authority, span of control and formal organizational relationships (see Chapter 2). An additional important dimension of structure is the impact of information technology, which naturally affects the flow of information through the structure.

The structure of an organization affects not only productivity and economic efficiency, but also the morale and job satisfaction of its members. The overall effectiveness of the organization will be influenced both by structural design and by the behaviour of the employees. The "sociotechnical system" maintains and integrates the structural and technological requirements of the organization, and the needs and demands of the human part of the organization. A badly designed structure is in part likely to lead to inefficiency, low motivation and morale, late and inappropriate decisions, conflict, rising costs and lack of development.

There is always an underlying need to establish a framework of order and system of command through which the activities of the organization can be planned, organized, directed and controlled. This demands attention to certain basic considerations in the design of organization structure, such as the classic Weberian bureaucracy decisions: clarification of objectives, dimensions of structure, division of work and coordination of activities, centralization, task and element functions, principles of organization, span of control and scalar chain, and formal organizational relationships (see Chapter 2).

The essence of structure is the division of work among members of the organization and the coordination of their activities. Work can be divided and activities linked in various ways. Most organizations will contain examples of alternative combinations (formal versus informal; tall versus flat) for grouping activities and relating different jobs to each other. A particular form of structure that can cause difficulty is the line and staff organization. With the growth in newer, complex and technologically advanced systems, and the need to provide integration of a wide range of functional activities, greater attention has been given to more flexible forms of structure, such as matrix organization. According to Randolph & Blackburn (1989), the process approach to organizational structure specifies four dimensions relevant to describing and understanding structure:

1   *Complexity:* the degree of differentiation of jobs and work units. Large organizations are nearly always complex and hence there are communication, coordination, conflict and control problems.
2   *Formalization:* the extent to which there are explicit written rules, regulations and procedures to direct work activities. Sometimes they exist but are not enforced; and unwritten norms contradict the written documents. The level of formalization may also change significantly within the organization, with many more at the bottom than at the top.
3   *Centralization:* the location or dispersion of decision-making authority within an organization. It is frequently not the case that an organization is either centralized or decentralized. It can easily be both at the same time. For instance, management may decentralize routine decisions but retain control of what they see as crucial decisions. However, decentralized decision authority may be constrained by formalized regulations. Sophisticated on-line computer systems can often encourage a false sense of real decision decentralization.
4   *Coordination:* this is the strategy process or procedure that attempts to ensure that various jobs are accomplished in the proper order. This includes regular communication needed to accomplish tasks involving various people, direct supervision as well as an attempt to standardize work processes, outputs and skills fully.

According to Mintzberg (1979), the basic structure of all organizations has five elements:

- a *strategic apex* of executives who attempt to ensure that the organization fulfils its primary purpose;
- the *operating core* of the bulk of employees who perform the basic work related directly to the production of products and services;
- the *middle line* of managers who connect core and apex;
- a *technostructure* that designs, plans and changes the workflow (engineers, accountants, human resource experts);
- *support staff* who provide support to the organization outside the operating workflow (legal experts, public relations, research department).

The structure of an organization is depicted usually in the form of an organization chart (organogram), which provides, at a given moment in time, a pictorial representation of the structural framework of an organization. Charts may be used as a basis for the analysis and review of structure, and may indicate apparent weaknesses. They can look very different from one another (Senior, 2000).

There are some classic bureaucratic principles that may be used to dictate a particular structure: a clear division of labour; employment decisions based solely on merit; a formal, explicit hierarchy of authority; the job and the job-holder remaining separate;

impersonal (fair, non-favouritism-orientated) approaches to all interpersonal activities; and the setting down of rules and regulations. The anticipated outcomes of these procedures are fair treatment of employees, judicious allocation of resources and maximally efficient task completion, but unintended outcomes can include inflexibility, customer alienation and frustration, and goal displacement (Randolph & Blackburn, 1989). Naturally, different principles lead to different priorities and different structures. But these principles are not mutually exclusive and it is quite possible to use more than one at the same time to design an organizational structure. Four are shown in Table 14.3 (Gordon, Mondy, Sharplin, & Premeaux, 1990).

Over the years, there has been something of a change in thinking about many of these basic organizational concepts. For instance, the classic view of the division of labour was nearly always positive, whereas the contemporary view is that the dis-economies of the division of labour, which manifest themselves as boredom, fatigue, stress, and so on, exceed the economic advantages. Equally, the classic view of unity of command was clear; but in complex and dynamic organizations, people may have different bosses, depending on the particular task they are carrying out. The classic view of authority distinguished between line and staff authority, and took the view that managers were all-powerful. Organizations today stress teamwork and participation, and downplay authoritative, superior–subordinate relationships. The span of control concept (Figure 14.1) usually dictates "tall", multilayered organizations, whereas

Table 14.3 Organizing principles

Principle	Definition of	Reason for	Possible cases of violation	Possible results of violation
Unity of command	A person should report to only *one* boss	Clarity and understanding, to ensure unity of effort and direction, and to avoid conflicts	Unclear definition of authority figure and role	Dissatisfaction or frustration of employees and lower efficiency
Equality of authority and responsibility	The amount of authority and responsibility should be equal	Allows work to be accomplished more efficiently; develops people; reduces frustration	Fear on the part of some managers that subordinates might "take over"	Waste of energies and dissatisfaction of employees, thereby reducing effectiveness
Scalar principle	There should be a clear definition of authority in the organization ("to go through channels")	Clarity of relationship avoids confusion and improves decision-making and performance	Uncertainty on the part of the employee or a direct effort by the employee to avoid chain of command	Poor performance, confusion and/or dissatisfaction
Span of management control	There is a limit to the number of employees a manager can effectively supervise	Increased effectiveness in direction and control of a manager	Overloading a manager because of growth in number of personnel	Lack of efficiency and control, resulting in poor performance

Source: Reproduced from Gordon *et al.* (1990) with the permission of Prentice-Hall, Inc.

Members of each level

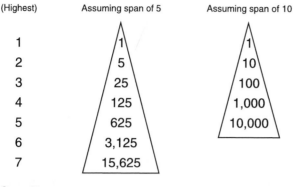

Span of 5:
Workers = 15,625
Managers (levels 1–6) = 3,905

Span of 10:
Workers = 10,000
Managers (levels 1–4) = 1,110

Figure 14.1 Contrasting spans of control. Note that, with a span control of 5, one needs about three times as many levels.

contemporary theorists favour flat organizations. Even views on departmentalization are being challenged. Now customer departmentalization (customers in each department have common problems that require specialists for each) is being emphasized. Furthermore, rigid departmentalization is being complemented by the use of cross-departmental teams or task forces that ignore departmental boundaries (Robbins, 1991).

As a consequence, organizations are "designed" rather differently now from the way in which they were in the past. Often, the design is rather *ad hoc* and never planned carefully. Each particular principle needs to be applied very sensitively, given the nature of the organization. For instance, various factors affect the span of management:

- In general, the more complex the work, the shorter the optimum span of management.
- The span can be longer if the manager is supervising employees performing similar jobs.
- If jobs are closely linked and interdependent, the manager may have greater problems with coordination, creating the need for a rather limited span of management.
- If the organization is operating in an unstable environment, a narrow span may prove to be more effective.
- The establishment of many standards increases predictability and provides the basis for effective control, thereby resulting in a wider effective span.
- Managers and employees who are highly skilled, experienced and motivated generally can operate with wider spans of management and with less supervision.
- Where high commitment to the organization is as important as technical efficiency, such commitment can be enhanced through wider spans of management. (Gordon *et al.*, 1990: 246)

Any organizational chart specifies quite different relationships. These include:

- *Line relationships:* between senior and subordinate and are found *within* departments and functions.
- *Staff relationships:* these occur when people offer specialist advice but have *no* specific personal *authority*.
- *Functional relationships:* these occur where a particular specialist is designated to provide a service which a line manager is *compelled to accept*.
- *Authority relationships:* these reflect the formal authority assigned to positions, not people.

Authority relationships can be traced on an organizational chart by following the lines downwards. Responsibility relationships can be traced by following those same lines upwards. Although these charts are often redrawn and sometimes overlooked, in terms of how people report to one another they do highlight how the organization is structured. Apart from the annual balance sheet, the organizational chart probably represents one of the simplest but most important documents that tell the outsider (consultant), or insider for that matter, how the organization is run.

Departmentalization

The process of grouping related work activities into manageable units is known as *departmentalization*. It is concerned with the processes of differentiation and integration. Its purpose is to contribute to more effective and efficient use of organizational resources. This may be done in many different ways. Probably the most popular is functional similarity. Ideally, each department or division in the organization should be made up of people performing similar tasks or functions. Jobs with similar objectives and requirements are grouped to form a section, and the person with the background necessary to supervise these functions effectively is assigned as the manager. The achievement of functional similarity nevertheless depends on several factors (Gordon *et al.*, 1990).

The first is *volume of work*. Sometimes the volume of work does not allow for specialization. In small firms, personnel have to cope with a wide assortment of jobs. For example, compare the operations of a small corner-shop grocery store with those of a large supermarket. In the small store, one person might be responsible for stocking shelves and the checking-out function. In the large supermarket, personnel will tend to specialize in one or only a few of the basic functions. It is common for individual managers to oversee the produce section and the stocking and checking functions. The larger the organization, the more specialization occurs. Second, *traditions, preference* and *work rules* may dictate departmentalization. Although two tasks may be similar, traditions, work rules (union- or simply historically based) and personal preferences may prevent their assignment to one individual. In some countries, strong trade unions prevent functional similarity from dictating departmentalization. Third, *similar functions may occur in different departments*. Another complicating factor is that a particular function often occurs in different independent departments. For example, inventory control would appear to fit logically in the purchasing department, which buys materials and keeps records. However, the production department uses the same materials and, in scheduling, must work with these same inventory records. Some organizations prefer not to have a human resources or personnel department, encouraging line managers to take over that function. Fourth, *separation of functions may occur to prevent conflicts of interest*. Sometimes similar functions are not combined because doing so might create conflicts of interest. Quality control is intimately involved in production; inspectors frequently work side by side with production employees. Finally, there may be a *combining of dissimilar functions to promote coordination*. There are occasions when two dissimilar functions must be combined for purposes of effective action and control (Gordon *et al.*, 1990).

There are both advantages and disadvantages to differentiation by function (Randolph & Blackburn, 1989). The advantages include: resources are used more efficiently; decisions and directions are centralized at the top level; there is better coordination of activities within the function; there are usually opportunities for supervision and training by specialists; and career development activities can occur within the professional speciality. The disadvantages include: coordination across functions can be difficult; centralization can overburden top management; response times and innovation can be very slow; responsibility for unit success or failure is frequently difficult to determine; and there is little training for general management positions.

Similarly, structuring organizations by divisions (often self-contained units such as profit centres) has its pluses and minuses. Those who favour divisional organization note that employees feel communication and coordination are good, they can more easily identify with divisional goals and outcomes, and there is usually reduced time in adapting to environmental changes. Those critics of this way of structuring an organization point out that it has the potential to use resources inefficiently, that divisional goals may displace organizational goals, that coordination problems are frequently made more serious by decentralized, divisional design, and that within each division there tends to be less specialized professional interaction.

Kinds of departments

There is no simple uniform standard way to divide an organization. Even companies in the same industry often have vastly different kinds of departments. However, it is possible to identify five bases on which departmentalization normally occurs: function, product, customer, geographical territory and project. Additionally, a combination approach may be utilized.

- *Departmentalization by function*: Departmentalization by function is perhaps the most common means of dividing an organization (see above). By grouping related functions, organizations form their departments on the basis of specialized activities such as finance, marketing, production, engineering and personnel. Grouped together, it is often believed that specialists become more efficient, although various people now challenge this view. Departmentalization by function is especially useful in stable environments where technical efficiency and quality are important. Certainly, functional specialists feel comfortable working with others of similar background and experience. However, departmentalization by function may create certain problems for management. Employees in specialized departments may become more concerned with their own department than with the overall company. They develop their own jargon and values, and have a competitive "us" versus "them" attitude to other departments. In the terminology of social science, ingroup homogeneity often leads to outgroup bias and preju-dice. Because of the sometimes conflicting purposes of various departments, upper management must ensure that an effective means of coordination exists (Gordon *et al.*, 1990: 216).

- *Departmentalization by customer*: Departmentalization by type of customer is used by organizations that have a special need to provide better service to different types of customers. A diversified manufacturing company may have industrial, govern-ment and consumer sales divisions, depending on the type of customer and their particular requirements. Customers can be segmented by all sorts of methods, including demographics, psychographics and source of income.

- *Departmentalization by geographical territory or location*: Grouping activities according to geographical territory is used by organizations that have physically dispersed and/or non-interdependent operations or markets to serve. Geographical departmentalization offers the advantages of better services with local regional personnel, often at less cost. Division by geography is the single most common structure for international and global companies, although countries may be com-bined and others differentiated according to their size and the company's product.

- *Departmentalization by project*: When the work of an organization consists of a continuing series of major projects, departmentalization by project normally occurs. This is relatively infrequent except in construction, computer and consult-ancy companies.

Centralization versus decentralization

Management has among other things to determine the appropriate levels of responsi-bility and authority to be delegated. This has a fundamental impact on organizations. Centralization is the degree to which authority is retained by higher-level managers within an organization. If a limited amount of authority is delegated, the organization is described as being *centralized*, but if a significant amount of authority is delegated to lower levels, the enterprise is described as being *decentralized*. However, there are many degrees of centralization. The major question is not whether a company should decentralize, but *what degree* of decentralization is appropriate, and indeed *what* (i.e. decisions) should be decentralized.

In a highly centralized structure, individual managers and workers at lower levels in the organization take a narrow range of decisions. By contrast, in decentralized organ-izations, the scope of authority to make decisions and take actions is broader for lower-level managers and employees. In a highly centralized organizational structure, top management usually makes all major decisions; in a decentralized structure, lower-level management may make these decisions (Gordon *et al.*, 1990: 248).

Decentralization is advocated by many who believe that a greater share in manage-ment decision-making should be given to lower organizational levels. Advocates of the modern ideas of *empowerment* and *delayering* argue strongly for it. Decentralization tends to create a climate for more rapid growth and development of personnel. If virtually all decisions and orders come from "the top", organization members and employees tend to act as unthinking executors of someone else's commands. Yet, many employees and lower-level managers do not wish to be involved at high levels in the organization because of the responsibility that goes with decision-making. Freedom to decide means the possibility of accepting personal failure.

According to Gordon *et al.* (1990), centralization tends to:

- produce great uniformity of policy and action;
- result in fewer errors by subordinates who lack either information or skill;
- utilize better the skills of central and specialized experts;
- facilitate closer control of all operations.

By contrast, decentralization:

- tends to make for speedier decisions and actions without having to consult higher levels;
- results in decisions that are more likely to be adapted to local conditions;
- usually results in greater interest and enthusiasm on the part of the subordinate to whom the authority has been entrusted (these expanded jobs provide excellent training experiences for possible promotion to higher levels);
- allows top management to utilize time for strategic research and decision.

It is not a case of which is best but rather under what conditions the one seems preferable. The following factors need to be taken into account when considering centralization or decentralization in an organization:

- *Size and complexity of the organization*: The larger the organization, the more authority the central manager is forced to delegate. Inevitably, limitations of expertise will usually lead to decentralization within any organization. Authority will be delegated to the heads of units or departments. Each major "product group" is likely to have different product problems, various kinds of customers and different marketing channels. If speed and adaptability to change are necessary for success, decentralization will be preferable, although it reduces homogeneity within an organization.
- *Dispersion of the organization*: When the difficulties of size are compounded by geographical dispersion, it is evident that a greater degree of decentralization will be necessary. Control of operations may have to be pushed down to lower levels in the organization, even though control of financing may be centralized. However, the speed and cost of electronic communications do mean that geographical dispersion is less and less of a problem.
- *Competence of personnel available*: A major limiting factor in centralization is the degree of competence (abilities, motivation) of employees. If an organization has grown up under centralized decision-making and control, employees are often poorly equipped to start making major decisions. People are promoted to supervisory positions not because of their decision-making ability but because of experience, loyalty and a good track record (Gordon *et al.*, 1990: 249).

Mechanistic versus organic structures

As new technology changes more rapidly and comes down in price, organizations tend to evolve from "mechanistic" to "organic" structures, although occasionally the reverse is true.

Mechanistic organizations emphasize relatively less flexible and more stable organizational structures (Gordon *et al.*, 1990: 258):

- Activities are specialized into clearly defined jobs and tasks. A manufacturing organization with a single assembly line is typically a mechanistic structure.
- Persons of higher rank typically (should) have greater knowledge of the problems facing the organization than those at lower levels. All problems are thus passed up the hierarchy until they reach a person with both the knowledge and skill to deal with it.
- Standardized policies, procedures and rules guide much of the decision-making in the organization. Mechanistic organizations often have detailed manuals of organizational policies. Rules are followed rigidly, and the punishment for breaking them is often harsh.
- Rewards are chiefly obtained through obedience to the directions of supervisors. Mechanistic organizations encourage conformity and discourage innovation, since innovation often means not obeying company regulations.

Organic organizations, on the other hand, have flexible organizational designs and can adjust rapidly to change (Gordon *et al.*, 1990: 258–259):

- There is less emphasis on job descriptions and specialization. People become involved in problem-solving when they have the knowledge or skill that will help solve the problem. It is skill, ability and knowledge rather than rank which dictates participation in problem-solving.
- People holding higher positions are not necessarily assumed to be better informed than employees at lower levels. Such organizations emphasize decentralization of decision-making, where responsibility and accountability are pushed as low in the organization as is feasible.
- Horizontal and lateral organization relationships are given as much or more attention than vertical relationships. Project teams, matrix structures, integrating or liaison roles, and task forces, which bring together individuals with diverse functional expertise, are frequently introduced.
- Status and rank differences are de-emphasized. Individuals are ideally valued for their expertise rather than for their position in the hierarchy.
- The formal structure of the organization is less permanent, more changeable. Integrating (such as a matrix organization) and *ad hoc* structures (which use a variety of liaison devices, such as project teams) are organic.

Despite the above description, which implies that organic structures have to be better, much depends on the organization itself. Mechanistic structures work well in particular circumstances.

It could appear to the educated, liberal reader that organic structures must be happier, healthier, more profitable and more successful. This does not have to be the case. A surprising number of people socialized in hierarchical and authoritarian schools and families shun them and are most unhappy in them. Naturally, the cultures and climates of the two types are radically different (see Chapter 13). Furthermore, it is quite possible that people with different personalities and values seek out the one type or the other. There is considerable evidence that the fit between person and organization is partly attributable to people seeking out organizations that fit with their values (Argyle, Furnham, & Graham, 1981).

Matrix organizations

For some time, there have been strong and enthusiastic advocates of the matrix organization (Davis & Lawrence, 1977; Senior, 2000). They are characterized by two things: *dual hierarchies*, where a functional hierarchy is overlain by a product hierarchy, so that each person has two bosses; and a *balance of power* between these hierarchies. Thus, the responsibilities of the function manager include recruiting and hiring functional specialists, maintaining their expertise by training, and ensuring that products meet technical specifications. Product managers need to recruit specialists for each product, ensure that each product is completed on time and within budget, and that functional specialists comply with the product goals.

Matrix organizations have clear advantages. Since resources can be shifted between products or projects, there is good use of limited resources. Matrix organizations also respond relatively quickly to changing environmental demands. Individuals within these organizations gain experience from both a functional and a general management perspective. However, as might be predicted, there are also clear disadvantages of these organizations. The dual lines of authority do lead to conflicts, which can exacerbate frustration, anxiety and stress. More time is spent in meetings, and matrix managers appear to need a particular set of skills. Much depends on the balance of power between the two hierarchies.

Big versus small: Over- versus understaffing

The number of people in any work situation is clearly going to affect the quality and quantity of the interaction in that situation. This is especially true when inappropriate staffing levels can cause industrial and political disputes about staffing and job specification in certain job situations.

Barker (1968) has shown that occupants in undermanned settings:

- work harder and longer to support the setting and its function;
- get involved in more difficult and important tasks;
- participate in a greater diversity of tasks and roles;
- become less sensitive to differences between people;
- have a lower level of maximal or best performance;
- have a great functional importance as individuals within the setting;
- become more responsible in the sense that the setting and what others gain from it depend on the individual occupant;
- view themselves and others more in terms of task-related than socio-emotional characteristics;
- set lower standards and fewer tests for admission into a setting;
- have greater insecurity about the eventual maintenance of the setting;
- have more frequent occurrences of success and failure, depending upon the outcome of the setting's functions.

Some research has shown that members of small churches contribute more money, attend Sunday worship more frequently, spend more time in church settings and are more approving of high levels of support for church activities than members of a large church.

Later work made a number of important distinctions in this area. The traditional index of manning levels in an organization was replaced by a more precise measure, which takes account of the capacity and the number of applications for organizational settings. Second, a more complex specification of manning levels: in terms of two mutually exclusive sets of organizational setting occupants (performers and non-performers) and the minimum/maximum capacity for maintenance of an organizational setting.

There is a trade-off between being over- or understaffed. In big, overstaffed organizations (these two terms are not synonymous, however), the induction period may be long but there may be years of menial work before skills are developed. On the other hand, the new person joining the understaffed organization is greeted with joy and relief and literally put to work immediately. The newcomer in the understaffed organization learns more quickly – the learning curve is steep. They have to have a go at practically everything – there is nobody else to do the various jobs.

For the manager/owner of an organization, the understaffed organization, of course, means a lower payroll. The trade-off can be seen above in points 5, 9 and 10: the work is often not as good and the staff experience more stress and insecurity. So the answer is the *via media*: the *optimally* staffed organization.

The consequences of a poor structure

Mintzberg (1979) argued that there were essentially only five structural configurations in organizations:

- The *simple structure* was characterized by little complexity and formality, but high centralization. It worked well for small companies in a simple but dynamic environment.
- The *machine bureaucracy* seemed to work best in a simple stable environment, because large, complex organizations, high on formalization and centralization, needed to standardize their work.
- The *professional bureaucracy* structure has many specialists with a high degree of specialized training and skill, which encourages substantial autonomy and decentralization. It is best suited to complex, stable working environments.
- The *divisional structure* has several semi-independent units that may have machine bureaucracy structures working as profit centres. Typical of large organizations with multiple product lines, it seems best suited to relatively simple stable environments.
- The *adhocracy* is usually found in organizations with specialized professionals working on different aspects of a project. It is best suited to the complex dynamic environment.

The point is not that there are good and bad structures but that the business environment and the organization's product should in part determine the structure. A poor structure is one that is highly inappropriate for that organization attempting to achieve its specific goal.

It is common for organizations to frequently restructure. Cynics argue this is done out of desperation or naïve hope to improve productivity. Many also believe it is an attempt to destabilize and downgrade specific groups or individuals. Others argue that business necessities require different structures that have to adapt constantly.

What are the results for an organization if its formal structure is inappropriate or poorly designed?

- *It may be illogical.* No member of the organization should be appointed to a senior position without identification of the responsibilities and relationships attached to that position and its role within the social pattern of the organization. Structure should not follow the skills profile available. A careful and comprehensive analysis of the task and processes should dictate an ideal structure, which is then filled with appropriate people. What often happens is that powerful individuals create structures that suit their aims and personality, not necessarily the needs of the organization.
- *It may be stress-inducing*, because it is the individual members of the organization who suffer most from inappropriate structure. If members are appointed to the organization without a clear definition of their duties or the qualifications required to perform those duties, it is these members who are likely to be blamed for the poor results that do not match the vague ideas of what was expected of them. Structure needs to be clear and explicit. All employees need to know who they report to, what they are responsible for, and the criteria upon which they are judged.
- *It can be wasteful*, because if jobs are structured along the lines of functional specialization, then new members of the organization cannot be trained effectively to take over those jobs. If jobs have to be fitted *to members* of the organization, rather than members of the organization *to jobs*, then every new member has to be trained in such a way as to aim to replace the special personal experience of the previous job incumbent. Job specifications must precede person specification.
- *It is ultimately inefficient*, because if the organization is not founded on principles, managers are forced to fall back on "personalities". Unless there are clearly established principles, which are understood by everyone in the organization, managers may put self- and departmental interest above that of the organization.

The consequences of structural deficiencies are more than manifest in many organizations (Child, 1964):

- *Low motivation and morale* result from apparently inconsistent and arbitrary decisions, insufficient delegation of decision-making, lack of clarity in job definition and assessment of performance, competing pressures from different parts of the organization, and managers and supervisors overloaded through inadequate support systems. Of course, there are many other causes of inappropriate or unclear structures, and many other causes of low morale, but this is clearly most important.
- *Late and inappropriate decisions* result from lack of relevant timely information to the right people, poor coordination of decision-makers in different units, overloading of decision-makers because of insufficient delegation, and inadequate procedures for evaluation of past decisions.

- *Conflict and lack of coordination* result from conflicting goals and people working at cross-purposes because of lack of clarity on objectives and priorities, a failure to bring people together into teams or through lack of liaison, and a breakdown between planning and actual operational work. A badly thought out, contradictory or unclear communication structure can very easily be the cause of significant problems.
- *Poor response to new opportunities and external change* results from failure to establish specialist jobs concerned with forecasting environmental change, failure to give adequate attention to innovation and planning of change as main management activities, or inadequate coordination between identification of market changes and research into possible technological solutions.
- *Rising costs* may result from an extended hierarchy of authority with a high proportion of senior positions, an excess of administrative work at the expense of production work, and the presence of some, or all, of the other organizational problems. One may argue for "rightsizing" and re-engineering organizations to save on cash.

Johns (1992) proposed five major symptoms of structural problems:

- poor job design;
- the fact that the right hand does not know what the left hand is doing;
- persistent inter-departmental conflict;
- slow response times;
- decisions made frequently with incomplete information, and a proliferation of committees.

Of course, these may be symptoms of other organizational problems, but if, say, three to six occur simultaneously, it appears to imply structural problems.

Devising, and where appropriate changing, the formal and explicit structure of an organization is clearly of crucial importance. For some, the very idea of structure implies bureaucratic restrictions, but structure is clearly necessary. Furthermore, just as in the case of leadership there may well be formal and informal structures. Informal structures often arise when the formal structures fail. Structure can be flexible and must change to meet the requirements of the organization.

What is the optimal organizational structure? The answer to the question is inevitably contingent on such things as the size, goals and technology of the organization. Once the environmental factors have been closely considered, the organization may be designed and specific decisions made about the span of control, the bias of differentiation and integration. The design may be functional, divisional or matrix, and inevitably it will have particular characteristics that may be described in terms of complexity, formality and centralization (Randolph & Blackburn, 1989). Each structure will inevitably have particular outcomes that are a happy fit or misfit between internal and external requirements.

Senior (2000) has argued that organizational structure and culture are closely interwoven. Furthermore, that these lead to very different attitudes to, and capacity for, change.

Segmentalist cultures

- compartmentalize actions, events and problems;
- see problems as narrowly as possible;
- have segmented structures with large numbers of departments walled off from one another;
- assume problems can be solved by carving them up into pieces, which are then assigned to specialists who work in isolation;
- divide resources up among the many departments;
- avoid experimentation;
- avoid conflict and confrontation;
- have weak co-ordinating mechanisms;
- stress precedent and procedures.

Integrative cultures

- are willing to move beyond received wisdom;
- combine ideas from unconnected sources;
- see problems as wholes, related to larger wholes;
- challenge established practices;
- operate at the edge of competencies;
- measure themselves by looking to visions of the future rather than by referring to the standards of the past;
- create mechanisms for exchange of information and new ideas;
- recognize and even encourage differences, but then be prepared to co-operate;
- are outward looking;
- looking for novel solutions to problems. (Senior, 2000: 360–361)

Organizational change

Rapid changes in technology, markets and the world economy have meant that organizations have been forced to change dramatically not only in what they do but how they do it (Furnham, 2002). A major task for all organizations is managing change effectively (Carnall, 1990).

There have been substantial shifts in supply and demand (Heller, 2002). Changes have taken place in working practices, processes, design and materials management. In the private sector, Heller (2002) has identified seven major changes that have directly impacted on the profitability of firms: changes in the desirability (fashion) for particular products and services; changes in product price; changes in market size; changes in promotion awareness and availability; changes in the distribution of goods and service; changes in field support from suppliers; and changes in labour and operating costs.

The targets of change are frequently the organizational structure, the technology and the people. There are often both internal and external pressures for change. Organizations must have the *courage* to change the things they can change, the *tolerance* and adaptability to leave unchanged the things they cannot change, and the *wisdom* to know the difference. Many hope to be adaptive and flexible. A major determinant is attitude to risk (Senior, 2000). One objective is to eliminate the typical structure in favour of an ever-changing network of teams, projects, alliances and coalitions, which adapt appropriately to internal and external forces. Organizations cannot change everything. They can, with difficulty, persistence and determination, change their goals and strategies, technology, structure and people.

It is useful to distinguish between planned, intentional, goal-orientated change and that which inevitably occurs. Change may be at different levels and applied to structure, technology and products, as well as individual behaviours. Perhaps the four most common pressures to change are:

- *Globalization:* there is an increasing global market for products, but to compete effectively in it, many organizations have to change their culture, structure and operations.
- *Changing technology:* the rapid expansion of information systems technology, computer-integrated manufacturing, virtual reality technology and robots; the speed, power and cost of various operations have changed remarkably.
- *Rapid product obsolescence:* the shortened life-cycle of products occurs because of innovations, requiring a shortening of production lead times. Hence, organizations have to adapt quickly and constantly to new information, and facilitate transitions to new forms of operations.
- *Changing nature of the workforce:* depending on the demographic nature of the country, there are many important and noticeable changes.

Hartley (2002) has provided a useful framework for understanding organizational change that has four mutually interacting parts:

- *Context:* external, including political, social and economic forces; and internal, including organizational size, culture, resource and history.
- *Leadership:* whether the key agents of change tend to be change strategists, implementers or recipients.
- *Management of the change process:* the strategy and vision for change, the engagement of the different stakeholders, the timing and phasing of change, and whether the change is essentially cultural or structural.
- *Outcomes of change:* intended and unintended and how easy they are to measure.

Change is both ubiquitous and constant. It can be planned or not planned and, as such, some organizations are *proactive* and others are *reactive*. Change can also come from the inside or the outside, or both. One could also categorize reactions to change, as in Table 14.4. Equally, it is possible to categorize or list various factors that mitigate against changes (see Box 14.1).

Table 14.4 Type of change

	"Chango-philes"	"Chango-phobes"
People	Love psychological, human resource programmes aimed at changing attitudes, beliefs, behaviour and values.	Hate attempting to change others (and probably themselves).
Things	Love changing "systems", be they organizational charts, structure, process or gadgets.	Against "rocking the boat" in any way whatsoever.

Box 14.1 Organizational factors for and against change

Factors

For change (that facilitate, drive, encourage)

- repealed or revised laws or regulations (often government-based) that lead to new opportunities, markets or ways of operating;
- rapidly changing environment (geographic, market, political situation) that makes old methods, processes or products redundant;
- improved technology or technology that can do things faster, cheaper and more reliably;
- new product development or selection by consumers;
- changed workforce (for example, more educated, more women) with different demands and skills;
- more technically trained management who appreciate the possibilities of, and for, the new technology;
- organizational crisis (for example, impending bankruptcy, purchase) that requires change of necessity;
- reduced productivity or product quality that leads to a change;
- reduced satisfaction or commitment by staff, which ultimately forces a crisis of morale and reduced productivity;
- increased turnover, absenteeism and other signs of organizational stress.

Against change

- individual distrust of change agents, be they consultants, new managers or technocrats;
- individual fear of change, especially fear of the unknown or fear that personal or occupational security will be challenged;
- individual desires for maintaining power in the present structure;
- individual complacency and believing all is well;
- lack of resources to support change so that early efforts collapse;
- conflict between individual and organizational goals;
- organizational inertia against changing the *status quo*.

There are a variety of things that can (and need) to be changed in an organization (Randolph & Blackburn, 1989). At the environmental level, these include an attempt to change laws, entry requirements to the market, one's niche in the market or indeed the competition. At the organizational level, one can change (with difficulty) the organization's goals, strategies, culture, technology, processes and structure. At the group level, it may be possible to change group composition and cohesiveness, as well as leadership and conflict management styles. Finally, at the individual level, most managers have attempted to change attitudes, commitment, performance, skills and motivation.

Change tactics can be described on various dimensions: quick versus slow, unilateral versus participative, planned versus evolving, and aiming to eliminate resistance versus pacification. The choice of strategy inevitably depends on many things, including the importance of the required change, the distribution of power in the organization, the management culture and style, as well as the perceived strength and source of the resistance forces.

Individuals don't change themselves; they are changed by others. They tend to be more accepting of change when:

- it is understood;

- it does not threaten security;
- those affected have helped to create it;
- it follows other successful changes;
- it genuinely reduces a work burden;
- the outcome is reasonably certain;
- the implementation has been mutually planned;
- top management support is strongly evident.

Individuals and groups, like organizations as a whole, need to experience different things during the process of change. Old beliefs and behaviours need to be challenged, rejected, unfrozen and the new patterns established. Change involves the unfreezing of old ways, changes established and the refreezing into a normative pattern. When does change occur and when not? Whether or not an organizational change will be made depends on members' beliefs regarding the relative benefits and costs of making the change. The benefits are reflected by three considerations, reviewed below (Greenberg & Baron, 1992) (see Figure 14.2).

To evaluate the efficiency of an intervention programme, researchers often give questionnaires to those involved *before* and *after* the change process. Golembiewski, Billingsley & Yeager (1976) proposed that changes in numerical ratings on questionnaires typically used in evaluating interventions confound three types of change: alpha, beta and gamma change. *Alpha change* is a shift in the numerical rating that reflects real change in the target of the intervention. *Beta change* is a recalibration of the scale. *Gamma change* is the redefinition of the construct underlying the scale. Consider a team-building programme intended to increase the openness of group members in communicating with each other. To evaluate the effectiveness of the programme, members of the group are asked to rate how open the group is in its communications, with 1 indicating "very closed" and 7 "very open". Assume that *before* the team-building intervention the average response was 6, and after it is 4. Should we conclude that the team-building intervention failed and actually led to more closed communications within the group?

In an alpha change, the extent of real change is often masked by two other types of changes. The shift from 6 to 4 could reflect the beta change in the form of a redefinition of the scale on which the group evaluated openness. Thus, after going through the team-building intervention, members might decide that the 6 they gave to openness of

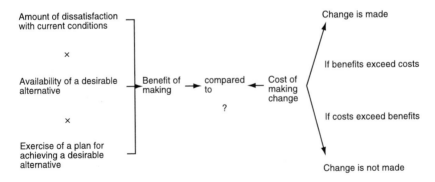

Figure 14.2 Organizational change – when will it occur? Reproduced from Greenberg & Baron (1992) with the permission of Prentice-Hall, Inc.

communication prior to the training was actually a 3. This might reflect the fact that, before the team-building, members perceived the group to be moderately high on open communications, but afterwards they have seen the extent to which people *can* achieve open communication and the previous state of the group's communications seems pretty dismal.

A third type of change, gamma change, reflects a shift attributable to redefinition of the construct underlying the scale. Thus, before the team-building intervention, the group may have conceived of openness in communications as simply providing information when asked. The group was seen as open in terms of this definition of the construct, yet the team-building intervention led members to redefine open communications as including actively giving feedback, expressing emotions, confronting the boss and taking emotional risks. In reference to this redefined construct, group communications after the intervention are now seen as more open than before the intervention.

Factors associated with organizational change

Some factors make organizations ripe for, and amenable to, change, but render others much more difficult to change in fundamental ways. Although these factors may include wider macroeconomic reasons (such as increased competition from the Third World), legal changes (protecting certain groups or markets or prohibiting products) or sociological changes (in attitudes to particular issues), it is simplest to divide these into various organizational and personal characteristics (Westwood, 1992).

Organizational factors

- *Centralization of decision-making.* Where decisional prerogatives are concentrated at the highest levels of the organization, there is a natural tendency for those in authority to try to maintain and protect their position of power and to resist change. However, the likelihood of change in organizations, especially small ones run by owner-managers, depends in large measure on the personality characteristics of the person(s) at the top. In the hands of progressive and dynamic leaders, organizations tend to be quite flexible and adaptable. Radical individual leaders can also change large organizations, but centralization is usually a result of, and a contributor to, anti-change bureaucracy.
- *Organizational hierarchy.* Tall organizations with high degrees of differentiation in terms of social status, administrative position and compensation levels tend to exhibit less change than do organizations with flat structures. In highly hierarchical organizations, people who are high up on the administrative ladder are typically insulated from operational problems that may require change. They have also spent a long time getting there and feel they deserve their current status. Such organizations tend to be unresponsive to changing forces within, and sometimes outside, the organization. This may account for the current enthusiasm for de-layering and downsizing middle-management jobs, although there is now much doubt about the wisdom of downsizing.
- *Degree of formalization.* The greater the extent to which organizational activities are governed by formal rules and procedures, the less flexible the organization and the less likely it is to respond readily to external changes. Local, national and international laws and customs may well inhibit change.

- *Degree of professionalization.* The degree of professionalization of organizational members is understandably high in such organizations as law offices, medical clinics and engineering firms, and comparatively low in most mass-production manufacturing companies. Sometimes, because of their commitment to knowledge and quality of performance, professionals tend to favour continuous adaptation to changing technologies, and therefore exert a slow but positive influence on organizational change. But many are independently minded and can cause much internal disagreement. Thus, advertising and engineering firms tend to be more receptive to change than are law firms and financial institutions, which tend to be more tradition-bound, partly because of the speed and nature of change in the profession. In fact, because they have more to lose (years of poorly paid training), some professionals are strongly against change of any sort, because they want to recoup their losses.

- *Complexity.* Organizations that undertake wide-ranging tasks or produce multiple products usually perceive a greater need for change than do organizations with simple structures and processes. Complex systems interact with many segments of the external environment, and the adaptive process therefore requires many and more frequent organizational changes. Furthermore, they assume the habit of change more easily. But complexity of operation and structure certainly mitigates against speed and ease of change.

- *Organizational size.* Small organizations tend to be less formal and less differentiated and therefore more flexible. Moreover, smaller organizations typically have fewer resources committed to specific activities or processes, and therefore incur relatively few sunk costs of change compared with large organizations.

- *Age of the organization.* The older the organization, typically the greater the degree of formalization and standardization of procedures, and therefore older organizations tend to be less flexible. They have more formal and established commitments to their external environments (in the form of contracts or working arrangements with trade unions, suppliers, competitors, regulatory agencies and other entities with which they regularly interact), thereby limiting their opportunities for change. But having seen the need for change previously, and having done so (simply in order to survive), they may have accumulated the experience necessary to cope with change more effectively. Indeed, it may be that, being in an old organization (staying alive in the business world), one has to be change-orientated.

Personal characteristics

- *Age.* Normally, younger people are more inclined to initiate and accept change than are older people. They tend to be less risk-averse and are more willing to try new things. More importantly, new and low-ranking in the organization, young people have little to lose from change. For their part, older members of organizations tend to be more set in their ways, have a greater stake in the *status quo*, and therefore tend to be more wary about change. Along with chronological age is *deference to age*, which may inhibit change. To the extent that older, more conservative people occupy leadership roles in organizations, and to the extent that organizational members acquiesce to or despise them, organizational change may be slow to materialize. A company's age profile may give some indication as to its attitude to change, and more particularly the age profile of its decision-makers.

- *Training and education.* Well trained and better educated people tend to be more progressive in outlook and have a better appreciation of the need for the most appropriate time to set in motion effective strategies of change. They can be aware of the potential impact of change on the organization and have a clear understanding of the cost of implementing change. They base their judgements more on facts and analysis than on personal values and sentiments, and usually have more confidence in their ability to learn new skills.
- *Rank.* People of rank and status at the upper reaches of the administrative hierarchy, together with those who wield power and authority, tend to be quite cautious in adopting change for fear of losing their power and resulting rewards. Yet, the successful implementation of change in organizations requires the active involvement and support of the people who make the major decisions in the organization. For good or bad, organizational managers play a key role in the change process.
- *Values and beliefs.* As noted in Chapter 5, certain values, such as conservatism, belief in a just world and work locus of control, may be expected to relate quite specifically to attitudes to, and indeed phobia about, change.
- *Management courage.* To be successful, organizational change takes courage. Furnham (2002) argues that successful change-oriented managers need three types of courage: the *courage* to accept failure when their change efforts fail for whatever reason; interpersonal *courage* to confront poor performers and where necessary deliver bad news; and the moral *courage* to uphold ethical and moral decisions, and eliminate various forms of corruption and counter-productive behaviour.

Quite simply, habit, fear, need for security, self-interest, a different assessment of the selection and natural conservatism often drive people to resist change. But it may be that attitudes to change are culture- and sector-dependent. Consider the following four questions and the extent to which they are culturally determined:

- Do people believe that change is possible (let alone desirable)? Some fatalistic cultures may not believe it as strongly as those infused with instrumentalist beliefs. That is, for some, change is instituted externally and one must wait patiently for it to happen.
- If change is possible, how long will it take and when will it be necessary to change gain? This relates to cultural difference in reactions to time.
- Do some cultures resist more than others? This may be determined by how much a culture values tradition and is past- as opposed to future-orientated.
- Do cultures influence *how* changes can or should be implemented? This refers to top-down autocratic versus bottom-up democratic attitudes to change.

In some countries, change is managed at the organizational level through restructuring, the introduction of new reward systems, and attempts to change the corporate culture. Other interventions may be based on technology, job design and concern about sociotechnical systems. Finally, some organizations prefer to focus on the individual through such things as sensitivity training, feedback, personal performance and team-building.

Characteristics of the change situation

Certain aspects of the change itself affect the likelihood of its being proposed and the chances of its successful implementation. Some of these are objective and can be reasonably well managed, whereas others are based more on perceptions and attitude (Westwood, 1992).

- *Cost*. Other things being equal, the higher the costs associated with a particular change proposal, the less likely that it will be put into effect. Cost is a major consideration in the installation of a computer-based management information system, or in the expansion of plant capacity. But once cost–benefit calculations are done, over a particular time period even the highest-cost programme may look reasonable if not essential. Ultimately, the cost of not changing may be higher than the cost of change, although this calculation is difficult, speculative and often avoided.
- *Riskiness*. The resource requirements and ultimate results of a change proposal are often difficult to ascertain well in advance. As a rule, the less certainty surrounding a particular change, the less likely that it will be considered. This follows from the fact that people and organizations are all risk-averse to varying degrees. The "no-pain, no-gain" philosophy of the 1980s has made more organizations less overtly risk-averse, but once they have introduced a costly and unsuccessful change, the experience of "having their fingers burnt" makes them very cautious.
- *Adaptability*. Changes that are irreversible, or those which are difficult to modify once started, stand less chance of being adopted than changes that are easily adaptable. Adaptability is easier than innovation. Note the way some countries make changes – in their currency or use of the metric system. Some have a period when the "dual system operates", tending to favour adaptation, whereas sudden change favours innovation. Many argue that adaptability is an enemy of change because it allows those who resist change never fully to come to grips with changed circumstances.
- *Magnitude of the change*. Changes that require substantial time and resources to implement, and those that result in major transformation of organizational structure and processes, are more difficult to adopt than those that entail little effort and few resources, or have minimal impact on organizational life. Moreover, the larger the size of the change, the greater the degree of risk associated with it. In this sense, all the factors listed above are interrelated.
- *Type of change*. Administrative changes are those that alter positions, responsibilities, reporting relationships and compensation, whereas technological changes are those that affect the process by which inputs are transformed into outputs. These two types of change are, typically, implemented through different procedures. Administrative changes are typically initiated and enforced by the organization's top decision-makers, and technical changes are conceived and implemented by its technical, professional and operational staff. Administrative changes elicit more objections and controversy than do technological changes, and are therefore more difficult to implement.

Reactions to change

Inevitably, organizations are most concerned with resistance to change, which will be manifest in everything from strikes and sabotage, to a drop in motivation and morale, to no participation in, and commitment to, change initiatives. There is both individual resistance and organizational resistance for a variety of well-known and anticipatory reasons.

Organizational change causes powerful emotions from a sense of liberation to depression and humiliation. People's support of, or resistance to, change depends heavily on how they answer the following questions:

- Will this change cause me to gain or lose something of value?
- Do I understand the nature of this change?
- Do I trust the initiators of this change?
- Do I agree with the advisability of this change?
- Given my personality, personal values and attitudes, how do I feel about this change?

How they answer these questions may lead to one of seven responses (Greenberg & Baron, 1992):

- *Quitting*: The most extreme reaction an employee shows to a change is to leave the organization. For example, following the introduction of a major organizational change, such as a merger or a transfer in job assignment, many workers leave because they believe the change is so obnoxious that staying would be intolerable. Sometimes organization members depart even if the change is a good one, because they find it personally difficult to cope with the change. Early retirement is a convenient and acceptable way to "let people go" who are unhappy with organizational change. Although leaving an organization may be the most extreme reaction to change, it is not necessarily the most damaging one to the organization. Indeed, things probably proceed more smoothly if the most adamant opponents of a change leave rather than stay to fight it.
- *Active resistance*: Workers who actively resist a change may try either to prevent it from occurring or to modify its nature. At its extreme, active resistance sends the message "No, I will not do this". Active resistance often goes beyond personal defiance and includes attempts to encourage others to resist the change. Many organizational changes have been scuttled by active employee resistance. A strike is a good example of group-orientated active resistance.
- *Opposition*: Somewhat less extreme than active resistance is behaviour that can be labelled "opposition". Usually somewhat passive in nature, opposition behaviour might result in no more than simple "foot dragging" to delay implementation or to bring about a scaled-down version of a proposed change. Opposition is a tactic commonly used by those who control resources that are necessary for the change to be made. By withholding essential resources, people can slow or modify a change quietly without having to make their dislike for the change known actively or aggressively.
- *Acquiescence*: Opposition reactions tend to occur when those affected dislike a change and engage in passive resistance to delay or modify it. Sometimes, however,

those opposed to a change feel powerless to prevent or alter it and they allow the change to occur without interference. This acquiescence to an unwanted change may arise from an impending sense of its inevitability – like death or taxes. People put up with the inevitable as best they can, shrugging their shoulders, gritting their teeth, and steeling themselves to face the inevitable. They hardly welcome the change but understand its inevitability.

- *Acceptance/modification*: Employers who demonstrate an acceptance/modification response accept a change to a certain extent but have some reservations about it. For example, suppose a manager has been told that her employer intends to move the company's headquarters to another European capital. She supports the idea of moving operations because local taxes and other restrictive ordinances are hurting the company's ability to compete in the marketplace. On the other hand, she is worried that the change may alienate many of its major customers and adversely affect its supply and delivery systems. At a personal level, she would rather not move her family too far from friends and relatives. One option available is to try to persuade her employer that there are sound reasons for finding a different site in the same country. Acceptance/modification responses to change usually can be characterized as bargaining over details (albeit, perhaps, important ones), rather than over principles.

- *Acceptance*: This type of reaction is likely when people are either indifferent towards the change (that is, they do not *dislike* it) or they agree with it. Acceptance reactions to change are characterized by passive support. If asked whether they like the change, for example, workers might agree that they do – but they are unlikely to volunteer such information. If asked to participate in the change, they will cooperate – but they probably will not initiate participation. They may see change as inevitable or that their jobs ultimately depend on it.

- *Active support*: In this situation, organization members choose to engage actively in behaviours that increase the change's chances of success. Active supporters often initiate conversations, explaining why they support the change and think it is a good idea. They embrace, welcome and even rejoice in change.

Resistance to innovation and change occurs for different reasons. Managers may consciously or unconsciously resist the relearning and adaptation process that is part and parcel of change.

Human beings tend to become satisfied with the *status quo*. Insecurity develops when changes occur. Sometimes this insecurity is caused by economic factors. Lower-level workers fear that automation will result in unemployment. Higher-level employees might view change as a threat to their status and eventually to their economic well-being. For example, doctors might resist the professional acceptance of paramedical personnel for fear that the increased volume of work paramedics could handle would reduce the amount of work performed by physicians.

The following is a checklist of factors that account for why people don't change, although it may be in their best interests:

- *Because of ignorance*: Often, concerned individuals are simply not aware of the changes taking place. Manufacturers may continue to use a certain production process because they are unaware of a better method.
- *By default*: Sometimes people may reject a change, even though they are aware of

another better technique, with little justification except a desire not to learn to use a new method.

- *On the basis of the status quo*: Change is rejected because it will alter the way in which things have traditionally been done.
- *Because of social reasons*: A manager may refuse to change because of a rationalization that the people within, and society outside, the organization will not accept it.
- *On the basis of interpersonal relations*: Because friends and even competitors have not accepted the change or are threatened by it.
- *Through substitution*: Another process or technique is selected in favour of the proposed change, because it seems easier, safer and less threatening.
- *Because of experience*: People reject a change when they try it but do not like it, or do it badly, wrongly or half-heartedly, thus self-fulfilling their prophesies.
- *Through incorrect logic*: People may reject a change on supposedly "logical" grounds without having well-founded reasons. Collective rationalization is strong when passion is involved.

In short, people resist change through habit and the inconvenience of having to do things differently. Fearing the unknown, insecurity or indeed economic implications (having to work harder) are main causes of individuals resisting change. In his force-field analysis, Lewin (1951) believed all organizations were in a state of equilibrium as a consequence of various forces, some pushing for change and others resisting it. His technique was to attempt to identify *all* the salient forces for and against change, and next identify those that seemed controllable. Once the most important controllable forces were identified, they could at least be worked on. Lewin's process was then a three-step procedure: first to unfreeze the organization by reducing the forces holding the behaviour in the organization as stable; next to change structures and procedures; and then to refreeze by stabilizing the organization at a new state of equilibrium.

Various methods for resisting change have been considered (see Table 14.5).

Organization development

The term "organization development" has been used generically to describe a wide range of approaches to organizational change. It is a planned, continuing effort to change organizations to be more effective and, where appropriate, humane. In essence, it tries to obtain better use of human and other resources. Senior (2000) claims that the defining characteristics of organization development is an emphasis on processes and planned change over the medium period. It involves an analysis of the desired future and the actual present. The aim of organization development is to gain commitment to the vision and need for change. The next crucial stage is to develop an action plan that specifies goals, roles, communication strategy, negotiation strategy, responsibility charting, and so on. Action plans should ideally be adaptable, chronologically detailed, integrated, relevant and specific. The next stage is to implement the change hopefully with various "short-term wins" and, finally, to assess and reinforce the change.

More specifically, organization development may be defined as:

- a long-range effort to improve an organization's problem-solving and renewal processes, through a more effective and collaborative management of organizational culture – formal workteams – with the assistance of a change agent or catalyst;

Table 14.5 Methods of reducing resistance to change

Approach	Situational use	Advantages	Drawbacks
Education and communication	Where there is lack of information or inaccurate information about the change.	Once persuaded, people often will help with the implementation of the change.	Can be very time-consuming if many people are involved.
Participation and involvement	Where the initiators do not have all the information they need to design the change, and where others have considerable power to resist.	People who participate will be committed to implementing change, and any relevant information they have will be integrated into the change plan.	Can be very time-consuming if participators design an inappropriate change.
Facilitation and support	Where people are resisting because of adjustment problems.	No other approach works as well with adjustment problems.	Can be time-consuming, expensive, and still fail.
Negotiation and agreement	Where someone or some group will clearly lose out in a change, and where that person/group has considerable power to resist.	Sometimes it is a relatively easy way to avoid major resistance.	Can be too expensive for others to negotiate for compliance.
Manipulation and co-optation	Where other tactics will not work or are too expensive.	It can be a relatively quick and inexpensive solution to resistance problems.	Can lead to future problems if people feel manipulated.
Explicit and implicit coercion	Where speed is essential, and the change initiators possess considerable power.	It is speedy, and can overcome any kind of resistance.	Can be risky if it leaves initiators discredited.

Source: Reproduced from Kotter & Schlesinger (1979) with the permission of the President and Fellows of Harvard College.

- an effort, planned, organization-wide and managed from the top, to increase organizational effectiveness and health through planned interventions in the organization's "processes", using behavioural science knowledge.

For Beer (1980), the basic terms of organization development are:

- Organization development seeks to create self-directed change to which people are committed. The problems and issues to be solved are those identified by the organization members directly concerned.
- Organization development is system-wide change effort. Making lasting changes that create a more effective organization requires an understanding of the entire organization. It is not possible to change part of the organization without changing the whole organization in some sense.
- Organization development typically places equal emphasis on solving immediate problems and the long-term development of an adaptive organization. The most

effective change programme is not just one that solves present problems but one that also prepares employees to solve future problems.

- Organization development (OD) places more emphasis than do other approaches on a collaborative process of data collection, diagnosis and action for arriving at solutions to problems. Action research, discussed in the previous section, is a primary change process used in most OD programmes.
- Organization development often leads to new organizational structures, job designs and working relationships that break with traditional bureaucratic patterns.

Typically, OD techniques are structural, task-technology and people-focused. Structural interventions are typically concerned with structural reorganization, the introduction of new reward systems such as performance-related pay, and attempts to change the corporate culture. Task-technology interventions typically look at job redesign and the development of sociotechnical systems which optimize the social and technological demands of the job, as well as paying attention to quality of working life issues. People-focused interventions include sensitivity training, survey feedback (360° feedback; see p. 451) and team-building.

How does one implement changes? Usually, a number of quite specific steps are followed, such as:

1 Hearing the different members' perception of the organization and their attitudes to and goals for change.
2 Extensive data-gathering from many sources.
3 Diagnosis based on providing an in-depth analysis of all the options available.
4 Feedback on results and future plans.
5 Action – implementing the change.
6 Monitoring and evaluation of that change – particularly affective (emotional reactions, the learning that took place, actual behavioural changes occurring and perhaps, most importantly of all, performance changes).

All sorts of techniques are used in this process. Doing a SWOT (strengths, weaknesses, opportunities, threats) analysis is common. This involves looking at any organization or procedure and attempting to ascertain the four qualities specified by SWOT. Another is force-field analysis.

These ideas go back to Lewin, who talked about a three-step process of unfreezing, moving and then refreezing the organization. Often managers and OD consultants have a specific model, process or checklist that they use to go about their business. Many begin with pretty fundamental but ignored, forgotten or repressed questions like: What business are we in? How do we manage conflict? How do we divide up the work?

Often OD work is experimental. Thus by using autonomous working groups that participate in setting their own goals, OD consultants have tried to motivate blue-collar workers (Lowenberg & Conrad, 1998). Organization development experts tend to focus on specific issues such as: the individual autonomy that workers have; whether the group, division or organizational structure is appropriate; the whole business of rewards; teamwork and cooperation.

The idea is nearly always conceptualized in terms of forming high-performance teams with participative leadership, alignment, task and future focus, rapid response, shared responsibility, and so on.

Table 14.6 Advantages and disadvantages of internal and external change agents

	Internal agents	*External agents*
Advantages	Possess better knowledge of organization; are more quickly available; require lower out-of-pocket costs; are a known quantity; have more control and authority.	Have more objective view of organization; have more experience in dealing with diverse problems; can call on more individuals with diverse expertise.
Disadvantages	May be too close to problems; may hold biased views; may create additional resistance if viewed as part of the problem.	Have less knowledge of organization; require higher out-of-pocket costs; are an unknown quantity; have longer start-up time.

Organizational development is the implementation of planned change. This is done by people within the organization, as well as those lured in from the outside (Table 14.6). Some techniques are well established, such as clarifying organizational goals by a "management objective" exercise.

Currently, a variety of techniques are popular. These include the following.

Quality circles

Quality circles originated in Japan but have spread extensively (Munchus, 1983). They are small groups of volunteers (usually around ten) who meet regularly (usually weekly) to identify and solve problems related to the quality of work they perform and the conditions under which people do their jobs. An organization may have several quality circles operating at once, each dealing with a particular work area about which it has the most expertise. To help the members of the circle work effectively, they usually receive some form of training. Groups deal with such issues as customer relations, how to create safer and more comfortable working environments, and how to improve product quality. Research has shown that, although quality circles are very effective at bringing about short-term improvements in quality of working life (i.e. those lasting up to 18 months), they are less effective at creating more permanent changes (Meyer & Scott, 1985).

There are two major potential pitfalls that must be avoided for quality of working life programmes to be successfully implemented. First, it is essential that both management and labour cooperate in designing their programme. Should either believe that the programme is really just a method of gaining an advantage over the other, it is doomed to fail. Second, it is essential that the plans agreed to by all concerned parties are fully implemented (Greenberg & Baron, 1992).

Team-building

This is not very different from the above. It involves forming a self-managing team that takes responsibility for its development and output. Usually, the team is set up to investigate and solve some organizational problems. The team is tasked to diagnose its own strengths and weaknesses, then develop clear goals for change. Once these realistic, achievable goals have been developed, the team needs to develop and implement the action plan. Finally, it should aim to evaluate the process. Much depends on the ability, motives and preferred role of the people in the team (Furnham & Gunter, 1994).

There is now considerable emphasis on team performance and hence team training. Teams are encouraged to devise and then re-examine their mission statements; their informal structure and interaction pattern; their cohesiveness and the way they can develop their skills; and perhaps most importantly how they solve problems and resolve conflict.

The aim is nearly always to develop high performing teams. They have characteristics like shared responsibility, alignment of purpose, effective communication, future focus, a continued focus on task, creativity and rapid response (Lowenberg & Conrad, 1998).

Survey feedback

This is a simple, powerful, effective and ubiquitous technique used in the OD world. It is quick, flexible and fairly cheap. It is based on the premise that all decision-makers need regular, detailed data before they can plan. Because information flows down rather than up organizations, and that managers tend to pay more attention to financial and production/output data than to attitudinal data, it is argued that too few senior managers really know what their staff want, feel and believe.

Hence, organization-wide surveys (climate or culture surveys; see Chapter 13) are used to collect information showing decision-makers how employees think and feel. They acquire data on morale, attitudes to customers, or indeed any issue that really interests them. Currently, 360° feedback techniques are in vogue. These are so named because they require different people to rate individual managers: their superiors (0°), their peers (90°), their subordinates (180°) and their clients, customers or shareholders (270°). Because senior managers rarely have such specific and detailed feedback from so many different and interested parties who experience the consequences of their management style and procedures, they are often surprised and they act positively in response to those results. Although the effect "wears off" over time, such feedback techniques are potentially very powerful to initiate and sustain organization development.

But does organization development work? Are the benefits worth the cost and effort? Is it simply a new but spreading fad? This question is difficult to answer because so few studies have attempted a full dispassionate evaluation of OD efforts. White & Mitchell (1976) have noted three classic problems:

- Efforts at organization development usually involve a complex series of changes that occur simultaneously. It becomes very difficult to determine which procedures have what effect. Indeed, it is quite possible that two procedures introduced at much the same time actually "cancel each other out".
- The novelty of new procedures, as well as the Hawthorne effect (see Chapter 2), means that employees receive special treatment which does not last, so that all observed effects are short term and do not endure over time.
- To a large extent, researchers rely on the self-report of employees to measure effect. All sorts of biases occur, with some people trying to please the change agents, and thus reporting significant helpful change, and others doing the precise opposite.

However, in a very comprehensive review of 15 different studies, looking at many different "hard" measures of change such as turnover, absenteeism, cost, profits, sales, and so on, Nicholas (1982) showed well over half did demonstrate change. However, this varied from 0 to 100%, showing clearly how some measures are much easier to change than others.

The generation, implementation and diffusion of new ideas and processes in an organization are particularly difficult. Organization development change agents find many obstacles to their efforts. Sometimes there is a lack of support and commitment from top management. Management reward systems that concentrate on traditional performance, not new-style performance, can thwart any OD programme if not changed themselves. Union resistance is common, along with those in the more administrative sections of organizations. Often, an OD pilot project fails because of the differences between the technology and setting of the project and those of the other units in the organization. There is no doubt that being an OD change agent, whether an internal or external consultant, is far from easy.

Assessment of change checklist

Heller (2000: 214–215) provide the following useful checklist to evaluate the success of change initiative:

Definition of the dilemma to be resolved or opportunity to be taken

1. Is there a clear statement setting out what is to be changed and why?		YES/NO
2. Has this been discussed with all involved to gain understanding and agreement?		YES/NO
3. Is the focus on problems, not symptoms?		YES/NO

Statement of the desired outcomes

4. Is there a clear statement setting out what will be different at the end of the change process?		YES/NO
5. Has this been discussed with all involved to gain understanding and agreement?		YES/NO
6. Has a benchmark organization been identified?		YES/NO

Commitment of the senior management team to the leadership of the initiative

7. Is the senior management team really committed to change?		YES/NO
8. Do all members understand the implications for them?		YES/NO
9. Will they all survive the process?		YES/NO
10. Does the desired outcome have a direct relationship to a valued business goal?		YES/NO

Stakeholder involvement through creating the motivation and commitment to change

11. Have the key stakeholders been identified?		YES/NO
12. Have they been involved in designing the change?		YES/NO
13. Is there evidence of this?		YES/NO
14. Is it likely they will cooperate?		YES/NO
15. Is there evidence that their views have been taken into account?		YES/NO
16. Have both plus and minus motivators been identified and built into the plan?		YES/NO

Choice of the "tool"

17. Has the change been categorized as innovative or strategic?		YES/NO
18. Has a suitable tool been selected to implement the change?		YES/NO
19. Does everybody know what it is?		YES/NO
20. Does everybody know how it will work?		YES/NO
21. Is it known who has used it before?		YES/NO

22. Is it known what their experience was like?	YES/NO
23. Would you recommend it?	YES/NO

Use of a disciplined, action learning-based implementation strategy

24. Is there a composite programme covering the change?	YES/NO
25. Does it have milestones, time-scales, costs?	YES/NO
26. Has it been communicated to all concerned?	YES/NO
27. Is someone at senior level taking responsibility for managing the implementation?	YES/NO
28. Does it embrace learning opportunities and have the capability for change?	YES/NO
29. Is it based on "action learning"?	YES/NO

Focus on measuring success

30. Have performance indicators been identified and targets agreed?	YES/NO
31. Is there an effective monitoring and control structure in place?	YES/NO
32. Is the information being used to control the implementation?	YES/NO
33. Are the necessary changes being made?	YES/NO

Conclusion

All organizations have a structure, usually based on the classic pyramid-shape organizational chart. This is often based on particular principles, such as span of control, chain of command, and so on. Nearly every organization has anomalies that do not follow explicit principles. However, the lines joining the people in the official chart provide little information about what decisions are made where. The structure is partly a function of such things as complexity (the degree of differentiation of jobs and work units), formalization (the extent to which written rules guide or direct employees' activities) and centralization (the location or dispersal of decision-making authority within the organization). The aim of a formal structure is to maximize coordination and standardization.

The application of various principles, such as unity of command and span of control, can be used to dictate structure. A central question is the nature and size of the divisions or departments in the structure, and the principle by which they can be categorized. Categorization by function is the most common, although more frequently this is being done by division or profit centre. Organizations may be described as mechanistic or organic in terms of their structures, both being appropriate in particular circumstances. Certainly, the consequences of having a poor or inappropriate structure for the welfare of the employees and the ultimate "health" of the organization mean it needs to be designed carefully.

Managers must plan and manage change. The "calm waters" metaphor in management has been replaced by the "whitewater rapids" metaphor, indicating the speed and exhilaration, but also danger, involved in change. It is not the planning of change that proves so often the problem but rather resistance to change. At the individual level, this is often based on habit, fear of the unknown and investment in the past. There are also resistance factors at the organizational level, such as structural and group inertia, as well as threats to established power relationships and resource allocation procedures. Through education, participation, facilitation and negotiation, as well as manipulation and coercion, managers attempt to facilitate the change process.

Some factors seem to facilitate change within the organization and it is clearly important to know what they are. These are both structural and organizational. Those in organizations have to attempt to marshall all factors that facilitate change while suppressing those that oppose it. Inevitably, there are typical resistance responses to be anticipated.

Organizational development is the name given to strategies companies use to be proactive and grow. Everyone recognizes that development is desirable and large organizations employ internal and/or external change agents to attempt to bring about positive development. Various techniques such as quality circles, team-building and survey feedback are used to achieve this end. Although many recognize how important this is, evidence is scarce as to whether it works and is thus cost-effective.

A research perspective

Dealing with and pushing through change

Managers are frequently told that the only constant is change. Certainly, the electronic revolution has signalled rapid, dramatic and continuing change in the workplace. As a consequence, there are various possible approaches they might use. Tannenbaum & Schmidt (1973) suggested an *escalation* model, using:

- *education and communication* for change where there is a lack of accurate information; *participation and involvement* where the change agents need more information to design change or more power;
- *facilitation and support* because employees resist change because of adjustment problems; *negotiation and incentives* when those who resist changes have power to resist and may lose out in the change;
- *manipulation and co-option* where other tactics won't work, so resisting individuals are asked to participate in designing change in a superficial way;
- *coercion*, where threats of job loss, pay cuts, demotions or undesirable transfers are the only options left.

Furnham & Gunter (1994) have suggested a rather different range of options.

- *The fellowship strategy*. The fellowship strategy relies heavily on interpersonal relations, using seminars, dinners and events to announce and discuss what needs to be changed and how. People at all levels are listened to, supposedly treated equally, and conflicting opinions are expressed. This "warm and fuzzy" approach emphasizes personal commitment over ideas; as a consequence, the change process may have serious problems getting under way. Because this strategy is averse to conflict, it can miss crucial issues and even waste time. Many fellowship types leave the organization and can be replaced only by those who have a need to belong.
- *The political struggle*. Here the power structure is targeted by attempting to influence the official and unofficial leaders. The strategy seeks to identify and persuade those in the organization who are most respected and who have large constituencies. Political strategists flatter, bargain and compromise to achieve their ends. But this destabilizes the organization because of continuing shifts in people's political stances. Maintaining credibility can be difficult because the strategy is so obviously devious. Persuading people to show their true colours in this way is never simple.
- *The economic strategy*. The cynical economist believes that money is the best persuader. The person who controls the purse strings can buy or change anything. Everyone has a price. This is the rational "*Homo economicus*" approach that assumes people act more or less logically but that their logic is based on economic motives. But "buying people off" can be

costly and the effects short term in nature. The strategy also ignores emotional issues and all questions besides bottom-line profit.

- *The academic strategy*. The academic strategy assumes that, if you present people with enough information and the correct facts, they will accept the need to change. The academic strategist commissions studies and reports from employees, experts and consultants. Although such strategists are happy to share their findings, it is difficult to mobilize energy and resources after the analysis phase. "Analysis paralysis" often results because the study phase lasts too long and the results and recommendations are often out of date when they are published.

- *The engineering strategy*. This technocratic approach assumes that, if the physical nature of a job is changed, enough people will be forced to change. The strong emphasis on the structural aspects of problems leads to a sensitivity to the environment which is particularly helpful in unstable situations. The concern over channels of communication can prompt structural change, but fails to commit most people. Most people do not like being treated as machines and hence do not feel committed. Such change can also break up happy and efficient teams. The strategy is limited because only high-level managers can really understand it, it is impersonal and it ignores the question: "What is in this for me?"

- *The military strategy*. The military strategy is reliant on brute force and sometimes ignorance. It is at times used by the military, the police, students, pressure groups and political parties. The emphasis is on learning to use the weapons for the fight. Physical strength and agility are required and following the plan is rewarded. But the change-enforcer cannot relax, in case the imposed change disappears. Furthermore, force is met by force and the result is continuously escalating violence.

- *The confrontational strategy*. The confrontational strategy holds that, if you can arouse and then mobilize anger in people to confront the problem, they will change. Much depends on the strategists' ability to argue the points, as well as being able to stir up anger without promoting violence. This approach encourages people to confront problems they would prefer not to address, but tends to focus too much on the problem and not on the solution. Anger and conflict tend to polarize people and can cause a backlash.

Few of these strategies occur in isolation. But they do have different basic assumptions about who to influence, how to proceed and what to focus on. Each tends to be effective at addressing certain change problems but very poor at dealing with others. The political strategy has problems with credibility, the economic approach with maintaining change, and the academic with implementing findings. But for the professional who must demonstrate his worth to the organization by implementing change, any of the above might help him.

The trouble is that strategies tend to be chosen by chief executives for personal reasons rather than as a result of any well-considered set of options. An inappropriate strategy may cause more trouble than the initial reason for change. Research is required to investigate these strategies further, in particular to determine which is more effective and when.

A cross-cultural perspective

Culture values and organizational development

Do cultural values determine both to what extent and which organization development intervention is preferred? Perhaps the powerful economic influence of the USA has blinded American work psychologists to the cultural boundaries of their perspectives.

Head & Sorensen (1993) compared seven very different countries, namely Bangladesh, Britain, the People's Republic of China (PRC), Denmark, Japan, Taiwan and Venezuela. First, these seven countries were classified using Hofstede's (1980) four dimensions:

- *Power distance:* the extent to which a society accepts the fact that power in institutions and organizations is distributed unequally.
- *Uncertainty avoidance:* the extent to which a society feels threatened by uncertain and ambiguous situations, by providing career stability, establishing more formal rules, not tolerating deviant ideas and behaviours, and believing in absolute truths and the attainment of expertise.
- *Individualism:* implies a loosely knit social framework in which people are supposed to take care of themselves and their immediate families only, whereas collectivism is characterized by a tight social framework in which people distinguish between ingroups and outgroups; they expect their ingroups (relatives, clans, organizations) to look after them and, in exchange for that, they feel that they owe absolute loyalty to those groups.
- *Masculinity:* the extent to which the dominant values in society are "masculine" – that is, assertiveness, the acquisition of money and things, and not caring for others – tough analytical "muscular Christianity" ideals.

The classification, by country, is shown in Table 14.7.

Organization development interventions were loosely classified into four groups: individual task (role analysis, career planning), individual process (T-groups, transactional analysis), group task (quality circles, survey feedback) and group process. They found the Danish companies used most interventions and claimed them to be most effective, whereas the Taiwanese used them least. The authors had various hypotheses based on Hofstede's four dimensions. Thus:

> countries high on the masculinity dimensions might be expected to be characterized by task-orientated interventions, while countries higher on the femininity dimensions would be expected to be characterized by more process-orientated interventions. Individualistic cultures would employ interventions focusing on the individual, while more collectivist cultures would be orientated towards group interventions. Cultures high on uncertainty avoidance might be expected to be orientated towards task interventions, while cultures higher in tolerance for uncertainty would use process interventions more frequently. Cultures high on power distance would be inclined towards task interventions, and cultures low on power distance orientated towards process interventions. (Head & Sorensen, 1993: 5)

Head & Sorensen found that the most widely used organization development techniques, based on the combined samples, include team-building, management by objectives and survey feedback. Other widely used techniques include transactional analysis, quality of work life, process consultation and job design. Less frequently cited interventions include confrontation meetings, T-groups and career planning.

Table 14.7 Classification of countries by Hofstede's dimensions

Country	Power	Masculinity	Uncertainty avoidance	Individualism
Denmark	Very low	Very low	Very low	High
Japan	Moderate	Very high	Very high	Low
UK	Low	High	Low	Very high
Venezuela	Very high	Very high	High	Very low
PRC*	Moderate	Low	Moderate	Very low
Bangladesh*	Very high	Moderate	High	Low
Taiwan	High	Low	High	Very low

* Based on estimates by experts; other values established by Hofstede (1980).

Source: Reproduced from Head & Sorensen (1993) with the permission of MCB University Press Ltd.

The central hypothesis that the more a country's dominant culture was compatible with the values of organization development, the greater the use and effectiveness of the interventions, did receive partial support. Certainly, there was clear evidence that national culture plays a role in determining which intervention strategy is used. Thus, masculine cultures with low tolerance for ambiguity choose task-orientated interventions, whereas feminine cultures, which are tolerant of ambiguity, use process techniques quite happily. In other words, there needs to be a congruency between national (and corporate) culture and the organization development intervention used if it is to be successful.

This had many limitations. The sample was small and not representative. Furthermore, it was not clear that the various organizations in the different countries were in any sense comparable in terms of size and product, or typical for the country. It is all the more impressive that many of the results were confirmed.

However, what this study did clearly indicate was that, when looking at all aspects of an organization – its structure, how it changes and what developmental procedures it employs – it is important to take into consideration national culture. Thus, some strategies would seem immediately to have a better chance than others if they are fitted into the cultural values of that organization. To disregard culture, therefore, is to invite failure.

A human resources perspective

Experts and consultants

Because the business of management is difficult, it is not uncommon for organizations to call in experts – consultants, advisers, academics – to help them. One of the main reasons to call in outsiders is that they are politically, financially and administratively independent. In other words, although their view and opinion may not exactly be objective, at least it is not necessarily seen as biased.

So, why use experts? They may be used for a variety of reasons:

- Because they have a *particular knowledge or skill* that the organization does not have "in-house" in sufficient depth.
- Because professional help may be needed *intensively* on a *temporary basis*, either because a problem is project-based or the organization finds itself "caught short" by insufficient trained personnel.
- Because an *impartial outside view* is required to give fresh and untainted insights into the nature of problems.
- To *justify decisions and analysis* made by powerful political forces in the organization. Hence, the outsider may be a naïve scapegoat for some nasty in-company politicking.
- To *learn* through consultants, who can be powerful educators.

Who uses these experts? Most people believe consultants are only called in to ailing, failing or incompetent organizations. Thus, consultants may be seen as doctors, healers, troubleshooters. However, it may be just as necessary to call in consultants to highly successful organizations, in part to understand the causes of their success. Human resource consultants are often employed.

But what do human resources consultants do? Why spend up to £2000 per day on some outsider coming into your organization and telling you how to run it? Why divulge highly sensitive organizational data to some human resources consultant who might have worked, does work or will work for your direct competitor? What have these people to offer? What are their skills?

Human resources consultants offer several types of skills, many of which are surprisingly absent from most large organizations' personnel departments. This is mainly because the nature and function of "personnel" has changed and training is often woefully inadequate. Five different and specific skills of human resources consultants have been identified (Furnham & Gunter, 1994).

Diagnostic skills

Human resources consultants can offer a "second opinion". They can bring the objectivity and disinterest of the outsider, but also the potential experience of having seen the problem before. However, the disadvantage of diagnostician human resources consultants is that they align their diagnostics with their preferred "skill solution". In other words, having various expensive solutions (programmes) available, they will force the diagnostics of the problem to fit their products. But a major advantage of using experienced and insightful human resources consultants is that they can show the organization to be fundamentally flawed in either its own diagnosis of the malady or in the proposed solutions. Organizations like to believe that easy solutions are possible; they are also often unable to distinguish between explicit and implicit messages from clients, customers or their own staff, whom they meet every day.

For instance, managers' complaints about the number of staff they have in their department to complete workloads could have as much to do with problems in organizational structure, or a particular manager's ambitions, as with staffing. Equally, staff complaints about the physical working environment may be more a function of the psychological climate of the office about which they feel uncomfortable, or incapable of articulating.

Human resources consultants will tell you that diagnosis is more difficult and important than cure and therefore getting it right easily merits the "modest" fee. In this they might be right.

Measurement

Many personnel managers are not highly trained in measuring human performance, abilities, needs or personal preferences (e.g. intelligence, personality, team-role preferences). After gullible, but enthusiastic and peer-pressured, purchases of flashy but not necessarily valid tests, personnel managers often set about measuring the line manager's personality or the board's team-role preference. When the only tool you have is a hammer, you tend to treat everything as if it were a nail. Hence, organizations measure what they can more often than what they need to. And this is where the well-trained human resources consultant can bring to bear a formidable array of well-tested measures. Over 100,000 tests are in print and a good human resources consultant will know where to look for the most appropriate measure.

There is a tendency to use inappropriate tests just because the organization has bought them. Rather than spend all one's effort measuring the personalities of directors, the human resources consultant may wisely recommend the measurement of organizational culture (the values and norms of the organization), the climate (the perception of employees), the communication networks, the clients', customers' or competitors' perceptions. Organizational problems require audits, just like those done by the finance department. Measuring instruments (questionnaires, tests) need to be robust, reliable, valid, multidimensional, sensitive to faking, and "normed" for the appropriate population. Human resources consultants must, of course, not only choose and administer good tests, but know how to analyse them appropriately and interpret the data.

As human resources consultants know, many personnel officers often shy away from objective hard data, preferring softer interviews, reports or selected quotes from "key players". This may be one reason why they are often despised by their hard-headed colleagues in accounts, strategic planning and even marketing. Some human resources consultants are experienced and trained psycho- and organometricians, and are well able to measure important organizational variables.

Instruction

There is, and there will probably always be, a place for "chalk-and-talk" training. Now more likely to be run with impressive videos, self-instruction and completion booklets, and elaborate feedback reports, the business of education remains a central task of some human resources consultants. Training adults is a challenging task for the human resources consultant. There are those in organizations, who are themselves very bright and highly educated, who may be extremely critical of any outside consultant. Equally, there are those with chips on their shoulders because they never went to university, or did and performed rather poorly; they may make poor students, flipping between the sycophantic and the cynical. But there are others who are deeply appreciative and very good students.

The good human resources consultant soon realizes that training adults is rather different from educating students. Training managers must be practical and concrete, with plenty of memorable examples and helpful models. Whereas academics are trained to be critical and sceptical, human resources consultants soon realize they are appreciated more if they are enthusiastic and zealous about the cause. Human resources consultants are frequently extraverts with a self-confidence that extends somewhat beyond the bounds of their ability. As a result, they rarely fear the role of teaching, training or instructing, although they may not be good at it. Good teaching is a rare combination of intellectual ability and knowing how to put it across.

Certainly, instructing or teaching is a crucial function for many human resources consultants. For many, alas, the term "training" has a poor reputation, and trainers are considered rather lowly (paid) sorts of consultants, especially when teachers are trained to deliver "packaged" courses.

Process

Some human resources consultants specialize in process or interpretation as opposed to product. When, for instance, a management team is underperforming or suffering low morale, the process-orientated human resources consultant might be called in not only for diagnosis but also to cure. Process skills are closely akin to group psychotherapy, and indeed that may be how the consultant was originally trained.

Just as most accidents are the result of human error, so poor business operations are often the result of human frailty. Whether one prefers to use meaningless euphemisms such as "personality clash" or not, many people recognize that the quality of human relationships in offices, teams and departments contributes to business success or failure. It is the intangible psychological factors of morale, conflict and lack of commitment that the process consultant hopes to make manifest and explicit. Good human resources consultants, especially those with psychoanalytic training, are frequently able to reveal unexpected or paradoxical findings, such as depression among employees being a consequence of their anger.

To some, "process consultants" represent the consultants who ask both intrusive and daft questions primarily to embarrass. Furthermore, they may not even come to a conclusion, write a report or deliver any tangible outcome. Insight alone is often the orally explicit goal of the process consultant. It is nearly always the case that process work has to be done by the outside consultant. Politically, the personnel department may wisely judge it necessary to lure in consultants, albeit at some critical (and financial) cost.

Systems

Some human resources consultants are specialists in devising, operating or tweaking systems, such as performance management systems, selection systems or staff development systems. More often than not this involves the development of fairly sophisticated computer-based statistical software. As a result, these human resources consultants are not the warm and cuddly process type, but hardened fellows.

Because writing software and developing systems is very time-consuming, these human resources consultants tend to offer a relatively fixed package. Although it is true that it can be personalized or adapted to suit each organization, these modifications are usually pretty minimal. In this sense, the human resources consultant sells packages used by the personnel department.

Some computer-illiterate and number-phobic personnel directors are highly gullible to the hard sell of systems human resources consultants for two reasons. First, they may not be able to make an intelligent judgement on the usefulness, limitations or appropriateness of the system. Second, and perhaps more importantly, personnel managers are eager to show that they are up to date, "scientific" and sophisticated, and hence impressed by the largely irrelevant packaging rather than the content. However, all organizations need efficient computer-assisted systems. Some systems experts can devise very useful systems that serve organizations for many years.

References

Argyle, M., Furnham, A., & Graham, J. (1981). *Social situations*. Cambridge: Cambridge University Press.

Barker, R. (1968). *Ecological psychology*. Stanford, CA: Stanford University Press.

Beer, M. (1980). *Organizational change and development*. Santa Monica, CA: Goodyear.

Carnall, C. (1990). *Managing change in organizations*. Englewood Cliffs, NJ: Prentice-Hall.

Cascio, W. (1998). The virtual workplace: A reality now. *The Industrial-Organizational Psychologist, 35*, 32–36.

Cascio, W. (2000). Managing a virtual workplace. *Academy of Management Executive, 14*, 81–90.

Cherrington, D. (1989). *Organizational behaviour*. Boston, MA: Allyn & Bacon.

Child, J. (1964). *Organization: A guide to problems and practice*. London: Harper & Row.

Davis, S., & Lawrence, P. (1977). *Matrix*. Reading, MA: Addison-Wesley.

Furnham, A. (1994). *Personality at work*. London: Routledge.

Furnham, A. (2000). *The hopeless, hapless and helpless manager*. London: Whurr Publishers.

Furnham, A. (2002). Managers as change agents. *Journal of Change Management, 3*, 21–29.

Furnham, A., & Gunter, B. (1994). *Business watching*. London: ABRA Press.

Golembiewski, R., Billingsley, K., & Yeager, S. (1976). Measuring change and persistence in human affairs. *Journal of Applied Behavioral Science, 12*, 133–157.

Gordon, J., Mondy, R., Sharplin, A., & Premeaux, S. (1990). *Management and organizational behaviour*. Boston, MA: Allyn & Bacon.

Greenberg, J., & Baron, R. (1990). *Behavior in organizations*. Boston, MA: Allyn & Bacon.

Handy, C. (1994). *The empty raincoat*. London: Arrow.

Hartley, J. (2002). Organizational change and development. In P. Warr. (Ed.), *Psychology at work* (pp. 399–425). Harmondsworth, UK: Penguin.

Head, T., & Sorensen, P. (1993). Cultural values and organizational development. *Leadership and Organizational Development, 14*, 3–7.

Heller, R. (Ed.) (2002). *Manager's handbook*. London: Dorling Kindersley.

Hellriegel, D., Slocum, J., & Woodman, J. (1992). *Organizational behaviour*. St Paul, MN: West Publishing Co.

Hofstede, G. (1980). *Culture's consequences*. Los Angeles, CA: Sage.

Holland, B., & Hogan, R. (1998). Remodelling the electronic cottage. *The Industrial-Organizational Psychologist, 36*, 15–17.

Johns, G. (1991). *Organizational behavior: Understanding life at work*. New York: HarperCollins.

Johns, G. (1992). *Organizational behaviour*. New York: HarperCollins.

Kotter, J., & Schlesinger, L. (1979). Choosing strategies for change. *Harvard Business Review*, March–April, pp. 106–114.

Lewin, K. (1951). *Field theory in social science*. New York: Harper & Row.

Lowenberg, G., & Conrad, K. (1998). *Current perspectives in industrial/organizational psychology*. Boston, MA: Allyn & Bacon.

Meyer, G., & Scott, R. (1985). Quality circles: Panacea or Pandora's box. *Organizational Dynamics, 11*, 34–50.

Mineham, M. (1996). Consider all possibilities for telecommuters. *HR Magazine* (online) (available at: http//www.shrm.org/hrmagazine/articles/aa96fut.htm).

Mintzberg, H. (1979). *The structuring of organizations*. Englewood Cliffs, NJ: Prentice-Hall.

Munchus, G. (1983). Employer–employee based quality circles in Japan. *Academy of Management Review, 8*, 255–261.

Nicholas, J. (1982). The comparative impact of organizational development interventions on hard criteria measures. *Academy of Management Review, 7,* 530–545.

Peters, T. (1987). A world turned upside down. *Academy of Management Executive,* **1**, 231–241.

Ramsower, R. M. (1985). *Telecommuting: The organizational and behavioural effects of working at home.* Ann Arbor, MI: UMI Research Press.

Randolph, W., & Blackburn, R. (1989). *Managing organizational behavior.* Homewood, IL: Irwin.

Robbins, S. (1991). *Organizational behaviour: Concepts, controversies, and applications.* Englewood Cliffs, NJ: Prentice-Hall.

Rogers, E. (1983). *Diffusion of innovations.* New York: Free Press.

Senior, B. (2000). Organizational change and development. In N. Chmiel (Ed.), *Introduction to work and organizational psychology* (pp. 347–383). Oxford: Blackwell.

Strobel, P. (1997). Choosing the right change path. In T. Dickson (Ed.), *Mastering management* (pp. 538–543). London: Financial Times.

Tannenbaum, R., & Schmidt, W. (1973). How to choose a leadership pattern. *Harvard Business Review,* May–June, pp. 95–101.

Toffler, A. (1984). *Previews and premises.* London: Pan.

Westwood, R. (Ed.) (1992). *Organizational behaviour.* Hong Kong: Longman.

White, S., & Mitchell, T. (1976). Organizational development: A review of research content and research design. *Academy of Management Review, 1,* 57–73.

15 Working abroad

Introduction

The world is shrinking all the time. There are fewer and fewer purely domestic organizations and more that operate in a global market. Indeed, it has been suggested that there are at least four types of organizations today (see Table 15.1), more of which are becoming global.

There seems an inevitable drift from left to right – that is, from domestic to global – no matter how small the organization. Electronic media and cheaper transportation mean that people and goods can and do travel more easily. Even small businesses interested only in the domestic market find themselves becoming international. There remain few truly global organizations (such as the United Nations), but their numbers are growing. This has naturally led to an interest in the management of multicultural workforces (Tayeb, 1996). For instance, it has been shown that work groups' ethnic diversity influences all aspects of group processes, leadership style and performance (Watson, Johnson, & Zgourides, 2002).

More importantly, it is increasingly common for people from all backgrounds to work abroad for a period. Equally improved communications means a great increase in short overseas business trips for executives (Westman & Etzion, 2002). They may be

Table 15.1 Four types of organizations and the traditional phases they pass through

	Phase I: Domestic	Phase II: International	Phase III: Multinational	Phase IV: Global
Primary orientation	Product/service	Market	Price	Strategy
Strategy	Domestic	Multi-domestic	Multinational	Global
Perspective	Ethnocentric	Polycentric/ regiocentric	Multinational	Global/ multicentric
Cultural sensitivity	Marginally important	Very important	Somewhat important	Critically important
With whom	No one	Clients	Employees	Employees and clients
Level	No one	Workers and clients	Managers	Executives
Strategic assumption	"One way"/ "One best way"	"Many good" ways", equifinality	"One least-cost way"	"Many good ways" simultaneously

Source: Reproduced from Adler (1991) with the permission of Kent Publishers.

relatively unskilled people moving from regions of economic decline to those with more booming economies. They may be young people simply out to see the world, or they may be specialists and managers specially selected by their companies to take their particular skill abroad. The cost of travel and ease of migration has meant a large increase in the number of people working abroad. Hence the great interest in cross-cultural psychology, particularly national and cultural differences in organization behaviour, including styles of leadership and negotiation, as well as motivation and reward allocation (Smith & Bond, 1998).

In northern Europe, most migrant workers are from poorer southern, Mediterranean countries. For the most part, they are semi-skilled or unskilled workers who are employed in the declining and highly competitive manufacturing sector. They are also employed in "dirty" jobs such as street cleaning, or in service industries such as transportation, tourism and health. They are economic migrants who hope for a better life for themselves and their families. Not all migrant workers are welcomed by the native population, particularly if they are from a different racial group. Many of these migrants choose a particular country for historical or geographical reasons. Thus, Indonesians would choose Holland, Indians and Pakistanis Britain, Algerians France, and Angolans Portugal. Not all, but certainly most, migrant workers from underdeveloped countries seeking to work abroad in the high-income welfare-state supported countries end up in lower skilled jobs. A huge increase in "asylum seekers" in Europe has increased the complex mix of newcomers seeking assistance, assimilation and employment.

This chapter will look at two things: the problems and reactions of expatriate managers and workers who work in foreign countries (or occasionally foreign companies), and the growth and nature of multinational and global companies.

It is extremely difficult to ascertain the number of expatriates living in any one country. Figures are unreliable for several reasons: some countries can and do attempt to keep reliable records; other countries are loath to disclose the precise number of the nationals living abroad; others still might be prone to exaggerate the number for political reasons. Furthermore, expatriates are made up of a very diverse and heterogeneous population of individuals: businessmen and women, diplomats, military personnel, missionaries and students, as well as a host of others who have left their country of birth for a wide variety of reasons. Hence, research in the area is scattered and limited.

First, an attempt will be made to categorize or classify the many different types of expatriates. The motives for movement inevitably relate directly to the personal experience of change, hence the issue is of fundamental importance. Second, the concept of culture shock – a popular lay description of the experience of all sojourners – will be discussed from a psychological perspective. Adaptation to a new country, culture and environment clearly goes through different phases; the U- and W-curve hypothesis for adaptation will then be considered. Some of the more simple but important cultural differences that prove problematic for the expatriate will be addressed, as well as the important issue of selecting and preparing expatriates for their move. Also, different methods for reducing expatriate stress will be discussed.

Types of expatriates

Most scientific enterprise begins with initial classification and later refined taxonomization. The study of expatriates is no exception. Dictionary definitions are of little use, since the term "expatriate" appears to have two related meanings: there is a neutral reference to one who lives, probably voluntarily, in a foreign country (specifically one who has renounced his or her native country), as well as a negative reference to someone banished and exiled to a foreign country, presumably involuntarily, and who subsequently withdraws his or her allegiance to the native country. Hence, the former definition simply implies change of status, whereas the second stresses the change in affection, specifically patriotism or love of country. Curiously, the term is often used by expatriates themselves, not to indicate disaffection from country-of-origin but the precise opposite – increased loyalty to one's home country. "Expat" gatherings and entertainments are often characterized by affectionate nostalgia for the home country, its traditions and values.

Various attempts have been made to classify or categorize travellers, using different dimensions. For instance, Bochner (1982) classified expatriates and sojourners according to their psychological response to the host culture (Table 15.2). Clearly, the model supports the mediating response as the most healthy and adaptive. This is essentially the bi- or multicultural response that allows the individual to accept and translate the values and behaviours of one culture into the other.

This is clearly a useful way of distinguishing expatriates, but it tends to concentrate on reactions to migration. However, motives are complex, numerous and not always explicit. Some have categorized them into *pull* and *push* motives – features of the second country or culture, such as the climate or a higher standard of living that pulls one to that culture. On the other hand, certain factors, such as discrimination or political uncertainty, push one away from one's country of origin. Certainly, it seems implicitly the case that "expats" who are pulled would adapt more readily than expats who are pushed.

Table 15.2 Outcomes of cultural contact at the individual level: Psychological responses to "second culture" influences

Response	Type	Multiple-group membership affiliation	Effect on individual	Effect on society
Reject culture of origin, embrace second culture	"Passing"	Culture I norms lose salience Culture II norms become salient	Loss of ethnic identity Self-denigration	Assimilation Cultural erosion
Reject second culture, exaggerate first culture	Chauvinistic	Culture I norms increase in salience Culture II norms decrease in salience	Nationalism Racism	Intergroup friction
Vacillate between the two cultures	Marginal	Norms of both cultures salient but perceived as mutually incompatible	Conflict Identity confusion Over-compensation	Reform Social change
Synthesize both cultures	Mediating	Norms of both cultures salient and perceived as capable of being integrated	Personal growth	Intergroup harmony Pluralistic societies Cultural preservation

Source: Reproduced from Bochner (1982) with the permission of Pergamon Press.

Black, Gregerson & Mendenhall (1992) have also come up with a typology of expatriates in terms of how they see themselves, which may be a very good indicator of how they behave at work and adapt to the local setting. Four types may be described by looking at how they react on two dimensions: *allegiance to the parent firm* and *allegiance to the local operation*. If both allegiances are strong, they see themselves and react as *dual citizens* equally committed to both; if their allegiance is low on both, they are likely to see themselves as *free agents* with relatively little organizational commitment. If their commitment to the parent firm is high and the local operation (to which they have moved) is low, they have clearly *left their heart and their real commitment behind*. Finally, if they become highly committed to the local organization while losing their commitment and allegiance to the parent head office, they may be seen as *going native*. All four reactions are fairly common.

Furnham & Bochner (1986) suggest various dimensions on which groups of ex-patriots could be classified. These include:

- geographical distance – between "home" and second culture, implying various climate and cultural differences;
- amount of change required – this is both qualitative and quantitative and suggests both behavioural and cognitive aspects;
- length of time spent – this could be categorized into meaningful time zones such as five-year periods;
- "voluntariness" of the move – the idea that the move itself may not be voluntary but may be the result of various constraints and prescriptions.

There are many other dimensions that could be used to categorize expatriates into quite different groups. One such group is proposed by Gudykunst (1983) in his typology of stranger–host relationships. However, the point is an important but simple one: description usually precedes explanation, and taxonomization is frequently the first step to an adequate description. To understand the psychological perspectives, preferences and reactions of expatriates, it is first necessary to classify them into various groups or types. These taxonomies may differ according to the particular phenomena considered. Thus, for instance, the taxonomy for looking at expatriate stress may be rather different from that focusing on expatriate–native interactions, although the two may be related. Hence, no one exhaustive typology shall be offered here.

However, there are some useful dimensions or factors that may be used to distinguish one type of expatriate move from another. These include:

- distance – how far a person is transferred;
- country – whether the move involves leaving one's own country, continent, linguistic area, or not;
- job – whether the person is expected to do much the same or a different type of job, or at the same or at a different level;
- social support – whether the person moves alone, with others from the workplace, with or without family;
- time – how long the persons are likely to spend in this other place and when can they expect to return or move to another posting;
- returns – benefits and costs of the move, including the possibility of being dismissed or demoted if not agreeing to the transfer;

- volunteering – to what extent the individuals believe that they had a choice in the move.

These and indeed other factors may be important for the adjustment of the expatriate. For instance, a six-month sideways transfer, alone and to an unknown and distant country, is likely to have consequences quite different from a two-year sojourn in another part of the same country, accompanied by one's spouse, family and provided with generous financial and social support. Stokols & Shumaker (1982) proposed that the health effects of location depend not only on the immediate circumstances surrounding a move, but also on the broader context of the individual's residential history, current life situation and aspirations for the future.

According to Torbiorn (1982), multinationals have three basic motives for posting people to foreign countries: *the control function* (to ensure that operations in other countries are being carried out as planned and to secure staff loyalty); *the know-how function* (to provide technological and administrative services); and *the contact/ coordination function* (to evaluate and transmit salient information between company operations). Thus, business expats have a difficult role in that they are required to act in accordance with the expectations of the parent company *and* also fulfil local expectations: the two are often incompatible. Problems with these professional roles include unclear, ambiguous or even incompatible expectations on the part of the parent company, communication difficulties, a clash between company and personal interests and values, uncertainty about the future, and problems with the adjustment of the spouse and family.

In a large empirical study, Torbiorn (1982) set out to establish the determinants of business expatriate satisfaction. In doing so, he questioned more than 1000 Swedish expat businessmen and women in 26 host countries, looking at their personal circumstances (age, education, status), motives for moving abroad, who initiated the move, previous overseas experience, the nature of the country they came from and the country they moved to, their chosen lifestyle, and spouse satisfaction. He found that men more than women, and better educated rather than less well educated people, adapt better; that the motive for moving most strongly associated with adjustment was "a special interest in the particular host country"; that previous overseas experience had no effect on adjustment; that expatriates who spent most of their free time with host country nationals were happier on average than those who turned to their own countrymen; and that the satisfaction of the spouse was a major factor in determining adjustment. By and large, whichever variable was plotted against adjustment over time (sex, age, previous experience, friends, or attitudes to the host country), the pattern was much the same – a steady increase in satisfaction, although there was sometimes the indication of a flat U-curve (discussed later).

The study also covered variables such as the most popular countries to work in, knowledge and adoption of host country conditions, the adaptation of children, and the experience of work in other countries. However, Torbiorn was unable to explain much of the variance in business expatriates' satisfaction and adjustment, the 30 variables he examined together accounting for between 25 and 50% of the variance. Happiness of spouse was by far the most important factor, followed by various features of the external environment, such as food and climate. Women tended to feel more isolated than men, which in turn greatly affected men's satisfaction. Some cultural barriers – religion, language and socioeconomic development – were good predictors of the business people's happiness, adjustment and lifestyle, and hence showed enormous variation between countries – the more the barriers, the less the satisfaction.

It is difficult not to overemphasize this point too strongly. When people go to work abroad for any length of time, they nearly always take partners and possibly family – even the extended family. Little research attention has been paid to the family aspect of the work sojourn, but it is clearly very important. If the poor adaptation and unhappiness of the sojourning worker's partner and family increases, rather than reduces, his or her stress, it must be an extremely important factor in predicting their overall effectiveness. Many organizations are becoming aware of this and taking into consideration partner and family issues when considering selecting people for overseas assignments.

Studies on expat businessmen and women who have moved from one area or country to another have revealed evidence of unhappiness, distress and poor adjustment. Of course, this is not always the case and, as research has shown, there are many complex variables determining the actual adjustment of particular individuals. At the same time, it is probably safe to say that, overall, business expats experience less difficulty than migrants, missionaries or other sojourners (particularly students) moving to new environments. There may be several reasons for this. First, business people are usually posted elsewhere for a set, specific and relatively *short period of time* (two to five years). Hence, they may see their move as relatively temporary and not requiring much adaptation and change. Second, businessmen and women are posted abroad for a *specific purpose*, usually to deal with particular technical and managerial problems. This is not to say that the problems are simple – indeed, they are often complex and highly intractable – but rather that many of their problems are confined to work. They do not, as a rule, have to worry about transportation, accommodation and other "housekeeping" problems. Third, business people usually have *strong sponsorship*. Many are given financial incentives for working abroad and often their life overseas is an improvement on their previous lifestyles. Furthermore, the sponsorship is not only financial but may include social and political beliefs that increase rather than decrease a person's social standing, political power and influence in the new society. Similarly, a tour abroad often increases opportunities for *advancement on return*. Many business people travel specifically to enhance their chances for promotion, therefore any hardships on the trip may be seen as a small price to pay for the rewards to be gained later.

In contrast to students, military people and some migrants, business "expats" tend to be *older and are usually more mature*. Although the literature is equivocal on this point, it is generally the case that older, more experienced and better educated people can cope with the problems of geographical movement (Furnham & Bochner, 1986). Businesses often provide accommodation enclaves, "old-hand" guides and a *social support network* that insulate the foreigner against the initial difficulties and surprises of movement. However, the long-term benefits associated with these "ghettos" are debatable, as they reduce contact with the locals from whom the skills of intercultural communication are best learned. Furthermore, because businesses are primarily interested in the work their employees do, the employees' *time is carefully structured and scheduled*. As unemployment researchers have shown, this is directly related to a reduction in mental illness. Finally, the *social relationships* both inside and outside the workplace are probably more likely to be on an *equal footing for businessmen* than for students. Such equal-status peer-group interaction probably goes some way to account for the better adjustment of business people compared with students, whose social relationships put them in the dependent role.

Culture shock

Experts talk much about culture shock, which is a sort of shorthand for their early and profound experiences in the new culture. The concept implies that the experience of visiting or living in a new culture is an unpleasant surprise or shock, partly because it is unexpected, and partly because it may lead to a negative evaluation of one's own and/ or the other culture.

The anthropologist Oberg (1960) was the first to use the term. In a brief and largely anecdotal article, he mentions at least six aspects of culture shock:

- *strain* because of the effort required to make necessary psychological adaptations;
- *a sense of loss* and *feelings of deprivation* about friends, status, profession and possessions;
- being *rejected* by/and or rejecting members of the new culture;
- *confusion* in role, role expectations, values, feelings and self-identity;
- *surprise, anxiety,* even *disgust* and *indignation* after becoming aware of cultural differences;
- *feelings of impotence* because of not being able to cope with the new environment.

Cleveland, Mangone & Adams (1960) offered a similar analysis that relied heavily on the personal experience of businessmen and other travellers, especially those at the two extremes of the adaptation continuum: individuals who act as if they had "never left home" and those who immediately "go native". These descriptions are nearly always qualitative rather than quantitative and they rarely attempt to explain *why* some expatriates experience culture shock and others do not.

Researchers since Oberg have seen culture shock as a normal and expected reaction; as part of the routine process of adaptation to cultural differences and the manifestation of a longing for a more predictable, stable and understandable environment. Others have attempted to improve and extend Oberg's definition and concept of culture shock. Guthrie (1975) has used the term *culture fatigue*, Smalley (1963) *language shock*, Byrnes (1966) *role shock* and Ball-Rokeach (1973) *pervasive ambiguity*. In doing so, different researchers have simply replaced the emphasis on different problems – language, physical irritability, role ambiguity – but have tended to deal with it in roughly similar ways.

Bock (1970) has described culture shock as primarily an emotional reaction that follows from not being able to understand, control and predict another's behaviour. When customary experiences no longer seem relevant or applicable, people's behaviour becomes "unusual". A lack of familiarity with both the physical setting (design of homes, shops, offices) and the social environment (etiquette, ritual) have this effect, as do the experiences with the use of time (Hall, 1959). This theme is reiterated by all the writers in the field (Hays, 1972; Lunstedt, 1963). Culture shock is seen as a stress reaction where salient psychological and physical rewards are generally uncertain and hence difficult to control or predict. Thus, a person is anxious, confused and apparently apathetic, until he or she has had time to develop a new set of cognitive constructs to understand and enact the appropriate behaviour. In the business world, for example, a manager who has been successful and developed all the requisite skills for dealing with peers, subordinates, supervisors and clients in his or her own culture, may find that all or many of these skills, strategies and techniques may become ineffective or irrelevant in the new culture. Hence, the anxiety and confusion until new techniques, skills and concepts are learned.

Culture shock includes an individual's lack of points of reference, social norms and rules to guide their actions and understand others' behaviour. This is very similar to the attributes studied under the heading of *alienation* and *anomie*, which include powerlessness, meaninglessness, normlessness, self- and social estrangements and social isolation. Certainly, many poorly adapted expats react to their new environment like alienated people do in their native environment.

In addition, ideas associated with *anxiety* pervade the culture shock literature. Observers have pointed to a continuous general "free-floating" anxiety that affects people's normal behaviour. A lack of self-confidence, distrust of others and mild psychosomatic complaints are also common (May, 1970). Furthermore, people appear to lose their inventiveness and spontaneity and become obsessively concerned with orderliness (Nash, 1967).

The concept of culture shock is similar to that of *reality shock*, conceived by Schein (1978) to describe what it is like when joining or entering a new organization. This, too, is a stage-wise concept with three phases – entry, socialization and mutual acceptance (see Chapter 3).

Most studies of culture shock have been descriptive, in that they have attempted to list the various difficulties that sojourners experience and their typical reactions. Less attention has been paid to explain for whom the shock will be more or less intense (e.g. the old or the less educated); what determines which reaction a person is likely to experience; how long they remain in a period of shock, and so forth. The literature suggests that all people will suffer culture shock to some extent, which is always thought of as being unpleasant and stressful. However, this assumption needs to be empirically supported. In theory, some people need not experience any negative aspects of shock; instead, they may seek out these experiences for their enjoyment. Sensation-seekers, for instance, might be expected not to suffer any adverse effects but to enjoy the highly arousing stimuli of the unfamiliar (Zuckerman, 1979). People with multicultural backgrounds or experiences may also adapt more successfully. For instance, Adler (1975) and David (1971) have stated that, although culture shock is most often associated with negative consequences, it may, in mild doses, be important for self-development and personal growth. Culture shock is seen as a transitional experience that can result in the adoption of new values, attitudes and behaviour patterns:

> In the encounter with another culture the individual gains new experiential knowledge by coming to understand the roots of his or her own ethnocentrism, and by gaining new perspectives and outlooks on the nature of culture . . . Paradoxically, the more one is capable of experiencing new and different dimensions of human diversity, the more one learns of oneself. (Adler, 1975: 22)

Mumford (1998) attempted to develop and validate a simple, but useful measure of culture shock (see Box 15.1). The questionnaire was validated on 380 British volunteer workers who had gone to 27 different countries. The alpha-value (internal realiability) for each part was not particularly impressive (.75 and .52), although overall it was an acceptable .79. External criterion validity was established by using the culture difference index (Babiker, Cos, & Miller, 1980). As predicted, the greater the cultural difference between Britain and the country visited, the greater the culture shock. It appears to be a

Box 15.1 Culture shock questionnaire

A. *"Core" culture shock items*

1. Do you feel strain from the effort to adapt to a new culture?
   Most of the time
   Occasionally
   Not at all

2. Have you been missing your family and friends back home?
   Most of the time
   Occasionally
   Not at all

3. Do you feel generally accepted by the local people in the new culture?
   No
   Not sure
   Yes

4. Do you ever wish to escape from your environment altogether?
   Most of the time
   Occasionally
   Not at all

5. Do you ever feel confused about your role or identity in the new culture?
   Most of the time
   Occasionally
   Not at all

6. Have you ever found things in your new environment shocking or disgusting?
   Many things
   A few things
   None

7. Do you ever feel helpless or powerless when trying to cope with the new culture?
   Most of the time
   Occasionally
   Not at all

B. *Interpersonal stress items*

1. Do you feel anxious or awkward when meeting local people?
   Most of the time
   Occasionally
   Not at all

2. When talking to people, can you make sense of their gestures or facial expressions?
   Not at all
   Occasionally
   Most of the time

3. Do you feel uncomfortable if people stare at you when you go out?
   Very uncomfortable
   Slightly uncomfortable
   Not at all

4. When you go out shopping, do you feel as though people may be trying to cheat you?
   Most of the time
   Occasionally
   Not at all

Scoring: First response = 2, Second response = 1, Third response = 0. If combined 12-item version is used, it is recommended to alternate the items from sections A and B.

Source: Adapted from Mumford (1998: 154) with the permission of Springer.

simple, albeit fakeable, instrument to get a "rough-and-ready" self-report with little difficulty.

Thus, although different writers have emphasized different aspects of culture shock, there is by and large agreement that exposure to new cultures is stressful. Fewer researchers have seen the positive side of culture shock, either for those individuals who revel in exciting and different environments, or for those whose initial discomfiture leads to personal growth. The quality and quantity of culture shock has been shown to be related to the amount of *difference* between the visitor's (sojourner's or manager's) culture and the culture of the country they are visiting or working in. These differences refer to the many cultural differences in social beliefs and behaviours.

Furnham & Bochner (1986) have proposed eight different explanations for culture shock and evaluated the power of each "theory" to explain the phenomenon. Briefly, the eight explanations are:

- Culture shock is the psychology of loss and the phenomenon is akin to that of grief or grieving. Therefore, it is experienced by most people but depends mainly on how much one loved, and was attached to, one's mother country.
- Locus-of-control type beliefs in fatalism or instrumentation best predict culture shock. The more fatalistic, the less adaptive people are.
- Social Darwinism or selective migration forces are some of the best predictors of culture shock. That is, the more carefully migrants are self-selected or selected by other forces (economic) for their ability and strength, the better they will be able to adapt.
- Realistic expectations about what will be encountered are the most important factors in adaptation. The closer the sojourner's expectations about *all* aspects of their new life and job approximate to reality, the happier they will be.
- Culture shock should be seen as, and calculated by, negative life events, such that the more actual change people experience and have to adapt to, the more likely it is they will experience culture shock. The sheer number of major life differences experienced is a good (negative) predictor of adaptation and happiness.
- The better one's social support network of friends, family and co-nationals – both quantitatively and qualitatively – the better will be one's ability to overcome culture shock.
- Value differences between native and foreign culture are the most powerful predictors of adaptation and shock. The closer one approaches the fundamental values and behaviours that drive them, the easier it is to adapt.
- The actual social skills one possesses in dealing with people from the native culture are the best predictor of adaptation and shock.

Furnham & Bochner (1986) attempt to point out the insights and limitations of each "explanation", favouring the latter four as having most explanatory power. Certainly, each explanation has important implications for how one deals with culture shock and the psychological effects of change and transition.

Ward, Bochner & Furnham (2001) note three theoretical approaches to culture shock. The first is the *culture learning perspective*, which stresses the importance of acquiring culturally relevant social knowledge to cope with, and thrive in, any new society. This involves knowledge of social etiquette, conflict resolution, non-verbal communication, rules and conventions, forms of polite address, and so on. Thus to minimize culture shock, sojourners need to become communicatively competent in the new culture. They need to master the subtleties and nuances of the "hidden language" of cross-cultural interaction to prevent friction and misunderstanding.

The second approach is the *stress, coping and adjustment process*, which focuses on the coping styles of individual sojourners as they attempt to adjust to the new culture. Thus their personality, social support network, knowledge and skills, and personal demography (age, sex) will, in part, determine how quickly and thoroughly they adapt. As they note, "Both macro and micro level variables affect transition and adjustment and characteristics of both the individual and the situation mediate and moderate the appraisal of stress, coping responses and long and short term outcomes" (p. 96).

The third approach focuses on *social identity and inter-group relations*. The idea is that how people see themselves and their group affects how they deal with those from a different group. Stereotyped attributions for the cause of behaviour and discrimination against out-groups but in favour of in-groups are seen to be a functions of a person's self-identity. It is argued that various individual and social forces influence a person's sense of themselves, which, in turn, influences their adaptation to, and acculturation in, the new society.

The U-curve hypothesis

Since Oberg (1960), it has been fashionable to describe the "disease" of culture shock in terms of several stages (Smalley, 1963). These attempts have all been descriptive and tend to overlap. Oberg (1960) listed four stages of shock:

1   *Honeymoon stage*: An initial reaction of enchantment, fascination, enthusiasm, admiration and cordial, friendly, superficial relationships with hosts.
2   *Crisis*: Initial differences in language, concepts, values, familiar signs and symbols lead to feelings of inadequacy, frustration, anxiety and anger.
3   *Recovery*: The crisis is resolved by several methods, such that the person ends up learning the language and culture of the host country.
4   *Adjustment*: The sojourner begins to work in and enjoy the new culture, although there may be occasional instances of anxiety and strain.

Others such as Adler (1975) have set out a much more elaborate theory (Table 15.3).

One of the more consequential of these stage-wise theories is the debate on the U- or W-curve. The idea of the U-curve has been attributed to Lysgaard (1955). He concluded from his study of over 200 Norwegian Fulbright scholars in the USA that people go through three phases: initial adjustment, crisis and regained adjustment. Nowhere in the paper does Lysgaard describe the shape of the U, although he did imply that the period of adjustment took about 20 months, with some point between 6 and 18 months being the bottom of the U. If one traces the sojourner's level of adjustment, adaptation and well-being over time, a U-shape occurs, such that satisfaction and well-being gradually decline but then increase again. The W-curve is an extension proposed by Gullahorn & Gullahorn (1963), who found that once sojourners return to their home country, they often undergo a similar re-acculturation process, again in the shape of a U, hence the double-U. Furnham & Bochner (1986) have highlighted various problems with this literature, notably the vagueness of the description and definition (when is a U not a U?).

Table 15.3 Adler's five-stage theory of culture-shock development

Stage	Perception	Emotional range	Behaviour	Interpretation
Contact	Differences are intriguing. Perceptions are screened and selected.	Excitement Stimulation Euphoria Playfulness Discovery	Curiosity Interest Impressionistic	The individual is insulated by his or her own culture. Differences as well as similarities provide rationalization for continuing confirmation of status, role and identity.
Disintegration	Differences are impactful. Contrasted cultural reality cannot be screened out.	Confusion Disorientation Loss Apathy Isolation Loneliness Inadequacy	Depression Withdrawal	Cultural differences begin to intrude. Growing awareness of being different leads to loss of self-esteem. Individual experiences loss of cultural support ties and misreads new cultural cues.
Reintegration	Differences are rejected.	Anger Rage Nervousness Anxiety Frustration	Rebellion Suspicion Rejection Hostility Exclusive Opinionated	Rejection of second culture causes preoccupation with likes and dislikes; differences are projected. Negative behaviour, however, is a form of self-assertion and growing self-esteem.
Autonomy	Differences and similarities are legitimized.	Self-assured Relaxed Warm Empathic	Assured Controlled Independent "Old hand" Confident	The individual is socially and linguistically capable of negotiating most new and different situations; he or she is assured of ability to survive new experiences.
Independence	Differences and similarities are valued and significant.	Trust Humour Love Full range of previous emotions	Expressive Creative Actualizing	Social, psychological and cultural differences are accepted and enjoyed. The individual is capable of exercising choice and responsibility and able to *create* meaning for situations.

Source: Reproduced from Adler (1975: 13–23) with permission of Sage Publications, Inc.

In a review of the U-curve literature, Church (1982) reports seven studies that found some evidence for the hypothesis but a similar number that did not. He concluded that support for the U-curve hypothesis is weak, inconclusive and over-generalized. For instance, not all sojourners start off in the phase of supposed adjustment, elation and optimism – some are unhappy, depressed and anxious right from the start (if not before). Second, some never become depressed or anxious, enjoying the experience and adjusting to the culture right from the start. Third, where there are U-curves, they are of a dramatically different shape – some are flat, others tall, and all are irregular. As Church (1982: 542) has noted, there are many problems with these simple descriptive theories:

> Is the order of stages invariant? Must all stages be passed through or can some be skipped by some individuals? In order to classify individuals, key indicators of each stage are needed, indicators that may vary with the culture of origin or be indicative of more than one stage, reflecting superficial adjustment in an early stage but a true "coming to terms" with the new culture in a later stage.

Bochner, Lin & McLeod (1980) argued that so-called adjustments entail the acquisition, over time, of behaviours, skills and norms that are appropriate to the social roles that expatriates are required to enact. In particular, this involves entering into new relationships with significant people in the host country and resuming relationships with significant people after returning home. The sojourn U-shape can be derived from the distinction between observing a new culture and participating in it. When the sojourner's role as an observer shifts to that of a participant, a transition that is inevitable, the initial fascination with the new culture similarly shifts to now having to cope with it, which in Bochner's terms means learning its salient features. Some sojourners never learn the new culture, or develop reciprocal role relationships with their hosts. Other sojourners do acquire the social skills of the new society and develop genuine contacts with their hosts. Still others stand somewhere between the two extremes. Thus, the rate of culture-learning is not uniform across sojourners but depends on all the contact variables described earlier. This may explain why the U-curve is not supported in some studies, since some individuals may not experience it, such as sophisticated culture travellers who immediately become full participants and hence their curve never drops. Similarly, there are some very poor culture-learners who fail to participate in their new society, and their curve of satisfaction would therefore never rise.

The re-entry U-curve can be derived from the notion of contradictory role demands. In one study, Gaw (2000) looked at reverse culture shock in American students returning home. Many felt alienated, lonely, depressed and confused. Bochner *et al.* (1980) have shown that returning expats anticipate that they will be subjected to contradictory social expectations. In particular, they think that there will be some ambivalence in the treatment they will receive from their professional, peer and family groups. Again, the rate of resolving these role conflicts may vary with certain circumstances and could account for the absence of a W-curve in some studies. Furnham & Bochner (1986) have maintained that the advantage of the social psychological model of temporal adjustment is that it can predict and explain different "adjustment" profiles as a function of quite significant determinants. Thus, the successful culture-learner should exhibit a typical U-curve and, after re-entry, a W-curve. Experienced culture travellers should show a flat "curve" and unsuccessful ones a declining curve during sojourn and a rising one after re-entry.

Figure 15.1 shows some of these possible relationships, all of which can be tested empirically. This model is not restricted to the adjustment patterns of sojourners, but it has general implications. For instance, the model predicts that all persons entering into new relationships or social situations can be expected to develop sequential feelings

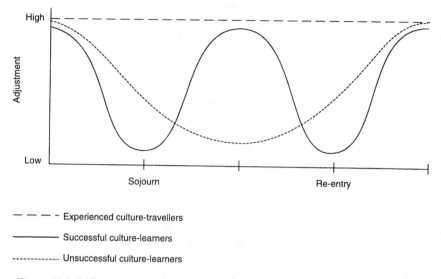

Figure 15.1 Different adjustment profiles of culture learners and travellers. Reproduced from Furnham & Bochner (1986) with the permission of Methuen.

of satisfaction or dissatisfaction. The shapes of these curves will depend on how well the persons acquire the relevant behaviours, and to what extent they can clarify their new roles, avoid role ambiguity and resolve any contradictory role demands in their relationships with significant persons in these new situations. The model suggests that coping successfully with any life-event changes has an interpersonal aspect, which depends upon processes similar to those involved in learning a new culture and may explain why some people cope with change better than others. Van Oudenhoven, Van der Zee and Van Kooten (2001) studied the successful adaptation strategies of expatriates. They found four types depending on their allegiance to their local or parent company. Some believed in "going native", while others thought of themselves as dual citizens. Open-mindedness, adventurousness, action-orientation and commitment to the company were the best predictors of how individuals tried to adapt.

Migrants and travellers hold a variety of beliefs and assumptions about how to deal with cultural differences. There are various books and pamphlets that attempt to specify these differences. Consider persuasion, for instance (Table 15.4). Note the many differences between the factual, the affective and the axiomatic approaches, and how frustrating it must be dealing with individuals who favour a different approach. Negotiation and persuasion are very fundamental aspects of management. Hence, it can be deeply frustrating and extremely inefficient if negotiators or persuaders clash constantly because of their style or implicit understanding of how to do business.

Hofstede (1984) (see Chapter 5) found that managers from different cultures are likely to have quite different concerns (see Table 15.5). Furthermore, it has been suggested that organizations actually reflect their national culture (Van Oudenhoven, 2001).

Different concerns, styles and values can cause significant problems at work. As a

Table 15.4 Natural styles of persuasion

Primary negotiating style and process	*Factual:* Appeals made to logic	*Affective:* Appeals made to emotions	*Axiomatic:* Appeals made to ideals
Conflict: opponent's arguments countered with . . .	Objective facts	Subjective feelings	Asserted ideals
Making concessions	Small concessions made early to establish a relationship	Concession made throughout as a part of the bargaining process	Few, if any, concessions made
Response to opponent's concessions	Usually reciprocate opponent's concessions	Almost always reciprocate opponent's concessions	Opponent's concessions viewed as weakness and almost never reciprocated
Relationship	Short term	Long term	No continuing relationship
Authority	Broad	Broad	Limited
Initial position	Moderate	Extreme	Extreme
Deadline	Very important	Casual	Ignored

Source: Reproduced from Glenn, Witneyer, & Stevenson (1984) with the permission of Elsevier Science.

Table 15.5 Concerns of managers in different countries

Managers in low-collectivism countries place much emphasis on: • contribution to society • independence at work • influence in the organization	Managers in moderate-collectivism countries place much emphasis on: • independence at work • job status • meaningful work
Managers from high-collectivism countries place much emphasis on: • benefits, vacation, sick leave, pension, insurance, etc. • fellow workers who are pleasant and agreeable • job security • pay input • recognition for doing a good job • work conditions	but put the least value on: • achievement at work • contribution to society • esteem • feedback concerning the result of work • opportunity for personal growth • use of ability and knowledge in work

Source: Hui (1992).

result, there is an increasing interest in how managers and workers from different countries perceive similar issues quite differently. Trompenaars (1993) has reported fascinating data for managers from 47 different countries which show how much individuals differ. To all intents and purposes, the business world is dominated by four sub-civilizations: the Saxon, Teutonic, Gallic and Nipponic (Galting, 1981). Partly because of the formal education and informal socialization that every culture affords, they have diverse ways of reaching decisions.

The *Saxon* style fosters and encourages debate and discourse. Pluralism and compromise are overriding values, and there is often the belief, particularly in America, that the individual should be built up not put down. Accepting that there are different perspectives and convictions, the general approach is that these should be debated and openly confronted, so that not only a compromise but a synergism is produced – a sum greater than its parts. The price of ecumenism is anodyne blandness.

This is quite different in the *Teutonic* and *Gallic* traditions. First, less conflict is likely to arise, because groups are often more homogeneous, being selected and socialized for being "sound on the silent issues". Teutons and Gauls love to debate, but not with antagonists, which would be considered a hopeless waste of time or an act of condescension. There is less tension-relieving humour – the tone is stiff and caustic.

The Japanese from the *Nipponic* tradition do not debate, partly through lack of experience and partly because their first rule is not to upset pre-established social relations. They respect authority and collectivist solidarity. Questions are for clarification and debate is a social rather than an intellectual act.

The British have a penchant for documentation, the Americans for statistics. Both believe that data (reality) unite and theory divides. The British are distrustful of theories, "-isms" and "-ologies": these are considered to be "sweeping generalizations". Reports, graphs and tables are seen as necessary back-up to support decisions.

The Germans like theories which are deductive in both senses of the word: that the theory may be deduced from other more fundamental principles and that it is fecund for practical deductions. It is not that they eschew data – quite the contrary – but they like to know the philosophical or economic model or theory that drives both data collection and decision-making. The Gauls are impressed by the elegance of theories and approaches. The aesthetic nature of the argument is appreciated. The use of *bon mots*, double entendres, alliterations and allusions to obscure cultural artefacts is celebrated, not shunned. For the Teutons it is rigour before elegance, but for the Gauls it is the other way round – the sound of words can be more important than their meaning.

The Nipponese might fear inconsistency, ambiguity and contradiction, but seem able to live with it. Arguments are less categorical and it is perfectly acceptable to see things as tentative, not fully formed. Ideas and theories are very cautiously elaborated with various kinds of excuses and apologies for their incompleteness.

In decision-making groups, the Anglo-Saxons pretend they are all equal but different; the Teutonic leaders have to pretend that they have nothing much to learn; the Gauls that they are all irrelevant to each other; and the Nipponese that they all agree.

Given a proposition, the Saxons ask "How can you document or measure this?"; the Teutons want to know "How can this be deduced from first principles?"; the Gauls, of course, wonder "Can this be expressed in French?"; while the Nipponese approach is to ask "Who is the proposer's boss?" It is no surprise, therefore, that courses on international management styles are so popular.

Preparing, selecting, training, evaluating and repatriating managers

Although somewhat scattered in the literature, there are some references concerned with effective performance in overseas work assignments. In their study, Bores & Rothstein (2002) found that not all managers want to work overseas. The more satisfied managers were (with salary, co-workers, etc.), the less likely they were interested in going abroad except if they saw the international assignment as being particularly beneficial for their careers. Cleveland *et al.* (1960) found that expatriates who performed well tended to be rated relatively high on technical skill, belief in their mission, a sense of politics, evidence of cultural empathy, and clear organizational ability. In a smaller but more intensive study, Stoner, Aram & Rubin (1972) recruited more than 50 men who had worked in Africa and Mauritius over an eight-year period. Using supervisors' and subordinates' ratings as the measure of performance, they attempted to delineate the factors associated with high performance. Whereas previous overseas travel and work experience, age at the start of the overseas tour, academic education and reasons for leaving were not related to overseas performance, previous ability (at time of interview) and marital status (married as opposed to single) were positively correlated with success. Also, the early reactions of the men to their new jobs appeared to be a powerful predictor of their subsequent success in developing a satisfactory working environment. Another predictor of success was the job-holder's rating of the similarity between his own and his organization's expectations about the job he would be performing. They concluded that:

> In the staffing of overseas positions, in which the opportunity for direct contact between the new employee and the organization are likely to be quite limited, the task of matching individuals to positions and helping establish constant expectations would seem to be both especially difficult and particularly critical for the subsequent evolution of the work situation. (Stoner *et al.*, 1972: 318)

Others have concentrated much more significantly on how to prepare potential expatriates for overseas transfer. For instance, Lanier (1979) recommends seven steps to be taken when preparing personnel:

1   A well-planned, realistic, pre-visit to the site (country).
2   Early language training, prior to departure.
3   Intensive study on issues such as history, culture and etiquette.
4   The provision of country-specific handbooks, including useful facts.
5   Efficient, explicit provision of inter-company counselling facilities.
6   Meeting returnees for "old hand" tips.
7   Notification of personnel office and spouses' committee on arrival.

Sievenking, Anchor & Marston (1981) stressed the importance of orientation programmes before expatriation, which aim to:

- Develop an understanding of personal and family values so that employees can anticipate and cope with the inevitably unsettling emotions that accompany culture shock.
- Develop an appreciation of the important ways in which the host culture will differ from the employee's own culture, so that the employee can guide his or her behaviour accordingly.
- Show the expatriate how he or she can be rewarded in ways other than income and travel, such as novelty, challenge and the opportunity to learn new skills.
- Help expatriates anticipate and begin to plan for hardships, delays, frustrations, material inconveniences, and the consequences of close living and working with others.

- Help expatriates to anticipate that, although they may have been superior employees in their own culture, they may need to gain greater satisfaction from experiences other than those that are work-related.

In a more considered and thoughtful paper on the selection and training of personnel for overseas, Tung (1981) outlines a contingency approach and notes four factors crucial to success in foreign assignments: technical competence on the job, relational abilities (social skills), an ability to deal with environmental constraints (government, labour issues) and family situation. Tung argued that:

> This practice of basing the selection decision on technical competence criteria – regardless of the country of foreign assignment, may account for the high failure rate among expatriates. This practice should not be continued when research findings indicate that other factors may increase the chances of successful performance abroad. (Tung, 1981: 30)

Tung outlines five types of training programmes: environmental briefings (giving extensive background knowledge), culture assimilation (testing cross-cultural communication), language training, sensitivity training (focusing on affect) and field experiences in a microculture. These programmes have very different emphases and can be costly and inefficient. A study of 26 organizations showed that many organizations used language training and the environmental briefing (both non-psychological), but very few used a culture assimilator (a training programme examining cultural differences in attribution), sensitivity training or field experience.

Instead, Tung offers a way of coping with the process based on a sensitive selection process (see Figure 15.2). The flow chart is self-explanatory. It was agreed that organizations that – experience lower expatriate failure rates adopt different criteria for selecting candidates and sponsor different types of training programmes for personnel in each of the job categories. Clearly, no one test, selection criterion or training programme is appropriate for all job categories.

A contingency framework states that in practice there is no one criterion that could be used in all situations. Rather, each assignment should be viewed on its own. In each instance, the selection of the "right person" to fill the position should be made only after a careful analysis of the task (in terms of interaction with the social community) and the country of assignment (in terms of the degree to which it is similar/dissimilar to that of the home country), and the personality characteristics – of the candidate (in terms of the candidate's and spouse's ability to live and work in a different cultural environment). (Tung, 1981: 77–78)

There has been something of an upsurge in this literature recently with the establishment of various new journals (Black, 1988). Many articles, however, have concentrated quite specifically on multinational corporate policies for expatriates, most of which appear to accept, somewhat uncritically, lists of traits and abilities that supposedly distinguish successful expatriate managers. Thus, for instance, Baliga & Baker (1985) accept *Business International*'s list in Box 15.2.

It is uncertain to what extent there are research data to support these lists, or whether indeed they are simply hypotheses or "hunches". Moreover, there are more obvious problems: how to measure these variables, the relationship between them, which are the most powerful predictors of which expatriate behaviour, and so on. Nevertheless, such

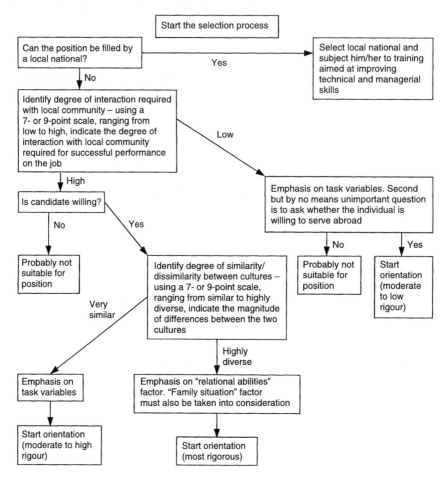

Figure 15.2 Flow chart of the selection–decision process. Reproduced from Tung (1981) with the permission of Elsevier.

attempts to understand the problem do provide a rich source of hypotheses which one may test.

In an empirical study, Harvey (1989) looked at the problems in repatriating corporate expatriate executives. In his study of over 175 executives, less than a third had repatriation programmes, although over three-quarters had programmes before expatriation. Those programmes that did exist tended to stress legal, organizational and economic issues rather than "psychological" issues and problems. Some of the aspects of an "ideal" repatriation that executives and their spouses wanted led to family disorientation and dissatisfaction. Harvey recognizes that his survey provides more questions than answers and he himself poses various questions, such as:

> To what degree does the lack of cultural "signposts" increase the difficulty and stress upon repatriating? . . . Are the differences observed in Japanese, European and US expatriates an indication or clue as to which nationalities might need more structured re-entry programs? (Harvey, 1989: 142)

Box 15.2 Characteristics of successful expatriate managers

Basic characteristics

Zeal for work	Ability to make decisions
Ability to develop others	Alertness
Persuasiveness	Foresight
Resourcefulness	Ability to learn foreign languages
Initiative and imagination	Flexibility
Self-sufficiency	Adaptability to new ideas, new cultures and new challenges

Experience factors

Technical competence	Knowledge of job to which he or she
Professional management and	is to be assigned
business experience	Open-mindedness to new ideas
Knowledge of company policies, markets	Attitude towards foreigners
and goals	Lack of fixed prejudices

Environmental factors

Knowledge of firm's international	Knowledge of local language
operations	Contacts in foreign market
Knowledge of foreign market	

Personal factors

Motivation for seeking or accepting	Personal attitudes
foreign assignment	Emotional stability
Nationality	Sociability
Family status	Dignity and integrity
Personal appeal	

Source: Reproduced from Baliga & Baker (1985) with the permission of The Society for the Advancement of Management.

More recently, Harvey, Novicevic & Kiessling, (2002) have provided good evidence that expatriate managers need eight "intelligences" grouped under three categories: analytic, practical and creative intelligence:

MULTIPLE IQs

COGNITIVE IQ: The traditional measure of intellectual ability. This IQ measures the ability to reason, learn and think analytically.

I. EMOTIONAL IQ: The ability to use one's own affective state to tap the affective state of others to accomplish objectives. The ability to display an appropriate emotional state and to respond to others' emotions in an effective manner.

POLITICAL IQ: The ability to use the formal and informal power in the company to accomplish objectives. The ability to know how to prudently, judiciously and artfully use power in the organization.

SOCIAL/CULTURAL IQ: The extent to which one is adequately socialized in a society, an organization, or a subculture. Recognition and understanding of roles, norms, routines and taboos in various settings.

II. ORGANIZATIONAL IQ: Having a detailed and accurate understanding of how the organization operates functionally and the time that is needed to accomplish certain tasks in the company. The detailed knowledge of how to get "things" done in the company.

NETWORK IQ: The ability to get things done when working with multiple organizational units. Accomplishing the goals of the company by effectively recognizing, understanding and managing inter-organizational relations.

CREATIVE IQ: The ability to diverge/innovate in thinking and create fresh novel ideas and solutions to problems. The ability to address problems/issues with insight and resourcefulness and to find unique solutions.

III. INTUITIVE IQ: The ability to have quick insights into how to solve problems or to address situations without past experience with the problem and without actively or formally processing information (i.e. street smart). (Harvey *et al.*, 2002: 502)

The issue of selecting and preparing both ex- and repatriates is at last meriting the attention and research it deserves for many reasons, not least of which is the cost of poor decision-making.

Until recently, a very important and neglected issue in manager adjustment was the adjustment of the spouse, who was often in the role of providing social support. Indeed, it has been suggested that the best/strongest predictor of an expatriate manager's adjustment is that of his or her spouse. Copeland and Norell (2002) found that five factors predicted the adaptation of the wives of expatriate managers: (1) how cohesive the family was, (2) the extent to which they were involved in the decision to move, (3) the extent to which they felt they had lost a friendship network, (4) the extent to which they felt supported and (5) the extent to which they received their support from local as opposed to long-distance providers.

One major aim is to prevent or correct stereotypes of other people or countries. Stereotypes, like other forms of categories, can be helpful or harmful depending on how we use them. Effective stereotyping allows people to understand and act appropriately in new situations. A stereotype may be helpful when it is:

* *consciously held:* the person should be aware that they are describing a group norm rather than the characteristics of a specific individual;
* *descriptive rather than evaluative:* the stereotype should describe what people from this group will probably be like (actual behaviour) and not evaluate those people as good or bad;
* *accurate:* the stereotype should accurately describe the norm for the group to which the person belongs;
* *the first best guess* about a group prior to having direct information about the specific person or persons involved;
* *modified:* based on further observation and experience with the actual people and situations. To this extent, however, it is not a stereotype.

Reducing expatriate stress

Attempts to reduce ex- and repatriate stress and to improve the skills and coping mechanisms of those preparing to move have been at the centre of research in this area. Opinions differ as to which is the most effective method. Few would disagree with the idea that men and women working in culturally different environments require some sort of orientation programme, and many techniques are available that differ according to theoretical orientation, length and type of training, and personnel involved. For instance, Brislin (1979) has listed five non-mutually exclusive programmes: self-awareness training (learning about the cultural basis of one's own behaviour), cognitive training (being given various facts about other cultures), attribution training (learning the explanation of behaviour from the point of view of people in other cultures), behaviour modification (individuals are asked to analyse the aspects of their culture that they find rewarding or punishing) and experiential learning (actively participating in realistic simulation). Furnham & Bochner (1986) have examined some of these in greater detail.

Information-giving

The most common type of cross-cultural orientation usually involves providing pro-spective sojourners with specific information about their new culture. Prospective expatriates are presented with all sorts of facts and figures, in written form, lectures or films, about such topics as the climate, food, sexual relations, religious customs and anything else the trainer may consider important. However, the effectiveness of such illustrative programmes is limited in four ways. First, the facts are often too general to have any clear and specific application, except when discussing tax or organizational structure. Second, the facts emphasize the exotic, yet tend to ignore the mundane but more common things, such as how to hail or pay for a taxi. Third, such programmes give the false impression that a culture can be learned in a few easy lessons, whereas all that they mostly convey is a superficial, incoherent and often misleading picture, which glosses over the culture's hidden agenda. Finally, even if the facts are remembered, they do not necessarily lead to action, or to the current action. It would be absurd to teach people how to drive a car by *only* giving them information about how to do it. If cognitive informational training is to be of any practical use, it must be combined with some sort of practical experiential learning in the appropriate setting – amusing lec-tures, helpful guidebooks and well-prepared videos are not enough.

Cultural sensitization

Programmes based on this approach set out to provide trainees with information about other cultures, as well as how to heighten their awareness about the cultural bias of their own behaviour, and how the practices of their society differ from those of the host country. The aim is therefore to *compare* and *contrast* the different cultures, look at various behaviours from the perspective of each society, and thus develop a sensitivity to, and awareness of, cultural relativity. This view holds that very few human values, beliefs and behaviours are absolute and universal, and that what a particular individual believes to be true and good will depend on the norms prevailing in that person's society, norms that other societies may reject. Such programmes often operate at two levels: they aim to achieve self-awareness about the modal values and attitudes that are typically held by members of one's own society; and to gain insight into one's own personal traits, attitudes and prejudices. Cultural sensitization and self-awareness programmes, being essentially cognitive techniques, suffer from many of the same limitations as information-giving. For instance, it is all very well for a Westerner to accept intellectually that, in some cultures, ceremonies featuring ritual animal slaughter have the same socially cohesive function as, say, the Trooping of the Colour in England, but it is another matter to then willingly observe such occasions and regard them in the same light as indigenous spectators do.

Isomorphic attributions

Many researchers have pointed out that a potential obstacle to effective cross-cultural communication is the inability of the participants to understand the causes of each other's behaviour – that is, to make correct attributions about the other's actions. Effective intercultural relations require isomorphic attributions, so that observers offer the same cause or reason for actors' (others) behaviour as they would for their own. The likelihood of making isomorphic attributions decreases as the divergence between the subjective cultures of the participants increases, and explains why intercultural relations are often characterized by mutual hostility and misunderstanding. One solution is to train individuals to understand the subjective culture of the other group, which in practice means teaching them how to make "correct" behavioural attributions. This is done through a device called the "culture assimilator", which, in effect, is a programmed learning manual. The booklet contains descriptions of episodes in which two culturally disparate individuals meet. The interactions are unsuccessful, in that each incident terminates in embarrassment, misunderstanding or interpersonal hostility. The trainee is then presented with four or five alternative explanations of what went wrong, which correspond to different attributions of the observed behaviour. Only one of these attributions is "correct" from the perspective of the culture being learned. The trainees select the answer they regard as correct, and are then instructed to turn to a subsequent page, where they are either praised if they selected the "right" answer or are told why they were wrong if they selected an "incorrect" answer. A great deal also depends on which particular critical incidents are selected to form the basic curriculum. Inevitably, exotic, strange and hence less common events tend to be given greater prominence than the less interesting but more frequent day-to-day problems that make up the "bread and butter" content of intercultural contacts.

Learning by doing

The limitations of information-based orientation programmes led to various attempts to expose trainees to supervised second cultural experiences, real or simulated. Most organizations do not have, or are unwilling to commit, such massive resources for experimental culture training. More typically, behaviourally based culture training programmes rely on role-playing encounters between trainees and persons pretending to come from some other culture, or if professional personnel from the other culture are actually available, with them. In this respect, the techniques are similar to those employed in social skills training. Some programmes also contain a behavioural evaluation component, which may take the form of a team of psychologists evaluating and training the performance of the candidates in the field.

Finally, the vast majority of sojourners, or those who come into contact with members of other cultures in their own societies, receive no systematic culture training whatsoever. The little "training" that does occur is done informally by experienced migrants who pass on useful information to the new visitors. This in itself may not be such a bad thing. One of the requirements of a successful culture trainer is to be a mediating person – that is, a person who is intimately familiar with both cultures and can act as a link between them, representing each to the other. In theory experienced sojourners should have that rare capacity, but in practice some may have highly specialized, distorted or even prejudiced views of one or both of their cultures, and perpetuate these distortions in the informal training they impart to highly impressionable newcomers.

Intercultural (social) skills training

Although there are various different approaches to social skills training, they have various elements in common. The first is an *assessment* or *diagnosis* of a particular problem (e.g. assertiveness) or situation (e.g. chairing meetings) that the person has or is likely to encounter. The second stage is an *analysis* or *discussion* of the elements in these problem areas, possibly followed by a modelling exercise where a trainer enacts the role. This in turn is followed by a *role-play* by the trainee, with critical *feedback* at length after each practice. The number, range and variety of contexts in which the role-plays are enacted add to the generalizability of the training. Trainees are also encouraged to do homework exercises between role-play and feedback sessions. For Ellis & Whittington, the following strategies may be useful in helping individual trainees to obtain maximum benefit:

> The programme should be carefully introduced to trainees and something of its rationale should be explained; trainees should be allowed ample time for "practice" practices so that any cosmetic effect of video or other feedback can be got over; models should be as closely related to individual trainee characteristics as possible; trainees should participate as much as possible in the sensitization phase and every effort should be made to accommodate individual learning differences in the activities provided; practice talks and situations should be readily comprehensible and should have validity for trainee; feedback should be at an appropriate intellectual level and should have a supportive emotional tone. (Ellis & Whittington, 1981: 73)

The advantages of the intercultural skills approach include:

- Training procedures are based on a *specific theory*, thereby avoiding vague statements about "mutual understanding" and instead emphasizing behavioural skill deficits.
- "*Practical*" aspects are covered in the sense that the approach has at its centre everyday common – as well as business – situations, which, nevertheless, cause friction, misunderstanding and interpersonal hostility; this avoids vague statements about culture shock by attempting to quantify social difficulty on various dimensions and then reduce it.
- The approach has the possibility of *tailor-made* aspects for the idiosyncratic features of the trainee, in that a particular person's social skills deficiencies are

diagnosed and the person is then given culturally appropriate remedial training aimed at removing those specific deficiencies. The training programme avoids general non-specific lectures and films about superficial and/or exotic aspects of the host culture, preferring to concentrate on those specific features of culture that the clients find problematic.

- The approach employs well-tried *behavioural techniques* such as video feedback, role-playing and modelling to simulate real-life situations realistically. The training does not rely exclusively on cognitive or information-giving procedures alone, partly because they do not generalize readily across to real-life situations and partly because they are readily forgotten.

- It involves *management* of interpersonal encounters. Its emphasis, therefore, is on the social psychology of the sojourner and it avoids vague assumptions about achieving personal growth and insight; the stress is on the acquisition and execution of skills.

- *Evaluating* the theory, training content, training techniques and impact of the programme – this can be built into a project from the start, and not tacked on as an afterthought at its completion. It is possible to indicate if, and exactly how well, the various aspects of the project were performed in accordance with expectations.

The disadvantage of this approach is that, because of the systematic nature of such programmes, they are likely to cost more, intrude into and disrupt the activities of the institution whose members are being trained, and require an interdisciplinary team of trainers, unless relevant bi-cultural mediating trainers (Bochner, 1982) are available.

Black *et al.* (1992) have proposed various important policy explanations for dealing with expatriate businessmen and women. For instance, to prevent employees "going native", they recommend only a limited time away from the organization; sending only managers with strong organizational ties, and having good sponsor (old-hand tutor) links. On the other hand, to avoid sending managers who "leave their hearts at home" and do not adapt, it is preferable to send younger managers, facilitate cross-cultural adjustment and provide cross-cultural training. The ultimate aim of any organization should be to create "dual-national" or "multinational" citizens who need to be carefully selected, trained and rewarded.

Globalization and international relocation

It is becoming increasingly frequent, particularly for people in developed countries, to move from job to job and/or to be geographically transferred in the course of their working lives. Business movement is related to the process of internationalization by large employers as they evolve their corporate business structures. Indeed, some businesses, for a variety of reasons, have an active (and expensive) policy of regular job transferral, while for some occupations (e.g. travelling salesperson, diplomat) the job almost by definition involves travel. It was not until comparatively recently that social scientists begun to consider some of the psychological consequences of business transfer. What businesses and developmental agencies want to know as a matter of urgency and priority is what are the best predictions of work efficacy while abroad.

Over the past decade or so, there has been a flourishing of research on the adaptation of expatriates (Gregersen & Stroh, 1997). Much of this research has very clearly an applied flavour, as the psychological and monetary costs of relocation are high.

McDonald (1993) found that 25–40% of expatriate managers failed in their objective in the years 1965 to 1985, which cost their companies about US$100,000 each. Hence there is increasing interest in better expatriate selection (Mendenhall, Dunbar, & Oddon, 1987), preparation, acculturation and repatriation. The cost of maintaining a British executive in Japan is more than two-and-a-half times that of doing so in Britain. There is even a debate as to whether to use expatriate managers at all (McDonald, 1993). The cultural background of the expatriate sojourner (i.e. Japanese or American) is often more important than the particular country-specific environment to which they went in predicting their cross-cultural adaptation.

These factors are important for the adjustment of the business person. For instance, a six-month sideways transfer, alone to an unknown and distant country, is likely to have quite different consequences than a two-year sojourn in another part of the same country when one is accompanied by one's spouse or family and provided with generous financial and social support. A major theoretical and research problem in this area is to distinguish which of a number of concurrent changes account for the variety of psychological consequences observed. Job transfer within or between different countries nearly always entails some differences in the work itself (e.g. change of status, income, skill utilization), different living arrangements (family, physical environment) and different organizational variables (size, structure), all or none of which may account for change or no change in a person's adjustment, health or performance. Thus Brett, Stroh & Reilly (1993) asked the simple question of more than 800 employees of twenty American-500 corporations, "who is willing to relocate". The single most important predictor of willingness to relocate was spouse's willingness to move.

In their review of the expatriation literature, Hilltop and Janssen (1995) list what they argue are known facts about expatriation. These include:

1 The demand for expatriates is increasing.
2 Expatriates are expensive to employ.
3 International assignments present expatriate managers and their families with a variety of difficulties and challenges.
4 The failure rate of expatriate managers is high.
5 Premature repatriation is costly both to the manager and the company.
6 Personal characteristics associated with successful expatriation include technical ability, stress tolerance, flexibility, communication skills and cultural empathy.
7 The adaptability of the spouse is a crucial factor in a manager's adaptation.
8 The subsidiary–parent company relations are an important factor in expatriate adaptation.
9 Selection, training and support during the assignment are crucial.
10 How companies are dealing with repatriation problems is perhaps not the most important question. The key issue is to involve the expatriate in determining what position will be most suited to his/her needs after the international assignment. (Hilltop & Janssen, 1995: 365)

The last point is clearly supported by Guzzo, Noonan & Elron (1994), who found that expatriates' attitudes and perceptions at work are related to the extent to which they have control over their best and worst experiences, many of which are, by definition, beyond the control of the employer. The need for perceived control is common across cultural travellers as previously mentioned. An inner locus of control is associated with better psychological adaptation during cross-cultural transitions.

Various attempts have been made to develop a comprehensive, multifaceted model of the expatriate adjustment experience (Aycan, 1997). One of the most influential has been that of Black, Mendenhall & Oddon (1991), which allowed them to formulate specific propositions. Four hypotheses concerned anticipatory adjustment before departure (e.g. "Previous work-related experiences will facilitate the formation of accurate work expectations and previous non-work experiences will facilitate the formation of accurate non-work expectations"). They also drew up a list of *personal* skills (self-efficacy, relational skills, perceptual skills), *job* factors (role clarity, conflict, discretion, novelty), *organizational culture* factors (novelty, support) and *socialization* factors as well as *non-work* factors that related to adjustment. At the centre of their influential model is the idea that there is no discontinuity between the international and domestic adjustment process. How organizations socialize their staff, help with career decisions and are concerned with work role transitions and transfers is as relevant to the domestic as the international literature. Looking at this and other models, one is struck by the fact that so little in this area is counter-intuitive. Also, the level of psychological as opposed to organizational theorizing is clearly not great.

The international breakdown of economic and political barriers all over the world, combined with the massive increase in cheap and efficient communication through electronic information flow, has led to globalization in production and markets. Joint ventures, expansion into developing countries and the dispersal of production have meant employees are now frequently asked to relocate abroad (Coyle & Shortland, 1992).

Companies use expatriates essentially for three reasons: for staffing when locals cannot fulfil current job requirements, for management development experience specifically for high-fliers, and for organization development in developing international networks and contacts. Expatriates also provide "diplomatic" representation and can ensure better "control from headquarters".

Brewster (1991) asked unprompted international personnel executives from European multinational companies for the key criteria used by their corporation in selecting expatriates. Sixteen separate criteria were identified, listed in order in Table 15.6.

Table 15.6 Key selection criteria used by multinational corporations

Criteria	Companies mentioning
• Technical expertise	18
• Language	12
• Family support	12
• Potential	9
• Knowing company systems	7
• Experience	5
• Marital status	5
• Medical status	3
• Independence	3
• Motivation	3
• Age	3
• Liaison skills	3
• Sex	2
• Seniority	2
• Helping high potential employees avoid military conscription	1

The workforce in most large companies is, as a result of demographic changes, international movement and relocated sojourning managers, becoming much more *diverse*. In this sense, individuals can experience adjustment problems in their own organization as it changes around them. Many companies have moved from a national through international (polycentric) to a global or geocentric perspective. Hence, they are on the look-out for multilingual, adaptable, socially skilled managers who can operate as a sojourning expatriate. Companies and consultants have often described a "wish-list" of the characteristics they are seeking, all of which are pretty similar and to do with adaptiveness, intellectual and social curiosity, tolerance for ambiguity, business acumen and intelligence. Unfortunately, little attempt is made to rank-order these skills or to suggest how they may be related to each other. The resources devoted to expatriates are often greater than those devoted to any other comparable group of employees.

It is not clear whether the number of expatriate businessmen and women is increasing or decreasing. Business expansion and globalization suggest the former, while others point to the evidence that expatriates everywhere are being replaced by cheaper locals. Larger companies are reducing the number of expatriates that they employ, while smaller companies appear to be doing the opposite: "Overall there may be more expatriates than there were; and many of them will be employed by organizations with little international know-how, and little expertise in the area of expatriation" (Brewster, 1991: 11)

Employing organizations need to consider when, if and why they need expatriate managers; the kind of expatriate they want to foster, and to develop a coherent approach to recruitment and selection. They need to develop an equitable compensation package and have clearly formulated policies of performance evaluation while abroad and repatriation policies.

The trends in relocation seem quite clear. Relocation, once the exclusive province of technical or managerial staff, is now being used to counter labour shortages in particular specialist operations. Resistance to relocation is diminishing as several positive incentives have been described. These include a possible improvement in career prospects and job security; the provision of new work experiences and training; the establishment of new (better) working relationships; and often a higher (lower tax) salary in the new job.

In reviewing their overseas experiences, Adler (1986) found that returnees reported enhanced managerial skills, though not technical skills. Returnees reported being better able to: make decisions under ambiguous and uncertain conditions, be patient, ask the right questions (as opposed to know the right answers), see situations from a number of perspectives, tolerate ambiguity and work successfully with a wider range of people.

From a business point of view, the most common reasons for arranging overseas assignments for expatriates are

- the transfer of new technology by an expert;
- absorption of expertise by a specialist from a developing country;
- supervision of a start-up unit in a new region;
- personal career planning for international management;
- filling a vacancy;
- promotion from a flat home organization.

The employer's objectives need not be those of the employee. It is clearly important that there is explicit identification of the varying priorities among objectives, both between employee and expatriate and between assignments in different environments. Expatriates need to know the philosophy and logic of the remuneration package, not just the actual numbers involved. Non-parity with other expatriates, with locals and between assignments is an important source of dissatisfaction. Furthermore, where possible problems need to be anticipated and monetary solutions or compensations need to be resisted.

As Brewster (1991) noted, the objectives of any company's compensation package are essentially fourfold:

- to attract and retain the right quality of staff for the organization;
- to ensure that the employee feels fairly and equatably treated in comparison to reference groups both within and outside the organization;
- to motivate the employee to an acceptable, and hopefully ever improving, standard of performance;
- to fit with policies in other areas of human resource management.

Various practical guides are available, both for individuals and companies, on some of the crucial issues concerned with relocation. These include:

- The direct costs to companies: disturbance allowances, temporary accommodation, spouse's income compensation, two-home allowances, tax issues.
- Group moves of whole companies: because of rents, markets or labour shortages, or mergers and acquisitions.
- Develop high flyers, fill skills gap and transfer expertise or to develop new teams.

The problems for any expatriate are considerable. They have to fully understand how business is done (officially/unofficially; explicitly/implicitly) locally, and they have to understand the varied motives and habits of their new colleagues, clients, subordinates and supervisors. They must come to realize that local management styles vary considerably and that social values impinge on all aspects of work and decision-making. Understanding attitudes to time, communication patterns and beliefs about bribery, nepotism, and so on are crucially important. Expatriates have to judge the increases in job responsibility and accountability and, possibly, the unusual experience of dealing with head office. They need to be aware of prejudice towards themselves in some cases, as well as the claustrophobia of working and living in compounds.

It is therefore essential that all salient people involved are aware of their particular responsibilities. The expatriate, as well as his or her host and home country manager, have specific responsibilities to ensure adaptation is successful as well as possible. Companies have to develop clear policies about the number and length of the postings abroad (Brewster, 1991).

In a descriptive study and review, Brewster (1991) attempted to answer some of the more obvious, but unanswered, questions about expatriates:

1   *Who are they?* Older, married expatriates tend to be senior managers, while younger, single managers are more likely to be technical specialists. There seems to be a double wave – in their twenties and thirties, and in their fifties and sixties. Less than a fifth are women, and about the same total number go abroad of their own accord looking for work. As might be expected, a substantial number have some

sort of links with foreign countries before their assignment (e.g. family). The typical length of each posting is 3–4 years.

2   *Why do they go?* Single men stress higher incomes, while women stress the importance of experiencing a different culture, lifestyle and opportunity to travel. Married people seem particularly sensitive to the distinction. Overall, the job-sense of vocation and the lure of financial rewards are consistently rated as the most important factors. At the beginning of careers, personal development and advancement are seen as important, but as careers do advance through multiple overseas postings, the destination ascends the ranking for motivation.

3   *Perception of contracts.* Expatriates are extremely expensive: well-paid workers in first-class accommodation with additional perks. What expatriates seem to value most, in rank-order, are provision of medical care, continued pension rights, provision of accommodation, freight of possessions, return leave flights paid for, emergency return provided if necessary, and salary paid in hard currency.

4   *Preparation for the expatriate assignment.* Despite recommendations, companies appear to offer little in addition to informal briefings and language training. Because of cost, lack of availability or not realizing the need, surprisingly little training is actually offered to expatriates before they go.

5   *The experience of work.* Two factors appear to merit the most common problems: attitudes to time (time-keeping and time-frames) and unmeritocratic behaviour (nepotism, etc). Other factors were frequently mentioned, including language difficulties, different motivation factors, impingement on religion and ethics at work, frustration with fatalism and a low respect for life, problems with attitudes to the family, different approaches to handling emotional issues as work, different commitment to objectives, apparent lack of professionalism and, more profanely, the slow process of leaving the ground rules of the new culture. The five most helpful coping strategies were cultivating local activities, mixing with the locals, taking up a new hobby, involvement with the expat community and gaining language fluency.

There is naturally great concern about what is described as "expatriate failure rates", usually defined as early return. Naturally, companies and individuals do not like to admit "failure", and they rarely break down the data showing what type of person (in terms of demography, management level, etc.) has most difficulty in what country. It is easy to ignore, obscure or reinterpret underperformance. The cost and loss of face may prevent certain companies having a recall process, while others may send out further help. Underperformance (due in part to inadequate cultural skills) may be two or three times as common as the numbers deemed required to be sent home. Brewster (1991) found that for American companies the estimated rate of failure (early recall) was 20–50%. The rates are much higher in certain countries (e.g. Japan, Iran) and certain sectors (i.e. the construction industry). Better quality studies suggest, however, that some figures are over-exaggerated and the real figure may be more like 10%. European expatriates appear to fare better with failure rates closer to 5%.

Brewsters' (1991) research and review suggested it may confidently be assumed that about three-quarters of companies have failure rates of less than 5%, while a quarter see between 5 and 10% of staff being "brought home early". But failure rates decline over time as companies learn to select, prepare and manage their expatriates more successfully.

Coping with job transfers

The problems of the business sojourn, transfer or short-term posting have been apparent for some time. Studies have recognized the importance also of examining the adaptation of spouses (Stone-Feinstein & Ward, 1990). After the Second World War, multinational industrial and manufacturing companies found their overseas operations hampered and rendered inefficient by staff not being able to adjust and work efficiently in their new surroundings. Forster (1997) noted that there is now a "mature literature" on expatriate failure rates, defined as returning home before the agreed end of the international assignment. Using this definition, it would appear that the rate is around 10% for British managers, but this figure disguises the true nature of the problems caused by business expatriation. Even military personnel have shown evidence of problems in foreign countries. In an early study, Stoner *et al.* (1972) set out to assess the determinants of effective work performance among young Americans in Africa. Various individual, organizational and environmental factors were considered. Age, travel experience and qualifications were not related to performance, but perceived ability and marital status were. Early success in the job, similarity between own and organizational expectations and specific task-needs were all correlated with good performance. Furthermore, the closer the country was to independence, the better the Americans performed in it.

Despite the paucity of early psychological research on the consequences of job transfers, popularists have been quick to point to the negative consequences of transfer: heart attacks in men, depression in women, maladjustment in children. Brett (1982) tested some specific hypotheses about the effects of job transfer in five different areas of life:

1   *Work.* Mobile employees should be more satisfied (with pay, security, fringe benefits, promotion) than less mobile employees, whereas working wives of mobile employees are likely to be less satisfied than less mobile working women.
2   *Self.* Mobile employees should have better, and their wives worse, self-concepts and mental health than their less mobile counterparts. Furthermore, mobile parents are likely to perceive their children as less mature but more adaptable to new environments.
3   *Marriage/family life.* Because of the conflict of interests in transfer, it is expected that marital instability would be higher in mobile than non-mobile families.
4   *Friendships.* Mobile employees, their wives and children should all have less stable friendship patterns than their counterparts in less mobile families.
5   *Standard of living.* Mobile families should have a higher standard of living than less mobile families.

Despite the apparent reasonableness of the above hypotheses, many of which had been entertained by other writers, Brett (1982) was able to confirm only the hypothesis relating to social relationships – that is, mobile families are less satisfied with their friendship networks than immobile families. She comments on her findings thus:

The challenge of moving may make life interesting. The experience of reestablishing a household after a move may contribute to feelings of competency. Dissatisfaction with social relationships may be due as much or more to the trauma of relinquishing old friends as to the difficulty of making new ones. This interpretation is particularly supported in the children's data. Further, the fact that the family members go through the disruption of the move together and must provide social support for each other until new friendships can be made explains the mobile adults' relative satisfaction with family life and marriage.

Few families in the transfer sample believed moving is easy. However, the data from this study show that despite their mobility, these families were as satisfied with all aspects of their lives, except social relationships, as were stable families. (Brett, 1982: 462)

Not all researchers, however, come to this conclusion. Stokols and Shumaker (1982) developed a new theoretical framework for the study of residential mobility and mental health. They state that previous research on the topic has assumed that geographic movement is inherently stressful. Yet findings suggest that most people change residence voluntarily and regularly without any obviously detrimental consequences for mental or physical health. Prior theoretical analyses were simplistic and misleading because they provided an inadequate conceptualization of mobility, failed to delineate the psychological context of relocation, and oversimplified health outcomes. Only when there is prolonged exposure to undesirable places or separation from familiar ones are psychological and health problems likely to occur. The antecedents of place dependence include the quality of the current residential situation and the relative quality of alternative (past/future) residential situations. Hence moves to lower levels promote stress and illness, whereas moves to higher levels do not. Stokols & Shumaker also note that current residential satisfaction depends on many factors both within and outside the residence.

In summary, the model of Stokols & Shumaker (1982) says that staying in a place that does not meet one's needs is associated with negative health outcomes, whereas staying in a place that does meet one's needs is associated with positive health outcomes. The consequences of moving depend on how well the new location compares with previously experienced environments in meeting important needs. Furthermore, various psychological and material benefits of residential change are able to reduce or ameliorate any negative effects.

This may explain why some people find geographic mobility stressful, while the opposite is true for others. Neither simple, upward, social nor geographic mobility is of itself sufficient to explain an individual's reaction. It is the perception of the changes and how these affect the person's needs and the congruence between these needs and the environment that ultimately determine the relationship between mobility and adjustment.

So far, most of the studies considered in-depth have been concerned primarily with job transfer *within* countries. There is now much more interest in business people living abroad: expatriates (Ward *et al.*, 2001). Several studies have attempted to determine which factors predict success as an expatriate manager (international assignee). Some papers have been speculative, simply listing obvious factors thought to be relevant. Arthur and Bennett (1995) identified six factors in descending order of importance: family situations, spouse relationship, personal flexibility/adaptability, job knowledge and motivation, interpersonal/relational skills, and extra-cultural openness. However, they found that the predictive power of these factors differed greatly depending on the nature of the organization (i.e. service versus manufacturing).

Fisher and Shaw (1994) listed role ambiguity and conflict in the job, the degree of advancement in the job, as well as community and job satisfaction. Interestingly, the best predictor of adjustment difficulty in the new setting was the amount of difficulty the managers had in adjusting to other foreign locations. Equally important, pre-move expectations appeared to have no impact on adjustment – contrary to many other speculations.

In a very interesting and important study, Spreitzer, McCall and Mahoney (1997) looked at the predictors of "international executive potential" among 838 managers from six international firms in 21 countries. Their study was based on the premise that what is important is the ability to learn from experience. The 14 factors that they identified were classified into two groups. Some were about end-state competency like *sensitivity to cultural differences, business knowledge*, has the *courage to take a stand*, and *brings the best out in people*, while others were labelled learning-oriented dimensions and included such items as *uses feedback*, is *culturally adventurous*, and *seeks opportunities to learn*. As expected, they found cross-cultural adventurousness was a good predictor of the international criteria outlined. Their results led them to consider why some managers are likely to develop into successful international executives. They first asked what is the price of admission, or what traits does one need to attract attention and investment? The answer appeared to be: committed to success, is insightful, has courage, has broad business experience and takes risks. The second question was do expatriate managers actively take or make opportunities to learn, and is this related to cross-cultural adventurousness and seeking feedback? The answer was "yes". Other questions concerned responsiveness in learning contexts and the ability to change as a result of experience.

The extensive literature on problems associated with job transfers within and between countries has concentrated on specific issues or processes that appear to relate to adaptation, functioning and productivity in the new setting. Thus Kramer (1993) emphasized the importance of open and honest *communication* with peers and supervisors as an important aspect of adjusting to job transfers. Martin (1995) showed how *prior moves* related to relocation adjustment and stress. Interestingly, those with fewest and those with many moves reported most stress. Janssen (1995) found the amount of intercultural interaction (contact with hosts) to be an important predictor of adjustment of managers on a foreign assignment. Martin (1996) also demonstrated that *attributional* style (optimistic versus pessimistic) is a good predictor of psychological reaction to job relocation.

Some studies have highlighted the importance of pre-expatriation and the early stages of the way a company internationalizes. Black and Gregersen (1991) looked at three types of expatriate adjustment: work, interaction and general. Work adjustment was best predicted by role discretion, role ambiguity, role conflict and interaction with home nationals. Interaction adjustment was best predicted by interaction with host national, spouse interaction adjustment, company-provided cross-cultural training and self-initiated cross-cultural training. General adjustment was best predicted by spouse general adjustment and interaction with host nationals. Clearly, the results demonstrate very different antecedents depending on which type of adjustment one is considering. This study was replicated, examining specifically the adjustment of Finnish expatriates (Gregersen & Stroh, 1997). Many but not all of the results were replicated, suggesting cross-cultural differences in the repatriation experience.

A few studies have concentrated on the problem for expatriates when returning home.

As Black (1992) notes, the returning expatriate must adjust on return to interacting with home nationals on a full-time and broad basis as well as to the general non-work environment in their home country. He hypothesized and found a "fit" between the expectations of repatriation readjustment and job performance. The assumption is that met assumptions are accurate and appropriate adjustments are made to cope with change. As others have found, this was the established spillover from job expectations to general non-work repatriation adjustment and from general non-work expectations to job performance. He argues:

> The results from this study suggest that shaping accurate expectations relative to *both* work and non-work issues can have positive separate and spillover effects. Consequently, firms that choose to offer programs in an effort to shape expectations may want to provide information and counselling on *both* work and non-work issues. (Black, 1992: 190)

Forster (1994) also believe that repatriates need to be fully committed to their move and develop realistic expectations of both the sojourn and the return. However, he argues that "there is only so much that organizations can do to help their staff. They need to be as proactive as possible during the transition" (p. 422).

By and large, studies on business people who have moved from one area or country to another have come up with evidence of unhappiness, distress and poor adjustment. Of course, this is not always the case and, as research has shown, there are many complex variables determining the actual adjustment of particular individuals. At the same time, it is probably safe to say that, overall, business people experience less difficulty than, say, students or other sojourners moving to new environments.

The literature on the movement of working people is, like all research concerned with the psychological consequences of geographic movement, complex and equivocal. Commonsense ideas have not proved particularly reliable in predicting adjustment or performance. There also remain some fairly puzzling results. Overall, it would appear that the relative quality of life (social, occupational, familial) between the point of departure and the point of arrival best predicts the adjustment of business people, though there may be initial distress or strain. This is hardly a startling finding. Nevertheless, it does have practical implications. In particular, companies must ensure that their overseas employees are no worse off than they would have been had they stayed at home. However, as we have seen, this is not simply a matter of pecuniary reward, but involves a variety of social, psychological and familial considerations that together influence the well-being of the sojourner.

Managing cross-culturally

Because of migration pressures and practices in most Western, developed countries and because of the globalization of so many companies, many people at work either soon discover that they have to manage an increasingly culturally diverse workforce or themselves have to work abroad. Hence there has developed in the business management and work psychology literature an increasing interest in the solutions to the problems of cross-cultural management. Recent attention has been drawn to the particular problem of cultural differences in work motivation as well as the influence of national culture on work values.

Tayeb (1996) has highlighted the importance of national and corporate culture in multinational teams as well as companies attempting to start alliances. Clearly, when managers move from one country to another, they frequently have to understand and adapt to a different economic, educational, politico-legal and sociocultural environment. All functions such as planning, organizing, staffing, leading and controlling may be different. Hence, the growth of a field called "comparative management". Thus, for instance, a Japanese manager who takes a temporary sojourn in an American-based factor is required to learn how to do the task differently. In Japan, leaders/managers act as a social facilitator and group member, whereas in America the role is primarily that of decision-maker and group head. The style in Japan tends to be paternalistic and confrontation-avoidant; in America, managers often have a more directive, confrontational style. Japanese organizational structures are more implicit and informal, whereas in America they can be very formal and bureaucratic.

Harris and Moran (1987) have highlighted the cultural knowledge and sensitivity, as well as behavioural and cognitive flexibility, required of managers sent on "foreign deployment". They argue that successful economic cooperation starts with cultural sensitivity and with understanding people:

- Whose beliefs we may not share, but must respect.
- Whose cultures and societies may demand different patterns of economic and social development.
- Who may refuse to accept our own beliefs and assumptions.
- Who may or may not share our own views on equitable distribution of wealth within their national borders.
- Who may not have forgotten hundreds of years of colonial domination, and may be suspicious of our motives even when we believe our intentions are pure.
- Who may be struggling to free themselves from some part of their cultural past. (Harris & Moran, 1987: 524)

While the number of studies looking at the stressed and then repatriated manager has increased, the most important and interesting work has been directed at attempting to taxonomize national (and corporate) culture. As noted earlier, two overlapping systems, both devised by Dutchmen, have been very influential. Hofstede (1980), in a study of 116,000 people from 70 different countries, argued that there are four basic cultural dimensions that inevitably affect the way people behave at work. All four are relevant to the world of work, but some more than others.

Power-distance refers to the fact that people accept that both power and influence are not equally distributed in organizations. Decentralized, flatter organizations with less supervisory personnel tend to have lower distance scores. A comparison of high- versus low-power-distance countries/cultures is given in Table 15.7. The manager used to one style but confronted by employees' demands for the other will necessarily have problems. It is intuitively the case that a low-power-distance manager could adapt to a high-power-distance culture more readily than a high-power-distance manager having to work in a culture and country that prefers low-power-distance values.

Uncertainty avoidance refers to tolerance of ambiguity and the extent to which people and organizations attempt to avoid or reduce uncertainty. People with strong uncertainty avoidance needs tend to like experts and be risk-averse. High uncertainty avoidance cultures are more rule-oriented. The manager socialized in a high

Table 15.7 Power-distance

Low-power distance countries	High-power distance countries
Employees put high value on independence.	Employees put high value on conformity.
Employees are less afraid of disagreeing with their boss.	Employees do not disagree with their boss.
Signs of rank at work are minimal.	There are often clear signs of rank and power.
Mangers are seen as making decisions only after consulting subordinates.	Managers are seen as making decisions alone: autocratically and paternalistically.
Close supervision is not liked by subordinates.	Close supervision is expected by subordinates.
A stronger perceived work ethic exists but a strong disbelief that people dislike work.	A weaker perceived work ethic exists and a more frequent belief that people dislike work.
Managers like seeing themselves as practical, supportive but requiring support.	Managers like seeing themselves as benevolent and wise decision-makers.
Employees tend to be more cooperative.	Employees are reluctant to trust each other.
Informal employee consultation often occurs.	Formal employee participation is rare.

Source: Adapted from Hofstede (1980) with the permission of Sage Publications, Inc.

uncertainty avoidance culture and company may be perplexed by the values and behaviour of those in a different culture, and may have considerable difficulty in adjusting to his or her new environment (Table 15.8).

Individualism–collectivism is in many ways a West–East difference. Individualism and collectivism are deeply rooted in cultural values and consciousness. Managers moving from Europe and America, both highly individualistic cultures, to the Pacific Rim are often surprised and puzzled by the organizational consequence of their own particular culture on this dimension (Table 15.9).

The final dimension, *masculinity–femininity*, reflects different values. Masculinity refers to maleness of dominant values like money, possessions and status, while femininity refers to female values of caring and quality of life. Arguably this has less impact on the expatriate manager than the other dimensions.

Table 15.8 Uncertainty avoidance

Low uncertainty avoidance	High uncertainty avoidance
Uncertainty in general is more easily accepted.	Uncertainty is seen as a continuous threat that must be fought.
Desire for generalists and common sense.	Desire for experts and their knowledge.
More acceptance of dissent.	Strong need for consensus.
Low anxiety and stress.	High anxiety and stress.
Hard work not a virtue *per se*.	Inner urge to work hard.
Less display of positive and negative emotions.	More show of all sorts of emotions.
Less in-group favouritism.	More in-group favouritism.
More willingness to take risks in business.	Concern with security in all business operations.

Source: Adapted from Hofstede (1983) with the permission of Sage Publications, Inc.

Table 15.9 Individualism–collectivism

Low individualism	High individualism
External locus of control.	Internal locus of control.
Extended families that protect individuals in exchange for loyalty (nepotism).	Employees are required to take care of himself or herself and her or his immediate family.
"We" consciousness favouring in a group.	"I" consciousness stressing personal needs.
Emotional dependence on organization and institutions.	Emotional independence from work.
Emphasis on belonging to organization: total identification.	Emphasis on individual initiative and personal achievement.
Expertise, order, duty, security seen to derive from organization.	Autonomy, variety, pleasure, individual financial security are valued above loyalty.
Belief in group decisions.	Belief in individual decisions.

Source: Adapted from Hofstede (1980) with the permission of Sage Publications, Inc.

Triandis (1994), in a consideration of Hofstede's (1980) work, listed a number of what he felt to be important psychological implications:

- Family involvement (nepotism) is acceptable in low-individualism countries.
- Harmony is more important in low-individualism countries.
- Paternalistic management is acceptable in high-power-distance countries.
- Status differences are more accepted in high-power-distance countries.
- Task has a higher priority than relationship in high-individualism countries.
- Older individuals are more respected in high-power-distance countries.
- Channels for handling grievances are found only in low-power-distance countries.
- Management by objectives, the managerial grid, theory Y and theory Z (which combines emphasis on production with emphasis on people) management styles do not work well in high-power-distance countries.
- Planning is more popular in low-uncertainty-avoidance countries.
- Time is more important in high-uncertainty-avoidance countries.
- Achievement motivation is high in high-masculinity countries and low in low-uncertainty-avoidance countries.
- A machismo style of management is acceptable in high-power-distance and high-masculinity cultures.
- Job differentiation according to sex roles is rigid in high-masculinity cultures.
- Appraisal systems require low-power-distance, high-individualism cultures.
- High-masculinity cultures have a need for formal rules.

Trompenaars (1997) presented a similar way of classifying cultures (see Chapter 14). Furthermore, it is his avowed aim to help people in international management.

Trompenaars (1993) dealt specifically with the topic of cross-cultural management and identified seven dimensions and how they relate to cultural issues:

Dimension 1: UNIVERSALISM AND PARTICULARISM

Universalism: A universalistic corporate culture occurs when the organization shares a predominate belief that the rights of the organization prevail over the rights of a specific individual. Rules apply equally to everybody.

Particularism: In a particularistic organization the rights of individuals are seen to be more important than the rights of the larger community. General or formal rules and laws; are likely to be broken for the sake of friendship or family members, even at the cost of order within the large society.

Universalists	*Particularists*
• Strive for consistency and uniform procedures • Institute formal ways of changing the way business is conducted • Modify the system so that the system will modify you • Signal changes publicity • Seek fairness by treating all like cases in the same way	• Build informal networks and create private understanding • Try to alter informally accustomed patterns of activity • Modify relations with you so that you will modify the system • Pull levers privately • Seek fairness by treating all cases on their special merits (Trompenaars, 1993: 10)

Dimension 2: INDIVIDUALISM AND COMMUNITARIANISM

Individualism: In an individualistic organization people are expected to make their own decisions and to take care of themselves. Success in society is assumed to result from the personal freedom and individual development of its members.

Communitarianism: Members of a communitarian organization are integrated into groups which provide help and protection in exchange for a sense of loyalty.

Individualists	*Communitarians*
• Try to adjust individual needs to organizational needs • Introduce methods of individual incentives like pay-for-performance, individual assessment, managing by objectives • Expect job turnover and mobility to be high • Seek out high performers, heroes and champions for special praise	• Seek to integrate personality with authority within the group • Give attention to *esprit de corps*, morale and cohesiveness • Have low job turnover and mobility • Extol the whole group and avoid showing favouritism • Hold up superordinate goals for all to meet (Trompenaars, 1993: 16)

Dimension 3: SPECIFIC AND DIFFUSE

Specific orientation: An employee with a specific orientation can make close contact with others and knows what to share with others and what not. This helps being flexible when dealing with different people. Successes and failures are seen to result from his or her personal competencies or weaknesses.

Diffuse orientation: An employee with a diffuse orientation is less explicit in what he or she expects from relationships. Because of the reluctance to get close to others, diffusely orientated people are less likely to become socially aware or skilled. Successes and failures at work are seen as resulting from him or her being the person he or she is.

Practical Tips for Specifically and Diffusively Oriented Cultures

WHEN MANAGING AND BEING MANAGED

Specifically oriented people	*Diffusely oriented people*
• Management is the realization of objectives and standards with rewards attached • Private and business agendas are kept separate from each other • Conflicts of interest are frowned upon • Clear, precise and detailed instructions are seen as assuring better compliance, or allowing employees to dissent in clear terms • Begin reports with an executive summary	• Management is a continuously improving process by which quality improves • Private and business issues interpenetrate • Consider an employee's whole situation before you judge him or her • Ambiguous and vague instructions are seen as allowing subtle and responsive interpretations through which employees can exercise personal judgement • End reports with a concluding overview (Trompenaars, 1993: 23)

Dimension 4: NEUTRAL AND AFFECTIVE

Neutral orientation: Employees with a neutral orientation are reluctant to show what they feel, even if it involves a considerable amount of self-control. They tend to be stoical.
Affective orientation: People with an affective orientation prefer to show spontaneously how they feel and to act accordingly. They may be known for their high emotional intelligence.

Practical Tips for Neutrally and Affectively Oriented Cultures

WHEN MANAGING AND BEING MANAGED

Neutrally oriented people	*Affectively oriented people*
• Avoid warm, expressive or enthusiastic behaviour. This is interpreted as lack of control over your feelings and inconsistent with high status • If you prepare extensively beforehand, you will find it easier to "stick to the point" – that is, the neutral topics being discussed • Look for subtle indications that the person is pleased or angry and amplify their importance	• Avoid detached, ambiguous and cool demeanour. This will be interpreted as negative evaluation, as disdain, dislike and social distance. You are excluding them from "the family" • If you discover whose work, energy and enthusiasm has been invested in which projects, you are more likely to appreciate tenacious positions • Tolerate great "surfeits" of emotionality without getting intimidated or coerced and moderate their importance (Trompenaars, 1993: 20)

Dimension 5: ACHIEVEMENT AND ASCRIPTION

Achievement orientation: Social status results from the individual's success in building up a personal portfolio of success through individual effort and ability.
Ascription orientation: Social status depends on one's descent, sex, age or affluence that one somehow finds oneself with.

Practical Tips for Achievement- and Ascription-Oriented Cultures
WHEN MANAGING AND BEING MANAGED

Achievement-oriented people	*Ascription-oriented people*
• Respect for a manager is based on knowledge and skills • Management-by-objectives and pay-for-performance are effective tools • Decisions are challenged on technical and functional grounds	• Respect for a manager is based on seniority • Management-by-objectives and pay-for-performance are less effective than direct rewards from the manager • Decisions are only challenged by people with higher authority (Trompenaars, 1993: 39)

Dimension 6: TIME ORIENTATION

Subdimension 6a: TIME ORIENTATION – PAST, PRESENT, FUTURE
Past orientation: A past-oriented organization bases its future on past events.
Present and future orientation: An organization oriented towards the future cares less about past events and views the present only as the first step towards the future.

Practical Tips for Past-, Present- and Future-Oriented Cultures
TIPS FOR DOING BUSINESS WITH

Past and present-oriented people (for present- and future-oriented individuals)	*Future-oriented people (for past- and present-oriented individuals)*
• Emphasize the history, tradition and rich cultural heritage of those you deal with as evidence of their great potential • Discover whether internal relationships will sanction the kind of changes you seek to encourage • Agree future meetings in principle but do not fix deadlines for completion • Do your homework on the history, traditions of the glories of the company; consider what re-enactments you might propose	• Emphasize the freedom, opportunity and limitless scope for that company and its people in the future • Discover what core competence or continuity the company intends to carry with it into the envisaged future • Agree specific deadlines and do not expect work to be complete unless you have set such a deadline • Do your homework on the future, the prospects and the technological potentials of the company; consider mounting a sizeable challenge (Trompenaars, 1993: 39)

Subdimension 6b: TIME ORIENTATION – SEQUENTIAL AND SYNCHRONIC
Sequential orientation: Employees structuring time sequentially tend to do one thing at a time. Time is a line consisting of discrete, consecutive portions. Time is

tangible and divisible. Time commitments are taken seriously and keeping to a schedule is crucial.

Synchronic orientation: Employees who structure time synchronically do several things at the same time. Time is a wide ribbon, time is flexible and intangible. Time commitments as desirable rather than as absolute, change plans easily and place more value on the satisfactory completion of interactions with others. Promptness depends on the type of relationship in question.

Practical Tips for Sequential and Synchronically Oriented Cultures

WHEN MANAGING AND BEING MANAGED

Sequentially oriented people	*Synchronically oriented people*
• Employees feel rewarded and fulfilled by achieving planned future goals as in management-by-objectives • Employees' most recent performance is the major issue, along with whether their commitments for the future can be relied upon • Plan the career of an employee jointly with him/her, stressing landmarks to be reached by certain times • The corporate ideal is the straight line and the most direct, efficient and rapid route to your objectives	• Employees feel rewarded and fulfilled by achieving improved relationships with supervisors/customers • Employees' whole history with the company and future potential is the context in which their current performance is viewed • Discuss with the employee his/her final aspirations in the context of the company; in what ways can these be realised? • The corporate ideal is the interacting circle in which past experience, present opportunities and future possibilities interact (Trompenaars, 1993: 43)

Dimension 7: INTERNAL AND EXTERNAL

Internal orientation: Internals believe we are each captain of our ship and master of our fate. What happens to us is primarily a function of personal effort and ability.

External orientation: Externals believe their working lives are controlled by chance, luck, fate and other powerful forces.

Practical Tips for Internally and Externally Oriented Cultures

WHEN MANAGING AND BEING MANAGED

Internally oriented people	*Externally oriented people*
• Get agreement on and ownership of clear objectives • Make sure that tangible goals are clearly linked to tangible rewards • Discuss disagreements and conflict openly; these show that everyone is determined • Management-by-objectives works if everyone is genuinely committed to directing themselves towards shared objectives and if these persist	• Achieve congruence among various people's goals • Try to reinforce the current directions and facilitate the work of employees • Give people time and opportunity to quietly work through conflicts; these are distressing • Management-by-environments works if everyone is genuinely committed to adapting themselves to fit external demands as these shift (Trompenaars, 1993: 49)

Considerations for successful relocation

Inevitably, relocation transforms lives and the shock waves resulting can last for years. It is not merely the executive who is affected: his or her spouse, family, friends and work colleagues are also affected. The process begins with the offer of a relocated job, then making the decision to move, the move itself and, finally (where appropriate), either the return home or indeed another move. Relocation inevitably places stress on the family unit as it has to adjust to new roles and relationships. This also occurs when returning home to discover the loss in the desirable expatriate lifestyle. The breaking of social bonds, the feeling of loss and the requirement to restructure routine and look at the world differently are all major sources of stress.

Coyle and Shortland (1992) recommend various steps in preparation for expatriation. These include (where possible):

- A pre-move to establish such things as house prices, local schools, etc.
- Comprehensive and practical information on the country or residential town and related issues.
- Financial counselling to understand the nature of the relocation/salary package, tax implications.
- Pre-move counselling to help expatriates develop a positive attitude and think through the adaptation strategy.
- Language training for all members of the family.
- Cultural awareness training in the etiquette, norms and values of the new culture.
- Post-move counselling, often by "old hands" who show the ropes, helping with group activities and support as well as moving out into the community.

Others have written practical books for expatriates. Pascoe (1992) aimed her book specifically at the expatriate wife. She warns readers of the emotional "roller coaster" that precedes the move as well as simple but practical issues as: how, when and who to say goodbye to; how and when to meet the new boss and wife; writing wills. Readers are warned that it is not unnatural to feel resentment about the isolation and sacrifice in personal career; the absent husband; the sudden change in living standards; as well as dealing with the culture shock of other family members. She recommends developing family routines, having some familiar foods and other signs of home, learning the new language together, and sharing personal experiences of shock and disorientation.

Pascoe (1992) notes that many expatriate wives soon get bored and fall victim to the "nothing to do" syndrome. This can lead to problems with alcohol, questioning personal identity and inevitable problems in the marriage. Hypochondria is frequently a major concomitant of the bored expatriate wife. Pascoe recommends, wisely, the possibility of some type of work to give meaning, structure, money and support. She also discusses the delicate but important problem of dealing with servants, which is something of a taboo subject. Issues include losing privacy with live-in servants and how to avoid being controlled by them. One's children's relationships with servants are often a cause of stress, as is how to effectively discipline servants when necessary.

Learning the protocol and pecking order in expatriate life is clearly important, as the social network can be an important source of social support (or stress). Etiquette at dinner, cocktails and tennis parties can be most important in ensuring that they function effectively.

Wilkinson (1989) found that wives are also quite clear about the positive and negative effects of the posting for accompanying children. Positive effects included: the experience of different cultures and environments; increased tolerance of other culture and races; more time spent with the mother and often the father; greater family solidarity; a growth of confidence, independence and maturity. Negative effects included: the child misses out on extended family relationships; they sometimes lose touch with their own culture or ways of life, even (for example, with Scandinavian children being educated in "American" schools in Malaysia) their native language; they can easily become spoilt and selfish.

The literature on international management issues is comparatively recent. It is also frequently poor, being too descriptive and lacking in analytic rigour. It is often *ad hoc*, expedient and opportunistic rather than being planned. And it still retains an unfortunate air of ethnocentricity, ignoring what little other research has been done in the area. More recent work has turned to the selection and training of expatriates and managers of multicultural teams. Tung (1981) has argued that the piecemeal approach to expatriate selection and training needs to be more holistic and integrated, including area studies programmes, culture assimilator exercises, language training, sensitivity training and field experiences. Thus appraisal, compensation, selection and training need to be integrated when considering the training needs of ex- and repatriated managers.

Conclusion

Because of the relative ease and cheapness of travel, more and more people are spending a sojourn working abroad. Young people between school and university, or university and a full-time job, enjoy working in a foreign country for experience. More commonly, international and multinational companies require that their staff work at one of their many offices or plants in, what is for them, a foreign country. Although the costs to the organization are high (travel, accommodation), many believe it is good for them and their employees.

People move and work abroad for all sorts of reasons. Some are *pushed* by poverty, political instability and few educational opportunities; others are *pulled* by family, certain organizations or the promise of a better life. Students, missionaries, diplomats, business people and the military are groups that regularly "do a stint" abroad. It is possible to classify people working abroad in terms of types or along dimensions. Because of the number of subtle factors involved, it is probably more useful to describe people working abroad in terms of several factors, such as how long their spell of duty is, whether they go voluntarily and the support network available to them.

Students have an experience quite different from that of business people, who often go abroad for a shorter time, with stronger support and sponsorship, and with a more structured work schedule. Furthermore, being older and given better pre-trip training, they tend to adapt more successfully than younger students with fewer facilities.

Both students and business people experience *culture shock*, which is a multidimensional phenomenon that has been extensively considered. Because the experience of another country is a shock or surprise, it is usually but not always a negative, albeit temporary, experience. There is a rich and diverse literature on culture shock, which focuses on why certain groups suffer considerable difficulty, unhappiness and even health problems.

There is an interesting debate over the *stages* of adaptation through which the sojourner usually goes. Many people claim evidence of a U-curve, which suggests that, after initial surprise, even joy at the experience of the new way of life, people's happiness and well-being drop steadily as they learn to adapt. After a fairly long period, however, their well-being returns to initial levels and may even exceed them. The number of stages and the length and depth of the curve are, however, much debated.

As we have seen in the cross-cultural section at the end of every chapter, there are clear differences in the ways in which people from different cultures understand and behave in the business world. It is those differences in attitudes to time, negotiation styles, and so on, that cause the shock in the first place. Hence, to be most cost-efficient, organizations put considerable effort into selecting and training those sent abroad. As yet there is no very clear list of individual difference factors (such as ability to speak the language or personality) that are good predictors of adaptation success and therefore important to look for in selection. Furthermore, there is no agreement as to which method of helping sojourning expatriates is most useful. A combination of methods is probably the best, with a significant emphasis on acquiring skills.

A research perspective

Homesickness and the student

References to homesickness occur in all languages over many countries. In the eighteenth century, medical texts occasionally explained pathology in terms of homesickness. It is, of course, also experienced by people who move *within* rather than *between* countries, as they too have left their home. The key psychological features of homesickness appear to be a strong preoccupation with thoughts of home, a perceived need to go home, a sense of grief for the home (people, place and things), and a concurrent feeling of unhappiness, disease and disorientation in the new place, which, conspicuously, is not home.

In several studies, Fisher investigated the causes and correlates of homesickness (Fisher & Hood, 1987; Fisher, Murray, & Frazer, 1985). She found that 60% of her mainly native sample of students at a small Scottish university reported homesickness. To tease out the experience of the homesick versus the non-homesick, she asked them various questions, the results of which are given in Table 15.10.

She did not find age, sex or home-environment factors (i.e. city versus country) to be good predictors of homesickness. However, she did find a clear number of factors that discriminated. Compared with those who did not report homesickness, the homesick students:

- lived further from home;
- said that the university they were attending was not their first choice;
- were less satisfied with their current residence;
- were less satisfied with present, relative to past, friendships;
- expect their friendships to be better in the future than at present.

Fisher also found an association between homesickness reporting and a greater number of cognitive failures, poor concentration, handing in work late and decrements in work quality. These data suggest that homesickness is a potentially important phenomenon that may have a considerable impact on academic performance, at least over the short term.

More recently, Brewin, Furnham & Howe (1989) investigated some of the determinants of homesickness and reactions to homesickness in two samples of first-year English psychology students who had left home for the first time. Homesickness was found to be a reasonably

Table 15.10 Features utilized in definitions of homesickness and non-homesick first-year students

Feature categories from definitions provided	Frequency of reporting and percentage of subjects reporting each feature	
	Homesick (N=60) f (%)	Non-homesick (N=40) f (%)
Missing home environment: missing house, home, area etc.	18 (30.0)	16 (40.0)
Missing parents/family: longing for people at home	20 (33.3)	12 (10.0)
Missing friends; longing for friends	18 (30.0)	5 (12.5)
Feelings of loneliness	3 (5.0)	7 (17.5)
Feeling depressed	3 (5.0)	3 (7.5)
Missing someone close to talk to	4 (6.7)	1 (2.5)
Feeling insecure	3 (5.0)	2 (5.0)
Obsession with thoughts of home; thoughts about home	3 (5.0)	3 (7.5)
Feeling unhappy	1 (1.7)	3 (7.5)
Feeling unloved	2 (3.3)	1 (2.5)
Disorientation; feeling lost in new environment	2 (3.3)	1 (2.5)
A longing for familiar company and places	1 (1.7)	1 (2.5)
Thinking of the past	1 (1.7)	2 (5.0)
Feeling of not belonging	1 (1.7)	1 (2.5)
Regret that life had changed: a feeling of regret	3 (5.0)	0 (0.0)
Feeling isolated; cut off from the world	2 (3.3)	1 (2.5)
Feeling uneasy	0 (0.0)	2 (5.0)
Feeling ill	1 (1.7)	0 (0.0)
Dissatisfaction with present situation	1 (1.7)	0 (0.0)
Unable to cope	1 (1.7)	0 (0.0)
Unable to do anything	1 (1.7)	0 (0.0)
Hating the present place	0 (0.0)	1 (2.5)

The following features were endorsed by only one person in the following groups:
Homesick: thinking that home was better than here; feeling of making a mistake; sinking feeling in stomach; loss of appetite; feeling of desperation; crying.
Non-homesick: new self-reliance; feeling of desolation; feeling unsettled.

Source: Reproduced from Fisher & Hood (1987) with the permission of the British Psychological Society.

common but short-lived phenomenon, and was predicted longitudinally by greater self-reported dependency on other people and by higher estimates of the frequency of homesickness among students in general. Although homesickness was equally common in men and women, women were much more likely to discuss their feelings with others and to respond by being more affiliative. Greater anxiety and depression about homesickness were also associated with more confiding behaviour. There was a suggestion that homesick male students were more likely to seek out others the more common they perceived homesickness to be. The authors note:

> Like examination failure, homesickness appears to be a consistent source of stress to a considerable number of students, and lends itself to the testing of hypotheses about aetiology and coping behaviours. The present study has identified attitudinal precursors of homesickness that implicate attachment style and expectations about the transition to university. It has also identified large sex differences in reactions to homesickness, and has suggested that consensus beliefs may be an important determinant of confiding and affiliation among men, although they do not appear to be so among women. Further research is necessary to confirm these findings and to clarify the meaning of homesickness. For

example, although it is often assumed to be a wholly negative experience, for some individuals homesickness may represent a positive affirmation of the importance of their personal relationships rather than an unwanted interference in the transition to a new environment. (Brewin *et al.*, 1989: 476)

We need to find out more about homesickness, partly because of the costs to the happiness and functioning of the individual, but also because of the costs to organizations, particularly when very homesick people have to be repatriated.

A cross-cultural perspective

Is management science applicable internationally

A certain feature of science is external validity – the extent to which behaviours observed in one setting (organization, culture, country) can be generalized to others. Physics, physiology, zoology and biology assume, and can demonstrate, the universality of laws.

Management science as a whole is concerned with the export and import of theories. Overall, management sciences are concerned with both technical (inventory systems, linear programming, accounting procedures) and social (decision-making, leadership) systems, the former being less sensitive to cultural influences.

Rosenzweig (1994: 29–30) has argued that cultural variables have an impact on six questions in the scientific enterprise:

- *Is the definition of variables conceptually equivalent between countries?*
  If *yes*, universal generalization may be possible.
  If *no*, generalization is possible only over the range where conceptual equivalence exists.
- *Is the operationalization of variables equivalent between countries?*
  If *yes*, universal generalization may be possible.
  If *no*, generalization is possible only over the range where the operationalization of variables is equivalent.
- *Is the theorized relationship among focal variables the same across countries?*
  If *same*, universal generalization may be possible.
  If *different*, generalization is possible only over the range where theorized relationships among variables are the same.
- *Is the system closed or open?*
  If *closed*, universal generalization may be possible.
  If *open*, generalization is possible only over the range where critical features of the external environment are identical.
- *Are the data affected by observer bias?*
  If *no*, universal generalization may be possible.
  If *yes*, generalization is possible only over the range where observer behaviour is comparable.
- *Are the data affected by respondent bias?*
  If *no*, universal generalization may be possible.
  If *yes*, generalization is possible only over the range where respondent behaviour is comparable.

If our desire is to make management science as valuable as possible, it is important that we consider relevance as well as validity. It is not enough simply to ask whether the research of one country is valid in a second country; rather, it is important to begin by identifying the concerns and particular circumstances in a given country, to ask what are the most interesting and import-ant questions for study and to determine how best to study them. The question should not merely be "Are management theories that interest us valid elsewhere?", but "How can we best understand management as it exists around the world?"

As a related point, some may conclude that, precisely because of their broad validity, models of closed technical systems are the most powerful or valuable kinds of management science research to undertake. Indeed, it is tempting to infer that the broader a study's range of external validity, the stronger the claim to "truth", and therefore the greater its importance. Conversely, studies with narrowly bounded generalizability may be discounted as weak or of limited value. In fact, a study's range of generalizability and its importance are quite separate matters. A study can have broad generalizability but may be neither important nor interesting, whereas, as noted by the philosopher Kuhn, the most pressing problems of the day often do not lend themselves to high external validity. Research in management science would do well to concentrate on the most important issues of theory and of practice, keeping in mind the need for appropriate generalization, but with breadth of generalizability as a secondary objective.

If management science is to continue to make a global contribution, it must address explicitly the generalizability of research across countries.

A human resources perspective

To adapt to managing, or indeed working, abroad requires various skills, some of which can be taught. The working sojourner in a foreign country needs training in culture differences and sensitivities, political and economic awareness, language, lifestyle and health issues, as well as in the more mundane, but equally important, technical and managerial competencies to do the job. Sojourners are often faced by technical difficulties associated with attitudes to time and work. Other typical problems include:

- *Language: both vocabulary and semantics*. Although higher-order jobs often mean people share a common technical vocabulary (often in English), less skilled workers share far fewer mutually understood words. Furthermore, the meanings of words (semantics) differ subtly, so much so that even simple everyday concepts do not translate easily.
- *Psychological*. These include well-known problems, such as the selection and distortion of information as a function of preconceived ideas, as well as lack of trust and openness, jealousy, and so on.

Ratnu (1983) has come up with a very useful list (Table 15.11).

Explaining ourselves to others
In the English language at least, there are a plethora of books that attempt to explain "funny foreigners'" beliefs, behaviours and values. There are far fewer, but perhaps more interesting and important books on explaining ourselves to others.

Americans are informal, direct, but rather insular. They are keen on numbers, on planning and on packaging. In their book subtitled "A practical guide for Asians on how to succeed with US managers", Wallach and Metcalf (1995) offer simple pieces of advice to Asian business people. Consider the following:

> If an American asks a question, it is probably not a challenge to your authority or knowledge but rather an attempt to gain information. When you don't understand something or need more information, the American expects you will ask a question. (p. 42)
>
> If you are uncomfortable in a problem-solving or brainstorming session, or when asked to state your opinion in front of a group, recognize that this behaviour may be out of your comfort zone. You can build your skills in these areas through practice. Work to develop your "thinking muscles" in areas that directly affect your job performance. (p. 44)
>
> Americans will respect your privacy. They will knock before entering your office. They will ask if they can interrupt a conversation. They expect you to do the same with them. (p. 58)
>
> To be perceived as trustworthy by an American manager, do not share any information that

Table 15.11 A comparison of managers who are more able and less able to think internationally

Characteristic	More able managers	Less able managers
Personal objectives	Be able to adapt to individual people	Be able to adapt to society
Perceived requirements for successful interaction with others	No special skills are needed; effective adaptation depends on the demands of the situation	Special skills are needed such as patience, empathy, honesty, broadmindedness and flexibility
Question to ask in adapting to a new culture	What is happening? Search for descriptions, interpretations, and meanings	Why is this happening? Search for explanations and reasons
Relevant data in making decisions	Feelings and impressions are most important	Facts and information are most important
Process of analysing culturally related information	Try to describe qualitatively cultures in an attempt to differentiate between them	Try to compare quantitatively and evaluate cultures
Internal impact on the manager	Modify stereotypes and clarify impressions and interpretations	Confirm stereotypes and impressions
Behavioural impact on the manager	Socially flexible and open	Socially judgemental and withdrawn

Source: Reproduced from Ratnu (1983: 148) with the permission of M.A. Sharpe, Inc.

has been conveyed to you confidentially with anyone else, without direct permission from the person who told you. Also, never gossip or talk to colleagues at work about other colleagues. This is one of the surest ways to get into trouble in an American company. (p. 59)

Americans separate their "work life" from their "private life", that is their family and friend-ships. After working hours, they are less likely to spend time socializing with people from the office than their Asian colleagues. (p. 63)

You can do business with an American without having a strong personal relationship. In a first meeting with an American manager, start the process by clearly stating your goals and what you want to achieve. Keep the focus on these goals. At the end of the meeting, summar-ize what has been agreed upon and the next steps to be taken by both sides. This will increase the American's confidence in you. (p. 65)

Americans, particularly when under stress, may neglect the small courtesies at work, such as saying "Good morning". Americans see these as polite gestures, nice to do, but not really critical. While this may be rude and uncaring from your perspective, try to remember that such behaviour is not intended to offend you. (p. 67)

Americans may be critical of how things are done in your culture and not realize that such comments may be very offensive. Rather than become resentful, try to help the American, who may only be looking at the world through American cultural glasses, to see how your culture makes sense. (p. 60)

References

Adler, P. (1975). The transitional experience: An alternative view of culture shock. *Journal of Humanistic Psychology, 15*, 13–23.

Adler, N. (1986). *International dimensions of organizational behaviour*. Boston, MA: Kent.

Arthur, W., & Bennett, W. (1995). The international assignee: The relative importance of factors perceived to contribute to success. *Personnel Psychology, 48,* 99–114.

Aycan, Z. (1997). Expatriate adjustment as a multi-faceted phenomenon. *International Journal of Human Resource Management, 8,* 434–456.

Babiker, I., Cox, J., & Miller, P. (1980). The measurement of culture distance and its relationship to medical consultations, symptomatology, and examination performance of overseas students at Edinburgh University. *Social Psychiatry, 15,* 109–116.

Baliga, C., & Baker, J. (1985). Multinational corporate policies for expatriate managers: Selection, training, evaluation. *SAM Advanced Management Journal, 50,* 31–50.

Ball-Rokeach, S. (1973). From pervasive ambiguity to a definition of the situation. *Sociometry, 36,* 3–13.

Black, J. (1988). Work role transitions: A study of American expatriate managers in Japan. *Journal of International Business Studies, 19,* 277–294.

Black, J. (1992). Socializing American expatriate managers overseas. *Group and Organization Management, 17,* 171–192.

Black, J., & Gregerson, H. (1991). Antecedents to cross-cultural adjustment for expatriates in Pacific rim assignments. *Human Relations, 44,* 497–515.

Black, J., Gregersen, H., & Mendenhall, M. (1992). *Global assignments.* San Francisco, CA: Jossey-Bass.

Black, J., Mendenhall, M., & Oddon, E. (1991). Toward a comprehensive model of international adjustment. *Academy of Management Review, 16,* 291–317.

Bochner, S. (1982). The social psychology of cross-cultural relations. In S. Bochner (Ed.), *Cultures in contact: Studies in cross-cultural interaction* (pp. 5–44). Oxford: Pergamon Press.

Bochner, S., Lin, A., & McLeod, B. (1980). Cross-cultural contact and the development of an international perspective. *Journal of Social Psychology, 107,* 29–41.

Bock, P. (Ed.) (1970). *Culture shock: A reader in modern anthropology.* New York: Knopf.

Bores, K., & Rothstein, M. (2002). Managers' interest in intercultural assignments: The role of work and career satisfaction. *International Journal of Intercultural Relations, 26,* 233–253.

Brett, J. (1982). Job transfer and well-being. *Journal of Applied Psychology, 67,* 450–467.

Brett, J., Stroh, L., & Reilly, A. (1993). Pulling up roots in the 1990's. *Journal of Organizational Behaviour, 14,* 49–60.

Brewin, C., Furnham, A., & Howe, M. (1989). Demographic and psychological determinants of homesickness and confiding among students. *British Journal of Psychology, 80,* 467–477.

Brewster, C. (1991). *The management of expatriates.* London: Kogan Page.

Brislin, R. (1979). Orientation programs for cross-cultural preparation. In A. Marsella, R. Thorpe, & I. Ciborowski (Eds.), *Perspectives on cross-cultural psychology* (pp. 137–174). New York: Academic Press.

Byrnes, F. (1966). Role shock: An occupational hazard of American technical assistants abroad. *Annals of the American Academy of Political and Social Science, 368,* 95–108.

Church, A. (1982). Sojourner adjustment. *Psychological Bulletin, 91,* 540–572.

Cleveland, H., Mangone, G., & Adams, J. (1960). *The overseas Americans.* New York: McGraw-Hill.

Copeland, A., & Norell, S. (2002). Spousal adjustment of international assignments: The role of social support. *International Journal of Intercultural Relations, 26,* 255–271.

Coyle, W., & Shortland, S. (1992). *International relocation.* London: Butterworth.

David, K. (1971). Culture shock and the development of self-awareness. *Journal of Contemporary Psychotherapy, 4,* 44–48.

Ellis, R., & Whittington, D. (1981). *A guide to social skills training.* London: Croom Helm.

Fisher, S., & Hood, B. (1987). The stress of the transition to university: A longitudinal study of psychological disturbance, absent-mindedness and vulnerability to homesickness. *British Journal of Psychology, 78,* 425–441.

Fisher, C., & Shaw, J. (1994). Relocation attitudes and adjustment: A longitudinal study. *Journal of Organizational Behaviour, 15*, 209–222.

Fisher, S., Murray, K., & Frazer, N. (1985). Homesickness, health and efficiency in first year students. *Journal of Environmental Psychology, 5*, 181–195.

Forster, N. (1994). The forgotten employees? The experiences of expatriate staff returning to the UK. *International Journal of Human Resource Management, 5*, 405–425.

Forster, N. (1997). The persistent myth of high expatriate failure rates. *International Journal of Human Resource Management, 8*, 414–433.

Furnham, A., & Bochner, S. (1986). *Culture shock*. London: Methuen

Galting, J. (1981). Structure, culture, and intellectual style. *Social Science Information, 6*, 817–856.

Gaw, K. (2000). Reverse culture shock in students returning from overseas. *International Journal of Intercultural Relations, 24*, 83–104.

Glenn, E., Witmeyer, D., & Stevenson, N. (1984). Culture systems of persuasion. *International Journal of International Relations, 1*, 52–66.

Gregersen, H., & Stroh, L. (1997). Coming home to the arctic cold. *Personnel Psychology, 50*, 635–654.

Gudykunst, W. (1983). Toward a typology of stranger–host relationships. *International Journal of Intercultural Relations, 7*, 401–413.

Gullahorn, J., & Gullahorn, J. (1963). An extension of the U-curve hypotheses. *Journal of Social Issues, 19*, 33–47.

Guthrie, G. (1975). A behavioural analysis of culture learning. In R. Brislin, S. Bochner, & W. Lonner (Eds.), *Cross-cultural perspectives on learning* (pp. 95–1150). New York: Wiley.

Guzzo, R., Noonan, K., & Elron, E. (1994). Expatriate managers and the psychological contract. *Journal of Applied Psychology, 79*, 617–626.

Hall, E. (1959). *The silent language*. New York: Doubleday.

Harris, P., & Moran, R. (1991). *Managing cultural differences*. Houston, TX: Gulf Publishing.

Harvey, M. (1989). Repatriation of corporate executives: An empirical study. *Journal of International Business Studies, 20*, 131–144.

Harvey, M., Novicevic, M., & Kiessling, T. (2002). Development of multiple IQ maps for use in the selection of inpatriate managers: A practical theory. *International Journal of Intercultural Relations, 26*, 493–524.

Hays, R. (1972). *International business: An introduction to the world of the firm*. Englewood Cliffs, NJ: Prentice-Hall.

Hilltop, J.-M., & Janssen, M. (1995). Expatriation: Challenges and recommendations. In T. Jackson (Ed.), *Cross-cultural management* (pp. 141–160). London: Butterworth-Heinemann.

Hofstede, G. (1980). *Culture's consequences*. Beverly Hills, CA: Sage.

Hofstede, G. (1983). National cultures in four dimensions. *International Studies of Management and Organization*, Spring/Summer, pp. 335–355.

Hui, C. (1992). Values and attitudes. In R. Westwood (Ed.), *Organizational behaviour: Southeast Asian perspective* (pp. 63–90). Hong Kong: Longman.

Janssen, M. (1995). Intercultural interaction: A burden on international managers. *Journal of Organizational Behaviour, 16*, 155–167.

Kramer, M. (1993). Communication and uncertainty reduction during job transfers. *Communication Monographs, 60*, 178–198.

Lanier, A. (1979). Selecting and preparing personnel for overseas transfers. *Personnel Journal, 58*, 160–163.

Lunstedt, S. (1963). An introduction to some evoking problems in cross-cultural research. *Journal of Social Issues, 19*, 1–9.

Lysgaard, S. (1955). Adjustment in a foreign society: Norwegian Fulbright grantees visiting the United States. *International Social Science Bulletin, 7*, 45–51.

Martin, R. (1995). The effects of prior moves on job relocation stress. *Journal of Occupational and Organizational Psychology, 68*, 49–56.

Martin, R. (1996). A longitudinal study examining the psychological reactions of job relocation. *Journal of Applied Social Psychology, 26*, 265–282.

May, R. (1970). The nature of anxiety and its relation to fear. In A. Elbing (Ed.), *Behavioural decisions in organizations* (pp. 43–60). New York: Scott, Foresman.

McDonald, G. (1993). ET go home? The successful management of expatriate transfers. *Journal of Managerial Psychology, 8*, 18–29.

Mendenhall, M., Dunbar, E., & Oddon, G. (1987). Expatriate selection: Training and career-patting. *Human Resource Management, 26*, 331–346.

Mumford, D. (1998). The measurement of culture shock. *Social Psychiatry and Psychiatric Epidemiology, 33*, 149–154.

Nash, D. (1967). The fact of Americans in a Spanish setting: A study of adaption. *Human Organization, 26*, 3–17.

Oberg, K. (1960). Culture shock: Adjustment to new cultural environments. *Practical Anthropology, 7*, 177–182.

Pascoe, R. (1992). *Culture shock! Successful living abroad: A wife's guide*. Singapore: Singapore Times.

Ratnu, I. (1983). Thinking internationally. *International Studies of Management and Organization, 6*, 148–156.

Rosenzweig, P. (1994). When can management science research be generalized internationally? *Management Science, 40*, 28–35.

Schein, E. (1978). *Career dynamics: Matching individual and organizational needs*. Reading, MA: Addison-Wesley.

Sievenking, N., Anchor, K., & Marston, R. (1981). Selecting and preparing expatriate employees. *Personnel Journal, 18*, 197–202.

Smalley, W. (1963). Culture shock, language shock, and the shock of self-discovery. *Practical Anthropology, 10*, 49–56.

Smith, P., & Bond, M. (1998). *Social psychology across cultures*. London: Prentice-Hall.

Spreitzer, G., McCall, M., & Mahoney, J. (1997). Early identification of international executive potential. *Journal of Applied Psychology, 82*, 6–29.

Stokols, D., & Shumaker, S. (1982). The psychological context of residential mobility and well-being. *Journal of Social Issues, 38*, 149–170.

Stone-Fernstein, E., & Ward, C. (1990). Loneliness and psychological adjustment of sojourners. In D. Keats, D. Munro, & C. Mann (Eds.), *Heterogeneity in cross-cultural psychology* (pp. 537–547). Lisse: Swats & Zeitlinger.

Stoner, J., Aram, J., & Rubin, J. (1972). Factors associated with effective performance in overseas work assignments. *Personnel Psychology, 25*, 303–318.

Tayeb, M. (1996). Organizations and national culture: Methodology considered. *Organizational Studies, 15*, 429–446.

Torbiorn, I. (1982). *Living abroad: Personal adjustment and personnel policy in the overseas setting*. Chichester, UK: Wiley.

Triandis, H. (1994). *Culture and social behavior*. New York: McGraw-Hill.

Trompenaars, F. (1993). *Riding the waves of culture: Understanding cultural diversity in business*. London: Nicholas Brealey.

Trompenaars, F. (1997). *The better business guide to international management*. Amsterdam: Intercultural Management Publishers.

Tung, R. (1981). Selection and training of personnel for overseas assignments. *Columbia Journal of World Business, 16*, 66–68.

Van Oudenhoven, J. (2001). Do organizations reflect national cultures? A 10 nation study. *International Journal of Intercultural Relations, 25*, 89–101.

Van Oudenhoven, J., Van der See, K., & Van Kooten, M. (2001). Successful adaptation strategies according to expatriates. *International Journal of Intercultural Relations, 25*, 467–482.

Wallach, J., & Metcalf, E. (1995). *Working with Americans*. Singapore: McGraw-Hall.

Ward, C., Bochner, S., & Furnham, A. (2001). *The psychology of culture shock*. London: Routledge.

Watson, W., Johnson, L., & Zgourides, G. (2002). The influence of ethnic diversity on leadership, group processes and performance. *International Journal of Intercultural Relations, 26*, 1–16.

Westman, M., & Etzion, D. (2002). The impact of short overseas business trips on job stress and burnout. *Applied Psychology, 51*, 582–592.

Wilkinson, J. (1989). *Expatriate families in Malaysia*. HRRC Working Paper, Cranfield School of Management.

Zuckerman, M. (1979). *Sensation seeking: Beyond the optimal level of arousal*. Chichester, UK: Wiley.

16 The future of work

Introduction

If the nature of work changes as a function of the developments in technology, the economic conditions (e.g. oil shortage, inflation, etc.) or the way society is ordered, it will inevitably have profound effects on the way organizations are structured and how they operate. Consider the dramatic rise in e-commerce and the effect of buying and selling on individuals. Medical and political changes can also have massive impacts on the world of work. One epidemiological phenomenon to profoundly affect work in some Third World countries is AIDS. Porteous (1997) has shown how AIDS has had significant consequences in both developed countries (through insurance) and developing countries (through productivity).

Some commentators believe we are going to see more changes in the world of work in the next 20 years than we have seen in the last 10,000 years. The idea of a stable job in a local community with set tasks perhaps dictated by the seasons will be replaced my nomadic workers, working on line all hours of the day for many different customers, clients and bosses. The new workers will have to be educated, highly literate and with lots of "soft" skills around communication, influencing and self-management. Their boss will not be a score-keeper or supervisor but a leader and a coach. They will, in any case, have to be more attentive to their customers than their boss. They will work in teams rather than departments and be paid not for their attendance but their output.

They will in every sense be knowledge workers in an unwired world. They might work for a company that has no CEO, no head office, even no IT facility and whose major asset is its reputation. They will be digital nomads working in data hotels located in high-technology archipelagos. As a result, they will have to be self-motivated and reliant. They will have to manage their own career portfolios and work out their own work–life balance.

According to Crainer (1996), there are several key drivers behind globalization: communication and manufacturing technology; cost savings and the use of worldwide homogeneous markets. All aspects of a company – research and development, purchasing, production, marketing and distribution/sales – can benefit from globalization. We have seen the rise of global brands and with them the rise of the global workforce, which requires careful management. There are, however, worries about globalization and a backlash against some of the implications of it. Capital, technology and know-how move quickly from country to country seeking workers and sites that command the lowest prices.

Casio (2003) has noted eight shifts in the psychological contract at work: from stability and predictability to change and uncertainty; from work permanence to temporariness; from standard work patterns to flexible work; from valuing loyalty to valuing performance and skills; from paternalism at work to self-reliance; from job security to employment security; from linear (same) career growth to multiple careers; and from one-time learning to life-long learning. He also notes the importance of attempts of companies to retain young, talented mobile workers. The new workplace is fast, global and virtual. In the new world of work, flexibility and change are strengths. People are networked, interdependent and integrated more than they were in the past. Leaders have to be more inspirational and less dogmatic because information and influence flow up as much as down within an organization.

Even practical books for managers start with what is changing in the world of work, though they can become dated very quickly. Pell (1995) noted seven important changes: flatter organizational structures; greater participative decision-making; greater use of teamwork; more total project management; greater outsourcing; the just-in-time delivery idea; and re-engineering. In 1998, the Henley Centre – a dedicated forecasting centre – made predictions about work. Their predictions were about a number of specific work-related issues and, being more recent and more data-based, are probably more useful:

- *Working hours.* They believe people will have a shorter working day (5 hours = 25 hours per week) but that many businesses will be open 24 hours a day. People will work three- to four-day weeks, the remaining time will be absorbed by leisure and community work.
- *Travel.* Their vision is one of rail renaissance and privatized automated roads: "we might go to work in our solar-powered, eco-friendly, self-driving car along privatized roads employing automated highway systems which control the speed and direction of the car. Congestion should be a thing of the past as the on-board global positioning system automatically redirects and navigates . . . The longest commuter journey will be just under two hours, mainly for the wealthy using the space shuttle (to travel outside the world's atmosphere and back again) to Sydney or San Francisco" (Barclays Life, 1998: 12–13).
- *Communication.* Personal computers will become all the more powerful: "virtual glasses receiving wireless digital video will enable us to talk and see anybody in the world whilst still on the move" (Barclays Life, 1998: 13). Yet they do not believe there will be information overload.
- *Home working.* They argue that a quarter of all people will work from home and that 10% of top companies will be virtual companies, which will be very flat organizations.
- *Careers.* They acknowledge little job tenure, and therefore the need for precautionary saving for no-work periods. "There will also be vast armies of self-employed, stimulated by the on-line world and the ease with which the next generation internet matches the supply and demand for funds to start up businesses" (Barclays Life, 1998: 12).

The Henley Centre argue that the most likely scenario for the year 2020, specifically in the UK, is characterized by some fluctuation in economic cycles. They believe real incomes will have increased by over 40% compared with those we currently enjoy, but that those disposable income gains will be absorbed by "personal welfare" costs that cover health, education and pensions. Globalization, they feel, may undermine the national tax base because of "footloose companies" and electronic commerce. On a more negative note, they speculate about permanent labour market uncertainty, strains on social cohesion and a widening skills imbalance, based on education and high unemployment. They also believe that a widening income distribution may force an electoral backlash and a limited increase in higher tax rates.

Finally, they note that there are both "drivers" and "constraints" to the whole business of globalization. They believe there are eight factors that are likely to increase the pace of globalization: increasing affluence, the removal of trade barriers, the triumph of capitalism over communism, innovations in transport, the well-recorded evolution in communications, the powerful role of international finance, changes in corporate restructuring and exchange rate volatility. On the other hand, they list half-a-dozen factors that are likely to constrain the movement to globalization: the trade impact on welfare costs, nationalist sentiments, government needs for structure, religious fundamentalism, protectionist politics and the lack of economic convergence between particular countries.

There is considerable agreement on the *globalization* of marketing, manufacturing, research and development, support services, as well as management infrastructures. There seems to be a strong trend for the strengthening of cross-border links to create greater coherence. There is also agreement about the widespread effect of computer technology in the "information age". The information superhighway, virtual reality machines and widespread electronic link-up between all people in the community means that fewer people will need to "go to work" and instead will work from home. Some speculators believe that large company head offices will close as fewer people will need to journey to work. It is difficult to over-estimate the impact of information and communication technology on the future of work. People all over the world are being asked to work in teams. Because of the nature of modern work tasks (see Chapter 5), multi-skilling and cross-functional teams, more and more workers are becoming interdependent on each other.

Most speculators believe that increases in population and automation will mean a decrease in the amount of actual work to be done. There are various ways in which one might create jobs under these conditions, such as banning overtime, implementing a shorter working week or a shorter working life, or splitting jobs into part-time jobs. Whereas automation may lead to the elimination of routine, dirty, dangerous and physically strenuous jobs, it may also de-skill those craft people with specialist skills. Thus, automation will empower some, such as computer specialists, but render others powerless and redundant. Hence, people may opt for more self-employment in the black or grey economy (Argyle, 1989).

Optimism and pessimism

Those who portend, presage and prophesy the future clearly fall into two groups. On the one hand, naïve, enthusiastic *optimists* paint a glowing picture of the future where technology liberates one from drudgery. Many dirty, dangerous and degrading jobs, they argue, will be done by machines, which will increase the intrinsic job satisfaction of many workers. More cautious and considered optimists see a cost to the change in jobs. The cost is twofold: first the good life will be available only to those in wealthy, developed countries; and second, it will often be at the cost of social factors – a less cohesive society, an increase in loneliness, and so on.

On the other hand, sceptical, cynical *pessimists* see technology as alienating and perceive the speed of change as unnecessary. They see a trade-off between speed and quality and a growing schism in previously coherent societies between the "haves" (with skills, knowledge, jobs) and the "have nots" (without all of the above). They feel the virtual organization of teleworkers is a poor substitute for the camaraderie of office gossip, contact with staff and the opportunity to use one's talents.

Optimism, not pessimism, about the future sells. One has only to look at the business section of bookshops to see this. They are full of "one-minute-manager, secrets of highly successful people techniques". They maintain that human behaviour (of employees) is easily changeable and that good managers have the ability to control it. They stress the power of technology and techniques that have an immediate short-term pay-off.

Enthusiasts are engineering technocrats. They believe that they invent technology, but it often invents us. The invention of technology created the suburbs, computers and the possibility of virtual companies. We cannot always see the result of the technology, but optimistic soothsayers think they can.

Pessimists stress the costs of change and those who will not benefit from it. They know that human behaviour and human needs have not changed much over the millennia and do not see how smart computers make much difference. They are often social scientists who know how difficult it is to change people.

Handy (1995) argued a decade ago that those in work will work harder – longer hours for instance – and more people will be outside the orthodox employment categories. There will be less work to go around, but it will be more specialist and technical, and therefore there will be fewer people qualified to do it. Those in work will be well rewarded and those out of work much less so, creating a more unequal society.

But optimists point out that these changes may herald an opportunity to create better working conditions, such as: more varied and meaningful work; more freedom to choose the pace of working conditions; reduced stress; better incentives, such as pay, promotion and security; the formation of small, happy, functional cohesive groups and more humane organizational structures with more decentralization, fewer hierarchical levels and reduced role conflict.

Researchers in this area tend to list the changes they expect. These include:

- Changes in the workforce in terms of *cultural diversity, skill, experience and expectations*, which probably differ significantly from one country to another.
- Changes in *customer expectations*, which normally means a rise in the quality and reliability of products, and the excellence of service demanded.
- Changes in the *size, structure and international focus of companies*, and the managers needed to run them. Economics, legal, social and competitive forces mean that companies have to adapt, reinvent themselves and re-engineer simply to survive, let alone prosper.
- Changes in *economic conditions* governed by new inventions (the electronic revolution), raw materials (the exhaustion of certain assets) and political cooperation and competition (e.g. the European Union).

Forecasting

Forecasting the future is a difficult business, as the following quotes show:

> This telephone has too many shortcomings . . . as a means of communication . . . the device is inherently of no value. (Western Union internal memo, 1876)

> The light bulb . . . unworthy of the attention of practical or scientific men. (British Parliamentary Committee, 1883)

> Heavier than air flying machines are impossible. (Lord Kelvin, President, The Royal Society, 1895)

> I think there is a world market for maybe five computers. (Thomas Watson, Chairman of IBM, 1943)

> Space travel is utter bilge. (Richard Riet Woolley, British Astronomer Royal, 1956)

> There is no reason for any individuals to have a computer in their home. (Ken Olsen, President and Founder of Digital Equipment Corporation, 1977)

> Everything that can be invented has been invented. (US Office of Patents, 1899)

> Airplanes are interesting toys but of no military power. (Marshal Foch, Professor of Strategy, Ecole Superieure de Guerre, undated)

> Who the hell wants to hear actors talk? (Harry Warner, Warner Bros, 1927)

But there are some obvious things that have changed at work, such as:

1   The way we think about:
    –   ourselves at work
    –   our boss, colleagues
    –   our customers
    –   our shareholders
2   The expectations of customers.
3   The speed, openness and cheapness of communication.
4   The cost, shelf-life, size and portability of technology.
5   Our use of time.
6   The working life in a time of greater longevity.
7   Globalization of workforce and markets.

Individuals are now faced with new pressures and changes, including:

* No more jobs for life: change of emphasis from being employed to being employable.
* Job security based on performance: individuals need to take responsibility for their own learning.
* Greater global competition: greater speed of reaction, reducing product life-cycles, increasing focus on core business and delivery.
* Recruitment: reducing permanent workforce; 41% of today's workforce is temporary/contract.

Naturally, there have been business responses to these changes:

* Continual reorganization of various divisions.

- Subcontracting to other non-core services and operations.
- Developing good relationships with key constituencies.
- Streamlining and rationalizing processes (process engineering).
- Subscribing to continuous improvement of processes.
- Creating flatter structures.
- Creating more teamwork.
- Developing core competencies.
- Recognizing workforce diversity.
- Creating a flexible workforce.
- Acknowledging the end of the era.
- "Empowering" people at work.
- Promoting the concept of the manager as a facilitator and coordinator.
- Recognizing a need for employees to continually update their knowledge and skills.

In their book *Tomorrow's Office*, Raymond and Cunliffe (2000) sketch out why changes in business have to be reflected in changes in the office (see Figure 16.1).

Future shock – the discomfort experienced in times of continual and uncertain change – is a characteristic of the modern office. The *global economy* means a global workforce, with all the competition and cultural issues which that involves. As a result, *human rights in the workplace* are asserted, as there is increasing pressure for employee (rather than employer) rights and for equality of opportunity. The development of the *information technologies* makes data analysis easier and decisional power greater while both creating some new jobs and making others unnecessary. In fact, it has been proposed that what we shall see more often in the future is a *contingency* of permanent temporary employees. These are people hired (for their skills) to perform a temporary role caused by unexpected or temporary changes in the outside world.

Perhaps most importantly, the new workplace has meant more organizational transitions (Schermerhorn, Hunt, & Osborn, 1994). What many organizations are trying to instill in their members are new values, including the following:

- It is customers, not your boss, who pay your salary, so keep them happy.
- All jobs depend on the value they create, so if new ideas and working practices are apparent, it is important to try them to see if they add value.
- Accept personal ownership of problems and share in solving them rather than pass them up or down.
- Everyone is part of a team: a good manager builds a cooperative team, not a large empire.
- Because the future is uncertain, constant learning is the key to success.

Some have talked of the *virtual organization* (Davidow & Malone, 1993). This is a temporary alliance or network based on specific interests – partnerships based on electronic linkage and core competencies. In these new workplaces, managers are seen as helpers, trainers and supporters, not controllers.

Certainly, the *quality of work life* (QWL) is becoming a very important issue that will probably intensify. This is concerned with participation, trust and responsiveness. What QWL writers mention is that more and more employees want greater participation in management decisions; more sensitivity to family (extracurricular) issues, a more equitable sharing of the wealth, and a feeling that the workplace is a desirable place to be.

MORAL
corporate ethos + self interest
formal hierarchy (West) + intimate hierarchy (East)
exploiting natural resources → conserving natural resources
exploiting the workforce → nurturing the workforce
personal responsibilities → personal rights

ECONOMIC
competition + collaboration
maximum profit → sustainable success
growth (quantitative) → growth (qualitative)
protectionism + global sourcing

outputs → outcomes
work = place → work = person
cost reduction → revenue generation
competence → excellence
stockpiles → just-in-time

confrontation → partnership
military model → jazz ensemble
line management + project management
permanent hierarchy + project team
doubting people → trusting people

inner cities → surburban centres
producer orientation → consumer orientation   *BUSINESS*
local general markets → global niche markets
regional competition → global competition

status → equality
vertical structure → horizontal structure
nose to the grindstone + eyes on the horizon
corporate paternalism → individualism
controlling → leading

job security → outsourcing
who you know (old boy net) → who you know who knows (networking)
doing things right (efficiency)   → doing the right things (effectiveness)

SOCIO-POLITCAL
male ethos → gender spectrum
half a century of peace → terrorism and civil war
unions of nations (Europe) + tribal loyalties (Bosnia)
change for change sake + change fatigue
'stiff upper lip' → litigiousness and protest

KNOWLEDGE AND EDUCATION
know-all + know-nots
left brain (logical thought) + right brain (intuitive thought)
learning curve (acquisition) + forgetting curve (letting go)
growth of knowledge + knowledge obsolescence
college education + continuing education

TECHNOLOGY
private office → mobile working
city centre skyscraper + home office
commuting (person to workplace) + telecommuting (information to person)
face to face meetings + video-conferencing

Figure 16.1 Polarities of change as they affect business. From Yesterday to Tomorrow change can be both/and (shown as +) or from/to (shown as →). Reprinted with permission from Taylor and Francis.

Focus has moved from the *legal contract* people sign when taking a job, to the *psychological contract* between employer and employee. A legal contract is a written document covering such things as pay, hours and vacation. A *psychological* contract is a set of expectations held by individuals specifying what the individual and organization expect to give and receive from each other in the full course of the working relationship.

These psychological contracts take many forms – they tend to be long, open-ended and dynamic, and take into consideration diffuse responsibilities. Whether they have ever thought of it or not, most employees have some sort of psychological contract with their employer. The problem with having these rather vague, implicit contracts is that the employer may not know when he or she has broken the contract. The hurt, alienation and perception of deep injustice by the employee may be the result (Parks & Kidder, 1994). It may well be, in the organization of the future, that both employer and employee will discuss more openly and explicitly the psychological contract between them.

Many observers have suggested that all organizations go through cycles (see Table 16.1). Indeed, it may be possible that whole industries, and the regions that depend on them, go through similar predictable cycles. In this sense, it may be possible to make fairly accurate predictions about the future, given that we know where we are in the cycle. Table 16.1 shows the "typical" pattern of an organization. It may well be that whole sectors of the economy go through similar cycles of growth and decay.

What are organizations trying to achieve? Clearly, they have several goals. All must and do have *economic* goals – concerned with the production of goods and services. They also have *sociocultural* goals concerned with supporting a particular type of society.

Organizations have general and specific goals. Most are in the business of satisfying all their *stakeholders' interests* (employees, shareholders, customers, owners, etc.). They are concerned with the *output of goods and services* and with *efficiency or profitability*, whichever is the more relevant. They have goals regarding development, growth and *investment in long-term viability*. They also have more mundane but extremely important production, inventory, sales, market-share, profit and operational targets or goals.

At the most fundamental level, organizations strive to stay in existence. They have to monitor and adapt to changes in their workforce, customers and products. Most want not only to change and adapt but to influence the future – to be the first innovator. In doing so, they often need to do strategic planning, which means gathering information to help to decide between future likely alternatives for structuring and managing an organization.

Obviously, some changes can be planned and anticipated, but sometimes they are thrust upon the organization. Furthermore, the changes may be internal or external to the organization. Thus, *planned internal change* may be about products or services, or the structure and size of the organization. *Planned external change* may be about the introduction of new technologies or communication patterns as a function of new products on the market and the behaviour of competitors. *Unplanned internal change* may concern the changing of employee demographics with the organizational

Table 16.1 Summary model of the organizational life-cycle

Entrepreneurial stage	*Collectivity stage*	*Formalization and control stage*	*Elaboration of structure stage*
Marshalling of resources	Informal communication and structure	Formalization of rules	Elaboration of structure
Lots of ideas	Sense of collectivity	Stable structure	Decentralization
Entrepreneurial activities	Long hours spent	Emphasis on efficiency and structure	Domain expansion
Little planning and co-ordination	Sense of mission	Conservatism	Adaptation
Formation of a "niche"	Innovation continues	Institutional procedures	Renewal
"Prime mover" has power		High commitment	

Reprinted by permission of Quinn & Cameron (1983).

workforce being older and with a greater proportion of females and ethnic minorities than before. Finally, organizations have to cope with *unplanned external change* in such things as new government regulations and increased external competition from foreign countries (Greenberg & Baron, 1995).

The changing nature of work

Frese (2000) warns that forecasts about the changing nature of work are often wrong or the speed of change specified is incorrect. But he also observed that small changes/developments can have enormous effects. There are also counter-movements against trends which can have a significant impact. Despite the fact that both human beings and organizations are conservative, changes do occur. Frese lists nine trends:

1   *Dissolution of the unit of work in time and space*: The internet has meant many people can work anywhere at any time. Not everyone likes teleworking and forms of it are illegal, but it continues to grow. There are, however, limitations to telework: problems of coordination; changes in communication; reduced commitment; information overload. But the old idea of a 9 to 5 job in the office is clearly on the wane.

2   *A faster rate of innovation*: There are greater pressures on rewards of innovation in a global market. Some innovations are done by groups, others by individuals incentivized to innovate both processes and products at work. One of the greatest pressures to innovate is the need to adapt to new conditions. Furthermore, organizations have to learn *and* support learning: they realize they need to reward curiosity and experimentalism.

3   *The increased complexity of work*: Factors that cause increased complexity are the need for customization and environmental turbulence. The workforce needs to be more intelligent than in the past to cope. This will leave an increasingly less-employable, semi- or unskilled workforce, which could cause social disruption. Attempts to solve the problem include inducing companies to employ these people, state-supported education, as well as training in self-esteem and self-efficacy.

4   *Global competition*: The web, the European Union and a fall in the cost of travel means that individuals have to compete for jobs with others all over the world. Highly paid workers in developed countries have to be more reliable, up-to-date, pro-active, creative and skilful to hope to compete with their competitors from developing countries. Companies will have to stimulate the self-reliance and initiative of their staff. They will also need to encourage international cooperation. Unions will need to adapt and find better ways to ensure justice in organizations.

5   *Development of larger and smaller units*: At the same time that organizations are getting bigger because of mergers and acquisitions, within organizations units are becoming smaller. Smaller units are thought to be more flexible and efficient. Being big helps with the economics of scale but can become bureaucratic.

6   *Changing job and career concepts*: The fad for re-engineering in the 1990s saw a large reduction in jobs of all kinds. Companies often outsource to specialists. Also, in some companies employees are assigned to a project (team) rather than a job. Thus for individuals the concept of employability is all important. Yet inevitably they will be less committed to, and identify with less strongly, an organization they will not work for long. People will have to become more entrepreneurial and more

strategic with regard to their own careers. Career advice and mentoring thus become important throughout life.

7   *More teamwork*: Groupwork is becoming more common and important for five reasons: production responsibility is given back to the shop floor where team decisions have to be made; new production methods do not have supervising personnel; job complexity increases the need for coordinated efforts; interdisciplinary work requires greater efforts to understand each other; teams deal with turbulence better than individuals. Teamwork requires such social skills as perceptiveness, emotional regulation and empathy.

8   *Reduced supervision*: Many factors have led to the reduction in supervisory roles and responsibilities: more personal responsibility for production, standardization, greater professionalism and more enriched, satisfying tasks. However, the functions of traditional supervisors should not be forgotten, which include monitoring, implementing changes and maintaining the corporate culture.

9   *Increased cultural diversity*: Increased migration and changes in the demographic profile of the workforce have led to much greater diversity at work.

Thus according to Frese (2000), the jobs of the future differ from those of the past by showing a greater degree of learning by oneself, working in groups, communication with co-workers, interdisciplinary work and self-determination. Workers will need to show more self-reliance, personal initiative, entrepreneurship and professionalism.

Alternative work arrangements

Armstrong-Stassen (1998) focused on five developments at work called "alternative work arrangements". For each form she helpfully examines the definition and form of these alternative arrangements, their prevalence and predicted future status (exclusively in Canada) and the challenges they provide.

- *Part-time employment*, defined as working less than 30 hours per week. These jobs can be very varied and may be distinguished as permanent versus casual, good versus bad, voluntary versus involuntary. Nearly one-quarter of jobs in Canada fell into this category. They clearly provide real challenges, which include establishing policies, practices and procedures for part-timers with their preferred work status if possible; promoting part-time work as a legitimate alternative to full-time work; and promoting part-time work for older workers.
- *Contingent employment*, defined as when an individual is working for an organization but is not considered a regular employee. These include temporary, casual and technical contingent workers. For Armstrong-Stassen (1998), there are three specific challenges for this group: designing new ways of managing and motivating contingent workers; providing equitable treatment of contingent-workers; and protecting their interests.
- *Flextime*, defined as when employees vary their starting and quitting times but are required to work a standard number of hours within a specific time period. Around a quarter of Canadians reported having these arrangements, which most appeared to like and see as a stress reliever. Challenges noted included: establishing selection and eligibility criteria and successful implementation procedures; promoting the use of flextime; and ensuring its compatibility with other organization initiatives.

- *Compressed work weeks*, defined as reallocating the work time by condensing the total hours in the traditional five-day work week into fewer days. This is popular, though its effects on productivity are unknown. Four challenges are specified: identifying jobs that are appropriate for compressed work weeks; identifying which compressed work week form is best; preparing employees for compressed work weeks; and preparing managers and supervisors to manage these workers.
- *Teleworking*, defined as working at a location away from the traditional place of work, full- or part-time, and involving the use of telecommunications and the electronic processing of information. Again four challenges of this working type are identified: ensuring a supportive environment; identifying jobs that are appropriate for teleworking; establishing selection procedures and eligibility criteria; and training both telemanagers and teleworkers.

Armstrong-Stassen believes there are other general applied academic challenges, such as developing an integrative, conceptual model to help us understand the processes underlying alternative work arrangements. She argues researchers "should take a more proactive role in the planning, implementation and evaluation phases of these alternative work arrangements. I-O psychologists can be instrumental in making policy-makers, top management, employees, and union leaders aware of the potential benefits as well as the possible drawbacks of a particular work arrangement" (Armstrong-Stassen, 1998: 119).

The development of technology has led to the possibility of teleworkers working from home, in what is called the *electronic cottage* (Holland & Hogan, 1999). While some are extremely enthusiastic about the benefits of this new working arrangement, other have been much more cautious (Cascio, 1998; Holland & Hogan, 1999).

The concept of *work-life balance* is increasingly coming to the fore. It is in many ways an unfortunate term. The opposite of work is not life, but could be leisure or home-life. It refers to the stresses and strains caused by a lack of equilibrium between work-related tasks and non-worked related tasks like maintaining family relationships. The tired, irritable worker makes a bad parent, and partner. Thus instead of finding social and emotional support in the home they bring only friction and thus return to work unrested and often frustrated. Thus we have a vicious cycle where work pressures cause relationship pressures which impact on work.

Every employer wants a happy, healthy, loyal and engaged work-force. They want healthy, not unhealthy, job turn-over and they want to keep their best workers. All employers want committed and engaged staff who identify with the goals, values and products of the organization, staff that are interested and involved; staff that are loyal with a genuine fondness for their workplace and real value alignment; and staff with a wish to continue working there. Yet everyone has a life outside work. And that "other life" has its benefits and demands. The concept of work-life balance is essentially about allowing employees some choice in *where* and *how* they work. The idea of balance and equilibrium or stability in allowing employees with very different private lives (i.e. with or without spouses, children, elderly parents) to find a work style to suite them.

To some extent this is also about trade-off. People are often happy to trade-off a high salary for less stressful work; or promotion for not having to move. But not everybody has choice, and they can feel that their employers are deeply unsympathetic to certain groups of people who at certain stages of their personal and professional lives perhaps need more time out, without cost or punishment, because of their circumstances.

It is probably true that the work-life balance can be more of an issue for women particularly in jobs where there are large numbers of married women. Currently around three-quarters of British women work outside the home. Of working women, around 15% have children under the age of 16 years. Still, in most homes, a great deal of the home making responsibilities fall on the woman whether she is working or not. Hence the problem of being fully committed in two places at once. This added to the fact that women seem more poorly paid and more often passed over for senior jobs compared to men, means that they are likely to experience stress, go absent and withdraw from jobs or sectors with a "long hours" culture.

In the interest of attempting to put into place work-life balance policies and procedures, the following can be put into place:

- full-time/part-time working
- job share
- special shift arrangements
- non-standard working weeks
- flexi-time
- compressed working hours
- voluntary reduced hours
- term time and variable hours
- home working
- emergency leave
- study leave

- public/community service leave
- career leave
- parental leave
- maternity phase back
- sick childleav
- childcare arrangements
- winding down to retirement
- career breaks

Work-life balance is about flexible working. But the issue begs some fundamental questions: "Is it suitable, desirable, possible for all jobs and all employees? Does it (ever, really) matter when, where, or how, employees work? Who is selected or volunteered for flexibility and why? What are the line managers' central concerns? Most importantly can one build a good business case for introducing work-life balance procedures?"

The argument from a business perspective is that offering work-life balance packages;

- encourages and improves worker retention/turnover.
- reduces recruitment and training costs.
- reduces all forms of absenteeism.
- provides positive publicity for organizations.
- improves motivation and loyalty, and thence productivity.
- increases customer satisfaction.

Essentially all this means that organizations choose to be flexible in their demands on the worker. It is all about giving the individual latitude to choose his/her work style as much as their life style. It is a form of subjective-ergonomics that encourages the individual to maximize the time they spend at work and outside it. Organizations have to consider this issue carefully.

But there are prominent case studies in both the private and public sector to support introducing work-life balance policies. Some public sector companies claimed all of the above were true and even that they were able to recruit more married women with children because of their "family friendly initiatives and benefit."

It seems then, that everybody wants to balance the needs of work and family/personal life. Few would dispute that, but many may be sceptical of the evidence and data available. For ambitious, need-achieving executives the task at work is *getting along with*, but also *ahead of* others. Success requires sacrifice which may be personal, leisure, or family time. The work ethic and many organizations make it clear that you get ahead only with ability and effort, dedication and discipline. Further, some executives find being at work preferable to life outside work. They have power, respect and control. Their day is structured and they have lots of help in their many tasks. Some may look like workaholics.

It would be unfair to suggest that there are robust and consistent gender differences in the interest in and call for, work-life balance procedures at work. One can be certain that if the business case is clear and proven organizations will implement appropriate procedures and the culture will follow. If there is a skill or labour shortage that is relatively easily solved by introducing work-life balance procedures, they are sure to be implemented. However, there remain many who still retain some hesitation and scepticism about whether, when and how an organization should go down the track of trying to introduce a whole raft of work-life balance procedures.

Demographic changes in the workforce

There is evidence that the gender, age and ethnic make-up of the workforce is changing. More women in particular work in white-collar jobs. In the West, the workforce is ageing. Further mass migration has meant that the workforce is now both multinational and multiracial. What is the implication for the world of work?

In the West, a decline in the birth rate and greater longevity means the average age of the workforce is increasing. Are people too old at 40 or 50 years for certain jobs? What is the appropriate dividing line between younger and older workers? Are older workers stereotyped and discriminated against.

Warr (2000), who has conducted extensive research in this area, posed and answered five questions about job performance and the ageing workforce:

1 *Are older workers less effective than younger ones?* Across jobs in general there is no evidence of age differences. Older workers are thought of as more careful, reliable, loyal, knowledgeable and socially skilled but less willing to change. Furthermore, absenteeism, accidents and turnover rates are higher with younger staff.

2 *Why might one expect older workers to be less effective?* Older people do less well on fluid intelligence tests (solving new problems), have poorer working memories, poorer information-processing strategies – indeed, slower mental processes overall. These deficits are naturally apparent with job tasks that are complex and new. Of course, systems can be established to help older workers.

3 *Does experience help older workers?* Older workers do, almost inevitably, have greater experiences and expertise, and since these are related to work performance may make excellent workers. Age is positively related to crystallized intelligence, particular vocabulary and verbal ability. Older people have often automatized work processes. Expertise is, however, domain-specific and there are some areas, such as computer technology, where younger workers out-perform older workers.

4 *Under what conditions are young–old similarities/differences expected?* Warr (2000) noted that younger people do better than older people in complex mental activities

with no environmental support. He examined eight tasks, four in which young workers do better, three of which are age-neutral and one in which older workers do better. Younger people do much better on complex information tasks where they already have expertise but perform worse on simple tasks (with simple routines, relaxed pace).

5 *Are there age differences in learning?* Older people tend to have lower educational qualifications, less confidence in their ability and therefore less motivation to take part in training. But when they do undertake training, older people are slower and have more difficulty remembering. However, training can be adapted to an older person's limitations and expertise.

However, when comparing older and younger employees, it is important to realize that other factors powerfully influence effectiveness at work: cognitive ability (intelligence), expertise, personality (conscientiousness) and motivation/interests. Clearly, in a world where retirement ages are extended or abolished and the workforce is ageing, it becomes more important to understand the strengths and limitations of the older worker.

Forecasting the present: The view from 30 years ago

It is always interesting when speculating on the future of work to examine the success of past prognosticators (Katzell, 1979; Kerr & Rosnow, 1979; Rosnow, 1979). Indeed, the process of predicting future trends, even based on sound empirical sources, is fraught with danger, given that quite unexpected and novel occurrences (inventions, wars, economic crises) with substantial wide-ranging effects upset reasonable, rational forecasts. Many forecasts were wrong: the 20 hour week, the paperless office, the leisure economy.

For Yankelovich (1979), six "old values" at the workplace were changing: women not working; men putting up with bad jobs just for economic security; a "negative" system based mainly on money and status; loyalty to particular organizations; identity primarily achieved through organizations; work was a paid activity that provided steady full-time employment. Old symbols of success, he believed, would be rejected in favour of self-development and enlightenment, which is so difficult to define that it leaves people restless, narcissistic and self-obsessed. He believed changes would include a recognition of the increasing importance of leisure; the important symbolic importance of a "paid job", and the refusal of people to subordinate their personalities and needs to the work role. For Yankelovich, rather than lose the enthusiasm for work – a well-paid job – the future will see an increase in the demand for employment. However, the incentives in these new paid jobs will have to be less materialistic and more psychological, more diverse and more equitable. To a large extent, this scenario for the 1980s proved true.

Also, Etzioni (1979) foresaw a "quality-of-life" society, which was more "continental" and which focused more on culture and recreation than materialism. However, one should bear in mind that all these writers were thinking about the future of working attitudes and preferences in rich post-industrial Western democracies. There were far fewer speculations about the new booming economies of the Pacific Rim (such as Singapore, Malaysia and Indonesia) or the changes in work in poor developing countries in Africa, for example. Many foresaw the greater stress on intrinsic values rather than the extrinsic values at work. Some, but not all, of these speculations have come true. The factors thought to influence work attitudes and hence the future of work were:

- Reduced concern over economic insecurity (which has certainly proved wrong; if anything, the opposite has occurred as a function of recession).
- Revised definition of less (less material, more psychological) reward or benefits of work. (In fact people do not want a trade-off; they want both more material reward *and* better quality of life.)
- More flexible and equal sexual role, division of work. (Certainly, many want this, but there has been a "backlash" of unskilled White men or those who see themselves as victims of reverse discrimination.)
- Belief in the entitlement to the good life. (True; note that entitlement/rights does not mention reciprocal responsibilities.)
- Increasing questions about efficiency as a criterion of goodness. (This depends on who one approaches: as many stress efficiency now as shun it. The question is always what is "traded-off" in the quest for total efficiency.)
- Less emphasis on growth and more on conservation. Increased ecological and environmental concerns. (Partly true, but definitely a function of rich countries. The green or ecological issues that impact on work are growing, but are still seen as the issues of rich countries.)
- A belief that work organizations should contribute to the quality of life. (True, although the costs can occasionally cause the organization to fail.)
- Increased concern with the welfare of consumers. (In part true, although not just their welfare but trying to satisfy their complex changing and ever-growing expectations.)
- Greater awareness of issues relating to mental and physical health. (True, but not always a will or an ability to deal with these issues.)
- Greater acceptance of ethnic minorities and migrants. (True.)

It could be argued that the reasons why these speculations and predictions were by-and-large accurate were that they were considered over a ten-year period (the 1970s, which was a time of great change) and largely data-based. Some would argue that it is not very difficult to extrapolate accurately from extensive data banks over a period such as this. Furthermore, most of the forecasters came up with similar scenarios and hence they were more than likely all right (or wrong). Nevertheless, various fairly dramatic economic and sociological changes have now occurred, as well as technological advances, yet the predictions remain mostly true. This, therefore, may lead one to believe that other (more recent) speculations about the future of work – given that they are as carefully and thoughtfully based – might indeed come true.

There have been many speculations about the future of work, leisure and unemployment. One of the earliest and most influential writers on the future of work (and leisure) was Parker (1972), who distinguished six "components of life-space" that fitted nicely into a two-dimensional structure: work, working/sold/subsistence time; work-related time, work obligations; leisure at work; existence time meeting psychological needs; non-work obligations, semi-leisure; leisure; free/spare/uncommitted/discretionary time. For Parker, the future of work and leisure will depend on both personal values and personality and on the social structure of society. He painted two alternative scenarios of the future confrontation of work and leisure:

- The *differentiation* of work and leisure into different segments: this polarity will be of structure, and function can involve changes in both.
- The *integration* of work and leisure: "In this fusion, work may lose its present characteristic feature of constraint and gain the creativity now associated mainly with leisure, while leisure may lose its present characteristic feature of opposition to work and gain the status – now associated mainly with the *product* of work – of a resource worthy of planning to provide the greatest possible human satisfaction". (Parker, 1972: 122)

Parker was able to identify both segmentalist and holistic social policies and was quite clear on favouring the former. However, 11 years later, he (Parker, 1983) updated his text, considering such things as the microelectronics revolution. This naturally had some very important and wide-ranging implications:

- a continuous and accelerating process of specialization, meaning the destruction of some jobs but the development of others;
- considerable occupational change during a lifetime;
- more application of the principles of science and technology to organizational behaviour;
- a decline in working hours and the simultaneous rise in the level of formal education;
- a shift from manufacturing to service occupations.

Just as this revolution affects work, so it will affect leisure and the relationship between work and leisure.

Paradoxically, Parker believed that leisure will take on more of the character of work in the sense that it will be more central to life, and the culture and economy will be dominated more by leisure values. Equally, there will be less distinction between work and leisure, as the two will become integrated. Parker reiterates his distinction between segmentalist and holistic viewpoints:

> Segmentalists will want to tackle the problems of work and leisure in relative isolation from each other, on the assumption that differentiation of spheres makes this possible; holists will want to pursue a more difficult and longer-term policy of integration, on the assumption that the interdependence of spheres makes this necessary. At the level of general theories of society there are again implications for this policy. Segmentalists will want to make "practical" reforms to the existing work and leisure spheres starting with the experiences and immediate environments of individuals. Holists will insist that more far-reaching policies aimed at changes in the social and economic structure as a whole are necessary. (Parker, 1983: 136)

Some of the following future speculations are fairly global, others more specific. On the global level, for instance, Naisbitt (1984) has speculated on ten major trends that he sees as a "road map to the 21st century". These include trends from:

- an industrial society to an informational society where the new wealth is know-how with adaptable generalists;

- "forced" technology to high tech/high touch that is high technology designed with and for the human touch;
- national to world economy and hence the globalization of economies, languages and greater interdependence;
- short-term to long-term planning, investment and development, with strategic vision as well as planning;
- centralized to decentralized societies, with an aggressive bidding from the bottom-up regionalism;
- institutional to self-help, particularly in the areas of health, education and unemployment;
- representative to participative democracy in occupational, political and business spheres;
- hierarchies to networking in the structure of organizations and communities sharing knowledge;
- North to South, meant in terms of America, but probably applying to the world in general;
- either/or to multiple options in terms of nuclear family, options for women, work, leisure.

Naisbitt is clearly an optimist, having the vision of a democratic, egalitarian and healthy society. Although this list has been updated in the 1990s and rearranged, it remains essentially the same.

These futurological speculations make interesting reading, almost as interesting as the readings of older futurologists predicting the present. Orwell's *1984* fortunately did not come to fruition, at least in many of its manifestations. It is, of course, impossible to determine the accuracy of these general predictions for many years.

Handy (1985) noted eight major changes in the pattern of work in post-industrialized countries:

- a full-employment society was becoming part-employment;
- manual skills were being replaced by knowledge as the basis of work;
- industry was declining and services growing;
- hierarchies and bureaucracies were being replaced by networks and partnerships;
- one-organization careers were being replaced with job mobility and career change;
- the "third stage" of life (post-employment) was becoming more and more important;
- sex roles at work and at the home are no longer rigid;
- work was shifting southwards, inside countries and between countries.

Handy (1985, 1995) argued that the world of work in the future will be different and needs to be planned for. He stated that, if the trends he envisioned turn out to be significant, one can expect some important changes, including:

- more people than at present *not* working for an organization;
- shorter working lives for many people;
- fewer mammoth bureaucracies and more tiny businesses;
- more requirements for specialists and professionals in organizations;
- more importance given to the informal untaxed economy;
- a smaller manufacturing sector larger in output;

- a smaller earning population with a larger dependent population;
- a greatly increased demand for education;
- new forms of social organization to complement the employment organization.

Handy concentrated not on the market or state economy but the *informal* economy (black, voluntary and household) and the *information* (as opposed to industrial, services or agriculture) job sector where most future jobs will lie. Work, he argued, will change: there will be new worlds of work (in the black and grey economies), new meanings of work (job, marginal and gift) and new patterns of work (shorter working week, year and earlier retirement). In the new reorganized work, dials will replace tools (i.e. machines will do all heavy labour), terminals will replace trains (people will work from home), fees will replace wages (we will be paid for services, not time).

Handy (1985) argued for more flexibility, variety, choice and participation in education. He believed that education is an investment, not a cost that can be measured on various scales. He argued that education happens not only in one place (school, university) and that people should be able to choose what and where to learn. He appeared to approve of entrepreneurship and enterprise and to rejoice in "choice and responsibility".

From the humanist ecological perspective, Robertson (1985) dichotomized the future of work into three opposing camps: BAU (business as usual), HE (hyper-expansionist) and SHE (sane, humane, ecological). From these acronyms alone it is quite clear which alternative the author favours. He then systematically draws out the implications of these three quite different scenarios for the economy, technology, and so on, but also for work. He argues, as of course have many others, that industrial and post-industrial forms of work will have to change. It will become more autonomous, self-controlled and directly related to the needs and purposes of those doing the work.

According to Robertson, supporters of the HE vision of the future see the work ethic being replaced by the leisure ethic, whereas SHE visionaries believe a new work ethic will be central to the new type of work. The new work ethic, thought to be more powerful than either the job or leisure ethic, will be based on the new, more meaningful "own work". The old work ethic based on the values of achievement, money and time will change as the new ecological values are acquired. The new ethic, like the old one, will be pioneered by non-conforming minorities supporting the SHE communal vision of the future. And, like the old work ethic, the new one will liberate people, but with the latter ethic it will liberate *all* people, enabling them to become more self-reliant.

This optimistic view of the future sees major changes in values. For Robertson there are three eras of success symbols. The future will see such things as the feminization of work, completely different criteria used in the valuation of work (qualitative rather than quantitative), and the end of the employment empire. There will be a paradigm shift to the SHE vision of own work with its own specific agenda.

Others see the future of work in terms of the symbols of success (Table 16.2), although this is highly speculative. Furthermore, it remains quite uncertain as to precisely who shares these values and how they change.

This vision of future work is essentially optimistic, humanist and sociological. It shares in many ways, which the author recognizes, the vision of the early Protestants: the belief that small groups of people, with the same beliefs and vision of the role of

Table 16.2 Symbols of success

Past symbols of success	Present symbols of success	Future symbols of success
Fame	Unlisted phone number	Free any time
Being in *Who's Who*	Swiss bank account	Recognition as a creative person
Five-figure salary	Connections with celebrities	One-ness of work and play
College degree	Deskless office	Regarded less by money than by respect and affection
Splendid home	Second and third home	
Executive position	Being a vice-president	Major societal commitments
Live-in servants	Being published	Philosophical independence
New car every year	Frequent world travel	Being "in touch with self"

Source: Adapted from Robertson (1985).

work, find ways of organizing work for themselves and develop a coherent and explicit philosophy for it.

Theologians, too, have been interested in the future of work. Davis & Gosling (1985) have suggested that the Church has a major responsibility to search for an *ethic for living* which will replace the inherited ethic of *working to make a living*. They argue for a new work ethic, but believe this can only be achieved once greater workforce involvement and participation have been achieved. However, they are pessimistic about the development of a new humanized alternative work ethic for several reasons:

- job insecurity has made protectionism the primary issue, rendering more important issues less relevant;
- recession has led to a strengthening of hierarchical forms of management;
- workers remain involved in sectional struggles;
- market criteria are more important than paternalism or welfare;
- less partnership between management and workers.

Collste (1985) believed that, although the possibilities for gratifying material demands have increased as a result of new technology, the opposite has occurred for psychological and social needs. We therefore need a new attitude in the new technological age.

Over the past 25 years, a host of writers have speculated on the future of work. What is perhaps most noticeable about these various attempts to analyse current and future changes is the relatively weak consensus that has been reached. Thus, although all researchers expect considerable change, some are optimistic, others pessimistic and some neutral. Some expect only superficial changes, others massive sociological change. For some the beliefs, ethics and values established over the past two centuries will be altered completely, whereas others see slow, imperceptible and minimal change.

Hence, there are various rather different scenarios. For instance, it has been argued that there is, and will be, little decline in the attachment to work. Littler (1985) has suggested that an inspection of the available evidence suggests the desire to obtain paid work for economic, personal or social reasons seems to be ingrained in most members of society. He cites as evidence all sorts of studies: Japanese firms recruiting working-class British workers finding a strongly rooted work-ethic; working women being extra-ordinarily attached to paid employment, regardless of the quality of work experience;

men finding that work is an integral part of their daily social relations as men: "At the level of society, there seems to be *more* emphasis, not less, on the work ethic during the 1980s depression, and unemployment still carries the social stigma as during the years of full employment" (Littler, 1985: 81). There will always be a need for jobs that demand a degree of knowledge, skill and fairly lengthy socialization, and it seems too difficult to imagine how they will change dramatically.

There is no shortage of recent books, particularly those written by trade unionists and politicians, which seem intensely pessimistic about the future of work. Their scenarios might have slightly different emphases, but all see inevitable and inexorable changes as deeply undesirable. Jenkins & Sherman (1979) argued that modern societies will be unable to provide enough work for people and that the resultant high under- or unemployment will not change. These analyses are often long on polemic and short on data or analysis.

Various forms of state intervention are suggested to share jobs and revolutionize attitudes to work and leisure. Moynagh (1985: 71) states the question most clearly:

> No one can be sure exactly what new industries will flourish in the next century as a result of new technologies. What is clear is that these technologies are combining to reveal both undreamed of opportunities and the possibility of an unprecedented destruction of jobs. What people want to know is whether the jobs created by these opportunities will exceed the number destroyed.

Williams (1985) notes that service jobs will not replace old production jobs, because without an efficient competitive manufacturing industry the demand for the services will decline. She argues that there are essentially three possibilities:

- the return of work – based on Kondratiev cycles, some argue that an upturn in the economy will lead to the return of work (after the slump in the late 1980s and 1990s);
- the collapse of work – the scenario, it is argued, exaggerates the speed of change, the number of jobs lost and the absence of new work;
- the change of work – this includes changes in the number, length and importance of jobs.

Moynagh (1985) appears agnostic as to which of these various scenarios is most likely to occur. However, he does argue that there will be definite changes in the nature of work that we can both anticipate and plan for. These include changing the meaning of work and believing that work is not the basis of worth.

Speculations on the future of work are many and varied, although there do seem to be some common threads. But along with specific sociological and political speculations about the future of work *per se*, there are many futurological views of life in general. British futurologists appear to believe that pessimism is profound; US futurologists optimistically see the future as having limitless opportunities. There is no shortage of people interested in speculating about the future of work, leisure, employment, and so on.

Education and the future of work

It is of course not only vocational guidance counsellors, personnel selectors and human resource specialists who have been forced to rethink their jobs in the light of current changes and unemployment. All involved in education have had to consider the relevance, salience and usefulness of what they teach to young people. Watts (1983) has argued that education functions in several ways, both overtly and covertly, to prepare young people for employment or unemployment. Education functions to:

- select people for education in particular skills and avenues of work;
- socialize people into attitudes appropriate for the world of work;
- orientate people to understand the world of employment, and to prepare for the choices and transitions they will have to make on entering it;
- prepare them with specific skills and knowledge to apply in a direct way after entering employment.

Given these and presumably other important functions, it remains crucial that educationalists prepare pupils for hire outside school. But the question remains, what does the future hold? Watts speculated on four quite different scenarios:

- *unemployment* would continue to grow;
- a *leisure class* (non-stigmatized) outside unemployment would emerge;
- *unemployment* would remain but income and status would be distributed more evenly;
- *work* would change in that there would be greater attachment to self-employment and to forms of work outside the formal economy.

Watts (1987) later seemed to believe the unemployment scenario to be most likely, as computers and mechanization reduce the need for many jobs. He believed countries are faced with artificially or corporately sustaining full employment (and with it social harmony and economic growth), and the fact that both work and unemployment will become more and more skewed. Watts appeared to favour the idea of destroying the concept of unemployment by offering a basic guaranteed income for all, received as a right, with no sense of stigma and guilt and with many other possible advantages.

However, along with this Utopian speculation, Watts (1987) speculated on the implication for education. He sees education for leisure not as an alternative to education for work but complementary to it. But he did believe educational practices should change to reflect present and future employment opportunities. These include:

- more emphasis on criterion-referenced forms of assessment, with explicit definitions of skills and levels of competence in performing them;
- more varied forms of learning for more varied purposes;
- more attempts to educate in enterprise or cooperative principles so as to instil the notion of creating and managing one's own work;
- affirming the importance of the use of, rather than the further acquisition of, knowledge;
- more subtle and useful political education.

Table 16.3 Changes in work-related education

From	To
As narrowly preparing for vocational and other "slots" with little concern for developing a critical awareness.	As a broad preparation for life, including social understanding and awareness and social criticism.
As a discrete experience, probably within and end-on to schooling.	As a continuous life-long process of learning.
As based on limited access, involving selection of, rather than choice by, individuals.	As based on open access, widely available in varied forms within which choices can be made.
As a determinant of life-chances from an early age, on a basis which largely reproduces existing differentials and inequalities.	As a catalyst for social mobility throughout life.
As the prerogative of professionals based within the formal education institutions.	As a task shared by and sometimes led by non-professional educators.
As a centralized activity based on "core curricula" and centrally controlled standards.	As a decentralized activity with curricula which are negotiated and evaluated locally.

Source: Reproduced from Watts (1987) with the permission of Blackwell Publishers Ltd/Standing Conference on Studies in Education.

He offered six major changes anticipated within the world of work-related education (Table 16.3).

Education is a sensitive and volatile area. It is often state-funded and hence open to rapid and significant changes. This makes speculation in this area particularly unreliable. However, it is very important to realize the role of tertiary education in the development of successful organizations of the future. Yet everyone acknowledges that education and training do not stop once people have a job. Indeed, there is a need for life-time learning, truly continuous education and the opportunity to practise and increase one's skills all the time.

The limitations of past approaches

How disinterested and objective is work psychology and the research of work psychologists? Holloway (1991) offers a sociological critique of current work or work psychology. She asks the following questions:

- If work psychology is scientific in terms of theory-building and research, what does scientific mean in the context of application? Is it as disinterested and value-free as it often suggests?
- To what end, and on whose behalf, do psychologists study organizations and their employees and what effects do they have? Are psychologists interested in happier or more efficient workers and are they compatible? Do they represent the interests primarily of employee or management?
- What do the different activities of work psychology have in common – selection, skills training, scientific measurement? Is their focus on the individual to the exclusion of social and organizational factors?

Holloway (1991: 187) argues that:

> Work psychology's legitimacy hinges on its claim to be scientific and therefore neutral. The historical evidence demonstrates, however, that this very claim was part of a wider set of power relations which meant that work psychology has predominantly been produced from a vantage point of management's concern with the regulation of individual employees. The extent to which this functions on behalf of employees is a question that can be answered only by looking at specific practices in specific locations. None-the-less, work psychology's utility to management hinges on its claim to be in the interests of both efficiency and welfare simultaneously.

Certainly, sociologists and others have argued that work psychology is far from value-free and serves specific interest groups.

A review of old work psychology, industrial/organizational and occupational/vocational psychology textbooks can make for pretty depressing reading. The optimist, who sees the glass as being half full, and the critical academic reader may point to the growth and popularity of work psychology and the fat glossy books available on this topic. The pessimist, who sees the glass as being half empty, points to the thinness of the contents in contrast to the fatness of the binding. At least six criticisms could be made of older approaches in books published in the 1960s and 1970s. Any students of this topic should consider these carefully and see what evidence they can marshall against such attacks in current texts.

1. *Largely ethnocentric and parochial.* Textbooks in work psychology tend to focus on, quote and review studies, theories and case histories from the perspective of Western industrial countries. They grossly under-represent, downplay or neglect the contribution of scholars from other predominantly developing countries. Worse than that, they remain resolutely monoglot, ignoring all writing that is not in English. Hence, the subject is viewed and represented from a narrow, albeit important, perspective. National cultures do influence behaviour at work and it is important that they are taken into consideration. Too many textbooks are too provincial, but it is to the credit of American and European workers that their ideas and concepts are imported so uncritically, even if they find they do not "fit" the local culture well. Indeed, it may not be that Euro-Americans are enthusiastic exporters so much as that others are eager *importers* of Euro-American know-how and procedures. What is more likely, however, is that there are few competitors in the market with more buyers than producers. This pattern may be changing. In fact, the topic of international business management is now booming, which attempts quite specifically to examine, compare and contrast national differences in management practices and theories.

2. *A-theoretical contributions.* Of all the branches of psychology, work psychology has perhaps been least concerned with theory development. There are no grand theories in this area, unlike, for example, psychoanalysis or behaviourism. Some topics of concern in work psychology, such as job motivation or satisfaction, do boast various different theoretical perspectives, but they have been borrowed or adapted from other branches of psychology and economics (see equity theory). There is nothing wrong with this, of course, but it does reflect little interest in theory development. There are some unique theories in the area, such as Herzberg's celebrated two factor theory, but they are few and far between. Because of both the pragmatism and the applied focus of

their endeavours, work psychology researchers have downplayed the origin, intricacies, inconsistencies and implication of theories. It remains important to examine the theoretical underpinning and origins of concepts.

3. *An a-historical understanding.* Work psychology, like psychology as a whole, has a short history but a long past, yet for most of this century researchers and theoreticians have been very active and the number of journals and books produced voluminous. A discipline with no memory keeps rediscovering itself. Fads, fashions and folderol seem particularly prevalent in work psychology, perhaps precisely because researchers have no historical insight, no knowledge of where they have been. Any cursory glance at textbooks in the area shows how little attention is devoted to history.

4. *Neglect the effect of pre-, post- and outside-work activities.* To understand the behaviour of people at work, one must know what they did before work and what they do while not working. Inevitably, the eight hours spent working each day are strongly influenced by the eight waking hours spent not working. There is a considerable, but largely neglected, literature on the interface between work and leisure that needs to be considered at length. Furthermore, discovering some of the frustrations of unemployment throws important light on the benefits, and also the frustrations, of the world of work. Work, while important, is not everything. Behaviour in organizations may not be very different from behaviour outside organizations. These organizational behaviours may not be very different from non- or extra-organizational behaviours. In this case, the science of behaviour should have most to say in how people behave at work. Too much highly relevant general psychology (and sociology) has been neglected in previous textbooks.

5. *Simplification rather than clarification.* Perhaps an index of a textbook's limitation is the number of cartoons or illustrative stories/case histories. The fact that young people have been brought up on comic books and that cartoons may present truisms in a way, even memorably, does not necessarily justify their inclusion in textbooks. Too often, theories and data are presented in a simplified rather than clasified way. The difference is important: the former cuts corners, ignores complexity, renders bland and facile. The latter hopes to present the ideas and data such that important distinctions are made; *non sequiturs*, contradictory inconsistencies and fallacious logic are exposed.

6. *A tendency to benevolent eclecticism (relativism) or partisan zealotry (absolutism).* Where different theories or approaches exist, as in personality theories, two opposed but equally wrong approaches are taken. Benevolent eclectics present critically all the approaches, ideas and theories as if they were equally valid; partisan zealots will accept only one approach as valid and veridical. Both neglect an appropriate review of the evidence upon which the theory is based. For the field to progress, ideas need to be tested and those found wanting dropped. After all, chemistry books have no detailed sections on alchemy.

But the past is another country: they did things differently there. Organizational psychology is today very sensitive to cultural issues, interested in theory building, aware of its past and the effect it has on the future, and eager to see organizational behaviour within the context of social behaviour. Furnham (2001) has made various specific accusations that can be made against the business school discipline of organizational behaviour as currently taught:

1   *Political correctness.* This involves anything from a doctrinaire denial of biological

influences on human behaviour to laments about the fashionably oppressed. Organizational behaviour seems particularly eager to jump on any politically correct bandwagon, like diversity, espousing the accepted view or following lay enthusiasms like emotional intelligence. Fashion and managerial acceptance, not veridicality, appear to be the important criteria for researching and writing about a topic, which is not how science should or does proceed.

2   *Anecdotes, not data*. There is too much emphasis on stories, case studies, parables and anecdotes and not enough emphasis on the data to substantiate theories and concepts. Case studies make interesting reading and they are extremely useful for teaching. But science develops from hunch to hypothesis to theory to law. We move from observation and induction to verification and falsification. Organizational behaviour researchers need to develop and test theories more.

3   *No powerful theories*. A theory is a network of falsifiable causal generalizations. But organizational behaviour has a messy stew of ideology, buzz words and doctrinaire statements. What theory regularly leads to is the prediction of empirical relationships and generalization across topics/phenomena. Theories in psychology and economics – dissonance theory, equity theory, social exchange theory – are warmly embraced but never bettered by organizational behaviour theories.

4   *Derivative methodology*. Most psychologists collect their own data to test hypotheses. They choose the most appropriate methods to do so. Many economists analyse others' large data sets with sophisticated econometric models. Organizational behaviour does neither. The focus should be on what we know rather than how we found out about it. Methodology is a tool, but an important one for doing research. Organizational behaviour research is difficult – there are lots of related and confounding factors, but organizational behaviour really needs to explore them sensitively and thoroughly.

5   *Identity*. Organizational behaviour does not know what it is and what it isn't. Its incoherence means it never rejects ideas, many of which are pretentious bunk. Marxists, feminists, psycho-biologists, ethno-methodologists, all can find a cosy nest in organizational behaviour. Everybody is welcome, all ideas are equally important and all approaches are equally good. There are no rules, no limits and no quality control. All this exacerbates the identity problem.

6   *Marketing*. Work psychologists know about marketing their ideas. They know the power of the press, the virtue of spin and they use it to the full to further their cause. Organizational behaviour courses are well attended and organizational behaviour departments are often highly rated within business schools because of the business that they attract. Marketing is important because often the ideas are ephemeral and vaporous – there is a constant need for marketing because new products are continuously brought to the market.

7   *Attempting tractable rather than important problems*. Work psychologists know the difference between tractable, and those intractable, but perennial, problems of business that are pretty unsolvable. So they go for those pretty important ones where they can make a difference. And this is a fairly good strategy. To make a small but significant difference is surely the right thing to do.

However, it would be entirely wrong to be gloomy, despondent or depressed about the future. Indeed, the opposite is true. Increasingly, work psychology is becoming a theoretically coherent, methodologically sophisticated, applied field of psychology.

Just like all applied psychologists – clinical, educational, ergonomic – work psychologists have a foot in both the world of science and in that of the application of science. In the ideal world, these two experiences are complementary and enriching. The scientist is trained to formulate and test hypotheses; to challenge assertions and to develop strong theoretical foundation to their area. The practitioner uses the scientific knowledge to understand issues and solve organizational problems. As Belar (2000) has noted, the science–practitioner model is fundamental to the growth of professional psychology. Practitioners have innovative scientific ideas and the marketplace impacts on science. Thus the work psychologist needs training in science and its application.

The future of work psychology

An understanding of both historical factors and current conditions is necessary for a realistic prognostication into the future (Parker, Wall, & Cordery, 2001). Two factors of obvious – and no doubt dramatic – importance are the *globalization of business* and the increasing perception of the *importance of corporate and national culture*. The internet has opened up many new possibilities for work psychologists. Spector (2003) lists 10 websites of interest to students and practitioners who can quickly and efficiently obtain the latest thinking in particular areas. To a large extent, management science and organizational behaviour have been parochial and ethnocentric. This may have been acceptable during colonial and "post-colonial" phases of growth when the "rest of the world" imported organizational behaviour ideas from Europe or America. But the world economy is becoming increasingly integrated and more people are able and willing to adopt a global perspective. There was too much assumed universality and a downplaying of cultural factors. The US and European preference for belief in free will over determinism, of individualism over collectivism, of explicit over implicit communication, has been challenged. Hence, Boyacigiller & Adler (1991) believe work psychology should address itself to whether theories, ideas and practices are:

* universally applicable across widely different organizational and national cultures;
* regiocentre theories that may apply to contiguous geographical areas or those experiencing similar levels of economic development;
* intercultural theories that help to explain the interaction among people from different cultures;
* intracultural theories that explain processes that occur exclusively in one culture.

Future work psychology, then, is likely to take cognizance of its own historical, epistemological but often implicit values. Also, it will focus much more on the economic and sociological factors that influence behaviour, so making theories ultimately more powerful, because of their ability to travel further across geographical areas and time.

A second change may be an *increasing separation of pure and applied* organizational behaviour and work psychology. According to Schönpflug (1992), applied and pure or basic research have never been very close and that rather than seeing technical innovations resulting from theoretical discoveries, applied organizational behaviour has stimulated basic theorizing (i.e. application has driven theory, not the reverse). Applied psychology and management science have a fairly autonomous status, separate from the pure disciplines of psychology and sociology. Pure or basic psychology has isolated, excluded and ignored the economic, social and technical environment within which processes occur, whereas the pragmatic tradition of applied researchers meant they had to be problem-driven and hence take account of contextual variables. However, according to Schönpflug, the coalition between the two is breaking down. Whereas both had mutual benefits – applied researchers, for instance, were able to clothe themselves in the mantle of science – the two are increasingly uncomfortable bedfellows. There are theoretical, historical and political reasons why pure and applied research fail to stimulate and help each other, making this potentially dynamic and bi-directional relationship one of hesitant mistrust.

But the position may be changing. Academic occupational, organizational and work psychologists are being encouraged to work more closely with industry to obtain grants and "real-life" data. This is true even of those psychologists from an experimental tradition, whose interests and methods are pure in the sense that they are relatively unconcerned with whether or how their research is applied. Equally, psychologists and human resource specialists in applied settings are turning in part through frustration but also curiosity to the "first principles" of pure research to help them answer some particularly difficult problems. This cross-fertilization and *rapprochement* must be good for both parties.

There are clear trends in the study of organizations. Some, according to Kolb, Rubin & McIntyre (1992), are realized, others active and still others emerging. Thus, Table 16.4 could, of course, be expanded to look at theoretical and methodological issues. Not everyone will agree with these trends as set out, but the exercise is an important one for organizational psychology.

Work psychology is expanding quickly in most countries in the world. No longer confined to selection and ergonomic issues, work psychologists are diversifying their interests and skills in a wide variety of industries in both the public and private sectors. In America alone, there are 55 postgraduate courses in work (industrial/organizational) psychology (Lower, 1993).

Patterson (2001) has identified five themes that, she argues, have very important consequences for work and organizational psychology:

1   The transformation of the organizational context, including an increase in the *service sector* in most Western countries and an increasing *skills gap*.
2   Employer demands versus employee choice – that is, from a buyer's to a seller's market, and the "war for talent". The concept of *employer of choice* is now very important, as is that of the *psychological contract*, which is an implicit agreement between the employer and employee.
3   The psychological impact of the changing nature of work, with more emphasis on *employee well-being, work–life balance* and *customer service skills*.
4   Theoretical and methodological advances in, for example, *meta-analysis* and *structural equation modelling* to analyse the complexity of the data.
5   Developments in the profession, with greater professionalism and opportunities to study and practise organizational psychology.

Conclusion

This chapter looked at the future of work and the organizations we may expect to find in the next decade or so. There was general agreement that various factors already apparent would have a considerable influence on these changes. These involved the

Table 16.4 Trends in the study of organization

	Realized trends		Active trends		Emerging trends	
	From	*To*	*From*	*To*	*From*	*To*
1. Definition of the field	Behavioural science discipline orientation	Professional experiential orientation	Industrial/business economic focus	Management focus	Psychological emphasis	Sociopolitical, systems focus
2. Management education and training	Academic	Experiential on-the-job training	Creating awareness	Skills-building	Performance orientation	Learning and developing orientation
3. Perspective on employees	Tender (communication, intimacy, growth)	Tough (power and influence)	Socio-emotional factors	Cognitive problem-solving factors	Deficiency orientation (adjustment)	Appreciation orientation (development)
4. Human resource management	Human relations	Human resources	Management of people	Management of work processes	Career development	Organization development
5. Perspective on organizations and their purpose	Job satisfaction, human fulfilment	Organization productivity overall	Internal organizational functioning	Organization, environment adaptation	Organizations as the dominant stable structures	Flexible relationship among professional careers, institutions, and organizations
6. Change processes	Expert, content consultation	Process consultation	Change created by change agents Simple, global techniques	Management of change by the system itself Highly differentiated problem-specific techniques	Change via intervention (action research)	Change via organizational analysis (research action)

Source: Based on Kolb *et al.* (1992).

rapid development and spread of electronic communication and information technology, the globalization of all economies, changes in the workforce and the market, and changes in how organizations choose to operate. Some of these changes can be foreseen and planned; others are, by definition, impossible to predict.

Certainly, in the Western developed and democratic countries, there will be more concern with the quality of life and the legal as well as psychological contract between the employing organization and the employee. However, it will be rare for a person to work for one, or even a few, organizations all their (shortened) working lives. Most jobs, many argue, will be contingent upon circumstance.

Organizations and industries go through cycles and it is quite possible that some industries and sectors will decline as social, economic and political forces dictate. The larger the industry, the greater the impact on the region and related organizations.

One way to test the truthfulness of these predictions about the future is to examine how good speculations have been in the past. Looking back 25 years to those who tried to predict the present, we find that most speculations were fairly accurate. There was some degree of consensus among them, although some speculations were either overtly optimistic or pessimistic. There must inevitably be good reasons to be both. Pessimists see the end to many jobs and the rise of unemployment, with only menial part-time jobs being created. Optimists see the quality of working life improving significantly.

The expansion of work psychology and the increase in the number of work psychologists is in part an indication of change in the workplace. The close association between the academic world of pure research and the applied world of the human resources practitioner is, and no doubt will continue to be, good for work psychology.

There is also a rejuvenation of the disciplines of work psychology and organizational behaviour. A rapid increase in popularity of university courses in this topic and professionally trained and chartered work psychologists have been the catalyst to improve books, teaching and research in this area. It is now one of the most vibrant areas in psychology, and long may it remain so.

A research perspective

Sweat shop to virtual organization

The world of work is changing. It is quite possible that your grandfather *slaved* in a Victorian workshop, your father *laboured* in standard post-war office, you *work* in an *open-planned office* and your children *explore* in a *virtual organization*.

In the good old days of mass production, there was command-and-control management. There were few suppliers, a relatively stable market and very low labour flexibility. Fashions for centralization and decentralization came and went with periods of integration and disintegration.

A period of lean-management production started in the 1990s. There were those dreaded ideas of de-layered management, process redesign and horizontal integration. And now we have what is called *agile* production, with all employees having a self-employment mindset with carefully selected and updated core competences, with many alliances all over the world.

It is possible that every generation experiences work quite differently as a function of management theories and the demands of current technology. Consider the six examples in Table 16.5 drawn up by Furnham (2001). They are speculative and possibly something of a caricature. But the real question is whether the columns represent progress. Is the world of work tomorrow going to be better than that of today? Only research can answer the question.

Table 16.5 Sweatshop to virtual organization

	Grandfather's workshop 1920s	Father's office 1950s	Your open-plan work environment 2000	Your child's virtual organization
The boss's office	The foreman has a functional office with tea-making facilities, personnel files and all the valuable equipment	A dark-panelled sober office dominated by a high desk, which has executive toys and an ashtray on it	The boss's glass-panelled enclosure has a door that is always open. A coffee table dominates	Nobody has an office. But the building has "meeting stations" for stand-up meetings and mass visual display areas
Incentive schemes	Knowing that after 40 years of dedicated service you were least likely to be laid off	Meet your pre-set goals (management by objectives) and you keep your job	Training courses to "upskill" yourself and performance-related pay	Equity in the company. Total freedom to plan own career; go part-time, etc
Appraisal systems	If your boss never shouted at you or demanded you to see him in his office, you were OK	Annual, staff department driven by bureaucratic process of no consequence	Mandatory, three times a year progress reviews that bosses have been trained to give	360 degree feedback data, fed into development and assessment-centre and biannual 20-page report delivered
Skills valued	Manual and engineering skills	Knowledge of systems	Computing	Knowledge and know-how at the cutting edge of biotechnology
Career opportunities	None, unless you married the boss's daughter	In the service-based system, loyalty was rewarded by the "Buggins turn" system	Performance-based but liable to erratic but enthusiastic restructuring, downsizing and re-appraising	The work "career" went out of fashion. Workers each carry and compose portfolios of work experience and skills
Working hours	07.00–18.00 with a short dinner break and the odd tea break	08.00–17.00 with fixed, negotiated breaks	Half an hour before the boss, an hour after he or she leaves. Sandwich or desk lunch	Personal circadian rhythms dictate flexitime pattern chosen

Source: Furnham (2001).

A cross-cultural perspective

The Japanese experience

The management guru William Ouchi (1981) tried to explain to increasingly envious and paranoid Americans and Europeans the cause of Japanese manufacturing success. What accounts for
Japanese quality, productivity, industrial relations and export success?

- *Lifetime employment*: Employees in many (but by no means all) Japanese companies are or
  were virtually assured a position for life. Feeling that their future is intimately linked with
  that of their company, they become deeply committed to it and unwilling to strike.
- *Slow evaluation and promotion*: Evaluation and promotion are both relatively slow in most
  Japanese companies. Thus, an individual's performance can be appraised by many persons
  over a period of several years. This leads employees to realize that the company has a
  "memory" and will ultimately reward faithful service. It also instills great confidence that
  their performance will be fairly and accurately evaluated.
- *Non-specialized career paths*: Many employees in Japanese companies – especially those at
  high levels – perform several different jobs during their careers. This leads to lessened commitment or identification with their own speciality or field, and to greater involvement with
  the company. This reduces departmental squabbles.
- *Consensual decision-making*: Decisions in most Japanese companies are made collectively,
  through a process in which all persons affected have a chance to provide input. This
  strengthens feelings of involvement within the organization because it is easier to own a
  decision when you have taken part in it.
- *Collective responsibility*: Responsibility for success and failure is spread among all members
  of a work unit or department. Since each person's fate is intimately linked with that of many
  others, feelings of general commitment are enhanced.
- *Holistic concern for employees*: Finally, Japanese companies are not simply interested in their
  employees during working hours and in work contexts. Rather, they show concern for their
  welfare off the job. Such concern fosters a high degree of intimacy between employees and
  enhances involvement with the organization.

These patterns and preferences were, and for most remain, quite different from those in the
West, where evaluation and promotion tend to occur rapidly. Decision-making and responsibility
are largely individual matters. Career paths are highly specialized and there is segmented concern
– the organization is interested in employees only within the scope of company business.

But things are changing. In the early 1990s, the Japanese experienced a major recession. The
Americans restructured and slimmed down through "right-sizing" and "re-engineering". The
most obvious problem for the Japanese is how to manage the lifetime employment promise in a
time of recession. First, it must be acknowledged that only 30% of Japanese companies (exclud-
ing the smallest) had lifetime guarantees. Second, because compulsory lay-offs lead to declining
morale, recruitment problems and stigmatization within the business community, Japanese
organizations have attempted classic "solutions". These include voluntary retirement with
attractive packages, as well as promotion to the presidency of minor subsidiaries.

Slow promotion and the non-specialized career path remain. The *crème de la crème* of the
workforce go into government departments, such as the Ministry of Finance. What seems to
characterize so much of Japanese industry is consensus and strong strategic alliances. There is an
"iron triangle" of cooperation and respect between bureaucrats, industry and politicians. Even
company shareholders are stable and friendly. Middle managers, reduced in numbers in the West,
play an important facilitative and communicative role. Communication in large Japanese companies is neither top-down nor bottom-up. The middle manager communicates what is and what
ought to be, both explicitly and implicitly.

The problem – or one of many problems – facing Japan is that their operational efficiency is near its ceiling. Where do you go after that? Furthermore, the competitors have stolen and copied many of the good management ideas, such as "quality circles" and "just-in-time" management.

Many myths abound regarding Japanese success, such as joint R&D, benevolent (indeed protectionist) government regulation, and a superhuman work ethic. Japan has never been especially committed to Asia, and their imperial adventures 50 years ago are still not forgotten.

To maintain their position, the Japanese have had to do some rethinking. Outsourcing is much more common. But their ultimate strategy remains shrouded in secrecy. Strategic thinking is long term and the Japanese are good at that. But although their products and processes continually evolve, their basic management philosophy remains the same.

A human resources perspective

What are the major issues or concerns for human resources specialists? Bernardin & Russell (1993: 38) offer the examples in Box 16.1. They were important in the past and remain relevant for the future. The question for the future is which of these changes and how.

Box 16.1 Sample of issues and choices for HRM practices

Organization design

- The extent to which the organization should formalize how work is to be accomplished through a set of standardized operating procedures, formal chains of command, extensive rules and regulations, and detailed job descriptions.
- The extent to which different organizational units maintain their independence and responsiveness to their unique market niches while integrating their work with other organizational units through liaison teams, matrix organizations, etc.
- The design of jobs so that individuals within the organization work on tasks which are rewarding and self-reinforcing.
- The processes used to shape the organizational structure (e.g. how decisions are made, how widely accountability is distributed, how clearly roles and responsibilities are defined).

Staffing

- The type of criteria to set for bringing in new employees (e.g. short-term versus long-term, full-time versus part-time, contract versus leased employees, job-focused versus career-focused, customer perspective).
- Design for career paths and ladders in the organization (e.g. within one function versus across different functions).
- Processes for succession planning (e.g. formalized systems, involvement of senior managers, integration with strategic planning, link to developmental programmes, emphasis on internal versus external candidates).
- Types of programmes for terminated employees (e.g. during lay-offs, downsizing, early retirements).

Employee and organizational development

- Desired outcomes of development (e.g. conceptual understanding, skill-building, attitude change, team-building, problem-solving).
- Types of participants in developmental programmes (e.g. new employees, first-line supervisors, middle-level managers, top executives).
- The natural of the content built into developmental programmes, and how programmes are integrated with the strategic direction of firms.

Box 16.1 continued

- Types of performance review feedback sessions offered (e.g. frequency, nature of feedback, monitoring of feedback sessions, forms used, formal reporting systems in existence, managerial accountability).
- Processes used to ensure that feedback occurs continually (e.g. quarterly reviews).
- Sources of data for measurement and criterion development (e.g. clients, customers, peers, subordinates).

Reward systems, benefits and compliance

- Types of financial incentives existing (e.g. short-term versus long-term, base versus incentive pay, pay for performance versus pay for seniority).
- The extent to which reward systems are linked to strategic plans and encourage employees to work towards accomplishing business needs and meeting customer requirements.
- The extent to which rewards are based on individual versus group or corporate performance.
- Structure of non-financial rewards (e.g. recognition programmes, titles, informal status symbols).

Communications and public relations

- Types of information presented to employees, manner of presentation (e.g. confidential versus public).
- Types of communication channels; dissemination of information inside and outside the organization; opinion surveys; open-door policies.
- Design of communication programmes (e.g. public meetings, management forums for discussion, videos, written communications, bulletins).

Source: Bernardin & Russell (1993).

References

Argyle, M. (1989). *Social psychology of work*. Harmondsworth, UK: Penguin.

Armstrong-Stassen, M. (1998). Alternative work arrangements: Meeting the challenge. *Canadian Psychology, 39*, 108–123.

Barclays Life (1998). *The Haley Centre 2020 Vision*. London: Barclays Life.

Belar, C. (2000). Science practitioner ≠ science + practice. Boulder is bolder. *American Psychologist, 55*, 249–250.

Bernardin, H., & Russell, J. (1993). *Human resource management: An experimental approach*. New York: McGraw-Hill.

Boyacigiller, N., & Adler, N. (1991). The parochial dinosaur: Organizational science in a global context. *Academy of Management Review, 16*, 262–290.

Cacsio, W. (1998). The virtual workplace: A reality now. *The Industrial-Organizational Psychologist, 35*, 32–36.

Casio, W. (2003). Changes in workers, work and organizations. In W. Borman, D. Ilgen, & R. Klimoski (Eds.), *Handbook of psychology* (Vol. 12, pp. 401–422). New York: Wiley.

Collste, G. (1985). Towards a normative work ethic. In H. Davis & D. Gosling (Eds.), *Will the future work?* (pp. 94–100). Geneva: World Council of Churches.

Crainer, S. (1996). *Key management ideas*. London: Pitman.

Davidow, W., & Malone, M. (1993). *The virtual corporation*. New York: Harper Business.

Davis, H., & Gosling. D. (1985). *Will the future work? Values for emerging patterns of work and employment*. Geneva: World Council of Churches.

Etzioni, A. (1979). Work in the American future: Reindustrialization or quality of life. In C. Kerr & J. Rosow (Eds.), *Work in America: The decade ahead* (pp. 27–34). New York: Van Nostrand.

Frese, M. (2000). The changing nature of work. In N. Chmiel (Ed.), *Introduction to work and organizational psychology* (pp. 424–439). Oxford: Blackwell.

Furnham, A. (1990). *The Protestant work ethic*. London: Routledge.

Furnham, A. (2000). Work in 2020: Prognostications about the world of work 20 years into the millennium. *Journal of Managerial Psychology, 15*, 242–254.

Furnham, A. (2001). *The 3D manager: Dangerous, derailed and deranged*. London: Whurr Publishers.

Greenberg, J., & Baron, R. (1995). *Behavior in organizations*. Englewood Cliffs, NJ: Prentice-Hall.

Handy, C. (1985). *The future of work*. Oxford: Blackwell.

Handy, C. (1995). *The empty raincoat*. London: Arrow.

Holland, B., & Hogan, R. (1999). Remodelling in the electronic cottage. *The Industrial-Organizational Psychologist, 36*, 18–22.

Holloway, W. (1991). *Work psychology and organizational behaviour*. London: Sage.

Jenkins, C., & Sherman, B. (1979). *The collapse of work*. London: Methuen.

Katzell, R. (1979). Changing attitudes to work. In C. Kerr & J. Rosow (Eds.), *Work in America: The decade ahead* (pp. 35–57). New York: Van Nostrand.

Kerr, C., & Rosow, J. (Eds.) (1979). *Work in America: The decade ahead*. New York: Van Nostrand.

Kolb, D., Rubin, I., & McIntyre, J. (1992). *Organizational psychology*. Englewood Cliffs, NJ: Prentice-Hall.

Littler, C. (Ed.) (1985). *The experience of work*. Aldershot, UK: Gower.

Lower, R. (1993). Master's programme in industrial/organizational psychology. *Professional Psychology, 24*, 27–34.

Moynagh, M. (1985). *Making unemployment work*. Reading: Lion.

Naisbitt, J. (1984). *Megatrends: Ten new directions transforming our lives*. New York: Warner.

Ouchi, W. (1981). *Theory Z: How American business can meet the Japanese challenge*. Reading, MA: Addison-Wesley.

Parker, S. (1972). *The future of work and leisure*. London: Granada.

Parker, S. (1983). *Leisure and work*. London: Allen & Unwin.

Parker, S., Wall, T., & Cordery, J. (2001) Future work design and practice. *Journal of Occupational and Organizational Psychology, 74*, 413–440.

Parks, J., & Kidder, D. (1994). Changing work relationships in the 1990s. In C. Cooper & D. Rousseau (Eds.), *Trends in organization behaviour* (pp. 111–136). Chichester, UK: Wiley.

Patterson, F. (2001). Developments in working psychology: Emerging issues and future trends. *Journal of Occupational and Organizational Psychology, 74*, 381–390.

Pell, A. (1995). *The complete idiot's guide to managing people*. New York: Alpha Books.

Porteous, M. (1997). *Occupational psychology*. London: Prentice-Hall.

Raymond, S., & Cunliffe, R. (2000). *Tomorrow's office*. London: E & FN Spon.

Robertson, J. (1985). *Future work: Jobs, self-employment and leisure after the industrial age*. Aldershot, UK: Gower.

Rosow, J. (1979). Quality-of-work-life issues for the 1980s. In C. Kerr & J. Rosow (Eds.), *Work in America: The decade ahead* (pp. 157–203). New York: Van Nostrand.

Schönpflug, W. (1992). Applied psychology: Newcomer with a long tradition. *Applied Psychology: An International Review, 42*, 5–66.

Schermerhorn, J., Hunt, J., & Osborn, R. (1994). *Managing organizational behavior*. New York: Wiley.

Spector, P. (2003). *Industrial and organizational psychology*. New York: Wiley.

Warner, M. (1997). *Working at home*. Unpublished paper.

Warr, P. (2000). Job performance and the ageing workforce: In N. Chmiel (Ed.), *Introduction to work and organizational psychology* (pp. 407–423). Oxford: Blackwell.

Watts, A. (1983). *Education, unemployment and the future of work*. Milton Keynes, UK: Open University Press.

Watts, A. 1987. Beyond unemployment? Schools and the future of work. *British Journal of Educational Studies, 35*, 3–18.

Williams, S. (1985). *A job to live*. Harmondsworth, UK: Penguin.

Yankelovich, D. (1979). Work, values, and the new breed. In C. Kerr & J. Rosow (Eds.), *Work in America: The decade ahead* (pp. 3–26). New York: Van Nostrand.

Author index

Subject index